RON SHANDLER'S **2015**

BASEBALL FORECASTER

AND ENCYCLOPEDIA OF FANALYTICS

TRIUMPH
BOOKS

Triumph Books and colophon are registered trademarks of Random House, Inc.

This book is available in quantity at special discounts for your group or organization. For further information, contact:

Triumph Books LLC
814 North Franklin Street
Chicago, Illinois 60610
(312) 337-0747
www.triumphbooks.com

Printed in U.S.A.
ISBN: 978-1-62937-013-2

Rotisserie League Baseball is a registered trademark of the
Rotisserie League Baseball Association, Inc.

Statistics provided by Baseball Info Solutions

Cover design by Brent Hershey
Front cover photograph by Jayne Kamin-Oncea/USA TODAY Sports Images
Author photograph by Kevin Hurley

Ron Shandler's
BASEBALL FORECASTER

Editors
Ray Murphy
Brent Hershey

Associate Editor
Brandon Kruse

• • • • • •

Technical Wizard
Rob Rosenfeld

Design
Brent Hershey

Data and Charts
Matt Cederholm

Player Commentaries
Ryan Bloomfield
Rob Carroll
Matt Cederholm
Brent Hershey
Ray Murphy
Stephen Nickrand
Greg Pyron
Kristopher Olson
Josh Paley
Brian Rudd
Jock Thompson
Rod Truesdell

Research and Articles
Jason Collette
Patrick Davitt
David Martin
Vlad Sedler
Todd Zola

Prospects
Rob Gordon
Jeremy Deloney
Tom Mulhall

Injury Chart
Rick Wilton

Acknowledgments

Producing the *Baseball Forecaster* has been a team effort for a number of years now; the list of credits to the left is where the heavy lifting gets done. On behalf of Ron, Brent, and Ray, our most sincere thanks to each of those key contributors.

We are just as grateful to the rest of the BaseballHQ.com staff, who do the yeoman's work in populating the website with 12 months of incredible online content: Dave Adler, Andy Andres, Matt Beagle, Dan Becker, Alex Beckey, Rob Berger, Brian Brickley, Ed DeCaria, Doug Dennis, Matt Dodge, Greg Fishwick, Neil FitzGerald, Colby Garrapy, Matt Gelfand, Phil Hertz, Joe Hoffer, Ed Hubbard, Tom Kephart, Chris Lee, Chris Mallonee, Troy Martell, Craig Neuman, Harold Nichols, Frank Noto, Nick Richards, Mike Shears, Peter Sheridan, Skip Snow, Matthew St-Germain, Jeffrey Tomich and Michael Weddell.

Thank you to our behind-the-scenes troopers: our technical dynamic duo of Mike Krebs and Rob Rosenfeld; and to Lynda Knezovich, the patient and kind voice at the other end of your phone or email inquiries.

Thank you to all our industry colleagues, a truly impressive group. They are competitors, but they are also colleagues working to grow this industry, which is never a more evident than at our annual First Pitch Arizona gathering each November.

Thank you to Dave Morgan, Chris Pirrone, Dan Fogarty and the entire team at USA Today Sports Media Group.

Thank you for all the support from the folks at Triumph Books and Action Printing.

And of course, thank *you*, readers, for your interest in what we all have to say. Your kind words, support and (respectful) criticism move us forward on the fanalytic continium more than you know. We are grateful for your readership.

From Ray Murphy Ron and Brent each possess a rare combination of talent and dedication that make it a distinct pleasure to collaborate with them. In fact, the full BaseballHQ.com roster is a collection of talent and depth that would be the envy of any MLB GM. Particular thanks go to our sometimes-overlooked tech team: Rob Rosenfeld's wizardry has completely transformed our production process for this book, and Mike Krebs saved this edition from falling into the hands of nefarious online entities. Most importantly, thanks to my wife (and best friend) Jennifer, and our daughters Bridget and Grace, for patiently indulging my obsession with this game.

From Brent Hershey This year's cover photo symbolizes several layers of my gratitude. First, it represents two colleagues at the top their game: my partner Ray, whose insight contains all the depth of a Clayton Kershaw curveball; and Ron, the one "before" and so similar to the current ace, who set the standard of excellence at a nearly unreachable height for the franchise. Thanks to you both. Second, the photo emanates that end-of-event feeling, when, as you survey the results of the hard work of your team—in this case, every name in the box to the left—you let yourself believe that "We nailed it." *Gracias*, all. And third—and most importantly—that Kershaw scream of elation is probably what you heard from my family as we put the wraps on this edition. To my wife Lorie, and daughters Dillon and Eden: Thank you for supporting me in doing what I love.

From Ron Shandler It has been an honor to have my name attached to this work now for nearly three decades. THANK YOU to the amazing group of analysts who build this great structure, so ably helmed by Ray and Brent.

All three of us are outscored by the supportive women in our lives, 3-1. That's fair. My annual update: Darielle now lives the theatre dream in Manhattan, doing light design, stage management and riding the subway at ungodly hours. I just made my final tuition payment for Justina (yay!), who finished recording her second EP and is headed out to LA after graduation (boo!). For Sue and I, it's now winters in south Florida. If you're at Tradition Stadium in March, look for us.

As always, I'm incredibly grateful for your support all these years. Good luck in 2015!

TABLE OF CONTENTS

Benchmarks

by Ron Shandler

Imagine that you are sitting in the first car of a rollercoaster at an amusement park. You're taking that slow climb up the lift-hill to the precipice. You wait in eager anticipation for that point when you catch the first glimpse of open air below you.

And then…. whooooosh!

Down you plummet, picking up speed, faster and faster, while your brain tries to gauge how much longer your stomach will stay in your throat. If we were to graph the journey, it might look something like this:

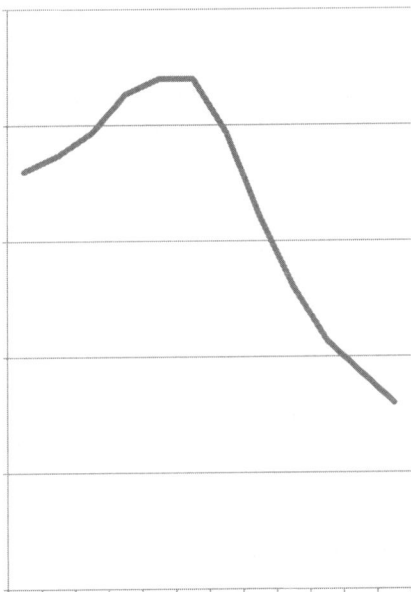

Coincidentally, this is also a graph of league-wide batting averages over the past 12 years. It is presented as a 3-year rolling average to smooth out a few extraneous bumps in the track. But make no mistake—the annual trajectory is just as precipitous (actually, even moreso).

There is one key difference between this trend and the rollercoaster analogy… on a rollercoaster, you can see where the drop ends and the track levels off. For those of us on this batting average ride, there is no telling when BAs will bottom out. Will it be 2015? How about 2016?

Last year's major league batting average was only .251. That was the lowest level since 1972, when batters hit .244 league-wide. Will the current trend continue to that point? Or maybe it will plummet all the way to .237, which is where offense settled in 1968. That's baseball's all-time low.

You're shaking your head. (Yes, I can see you.) You're thinking, "No, it won't go down that far." That's a logical reaction, but how do you know?

The current trajectory is pretty steep. The down slope covers an 8-year period. At the current trajectory, it would take only three more years to reach .244, and about another three to reach .237.

Let's take a deeper look:

	BATTING		PITCHING	
	BA	Iso	ERA	K/BB
2001-02	.263	.160	4.35	1.99
2003-04	.265	.160	4.43	1.95
2005-06	.267	.159	4.41	2.01
2007-08	.266	.154	4.40	2.01
2009-10	.260	.151	4.20	2.10
2011-12	.255	.147	3.98	2.39
2013-14	.252	.139	3.81	2.59

Typically, we look at data one year at a time. But really, each data point can be considered a small sample, and thus prone to some normal year-to-year volatility. To the undiscerning eye, this might even obscure a notable trend. But all we need to do is group the years into pairs and suddenly the trends are nothing short of striking.

Needless to say, this all filters down to the distribution of talent on an individual player basis.

Number of hitters with 35+ home runs

2001-02	39
2003-04	39
2005-06	37
2007-08	20
2009-10	19
2011-12	17
2013-14	12

Number of pitchers with an ERA under 3.50 (120+ IP)

2001-02	54
2003-04	46
2005-06	39
2007-08	47
2009-10	61
2011-12	80
2013-14	103

And while nobody wants to point a finger at any one variable, perhaps for fear of being accused of confusing correlation with causation, please explain to me how *this* happens:

Number of pitchers with an average FB velocity of 95+ mph (30+ IP)

2003-04	24
2005-06	29
2007-08	27
2009-10	53
2011-12	68
2013-14	77

Where did these bionic arms come from? That's a huge increase in super-human performance over such a short period of time.

What is going to put the brakes on this free fall? You can't just say, "It'll stop on its own. Baseball always runs in cycles." You can't say that because there has always been some type of external event or intervention to interrupt past cycles. An adjustment to the pitching mound put the brakes on 1968's plummet. PEDs drove the offensive explosion of the 1990s. MLB's fear-instilling drug testing P.R. campaign likely helped reverse that cycle during the past decade.

But with pitching dominance continuing to pick up speed, what is going to stop *this* runaway car? Maybe MLB will give us livelier baseballs next year. Maybe MLB will enact the time-saving measures they tried out in the Arizona Fall League (ha!), thus disrupting pitchers' timing. Or maybe the rate of Tommy John surgeries will continue to rise, thus wiping out all of baseball's young pitching talent.

It's fun to speculate.

Actually, there is one real variable that MLB might consider addressing. The following data was published by Jon Roegele of *The Hardball Times*:

Average size of the called strike zone (in square inches)

2008	436
2009	435
2010	436
2011	448
2012	456
2013	459
2014	475

Roegele wrote: "The strike zone has been changing since the possibility arose of grading umpires with newly installed pitch-tracking technology.... In the PITCHf/x era (beginning in 2007), the bottom of the strike zone has been expanding at a higher rate than the edges have been contracting, leading to a larger strike zone. This imbalance has paved the way for higher strikeout totals and lower walk totals. The changes have altered more pitch counts in favor of the pitcher, leading in total to a larger number of less successful plate appearances from batters and fewer runs scored."

Unless MLB decides to address this issue, odds are the current levels will persist.

Right now, there are probably some of you thinking, "So what? What's the harm of us just sitting back and being a spectator to all this exhilarating chaos?" I would respond with one word:

Plastics.

No, no, wrong word.

Benchmarks.

There was a time when 30/100/.300 meant something. Those were the benchmarks for stardom; a point of reference around which we could evaluate performance. Thirty home runs, 100 RBIs and a .300 batting average. When PEDs were peaking 15 years ago, at least *two dozen players* were reaching those numbers *every year*.

And now? Without looking, how many players reached that triumvirate of offensive accomplishment in 2014?

No looking. I mean it.

Last year, the only players to accomplish 30/100/.300 were a 27-year-old rookie who had never before faced major league pitching and a 35-year-old veteran who had never seen even 26 HRs in 10 previous years, let alone 30.

Jose Abreu and Victor Martinez.

Benchmarks.

There was also a time when a sub-2.00 ERA was virtually unachievable. *Thirty-one pitchers* (min. 30 IP) accomplished that feat in 2014.

A strikeout-to-walk ratio of 2.0 used to be our delimiter of success; it was one of the foundation filters of the LIMA Plan. Today, pitchers with that ratio are in the bottom 25%. Starting pitchers (min. 120 IP) with that ratio are in the bottom 15%!

There was a time when you could just mentally filter your pitcher list by ERA. Anyone under 4.00 had to have *some* redeeming quality and was worth at least considering. Today, you legitimately have to start your search at 3.50. In analyzing the hundreds of pitcher boxes in this book, if I saw someone falling off to a 3.75 ERA, I'd think, "heck, that's not so bad." But those 3.75 guys are barely league average these days.

So, what's "good" any more?

I don't know; certainly, the old benchmarks are of no help. I suppose we could arbitrarily set new benchmarks based on current conditions—30/100/.300 becomes 25/90/.290—but how long would *they* remain relevant?

Over the years, we've presented several of our metrics in this book normalized to the league average level. PX (linear weighted power index) and Spd (statistically scouted speed) have always been presented as an index with 100 representing league average. Batters with a 120 PX, for instance, were producing power 20% above league average; batters with a 65 PX were 35% below league average.

This was intended to provide a better measure of "good" for those skills that had a tendency to shift over time. And 100 could bounce off the walls for all we cared, but it didn't matter because everyone was benched to that league average.

Now, nearly everything is shifting. The use of indices to normalize metrics to a league average is more important that ever.

Given all of this, it has become time for the Mayberry Method to acquiesce to the changing times and transition *all of its components* to normalized metrics.

Mayberry Method 4.0

Some background: The foundation of the Mayberry Method (MM) is the assertion that we really can't project player performance with the level of precision that advanced metrics and modeling systems would like us to believe.

MM is named after the fictional TV village where life was simpler. MM evaluates skill by embracing the imprecision of the forecasting process and projecting performance in broad strokes rather than with hard statistics.

Here is an excerpt from my original article back in 2009:

> Tonight, the friendly weather forecaster on my local television station has told me that it is going to be partly cloudy tomorrow with a high of 78 degrees.
>
> I suspect that the meteorologist's advanced modeling system spit out that fancy number—78. I often think, why not 77? Or 79? The truth is, if I were to walk outside right now, I'd feel no difference if it was 77, or 78, or 79.
>
> In fact, it probably requires a good five degrees for me to feel any noticeable difference, and even then, it would be slight. 79 versus 74? 46 versus 41? 97 versus 92? More important, a five degree difference wouldn't likely make me change my behavior. If I'm not wearing a light jacket at 79, I'm not likely going to do so at 74.
>
> The 10-day forecast seems to be an exercise in excessive precision: 80, 82, 81, 82, 80, 77, 77, 77, 74, 76. What does

this tell me? The first half of the week is going to be warm. The second half of the week is going to be marginally cooler.

In fact, they could just say that the temp will be in the low 80s and I would be perfectly okay with that. High 70s, low 80s, high 80s, low 90s... that's all I need. They wouldn't even have to bother with mid-70s or mid-80s because that won't change what I am going to wear anyway.

What do we gain from the extra precision? We delude ourselves into believing we are gaining accuracy when in fact we are gaining an increased probability of being wrong. We're just not good enough to predict the temperature to the exact degree on a daily basis. We need to come to terms with that. And most important... there's no great need to be so perfect.

From here, it's an easy leap to replace temperatures with home runs, or stolen bases, or even strikeouts.

Remember that our unit of measure when comparing 25 home runs to 22 is "errant gusts of wind."

MM reduces every player to a 7-character code. The format of the code is 5555 AAA, where the first four characters describe elements of a player's skill on a scale of 0 to 5. The three alpha characters are our reliability grades (Health, Experience and Consistency) on the standard A-to-F scale. The skills numerics are forward-looking; the alpha characters grade reliability based on past history.

MM has gone through several iterations over the years, adjusting some of the factors. We are now at version 4.0.

Batting

The first character in the MM code measures a batter's **power** skills. It is assigned using the following table:

PX	MM
0 - 49	0
50 - 79	1
80 - 99	2
100 - 119	3
120 - 159	4
160+	5

Given that PX is already a normalized metric, it fits in perfectly with our goals for MM 4.0.

The second character measures a batter's **speed** skills. RSpd takes our Statistically Scouted Speed metric (Spd) and adds the elements of opportunity and success rate, to construct the formula of RSpd = Spd x (SBO + SB%).

RSpd	MM
0 - 39	0
40 - 59	1
60 - 79	2
80 - 99	3
100 - 119	4
120+	5

Here, too, speed is already normalized to league average. You'll note, however, that "average"—100—ranks pretty high on the scale. That's because the pool of baseball's most prolific speedsters is small and the distribution of stolen bases does not form a normal bell curve.

The third character measures expected **batting average**.

xBA	MM
.000 - .239	0
.240 - .254	1
.255 - .269	2
.270 - .284	3
.285 - .299	4
.300+	5

This is where we start running into trouble. Given the decline in batting averages—and xBA as well—assigning scores based on raw data does not work anymore. Check out the distribution of players in 2014 under the existing table:

xBA	MM	Pct.
.000 - .239	0	34.0
.240 - .254	1	22.6
.255 - .269	2	20.9
.270 - .284	3	13.8
.285 - .299	4	6.3
.300+	5	2.4

More than 77% of batters earned a MM score of 0, 1 or 2. Only 22.5% earned scores of 3, 4 or 5. We need to find a better balance.

If we index xBA levels to league average, we can create a much more useful table:

xBA Index	MM	Pct.
0-87	0	16.3
88-92	1	13.3
93-97	2	19.7
98-102	3	17.0
103-107	4	17.7
108+	5	16.0

Now, 49.3% of batters earn a MM score of 0, 1 or 2 and 50.7% earn a score of 3, 4 or 5.

The fourth character measures **playing time**. This can remain unchanged.

Role	PA	MM
Potential full-timers	450+	5
Mid-timers	250-449	3
Fringe/bench	100-249	1
Non-factors	0-99	0

Pitching

The first character in the pitching MM code measures xERA, which captures a pitcher's overall ability and is a proxy for **ERA**, and even **WHIP**. Once again, pitching dominance completely skews the distribution in the current chart.

xERA	MM	Pct.
4.81+	0	3.1
4.41 - 4.80	1	9.8
4.01 - 4.40	2	19.3
3.61 - 4.00	3	23.9
3.21 - 3.60	4	23.4
3.20-	5	20.6

More than two thirds of pitchers earned a MM score of 3, 4 or 5. Only 32.1% earned scores of 0, 1 or 2. We need to find a better balance, but this time the task is more difficult.

Similar to speed, this skill is distributed in such a way that it's impossible to create a normal bell curve. The group of pitchers at the top are too far ahead of the pack. Even normalizing to league average can't flatten the distribution. But we can come close.

xERA Index	MM	Pct.
0-80	0	5.9
81-90	1	19.8
91-100	2	26.0
101-110	3	18.5
111-120	4	14.9
121+	5	14.9

While it's nearly an even split between the top three scores and bottom three scores, you can see that there is still imbalance within the bottom group.

The second character measures **strikeout** ability. And again, a gross imbalance.

K/9	MM	Pct.
0.0 - 5.3	0	7.5
5.4 - 6.3	1	15.2
6.5 - 7.3	2	20.6
7.4 - 8.3	3	21.3
8.4 – 9.3	4	13.1
9.4+	5	21.9

And fixing it as best as we can:

K/9 Index	MM	Pct.
0-76	0	15.9
77-88	1	16.2
89-100	2	19.5
101-112	3	18.3
113-124	4	12.3
125+	5	17.7

The third character measures **saves** potential.

Description	Saves est.	MM
No hope for saves; starting pitchers	0	0
Speculative closer	1-9	1
Closer in a pen with alternatives	10-24	2
Frontline closer with firm bullpen role	25+	3

The fourth character measures **playing time**.

Role	IP	MM
Potential #1-2 starters	180+	5
Potential #3-4 starters	130-179	3
#5 starters/swingmen	70-129	1
Relievers	0-69	0

Overall Mayberry Scores

I think that the real value of Mayberry is to provide a skills profile on a player-by-player basis. I want to be able to see this…

Player A	4455 AAB
Player B	5245 BBD
Player C	5255 BAB
Player D	5155 BAF

…and make an objective, unbiased determination about these four players without being swayed by preconceived notions and baggage. In fact, the above provides an interesting case study in four players who have been vying for the #2 spot in early mock drafts, behind Mike Trout. Who would you pick from these Mayberry codes alone?

You can tell that Players B, C and D offer up better power than Player A, but Player A has significantly more speed. Player B trails

slightly when it comes to batting average. And Players B and D have both shown inconsistent output on a year-to-year basis. Any idea of the players who make up this quartet? (Answers shortly. Don't peek.)

While we need to rank players for our draft lists, the truth is, given normal statistical volatility, any of these players could probably hit 30 HRs or bat .300. MM provides a quick-glance assessment so you can opt for the player with the particular skill you find most valuable for your team. For instance, if you believe that building a solid batting average foundation is paramount, you might stay away from Player B. If you want to draft a player who has at least some speed, you'd likely stay away from Player D.

For what it's worth, the calculation for creating an overall rating for players is somewhat fuzzy, and I rarely use it myself. I'm not sold that MM gains its greatest utility as an overall measure for ranking purposes; I prefer to use it as an individual player profiler. But the calcs exist, so let's plow ahead.

This is the calculation for the overall MM batting score:

MM Score =
(PX score + Spd score + xBA score + PA score)
x PA score

An overall MM pitching score is calculated as:

MM Score =
((xERA score x 2) + K/9 score + Saves score + IP score)
x (IP score + Saves score)

The highest score you can get for either is 100. That makes the result of the formula easy to assess.

BaseballHQ.com analyst Patrick Davitt did some great research about using Reliability Grades to adjust the Mayberry scores. His research showed that "higher-reliability players met their Mayberry targets more often than their lower-reliability counterparts, and players with all "D" or "F" reliability scores underperform Mayberry projections far more often. Those results can be reflected by multiplying a player's MM Score by each of three reliability bonuses or penalties:"

I've taken his work a minor step further and applied slightly different multipliers to each Reliability element.

	Health	Experience	Consistency
A	x 1.10	x 1.10	x 1.10
B	x 1.05	x 1.05	x 1.05
C	x 1.00	x 1.00	x 1.00
D	x 0.90	x 0.95	x 0.95
F	x 0.80	x 0.90	x 0.90

So, let's perform the overall calculations for our quartet, using these Reliability adjustments.

Player A: 4455 AAB
= (4+4+5+5) x 5
= 90 x 1.10 x 1.10 x 1.05
= 114.3

Player B: 5245 BBD
= (5+2+4+5) x 5
= 80 x 1.05 x 1.05 x 0.95
= 83.8

Player C: 5255 BAB

= (5+2+5+5) x 5

= 85 x 1.05 x 1.10 x 1.05

= 103.0

Player D: 5155 BAF

= (5+1+5+5) x 5

= 80 x 1.05 x 1.10 x 0.90

= 83.2

Last chance to guess who these players are before I reveal the answers. (Cover up the next paragraph if you really want to try.)

Player A is Andrew McCutchen. Player B is Giancarlo Stanton. Player C is Paul Goldschmidt. Player D is Miguel Cabrera. While each player has his strengths and weaknesses, perhaps this methodology helps provide some clarity as to who to draft at #2.

You don't agree?

Okay, I get it. You might be thinking, "All like values are not equivalent skill sets. For instance, there's no way that Goldschmidt hits as many home runs as Stanton." But given each of their underlying power skills, there is not enough of a difference to separate them. They are both "5s." Maybe Stanton hits 38 and Goldschmidt hits 34, but that could easily be four "errant gusts of wind." Are you willing to bet with absolute, gun-to-your-head certainty that one is clearly better than the other?

I thought not.

The Portfolio3 Plan

I have to be honest. As I've been using Mayberry more and more over the years, I've been using the Portfolio3 Plan (P3) less and less. Seems like a lot of work.

Let's change that.

First, a review.

The foundation of Portfolio3 was the assertion that, when it comes to profitability, all players are not created equal. Every player has a different role on your team by virtue of his skill set, dollar value/draft round, position and risk profile. When it comes to a strategy for how to approach a specific player, one size does not fit all.

We need some players to return fair value more than others. A $40/first round player going belly-up is going to hurt you far more than a $1/23rd round bust. End-gamers are easily replaceable.

We rely on some players for profit more than others. First-rounders do not provide the most profit potential; that comes from players further down the value rankings.

We can afford to weather more risk with some players than with others. Since high-priced early-rounders need to return at least fair value, we cannot afford to take on excessive risk. Our risk tolerance opens up with later-round/lower cost picks.

Players have different risk profiles based solely on what roster spot they are going to fill. Catchers are more injury prone. A closer's value is highly dependent on managerial decision. These types of players are high risk even if they have great skills. That needs to affect their draft price or draft round.

For some players, the promise of providing a scarce skill, or productivity at a scarce position, may trump risk. Not always, but sometimes. The determining factor is usually price. A $3, 20th

round Michael McKenry is not something you pass up in an NL-only league, even with a Reliability Grade of BFF.

In the end, we need a way to integrate all these different types of players, roles and needs. We need to put some structure to the concept of a diversified draft approach. Thus:

The Portfolio3 Plan provides a three-tiered structure to the draft. Just like most folks prefer to diversify their stock portfolio, P3 advises to diversify your roster with three different types of players. Depending upon the stage of the draft (and budget constraints in auction leagues), P3 uses a different set of rules for each tier that you'll draft from. The three tiers are:

1. Core Players
2. Mid-Game Players
3. End-Game Players

In the original P3 structure, we used our sabermetrics to help filter the player pool. Now that we need to shift away from the raw gauges, it becomes more useful to integrate Mayberry into the process. Thus:

The Mayberry Portfolio3 Plan (MP3)

Mayberry scores can be used as a proxy for the original Portfolio3 filters, and they make more sense now. Most of the below will not be new, but I've made several tweaks to fine-tune the process.

When planning your draft, pretty much all you need to remember is the number "3". That essentially represents "just over league average" and makes it easy to set your targets.

TIER 1: CORE PLAYERS
General Roster Goals

Auction target: Budget a maximum of $160. Any player purchased for $20 or more should meet the Tier 1 skills criteria

Snake draft target: 5-8 players, with an emphasis on those drafted in the earlier rounds

Reliability grades: No worse than "B" for each variable (Health, Experience and Consistency)

Playing time: No restrictions, however, pricier early round players should have more guaranteed playing time

Batter skills: Minimum MM scores of 3 in xBA *plus* either PX or RSpd

Pitcher skills: Minimum MM scores of 3 in xERA *and* K/9

Tier 1 players provide the foundation to your roster. These are your prime stat contributors and where you will likely invest the largest percentage of your budget or early round picks. There is no room for risk here, so the majority of these core players should be batters.

These are going to be among the most important players on your roster, so their presence provides a report card, of sorts, for your draft. For instance, if you leave the table with only three Tier 1 players, then you know you have likely rostered too much risk or not enough skill. If you manage to draft nine Tier 1 players, that doesn't necessarily mean you've got a better roster, just a better core. There still may be more work to do in the other tiers.

TIER 2: MID-GAME PLAYERS
General Roster Goals

Auction target: Budget between $50 and $100; players should be under $20

Snake draft target: 7-13 players

Reliability grades: No worse than "B" for Health, no worse than "C" for Experience and Consistency

Playing time: Must have a MM score of 5 for batters (meaning full-time batters) and minimum 3 for pitchers (meaning at least mid-rotation starting pitchers)

Batter skills: Minimum MM scores of 3 in xBA or PX or RSpd

Pitcher skills: Minimum MM score of 3 in xERA or K/9

Tier 1 players are all about skill. Tier 2 is all about accumulating playing time, particularly on the batting side, with lesser regard to skill. This is where you can beef up on runs and RBI. If a player is getting 500 AB, he is likely going to provide positive value in those categories just from opportunity alone. And given that his team is seeing fit to give him those AB, he is probably also contributing somewhere else.

For pitchers, we use Tier 2 to accumulate arms whose innings provide some level of positive support, either by stockpiling strikeouts or by building your ERA foundation. If your Tier 1 pitchers are strong, you can afford to roster a few arms like Hiroki Kuroda (3105 BAA) or Jake Odorizzi (2303 ACA) who may not provide a complete skills/risk package.

TIER 3: END-GAME PLAYERS
General Roster Goals

Auction target: Budget up to $50; players should be under $10

Snake draft target: 5-10 players

Reliability grades: No restrictions, except no "F" Health grades.

Playing time: No restrictions

Batter skills: Minimum MM scores of 3 in xBA plus either PX or RSpd (same as Tier 1)

Pitcher skills: Minimum MM score of 3 in xERA

Tier 3 players are your gambling chips, but every end-gamer must provide the promise of upside. For that reason, the focus must remain on skill and conditional opportunity. MP3 drafters should fill the majority of their pitching slots from this group.

By definition, end-gamers are typically high risk players, but risk is something you'll want to embrace here. You don't want a low-risk Travis Wood-type player (1205 AAA) at the end of the draft; there is no upside or promise of profit. If a Tier 3 player does not pan out, he can be easily replaced.

As such, the best Tier 3 options should possess the MM skill levels noted above, and at least one of the following:

- playing time upside as a back-up to a risky front-liner
- an injury history that has depressed his value (but not chronically injured players)
- solid skills demonstrated at some point in the past
- minor league potential even if he has been more recently a major league bust

A complete list of players in each tier appears in the back of the book starting on page 269. This list pares down the draftable player pool to 213 players. There are 62 in Tier 1, 65 in Tier 2 and 86 in Tier 3. Unlike the past few years of P3, it's a sufficient pool at each tier from which to assemble your roster.

One of the major benefits of the MP3 process is that any player failing to find a home in one of the tiers can be safely ignored. Either his skills are not draft-worthy or his risk-profile too dangerous, regardless of skill.

So that means you are not going to find players like Troy Tulowitzki (5255 FDD) and Matt Kemp (5245 FCD) in that draftable Tier 1 pool. As near-$30 buys, their risk profile is too high to be considered at that price; players at that level need to be safer. Similarly, you are not going to find speculative upside plays in Tier 3 like Dylan Bundy (2201 FFF) or Robert Erlin (2201 DDB) either. We need to see better skills before we jump in.

By shrinking the draftable player pool, it makes the roster planning and construction process easier.

Category Targets

This is the final piece of the puzzle, setting MM targets for each category.

If you are in a league with good trading activity, this may not be important—you can always deal away excesses to beef up weak categories. But for those in leagues with little or no trading, drafting a balanced team is critical.

For skills budgeting purposes, here are targets for several standard leagues:

BATTING	PX	RSpd	xBA	PA
12-team mixed	41	28	40	66
15-team mixed	41	26	39	64
12-team AL/NL	37	23	32	54

PITCHING	xERA*	K/9*	Sv	IP
12-team mixed	23	33	7	29
15-team mixed	20	30	6	30
12-team AL/NL	17	27	5	25

* Make sure the majority of these points come from starting pitchers.

As you draft players, track each MM score and keep a running total of all the categories. With the above goals, you'll be able to easily shift your in-draft targets if you see you are falling behind in any area.

And that's it.

So, it almost doesn't matter where this rollercoaster is headed. It could keep spiraling into the abyss. It could take a temporary reprieve. Or it could completely reverse direction. MP3 will keep your draft planning grounded. It's a process that will keep benchmarking to wherever the ride takes us in 2015.

If you have any relevant questions, random suggestions, insightful (or inciteful) comments, lucrative proposals, second opinions, idle threats or are lonely tonight and need a friend, feel free to become my Twitter follower @RonShandler.

Welcome to the 29th Edition

If you are new to the *Baseball Forecaster*, the sheer volume of information in this book may seem daunting. We don't recommend you assessing its contents over a single commute to work, particularly if you drive. But take your time to let it all sink in. The payoff—Yoo-Hoo or otherwise—is worth it.

But where to begin?

The best place to start is with the Encyclopedia of Fanalytics, which provides the foundation concepts for everything else that appears in these pages. It's our research archive and collective memory, just as valuable for veterans as it is for rookies. Take a cursory read-through, lingering at any section that looks interesting. You'll keep coming back here frequently.

Then just jump in. Close your eyes, flip to a random page, and put your finger down anywhere. Oh, look—Marcell Ozuna hit 23 HR in 2014 but with a 49% ground-ball rate. Without some more fly balls, don't bet the farm on a HR repeat.

See, you've learned something already!

What's New in 2015?

2015 First-Round Analysis: With a turn of the page, you'll find one of our big new features: Ron Shandler's analysis of the 2015 first-round player pool. As always, some interesting takes and even a few surprises.

First-Pitch Strikes: Pitcher boxes now contain data on First-Pitch Strike % (denoted as FpK in the box). Based on our research (see page 61), FpK serves as a useful validation of Ctl (bb/9).

Hard Contact Index: Batter boxes now contain hard contact data (HctX) that combines hard-hit ball data with contact rates, indexed to league average. For additional information, see page 24.

Potential Gainers and Faders: New charts that identify upcoming changes in performance by highlighting 2014 results that were in conflict with their corresponding skill indicators. For batters, Power Index (PX) vs. Expected Power Index (xPX) and hit rate (h%) vs. Hard Contact Index (HctX). For pitchers, BB/9 vs. First Pitch Strike percentage (FpK%) and K/9 vs. Swinging Strike percentage (SwK%).

Answers to questions, such as: Is walk rate a reliable leading indcator for batting average? Does pitch velocity really matter? Is there age discrimination at the top of the ADPs? What is a "composite player"? And much more.

Updates

The Baseball Forecaster page at BaseballHQ.com is at http://www.baseballhq.com/content/ron-shandlers-2015-baseball-forecaster. This is your headquarters for all information and updates regarding this book. Here you will find links to the following:

Content Updates: In a project of this magnitude, there are occasionally items that need clarification or correction. You can find them here.

Free Projections Update: As a buyer of this book, you get one free 2015 projections update. This is a set of Excel spreadsheet files that will be posted on or about March 1, 2015. Remember to keep the book handy when you visit as the access codes are hidden within these pages.

Electronic book: The complete PDF version of the *Forecaster*—plus Excel versions of most key charts—is available free to those who bought the book directly through the BaseballHQ.com website. These files will be available in January 2015 for most of you; those who have an annual standing order should have received the files just before Thanksgiving. Contact us if you do not receive information via e-mail about accessing them. Information about the e-book version can be found at the above website.

If you purchased the book through an online vendor or bookstore, or would like these files earlier, you can purchase them from us for $9.95. Call 1-800-422-7820 for more information.

Beyond the Forecaster

The *Baseball Forecaster* is just the beginning. The following companion products and services are described in more detail in the back of the book.

BaseballHQ.com is our home website. It provides regular updates to everything in this book, including daily updated statistics and projections. A subscription to BHQ gets you more than 1,000 articles over the course of a year, customized tools, access to data going back over a decade, plus much more.

First Pitch Forums are a series of conferences we run all over the country, where you can meet top industry analysts and network with fellow fantasy leaguers in your area. We'll be in cities from coast to coast in February and March. Our big annual symposium at the Arizona Fall League is the first weekend in November.

The 10th edition of the *Minor League Baseball Analyst*, by Rob Gordon and Jeremy Deloney, is the minor league companion to this book, with stat boxes for 1,000-plus prospects, essays on prospects, lists upon lists, and more. It is available in January.

We still have copies available of *How to Value Players for Rotisserie Baseball*, Art McGee's ground-breaking book on valuation theory. They are still on closeout at 50% off.

RotoLab is the best draft software on the market and comes pre-loaded with our projections.

Even further beyond the Forecaster

Visit us on *Facebook* at http://www.facebook.com/baseballhq. "Like" the BaseballHQ page for updates, photos from events and links to other important stuff.

Follow us on *Twitter*. Site updates are tweeted from @BaseballHQ and many of our writers share their insights from their own personal accounts. We even have a list to follow: www.twitter.com/BaseballHQ/lists/hq-staff.

But back to baseball. Almost 300 pages await.

—*Brent Hershey and Ray Murphy*

A Critical Analysis of the $30/First Round Player Pool

by Ron Shandler

Each year's Average Draft Position (ADP) rankings represent the public consensus of how players are going to perform in the upcoming season.

Based on the 11-year report card of this pre-season effort, our success rate for correctly identifying the top 15 players has been a dismal 35%.

This is our track record on the game's best players. One would think these should be the *most* projectable. Yet, you can scan the lists on pages 51-52 and see that the public has been wrong on an average of 10 of the 15 players, every single year.

We're not any better with the $30-plus investments in auction leagues.

Many analysts rationalize this phenomenon. They say that the players ranked in the top 15 are just the ones with the *highest odds* of earning first round/$30 value. Still, can we be happy with 35% odds? It's tough to relinquish the other 65% to the rest of field and be satisfied that we've done the best possible job.

Why is our success rate so low? It's primarily because of each year's surprise performances (which we can't control) and the irresistible pull of "recency bias" (which we can).

How do we fight it? One way is to construct an objective list of the best players, and then conduct a critical analysis to uncover hidden pockets of profitability and risk. That's what I've done here.

The following are the projected top 15 players for 2015 based on an integrated ranking of projected Rotisserie values and reliability-adjusted Mayberry scores. This is not necessarily where you should draft them; it's where the dollars and Mayberry say they belong. In the next step, I get to toss in my two cents.

(Mayberry scores and projected Rotisserie values appear in parentheses.)

#1
(Finished 2014 ranked #4): In Rotisserie terms, **Mike Trout**'s (5545 AAB; $41) numbers have declined in each of the two years since his 2012 breakout explosion. But that explosion set a pretty high bar, and even his 2014 comedown has set a higher floor than any other player. It's tough to find a way—sans injury—that he would finish out of the first round. He seems like a lock, if not in the top 3 then surely in the top 15. *Recommendation:* There is nobody else that fits here.

#2
(#10): An August rib injury nearly slowed down **Andrew McCutchen** (4455 AAB; $38). But he remains one of the highest skilled, lowest risk players around. *Recommendation:* There will be some mixed opinion about this slot—expect votes for Kershaw and Stanton, maybe Miggy—but McCutchen provides the best balance of skill, track record and risk.

#3
(#2): I would never draft a pitcher in the first round. The early rounds are the only chances you get to stockpile big counting stats for batters, an increasingly scarce commodity. You can backfill your roster with LIMA-caliber relievers and still fare very well in ERA and WHIP. But HRs, Runs, RBI and to a lesser extent steals, need to be built up early.

That said, **Clayton Kershaw** (5505 BAA; $38) does represent a highly dominant commodity among pitchers. He gives you strikeouts. His big innings provide a strong ERA/WHIP foundation, which allows you to take on more risk later on. An argument can be made to draft him here. For some, he could be justifiable at #2. For me, he'd have to drop to the second round; I won't give up the chance to roster a 4-5 category banger in the top 15. *Recommendation:* I'm not going to stop you if you're committed, but the above arguments remain.

#4
(#62): Had **Paul Goldschmidt** (5255 BAB; $34) not gotten hurt, he was on pace to post a 28/101/13/.300 season. Yes, not quite the 36-HR output he posted in 2013, but still about $34 in earnings. The broken hand allegedly won't be an issue in 2015. *Recommendation:* There is a little bit of risk here—you never know with injuries—but this still looks like a $30+ first-rounder to me.

#5
(#12): **Carlos Gomez** (4535 BBB; $36) still draws his fair share of naysayers, but there is little in his profile that disputes his presence in the top 15. This ranking may be a bit high for some, but there are not too many 25/40 guys out there. *Recommendation:* Odds are he will go lower, but the only difference between him and Trout in 2014 were his situation-dependent runs and RBIs. Any additional help from his teammates could pump up those totals. Grab him any lower than 5th/$36 and you're looking at potential profit.

#6
(#6): I personally would not include two pitchers in the first round, but **Felix Hernandez** (5405 AAA; $33) kept rising to the top no matter what evaluation method I used. However, it makes sense. He's posted that AAA reliability grade for *six straight years!* Add in the possibility that Seattle could build on this year's showing and you can see where there could be more upside here. *Recommendation:* Felix will not likely go in many first rounds, or perhaps not exceed $30, because owners will see 2014 as just a random great season by a consistently good pitcher (read: he'll regress). You might consider him in the early 2nd round if Kershaw is gone. In auctions, go an extra buck.

#7
(#3): At a mock draft at First Pitch Arizona 2014, Mastersball's Lawr Michaels selected **Michael Brantley** (3355 AAC; $33) with the 6th pick and everyone gave him crap. But given today's dearth of offense, any supportable .300 BA with some pop and speed holds great value. He's in this discussion even if he regresses normally. *Recommendation:* This is a clear profit opportunity if his ADP slips, which I suspect it will. Most players are expected to regress after career years, but we often overestimate the extent of that regression. At 28, this is not Victor Martinez.

#8
(#43): Yes, we are bullish on **Starling Marte** (4535 BBB; $33), perhaps more than most. But you can experience the excitement emanating from his player box for yourself. *Recommendation:* I can guarantee that dozens of people are going to write me and say, "Ron, you idiot. Now that he's on this list

I'll never be able to sneak him onto my roster." The appropriate response if you're sniped should be, "Since when do you take advice from the guy who dissed Mike Trout?"

#9
(#1): **Jose Altuve** (1545 AAD; $38) is only the second pure speedster since 2004 to finish #1; Jose Reyes in 2006, was the other. It's tough to see Altuve as a top player because he doesn't put up the sexy power stats. But stolen bases (and BA!) are scarce commodities concentrated within a small group of players. For what it's worth, Reyes did follow up with strong earnings the next two years, finishing 8th in 2007 and 2nd in 2008. So there's that. *Recommendation:* That "D" in consistency makes him somewhat risky for the first round. But he's a reasonable grab early in the 2nd and could give you some profit.

#10
(#11): It's tough to think of **Miguel Cabrera** (5155 BAF; $37) as anything other than a first rounder. But last year's power outage begs the question as to whether nagging injuries might start becoming a part of his profile at age 32. I think his track record trumps that "F" in consistency, but I'd be more concerned with his current foot injury. *Recommendation:* I've been wrong before, but I consider him a risky pick here, and even moreso if he goes higher. His ADP and auction price will likely be driven too much by his reputation. For some players, we're swayed by the recency bias; for others, by the many years of stars in our eyes. The player pool is getting younger; you can find a more agile 27-year-old to draft here.

#11
(#26): The story is pretty much the same for **Robinson Cano** (3255 AAB; $32), as far as reputation driving value. The power outage here is a little more concerning, especially given his 53% ground ball rate, but the .300+ BA is the commodity we're chasing. *Recommendation:* When it comes to middle infielders, I want to always go young. Cano may be more proven, but I think I'd pass on him here and opt for a younger, less-expensive player later in the draft, like Rendon or Desmond, maybe even Dozier or Kipnis.

#12
(#24): **Jacoby Ellsbury**'s (2545 DBC; $31) questionable reliability grades are what push him this far down the rankings, but his numbers compare favorably with others among the elite. We just don't know whether the player with double-digit power is going to show up in 2015. And will he flirt with .300 or settle in at .270? That's a huge difference these days. *Recommendation:* Realistically, you should be happy with the 9-HR, .270 Ellsbury so long as he steals 40 bases and puts up 575 AB. Those are acceptable numbers at the end of the 1st round or early 2nd.

#13
(#8): You can typically pick holes in the performance of a player who comes out of nowhere. But **Jose Abreu** (5155 ACF; $31) is different. At 27, he arrived as a fully-formed commodity. What's more, he got better as the year went on. That is exceedingly rare for a "rookie" (not even Trout could claim that). *Recommendation:* Recency bias guarantees that someone is going to draft him in the first round, or go $30+. But here's the risk: he's still new and opposing teams had the entire off-season to review film to try to uncover a flaw. (Of course, I once said the

same thing about an Angels outfielder.) Heck, if I'm drafting 13th, I'm happy with him here. Given the names up this list, I might go as high as 9th. I live on the edge.

#14
(#9): It's surprising to find **Giancarlo Stanton** (5245 BBD; $30) ranked this far down. He will likely end up with an ADP in the top 5 and maybe as high as #2. Perhaps he deserves it, but he still only ranked 9th last year. And you can't ignore the reliability grades. *Recommendation:* If I'm drafting 3rd, and Trout and McCutchen are already gone, I will have a tough time not grabbing him. But I will have forgotten that I can't count on double-digit steals again. Or that 2014 was his first 500-AB season in three years. Or that I don't know how well he's recovered from the late season beaning (despite what the media noise tells us). And I might draft him anyway, because I won't be the idiot that passes on a guy who could hit 45 HRs.

#15
There are two players who are both deserving of the final slot, each for different reasons.

(#21) **Adam Jones** (4345 AAA; $28) is about the most overlooked, unsexy player there is. All he does is put up excellent, across-the-board numbers (4345), year after year (AAA). I'd be very happy with him in the 1st round.

(#15) **Anthony Rendon** (4445 ACD; $29) took a nice step up in 2014 and is still a good ways from his ceiling. I'd be happy drafting him in the 1st round too.

Odds are that public opinion—this spring's ADPs—will push others into the first round/$30 discussion. But exercise caution…

Be careful with players who are health or consistency risks, like Edwin Encarnacion (#41, 5155 CAA), Jose Bautista (#13, 5255 CBB) and Hanley Ramirez (#95, 4355 DBF).

Other upwardly-mobile players who might sneak into the discussion are Yasiel Puig (#44, 4445 ACB) and Anthony Rizzo (#32, 5145 AAF), but it's always risky to pay for a level of performance that a player has never achieved. Owners of Bryce Harper (#282, 4235 DBC) have gotten burned by that multiple times (but seem intent on jumping into the fire each year anyway).

Of course, the variable with the biggest impact will always be health. Given perfect health, players like Ryan Braun (#79, 4345 BBD), Matt Kemp (#34, 5245 FCD) and Troy Tulowitzki (#76, 5255 FDD) become immediate first round considerations. But we can't count on that.

And despite position scarcity, catchers are bad first round investments due to poor year-to-year consistency. Many of us chased Buster Posey (#35, 3155 BAD) two years ago and he disappointed, but he's appearing in first rounds yet again this year. Note that his 3155 MM score pales in comparison to every other player mentioned above.

This is how I see the $30+/first round pool as I sit here today. As events impact the baseball landscape over the winter, these may change. For instance, we're pretty bullish on Ryan Braun retaining much of his skill, assuming he's healthy. With a solid March, he might sneak into my first round. Similarly, if we see Goldchmidt nursing his hand, or Miggy limping, or Altuve moved from the lead-off spot… all bets are off.

I'll have a follow-up piece this spring at BaseballHQ.com.

CONSUMER ADVISORY

AN IMPORTANT MESSAGE FOR FANTASY LEAGUERS
REGARDING PROPER USAGE OF THE *BASEBALL FORECASTER*

This document is provided in compliance with authorities to outline the prospective risks and hazards possible in the event that the Baseball Forecaster is used incorrectly. Please be aware of these potentially dangerous situations and avoid them. The publisher assumes no risk related to any financial loss or stress-induced illnesses caused by ignoring the items as described below.

1. The statistical projections in this book are intended as general guidelines, not as gospel. It is highly dangerous to use the projected statistics alone, and then live and die by them. That's like going to a ballgame, being given a choice of any seat in the park, and deliberately choosing the last row in the right field corner with an obstructed view. The projections are there, you can look at them, but there are so many better places to sit.

We have to publish those numbers, but they are stagnant, inert pieces of data. This book focuses on a live forecasting process that provides the tools so that you can understand the leading indicators and draw your own conclusions. If you at least attempt your own analyses of the data, and enhance them with the player commentaries, you can paint more robust, colorful pictures of the future.

In other words...

If you bought this book purely for the projected statistics and do not intend to spend at least some time learning about the process, then you might as well just buy an $8 magazine.

2. The player commentaries in this book are written by humans, just like you. These commentaries provide an overall evaluation of performance and likely future direction, but 60-word capsules cannot capture everything. Your greatest value will be to use these as a springboard to your own analysis of the data. Odds are, if you take the time, you'll find hidden indicators that we might have missed. Forecaster veterans say that this self-guided excursion is the best part of owning the book.

3. This book does not attempt to tackle playing time. Rather than making arbitrary decisions about how roles will shake out, the focus is on performance. The playing time projections presented here are merely to help you better evaluate each player's talent. Our online preseason projections update provides more current AB and IP expectations based on how roles are being assigned.

4. The dollar values in this book are intended solely for player-to-player comparisons. They are not driven by a finite pool of playing time—which is required for valuation systems to work properly—so they cannot be used for bid values to be used in your own draft.

There are two reasons for this:

a. The finite pool of players that will generate the finite pool of playing time will not be determined until much closer to Opening Day. And, if we are to be brutally honest, there is really no such thing as a finite pool of players.

b. Your particular league's construction will drive the values; a $10 player in a 10-team mixed league will not be the same as a $10 player in a 12-team NL-only league.

Note that book dollar values also cannot be compared to those published at BaseballHQ.com as the online values are generated by a more finite player pool.

5. Do not pass judgment on the effectiveness of this book based on the performance of a few individual players. The test, rather, is on the collective predictive value of the book's methods. Are players with better base skills more likely to produce good results than bad ones? Years of research suggest that the answer is "yes." Does that mean that every high skilled player will do well? No. But many more of them will perform well than will the average low-skilled player. You should always side with the better percentage plays, but recognize that there are factors we cannot predict. Good decisions that beget bad outcomes do not invalidate the methods.

6. If your copy of this book is not marked up and dog-eared by Draft Day, you probably did not get as much value out of it as you might have.

7. This edition of the Forecaster is not intended to provide absorbency for spills of more than 7.5 ounces.

8. This edition is not intended to provide stabilizing weight for more than 18 sheets of 20 lb. paper in winds of more than 45 mph.

9. The pages of this book are not recommended for avian waste collection. In independent laboratory studies, 87% of migratory water fowl refused to excrete on interior pages, even when coaxed.

10. This book, when rolled into a cylindrical shape, is not intended to be used as a weapon for any purpose, including but not limited to insect extermination, canine training or to influence bidding behavior at a fantasy draft.

For new readers...

Everything begins here. The information in the following pages represents the foundation that powers everything we do.

You'll learn about the underlying concepts for our unique mode of analysis. You'll find answers to long-asked questions, interesting insights into what makes players tick, and innovative applications for all this newfound knowledge.

This Encyclopedia is organized into several logical sections:

1. Fundamentals
2. Batters
3. Pitchers
4. Prospects
5. Gaming

Enough talking. Jump in. Remember to breathe.

For veteran readers...

As we do in each edition, this year's ever-expanding Encyclopedia includes relevant research results we've published over the past year. We've added some of the essays from the Research Abstracts and Gaming Abstracts sections in the 2014 *Forecaster* as well as some other essays from BaseballHQ.com.

And we continue to mold the content to best fit how fantasy leaguers use their information. Many readers consider this their fantasy information bible.

Okay, time to jump-start the analytical process for 2015. Remember to breathe—it's always good advice.

Abbreviations

Fundamentals

What is Fanalytics?

Fanalytics is the scientific approach to fantasy baseball analysis. A contraction of "fantasy" and "analytics," fanalytic gaming might be considered a mode of play that requires a more strategic and quantitative approach to player analysis and game decisions.

The three key elements of fanalytics are:

1. Performance analysis
2. Performance forecasting
3. Gaming analysis

For performance analysis, we tap into the vast knowledge of the sabermetric community. Founded by Bill James, this area of study provides objective and progressive new ways to assess skill. What we do in this book is called "component skills analysis." We break down performance into its component parts, then reverse-engineer it back into the traditional measures with which we are more familiar.

Our forecasting methodology is one part science and one part art. We start with a computer-generated baseline for each player. We then make subjective adjustments based on a variety of factors, such as discrepancies in skills indicators and historical guidelines gleaned from more than 20 years of research. We don't rely on a rigid model; our method forces us to get our hands dirty.

You might say that our brand of forecasting is more about finding logical journeys than blind destinations.

Gaming analysis is an integrated approach designed to help us win our fantasy leagues. It takes the knowledge gleaned from the first two elements and adds the strategic and tactical aspect of each specific fantasy game format.

Definitions

Base Performance Indicator (BPI): A statistical formula that measures an isolated aspect of a player's situation-independent raw skill or a gauge that helps capture the effects that random chance has on skill.

Leading Indicator: A statistical formula that can be used to project potential future performance.

Noise: Irrelevant or meaningless pieces of information that can distort the results of an analysis. In news, this is opinion or rumor that can invalidate valuable information. In forecasting, these are unimportant elements of statistical data that can artificially inflate or depress a set of numbers.

Situation Independent: Describing performance that is separate from the context of team, ballpark, or other outside variables. Strikeouts and walks, as they are unaffected by the performance of a batter's team, are often considered situation independent stats. Conversely, RBIs are situation dependent because individual performance varies greatly by the performance of other batters on the team (you can't drive in runs if there is nobody on base). Situation independent gauges are important for us to be able to isolate and judge performance on its own merits.

Soft Skills: BPIs with levels below established minimums for acceptable performance.

Surface Stats: Traditional gauges that the mainstream media uses to measure performance. Stats like batting average, wins, and ERA only touch the surface of a player's skill and often distort the truth. To uncover a player's true skill, you have to look at component skills statistics.

Component Skills Analysis

Familiar gauges like HR and ERA have long been used to measure skill. In fact, these gauges only measure the outcome of an individual event, or series of events. They represent statistical output. They are "surface stats."

Raw skill is the talent beneath the stats, the individual elements of a player's makeup. Players use these skills to create the individual events, or components, that we record using measures like HR and ERA. Our approach:

1. It's not about batting average; it's about seeing the ball and making contact. We target hitters based on elements such as their batting eye (walks to strikeouts ratio), how often they make contact and the type of contact they make. We then combine these components into an "expected batting average." By comparing each hitter's actual BA to how he should be performing, we can draw conclusions about the future.

2. It's not about home runs; it's about power. From the perspective of a round bat meeting a round ball, it may be only a fraction of an inch at the point of contact that makes the difference between a HR or a long foul ball. When a ball is hit safely, often it is only a few inches that separate a HR from a double. We tend to neglect these facts in our analyses, although the outcomes—the doubles, triples, long fly balls—may be no less a measure of that batter's raw power skill. We must incorporate all these components to paint a complete picture.

3. It's not about ERA; it's about getting the ball over the plate and keeping it in the park. Forget ERA. You want to draft pitchers who walk few batters (Control), strike out many (Dominance) and succeed at both in tandem (Command). You also want pitchers who keep the ball on the ground (because home runs are bad). All of this translates into an "expected ERA" that you can use to compare to a pitcher's actual performance.

4. It's never about wins. For pitchers, winning ballgames is less about skill than it is about offensive support. As such, projecting wins is a very high-risk exercise and valuing hurlers based on their win history is dangerous. Target skill; wins will come.

5. It's not about saves; it's about opportunity first and skills second. While the highest-skilled pitchers have the best potential to succeed as closers, they still have to be given the ball with the game on the line in the 9th inning, and that is a decision left to others. Over the past 10 years, about 40% of relievers drafted for saves failed to hold the role for the entire season. The lesson: Don't take chances on draft day. There will always be saves in the free agent pool.

Accounting for "luck"

Luck has been used as a catch-all term to describe random chance. When we use the term here, we're talking about unexplained variances that shape the statistics. While these variances may be random, they are also often measurable and projectable.

To get a better read on "luck," we use formulas that capture the external variability of the data.

Through our research and the work of others, we have learned that when raw skill is separated from statistical output, what's remaining is often unexplained variance. The aggregate totals of many of these variances, for all players, is often a constant. For instance, while a pitcher's ERA might fluctuate, the rate at which his opposition's batted balls fall for hits will tend towards 30%. Large variances can be expected to regress towards 30%.

Why is all this important? Analysts complain about the lack of predictability of many traditional statistical gauges. The reason they find it difficult is that they are trying to project performance using gauges that are loaded with external noise. Raw skills gauges are more pure and follow better defined trends during a player's career. Then, as we get a better handle on the variances—explained and unexplained—we can construct a complete picture of what a player's statistics really mean.

Baseball Forecasting

Forecasting in perspective

Forecasts. Projections. Predictions. Prognostications. The crystal ball aura of this process conceals the fact it is a process. We might define it as "the systematic process of determining likely end results." At its core, it's scientific.

However, the *outcomes* of forecasted events are what is most closely scrutinized, and are used to judge the success or failure of the forecast. That said, as long as the process is sound, the forecast has done the best job it can do. *In the end, forecasting is about analysis, not prophecy.*

Baseball performance forecasting is inherently a high-risk exercise with a very modest accuracy rate. This is because the process involves not only statistics, but also unscientific elements, from random chance to human volatility. And even from within the statistical aspect there are multiple elements that need to be evaluated, from skill to playing time to a host of external variables.

Every system is comprised of the same core elements:

- Players will tend to perform within the framework of past history and/or trends.
- Skills will develop and decline according to age.
- Statistics will be shaped by a player's health, expected role and venue.

While all systems are built from these same elements, they also are constrained by the same limitations. We are all still trying to project a bunch of human beings, each one...

- with his own individual skill set
- with his own rate of growth and decline
- with his own ability to resist and recover from injury
- limited to opportunities determined by other people
- generating a group of statistics largely affected by external noise.

Research has shown that the best accuracy rate that can be attained by any system is about 70%. In fact, a simple system that uses three-year averages adjusted for age ("Marcel") can attain a success rate of 65%. This means all the advanced systems are fighting for occupation of the remaining 5%.

But there is a bigger question... *what exactly are we measuring?* When we search for accuracy, what does that mean? In fact, any quest for accuracy is going to run into a brick wall of paradoxes:

- If a slugging average projection is dead on, but the player hits 10 fewer HRs than expected (and likely, 20 more doubles), is that a success or a failure?
- If a projection of hits and walks allowed by a pitcher is on the mark, but the bullpen and defense implodes, and inflates his ERA by a run, is that a success or a failure?
- If the projection of a speedster's rate of stolen base success is perfect, but his team replaces the manager with one that doesn't run, and the player ends up with half as many SBs as expected, is that a success or a failure?
- If a batter is traded to a hitters' ballpark and all the touts project an increase in production, but he posts a statistical line exactly what would have been projected had he not been traded to that park, is that a success or a failure?
- If the projection for a bullpen closer's ERA, WHIP and peripheral numbers is perfect, but he saves 20 games instead of 40 because the GM decided to bring in a high-priced free agent at the trading deadline, is that a success or a failure?
- If a player is projected to hit .272 in 550 AB and only hits .249, is that a success or failure? Most will say "failure." But wait a minute! The real difference is only two hits per month. That shortfall of 23 points in batting average is because a fielder might have made a spectacular play, or a screaming liner might have been hit right at someone, or a long shot to the outfield might have been held up by the wind... once every 14 games. Does that constitute "failure"?

Even if we were to isolate a single statistic that measures "overall performance" and run our accuracy tests on it, the results will still be inconclusive.

According to OPS, these players are virtually identical:

BATTER	HR	RBI	SB	BA	OBA	SLG	OPS
Gomez,C	23	73	34	.284	.356	.477	.833
Upton,J	29	102	8	.270	.342	.491	.833
Altuve,J	7	56	56	.341	.377	.453	.830
Duda,L	30	92	3	.253	.349	.481	.830

If I projected Altuve-caliber stats and ended up with Lucas Duda's numbers, I'd hardly call that an accurate projection, especially if my fantasy team was in dire need of steals and batting average.

According to Roto dollars, these players are also dead-on:

BATTER	HR	RBI	Runs	SB	BA	R$
Puig,Y	16	69	92	11	.296	$22
Harrison,J	13	52	77	18	.315	$22
Donaldson,J	29	98	93	8	.255	$22
Desmond,I	24	91	73	24	.255	$22

It's not so simple for someone to claim they have accurate projections. And so, it is best to focus on the bigger picture, especially when it comes to winning at fantasy baseball.

More on this: "The Great Myths of Projective Accuracy"

http://www.baseballhq.com/great-myths-projective-accuracy

Baseball Forecaster's forecasting process

We are all about component skills. Our approach is to assemble these evaluators in such a way that they can be used to validate our observations, analyze their relevance and project a likely future direction.

In a perfect world, if a player's raw skills improve, then so should his surface stats. If his skills decline, then his stats should follow as well. But, sometimes a player's skill indicators increase while his surface stats decline. These variances may be due to a variety of factors.

Our forecasting process is based on the expectation that events tend to move towards universal order. Surface stats will eventually approach their skill levels. Unexplained variances will regress to a mean. And from this, we can identify players whose performance may potentially change.

For most of us, this process begins with the previous year's numbers. Last season provides us with a point of reference, so it's a natural way to begin the process of looking at the future. Component skills analysis allows us to validate those numbers. A batter with few HRs but a high linear weighted power level has a good probability of improving his future HR output. A pitcher whose ERA was poor while his command ratio was solid is a good bet for ERA improvement.

Of course, these leading indicators do not always follow the rules. There are more shades of grey than blacks and whites. When indicators are in conflict—for instance, a pitcher who is displaying both a rising strikeout rate and a rising walk rate— then we have to find ways to sort out what these indicators might be saying.

It is often helpful to look at leading indicators in a hierarchy, of sorts. In fact, a hierarchy of the most important pitching base performance indicators might look like this: Command (k/bb), Dominance (k/9), Control (bb/9) and GB/FB rate. For batters, contact rate might top the list, followed by power, walk rate and speed.

Assimilating additional research

Once we've painted the statistical picture of a player's potential, we then use additional criteria and research results to help us add some color to the analysis. These other criteria include the player's health, age, changes in role, ballpark and a variety of other factors. We also use the research results described in the following pages. This research looks at things like traditional periods of peak performance and breakout profiles.

The final element of the process is assimilating the news into the forecast. This is the element that many fantasy leaguers tend to rely on most since it is the most accessible. However, it is also the element that provides the most noise. Players, management and the media have absolute control over what we are allowed to know. Factors such as hidden injuries, messy divorces and clubhouse unrest are routinely kept from us, while we are fed red herrings and media spam. *We will never know the entire truth.*

Quite often, all you are reading is just other people's opinions... a manager who believes that a player has what it takes to be a regular or a team physician whose diagnosis is that a player is healthy enough to play. These words from experts have some element of truth, but cannot be wholly relied upon to provide an accurate expectation of future events. As such, it is often helpful to develop an appropriate cynicism for what you read.

For instance, if a player is struggling for no apparent reason and there are denials about health issues, don't dismiss the possibility that an injury does exist. There are often motives for such news to be withheld from the public.

And so, as long as we do not know all the facts, we cannot dismiss the possibility that any one fact is true, no matter how often the media assures it, deplores it, or ignores it. Don't believe everything you read; use your own judgment. If your observations conflict with what is being reported, that's powerful insight that should not be ignored.

Also remember that nothing lasts forever in major league baseball. *Reality is fluid.* One decision begets a series of events that lead to other decisions. Any reported action can easily be reversed based on subsequent events. My favorite examples are announcements of a team's new bullpen closer. Those are about the shortest realities known to man.

We need the media to provide us with context for our analyses, and the real news they provide is valuable intelligence. But separating the news from the noise is difficult. In most cases, the only thing you can trust is how that player actually performs.

Embracing imprecision

Precision in baseball prognosticating is a fool's quest. There are far too many unexpected variables and noise that can render our projections useless. The truth is, the best we can ever hope for is to accurately forecast general tendencies and percentage plays.

However, even when you follow an 80% percentage play, for instance, you will still lose 20% of the time. That 20% is what skeptics use as justification to dismiss prognosticators; they conveniently ignore the more prevalent 80%. The paradox, of course, is that fantasy league titles are often won or lost by those exceptions. Still, long-term success dictates that you always chase the 80% and accept the fact that you will be wrong 20% of the time. Or, whatever that percentage play happens to be.

For fantasy purposes, playing the percentages can take on an even less precise spin. The best projections are often the ones that are just far enough away from the field of expectation to alter decision-making. In other words, it doesn't matter if I project Player X to bat .320 and he only bats .295; it matters that I project .320 and everyone else projects .280. Those who follow my less-accurate projection will go the extra dollar to acquire him in their draft.

Or, perhaps we should evaluate the projections based upon their intrinsic value. For instance, coming into 2014, would it have been more important for me to tell you that Adam Jones was going to hit 30 HRs or that Devin Mesoraco would hit 15 HRs? By season's end, the Jones projection would have been more accurate, but the Mesoraco projection—even though it was off by 10 HRs—would have been far more *valuable*. The Mesoraco projection might have persuaded you to go an extra buck on Draft Day, yielding far more profit.

And that has to be enough. Any tout who projects a player's statistics dead-on will have just been lucky with his dart throws that day.

Perpetuity

Forecasting is not an exercise that produces a single set of numbers. It is dynamic, cyclical and ongoing. Conditions are constantly changing and we must react to those changes by adjusting our expectations. A pre-season projection is just a snapshot in time. Once the first batter steps to the plate on Opening Day, that projection has become obsolete. Its value is merely to provide a starting point, a baseline for what is about to occur.

During the season, if a projection appears to have been invalidated by current performance, the process continues. It is then that we need to ask... What went wrong? What conditions have changed? In fact, has *anything* changed? We need to analyze the situation and revise our expectation, if necessary. This process must be ongoing.

When good projections go bad

Although we'd like to think otherwise, we cannot predict the future. All we can do is provide a sound process for constructing a "most likely expectation for future performance." If we've captured as much information as is available, used the best methodology and analyzed the results correctly, that's the best we can do.

All we can control is the process. We simply can't control outcomes.

However, one thing we *can* do is analyze the misses to see *why* they occurred. This is always a valuable exercise each year. It puts a proper focus on the variables that were out of our control as well as providing perspective on those players with whom we might have done a better job.

In general, we can organize these forecasting misses into several categories.

To demonstrate, here are all the players whose 2014 Rotisserie earnings varied from projections by at least $10.

The performances that exceeded expectation

Development beyond the growth trend: These are young players for whom we knew there was skill. Some of them were prized prospects in the past who have taken their time ascending the growth curve. Others were a surprise only because their performance spike arrived sooner than anyone anticipated... Jose Altuve, Michael Brantley, Todd Frazier, Corey Kluber, Devin Mesoraco, Marcell Ozuna, Anthony Rendon, Garrett Richards, Anthony Rizzo, Tyson Ross, Julio Teheran, Christian Yelich.

We'll toss Dallas Keuchel in this group as well. Although most people didn't see him coming—and our official projections were equally unimpressive—attendees to the First Pitch Forum 2014 spring tour heard us talk about how his swinging strike rate jumped from 6% in 2012 to 9% in 2013—the biggest jump in the AL. That along with his high 56% ground ball rate would put an end to his 5.00-plus ERAs. Now if only our projections would heed our First Pitch analyses.

Skilled players who just had big years: We knew these guys were good too; we just didn't anticipate they'd be this good... Dellin Betances, Chris Carter, Johnny Cueto, Brian Dozier, Wade Davis, Felix Hernandez, Jon Lester, Denard Span, Giancarlo Stanton.

Unexpected health: We knew these players had the goods; we just didn't know whether they'd be healthy or would stay healthy all year... Lorenzo Cain, Danny Duffy, Justin Morneau, Michael Morse, Albert Pujols, Ben Revere.

Unexpected playing time: These players had the skills—and may have even displayed them at some time in the past—but had questionable playing time potential coming into this season. Some benefited from another player's injury, a rookie who didn't pan out or leveraged a short streak into a regular gig... Dustin Ackley, Charlie Blackmon, Lonnie Chisenhall, Corey Dickerson, Lucas Duda, Scooter Gennett, Josh Harrison, J.D. Martinez, Tanner Roark.

Unexpected return to form: These players had the skills, having displayed them at some point in the past. But those skills had been M.I.A. long enough that we began to doubt that they'd ever return; our projections model got tired of waiting. Or those previous skills displays were so inconsistent that projecting an "up year" would have been a shot in the dark; our projections model got tired of guessing. Yes, "once you display a skill, you own it" but still... Dee Gordon, Phil Hughes, Casey McGehee, Drew Stubbs.

Unexpected role: This category is reserved for 2014's surprise closers. There are always some every year, relievers who are on nearly nobody's radar for front-line saves and are suddenly thrust into the role with great success (some did not clear the $10 hurdle but are worth mentioning anyway)... Cody Allen, Joaquin Benoit, Zach Britton, Santiago Casilla, Sean Doolittle, Neftali Feliz, Jake McGee, Mark Melancon, Jenrry Mejia, Jacob Petricka, Chad Qualls, Hector Rondon, Francisco Rodriguez, Joe Smith.

Unexpected discovery of the Fountain of Youth: These players should have been done, or nearly done, or at least headed down the far side of the bell curve. That's what the trends were pointing to. The trends were wrong... Jose Bautista, Marlon Byrd, Adam LaRoche, Victor Martinez, Pat Neshek, Jimmy Rollins.

Unexpected post-PED performance: Yeah, we didn't know how the Biogenesis bustees would fare in their first year back. But Nelson Cruz and Jhonny Peralta both exceeded projections by more than $10, as did post-post-PEDer Melky Cabrera. Everth Cabrera and Ryan Braun? Not so much.

Celebrate and claim we're geniuses: How these players put up the numbers they did is a mystery, but fantasy owners will likely chalk it up to their own superior scouting skills as they count their winnings. The truth is, who knows? However, the odds of a comparable follow-up for these players—particularly those with soft peripherals—will be small:

Let's start with Jose Abreu and Masahiro Tanaka. Both came with impressive foreign resumes but we all hedged on our projections, which was the prudent thing to do. After all, Abreu might have struggled in the cold Chicago April and been benched. Nobody took Tanaka's 24-0 record in Japan seriously. The duo blew all our expectations out the window.

Jake Arrieta was one of several former Orioles prospects who were supposed to make up the core of their rotation by now. Only Chris Tillman made it, though Zach Britton did find a role. Brian Matusz fell short, and Dylan Bundy and Kevin Gausman are still on the outside looking in. Arrieta was one of the lesser-skilled members of this group, yet he's the only one to taste a 100+ BPV as a starter. We're so smart.

Collin McHugh was rated as a 7D prospect by our Minor League Baseball Analyst in 2012. In 2013, he was downgraded to a 6B. And as he was about to enter the Astros rotation for real this year, he was further downgraded to a 6C. For all those scoring at home, a 6C is a "platoon player" (one step down from an "average regular") with a "50% probability of reaching that potential." Jeff Luhnow is a genius.

Jacob DeGrom and Matt Shoemaker weren't on our radar either. They just weren't. It's so easy these days to put up good pitching numbers. </sarcasm>

The performances that fell short of expectation

The DL denizens: These are players who got hurt, may not have returned fully healthy, or may have never been fully healthy (whether they'd admit it or not)... Homer Bailey, Brandon Belt, Carlos Beltran, Michael Bourn, Ryan Braun, Jay Bruce, Everth Cabrera, Matt Cain, Shin-Soo Choo, Tony Cingrani, Gerrit Cole, Allen Craig, Michael Cuddyer, Yu Darvish, Jose Fernandez, Prince Fielder, Paul Goldschmidt, Carlos Gonzalez, Gio Gonzalez, Josh Hamilton, Bryce Harper, Corey Hart, Eric Hosmer, Casey Janssen, Jason Kipnis, Mat Latos, Brett Lawrie, Cliff Lee, Will Middlebrooks, Mike Minor, Yadier Molina, Will Myers, Bobby Parnell, Brandon Phillips, Wilin Rosario, Jarrod Saltalamacchia, Anibal Sanchez, Nick Swisher, Mark Trumbo, Shane Victorino, Joey Votto, Michael Wacha, Matt Wieters, David Wright, Ryan Zimmerman.

(Some of these players seemed to be putting up sub-par numbers before they actually hit the DL. Some may have been playing through the hurt before breaking down.)

Note that there are 45 players on this list (up from 39 last year). These were the DL denizens who lost at least $10 of value. There were dozens more that lost less. In all of the Top 300 coming into the season, 143 players lost time to the DL (and another 15 to demotion or release). The 53% attrition set a new record for losses.

Accelerated skills erosion: These are players who we knew were on the downside of their careers or had soft peripherals but who we did not think would plummet so quickly. In some cases, there were injuries involved, but all in all, 2014 might be the beginning of the end for some of these guys... Grant Balfour, Carlos Beltran, Matt Holliday, Dustin Pedroia (presumably, unless you think his thumb injury has been long-term and chronic), Alex Rios, Joe Nathan, Alfonso Soriano.

And Justin Verlander? Can we put Verlander in here? I don't know. This season looks remarkably similar to 2008, a performance he bounced back from with a vengeance. At 31, it's tough to say his southern trajectory is permanent, but that arm has weathered an average of nearly 220 IP for nine straight years, not including post-season play.

Inflated expectations: Here are players who we really should not have expected much more than what they produced. Some had short or spotty track records, others had soft peripherals coming into 2014, and still others were inflated by media hype. Yes, for some of these, it was "What the heck was I thinking?" For others, we've almost come to expect players to ascend the growth curve faster these days. (You're 23 and you haven't broken out yet? What's the problem??) The bottom line is that player performance trends simply don't progress or regress in a straight line; still, the BPI trends were intriguing enough to take a leap of faith. We were wrong... Domonic Brown, Clay Buchholz, Matt Carpenter, Chris Davis (who surpassed even our most pessimistic regression scenario), Alejandro De Aza, Chris Denorfia, Marco Estrada, Freddie Freeman, Jedd Gyorko, Aaron Hill, Jed Lowrie, Brad Miller, Shelby Miller, Daniel Nava, Danny Salazar, Nate Schierholtz, Jean Segura (though there were additional mitigating circumstances in his case), Dan Straily, Will Venable.

If you want to witness the recency bias in action, count how many of the above names had just one great season—in 2013. We count... nearly all of them. Perhaps that begs for a forecasting model that does not place so much weight on the immediate past season's performance.

Misplaced regression: Sometimes, we're so bullish on a player that we ignore the potential for regression within the bounds of normal random variance. Gravity is a powerful force, for... Elvis Andrus, Miguel Cabrera, Kenley Jansen, Stephen Strasburg.

Unexpected loss of role: This category is usually composed of closers who lost their job, sometimes through no fault of their own... Grant Balfour (again), Ernesto Frieri, Jason Grilli, Jim Johnson, Nate Jones, Joakim Soria, Jose Veras. I suppose we can also toss Kendrys Morales in here, who neither had a role, nor a team, until June.

Throw our hands up and yell at the TV: These are the players for whom there is little explanation for what happened. We can speculate that they hid an injury, went off of PEDs, or just didn't have their head on right in 2014. For some, it was just the turn of an unlucky card this year:

Billy Butler finally saw his home run output achieve harmony with his 50% ground ball rate. His plate patience also tumbled, leaving him with the lowest OBP of his career. At the ripe old age of 28, he's fast becoming irrelevant.

We've already listed Jim Johnson among the failed closers who lost the role (sometimes through no fault but their own), but let's get real here. Yes, he did not have the perfect skills set to close, but he did post BPVs of 84 and 103 in his two 50-save seasons. Who would've thought he'd completely collapse while moving to a better team and ballpark?

We could have made an excuse for Joe Mauer and listed him among the DL Denizens. However, his season was so out of character even before the 1-month DL stint that it can't just be written off. We were convinced that moving out from behind the plate full-time would be the elixir to boost his offensive numbers.

About fantasy baseball touts

As a group, there is a strong tendency for all pundits to provide numbers that are publicly palatable, often at the expense of realism. That's because committing to either end of the range of expectation poses a high risk. Few touts will put their credibility on the line like that, even though we all know that those outliers are inevitable. Among our projections, you will find few .350 hitters and 70-steal speedsters. *Someone* is going to post a sub-2.50 ERA next year, but damned if any of us will commit to that. So we take an easier road. We'll hedge our numbers or split the difference between two equally possible outcomes.

In the world of prognosticating, this is called the *comfort zone*. This represents the outer tolerances for the public acceptability of a set of numbers. In most circumstances, even if the evidence is outstanding, prognosticators will not stray from within the comfort zone.

As for this book, occasionally we do commit to outlying numbers when we feel the data support it. But on the whole, most of the numbers here can be nearly as cowardly as everyone else's. We get around this by providing "color" to the projections in the capsule commentaries. That is where you will find the players whose projection has the best potential to stray beyond the limits of the comfort zone.

As analyst John Burnson once wrote: "The issue is not the success rate for one player, but the success rate for all players. No system is 100% reliable, and in trying to capture the outliers, you weaken the middle and thereby lose more predictive pull than you gain. At some level, everyone is an exception!"

Formula for consistent success

Anyone can win a league in any given season. Winning once proves very little, especially in redraft leagues. True success has to be defined as the ability to win consistently. It is a feat in itself to reach the mountaintop, but the battle isn't truly won unless you can stay atop that peak while others keep trying to knock you off.

What does it take to win that battle? We surveyed 12 of the most prolific fantasy champions in national experts league play. Here is how they rated six variables:

	Percent ranked			
	1-2	3-4	5-6	Score
Better in-draft strategy/tactics	77%	15%	7%	5.00
Better sense of player value	46%	46%	7%	4.15
Better luck	46%	23%	31%	3.85
Better grasp of contextual elements that affect players	31%	38%	31%	3.62
Better in-season roster management	31%	38%	31%	3.54
Better player projections	12%	31%	54%	2.62

Validating Performance

Performance validation criteria

The following is a set of support variables that helps determine whether a player's statistical output is an accurate reflection of his skills. From this we can validate or refute stats that vary from expectation, essentially asking, is this performance "fact or fluke?"

1. Age: Is the player at the stage of development when we might expect a change in performance?

2. Health: Is he coming off an injury, reconditioned and healthy for the first time in years, or a habitual resident of the disabled list?

3. Minor league performance: Has he shown the potential for greater things at some level of the minors? Or does his minor league history show a poor skill set that might indicate a lower ceiling?

4. Historical trends: Have his skill levels over time been on an upswing or downswing?

5. Component skills indicators: Looking beyond batting averages and ERAs, what do his support ratios look like?

6. Ballpark, team, league: Pitchers going to Texas will see their ERA spike. Pitchers going to PETCO Park will see their ERA improve.

7. Team performance: Has a player's performance been affected by overall team chemistry or the environment fostered by a winning or losing club?

8. Batting stance, pitching style: Has a change in performance been due to a mechanical adjustment?

9. Usage pattern, lineup position, role: Has a change in RBI opportunities been a result of moving further up or down in the batting order? Has pitching effectiveness been impacted by moving from the bullpen to the rotation?

10. Coaching effects: Has the coaching staff changed the way a player approaches his conditioning, or how he approaches the game itself?

11. Off-season activity: Has the player spent the winter frequenting workout rooms or banquet tables?

12. Personal factors: Has the player undergone a family crisis? Experienced spiritual rebirth? Given up red meat? Taken up testosterone?

Skills ownership

Once a player displays a skill, he owns it. That display could occur at any time—earlier in his career, back in the minors, or even in winter ball play. And while that skill may lie dormant after its initial display, the potential is always there for him to tap back into that skill at some point, barring injury or age. That dormant skill can reappear at any time given the right set of circumstances.

Caveats:

1. The initial display of skill must have occurred over an extended period of time. An isolated 1-hit shut-out in Single-A ball amidst a 5.00 ERA season is not enough. The shorter the display of skill in the past, the more likely it can be attributed to random chance. The longer the display, the more likely that any re-emergence is for real.

2. If a player has been suspected of using performance enhancing drugs at any time, all bets are off.

Corollaries:

1. Once a player displays a vulnerability or skills deficiency, he owns that as well. That vulnerability could be an old injury problem, an inability to hit breaking pitches, or just a tendency to go into prolonged slumps.

2. The probability of a player correcting a skills deficiency declines with each year that deficiency exists.

Normal Production Variance *(Patrick Davitt)*

Even if we have a perfectly accurate understanding of a player's "normal" performance level, his actual performance can and does vary widely over any particular 150-game span—including the 150-game span we call "a season." A .300 career hitter can perform in a range of .250-.350, a 40-HR hitter from 30-50, and a 3.70/1.15 pitcher from 2.60/0.95 to 6.00/1.55. And all of these results must be considered "normal."

Contract year performance *(Tom Mullooly)*

There is a contention that players step up their game when they are playing for a contract. Research looked at contract year players and their performance during that year as compared to career levels. Of the batters and pitchers studied, 53% of the batters performed as if they were on a salary drive, while only 15% of the pitchers exhibited some level of contract year behavior.

How do players fare *after* signing a large contract (minimum $4M per year)? Research from 2005-2008 revealed that only 30% of pitchers and 22% of hitters exhibited an increase of more than 15% in BPV after signing a large deal either with their new team, or re-signing with the previous team. But nearly half of the pitchers (49%) and nearly half of the hitters (47%) saw a drop in BPV of more than 15% in the year after signing.

Risk management and reliability grades

Forecasts are constructed with the best data available, but there are factors that can impact the variability. One way we manage this risk is to assign each player Reliability Grades. The more certainty we see in a data set, the higher the reliability grades assigned to that player. The following variables are evaluated:

Health: Players with a history of staying healthy and off the DL are valuable to own. Unfortunately, while the ability to stay healthy can be considered skill, it is not very projectable. We can track the number of days spent on the disabled list and draw rough conclusions. The grades in the player boxes also include an adjustment for older players, who have a higher likelihood of getting hurt. That is the only forward-looking element of the grade.

"A" level players would have accumulated fewer than 30 days on the major league DL over the past five years. "F" grades go to those who've spent more than 120 days on the DL. Recent DL stays are given a heavier weight in the calculation.

Playing Time and Experience (PT/Exp): The greater the pool of MLB history to draw from, the greater our ability to construct a viable forecast. Length of service—and consistent service—is important. So players who bounce up and down from the majors to the minors are higher risk players. And rookies are all high risk.

For batters, we simply track plate appearances. Major league PAs have greater weight than minor league PAs. "A" level players would have averaged at least 550 major league PAs per year over the past three years. "F" graded players averaged fewer than 250 major league PA per year.

For pitchers, workload can be a double-edged sword. On one hand, small IP samples are deceptive in providing a read on a pitcher's true potential. Even a consistent 65-inning reliever can be considered higher risk since it would take just one bad outing to skew an entire season's work.

On the flipside, high workload levels also need to be monitored, especially in the formative years of a pitcher's career. Exceeding those levels elevates the risk of injury, burnout, or breakdown. So, tracking workload must be done within a range of innings. The grades capture this.

Consistency: Consistent performers are easier to project and garner higher reliability grades. Players that mix mediocrity with occasional flashes of brilliance or badness generate higher risk projections. Even those who exhibit a consistent upward or downward trend cannot be considered truly consistent as we do not know whether those trends will continue. Typically, they don't.

"A" level players are those whose runs created per game level (xERA for pitchers) has fluctuated by less than half a run during each of the past three years. "F" grades go to those whose RC/G or xERA has fluctuated by two runs or more.

Remember that these grades have nothing to do with quality of performance; they strictly refer to confidence in our expectations. So a grade of **AAA** for Kyle Kendrick, for instance, only means that there is a high probability he will perform as poorly as we've projected.

Reliability and age

Peak batting reliability occurs at ages 29 and 30, followed by a minor decline for four years. So, to draft the most reliable batters, and maximize the odds of returning at least par value on your investments, you should target the age range of 28-34.

The most reliable age range for pitchers is 29-34. While we are forever looking for "sleepers" and hot prospects, it is very risky to draft any pitcher under 27 or over 35.

Evaluating Reliability *(Bill Macey)*

Fantasy baseball owners are like investors who are always looking for a good return. Calculating our expected return includes assessing the risk of our draft-day investment.

Managing risk leads to two kinds of valuation adjustments. We downgrade talented players we believe to be higher injury risks, who have a history of inconsistent performance, or whose playing time (PT) is less certain. But we upgrade players we deem more reliable with respect to health, consistency, PT, or all three.

When you head into an upcoming auction or draft, consider the following with regard to reliability:

- Reliability grades do help identify more stable investments: players with "B" grades in both Health and PT/Experience are more likely to return a higher percentage of their projected value.
- While top-end starting pitching may be more reliable than ever, the overall pool of pitchers is fraught with uncertainty and the position represents a less reliable investment than batters.
- There does not appear to be a significant market premium for reliability, at least according to the criteria measured by BaseballHQ.com.
- There are only two types of players: risky and riskier. So while it may be worth going the extra buck for a more reliable player, be warned that even the most reliable player can falter—don't go overboard bidding up a AAA-rated player simply due to his Reliability grades.

Using 3-year trends as leading indicators *(Ed DeCaria)*

It is almost irresistibly tempting to look at three numbers moving in one direction and expect that the fourth will continue that progression. However, for both hitters and pitchers riding positive trends over any consecutive three-year period, not only do most players not continue their positive trend into a fourth year, their Year 4 performance usually regresses significantly. This is true for every metric tested (whether related to playing time, batting skills, pitching skills, running skills, luck indicators, or valuation). Negative trends show similar reversals, but tend to be more "sticky," meaning that rebounds are neither as frequent nor as strong as positive trend regressions. Challenge any analysis that hints at a player's demise coming off of a negative trend or that suggests an imminent breakout following a positive trend; more often than not, such predictions do not pan out.

Health Analysis

Disabled list statistics

Year	#Players	3yr Avg	DL Days	3yr Avg
2002	337	-	23,724	-
2003	351	-	22,118	-
2004	382	357	25,423	23,755
2005	356	363	24,016	23,852
2006	347	362	22,472	23,970
2007	404	369	28,524	25,004
2008	422	391	28,187	26,394
2009	408	411	26,252	27,654
2010	393	408	22,911	25,783
2011	422	408	25,610	24,924
2012	409	408	30,408	27,038
2013	442	419	29,551	28,523
2014	422	424	25,839	28,599

D.L. days as a leading indicator *(Bill Macey)*
Players who are injured in one year are likely to be injured in a subsequent year:

% DL batters in Year 1 who are also DL in year 2	38%
Under age 30	36%
Age 30 and older	41%
% DL batters in Year 1 and 2 who are also DL in year 3	54%
% DL pitchers in Year 1 who are also DL in year 2	43%
Under age 30	45%
Age 30 and older	41%
% DL pitchers in Yr 1 and 2 who are also DL in year 3	41%

Previously injured players also tend to spend a longer time on the DL. The average number of days on the DL was 51 days for batters and 73 days for pitchers. For the subset of these players who get hurt again the following year, the average number of days on the DL was 58 days for batters and 88 days for pitchers.

Spring training spin *(Dave Adler)*
Spring training sound bites raise expectations among fantasy leaguers, but how much of that "news" is really "noise"? Thanks to a summary listed at RotoAuthority.com, we were able to compile the stats for 2009. Verdict: Noise.

BATTERS	No.	IMPROVED	DECLINED
Weight change	30	33%	30%
Fitness program	3	0%	67%
Eye surgery	6	50%	33%
Plans more SB	6	17%	33%
PITCHERS	**No.**	**IMPROVED**	**DECLINED**
Weight change	18	44%	44%
Fitness program	4	50%	50%
Eye surgery	2	0%	50%
New pitch	5	60%	40%

In-Season Analysis

April performance as a leading indicator
We isolated all players who earned at least $10 more or $10 less than we had projected in March. Then we looked at the April stats of these players to see if we could have picked out the $10 outliers after just one month.

	Identifiable in April
Earned $10+ more than projected	
BATTERS	39%
PITCHERS	44%
Earned -$10 less than projected	
BATTERS	56%
PITCHERS	74%

Nearly three out of every four pitchers who earned at least $10 less than projected also struggled in April. For all the other surprises—batters or pitchers—April was not a strong leading indicator. Another look:

	Pct.
Batters who finished +$25	45%
Pitchers who finished +$20	44%
Batters who finished under $0	60%
Pitchers who finished under -$5	78%

April surgers are less than a 50/50 proposition to maintain that level all season. Those who finished April at the bottom of the roto rankings were more likely to continue struggling, especially pitchers. In fact, of those pitchers who finished April with a value *under -$10*, 91% finished the season in the red. Holes are tough to dig out of.

The weight of early season numbers
Early season strugglers who surge later in the year get no respect because they have to live with the weight of their early numbers all season long. Conversely, quick starters who fade late get far more accolades than they deserve.

For instance, take Lonnie Chisenhall's month-by-month batting averages. Based solely on his final .280 mark, the perception is that he had a nice breakout season. Reality is different. It's not readily apparent, but from June 13 on—over 310 AB—he batted a horrible .219.

Month	BA	Cum BA
April	.362	.362
May	.373	.369
June	.311	.345
July	.209	.307
August	.250	.296
September	.219	.280

Seasonal trends in hitting and pitching *(Bob Berger)*
A study of monthly trends in traditional statistical categories found:
- Batting average, HR/game and RBI/game rise from April through August, then fall in September/October.
- Stolen bases decline in July and August before rebounding in September.
- ERA worsens in July/August and improves in September.
- WHIP gets worse in July/August.
- K/9 rate improves all season.

The bold statement that hitters perform better in warmer weather seems to be true broadly.

Courtship period

Any time a player is put into a new situation, he enters into what we might call a courtship period. This period might occur when a player switches leagues, or switches teams. It could be the first few games when a minor leaguer is called up. It could occur when a reliever moves into the rotation, or when a lead-off hitter is moved to another spot in the lineup. There is a team-wide courtship period when a manager is replaced. Any external situation that could affect a player's performance sets off a new decision point in evaluating that performance.

During this period, it is difficult to get a true read on how a player is going to ultimately perform. He is adjusting to the new situation. Things could be volatile during this time. For instance, a role change that doesn't work could spur other moves. A rookie hurler might buy himself a few extra starts with a solid debut, even if he has questionable skills.

It is best not to make a decision on a player who is going through a courtship period. Wait until his stats stabilize. Don't cut a struggling pitcher in his first few starts after a managerial change. Don't pick up a hitter who smacks a pair of HRs in his first game after having been traded. Unless, of course, talent and track record say otherwise.

Half-season fallacies

A popular exercise at the midpoint of each season is to analyze those players who are consistent first half to second half surgers or faders. There are several fallacies with this analytical approach.

1. Half-season consistency is rare. There are very few players who show consistent changes in performance from one half of the season to the other.

Research results from a three-year study conducted in the late-1990s: The test groups... batters with min. 300 AB full season, 150 AB first half, and pitchers with min. 100 IP full season, 50 IP first half. Of those groups (size noted):

3-year consistency in	BATTERS (98)	PITCHERS (42)
1 stat category	40%	57%
2 stat categories	18%	21%
3 stat categories	3%	5%

When the analysis was stretched to a fourth year, only 1% of all players showed consistency in even one category.

2. Analysts often use false indicators. Situational statistics provide us with tools that can be misused. Several sources offer up 3- and 5-year stats intended to paint a picture of a long-term performance. Some analysts look at a player's half-season swing over that multi-year period and conclude that he is demonstrating consistent performance.

The fallacy is that those multi-year scans may not show any consistency at all. They are not individual season performances but *aggregate* performances. A player whose 5-year batting average shows a 15-point rise in the 2nd half, for instance, may actually have experienced a BA decline in several of those years, a fact that might have been offset by a huge BA rise in one of the years.

3. It's arbitrary. The season's midpoint is an arbitrary delineator of performance swings. Some players are slow starters and might be more appropriately evaluated as pre-May 1 and post-May 1. Others bring their game up a notch with a pennant chase and might see a performance swing with August 15 as the cut-off. Each player has his own individual tendency, if, in fact, one exists at all. There's nothing magical about mid-season as the break point, and certainly not over a multi-year period.

Half-season tendencies

Despite the above, it stands to reason logically that there might be some underlying tendencies on a more global scale, first half to second half. In fact, one would think that the player population as a whole might decline in performance as the season drones on. There are many variables that might contribute to a player wearing down—workload, weather, boredom—and the longer a player is on the field, the higher the likelihood that he is going to get hurt. A recent 5-year study uncovered the following tendencies:

Batting

Overall, batting skills held up pretty well, half to half. There was a 5% erosion of playing time, likely due, in part, to September roster expansion.

Power: First half power studs (20 HRs in 1H) saw a 10% drop-off in the second half. 34% of first half 20+ HR hitters hit 15 or fewer in the second half and only 27% were able to improve on their first half output.

Speed: Second half speed waned as well. About 26% of the 20+ SB speedsters stole *at least 10 fewer bases* in the second half. Only 26% increased their second half SB output at all.

Batting average: 60% of first half .300 hitters failed to hit .300 in the second half. Only 20% showed any second half improvement at all. As for 1H strugglers, managers tended to stick with their full-timers despite poor starts. Nearly one in five of the sub-.250 1H hitters managed to hit *more than* .300 in the second half.

Pitching

Overall, there was some slight erosion in innings and ERA despite marginal improvement in some peripherals.

ERA: For those who pitched at least 100 innings in the first half, ERAs rose an average of 0.40 runs in the 2H. Of those with first half ERAs less than 4.00, only 49% were able to maintain a sub-4.00 ERA in the second half.

Wins: Pitchers who won 18 or more games in a season tended to pitch *more* innings in the 2H and had slightly better peripherals.

Saves: Of those closers who saved 20 or more games in the first half, only 39% were able to post 20 or more saves in the 2H, and 26% posted fewer than 15 saves. Aggregate ERAs of these pitchers rose from 2.45 to 3.17, half to half.

Teams

Johnson Effect *(Bryan Johnson)*: Teams whose actual won/loss record exceeds or falls short of their statistically projected record in one season will tend to revert to the level of their projection in the following season.

Law of Competitive Balance *(Bill James)*: The level at which a team (or player) will address its problems is inversely related to its current level of success. Low performers will tend to make changes to improve; high performers will not. This law explains the existence of the Plexiglass and Whirlpool Principles.

Plexiglass Principle *(Bill James)*: If a player or team improves markedly in one season, it will likely decline in the next. The opposite is true but not as often (because a poor performer gets fewer opportunities to rebound).

Whirlpool Principle *(Bill James)*: All team and player performances are forcefully drawn to the center. For teams, that center is a .500 record. For players, it represents their career average level of performance.

Other Diamonds

The Fanalytic Fundamentals

1. This is not a game of accuracy or precision. It is a game of human beings and tendencies.
2. This is not a game of projections. It is a game of market value versus real value.
3. Draft skills, not stats. Draft skills, not roles.
4. A player's ability to post acceptable stats despite lousy BPIs will eventually run out.
5. Once you display a skill, you own it.
6. Virtually every player is vulnerable to a month of aberrant performance. Or a year.
7. Exercise excruciating patience.

Aging Axioms

1. Age is the only variable for which we can project a rising trend with 100% accuracy. (Or, age never regresses.)
2. The aging process slows down for those who maintain a firm grasp on the strike zone. Plate patience and pitching command can preserve any waning skill they have left.
3. Negatives tend to snowball as you age.

Steve Avery List

Players who hang onto MLB rosters for six years searching for a skill level they only had for three.

Bylaws of Badness

1. Some players are better than an open roster spot, but not by much.
2. Some players have bad years because they are unlucky. Others have *many* bad years because they are bad... and lucky.

George Brett Path to Retirement

Get out while you're still putting up good numbers and the public perception of you is favorable. Like Mike Mussina and Billy Wagner. And Chipper Jones, Mariano Rivera and Andy Pettitte.

Steve Carlton Path to Retirement

Hang around the majors long enough for your numbers to become so wretched that people begin to forget your past successes.

Classic cases include Jose Mesa, Doc Gooden, Nomar Garciaparra and of course, Steve Carlton. Recent players who have taken this path include Miguel Tejada, Travis Hafner, Jason Bay, Brian Roberts and Kevin Youkilis. Current players who could be on a similar course include Raul Ibanez, Carlos Pena, and Dan Uggla.

Christie Brinkley Law of Statistical Analysis

Never get married to the model.

Employment Standards

1. If you are right-brain dominant, own a catcher's mitt and are under 40, you will always be gainfully employed.
2. Some teams believe that it is better to employ a player with any experience because it has to be better than the devil they don't know.
3. It's not so good to go *pffft* in a contract year.

Laws of Prognosticating Perspective

- *Berkeley's 17th Law:* A great many problems do not have accurate answers, but do have approximate answers, from which sensible decisions can be made.
- *Ashley-Perry Statistical Axiom #4:* A complex system that works is invariably found to have evolved from a simple system that works.
- *Baseball Variation of Harvard Law:* Under the most rigorously observed conditions of skill, age, environment, statistical rules and other variables, a ballplayer will perform as he damn well pleases.

Brad Fullmer List

Players whose leading indicators indicate upside potential, year after year, but consistently fail to reach that full potential. Players like Justin Smoak, Josh Rutledge, Brett Lawrie are on the list right now.

Ceiling

The highest professional level at which a player maintains acceptable BPIs. Also, the peak performance level that a player will likely reach, given his BPIs.

Good Luck Truism

Good luck is rare and everyone has more of it than you do. That's the law.

The Gravity Principles

1. It is easier to be crappy than it is to be good.
2. All performance starts at zero, ends at zero and can drop to zero at any time.
3. The odds of a good performer slumping are far greater than the odds of a poor performer surging.
4. Once a player is in a slump, it takes several 3-for-5 days to get out of it. Once he is on a streak, it takes a single 0-for-4 day to begin the downward spiral. *Corollary:* Once a player is in a slump, not only does it take several 3-for-5 days to get out of it, but he also has to get his name back on the lineup card.
5. Eventually all performance comes down to earth. It may take a week, or a month, or may not happen until he's 45, but eventually it's going to happen.

Health Homilies

1. Staying healthy is a skill (and "DL Days" should be a Rotisserie category).
2. A $40 player can get hurt just as easily as a $5 player but is eight times tougher to replace.
3. Chronically injured players never suddenly get healthy.
4. There are two kinds of pitchers: those that are hurt and those that are not hurt... yet.
5. Players with back problems are always worth $10 less.
6. "Opting out of surgery" usually means it's coming anyway, just later.

The Health Hush

Players get hurt and potentially have a lot to lose, so there is an incentive for them to hide injuries. HIPAA laws restrict the disclosure of health information. Team doctors and trainers have been instructed not to talk with the media. So, when it comes to information on a player's health status, we're all pretty much in the dark.

Hidden Injury Progression

1. Player's skills implode.
2. Team and player deny injury.
3. More unexplained struggles.
4. Injury revealed; surgery follows.

Law of Injury Estimation (Westheimer's Rule)

To calculate an accurate projection of the amount of time a player will be out of action due to injury, first take the published time estimate, double it and change the unit of measure to the next highest unit. Thus, a player estimated to be out two weeks will actually be out four months.

The Livan Level

The point when a player's career Runs Above Replacement level has dropped so far below zero that he has effectively cancelled out any possible remaining future value. (Similarly, the Dontrelle Demarcation.)

The Momentum Maxims

1. A player will post a pattern of positive results until the day you add him to your roster.
2. Patterns of negative results are more likely to snowball than correct.
3. When an unstoppable force meets an immovable object, the wall always wins.

Monocarp

A player whose career consists of only one productive season.

Paradoxes and Conundrums

1. Is a player's improvement in performance from one year to the next a point in a growth trend, an isolated outlier or a complete anomaly?
2. A player can play through an injury, post rotten numbers and put his job at risk… or… he can admit that he can't play through an injury, allow himself to be taken out of the lineup/rotation, and put his job at risk.
3. Did irregular playing time take its toll on the player's performance or did poor performance force a reduction in his playing time?
4. Is a player only in the game versus right-handers because he has a true skills deficiency versus left-handers? Or is his poor performance versus left-handers because he's never given a chance to face them?
5. The problem with stockpiling bench players in the hope that one pans out is that you end up evaluating performance using data sets that are too small to be reliable.
6. There are players who could give you 20 stolen bases if they got 400 AB. But if they got 400 AB, they would likely be on a bad team that wouldn't let them steal.

Process-Outcome Matrix *(Russo and Schoemaker)*

	Good Outcome	Bad Outcome
Good Process	Deserved Success	Bad Break
Bad Process	Dumb Luck	Poetic Justice

Quack!

An exclamation in response to the educated speculation that a player has used performance enhancing drugs. While it is rare to have absolute proof, there is often enough information to suggest that, "if it looks like a duck and quacks like a duck, then odds are it's a duck."

Tenets of Optimal Timing

1. If a second half fader had put up his second half stats in the first half and his first half stats in the second half, then he probably wouldn't even have had a second half.
2. Fast starters can often buy six months of playing time out of one month of productivity.
3. Poor 2nd halves don't get recognized until it's too late.
4. "Baseball is like this. Have one good year and you can fool them for five more, because for five more years they expect you to have another good one." — Frankie Frisch

The Three True Outcomes

1. Strikeouts
2. Walks
3. Home runs

The Three True Handicaps

1. Has power but can't make contact.
2. Has speed but can't hit safely.
3. Has potential but is too old.

UGLY (Unreasonable Good Luck Year)

The driving force behind every winning team. It's what they really mean when they say "winning ugly."

Walbeckian

Possessing below replacement level stats, as in "Dan Uggla's season was downright Walbeckian." Alternate usage: "Dan Uggla's stats were so bad that I might as well have had Matt Walbeck in there."

Wasted talent

A player with a high level skill that is negated by a deficiency in another skill. For instance, base path speed can be negated by poor on base ability. Pitchers with strong arms can be wasted because home plate is an elusive concept to them.

Zombie

A player who is indestructible, continuing to get work, year-after-year, no matter how dead his BPIs are. Like Edwin Jackson, Joe Saunders, and Jerome Williams.

Batters

Batting Eye, Contact and Batting Average

Batting average (BA, or Avg)

This is where it starts. BA is a grand old nugget that has long outgrown its usefulness. We revere .300 hitting superstars and scoff at .250 hitters, yet the difference between the two is one hit every 20 ABs. This one hit every five games is not nearly the wide variance that exists in our perceptions of what it means to be a .300 or .250 hitter. BA is a poor evaluator of performance in that it neglects the offensive value of the base on balls and assumes that all hits are created equal.

Walk rate (bb%)

(BB / (AB + BB))

A measure of a batter's plate patience. **BENCHMARKS:** The best batters will have levels more than 10%. Those with poor plate patience will have levels of 5% or less.

On base average (OB)

(H + BB) / (AB + BB)

Addressing a key deficiency with BA, OB gives value to events that get batters on base, but are not hits. An OB of .350 can be read as "this batter gets on base 35% of the time." When a run is scored, there is no distinction made as to how that runner reached base. So, two-thirds of the time—about how often a batter comes to the plate with the bases empty—a walk really is as good as a hit.

The official version of this formula includes hit batsmen. We do not include it because our focus is on skills-based gauges; research has shown that HBP is not a measure of batting skill but of pitching deficiency. **BENCHMARKS:** We know what a .300 hitter is, but what represents "good" for OB? That comparable level would likely be .400, with .275 representing the comparable level of futility.

Ground ball, line drive, fly ball percentages (G/L/F)

The percentage of all balls in play that are hit on the ground, as line drives and in the air. For batters, increased fly ball tendency may foretell a rise in power skills; increased line drive tendency may foretell an improvement in batting average. For a pitcher, the ability to keep the ball on the ground can contribute to his statistical output exceeding his demonstrated skill level.

*BIP Type	Total%	Out%
Ground ball	45%	72%
Line drive	20%	28%
Fly ball	35%	85%
TOTAL	*100%*	*69%*

*Data only includes fieldable balls and is net of HRs.

Line drives and luck *(Patrick Davitt)*

Given that each individual batter's hit rate sets its own baseline, and that line drives (LD) are the most productive type of batted ball, a study looked at the relationship between the two. Among the findings were that hit rates on LDs are much higher than on FBs or GBs, with individual batters consistently falling into the 72-73% range. Ninety-five percent of all batters fall between the range of 60%-86%; batters outside this range regress very quickly, often within the season.

Note that batters' BAs did not always follow their LD% up or down, because some of them enjoyed higher hit rates on other batted balls, improved their contact rates, or both. Still, it's justifiable to bet that players hitting the ball with authority but getting fewer hits than they should will correct over time.

Batting eye (Eye)

(Walks / Strikeouts)

A measure of a player's strike zone judgment. **BENCHMARKS:** The best hitters have Eye ratios more than 1.00 (indicating more walks than strikeouts) and are the most likely to be among a league's .300 hitters. Ratios less than 0.50 represent batters who likely also have lower BAs.

Batting eye as a leading indicator

There is a strong correlation between strike zone judgment and batting average. However, research shows that this is more descriptive than predictive:

	Batting Average				
Batting Eye	2010	2011	2012	2013	2014
0.00 - 0.25	.235	.232	.243	.242	.238
0.26 - 0.50	.260	.254	.255	.253	.253
0.51 - 0.75	.264	.267	.268	.265	.268
0.76 - 1.00	.272	.276	.276	.277	.270
1.01 and over	.280	.298	.292	.284	.304

We have been running the above chart for years and have always had large enough samples to make each group statistically significant. But not this year. The last group—1.01 and over—contained only six players. Only two—Jose Bautista and Victor Martinez—had more than 150 AB. The correlation held, but the downward pressure on batting averages is changing the game.

We can create percentage plays for the different levels:

For Eye	Pct who bat	
Levels of	.300+	.250-
0.00 - 0.25	7%	39%
0.26 - 0.50	14%	26%
0.51 - 0.75	18%	17%
0.76 - 1.00	32%	14%
1.01 - 1.50	51%	9%
1.51 +	59%	4%

Any batter with an eye ratio more than 1.50 has about a 4% chance of hitting less than .250 over 500 at bats.

Of all .300 hitters, those with ratios of at least 1.00 have a 65% chance of repeating as .300 hitters. Those with ratios less than 1.00 have less than a 50% chance of repeating.

Only 4% of sub-.250 hitters with ratios less than 0.50 will mature into .300 hitters the following year.

In a 1995-2000 study, only 37 batters hit .300-plus with a sub-0.50 eye ratio over at least 300 AB in a season. Of this group, 30% were able to accomplish this feat on a consistent basis. For the other 70%, this was a short-term aberration.

Contact rate (ct%)

((AB - K) / AB)

Measures a batter's ability to get wood on the ball and hit it into the field of play. BENCHMARKS: Those batters with the best contact skill will have levels of 90% or better. The hackers of society will have levels of 75% or less.

Contact rate as a leading indicator

The more often a batter makes contact with the ball, the higher the likelihood that he will hit safely.

	Batting Average				
Contact Rate	2010	2011	2012	2013	2014
0% - 60%	.187	.171	.197	.203	.176
61% - 65%	.235	.199	.226	.211	.217
66% - 70%	.236	.229	.231	.232	.230
71% - 75%	.254	.243	.252	.246	.243
76% - 80%	.256	.260	.255	.261	.257
81% - 85%	.271	.268	.268	.268	.266
86% - 90%	.273	.272	.278	.272	.276
Over 90%	.270	.290	.282	.270	.324

Once again, the size of the highest-skilled group has dwindled, here to only 17 players, only four of whom had more than 50 AB.

Perhaps most notable here are the trends. Follow along the 81%-85% group, which represents what we used to consider as the lowest acceptable contact rate level. The decline is consistent, especially considering that the batting average for this group was .275 in 2009 and as high as .277 in 2007. It's dropped 10 points in seven years.

Contact rate and walk rate as leading indicators

A matrix of contact rates and walk rates can provide expectation benchmarks for a player's batting average:

	Walk rate (bb%)			
Contact rate (ct%)	0-5	6-10	11-15	16+
65-	.179	.195	.229	.237
66-75	.190	.248	.254	.272
76-85	.265	.267	.276	.283
86+	.269	.279	.301	.309

A contact rate of 65% or lower offers virtually no chance for a player to hit even .250, no matter how high a walk rate he has. The .300 hitters most often come from the group with a minimum 86% contact and 11% walk rate.

HCt and HctX *(Patrick Davitt)*

HCt= hard hit ball rate x contact rate

HctX= Player HCt divided by league average Hct, normalized to 100

The combination of making contact and hitting the ball hard might be the most important skills for a batter. HctX correlates very strongly with BA, and at higher BA levels often does so with high accuracy. Its success with HR was somewhat limited, probably due to GB/FB differences. BENCHMARKS: The average major-leaguer in a given year has a HctX of 100. Elite batters have an HctX of 135 or above; weakest batters have HctX of 55 or below.

Balls in play (BIP)

(AB – K)

The total number of batted balls that are hit fair, both hits and outs. An analysis of how these balls are hit—on the ground, in the air, hits, outs, etc.—can provide analytical insight, from player skill levels to the impact of luck on statistical output.

Batting average on balls in play *(Voros McCracken)*

(H – HR) / (AB – HR – K)

Also called hit rate (h%). The percent of balls hit into the field of play that fall for hits. BENCHMARK: Every hitter establishes his own individual hit rate that stabilizes over time. A batter whose seasonal hit rate varies significantly from the h% he has established over the preceding three seasons (variance of at least +/- 3%) is likely to improve or regress to his individual h% mean (with over-performer declines more likely and sharper than under-performer recoveries). Three-year h% levels strongly predict a player's h% the following year.

P/PA as a leading indicator for BA *(Paul Petera)*

The art of working the count has long been considered one of the more crucial aspects of good hitting. It is common knowledge that the more pitches a hitter sees, the greater opportunity he has to reach base safely.

P/PA	OBA	BA
4.00+	.360	.264
3.75-3.99	.347	.271
3.50-3.74	.334	.274
Under 3.50	.321	.276

Generally speaking, the more pitches seen, the lower the BA, but the higher the OBA. But what about the outliers, those players that bucked the trend in year #1?

	YEAR TWO	
	BA Improved	BA Declined
Low P/PA and Low BA	77%	23%
High P/PA and High BA	21%	79%

In these scenarios, there was a strong tendency for performance to normalize in year #2.

Expected batting average *(John Burnson)*

*xCT% * [xH1% + xH2%]*

where

$$xH1\% = GB\% \times [0.0004\ PX + 0.062\ ln(SX)]$$
$$+ LD\% \times [0.93 - 0.086\ ln(SX)]$$
$$+ FB\% \times 0.12$$

and

$$xH2\% = FB\% \times [0.0013\ PX - 0.0002\ SX - 0.057]$$
$$+ GB\% \times [0.0006\ PX]$$

A hitter's batting average as calculated by multiplying the percentage of balls put in play (contact rate) by the chance that a ball in play falls for a hit. The likelihood that a ball in play falls for a hit is a product of the speed of the ball and distance it is hit (PX), the speed of the batter (SX), and distribution of ground balls, fly balls, and line drives. We further split it out by non-homerun hit rate (xH1%) and homerun hit rate (xH2%). BENCHMARKS: In general, xBA should approximate batting average fairly closely.

Those hitters who have large variances between the two gauges are candidates for further analysis. LIMITATION: xBA tends to understate a batter's true value if he is an extreme ground ball hitter (G/F ratio over 3.0) with a low PX. These players are not inherently weak, but choose to take safe singles rather than swing for the fences.

Expected batting average variance
xBA – BA

The variance between a batter's BA and his xBA is a measure of over- or under-achievement. A positive variance indicates the potential for a batter's BA to rise. A negative variance indicates the potential for BA to decline. BENCHMARK: Discount variances that are less than 20 points. Any variance more than 30 points is regarded as a strong indicator of future change.

Power

Slugging average (Slg)
(Singles + (2 x Doubles) + (3 x Triples) + (4 x HR)) / AB

A measure of the total number of bases accumulated (or the minimum number of runners' bases advanced) per at bat. It is a misnomer; it is not a true measure of a batter's slugging ability because it includes singles. Slg also assumes that each type of hit has proportionately increasing value (i.e. a double is twice as valuable as a single, etc.) which is not true. For instance, with the bases loaded, a HR always scores four runs, a triple always scores three, but a double could score two or three and a single could score one, or two, or even three. BENCHMARKS: Top batters will have levels over .500. The bottom batters will have levels less than .300.

Fly ball tendency and power *(Mat Olkin)*

There is a proven connection between a hitter's ground ball/fly ball tendencies and his power production.

1. *Extreme ground ball hitters generally do not hit for much power.* It's almost impossible for a hitter with a ground/fly ratio over 1.80 to hit enough fly balls to produce even 25 HRs in a season. However, this does not mean that a low G/F ratio necessarily guarantees power production. Some players have no problem getting the ball into the air, but lack the strength to reach the fences consistently.

2. *Most batters' ground/fly ratios stay pretty steady over time.* Most year-to-year changes are small and random, as they are in any other statistical category. A large, sudden change in G/F, on the other hand, can signal a conscious change in plate approach. And so...

3. *If a player posts high G/F ratios in his first few years, he probably isn't ever going to hit for all that much power.*

4. *When a batter's power suddenly jumps, his G/F ratio often drops at the same time.*

5. *Every so often, a hitter's ratio will drop significantly even as his power production remains level.* In these rare cases, impending power development is likely, since the two factors almost always follow each other.

Home runs to fly ball rate (hr/f)
The percent of fly balls that are hit for HRs.

hr/f rate as a leading indicator *(Joshua Randall)*

Each batter establishes an individual home run to fly ball rate that stabilizes over rolling three-year periods; those levels strongly predict the hr/f in the subsequent year. A batter who varies significantly from his hr/f is likely to regress toward his individual hr/f mean, with over-performance decline more likely and more severe than under-performance recovery.

Hard-hit flies as a sustainable skill *(Patrick Davitt)*

A study of data from 2009-2011 found that we should seek batters with a high Hard-Hit Fly Ball percentage (HHFB%). Among the findings:

- Avoiding pop-ups and hitting HHFBs are sustainable core power skills.
- Consistent HHFB% performance marks batters with power potential.
- When looking for candidates to regress, we should look at individual past levels of HR/HHFB, perhaps using a three-year rolling average.

Linear weighted power (LWPwr)
((Doubles x .8) + (Triples x .8) + (HR x 1.4)) / (At bats- K) x 100

A variation of the linear weights formula that considers only events that are measures of a batter's pure power. BENCHMARKS: Top sluggers typically top the 17 mark. Weak hitters will have a LWPwr level of less than 10.

Linear weighted power index (PX)
(Batter's LWPwr / League LWPwr) x 100

LWPwr is presented in this book in its normalized form to get a better read on a batter's accomplishment in each year. For instance, a 30-HR season today is much more of an accomplishment than 30 HRs hit in a higher offense year like 2003. BENCHMARKS: A level of 100 equals league average power skills. Any player with a value more than 100 has above average power skills, and those more than 150 are the Slugging Elite.

Expected LW power index (xPX) *(Bill Macey)*
2.6 + 269*HHLD% + 724*HHFB%

Previous research has shown that hard-hit balls are more likely to result in hits and hard-hit fly balls are more likely to end up as HRs. As such, we can use hard-hit ball data to calculate an expected skills-based power index. This metric starts with hard-hit ball data, which measures a player's fundamental skill of making solid contact, and then places it on the same scale as PX (xPX). In the above formula, HHLD% is calculated as the number of hard hit-line drives divided by the total number of balls put in play. HHFB% is similarly calculated for fly balls.

P/PA as a leading indicator for PX *(Paul Petera)*
Working the count has a positive effect on power.

P/PA	PX
4.00+	123
3.75-3.99	108
3.50-3.74	96
Under 3.50	84

As for the year #1 outliers:

	YEAR TWO	
	PX Improved	PX Declined
Low P/PA and High PX	11%	89%
High P/PA and Low PX	70%	30%

In these scenarios, there was a strong tendency for performance to normalize in year #2.

Doubles as a leading indicator for home runs *(Bill Macey)*

There is little support for the theory that hitting many doubles in year x leads to an increase in HR in year x+1. However, it was shown that batters with high doubles rates (2B/AB) also tend to hit more HR/AB than the league average; oddly, they are unable to sustain the high 2B/AB rate but do sustain their higher HR/AB rates. Batters with high 2B/AB rates and low HR/AB rates are more likely to see HR gains in the following year, but those rates will still typically trail the league average. And, batters who experience a surge in 2B/AB typically give back most of those gains in the following year without any corresponding gain in HR.

Opposite field home runs *(Ed DeCaria)*

From 2001-2008, nearly 75% of all HRs were hit to the batter's pull field, with the remaining 25% distributed roughly evenly between straight away and opposite field. Left-handers accomplished the feat slightly more often than right-handers (including switch-hitters hitting each way), and younger hitters did it significantly more often than older hitters. The trend toward pulled home runs was especially strong after age 36.

Power Quartile	AB/HR	Opp. Field	Straight Away	Pull Field
Top 25%	17.2	15.8%	16.0%	68.2%
2nd 25%	28.0	10.7%	12.2%	77.0%
3rd 25%	44.1	8.9%	10.0%	81.1%
Bot 25%	94.7	5.4%	5.9%	88.7%

Opposite field HRs serve as a strong indicator of overall home run power (AB/HR). Power hitters (smaller AB/HR rates) hit a far higher percentage of their HR to the opposite field or straight away (over 30%). Conversely, non-power hitters hit almost 90% of their home runs to their pull field.

	Performance in Y2-Y4 (% of Group)		
Y1 Trigger	<=30 AB/HR	5.5+ RC/G	$16+ R$
2+ OppHR	69%	46%	33%
<2 OppHR	29%	13%	12%

Players who hit just two or more OppHR in one season were 2-3 times as likely as those who hit zero or one OppHR to sustain strong AB/HR rates, RC/G levels, or R$ values over the following three seasons.

	Y2-Y4 Breakout Performance		
	(% Breakout by Group, Age <=26 Only)		
	AB/HR	RC/G	R$
Y1 Trigger	>35 to <=30	<4.5 to 5.5+	<$8 to $16+
2+ OppHR	32%	21%	30%
<2 OppHR	23%	12%	10%

Roughly one of every 3-4 batters age 26 or younger experiences a *sustained three-year breakout* in AB/HR, RC/G or R$ after a season in which they hit 2+ OppHR, far better odds than the one in 8-10 batters who experience a breakout without the 2+ OppHR trigger.

Home runs in bunches *(Patrick Davitt)*

A study from HR data from 2010-2012 showed that batters hit HRs in a random manner, with game-gaps between HRs that correspond roughly to their average days per HR. Thus, the theory that batters hit HRs in "bunches" is a fallacy. It appears pointless to try to "time the market" by predicting the beginning or end of a drought or a bunch, or by assuming the end of one presages the beginning of the other, despite what the ex-player in the broadcast booth tells you.

Power breakout profile

It is not easy to predict which batters will experience a power spike. We can categorize power breakouts to determine the likelihood of a player taking a step up or of a surprise performer repeating his feat. Possibilities:

- Increase in playing time
- History of power skills at some time in the past
- Redistribution of already demonstrated extra base hit power
- Normal skills growth
- Situational breakouts, particularly in hitter-friendly venues
- Increased fly ball tendency
- Use of illegal performance-enhancing substances
- Miscellaneous unexplained variables

Speed

Wasted talent on the base paths

We refer to some players as having "wasted talent," a high level skill that is negated by a deficiency in another skill. Among these types are players who have blazing speed that is negated by a sub-.300 on base average.

These players can have short-term value. However, their stolen base totals are tied so tightly to their "green light" that any change in managerial strategy could completely erase that value. A higher OB mitigates that downside; the good news is that plate patience can be taught.

Players in 2014 who had at least 20 SBs with an OBP less than .300, and whose SB output could be at risk, are Billy Hamilton (56 SB, .292 OBP), Eric Young Jr. (30, .299), James Jones (27, .278), B.J. Upton (20, .287), Kolten Wong (20, .292) and Jean Segura (20, .289).

Speed score *(Bill James)*

A measure of the various elements that comprise a runner's speed skills. Although this formula (a variation of James' original version) may be used as a leading indicator for stolen base output, SB attempts are controlled by managerial strategy which makes speed score somewhat less valuable.

Speed score is calculated as the mean value of the following four elements:

1. Stolen base efficiency = $(((SB + 3)/(SB + CS + 7)) - .4) \times 20$
2. Stolen base freq. = $\textit{Square root of } ((SB + CS)/(Singles + BB))/.07$

3. Triples rating = *(3B / (AB - HR - K))* and the result assigned a value based on the following chart:

< 0.001	*0*	*0.0105*	*6*
0.001	*1*	*0.013*	*7*
0.0023	*2*	*0.0158*	*8*
0.0039	*3*	*0.0189*	*9*
0.0058	*4*	*0.0223+*	*10*
0.008	*5*		

4. Runs scored as a percentage of times on base =
(((R - HR) / (H + BB - HR)) - .1) / .04

Speed score index (SX)

(Batter's speed score / League speed score) x 100

Normalized speed scores get a better read on a runner's accomplishment in context. A level of 100 equals league average speed skill. Values more than 100 indicate above average skill, more than 200 represent the Fleet of Feet Elite.

Statistically scouted speed (Spd) *(Ed DeCaria)*

(104 + {[(Runs–HR+10*age_wt)/(RBI-HR+10)]/lg_av*100} / 5
+ {[(3B+5*age_wt)/(2B+3B+5)]/lg_av*100} / 5
+ {[(SoftMedGBhits+25*age_wt)/(SoftMedGB+25)]/lg_av*100} / 2
- {[Weight (Lbs)/Height (In)^2 * 703]/lg_av*100}

A skills-based gauge that measures speed without relying on stolen bases. Its components are:

- *(Runs – HR) / (RBI – HR)*: This metric aims to minimize the influence of extra base hit power and team run-scoring rates on perceived speed.

- *3B / (2B + 3B)*: No one can deny that triples are a fast runner's stat; dividing them by 2B+3B instead of all balls in play dampens the power aspect of extra base hits.

- *(Soft + Medium Ground Ball Hits) / (Soft + Medium Ground Balls)*: Faster runners are more likely than slower runners to beat out routine grounders. Hard hit balls are excluded from numerator and denominator.

- *Body Mass Index (BMI)*: Calculated as *Weight (lbs) / Height (in)2 * 703*. All other factors considered, leaner players run faster than heavier ones.

In this book, the formula is scaled as an index with a midpoint of 100.

Stolen base opportunity percent (SBO)

(SB + CS) / (BB + Singles)

A rough approximation of how often a baserunner attempts a stolen base. Provides a comparative measure for players on a given team and, as a team measure, the propensity of a manager to give a "green light" to his runners.

Roto Speed (RSpd)

(Spd x (SBO + SB%))

An adjustment to the measure for raw speed that takes into account a runner's opportunities to steal and his success rate. This stat is intended to provide a more accurate predictive measure of stolen bases for the Mayberry Method.

Stolen base breakout profile *(Bob Berger)*

To find stolen base breakouts (first 30+ steal season in the majors), look for players that:

- are between 22-27 years old
- have 3-7 years of professional (minors and MLB) experience
- have previous steals at the MLB level
- have averaged 20+ SB in previous three seasons (majors and minors combined)
- have at least one professional season of 30+ SB

Overall Performance Analysis

On base plus slugging average (OPS)

A simple sum of the two gauges, it is considered one of the better evaluators of overall performance. OPS combines the two basic elements of offensive production—the ability to get on base (OB) and the ability to advance baserunners (Slg). BENCHMARKS: The game's top batters will have OPS levels more than .900. The worst batters will have levels less than .600.

Base Performance Value (BPV)

(Walk rate - 5) x 2)
+ ((Contact rate - 75) x 4)
+ ((Power Index - 80) x 0.8)
+ ((Spd - 80) x 0.3)

A single value that describes a player's overall raw skill level. This is more useful than traditional statistical gauges to track player performance trends and project future statistical output. The BPV formula combines and weights several BPIs.

This formula combines the individual raw skills of batting eye, contact rate, power and speed. BENCHMARKS: The best hitters will have a BPV of 50 or greater.

Base Performance Index (BPX)

BPV scaled to league average to account for year-to-year fluctuations in league-wide statistical performance. It's a snapshot of a player's overall skills compared to an average player. BENCHMARK: A level of 100 means a player had a league-average BPV in that given season.

Linear weights *(Pete Palmer)*

((Singles x .46) + (Doubles x .8) + (Triples x 1.02)
+ (Home runs x 1.4) + (Walks x .33) + (Stolen Bases x .3)
- (Caught Stealing x .6) - ((At bats - Hits) x Normalizing Factor)

(Also referred to as Batting Runs.) Formula whose premise is that all events in baseball are linear; that is, the output (runs) is directly proportional to the input (offensive events). Each of these events is then weighted according to its relative value in producing runs. Positive events—hits, walks, stolen bases—have positive values. Negative events—outs, caught stealing—have negative values.

The normalizing factor, representing the value of an out, is an offset to the level of offense in a given year. It changes every season, growing larger in high offense years and smaller in low offense years. The value is about .26 and varies by league.

LW is not included in the player forecast boxes, but the LW concept is used with the linear weighted power gauge.

Runs above replacement (RAR)

An estimate of the number of runs a player contributes above a "replacement level" player. "Replacement" is defined as the level of performance at which another player can easily be found at little or no cost to a team. What constitutes replacement level is a topic that is hotly debated. There are a variety of formulas and rules of thumb used to determine this level for each position (replacement level for a shortstop will be very different from replacement level for an outfielder). Our estimates appear below.

One of the major values of RAR for fantasy applications is that it can be used to assemble an integrated ranking of batters and pitchers for drafting purposes.

To calculate RAR for batters:

- Start with a batter's runs created per game (RC/G).
- Subtract his position's replacement level RC/G.
- Multiply by number of games played: (AB - H + CS) / 25.5.

Replacement levels used in this book:

POS	AL	NL
C	3.33	3.46
1B	4.14	4.19
2B	3.39	3.39
3B	3.67	3.72
SS	3.18	3.30
LF	3.69	3.79
CF	3.89	3.83
RF	3.90	4.10
DH	4.05	

RAR can also be used to calculate rough projected team won-loss records. *(Roger Miller)* Total the RAR levels for all the players on a team, divide by 10 and add to 53 wins.

Runs created *(Bill James)*

$(H + BB - CS) \times (Total\ bases + (.55 \times SB)) / (AB + BB)$

A formula that converts all offensive events into a total of runs scored. As calculated for individual teams, the result approximates a club's actual run total with great accuracy.

Runs created per game (RC/G)

Bill James version: *Runs Created / ((AB - H + CS) / 25.5)*

RC expressed on a per-game basis might be considered the hypothetical ERA compiled against a particular batter. Another way to look at it: A batter with a RC/G of 7.00 would be expected to score 7 runs per game if he were cloned nine times and faced an average pitcher in every at bat. Cloning batters is not a practice we recommend. BENCHMARKS: Few players surpass the level of a 10.00 RC/G, but any level more than 7.50 can still be considered very good. At the bottom are levels less than 3.00.

Plate Appearances as a leading indicator *(Patrick Davitt)*

While targeting players "age 26 with experience" as potential breakout candidates has become a commonly accepted concept, a study has found that cumulative plate appearances, especially during the first two years of a young player's career, can also have predictive value in assessing a coming spike in production. Three main conclusions:

- When projecting players, MLB experience is more important than age.

- Players who amass 800+ PAs in their first two seasons are highly likely to have double-digit value in Year 3.
- Also target young players in the season where they attain 400 PAs, as they are twice as likely as other players to grow significantly in value.

Handedness

1. While pure southpaws account for about 27% of total ABs (RHers about 55% and switch-hitters about 18%), they hit 31% of the triples and take 30% of the walks.

2. The average lefty posts a batting average about 10 points higher than the average RHer. The on base averages of pure LHers are nearly 20 points higher than RHers, but only 10 points higher than switch-hitters.

3. LHers tend to have a better batting eye ratio than RHers, but about the same as switch-hitters.

4. Pure righties and lefties have virtually identical power skills. Switch-hitters tend to have less power, on average.

5. Switch-hitters tend to have the best speed, followed by LHers, and then RHers.

6. On an overall production basis, LHers have an 8% advantage over RHers and a 14% edge over switch-hitters.

Skill-specific aging patterns for batters *(Ed DeCaria)*

Baseball forecasters obsess over "peak age" of player performance because we must understand player ascent toward and decline from that peak to predict future value. Most published aging analyses are done using composite estimates of value such as OPS or linear weights. By contrast, fantasy GMs are typically more concerned with category-specific player value (HR, SB, AVG, etc.). We can better forecast what matters most by analyzing peak age of individual baseball skills rather than overall player value.

For batters, recognized peak age for overall batting value is a player's late 20s. But individual skills do not peak uniformly at the same time:

Contact rate (ct%): Ascends modestly by about a half point of contact per year from age 22 to 26, then holds steady within a half point of peak until age 35, after which players lose a half point of contact per year.

Walk rate (bb%): Trends the opposite way with age compared to contact rate, as batters tend to peak at age 30 and largely remain there until they turn 38.

Stolen Base Opportunity (SBO): Typically, players maintain their SBO through age 27, but then reduce their attempts steadily in each remaining year of their careers.

Stolen base success rate (SB%): Aggressive runners (>14% SBO) tend to lose about 2 points per year as they age. However, less aggressive runners (<=14% SBO) actually improve their SB% by about 2 points per year until age 28, after which they reverse course and give back 1-2 pts every year as they age.

GB%/LD%/FB%: Both GB% and LD% peak at the start of a player's career and then decline as many hitters seemingly learn to elevate the ball more. But at about age 30, hitter GB% ascends toward a second late-career peak while LD% continues to plummet and FB% continues to rise through age 38.

Hit rate (h%): Declines linearly with age. This is a natural result of a loss of speed and change in batted ball trajectory.

Isolated Power (ISO): Typically peaks from age 24-26. Similarly, home runs per fly ball, opposite field HR %, and Hard Hit % all peak by age 25 and decline somewhat linearly from that point on.

Catchers and late-career performance spikes *(Ed Spaulding)*
Many catchers—particularly second line catchers—have their best seasons late in their careers. Some possible reasons why:

1. Catchers, like shortstops, often get to the big leagues for defensive reasons and not their offensive skills. These skills take longer to develop.
2. The heavy emphasis on learning the catching/ defense/ pitching side of the game detracts from their time to learn about, and practice, hitting.
3. Injuries often curtail their ability to show offensive skills, though these injuries (typically jammed fingers, bruises on the arms, rib injuries from collisions) often don't lead to time on the disabled list.
4. The time spent behind the plate has to impact the ability to recognize, and eventually hit, all kinds of pitches.

Spring training Slg as leading indicator *(John Dewan)*
A hitter's spring training Slg .200 or more above his lifetime Slg is a leading indicator for a better than normal season.

Overall batting breakout profile *(Brandon Kruse)*
We define a breakout performance as one where a player posts a Roto value of $20+ after having never posted a value of $10. These criteria are used to validate an apparent breakout in the current season but may also be used carefully to project a potential upcoming breakout:

- Age 27 or younger
- An increase in at least two of: h%, PX or Spd
- Minimum league average PX or Spd (100)
- Minimum contact rate of 75%
- Minimum xBA of .270

In-Season Analysis

Batting order facts *(Ed DeCaria)*
Eighty-eight percent of today's leadoff hitters bat leadoff again in their next game, 78% still bat leadoff 10 games later, and 68% still bat leadoff 50 games later. Despite this level of turnover after 50 games, leadoff hitters have the best chance of retaining their role over time. After leadoff, #3 and #4 hitters are the next most likely to retain their lineup slots.

On a season-to-season basis, leadoff hitters are again the most stable, with 69% of last year's primary leadoff hitters retaining the #1 slot next year.

Plate appearances decline linearly by lineup slot. Leadoff batters receive 10-12% more PAs than when batting lower in the lineup. AL #9 batters and NL #8 batters get 9-10% fewer PAs. These results mirror play-by-play data showing a 15-20 PA drop by lineup slot over a full season.

Walk rate is largely unaffected by lineup slot in the AL. Beware strong walk rates by NL #8 hitters, as much of this "skill" will disappear if ever moved from the #8 slot.

Batting order has no discernable effect on contact rate.

Hit rate slopes gently upward as hitters are slotted deeper in the lineup.

As expected, the #3-4-5 slots are ideal for non-HR RBIs, at the expense of #6 hitters. RBIs are worst for players in the #1-2 slots. Batting atop the order sharply increases the probability of scoring runs, especially in the NL.

The leadoff slot easily has the highest stolen base attempt rate. #4-5-6 hitters attempt steals more often when batting out of those slots than they do batting elsewhere. The NL #8 hitter is a SB attempt sink hole. A change in batting order from #8 to #1 in the NL could nearly double a player's SB output due to lineup slot alone.

DOMination and DISaster rates
Week-to-week consistency is measured using a batter's BPV compiled in each week. A player earns a DOMinant week if his BPV was greater or equal to 50 for that week. A player registers a DISaster if his BPV was less than 0 for that week. The percentage of Dominant weeks, DOM%, is simply calculated as the number of DOM weeks divided by the total number of weeks played.

Is week-to-week consistency a repeatable skill? *(Bill Macey)*
To test whether consistent performance is a repeatable skill for batters, we examined how closely related a player's DOM% was from year to year.

YR1 DOM%	AVG YR2 DOM%
< 35%	37%
35%–45%	40%
46%–55%	45%
56%+	56%

Quality/consistency score (QC)
(DOM% – (2 x DIS%)) x 2
Using the DOM/DIS percentages, this score measures both the quality of performance as well as week–to-week consistency.

Sample size reliability *(Russell Carleton)*
At what point during the season do statistics become reliable indicators of skill? Measured in plate appearances:

- 100: Contact rate
- 150: Strikeout rate, line drive rate, pitches/PA
- 200: Walk rate, ground ball rate, GB/FB
- 250: Fly ball rate
- 300: HR rate, hr/f
- 500: OBP, Slg, OPS
- 550: Isolated power

Unlisted stats did not stabilize over a full season of play.

Projecting RBIs *(Patrick Davitt)*

Evaluating players in-season for RBI potential is a function of the interplay among four factors:

- Teammates' ability to reach base ahead of him and to run the bases efficiently
- His own ability to drive them in by hitting, especially XBH
- Number of Games Played
- Place in the batting order

3-4-5 Hitters:
(0.69 x GP x TOB) + (0.30 x ITB) + (0.275 x HR) − (.191 x GP)

6-7-8 Hitters:
(0.63 x GP x TOB) + (0.27 x ITB) + (0.250 x HR) − (.191 x GP)

9-1-2 Hitters:
(0.57 x GP x TOB) + (0.24 x ITB) + (0.225 x HR) − (.191 x GP)

...where GP = games played, TOB = team on-base pct. and ITB = individual total bases (ITB).

Apply this pRBI formula after 70 games played or so (to reduce the variation from small sample size) to find players more than 9 RBIs over or under their projected RBI. There could be a correction coming.

You should also consider other factors, like injury or trade (involving the player or a top-of-the-order speedster) or team SB philosophy and success rate.

Remember: the player himself has an impact on his TOB. When we first did this study, we excluded the player from his TOB and got better results. The formula overestimates projected RBI for players with high OBP who skew his teams' OBP but can't benefit in RBI from that effect.

Ten-Game hitting streaks as a leading indicator *(Bob Berger)*

Research of hitting streaks from 2011 and 2012 showed that a 10-game streak can reliably predict improved longer-term BA performance during the season. A player who has put together a hitting streak of at least 10 games will improve his BA for the remainder of the season about 60% of the time. This improvement can be significant, on average as much as .020 of BA.

Other Diamonds

It's a Busy World Shortcut

For marginal utility-type players, scan their PX and Spd history to see if there's anything to mine for. If you see triple digits anywhere, stop and look further. If not, move on.

Chronology of the Classic Free-Swinger with Pop

1. Gets off to a good start.
2. Thinks he's in a groove.
3. Gets lax, careless.
4. Pitchers begin to catch on.
5. Fades down the stretch.

Errant Gust of Wind

A unit of measure used to describe the difference between your home run projection and mine.

Hannahan Concession

Players with a .218 BA rarely get 500 plate appearances, but when they do, it's usually once.

Mendoza Line

Named for Mario Mendoza, it represents the benchmark for batting futility. Usually refers to a .200 batting average, but can also be used for low levels of other statistical categories. Note that Mendoza's lifetime batting average was actually a much more robust .215.

Old Player Skills

Power, low batting average, no speed and usually good plate patience. Young players, often those with a larger frame, who possess these "old player skills" tend to decline faster than normal, often in their early 30s.

Small Sample Certitude

If players' careers were judged based what they did in a single game performance, then Tuffy Rhodes and Mark Whiten would be in the Hall of Fame.

Esix Snead List

Players with excellent speed and sub-.300 on base averages who get a lot of practice running down the line to first base, and then back to the dugout. Also used as an adjective, as in "Esix-Sneadian."

Pitchers

Strikeouts and Walks

Fundamental skills

Unreliable pitching performance is a fallacy driven by the practice of attempting to project pitching stats using gauges that are poor evaluators of skill.

How can we better evaluate pitching skill? We can start with the three statistical categories that are generally unaffected by external factors. These three stats capture the outcome of an individual pitcher versus batter match-up without regard to supporting offense, defense or bullpen:

Walks Allowed, Strikeouts and Ground Balls

Even with only these stats to observe, there is a wealth of insight that these measures can provide.

Control rate (Ctl, bb/9), or opposition walks per game
BB allowed x 9 / IP

Measures how many walks a pitcher allows per game equivalent. BENCHMARK: The best pitchers will have bb/9 levels of 2.8 or less.

Dominance rate (Dom, k/9), or opposition strikeouts/game
Strikeouts recorded x 9 / IP

Measures how many strikeouts a pitcher allows per game equivalent. BENCHMARK: The best pitchers will have k/9 levels of 7.0 or higher.

Command ratio (Cmd)
(Strikeouts / Walks)

A measure of a pitcher's ability to get the ball over the plate. There is no more fundamental a skill than this, and so it is used as a leading indicator to project future rises and falls in other gauges, such as ERA. BENCHMARKS: Baseball's best pitchers will have ratios in excess of 3.0. Pitchers with ratios less than 1.0—indicating that they walk more batters than they strike out—have virtually no potential for long-term success. If you make no other changes in your approach to drafting pitchers, limiting your focus to only pitchers with a command ratio of 2.5 or better will substantially improve your odds of success.

Command ratio as a leading indicator

The ability to get the ball over the plate—command of the strike zone—is one of the best leading indicators for future performance. Command ratio (K/BB) can be used to project potential in ERA as well as other skills gauges.

1. Research indicates that there is a high correlation between a pitcher's Cmd ratio and his ERA.

| | Earned Run Average | | | | |
Command	2010	2011	2012	2013	2014
0.0 - 1.0	5.86	5.45	6.22	5.98	6.81
1.1 - 1.5	5.14	4.84	5.03	4.91	4.97
1.6 - 2.0	4.34	4.35	4.48	4.42	4.37
2.1 - 2.5	3.95	3.89	4.09	3.96	3.80
2.6 - 3.0	3.71	3.66	3.88	3.81	3.78
3.1 - 3.5	3.36	3.58	3.67	3.46	3.43
3.6 - 4.0	3.47	3.00	3.34	3.32	3.16
4.1+	2.80	2.95	3.12	2.86	2.92

On the pitching flipside, the number of arms comprising the 4.1+ group has nearly doubled in two years. In 2012, 58 pitchers made up that group; this year, 93.

We can create percentage plays for the different levels:

| For Cmd | % with ERA of | |
Levels of	3.50-	4.50+
0.0 - 1.0	0%	87%
1.1 - 1.5	7%	67%
1.6 - 2.0	7%	57%
2.1 - 2.5	19%	35%
2.6 - 3.0	26%	25%
3.1 +	53%	5%

Pitchers who maintain a Cmd over 2.5 have a high probability of long-term success. For fantasy drafting purposes, it is best to avoid pitchers with sub-2.0 ratios. Avoid bullpen closers if they have a ratio less than 2.5.

2. A pitcher's Command in tandem with Dominance (strikeout rate) provides even greater predictive abilities.

| | Earned Run Average | |
Command	-5.6 Dom	5.6+ Dom
0.0-0.9	5.36	5.99
1.0-1.4	4.94	5.03
1.5-1.9	4.67	4.47
2.0-2.4	4.32	4.08
2.5-2.9	4.21	3.88
3.0-3.9	4.04	3.46
4.0+	4.12	2.96

This helps to highlight the limited upside potential of soft-tossers with pinpoint control. The extra dominance makes a huge difference.

3. Research also suggests that there is a strong correlation between a pitcher's command ratio and his propensity to win ballgames. Over three quarters of those with ratios over 3.0 post winning records, and the collective W/L record of those command artists is nearly .600.

The command/winning correlation holds up in both leagues, although the effect was more pronounced in the NL. Over four times more NL hurlers than AL hurlers had Cmd over 3.0, and higher ratios were required in the NL to maintain good winning percentages. A ratio between 2.0 and 2.9 was good enough for a winning record for over 70% of AL pitchers, but that level in the NL generated an above-.500 mark slightly more than half the time.

In short, in order to have at least a 70% chance of drafting a pitcher with a winning record, you must target NL pitchers with at least a 3.0 command ratio. To achieve the same odds in the AL, a 2.0 command ratio will suffice.

Swinging strike rate as leading indicator *(Stephen Nickrand)*

An emerging indicator for predicting starting pitching performance is swinging strike rate (SwK%), which measures the percentage of total pitches against which a batter swings and misses. SwK% can help us validate and forecast a SP's Dominance (K/9) rate, which in turn allows us to identify surgers and faders with greater accuracy.

Follow these rules of thumb when targeting starting pitchers based on SwK%: SwK% baselines for SP are 8.0% in AL, 8.4% in

NL; Expected Dom (xDom) can be estimated from SwK%; and a pitcher's individual SwK% does not regress to league norms.

The few starters per year who have a 12.0% or higher SwK% are near-locks to have a 9.0 Dom or greater. In contrast, starters with a 7.0% or lower SwK% have nearly no chance at posting even an average Dom. Finally, use an 8.5% SwK% as an acceptable threshold when searching for SP based on this metric; raise it to 9.5% to begin to find SwK% difference-makers.

Fastball velocity and Dominance rate *(Stephen Nickrand)*

It is intuitive that an increase in fastball velocity for starting pitchers leads to more strikeouts. But how much? We analyzed the historical link between fastball velocity and Dominance (K/9) rate. Among the findings:

The vast majority of SP with significant fastball velocity gains

- experience a significant Dom gain during the same season.
- are likely to give back those gains during the following season.
- are likely to increase their Dom the following season, but the magnitude of the Dom increase usually is small.

The vast majority of SP with significant fastball velocity losses

- are likely to experience a significant Dom decrease during the same season.

Those SP with significant fastball velocity losses from one season to the next are just as likely to experience a fastball velocity or Dom increase as they are to experience a fastball or Dom decrease, and the amounts of the increase/decrease are nearly identical.

Power/contact rating

(BB + K) / IP

Measures the level by which a pitcher allows balls to be put into play. In general, extreme power pitchers can be successful even with poor defensive teams. Power pitchers tend to have greater longevity in the game. Contact pitchers with poor defenses behind them are high risks to have poor W-L records and ERA. BENCHMARKS: A level of 1.13+ describes pure throwers. A level of .93 or less describes high contact pitchers.

Balls in Play

Balls in play (BIP)

(Batters faced − (BB + HBP + SAC)) + H − K

The total number of batted balls that are hit fair, both hits and outs. An analysis of how these balls are hit—on the ground, in the air, hits, outs, etc.—can provide analytical insight, from player skill levels to the impact of luck on statistical output.

Batting average on balls in play *(Voros McCracken)*

(H − HR) / (Batters faced − (BB + HBP + SAC)) + H − K − HR

Abbreviated as BABIP; also called hit rate (H%). The percent of balls hit into the field of play that fall for hits. BENCHMARK: The league average is 30%, which is also the level that individual performances will regress to on a year to year basis. Any +/- variance of 3% or more can affect a pitcher's ERA.

BABIP as a leading indicator *(Voros McCracken)*

In 2000, Voros McCracken published a study that concluded that "there is little if any difference among major league pitchers in their ability to prevent hits on balls hit in the field of play." His assertion was that, while a Johan Santana would have a better ability to prevent a batter from getting wood on a ball, or perhaps keeping the ball in the park, once that ball was hit in the field of play, the probability of it falling for a hit was virtually no different than for any other pitcher.

Among the findings in his study were:

- There is little correlation between what a pitcher does one year in the stat and what he will do the next. This is not true with other significant stats (BB, K, HR).
- You can better predict a pitcher's hits per balls in play from the rate of the rest of the pitcher's team than from the pitcher's own rate.

This last point brings a team's defense into the picture. It begs the question, when a batter gets a hit, is it because the pitcher made a bad pitch, the batter took a good swing, or the defense was not positioned correctly?

Pitchers will often post hit rates per balls-in-play that are far off from the league average, but then revert to the mean the following year. As such, we can use that mean to project the direction of a pitcher's ERA.

Subsequent research has shown that ground ball or fly ball propensity has some impact on this rate.

Hit rate *(See Batting average on balls in play)*

Opposition batting average (OBA)

Hits allowed / (Batters faced − (BB + HBP + SAC))

The batting average achieved by opposing batters against a pitcher. BENCHMARKS: The best pitchers will have levels less than .250; the worst pitchers levels more than .300.

Opposition on base average (OOB)

(Hits allowed + BB) / ((Batters faced − (BB + HBP + SAC)) + Hits allowed + BB)

The on base average achieved by opposing batters against a pitcher. BENCHMARK: The best pitchers will have levels less than .300; the worst pitchers levels more than .375.

Walks plus hits divided by innings pitched (WHIP)

Essentially the same measure as opposition on base average, but used for Rotisserie purposes. BENCHMARKS: A WHIP of less than 1.20 is considered top level; more than 1.50 indicative of poor performance. Levels less than 1.00—allowing fewer runners than IP—represent extraordinary performance and are rarely maintained over time.

Ground ball, line drive, fly ball percentage (G/L/F)

The percentage of all balls-in-play that are hit on the ground, in the air and as line drives. For a pitcher, the ability to keep the ball on the ground can contribute to his statistical output exceeding his demonstrated skill level.

Ground ball tendency as a leading indicator *(John Burnson)*
Ground ball pitchers tend to give up fewer HRs than do fly ball pitchers. There is also evidence that GB pitchers have higher hit rates. In other words, a ground ball has a higher chance of being a hit than does a fly ball that is not out of the park.

GB pitchers have lower strikeout rates. We should be more forgiving of a low strikeout rate (under 5.5 K/9) if it belongs to an extreme ground ball pitcher.

GB pitchers have a lower ERA but a higher WHIP than do fly ball pitchers. On balance, GB pitchers come out ahead, even when considering strikeouts, because a lower ERA also leads to more wins.

Groundball and strikeout tendencies as indicators
(Mike Dranchak)
Pitchers were assembled into 9 groups based on the following profiles (minimum 23 starts in 2005):

Profile	Ground Ball Rate
Ground Ball	higher than 47%
Neutral	42% to 47%
Fly Ball	less than 42%

Profile	Strikeout Rate (k/9)
Strikeout	higher than 6.6 k/9
Average	5.4 to 6.6 k/9
Soft-Tosser	less than 5.4 k/9

Findings: Pitchers with higher strikeout rates had better ERAs and WHIPs than pitchers with lower strikeout rates, regardless of ground ball profile. However, for pitchers with similar strikeout rates, those with higher ground ball rates had better ERAs and WHIPs than those with lower ground ball rates.

Pitchers with higher strikeout rates tended to strand more baserunners than those with lower K rates. Fly ball pitchers tended to strand fewer runners than their GB or neutral counterparts within their strikeout profile.

Ground ball pitchers (especially those who lacked high-dominance) yielded more home runs per fly ball than did fly ball pitchers. However, the ERA risk was mitigated by the fact that ground ball pitchers (by definition) gave up fewer fly balls to begin with.

Extreme GB/FB pitchers *(Patrick Davitt)*
Among pitchers with normal strikeout levels, extreme GB pitchers (>3–7% of all batters faced) have ERAs about 0.4 runs lower than normal-GB% pitchers but only slight WHIP advantages. Extreme FB% pitchers (32% FB) show no ERA benefits.

Among High-K (>=24% of BF), however, extreme GBers have ERAs about 0.5 runs lower than normal-GB pitchers, and WHIPs about five points lower. Extreme FB% pitchers have ERAs about 0.2 runs lower than normal-FB pitchers, and WHIPs about 10 points lower.

Line drive percentage as a leading indicator *(Seth Samuels)*
Also beyond a pitcher's control is the percentage of balls-in-play that are line drives. Line drives do the most damage; from 1994-2003, here were the expected hit rates and number of total bases per type of BIP.

	Type of BIP		
	GB	FB	LD
H%	26%	23%	56%
Total bases	0.29	0.57	0.80

Despite the damage done by LDs, pitchers do not have any innate skill to avoid them. There is little relationship between a pitcher's LD% one year and his rate the next year. All rates tend to regress towards a mean of 22.6%.

However, GB pitchers do have a slight ability to prevent LDs (21.7%) and extreme GB hurlers even moreso (18.5%). Extreme FB pitchers have a slight ability to prevent LDs (21.1%) as well.

Home run to fly ball rate (hr/f)
HR / FB
The percent of fly balls that are hit for home runs.

hr/f as a leading indicator *(John Burnson)*
McCracken's work focused on "balls in play," omitting home runs from the study. However, pitchers also do not have much control over the percentage of fly balls that turn into HR. Research shows that there is an underlying rate of HR as a percentage of fly balls of about 10%. A pitcher's HR/FB rate will vary each year but always tends to regress to that 10%. The element that pitchers do have control over is the number of fly balls they allow. That is the underlying skill or deficiency that controls their HR rate.

Pitchers who keep the ball out of the air more often correlate well with Roto value.

Opposition home runs per game (hr/9)
(HR Allowed x 9 / IP)
Also, expected opposition HR rate = (FB x 0.10) x 9 / IP
Measures how many HR a pitcher allows per game equivalent. Since FB tend to go yard at about a 10% rate, we can also estimate this rate off of fly balls. **BENCHMARK:** The best pitchers will have hr/9 levels of less than 1.0.

Runs

Expected earned run average (xERA)
Gill and Reeve version: *(.575 x H [per 9 IP]) + (.94 x HR [per 9 IP]) + (.28 x BB [per 9 IP]) – (.01 x K [per 9 IP]) – Normalizing Factor*

John Burnson version (used in this book):
(xER x 9)/IP, where xER is defined as
xER% x (FB/10) + (1-xS%) x [0.3 x (BIP – FB/10) + BB]
where xER% = 0.96 – (0.0284 x (GB/FB))
and
xS% = (64.5 + (K/9 x 1.2) – (BB/9 x (BB/9 + 1)) / 20)
+ ((0.0012 x (GB%^2)) – (0.001 x GB%) - 2.4)

xERA represents the an equivalent of what a pitcher's real ERA might be, calculated solely with skills-based measures. It is not influenced by situation-dependent factors.

Expected ERA variance
xERA – ERA
The variance between a pitcher's ERA and his xERA is a measure of over or underachievement. A positive variance indicates the potential for a pitcher's ERA to rise. A negative variance indicates

the potential for ERA improvement. **BENCHMARK:** Discount variances that are less than 0.50. Any variance more than 1.00 (one run per game) is regarded as a indicator of future change.

Projected xERA or projected ERA?

Which should we be using to forecast a pitcher's ERA? Projected xERA is more accurate for looking ahead on a purely skills basis. Projected ERA includes *situation-dependent* events—bullpen support, park factors, etc.—which are reflected better by ERA. The optimal approach is to use both gauges as *a range of expectation* for forecasting purposes.

Strand rate (S%)

(H + BB − ER) / (H + BB − HR)

Measures the percentage of allowed runners a pitcher strands (earned runs only), which incorporates both individual pitcher skill and bullpen effectiveness. **BENCHMARKS:** The most adept at stranding runners will have S% levels over 75%. Those with rates over 80% will have artificially low ERAs which will be prone to relapse. Levels below 65% will inflate ERA but have a high probability of regression.

Expected strand rate *(Michael Weddell)*

$73.935 + K/9 - 0.116 * (BB/9*(BB/9+1))$
$+ (0.0047 * GB\%^2 - 0.3385 * GB\%)$
$+ (MAX(2,MIN(4,IP/G))/2-1)$
$+ (0.82$ if left-handed$)$

This formula is based on three core skills: strikeouts per nine innings, walks per nine innings, and groundballs per balls in play, with adjustments for whether the pitcher is a starter or reliever (measured by IP/G), and his handedness.

Strand rate as a leading indicator *(Ed DeCaria)*

Strand rate often regresses/rebounds toward past rates (usually 69-74%), resulting in Year 2 ERA changes:

% of Pitchers with Year 2 Regression/Rebound

Y1 S%	RP	SP	LR
<60%	100%	94%	94%
65	81%	74%	88%
70	53%	48%	65%
75	55%	85%	100%
80	80%	100%	100%
85	100%	100%	100%

Typical ERA Regression/Rebound in Year 2

Y1 S%	RP	SP	LR
<60%	-2.54	-2.03	-2.79
65	-1.00	-0.64	-0.93
70	-0.10	-0.05	-0.44
75	0.24	0.54	0.75
80	1.15	1.36	2.29
85	1.71	2.21	n/a

Starting pitchers (SP) have a narrower range of strand rate outcomes than do relievers (RP) or swingmen/long relievers (LR). **Relief pitchers** with Y1 strand rates of <=67% or >=78% are likely to experience a +/- ERA regression in Y2. **Starters and swingmen/long relievers** with Y1 strand rates of <=65% or >=75% are likely to experience a +/- ERA regression in Y2. Pitchers with strand rates that deviate more than a few points off of their individual expected strand rates are likely to experience some degree of ERA regression in Y2. Over-performing (or "lucky") pitchers are more likely than underperforming (or "unlucky") pitchers to see such a correction.

Wins

Projecting/chasing wins

There are five events that need to occur in order for a pitcher to post a single win...

1. He must pitch well, allowing few runs.
2. The offense must score enough runs.
3. The defense must successfully field all batted balls.
4. The bullpen must hold the lead.
5. The manager must leave the pitcher in for 5 innings, and not remove him if the team is still behind.

Of these five events, only one is within the control of the pitcher. As such, projecting or chasing wins based on skills alone can be an exercise in futility.

Home field advantage *(John Burnson)*

A 2006 study found that home starting pitchers get credited with a win in 38% of their outings. Visiting team starters are credited with a win in 33% of their outings.

Usage

Batters faced per game *(Craig Wright)*

((Batters faced − (BB + HBP + SAC)) + H + BB) / G

A measure of pitcher usage and one of the leading indicators for potential pitcher burnout.

Workload

Research suggests that there is a finite number of innings in a pitcher's arm. This number varies by pitcher, by development cycle, and by pitching style and repertoire. We can measure a pitcher's potential for future arm problems and/or reduced effectiveness (burnout):

Sharp increases in usage from one year to the next. Common wisdom has suggested that pitchers who significantly increase their workload from one year to the next are candidates for burnout symptoms. This has often been called the Verducci Effect, after writer Tom Verducci. BaseballHQ.com analyst Michael Weddell tested pitchers with sharp workload increases during the period 1988-2008 and found that no such effect exists.

Starters' overuse. Consistent "batters faced per game" (BF/G) levels of 28.0 or higher, combined with consistent seasonal IP totals of 200 or more may indicate burnout potential. Within a season, a BF/G of more than 30.0 with a projected IP total of 200 may indicate a late season fade.

Relievers' overuse. Warning flags should be up for relievers who post in excess of 100 IP in a season, while averaging fewer than 2 IP per outing.

When focusing solely on minor league pitchers, research results are striking:

Stamina: Virtually every minor league pitcher who had a BF/G of 28.5 or more in one season experienced a drop-off in BF/G the following year. Many were unable to ever duplicate that previous level of durability.

Performance: Most pitchers experienced an associated drop-off in their BPVs in the years following the 28.5 BF/G season. Some were able to salvage their effectiveness later on by moving to the bullpen.

Protecting young pitchers *(Craig Wright)*
There is a link between some degree of eventual arm trouble and a history of heavy workloads in a pitcher's formative years. Some recommendations from this research:

Teenagers (A-ball): No 200 IP seasons and no BF/G over 28.5 in any 150 IP span. No starts on three days rest.

Ages 20-22: Average no more than 105 pitches per start with a single game ceiling of 130 pitches.

Ages 23-24: Average no more than 110 pitches per start with a single game ceiling of 140 pitches.

When possible, a young starter should be introduced to the majors in long relief before he goes into the rotation.

Overall Performance Analysis

Base Performance Value (BPV)
((Dominance Rate - 5.0) x 18)
+ ((4.0 - Walk Rate) x 27))
+ (Ground ball rate as a whole number - 40%)

A single value that describes a player's overall raw skill level. This is more useful than traditional statistical gauges to track player performance trends and project future statistical output. The formula combines the individual raw skills of power, control and the ability to keep the ball down in the zone, all characteristics that are unaffected by most external factors. In tandem with a pitcher's strand rate, it provides a more complete picture of the elements that contribute to ERA, and therefore serves as an accurate tool to project likely changes in ERA. **BENCHMARKS:** A BPV of 50 is the minimum level required for long-term success. The elite of the bullpen aces will have BPVs in excess of 100 and it is rare for these stoppers to enjoy long term success with consistent levels under 75.

Base Performance Index (BPX)
BPV scaled to league average to account for year-to-year fluctuations in league-wide statistical performance. It's a snapshot of a player's overall skills compared to an average player. **BENCHMARK:** A level of 100 means a player had a league-average BPV in that given season.

Runs above replacement (RAR)
An estimate of the number of runs a player contributes above a "replacement level" player.

Batters create runs; pitchers save runs. But are batters and pitchers who have comparable RAR levels truly equal in value? Pitchers might be considered to have higher value. Saving an additional run is more important than producing an additional run. A pitcher who throws a shutout is guaranteed to win that game, whereas no matter how many runs a batter produces, his team can still lose given poor pitching support.

To calculate RAR for pitchers:
1. Start with the replacement level league ERA.
2. Subtract the pitcher's ERA. (To calculate projected RAR, use the pitcher's xERA.)
3. Multiply by number of games played, calculated as plate appearances (IP x 4.34) divided by 38.
4. Multiply the resulting RAR level by 1.08 to account for the variance between earned runs and total runs.

Handedness
1. LHers tend to peak about a year after RHers.
2. LHers post only 15% of the total saves. Typically, LHers are reserved for specialist roles so few are frontline closers.
3. RHers have slightly better command and HR rate.
4. There is no significant variance in ERA.
5. On an overall skills basis, RHers have ~6% advantage.

Skill-Specific Aging Patterns for Pitchers *(Ed DeCaria)*
Baseball forecasters obsess over "peak age" of player performance because we must understand player ascent toward and decline from that peak to predict future value. Most published aging analyses are done using composite estimates of value such as OPS or linear weights. By contrast, fantasy GMs are typically more concerned with category-specific player value (K, ERA, WHIP, etc.). We can better forecast what matters most by analyzing peak age of individual baseball skills rather than overall player value.

For pitchers, prior research has shown that pitcher value peaks somewhere in the late 20s to early 30s. But how does aging affect each demonstrable pitching skill?

Strikeout rate (k/9): Declines fairly linearly beginning at age 25.

Walk rate (bb/9): Improves until age 25 and holds somewhat steady until age 29, at which point it begins to steadily worsen. Deteriorating k/9 and bb/9 rates result in inefficiency, as it requires far more pitches to get an out. For starting pitchers, this affects the ability to pitch deep into games.

Innings Pitched per game (IP/G): Among starters, it improves slightly until age 27, then tails off considerably with age, costing pitchers nearly one full IP/G by age 33 and one more by age 39.

Hit rate (H%): Among pitchers, H% appears to increase slowly but steadily as pitchers age, to the tune of .002-.003 points per year.

Strand rate (S%): Very similar to hit rate, except strand rate decreases with age rather than increasing. GB%/LD%/FB%: Line drives increase steadily from age 24 onward, and outfield flies increase beginning at age 31. Because 70%+ of line drives fall for hits, and 10%+ of fly balls become home runs, this spells trouble for aging pitchers.

Home runs per fly ball (hr/f): As each year passes, a higher percentage of a pitcher's fly balls become home runs allowed increases with age.

Catchers' effect on pitching *(Thomas Hanrahan)*
A typical catcher handles a pitching staff better after having been with a club for a few years. Research has shown that there is an improvement in team ERA of approximately 0.37 runs from a catcher's rookie season to his prime years with a club. Expect a pitcher's ERA to be higher than expected if he is throwing to a rookie backstop.

First productive season *(Michael Weddell)*

To find those starting pitchers who are about to post their first productive season in the majors (10 wins, 150 IP, ERA of 4.00 or less), look for:

- Pitchers entering their age 23-26 seasons, especially those about to pitch their age 25 season.
- Pitchers who already have good skills, shown by an xERA in the prior year of 4.25 or less.
- Pitchers coming off of at least a partial season in the majors without a major health problem.
- To the extent that one speculates on pitchers who are one skill away, look for pitchers who only need to improve their control (bb/9).

Overall pitching breakout profile *(Brandon Kruse)*

A breakout performance is defined here as one where a player posts a Rotisserie value of $20 or higher after having never achieved $10 previously. These criteria are primarily used to validate an apparent breakout in the current season but may also be used carefully to project a potential breakout for an upcoming season.

- Age 27 or younger
- Minimum 5.6 Dom, 2.0 Cmd, 1.1 hr/9 and 50 BPV
- Maximum 30% hit rate
- Minimum 71% strand rate
- Starters should have a H% no greater than the previous year; relievers should show improved command
- Maximum xERA of 4.00

Career year drop-off *(Rick Wilton)*

Research shows that a pitcher's post-career year drop-off, on average, looks like this:

- ERA increases by 1.00
- WHIP increases by 0.14.
- Nearly 6 fewer wins

Pitchers crossing leagues *(Bob Berger)*

The AL has higher league-wide ERA and lower K/9 when compared to the NL. Fantasy owners should consider adjusting their ERA, WHIP, and K/9 expectations for pitchers moving to the "other" league. Pitchers moving to the NL may perform better than expected based on their recent career trends; pitchers moving to the AL may perform worse than expected.

Closers

Saves

There are six events that need to occur in order for a relief pitcher to post a single save:

1. The starting pitcher and middle relievers must pitch well.
2. The offense must score enough runs.
3. It must be a reasonably close game.
4. The manager must put the pitcher in for a save opportunity.
5. The pitcher must pitch well and hold the lead.
6. The manager must let him finish the game.

Of these six events, only one is within the control of the relief pitcher. As such, projecting saves for a reliever has little to do with skill and a lot to do with opportunity. However, pitchers with excellent skills may create opportunity for themselves.

Saves conversion rate (Sv%)

Saves / Save Opportunities

The percentage of save opportunities that are successfully converted. **BENCHMARK:** We look for a minimum 80% for long-term success.

Leverage index (LI) *(Tom Tango)*

Leverage index measures the amount of swing in the possible change in win probability indexed against an average value of 1.00. Thus, relievers who come into games in various situations create a composite score and if that average score is higher than 1.00, then their manager is showing enough confidence in them to try to win games with them. If the average score is below 1.00, then the manager is using them, but not showing nearly as much confidence that they can win games.

Saves chances and wins *(Craig Neuman)*

Should the quality of a pitcher's MLB team be a consideration in drafting a closer? One school of thought says that more wins means more save opportunities. The flipside is that when poor teams win they do so by a small margin, which means more save opportunities.

A six-season correlation yielded these results for saves, save opportunities, save percentage, wins, quality starts and run differential. (Any value above .50 suggests at least a moderate correlation.)

	Sv	SvO	W	Sv%	RD	QS
SV	1					
SVO	.78	1				
W	.66	.41	1			
S%	.66	.05	.56	1		
RD	.48	.26	.92	.44	1	
QS	.41	.24	.58	.34	.60	1

Saves do correlate with wins. As for the theory that teams who play in close games would accumulate more saves, the low correlation between saves and run differential seems to dispel that a bit.

On average, teams registered one save for every two wins. However, there is a relationship between wins and the number of saves per win a team achieves:

Win Total	Saves/Win
>90	.494
80-89	.492
70-79	.505
<69	.525

Teams with fewer wins end up with more saves per win. So, when poor teams win, they are more likely to have a save chance.

Origin of closers

History has long maintained that ace closers are not easily recognizable early on in their careers, so that every season does see its share of the unexpected. Cody Allen, Zach Britton, Sean Doolittle,

Jake McGee, Jenrry Mejia, Jacob Petricka, Hector Rondon, Joe Smith… who would have thought it a year ago?

Accepted facts, all of which have some element of truth:

- You cannot find major league closers from pitchers who were closers in the minors.
- Closers begin their careers as starters.
- Closers are converted set-up men.
- Closers are pitchers who were unable to develop a third effective pitch.

More simply, closers are a product of circumstance.

Are the minor leagues a place to look at all?

From 1990-2004, there were 280 twenty-save seasons in Double-A and Triple-A, accomplished by 254 pitchers.

Of those 254, only 46 ever made it to the majors at all.

Of those 46, only 13 ever saved 20 games in a season.

Of those 13, only 5 ever posted more than one 20-save season in the majors: John Wetteland, Mark Wohlers, Ricky Bottalico, Braden Looper and Francisco Cordero.

Five out of 254 pitchers, over 15 years—a rate of 2%.

One of the reasons that minor league closers rarely become major league closers is because, in general, they do not get enough innings in the minors to sufficiently develop their arms into big-league caliber.

In fact, organizations do not look at minor league closing performance seriously, assigning that role to pitchers who they do not see as legitimate prospects. The average age of minor league closers over the past decade has been 27.5.

Elements of saves success

The task of finding future closing potential comes down to looking at two elements:

Talent: The raw skills to mow down hitters for short periods of time. Optimal BPVs over 100, but not under 75.

Opportunity: The more important element, yet the one that pitchers have no control over.

There are pitchers that have Talent, but not Opportunity. These pitchers are not given a chance to close for a variety of reasons (e.g. being blocked by a solid front-liner in the pen, being left-handed, etc.), but are good to own because they will not likely hurt your pitching staff. You just can't count on them for saves, at least not in the near term.

There are pitchers that have Opportunity, but not Talent. MLB managers decide who to give the ball to in the 9th inning based on their own perceptions about what skills are required to succeed, even if those perceived "skills" don't translate into acceptable BPI levels.

Those pitchers without the BPIs may have some initial short-term success, but their long-term prognosis is poor and they are high risks to your roster. Classic examples of the short life span of these types of pitchers include Matt Karchner, Heath Slocumb, Ryan Kohlmeier, Dan Miceli, Joe Borowski and Danny Kolb. More recent examples include Tom Wilhelmsen, Kevin Gregg and Brian Fuentes.

Closers' job retention *(Michael Weddell)*

Of pitchers with 20 or more saves in one year, only 67.5% of these closers earned 20 or more saves the following year. The variables that best predicted whether a closer would avoid this attrition:

- *Saves history:* Career saves was the most important factor.
- *Age:* Closers are most likely to keep their jobs at age 27. For long-time closers, their growing career saves totals more than offset the negative impact of their advanced ages. Older closers without a long history of racking up saves tend to be bad candidates for retaining their roles.
- *Performance:* Actual performance, measured by ERA+, was of only minor importance.
- *Being right-handed:* Increased the odds of retaining the closer's role by 9% over left-handers.

How well can we predict which closers will keep their jobs? Of the 10 best closers during 1989-2007, 90% saved at least 20 games during the following season. Of the 10 worst bets, only 20% saved at least 20 games the next year.

Closer volatility history

Year	Closers Drafted	Avg R$	Closers Failed	Failure %	New Sources
1999	23	$25	5	22%	7
2000	27	$25	10	37%	9
2001	25	$26	7	28%	7
2002	28	$22	8	29%	12
2003	29	$21.97	17	59%	14
2004	29	$19.78	11	38%	15
2005	28	$20.79	12	43%	15
2006	30	$17.80	10	33%	12
2007	28	$17.67	10	36%	11
2008	32	$17.78	10	31%	11
2009	28	$17.56	9	32%	13
2010	28	$16.96	7	25%	13
2011	30	$15.47	11	37%	8
2012	29	$15.28	19	66%	18
2013	29	$15.55	9	31%	13
2014	28	$15.54	11	39%	15

Drafted refers to the number of saves sources purchased in both LABR and Tout Wars experts leagues each year. These only include relievers drafted for at least $10, specifically for saves speculation. *Avg R$* refers to the average purchase price of these pitchers in the AL-only and NL-only leagues. *Failed* is the number (and percentage) of saves sources drafted that did not return at least 50% of their value that year. The failures include those that lost their value due to ineffectiveness, injury or managerial decision. *New Sources* are arms that were drafted for less than $10 (if drafted at all) but finished with at least double-digit saves.

The failed saves investments in 2014 were John Axford, Grant Balfour, Neftali Feliz, Ernesto Frieri, Jason Grilli, Jim Henderson, Casey Janssen, Jim Johnson, Nate Jones, Joe Nathan and Bobby Parnell. The new sources in 2014 were Cody Allen, Joaquin Benoit, Zach Britton, Santiago Casilla, Sean Doolittle, LaTroy Hawkins, Jake McGee, Jenrry Mejia, Mark Melancon, Jacob Petricka, Chad Qualls, Francisco Rodriguez, Hector Rondon, Joe Smith and Drew Storen.

BPV as a leading indicator *(Doug Dennis)*

Research has shown that base performance value (BPV) is an excellent indicator of long-term success as a closer. Here are 20-plus saves seasons, by year:

Year	No.	100+	75+	<75
1999	26	27%	54%	46%
2000	24	25%	54%	46%
2001	25	56%	80%	20%
2002	25	60%	72%	28%
2003	25	36%	64%	36%
2004	23	61%	61%	39%
2005	25	36%	64%	36%
2006	25	52%	72%	28%
2007	23	52%	74%	26%
MEAN	*25*	*45%*	*66%*	*34%*

(Header spans: |------BPV------| over 100+, 75+, <75)

Though 20-saves success with a 75+ BPV is only a 66% percentage play in any given year, the below-75 group is composed of closers who are rarely able to repeat the feat in the following season:

Year	No. with BPV < 75	No. who followed up 20+ saves <75 BPV
1999	12	2
2000	11	2
2001	5	2
2002	7	3
2003	9	3
2004	9	2
2005	9	1
2006	7	3
2007	6	0

Other Relievers

Projecting holds *(Doug Dennis)*

Here are some general rules of thumb for identifying pitchers who might be in line to accumulate holds. The percentages represent the portion of 2003's top holds leaders who fell into the category noted.

1. Left-handed set-up men with excellent BPIs. (43%)
2. A "go-to" right-handed set-up man with excellent BPIs. This is the one set-up RHer that a manager turns to with a small lead in the 7th or 8th innings. These pitchers also tend to vulture wins. (43%, but 6 of the top 9)
3. Excellent BPIs, but not a firm role as the main LHed or RHed set-up man. Roles change during the season; cream rises to the top. Relievers projected to post great BPIs often overtake lesser set-up men in-season. (14%)

Reliever efficiency percent (REff%)

(Wins + Saves + Holds) / (Wins + Losses + SaveOpps + Holds)

This is a measure of how often a reliever contributes positively to the outcome of a game. A record of consistent, positive impact on game outcomes breeds managerial confidence, and that confidence could pave the way to save opportunities. For those pitchers suddenly thrust into a closer's role, this formula helps gauge their potential to succeed based on past successes in similar roles. **BENCHMARK:** Minimum of 80%.

Vulture

A pitcher, typically a middle reliever, who accumulates an unusually high number of wins by preying on other pitchers' misfortunes. More accurately, this is a pitcher typically brought into a game after a starting pitcher has put his team behind, and then pitches well enough and long enough to allow his offense to take the lead, thereby "vulturing" a win from the starter.

In-Season Analysis

Pure Quality Starts

We've always approached performance measures on an aggregate basis. Each individual event that our statistics chronicle gets dumped into a huge pool of data. We then use our formulas to try to sort and slice and manipulate the data into more usable information.

Pure Quality Starts (PQS) take a different approach. It says that the smallest unit of measure should not be the "event" but instead be the "game." Within that game, we can accumulate all the strikeouts, hits and walks, and evaluate that outing as a whole. After all, when a pitcher takes the mound, he is either "on" or "off" his game; he is either dominant or struggling, or somewhere in between.

In PQS, we give a starting pitcher credit for exhibiting certain skills in each of his starts. Then by tracking his "PQS Score" over time, we can follow his progress. A starter earns one point for each of the following criteria:

1. *The pitcher must go a minimum of 6 innings. This measures stamina. If he goes less than 5 innings, he automatically gets a total PQS score of zero, no matter what other stats he produces.*
2. *He must allow no more than an equal number of hits to the number of innings pitched. This measures hit prevention.*
3. *His number of strikeouts must be no fewer than two less than his innings pitched. This measures dominance.*
4. *He must strike out at least twice as many batters as he walks. This measures command.*
5. *He must allow no more than one home run. This measures his ability to keep the ball in the park.*

A perfect PQS score is 5. Any pitcher who averages 3 or more over the course of the season is probably performing admirably. The nice thing about PQS is it allows you to approach each start as more than an all-or-nothing event.

Note the absence of earned runs. No matter how many runs a pitcher allows, if he scores high on the PQS scale, he has hurled a good game in terms of his base skills. The number of runs allowed—a function of not only the pitcher's ability but that of his bullpen and defense—will tend to even out over time.

It doesn't matter if a few extra balls got through the infield, or the pitcher was given the hook in the fourth or sixth inning, or the bullpen was able to strand their inherited baserunners. When we look at performance in the aggregate, those events do matter, and will affect a pitcher's BPIs and ERA. But with PQS, the minutia is less relevant than the overall performance.

In the end, a dominating performance is a dominating performance, whether Clayton Kershaw is hurling a 3-hit shutout or giving up three runs while striking out 8 in 7 IP. And a disaster is still a disaster, whether Brandon Cumpton gets a 4th inning hook after giving up 4 runs on 9 hits, or "takes one for the team" and gets shelled for 10 runs in 3.2 innings.

Skill versus consistency

Two pitchers have identical 4.50 ERAs and identical 3.0 PQS averages. Their PQS logs look like this:

PITCHER A: 3 3 3 3 3
PITCHER B: 5 0 5 0 5

Which pitcher would you rather have on your team? The risk-averse manager would choose Pitcher A as he represents the perfectly known commodity. Many fantasy leaguers might opt for Pitcher B because his occasional dominating starts show that there is an upside. His Achilles Heel is inconsistency—he is unable to sustain that high level. Is there any hope for Pitcher B?

- If a pitcher's inconsistency is characterized by more poor starts than good starts, his upside is limited.
- Pitchers with extreme inconsistency rarely get a full season of starts.
- However, inconsistency is neither chronic nor fatal.

The outlook for Pitcher A is actually worse. Disaster avoidance might buy these pitchers more starts, but history shows that the lack of dominating outings is more telling of future potential. In short, consistent mediocrity is bad.

PQS DOMination and DISaster rates *(Gene McCaffrey)*

DOM% is the percentage of a starting pitcher's outings that rate as a PQS-4 or PQS-5. DIS% is the percentage that rate as a PQS-0 or PQS-1.

DOM/DIS percentages open up a new perspective, providing us with two separate scales of performance. In tandem, they measure consistency.

PQS ERA (qERA)

A pitcher's DOM/DIS split can be converted back to an equivalent ERA. By creating a grid of individual DOM% and DIS% levels, we can determine the average ERA at each cross point. The result is an ERA based purely on PQS.

Quality/consistency score (QC)

(DOM% – (2 x DIS%)) x 2

Using PQS and DOM/DIS percentages, this score measures both the quality of performance as well as start-to-start consistency.

PQS correlation with Quality Starts *(Paul Petera)*

PQS	QS%
0	0%
1	3%
2	21%
3	51%
4	75%
5	95%

Forward-looking PQS *(John Burnson)*

PQS says whether a pitcher performed ably in a *past* start—it doesn't say anything about how he'll do in the *next* start. We built a version of PQS that attempts to do that. For each series of five starts for a pitcher, we looked at his average IP, K/9, HR/9, H/9, and K/BB, and then whether the pitcher won his next start. We

catalogued the results by indicator and calculated the observed future winning percentage for each data point.

This research suggested that a forward-looking version of PQS should have these criteria:

- The pitcher must have lasted at least 6.2 innings.
- He must have recorded at least IP – 1 strikeouts.
- He must have allowed zero home runs.
- He must have allowed no more hits than IP+2.
- He must have had a Command (K/BB) of at least 2.5.

In-season ERA/xERA variance as a leading indicator

(Matt Cederholm)

Pitchers with large first-half ERA/xERA variances will see regression towards their xERA in the second half, if they are allowed (and are able) to finish out the season. Starters have a stronger regression tendency than relievers, which we would expect to see given the larger sample size. In addition, there is substantial attrition among all types of pitchers, but those who are "unlucky" have a much higher rate.

An important corollary: While a pitcher underperforming his xERA is very likely to rebound in the second half, such regression hinges on his ability to hold onto his job long enough to see that regression come to fruition. Healthy veteran pitchers with an established role are more likely to experience the second half boost than a rookie starter trying to make his mark.

Pure Quality Relief *(Patrick Davitt)*

A system for evaluating reliever outings. The scoring :

1. Two points for the first out, and one point for each subsequent out, to a maximum of four points.
2. One point for having at least one strikeout for every four full outs (one K for 1-4 outs, two Ks for 5-8 outs, etc.).
3. One point for zero baserunners, minus one point for each baserunner, though allowing the pitcher one unpenalized runner for each three full outs (one baserunner for 3-5 outs, two for 6-8 outs, three for nine outs)
4. Minus one point for each earned run, though allowing one ER for 8– or 9-out appearances.
5. An automatic PQR-0 for allowing a home run.

Avoiding relief disasters *(Ed DeCaria)*

Relief disasters (defined as ER>=3 and IP<=3), occur in 5%+ of all appearances. The chance of a disaster exceeds 13% in any 7-day period. To minimize the odds of a disaster, we created a model that produced the following list of factors, in order of influence:

1. Strength of opposing offense
2. Park factor of home stadium
3. BB/9 over latest 31 days (more walks is bad)
4. Pitch count over previous 7 days (more pitches is bad)
5. Latest 31 Days ERA>xERA (recent bad luck continues)

Daily league owners who can slot relievers by individual game should also pay attention to days of rest: pitching on less rest than one is accustomed to increases disaster risk.

Sample size reliability *(Russell Carleton)*

At what point during the season do statistics become reliable indicators of skill? Measured in batters faced:

150: K/PA, ground ball rate, line drive rate

200: Fly ball rate, GB/FB

500: K/BB

550: BB/PA

Unlisted stats did not stabilize over a full season of play. *(Note that 150 BF is roughly equivalent to six outings for a starting pitcher; 550 BF would be 22 starts, etc.)*

Pitching streaks

It is possible to find predictive value in strings of DOMinating (PQS 4/5) or DISaster (PQS 0/1) starts:

Once a pitcher enters into a DOM streak of any length, the probability is that his next start is going to be better than average. The further a player is into a DOM streak, the higher the likelihood that the subsequent performance will be high quality. In fact, once a pitcher has posted six DOM starts in a row, there is greater than a 70% probability that the streak will continue. When it does end, there is less than a 10% probability that the streak-breaker is going to be a DISaster.

Once a pitcher enters into a DIS streak of any length, the probability is that his next start is going to be below average, even if it breaks the streak. However, DIS streaks end quickly. Once a pitcher hits the skids, odds are low that he will post a good start in the short term, though the duration itself should be brief.

5-game PQS predictability *(Bill Macey)*

5-Game avg PQS	Avg PQS	DOM%	DIS%
Less than 1	2.1	27%	40%
Between 1 and 2	2.4	32%	32%
Between 2 and 3	2.6	36%	26%
Between 3 and 4	3.0	47%	19%
4 or greater	3.5	61%	12%

Pitchers with higher PQS scores in their previous 5 starts tended to pitch better in their next start. But the relative parity of subsequent DOM and DIS starts for all but the hottest of streaks warn us not to put too much effort into predicting any given start. That more than a quarter of pitchers who had been awful over their previous 5 starts still put up a dominating start next shows that anything can happen in a single game.

High pitch counts and PQS *(Patrick Davitt)*

Starting pitcher matchups are vital for both daily fantasy owners and owners in longer formats that allow "streaming" of starters. In making SP decisions, owners might be tempted to sit a starter coming off a high-pitch-count (PC) start, even a good start, believing his next-game performance is bound to suffer from fatigue.

We studied starts from 2010-12 that had both high PCs (100+, 110+ and even 120+) and high scores in the Pure Quality Start (PQS) metric. The study showed such starters had good results in starts after high-PC starts:

1st Game Pitches	Next PQS Ave
90-99	3.0
100-109	3.1
110-119	3.3
120+	3.6

And 120+ pitch-count starters were actually better than their peers after posting high PQS scores:

1st PQS	2nd All	2nd 120+
3	3.0	3.6
4	3.1	3.6
5	3.3	3.7

Thus, we can safely ignore the conventional wisdom that a high-PC game will make a pitcher "tired" or "worn out" and therefore less likely to be effective. The opposite is true—especially if the high-PC outing was also a strong PQS performance. It appears these workhorse starters and their teams know what they're doing, and that they are highly likely to deliver a solid outing the next time out.

Days of rest as a leading indicator

Workload is only part of the equation. The other part is how often a pitcher is sent out to the mound. For instance, it's possible that a hurler might see no erosion in skill after a 120+ pitch outing if he had enough rest between starts:

PITCH COUNTS		NEXT START			
Three days rest	Pct.	PQS	DOM	DIS	qERA
< 100	72%	2.8	35%	17%	4.60
100-119	28%	2.3	44%	44%	5.21
Four Days rest					
< 100	52%	2.7	36%	27%	4.82
100-119	45%	2.9	42%	22%	4.56
120+	3%	3.0	42%	20%	4.44
Five Days rest					
< 100	54%	2.7	38%	25%	4.79
100-119	43%	3.0	44%	19%	4.44
120+	3%	3.2	48%	14%	4.28
Six Days rest					
< 100	58%	2.7	39%	30%	5.00
100-119	40%	2.8	40%	26%	4.82
120+	3%	1.8	20%	60%	7.98
20+ Days rest					
< 100	85%	1.8	20%	46%	6.12
100-119	15%	2.3	33%	33%	5.08

Managers are reluctant to put a starter on the mound with any fewer than four days rest, and the results for those who pitched deeper into games shows why. Four days rest is the most common usage pattern and even appears to mitigate the drop-off at 120+ pitches.

Perhaps most surprising is that an extra day of rest improves performance across the board and squeezes even more productivity out of the 120+ pitch outings.

Performance begins to erode at six days (and continues at 7-20 days, though those are not displayed). The 20+ Days chart represents pitchers who were primarily injury rehabs and failed call-ups, and the length of the "days rest" was occasionally well over 100 days. This chart shows the result of their performance in their first start back. The good news is that the workload was limited for 85% of these returnees. The bad news is that these are not pitchers you want active. So for those who obsess over getting your DL returnees activated in time to catch every start, the better percentage play is to avoid that first outing.

April ERA as a leading indicator *(Stephen Nickrand)*

A starting pitcher's April ERA can act as a leading indicator for how his ERA is likely to fare during the balance of the season. A study looked at extreme April ERA results to see what kind of in-season forecasting power they may have. From 2010-2012, 42 SP posted an ERA in April that was at least 2.00 ER better than their career ERA. The findings:

- Pitchers who come out of the gates quickly have an excellent chance at finishing the season with an ERA much better than their career ERA.
- While April ERA gems see their in-season ERA regresses towards their career ERA, their May-Sept ERA is still significantly better than their career ERA.
- Those who stumble out of the gates have a strong chance at posting an ERA worse than their career average, but their in-season ERA improves towards their career ERA.
- April ERA disasters tend to have a May-Sept ERA that closely resembles their career ERA.

Second-half ERA Reduction Drivers *(Stephen Nickrand)*

It's easy to dismiss first-half-to-second-half improvement among starting pitchers as an unpredictable event. After all, the midpoint of the season is an arbitrary cutoff. Performance swings occur throughout the season.

A study of SP who experienced significant 1H-2H ERA improvement from 2010-2012 examined what indicators drove second-half ERA improvement. Among the findings for those 79 SP with a > 1.00 ERA 1H-2H reduction:

- 97% saw their WHIP decrease, with an average decrease of 0.26
- 97% saw their strand (S%) rate improve, with an average increase of 9%
- 87% saw their BABIP (H%) improve, with an average reduction of 5%
- 75% saw their control (bb/9) rate improve, with an average reduction of 0.8
- 70% saw their HR/9 rate improve, with an average decrease of 0.5
- 68% saw their swinging strike (SwK%) rate improve, with an average increase of 1.4%
- 68% saw their BPV improve, with an average increase of 37
- 67% saw their HR per fly ball rate (hr/f) improve, with an average decrease of 4%
- 53% saw their ground ball (GB%) rate improve, with an average increase of 5%
- 52% saw their dominance (k/9) rate improve, with an average increase of 1.3

These findings highlight the power of H% and S% regression as it relates to ERA and WHIP improvement. In fact, H% and S% are more often correlated with ERA improvement than are improved skills. They also suggest that improved control has a bigger impact on ERA reduction than does increased strikeouts.

Pitcher Home/Road Splits *(Stephen Nickrand)*

One overlooked strategy in leagues that allow frequent transactions is to bench pitchers when they are on the road. Research reveals that several pitching stats and indicators are significantly and consistently worse on the road than at home.

Some home/road rules of thumb for SP:

- If you want to gain significant ground in ERA and WHIP, keep all your average or worse SP benched on the road.
- A pitcher's win percentage drops by 15% when on the road, so don't bank on road starts as a means to catch up in wins.
- Control erodes by 10% on the road, so be especially careful with keeping wild SP in your active lineups when they are away from home.
- NL pitchers at home produce significantly more strikeouts than their AL counterparts and vs. all pitchers on the road.
- hr/9, groundball rate, hit rate, strand rate, and hr/f do not show significant home vs. road variances.

Post-DL Pitching Performance *(Bill Macey)*

One question that fantasy baseball managers frequently struggle with is whether or not to start a pitcher when he first returns from the disabled list. A 2011 study compared each pitcher's PQS score in their first post-DL start against his average PQS score for that year (limited to pitchers who had at least 15 starts during the year and whose first post-DL appearance was as a starter). The findings:

- In general, exercise caution with immediate activations. Pitchers performed worse than their yearly average in the first post-DL start, with a high rate of PQS-DIS starts.
- Avoid pitchers returning from the DL due to an arm injury, as they perform significantly worse than average.
- If there are no better options available, feel comfortable activating pitchers who spent near the minimum amount of time on the DL and/or suffered a leg injury, as they typically perform at a level consistent with their yearly average.

Other Diamonds

The Pitching Postulates

1. Never sign a soft-tosser to a long-term contract.
2. Right-brain dominance has a very long shelf life.
3. A fly ball pitcher who gives up many HRs is expected. A GB pitcher who gives up many HRs is making mistakes.
4. Never draft a contact fly ball pitcher who plays in a hitter's park.
5. Only bad teams ever have a need for an inning-eater.
6. Never chase wins.

Dontrelle Willis List
Pitchers with BPIs so incredibly horrible that you have to wonder how they can possibly draw a major league paycheck year after year.

Chaconian
Having the ability to post many saves despite sub-Mendoza BPIs and an ERA in the stratosphere.

Vintage Eck Territory
A BPV greater than 200, a level achieved by Dennis Eckersley for four consecutive years.

Edwhitsonitis
A dreaded malady marked by the sudden and unexplained loss of pitching ability upon a trade to the New York Yankees.

ERA Benchmark
A half run of ERA over 200 innings comes out to just one earned run every four starts.

Gopheritis (also, Acute Gopheritis and Chronic Gopheritis)
The dreaded malady in which a pitcher is unable to keep the ball in the park. Pitchers with gopheritis have a FB rate of at least 40%. More severe cases have a FB% over 45%.

The Knuckleballers Rule
Knuckleballers don't follow no stinkin' rules.

Brad Lidge Lament
When a closer posts a 62% strand rate, he has nobody to blame but himself.

LOOGY (Lefty One Out GuY)
A left-handed reliever whose job it is to get one out in important situations.

Vin Mazzaro Vindication
Occasional nightmares (2.1 innings, 14 ER) are just a part of the game.

Meltdown
Any game in which a starting pitcher allows more runs than innings pitched.

Lance Painter Lesson
Six months of solid performance can be screwed up by one bad outing. (In 2000, Painter finished with an ERA of 4.76. However, prior to his final appearance of the year—in which he pitched 1 inning and gave up 8 earned runs—his ERA was 3.70.)

The Five Saves Certainties
1. On every team, there will be save opportunities and someone will get them. At a bare minimum, there will be at least 30 saves to go around, and not unlikely more than 45.
2. Any pitcher could end up being the chief beneficiary. Bullpen management is a fickle endeavor.
3. Relief pitchers are often the ones that require the most time at the start of the season to find a groove. The weather is cold, the schedule is sparse and their usage is erratic.
4. Despite the talk about "bullpens by committee," managers prefer a go-to guy. It makes their job easier.
5. As many as 50% of the saves in any year will come from pitchers who are unselected at the end of Draft Day.

Soft-tosser
A pitcher with a strikeout rate of 5.5 or less.

Soft-tosser land
The place where feebler arms leave their fortunes in the hands of the defense, variable hit and strand rates, and park dimensions. It's a place where many live, but few survive.

Prospects

General

Minor league prospecting in perspective

In our perpetual quest to be the genius who uncovers the next Mike Trout when he's still in high school, there is an obsessive fascination with minor league prospects. That's not to say that prospecting is not important. The issue is perspective:

1. During the 10 year period of 1996 to 2005, only 8% of players selected in the first round of the Major League Baseball First Year Player Draft went on to become stars.

2. Some prospects are going to hit the ground running (Jake DeGrom) and some are going to immediately struggle (Gregory Polanco), no matter what level of hype follows them.

3. Some prospects are going to start fast (since the league is unfamiliar with them) and then fade (as the league figures them out). Others will start slow (since they are unfamiliar with the opposition) and then improve (as they adjust to the competition). So if you make your free agent and roster decisions based on small early samples sizes, you are just as likely to be an idiot as a genius.

4. How any individual player will perform relative to his talent is largely unknown because there is a psychological element that is vastly unexplored. Some make the transition to the majors seamlessly, some not, completely regardless of how talented they are.

5. Still, talent is the best predictor of future success, so major league equivalent base performance indicators still have a valuable role in the process. As do scouting reports, carefully filtered.

6. Follow the player's path to the majors. Did he have to repeat certain levels? Was he allowed to stay at a level long enough to learn how to adjust to the level of competition? A player with only two great months at Double-A is a good bet to struggle if promoted directly to the majors because he was never fully tested at Double-A, let alone Triple-A.

7. Younger players holding their own against older competition is a good thing. Older players reaching their physical peak, regardless of their current address, can be a good thing too. The Steve Pearce and Jordy Mercers can have some very profitable years.

8. Remember team context. A prospect with superior potential often will not unseat a steady but unspectacular incumbent, especially one with a large contract.

9. Don't try to anticipate how a team is going to manage their talent, both at the major and minor league level. You might think it's time to promote Joey Gallo and give him an everyday role. You are not running the Rangers.

10. Those who play in shallow, one-year leagues should have little cause to be looking at the minors at all. The risk versus reward is so skewed against you, and there is so much talent available with a track record, that taking a chance on an unproven commodity makes little sense.

11. Decide where your priorities really are. If your goal is to win, prospect analysis is just a *part* of the process, not the entire process.

Factors affecting minor league stats *(Terry Linhart)*

1. Often, there is an exaggerated emphasis on short-term performance in an environment that is supposed to focus on the long-term. Two poor outings don't mean a 21-year-old pitcher is washed up.

2. Ballpark dimensions and altitude create hitters parks and pitchers parks, but a factor rarely mentioned is that many parks in the lower minors are inconsistent in their field quality. Minor league clubs have limited resources to maintain field conditions, and this can artificially depress defensive statistics while inflating stats like batting average.

3. Some players' skills are so superior to the competition at their level that you can't get a true picture of what they're going to do from their stats alone.

4. Many pitchers are told to work on secondary pitches in unorthodox situations just to gain confidence in the pitch. The result is an artificially increased number of walks.

5. The #3, #4, and #5 pitchers in the lower minors are truly longshots to make the majors. They often possess only two pitches and are unable to disguise the off-speed offerings. Hitters can see inflated statistics in these leagues.

Minor league level versus age

When evaluating minor leaguers, look at the age of the prospect in relation to the median age of the league he is in:

Low level A	*Between 19-20*
Upper level A	*Around 20*
Double-A	*21*
Triple-A	*22*

These are the ideal ages for prospects at the particular level. If a prospect is younger than most and holds his own against older and more experienced players, elevate his status. If he is older than the median, reduce his status.

Triple-A experience as a leading indicator

The probability that a minor leaguer will immediately succeed in the majors can vary depending upon the level of Triple-A experience he has amassed at the time of call-up.

	BATTERS		PITCHERS	
	< 1 Yr	Full	< 1 Yr	Full
Performed well	57%	56%	16%	56%
Performed poorly	21%	38%	77%	33%
2nd half drop-off	21%	7%	6%	10%

The odds of a batter achieving immediate MLB success was slightly more than 50-50. More than 80% of all pitchers promoted with less than a full year at Triple-A struggled in their first year in the majors. Those pitchers with a year in Triple-A succeeded at a level equal to that of batters.

Major League Equivalency (MLE) *(Bill James)*

A formula that converts a player's minor or foreign league statistics into a comparable performance in the major leagues. These are not projections, but conversions of current performance. MLEs contain adjustments for the level of play in individual leagues and teams. They work best with Triple-A stats, not quite as well with Double-A stats, and hardly at all with the lower levels. Foreign conversions are still a work in process. James' original formula only addressed batting. Our research has devised conversion formulas for pitchers, however, their best use comes when looking at BPIs, not traditional stats.

Adjusting to the competition

All players must "adjust to the competition" at every level of professional play. Players often get off to fast or slow starts. During their second tour at that level is when we get to see whether the slow starters have caught up or whether the league has figured out the fast starters. That second half "adjustment" period is a good baseline for projecting the subsequent season, in the majors or minors.

Premature major league call-ups often negate the ability for us to accurately evaluate a player due to the lack of this adjustment period. For instance, a hotshot Double-A player might open the season in Triple-A. After putting up solid numbers for a month, he gets a call to the bigs, and struggles. The fact is, we do not have enough evidence that the player has mastered the Triple-A level. We don't know whether the rest of the league would have caught up to him during his second tour of the league. But now he's labeled as an underperformer in the bigs when in fact he has never truly proven his skills at the lower levels.

Rookie playing time

Weaker-performing teams have historically (1976-2009) been far more dependent on debut rookies than stronger-performing teams. This makes sense, as non-contenders have greater incentive and flexibility to allow young players to gain experience at the MLB level. Additionally, individual player characteristics can provide clues as to which debut rookies will earn significant PA or IP:

- Rookies who can play up-the-middle (CF, 2B, SS) or on the left side (LF, 3B) are likely to see more debut playing time than those at 1B, RF, C, or DH.
- LH batters and pitchers are slightly more likely than righties to earn significant PA or IP in their debuts.
- Rookies under age 22 earn nearly twice the PAs of those aged 25-26 in their debut season. Pitchers under age 23 earn twice the innings of those aged 26-27.

Bull Durham prospects

There is some potential talent in older players—age 26, 27 or higher—who, for many reasons (untimely injury, circumstance, bad luck, etc.), don't reach the majors until they have already been downgraded from prospect to suspect. Equating potential with age is an economic reality for major league clubs, but not necessarily a skills reality.

Skills growth and decline is universal, whether it occurs at the major league level or in the minors. So a high-skills journeyman

in Triple-A is just as likely to peak at age 27 as a major leaguer of the same age. The question becomes one of opportunity—will the parent club see fit to reap the benefits of that peak performance?

Prospecting these players for your fantasy team is, admittedly, a high risk endeavor, though there are some criteria you can use. Look for a player who is/has:

- Optimally, age 27-28 for overall peak skills, age 30-31 for power skills, or age 28-31 for pitchers.
- At least two seasons of experience at Triple-A. Career Double-A players are generally not good picks.
- Solid base skills levels.
- Shallow organizational depth at their position.
- Notable winter league or spring training performance.

Players who meet these conditions are not typically draftable players, but worthwhile reserve or FAAB picks.

Batters

MLE PX as a leading indicator *(Bill Macey)*

Looking at minor league performance (as MLE) in one year and the corresponding MLB performance the subsequent year:

	Year 1 MLE	Year 2 MLB
Observations	496	496
Median PX	95	96
Percent PX > 100	43%	46%

In addition, 53% of the players had a MLB PX in year 2 that exceeded their MLE PX in year 1. A slight bias towards improved performance in year 2 is consistent with general career trajectories.

Year 1 MLE PX	Year 2 MLB PX	Pct. Incr	Pct. MLB PX > 100
<= 50	61	70.3%	5.4%
51-75	85	69.6%	29.4%
76-100	93	55.2%	39.9%
101-125	111	47.4%	62.0%
126-150	119	32.1%	66.1%
> 150	142	28.6%	76.2%

Slicing the numbers by performance level, there is a good amount of regression to the mean.

Players rarely suddenly develop power at the MLB level if they didn't previously display that skill at the minor league level. However, the relatively large gap between the median MLE PX and MLB PX for these players, 125 to 110, confirms the notion that the best players continue to improve once they reach the major leagues.

MLE contact rate as a leading indicator *(Bill Macey)*

There is a strong positive correlation (0.63) between a player's MLE ct% in Year 1 and his actual ct% at the MLB level in Year 2.

MLE ct%	Year 1 MLE ct%	Year 2 MLB ct%
< 70%	69%	68%
70% - 74%	73%	72%
75% - 79%	77%	75%
80% - 84%	82%	77%
85% - 89%	87%	82%
90% +	91%	86%
TOTAL	**84%**	**79%**

There is very little difference between the median MLE BA in Year 1 and the median MLB BA in Year 2:

MLE ct%	Year 1 MLE BA	Year 2 MLB BA
< 70%	.230	.270
70% - 74%	.257	.248
75% - 79%	.248	.255
80% - 84%	.257	.255
85% - 89%	.266	.270
90% +	.282	.273
TOTAL	.261	.262

Excluding the <70% cohort (which was a tiny sample size), there is a positive relationship between MLE ct% and MLB BA.

Pitchers

BPIs as a leading indicator for pitching success

The percentage of hurlers that were good investments in the year that they were called up varied by the level of their historical minor league BPIs prior to that year.

Pitchers who had:	Fared well	Fared poorly
Good indicators	79%	21%
Marginal or poor indicators	18%	82%

The data used here were MLE levels from the previous two years, not the season in which they were called up. The significance? Solid current performance is what merits a call-up, but this is not a good indicator of short-term MLB success, because a) the performance data set is too small, typically just a few month's worth of statistics, and b) for those putting up good numbers at a new minor league level, there has typically not been enough time for the scouting reports to make their rounds.

Minor league BPV as a leading indicator *(Al Melchior)*

There is a link between minor league skill and how a pitching prospect will fare in his first 5 starts upon call-up.

PQS Avg	MLE BPV < 50	50-99	100+
0.0-1.9	60%	28%	19%
2.0-2.9	32%	40%	29%
3.0-5.0	8%	33%	52%

Pitchers who demonstrate sub-par skills in the minors (sub-50 BPV) tend to fare poorly in their first big league starts. Three-fifths of these pitchers register a PQS average below 2.0, while only 8% average over 3.0.

Fewer than 1 out of 5 minor leaguers with a 100+ MLE BPV go on to post a sub-2.0 PQS average in their initial major league starts, but more than half average 3.0 or better.

Late season performance of rookie starting pitchers *(Ray Murphy)*

Given that a rookie's second tour of the league provides insight as to future success, do rookie pitchers typically run out of gas? We studied 2002-2005, identified 56 rookies who threw at least 75 IP and analyzed their PQS logs. The group:

All rookies	#	#GS/P	DOM%	DIS%	qERA
before 7/31	56	13.3	42%	21%	4.56
after 7/31	56	9.3	37%	29%	4.82

There is some erosion, but a 0.26 run rise in qERA is hardly cause for panic. If we re-focus our study class, the qERA variance increased to 4.44-5.08 for those who made at least 16 starts before July 31. The variance also was larger (3.97-4.56) for those who had a PQS-3 average prior to July 31. The pitchers who intersected these two sub-groups:

PQS>3+GS>15	#	#GS/P	DOM%	DIS%	qERA
before 7/31	8	19.1	51%	12%	4.23
after 7/31	8	9.6	34%	30%	5.08

While the sample size is small, the degree of flameout by these guys (0.85 runs) is more significant.

Japanese Baseball *(Tom Mulhall)*

Comparing MLB and Japanese Baseball

The Japanese major leagues are generally considered to be equivalent to Triple-A ball and the pitching is thought to be even better. However, statistics are difficult to convert due to differences in the way the game is played in Japan.

1. While strong on fundamentals, Japanese baseball's guiding philosophy is risk avoidance. Mistakes are not tolerated. Runners rarely take extra bases, batters focus on making contact rather than driving the ball, and managers play for one run at a time. Bunts are more common. As a result, offenses score fewer runs per number of hits, and pitching stats tend to look better than the talent behind them.

2. Stadiums in Japan usually have much shorter fences. This should mean more HRs, but given #1 above, it is the American players who make up the majority of Japan's power elite. No power hitters have made an equivalent transition to the MLB.

3. There are more artificial turf fields, which increases the number of ground ball singles. Only a small number of stadiums have infield grass and a few still use all dirt infields.

4. The quality of umpiring is questionable and even inept. Fewer errors are called, reflecting the cultural philosophy of low tolerance for mistakes and the desire to avoid publicly embarrassing a player. Moreover, umpires are routinely intimidated, even physically.

5. Teams have smaller pitching staffs and use a six-man rotation. Starters usually pitch once a week, typically on the same day since Monday is an off-day for the entire league. Many starters will also occasionally pitch in relief between starts. Moreover, managers push for complete games, no matter what the score or situation. Because of the style of offense, higher pitch counts are common. Despite superior conditioning, Japanese pitchers tend to burn out early due to overuse.

6. The ball is smaller and lighter, and the strike zone is closer to the batter. A new ball was introduced in 2011 with lower-elasticity rubber surrounding the cork, which limited offense and inflated pitching stats. A more hitter-friendly ball was used in 2013 and home runs increased. But continue to exercise some skepticism when analyzing pitching stats and look for possible

signs of optimism in hitting stats other than the power categories.

7. Tie games are allowed. If the score remains even after 12 innings, the game goes into the books as a tie.

8. There are 18 fewer games in the Japanese schedule.

Japanese players as fantasy farm selections

Many fantasy leagues have large reserve or farm teams with rules allowing them to draft foreign players before they sign with a MLB team. With increased coverage by fantasy experts, the internet, and exposure from the World Baseball Classic, anyone willing to do a modicum of research can compile an adequate list of good players.

However, the key is not to just identify the best Japanese players—the key is to identify impact players who have the desire and opportunity to sign with a MLB team. With the success of Darvish and Tanaka, it is easy to overestimate the value of drafting these players. But since 1995, less than four dozen Japanese players have made a big league roster, and about half of them were middle relievers. Still, for owners who are allowed to carry a large reserve or farm team at reduced salaries, these players could be a real windfall, especially if your competitors do not do their homework.

A list of Japanese League players who could jump to the majors appears in the Prospects section.

Other Diamonds

Age 26 Paradox

Age 26 is when a player begins to reach his peak skill, no matter what his address is. If circumstances have him celebrating that birthday in the majors, he is a breakout candidate. If circumstances have him celebrating that birthday in the minors, he is washed up.

A-Rod 10-Step Path to Stardom

Not all well-hyped prospects hit the ground running. More often they follow an alternative path:

1. Prospect puts up phenomenal minor league numbers.
2. The media machine gets oiled up.
3. Prospect gets called up, but struggles, Year 1.
4. Prospect gets demoted.
5. Prospect tears it up in the minors, Year 2.
6. Prospect gets called up, but struggles, Year 2.
7. Prospect gets demoted.
8. The media turns their backs. Fantasy leaguers reduce their expectations.
9. Prospect tears it up in the minors, Year 3. The public shrugs its collective shoulders.
10. Prospect is promoted in Year 3 and explodes. Some lucky fantasy leaguer lands a franchise player for under $5.

Some players that are currently stuck at one of the interim steps, and may or may not ever reach Step 10, include Trevor Bauer, Jesus Montero and Jackie Bradley.

Developmental Dogmata

1. Defense is what gets a minor league prospect to the majors; offense is what keeps him there. *(Deric McKamey)*

2. The reason why rapidly promoted minor leaguers often fail is that they are never given the opportunity to master the skill of "adjusting to the competition."

3. Rookies who are promoted in-season often perform better than those that make the club out of spring training. Inferior March competition can inflate the latter group's perceived talent level.

4. Young players rarely lose their inherent skills. Pitchers may uncover weaknesses and the players may have difficulty adjusting. These are bumps along the growth curve, but they do not reflect a loss of skill.

5. Late bloomers have smaller windows of opportunity and much less chance for forgiveness.

6. The greatest risk in this game is to pay for performance that a player has never achieved.

7. Some outwardly talented prospects simply have a ceiling that's spelled "A-A-A."

Rule 5 Reminder

Don't ignore the Rule 5 draft lest you ignore the possibility of players like Jose Bautista, Josh Hamilton, Johan Santana, Joakim Soria, Dan Uggla, Shane Victorino and Jayson Werth. All were Rule 5 draftees.

Trout Inflation

The tendency for rookies to go for exorbitant draft prices following a year when there was a very good rookie crop.

Gaming

Standard Rules and Variations

Rotisserie Baseball was invented as an elegant confluence of baseball and economics. Whether by design or accident, the result has lasted for more than three decades. But what would Rotisserie and fantasy have been like if the Founding Fathers knew then what we know now about statistical analysis and game design? You can be sure things would be different.

The world has changed since the original game was introduced yet many leagues use the same rules today. New technologies have opened up opportunities to improve elements of the game that might have been limited by the capabilities of the 1980s. New analytical approaches have revealed areas where the original game falls short.

As such, there are good reasons to tinker and experiment; to find ways to enhance the experience.

Following are the basic elements of fantasy competition, those that provide opportunities for alternative rules and experimentation. This is by no means an exhaustive list, but at minimum provides some interesting food-for-thought.

Player pool

Standard: American League-only, National League-only or Mixed League.

AL/NL-only typically drafts 8-12 teams (pool penetration of 49% to 74%). Mixed leagues draft 10-18 teams (31% to 55% penetration), though 15 teams (46%) is a common number.

Drafting of reserve players will increase the penetration percentages. A 12-team AL/NL-only league adding six reserves onto 23-man rosters would draft 93% of the available pool of players on all teams' 25-man rosters.

The draft penetration level determines which fantasy management skills are most important to your league. The higher the penetration, the more important it is to draft a good team. The lower the penetration, the greater the availability of free agents and the more important in-season roster management becomes.

There is no generally-accepted optimal penetration level, but we have often suggested that 75% (including reserves) provides a good balance between the skills required for both draft prep and in-season management.

Alternative pools: There is a wide variety of options here. Certain leagues draft from within a small group of major league divisions or teams. Some competitions, like home run leagues, only draft batters.

Bottom-tier pool: Drafting from the entire major league population, the only players available are those who posted a Rotisserie dollar value of $5 or less in the previous season. Intended as a test of an owner's ability to identify talent with upside. Best used as a pick-a-player contest with any number of teams participating.

Positional structure

Standard: 23 players. One at each defensive position (though three outfielders may be from any of LF, CF or RF), plus one additional catcher, one middle infielder (2B or SS), one corner infielder (1B or 3B), two additional outfielders and a utility player/designated hitter (which often can be a batter who qualifies anywhere). Nine pitchers, typically holding any starting or relief role.

Open: 25 players. One at each defensive position (plus DH), 5-man starting rotation and two relief pitchers. Nine additional players at any position, which may be a part of the active roster or constitute a reserve list.

40-man: Standard 23 plus 17 reserves. Used in many keeper and dynasty leagues.

Reapportioned: In recent years, new obstacles are being faced by 12-team AL/NL-only leagues thanks to changes in the real game. The 14/9 split between batters and pitchers no longer reflects how MLB teams structure their rosters. Of the 30 teams, each with 25-man rosters, not one contains 14 batters for any length of time. In fact, many spend a good part of the season with only 12 batters, which means teams often have more pitchers than hitters.

For fantasy purposes in AL/NL-only leagues, that leaves a disproportionate draft penetration into the batter and pitcher pools:

	BATTERS	PITCHERS
On all MLB rosters	195	180
Players drafted	168	108
Pct.	86%	60%

These drafts are depleting 26% more batters out of the pool than pitchers. Add in those leagues with reserve lists—perhaps an additional six players per team removing another 72 players—and post-draft free agent pools are very thin, especially on the batting side.

The impact is less in 15-team mixed leagues, though the FA pitching pool is still disproportionately deep.

	BATTERS	PITCHERS
On all rosters	381	369
Drafted	210	135
Pct.	55%	37%

One solution is to reapportion the number of batters and pitchers that are rostered. Adding one pitcher slot and eliminating one batter slot may be enough to provide better balance. The batting slot most often removed is the second catcher, since it is the position with the least de

Beginning in the 2012 season, the Tout Wars AL/NL-only experts leagues opted to eliminate one of the outfield slots and replace it with a "swingman" position. This position could be any batter or pitcher, depending upon the owner's needs at any given time.

Selecting players

Standard: The three most prevalent methods for stocking fantasy rosters are:

Snake/Straight/Serpentine draft: Players are selected in order with seeds reversed in alternating rounds. This method has become the most popular due to its speed, ease of implementation and ease of automation.

In these drafts, the underlying assumption is that value can be ranked relative to a linear baseline. Pick #1 is better than pick #2, which is better than pick #3, and the difference between each pick is assumed to be somewhat equivalent. While a faulty assumption, we must believe in it to assume a level playing field.

Auction: Players are sold to the highest bidder from a fixed budget, typically $260. Auctions provide the team owner with the most control over which players will be on his team, but can take twice as long as snake drafts.

The baseline is $0 at the beginning of each player put up for bid. The final purchase price for each player is shaped by many wildly variable factors, from roster need to geographic location of the draft. A $30 player can mean different things to different drafters.

One option that can help reduce the time commitment of auctions is to force minimum bids at each hour mark. You could mandate $15 openers in hour #1; $10 openers in hour #2, etc.

Pick-a-player / Salary cap: Players are assigned fixed dollar values and owners assemble their roster within a fixed cap. This type of roster-stocking is an individual exercise which results in teams typically having some of the same players.

In these leagues, the "value" decision is taken out of the hands of the owners. Each player has a fixed value, pre-assigned based on past season performance.

Hybrid snake-auction: Each draft begins as an auction. Each team has to fill its first seven roster slots from a budget of $154. Opening bid for any player is $15. This assures that player values will be close to reality. After each team has filled seven slots, it becomes a snake draft.

If you like, you can assign fixed salaries to the snake-drafted players in such a way that rosters will still add up to about $260.

Round	Salary		Round	Salary
8	$14		16	$6
9	$13		17	$5
10	$12		18	$4
11	$11		19	$3
12	$10		20	$2
13	$9		21	$1
14	$8		22	$1
15	$7		23	$1

You can also use this chart to decide how deep you want to auction. If you want to auction the first 15 players, for instance, you'd use a budget of $238. Though not shown, if you only wanted to auction the first 5 players, your budget would be $121.

This method is intended to reduce draft time while still providing an economic component for selecting players.

Stat categories

Standard: The standard statistical categories for Rotisserie leagues are:

4x4: HR, RBI, SB, BA, W, Sv, ERA, WHIP

5x5: HR, R, RBI, SB, BA, W, Sv, K, ERA, WHIP

6x6: Categories typically added are Holds and OPS.

7x7, etc.: Any number of categories may be added.

In general, the more categories you add, the more complicated it is to isolate individual performance and manage the categorical impact on your roster. There is also the danger of redundancy; with multiple categories measuring like stats, certain skills can get over-valued. For instance, home runs are double-counted when using the categories of both HR and slugging average. (Though

note that HRs are actually already triple-counted in standard 5x5—HRs, runs, and RBIs)

If the goal is to have categories that create a more encompassing picture of player performance, it is actually possible to accomplish more with less:

Modified 4x4: HR, (R+RBI-HR), SB, OBA, (W+QS), (Sv+Hld), K, ERA

This provides a better balance between batting and pitching in that each has three counting categories and one ratio category. In fact, the balance is shown to be even more notable here:

	BATTING	PITCHING
Pure skill counting stat	HR	K
Ratio category	OBA	ERA
Dependent upon managerial decision	SB	(Sv+Hold)
Dependent upon team support	(R+RBI-HR)	(W+QS)

3x3: In an attempt to make the game cleaner and rosters more manageable, this format uses HR, SB, OBA, K, ERA, (Svs + Holds + Quality Starts).

Replacing saves: The problem with the Saves statistic is that we have a scarce commodity that is centered on a small group of players, thereby creating inflated demand for those players. With the rising failure rate for closers these days, the incentive to pay full value for the commodity decreases. The higher the risk, the lower the prices.

We can increase the value of the commodity by reducing the risk. We might do this by increasing the number of players that contribute to that category, thereby spreading the risk around. One way we can accomplish this is by changing the category to Saves + Holds.

Holds are not perfect, but the typical argument about them being random and arbitrary can apply to saves these days as well. In fact, many of the pitchers who record holds are far more skilled and valuable than closers; they are often called to the mound in much higher leverage situations (a fact backed up by a scan of each pitcher's Leverage Index).

Neither stat is perfect, but together they form a reasonable proxy for overall bullpen performance.

In tandem, they effectively double the player pool of draftable relievers while also flattening the values allotted to those pitchers. The more players around which we spread the risk, the more control we have in managing our pitching staffs.

Replacing wins: Using reasons similar to replacing Saves with Saves + Holds, some have argued for replacing the Wins statistic with W + QS (quality starts). This method of scoring gives value to a starting pitcher who pitches well, but fails to receive the win due to his team's poor offense or poor luck.

Keeping score

Standard: These are the most common scoring methods:

Rotisserie: Players are evaluated in several statistical categories. Totals of these statistics are ranked by team. The winner is the team with the highest cumulative ranking.

Points: Players receive points for events that they contribute to in each game. Points are totaled for each team and teams are then ranked.

Head-to-Head (H2H): Using Rotisserie or points scoring, teams are scheduled in daily or weekly matchups. The winner of each matchup is the team that finishes higher in more categories (Rotisserie) or scores the most points.

Hybrid H2H-Rotisserie: Rotisserie's category ranking system can be converted into a weekly won-loss record. Depending upon where your team finishes for that week's statistics determines how many games you win for that week. Each week, your team will play seven games.

*Place	Record	*Place	Record
1st	7-0	7th	3-4
2nd	6-1	8th	2-5
3rd	6-1	9th	2-5
4th	5-2	10th	1-6
5th	5-2	11th	1-6
6th	4-3	12th	0-7

* Based on overall Rotisserie category ranking for the week.

At the end of each week, all the statistics revert to zero and you start over. You never dig a hole in any category that you can't climb out of, because all categories themselves are incidental to the standings.

The regular season lasts for 23 weeks, which equals 161 games. Weeks 24, 25 and 26 are for play-offs.

Free agent acquisition

Standard: Three methods are the most common for acquiring free agent players during the season.

First to the phone: Free agents are awarded to the first owner who claims them.

Reverse order of standings: Access to the free agent pool is typically in a snake draft fashion with the last place team getting the first pick, and each successive team higher in the standings picking afterwards.

Free agent acquisition budget (FAAB): Teams are given a set budget at the beginning of the season (typically, $100 or $1000) from which they bid on free agents in a closed auction process.

Vickrey FAAB: Research has shown that more than 50% of FAAB dollars are lost via overbid on an annual basis. Given that this is a scarce commodity, one would think that a system to better manage these dollars might be desirable. The Vickrey system conducts a closed auction in the same way as standard FAAB, but the price of the winning bid is set at the amount of the second highest bid, plus $1. In some cases, gross overbids (at least $10 over) are reduced to the second highest bid plus $5.

This method was designed by William Vickrey, a Professor of Economics at Columbia University. His theory was that this process reveals the true value of the commodity. For his work, Vickrey was awarded the Nobel Prize for Economics (and $1.2 million) in 1996.

Double-Bid FAAB: One of the inherent difficulties in the current FAAB system is that we have so many options for setting a bid amount. You can bid $47, or $51, or $23. You might agonize over whether to go $38 or $39. With a $100 budget, there are 100 decision points. And while you may come up with a rough guesstimate of the range in which your opponents might bid, the results for any individual player bidding are typically random within that range.

The first part of this process reduces the number of decision points. Owners must categorize their interest by bidding a fixed number of pre-set dollar amounts for each player. In a $100 FAAB league, for instance, those levels might be $1, $5, $10, $15, $20, $30, $40 or $50. All owners would set the general market value for free agents in these eight levels of interest. (This system sets a $50 maximum, but that is not absolutely necessary.)

The initial stage of the bidding process serves to screen out those who are not interested in a player at the appropriate market level. That leaves a high potential for tied owners, those who share the same level of interest.

The tied owners must then submit a second bid of equal or greater value than their first bid. These bids can be in $1 increments. The winning owner gets the player; if there is still a tie, then the player would go to the owner lower in the standings.

An advantage of this second bid is that it gives owners an opportunity to see who they are going up against, and adjust. If you are bidding against an owner close to you in the standings, you may need to be more aggressive in that second bid. If you see that the tied owner(s) wouldn't hurt you by acquiring that player, then maybe you resubmit the original bid and be content to potentially lose out on the player. If you're ahead in the standings, it's actually a way to potentially opt out on that player completely by resubmitting your original bid and forcing another owner to spend his FAAB.

Some leagues will balk at adding another layer to the weekly deadline process; it's a trade-off to having more control over managing your FAAB.

Fixed price free agents: In the same way as salary cap games have pre-assigned prices for players at the draft, free agents can be assigned a fixed price as well. For a player who has been in the free agent pool and available for at least two weeks, his price would be his current Rotisserie dollar value. For a player who is a recent call-up or in the pool for less than two weeks, he would be assigned a baseline (e.g. $5 in a $100 FAAB league) augmented by a pre-determined amount based on contextual factors.

For instance, claiming a current minor league call-up would cost an owner the $5 baseline, plus an additional $5 for each month the player is expected to be a full-timer, plus perhaps another $5 if he is on a .500 or better ballclub, in a favorable ballpark, etc. The final pre-set price will serve to screen out only the most interested owners. Multiple like claims would be awarded to the team lower in the standings.

The season

Standard: Leagues are played out during the course of the entire Major League Baseball season.

Split-season: Leagues are conducted from Opening Day through the All-Star break, then re-drafted to play from the All-Star break through the end of the season.

50-game split-season: Leagues are divided into three 50-game seasons with one-week break in between. The advantages:

- With dwindling attention spans over the long 162-game season, 50 games is a more accessible time frame to maintain interest. There would be fewer abandoned teams.

- There would be four shots at a title each year; the first place team from each split, plus the team with the best overall record for the entire year.
- Given that drafting is considered the most fun aspect of the game, these splits triple the opportunities to participate in some type of draft. Leagues may choose to do complete re-drafts and treat the year as three distinct mini-seasons. Or, leagues might allow teams to drop their five worst players and conduct a restocking draft at each break.

Monthly leagues: The introduction of one-month leagues at ShandlerPark.com was a recognition of our industry's dwindling attention spans and growing need for immediate gratification. But the time frame does make some analytical sense.

We have greater accuracy projecting skill over a longer time horizon, but greater accuracy projecting playing time over a shorter time horizon. Full-season leagues and daily contests feed into opposite ends of that dichotomy. One-month leagues provide a balance.

Among the benefits of the one-month time horizon are more drafts and pennant races, and the opportunity to start over if your team is hit with injuries or underperformance. Unlike daily contests, the one-month game provides the continuity and drama of daily standings.

The major objection to the one-month time frame is that it is too short a time period to have statistical relevance. However, statistics do tend to stabilize over an entire roster in one month. In fact, research has shown that 80% of eventual 6-month winners finish April in 1st, 2nd, 3rd or 4th place.

Daily games: Participants select a roster of players from one day's MLB schedule. Scoring is based on an aggregate points-based system rather than categories, with cash prizes awarded based on the day's results. The structure and distribution of that prize pool varies across different types of events, and those differences can affect roster construction strategies. Although scoring and prizes are based on one day's play, the season-long element of bankroll management provides a proxy for overall standings.

In terms of projecting outcomes, daily games are drastically different than full-season leagues. Playing time is one key element of any projection, and daily games offer near-100% accuracy in projecting playing time: you can check pre-game lineups to see exactly which players are in the lineup that night. The other key component of any projection is performance, but that is plagued by variance in daily competitions. Even if you roster a team full of the most advantageous matchups (for instance, Mike Trout facing Franklin Morales at Coors Field), Trout will sometimes go 0-for-4 on that one night.

Single game (Quint-Inning): A game that drafts from the active rosters of two major league teams in a single game. The rules:

1. Start with five owners.

2. Prior to first pitch, conduct a simple snake draft where each owner selects five players. If you're more ambitious, auction off the 25 players giving each owner a budget of $50 of real or fake money.

3. Scoring is simple. For batters, singles, walks, hit-by-pitches and stolen bases are one point each. Doubles are 2 points. Triples

are 3 points. Home runs are 4 points. Pitchers get one point for each complete inning pitched but lose one point for every run they allow.

4. At the beginning of the 5th inning, each owner has the option of doubling any future points for one player on his roster. We call that player the Quint. Points for all batters are doubled beginning in the 9th inning. That means the Quint's points would be quadrupled.

5. At the end of each inning, you can cut players, claim players from the free agent pool or trade players. You must maintain five players at all times, so all adds, drops and trades must keep your roster square. Free agent claims are done in reverse order of the standings. If two teams are tied and both want the same player, it can be helpful to have a deck of cards handy - the owner who draws high card would get the player.

6. Quint-Inning is a betting game (which makes it technically illegal). Owners need to ante up to play, typically $5, though if you're using a $50 auction budget, that works fine. It then costs $1 per inning to stay in the game for the second through fourth innings. Beginning in the 5th inning, the stakes increase to $2 per inning to stay in the game. You can use higher or lower stakes if you prefer.

7. Owners can fold at any time, forfeiting any monies they contributed to the pot. Their players are released into the free agent pool and are available to the remaining owners in reverse order of the standings.

8. The owner with the most points at the end of the game wins the pot.

Post-season league: Some leagues re-draft teams from among the MLB post-season contenders and play out a separate competition. It is possible, however, to make a post-season competition that is an extension of the regular season.

Start by designating a set number of regular season finishers as qualifying for the post-season. The top four teams in a league is a good number.

These four teams would designate a fixed 23-man roster for all post-season games. First, they would freeze all of their currently-owned players who are on MLB post-season teams.

In order to fill the roster holes that will likely exist, these four teams would then pick players from their league's non-playoff teams (for the sake of the post-season only). This would be in the form of a snake draft done on the day following the end of the regular season. Draft order would be regular season finish, so the play-off team with the most regular season points would get first pick. Picks would continue until all four rosters are filled with 23 men.

Regular scoring would be used for all games during October. The team with the best play-off stats at the end of the World Series is the overall champ.

Snake Drafting

Snake draft first round history

The following tables record the comparison between pre-season projected player rankings (using Average Draft Position data from Mock Draft Central) and actual end-of-season results. The 11-year success rate of identifying each season's top talent is only 35%.

2004	ADP		ACTUAL = 6
1	Alex Rodriguez	1	Ichiro Suzuki
2	Albert Pujols	2	Vlad Guerrero (5)
3	Carlos Beltran	3	Randy Johnson
4	Todd Helton	4	Albert Pujols (2)
5	Vlad Guerrero	5	Johan Santana
6	Alfonso Soriano	6	Bobby Abreu
7	N. Garciaparra	7	Adrian Beltre
8	Barry Bonds	8	Barry Bonds (8)
9	Pedro Martinez	9	Carlos Beltran (3)
10	Mark Prior	10	Ben Sheets
11	Manny Ramirez	11	Melvin Mora
12	Roy Halladay	12	Carl Crawford
13	Magglio Ordonez	13	Manny Ramirez (11)
14	Edgar Renteria	14	Miguel Tejada
15	Sammy Sosa	15	Todd Helton (4)

2005	ADP		ACTUAL = 7
1	Alex Rodriguez	1	Derrek Lee
2	Carlos Beltran	2	Alex Rodriguez (1)
3	Albert Pujols	3	Albert Pujols (3)
4	Vlad Guerrero	4	David Ortiz
5	Manny Ramirez	5	Mark Teixeira
6	Bobby Abreu	6	Carl Crawford (12)
7	Miguel Tejada	7	Chone Figgins
8	Johan Santana	8	Jason Bay
9	Todd Helton	9	Miguel Cabrera
10	Jason Schmidt	10	Manny Ramirez (5)
11	Randy Johnson	11	Michael Young
12	Carl Crawford	12	Vlad Guerrero (4)
13	Alfonso Soriano	13	Ichiro Suzuki
14	Ben Sheets	14	Bobby Abreu (6)
15	Curt Schilling	15	Johan Santana (8)

2006	ADP		ACTUAL = 4
1	Albert Pujols	1	Jose Reyes
2	Alex Rodriguez	2	Derek Jeter
3	Vlad Guerrero	3	Albert Pujols (1)
4	Mark Teixeira	4	Ryan Howard
5	Manny Ramirez	5	Johan Santana
6	Miguel Cabrera	6	Alfonso Soriano
7	Derrek Lee	7	Carl Crawford (10)
8	Bobby Abreu	8	Matt Holliday
9	Miguel Tejada	9	Vlad Guerrero (3)
10	Carl Crawford	10	Miguel Cabrera (6)
11	Michael Young	11	Ichiro Suzuki
12	Carlos Beltran	12	Chase Utley
13	Jason Bay	13	Garrett Atkins
14	David Ortiz	14	Jermaine Dye
15	David Wright	15	Lance Berkman

2007	ADP		ACTUAL = 5
1	Albert Pujols	1	Alex Rodriguez (4)
2	Alfonso Soriano	2	Hanley Ramirez
3	Jose Reyes	3	Matt Holliday
4	Alex Rodriguez	4	Magglio Ordonez
5	Ryan Howard	5	David Wright (12)
6	Johan Santana	6	Jimmy Rollins
7	Carl Crawford	7	Ichiro Suzuki
8	Chase Utley	8	Jose Reyes (3)
9	Carlos Beltran	9	Jake Peavy
10	David Ortiz	10	David Ortiz (10)
11	Vlad Guerrero	11	Carl Crawford (7)
12	David Wright	12	Eric Byrnes
13	Miguel Cabrera	13	Brandon Phillips
14	Lance Berkman	14	Chipper Jones
15	Carlos Lee	15	Prince Fielder

2008	ADP		ACTUAL = 7
1	Alex Rodriguez	1	Albert Pujols (10)
2	Hanley Ramirez	2	Jose Reyes (4)
3	David Wright	3	Hanley Ramirez (2)
4	Jose Reyes	4	Manny Ramirez
5	Matt Holliday	5	Matt Holliday (5)
6	Jimmy Rollins	6	David Wright (3)
7	Miguel Cabrera	7	Lance Berkman
8	Chase Utley	8	Dustin Pedroia
9	Ryan Howard	9	Roy Halladay
10	Albert Pujols	10	Josh Hamilton
11	Prince Fielder	11	Alex Rodriguez (1)
12	Ryan Braun	12	C.C. Sabathia
13	Johan Santana	13	Carlos Beltran
14	Carl Crawford	14	Grady Sizemore
15	Alfonso Soriano	15	Chase Utley (8)

2009	ADP		ACTUAL = 5
1	Hanley Ramirez	1	Albert Pujols (2)
2	Albert Pujols	2	Hanley Ramirez (1)
3	Jose Reyes	3	Tim Lincecum
4	David Wright	4	Dan Haren
5	Grady Sizemore	5	Carl Crawford
6	Miguel Cabrera	6	Matt Kemp
7	Ryan Braun	7	Joe Mauer
8	Jimmy Rollins	8	Derek Jeter
9	Ian Kinsler	9	Zach Greinke
10	Josh Hamilton	10	Ryan Braun (7)
11	Ryan Howard	11	Jacoby Ellsbury
12	Mark Teixeira	12	Mark Reynolds
13	Alex Rodriguez	13	Prince Fielder
14	Matt Holliday	14	Chase Utley (15)
15	Chase Utley	15	Miguel Cabrera (6)

2010	ADP		ACTUAL = 5
1	Albert Pujols	1	Carlos Gonzalez
2	Hanley Ramirez	2	Albert Pujols (1)
3	Alex Rodriguez	3	Joey Votto
4	Chase Utley	4	Roy Halladay
5	Ryan Braun	5	Carl Crawford (15)
6	Mark Teixeira	6	Miguel Cabrera (9)
7	Matt Kemp	7	Josh Hamilton
8	Prince Fielder	8	Adam Wainwright
9	Miguel Cabrera	9	Felix Hernandez
10	Ryan Howard	10	Robinson Cano
11	Evan Longoria	11	Jose Bautista
12	Tom Lincecum	12	Paul Konerko
13	Joe Mauer	13	Matt Holliday
14	David Wright	14	Ryan Braun (5)
15	Carl Crawford	15	Hanley Ramirez (2)

2011	ADP		ACTUAL = 6
1	Albert Pujols	1	Matt Kemp
2	Hanley Ramirez	2	Jacoby Ellsbury
3	Miguel Cabrera	3	Ryan Braun (10)
4	Troy Tulowitzki	4	Justin Verlander
5	Evan Longoria	5	Clayton Kershaw
6	Carlos Gonzalez	6	Curtis Granderson
7	Joey Votto	7	Adrian Gonzalez (8)
8	Adrian Gonzalez	8	Miguel Cabrera (3)
9	Robinson Cano	9	Roy Halladay (15)
10	Ryan Braun	10	Cliff Lee
11	David Wright	11	Jose Bautista
12	Mark Teixeira	12	Dustin Pedroia
13	Carl Crawford	13	Jered Weaver
14	Josh Hamilton	14	Albert Pujols (1)
15	Roy Halladay	15	Robinson Cano (9)

2012	ADP		ACTUAL = 4	
1	Matt Kemp	1	Mike Trout	
2	Ryan Braun	2	Ryan Braun (2)	
3	Albert Pujols	3	Miguel Cabrera (4)	
4	Miguel Cabrera	4	Andrew McCutchen	
5	Troy Tulowitzki	5	R.A. Dickey	
6	Jose Bautista	6	Clayton Kershaw	
7	Jacoby Ellsbury	7	Justin Verlander (8)	
8	Justin Verlander	8	Josh Hamilton	
9	Adrian Gonzalez	9	Fernando Rodney	
10	Justin Upton	10	Adrian Beltre	
11	Robinson Cano	11	Alex Rios	
12	Joey Votto	12	David Price	
13	Evan Longoria	13	Chase Headley	
14	Carlos Gonzalez	14	Robinson Cano (11)	
15	Prince Fielder	15	Edwin Encarnacion	

2013	ADP		ACTUAL = 5	
1	Ryan Braun	1	Miguel Cabrera (2)	
2	Miguel Cabrera	2	Mike Trout (3)	
3	Mike Trout	3	Clayton Kershaw (15)	
4	Matt Kemp	4	Chris Davis	
5	Andrew McCutchen	5	Paul Goldschmidt	
6	Albert Pujols	6	Andrew McCutchen (5)	
7	Robinson Cano	7	Adam Jones	
8	Jose Bautista	8	Jacoby Ellsbury	
9	Joey Votto	9	Max Scherzer	
10	Carlos Gonzalez	10	Carlos Gomez	
11	Buster Posey	11	Hunter Pence	
12	Justin Upton	12	Robinson Cano (7)	
13	Giancarlo Stanton	13	Alex Rios	
14	Prince Fielder	14	Adrian Beltre	
15	Clayton Kershaw	15	Matt Harvey	

2014	ADP		ACTUAL = 4	
1	Mike Trout	1	Jose Altuve	
2	Miguel Cabrera	2	Clayton Kershaw (6)	
3	Paul Goldschmidt	3	Michael Brantley	
4	Andrew McCutchen	4	Mike Trout (1)	
5	Carlos Gonzalez	5	Johnny Cueto	
6	Clayton Kershaw	6	Felix Hernandez	
7	Chris Davis	7	Victor Martinez	
8	Ryan Braun	8	Jose Abreu	
9	Adam Jones	9	Giancarlo Stanton	
10	Bryce Harper	10	Andrew McCutchen (4)	
11	Robinson Cano	11	Miguel Cabrera (2)	
12	Hanley Ramirez	12	Carlos Gomez	
13	Jacoby Ellsbury	13	Jose Bautista	
14	Prince Fielder	14	Dee Gordon	
15	Troy Tulowitzki	15	Anthony Rendon	

ADP attrition

Why is our success rate so low in identifying what should be the most easy-to-project players each year? We rank and draft players based on the expectation that those ranked higher will return greater value in terms of productivity and playing time, as well as being the safest investments. However, there are many variables affecting where players finish.

Earlier, it was shown that players spend an inordinate number of days on the disabled list. In fact, of the players projected to finish in the top 300 coming into each of the past four seasons, the number who lost playing time due to injuries, demotions and suspensions has been extreme:

Year	Pct. of top-ranked 300 players who lost PT
2009	51%
2010	44%
2011	49%
2012	45%
2013	51%
2014	53%

When you consider that about half of each season's very best players had fewer at-bats or innings pitched than we projected, it shows how tough it is to rank players each year.

The fallout? Consider: It is nearly a foregone conclusion that Joses Altuve and Abreu—players who finished in the top 15 for the first time last year—will rank as first round picks in 2015. The above data provide a strong argument against them returning first-round value.

Yes, they are excellent players, two of the best in the game, in 2014 anyway. But the issue is not their skills profile. The issue is the profile of what makes a worthy first rounder. Note:

- Two-thirds of players finishing in the Top 15 were not in the Top 15 the previous year. There is a great deal of turnover in the first round, year-to-year.

- Of those who were first-timers, only 14% repeated in the first round the following year.

- Established superstars who finished in the Top 15 were no guarantee to repeat but occasionally reappear in a later year. These were players like David Ortiz (twice in 1st round, twice unable to repeat), Mark Teixeira (#5, 2005), Ryan Howard (#4, 2006) and Chase Utley (3 times in 1st round, only repeated once). First-time stars like Josh Hamilton (2008), Joe Mauer (2009) and Buster Posey (2012) are even less likely to repeat. Note that Carlos Gonzalez was baseball's top-ranked player in 2010. He has been drafted in the first round in each season since but has yet to return first round value again.

- From 2005 to 2007, 14 of the top 15 players were batters. In 2008, that dropped to 13. In 2009 and 2010, it dropped again to 12. In 2011 and 2012, only 10 of 15 were batters. The past two seasons, 12 of 15 first-rounders were batters, however, the pitchers ranked higher and populated more of the second round. As player value shifts toward pitching, there are fewer spots in the first few rounds for batters.

As such, the odds are against Altuve and Abreu repeating in the first round, as counter-intuitive as it may seem. In past years, sudden stars like Zack Greinke, Curtis Granderson and Dustin Pedroia have failed to repeat. Last year in this very space, I wrote the same thing about Chris Davis and Paul Goldschmidt. As talented as these players are, it's not just about skill; it's also about skill relative to the rest of a volatile player pool.

Importance of the Early Rounds *(Bill Macey)*

It's long been said that you can't win your league in the first round, but you can lose it there. An analysis of data from actual drafts reveals that this holds true—those who spend an early round pick on a player that severely under-performs expectations rarely win their league and seldom even finish in the top 3.

At the same time, drafting a player in the first round that actually returns first-round value is no guarantee of success. In fact, those that draft some of the best values still only win their league about a quarter of the time and finish in the top 3 less than half the time. Research also shows that drafting pitchers in the first round is a risky proposition. Even if the pitchers deliver first-round value, the opportunity cost of passing up on an elite batter makes you less likely to win your league.

What is the best seed to draft from?

Most drafters like mid-round so they never have to wait too long for their next player. Some like the swing pick, suggesting that getting two players at 15 and 16 is better than a 1 and a 30. Many drafters assume that the swing pick means you'd be getting something like two $30 players instead of a $40 and $20.

Equivalent auction dollar values reveal the following facts about the first two snake draft rounds:

In an AL/NL-only league, the top seed would get a $44 player (at #1) and a $24 player (at #24) for a total of $68; the 12th seed would get two $29s (at #12 and #13) for $58.

In a mixed league, the top seed would get a $47 and a $24 ($71); the 15th seed would get two $28s ($56).

Since the talent level flattens out after the 2nd round, low seeds never get a chance to catch up:

Dollar value difference between first player selected and last player selected		
Round	12-team	15-team
1	$15	$19
2	$7	$8
3	$5	$4
4	$3	$3
5	$2	$2
6	$2	$1
7-17	$1	$1
18-23	$0	$0

The total value each seed accumulates at the end of the draft is hardly equitable:

Seed	Mixed	AL/NL-only
1	$266	$273
2	$264	$269
3	$263	$261
4	$262	$262
5	$259	$260
6	$261	$260
7	$260	$260
8	$261	$260
9	$261	$258
10	$257	$260
11	$257	$257
12	$258	$257
13	$254	
14	$255	
15	$256	

Of course, the draft is just the starting point for managing your roster and player values are variable. Still, it's tough to imagine a scenario where the top seed wouldn't have an advantage over the bottom seed.

Using ADPs to determine when to select players *(Bill Macey)*

Although average draft position (ADP) data gives us a good idea of where in the draft each player is selected, it can be misleading when trying to determine how early to target a player. This chart summarizes the percentage of players drafted within 15 picks of his ADP as well as the average standard deviation by grouping of players.

ADP Rank	% within 15 picks	Standard Deviation
1-25	100%	2.5
26-50	97%	6.1
51-100	87%	9.6
100-150	72%	14.0
150-200	61%	17.4
200-250	53%	20.9

As the draft progresses, the picks for each player become more widely dispersed and less clustered around the average. Most top 100 players will go within one round of their ADP-converted round. However, as you reach the mid-to-late rounds, there is much more uncertainty as to when a player will be selected. Pitchers have slightly smaller standard deviations than do batters (i.e. they tend to be drafted in a narrower range). This suggests that drafters may be more likely to reach for a batter than for a pitcher.

Using the ADP and corresponding standard deviation, we can to estimate the likelihood that a given player will be available at a certain draft pick. We estimate the predicted standard deviation for each player as follows:

$$Stdev = -0.42 + 0.42*(ADP - Earliest\ Pick)$$

(That the figure 0.42 appears twice is pure coincidence; the numbers are not equal past two decimal points.)

If we assume that the picks are normally distributed, we can use a player's ADP and estimated standard deviation to estimate the likelihood that the player is available with a certain pick (MS Excel formula):

$$=1-normdist(x,ADP,Standard\ Deviation,True)$$
where «x» represents the pick number to be evaluated.

We can use this information to prepare for a snake draft by determining how early we may need to reach in order to roster a player. Suppose you have the 8th pick in a 15-team league draft and your target is 2009 sleeper candidate Nelson Cruz. His ADP is 128.9 and his earliest selection was with the 94th pick. This yields an estimated standard deviation of 14.2. You can then enter these values into the formula above to estimate the likelihood that he is still available at each of the following picks:

Pick	Likelihood Available
83	100%
98	99%
113	87%
128	53%
143	16%
158	2%

ADPs and scarcity *(Bill Macey)*

Most players are selected within a round or two of their ADP with tight clustering around the average. But every draft is unique and every pick in the draft seemingly affects the ordering of subsequent picks. In fact, deviations from "expected" sequences can sometimes start a chain reaction at that position. This is most often seen in runs at scarce positions such as the closer; once the first one goes, the next seems sure to closely follow.

Research also suggests that within each position, there is a correlation within tiers of players. The sooner players within a generally accepted tier are selected, the sooner other players within the same tier will be taken. However, once that tier is exhausted, draft order reverts to normal.

How can we use this information? If you notice a reach pick, you can expect that other drafters may follow suit. If your draft plan is to get a similar player within that tier, you'll need to adjust your picks accordingly.

Mapping ADPs to auction value *(Bill Macey)*

Reliable average auction values (AAV) are often tougher to come by than ADP data for snake drafts. However, we can estimate predicted auction prices as a function of ADP, arriving at the following equation:

y = -9.8ln(x) + 57.8
where ln(x) is the natural log function, x represents the actual ADP, and y represents the predicted AAV.

This equation does an excellent job estimating auction prices (r2=0.93), though deviations are unavoidable. The asymptotic nature of the logarithmic function, however, causes the model to predict overly high prices for the top players. So be aware of that, and adjust.

Auction Value Analysis

Auction values (R$) in perspective

R$ is the dollar value placed on a player's statistical performance in a Rotisserie league, and designed to measure the impact that player has on the standings.

There are several methods to calculate a player's value from his projected (or actual) statistics.

One method is Standings Gain Points, described in the book, *How to Value Players for Rotisserie Baseball*, by Art McGee (2nd edition available at BaseballHQ.com). SGP converts a player's statistics in each Rotisserie category into the number of points those stats will allow you to gain in the standings. These are then converted back into dollars.

Another popular method is the Percentage Valuation Method. In PVM, a least valuable, or replacement performance level is set for each category (in a given league size) and then values are calculated representing the incremental improvement from that base. A player is then awarded value in direct proportion to the level he contributes to each category.

As much as these methods serve to attach a firm number to projected performance, the winning bid for any player is still highly variable depending upon many factors:

- the salary cap limit
- the number of teams in the league
- each team's roster size
- the impact of any protected players
- each team's positional demands at the time of bidding
- the statistical category demands at the time of bidding
- external factors, e.g. media inflation or deflation of value

In other words, a $30 player is only a $30 player if someone in your draft pays $30 for him.

Roster slot valuation *(John Burnson)*

Tenets of player valuation say that the number of ballplayers with positive value—either positive projected value (before the season) or positive actual value (after the season)—must equal the total number of roster spots, and that, before the season, the value of a player must match his expected production. These propositions are wrong.

The unit of production in Rotisserie is not "the player" or "the statistic" but the player-week. If you own a player, you must own him for at least one week, and if you own him for more than one week, you must own him for multiples of one week. Moreover, you cannot break down his production—everything that a player does in a given week, you earn. (In leagues that allow daily transactions, the unit is the player-day. The point stays.)

When you draft a player, what have you bought?
"You have bought the stats generated by this player."

No. You have bought the stats generated by his slot. Initially, the drafted player fills the slot, but he need not fill the slot for the season, and he need not contribute from Day One. If you trade the player during the season, then your bid on Draft Day paid for the stats of the original player plus the stats of the new player. If the player misses time due to injury or demotion, then you bought the stats of whomever fills the weeks while the drafted player is missing. At season's end, there will be more players providing positive value than there are roster slots.

Before the season, the number of players projected for positive value has to equal the total number of roster slots—after all, we can't order owners to draft more players than can fit on their rosters. However, the projected productivity should be adjusted by the potential to capture extra value in the slot. This is especially important for injury-rehab cases and late-season call-ups. For example, if we think that a player will miss half the season, then we would augment his projected stats with a half-year of stats from a replacement-level player at his position. Only then would we calculate prices. Essentially, we want to apportion $260 per team among the slots, not the players.

Average player value by draft round

Rd	AL/NL	Mxd
1	$34	$34
2	$26	$26
3	$23	$23
4	$20	$20
5	$18	$18
6	$17	$16
7	$16	$15
8	$15	$13
9	$13	$12
10	$12	$11
11	$11	$10
12	$10	$9
13	$9	$8
14	$8	$8
15	$7	$7
16	$6	$6
17	$5	$5
18	$4	$4
19	$3	$3
20	$2	$2
21	$1	$2
22	$1	$1
23	$1	$1

Benchmarks for auction players:

- All $30 players will go in the first round.
- All $20-plus players will go in the first four rounds.
- Double-digit value ends pretty much after Round 11.
- The $1 end game starts at about Round 21.

Dollar values by lineup position *(Michael Roy)*

How much value is derived from batting order position?

Pos	PA	R	RBI	R$
#1	747	107	72	$18.75
#2	728	102	84	$19.00
#3	715	95	100	$19.45
#4	698	93	104	$19.36
#5	682	86	94	$18.18
#6	665	85	82	$17.19
#7	645	81	80	$16.60
#8	623	78	80	$16.19
#9	600	78	73	$15.50

So, a batter moving from the bottom of the order to the clean-up spot, with no change in performance, would gain nearly $4 in value from runs and RBIs alone.

Dollar values: expected projective accuracy

There is a 65% chance that a player projected for a certain dollar value will finish the season with a final value within plus-or-minus $5 of that projection. That means, if you value a player at $25, you only have about a 2-in-3 shot of him finishing between $20 and $30.

If you want to get your odds up to 80%, the range now becomes +/- $9. You have an 80% shot that your $25 player will finish somewhere between $16 and $34.

How likely is it that a $30 player will repeat? *(Matt Cederholm)*

From 2003-2008, there were 205 players who earned $30 or more (using single-league 5x5 values). Only 70 of them (34%) earned $30 or more in the next season.

In fact, the odds of repeating a $30 season aren't good. As seen below, the best odds during that period were 42%. And as we would expect, pitchers fare far worse than hitters.

	Total>$30	# Repeat	% Repeat
Hitters	167	64	38%
Pitchers	38	6	16%
Total	205	70	34%
*High-Reliability**			
Hitters	42	16	38%
Pitchers	7	0	0%
Total	49	16	33%
100+ BPV			
Hitters	60	25	42%
Pitchers	31	6	19%
Total	91	31	19%
*High-Reliability and 100+ BPV**			
Hitters	12	5	42%
Pitchers	6	0	0%
Total	18	5	28%

Reliability figures are from 2006-2008

For players with multiple seasons of $30 or more, the numbers get better. Players with consecutive $30 seasons, 2003-2008:

	Total>$30	# Repeat	% Repeat
Two Years	62	29	55%
Three+ Years	29	19	66%

Still, a player with two consecutive seasons at $30 in value is barely a 50/50 proposition. And three consecutive seasons is only a 2/3 shot. Small sample sizes aside, this does illustrate the nature of the beast. Even the most consistent, reliable players fail 1/3 of the time. Of course, this is true whether they are kept or drafted anew, so this alone shouldn't prevent you from keeping a player.

How well do elite pitchers retain their value? *(Michael Weddell)*

An elite pitcher (one who earns at least $24 in a season) on average keeps 80% of his R$ value from year 1 to year 2. This compares to the baseline case of only 52%.

Historically, 36% of elite pitchers improve, returning a greater R$ in the second year than they did the first year. That is an impressive performance considering they already were at an elite level. 17% collapse, returning less than a third of their R$ in the second year. The remaining 47% experience a middling outcome, keeping more than a third but less than all of their R$ from one year to the next.

Valuing closers

Given the high risk associated with the closer's role, it is difficult to determine a fair draft value. Typically, those who have successfully held the role for several seasons will earn the highest draft price, but valuing less stable commodities is troublesome.

A rough rule of thumb is to start by paying $10 for the role alone. Any pitcher tagged the closer on draft day should merit at least $10. Then add anywhere from $0 to $15 for support skills.

In this way, the top level talents will draw upwards of $20-$25. Those with moderate skill will draw $15-$20, and those with more questionable skill in the $10-$15 range.

Profiling the end game

What types of players are typically the most profitable in the end-game? First, our overall track record on $1 picks:

Avg Return	%Profitable	Avg Prof	Avg. Loss
$1.89	51%	$10.37	($7.17)

On aggregate, the hundreds of players drafted in the end-game earned $1.89 on our $1 investments. While they were profitable overall, only 51% of them actually turned a profit. Those that did cleared more than $10 on average. Those that didn't—the other 49%—lost about $7 apiece.

Pos	Pct.of tot	Avg Val	%Profit	Avg Prof	Avg Loss
CA	12%	($1.68)	41%	$7.11	($7.77)
CO	9%	$6.12	71%	$10.97	($3.80)
MI	9%	$3.59	53%	$10.33	($4.84)
OF	22%	$2.61	46%	$12.06	($5.90)
SP	29%	$1.96	52%	$8.19	($7.06)
RP	19%	$0.35	50%	$11.33	($10.10)

These results bear out the danger of leaving catchers to the end; only catchers returned negative value. Corner infielder returns say leaving a 1B or 3B open until late.

Age	Pct.of tot	Avg Val	%Profit	Avg Prof	Avg Loss
< 25	15%	($0.88)	33%	$8.25	($8.71)
25-29	48%	$2.59	56%	$11.10	($8.38)
30-35	28%	$2.06	44%	$10.39	($5.04)
35+	9%	$2.15	41%	$8.86	($5.67)

The practice of speculating on younger players—mostly rookies—in the end game was a washout. Part of the reason was that those that even made it to the end game were often the long-term or fringe type. Better prospects were typically drafted earlier.

	Pct.of tot	Avg Val	%Profit	Avg Prof	Avg Loss
Injury rehabs	20%	$3.63	36%	$15.07	($5.65)

One in five end-gamers were players coming back from injury. While only 36% of them were profitable, the healthy ones returned a healthy profit. The group's losses were small, likely because they weren't healthy enough to play.

Realistic expectations of $1 endgamers *(Patrick Davitt)*

Many fantasy articles insist leagues are won or lost with $1 batters, because "that's where the profits are." But are they?

A 2011 analysis showed that when considering $1 players in deep leagues, managing $1 endgamers should be more about minimizing losses than fishing for profit. In the cohort of batters projected $0 to -$5, 82% returned losses, based on a $1 bid. Two-thirds of the projected $1 cohort returned losses. In addition, when considering $1 players, speculate on speed.

Advanced Draft Strategies

Stars & Scrubs v. Spread the Risk

Stars & Scrubs (S&S): A Rotisserie auction strategy in which a roster is anchored by a core of high priced stars and the remaining positions filled with low-cost players.

Spread the Risk (STR): An auction strategy in which available dollars are spread evenly among all roster slots.

Both approaches have benefits and risks. An experiment was conducted in 2004 whereby a league was stocked with four teams assembled as S&S, four as STR and four as a control group. Rosters were then frozen for the season.

The Stars & Scrubs teams won all three ratio categories. Those deep investments ensured stability in the categories that are typically most difficult to manage. On the batting side, however, S&S teams amassed the least amount of playing time, which in turn led to bottom-rung finishes in HRs, RBIs and Runs.

One of the arguments for the S&S approach is that it is easier to replace end-game losers (which, in turn, may help resolve the playing time issues). Not only is this true, but the results of this experiment show that replacing those bottom players is critical to success.

The Spread the Risk teams stockpiled playing time, which in turn led to strong finishes in many of the counting stats, including clear victories in RBIs, wins and strikeouts. This is a key tenet in drafting philosophy; we often say that the team that compiles the most ABs will undoubtedly be among the top teams in RBI and Runs.

The danger is on the pitching side. More innings did yield more wins and Ks, but also destroyed ERA/WHIP.

So, what approach makes the most sense? **The optimal strategy might be to STR on offense and go S&S with your pitching staff.** STR buys more ABs, so you immediately position yourself well in four of the five batting categories. On pitching, it might be more advisable to roster a few core arms, though that immediately elevates your risk exposure. Admittedly, it's a balancing act, which is why we need to pay more attention to risk analysis and look closer at strategies like the RIMA Plan and Portfolio3.

The LIMA Plan

The LIMA Plan is a strategy for Rotisserie leagues (though the underlying concept can be used in other formats) that allows you to target high skills pitchers at very low cost, thereby freeing up dollars for offense. LIMA is an acronym for Low Investment Mound Aces, and also pays tribute to Jose Lima, a $1 pitcher in 1998 who exemplified the power of the strategy. In a $260 league:

1. Budget a maximum of $60 for your pitching staff.
2. Allot no more than $30 of that budget for acquiring saves. In 5x5 leagues, it is reasonable to forego saves at the draft (and acquire them during the season) and re-allocate this $30 to starters ($20) and offense ($10).
3. Ignore ERA. Draft only pitchers with:
   - Command ratio (K/BB) of 2.5 or better.
   - Strikeout rate of 7.0 or better.
   - Expected home run rate of 1.0 or less.
4. Draft as few innings as your league rules will allow. This is intended to manage risk. For some game formats, this should be a secondary consideration.
5. Maximize your batting slots. Target batters with:
   - Contact rate of at least 80%
   - Walk rate of at least 10%
   - PX or Spd level of at least 100

Spend no more than $29 for any player and try to keep the $1 picks to a minimum.

The goal is to ace the batting categories and carefully pick your pitching staff so that it will finish in the upper third in ERA, WHIP and saves (and Ks in 5x5), and an upside of perhaps 9th in wins. In a competitive league, that should be enough to win, and definitely enough to finish in the money. Worst case, you should have an excess of offense available that you can deal for pitching.

The strategy works because it better allocates resources. Fantasy leaguers who spend a lot for pitching are not only paying for expected performance, they are also paying for better defined roles—#1 and #2 rotation starters, ace closers, etc.—which are expected to translate into more IP, wins and saves. But roles are highly variable. A pitcher's role will usually come down to his skill and performance; if he doesn't perform, he'll lose the role.

The LIMA Plan says, let's invest in skill and let the roles fall where they may. In the long run, better skills should translate into more innings, wins and saves. And as it turns out, pitching skill costs less than pitching roles do.

In *snake draft leagues,* don't start drafting starting pitchers until Round 10. In *shallow mixed leagues,* the LIMA Plan may not be necessary; just focus on the BPI benchmarks. In *simulation leagues,* build your staff around BPI benchmarks.

Variations on the LIMA Plan

LIMA Extrema: Limit your total pitching budget to only $30, or less. This can be particularly effective in shallow leagues where LIMA-caliber starting pitcher free agents are plentiful during the season.

SANTANA Plan: Instead of spending $30 on saves, you spend it on a starting pitcher anchor. In 5x5 leagues where you can reasonably punt saves at the draft table, allocating those dollars to a high-end LIMA-caliber starting pitcher can work well as long as you pick the right anchor.

Total Control Drafting (TCD)

On Draft Day, we make every effort to control as many elements as possible. In reality, the players that end up on our teams are largely controlled by the other owners. Their bidding affects your ability to roster the players you want. In a snake draft, the other owners control your roster even more. We are really only able to get the players we want within the limitations set by others.

However, an optimal roster can be constructed from a fanalytic assessment of skill and risk combined with more assertive draft day demeanor.

Why this makes sense

1. Our obsession with projected player values is holding us back. If a player on your draft list is valued at $20 and you agonize when the bidding hits $23, odds are about two chances in three that he could really earn anywhere from $15 to $25. What this means is, in some cases, and within reason, you should just pay what it takes to get the players you want.

2. There is no such thing as a bargain. Most of us *don't* just pay what it takes because we are always on the lookout for players who go under value. But we really don't know which players will cost less than they will earn because prices are still driven by the draft table. The concept of "bargain" assumes that we even know what a player's true value is.

3. "Control" is there for the taking. Most owners are so focused on their own team that they really don't pay much attention to what you're doing. There are some exceptions, and bidding wars do happen, but in general, other owners will not provide that much resistance.

How it's done

1. Create your optimal draft pool.

2. Get those players.

Start by identifying which players will be draftable based on the LIMA or Portfolio3 criteria. Then, at the draft, focus solely on your roster. When it's your bid opener, toss a player you need at about 50%-75% of your projected value. Bid aggressively and just pay what you need to pay. Of course, don't spend $40 for a player with $25 market value, but it's okay to exceed your projected value within reason.

From a tactical perspective, mix up the caliber of openers. Drop out early on some bids to prevent other owners from catching on to you.

In the end, it's okay to pay a slight premium to make sure you get the players with the highest potential to provide a good return on your investment. It's no different than the premium you might pay for a player with position flexbility or to get the last valuable shortstop. With TCD, you're just spending those extra dollars up front to ensure you are rostering your targets. In fact, TCD almost asssures that you don't leave money on the table.

The Portfolio3 Plan & Mayberry Method

For more information on these draft aids, please refer to this edition's Introduction.

For those who still use the current version of Portfolio3, these are the tier charts:

TIER 1: CORE PLAYERS

Roster			BATTERS		PITCHERS	
Slots	Budget	Rel	Ct%	PX or Spd	Rel	BPV
5-8	Max $160	BBB	80%	100 / 100	BBB	75

TIER 2: MID-GAME PLAYERS

Roster			BATTERS		PITCHERS	
Slots	Budget	Rel	Ct% or	PX or Spd	Rel	BPV
7-13	$50-$100	BBB	80%	100 100	BBB	50

All players must be less than $20
Batters must be projected for at least 500 AB

TIER 3: END-GAME PLAYERS

Roster			BATTERS		PITCHERS	
Slots	Budget	Rel	Ct%	PX or Spd	Rel	BPV
5-10	Up to $50	n/a	80%	100 100	n/a	75

All players must be less than $10

Building a Homogeneous Head-to-Head Team *(David Martin)*

Though variety is the spice of life, it has no place in the type of players rostered on head-to-head teams. Teams in head-to-head leagues need players cut from the same cloth—players that are completely homogenous.

Focusing on certain metrics helps build a homogenous team; Drafting a homogenous team inherently builds consistency into your roster. Our filters for such success are:

- Contact rate = minimum 80%
- xBA = minimum .280
- PX (or Spd) = minimum 120
- RC/G = minimum 5.00

Research shows that a homogeneous team based on these metrics is more likely to be a consistent team, which is the roster holy grail for head-to-head players.

Ratio Insulation in Head-to-Head Leagues *(David Martin)*

On a week-to-week basis, inequities are inherent in the head-to-head game. One way to eliminate your competitor's advantage in the pure numbers game is to build your team's foundation around the ratio categories.

One should normally insulate at the end of a draft, once your hitters are in place. To obtain several ratio insulators, target players that have:

- Cmd greater than 3.0
- Dom greater than 7.5
- xERA less than 3.30

While adopting this strategy may compromise wins, research has shown that wins come at a cost to ERA and WHIP. Roster space permitting, adding two to four insulators to your team will improve your team's weekly ERA and WHIP.

In-Season Analyses

The efficacy of streaming *(John Burnson)*

In leagues that allow weekly or daily transactions, many owners flit from hot player to hot player. But published dollar values don't capture this traffic—they assume that players are owned from April to October. For many leagues, this may be unrealistic.

We decided to calculate these "investor returns." For each week, we identified the top players by one statistic—BA for hitters, ERA for pitchers—and took the top 100 hitters and top 50 pitchers. We then said that, at the end of the week, the #1 player was picked up (or already owned) by 100% of teams, the #2 player was picked up or owned by 99% of teams, and so on, down to the 100th player, who was on 1% of teams. (For pitchers, we stepped by 2%.) Last, we tracked each player's performance in the next week, when ownership matters.

We ran this process anew for every week of the season, tabulating each player's "investor returns" along the way. If a player was owned by 100% of teams, then we awarded him 100% of his performance. If the player was owned by half the teams, we gave him half his performance. If he was owned by no one (that is, he was not among the top players in the prior week), his performance was ignored. A player's cumulative stats over the season was his investor return.

The results...

- 60% of pitchers had poorer investor returns, with an aggregate ERA 0.40 higher than their true ERA.
- 55% of batters had poorer investor returns, but with an aggregate batting average virtually identical to the true BA.

Sitting stars and starting scrubs *(Ed DeCaria)*

In setting your pitching rotation, conventional wisdom suggests sticking with trusted stars despite difficult matchups. But does this hold up? And can you carefully start inferior pitchers against weaker opponents? Here are the ERA's posted by varying skilled pitchers facing a range of different strength offenses:

	OPPOSING OFFENSE (RC/G)				
Pitcher (ERA)	5.25+	5.00	4.25	4.00	<4.00
3.00-	3.46	3.04	3.04	2.50	2.20
3.50	3.98	3.94	3.44	3.17	2.87
4.00	4.72	4.57	3.96	3.66	3.24
4.50	5.37	4.92	4.47	4.07	3.66
5.00+	6.02	5.41	5.15	4.94	4.42

Recommendations:

1. Never start below replacement-level pitchers.
2. Always start elite pitchers.
3. Other than that, never say never or always.

Playing matchups can pay off when the difference in opposing offense is severe.

Two-start pitcher weeks *(Ed DeCaria)*

A two-start pitcher is a prized possession. But those starts can mean two DOMinant outings, two DISasters, or anything else in between, as shown by these results:

PQS Pair	% Weeks	ERA	WHIP	Win/Wk	K/Wk
DOM-DOM	20%	2.53	1.02	1.1	12.0
DOM-AVG	28%	3.60	1.25	0.8	9.2
AVG-AVG	14%	4.44	1.45	0.7	6.8
DOM-DIS	15%	5.24	1.48	0.6	7.9
AVG-DIS	17%	6.58	1.74	0.5	5.7
DIS-DIS	6%	8.85	2.07	0.3	5.0

Weeks that include even one DISaster start produce terrible results. Unfortunately, avoiding such disasters is much easier in hindsight. But what is the actual impact of this decision on the stat categories?

ERA and WHIP: When the difference between opponents is extreme, inferior pitchers can actually be a better percentage play. This is true both for one-start pitchers and two-start pitchers, and for choosing inferior one-start pitchers over superior two-start pitchers.

Strikeouts per Week: Unlike the two rate stats, there is a massive shift in the balance of power between one-start and two-start pitchers in the strikeout category. Even stars with easy one-start matchups can only barely keep pace with two-start replacement-level arms in strikeouts per week.

Wins per week are also dominated by the two-start pitchers. Even the very worst two-start pitchers will earn a half of a win on average, which is the same rate as the very best one-start pitchers.

The bottom line: If strikeouts and wins are the strategic priority, use as many two-start weeks as the rules allow, even if it means using a replacement-level pitcher with two tough starts instead of a mid-level arm with a single easy start. But if ERA and/or WHIP management are the priority, two-start pitchers can be very powerful, as a single week might impact the standings by over 1.5 points in ERA/WHIP, positively or negatively.

Six Tips on Category Management *(Todd Zola)*

1. Disregard whether you are near the top or the bottom of a category; focus instead on the gaps directly above and below your squad.
2. Prorate the difference in stats between teams.
3. ERA tends to move towards WHIP.
4. As the season progresses, the number of at-bats and innings pitched do not preclude a gain/loss in the ratio categories.
5. An opponent's point lost is a point earned.
6. *Most important!* Come crunch time, forget value, forget names, and forget reputation. It's all about stats and where you are situated within each category.

Consistency *(Dylan Hedges)*

Few things are as valuable to head-to-head league success as filling your roster with players who can produce a solid baseline of stats, week in and week out. In traditional leagues, while consistency is not as important—all we care about are aggregate numbers—filling your team with consistent players can make roster management easier.

Consistent batters have good plate discipline, walk rates and on base percentages. These are foundation skills. Those who add power to the mix are obviously more valuable, however, the ability to hit home runs consistently is rare.

Consistent pitchers demonstrate similar skills in each outing; if they also produce similar results, they are even more valuable.

We can track consistency but predicting it is difficult. Many fantasy leaguers try to predict a batter's hot or cold streaks, or individual pitcher starts, but that is typically a fool's errand. The best we can do is find players who demonstrate seasonal consistency over time; in-season, we want to manage players and consistency tactically.

Consistency in points leagues *(Bill Macey)*

Previous research has demonstrated that week-to-week statistical consistency is important for Rotisserie-based head-to-head play. But one can use the same foundation in points-based games. A study showed that not only do players with better skills post more overall points in this format, but that the format caters to consistent performances on a week-to-week basis, even after accounting for differences in total points scored and playing-time.

Therefore, when drafting your batters in points-based head-to-head leagues, ct% and bb% make excellent tiebreakers if you are having trouble deciding between two players with similarly projected point totals. Likewise, when rostering pitchers, favor those who tend not to give up home runs.

Other Diamonds

Cellar value
The dollar value at which a player cannot help but earn more than he costs. Always profit here.

Crickets
The sound heard when someone's opening draft bid on a player is also the only bid.

Scott Elarton List
Players you drop out on when the bidding reaches $1.

End-game wasteland
Home for players undraftable in the deepest of leagues, who stay in the free agent pool all year. It's the place where even crickets keep quiet when a name is called at the draft.

FAAB Forewarnings
1. Spend early and often.
2. Emptying your budget for one prime league-crosser is a tactic that should be reserved for the desperate.
3. If you chase two rabbits, you will lose them both.

Fantasy Economics 101
The market value for a player is generally based on the aura of past performance, not the promise of future potential. Your greatest advantage is to leverage the variance between market value and real value.

Fantasy Economics 102
The variance between market value and real value is far more important than the absolute accuracy of any individual player projection.

Hope
A commodity that routinely goes for $5 over value at the draft table.

JA$G
Just Another Dollar Guy.

Professional Free Agent (PFA)
Player whose name will never come up on draft day but will always end up on a roster at some point during the season as an injury replacement.

RUM pick
A player who is rosterable only as a Reserve, Ultra or Minors pick.

Standings Vantage Points
First Place: It's lonely at the top, but it's comforting to look down upon everyone else.
Sixth Place: The toughest position to be in is mid-pack at dump time.
Last Place in April: The sooner you fall behind, the more time you will have to catch up.
Last Place, Yet Again: If you can't learn to do something well, learn to enjoy doing it badly.

Mike Timlin List
Players who you are unable to resist drafting even though they have burned you multiple times in the past.

Seasonal Assessment Standard
If you still have reason to be reading the boxscores during the last weekend of the season, then your year has to be considered a success.

The Three Cardinal Rules for Winners
If you cherish this hobby, you will live by them or die by them...
1. Revel in your success; fame is fleeting.
2. Exercise excruciating humility.
3. 100% of winnings must be spent on significant others.

Starting Pitcher First-Pitch Strike Rates

by Stephen Nickrand

Our 2013 research on swinging strike rate (SwK%) illustrated the strong correlation between a pitcher's level of swinging strikes and one of the staple pitching metrics we have used for years—Dominance (K/9) rate. SwK% is a metric often used today to validate strikeout levels and to forecast the potential for a pitcher to experience a surge or decline in strikeouts.

Like Dominance rate, Control (BB/9) rate is another indicator in our toolbox that has driven our pitching roster decisions for a long time. In fact, it is a significant component of our base performance value (BPV) metric for pitchers. However, we haven't been able to incorporate a sub-measurement to validate a pitcher's control rate—nor anticipate changes in a pitcher's future level of walks—using a comparable indicator to SwK% for strikeouts.

Here, our research will show that first-pitch strike rate (FpK%)—the percentage of first-pitch strikes a pitcher throws—can serve as this indicator.

Hypothesis

It seems intuitive that pitchers with a high FpK% would tend to have low control rates—and therefore lower WHIPs—than those with a higher FpK%. And perhaps pitchers who are allowing a lot of walks—even though they are getting a lot of first-pitch strikes—could be forecasted to expect a reduction in their control rate in the future, and vice-versa.

In fact, our initial research on stats and skills by starting pitcher ball-strike counts confirms the significant positive impact on a pitcher when starting the count 0-1. We found that ball-strike counts that started 0-1 resulted in a walk in just four percent of plate appearances. (See page 67 for more details.)

Method

Let's take a closer look at FpK% to see how strongly it is correlated with the common pitching metrics you will find at BaseballHQ.com and the *Baseball Forecaster*.

To do this, we took a look at starting pitchers that posted 40 IP or more per season from 2010 to 2013. This threshold was reached a total of 775 times during this period.

As a reminder, correlations can range from +1.0 to -1.0. Let's segregate them into the following groups to describe how strong they are:

+0.70 to +1.00	Strong positive relationship
+0.40 to +0.69	Moderate positive relationship
+0.20 to +0.39	Weak positive relationship
+0.19 to -0.19	No or negligible relationship
-0.20 to -0.39	Weak negative relationship
-0.40 to -0.69	Moderate negative relationship
-0.70 to -1.00	Strong negative relationship

Results

From 2010 to 2013, the average FpK% of pitchers by type of pitcher and league were as follows:

Pitcher	League	FpK%
Starters	AL	59.8%
Starters	NL	60.4%
Starters	All	60.1%
Relievers	AL	58.4%
Relievers	NL	58.8%
Relievers	All	58.6%
All pitchers	AL	59.3%
All pitchers	NL	59.9%
All pitchers	All	59.6%

The following indicators had positive correlations with FpK%, meaning that they had a tendency to move in the same direction as FpK%:

Indicator	Correlation
BPV	+0.49
Age	+0.19
Win Pct	+0.19
SwK%	+0.17
S%	+0.13
Dom (K/9)	+0.13

Here is a graphical look at the above table:

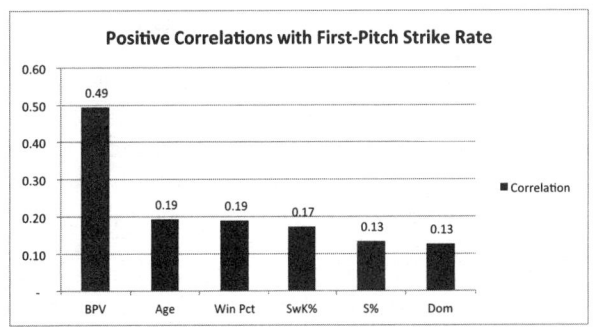

Conversely, these indicators had negative correlations with FpK%, meaning they tended to move in the opposite direction of FpK%:

Indicator	Correlation
Ctl (BB/9)	-0.62
WHIP	-0.42
ERA	-0.26
GB%	-0.18
FAv	-0.12
hr/f	-0.11
HR/9	-0.05
H%	-0.01

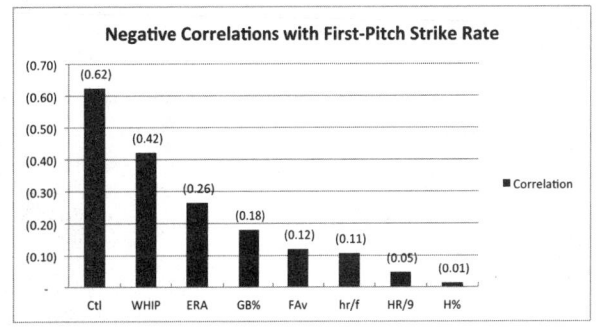

FpK% has the strongest correlations with the following three BHQ metrics:

Indicator	Type of Correlation	Strength of Correlation
Control rate	Negative	r = -0.62
BPV	Positive	r = +0.49
WHIP	Negative	r = -0.42

In summary:

- There is a moderate-to-strong negative correlation between control rate and FpK%, meaning as a SP's first-pitch strike rate goes up, his walks are likely to go down.

- As control rate is a significant component in our pitching BPV calculation, it should not come as a surprise that there is a moderate positive correlation between BPV and FpK%. This means that as a starting pitcher's first-pitch strike rate increases, so too will his BPV.

- Given that walks drive up WHIP, it is also logical that there is a moderate negative correlation between WHIP and FpK%, meaning his WHIP will go down as a pitcher's rate of first-pitch strikes goes up.

FpK% Stability

What about FpK% from season to season? How much is it likely to vary for starting pitchers?

A total of 82 starting pitchers threw at least 40 IP in each season from 2010 to 2013.

The average FpK% variance by starting pitcher from one season to another during this period was only +0.6%. Large increases in FpK% from one season to the next typically were offset by similarly large reductions within the same three-year period.

This is confirmation that FpK% does not regress towards league norms—it is in control of the pitcher.

We also wondered if FpK% tends to regress to a pitcher's three-year rolling average, similar to how batters set their own hit rate level.

- 41% of starting pitchers tended to approach their prior season's FpK% more so than their three-year FpK% or career FpK%.

- 42% of starting pitchers tended to approach their three-year FpK% more so than their prior season's FpK% or career FpK%.

- Only 17% of starting pitchers tended to approach their career FpK% more so than their prior season's FpK% or three-year FpK%.

This means that a starting pitcher's FpK% is much more likely to approach their prior season or three-year FpK% levels than their career FpK%.

Now let's look at extreme FpK% changes from one season to the next.

There were 19 instances of SP whose FpK% increased by 5% or more from one season to the next from 2010 to 2013.

Our research found that there is an extremely strong tendency for big FpK% surgers from one year to the next to keep most of those gains in year three, rather than regressing to the SP's prior career FpK% norm:

FpK% Season-to-Season Increase > 5%: Period 2010 to 2013
First-Pitch Strike Rate (FpK%)

Name	Year 1	Year 2	Career	Year 3
Lohse, Kyle	56%	68%	57%	69%
Morrow, Brandon	53%	61%	53%	60%
Hudson, Tim	54%	62%	44%	62%
Capuano, Chris	57%	64%	60%	67%
Guthrie, Jeremy	53%	59%	57%	60%
Garza, Matt	58%	64%	57%	63%
Hughes, Phil	63%	68%	61%	66%
Sanchez, Anibal	58%	63%	56%	66%
Sabathia, C.C.	58%	62%	55%	63%
Westbrook, Jake	56%	61%	57%	61%
Cueto, Johnny	56%	63%	57%	62%
Happ, J.A.	56%	63%	57%	60%
Buchholz, Clay	56%	63%	59%	60%
Morton, Charlie	55%	61%	55%	59%
Garcia, Jaime	58%	64%	56%	68%
Arroyo, Bronson	62%	68%	57%	66%
Gonzalez, Gio	53%	59%	53%	61%
Cahill, Trevor	57%	63%	56%	60%
Leake, Mike	58%	63%	58%	59%

If we expand the FpK% increase threshold to +3% or greater, we find that 70 starting pitchers saw a FpK% increase of 3.0% or higher from one season to the next between 2010 and 2013. Fifty of them (70%) experienced a reduction in their control rate during the same season with an average reduction of 0.7.

For guys whose FpK% reduced by more than 5% from one season to the next, all but one saw their FpK% rebound the following season, although it was slightly more common for their FpK% to revert to their prior career FpK% norms:

FpK% Season-to-Season Decline > 5%: Period 2010 to 2013
First-Pitch Strike Rate (FpK%)

Name	Year 1	Year 2	Career	Year 3
Liriano, Francisco	62%	49%	57%	53%
Johnson, Josh	65%	55%	61%	58%
Buehrle, Mark	62%	56%	54%	61%
Lee, Cliff	70%	65%	64%	72%
Wood, Travis	59%	54%	59%	58%
Danks, John	63%	56%	60%	62%
Marquis, Jason	61%	54%	54%	54%
Gallardo, Yovani	63%	57%	59%	56%
Harang, Aaron	62%	56%	62%	59%

Expanding this FpK% decline threshold to -3% or greater, we find that 40 starting pitchers saw an erosion of at least 3% in their FpK% from one season to the next between 2010 and 2013. Twenty-four (60%) experienced an increase in their control rate during the same season with an average control rate increase of 0.8.

Predicting Control Rate from FpK%

We can forecast future changes of control rate when a pitcher's FpK% is not associated with a control rate that is normally associated with that level of FpK%.

The following table shows the range of control rates over the last four seasons for different levels of FpK%, and that there is a steady erosion in control as a SP's FpK% declines.

The 50th percentile data means that 50% of pitchers will have control rates below the value listed, and 50% of pitchers will have control rates above the value listed.

For example, a pitcher with a FpK% of 60% (average level for a starting pitcher) is expected to have a 2.9 Ctl. Only 10% of pitchers with a FpK% of 60% will have a 2.1 Ctl or lower, and only 10% will have a 4.0 Ctl or higher.

Control (BB/9) Rate by Percentile

FpK%	10th	25th	50th	75th	90th
>68%	1.1	1.3	1.7	2.3	2.7
66-67%	1.3	1.7	2.2	2.5	2.5
65%	1.4	1.6	2.1	2.4	2.9
64%	1.9	2.1	2.4	2.7	3.2
63%	2.0	2.2	2.5	2.9	3.3
62%	1.9	2.1	2.6	3.0	3.3
61%	2.0	2.3	2.7	3.2	3.5
60%	2.1	2.4	2.9	3.4	4.0
59%	2.1	2.6	3.0	3.4	3.7
58%	2.3	2.7	3.2	3.5	4.0
57%	2.1	2.8	3.2	3.8	4.5
56%	2.2	2.8	3.3	3.9	4.3
55%	2.8	3.1	3.8	4.3	4.8
53-54%	3.0	3.3	3.6	4.9	5.3
<52%	3.3	3.5	4.5	5.0	5.9

Let's wrap up our findings by highlighting the takeaways of this research.

Conclusions

- There is a moderate-to-strong negative correlation between control rate and FpK%.
- There is a moderate positive correlation between BPV and FpK%.
- There is a moderate negative correlation between WHIP and FpK%.
- Big FpK% surgers from one year to the next tend to hold on to those gains in the third year or revert to their three-year FpK% average rather than regress to their prior career FpK% norm.
- Big FpK% decliners from one year to the next tend to recoup those losses in the third year, but there is a slightly greater tendency for the decliners to revert back to their prior career FpK% norms.
- Levels of control rate can be predicted based on levels of FpK%. For example, only 10 percent of pitchers with a FpK% of 65% will have a control rate of greater than 2.9.

It also seems intuitive that the total percentage of strikes that a pitcher throws—as well as the percentage of pitches that he throws within the strike zone—would also be predictive indicators of his walk rate.

As we do with the SwK% metric when validating a pitcher's Dominance rate, we can use FpK% as a measure to validate a pitcher's Control rate. As first-pitch strike rate increases, walks are very likely to go down, and WHIP will follow. As it goes up, walks are likely to increase, as will WHIP. So if you're wondering if a pitcher's newfound good control is likely to hold, check out his FpK%.

Walk Rate and Batting Average

by Patrick Davitt

Analysts often tell us a hitter's walk rate (bb%) is a reliable leading indicator of batting average (BA), and that changes in bb% are clues about improvements or declines in BA. The idea makes intuitive sense. But a review of the data shows that bb% and BA are as unconnected as they could be.

Method

We took every non-pitcher with >100 AB in any of the last five years. We had 735 different players and 2,151 player-seasons in all. Then we correlated each such qualified batter's BA with his bb%.

Results: Walk Rate/BA

To check the contention that bb% is related to BA, we correlated them. If they were positively correlated (rising bb% is correlated with rising BA), we would expect a score close to +1.0. If uncorrelated, we would expect a score closer to 0.0.

The correlation between bb% and BA was +0.01.

BAs were clustered around .250 at any given bb% decile level:

Decile	BB%			BA		
	Ave	Min	Max	Ave	Min	Max
1st	4%	1%	5%	.249	.145	.338
2nd	5%	5%	6%	.255	.167	.352
3rd	6%	6%	7%	.257	.150	.336
4th	7%	7%	7%	.257	.144	.346
5th	8%	7%	8%	.250	.157	.359
6th	9%	8%	9%	.258	.142	.345
7th	9%	9%	10%	.254	.156	.332
8th	10%	10%	11%	.256	.181	.342
9th	12%	11%	13%	.259	.175	.338
10th	15%	13%	20%	.254	.141	.365

In every decile, average BA was between .249 and .259, with no consistent increase or decrease as the bb% rose or declined.

Similarly, maximum and minimum BAs occurred randomly relative to bb% level: The .338 maximum BA in the 9th BB% decile (11%-13%) is matched by the maximum BA in the 2nd decile (5%-6%). Four different deciles have minimum BAs in the .140s

Look again at the third and seventh deciles: The seventh has bb% three points higher than the third, but their BA results are essentially identical.

Specific players illustrate the lack of connection. In 2012, for example, BAs within the 4% bb% cohort ranged from .309 to .193. In the 12% bb%, cohort, the BA range was .230 to .336. Turning it around, among .300+ hitters, bb% ranged from 4% to 14%.

The same sorts of results hold true for every other single year, and for all the years combined.

Conclusion

This study found little correlation between bb% and BA. With hitters >400 AB, the overall pattern holds with small differences: Slightly fewer low-bb% guys have high BAs, and slightly fewer high-bb% guys have low BAs.

Likely, the perceived "connection" between bb% and BA came about because analysts wanted a proxy for a hitter's ability to lay off pitches outside the zone and to swing at pitches in the zone. Now we have that data. And while swinging at pitches inside /outside the zone is also uncorrelated with BA, contact with those pitches is.

Strike Zone Metrics and Batting Average

by Patrick Davitt

So if walk rate (bb%) doesn't predict BA, what does?

We thought the "connection" between bb% and BA might have arisen because analysts were using bb% as a proxy for an ability to lay off pitches outside the zone and to swing at pitches in the zone.

Nowadays, however, we have data detailing how often each hitter swings (or doesn't) at pitches inside and outside the strike zone.

So we repeated the bb% study using those metrics, and we did find some stronger correlations. What we learned is that it isn't about swinging at balls in or out of the zone, it's about hitting them.

Method

We examined every non-pitcher with at least 100 ABs in any of the last five years, and correlated individual-season BA with:

- O-Swing% and Z-Swing% (the percentage of pitches a hitter swung at that were outside/inside the strike zone)
- Contact% (not the BHQ version, which is percentage of ABs without strikeouts, but the percentage of pitches swung at that resulted in contact)
- And O- and Z-Contact, which are the percentages of pitches swung at, outside and inside the zone, which resulted in contact

Each player-season was counted separately. We had 735 different players and 2,151 player-seasons in all. Correlations run on a scale from -1.00 (perfect inverse correlation), through 0.00 (no correlation) to +1.00 (perfect positive correlation).

Results 1: Swinging at Strikes

We first tested Z-Swing% and O-Swing%. The hypothesis was that batters with higher Z-Swing% should have a positive correlation with BA, while higher O-Swing should have a negative correlation with BA.

As with bb%, though, there were no correlations. Z-Swing% correlated with BA at +0.03 while O-Swing% correlated at -0.01.

Here is a table of Z- and O-Swing% levels at various BA levels:

BA Range	Z-Swing%		
	Ave	Max	Min
>.325	67%	83%	55%
.300-.324	65%	86%	49%
.275-.299	66%	85%	45%
.250-.274	65%	86%	36%
.225-.249	66%	81%	49%
.200-.224	65%	79%	51%
<.200	65%	81%	51%

No pattern, nor in BA performance by Z-Swing% decile:

Decile	Z-Swing%			BA		
	Ave	Min	Max	Ave	Min	Max
1st	55%	36%	58%	.260	.165	.365
2nd	59%	58%	61%	.253	.157	.337
3rd	62%	61%	62%	.253	.157	.338
4th	63%	63%	64%	.251	.142	.332
5th	65%	64%	66%	.250	.146	.325
6th	66%	66%	67%	.256	.141	.352
7th	68%	67%	69%	.255	.144	.329
8th	69%	69%	71%	.253	.144	.338
9th	72%	71%	73%	.256	.145	.345
10th	76%	73%	86%	.262	.157	.359

We saw similar results for O-Swing%.

Results 2: Contact

So swinging at good pitches and not swinging at bad ones is still not connected to BA. What we looked at last was O-Contact% and Z-Contact%—measures of hitters who wait not just for pitches in the zone but for pitches they can swing at and connect.

We expected—and got—positive correlations between contact and BA:

All Contact%: 0.32

Z-Contact%: 0.31

O-Contact%: 0.29

Not especially strong, but they do suggest some connection. We repeated the earlier exercises in looking at BA by metric and the reverse, starting with Z-Contact%:

	Z-Contact%		
	Ave	Max	Min
>.325	90%	97%	83%
.300-.324	90%	98%	77%
.275-.299	89%	98%	77%
.250-.274	88%	98%	70%
.225-.249	87%	98%	74%
.200-.224	86%	97%	67%
<.200	84%	98%	68%

Here is a definite pattern. As BA declined, average Z-Contact% declined, especially at the low end. And in the lowest BA cohorts, minimum Z-Contact% was below 70%.

Turning it around, we looked at Z-Contact% deciles and corresponding BA outcomes:

Decile	Z-Contact%			BA		
	Ave	Min	Max	Ave	Min	Max
1st	78%	67%	81%	.233	.141	.324
2nd	83%	81%	84%	.245	.144	.359
3rd	85%	84%	86%	.249	.142	.327
4th	86%	86%	87%	.251	.145	.344
5th	88%	87%	88%	.253	.150	.348
6th	89%	88%	90%	.260	.169	.345
7th	90%	90%	91%	.260	.167	.338
8th	91%	91%	92%	.263	.177	.365
9th	93%	92%	94%	.267	.167	.352
10th	95%	94%	98%	.269	.178	.337

In both average BA and minimum, the highest Z-Contact% decile had a 30-point BA advantage over the lowest.

Oddly, though, maximum BAs didn't follow a pattern at all. What gives? In a word, outliers—guys who just have the knack for hitting ball hard enough to get base hits despite swinging and missing a lot.

That bottom Z-Contact% decile had just eight batters >.300 and 87 <.225 (38 <.200). By contrast, the uppermost decile had 34 batters >.300, just 20 <.225, and four Mendozites.

Looking at O-Contact%:

	O-Contact%		
	Ave	Max	Min
>.325	73%	87%	60%
.300-.324	71%	89%	41%
.275-.299	69%	91%	42%
.250-.274	67%	88%	40%
.225-.249	65%	93%	25%
.200-.224	62%	87%	33%
<.200	61%	88%	30%

Here was another pattern: Average O-Contact% declined neatly through declining BA levels.

Reversing the metric and the BA outcome, we saw a similar pattern to Z-Contact, with big top-to-bottom differences in average and minimum BAs in the O-Contact% deciles, and a more orderly upward procession of maximum BAs as well.

Finally, a quick look at All Contact%:

| | |—O-Contact%—| |
	Ave	Max	Min
>.325	84%	93%	75%
.300-.324	84%	95%	65%
.275-.299	82%	96%	65%
.250-.274	81%	94%	50%
.225-.249	79%	94%	65%
.200-.224	78%	92%	62%
<.200	76%	92%	58%

This reinforces what we've already seen: Contact connects to good BA (or, more precisely, non-contact connects to poor BA).

Conclusions

It appears we can say contacting balls swung at is something worth looking at. We should be targeting batters with Z-Contact% over 90% and O-Contact% over 70%, especially if any of them has a BA too low for those skills.

Remember, however: the patterns are there, but the correlations are not super-strong in any of these metrics.

A batter's BA will depend on many other factors, especially how hard he hits the ball and his batted-ball trajectory mix.

Revisiting Flyballs

by Jason Collette

There is safety in groundballs when targeting and drafting pitchers. The *2014 Baseball Forecaster* reminded us about how groundball pitchers have lower ERAs, which also leads to more wins due to the correlation between ERA and wins. The lower ERA comes from the fact that groundball pitchers give up fewer home runs, even with a higher home run to flyball rate, simply because they allow fewer fly balls.

As the adage goes, when deciding between two pitchers with similar skills, lean toward the one with the higher groundball rate.

Or is it time to re-visit those tenets of analysis?

Data 1: More FBs are Becoming Outs

Over the past five seasons, the league-wide batting average on groundballs has remained extremely consistent. The same cannot be said about flyballs, whose BA has fallen from just under .240 to just under .220. That 20-point drop has quietly flown under the radar, for the most part.

Data 2: FB Out Efficiency Varies by Team

But while FB out efficiency overall has been improving, the effect is not uniform across the game.

Game-wide, 45,397 flyballs were hit in 2013, of which 35,672 (78.6%) were converted into outs. But some teams were way more efficient than others, as we see in this table, sorted by Out% on FB:

Team	FB	Outs	Out%	Team	FB	Outs	Out%
OAK	1,806	1,478	81.8%	WAS	1,491	1,169	78.4%
STL	1,325	1,069	80.7%	CLE	1,406	1,102	78.4%
TEX	1,506	1,211	80.4%	CHW	1,637	1,283	78.4%
MIA	1,476	1,182	80.1%	PIT	1,168	915	78.3%
NYY	1,536	1,229	80.0%	SD	1,474	1,152	78.2%
LAA	1,669	1,331	79.7%	BOS	1,578	1,231	78.0%
CHC	1,560	1,243	79.7%	MIL	1,513	1,178	77.9%
ATL	1,400	1,114	79.6%	ARI	1,467	1,142	77.8%
DET	1,452	1,155	79.5%	PHI	1,542	1,200	77.8%
KC	1,607	1,278	79.5%	MIN	1,685	1,300	77.2%
CIN	1,474	1,171	79.4%	TOR	1,608	1,240	77.1%
SF	1,506	1,196	79.4%	SEA	1,511	1,158	76.6%
LA	1,338	1,056	78.9%	HOU	1,657	1,260	76.0%
TAM	1,479	1,165	78.8%	BAL	1,627	1,228	75.5%
NYM	1,535	1,208	78.7%	COL	1,364	1,028	75.4%
				MLB	**1,513**	**1,189**	**78.6%**

So we see a broad change in FB outcomes combined with a wide range in outcomes for specific teams. That leads us to wonder why.

Possible Explanation

One theory is that the increased FB out efficiency is caused by an emphasis on defensive alignments, notably the willingness of teams to aggressively shift their outfield alignments in response to hitter "spray charts" showing flyball paths.

In late July 2013, ACTA Sports reported that the game was on pace to blow away its previous high-water mark for defensive shifts in a season since they started tracking such data in 2010. By late September, ESPN was reporting that the pace had been maintained throughout the summer, although the final 2013 data on team shift totals haven't been published online or in print.

The increased emphasis on defensive positioning is often associated with infield shifting, but it was just a matter of time until the same data influenced how outfielders were positioned. And sure enough, some managers are positioning OFs more aggressively than just the customary few steps given to batters because of right- or left-handed swinging.

We have long seen teams use no-doubles alignments or have OFs take a few steps left or right depending on the handedness of the batter.

Analysis of Explanation

Outfield shifting makes an interesting hypothesis, but the data do not point to positioning by itself.

For example, BAL is cited in the ACTA study as the leading team for aggressive OF shifting, but the table shows the Orioles ahead of only COL among the worst teams in baseball in FB out efficiency. Similarly, the aggressive Red Sox are only 21st in FB out efficiency.

On the flip side, STL is among the least aggressive positioners (manager Mike Matheny stopped the practice after his pitchers said they didn't like it), yet finished second overall in FB out efficiency. And most of the top and bottom out-efficiency clubs are neither aggressive nor non-aggressive.

Park effects stand up as a useful explanation for FB out efficiency.

Five of the top 10 efficiency teams—OAK, STL, MIA, LAA and KC—also have big parks among the top 10 in HR suppression, according to BaseballHQ.com's Ballpark Factors, and three more top-10 teams are in the top half of those tough hitter's parks. Only two teams, TEX and NYY, are top-10 in efficiency despite HR-friendly parks.

And it appears the A's are exploiting their park advantage by putting flyball pitchers on the mound. Their number of flyballs led baseball in 2013, more than 300 over league average and over 600 more than the groundball-heavy Pittsburgh staff.

Finally, defensive OF quality also makes sense as an important contributing factor.

TEX were third in FB out efficiency, even though their park is one of the most hitter-friendly in baseball (+22% for LH HR and +13% for RH HR). But flyballs that did not have the distance to get out were very efficiently hawked by a talented trio of outfielders. Leonys Martin, Alex Rios, and David Murphy all finished in the top five at their positions as graded by the SABR Defensive Index (SDI) in the year under study (2013).

Other top efficiency teams likewise had top defensive OFs:

- #1 OAK OFs Yoenis Cespedes and Josh Reddick both finished in the top three at their positions on the SDI, helping magnify the run-suppressing effects of the huge OAK park.
- #10 KC had LF Alex Gordon and CF Lorenzo Cain at the top of their positions in the SDI, again in a good pitcher's park.

Then there are the anomalies. BOS plays in a tough HR park, notwithstanding the Green Monster, and had two top defensive OFs in Jacoby Ellsbury and RF leader Shane Victorino. Yet the Sox were 21st in FB out efficiency.

Likewise, PIT had a good pitcher's park and top OFs Starling Marte (#1 LF on SDI) and Andrew McCutchen (#5 CF) but were 19th in FB out efficiency.

And STL did well converting FBs into outs despite three below-average defensive OFs.

Conclusion

So how can we use this information?

First, we should pay more attention to park factors and OF defensive talent before automatically dismissing flyball pitchers as toxic assets.

In particular, we should be a little more willing to roster FB pitchers who pitch both in front of good defensive OFs and in good pitchers' parks. Before their early 2014 injuries, OAK starters like Jarrod Parker and A.J. Griffin come to mind—not only did they have team advantages, but Griffin had the highest FB% of balls-in-play in MLB 2013, and Parker was top-5.

C.J. Wilson might also fit the model, with a top-20 FB% in a big park and Mike Trout.

Conversely, we might want to take even further caution or require even bigger discounts before rostering flyball pitchers in hitting-friendly parks with poor defensive OF support.

But it is not at all clear that we should give weight to aggressive defensive positioning, which does not appear to have had an effect on FB efficiency.

Pitch Velocity & Outcomes I: ERA, Dom and GB%

by Patrick Davitt

Does pitch velocity really matter?

This question has been the subject of a lot of interesting discussion behind the scenes here at BaseballHQ.com, as we work to figure out how best to manage the current torrent of on-field baseball data (not to mention the massive flood that's on the way).

The connection between velocity and pitcher success has powerful intuitive power—it seems obvious that throwing harder will mean more strikeouts, at least, and possibly all the other good stuff that goes with high-K pitching.

But using some of the more granular data that has come onstream the last few years, we tested that assumption—and found it wanting.

Method

We compiled PITCHf/x pitch-velocity data for 2013 from online sources, and compiled it into one large database of 568 pitchers. We ignored pitchers <10 IP.

We then applied correlation calculations to check connections between velocities and outcomes.

Correlations run from +1.0 to -1.0. We used this tiering method:

+0.70 to +1.00	Strong positive relationship
+0.40 to +0.69	Moderate positive relationship
+0.20 to +0.39	Weak positive relationship
+0.19 to -0.19	No or negligible relationship
-0.20 to -0.39	Weak negative relationship
-0.40 to -0.69	Moderate negative relationship
-0.70 to -1.00	Strong negative relationship

A positive relationship means variables rise or fall together, and a negative relationship means one variable rises as the other falls. At zero there is no correlation; the variables are moving independently of each other.

We looked at three particular outcomes: ERA, Dom (K/9) and GB%. We also looked at various cohorts of pitchers by velocity to see if they had patterns in their outcomes, and by outcomes to see if they had patterns in velocities.

Results 1: Overall

The first test was correlations between velocities and outcomes.

	ERA	K/9	GB%
4-seam	-0.23	+0.31	+0.06
2-seam	-0.22	+0.31	+0.07
Cutter	-0.14	+0.19	+0.21
Split	-0.18	+0.06	+0.20
Slider	-0.10	+0.13	+0.17
Curve	-0.18	+0.17	+0.22
Change	-0.15	+0.23	+0.17

Overall, there isn't much here to get excited about. Thirteen of the 21 correlation tests returned values in the "No or negligible relationship" category clustered around 0.00.

Six more are weak correlations in the low 20s, including three weak correlations between GB% and velocities of cutters, splitters and curves, a weak +0.23 with changeup speed and Dom, and weak correlations for both four- and two-seam fastball velocities (we would expect any correlation to be negative because ERA would fall as velocity rose).

The best correlations are two +0.31 correlations between Dom for four- and two-seamers. These are still in the "weak positive" category, and not results you would want to bet your house on.

Results 2: By result cohorts

We also looked at groups of pitchers by results (looking at the corresponding pitcher velocities) and by velocities (looking at the associated results).

Again, there was little evidence of a dependable connection. Here are a few pitcher cohorts by Dom:

		——FA Velocity——		
Cohort K/9	Max	Med	Min	Range
>=10.6	98	94	89	9
9.6 to10.5	97	92	88	9
8.6 to 9.5	95	92	86	9
7.6 to 8.5	95	92	87	8

We saw the same sorts of results no matter how we sliced the cohorts: Top-end velocities generally declined with Dom, but not a lot.

With ERA, breaking the pitchers into quintiles:

		——FA Velocity——		
Quintile ERA	Max	Med	Min	Range
Q5 0.45-2.86	98	92	85	13
Q4 2.86-3.56	98	93	86	12
Q3 3.58-4.16	97	92	84	13
Q2 4.17-5.30	98	91	82	16
Q1 5.32+	96	91	83	13

The range of max velocities from the worst quintile to the best is barely 2 mph, and the medians are tightly packed. In the top two cohorts, the gaps are even narrower. Velocity appears not to be contributing to ERAs.

Results 3: By Velocity Cohorts

Finally, we looked at the pitchers by velocity quintiles, to assess the connections between velocity and both Dom and ERA. If they are connected, we should see a pattern of improving Dom and ERA by quintiles (remember the 5th quintile is the best):

		|——Dom K/9——|		|——ERA——|	
Qn	MPH	Max	Med	Min	Min	Med	Max
5Q	94-98	15.8	8.1	2.6	0.45	3.46	8.60
4Q	92-94	13.3	7.6	3.7	0.66	3.57	9.37
3Q	91-92	13.5	7.7	4.1	0.82	3.75	9.00
2Q	90-91	12.2	7.3	3.8	0.61	4.03	11.85
1Q	82-90	12.2	6.8	2.8	1.09	4.40	10.80

Again we see the pattern seen in the previous tables: A general decline in results as velocity drops, but with plenty of variation within the cohorts. Individual pitchers in the lowest velocity quintiles can and do outperform their flamethrowing peers.

Conclusion

These results still seem counterintuitive, so we feel obliged to offer some theories about why.

First, looking solely at velocity of a pitch ignores location and movement. Throwing hard doesn't matter if the pitches miss the plate or are straight.

Second, differences in the calibration of radar equipment and its interaction with the particular conditions and operators can affect readings.

Third, the reported speed of a pitch type is necessarily an average of many pitches, thrown in many circumstances—it is possible that a pitcher is mowing 'em down at 97 mph in the first inning but giving up hits and runs at 91 mph in the seventh, but all outcomes get reported at the average of 94.

As well, we want to acknowledge that there have been more convincing studies on the change in velocity for individual pitchers. These show that increases in a particular pitcher's fastball velocity reliably lead to improvements in Dom, ERA and expected ERA, and that decreases in velocity lead to worse results.

Our research, however, shows it is almost surely incorrect to reason deductively from the individual examples of such pitchers to draw general conclusions about the connections between velocity and outcomes. If you find yourself considering two pitchers, fastball speed should not be the key factor in making your choice.

Pitch Velocity & Outcomes II: Accuracy, Swing Data

by Patrick Davitt

With fastball velocity alone only weakly correlated to Dominance (Dom, K/9) and even more weakly to ERA, we wanted to see if it might be more useful to assess measures of pitch accuracy and swing-and-miss data for their correlations to desired outcomes.

As well, we also wanted to check if we might improve the correlative connection to ERA and Dom by combining fastball velocity with those various second metrics.

Method

We compiled PITCHf/x pitch-velocity data, strike data, and count data for last season from various online sources into a database of 571 pitchers with >10 IP, using these metrics:

- Str% (Strikes/Pitches)
- S-M% (Swing-and-miss/All strikes)
- Con% (Foul+In-play)/(Foul+In-play+swing-and-miss)
- 1st% (First pitch strike/First pitches)
- 0-2% (0-2 counts/PA)
- Sw/Str (Swinging strikes/All Strikes)
- F/Str (Pitches fouled/total strikes)
- BIP/Str (Balls in play/All strikes)
- ASw/Str (All swings (BIP+Foul+Swing-miss)/All strikes)
- Sw/Pit (All swings/Pitches)
- 3-0% (3-0 counts/PA)
- Sw/K% (K swinging/All K)

We then correlated ERA and Dom outcomes and those other measures. The term "pitches" in these formulas excludes intentional balls.

Results 1: Overall/Basic Correlations

Our first test ran the correlations between the new variables and ERA and Dom. As a reminder, we left the fastball velocity correlation listed in the first row:

	ERA	Dom
vFA	-0.23	+0.31
Str%	-0.31	+0.21
S-M%	-0.25	+0.72
Con%	+0.28	-0.78
1st%	-0.16	+0.10
0-2%	-0.25	+0.48
Sw/Str	+0.07	-0.13
F/Str	-0.04	+0.12
BIP/Str	+0.33	-0.89
ASw/Pit	-0.16	+0.06
3-0%	+0.25	-0.06
Sw/K%	+0.06	+0.08

As we found earlier, most of these individual correlations are weak, many essentially random. No metric had even a moderately strong relationship to ERA, with the best being Str% at -0.31.

But there were a couple of noteworthy correlations to Dom:

1. S-M% had a strong correlation to Dom, as expected.

2. 0-2 percentage had a moderate correlation to Dom, also as expected.

Note that the seemingly high negative Dom correlations to Con% and BIP/Str are obvious—Con and BIP are by definition non-K events, so the more of them a pitcher has, the fewer strikeouts he will get.

Results 2: Correlations for Combined Measures

Since the hypothesis for this study was that we might generate stronger correlations by combining metrics, we tried that to see if the correlations would improve. We focused on combining metrics that had showed any strength in correlations with ERA and Dom.

For this table, we multiplied vFA by each listed metric and correlated the results with ERA and Dom. For comparison's sake, we again left vFA on the top of the list:

	ERA	Dom
vFA	-0.23	+0.31
xStr%	-0.38	+0.35
xS-M%	-0.26	+0.72
x1st%	-0.22	+0.20
x0-2%	-0.26	+0.50
x3-0%	+0.23	-0.04
xSw/K%	+0.01	+0.14
Multi*	-0.28	+0.43

Multi=* vFA x Str% x 1st% x 0-2%

The only combined metric that improved ERA correlation was vFA x Str%, which makes sense: Combining higher velocity with the ability to throw strikes seems bound to improve ERA, if only by reducing walks. Oddly, though, the expected improvement in correlation to Dom, while present, was modest at just four points (to 0.35 from 0.31 for vFA alone).

All the other combinations barely moved the ERA correlation.

The swing-and-miss metric combined with VFA to create a very strong 0.72 correlation with Dom, but that was the same Dom correlation as the swing-and-miss metric alone—combining it with fastball velocity didn't change anything. We also checked the correlation between the vFA and swing-and-miss variables, and it was only +0.31.)

Clearly there is a lot of interplay among these measures.

In this instance, velocity is slightly connected to swings-and-misses, and (though we didn't list it in the tables), also correlated at 0.40 to foul strikes—as we would suspect given eyeball evidence that it's harder to catch up with the big heat.

Foul strikes advance the cause of Dom by adding strikes to the count. So the correlation between vFA and Dom is partly explained by its connections to those individual pitch outcomes.

Analysis and Conclusions

We are only digging at the topsoil with these studies, which seem sure to get much deeper and more detailed as new data streams become available.

In the meantime, we might profitably assess pitchers using these more granular pitch metrics, by focusing on pitchers who get ahead in the count and throw lots of strikes. Of course, most of us have been doing that for a while anyway, based on popular truisms on the topic that, in this case at least, turn out to be actually pretty true.

Similarly, in leagues that count strikeouts, pitchers who get lots of swings-and-misses should generate more interest.

And while this sort of analysis will likely draw the response of, "Well, duh," it might well be possible to find outliers whose ERA and Dom outcomes are out of whack with their vFA and combination metrics as noted. Such pitchers could be projected to performance change.

We might even be able to make such changes to our in-season expectations with more confidence than we do now. One issue with making in-season reassessments has been that a season (or, especially, part of a season) is really too short to generate a useful sample to confidently predict regression for many of our current metrics.

But when are using pitch metrics, it isn't long before most pitchers get their counts up to the point where our confidence is greater. One-third of the way through a season, for example, a starter has only 60 innings and 350 or 400 batters on which to base analysis relating to outcomes like strikeouts and walks per inning. But he has well over 1,000 pitches.

And at full-season or multi-season levels, the same could be even more true. Instead of looking at 33 games in a season, or even 900 batters faced, we get to see the outcomes of 3,500 pitches. Over three seasons, that effect is even more important, as we now start to approach 10,000 pitches.

Interesting times ahead.

Closers: Team Wins and Saves

by Patrick Davitt

Some fantasy owners think good teams generate more wins, and therefore more saves. Other owners think that poor teams are likelier to have more of the close wins that generate save opportunities.

We looked at the situation and concluded that the good-team side is probably more correct than the poor-team side. But it is far from a betting certainty.

Method

Note: This study frequently uses the term "team-season," which simply means the result of one particular team for one particular season. The Giants' 2012 season is one team-season, their 2013 season another team-season, and so on for all 30 teams across all five seasons in the study. So there were 150 team-seasons in the study.

We looked at all MLB teams in the last five full seasons to assess the connection between high- and low-saves seasons with high- and low-wins seasons. We also looked at the individual games of the four winningest and losingest teams in 2013, to see if the good teams' extra wins overall generate more wins with save opportunities.

Results 1: General/Overall

Over the five seasons, essentially half of all wins were saved. The percentage of saved wins (Sv%W) grew slowly, from 49% in Year 1 to 52% in Year 5. Over the entire period, the median Sv%W was 52%, while 53% was the most common result. Half of all team-seasons fell in the Sv%W range of 48%-56%.

Results 2: Team Wins and Saves

Besides the general observation that saves were generally right around half of wins, we saw other evidence that more team wins means more team saves.

The study identified 41 team-seasons of 45+ saves. Of those:

Wins	Tms	%
95+	12	29%
90-94	14	34%
85-89	11	27%
80-84	1	2%
75-79	3	7%
70-	0	0%

In all, 37 of the 41 high-save team-seasons (90%) were by teams with 85+ wins—and none was by a team with fewer than 75 wins.

Similarly, team-seasons with the fewest saves tended to be those with the fewest wins. The bottom of the saves barrel was 28 team-seasons of 35 or fewer saves:

Wins	Tms	%
90+	2	7%
85-89	1	4%
80-84	3	11%
75-79	2	7%
70-74	3	11%
65-69	8	29%
60-64	4	14%
55-59	4	14%
50-54	1	4%

Teams under 80 wins account for 79% of low-save team-seasons.

Keep in mind, though: We also saw it is possible for a high-win team to generate low saves, and indeed it is much more common than the reverse. But at the same time, we can clearly infer that as wins decline, saves follow.

That inference is further borne out by these data: Teams with seasons of 90+ wins made up 29% of all team-seasons in the study, but accounted for:

- 63% of team-seasons with 45 saves or more
- 7% of team-seasons with 35 saves or fewer

Conversely, teams with fewer than 70 wins made up 18% of team-seasons, but they accounted for:

- 61% of team-seasons with 35 saves or fewer
- And none of the team-seasons with 45+ saves

Overall, when we looked at tiers of team-seasons by wins, the data showed fairly wide ranges of both Sv%W and actual saves:

		Sv%W			Saves		
Wins	n	MAX	MIN	MED	MAX	MIN	MED
90+	45	62%	34%	49%	58	32	46
80-89	40	67%	37%	49%	57	32	41
70-79	37	62%	33%	53%	45	25	40
69-	28	66%	38%	54%	44	25	35

Overall, it seems safe to say that you should get more saves from teams with more wins than from teams with fewer wins, but that you can't count on things turning out that way.

Results 3: The "More-blowouts" Theory

Finally, there's the argument that high-win teams have more blowout wins (and therefore fewer save opportunities), and low-win teams have more close victories (and therefore more with save opportunities).

We used game-log data for the four top and bottom wins teams in 2013. We determined what percentage of all their wins were within 3 runs, which of course is the definition of a Save opportunity. (We do understand this method misses certain save situations, most notably all the games in which a blown save led to losses. But as a first approximation, it will do.)

The results:

Tm	Wins	Close	%
Good	386	215	56%
Poor	242	176	73%

It is true that poorer teams had more close wins as a percentage of their overall wins. But that advantage was offset by the good teams' higher number of wins overall, which created more close wins even at the lower percentages.

Conclusions

- The argument "more wins leads to more saves" is correct at the macro level. Guesstimating that a team will get saves in roughly 50% of its wins will work reasonably well.

- At the micro level, however, we found many outliers, and the wins-saves connection was more tenuous (and therefore less predictable) than we'd hoped.

- And the theory about higher-win teams getting more blowouts is true, but it doesn't affect actual saves outcomes.

Closers and Multi-Year Performance

by Patrick Davitt

Closers matter. Or not.

We looked at how a team having a high-save closer in one season affects team saves in the next, and whether team saves leaders follow up with another season of similar saves performance.

Method

We used data from baseball-reference.com to identify team saves totals and team saves leaders in the last five seasons. We wanted to check:

- Whether a good or poor year for the team's saves leader led to a change in the percentage of wins that were saved (Sv%W) the next year
- Whether a big saves year (40+) for a teams' saves leader led to a Sv%W increase in the subsequent year
- Whether a poor such year (less than 20) led to a decline in Sv%W
- And whether a good or poor year for the team saves leader affected whether that pitcher stayed in the role the next year

Next-year assessments excluded the 2013 season because there was no way at the time of writing to check the following-year results. We broke the saves leaders into quintiles by save counts in a season with each quintile around 24 pitchers.

Results 1: Overall

First we wanted to see if just getting a lot of saves in a year led to getting a lot of saves the next year. Keeping in mind the fifth quintile is the cohort with the most saves, and the first quintile is the cohort with the least:

Q	n	Sv*	Sv%W**
5	25	45	52%
4	24	37	53%
3	24	31	50%
2	24	24	50%
1	23	12	52%

* average per team, first season
** overall, subsequent season

It appears that the presence of a saves leader in Year X does not affect the Sv%W in Year X+1.

This suggests that save opportunities create closers, rather than the other way around.

Results 2: Top Closers vs Bottom Closers

What about teams who had top-flight closers versus teams who didn't?

We again looked at subsequent-year Sv%W. We found that the poor-closer clubs (<20 Saves) had 54% Sv%W the following year, while the top-closer teams (>40) were around 51%, both within normal variation.

We also wanted to know how likely top closers were to retain their roles. We'd expect a top closer to be back the next season, and a low-saves closer to be at greater risk.

Sure enough, 65% of high-save closer reprised their roles, while 76% of the low-save closers did not close the following year.

Little wonder those closers who held the role for three straight seasons averaged 34.3 saves per season, and those who had it for two straight averaged about the same. Teams who changed closers averaged 27 saves.

Conclusion

In all, top closers do have a better track record for retaining their jobs, and the degree to which that's true is skewed downward by player movement via trade or free agency.

But saves will generally be higher on teams that win more games, and that fact does not depend on individual closers.

GAMING RESEARCH ABSTRACTS

2014 Trends, 2015 Responses

by Patrick Davitt

Near the end of 2013, BaseballHQ.com analyzed pitching trends over the four previous seasons. We found pitching outcomes and skills measures were improving—some suddenly, others gradually, some large and others incremental.

Understanding the trends, and their implications for production and skills expectations, helped us identify possible pitcher breakouts, including starters Jose Quintana, Corey Kluber, Sonny Gray and Rick Porcello, and relievers like Sean Doolittle.

So we're once more checking trends of key pitching rate stats to better understand the environment for players for 2015.

Trend #1: Strikeouts jumped. Again

Strikeouts had leveled off in 2013, but leaped again in 2014. In fact, for the first time in big-league history, pitchers fanned more than 20% of batters faced. The 20.3% mark was up 0.5% over 2013.

Analysts have explained increasing strikeouts in part by pointing to the increasing use of specialist relievers, who can go "all out" for Ks because they pitch as few as 70 innings in a season, to only three or four batters per appearance.

Indeed, for each of the last three seasons, strikeout rates for relievers (all games in relief, >20 IP) have been around 23%.

But even if we credit the overall strikeout increase primarily to relievers, it is also affecting starters. Starters' (>10 starts and >90% of games pitched as starters), K-rate was 19.9%, up 0.6% from last year and also a historic high.

Trend #2: Walks, Hits and WHIP Continued to Fall

Even as Ks were historically high, walks were historically low. The highest walk percentage since 1976 was 9.6% in 2000. Then came a roller-coaster ride falling to 7.7% this year, the lowest since Bob Gibson dominated batters in his 1968 MVP/Cy Young season.

More strikeouts and fewer walks has inevitably increased Command Ratio (Cmd), a critical measure of pitcher effectiveness. At 2.5 K/bb, overall Cmd in 2014 continued a nearly straight-line uptrend since 2002 and reached a modern high (the last time pitchers posted higher Cmd was in 1884, when balls were the color of mud and spitballs were legal).

Meanwhile, as walks were declining, so were hits, sinking to a 40-year low at 22.6% of BF, or 8.6 H/9 IP.

As a result of these declines, gamewide WHIP plummeted to 1.277, the lowest in the free-agent era. That, too, continued a steady decline, with minor rebounds, from 1.43 in 1994.

Trend #3: HRs are down

The saving grace for offensive baseball the last few years has been the power game, but that, too, has declined. During the PED era, HRs peaked at around 3.0% of plate appearances, and just two years ago the mark was still at about 2.7%. This year, after falling two straight years, that rate is down to 2.3%. Chicks will need something else to dig.

Trend #4: ERAs continued to fall

Finally, with hits, walks and HR down, and strikeouts way up, it's no surprise that ERAs are falling

In 2009, ERA was 4.32. That dipped below 4.00 in 2011, bounced back slightly over 4.00 in 2012, and has since dropped twice, to this year's 3.74 mark, the lowest since 1992. Strand rates rose to 73% gamewide, up a full percentage point from just three years ago. Fewer runners reaching base via hit or walk, and fewer of those baserunners coming around to score: an obvious recipe for lower ERAs.

So those are the main pitching trends: More Ks; fewer walks, hits and HR; and declining ERAs and WHIP. These changes strongly imply we need to rethink pitching and hitting in 2015, and probably beyond.

Response #1: Reset Expectations

The danger in these low ERAs, WHIPs and supporting metrics is that owners can fail to calibrate expectations.

Not long ago, an owner could anchor a successful fantasy rotation with a single elite starter whose ERA was under 3.00. As recently as 2009, only 11 starters met that standard. This year, 21 do, including Clayton Kershaw under 2.00 and six others under 2.50.

Ditto for WHIP. In 2009, six starters had WHIPs under 1.10, none of them under 1.00. This year, there are 12 under 1.10, with four under 1.00.

This obliges fantasy owners to rethink what we mean by "elite" starters. In 2009, only 19 starters beat the overall ERA of 4.32 by a full run or more. This year, if we set 3.32 as "elite," we'll have 31 to choose from.

But 3.32 won't help as much when the gamewide ERA is down to 3.74. All these stats are relative.

In the previous example, targeting starters with ERAs one full run better than the 2014 overall means under 2.74. Only 11 starters in 2014 are a full run better than overall ERA making them harder to find, not easier, than in 2009.

So elite pitchers are just as scarce as always. We just have to define them differently.

Response 2: Calibrate Skills Requirements

At the same time, since we at BaseballHQ.com believe in skills and not outcomes, we need to re-evaluate the metrics we use, because they're relative, too.

Look at the BHQ Dominance (Dom) metric. In 2009, the gamewide Dom was 7.0 K/9, and just 29 starters had Dom above that level. By contrast, this year saw 54 starters over 7.0.

Again, it would be easy to mistake this as meaning we have more choices in rostering "elite" pitchers. But 7.0 is no longer the gamewide standard. Dom is now up to 7.7, and 37 starters this year are above it, slightly more than managed with the 29 in 2009 who beat that year's mark.

Last year, we adjusted our skills filters to find the top 15% of all pitchers. We did the same this year, and took the extra step of calibrating SP and RP differently, because skills measures, especially Dom and Cmd, are generally a little better among RP.

Here are the adjusted elite skills levels:

- Dom: from 7.0 K/9 to 7.3 (SP) and 8.2 (RP)
- Ctl: from 3.0 bb/9 to 2.6 (SP) and 2.9 (RP)
- Cmd: from 2.0 K/bb to 2.8 (SP) and 3.4 (RP)
- HR/9: from 0.9 to 0.9 (SP) and 0.8 (RP)

These filters captured 27 of 183 qualifying starters, about 13%, and 26 of 189 relievers (35+ IP), or 14%.

You'd expect to see most of the names on list: Kershaw, Sale, Felix, Scherzer among SP, and Jansen, Papelbon, Doolittle and Street among RP.

Of course, we can't roster all those guys, or perhaps even any of them. But other pitchers who met the filters might be available because their results didn't reflect their high-level skills, or even good results might be perceived as fluky.

Among SPs, we found Phil Hughes of Minnesota (who set an all-time Cmd record for starters at 11.6 K/bb), Marcus Stroman, Matt Shoemaker, Jake Arrieta and regular fantasy heartbreaker Carlos Carrasco.

On the reliever side, we saw Jake McGee, Josh Fields, Chris Hatcher, Wade Davis, Ken Giles and Junichi Tazawa.

Response 3: Also reconsider hitter value

Of course, changes in pitching also affect hitter valuations. In particular, we might want to put asterisks on our cheat sheets beside batters who make contact, take walks, and hit HRs.

Much the same as the ERA example above, our idea of "elite" skills for batters should be different. In 2009, the median Contact Rate (ct%) for all batters 150+ PA was 80%, which is also our benchmark for rosterable batters. The mode (the ct% seen most often) was 84%. This season, the average ct% was 78% and the mode about the same.

We checked all 2014 batters (minimum 150 PA; 423 qualified) to find those at least 10% better than league average in K%, bb% and HR%. As we expected, far fewer batters (35%) met the K% threshold than walks (68%) or HR (66%). (Interestingly, only eight batters had K% under 10%, compared with 25 in 2009 and 44 in 1999.

And 16 batters in 2014 met all three thresholds:

Batter	SO% <18.4% n=147	BB% >8.4% n=288	HR% >2.5% n=281
Martinez,V	6.4%	10.9%	5.0%
Beltre	11.6%	9.3%	3.0%
Cabrera,A	13.4%	10.8%	2.7%
Bautista	14.1%	15.8%	5.3%
Betts	14.2%	9.5%	2.6%
Holliday	14.8%	10.8%	3.1%
Encarnacion	15.1%	11.7%	6.5%
Tulowitzki	15.2%	13.3%	5.6%
Ortiz	15.8%	12.5%	5.8%
Rollins	16.4%	10.5%	2.8%
Ramirez,H	16.4%	10.7%	2.6%
Cabrera,M	16.5%	9.0%	3.5%
McCutchen	17.1%	12.8%	3.8%
Peralta	17.9%	9.4%	3.4%
Werth	18.0%	13.2%	2.6%
Dozier	18.3%	12.9%	3.1%

As expected, this list of relatively high-skill hitters has many familiar names. But we draw your attention to Asdrubal Cabrera, Mookie Betts, Jhonny Peralta, Jayson Werth and Brian Dozier as potentially undervalued hitters whose skills play as "elite" in modern high-K baseball.

If we eliminate the power requirement, we add 28 more batters, including some with at least a little HR potential: Yangervis Solarte, (2.0% HR), Ryan Hanigan (2.0% HR), David DeJesus (2.3% HR), Adam Lind (2.0% HR), Seth Smith (2.4% HR) and Russell Martin (2.4% HR).

Conclusion

In all, the key takeaway is that stats are relative. As ERAs and WHIPs sink, it takes lower ERAs and WHIPs to get the same fantasy points, and for an individual to be genuinely better and more valuable than the norm. A 3.50 ERA used to be damn fine, and a 3.00 was elite. Not any more.

We also need to keep in mind that baseball might take steps to boost scoring. They can't lower the mound again, and they can't rely on PEDs as they did in the past, since the commissioner has tied the game's credibility to the issue.

They can, however, change the strike zone (possibly with automated camera/computer systems) to force pitchers to throw more hittable pitches. And/or they could juice the baseball.

Whatever they do, the balance could be reset yet again. In the meantime, be aware and let the trend be your friend.

Age Discrimination at the Top of the ADPs?

by Ron Shandler

One of the curiosities of the Average Draft Position (ADP) rankings this past year was the lack of love for Alex Rios. Rios had an accomplishment that only six other players could boast—he earned first round value in both 2012 and 2013. This was an elite group; the other members were Mike Trout, Miguel Cabrera, Clayton Kershaw, Andrew McCutchen, Robinson Cano and Adrian Beltre.

Yet Rios' ADP on Opening Day this year was #34—a third round pick!

Why was he drafted so low? Was it because he had been such an inconsistent performer prior to 2012? Or was it because he was 33, one of the older players at the top of the pyramid? Beltre was actually a year older, but he didn't fall nearly as far; his ADP was #17.

So I thought that, perhaps our annual desire for fresh young blood may be clouding our opinion of perfectly good first round studs. Do we have a bias towards younger players in the first round?

I looked back over the past 10 years of first round (top 15) ADPs and earnings to see if my suspicion was on target. Here are the results.

Year		Youngest Player	Oldest player
2004	ADP	Pujols/Prior (24)	B.Bonds (40)
	Earned	C.Crawford (23)	R.Johnson (41)
2005	ADP	C.Crawford (24)	R.Johnson (42)
	Earned	M.Cabrera (22)	Suzuki/Abreu (31)
2006	ADP	M.Cabrera (23)	M.Ramirez (34)
	Earned	Cabrera/Reyes (23)	Suzuki/Jeter/Dye (32)
2007	ADP	Cabrera/Reyes/Wright(24)	V.Guerrero/A-Rod (32)
	Earned	H.Ramirez/Fielder (23)	C.Jones (35)
2008	ADP	H.Ram/Fielder/Braun (24)	A.Rodriguez (33)
	Earned	H.Ramirez (24)	M.Ramirez (36)
2009	ADP	H.Ramirez/Braun (25)	A.Rodriguez (34)
	Earned	6 players (25)	D. Jeter (35)
2010	ADP	E.Longoria (24)	A.Rodriguez (35)
	Earned	CarGo/F.Hernandez (24)	P.Konerko (34)
2011	ADP	CarGo/E.Longoria (25)	R.Halladay (34)
	Earned	C.Kershaw (23)	R.Halladay (34)
2012	ADP	J.Upton (25)	A.Pujols (32)
	Earned	M.Trout (21)	R.A. Dickey (37)
2013	ADP	M.Trout (22)	J.Bautista (32)
	Earned	M.Trout (22)	A.Beltre (34)
2014	ADP	M.Trout (23)	R.Cano (32)
	Earned	M.Trout (23)	V.Martinez (36)

At the fringes, there is not a lot of insight here. If nothing else, it's another interesting exercise in the recency bias. Look how many top round earners in one year end up right back in the top round ADPs the following year.

But let's take a more analytical look:

Year	Average Age			No. 30+ Players	
	ADP	Earned	League	ADP	Earned
2004	29.9	29.7	29.2	7	7
2005	30.5	27.9	29.3	9	5
2006	28.7	27.7	29.0	7	6
2007	28.4	28.1	28.9	7	6
2008	27.3	28.5	28.7	2	5
2009	28.0	27.0	28.6	3	2
2010	28.0	28.2	28.7	5	4
2011	28.5	28.9	28.5	5	5
2012	28.4	29.1	28.5	3	5
2013	27.8	28.0	28.5	5	6
2014	28.3	28.4	28.4	6	3
MEAN	**28.6**	**28.3**	**28.8**	**5.4**	**4.9**

The takeaways...

The ADPs have skewed slightly younger than the actual earnings in six of the past seven years, so there does seem to be a trend. Still, the results are fairly close.

The player population as a whole has been trending younger over the past decade. In general, first round players tend to be aged at about the population mean, if not slightly younger.

About five of 15 first rounders will be 30 or older, so there is no reason to avoid them on draft day unless there has been a clear deterioration of skills.

As it turned out, the marketplace was correct about downgrading Rios and Beltre.

Playing the Game One Month at a Time

by Ron Shandler

Full-season fantasy leaguers are in it for the long haul. Daily gamers are in it for the immediate gratification. A monthly game seems like a concept without a home—too short for real analysis, too long to wait for a payoff.

But more than 2,000 teams participated in one-month leagues at ShandlerPark.com in 2014.

There is no question that it is a different kind of game, requiring different analysis of the data. It is a hybrid, combining longer-term skills assessment with short-term tactical analysis. Here are the key analytical components:

Games played: During a one-month period, not all Major League teams will play the same number of games. Some teams might have as many as 4-6 more games on their schedule. More games equals more counting stats.

Home games: Players do tend to perform better at home and some teams have extreme home-road splits in a given month. For instance, last May (the Shandler Park season ran May 5-29), the Yankees played less than 25% of their games at home. Their players were poor 1-month targets that month.

Opposition: The caliber of competition a team will face in a given month can vary widely. Back in July, Atlanta played 24 of their 27 games against teams with sub-.500 records -- The Mets, D-backs, Cubs, Padres, Phils and Marlins. Braves players were good percentage plays that month.

Skill: Yes, this should be at the top of the list. But the most controversial aspect of monthly analysis is the fallacy that the data samples are too small to be useful.

There is some truth to this, however, the over- and under-achieving players tend to even out over an entire roster. But there are different ways to look at skill when planning for a single month.

When we evaluate a player's performance, it is typically done on an annual basis. We can compare a 30-HR, .300 season over 550 AB against a 24 HR, .270 season over 550 AB and draw reasonable comparisons. The "year" has always been the traditional benchmark.

But when it comes to fantasy decision-making, we do not have the luxury of time. We have to make decisions using less projectable chunks of performance data.

Needless to say, bigger chunks are better. There is not a lot of projectability in a single day, but a week is better and a month even more. Of course, those are just arbitrary periods of time. Still, there is a long-standing sabermetric tenet that can provide interesting insight for even monthly data chunks.

Bill James' Plexiglass Principle states that "if a team improves markedly in one season, it will likely decline in the next." We've shown that this works on an individual player level as well. It's all about the two most powerful forces on earth: regression and gravity.

And it works in monthly chunks too.

As soon as May 1, there is enough data to start analyzing these chunks. In fact, even after one month, we have two data points to work with... April, and the original seasonal expectation.

That second data point can't be discounted; it represents the comprehensive off-season analysis of past history. That projection still has analytical value. And if monthly data is benched against the original expectation for the year, there are some interesting insights. In fact, if you consider the projection as each player's "potential destination" for the full year, it provides a baseline around which each month's performance can be evaluated.

I selected a group of players that started somewhat slow in April as compared to their projection and then had a huge May breakout that generated a Rotisserie dollar value at least twice what they earned in April. For these players, the Plexiglass Principle would project strong odds that they'd regress in June.

(Dollar values are based on the scoring system for the monthly leagues.)

BATTERS	Prj	Apr	May	Jun	Jul	Aug	Sep	2014
Puig, Yasiel	15	10	48	17	29	0	13	22
Martinez, Victor	12	8	36	28	18	30	35	30
Moss, Brandon	12	11	29	5	3	0	1	12
Stubbs, Drew	7	0	20	4	32	0	5	14
Teixeira, Mark	9	3	21	6	3	0	0	7
Murphy, Daniel	14	10	24	20	10	9	0	16
Granderson, Curtis	3	1	13	25	12	0	19	11
Kinsler, Ian	14	12	24	20	1	10	4	17
PITCHERS	**Prj**	**Apr**	**May**	**Jun**	**Jul**	**Aug**	**Sep**	**2014**
Hughes, Phil	1	0	20	8	0	18	13	9
Weaver, Jered	7	3	25	3	0	12	14	10
Clippard, Tyler	9	4	22	1	18	6	8	14
Leake, Mike	7	3	13	2	6	15	0	4

Every one except Granderson did regress in June, at least a little. For those playing in a May league, these players would not have necessarily been strong targets for May but they would have been reasonable plays. In June leagues, however, they would have been very strong targets to avoid.

Basically, most of these players just bounced back and forth between profit and loss as compared to their projection. In fact, 10 of the 12 finished with a full-season profit yet still spent anywhere from 1 to 4 months in the red.

The season-long takeaway is that it is rare for a player to post consistent productivity on a month-to-month basis. And that volatility can be leveraged when planning a 1-month draft strategy.

The Equalizer Format in Head-to-Head Play

by David Martin

In head-to-head play, your team can have a great week statistically, but still lose to a team that had an even better week. The Equalizer Format is one way to compensate for the bad luck inherent in head-to-head gaming.

The Theory

The Equalizer Format has two aims: first, to reward teams that play well but have the misfortune of playing a "hot" team on that given week, and second, to correct for some of the late season unfairness we often see in the fantasy baseball playoffs (think innings limits, star players on non-contending teams who are shut down with minor injuries, etc.).

Unlike the Rotisserie game, head-to-head gamers cannot "bank" stats. Every week, it's *tabula rasa* on Monday and a 0-0 score. Because statistics are not cumulative, and teams are judged on the small sample size of one week's performance, luck plays a notable role in the head-to-head game.

But an equalizer can reduce the role of luck and reward a team's actual season-long performance. An equalizer is simple to calculate: it's your team's average weekly score. In an Equalizer Format, each week you add the equalizer to your team's actual score. The winner has the higher overall score.

The Application

An equalizer can be used in points leagues and standard five-by-five category leagues alike. In points leagues, its application is fairly straightforward. For instance, in week 9, Team A outscores Team B, 161 to 145. But Team B's average weekly score is 160, and when this equalizer is added to 145, its resulting score is 305. In contrast, Team A's average weekly score is 140. When added to is actual score of 161, Team A's total score is 301. In the Equalizer Format, Team B would defeat Team A, 305 to 301.

Now let's try the Equalizer Format in a five-by-five category-based league. Going into week 9, Team A has a record of 1-6-1 with a category win-loss record of 26-54. Its equalizer is 3.25 (26 divided by 8). Team B is 4-3-1 with a category win-loss record of 49-31. Its equalizer is 6.13 (49 divided by 8). Based on standard scoring, Team A defeats Team B, 6-4. When the equalizers are added to the standard scores, Team B wins, 10.13 to 9.25.

In theory, Team B has been performing better than its 4-3-1 record indicates. The equalizer should balance out some of the team's unlucky matchups over the course of the season.

It is very important that the equalizer is calculated based solely on the actual number of category wins or points. Therefore, when calculating the new equalizers for week 10 in the five-by-five league above, the 6-4 score is used, not the 10.13-9.25 score. Despite the loss, Team A's equalizer increases from 3.25 to 3.55 (32 divided by 9), while Team B's decreases from 6.13 to 5.88 (53 divided by 9). Team A's actual performance has in fact been rewarded by virtue of an increased equalizer going forward.

In points leagues, the equalizer for week 10 should also be based on the actual score (161-145). Again, Team A will be rewarded going forward for its performance despite the loss.

Refining the Format

Your league's commissioner can opt to add equalizing scores every Sunday night (i.e. a season-long format) or just in the playoffs. To avoid distorting your league's standings early in the season, we advise you to wait a month to implement an equalizer if you are going to use it for the duration of the season. You should be able to use the Equalizer Format in any league where your commissioner can manually adjust scoring/standings or enters all results manually.

Conclusion

While it can be difficult to foster consensus on a league formatting change, the sensible league-mate will vote for a format that is more equitable. The Equalizer Format promotes fairness while still allowing for the camaraderie and rivalries that make the head-to-head game appealing.

The Analytics of Hope

by Ron Shandler

Research says that fantasy teams in fifth place or lower at the end of April have only a 20% chance of winning, at best. The further down you are in the standings, the lower your odds.

This research is backed up at the major league level. Since 2002, only 23% of teams that were more than three games out of first place on May 1 went on to win their division. Three games seems like nothing to overcome, but there it is.

So put yourself in Paul Goldschmidt's shoes back on May 1. You've just come off of a breakout season. Your whole career is ahead of you. Opening Day brings the promise of new beginnings and the chance for your team to contend.

And then the Diamondbacks went SPLAT. On May 1, they were 9-22, 9 1/2 games out of first.

This was not just a little splat, mind you. This was one big huge honkin' splat at the beginning of a season. If you're Goldschmidt, all you knew was that you still had to go out there every day for the next 22 weeks and your team couldn't see first place without a telescope.

Odds are, some Diamondbacks fans were probably thinking, "There is always a chance the team will turn it around, right? After all, it's only May. There's lots of time! There's always hope!"

Hope, yes. But realistically, the baseball season was already over in the Arizona desert.

You see, since 2002, there have been 24 teams that ended April at least 9 1/2 games out of first place. Guess how many made it to post-season?

None. Not a one.

Not exactly a ringing endorsement for hope.

But that's all we've got, right? That slim glimmer of a happy future that baseball fans have been clinging onto forever.

In the Fanalytic Encyclopedia, we define Hope as "a commodity that routinely goes for $5 over value at the draft table." Clearly, it was hope that pushed Bryce Harper into the first round in this year's drafts. Hope is what pushed perennially injured Troy Tulowitzki's auction price into the $30s. And it was hope that created a FAAB frenzy for Chris Colabello when he was hitting .359 with 19 RBIs after three weeks.

How'd that all work out for you?

Back on May 1, my Tout Wars team was in 12th place with 26 points, 10 points out of 11th. My teams often start slow and then I spend a Herculean effort to move up. I have never finished in last place in my life.

But I knew I was not going to win. I might grind it out for another five months to finish... 7th. In all the years of grinding out bad starts, I have finished as high as 2nd. Twice. I suppose that was worth the effort, but as former Tout and current Rays scout Jason Grey always said, "second place is first loser."

Everything we do is about percentage plays, and the standings on May 1 can tell you tons. Is it a 100% absolute guarantee of failure? No. But it's pretty darn close. And we know not to chase such terrible percentage plays.

It's a slap-in-the-face reality check. Yes, as early as May 1, many of us do know that we are not going to win. In Tout Wars, I knew. Odds are, Paul Goldschmidt and the Arizona Diamondbacks knew back then too.

So, what then?

Well, we all kept on playing.

Why?

Because we are idiots.

No, no... we kept on playing for the sake of sportsmanship.

Ugh.

I don't know. Why do we keep on playing if there is really no hope to win? If the percentage play is really so close to 0%, why bother?

Perhaps it's because there are occasional miracles. It's that "one-in-a-million" happenstance when the Red Sox come back from a 3-0 deficit, facing Mariano Rivera, to win four straight against the Yankees. It's that 9th place fantasy team, 40 points back at the All Star break, that makes a second half run to a title behind Javier Vazquez. And, I suppose it's the simple joy of "just playing," regardless of winning or losing.

"Just playing" has its own advantages too. As Todd Zola reminded us on BaseballHQ Radio, the skills you gain working an 11th place team up to 9th may come in handy that day when you're in 3rd place.

"Just playing" opens you up to trying things you haven't in the past. You can take more gambles and make higher risk plays. I placed some inflated FAAB bids with my Tout team and came away with players like Collin McHugh, C.J. Cron, Kennys Vargas and T.J. House. Had I been higher in the standings, I would have been more conservative with my bids.

I didn't just overcome my 12th place start. I finished 5th. Not a win, but a hell of a ride.

Finally, the line between hopelessness and hope can be very thin.

In our original example of teams 9 1/2 games out on May 1, let's cast out our net a little further and include teams that were 9 games out. That adds six more laggards, making 30 total. Of those, two actually did sniff October.

In 2006, Minnesota opened the season 9-16. They ended up backing into a division title by one game over the Tigers, which lost their last five in a row. Then the Twins went three-and-out in the ALDS.

The other team that made it into the post-season despite being 9 games out on May 1 was... this year's Pittsburgh Pirates.

Back on May 1, the Bucs were 10-18 and Andrew McCutchen was facing just as discouraging a season as Goldschmidt. Despite the similar views back then, the results for the two clubs were not the same.

But here too, the Pirates still went out with a whimper. For all intents and purposes, everyone spent October at home.

Even at 0.0001%—"one in a million"—Jim Carrey reminds us, "so you're telling me there's a chance." But realistically, most of us will end up playing this game for the journey, not the destination.

The Composite Player

by Todd Zola

Target drafting refers to setting statistical goals in each category for your team to meet or surpass to be competitive. The concern is that target drafting shifts focus from winning the *league* to winning the *draft*. Often, a target drafter overlooks latent upside or dismisses downside risk.

As an alternative, The Composite Player a new form of target drafting where the focus is on an expectation for each pick or auction purchase. As long as each pick or purchase meets its objective, then the total will follow. The key is to move from tracking stagnant numbers to examining a range of outcomes.

Introducing the Composite Hitter

Each pick (or auction purchase) has an inherent expectation, expressed in a dollar value. In a 12-team snake draft, the expectation for each round is the average of the 12 highest projected dollar values still available.

Obviously, there's an infinite combination of statistics that generate a specific value. The composite hitter contributes equally in all categories at each price point, and the stat line of the composite hitter is an average of all players drafted in that specific vicinity. With a sample of sufficient size, the distribution is smoothed such that each categorical contribution is roughly identical.

The average of 11-15 hitters is required to generate a representative composite hitter. The process requires three years' worth of end-of-season value, customized to your league. Using the 100th ranked player as an example, Composite Hitter #100 is computed by averaging the stats of all hitters finishing between 98 and 102 over that three-year span. Pitchers are omitted, but doing so usually leaves ample hitters for that spot.

Adjusting for Catchers

In terms of valuation theory, position scarcity for a replacement level player doesn't exist with the present player inventory. In short, a home run (as an example) is worth the same regardless of position—except catcher. In order for catchers to be included in the composite average, make the following adjustments:

	HR	RBI	RUNS	SB	AVG
AL&NL	+1	+3	+3	+1	+.002
15-mix	+3	+16	+16	+3	+.012
12-mix	+5	+20	+20	+5	+.016

Examples of Composite Hitters

Here are examples of composite hitters for 15-tm mixed leagues.

RANK	AB	RUNS	HITS	HR	RBI	SB	AVG	VALUE
1	572	108	189	35	109	22	.330	$43
10	598	89	175	26	90	24	.293	$28
25	577	94	168	23	82	14	.291	$22
50	503	76	149	20	79	9	.296	$17
75	509	77	140	20	64	17	.275	$15
100	540	77	144	16	67	17	.267	$14
150	524	70	141	17	69	7	.269	$10
200	476	62	123	14	56	10	.258	$6
250	377	49	100	10	45	10	.265	$3

Comparing Players with an Uneven Statistical Distribution

As you can see, the composite player contributes across-the-board, however, most players have an uneven distribution. We can adjust those uneven stats to provide a better comparison to the composite player by using a "points" system. Here are the factors, which you would divide into each category's variance.

HR	RBI	RUNS	SB	AVG
1	2.5	2.5	1	.002

Take the following hitters for example:

	HR	RBI	RUNS	SB	AVG
Composite	25	95	94	13	.308
PlayerA	21	105	94	13	.308
PlayerB	19	95	99	21	.300
PlayerC	27	95	94	16	.298

Comparing PlayerA to the Composite, he has 4 fewer HR (-4 / 1, or -4 points) but 10 more RBI (10 / 2.5, or +4 points). The net is 0, meaning that PlayerA is equivalent to the Composite. In fact, all four players are equivalent to the Composite. While the objective is to net out to 0, any +/- points will help gauge how far you are from your goal.

The following are examples of catchers identical in value to the same composite hitter (the previously noted adjustments).

HR	RBI	RUNS	SB	AVG
20	75	74	8	.292
27	84	70	2	.284
32	90	74	1	.270

Applications of the Composite Hitter

The composite hitter represents the minimum expectation for every pick. As you consider options for each pick, compare the player's stats the composite hitter's stats. You want to roster players with a plausible means to meet each expectation.

1. After adjusting the projection, the numbers may fall short from of the composite hitter's. But the key is plausibility. Projections are presented at static numbers, but they are usually the most probable expectation from a range of outcomes. At times, chasing the upside is advantageous. Using conventional target drafting, you may be inclined to bypass a hitter with upside, who, in fact, is useful for your squad. Similarly, a hitter may meet or exceed the requirements of the composite hitter but carry some downside risk that may have been missed with a static projection. Depending, adding the player could be detrimental to your roster even though the static numbers suggest he'll help.

2. Players who are injury-prone are usually projected to miss a portion of the season. Standard ranking of these players only accounts for their stats, so adding on the anticipated stats of their replacement renders a better estimation of what your team will receive. Others will devalue these injury-prone players, whereas you can sagely rank the player in the vicinity of the composite hitter who matches the sum of the injury-prone hitter and his replacement. If the player doesn't get hurt, chances are he beats the projection and is better than the composite player.

3. No one agrees with every projection. A simple way to compare your expectations with the rest of the pool is identify the composite hitter closest to your adjusted projection and rank accordingly.

SP-Centric Approach to Daily Fantasy Baseball

by Vlad Sedler

Daily Fantasy Sports (DFS) have evolved with immense popularity over the past couple of years, offering fantasy fanatics an opportunity to make a quick buck (or million!) by selecting a team of players for a single day of action. The *Baseball Forecaster* equips us with the proper guidance for a season-long, patient approach to the fantasy baseball season, but understanding the underlying metrics and skills of individual players can assist with building our DFS lineups. With so much unpredictability with offensive players on a daily basis, it's best to build a squad around the most predictable part of a lineup—the value starting pitcher.

A common notion that may have some statistical relevance says that hitters start off the season slower and heat up in the summer months; alternately, pitchers tend to get a jump on hitters by reporting to camp earlier and having the opportunity to work on their individual repertoires to gain an early edge. Weather plays a factor as well, as it is harder to hit in the colder weather early on. Though scoring systems vary across different DFS sites, dominant starting pitchers who go deep into games (7+ IP), with a high strikeout rate (7.5+ k/9) are universally valuable and the all-important piece to build DFS squad's around. One can certainly take a Clayton Kershaw (LHP, LA) or Felix Hernandez (RHP, SEA) on their rotation turns, but DFS sites are wise enough to set their salaries at a high enough price point to make it difficult to afford them while fielding a well-balanced offense. Due to this cost vs performance aspect of DFS games, being able to analyze a slate of pitching matchups and identify value plays can give us a leg up on our competition by coming within striking distance to ace-level pitching performances while allowing enough salary cap to fill hitter slots with more expensive, reliable options.

Four crucial factors to consider when selecting starting pitchers:

1. Run Totals and Wins

Targeting SPs on teams favored to win can add a few points to the total. Certain DFS setups value wins more than others while other sites penalize for losses. On a day where we want to fit in high-priced offense and avoid rostering an expensive ace in a Max Scherzer (RHP, DET) vs. Corey Kluber (RHP, CLE) battle, it may be wiser to look for a mid-range or cheap high-upside starter from a heavy favorite against a weaker offense. Keep in mind that DFS sites will do their best to inflate pitcher salaries to reflect a matchup against an easier opponent or likelihood of a win. Target pitchers from games with a combined projected run total under seven and avoid pitchers from games with a combined run total of nine or more. Most sites deduct points for earned runs allowed.

2. Split Analysis & Park Factors

There's no fantasy sport where splits are more relevant or better extrapolated than in baseball. Looking deep into a starting pitcher's home / away splits and adjusting to their strengths in different ballparks are vital keys to identifying value. BaseballHQ.com colleague Stephen Nickrand backed up with facts what many

of you may already assumed: that several pitching stats are significantly better at home than on the road, including ERA, WHIP, Ctl (bb/9) and Dom (k/9). Combined ERA for all pitchers in 2013 was 3.82 at home compared to 4.21 on the road, while WHIP was 1.29 at home compared to 1.37 on the road. Nickrand also noted that win percentages decrease by 15% on the road, and this certainly matters when you're looking to maximize DFS points from your starters. Since all formats of DFS deduct points for earned runs, avoiding fly ball pitchers in home run friendly parks is always a good bet. Keep in mind that ballpark factors can change drastically year to year.

3. IP and K/9 (Dom)

Wins are hard enough to predict. If you add in the fact that relievers can blow leads in the latter innings, it's best to just concentrate on what is most easily projectable. Innings pitched and strikeouts are where the bulk of your pitching points will come from, so target pitchers who consistently go deeper into games (90+ pitch count or 7+ IP) and average 7.5 or more strikeouts per 9 innings.

4. PQS DOM/DIS

Reviewing PQS logs and DOM/DIS figures are a great way to track consistency in starting pitchers and avoid potential land mines. In 2014, two of the most elite in this regard were Kershaw (93% DOM / 4% DIS) and Kluber (82% / 9%). Kluber was the ultimate value play early on in 2014 before his DFS salary caught up with his skill and performance. Target value-priced starting pitchers against week offenses with a DOM% last year above 65% and below 20% DIS%. We can set our own percentages as a guideline as long as this basic tenet is kept in mind when selecting starting pitchers.

One final interesting notion covered in the 2014 *Forecaster* is finding predictive value in strings of DOM or DIS starts. BHQ colleague Bill Macey illustrates how the probability of a pitcher's DOM streak continuing increases with each additional DOMinant start. There is no such thing as "pitcher X is due to get shelled" because pitcher X has had four PQS 4 or 5 starts in a row and is "due" for a bad start—in fact, his research proves otherwise.

There are several tenets that successful DFS players use when analyzing starting pitchers for their lineups and each player analyzes the day's slate of pitching options differently. Don't forget the strong role intuition plays, especially when you have a strong feel for a pitcher's set of skills and get to watch them consistently. The starting pitcher isn't the be-all, end-all of a DFS roster, but it is definitely a cornerstone slot that needs to produce. Couple that with a strong set of hitters for the day, and you might be the next person to win big.

The Value of Mock Drafts

by Todd Zola

The more puzzles you solve, the better you become at solving puzzles. Drafting a fantasy baseball team is akin to putting a puzzle together. Therefore, the more mock drafts you do, the better you are at assembling your fantasy baseball squad. Here are three specific reasons why mocks are integral for draft preparation.

1. Monkey in the Middle or Hamster on the Wheel

In a snake draft, the dynamics are different picking in the middle or at either end. There are advantages and disadvantages to all the spots.

Being at the wheel means you can initiate position or category runs. But sometimes you can be caught at the end of a run, leaving you devoid of a quality pitching anchor, closer or catcher. The more times you draft from the wheel, the better you'll become at sensing when it's time to start a run or to stay the course.

The challenges of a middle position also revolve around runs. Your ability to cause panic by initiating a run is lessened since you aren't able to double dip at the position. You're more likely to play fantasy chicken, daring others not to take players you may want since there is less of a wait half the time. The more times you make this type of decisions, the more comfortable you'll be doing it when it matters.

The danger with mocks is the preconception the flow will be the same as your real leagues. The trick is not to focus on individuals but rather arranging your list by tiers. If only one or two from a position are taken before your turn(s), it's safe to wait. If half are gone, it's time to jump in. If no one is taken you can wait or attempt to start a run, running the risk of no one joining often meaning you bypassed a better player. The experience gained from doing several mocks from the wheel or the middle facilitates making that crucial decision, since each entail unique nuances.

2. Ride into the Danger Zone

We all have our pet players and tactics. However, sometimes you're sniped or the dynamics are such that relying on your usual strategy is less effective. You're now in the danger zone forced to draft players you're not accustomed to or being forced to switch course on the fly.

Here's where a mock comes in handy. Regardless of your strategy or target players, do something different to push you out of your comfort zone. Mix it up. Put yourself in an unfamiliar spot.

The goal is not to judge your team at the end, rather to develop grace under pressure. If you deliberately put yourself in unchartered territory several times, you'll be able to navigate to safe grounds in the event your opponents veer you off course when it counts.

Pet players and pet tactics often lead to choosing similar players. Using an alternate plan forces consideration of players not on your typical short list. Who knows, maybe upon further inspection your short list expands.

3. By Failing to Prepare, You Are Preparing to Fail

Preparation extends beyond reading the Baseball Forecaster and customizing your cheat sheets. Organization is an integral, and often overlooked, aspect of preparation.

If your drafting platform doesn't track available players, rosters and auction salaries, most find it helpful to do it by hand or electronically, often using drafting software. The faster your draft board is updated, the more time can be spent studying it in an effort to plot accordingly. The less time it takes to retrieve information, the more it can be applied to the draft or auction.

If you're fortunate enough to mock draft using the same on-line room as your actual draft, it's just a matter of getting acclimated to the mechanisms. But chances are, where you mock is different than where you draft so it's best to ignore the provided tracking process and mimic the process you'll be using for real. This includes getting accustomed to draft software.

In summary:

- Alter the positions from which you mock.
- Use non-typical strategies and consider players you rarely target.
- Work out the most efficient means to track your draft or auction.
- Make sure you can seamlessly use an on-line drafting room or draft software.

The following section contains player boxes for every batter who had significant playing time in 2014 and/or is expected to get fantasy roster-worthy plate appearances in 2015. In most cases, high-end prospects who have yet to make their major league debuts will not appear here; you can find scouting reports for them in the Prospects section.

Snapshot Section

The top band of each player box contains the following information:

Age as of Opening Day 2015.

Bats shows which side of the plate he bats from—(L)eft, (R)ight or (B)oth.

Positions: Up to three defensive positions are listed and represent those for which he appeared a minimum of 20 games in 2014.

Ht/Wt: Each batter's height and weight.

Reliability Grades analyze each batter's forecast risk, on an A-F scale. High grades go to those who have accumulated few disabled list days (Health), have a history of substantial and regular major league playing time (PT/Exp) and have displayed consistent performance over the past three years, using RC/G (Consist).

LIMA Plan Grade evaluates how well a batter would fit into a team using the LIMA Plan draft strategy. Best grades go to batters who have excellent base skills, are expected to see regular playing time, and are in the $10-$30 Rotisserie dollar range. Lowest grades will go to poor skills, few AB and values less than $5 or more than $30.

Random Variance Score (Rand Var) measures the impact random variance had on the batter's 2014 stats and the probability that his 2015 performance will exceed or fall short of 2014. The variables tracked are those prone to regression—h%, hr/f and xBA to BA variance. Players are rated on a scale of −5 to +5 with positive scores indicating rebounds and negative scores indicating corrections. Note that this score is computer-generated and the projections will override it on occasion.

Mayberry Method (MM) acknowledges the imprecision of the forecasting process by projecting player performance in broad strokes. The four digits of MM each represent a fantasy-relevant skill—power, speed, batting average and playing time (PA)—and are all on a scale of 0 to 5.

Commentaries for each batter provide a brief analysis of BPIs and the potential impact on performance in 2015. MLB statistics are listed first for those who played only a portion of 2014 at the major league level. Note that these commentaries generally look at performance related issues only. Role and playing time expectations may impact these analyses, so you will have to adjust accordingly. Upside (UP) and downside (DN) statistical potential appears for some players; these are less grounded in hard data and more speculative of skills potential.

Player Stat Section

The past five years' statistics represent the total accumulated in the majors as well as in Triple-A, Double-A ball and various foreign leagues during each year. All non-major league stats have been converted to a major league equivalent (MLE) performance level. Minor league levels below Double-A are not included.

Nearly all baseball publications separate a player's statistical experiences in the major leagues from the minor leagues and outside leagues. While this may be appropriate for official record-keeping purposes, it is not an easy-to-analyze snapshot of a player's complete performance for a given year.

Bill James has proven that minor league statistics (converted to MLEs), at Double-A level or above, provide as accurate a record of a player's performance as major league statistics. Other researchers have also devised conversion factors for foreign leagues. Since these are adequate barometers, we include them in the pool of historical data for each year.

Team designations: An asterisk (*) appearing with a team name means that Triple-A and/or Double-A numbers are included in that year's stat line. Any stints of less than 20 AB are not included (to screen out most rehab appearances). A designation of "a/a" means the stats were accumulated at both AA and AAA levels that year. "for" represents a foreign or independent league. The designation "2TM" appears whenever a player was on more than one major league team, crossing leagues, in a season. "2AL" and "2NL" represent more than one team in the same league. Players who were cut during the season and finished 2014 as a free agent are designated as FAA (Free agent, AL) and FAN (Free agent, NL).

Stats: Descriptions of all the categories appear in the Encyclopedia.

- The leading decimal point has been suppressed on some categories to conserve space.
- Data for platoons (vL, vR), balls-in-play (G/L/F) and consistency (Wk#, DOM, DIS) are for major league performance only.
- Formulas that use BIP data, like xBA and xPX, only appear for years in which G/L/F data is available.

Batting average is presented alongside xBA. On base average and slugging average appear next, and the combined On Base Plus Slugging (OPS). OPS splits vs. left-handed and right-handed pitchers appear after the overall OPS column.

Batting eye and contact skill are measured with walk rate (bb%), contact rate (ct%). Eye is the ratio of walks to strikeouts.

Once the ball leaves the bat, it will either be a (G)round ball, (L)ine drive or (F)ly ball. Hit rate (h%), the also referred to as batting average on balls-in-play (BABIP), measures how often a ball put into play results in a base hit. Hard contact index (HctX) measures the frequency of hard contact, compared to overall league levels. Looking at the ratio of fly balls is a good springboard to the Power gauges. Linear weighted power index (PX) measures a batter's skill at hitting extra base hits as compared to overall league levels. xPX measures power by assessing how hard the ball is being hit (rather than the outcomes of those hits). And the ratio of home runs to fly balls shows the results of those hits.

To assess speed, first look at on base average (does he get on base?), then Spd (is he fast enough to steal bases?), then SBO (how often is he attempting to steal bases?) and finally, SB% (when he attempts, what is his rate of success?).

In looking at consistency, we use weekly Base Performance Value (BPV) levels. Starting with the total number of weeks the batter accumulated stats (#Wk), the percentage of DOMinating weeks (BPV over 50) and DISaster weeks (BPV under 0) is shown. The larger the variance between DOM and DIS, the greater the consistency.

The final section includes several overall performance measures: runs created per game (RC/G), runs above replacement (RAR), Base performance value (BPV), Base performance index (BPX, which is BPV indexed to each year's league average) and the Rotisserie value (R$).

2015 Projections

Forecasts are computed from a player's trends over the past five years. Adjustments were made for leading indicators and variances between skill and statistical output. After reviewing the leading indicators, you might opt to make further adjustments.

Although each year's numbers include all playing time at the Double-A level or above, the 2015 forecast only represents potential playing time at the major league level, and again is highly preliminary.

Note that the projected Rotisserie values in this book will not necessarily align with each player's historical actuals. Since we currently have no idea who is going to play first base for the Pirates, or whether Kris Bryant is going to break camp with the Cubs, it is impossible to create a finite pool of playing time, something which is required for valuation. So the projections are roughly based on a 12-team AL/NL league, and include an inflated number of plate appearances, league-wide. This serves to flatten the spread of values and depress individual player dollar projections. In truth, a $25 player in this book might actually be worth $21, or $28. This level of precision is irrelevant in a process that is driven by market forces anyway. So, don't obsess over it.

Be aware of other sources that publish perfectly calibrated Rotisserie values over the winter. They are likely making arbitrary decisions as to where free agents are going to sign and who is going to land jobs in the spring. We do not make those leaps of faith here.

Bottom line… It is far too early to be making definitive projections for 2015, especially on playing time. Focus on the skill levels and trends, then consult BaseballHQ.com for playing time revisions as players change teams and roles become more defined. A free projections update will be available online in March.

Do-it-yourself analysis

Here are some data points you can look at in doing your own player analysis:

- Variance between vLH and vRH OPS
- Growth or decline in walk rate (bb%)
- Growth or decline in contact rate (ct%)
- Growth or decline in G/L/F individually, or concurrent shifts
- Variance in 2014 hit rate (h%) to 2011-2013 three-year average
- Variance between Avg and xBA each year
- Growth or decline in HctX level
- Growth or decline in power index (PX) rate
- Variance between PX and xPX each year
- Variance in 2014 hr/f rate to 2011-2013 three-year average
- Growth or decline in statistically scouted speed (Spd) score
- Concurrent growth/decline of gauges like ct%, FB, PX, xPX, hr/f
- Concurrent growth/decline of gauges like OB, Spd, SBO, SB%
- Trends in DOM/DIS splits

Abreu,Jose	Health: A	LIMA Plan: C
Age: 28 Bats: R Pos: 1B DH	PT/Exp: C	Rand Var: 0
Ht: 6' 3" Wt: 255	Consist: F	MM: 5155

Terrific MLB debut from Cuban import. Power was expected, but 2H plate skill surge helped produce stunning year-end BA. Likely h% regression says some BA gains are fleeting, but HctX made him a force even with 2H FB dip. Platoon splits still in flux, but he'll be a legit .300/30/100 threat again. And with a FB uptick... UP: 45 HR.

Yr Tm	AB	R	HR	RBI	SB	BA	xBA	OBP	SLG	OPS	vL	vR	bb%	ct%	Eye	G	L	F	h%	HctX	PX	xPX	hr/f	Spd	SBO	SB%	#Wk	DOM	DIS	RC/G	RAR	BPV	BPX	R$
10 for	304	81	14	72	2	331		433	570	1003			15	82	0.98				37		151			121	2%	62%				9.34	27.2	116	252	$20
11 for	252	91	18	87	2	385		484	655	1138			16	85	1.28				40		161			84	3%	62%				13.01	43.2	128	284	$27
12 for	297	72	18	91	1	339		447	582	1029			16	85	1.28				35		138			89	1%	100%				10.06	36.2	111	278	$22
13 for	285	59	10	54	2	320		406	480	886			13	84	0.90				35		103			85	8%	21%				6.76	17.0	71	178	$16
14 CHW	556	80	36	107	3	317	307	383	581	964	1098	919	8	76	0.39	45	23	31	36	120	185	132	27%	71	3%	75%	24	71%	17%	8.09	59.0	94	254	$35
1st Half	272	44	25	64	0	279	324	328	625	953	825	998	6	74	0.24	44	21	35	29	118	241	163	35%	50	0%	0%	12	83%	8%	7.12	22.7	117	316	$36
2nd Half	284	36	11	43	3	352	292	433	539	971	1373	846	11	79	0.57	47	25	28	42	123	134	104	18%	95	4%	75%	12	58%	25%	8.92	34.5	75	203	$35
15 Proj	574	90	33	101	4	307	306	392	545	937	1071	893	11	80	0.60	46	24	31	34	121	162	128	24%	79	4%	51%				7.56	53.4	89	234	$31

Ackley,Dustin	Health: A	LIMA Plan: B+
Age: 27 Bats: L Pos: LF	PT/Exp: B	Rand Var: +2
Ht: 6' 1" Wt: 195	Consist: A	MM: 3335

More volatility. Survived another miserable 1H, then tattooed RHP during Jul/Aug before crumbling down the stretch (.149 BA in Sept). Once-patient approach disappeared (in power sell-out?), contact rate stagnant and speed metrics are trending poorly. Short on secondary skills, a career .236 BA v. LHP points to a platoon future.

Yr Tm	AB	R	HR	RBI	SB	BA	xBA	OBP	SLG	OPS	vL	vR	bb%	ct%	Eye	G	L	F	h%	HctX	PX	xPX	hr/f	Spd	SBO	SB%	#Wk	DOM	DIS	RC/G	RAR	BPV	BPX	R$
10 a/a	501	61	5	39	8	231		312	340	652			10	82	0.65				27		79			124	8%	70%				3.51		51	111	$4
11 SEA *	604	75	11	58	10	256	249	339	389	727	652	804	11	79	0.60	40	22	38	31	115	92	110	6%	148	8%	75%	16	50%	38%	4.51	-7.3	59	131	$13
12 SEA	607	84	12	50	13	226	234	294	328	622	675	593	9	80	0.48	45	19	35	27	97	67	74	7%	123	10%	81%	28	29%	36%	3.22	-24.9	28	70	$8
13 SEA *	488	54	5	41	2	262	254	330	354	685	664	659	9	82	0.55	51	22	27	31	106	69	62	5%	110	3%	40%	24	38%	42%	3.97	0.0	35	88	$8
14 SEA	502	64	14	65	8	245	265	293	398	692	553	749	6	82	0.36	45	18	36	27	108	106	105	9%	103	11%	67%	27	48%	33%	3.85	2.3	58	157	$13
1st Half	243	30	4	27	3	214	246	273	329	602	638	588	7	81	0.42	48	17	35	25	101	83	97	6%	101	9%	60%	14	36%	29%	2.84	-6.8	39	105	$4
2nd Half	259	34	10	38	5	274	281	313	463	776	485	912	5	83	0.29	43	20	37	30	115	127	113	13%	108	12%	71%	13	62%	38%	4.97	9.1	76	205	$22
15 Proj	453	56	12	49	6	249	262	307	393	700	609	739	8	82	0.45	45	20	35	28	107	101	91	9%	110	8%	67%				4.03	4.0	51	135	$12

Adams,Matt	Health: A	LIMA Plan: B+
Age: 26 Bats: L Pos: 1B	PT/Exp: C	Rand Var: -2
Ht: 6' 3" Wt: 260	Consist: B	MM: 4035

Repeat of his elevated h%, along with ct%, LD% upticks kept BA afloat, but xBA and 2H hint it won't last. Career PX/xPX say low HR totals are a mystery, and but that plus power still points to his upside. Issues v. LHP could cut into his AB at some point. But at his age, with FB on the rise... UP: 30 HR.

Yr Tm	AB	R	HR	RBI	SB	BA	xBA	OBP	SLG	OPS	vL	vR	bb%	ct%	Eye	G	L	F	h%	HctX	PX	xPX	hr/f	Spd	SBO	SB%	#Wk	DOM	DIS	RC/G	RAR	BPV	BPX	R$
10																																		
11 aa	463	51	18	64	0	234		276	398	674			5	78	0.26				26		109			86	1%	0%				3.61		36	80	$8
12 STL *	344	38	14	50	2	267	255	300	465	765	440	739	5	74	0.18	44	18	39	32	99	142	126	8%	60	5%	66%	5	20%	60%	4.81	-6.0	38	95	$9
13 STL	296	46	17	51	0	284	262	335	503	839	654	876	7	73	0.29	44	19	36	34	121	153	145	22%	71	1%	0%	26	54%	42%	5.93	11.2	52	130	$12
14 STL	527	55	15	68	3	288	265	321	457	779	528	854	5	78	0.23	35	24	41	34	109	124	130	9%	79	4%	60%	26	54%	23%	5.22	15.3	48	130	$19
1st Half	252	26	9	33	2	325	284	337	528	865	537	964	3	80	0.14	37	24	39	38	111	144	129	11%	86	5%	67%	13	69%	15%	6.79	17.6	67	181	$21
2nd Half	275	29	6	35	1	255	248	308	393	700	520	754	6	77	0.30	32	25	43	31	108	106	131	7%	72	3%	50%	13	38%	31%	4.02	-1.2	30	81	$16
15 Proj	530	63	21	76	2	276	264	316	464	780	507	852	5	76	0.24	38	22	40	33	112	138	135	13%	73	3%	51%				5.10	14.1	46	121	$20

Adduci,James	Health: D	LIMA Plan: F
Age: 30 Bats: L Pos: LF	PT/Exp: D	Rand Var: +2
Ht: 6' 2" Wt: 210	Consist: C	MM: 1301

1-8-.168 in 101 AB at TEX. A powerless 30-year-old journeyman OF who suddenly sees a career-high MLB AB despite that slash line speaks more to his team's issues than anything else. He had his own injuries, and his career .285 BA and minor league running game aren't awful. But nothing here points to any real fantasy value.

Yr Tm	AB	R	HR	RBI	SB	BA	xBA	OBP	SLG	OPS	vL	vR	bb%	ct%	Eye	G	L	F	h%	HctX	PX	xPX	hr/f	Spd	SBO	SB%	#Wk	DOM	DIS	RC/G	RAR	BPV	BPX	R$
10 aaa	367	40	2	22	15	202		239	243	481			5	75	0.19				26		32			115	31%	59%				1.73		-29	-63	$1
11 aa	237	30	3	14	14	251		304	343	647			7	83	0.46				29		65			114	31%	75%				3.56		36	80	$5
12 a/a	399	47	5	31	13	240		301	331	632			8	73	0.32				32		69			103	20%	60%				3.20		-3	-8	$7
13 TEX *	504	53	12	44	24	241	252	308	362	670	667	601	9	72	0.35	71	14	14	31	68	90	9	0%	113	26%	68%	4	0%	75%	3.64	-5.1	15	38	$15
14 TEX *	150	17	2	14	5	191	199	248	265	513	0	504	7	71	0.26	52	14	34	26	72	61	74	4%	102	22%	68%	11	27%	55%	2.05	-7.9	-19	-51	$0
1st Half	33	6	0	4	1	301	280	301	402	703	0	1167	0	79	0.00	55	27	18	38	31	81	8	0%	124	9%	100%	3	67%	0%	4.53	0.7	20	54	-$3
2nd Half	117	11	2	10	4	161	178	235	226	461	0	411	9	69	0.31	52	11	37	22	77	54	86	4%	83	25%	65%	8	13%	75%	1.59	-8.5	-36	-97	$0
15 Proj	97	10	1	7	4	215	196	272	287	560	37	602	8	73	0.33	52	11	37	28	69	61	77	4%	90	25%	66%				2.53	-3.7	-12	-30	$2

Adrianza,Ehire	Health: C	LIMA Plan: F
Age: 25 Bats: B Pos: 2B	PT/Exp: D	Rand Var: -2
Ht: 6' 1" Wt: 170	Consist: A	MM: 1400

.310/.409/.441 Triple-A line (145 AB) in 2013 and 3 HR in March vaulted slick-fielding, career .250-hitting MI into early 2B playing time contention. Reality and year-long hamstring issues intervened beginning in April. The moral: Small sample performance surges aren't always skills improvement, and hope isn't a plan.

Yr Tm	AB	R	HR	RBI	SB	BA	xBA	OBP	SLG	OPS	vL	vR	bb%	ct%	Eye	G	L	F	h%	HctX	PX	xPX	hr/f	Spd	SBO	SB%	#Wk	DOM	DIS	RC/G	RAR	BPV	BPX	R$
10																																		
11																																		
12 aa	451	46	2	28	14	200		259	279	539			7	78	0.36				25		59			113	19%	76%				2.34		10	25	$0
13 SF *	413	41	2	27	12	219	232	286	297	583	583	929	9	78	0.42	42	25	33	28	114	59	152	25%	134	20%	56%	4	50%	0%	2.63	-13.3	17	43	$3
14 SF	97	10	0	5	1	237	226	279	299	578	499	605	5	77	0.23	36	25	39	31	60	63	71	0%	109	9%	50%	15	27%	40%	2.66	-2.1	4	11	-$1
1st Half	75	7	0	4	1	213	217	259	267	526	417	561	5	79	0.25	35	23	42	27	60	53	73	0%	110	6%	100%	12	25%	50%	2.25	-2.6	2	5	-$1
2nd Half	22	3	0	1	0	318	253	348	409	757	714	775	4	73	0.17	38	31	31	44	59	98	64	0%	116	17%	0%	3	33%	0%	4.37	0.6	15	41	-$1
15 Proj	78	8	0	5	2	222	215	280	281	561	481	586	7	78	0.33	35	23	42	28	54	54	66	0%	119	14%	73%				2.55	-2.0	-3	-7	$1

Ahmed,Nick	Health: A	LIMA Plan: D
Age: 25 Bats: R Pos: SS	PT/Exp: D	Rand Var: -1
Ht: 6' 3" Wt: 205	Consist: A	MM: 1411

1-14-.200 in 70 AB at ARI. Another outstanding defensive MI who enjoyed his best offensive season in the hitter-friendly PCL (.312/.373/.425). Small sample MLB 86% ct% was decent, and can steal a base in a pinch. But zero power and poor patience leave little room for speculation.

Yr Tm	AB	R	HR	RBI	SB	BA	xBA	OBP	SLG	OPS	vL	vR	bb%	ct%	Eye	G	L	F	h%	HctX	PX	xPX	hr/f	Spd	SBO	SB%	#Wk	DOM	DIS	RC/G	RAR	BPV	BPX	R$
10																																		
11																																		
12																																		
13 aa	487	49	4	39	22	223		265	309	574			5	84	0.36				26		59			121	28%	74%				2.69		33	83	$9
14 ARI *	477	45	4	34	9	249	236	287	336	623	428	577	5	85	0.35	42	18	40	29	89	66	85	4%	126	15%	53%	9	22%	56%	3.12	-2.5	41	111	$7
1st Half	302	25	1	23	6	268	382	311	354	665	0	667	6	84	0.38	33	67	0	32	121	68	-14	0%	115	15%	52%	1	0%	0%	3.64	3.6	38	103	$10
2nd Half	175	20	2	11	3	215	229	246	304	550	428	569	4	86	0.29	42	16	42	24	88	63	91	4%	127	13%	54%	8	25%	63%	2.33	-5.0	42	114	$2
15 Proj	133	13	2	10	4	240	233	278	341	619	548	694	5	85	0.35	42	16	42	27	79	72	82	4%	126	20%	65%				3.10	-0.6	37	97	$3

Alcantara,Arismendy	Health: A	LIMA Plan: B+
Age: 23 Bats: B Pos: CF 2B	PT/Exp: D	Rand Var: 0
Ht: 5' 10" Wt: 170	Consist: A	MM: 4525

10-29-.205 with 8 SB in 278 AB at CHC. A real MI prospect, being groomed as an infield/OF utility. Power and speed metrics speak to legitimate secondary skills that, with positional versatility, could make him special. Inexperience, ct% and BA show short-term risk/downside. Expect adjustment period, but a fine keeper lg play.

Yr Tm	AB	R	HR	RBI	SB	BA	xBA	OBP	SLG	OPS	vL	vR	bb%	ct%	Eye	G	L	F	h%	HctX	PX	xPX	hr/f	Spd	SBO	SB%	#Wk	DOM	DIS	RC/G	RAR	BPV	BPX	R$
10																																		
11																																		
12																																		
13 aa	494	55	12	55	25	245		315	399	714			9	72	0.37				32		121			96	25%	79%				4.30		36	90	$17
14 CHC *	613	78	18	60	24	242	241	284	416	700	755	565	6	70	0.20	51	12	37	32	77	137	90	15%	143	26%	74%	13	38%	38%	3.92	1.7	44	119	$20
1st Half	302	44	8	29	14	270	259	307	461	768			5	72	0.19				35	0	147			142	27%	80%				4.95		60	162	$23
2nd Half	311	34	10	31	10	215	226	262	373	635	755	565	6	68	0.20	51	12	37	28	75	127	90	15%	127	25%	67%	13	38%	38%	3.08	-7.7	24	65	$17
15 Proj	455	54	15	47	19	240	253	297	422	719	863	658	7	71	0.26	48	17	35	31	68	144	81	13%	130	26%	75%				4.12	3.6	53	140	$15

JOCK THOMPSON

Almonte,Abraham

Age: 26 Bats: B Pos: CF | Ht: 5' 9" Wt: 205

Health: A | PT/Exp: C | Consist: C | LIMA Plan: D | Rand Var: 0 | MM: 2221

3-15-.230 with 4 SB in 204 AB at SEA and SD. Lost starting job, earned AAA demotion from SEA following .194 BA, 61% ct% in April. Fared slightly better after 2H trade to SD. But patience and running game were M.I.A. all season at all levels, and that 2013 power flash looks anomalous. It all points to a bench role at very best.

Yr	Tm	AB	R	HR	RBI	SB	BA	xBA	OBP	SLG	OPS	vL	vR	bb%	ct%	Eye	G	L	F	h%	HctX	PX	xPX	hr/f	Spd	SBO	SB%	#Wk	DOM	DIS	RC/G	RAR	BPV	BPX	R$
10																																			
11																																			
12	aa	319	38	4	20	24	245		310	344	654			9	80	0.46				30		69			114	34%	81%				3.74		27	68	$9
13	SEA *	512	73	13	62	21	259	248	332	398	731	475	872	10	74	0.43	50	20	30	33	67	102	29	14%	94	21%	70%	6	50%	50%	4.48	5.7	29	73	$20
14	2 TM *	481	47	7	35	9	219	224	265	310	575	670	573	6	71	0.21	50	21	28	30	86	76	108	8%	91	15%	53%	13	31%	62%	2.55	-19.1	-14	-38	$4
1st Half		290	25	3	21	6	197	196	239	279	518	687	467	5	66	0.17	50	16	34	29	87	72	126	5%	111	16%	63%	6	17%	83%	2.07	-16.6	-31	-84	$2
2nd Half		191	22	4	14	3	253	258	303	357	660	654	702	7	77	0.32	51	25	24	31	87	81	92	11%	70	15%	40%	7	43%	43%	3.41	-2.6	10	27	$6
15	**Proj**	**129**	**15**	**3**	**11**	**4**	**242**	**247**	**299**	**368**	**667**	**578**	**723**	**8**	**74**	**0.33**	**50**	**21**	**29**	**30**	**79**	**96**	**75**	**11%**	**90**	**20%**	**67%**				**3.64**	**-0.9**	**22**	**59**	**$1**

Alonso,Yonder

Age: 28 Bats: L Pos: 1B | Ht: 6' 1" Wt: 230

Health: C | PT/Exp: C | Consist: A | LIMA Plan: B+ | Rand Var: +5 | MM: 3133

Poor h% killed 1H, before more wrist and hand injuries ended season prematurely. Lots of positives still lurk behind the mediocre bottom line: Rising ct%, xBA and PX/xPX spikes, current FB% trajectory. With just platoon AB, age and handedness make him an undervalued asset. With health and a fast start: UP: .280, 20 HR.

Yr	Tm	AB	R	HR	RBI	SB	BA	xBA	OBP	SLG	OPS	vL	vR	bb%	ct%	Eye	G	L	F	h%	HctX	PX	xPX	hr/f	Spd	SBO	SB%	#Wk	DOM	DIS	RC/G	RAR	BPV	BPX	R$
10	CIN *	536	55	13	56	10	253	254	310	393	703	222	600	8	79	0.39	47	16	37	30	152	103	139	0%	77	10%	75%	6	17%	50%	4.15	-33.2	37	80	$11
11	CIN *	446	43	15	56	4	268	268	334	435	768	651	995	9	80	0.48	42	22	36	31	90	113	98	21%	84	8%	44%	10	40%	50%	4.85	-18.2	54	120	$12
12	SD	549	47	9	62	3	273	264	348	393	741	693	760	10	82	0.61	45	24	31	32	107	88	106	6%	58	2%	100%	27	48%	22%	4.83	-9.3	36	90	$11
13	SD	334	34	6	45	6	281	247	341	368	710	637	736	9	86	0.68	46	21	33	31	107	57	84	6%	64	6%	100%	19	26%	32%	4.62	0.3	28	70	$10
14	SD	267	27	7	27	6	240	279	285	397	682	607	699	6	87	0.47	43	19	38	25	120	110	121	8%	68	13%	86%	16	44%	13%	3.85	-2.6	69	186	$5
1st Half		229	19	5	22	6	210	267	250	341	591	496	615	5	86	0.41	43	19	38	22	116	95	120	7%	61	17%	86%	12	33%	17%	2.82	-9.6	51	138	$6
2nd Half		38	8	2	5	0	421	348	477	737	1214	1514	1160	10	89	1.00	40	17	43	44	144	196	128	13%	94	0%	0%	4	75%	0%	15.45	9.7	164	443	$1
15	**Proj**	**406**	**37**	**11**	**46**	**7**	**266**	**271**	**325**	**412**	**737**	**702**	**745**	**8**	**86**	**0.60**	**43**	**20**	**37**	**29**	**114**	**101**	**109**	**9%**	**60**	**8%**	**80%**				**4.64**	**5.6**	**59**	**156**	**$12**

Altuve,Jose

Age: 25 Bats: R Pos: 2B | Ht: 5' 6" Wt: 175

Health: A | PT/Exp: A | Consist: D | LIMA Plan: D+ | Rand Var: -5 | MM: 1545

Blew away expectations with a confluence of ct%, h%, PX and speed metrics spikes. Obviously, odds against maintaining this level; expect notable BA decline and SB% more in line with 2H performance. But top-of-the-lineup AB will pile up and keep him plenty valuable. Capable of repeating as only 2B with .300+ BA and 20+ SB.

Yr	Tm	AB	R	HR	RBI	SB	BA	xBA	OBP	SLG	OPS	vL	vR	bb%	ct%	Eye	G	L	F	h%	HctX	PX	xPX	hr/f	Spd	SBO	SB%	#Wk	DOM	DIS	RC/G	RAR	BPV	BPX	R$
10																																			
11	HOU *	365	42	6	31	11	297	278	316	415	731	766	618	3	88	0.23	50	20	30	33	65	77	54	4%	121	21%	56%	11	36%	27%	4.45	-1.5	57	127	$12
12	HOU	576	80	7	37	33	290	277	340	399	740	911	676	6	87	0.54	53	20	27	32	87	72	73	5%	140	27%	75%	27	44%	7%	4.79	10.3	63	158	$24
13	HOU	626	64	5	52	35	283	264	316	363	678	733	656	5	86	0.38	49	23	28	32	94	58	78	3%	101	28%	73%	27	33%	15%	4.05	5.8	34	85	$27
14	HOU	660	85	7	59	56	341	296	377	453	830	1013	775	5	92	0.68	48	23	30	36	95	81	77	4%	124	32%	86%	27	78%	7%	6.86	60.3	82	222	$50
1st Half		337	41	2	26	37	344	294	385	448	833	1012	763	6	93	0.91	46	23	31	37	94	76	71	2%	125	37%	93%	14	79%	7%	7.30	34.3	85	230	$50
2nd Half		323	44	5	33	19	337	297	368	458	827	1016	787	4	91	0.50	49	23	28	36	96	85	84	6%	118	26%	76%	13	77%	8%	6.41	26.0	77	208	$50
15	**Proj**	**646**	**90**	**7**	**55**	**42**	**309**	**284**	**344**	**412**	**757**	**885**	**715**	**5**	**89**	**0.48**	**49**	**22**	**29**	**34**	**91**	**75**	**75**	**4%**	**123**	**29%**	**78%**				**5.25**	**33.4**	**66**	**173**	**$38**

Alvarez,Pedro

Age: 28 Bats: L Pos: 3B | Ht: 6' 3" Wt: 235

Health: A | PT/Exp: B | Consist: A | LIMA Plan: B+ | Rand Var: +1 | MM: 5125

Plus power was just a touch off, and plate skills actually improved. Issues vs. LHP, poor 3B play and August stress fracture cost him AB. Did defensive woes follow him to the plate? With health and even platoon AB, he's a decent low-BA power source. As a full-timer, there's still this... UP: 40 HR, .250 BA

Yr	Tm	AB	R	HR	RBI	SB	BA	xBA	OBP	SLG	OPS	vL	vR	bb%	ct%	Eye	G	L	F	h%	HctX	PX	xPX	hr/f	Spd	SBO	SB%	#Wk	DOM	DIS	RC/G	RAR	BPV	BPX	R$
10	PIT *	589	74	25	104	3	250	246	320	450	770	644	858	9	67	0.32	46	15	40	33	111	156	135	18%	81	5%	40%	16	44%	38%	4.77	-26.0	40	87	$16
11	PIT *	360	30	8	33	1	201	214	281	311	592	545	565	10	65	0.32	55	19	25	28	95	92	89	10%	75	2%	47%	16	19%	56%	2.76	-39.5	-19	-42	-$2
12	PIT	525	64	30	85	1	244	244	317	467	784	648	833	10	66	0.32	47	19	34	31	97	164	144	25%	73	1%	100%	27	44%	37%	5.01	-6.4	38	95	$14
13	PIT	558	70	36	100	2	233	256	296	473	770	537	842	8	67	0.26	43	20	36	28	115	176	168	26%	77	2%	100%	27	48%	30%	4.64	0.8	49	123	$17
14	PIT	398	46	18	56	8	231	235	312	405	717	504	770	10	72	0.40	45	16	39	28	118	125	138	16%	75	10%	73%	23	39%	39%	4.13	-0.6	31	84	$11
1st Half		286	36	13	42	5	241	238	330	416	746	610	778	11	73	0.47	45	15	39	29	121	123	148	16%	82	7%	83%	14	43%	36%	4.60	3.7	40	108	$16
2nd Half		112	10	5	14	3	205	228	264	375	639	269	747	7	68	0.25	45	17	38	25	108	132	110	17%	70	22%	60%	9	33%	44%	3.03	-4.0	15	41	-$2
15	**Proj**	**511**	**62**	**29**	**81**	**7**	**237**	**252**	**305**	**453**	**758**	**521**	**828**	**9**	**69**	**0.31**	**44**	**18**	**38**	**29**	**110**	**163**	**137**	**22%**	**69**	**8%**	**67%**				**4.53**	**12.9**	**46**	**120**	**$17**

Amarista,Alexi

Age: 26 Bats: L Pos: SS 3B 2B | Ht: 5' 6" Wt: 150

Health: A | PT/Exp: C | Consist: A | LIMA Plan: D+ | Rand Var: 0 | MM: 1423

Health and versatility on an injury-plagued team were primarily responsible for his 400+ AB season. His ct% remains decent, and the improved SB% was a plus. But sub-par patience, power and HctX throughout his career point to a chronic inability to generate any consistent offensive value. 5-year OPS history tells the story.

Yr	Tm	AB	R	HR	RBI	SB	BA	xBA	OBP	SLG	OPS	vL	vR	bb%	ct%	Eye	G	L	F	h%	HctX	PX	xPX	hr/f	Spd	SBO	SB%	#Wk	DOM	DIS	RC/G	RAR	BPV	BPX	R$
10	a/a	256	29	1	22	6	277		305	333	638			4	92	0.49				30		34			129	13%	65%				3.50		43	93	$5
11	LAA *	415	35	3	39	10	227	223	258	318	576	0	491	4	83	0.24	43	14	43	27	27	68	53	0%	109	23%	53%	10	30%	20%	2.52	-25.7	28	62	$3
12	2 TM *	401	48	6	44	11	235	271	271	362	633	705	657	5	86	0.35	50	19	30	26	87	78	78	7%	135	18%	73%	22	55%	23%	3.25	-10.4	58	145	$6
13	SD	368	35	5	32	4	236	252	282	337	619	557	627	6	85	0.39	43	23	34	27	83	65	72	5%	120	7%	67%	27	52%	22%	3.12	-4.2	39	98	$3
14	SD	423	39	5	40	12	239	252	286	314	600	446	651	6	84	0.42	49	23	28	28	76	53	55	5%	110	12%	92%	27	30%	48%	3.15	-1.8	25	68	$7
1st Half		158	14	1	13	4	209	228	262	278	540	374	568	7	82	0.41	54	15	31	25	88	53	76	3%	103	14%	80%	14	43%	43%	2.42	-4.0	16	43	-$3
2nd Half		265	25	4	27	8	257	265	301	336	637	467	711	6	85	0.43	46	27	27	29	69	52	43	7%	117	11%	100%	13	15%	54%	3.64	3.1	30	81	$14
15	**Proj**	**264**	**26**	**3**	**25**	**6**	**238**	**253**	**281**	**331**	**611**	**490**	**641**	**6**	**85**	**0.39**	**47**	**21**	**32**	**27**	**75**	**64**	**63**	**5%**	**116**	**12%**	**80%**				**3.15**	**-0.7**	**32**	**84**	**$5**

Andrus,Elvis

Age: 26 Bats: R Pos: SS | Ht: 6' 0" Wt: 200

Health: A | PT/Exp: A | Consist: B | LIMA Plan: B | Rand Var: +1 | MM: 1435

Counting stats suffered amid team-wide implosion. Speed metrics remain volatile from year to year; his 2013 SB% now looks like an outlier. Overall skill set is mildy stagnant. Two-year slide vs. RHP bears watching. Age, athleticism, health, and a more productive lineup should fuel a modest rebound, maybe more.

Yr	Tm	AB	R	HR	RBI	SB	BA	xBA	OBP	SLG	OPS	vL	vR	bb%	ct%	Eye	G	L	F	h%	HctX	PX	xPX	hr/f	Spd	SBO	SB%	#Wk	DOM	DIS	RC/G	RAR	BPV	BPX	R$
10	TEX	588	88	0	35	32	265	256	342	301	643	642	644	10	84	0.67	61	19	20	32	78	28	34	0%	155	23%	68%	27	22%	37%	3.49	-12.0	25	54	$18
11	TEX	587	96	5	60	37	279	284	347	361	708	714	706	9	87	0.76	56	23	21	31	76	57	51	5%	113	26%	76%	27	48%	15%	4.41	3.9	49	109	$26
12	TEX	629	85	3	62	21	286	275	349	378	727	687	742	8	85	0.59	57	22	21	33	101	61	76	3%	141	16%	68%	27	48%	22%	4.59	12.2	49	123	$21
13	TEX	620	91	4	67	42	271	257	328	331	659	698	644	8	84	0.54	56	21	22	32	95	40	54	3%	139	26%	84%	27	30%	37%	3.99	10.1	29	73	$30
14	TEX	619	72	2	41	27	263	268	314	333	647	760	607	7	84	0.48	59	20	21	31	75	59	36	2%	106	25%	64%	27	37%	19%	3.49	5.7	33	89	$19
1st Half		318	45	2	19	18	267	283	316	343	659	831	602	7	85	0.49	63	21	16	31	82	62	31	5%	109	28%	72%	14	43%	14%	3.74	4.7	39	105	$22
2nd Half		301	27	0	22	9	259	252	312	322	634	694	612	7	84	0.47	55	20	26	31	67	56	40	0%	102	20%	53%	13	31%	23%	3.23	-0.1	27	73	$15
15	**Proj**	**614**	**79**	**3**	**51**	**34**	**269**	**267**	**326**	**339**	**665**	**719**	**645**	**8**	**85**	**0.53**	**57**	**21**	**22**	**31**	**83**	**56**	**47**	**2%**	**119**	**26%**	**71%**				**3.81**	**10.3**	**35**	**91**	**$24**

Aoki,Norichika

Age: 33 Bats: L Pos: RF | Ht: 5' 9" Wt: 180

Health: A | PT/Exp: A | Consist: B | LIMA Plan: B+ | Rand Var: 0 | MM: 1455

HR plunge wasn't surprising, given subterranean power metrics and move to less friendly venue. Despite 3-week DL stint (groin), managed to retain rest of his R$ thanks to excellent ct% paired with h% and LD upticks. Value is wrapped up in BA and moderate running game. SBs more at risk with age, but still good low-end speed buy.

Yr	Tm	AB	R	HR	RBI	SB	BA	xBA	OBP	SLG	OPS	vL	vR	bb%	ct%	Eye	G	L	F	h%	HctX	PX	xPX	hr/f	Spd	SBO	SB%	#Wk	DOM	DIS	RC/G	RAR	BPV	BPX	R$
10	for	583	90	8	61	17	334		387	457	844			8	90	0.88				36		85	-5		100	11%	79%				6.81	25.5	77	167	$30
11	for	583	71	2	43	7	272		320	342	661			7	91	0.79				30		43	2		134	6%	68%				3.80	-22.7	54	120	$11
12	MIL	520	81	10	50	30	288	294	355	433	787	711	828	8	89	0.78	55	17	28	31	98	91	81	8%	130	27%	79%	27	63%	15%	5.35	7.3	87	218	$24
13	MIL	597	80	8	37	20	286	282	356	370	726	781	703	8	93	1.38	60	18	22	30	102	50	69	7%	142	16%	63%	27	56%	4%	4.43	2.6	75	188	$22
14	KC	491	63	1	43	17	285	292	349	360	710	863	658	8	90	0.88	62	21	17	32	73	53	40	1%	134	16%	68%	25	48%	4%	4.34	6.2	61	165	$17
1st Half		262	36	0	14	7	263	280	326	324	651	851	583	7	89	0.70	66	18	16	30	65	47	28	0%	129	14%	64%	12	33%	8%	3.49	-3.9	47	127	$12
2nd Half		229	27	1	29	10	310	304	375	402	777	876	743	9	92	1.16	58	24	19	33	82	59	54	3%	133	18%	71%	13	62%	0%	5.44	9.2	74	200	$24
15	**Proj**	**515**	**69**	**4**	**45**	**18**	**287**	**292**	**353**	**378**	**731**	**802**	**702**	**8**	**91**	**0.98**	**60**	**20**	**21**	**31**	**88**	**62**	**58**	**4%**	**132**	**17%**	**66%**				**4.54**	**8.0**	**65**	**171**	**$21**

JOCK THOMPSON

Arcia,Oswaldo Celestino

Age: 24 Bats: L Pos: RF		Health	B	LIMA Plan	B+
Ht: 6' 0" Wt: 210		PT/Exp	D	Rand Var	+3
		Consist	B	MM	5125

20-51-.237 in 372 AB at MIN. Battled nagging injuries to finish strong, with 13 HR and a 200+ PX over the final 2 months. Sub-par contact looks chronic, but plus power is legit, and 2H hr/f, bb% spikes are promising. Won't help your BA, or benefit from home venue. And struggles vL cap his ceiling. But with health... UP: 30+ HR.

Yr	Tm	AB	R	HR	RBI	SB	BA	xBA	OBP	SLG	OPS	vL	vR	bb%	ct%	Eye	G	L	F	h%	HctX	PX	xPX	hr/f	Spd	SBO	SB%	#Wk	DOM	DIS	RC/G	RAR	BPV	BPX	R$
10																																			
11																																			
12	aa	262	45	8	56	2	305		362	500	862			8	75	0.36				38		136			105	6%	53%				6.49		57	143	$12
13	MIN *	479	54	21	67	3	257	231	315	446	761	659	769	8	67	0.25	42	17	41	34	93	145	131	15%	100	5%	45%	19	42%	37%	4.72	6.1	32	80	$14
14	MIN *	449	59	24	72	2	239	253	295	462	757	574	848	7	68	0.24	37	22	42	30	94	174	144	19%	91	4%	48%	20	45%	50%	4.50	8.1	53	143	$14
1st Half		203	26	9	31	1	234	242	277	431	709	406	747	6	69	0.19	32	21	48	29	84	157	156	13%	75	7%	29%	7	29%	71%	3.82	-1.1	38	103	$8
2nd Half		246	33	15	41	1	244	260	315	488	803	636	908	9	66	0.28	39	22	39	30	98	189	138	23%	104	2%	100%	13	54%	38%	5.10	8.0	67	181	$19
15	Proj	**484**	**63**	**25**	**78**	**3**	**250**	**256**	**318**	**475**	**793**	**639**	**870**	**8**	**68**	**0.27**	**39**	**20**	**42**	**31**	**93**	**176**	**140**	**18%**	**97**	**5%**	**51%**				**4.91**	**13.0**	**55**	**144**	**$15**

Arenado,Nolan

Age: 24 Bats: R Pos: 3B		Health	B	LIMA Plan	A
Ht: 6' 2" Wt: 205		PT/Exp	B	Rand Var	+1
		Consist	B	MM	4155

Lost 6 weeks to a finger injury and season ended early due to a chest contusion and pneumonia. But he boosted contact and BA skills while making across-the-board power gains. Patience is still an issue, and hit just 2 HR outside Coors, which is concerning. But with health, those 2H HctX and hr/f gains point to... UP: .300 BA, 25 HR.

Yr	Tm	AB	R	HR	RBI	SB	BA	xBA	OBP	SLG	OPS	vL	vR	bb%	ct%	Eye	G	L	F	h%	HctX	PX	xPX	hr/f	Spd	SBO	SB%	#Wk	DOM	DIS	RC/G	RAR	BPV	BPX	R$
10																																			
11																																			
12	aa	516	48	13	49	0	289		333	440	773			6	89	0.59				31		95			82	2%	0%				5.16		71	178	$13
13	COL *	552	58	12	65	2	273	284	306	424	730	846	652	5	85	0.32	43	24	34	30	101	103	103	7%	104	3%	47%	23	48%	17%	4.50	7.9	66	165	$14
14	COL	432	58	18	61	2	287	300	328	500	828	973	776	5	87	0.43	38	21	42	30	127	142	134	11%	97	3%	67%	20	80%	10%	5.80	25.3	102	276	$18
1st Half		192	27	6	28	1	302	297	330	484	814	777	830	4	86	0.33	40	22	38	33	117	131	90	10%	90	5%	50%	9	78%	22%	5.80	11.2	86	232	$14
2nd Half		240	31	12	33	1	275	302	327	513	839	1161	736	6	87	0.52	35	20	45	27	136	150	170	13%	106	2%	100%	11	82%	0%	5.80	14.4	115	311	$21
15	Proj	**585**	**69**	**21**	**74**	**2**	**289**	**297**	**327**	**481**	**808**	**954**	**753**	**5**	**87**	**0.40**	**39**	**22**	**39**	**31**	**119**	**130**	**123**	**11%**	**98**	**3%**	**55%**				**5.56**	**30.5**	**81**	**212**	**$23**

Arencibia,J.P.

Age: 29 Bats: R Pos: CA 1B		Health	A	LIMA Plan	D
Ht: 6' 0" Wt: 205		PT/Exp	C	Rand Var	+3
		Consist	B	MM	4103

10-35-.177 in 203 AB at TEX. Power-desperate owners who took a flyer on his mid-July recall lucked into a decent half-season of #2 catcher stats (7 HR, 22 RBI) over the next 3 weeks. The before and after were killers. Plus power in an otherwise complete skills vacuum is a timing crap-shoot. Now a positional question mark, too.

Yr	Tm	AB	R	HR	RBI	SB	BA	xBA	OBP	SLG	OPS	vL	vR	bb%	ct%	Eye	G	L	F	h%	HctX	PX	xPX	hr/f	Spd	SBO	SB%	#Wk	DOM	DIS	RC/G	RAR	BPV	BPX	R$
10	TOR *	447	48	22	54	0	225	242	265	438	703	77	772	5	74	0.21	29	13	58	25	114	153	161	14%	84	0%	0%	8	13%	75%	3.81	-24.7	57	124	$5
11	TOR	443	47	23	78	1	219	240	282	438	720	838	682	8	70	0.27	35	16	50	26	110	158	153	15%	103	2%	50%	27	44%	26%	3.94	-23.0	54	120	$8
12	TOR	347	45	18	56	1	233	233	275	435	710	774	688	5	69	0.17	37	18	45	29	98	144	128	17%	73	2%	100%	22	45%	45%	3.94	-14.0	25	63	$7
13	TOR	474	45	21	55	0	194	225	227	365	592	588	594	4	69	0.12	37	20	44	23	92	127	133	15%	75	3%	0%	27	33%	48%	2.52	-31.3	8	20	$1
14	TEX *	393	39	19	60	1	195	221	227	381	608	840	492	4	68	0.13	34	16	50	23	109	145	164	14%	67	1%	100%	18	39%	33%	2.75	-17.2	17	46	$4
1st Half		196	19	7	21	0	178	204	210	319	529	937	252	4	69	0.13	32	17	51	22	114	111	171	4%	73	0%	0%	7	29%	43%	2.07	-13.2	-5	-14	-$3
2nd Half		197	20	12	39	1	213	239	245	444	688	815	615	4	67	0.13	34	16	50	25	105	179	160	19%	74	2%	100%	11	45%	27%	3.53	-3.9	42	114	$10
15	Proj	**268**	**28**	**12**	**40**	**1**	**205**	**225**	**251**	**386**	**637**	**802**	**568**	**4**	**68**	**0.14**	**35**	**17**	**48**	**25**	**103**	**142**	**150**	**14%**	**74**	**2%**	**64%**				**2.96**	**-3.7**	**9**	**24**	**$4**

Arias,Joaquin

Age: 30 Bats: R Pos: 3B		Health	A	LIMA Plan	D+
Ht: 6' 1" Wt: 165		PT/Exp	F	Rand Var	-1
		Consist	B	MM	1521

Probably shouldn't be dismissed as easily as most weak-hitting bench infielders. With luck, that ct% and Spd may help him out-hit his xBA as a short-term fill-in. But if you're unlucky enough to find yourself in that position, don't let him overstay his roster welcome. The HctX, power metrics, SBs and OPS history speak volumes.

Yr	Tm	AB	R	HR	RBI	SB	BA	xBA	OBP	SLG	OPS	vL	vR	bb%	ct%	Eye	G	L	F	h%	HctX	PX	xPX	hr/f	Spd	SBO	SB%	#Wk	DOM	DIS	RC/G	RAR	BPV	BPX	R$
10	2 TM *	159	26	0	14	1	240	215	269	290	559	765	542	4	81	0.20	43	18	39	30	49	41	49	0%	159	3%	100%	23	13%	39%	2.65	-11.5	12	26	$0
11	aaa	241	24	2	16	5	186		216	276	492			4	87	0.28				21		59			121	15%	79%				1.88		39	87	-$3
12	SF *	389	39	6	45	5	275	262	302	391	693	768	625	4	85	0.25	47	22	32	31	83	71	84	6%	149	8%	68%	24	46%	25%	4.12	-5.4	51	128	$9
13	SF	225	17	1	19	1	271	249	284	342	627	618	636	2	85	0.12	52	21	28	31	85	50	73	2%	138	2%	100%	24	29%	46%	3.42	-3.6	28	70	$2
14	SF	193	18	0	15	1	254	239	281	301	581	720	413	4	88	0.35	52	18	30	29	62	42	48	0%	111	2%	100%	27	30%	33%	2.94	-4.3	29	78	$1
1st Half		93	5	0	8	0	183	184	214	183	397	399	395	4	89	0.40	56	14	30	20	73	0	51	0%	109	0%	0%	14	14%	36%	1.23	-7.3	0	0	-$4
2nd Half		100	13	0	7	1	320	275	343	410	753	949	436	4	87	0.31	49	22	30	37	51	81	45	0%	122	4%	100%	13	46%	31%	5.39	4.5	59	159	$5
15	Proj	**203**	**20**	**1**	**17**	**2**	**263**	**250**	**287**	**331**	**618**	**718**	**514**	**3**	**86**	**0.26**	**50**	**20**	**30**	**30**	**69**	**54**	**59**	**1%**	**128**	**6%**	**93%**				**3.35**	**-2.0**	**22**	**57**	**$4**

Asche,Cody

Age: 25 Bats: L Pos: 3B		Health	A	LIMA Plan	B
Ht: 6' 1" Wt: 200		PT/Exp	C	Rand Var	0
		Consist	A	MM	4125

Young, healthy, left-handed and could prove useful at a scarce position for a few years. But his contact and BA skills are stagnant, and a sneaky running game disappeared in 2014. Despite decent power, he doesn't hit enough FBs to turn that pop into value. Not awful, but he's a bit player whose playing time will always be at risk.

Yr	Tm	AB	R	HR	RBI	SB	BA	xBA	OBP	SLG	OPS	vL	vR	bb%	ct%	Eye	G	L	F	h%	HctX	PX	xPX	hr/f	Spd	SBO	SB%	#Wk	DOM	DIS	RC/G	RAR	BPV	BPX	R$
10																																			
11																																			
12	aa	263	33	8	37	1	269		315	450	765			6	76	0.28				32		127			93	3%	42%				4.87		49	123	$6
13	PHI *	566	58	17	75	10	252	246	304	411	715	608	710	7	73	0.28	44	21	35	32	91	116	109	12%	110	10%	74%	10	40%	40%	4.24	4.2	35	88	$16
14	PHI	397	43	10	46	0	252	249	309	390	699	733	690	8	74	0.32	41	24	35	32	95	113	102	10%	92	1%	0%	24	54%	25%	4.07	4.2	32	86	$7
1st Half		165	16	4	24	0	248	259	315	388	703	796	682	9	77	0.42	50	22	28	30	110	111	107	11%	90	2%	0%	11	55%	9%	4.04	1.7	43	116	$4
2nd Half		232	27	6	22	0	254	242	304	392	696	693	697	7	72	0.27	34	25	41	33	84	115	98	9%	98	0%	0%	13	54%	38%	4.09	2.7	27	73	$10
15	Proj	**454**	**50**	**13**	**57**	**2**	**255**	**253**	**310**	**406**	**716**	**703**	**719**	**7**	**74**	**0.30**	**42**	**23**	**36**	**32**	**93**	**120**	**105**	**11%**	**99**	**3%**	**56%**				**4.26**	**7.5**	**27**	**70**	**$12**

Avila,Alex

Age: 28 Bats: L Pos: CA		Health	B	LIMA Plan	D+
Ht: 5' 11" Wt: 210		PT/Exp	C	Rand Var	0
		Consist	A	MM	4013

Contact and BA continue to drift downward, dragging value along for the ride. Good power and patience only partly compensate, due to the lofty GB%. Struggles vs. LHP and continued concussion issues haven't helped. Buy for HR, hope for better ct% and an OBP surprise. But he needs health at a position that is taking a toll.

Yr	Tm	AB	R	HR	RBI	SB	BA	xBA	OBP	SLG	OPS	vL	vR	bb%	ct%	Eye	G	L	F	h%	HctX	PX	xPX	hr/f	Spd	SBO	SB%	#Wk	DOM	DIS	RC/G	RAR	BPV	BPX	R$
10	DET	294	28	7	31	2	228	239	316	340	656	502	676	11	76	0.51	43	22	35	28	117	82	127	9%	61	5%	50%	27	26%	48%	3.45	-6.8	11	24	$2
11	DET	464	63	19	82	3	295	264	389	506	895	779	939	14	72	0.56	38	22	40	38	115	160	154	14%	91	3%	75%	27	48%	22%	7.16	38.0	72	160	$20
12	DET	367	42	9	48	2	243	245	352	384	736	539	796	14	72	0.59	46	24	30	31	105	106	130	11%	80	2%	100%	26	35%	38%	4.57	4.7	26	65	$5
13	DET *	374	43	12	51	0	225	238	316	369	685	455	767	12	66	0.39	42	28	30	31	99	116	138	17%	72	0%	0%	24	25%	42%	3.84	1.4	5	13	$4
14	DET	390	44	11	47	0	218	222	327	359	686	589	720	14	61	0.40	45	25	30	32	105	136	147	15%	63	3%	0%	27	37%	44%	3.68	4.2	2	5	$3
1st Half		193	25	5	18	0	233	233	348	378	726	576	779	14	61	0.41	42	28	30	35	114	145	154	14%	73	5%	0%	14	36%	43%	4.02	3.7	12	32	$3
2nd Half		197	19	6	29	0	203	210	306	340	646	601	663	13	61	0.39	47	22	31	30	97	127	140	16%	65	0%	0%	13	38%	46%	3.36	-0.2	-5	-14	$4
15	Proj	**384**	**43**	**12**	**50**	**0**	**226**	**235**	**328**	**378**	**706**	**561**	**753**	**13**	**65**	**0.43**	**44**	**25**	**31**	**31**	**104**	**133**	**141**	**16%**	**67**	**1%**	**-46%**				**4.00**	**7.2**	**4**	**10**	**$6**

Aviles,Mike

Age: 34 Bats: R Pos: 3B 2B LF		Health	A	LIMA Plan	D+
Ht: 5' 10" Wt: 205		PT/Exp	C	Rand Var	0
		Consist	A	MM	1223

Aging utility player in slow decline. Can still steal a base, but now unremarkable Spd and SB% history say this is risky going forward. Contact still a plus, but BA and xBA have stuck in mediocrity for a while. And both HctX, power metrics are deteriorating rapidly. Still a versatile stopgap, but don't spend all your FAAB here.

Yr	Tm	AB	R	HR	RBI	SB	BA	xBA	OBP	SLG	OPS	vL	vR	bb%	ct%	Eye	G	L	F	h%	HctX	PX	xPX	hr/f	Spd	SBO	SB%	#Wk	DOM	DIS	RC/G	RAR	BPV	BPX	R$
10	KC *	494	68	9	37	14	291	257	322	396	718	642	787	4	88	0.37	43	19	38	32	89	65	70	6%	151	14%	74%	24	38%	38%	4.56	-3.4	58	126	$17
11	2 AL *	426	44	12	55	18	247	260	276	408	683	924	601	4	85	0.26	42	16	43	27	98	103	93	7%	111	33%	66%	22	55%	32%	3.61	-15.4	64	142	$12
12	BOS	512	57	13	60	14	250	254	282	381	663	753	626	4	85	0.30	41	19	40	27	100	84	90	7%	69	18%	70%	26	31%	19%	3.59	-14.6	38	95	$13
13	CLE	361	54	9	46	8	252	260	282	368	650	605	689	4	89	0.37	43	20	37	26	94	72	73	7%	60	16%	62%	27	44%	26%	3.42	-5.6	40	100	$10
14	CLE	344	38	5	39	14	247	255	273	343	616	645	596	4	86	0.27	44	21	35	28	61	69	45	5%	77	25%	74%	26	38%	31%	3.16	-5.2	31	84	$9
1st Half		184	23	3	21	7	261	243	281	348	629	635	625	3	84	0.21	43	21	36	30	56	62	45	5%	77	23%	70%	14	29%	43%	3.34	-1.9	18	49	$11
2nd Half		160	15	2	18	7	231	268	263	338	601	655	559	4	88	0.35	45	21	34	25	67	76	45	4%	76	28%	78%	12	50%	17%	2.97	-3.6	44	119	$8
15	Proj	**283**	**34**	**5**	**33**	**9**	**249**	**258**	**277**	**359**	**636**	**652**	**625**	**4**	**87**	**0.30**	**43**	**20**	**37**	**27**	**79**	**76**	**62**	**6%**	**77**	**20%**	**69%**				**3.31**	**-3.2**	**46**	**121**	**$8**

JOCK THOMPSON

Aybar,Erick

Age: 31 Bats: B Pos: SS | Ht: 5' 10" Wt: 180

Health B | PT/Exp A | Consist B | LIMA Plan A | Rand Var 0 | MM 1345

The bb% uptick, fewer nagging injuries and a productive lineup all factored into the R$ surge. Beyond the counting stat gains, his overall metrics remained planted within a narrow range. Declining Spd, SB% indicate SBs unlikely to rebound. But this ct%-driven skill set should stay reliable at a value-challenged SS position.

Yr	Tm	AB	R	HR	RBI	SB	BA	xBA	OBP	SLG	OPS	vL	vR	bb%	ct%	Eye	G	L	F	h%	HctX	PX	xPX	hr/f	Spd	SBO	SB%	#Wk	DOM	DIS	RC/G	RAR	BPV	BPX	R$
10	LAA	534	69	5	29	22	253	237	306	330	636	609	646	6	85	0.43	49	15	36	29	74	51	54	3%	147	21%	73%	26	35%	27%	3.36	-13.1	38	83	$12
11	LAA	556	71	10	59	30	279	287	322	421	743	607	807	5	88	0.46	48	21	31	30	85	91	66	7%	124	27%	83%	25	64%	12%	4.81	10.1	74	164	$23
12	LAA	517	67	8	45	20	290	279	324	416	740	879	690	4	88	0.36	52	19	29	32	91	79	63	6%	116	19%	83%	25	52%	20%	4.84	13.6	61	153	$19
13	LAA	550	68	6	54	12	271	287	301	382	683	723	666	4	89	0.39	50	23	27	29	93	75	63	5%	109	15%	63%	25	52%	16%	3.90	7.5	60	150	$16
14	LAA	589	77	7	68	16	278	282	321	379	700	622	727	6	89	0.58	49	23	28	30	88	69	54	5%	102	16%	64%	27	44%	15%	4.16	16.7	57	154	$21
1st Half		300	40	6	42	8	287	299	326	433	759	638	814	5	90	0.55	48	22	30	30	96	98	70	8%	99	18%	62%	14	64%	14%	4.84	13.7	80	216	$24
2nd Half		289	37	1	26	8	270	265	316	322	638	601	646	6	89	0.61	50	24	26	30	81	39	37	2%	104	14%	67%	13	23%	15%	3.49	2.1	34	92	$18
15	Proj	**572**	**73**	**6**	**58**	**15**	**276**	**283**	**315**	**378**	**692**	**682**	**696**	**5**	**89**	**0.47**	**50**	**23**	**27**	**30**	**88**	**71**	**56**	**5%**	**107**	**15%**	**67%**				**4.07**	**13.7**	**57**	**149**	**$18**

Baez,Javier

Age: 22 Bats: R Pos: SS 2B | Ht: 6' 0" Wt: 190

Health A | PT/Exp F | Consist F | LIMA Plan C+ | Rand Var 0 | MM 4205

9-20-.169, 5 SBs in 213 AB at CHC. Big-time prospect struggled early in Triple-A intro before turnaround, and again in 2H MLB debut. Offers huge power upside and similar contact-and-BA risk, at least in the short-term, which could result in more AAA time. But MI position and young legs help make him speculation-worthy now.

Yr	Tm	AB	R	HR	RBI	SB	BA	xBA	OBP	SLG	OPS	vL	vR	bb%	ct%	Eye	G	L	F	h%	HctX	PX	xPX	hr/f	Spd	SBO	SB%	#Wk	DOM	DIS	RC/G	RAR	BPV	BPX	R$
10																																			
11																																			
12																																			
13	aa	218	31	16	43	6	268		317	557	874			7	66	0.21				33		224			78	20%	75%				6.07		81	203	$11
14	CHC *	601	74	27	81	17	209	214	261	395	655	569	546	6	61	0.18	41	14	45	29	82	165	120	17%	97	24%	64%	9	33%	67%	3.18	-3.9	18	49	$15
1st Half		268	30	8	35	11	215	217	265	373	638			6	61	0.17				32	0	145			107	29%	71%				3.14		5	14	$9
2nd Half		333	44	18	46	7	205	223	257	413	670	569	546	7	61	0.18	41	14	45	27	82	181	120	17%	90	20%	55%	9	33%	67%	3.23	-1.8	29	78	$20
15	Proj	**457**	**60**	**18**	**73**	**11**	**223**	**219**	**278**	**397**	**674**	**667**	**677**	**7**	**63**	**0.19**	**41**	**16**	**43**	**31**	**74**	**156**	**108**	**14%**	**91**	**17%**	**70%**				**3.52**	**4.0**	**19**	**49**	**$13**

Baker,Jeff

Age: 34 Bats: R Pos: 1B 2B | Ht: 6' 2" Wt: 220

Health B | PT/Exp F | Consist F | LIMA Plan D | Rand Var 0 | MM 4431

Vanishing HRs not a shock given venue change. Power metrics say they'll rebound a tad, though timing is everything for a 200-AB reserve. That 2nd half h% compensated, making for a nice injury pickup if you were fortunate enough to add him in July. At very best, he's a deep league in-season flyer again.

Yr	Tm	AB	R	HR	RBI	SB	BA	xBA	OBP	SLG	OPS	vL	vR	bb%	ct%	Eye	G	L	F	h%	HctX	PX	xPX	hr/f	Spd	SBO	SB%	#Wk	DOM	DIS	RC/G	RAR	BPV	BPX	R$
10	CHC	206	29	4	21	1	272	256	326	413	739	945	302	7	76	0.32	42	22	36	34	87	106	92	7%	114	2%	100%	27	41%	33%	4.72	-9.0	38	83	$4
11	CHC	201	20	3	23	0	269	255	302	383	685	812	491	5	77	0.22	48	24	28	34	105	89	94	7%	109	0%	0%	25	48%	36%	4.05	-12.6	24	53	$2
12	3 TM	188	18	4	25	4	239	264	279	378	656	665	637	6	74	0.23	48	27	25	30	83	103	63	11%	90	13%	80%	27	26%	41%	3.58	-10.3	20	50	$2
13	TEX	154	21	11	21	1	279	271	360	545	905	1073	536	10	69	0.38	49	18	34	34	125	194	160	31%	102	2%	100%	22	50%	50%	6.89	10.0	84	210	$5
14	MIA	208	27	3	28	1	264	257	307	394	701	824	535	6	75	0.25	48	24	28	34	114	96	118	7%	142	2%	100%	26	35%	46%	4.23	0.3	35	95	$4
1st Half		111	15	2	14	1	198	246	252	306	558	569	546	7	77	0.31	52	20	27	24	106	79	105	8%	106	4%	100%	14	36%	50%	2.50	-5.8	17	46	$1
2nd Half		97	12	1	14	0	340	269	373	495	867	1087	520	5	74	0.20	43	29	28	45	125	117	135	5%	151	0%	0%	12	33%	42%	7.13	7.4	48	130	$7
15	Proj	**163**	**20**	**5**	**22**	**1**	**268**	**264**	**320**	**433**	**753**	**886**	**524**	**7**	**74**	**0.28**	**47**	**24**	**29**	**34**	**112**	**125**	**120**	**13%**	**124**	**3%**	**90%**				**4.84**	**3.1**	**37**	**98**	**$5**

Baker,John

Age: 34 Bats: L Pos: CA | Ht: 6' 1" Wt: 215

Health D | PT/Exp F | Consist C | LIMA Plan F | Rand Var -1 | MM 0001

We didn't know it then, but his career year, 373 AB peak—and last MLB HR—came in 2009, when a .271 BA, 10% bb% and average power prompted us to suggest here that you could do worse for your second catcher slot. Injuries and gravity have since taken over his career. But lefty catchers live forever.

Yr	Tm	AB	R	HR	RBI	SB	BA	xBA	OBP	SLG	OPS	vL	vR	bb%	ct%	Eye	G	L	F	h%	HctX	PX	xPX	hr/f	Spd	SBO	SB%	#Wk	DOM	DIS	RC/G	RAR	BPV	BPX	R$
10	FLA	78	7	0	6	0	218	238	307	282	589	250	625	10	77	0.50	53	22	25	28	73	50	37	0%	106	0%	0%	6	33%	50%	2.75	-3.8	2	4	-$2
11	FLA	13	0	0	1	0	154	73	267	154	421	0	421	13	77	0.67	80	10	10	20	106	0	2	0%	91	0%	0%	4	0%	75%	1.24	-1.3	-35	-78	-$3
12	SD	193	17	0	14	2	238	223	310	280	590	582	591	9	79	0.49	52	21	26	30	92	38	75	0%	89	5%	67%	25	16%	56%	2.90	-8.0	-6	-15	-$1
13	SD *	186	10	2	13	0	146	169	220	188	408	333	422	9	67	0.28	39	21	39	20	69	30	83	0%	74	3%	0%	8	13%	75%	1.19	-15.7	-66	-165	-$7
14	CHC	182	9	0	15	0	192	199	273	231	504	461	512	9	68	0.33	47	26	27	28	89	44	89	0%	71	0%	0%	25	16%	68%	1.96	-8.6	-49	-132	-$4
1st Half		100	5	0	8	0	180	192	245	210	455	458	455	7	66	0.24	54	25	21	27	93	36	71	0%	83	0%	0%	14	14%	71%	1.57	-5.9	-66	-178	-$5
2nd Half		82	4	0	7	0	207	209	305	256	561	464	581	12	71	0.46	40	26	34	29	85	54	110	0%	68	0%	0%	11	18%	64%	2.48	-2.3	-28	-76	-$3
15	Proj	**127**	**7**	**0**	**10**	**0**	**185**	**194**	**265**	**213**	**479**	**426**	**489**	**9**	**70**	**0.34**	**49**	**24**	**28**	**27**	**87**	**33**	**79**	**0%**	**76**	**2%**	**37%**				**1.73**	**-6.8**	**-68**	**-178**	**-$2**

Barnes,Brandon

Age: 29 Bats: R Pos: RF | Ht: 6' 2" Wt: 210

Health A | PT/Exp C | Consist B | LIMA Plan D | Rand Var -4 | MM 4311

Unsurprising hr/f, PX spikes accompanied Coors Field move; GB%, xPX history say this is tenuous. In fact, a .299/.338/.552 line and 7 HR at home accounted for all of his offensive value. He's a fine defender, but mediocre plate skills and poor SB% leave the prospect for power as his primary path to more ABs. Seems very unlikely.

Yr	Tm	AB	R	HR	RBI	SB	BA	xBA	OBP	SLG	OPS	vL	vR	bb%	ct%	Eye	G	L	F	h%	HctX	PX	xPX	hr/f	Spd	SBO	SB%	#Wk	DOM	DIS	RC/G	RAR	BPV	BPX	R$
10	aaa	21	1	1	1	1	244		270	396	666			3	67	0.10				33		119			109	18%	100%				3.78		3	7	-$1
11	a/a	432	43	11	39	8	200		253	347	600			7	70	0.24				26		115			104	16%	63%				2.73		17	38	$1
12	HOU *	497	63	9	54	15	246	244	290	376	666	578	458	6	71	0.21	49	22	29	33	89	107	114	5%	90	22%	65%	9	22%	67%	3.56	-23.8	11	28	$11
13	HOU	408	46	8	41	11	240	217	289	346	635	791	557	5	69	0.17	48	20	32	33	76	86	71	9%	115	24%	50%	26	19%	58%	2.94	-20.9	-8	-20	$8
14	COL	292	37	8	27	5	257	241	293	425	718	639	767	5	66	0.15	47	21	32	36	79	143	111	13%	135	15%	56%	27	44%	48%	4.10	0.0	30	81	$7
1st Half		158	20	3	12	4	272	245	315	418	733	545	861	6	67	0.19	41	29	30	39	68	128	97	10%	136	16%	67%	14	43%	50%	4.51	2.4	26	70	$7
2nd Half		134	17	5	15	1	239	238	266	433	699	763	660	4	64	0.10	54	12	35	33	93	162	128	17%	121	13%	33%	13	46%	46%	3.61	-1.6	32	86	$7
15	Proj	**166**	**20**	**4**	**16**	**3**	**243**	**237**	**287**	**395**	**682**	**712**	**664**	**5**	**68**	**0.17**	**47**	**20**	**33**	**33**	**81**	**129**	**100**	**12%**	**118**	**18%**	**54%**				**3.55**	**-2.2**	**17**	**46**	**$4**

Barney,Darwin

Age: 29 Bats: R Pos: 2B | Ht: 5' 10" Wt: 185

Health A | PT/Exp C | Consist B | LIMA Plan D | Rand Var +1 | MM 1321

3-23-.241 in 237 AB at CHC and LA. Despite decent ct%, plus defender seems far removed from AB-fueled 2011-12 watermarks. Still powerless, a sub-par HctX, falling GB% and non-existent running game make his speed a non-factor. Forced out by CHC prospect wave, LA added him for depth. Your league likely isn't this deep.

Yr	Tm	AB	R	HR	RBI	SB	BA	xBA	OBP	SLG	OPS	vL	vR	bb%	ct%	Eye	G	L	F	h%	HctX	PX	xPX	hr/f	Spd	SBO	SB%	#Wk	DOM	DIS	RC/G	RAR	BPV	BPX	R$
10	CHC *	558	60	1	35	7	244	249	272	304	576	699	528	4	87	0.29	54	16	30	28	85	45	40	0%	115	8%	67%	9	56%	33%	2.77	-32.3	28	61	$4
11	CHC	529	66	2	43	9	276	267	313	353	666	734	650	4	87	0.33	49	23	28	31	55	53	36	2%	144	8%	82%	26	31%	27%	3.83	-13.3	45	100	$12
12	CHC	548	73	7	44	6	254	273	299	354	653	636	659	6	89	0.57	48	22	30	27	81	62	58	5%	124	5%	86%	27	48%	22%	3.61	-11.8	58	145	$9
13	CHC	501	49	7	41	4	208	252	266	303	569	725	515	7	87	0.56	45	19	36	23	75	66	74	4%	92	6%	67%	24	38%	21%	2.53	-17.6	45	113	$0
14	2 NL *	272	27	3	24	1	232	243	281	323	604	707	614	6	85	0.46	43	20	37	26	94	64	79	4%	130	2%	100%	24	38%	21%	3.03	-2.9	45	122	$1
1st Half		165	15	2	15	1	194	245	239	279	517	606	483	5	84	0.35	39	23	39	22	98	65	80	4%	85	3%	100%	14	29%	36%	2.10	-6.7	27	73	$0
2nd Half		107	12	1	9	0	291	239	349	391	740	875	936	8	86	0.65	52	14	34	33	85	63	78	5%	170	0%	0%	10	50%	0%	4.90	4.5	65	176	$3
15	Proj	**105**	**11**	**1**	**9**	**1**	**242**	**252**	**299**	**338**	**637**	**694**	**614**	**6**	**87**	**0.50**	**47**	**19**	**34**	**27**	**83**	**67**	**70**	**4%**	**120**	**3%**	**78%**				**3.30**	**-0.3**	**37**	**97**	**$1**

Bautista,Jose

Age: 34 Bats: R Pos: RF | Ht: 6' 0" Wt: 205

Health C | PT/Exp B | Consist B | LIMA Plan A | Rand Var 0 | MM 5255

Nice rebound off two years of wrist and hip injuries. Plate skill and LD upticks pushed BA back in line with xBA history. Sure, he's now in his mid-30s and the PX/xPX and hr/f are no longer at peak levels. But they're plenty good enough, and as the HctX notes, he still hits the ball hard. If he's healthy again in March, pay full value.

Yr	Tm	AB	R	HR	RBI	SB	BA	xBA	OBP	SLG	OPS	vL	vR	bb%	ct%	Eye	G	L	F	h%	HctX	PX	xPX	hr/f	Spd	SBO	SB%	#Wk	DOM	DIS	RC/G	RAR	BPV	BPX	R$
10	TOR	569	109	54	124	9	260	322	378	617	995	843	1030	15	80	0.86	31	14	54	24	129	220	173	22%	99	7%	82%	27	85%	15%	7.89	45.1	156	339	$31
11	TOR	513	105	43	103	9	302	297	447	608	1056	1156	1025	20	78	1.19	37	16	47	31	155	191	158	23%	105	6%	64%	27	74%	7%	9.73	65.0	141	313	$35
12	TOR	332	64	27	65	5	241	280	358	527	886	718	942	15	81	0.94	37	14	49	22	130	165	145	20%	76	7%	71%	17	76%	12%	6.25	13.9	111	278	$14
13	TOR	452	82	28	73	7	259	281	358	498	856	910	842	13	81	0.82	41	16	43	26	129	150	138	18%	83	7%	78%	21	67%	5%	6.12	24.2	99	248	$20
14	TOR	553	101	35	103	6	286	290	403	524	928	1079	888	16	83	1.08	40	18	42	29	124	152	121	18%	89	4%	75%	27	81%	7%	7.46	55.4	112	303	$32
1st Half		273	54	15	49	3	304	288	432	524	956	1307	862	18	82	1.23	41	19	39	32	117	144	111	17%	97	4%	75%	14	86%	0%	8.20	31.5	112	303	$30
2nd Half		280	47	20	54	3	268	291	374	525	899	848	913	14	83	0.94	39	17	44	26	131	159	130	19%	81	5%	75%	13	77%	15%	6.74	22.1	113	305	$33
15	Proj	**523**	**96**	**35**	**96**	**5**	**270**	**289**	**384**	**523**	**908**	**944**	**898**	**15**	**82**	**0.98**	**39**	**16**	**44**	**27**	**129**	**163**	**134**	**19%**	**86**	**4%**	**68%**				**6.92**	**43.9**	**106**	**280**	**$28**

JOCK THOMPSON

Beckham,Gordon

Age: 28 Bats: R Pos: 2B | Ht: 6' 0" Wt: 185

Health: C | PT/Exp: C | Consist: B | LIMA Plan: D+ | Rand Var: +3 | MM: 2213

9-46-.226 in 446 AB at CHW/LAA. For CHW, it was the definition of insanity - trying the same thing over and over, expecting a different result. They finally gave up on Aug. 23 amidst Beckham's brutal 2H plummet, but then he hit a decent .268 with LAA the rest of the way, including .306 in Sept. That's how he lures you in. Resist.

Yr	Tm	AB	R	HR	RBI	SB	BA	xBA	OBP	SLG	OPS	vL	vR	bb%	ct%	Eye	G	L	F	h%	HctX	PX	xPX	hr/f	Spd	SBO	SB%	#Wk	DOM	DIS	RC/G	RAR	BPV	BPX	R$
10	CHW	444	58	9	49	4	252	249	317	378	695	667	705	8	79	0.40	46	17	37	30	106	91	90	7%	111	9%	40%	26	42%	31%	3.82	-10.3	41	89	$8
11	CHW	499	60	10	44	5	230	230	296	337	633	541	663	7	78	0.32	39	20	40	28	76	79	66	6%	110	7%	63%	27	33%	26%	3.10	-22.7	22	49	$5
12	CHW	525	62	16	60	5	234	245	296	371	668	689	659	7	83	0.45	38	20	42	25	92	86	90	9%	95	7%	56%	27	41%	30%	3.50	-10.6	46	115	$8
13	CHW*	407	51	5	28	5	267	247	317	367	684	510	745	7	84	0.47	35	23	41	31	96	73	105	4%	116	6%	83%	20	40%	30%	4.08	4.2	46	115	$8
14	2 AL *	489	56	10	48	4	217	242	255	336	591	780	560	5	82	0.28	45	16	39	25	98	89	85	6%	79	4%	100%	24	46%	29%	2.83	-8.4	34	92	$4
1st Half		281	32	8	27	3	240	266	285	385	670	920	665	6	83	0.37	45	19	35	27	108	105	102	10%	81	4%	100%	11	55%	0%	3.73	2.8	53	143	$8
2nd Half		208	24	2	21	1	188	210	221	269	490	630	437	3	81	0.18	45	12	44	22	86	68	65	3%	84	3%	100%	13	38%	54%	1.83	-10.4	11	30	-$2
15	Proj	297	35	6	28	3	230	242	280	345	625	660	613	6	82	0.33	41	18	41	26	94	87	87	6%	93	6%	77%				3.12	-2.5	32	84	$2

Belt,Brandon

Age: 27 Bats: L Pos: 1B | Ht: 6' 5" Wt: 220

Health: D | PT/Exp: C | Consist: C | LIMA Plan: B+ | Rand Var: 0 | MM: 4225

Began 2014 where he left 2013, selling out patience for HR and making it work. Broken thumb shelved him for 8 weeks in mid-May before concussion wrecked his 2H. Clean health is key, but with trending hr/f, the recent power gains are hopeful. His contact and BA/xBA outlooks are sketchier, but still... UP: 30 HR.

Yr	Tm	AB	R	HR	RBI	SB	BA	xBA	OBP	SLG	OPS	vL	vR	bb%	ct%	Eye	G	L	F	h%	HctX	PX	xPX	hr/f	Spd	SBO	SB%	#Wk	DOM	DIS	RC/G	RAR	BPV	BPX	R$
10	a/a	223	30	10	40	3	288		367	536	904			11	76	0.53				34		165			124	7%	75%				7.03		99	215	$9
11	SF *	352	42	14	39	6	236	220	325	405	730	934	648	12	68	0.42	42	14	44	31	87	130	111	16%	102	12%	46%	15	47%	47%	4.16	-22.6	33	73	$7
12	SF	411	47	7	56	12	275	247	360	421	781	768	786	12	74	0.51	38	26	37	36	95	107	112	6%	110	11%	86%	27	41%	37%	5.42	-0.1	41	103	$13
13	SF	509	76	17	67	5	289	266	360	481	841	755	867	9	75	0.42	34	24	41	35	115	143	130	11%	105	5%	71%	27	59%	22%	6.09	21.5	68	170	$21
14	SF	214	30	12	27	3	243	244	306	449	755	715	772	8	70	0.28	38	18	44	29	90	152	119	18%	109	8%	75%	14	71%	21%	4.54	2.3	52	141	$6
1st Half		129	18	9	18	3	264	262	317	504	820	821	821	6	71	0.21	41	19	41	30	97	171	98	24%	115	10%	100%	7	86%	14%	5.48	4.9	67	181	$10
2nd Half		85	12	3	9	0	212	216	292	365	656	471	710	11	69	0.38	34	17	49	27	80	123	150	10%	100	5%	0%	7	57%	29%	3.30	-2.3	29	78	$0
15	Proj	493	78	23	73	3	256	257	331	462	793	745	811	10	72	0.39	37	20	43	31	95	156	125	15%	107	5%	52%				5.10	13.6	59	156	$18

Beltran,Carlos

Age: 38 Bats: B Pos: DH RF | Ht: 6' 1" Wt: 210

Health: C | PT/Exp: B | Consist: C | LIMA Plan: B+ | Rand Var: +4 | MM: 4235

4-year decline vs. LHP accelerated. HctX, h% may have been affected by concussion and elbow issues dogging him all season. Elbow surgery will help, but health risk is scary at his age. Through it all, his plate skills and power have held up well. If his body doesn't betray him, a last hurrah looks very doable. Do you feel lucky?

Yr	Tm	AB	R	HR	RBI	SB	BA	xBA	OBP	SLG	OPS	vL	vR	bb%	ct%	Eye	G	L	F	h%	HctX	PX	xPX	hr/f	Spd	SBO	SB%	#Wk	DOM	DIS	RC/G	RAR	BPV	BPX	R$
10	NYM	220	21	7	27	3	255	271	341	427	768	1009	701	12	82	0.77	42	19	39	28	132	109	131	10%	101	6%	75%	12	58%	8%	5.03	-5.2	73	159	$4
11	2 NL	520	78	22	84	4	300	298	385	525	910	923	903	12	83	0.81	40	21	39	33	154	147	147	13%	98	4%	67%	26	73%	12%	7.30	21.0	105	233	$24
12	STL	547	83	32	97	13	269	274	346	495	842	867	832	11	77	0.52	42	20	38	29	115	142	124	20%	75	12%	68%	27	56%	22%	5.88	15.8	69	173	$25
13	STL	554	79	24	84	2	296	282	339	491	830	729	871	6	84	0.42	35	24	41	32	129	122	127	13%	94	2%	67%	27	63%	11%	6.05	23.7	76	190	$25
14	NYY	403	46	15	49	3	233	258	301	402	703	564	777	8	80	0.46	44	16	39	26	105	120	101	12%	76	4%	75%	23	43%	35%	3.98	-0.8	58	157	$8
1st Half		210	21	8	24	1	219	266	274	410	683	584	746	7	82	0.42	41	15	44	23	114	137	121	10%	70	3%	100%	12	50%	42%	3.69	-2.3	74	200	$5
2nd Half		193	25	7	25	2	249	247	329	394	723	536	806	10	78	0.50	48	18	34	28	95	100	79	13%	86	5%	67%	11	36%	27%	4.28	1.3	40	108	$11
15	Proj	447	58	19	63	4	260	271	327	445	771	670	816	9	81	0.50	42	19	39	29	115	127	112	13%	83	5%	70%				4.97	11.9	63	166	$16

Beltre,Adrian

Age: 36 Bats: R Pos: 3B | Ht: 5' 11" Wt: 220

Health: B | PT/Exp: A | Consist: A | LIMA Plan: B+ | Rand Var: -4 | MM: 3155

Power may be inching downward with age, but only if you're looking closely. Near rock-solid plate skills have never been better, while consistency keeps him at the top of H2H 3B wish-lists. If others are too preoccupied with age and counting stat declines, it's an opportunity to acquire elite production at a scarce position.

Yr	Tm	AB	R	HR	RBI	SB	BA	xBA	OBP	SLG	OPS	vL	vR	bb%	ct%	Eye	G	L	F	h%	HctX	PX	xPX	hr/f	Spd	SBO	SB%	#Wk	DOM	DIS	RC/G	RAR	BPV	BPX	R$
10	BOS	589	84	28	102	2	321	312	365	553	919	943	908	6	86	0.49	40	19	40	34	141	148	137	13%	65	2%	67%	26	73%	4%	7.54	42.9	97	211	$31
11	TEX	487	82	32	105	1	296	315	331	561	892	1075	836	5	89	0.47	38	18	44	28	156	156	160	16%	63	2%	50%	22	73%	5%	6.65	24.9	112	249	$27
12	TEX	604	95	36	102	1	321	299	359	561	921	737	985	6	86	0.44	39	21	40	33	135	136	139	17%	79	1%	100%	27	74%	7%	7.59	48.9	92	230	$33
13	TEX	631	88	30	92	1	315	287	371	509	880	948	857	7	88	0.64	38	22	40	32	129	115	127	14%	65	1%	100%	27	63%	7%	6.94	50.6	79	198	$32
14	TEX	549	79	19	77	1	324	286	388	492	879	984	845	9	87	0.77	42	22	36	35	125	111	122	11%	85	1%	50%	26	73%	12%	7.16	50.9	81	219	$28
1st Half		259	41	9	42	1	332	290	378	506	884	907	877	7	86	0.57	42	22	36	36	125	118	117	11%	76	3%	50%	13	77%	8%	7.26	24.3	80	216	$28
2nd Half		290	38	10	35	0	317	283	396	479	875	1043	815	11	87	0.95	42	23	35	34	124	105	126	11%	92	0%	0%	13	69%	15%	7.06	26.2	82	222	$29
15	Proj	567	82	22	85	1	311	288	367	487	854	909	836	8	87	0.66	41	22	37	33	130	116	129	12%	78	1%	64%				6.58	44.2	71	187	$28

Bethancourt,Christian

Age: 23 Bats: R Pos: CA | Ht: 6' 2" Wt: 205

Health: A | PT/Exp: D | Consist: C | LIMA Plan: D+ | Rand Var: -2 | MM: 1203

0-9-.248 in 113 AB at ATL. Defense-first catcher scuffled in first significant MLB exposure. Decent ct% kept him from being overmatched. Has time to become more selective and reduce that GB%; size, health, and athleticism all work in his favor. He's marginally profitable now at best, but it's too early to dismiss his future.

Yr	Tm	AB	R	HR	RBI	SB	BA	xBA	OBP	SLG	OPS	vL	vR	bb%	ct%	Eye	G	L	F	h%	HctX	PX	xPX	hr/f	Spd	SBO	SB%	#Wk	DOM	DIS	RC/G	RAR	BPV	BPX	R$
10																																			
11																																			
12	aa	268	26	2	23	7	227		254	270	524			3	82	0.19				27		28			103	21%	52%				2.10		-11	-28	$1
13	ATL *	359	37	10	40	10	256	260	284	397	681	0	0	4	82	0.22	44	20	36	29	0	97	-15	0%	85	23%	56%	1	0%	100%	3.62	-0.8	41	103	$10
14	ATL *	456	31	6	44	6	243	222	263	323	586	889	465	3	79	0.13	54	15	31	30	86	62	54	0%	88	8%	74%	8	0%	75%	2.86	-8.1	0	0	$6
1st Half		238	14	2	24	3	234	227	259	311	570	2000	452	3	81	0.18	50	17	33	28	59	60	27	0%	99	6%	100%	2	0%	100%	2.74	-4.7	11	30	$3
2nd Half		218	17	4	21	3	253	215	268	336	604	838	465	2	76	0.09	54	15	31	32	86	65	56	0%	87	11%	60%	6	0%	67%	2.99	-2.6	-11	-30	$8
15	Proj	407	35	5	41	8	247	227	270	327	596	965	504	3	80	0.16	54	15	31	30	77	63	50	5%	88	15%	59%				2.88	-6.3	-1	-3	$8

Betts,Mookie

Age: 22 Bats: R Pos: CF | Ht: 5' 9" Wt: 155

Health: A | PT/Exp: F | Consist: F | LIMA Plan: B+ | Rand Var: -3 | MM: 3545

5-18-.291 with 7 SB in 189 AB at BOS. Dominating every level, precocious 21-y/o fast-tracked to unexpected MLB debut. Eye-popping .346/.431/.529 and 33 SB over just 399 AA-AAA AB forced Red Sox' hand. Solid across-the-board skills held up just fine vs. MLB pitchers. Position is his only question; offers All-Star ceiling at 2B.

Yr	Tm	AB	R	HR	RBI	SB	BA	xBA	OBP	SLG	OPS	vL	vR	bb%	ct%	Eye	G	L	F	h%	HctX	PX	xPX	hr/f	Spd	SBO	SB%	#Wk	DOM	DIS	RC/G	RAR	BPV	BPX	R$
10																																			
11																																			
12																																			
13																																			
14	BOS *	588	106	14	72	34	317	281	390	480	870	843	798	11	86	0.83	41	21	39	35	133	114	117	8%	137	23%	76%	12	67%	8%	6.97	49.6	98	265	$40
1st Half		310	59	6	40	24	326	291	407	481	888	500	400	12	89	1.20	50	17	33	35	128	105	27	0%	131	27%	79%	1	100%	0%	7.47	29.3	104	281	$45
2nd Half		278	47	7	32	10	308	277	371	478	849	847	813	9	82	0.57	40	21	39	35	128	124	120	8%	131	17%	71%	11	64%	9%	6.43	18.7	88	238	$35
15	Proj	440	75	11	50	23	286	280	365	452	817	851	800	10	85	0.75	40	21	39	32	115	117	108	8%	138	24%	76%				5.79	24.2	94	247	$24

Blackmon,Charlie

Age: 29 Bats: L Pos: RF CF LF | Ht: 6' 3" Wt: 210

Health: D | PT/Exp: C | Consist: B | LIMA Plan: B+ | Rand Var: -2 | MM: 3435

That 1H ct% surge and top-of-the-lineup opportunity (.331/.391/.524 in Coors) were critical to probable career year. PRO: HctX trend hints at high BA floor; ditto SBs with continued SB% cooperation; OF versatility. CON: Mediocre plate skills, PX/xPX history, age. Unlikely to repeat. DOWN: 10-45-.260, 15 SB.

Yr	Tm	AB	R	HR	RBI	SB	BA	xBA	OBP	SLG	OPS	vL	vR	bb%	ct%	Eye	G	L	F	h%	HctX	PX	xPX	hr/f	Spd	SBO	SB%	#Wk	DOM	DIS	RC/G	RAR	BPV	BPX	R$
10	aa	337	40	9	42	15	273		320	441	761			7	87	0.52				29		106			112	27%	65%				4.71		80	174	$13
11	COL *	341	34	7	33	11	260	256	286	380	666	905	484	4	86	0.27	47	16	37	28	72	79	53	3%	103	24%	61%	5	20%	20%	3.54	-12.6	48	107	$8
12	COL *	341	47	6	29	7	260	266	302	392	694	853	701	6	81	0.32	49	21	30	31	88	93	86	7%	111	11%	77%	8	63%	25%	4.09	-5.9	46	115	$7
13	COL *	503	66	8	44	11	266	268	302	395	697	752	824	5	81	0.27	42	27	31	32	90	90	67	10%	135	15%	64%	16	38%	25%	4.04	-0.8	48	120	$14
14	COL	593	82	19	72	28	288	269	335	440	775	697	801	5	84	0.32	41	22	37	32	103	100	94	10%	101	25%	74%	27	52%	19%	5.02	20.1	58	157	$32
1st Half		311	47	12	46	15	296	283	339	466	806	734	832	5	87	0.46	45	19	36	31	98	107	93	12%	89	23%	79%	14	50%	7%	5.65	15.6	75	203	$37
2nd Half		282	35	7	26	13	280	253	330	411	741	648	769	4	80	0.23	37	25	38	33	109	92	96	8%	118	27%	68%	13	54%	31%	4.38	4.3	39	105	$27
15	Proj	566	75	14	58	20	270	269	316	413	729	718	733	5	82	0.29	42	23	35	31	95	100	82	9%	112	22%	70%				4.30	5.0	57	149	$23

JOCK THOMPSON

Blanco,Gregor

Age: 31 Bats: L Pos: CF LF	Health A	LIMA Plan D+	
Ht: 5' 11" Wt: 175	PT/Exp B	Rand Var -2	
	Consist A	MM 1513	

2H surge fueled by PX and HctX spikes at odds with a soft history—and that at his age, aren't likely sustainable longer term. Spd offers value, but only while volatile SB% hovers near acceptability. We'd be a tad more impressed by a GB% spike that might exploit his legs and put some lift into BA/xBA. But that didn't happen.

Yr Tm	AB	R	HR	RBI	SB	BA	xBA	OBP	SLG	OPS	vL	vR	bb%	ct%	Eye	G	L	F	h%	HctX	PX	xPX	hr/f	Spd	SBO	SB%	#Wk	DOM	DIS	RC/G	RAR	BPV	BPX	R$
10 2TM *	391	50	2	22	18	262	246	340	336	676	448	813	11	78	0.55	54	20	26	33	84	55	66	2%	146	18%	77%	19	37%	37%	4.02	-14.3	24	52	$10
11 aaa	199	29	2	10	17	159		268	254	522			13	70	0.50				22		81			117	40%	87%				2.32		8	18	$0
12 SF	393	56	5	34	26	244	227	333	344	676	694	667	11	74	0.49	44	24	32	32	73	69	73	6%	145	26%	81%	27	19%	59%	3.99	-8.7	18	45	$12
13 SF	452	50	3	41	14	265	250	341	350	690	650	696	10	79	0.55	44	28	28	33	87	60	69	3%	158	16%	61%	27	22%	30%	4.01	-0.6	34	85	$12
14 SF	393	51	5	38	16	260	241	333	374	707	730	697	9	80	0.53	40	21	39	31	93	81	93	4%	139	18%	76%	27	37%	37%	4.27	5.6	49	132	$13
1st Half	157	14	0	15	8	236	209	310	299	610	617	607	9	80	0.48	38	20	41	29	80	44	65	0%	144	24%	73%	14	29%	43%	3.04	-3.4	19	51	$2
2nd Half	236	37	5	23	8	275	263	348	424	772	777	770	10	81	0.57	41	22	37	32	101	106	112	7%	129	14%	80%	13	46%	31%	5.23	10.1	67	181	$20
15 Proj	270	34	3	24	12	254	242	333	355	688	675	693	10	78	0.53	43	23	34	31	87	75	81	4%	138	20%	75%				4.04	1.4	34	90	$7

Blanks,Kyle

Age: 28 Bats: R Pos: 1B	Health F	LIMA Plan D	
Ht: 6' 6" Wt: 265	PT/Exp F	Rand Var -2	
	Consist C	MM 4203	

2-7-.309 in 55 AB at SD and OAK. Has his own "3 true outcomes": 1) plus power-and-patience; 2) sub-standard contact-and-BA; and 3) DL time. Calf muscle tear made it 4 of 5 years with 80+ DL days, following a strained achilles, labrum tear and TJS. Window is closing because cheaper, younger talent won't wait.

Yr Tm	AB	R	HR	RBI	SB	BA	xBA	OBP	SLG	OPS	vL	vR	bb%	ct%	Eye	G	L	F	h%	HctX	PX	xPX	hr/f	Spd	SBO	SB%	#Wk	DOM	DIS	RC/G	RAR	BPV	BPX	R$
10 SD	102	14	3	15	1	157	202	283	324	607	865	526	13	55	0.33	41	14	45	25	72	165	93	12%	106	5%	100%	7	29%	57%	2.64	-10.0	11	24	-$2
11 SD *	481	65	16	65	4	231	229	288	404	692	528	789	7	69	0.25	40	16	45	30	109	137	115	13%	99	5%	76%	11	36%	45%	3.85	-34.9	30	67	$9
12 SD	5	0	0	0	0	200	25	333	200	533	833	0	17	60	0.50	33	0	67	33	0	0	-11	0%	94	0%	0%	2	0%	100%	2.13	-0.4	-95	-238	-$2
13 SD *	318	36	9	37	1	234	231	289	366	655	829	596	7	69	0.25	46	22	32	31	93	107	115	13%	86	3%	50%	18	22%	67%	3.49	-10.4	5	13	$3
14 2TM *	159	22	8	21	0	247	240	324	425	749	889	793	10	68	0.35	53	20	28	32	96	137	104	18%	96	0%	0%	8	25%	50%	4.67	2.5	33	89	$3
1st Half	138	19	7	19	0	237	243	308	429	736	889	793	9	66	0.30	53	20	28	30	93	153	104	18%	96	0%	0%	8	25%	50%	4.41	1.0	37	100	$4
2nd Half	21	3	1	2	0	322	213	427	404	832			16	81	0.97				38	0	47			87	0%	0%				6.49		21	57	-$5
15 Proj	243	32	8	33	1	235	229	312	398	711	743	691	9	66	0.28	45	18	37	32	95	139	108	14%	97	3%	79%				4.00	-1.2	15	39	$6

Boesch,Brennan

Age: 30 Bats: L Pos: DH	Health A	LIMA Plan D	
Ht: 6' 4" Wt: 235	PT/Exp D	Rand Var +1	
	Consist B	MM 4211	

2-7-.187 in 75 AB at LAA. PX history, FB% spike and 25 Triple-A HR underscore the power potential, though xPX and hr/f plunge are skeptical. Declining plate skills and susceptibility to breaking stuff during MLB stint don't help his case. Handedness guarantees him minor league AB, and perhaps more MLB chances. But has a lot to prove.

Yr Tm	AB	R	HR	RBI	SB	BA	xBA	OBP	SLG	OPS	vL	vR	bb%	ct%	Eye	G	L	F	h%	HctX	PX	xPX	hr/f	Spd	SBO	SB%	#Wk	DOM	DIS	RC/G	RAR	BPV	BPX	R$
10 DET *	522	54	16	80	9	265	254	321	428	748	951	673	8	77	0.36	45	15	40	31	101	114	97	10%	96	8%	80%	25	40%	36%	4.77	-6.0	47	102	$15
11 DET	428	75	16	54	5	283	266	341	458	799	752	814	8	81	0.42	43	18	39	32	119	119	110	12%	101	7%	63%	23	48%	30%	5.40	2.8	65	144	$17
12 DET	470	52	12	54	6	240	239	286	372	659	625	671	5	78	0.25	50	16	34	29	89	89	92	10%	85	9%	67%	27	26%	41%	3.46	-19.6	21	53	$8
13 NYY *	81	11	3	10	0	233	248	298	413	712	641	890	8	77	0.40	52	12	36	27	68	120	57	20%	110	0%	0%	9	67%	22%	4.10	-0.3	55	138	-$1
14 LAA *	449	43	15	53	8	220	213	249	377	626	1833	437	4	70	0.13	43	10	47	28	73	121	67	7%	104	18%	61%	9	22%	56%	2.96	-13.0	16	43	$7
1st Half	209	20	6	24	3	235	209	263	394	656	0	583	4	66	0.11	45	9	45	33	52	132	8	0%	109	12%	70%	2	50%	50%	3.40	-3.8	10	27	$5
2nd Half	240	23	9	29	5	208	217	237	362	599	2667	408	4	73	0.14	43	11	47	25	81	113	81	9%	91	23%	57%	7	14%	57%	2.61	-10.6	20	54	$10
15 Proj	199	22	7	24	3	238	239	278	400	679	823	646	5	74	0.21	47	14	40	29	88	121	85	12%	91	12%	64%				3.65	-2.4	31	81	$5

Bogaerts,Xander

Age: 22 Bats: R Pos: SS 3B	Health A	LIMA Plan B+	
Ht: 6' 1" Wt: 210	PT/Exp C	Rand Var +1	
	Consist D	MM 3215	

With just 536 AB in the high minors, highly-regarded 21-y/o scuffled in his rookie season. Wasn't completely overmatched, as you can tell from playing time and counting stats. But his patience crumbled in 2H—and a reversal is necessary to unlock power potential. He'll improve, but it all won't happen overnight. Baby steps.

Yr Tm	AB	R	HR	RBI	SB	BA	xBA	OBP	SLG	OPS	vL	vR	bb%	ct%	Eye	G	L	F	h%	HctX	PX	xPX	hr/f	Spd	SBO	SB%	#Wk	DOM	DIS	RC/G	RAR	BPV	BPX	R$
10																																		
11																																		
12 aa	92	10	4	15	1	326		332	581	913			1	77	0.04				39		187			80	12%	46%				7.00		84	210	$3
13 BOS *	488	64	12	58	7	277	291	349	427	777	1089	463	10	77	0.48	47	34	19	34	138	107	87	17%	114	7%	67%	7	43%	57%	5.22	25.0	48	120	$16
14 BOS	538	60	12	46	2	240	230	297	362	660	755	621	7	74	0.28	38	21	41	30	110	98	111	7%	97	4%	40%	26	38%	46%	3.47	4.7	21	57	$7
1st Half	290	36	6	19	2	248	231	328	376	704	772	673	9	74	0.37	36	21	43	32	122	105	120	7%	111	5%	50%	14	43%	43%	3.93	6.0	32	86	$8
2nd Half	248	24	6	27	0	230	227	259	347	606	729	562	4	75	0.18	40	20	40	28	97	91	100	8%	85	2%	0%	12	33%	50%	2.95	-2.1	9	24	$6
15 Proj	576	68	17	60	4	253	244	320	401	722	828	680	9	76	0.39	39	21	41	31	107	112	108	9%	106	5%	57%				4.29	17.9	33	86	$15

Bonifacio,Emilio

Age: 30 Bats: B Pos: CF 2B	Health D	LIMA Plan C	
Ht: 5' 11" Wt: 205	PT/Exp C	Rand Var 0	
	Consist B	MM 1513	

Classic profile of a zero-power, soft-contact player with mediocre plate skills—yet who remains valuable in this era of offensive decline due to established running game and defensive versatility. And by most reports, his glove has suddenly improved across the board, mitigating that Spd decline for now. Expect more of the same.

Yr Tm	AB	R	HR	RBI	SB	BA	xBA	OBP	SLG	OPS	vL	vR	bb%	ct%	Eye	G	L	F	h%	HctX	PX	xPX	hr/f	Spd	SBO	SB%	#Wk	DOM	DIS	RC/G	RAR	BPV	BPX	R$
10 FLA *	344	43	0	18	18	244	239	303	310	613	827	586	8	76	0.35	52	22	26	32	77	51	52	0%	164	23%	79%	20	25%	55%	3.25	-15.2	10	22	$6
11 FLA	565	78	5	36	40	296	259	360	393	753	863	714	9	77	0.46	53	24	23	38	73	73	53	5%	146	27%	78%	27	22%	33%	5.24	8.4	32	71	$26
12 MIA	244	30	1	11	30	258	225	330	316	645	503	714	9	79	0.48	58	17	26	32	86	33	56	2%	176	41%	91%	12	17%	58%	4.09	-1.7	14	35	$11
13 2AL	420	54	3	31	28	243	241	295	331	625	563	651	7	75	0.29	53	20	27	32	79	72	44	4%	128	35%	78%	26	19%	46%	3.33	-4.2	13	33	$14
14 2NL	394	47	3	24	26	259	250	305	345	650	959	539	6	78	0.31	53	22	26	32	72	67	46	4%	127	33%	76%	22	27%	36%	3.65	3.0	20	54	$14
1st Half	241	29	1	16	13	261	266	307	340	648	893	570	6	83	0.38	56	23	22	31	70	58	36	2%	127	29%	68%	11	18%	36%	3.51	0.8	29	78	$15
2nd Half	153	18	2	8	13	255	224	301	353	654	1040	484	6	72	0.23	48	19	33	34	75	82	65	6%	111	38%	87%	11	36%	36%	3.88	2.2	1	3	$13
15 Proj	391	48	3	23	28	250	240	302	335	637	772	583	7	76	0.32	53	20	27	32	77	67	51	4%	133	34%	81%				3.56	-3.5	19	49	$15

Bour,Justin

Age: 27 Bats: L Pos: 1B	Health A	LIMA Plan D	
Ht: 6' 4" Wt: 250	PT/Exp C	Rand Var 0	
	Consist B	MM 2001	

1-11-.284 in 74 AB at MIA. Minor league journeyman or late-bloomer? Small sample HctX is optimistic, and xPX likes his power upside. But while minor league splits don't scream "PCL creation!", plate skills and GB% need work. He'll have to move quickly, but he's another hitter that age, size and handedness keep watchable.

Yr Tm	AB	R	HR	RBI	SB	BA	xBA	OBP	SLG	OPS	vL	vR	bb%	ct%	Eye	G	L	F	h%	HctX	PX	xPX	hr/f	Spd	SBO	SB%	#Wk	DOM	DIS	RC/G	RAR	BPV	BPX	R$
10																																		
11																																		
12 aa	506	50	13	86	3	245		313	387	700			9	74	0.38				31		106			70	3%	73%				4.09		21	53	$10
13 aa	317	36	14	47	0	200		263	374	638			8	77	0.38				22		119			78	4%	0%				3.03		45	113	$2
14 MIA *	459	48	11	58	2	246	249	299	371	671	600	734	7	81	0.39	53	16	31	28	127	93	126	6%	70	3%	61%	12	33%	58%	3.74	-6.0	35	95	$9
1st Half	242	28	6	32	1	256	265	317	402	719	0	817	8	83	0.52	54	15	31	29	138	109	139	0%	76	4%	51%	5	40%	60%	4.30	1.0	60	162	$10
2nd Half	217	21	5	26	1	236	226	280	337	617	1000	704	6	78	0.28	52	17	31	28	121	74	122	8%	71	1%	100%	7	29%	57%	3.16	-6.5	7	19	$7
15 Proj	162	17	3	23	1	228	232	286	329	616	1008	593	8	78	0.37	52	17	31	28	109	82	110	7%	70	3%	48%				3.08	-5.3	7	19	$2

Bourjos,Peter

Age: 28 Bats: R Pos: CF	Health D	LIMA Plan D+	
Ht: 6' 1" Wt: 185	PT/Exp F	Rand Var 0	
	Consist A	MM 2513	

His legs can still help out-hit an xBA, as he did in the 2H. And recent SB% history still hints at a value spike with full-time AB. But despite warp speed and a great glove, sub-par patience, inconsistent ct%, and problems vs. RHP make him a part-timer until further notice.

Yr Tm	AB	R	HR	RBI	SB	BA	xBA	OBP	SLG	OPS	vL	vR	bb%	ct%	Eye	G	L	F	h%	HctX	PX	xPX	hr/f	Spd	SBO	SB%	#Wk	DOM	DIS	RC/G	RAR	BPV	BPX	R$
10 LAA *	595	77	15	50	29	242	237	269	382	651	480	679	4	78	0.17	51	10	39	29	79	86	96	12%	195	30%	77%	10	60%	20%	3.43	-24.3	50	109	$17
11 LAA	502	72	12	43	22	271	252	327	438	765	840	725	6	75	0.26	47	17	36	34	87	117	88	9%	192	26%	71%	26	38%	27%	4.70	-1.2	66	147	$18
12 LAA *	197	30	3	21	3	223	214	285	325	610	606	607	8	74	0.33	52	13	35	29	58	73	64	7%	138	8%	75%	25	8%	64%	3.04	-9.8	13	33	$1
13 LAA *	223	34	4	16	6	247	222	287	356	643	608	740	5	70	0.19	59	14	27	33	78	77	65	9%	184	11%	100%	12	17%	50%	3.60	-3.2	10	25	$4
14 STL	264	32	4	24	9	231	234	294	348	643	582	680	7	70	0.26	53	20	27	31	89	89	81	9%	185	19%	75%	27	30%	56%	3.30	-4.2	25	68	$5
1st Half	162	16	2	11	5	204	228	270	309	578	473	656	7	68	0.25	51	24	25	29	95	82	72	8%	171	19%	71%	14	21%	71%	2.58	-6.6	5	14	$2
2nd Half	102	16	2	13	4	275	245	333	412	745	809	715	6	75	0.27	56	15	29	35	81	98	92	9%	169	19%	80%	13	38%	38%	4.69	2.4	42	114	$8
15 Proj	302	43	6	28	10	244	235	303	367	670	632	689	6	72	0.24	54	16	30	32	80	92	77	9%	182	16%	80%				3.64	-2.1	21	55	$9

JOCK THOMPSON

Bourn,Michael

Age: 32 Bats: L Pos: CF | Ht: 5' 10" Wt: 180

Health C | PT/Exp A | Consist B | LIMA Plan B | Rand Var +1 | MM 1515

3-28-.257 with 10 SB in 444 AB at CLE. Cleared after Oct 2013 hamstring surgery, but trouble arose in March and followed him the entire season. Declining ct%, xBA and SB% aren't good signs, though if legs are healthy, there's some rebound potential. But a solemn reminder of how speed players need their wheels.

Yr	Tm	AB	R	HR	RBI	SB	BA	xBA	OBP	SLG	OPS	vL	vR	bb%	ct%	Eye	G	L	F	h%	HctX	PX	xPX	hr/f	Spd	SBO	SB%	#Wk	DOM	DIS	RC/G	RAR	BPV	BPX	R$
10	HOU	535	84	2	38	52	265	260	341	346	686	555	723	10	80	0.54	59	17	23	33	78	61	54	2%	142	38%	81%	25	28%	44%	4.28	-12.8	32	70	$25
11	2 NL	656	94	2	50	61	294	265	349	386	734	645	772	7	79	0.38	51	27	23	37	77	70	56	2%	147	38%	81%	27	33%	44%	5.01	-1.3	32	71	$35
12	ATL	624	96	9	57	42	274	251	348	391	739	728	745	10	75	0.45	54	22	25	35	100	80	86	8%	146	28%	76%	26	38%	42%	4.80	-1.0	31	78	$28
13	CLE	525	75	6	50	23	263	243	316	360	676	655	685	7	75	0.30	57	20	24	34	71	72	61	7%	154	24%	66%	25	28%	56%	3.79	-7.0	19	48	$19
14	CLE *	487	58	3	29	11	242	239	294	338	632	569	724	7	73	0.28	50	24	25	32	69	73	71	4%	157	14%	64%	19	26%	63%	3.27	-9.0	14	38	$7
1st Half		292	35	2	20	8	261	249	307	357	664	510	764	6	76	0.27	52	26	23	34	69	66	62	4%	164	14%	72%	12	33%	58%	3.76	-0.9	18	49	$12
2nd Half		195	23	1	9	3	213	224	276	309	585	635	650	8	70	0.29	48	22	30	30	70	84	86	3%	131	13%	50%	7	14%	71%	2.64	-7.5	3	8	$0
15	**Proj**	**542**	**72**	**5**	**39**	**22**	**250**	**243**	**311**	**351**	**662**	**612**	**686**	**8**	**74**	**0.32**	**52**	**22**	**26**	**33**	**75**	**79**	**72**	**5%**	**149**	**22%**	**70%**				**3.62**	**-4.0**	**18**	**48**	**$13**

Bradley,Jackie

Age: 25 Bats: L Pos: CF | Ht: 5' 10" Wt: 195

Health A | PT/Exp D | Consist C | LIMA Plan D | Rand Var +1 | MM 3311

1-30-.198 with 8 SB in 384 AB at BOS. Fell out of favor quickly (remember spring 2013?). A slow start spiraled into a swing-at-anything 2nd half, zero power (try slugging .262!) and a Sept tiff with management. Still young, his current HctX, speed game, and pre-2014 plate skills provide a foundation. But needs to secure AB.

Yr	Tm	AB	R	HR	RBI	SB	BA	xBA	OBP	SLG	OPS	vL	vR	bb%	ct%	Eye	G	L	F	h%	HctX	PX	xPX	hr/f	Spd	SBO	SB%	#Wk	DOM	DIS	RC/G	RAR	BPV	BPX	R$
10																																			
11																																			
12	aa	229	31	5	24	7	262		346	414	760			11	77	0.56				32		110			97	15%	68%				4.86		52	130	$5
13	BOS *	415	62	10	37	7	239	268	307	401	708	327	722	9	73	0.36	63	16	22	30	94	130	79	21%	108	16%	49%	11	36%	45%	3.90	-4.2	48	120	$8
14	BOS *	450	50	2	34	8	197	197	252	262	514	640	473	7	69	0.24	46	18	36	28	104	64	119	1%	89	9%	88%	25	16%	64%	2.14	-24.8	-30	-81	-$1
1st Half		241	32	1	24	5	207	209	289	295	583	650	539	9	68	0.31	48	17	35	30	99	85	106	2%	91	9%	100%	14	21%	57%	2.75	-8.3	-12	-32	$3
2nd Half		209	18	1	10	3	184	182	219	224	443	614	378	4	69	0.15	43	19	37	26	111	40	142	0%	90	10%	73%	11	9%	73%	1.54	-15.6	-53	-143	-$5
15	**Proj**	**181**	**23**	**4**	**15**	**4**	**230**	**238**	**299**	**356**	**655**	**617**	**671**	**8**	**71**	**0.30**	**52**	**17**	**30**	**30**	**101**	**107**	**108**	**9%**	**95**	**15%**	**71%**				**3.39**	**-2.6**	**18**	**48**	**$4**

Brantley,Michael

Age: 28 Bats: L Pos: LF CF | Ht: 6' 2" Wt: 200

Health A | PT/Exp A | Consist C | LIMA Plan C | Rand Var -2 | MM 3355

We knew about the elite contact and double-digit SBs. But now power joined the party and the results were a 2nd-tier MVP candidate. How? More LDs; hit everything hard, and more FBs reached the seats. Will regress some, but age and broad base of skills (hit tool, speed, power) should prevent a total collapse.

Yr	Tm	AB	R	HR	RBI	SB	BA	xBA	OBP	SLG	OPS	vL	vR	bb%	ct%	Eye	G	L	F	h%	HctX	PX	xPX	hr/f	Spd	SBO	SB%	#Wk	DOM	DIS	RC/G	RAR	BPV	BPX	R$
10	CLE *	570	79	6	44	20	260	263	318	342	659	467	665	8	88	0.69	48	20	32	29	99	53	57	4%	114	17%	72%	17	41%	29%	3.73	-20.1	45	98	$15
11	CLE	451	63	7	46	13	266	264	318	384	702	525	782	7	83	0.45	49	20	31	31	111	82	82	6%	111	15%	72%	22	45%	9%	4.20	-9.5	48	107	$13
12	CLE	552	63	6	60	12	288	286	348	402	750	680	785	9	90	0.95	49	23	29	31	100	75	76	4%	108	13%	57%	27	63%	0%	4.87	4.7	71	178	$17
13	CLE	556	66	10	73	17	284	277	332	396	728	664	757	7	88	0.60	47	23	30	31	91	72	76	7%	108	13%	81%	27	56%	19%	4.74	11.9	57	143	$23
14	CLE	611	94	20	97	23	327	324	385	506	890	826	923	8	91	0.93	46	26	28	34	133	116	105	13%	94	13%	96%	26	85%	4%	7.54	62.1	102	276	$42
1st Half		299	54	12	53	9	314	329	382	505	887	839	909	9	90	0.93	47	27	26	32	131	120	114	17%	88	10%	100%	14	79%	0%	7.24	28.1	101	273	$39
2nd Half		312	40	8	44	14	340	319	387	506	894	815	937	7	92	0.92	46	24	30	35	135	113	97	9%	103	16%	93%	12	92%	8%	7.84	33.2	104	281	$44
15	**Proj**	**601**	**81**	**16**	**82**	**20**	**305**	**304**	**360**	**457**	**817**	**745**	**852**	**8**	**90**	**0.79**	**47**	**24**	**29**	**32**	**115**	**101**	**89**	**10%**	**100**	**14%**	**84%**				**6.10**	**39.0**	**87**	**229**	**$33**

Braun,Ryan

Age: 31 Bats: R Pos: RF | Ht: 6' 2" Wt: 200

Health B | PT/Exp B | Consist D | LIMA Plan C | Rand Var +3 | MM 4345

Finally succumbed to thumb surgery in Oct after two years of having trouble gripping the bat. Is that, and not PEDs, the main reason for the sharp decline? Plate skills, HctX and PX have all slipped but are good enough to rebound, and his Spd his holding up. With health, it might be the season to buy low.

Yr	Tm	AB	R	HR	RBI	SB	BA	xBA	OBP	SLG	OPS	vL	vR	bb%	ct%	Eye	G	L	F	h%	HctX	PX	xPX	hr/f	Spd	SBO	SB%	#Wk	DOM	DIS	RC/G	RAR	BPV	BPX	R$
10	MIL	619	101	25	103	14	304	295	365	501	866	786	893	8	83	0.53	48	17	35	33	117	131	112	14%	108	10%	82%	27	67%	4%	6.66	25.8	88	191	$32
11	MIL	563	109	33	111	33	332	314	397	597	994	1049	979	9	83	0.62	42	21	37	35	154	165	154	19%	122	23%	85%	26	81%	4%	9.10	59.2	123	273	$47
12	MIL	598	108	41	112	30	319	296	391	595	987	1209	915	10	79	0.49	44	18	38	35	127	170	153	23%	113	21%	81%	27	74%	11%	8.57	55.6	105	263	$45
13	MIL	225	30	9	38	4	298	268	372	498	869	1053	777	11	75	0.48	52	16	32	36	120	142	150	16%	126	13%	44%	14	43%	14%	6.31	10.8	75	188	$10
14	MIL	530	68	19	81	11	266	277	324	453	777	823	760	7	79	0.36	47	20	33	31	115	130	125	14%	120	13%	69%	25	56%	24%	4.94	12.9	71	192	$21
1st Half		262	44	11	46	8	290	298	341	508	849	800	870	6	80	0.35	46	23	32	33	126	147	136	16%	126	17%	73%	12	58%	25%	6.02	15.0	91	246	$28
2nd Half		268	24	8	35	3	243	253	307	399	706	853	663	8	77	0.38	49	17	34	29	104	114	113	11%	107	8%	60%	13	54%	23%	3.99	0.0	50	135	$14
15	**Proj**	**576**	**80**	**26**	**94**	**15**	**285**	**280**	**350**	**496**	**846**	**964**	**801**	**9**	**78**	**0.43**	**47**	**17**	**36**	**33**	**119**	**148**	**135**	**16%**	**120**	**14%**	**67%**				**5.98**	**32.6**	**81**	**212**	**$30**

Brown,Domonic

Age: 27 Bats: L Pos: LF | Ht: 6' 5" Wt: 230

Health A | PT/Exp B | Consist F | LIMA Plan B | Rand Var +2 | MM 3235

The Ghost of May 2013 still haunts his fantasy owners. Smacked 12 HR that month, but only a shadow of that guy since. In 2014 a ground-ball bump sapped power, speed skills sagged, and mental lapses (defense/on bases) cost him AB. Still young with tools, but tough to escape expectations.

Yr	Tm	AB	R	HR	RBI	SB	BA	xBA	OBP	SLG	OPS	vL	vR	bb%	ct%	Eye	G	L	F	h%	HctX	PX	xPX	hr/f	Spd	SBO	SB%	#Wk	DOM	DIS	RC/G	RAR	BPV	BPX	R$
10	PHI *	405	60	18	67	16	279	274	335	485	820	148	732	8	74	0.32	41	22	37	34	132	145	159	13%	103	24%	64%	9	33%	44%	5.47	2.4	60	130	$19
11	PHI *	322	46	7	31	13	238	242	336	362	698	705	729	13	77	0.66	47	18	35	29	107	90	90	9%	105	18%	70%	13	46%	31%	4.03	-12.1	41	91	$7
12	PHI *	407	48	9	49	3	243	257	303	384	687	621	746	8	80	0.42	46	21	33	28	103	95	90	10%	82	10%	32%	10	50%	30%	3.68	-12.8	37	93	$6
13	PHI	496	65	27	83	8	272	288	324	494	818	724	857	7	80	0.40	42	23	35	29	111	137	112	19%	101	9%	73%	26	50%	15%	5.58	21.8	78	195	$22
14	PHI	473	47	10	63	7	235	247	285	349	634	536	662	7	81	0.37	50	17	33	27	93	83	79	8%	78	7%	88%	27	26%	30%	3.37	-5.9	28	76	$9
1st Half		280	26	5	38	5	221	244	275	321	596	600	595	7	80	0.40	54	17	29	26	84	72	64	8%	79	9%	83%	14	14%	29%	2.97	-6.6	19	51	$9
2nd Half		193	21	5	25	2	254	249	301	389	690	445	761	6	81	0.33	44	17	38	29	108	99	101	8%	87	4%	100%	13	38%	31%	4.01	1.5	44	119	$8
15	**Proj**	**422**	**49**	**13**	**59**	**7**	**251**	**262**	**305**	**404**	**709**	**588**	**748**	**7**	**80**	**0.39**	**46**	**20**	**34**	**29**	**104**	**108**	**97**	**11%**	**86**	**9%**	**70%**				**4.16**	**5.2**	**47**	**123**	**$13**

Bruce,Jay

Age: 28 Bats: L Pos: RF | Ht: 6' 3" Wt: 215

Health A | PT/Exp A | Consist C | LIMA Plan B | Rand Var +3 | MM 4225

A May knee injury took a bite out of his AB, maybe more. A GB/FB flip and a touch of h% bad luck were the main culprits; though his 2nd half approach proved disastrous. SB spike can be dismissed due to wacky 1st half green light. Healed, his pre-2014 stability and prime age point to profit potential in power-starved context.

Yr	Tm	AB	R	HR	RBI	SB	BA	xBA	OBP	SLG	OPS	vL	vR	bb%	ct%	Eye	G	L	F	h%	HctX	PX	xPX	hr/f	Spd	SBO	SB%	#Wk	DOM	DIS	RC/G	RAR	BPV	BPX	R$
10	CIN	509	80	25	70	5	281	261	353	493	846	899	821	10	73	0.43	36	20	44	34	111	145	139	15%	133	6%	56%	26	54%	35%	6.08	13.4	71	154	$20
11	CIN	585	84	32	97	8	256	251	341	474	814	804	818	11	73	0.45	36	17	47	30	124	151	150	16%	96	9%	53%	27	52%	26%	5.30	2.5	65	144	$22
12	CIN	560	89	34	99	9	252	270	327	514	841	754	879	10	72	0.40	35	20	44	29	118	178	162	19%	95	9%	75%	27	63%	26%	5.69	9.0	82	205	$22
13	CIN	626	89	30	109	7	262	264	329	478	807	734	841	9	70	0.34	37	24	39	33	101	165	132	17%	86	7%	70%	27	52%	30%	5.40	14.3	60	150	$25
14	CIN	493	71	18	66	12	217	240	281	373	654	556	685	8	70	0.30	45	21	34	27	99	122	109	15%	92	14%	80%	26	35%	46%	3.44	-9.9	23	62	$12
1st Half		232	41	7	31	9	241	256	330	414	743	658	771	11	69	0.41	44	23	32	32	104	149	117	13%	94	16%	90%	13	54%	46%	4.72	5.0	47	127	$14
2nd Half		261	30	11	35	3	195	223	235	337	572	455	607	5	71	0.18	46	18	36	23	95	99	103	17%	93	10%	60%	13	15%	46%	2.47	-12.7	3	8	$10
15	**Proj**	**589**	**85**	**26**	**90**	**8**	**251**	**252**	**314**	**440**	**754**	**686**	**780**	**9**	**71**	**0.32**	**41**	**21**	**38**	**31**	**104**	**146**	**126**	**16%**	**92**	**8%**	**70%**				**4.67**	**11.7**	**45**	**118**	**$22**

Bryant,Kris

Age: 23 Bats: R Pos: 3B | Ht: 6' 5" Wt: 215

Health A | PT/Exp F | Consist F | LIMA Plan C+ | Rand Var 0 | MM 5303

Current poster-boy prospect with a full dose of minor-league seasoning. MLEs point to some swing-and-miss; h% was kind to BA and he wasn't quite as explosive at Triple-A (2nd half line). But plate patience, elite power are are excellent starting points. Looks ready; from here it's all about adjustments at the highest level.

Yr	Tm	AB	R	HR	RBI	SB	BA	xBA	OBP	SLG	OPS	vL	vR	bb%	ct%	Eye	G	L	F	h%	HctX	PX	xPX	hr/f	Spd	SBO	SB%	#Wk	DOM	DIS	RC/G	RAR	BPV	BPX	R$
10																																			
11																																			
12																																			
13																																			
14	a/a	492	91	34	84	12	291		377	562	939			12	64	0.38				39		228			86	11%	72%				7.54		89	241	$32
1st Half		293	55	22	56	6	316		396	612	1008			12	65	0.38				42		247			88	9%	74%				8.96		109	295	$41
2nd Half		199	36	12	28	5	255		350	488	838			13	62	0.38				35		199			111	13%	71%				5.78		68	184	$19
15	**Proj**	**355**	**65**	**14**	**57**	**8**	**244**	**226**	**339**	**428**	**767**	**767**	**767**	**13**	**63**	**0.39**	**36**	**19**	**45**	**35**		**165**		**14%**	**102**	**11%**	**73%**				**4.88**	**12.6**	**41**	**109**	**$14**

BRENT HERSHEY

Buck,John

Age: 34	Bats: R	Pos: CA	Health	A	LIMA Plan	F
Ht: 6' 3"	Wt: 245		PT/Exp	D	Rand Var	+1
			Consist	B	MM	2101

1-6-.225 in 89 AB at SEA/LAA. One sign that the bell curve is nearing the bottom: the re-appearance of the asterisk year. But veteran backup CAs are still employable for MLB clubs, and his power, while waning, is a powerful lure. For you, RAR and R$ should be your warning. Don't want to get caught in the headlights.

Yr	Tm	AB	R	HR	RBI	SB	BA	xBA	OBP	SLG	OPS	vL	vR	bb%	ct%	Eye	G	L	F	h%	HctX	PX	xPX	hr/f	Spd	SBO	SB%	#Wk	DOM	DIS	RC/G	RAR	BPV	BPX	R$
10	TOR	409	53	20	66	0	281	254	314	489	802	1116	718	4	73	0.14	39	16	45	34	107	151	138	15%	76	0%	0%	25	36%	48%	5.35	13.1	44	96	$14
11	FLA	466	41	16	57	0	227	224	316	367	683	586	716	10	75	0.47	41	18	41	27	109	95	133	11%	67	1%	0%	27	41%	44%	3.69	-7.2	20	44	$5
12	MIA	343	29	12	41	0	192	217	297	347	644	564	680	13	70	0.48	43	17	40	24	90	111	123	13%	60	0%	0%	27	30%	56%	3.21	-10.0	14	35	-$1
13	2 NL	392	39	15	62	2	222	228	288	365	652	617	664	7	73	0.28	44	19	37	26	113	98	128	14%	70	3%	67%	27	33%	48%	3.28	-5.2	9	23	$6
14	2 AL *	208	16	2	14	0	209	229	261	273	534	613	533	7	73	0.26	49	27	24	28	121	56	93	7%	70	0%	0%	18	22%	72%	2.30	-6.6	-26	-70	-$3
1st Half		76	9	1	5	0	224	222	298	289	587	641	539	10	72	0.38	49	25	25	30	114	54	104	7%	80	0%	0%	14	29%	71%	2.83	-1.3	-22	-59	-$3
2nd Half		132	7	1	9	0	200	272	239	263	502	400	500	5	74	0.19	50	38	13	26	159	57	17	0%	66	0%	0%	4	0%	75%	2.00	-5.7	-29	-78	-$3
15	**Proj**	**97**	**9**	**3**	**10**	**0**	**214**	**224**	**281**	**337**	**617**	**609**	**621**	**8**	**73**	**0.31**	**44**	**20**	**36**	**26**	**106**	**94**	**121**	**11%**	**71**	**1%**	**63%**				**3.00**	**-1.2**	**-9**	**-23**	**-$1**

Butera,Drew

Age: 31	Bats: R	Pos: CA	Health	A	LIMA Plan	F
Ht: 6' 1"	Wt: 200		PT/Exp	F	Rand Var	+1
			Consist	D	MM	1001

Usually, we'd laud a player with an OBA 79 points higher than his BA. But with an average this low, and the sample size this small... eh, not so much. The highlight from 2014? Caught Josh Beckett's no-hitter. A fitting term, now that we think about it.

Yr	Tm	AB	R	HR	RBI	SB	BA	xBA	OBP	SLG	OPS	vL	vR	bb%	ct%	Eye	G	L	F	h%	HctX	PX	xPX	hr/f	Spd	SBO	SB%	#Wk	DOM	DIS	RC/G	RAR	BPV	BPX	R$
10	MIN	142	12	2	13	0	197	236	237	296	533	453	591	3	82	0.16	40	19	41	23	63	67	52	4%	102	0%	0%	26	23%	42%	2.06	-10.3	21	46	-$2
11	MIN	234	19	2	23	0	167	203	210	239	449	569	403	4	82	0.26	40	15	46	19	54	53	63	2%	91	0%	0%	27	26%	59%	1.49	-22.0	9	20	-$6
12	MIN *	154	11	2	9	0	205	225	259	293	552	336	644	7	76	0.30	34	24	42	26	55	71	37	3%	95	0%	0%	20	20%	45%	2.44	-8.8	4	10	-$3
13	2 TM *	149	7	1	8	0	129	186	148	182	330	0	400	2	71	0.08	40	20	40	17	118	43	135	0%	101	0%	0%	5	0%	80%	0.79	-14.7	-43	-108	-$8
14	LA	170	16	3	14	0	188	226	267	288	555	715	511	9	76	0.41	34	24	42	23	82	75	73	5%	107	0%	0%	25	24%	56%	2.37	-5.8	16	43	-$3
1st Half		111	13	2	11	0	207	223	280	306	586	883	496	9	76	0.40	33	26	42	26	94	70	84	6%	119	0%	0%	13	23%	54%	2.75	-2.2	14	38	-$1
2nd Half		59	3	1	3	0	153	226	242	254	497	322	537	9	76	0.43	36	22	42	18	59	83	52	5%	86	0%	0%	12	25%	58%	1.77	-3.2	18	49	-$6
15	**Proj**	**98**	**7**	**1**	**7**	**0**	**168**	**214**	**232**	**252**	**484**	**449**	**497**	**6**	**75**	**0.28**	**36**	**22**	**43**	**21**	**65**	**68**	**56**	**4%**	**92**	**0%**	**0%**				**1.72**	**-5.4**	**-19**	**-51**	**-$2**

Butler,Billy

Age: 29	Bats: R	Pos: DH 1B	Health	A	LIMA Plan	B+
Ht: 6' 1"	Wt: 240		PT/Exp	A	Rand Var	0
			Consist	C	MM	2035

Perspective, people. Easy to see now that 2012's power "breakout" was simply a hr/f outlier (as was 2014's). But as long as he sports that Jose Altuve G/L/F (really; look it up), his HR total will disappoint. Hit tool goods aplenty—HctX, ct%, h%—will preserve his plus BA, but it's time to accept that he's not a true thumper.

Yr	Tm	AB	R	HR	RBI	SB	BA	xBA	OBP	SLG	OPS	vL	vR	bb%	ct%	Eye	G	L	F	h%	HctX	PX	xPX	hr/f	Spd	SBO	SB%	#Wk	DOM	DIS	RC/G	RAR	BPV	BPX	R$
10	KC	595	77	15	78	0	318	278	388	469	857	727	888	10	87	0.88	48	18	34	35	129	104	112	8%	66	0%	0%	27	70%	7%	6.81	15.4	73	159	$24
11	KC	597	74	19	95	2	291	277	361	461	822	917	790	10	84	0.69	46	19	36	32	132	117	131	10%	57	2%	67%	27	67%	7%	5.99	2.4	69	153	$23
12	KC	614	72	29	107	2	313	288	373	510	882	1042	827	8	82	0.49	47	24	29	34	132	120	118	20%	58	2%	67%	27	52%	26%	6.94	34.1	59	148	$29
13	KC	582	62	15	82	0	289	251	374	412	787	797	783	12	82	0.77	53	20	26	33	111	84	92	12%	49	0%	0%	27	44%	37%	5.52	16.6	38	95	$19
14	KC	549	57	9	66	0	271	258	323	379	702	847	653	7	83	0.43	49	22	28	32	132	83	111	7%	54	0%	0%	27	37%	33%	4.27	3.4	29	78	$13
1st Half		297	33	2	34	0	273	255	328	354	682	674	684	8	81	0.49	51	24	25	33	139	70	107	3%	59	0%	0%	14	36%	50%	4.13	0.7	18	49	$12
2nd Half		252	24	7	32	0	270	261	317	409	726	1046	615	5	84	0.34	47	20	33	30	123	98	116	10%	56	0%	0%	13	38%	15%	4.40	2.5	43	116	$14
15	**Proj**	**578**	**62**	**15**	**79**	**0**	**285**	**266**	**347**	**418**	**764**	**884**	**724**	**8**	**83**	**0.53**	**49**	**21**	**29**	**32**	**125**	**96**	**109**	**11%**	**52**	**0%**	**67%**				**5.13**	**17.4**	**35**	**91**	**$20**

Buxton,Byron

Age: 21	Bats: R	Pos: CF	Health	D	LIMA Plan	D
Ht: 6' 2"	Wt: 190		PT/Exp	F	Rand Var	0
			Consist	F	MM	1501

Lost year due to injuries (wrist, concussion) for consensus #1 prospect heading into 2014. Tore through two levels of A-ball two seasons ago, with impressive plate patience, extra-base power and superior defense. SB ability (55 in 2013) should pay immediate dividends even if the bat takes time to adjust.

Yr	Tm	AB	R	HR	RBI	SB	BA	xBA	OBP	SLG	OPS	vL	vR	bb%	ct%	Eye	G	L	F	h%	HctX	PX	xPX	hr/f	Spd	SBO	SB%	#Wk	DOM	DIS	RC/G	RAR	BPV	BPX	R$
10																																			
11																																			
12																																			
13																																			
14																																			
1st Half																																			
2nd Half																																			
15	**Proj**	**127**	**20**	**5**	**15**	**8**	**252**	**213**	**321**	**373**	**695**	**695**	**695**	**9**	**74**	**0.39**	**44**	**17**	**39**	**30**		**76**		**14%**	**120**	**28%**	**73%**				**4.04**	**0.7**	**5**	**14**	**$7**

Byrd,Marlon

Age: 37	Bats: R	Pos: RF	Health	A	LIMA Plan	C+
Ht: 6' 0"	Wt: 245		PT/Exp	C	Rand Var	-3
			Consist	F	MM	3025

Let's have a little reality check here. In his first 10 MLB seasons, he managed 20 HRs ONCE. Only 100+ PX levels were 106 and 124. Never earned $20. Now, at age 36-37, he's suddenly discovered power skill? He redefines himself as a slugger NOW? If that was so easy, why doesn't everyone do it?

Yr	Tm	AB	R	HR	RBI	SB	BA	xBA	OBP	SLG	OPS	vL	vR	bb%	ct%	Eye	G	L	F	h%	HctX	PX	xPX	hr/f	Spd	SBO	SB%	#Wk	DOM	DIS	RC/G	RAR	BPV	BPX	R$
10	CHC	580	84	12	66	5	293	277	346	429	775	916	717	5	83	0.32	52	17	30	34	111	97	90	8%	83	4%	83%	27	44%	30%	5.11	-0.5	47	102	$19
11	CHC	446	51	9	35	3	276	266	324	395	719	649	740	5	83	0.32	50	22	28	32	78	82	68	9%	91	4%	60%	22	41%	32%	4.32	-10.5	35	78	$10
12	2 TM	143	10	1	9	0	210	224	243	245	488	761	348	3	78	0.16	50	26	25	26	86	24	57	4%	76	9%	0%	10	0%	80%	1.66	-15.8	-35	-88	-$3
13	2 NL	532	75	24	88	2	291	272	336	511	847	959	797	6	73	0.22	39	24	37	36	124	159	153	16%	113	5%	33%	26	65%	19%	5.91	19.4	66	165	$24
14	PHI	591	71	25	85	3	264	243	312	445	757	773	751	6	69	0.19	37	23	40	34	108	143	145	15%	74	4%	60%	27	30%	30%	4.66	9.6	25	68	$20
1st Half		310	40	15	48	1	268	257	319	487	806	939	767	6	69	0.22	35	21	44	34	115	173	163	16%	90	1%	100%	14	43%	14%	5.35	12.0	58	157	$23
2nd Half		281	31	10	37	2	260	228	305	399	703	642	732	5	68	0.16	39	25	36	35	99	109	124	14%	50	6%	50%	13	15%	46%	3.96	-0.4	-14	-38	$17
15	**Proj**	**498**	**59**	**17**	**65**	**2**	**264**	**247**	**309**	**419**	**728**	**799**	**698**	**5**	**73**	**0.20**	**41**	**23**	**36**	**33**	**106**	**119**	**125**	**13%**	**84**	**5%**	**38%**				**4.26**	**3.7**	**16**	**41**	**$15**

Cabrera,Asdrubal

Age: 29	Bats: B	Pos: SS 2B	Health	B	LIMA Plan	B+
Ht: 6' 0"	Wt: 205		PT/Exp	A	Rand Var	+1
			Consist	B	MM	3325

It's not supposed to work this way, retreating from 2011's high during his prime years. Truthfully, he's still productive—good contact, hits with authority, runs a little. And look: given the declining state of offense in the game, 2014 was actually better than 2011! (See RAR, BPX). Normalize hr/f and it's nearly the same player.

Yr	Tm	AB	R	HR	RBI	SB	BA	xBA	OBP	SLG	OPS	vL	vR	bb%	ct%	Eye	G	L	F	h%	HctX	PX	xPX	hr/f	Spd	SBO	SB%	#Wk	DOM	DIS	RC/G	RAR	BPV	BPX	R$
10	CLE	381	39	3	29	6	276	242	326	346	673	647	685	6	84	0.42	52	17	31	32	87	52	57	3%	96	9%	60%	18	33%	28%	3.82	-9.7	22	48	$7
11	CLE	604	87	25	92	17	273	269	332	460	792	777	799	7	80	0.37	44	17	39	30	109	123	115	13%	96	15%	77%	27	56%	26%	5.20	8.3	64	142	$26
12	CLE	555	70	16	68	9	270	269	338	423	762	796	745	9	82	0.53	41	23	36	30	117	101	105	10%	67	9%	69%	27	48%	30%	4.88	8.5	49	123	$17
13	CLE	508	66	14	64	9	242	256	299	402	700	639	730	6	78	0.31	36	23	41	29	108	118	139	9%	93	11%	75%	25	32%	20%	3.92	3.9	47	118	$13
14	2 TM	553	74	14	61	10	241	250	307	387	694	689	696	8	80	0.45	38	19	42	28	118	105	127	8%	107	9%	83%	27	48%	30%	3.97	9.5	56	151	$13
1st Half		298	46	8	33	6	245	253	310	396	706	662	728	7	80	0.39	38	19	42	28	116	113	125	8%	97	10%	86%	14	57%	29%	4.08	6.1	54	146	$16
2nd Half		255	28	6	28	4	235	247	304	376	680	727	661	9	82	0.53	39	19	42	27	121	96	128	7%	116	8%	80%	13	38%	31%	3.83	3.4	58	157	$10
15	**Proj**	**485**	**62**	**13**	**56**	**9**	**248**	**257**	**311**	**397**	**708**	**700**	**712**	**8**	**80**	**0.42**	**39**	**21**	**40**	**29**	**114**	**109**	**123**	**8%**	**96**	**10%**	**77%**				**4.12**	**12.7**	**54**	**143**	**$14**

Cabrera,Everth

Age: 28	Bats: B	Pos: SS	Health	D	LIMA Plan	C
Ht: 5' 10"	Wt: 190		PT/Exp	C	Rand Var	+1
			Consist	D	MM	1523

Wascally wabbits can be such a tease. 54 SB? Meep-meep! Not a 400-AB season since. 82% ct% and .355 OBA? Juuuust kidding! Draft-day investments die when leg injuries (knee, hamstring in 2014) fell one-trick ponies. And yet we'll chase those SB, ignoring the DCD reliability risk. Are we having fun yet?

Yr	Tm	AB	R	HR	RBI	SB	BA	xBA	OBP	SLG	OPS	vL	vR	bb%	ct%	Eye	G	L	F	h%	HctX	PX	xPX	hr/f	Spd	SBO	SB%	#Wk	DOM	DIS	RC/G	RAR	BPV	BPX	R$
10	SD *	243	27	1	24	12	207	229	278	272	550	607	545	9	71	0.34	54	22	23	29	70	50	70	3%	107	29%	67%	22	18%	45%	2.39	-16.4	-22	-48	$2
11	SD *	254	31	1	9	19	209	264	264	274	538	1000	143	7	78	0.34	100	0	0	26	0	48	2	0%	154	48%	65%	1	0%	100%	2.20	-19.0	14	31	$2
12	SD *	542	67	2	34	54	249	237	313	321	635	523	698	9	73	0.35	61	19	20	34	63	61	47	4%	123	37%	93%	21	10%	62%	3.88	-3.7	-2	-5	$21
13	SD	381	54	4	31	37	283	273	355	381	736	934	651	10	82	0.59	60	21	19	34	88	65	49	7%	147	39%	76%	18	39%	33%	4.80	14.5	45	113	$23
14	SD	357	36	3	20	18	232	254	272	300	572	642	551	5	76	0.23	67	21	12	30	60	56	31	9%	109	30%	69%	16	19%	56%	2.66	-6.9	-5	-14	$7
1st Half		317	30	3	16	13	218	248	256	290	546	590	533	5	74	0.21	67	20	14	28	59	61	36	9%	109	29%	65%	14	21%	57%	2.35	-8.9	-8	-22	$8
2nd Half		40	6	0	4	5	350	301	391	375	766	1056	684	7	88	0.60	69	28	3	40	68	22	0	0%	103	38%	83%	2	0%	50%	6.24	3.2	14	38	$0
15	**Proj**	**343**	**40**	**2**	**21**	**25**	**251**	**258**	**309**	**319**	**628**	**745**	**589**	**8**	**76**	**0.34**	**64**	**23**	**13**	**33**	**71**	**57**	**34**	**4%**	**123**	**34%**	**76%**				**3.38**	**1.5**	**4**	**12**	**$13**

BRENT HERSHEY

Cabrera,Melky

Age: 30	Bats: B	Pos: LF	Health	C	LIMA Plan	B+
Ht: 5' 10"	Wt: 210		PT/Exp	B	Rand Var	0
			Consist	F	MM	2255

Pressed the reset button on his career and rewarded owners with his second-highest hit, HR and RBI totals. Injuries and past allegations aside, this is an impressive 4-year run run of BPIs with consistent ct% and HctX, mature Eye, and solid L/R splits. Entering his 30's, running game looks like history, but the bat is very present.

Yr Tm	AB	R	HR	RBI	SB	BA	xBA	OBP	SLG	OPS	vL	vR	bb%	ct%	Eye	G	L	F	h%	HctX	PX	xPX	hr/f	Spd	SBO	SB%	#Wk	DOM	DIS	RC/G	RAR	BPV	BPX	R$
10 ATL	458	50	4	42	7	255	267	317	354	671	642	685	8	86	0.66	49	19	32	29	98	71	60	3%	87	6%	88%	26	38%	15%	3.91	-13.6	46	100	$7
11 KC	658	102	18	87	20	305	289	339	470	809	788	818	5	86	0.37	47	20	33	34	101	108	88	10%	109	18%	67%	27	63%	19%	5.70	14.1	74	164	$33
12 SF	459	84	11	60	13	346	298	390	516	906	1111	826	7	86	0.57	52	22	26	38	105	99	80	11%	143	12%	72%	20	65%	10%	7.84	39.1	84	210	$28
13 TOR	344	39	3	30	2	279	255	322	360	682	595	717	6	86	0.49	46	22	31	32	119	57	85	3%	99	4%	50%	15	27%	20%	4.07	0.9	35	88	$7
14 TOR	568	81	16	73	6	301	297	351	458	808	785	817	7	88	0.64	49	21	30	32	117	104	90	11%	93	5%	75%	23	61%	9%	5.84	33.6	80	216	$25
1st Half	344	52	11	42	4	299	296	344	465	809	807	810	6	87	0.50	48	22	30	32	112	109	83	12%	98	5%	80%	14	57%	0%	5.82	19.7	78	211	$30
2nd Half	224	29	5	31	2	304	296	360	446	807	749	827	8	91	0.95	51	20	29	32	124	96	102	8%	86	4%	67%	9	67%	22%	5.85	13.0	84	227	$18
15 Proj	**554**	**76**	**13**	**66**	**6**	**303**	**289**	**350**	**446**	**796**	**786**	**799**	**7**	**88**	**0.60**	**49**	**21**	**30**	**33**	**115**	**96**	**88**	**9%**	**101**	**6%**	**66%**				**5.66**	**29.3**	**69**	**182**	**$22**

Cabrera,Miguel

Age: 32	Bats: R	Pos: 1B DH	Health	B	LIMA Plan	C
Ht: 6' 4"	Wt: 240		PT/Exp	A	Rand Var	0
			Consist	F	MM	5155

In the context of 2010-13, is he still the Mighty Miggy? Naysayers would point to dips in bb%, ct% and Slg. Champions would cite flourishing HctX and xPX, crazy-low hr/f, and show that he's always far outhit his xBA. The missing variable is a foot injury that could well impact 2015. Projection is optimistic but don't ignore the risk.

Yr Tm	AB	R	HR	RBI	SB	BA	xBA	OBP	SLG	OPS	vL	vR	bb%	ct%	Eye	G	L	F	h%	HctX	PX	xPX	hr/f	Spd	SBO	SB%	#Wk	DOM	DIS	RC/G	RAR	BPV	BPX	R$
10 DET	548	111	38	126	3	328	327	420	622	1042	1000	1054	14	83	0.94	39	19	42	34	150	187	169	20%	66	3%	50%	26	81%	4%	9.83	61.0	130	283	$38
11 DET	572	111	30	105	2	344	317	448	586	1033	990	1047	16	84	1.21	44	22	34	37	157	158	140	18%	76	1%	67%	27	85%	0%	10.19	67.1	121	269	$39
12 DET	622	109	44	139	4	330	315	393	606	999	913	1027	10	84	0.67	42	22	36	34	159	161	161	23%	76	3%	80%	27	81%	7%	9.08	62.1	110	275	$42
13 DET	555	103	44	137	3	348	317	442	636	1078	1210	1038	14	83	0.96	39	24	37	36	155	170	165	25%	75	1%	100%	26	69%	19%	10.96	90.2	121	303	$46
14 DET	611	101	25	109	1	313	302	371	524	895	900	894	9	81	0.51	40	25	35	35	157	154	163	14%	80	1%	50%	27	70%	15%	7.23	51.0	90	243	$33
1st Half	306	47	14	65	0	314	312	366	546	912	806	948	8	83	0.51	40	23	36	34	149	166	157	15%	73	1%	0%	14	79%	7%	7.39	26.7	104	281	$34
2nd Half	305	54	11	44	1	311	290	376	502	877	990	839	10	79	0.52	40	26	34	37	166	141	169	13%	90	1%	100%	13	62%	23%	7.06	23.8	77	208	$33
15 Proj	**592**	**104**	**33**	**116**	**1**	**318**	**310**	**392**	**557**	**949**	**977**	**939**	**11**	**82**	**0.69**	**40**	**24**	**36**	**34**	**158**	**163**	**163**	**19%**	**77**	**1%**	**62%**				**8.16**	**63.3**	**97**	**254**	**$37**

Cain,Lorenzo

Age: 29	Bats: R	Pos: CF RF	Health	D	LIMA Plan	B
Ht: 6' 2"	Wt: 205		PT/Exp	C	Rand Var	-5
			Consist	C	MM	2525

Propelled himself into fantasy relevance by doubling lifetime SB total and hitting .300 in career-high AB. Recovered from 1H groin issues and ran wild in 2H. While BA tips its cap to h% and xBA history suggests some looming normalization, ct% and LD rate remain steady. If he can eke out a few more bb, then... UP: 40 SB.

Yr Tm	AB	R	HR	RBI	SB	BA	xBA	OBP	SLG	OPS	vL	vR	bb%	ct%	Eye	G	L	F	h%	HctX	PX	xPX	hr/f	Spd	SBO	SB%	#Wk	DOM	DIS	RC/G	RAR	BPV	BPX	R$
10 MIL *	478	61	3	33	27	283	233	343	379	722	668	805	8	77	0.40	43	21	37	36	123	70	104	2%	182	21%	86%	12	50%	25%	4.81	0.2	37	80	$18
11 KC *	509	62	10	57	11	262	260	301	393	695	167	765	5	77	0.24	50	22	28	32	65	95	57	0%	148	15%	61%	2	50%	50%	3.96	-16.9	40	89	$13
12 KC *	274	33	8	36	10	256	252	298	407	705	844	681	6	75	0.24	47	22	31	31	85	101	92	13%	119	16%	100%	12	42%	33%	4.37	-3.8	31	78	$8
13 KC	399	54	4	46	14	251	247	310	348	658	617	676	8	77	0.37	49	22	29	31	80	76	69	4%	126	19%	70%	24	38%	42%	3.61	-7.5	26	65	$11
14 KC	471	55	5	53	28	301	260	339	412	751	827	720	5	77	0.22	51	23	26	38	72	90	68	5%	130	26%	85%	25	28%	28%	5.20	17.1	31	84	$25
1st Half	216	23	3	35	7	315	266	351	440	790	855	767	5	78	0.23	50	23	27	39	67	99	65	7%	123	15%	78%	12	33%	17%	5.70	10.8	39	105	$20
2nd Half	255	32	2	18	21	290	255	328	388	717	805	679	5	76	0.22	52	23	25	37	76	83	70	4%	133	35%	88%	13	23%	38%	4.80	6.8	24	65	$29
15 Proj	**507**	**63**	**6**	**56**	**25**	**272**	**253**	**319**	**383**	**701**	**734**	**687**	**6**	**77**	**0.27**	**49**	**22**	**29**	**34**	**81**	**89**	**75**	**6%**	**130**	**23%**	**83%**				**4.33**	**6.9**	**31**	**82**	**$22**

Calhoun,Kole

Age: 27	Bats: L	Pos: RF	Health	B	LIMA Plan	B+
Ht: 5' 10"	Wt: 200		PT/Exp	C	Rand Var	-1
			Consist	B	MM	4245

17-58-.272 in 493 AB at LAA. Ankle injury and platoon rut kept him from full-time work until July, but 2H BPIs held steady in face of increased exposure to LHP. Impressive LD profile established in less than two seasons; a return to 2013 FB level could translate PX into more HR. His job-share days are over. A solid investment.

Yr Tm	AB	R	HR	RBI	SB	BA	xBA	OBP	SLG	OPS	vL	vR	bb%	ct%	Eye	G	L	F	h%	HctX	PX	xPX	hr/f	Spd	SBO	SB%	#Wk	DOM	DIS	RC/G	RAR	BPV	BPX	R$
10																																		
11																																		
12 LAA *	433	53	8	48	9	224	253	274	354	628	0	578	6	74	0.26	41	29	29	29	95	95	150	0%	94	14%	71%	9	0%	33%	3.16	-22.6	13	33	$5
13 LAA *	435	58	15	62	8	274	267	335	443	777	889	782	8	81	0.49	41	23	36	31	130	106	131	14%	98	10%	64%	10	70%	20%	5.10	10.2	58	145	$16
14 LAA *	515	94	18	61	5	276	281	326	455	782	710	793	7	79	0.35	44	24	32	32	99	129	94	13%	99	7%	53%	23	39%	13%	5.11	17.9	65	176	$20
1st Half	191	40	8	22	3	295	280	343	495	838	704	857	7	78	0.34	45	19	36	34	96	143	98	15%	105	9%	69%	10	50%	10%	6.07	11.0	75	203	$14
2nd Half	324	54	10	39	2	265	283	319	432	751	711	760	7	79	0.36	43	26	31	31	101	121	92	13%	94	6%	40%	13	31%	15%	4.59	5.6	58	157	$24
15 Proj	**570**	**90**	**21**	**72**	**8**	**278**	**277**	**330**	**462**	**792**	**792**	**792**	**7**	**79**	**0.38**	**43**	**23**	**34**	**32**	**111**	**128**	**109**	**14%**	**97**	**9%**	**61%**				**5.29**	**21.1**	**66**	**173**	**$24**

Callaspo,Alberto

Age: 32	Bats: B	Pos: 2B DH 1B	Health	B	LIMA Plan	D+
Ht: 5' 9"	Wt: 225		PT/Exp	B	Rand Var	+3
			Consist	B	MM	1023

When does a switch-hitting, multi-position guy stop providing value? In this case, when he became a sporadically used singles hitter, sans singles. As h% slipped and PX dropped, AB dwindled and 2H output plummeted. With still-solid Eye and ct%, a mini-bounceback is possible. But the bad outweighs the good at this point.

Yr Tm	AB	R	HR	RBI	SB	BA	xBA	OBP	SLG	OPS	vL	vR	bb%	ct%	Eye	G	L	F	h%	HctX	PX	xPX	hr/f	Spd	SBO	SB%	#Wk	DOM	DIS	RC/G	RAR	BPV	BPX	R$
10 2AL	562	61	10	56	5	265	270	302	374	675	576	701	5	93	0.74	45	18	38	27	90	67	64	5%	74	6%	63%	27	44%	11%	3.89	-11.4	58	126	$11
11 LAA	475	54	6	46	8	288	262	366	375	740	730	745	11	90	1.21	41	22	37	31	74	60	64	4%	69	5%	89%	27	48%	26%	4.99	5.2	52	116	$14
12 LAA	457	55	10	53	4	252	255	331	361	692	833	634	11	87	0.95	44	21	36	27	93	68	77	7%	57	5%	57%	27	48%	30%	4.05	-1.6	44	110	$8
13 2AL	453	52	10	58	0	258	272	333	369	702	763	672	10	90	1.13	40	25	36	27	93	70	66	7%	56	1%	0%	25	68%	12%	4.18	6.0	54	135	$9
14 OAK	404	37	4	39	0	223	237	290	290	580	518	616	9	88	0.80	42	21	37	25	80	49	67	3%	56	1%	0%	25	48%	36%	2.75	-7.8	27	73	$0
1st Half	246	27	3	26	0	244	244	329	317	646	494	725	11	88	1.03	43	22	35	27	87	52	76	4%	60	1%	0%	14	57%	29%	3.46	0.5	35	95	$5
2nd Half	158	10	1	13	0	190	225	228	247	475	550	425	5	87	0.45	41	20	39	21	69	44	54	2%	58	0%	0%	11	36%	45%	1.81	-7.9	15	41	-$6
15 Proj	**338**	**33**	**5**	**36**	**1**	**236**	**250**	**300**	**321**	**621**	**634**	**614**	**9**	**88**	**0.82**	**42**	**21**	**37**	**25**	**84**	**60**	**66**	**5%**	**57**	**2%**	**44%**				**3.21**	**-1.8**	**31**	**83**	**$4**

Campbell,Eric

Age: 28	Bats: R	Pos: LF	Health	A	LIMA Plan	D
Ht: 6' 3"	Wt: 205		PT/Exp	C	Rand Var	-4
			Consist	A	MM	2311

3-16-.263 in 190 AB at NYM. Distinguished himself during first cup of coffee with a .833 OPS before the All-Star Break. But he decomposed after that (.172 BA), and on balance struggled to make contact or hit the ball very hard. As the case with most older prospects, his best hope is roster filler, in real life and fantasy.

Yr Tm	AB	R	HR	RBI	SB	BA	xBA	OBP	SLG	OPS	vL	vR	bb%	ct%	Eye	G	L	F	h%	HctX	PX	xPX	hr/f	Spd	SBO	SB%	#Wk	DOM	DIS	RC/G	RAR	BPV	BPX	R$
10 aa	179	18	4	21	1	229		264	346	610			5	79	0.23				27		85			93	2%	100%				3.04		25	54	$0
11 aa	405	33	3	33	4	184		253	253	506			8	79	0.44				23		55			92	7%	65%				1.99		6	13	-$6
12 aa	394	40	7	38	8	243		319	354	673			10	77	0.47				30		80			89	12%	56%				3.68		19	48	$6
13 aaa	341	37	5	40	7	228		309	334	642			10	77	0.51				28		81			94	13%	59%				3.31		24	60	$4
14 NYM *	331	38	5	30	5	257	238	316	359	675	683	678	8	75	0.34	55	17	28	33	94	88	81	8%	115	7%	78%	22	32%	50%	3.91	-2.6	23	62	$7
1st Half	224	30	3	22	3	273	256	320	388	707	899	689	6	77	0.30	59	16	25	34	104	101	76	7%	118	7%	67%	9	44%	56%	4.31	0.9	39	105	$10
2nd Half	107	8	2	8	2	224	201	306	299	605	551	667	11	71	0.42	52	18	30	30	84	57	86	9%	113	6%	100%	13	23%	46%	3.14	-3.4	-13	-35	-$1
15 Proj	**203**	**20**	**3**	**19**	**4**	**236**	**235**	**306**	**336**	**641**	**643**	**640**	**9**	**75**	**0.42**	**55**	**17**	**28**	**30**	**92**	**81**	**82**	**8%**	**115**	**9%**	**71%**				**3.43**	**-1.9**	**7**	**18**	**$4**

Cano,Robinson

Age: 32	Bats: L	Pos: 2B	Health	A	LIMA Plan	C
Ht: 6' 0"	Wt: 210		PT/Exp	A	Rand Var	0
			Consist	B	MM	3255

Park effects? Hit all of TWO fewer HR at Safeco than he did at Yankee Stadium in 2013. But HctX, PX and Slg all dropped again, and hr/f was his lowest since 2008. Still elite ct%, Eye, textbook stroke keep h% elevated, providing more opportunities to reclaim lost power. In climate of depressed offense, he's still a top-tier MI.

Yr Tm	AB	R	HR	RBI	SB	BA	xBA	OBP	SLG	OPS	vL	vR	bb%	ct%	Eye	G	L	F	h%	HctX	PX	xPX	hr/f	Spd	SBO	SB%	#Wk	DOM	DIS	RC/G	RAR	BPV	BPX	R$
10 NYY	626	103	29	109	3	319	310	381	534	914	857	944	8	88	0.74	44	19	36	33	127	130	125	14%	91	3%	60%	27	70%	7%	7.47	48.1	101	220	$33
11 NYY	623	104	28	118	8	302	318	349	533	882	879	884	6	85	0.40	47	22	31	32	131	147	116	17%	91	7%	80%	27	67%	11%	6.65	35.2	97	216	$33
12 NYY	627	105	33	94	3	313	324	379	550	929	646	1108	9	85	0.64	49	26	26	33	141	145	115	24%	81	3%	60%	27	70%	7%	7.57	57.7	99	248	$32
13 NYY	605	81	27	107	7	314	312	383	516	899	788	969	10	86	0.76	44	26	30	33	137	128	115	17%	76	4%	88%	26	65%	19%	7.34	58.9	91	228	$34
14 SEA	595	77	14	82	10	314	301	382	454	836	746	891	9	89	0.90	53	23	25	34	109	95	82	11%	80	7%	77%	27	59%	11%	6.38	48.2	75	203	$29
1st Half	306	43	6	48	5	320	290	378	441	819	762	857	8	87	0.70	53	23	24	35	104	84	80	9%	84	7%	71%	14	43%	14%	6.21	23.2	59	159	$31
2nd Half	289	34	8	34	5	308	312	387	467	854	727	926	10	90	1.18	52	22	26	32	115	105	83	12%	78	6%	83%	13	77%	8%	6.57	25.0	91	246	$28
15 Proj	**605**	**84**	**20**	**92**	**8**	**311**	**309**	**378**	**483**	**861**	**742**	**934**	**9**	**87**	**0.78**	**49**	**24**	**27**	**33**	**124**	**116**	**99**	**14%**	**79**	**5%**	**78%**				**6.69**	**54.1**	**84**	**221**	**$32**

ROB CARROLL

Carp,Mike

Age: 29 Bats: L Pos: 1B | Ht: 6' 2" Wt: 210
Health D | PT/Exp F | Consist F
LIMA Plan D | Rand Var +5 | MM 2011

0-13-.175 in 126 AB in BOS and TEX. Season at-a-glance: Ineffective. Fractured foot. Ineffective. Idle. Trade demanded. Waived instead. Ineffective. PX history, rep as strong-side platoon mate (despite career .746 OPS vR and .736 OPS vL) may keep him around, but reliability grade recommends you look elsewhere.

Yr Tm	AB	R	HR	RBI	SB	BA	xBA	OBP	SLG	OPS	vL	vR	bb%	ct%	Eye	G	L	F	h%	HctX	PX	xPX	hr/f	Spd	SBO	SB%	#Wk	DOM	DIS	RC/G	RAR	BPV	BPX	R$
10 SEA *	446	50	19	56	1	207	229	264	377	642	556	496	7	73	0.29	31	17	52	24	93	117	124	0%	94	3%	24%	4	0%	50%	3.14	-34.8	31	67	$3
11 SEA *	541	61	24	85	4	267	267	314	455	769	884	761	6	73	0.25	43	25	32	32	142	136	152	18%	77	6%	45%	15	47%	33%	4.83	-12.6	39	87	$18
12 SEA *	303	26	6	31	2	191	220	262	292	554	722	631	9	72	0.34	50	21	29	24	98	75	94	14%	75	8%	31%	16	25%	38%	2.30	-29.0	-10	-25	-$2
13 BOS	216	34	9	43	1	296	273	362	523	885	745	904	9	69	0.33	41	24	34	39	116	181	140	17%	97	2%	100%	26	50%	35%	6.88	13.6	70	175	$9
14 2 AL *	147	12	1	15	0	178	212	262	246	507	361	553	10	73	0.42	46	21	33	24	78	59	53	0%	79	3%	0%	16	38%	50%	1.93	-10.5	-13	-35	-$4
1st Half	78	9	0	6	0	203	218	268	267	535	396	678	8	76	0.38	47	18	35	27	102	66	63	0%	76	6%	0%	8	38%	50%	2.15	-5.0	0	0	-$4
2nd Half	69	4	1	9	0	150	205	254	222	477	200	431	12	69	0.46	45	24	31	20	50	52	39	0%	99	0%	0%	8	38%	50%	1.69	-5.7	-24	-65	-$4
15 Proj	**127**	**15**	**2**	**19**	**0**	**242**	**234**	**325**	**362**	**686**	**627**	**698**	**10**	**72**	**0.37**	**45**	**22**	**32**	**32**	**93**	**98**	**89**	**8%**	**86**	**3%**	**34%**				**3.76**	**-1.5**	**5**	**14**	**$0**

Carpenter,Matt

Age: 29 Bats: L Pos: 3B | Ht: 6' 3" Wt: 215
Health A | PT/Exp A | Consist C
LIMA Plan B+ | Rand Var -1 | MM 2235

The difference between a .318 and .272 hitter? A slight dip in ct%, a few more GB/FB at the expense of LD, drops in both PX and Spd. But there is little in these BPIs that is truly notable; his value has been driven by volume (1400+ PA in 2013-14). For 2015, plant a flag someplace between the two years.

Yr Tm	AB	R	HR	RBI	SB	BA	xBA	OBP	SLG	OPS	vL	vR	bb%	ct%	Eye	G	L	F	h%	HctX	PX	xPX	hr/f	Spd	SBO	SB%	#Wk	DOM	DIS	RC/G	RAR	BPV	BPX	R$
10 aa	396	55	8	39	8	259		338	385	723			11	74	0.46				33		97			110	9%	77%				4.50		30	65	$9
11 STL *	449	41	7	48	3	228	178	323	338	661	500	378	12	81	0.74	45	0	55	27	0	80	2	0%	84	6%	41%	3	33%	67%	3.49	-22.1	39	87	$2
12 STL	296	44	6	46	1	294	268	365	463	828	784	846	10	79	0.54	40	24	36	36	118	116	114	7%	104	2%	50%	24	58%	21%	6.07	12.1	61	153	$9
13 STL	626	126	11	78	3	318	293	392	481	873	820	897	10	84	0.73	39	27	34	36	116	116	103	6%	124	3%	50%	27	63%	11%	6.89	48.8	90	225	$30
14 STL	595	99	8	59	5	272	253	375	375	750	722	762	14	81	0.86	41	24	35	32	117	80	98	5%	109	4%	63%	26	50%	27%	4.86	19.6	52	141	$17
1st Half	317	53	4	31	3	281	256	373	385	758	733	770	12	81	0.70	40	25	35	34	119	83	100	4%	113	4%	75%	14	50%	21%	5.01	11.8	49	132	$19
2nd Half	278	46	4	28	2	263	249	377	363	740	707	754	16	82	1.04	42	23	36	31	115	76	95	5%	102	4%	50%	12	50%	33%	4.69	8.1	53	143	$16
15 Proj	**582**	**97**	**9**	**67**	**4**	**283**	**266**	**374**	**411**	**785**	**748**	**801**	**12**	**81**	**0.77**	**40**	**25**	**35**	**33**	**117**	**98**	**102**	**6%**	**111**	**4%**	**57%**				**5.38**	**27.8**	**56**	**147**	**$21**

Carter,Chris

Age: 28 Bats: R Pos: DH | Ht: 6' 4" Wt: 250
Health A | PT/Exp B | Consist A
LIMA Plan B+ | Rand Var +2 | MM 5125

Three straight years with 20+% hr/f, with a FB% now surpassing 50%. 210 PX. (Let that marinate awhile.) Yes, the ct% is odorous and the BA has been stuck in the .220s, but he made real changes in 2H (HctX, xPX, LD) which can't be ignored. He could be a '15 monster but no less than a valuable power source. UP: 45 HR, .265

Yr Tm	AB	R	HR	RBI	SB	BA	xBA	OBP	SLG	OPS	vL	vR	bb%	ct%	Eye	G	L	F	h%	HctX	PX	xPX	hr/f	Spd	SBO	SB%	#Wk	DOM	DIS	RC/G	RAR	BPV	BPX	R$
10 OAK *	535	70	22	70	2	201	213	276	377	653	520	606	9	66	0.30	32	14	54	26	70	139	70	11%	75	2%	59%	6	33%	67%	3.30	-42.5	17	37	$3
11 OAK *	340	39	11	48	3	204	224	269	352	621	145	448	8	64	0.25	17	38	46	28	40	123	33	0%	82	6%	74%	6	0%	83%	3.03	-29.8	-2	-4	$2
12 OAK *	494	70	23	75	3	225	228	316	423	739	898	837	12	65	0.38	34	20	46	30	97	154	126	25%	67	4%	73%	15	47%	27%	4.39	-7.4	28	70	$10
13 HOU	506	64	29	82	2	223	226	320	451	770	782	765	12	58	0.33	31	22	47	32	94	197	171	21%	79	2%	100%	27	44%	33%	4.72	3.4	40	100	$12
14 HOU	507	68	37	88	5	227	252	308	491	799	869	772	10	64	0.31	27	22	51	27	106	210	171	22%	73	6%	71%	26	50%	31%	4.89	13.0	68	184	$18
1st Half	234	24	13	30	0	184	228	267	406	673	648	688	9	63	0.26	29	17	54	22	94	186	158	16%	90	2%	0%	14	43%	29%	3.19	-6.5	47	127	$0
2nd Half	273	44	24	58	5	264	272	342	564	906	1263	827	11	65	0.35	25	25	49	31	117	230	183	27%	60	8%	83%	12	58%	33%	6.73	21.2	86	232	$33
15 Proj	**531**	**81**	**39**	**100**	**4**	**241**	**256**	**323**	**508**	**831**	**876**	**812**	**11**	**64**	**0.34**	**28**	**22**	**50**	**29**	**99**	**214**	**155**	**23%**	**73**	**4%**	**76%**				**5.49**	**22.8**	**74**	**194**	**$23**

Casali,Curtis

Age: 26 Bats: R Pos: CA | Ht: 6' 2" Wt: 225
Health A | PT/Exp F | Consist F
LIMA Plan D | Rand Var 0 | MM 2001

0-3-.167 in 72 AB at TAM. Didn't show much during two-month major-league trial, but hit .303 in 350 AB in Double-A and Triple-A the past two seasons with 0.78 Eye. Power hasn't materialized, but catcher issues with the parent club all but guarantee a look-see in the spring.

Yr Tm	AB	R	HR	RBI	SB	BA	xBA	OBP	SLG	OPS	vL	vR	bb%	ct%	Eye	G	L	F	h%	HctX	PX	xPX	hr/f	Spd	SBO	SB%	#Wk	DOM	DIS	RC/G	RAR	BPV	BPX	R$
10																																		
11																																		
12																																		
13 aa	120	20	4	25	0	324		406	497	903			12	82	0.75				37		123			83	0%	0%				7.61		77	193	$5
14 TAM *	298	24	3	25	0	202	202	302	284	585	521	460	12	65	0.41	44	23	33	30	50	83	69	0%	72	0%	0%	11	9%	73%	2.74	-5.4	-22	-59	-$3
1st Half	198	12	3	22	0	236	198	339	340	679			13	66	0.46				34	0	101			72	0%	0%				3.85		-4	-11	$0
2nd Half	100	12	0	3	0	136	182	227	174	400	521	460	10	64	0.33	44	23	33	21	49	47	69	0%	94	0%	0%	11	9%	73%	1.16	-7.6	-55	-149	-$9
15 Proj	**155**	**15**	**2**	**19**	**0**	**238**	**227**	**341**	**340**	**682**	**756**	**657**	**12**	**72**	**0.46**	**44**	**23**	**33**	**32**	**44**	**93**	**62**	**6%**	**71**	**0%**	**0%**				**3.72**	**1.5**	**-8**	**-21**	**$2**

Castellanos,Nick

Age: 23 Bats: R Pos: 3B | Ht: 6' 4" Wt: 210
Health A | PT/Exp C | Consist B
LIMA Plan B+ | Rand Var -2 | MM 3125

Profile under construction with accent on Eye vR (0.18) and contact (70% in 2H). Size projects to prototypical slugger, but propensity for hitting the ball hard wasn't reflected by h%, BA or Slg. Also raises question of LD% sustainability. He's very young and going through on-the-job training at game's highest level. Patience.

Yr Tm	AB	R	HR	RBI	SB	BA	xBA	OBP	SLG	OPS	vL	vR	bb%	ct%	Eye	G	L	F	h%	HctX	PX	xPX	hr/f	Spd	SBO	SB%	#Wk	DOM	DIS	RC/G	RAR	BPV	BPX	R$
10																																		
11																																		
12 aa	322	29	6	21	4	245		270	345	616			3	76	0.15				30		71			98	12%	50%				3.02		0	0	$3
13 DET *	551	70	15	65	3	258	242	315	408	723	545	571	8	81	0.44	59	6	35	29	59	106	-15	0%	100	3%	76%	5	0%	20%	4.41	7.4	57	143	$13
14 DET	533	50	11	66	2	259	252	306	394	700	693	702	6	74	0.26	35	29	37	33	109	108	135	8%	104	3%	50%	27	37%	37%	4.10	6.6	27	73	$11
1st Half	261	24	6	30	2	272	263	312	418	730	878	669	6	77	0.27	32	28	40	33	117	115	137	7%	97	5%	67%	14	43%	29%	4.56	6.5	44	119	$11
2nd Half	272	26	5	36	0	246	242	300	371	671	482	731	7	70	0.25	38	29	32	33	100	102	133	8%	116	2%	0%	13	31%	46%	3.68	-0.1	13	35	$11
15 Proj	**556**	**58**	**12**	**63**	**3**	**255**	**250**	**304**	**388**	**692**	**654**	**705**	**6**	**76**	**0.29**	**38**	**25**	**38**	**31**	**107**	**104**	**135**	**8%**	**100**	**4%**	**55%**				**3.99**	**4.8**	**23**	**60**	**$13**

Castillo,Rusney

Age: 27 Bats: R Pos: CF | Ht: 5' 8" Wt: 186
Health A | PT/Exp D | Consist F
LIMA Plan B+ | Rand Var -5 | MM 3555

Adding 20 lbs of muscle after arriving in the US, he flashed broad range of skills during ten-game trial. The story is just unfolding, but here's a spoiler: Most scouting reports say he's a cut below recent Cuban imports (Cespedes, Puig, Abreu), but expectations will still be sky high and bidding will be extremely spirited.

Yr Tm	AB	R	HR	RBI	SB	BA	xBA	OBP	SLG	OPS	vL	vR	bb%	ct%	Eye	G	L	F	h%	HctX	PX	xPX	hr/f	Spd	SBO	SB%	#Wk	DOM	DIS	RC/G	RAR	BPV	BPX	R$
10 for	99	11	1	10	2	282		294	352	646			2	82	0.09				34		43	-5		134	25%	29%				3.03	-5.6	7	15	$1
11 for	441	89	13	93	29	298		324	484	808			4	89	0.34				31		112	2		114	36%	79%				5.66	8.9	88	196	$29
12 for	448	98	13	82	24	318		365	498	863			7	90	0.71				33		111	-11		93	26%	76%				6.72	23.9	91	228	$31
13 for	234	40	4	28	14	255		327	353	680			10	88	0.91				28		56	-15		140	33%	57%				3.59	-4.1	61	153	$9
14 BOS	36	6	2	6	3	333	286	400	528	928	500	1045	8	83	0.50	67	10	23	36	96	118	69	29%	93	25%	100%	3	33%	67%	8.44	4.3	73	197	$1
1st Half																																		
2nd Half	36	6	2	6	3	333	286	400	528	928	500	1045	8	83	0.50	67	10	23	36	96	118	69	29%	93	25%	100%	3	33%	67%	8.44	4.3	73	197	$1
15 Proj	**455**	**71**	**14**	**58**	**23**	**272**	**291**	**330**	**442**	**772**	**473**	**854**	**6**	**88**	**0.50**	**47**	**20**	**33**	**28**	**86**	**105**	**62**	**11%**	**131**	**33%**	**64%**				**4.54**	**9.2**	**91**	**241**	**$23**

Castillo,Welington

Age: 28 Bats: R Pos: CA | Ht: 5' 10" Wt: 210
Health C | PT/Exp C | Consist B
LIMA Plan D+ | Rand Var 0 | MM 3113

Sacrificed some patience and BA for PX, gaining loft with hr/f jumping by half. It's a tradeoff fantasy owners should accept, as (chronically low) xBA says 2013 BA was outlier. But here's the proper perspective... his 8-HR, .234 line in the 2nd half generated an above average BPX (114). The bar is very low these days.

Yr Tm	AB	R	HR	RBI	SB	BA	xBA	OBP	SLG	OPS	vL	vR	bb%	ct%	Eye	G	L	F	h%	HctX	PX	xPX	hr/f	Spd	SBO	SB%	#Wk	DOM	DIS	RC/G	RAR	BPV	BPX	R$
10 CHC *	259	27	11	46	0	224	218	264	423	687	708	1167	5	72	0.20	23	8	69	27	114	151	187	11%	89	5%	0%	5	60%	0%	3.51	-6.8	50	109	$3
11 CHC *	240	24	10	22	0	224	205	263	373	636	0	400	5	71	0.18	50	13	38	28	40	107	2	0%	84	0%	0%	3	0%	100%	3.22	-8.4	5	11	$1
12 CHC *	327	34	11	43	0	245	225	324	394	717	1199	604	10	70	0.39	46	20	34	32	92	111	99	12%	70	0%	0%	16	38%	38%	4.30	0.1	13	33	$5
13 CHC	380	41	8	32	2	274	240	349	397	746	707	758	8	74	0.35	44	22	34	35	113	99	110	8%	72	2%	100%	25	32%	40%	4.68	10.7	17	43	$8
14 CHC	380	28	13	46	0	237	228	296	389	686	855	631	6	73	0.25	41	19	40	29	103	118	121	12%	63	0%	0%	24	42%	33%	3.72	2.9	21	57	$5
1st Half	179	13	5	24	0	240	209	283	374	657	641	661	4	70	0.13	40	17	43	31	95	111	107	9%	66	0%	0%	12	33%	50%	3.38	-0.1	0	0	$4
2nd Half	201	15	8	22	0	234	245	308	403	711	998	602	9	76	0.39	41	21	38	27	111	124	132	14%	70	0%	0%	12	50%	17%	4.02	3.8	42	114	$6
15 Proj	**394**	**35**	**12**	**45**	**1**	**246**	**233**	**315**	**390**	**705**	**855**	**657**	**8**	**73**	**0.31**	**42**	**19**	**39**	**31**	**106**	**115**	**114**	**11%**	**65**	**1%**	**77%**				**4.00**	**7.1**	**9**	**23**	**$8**

ROB CARROLL

Castro,Jason

Age: 28 Bats: L Pos: CA	Health D	LIMA Plan D+
Ht: 6' 3" Wt: 215	PT/Exp C	Rand Var +2
	Consist D	MM 4215

Gave back 2013's h% and hr/f gains, which helped boost that apparent career year, but those were random fluctuations anyway. On the skills side, it was the second straight year that ct%, Eye, bb%, and LD% dropped. Did stay healthy, which is always good news for a catcher, but temper further growth expectations.

Yr	Tm	AB	R	HR	RBI	SB	BA	xBA	OBP	SLG	OPS	vL	vR	bb%	ct%	Eye	G	L	F	h%	HctX	PX	xPX	hr/f	Spd	SBO	SB%	#Wk	DOM	DIS	RC/G	RAR	BPV	BPX	R$
10	HOU *	406	49	5	28	1	218	236	298	296	594	223	670	10	80	0.58	41	22	37	26	91	56	62	4%	94	2%	40%	15	40%	27%	2.85	-16.9	17	37	-$1
11																																			
12	HOU	257	29	6	29	0	257	264	334	401	735	361	831	11	76	0.51	43	28	30	32	93	101	107	10%	91	0%	0%	22	55%	32%	4.63	3.7	37	93	$3
13	HOU	435	63	18	56	2	276	270	350	485	835	738	864	10	70	0.38	39	25	35	36	109	167	140	17%	85	3%	67%	23	61%	22%	5.96	27.8	62	155	$15
14	HOU	465	43	14	56	1	222	225	286	366	651	619	662	7	68	0.23	45	20	36	30	87	119	110	12%	98	1%	100%	26	42%	46%	3.30	-0.3	10	27	$5
1st Half		251	24	7	32	0	215	228	297	359	655	708	637	8	67	0.27	44	21	35	29	97	123	110	12%	105	0%	0%	14	43%	43%	3.24	-1.2	16	43	$4
2nd Half		214	19	7	24	1	229	221	272	374	646	507	690	5	68	0.18	46	18	37	30	76	114	109	13%	93	2%	100%	12	42%	50%	3.36	-0.2	5	14	$5
15	Proj	**417**	**46**	**13**	**48**	**1**	**241**	**244**	**308**	**394**	**702**	**564**	**745**	**8**	**71**	**0.31**	**43**	**22**	**35**	**31**	**93**	**124**	**112**	**12%**	**91**	**1%**	**77%**				**4.03**	**7.9**	**19**	**50**	**$6**

Castro,Starlin

Age: 25 Bats: R Pos: SS	Health A	LIMA Plan B
Ht: 6' 0" Wt: 190	PT/Exp A	Rand Var -3
	Consist D	MM 2235

Was en route to a career year when high ankle sprain ended his season on Sept. 4. H% regression helped BA return. Nice power gains. SBs may not come back, which is probably a good baseball decision (note mediocre success rate that's been getting worse), though a disappointing fantasy decision. UP: 20 HR

Yr	Tm	AB	R	HR	RBI	SB	BA	xBA	OBP	SLG	OPS	vL	vR	bb%	ct%	Eye	G	L	F	h%	HctX	PX	xPX	hr/f	Spd	SBO	SB%	#Wk	DOM	DIS	RC/G	RAR	BPV	BPX	R$
10	CHC *	572	69	4	57	13	310	282	351	428	779	897	701	6	86	0.43	51	20	29	36	97	83	78	3%	152	16%	49%	22	41%	32%	5.17	10.6	68	148	$21
11	CHC	674	91	10	66	22	307	273	341	432	773	847	751	5	86	0.36	49	20	31	35	100	82	79	5%	149	17%	71%	27	63%	15%	5.34	15.4	65	144	$29
12	CHC	646	78	14	78	25	283	271	323	430	753	775	746	5	85	0.36	47	21	32	32	99	87	100	8%	158	23%	66%	27	63%	19%	4.72	11.4	68	170	$26
13	CHC	666	59	10	44	9	245	249	284	347	631	619	635	4	81	0.23	51	20	29	29	105	75	99	6%	116	10%	60%	27	33%	41%	3.18	-6.5	28	70	$9
14	CHC	528	58	14	65	4	292	271	339	438	777	788	773	6	81	0.35	45	22	32	34	102	107	105	10%	94	6%	50%	23	52%	17%	5.17	27.8	53	143	$19
1st Half		321	38	11	47	2	283	289	331	467	799	747	811	6	81	0.33	46	22	33	32	109	133	112	13%	93	4%	67%	14	64%	14%	5.38	19.4	73	197	$25
2nd Half		207	20	3	18	2	304	244	351	391	742	836	710	7	81	0.38	45	23	32	37	91	67	95	6%	100	8%	40%	9	33%	22%	4.81	9.1	22	59	$11
15	Proj	**627**	**76**	**16**	**63**	**9**	**283**	**268**	**327**	**422**	**749**	**775**	**740**	**6**	**82**	**0.33**	**46**	**21**	**32**	**32**	**100**	**99**	**99**	**9%**	**120**	**10%**	**55%**				**4.69**	**26.1**	**44**	**117**	**$23**

Cervelli,Francisco

Age: 29 Bats: R Pos: CA	Health F	LIMA Plan D
Ht: 6' 1" Wt: 205	PT/Exp F	Rand Var -4
	Consist F	MM 2311

2-13-.301 in 146 AB at NYY. Strained hamstring cost him most of 1H. Was white-hot in the second, though unrepeatable h% may lead to talk of selling his soul to hit .300. Truth is, he's hit .278/.348/.381 in close to 700 lifetime AB... spread over 7 years. Seriously, not even a #2 catcher if you live in The Bronx.

Yr	Tm	AB	R	HR	RBI	SB	BA	xBA	OBP	SLG	OPS	vL	vR	bb%	ct%	Eye	G	L	F	h%	HctX	PX	xPX	hr/f	Spd	SBO	SB%	#Wk	DOM	DIS	RC/G	RAR	BPV	BPX	R$
10	NYY	266	27	0	38	1	271	237	359	335	694	846	617	11	84	0.79	47	18	34	32	81	47	52	0%	130	2%	50%	26	42%	42%	4.07	-0.9	37	80	$4
11	NYY	124	17	4	22	4	266	243	324	395	719	743	711	7	77	0.31	47	20	33	32	108	88	105	13%	95	15%	80%	19	32%	58%	4.37	0.6	21	47	$3
12	NYY *	355	34	2	30	5	205	75	268	262	531	1000	0	8	73	0.32	0	0	100	28	320	47	737	0%	101	5%	100%	2	50%	50%	2.32	-20.1	-21	-53	-$1
13	NYY	52	12	3	8	0	269	300	377	500	877	684	1017	13	83	0.89	30	28	42	28	143	145	148	17%	94	0%	0%	4	100%	0%	6.40	4.0	104	260	$0
14	NYY *	172	19	2	13	1	274	247	328	384	712	735	830	7	73	0.30	44	26	30	36	112	97	126	6%	99	2%	100%	17	47%	35%	4.46	5.5	18	49	$2
1st Half		49	5	0	2	0	165	168	225	206	431	222	804	7	76	0.32	38	13	50	22	185	42	282	0%	92	0%	0%	6	33%	17%	1.42	-3.2	-20	-54	-$7
2nd Half		123	14	2	11	1	317	264	387	455	842	859	835	8	72	0.29	45	28	27	43	99	119	98	8%	103	3%	100%	11	55%	45%	6.32	9.7	32	86	$6
15	Proj	**193**	**21**	**4**	**19**	**2**	**246**	**244**	**319**	**365**	**684**	**678**	**686**	**8**	**75**	**0.34**	**43**	**24**	**33**	**31**	**108**	**94**	**104**	**8%**	**99**	**5%**	**88%**				**3.81**	**2.4**	**15**	**39**	**$4**

Cespedes,Yoenis

Age: 29 Bats: R Pos: LF DH	Health A	LIMA Plan A
Ht: 5' 10" Wt: 210	PT/Exp A	Rand Var 0
	Consist C	MM 4335

Maybe it's the back-to-back HR Derby titles have him FB happy. In real games, though, fewer are clearing the fence, and his repressed LD% is taking BA with it. But power skill is steady as she comes. In friendlier home venue, projection may be understated. UP: 30-35 HR

Yr	Tm	AB	R	HR	RBI	SB	BA	xBA	OBP	SLG	OPS	vL	vR	bb%	ct%	Eye	G	L	F	h%	HctX	PX	xPX	hr/f	Spd	SBO	SB%	#Wk	DOM	DIS	RC/G	RAR	BPV	BPX	R$
10	for	342	85	13	65	5	322		383	529	912			9	88	0.79				34		121	-5		132	7%	57%				7.43	21.5	106	230	$21
11	for	354	87	20	97	10	311		380	536	915			10	89	1.04				30		128	2		92	12%	75%				7.47	22.9	109	242	$26
12	OAK	487	70	23	82	16	292	269	356	505	861	853	864	8	79	0.42	40	20	40	33	114	132	114	15%	113	15%	80%	26	58%	19%	6.36	24.5	74	185	$25
13	OAK	529	74	26	80	7	240	244	294	442	737	880	672	7	74	0.27	38	17	46	28	97	136	127	14%	119	12%	50%	24	46%	29%	4.11	2.2	56	140	$17
14	2AL	600	89	22	100	7	260	255	301	450	751	666	777	6	79	0.27	34	18	48	30	106	134	127	10%	113	7%	78%	27	56%	11%	4.66	16.9	69	186	$23
1st Half		308	50	14	55	1	273	273	326	497	823	808	828	8	80	0.40	33	18	49	30	103	155	125	11%	110	4%	33%	14	71%	0%	5.57	16.2	93	251	$25
2nd Half		292	39	8	45	6	247	236	273	401	673	483	725	3	77	0.15	34	19	47	29	109	111	129	7%	110	11%	100%	13	38%	23%	3.79	0.4	40	108	$20
15	Proj	**558**	**84**	**26**	**94**	**9**	**264**	**264**	**313**	**473**	**786**	**803**	**779**	**6**	**78**	**0.31**	**36**	**18**	**46**	**30**	**104**	**143**	**125**	**13%**	**115**	**10%**	**70%**				**5.02**	**20.8**	**76**	**201**	**$24**

Chavez,Endy

Age: 37 Bats: L Pos: RF	Health B	LIMA Plan D
Ht: 5' 11" Wt: 170	PT/Exp F	Rand Var -1
	Consist B	MM 1221

2-23-.276 in 232 AB at SEA. Hit five HR and stole 32 bases as an Expo ten years ago; has totals of eight and 36 since. He's forged a 13-year career by slapping singles against RHP and LHP equally, and his managers have lauded his makeup. Doubt if they'd draft him for their fantasy teams, though.

Yr	Tm	AB	R	HR	RBI	SB	BA	xBA	OBP	SLG	OPS	vL	vR	bb%	ct%	Eye	G	L	F	h%	HctX	PX	xPX	hr/f	Spd	SBO	SB%	#Wk	DOM	DIS	RC/G	RAR	BPV	BPX	R$
10																																			
11	TEX *	384	46	6	37	13	276	280	305	392	697	818	735	4	90	0.42	50	20	30	29	78	71	74	8%	139	20%	73%	21	43%	38%	4.16	-11.1	69	153	$12
12	BAL *	215	19	2	15	3	182	246	214	249	463	370	544	4	85	0.28	55	19	27	20	81	47	32	6%	91	13%	60%	16	13%	38%	1.62	-22.5	16	40	-$4
13	SEA *	294	27	2	15	1	272	251	298	329	627	530	646	4	88	0.31	53	22	25	30	97	42	74	3%	108	9%	15%	24	21%	42%	3.15	-9.7	27	68	$3
14	SEA *	346	31	2	27	5	249	240	295	317	612	232	753	6	85	0.42	49	19	31	29	71	51	51	3%	123	13%	41%	18	50%	28%	2.95	-9.8	31	84	$4
1st Half		205	18	1	11	1	225	248	263	291	554	0	811	5	85	0.34	49	23	29	26	60	46	32	4%	126	15%	14%	6	67%	17%	2.18	-11.8	26	70	$1
2nd Half		141	13	1	16	4	284	236	338	355	692	464	718	8	84	0.55	50	17	33	33	78	58	64	3%	109	11%	80%	12	42%	33%	4.35	1.4	34	92	$9
15	Proj	**166**	**15**	**2**	**13**	**3**	**253**	**253**	**291**	**331**	**622**	**406**	**665**	**5**	**86**	**0.40**	**51**	**20**	**29**	**28**	**80**	**57**	**56**	**4%**	**111**	**12%**	**50%**				**3.15**	**-4.2**	**22**	**58**	**$3**

Chirinos,Robinson

Age: 31 Bats: R Pos: CA	Health D	LIMA Plan D+
Ht: 6' 1" Wt: 205	PT/Exp F	Rand Var 0
	Consist C	MM 3111

Longtime minor leaguer provided major-league value in first extended action. Gunned down 40% of would-be base stealers and HR total was his second-highest at any level. Age, plate skills suggest this may be as good as it gets, but #2 catchers are all about damage control. Worth an extra buck.

Yr	Tm	AB	R	HR	RBI	SB	BA	xBA	OBP	SLG	OPS	vL	vR	bb%	ct%	Eye	G	L	F	h%	HctX	PX	xPX	hr/f	Spd	SBO	SB%	#Wk	DOM	DIS	RC/G	RAR	BPV	BPX	R$
10	a/a	319	42	13	50	1	266		328	460	788			8	84	0.58				28		128			87	9%	10%				4.86		83	180	$9
11	TAM *	337	22	5	25	1	208	174	265	296	561	833	576	7	71	0.26	54	7	39	28	43	71	44	6%	104	3%	38%	5	40%	60%	2.49	-18.0	-12	-27	-$3
12																																			
13	TEX *	293	26	6	27	1	199	194	269	305	574	445	583	9	75	0.37	24	19	57	25	98	77	175	0%	97	2%	100%	8	38%	38%	2.63	-9.9	9	23	-$2
14	TEX	306	36	13	40	0	239	259	290	415	705	759	682	5	77	0.24	42	21	37	27	100	126	130	15%	75	2%	0%	26	35%	35%	3.81	4.5	43	116	$6
1st Half		161	14	7	23	0	248	258	283	435	718	715	719	4	76	0.15	43	21	36	29	97	137	118	16%	79	0%	0%	14	29%	43%	4.06	3.2	46	124	$6
2nd Half		145	22	6	17	0	228	257	298	393	691	798	637	7	78	0.34	41	21	38	25	104	115	142	14%	80	3%	0%	12	42%	25%	3.55	0.7	44	119	$6
15	Proj	**228**	**25**	**8**	**26**	**1**	**238**	**237**	**299**	**385**	**684**	**809**	**651**	**7**	**76**	**0.32**	**46**	**16**	**38**	**28**	**78**	**109**	**97**	**11%**	**84**	**4%**	**58%**				**3.72**	**2.2**	**22**	**58**	**$5**

Chisenhall,Lonnie

Age: 26 Bats: L Pos: 3B	Health B	LIMA Plan B
Ht: 6' 2" Wt: 190	PT/Exp D	Rand Var -2
	Consist A	MM 3335

So completely out of his gourd in the 1st half and so earthbound in the second. The aggregate says it was a growth year for bb%, Eye and LD%, pumping up BA and OBA. But xPX and HctX are treading water. BPIs are painting a good player rather than a star, but he's young enough to change the palette.

Yr	Tm	AB	R	HR	RBI	SB	BA	xBA	OBP	SLG	OPS	vL	vR	bb%	ct%	Eye	G	L	F	h%	HctX	PX	xPX	hr/f	Spd	SBO	SB%	#Wk	DOM	DIS	RC/G	RAR	BPV	BPX	R$
10	aa	460	64	12	66	2	245		301	378	679			7	82	0.44				28		88			103	2%	100%				3.87		44	96	$9
11	CLE *	467	62	12	57	1	242	246	287	388	675	888	640	6	78	0.29	38	20	42	29	103	106	117	10%	107	2%	47%	14	50%	21%	3.72	-15.0	44	98	$8
12	CLE *	260	28	8	29	2	267	275	297	431	729	442	848	4	80	0.21	43	25	32	31	82	110	67	14%	95	5%	67%	9	44%	22%	4.43	-0.8	46	115	$5
13	CLE *	394	48	16	58	3	256	262	302	445	747	408	705	6	79	0.31	38	20	42	29	83	130	93	11%	107	3%	100%	22	68%	23%	4.64	7.9	65	163	$11
14	CLE	478	62	13	59	3	280	261	343	427	770	729	782	8	79	0.39	38	24	38	33	83	109	93	9%	100	3%	75%	27	56%	22%	5.06	18.7	51	138	$16
1st Half		220	33	8	36	2	345	303	399	555	954	946	956	7	82	0.41	35	26	39	39	103	152	126	11%	98	3%	100%	14	71%	7%	8.50	27.1	96	259	$24
2nd Half		258	29	5	23	1	225	224	295	318	613	599	617	8	77	0.38	40	22	38	27	65	70	63	7%	104	3%	50%	13	38%	38%	2.98	-5.6	13	35	$9
15	Proj	**490**	**61**	**15**	**62**	**3**	**265**	**262**	**320**	**422**	**742**	**655**	**766**	**7**	**79**	**0.34**	**39**	**22**	**39**	**31**	**83**	**116**	**89**	**10%**	**100**	**3%**	**78%**				**4.60**	**12.9**	**43**	**114**	**$15**

ROB CARROLL

Choice,Michael

Age: 25	Bats: R	Pos: LF	Health	A	LIMA Plan	D+
Ht: 6' 0"	Wt: 215		PT/Exp	C	Rand Var	+4
			Consist	B	MM	3103

9-36-.182 in 253 AB at TEX. It was an all or (mostly) nothing season; unexpressed HR power result of too little contact, high GB%. Showed he could work a walk, but paltry LD%, h% kept BA miniscule. Heralded rookie simply didn't hit with expected authority or frequency, but more opportunities await.

Yr	Tm	AB	R	HR	RBI	SB	BA	xBA	OBP	SLG	OPS	vL	vR	bb%	ct%	Eye	G	L	F	h%	HctX	PX	xPX	hr/f	Spd	SBO	SB%	#Wk	DOM	DIS	RC/G	RAR	BPV	BPX	R$
10																																			
11																																			
12	aa	359	45	7	43	4	241		292	342	634			7	72	0.26				32		73			97	5%	77%				3.36		-7	-18	$5
13	OAK *	528	65	9	62	1	246	198	311	347	658	583	700	9	73	0.36	58	8	33	32	101	81	131	0%	96	2%	23%	4	25%	50%	3.59	-6.0	6	15	$8
14	TEX *	403	36	14	56	2	195	213	262	335	597	709	505	8	69	0.29	50	13	37	24	77	107	103	13%	75	4%	66%	19	37%	53%	2.77	-11.7	4	11	$2
1st Half		189	16	8	28	1	180	220	252	328	580	699	527	9	75	0.40	52	13	34	20	88	100	102	16%	69	2%	100%	14	43%	57%	2.62	-6.8	19	51	$0
2nd Half		214	20	6	28	1	209	196	268	342	610	728	434	7	65	0.23	41	14	45	29	58	113	105	5%	85	5%	53%	5	20%	40%	2.90	-5.6	-7	-19	$4
15	Proj	322	34	9	41	2	221	210	298	349	646	810	564	8	71	0.30	45	13	41	28	70	101	104	10%	78	3%	60%				3.21	-5.2	0	-1	$2

Choo,Shin-Soo

Age: 32	Bats: L	Pos: LF DH	Health	C	LIMA Plan	B+
Ht: 5' 11"	Wt: 205		PT/Exp	A	Rand Var	0
			Consist	D	MM	3225

Felled by ankle and elbow injuries, the latter truncating his season. Notable was SBO with new team—was it the ankle or reluctance borne of 2013's SB%? Still walks a bunch and makes hard contact, but threat of 20/20 is what drives his value. Barring surprises, expect at least a partial rebound.

Yr	Tm	AB	R	HR	RBI	SB	BA	xBA	OBP	SLG	OPS	vL	vR	bb%	ct%	Eye	G	L	F	h%	HctX	PX	xPX	hr/f	Spd	SBO	SB%	#Wk	DOM	DIS	RC/G	RAR	BPV	BPX	R$
10	CLE	550	81	22	90	22	300	277	401	484	885	670	998	13	79	0.70	45	20	35	35	123	124	136	15%	78	15%	76%	24	63%	21%	6.89	26.4	65	141	$30
11	CLE	313	37	8	36	12	259	245	344	390	733	688	757	10	75	0.46	45	22	32	32	116	91	128	10%	97	18%	71%	17	35%	41%	4.44	-6.7	25	56	$9
12	CLE	598	88	16	67	21	283	268	373	441	815	605	926	11	75	0.49	50	23	27	35	99	118	107	13%	82	15%	75%	27	48%	33%	5.64	13.4	42	105	$24
13	CIN	569	107	21	54	20	285	273	423	462	885	612	1011	16	77	0.84	49	21	29	34	96	126	99	16%	114	14%	65%	27	59%	15%	6.46	35.6	76	190	$29
14	TEX	455	58	13	40	3	242	236	340	374	714	673	732	11	71	0.44	50	20	30	31	113	104	110	13%	91	5%	43%	21	33%	43%	4.01	1.5	20	54	$8
1st Half		275	41	7	29	3	251	245	368	382	750	740	754	13	74	0.58	50	21	30	32	114	102	115	11%	90	7%	50%	14	50%	36%	4.43	3.6	32	86	$13
2nd Half		180	17	6	11	0	228	217	295	361	656	570	696	8	67	0.27	51	20	30	30	111	107	100	17%	89	2%	0%	7	0%	57%	3.38	-3.4	-1	-3	$1
15	Proj	555	83	18	52	11	260	253	362	410	772	630	839	12	73	0.50	49	21	30	33	107	117	107	15%	95	10%	63%				4.83	17.8	37	96	$19

Clark,Matthew

Age: 28	Bats: L	Pos: 1B	Health	A	LIMA Plan	D
Ht: 6' 5"	Wt: 215		PT/Exp	C	Rand Var	-2
			Consist	B	MM	4003

3-7-.185 in 27 AB in MIL. Clubbed 150 HR during six seasons of organizational and international odyssey, so 2014 punch not a surprise. But low contact rate also tagged along, putting BA in peril. Late bloomer is far from a sure thing, but it's hard to ignore that power.

Yr	Tm	AB	R	HR	RBI	SB	BA	xBA	OBP	SLG	OPS	vL	vR	bb%	ct%	Eye	G	L	F	h%	HctX	PX	xPX	hr/f	Spd	SBO	SB%	#Wk	DOM	DIS	RC/G	RAR	BPV	BPX	R$
10	aa	498	51	21	81	0	223		282	387	669			8	65	0.23				30		129			88	0%	0%				3.59		5	11	$6
11	aaa	462	41	12	48	0	206		263	323	586			7	67	0.24				28		94			84	2%	0%				2.66		-13	-29	-$1
12	aaa	445	49	13	50	0	217		279	353	632			8	68	0.26				29		104			89	0%	0%				3.21		-1	-3	$3
13	for	407	55	15	68	0	222		291	367	658			9	70	0.32				28		107			78	0%	0%				3.50	-13.5	8	20	$6
14	MIL *	441	50	23	64	0	240	213	290	440	730	0	744	6	70	0.23	30	10	60	29	91	151	210	25%	73	0%	0%	5	40%	40%	4.28	1.2	38	103	$11
1st Half		219	22	8	32	0	238	243	296	397	692			8	74	0.31				29		122			84	0%	0%				3.92		35	95	$7
2nd Half		222	28	15	33	0	244	223	285	485	770	0	744	5	66	0.17	30	10	60	29	86	182	210	25%	79	0%	0%	5	40%	40%	4.66	3.2	48	130	$16
15	Proj	292	34	11	43	0	230	222	269	386	655		626	7	69	0.25	35	20	45	29	77	123	189	13%	77	0%	0%				3.65	-4.6	0	1	$6

Coghlan,Chris

Age: 30	Bats: L	Pos: LF	Health	F	LIMA Plan	D+
Ht: 6' 0"	Wt: 195		PT/Exp	D	Rand Var	-2
			Consist	C	MM	2333

9-41-.283 with 7 SB in 385 AB at CHC. Nice follow-up to ROY campaign—five years late. Responded to PT jump in 2nd half to work himself back onto rosters. LD are up, GB are down, and he amped up the power to complement good wheels. But be skeptical of full repeat; he's had us in this position before.

Yr	Tm	AB	R	HR	RBI	SB	BA	xBA	OBP	SLG	OPS	vL	vR	bb%	ct%	Eye	G	L	F	h%	HctX	PX	xPX	hr/f	Spd	SBO	SB%	#Wk	DOM	DIS	RC/G	RAR	BPV	BPX	R$
10	FLA	358	60	5	28	10	268	268	335	383	718	709	720	8	77	0.39	51	24	25	34	77	87	67	7%	125	13%	77%	17	35%	41%	4.42	-8.7	32	70	$10
11	FLA *	341	42	6	27	9	220	269	284	345	628	307	801	8	84	0.54	49	20	32	25	85	92	78	7%	85	22%	55%	12	50%	25%	3.02	-24.0	52	116	$3
12	MIA *	410	40	6	32	7	209	250	287	307	594	186	451	10	83	0.64	63	13	23	24	52	65	28	5%	94	11%	62%	9	11%	33%	2.79	-25.0	34	85	$0
13	MIA	195	10	1	10	2	256	242	318	354	672	861	641	8	78	0.40	50	21	29	32	84	73	65	2%	118	4%	100%	15	33%	53%	3.90	-0.8	24	60	$0
14	CHC *	455	56	9	45	11	268	271	338	419	757	709	832	10	77	0.46	43	26	31	33	100	118	80	9%	111	13%	67%	22	45%	41%	4.85	14.1	58	157	$14
1st Half		173	16	2	8	6	196	217	279	294	573	812	562	10	73	0.42	40	22	38	26	91	77	78	7%	119	17%	82%	9	33%	56%	2.67	-5.9	12	32	-$4
2nd Half		282	40	7	37	5	312	300	378	496	874	680	939	9	80	0.49	44	27	29	37	104	141	80	11%	106	11%	56%	13	54%	31%	6.64	22.5	84	227	$26
15	Proj	389	40	6	31	8	253	262	322	382	703	655	716	9	78	0.46	48	22	30	31	86	100	67	7%	107	11%	71%				4.14	4.6	43	114	$9

Colon,Christian

Age: 26	Bats: R	Pos: 2B	Health	A	LIMA Plan	D+
Ht: 5' 10"	Wt: 190		PT/Exp	C	Rand Var	+1
			Consist	B	MM	1453

0-6-.333 in 45 AB at KC. Fourth overall pick in 2010 and took his time getting to the big leagues. Pop hasn't developed (surprisingly few doubles) but supreme contact, LD bent and Spd should underwrite sound BA. Carries modest, situational value—a bit more if power comes. A big "if" at this stage.

Yr	Tm	AB	R	HR	RBI	SB	BA	xBA	OBP	SLG	OPS	vL	vR	bb%	ct%	Eye	G	L	F	h%	HctX	PX	xPX	hr/f	Spd	SBO	SB%	#Wk	DOM	DIS	RC/G	RAR	BPV	BPX	R$
10																																			
11	aa	491	51	5	45	13	226		276	291	567			6	89	0.63				24		41			103	16%	62%				2.57		35	78	$5
12	a/a	290	28	4	24	9	258		315	344	659			8	89	0.80				28		50			107	19%	57%				3.53		47	118	$5
13	aaa	512	57	9	46	12	242		287	326	613			6	88	0.52				26		49			121	12%	72%				3.14		41	103	$10
14	KC *	397	49	5	40	14	269	307	313	368	681	882	851	6	90	0.65	51	28	21	29	74	70	37	0%	105	17%	74%	9	56%	33%	4.01	7.1	63	170	$13
1st Half		294	33	3	25	10	243	248	290	309	599			6	90	0.68				26		48			88	17%	73%	1	100%	0%	3.02		41	111	$15
2nd Half		103	14	3	13	3	326	344	359	515	874	882	851	5	89	0.48	51	28	21	35	74	129	37	0%	114	18%	74%	8	50%	38%	6.90	9.7	107	289	$9
15	Proj	263	31	3	26	8	270	299	314	362	675	755	629	6	89	0.59	51	28	21	29	67	64	33	6%	123	16%	68%				3.90	3.9	50	133	$9

Conger,Hank

Age: 27	Bats: B	Pos: CA	Health	A	LIMA Plan	D
Ht: 6' 2"	Wt: 220		PT/Exp	F	Rand Var	0
			Consist	C	MM	2003

What was supposed to be a growth year didn't pan out. Eye, bb% did improve, but power regression and FB spike led to lots of lazy fly outs. He's past the prospect stage; things need to coalesce. Unfortunately, one step forward, two steps back doesn't forge a career--unless you're a moonwalker.

Yr	Tm	AB	R	HR	RBI	SB	BA	xBA	OBP	SLG	OPS	vL	vR	bb%	ct%	Eye	G	L	F	h%	HctX	PX	xPX	hr/f	Spd	SBO	SB%	#Wk	DOM	DIS	RC/G	RAR	BPV	BPX	R$
10	LAA *	416	41	8	39	0	245	252	315	365	680	333	587	9	82	0.57	55	15	30	28	101	84	82	0%	88	2%	0%	5	40%	60%	3.79	-5.1	43	93	$4
11	LAA *	277	23	9	36	0	221	230	285	361	646	539	644	8	79	0.43	39	18	44	25	76	95	92	10%	72	0%	0%	21	43%	33%	3.37	-7.0	32	71	$1
12	LAA *	282	32	6	29	1	226	189	260	336	597	0	405	4	79	0.22	58	0	42	27	52	77	28	0%	90	2%	100%	4	25%	0%	2.91	-10.4	16	40	$1
13	LAA	233	23	7	21	0	249	237	310	403	713	629	724	7	74	0.28	39	20	41	31	116	115	135	10%	87	2%	0%	27	44%	41%	4.03	2.1	29	73	$2
14	LAA	231	24	4	25	0	221	210	293	325	618	622	614	9	75	0.39	37	17	47	28	84	86	80	5%	63	4%	0%	27	37%	44%	2.95	-2.6	8	22	$0
1st Half		126	16	3	16	0	238	223	319	373	692	721	684	9	75	0.41	35	16	48	30	82	111	92	7%	70	0%	0%	14	43%	36%	3.86	1.8	29	78	$2
2nd Half		105	8	1	9	0	200	195	261	267	528	333	534	8	76	0.36	38	17	44	25	86	56	66	3%	75	8%	0%	13	31%	54%	2.04	-4.6	-10	-27	-$3
15	Proj	240	24	6	24	0	227	225	290	352	642	594	645	7	76	0.34	38	18	44	28	94	97	99	7%	71	3%	7%				3.20	-1.4	9	25	$3

Corporan,Carlos

Age: 31	Bats: B	Pos: CA	Health	A	LIMA Plan	D
Ht: 6' 2"	Wt: 245		PT/Exp	F	Rand Var	0
			Consist	A	MM	2011

Behold! What you just witnessed in 2014 was his likely peak career performance. At 31, you really can't expect further growth, so you have to live with the highs in ct%, xPX, RC/G, RAR, BPX and all three components of his slash line. Unfortunatetly, his high water mark for AB was 191 in 2013.

Yr	Tm	AB	R	HR	RBI	SB	BA	xBA	OBP	SLG	OPS	vL	vR	bb%	ct%	Eye	G	L	F	h%	HctX	PX	xPX	hr/f	Spd	SBO	SB%	#Wk	DOM	DIS	RC/G	RAR	BPV	BPX	R$
10	aaa	286	23	7	30	2	229		265	386	651			5	74	0.19				29		116			109	9%	50%				3.29		32	70	$1
11	HOU *	234	15	2	20	0	193	201	243	278	522	673	451	6	71	0.23	45	17	38	26	65	74	68	0%	69	3%	0%	16	13%	69%	2.08	-15.8	-22	-49	-$4
12	HOU *	284	27	8	32	1	229	248	264	359	623	433	855	5	72	0.17	32	32	37	29	83	96	89	18%	58	4%	55%	9	56%	22%	3.10	-8.9	-5	-13	$2
13	HOU	191	16	7	20	0	225	210	287	361	648	660	640	5	69	0.17	44	20	36	29	89	99	108	15%	65	0%	0%	25	20%	64%	3.13	-3.3	-14	-35	$0
14	HOU	170	22	6	19	0	235	242	302	376	678	606	730	8	78	0.38	39	21	40	27	82	97	108	11%	63	0%	0%	25	32%	44%	3.68	1.8	27	73	$2
1st Half		85	11	5	13	0	235	252	287	435	723	697	758	4	82	0.27	42	14	44	23	93	121	123	16%	68	0%	0%	14	43%	43%	3.91	1.3	58	157	$3
2nd Half		85	11	1	6	0	235	237	316	318	633	414	714	11	74	0.45	35	29	35	31	71	72	90	5%	68	0%	0%	11	18%	45%	3.34	-0.1	-2	-5	$0
15	Proj	164	18	5	17	0	229	236	291	361	652	590	687	7	74	0.27	39	23	38	28	81	99	99	11%	63	1%	45%				3.33	-0.3	1	3	$2

ROB CARROLL

Cowgill,Collin

Age: 29 Bats: R Pos: RF LF | Ht: 5' 9" Wt: 185
Health B | PT/Exp D | Consist B
LIMA Plan D | Rand Var -4 | MM 1401

It was a case of good luck/bad luck; LD rained until they stopped and balls found holes until they didn't. But the good times didn't produce THAT much, and the net result was a minus: further ct% erosion and the lack of punch leading to too many easy outs. That's where his chips usually fall.

Yr Tm	AB	R	HR	RBI	SB	BA	xBA	OBP	SLG	OPS	vL	vR	bb%	ct%	Eye	G	L	F	h%	HctX	PX	xPX	hr/f	Spd	SBO	SB%	#Wk	DOM	DIS	RC/G	RAR	BPV	BPX	R$
10 aa	502	73	13	68	20	263		325	427	752			8	84	0.58				29		108			107	24%	67%				4.64		74	161	$18
11 ARI *	487	60	8	48	21	270	248	319	391	710	716	518	7	79	0.34	48	19	33	33	81	85	115	5%	156	20%	78%	10	20%	60%	4.39	-12.4	45	100	$16
12 OAK *	364	32	3	34	8	216	241	266	290	556	844	510	6	76	0.28	55	23	22	28	47	57	30	6%	108	18%	57%	11	0%	64%	2.40	-24.7	-2	-5	$1
13 2 TM *	290	33	8	27	4	215	218	260	346	605	669	456	6	73	0.22	51	11	37	27	75	92	74	10%	124	7%	100%	21	24%	71%	2.98	-8.8	17	43	$2
14 LAA	260	37	5	21	4	250	214	330	354	684	790	586	9	72	0.35	49	16	36	33	61	83	42	8%	128	5%	100%	23	26%	48%	3.92	1.7	11	30	$5
1st Half	159	26	5	15	1	289	235	362	434	796	905	683	9	70	0.34	45	20	35	38	80	118	70	13%	116	2%	100%	14	36%	36%	5.56	8.1	31	84	$9
2nd Half	101	11	0	6	3	188	177	281	228	508	581	452	9	73	0.37	56	9	36	26	30	32	0	0%	134	12%	100%	9	11%	67%	2.00	-5.6	-21	-57	-$2
15 Proj	**226**	**27**	**4**	**19**	**5**	**227**	**218**	**293**	**323**	**616**	**721**	**512**	**8**	**74**	**0.32**	**52**	**15**	**34**	**29**	**59**	**76**	**49**	**6%**	**124**	**10%**	**84%**				**3.10**	**-6.2**	**4**	**10**	**$2**

Cozart,Zack

Age: 29 Bats: R Pos: SS | Ht: 6' 0" Wt: 195
Health A | PT/Exp A | Consist B
LIMA Plan C+ | Rand Var +3 | MM 2525

With 27 HR in 2012-13, the scarcity of much else was somewhat tolerable. But when BA and PX nosedived, he accrued an inordinate amount of empty AB in 2014. Reconciled GB bent by finding his legs again, but reclaiming his power stroke is what he needs to rise above the morass of middling middle infielders.

Yr Tm	AB	R	HR	RBI	SB	BA	xBA	OBP	SLG	OPS	vL	vR	bb%	ct%	Eye	G	L	F	h%	HctX	PX	xPX	hr/f	Spd	SBO	SB%	#Wk	DOM	DIS	RC/G	RAR	BPV	BPX	R$
10 aaa	553	68	14	50	22	216		257	349	606			5	77	0.24				26		93			112	25%	83%				2.98		29	63	$9
11 CIN *	360	47	8	26	6	260	248	292	389	681	667	880	4	81	0.24	58	10	32	30	115	92	163	20%	128	11%	73%	3	33%	33%	3.89	-6.4	47	104	$7
12 CIN	561	72	15	35	4	246	254	288	399	687	699	683	5	80	0.27	42	20	38	28	83	102	86	9%	135	3%	100%	26	35%	19%	3.89	-3.5	54	135	$8
13 CIN	567	74	12	63	0	254	255	284	381	665	686	658	4	82	0.25	50	18	32	29	83	88	63	8%	115	0%	0%	27	48%	19%	3.73	3.8	44	110	$11
14 CIN	506	48	4	38	7	221	231	268	300	568	702	532	5	84	0.32	45	18	38	26	84	55	77	3%	138	6%	100%	27	33%	33%	2.60	-10.6	34	92	$2
1st Half	276	25	2	21	2	228	237	276	304	580	658	557	5	83	0.30	45	20	35	27	87	60	83	2%	104	3%	100%	14	36%	36%	2.71	-4.5	24	65	$2
2nd Half	230	23	2	17	5	213	222	258	296	554	765	503	5	86	0.33	44	15	41	24	80	50	69	3%	170	10%	100%	13	31%	31%	2.48	-5.4	45	122	$3
15 Proj	**539**	**61**	**10**	**45**	**6**	**234**	**249**	**275**	**352**	**627**	**718**	**600**	**5**	**83**	**0.30**	**46**	**18**	**36**	**27**	**83**	**82**	**72**	**6%**	**133**	**6%**	**94%**				**3.22**	**-0.3**	**40**	**106**	**$9**

Craig,Allen

Age: 30 Bats: R Pos: RF 1B | Ht: 6' 2" Wt: 215
Health C | PT/Exp B | Consist F
LIMA Plan C+ | Rand Var +5 | MM 2225

Crappy year was made worse by injuries, but tumble has been percolating for a while. Even if you discount injury-marred 2nd half, FB, PX, and hr/f are on 3-year slides. Even so, he's been a precise hitter whose results always seemed to transcend his BPI. That gives credence to a rebound, however modest.

Yr Tm	AB	R	HR	RBI	SB	BA	xBA	OBP	SLG	OPS	vL	vR	bb%	ct%	Eye	G	L	F	h%	HctX	PX	xPX	hr/f	Spd	SBO	SB%	#Wk	DOM	DIS	RC/G	RAR	BPV	BPX	R$
10 STL *	420	50	13	72	1	249	262	302	407	710	674	739	7	77	0.33	38	22	39	30	120	115	141	11%	84	2%	40%	13	38%	38%	4.15	-12.3	41	89	$9
11 STL *	241	39	12	44	5	292	291	340	508	848	1000	875	7	81	0.39	44	19	37	32	129	144	111	18%	97	8%	100%	17	47%	41%	6.36	8.1	85	189	$11
12 STL	469	76	22	92	2	307	293	354	522	876	1011	827	7	81	0.42	44	23	33	34	104	140	112	17%	80	2%	67%	22	64%	5%	6.85	25.4	77	193	$23
13 STL	508	71	13	97	2	315	277	373	457	830	779	845	7	80	0.40	45	27	28	37	111	99	100	11%	93	1%	100%	23	48%	17%	6.23	26.6	45	113	$25
14 2 TM	461	41	8	46	2	215	242	279	315	594	693	559	7	75	0.31	54	21	25	27	100	79	105	9%	84	3%	67%	25	20%	56%	2.75	-16.2	7	19	$1
1st Half	318	32	6	40	1	255	259	305	368	673	753	647	6	80	0.33	55	21	24	30	107	85	103	10%	93	3%	50%	14	29%	43%	3.75	-2.3	30	81	$9
2nd Half	143	9	2	6	1	126	200	224	196	419	578	356	9	66	0.29	51	22	27	17	85	63	110	8%	72	4%	100%	11	9%	73%	1.19	-13.8	-45	-122	-$14
15 Proj	**421**	**47**	**10**	**56**	**2**	**264**	**256**	**327**	**392**	**719**	**789**	**693**	**8**	**77**	**0.35**	**48**	**23**	**29**	**32**	**103**	**99**	**108**	**11%**	**79**	**2%**	**84%**				**4.36**	**4.4**	**19**	**51**	**$12**

Crawford,Brandon

Age: 28 Bats: L Pos: SS | Ht: 6' 2" Wt: 215
Health A | PT/Exp B | Consist A
LIMA Plan B+ | Rand Var -3 | MM 2215

First-half PX and BA vL put him on course for career year (one of only two players with double-digit 2B, 3B, and HR). BA has been interminably flat, but jump in xPX and reversals of GB/FB could provide some upside if ct% rebounds. No longer stuck with the "deep leagues only" stigma.

Yr Tm	AB	R	HR	RBI	SB	BA	xBA	OBP	SLG	OPS	vL	vR	bb%	ct%	Eye	G	L	F	h%	HctX	PX	xPX	hr/f	Spd	SBO	SB%	#Wk	DOM	DIS	RC/G	RAR	BPV	BPX	R$
10 aa	291	37	6	19	3	223		303	342	645			10	71	0.40				29		89			133	6%	76%				3.41		19	41	$1
11 SF *	303	30	4	27	4	197	224	266	279	545	445	608	9	82	0.52	51	14	35	23	75	55	79	5%	109	13%	44%	14	36%	43%	2.22	-22.2	24	53	-$2
12 SF	435	44	4	45	1	248	246	304	349	653	631	661	7	78	0.35	47	23	30	31	98	77	85	4%	88	5%	20%	27	26%	37%	3.44	-8.6	17	43	$4
13 SF	499	52	9	43	1	248	246	311	363	674	546	727	8	81	0.44	49	19	32	29	83	80	78	7%	105	2%	33%	27	41%	41%	3.72	3.2	36	90	$6
14 SF	491	54	10	69	5	246	229	324	389	713	879	637	11	74	0.46	38	20	42	32	91	103	126	6%	127	6%	63%	27	48%	37%	4.26	14.1	39	105	$11
1st Half	259	34	7	36	2	251	247	329	444	773	1007	678	11	75	0.47	37	18	45	31	92	135	132	8%	143	6%	50%	14	64%	21%	4.90	12.7	72	195	$13
2nd Half	232	20	3	33	3	241	212	318	328	646	756	588	11	73	0.44	39	22	39	32	91	66	118	5%	96	6%	75%	13	31%	54%	3.57	2.3	-3	-8	$8
15 Proj	**552**	**58**	**11**	**64**	**4**	**252**	**237**	**322**	**379**	**701**	**750**	**681**	**9**	**76**	**0.44**	**43**	**20**	**38**	**31**	**89**	**93**	**102**	**7%**	**109**	**5%**	**54%**				**4.11**	**14.1**	**26**	**69**	**$12**

Crawford,Carl

Age: 33 Bats: L Pos: LF | Ht: 6' 2" Wt: 225
Health F | PT/Exp D | Consist B
LIMA Plan B | Rand Var -2 | MM 3545

On August 31, he was hitting .264/.305/.359. Then came September and talk of glory days. Truth is, his yearly BPI are remarkably consistent despite four straight seasons of missing 30+ games to injury. Entering his mid-30s, skills intact, a mini-Renaissance is possible—if he can avoid the trainer's room.

Yr Tm	AB	R	HR	RBI	SB	BA	xBA	OBP	SLG	OPS	vL	vR	bb%	ct%	Eye	G	L	F	h%	HctX	PX	xPX	hr/f	Spd	SBO	SB%	#Wk	DOM	DIS	RC/G	RAR	BPV	BPX	R$
10 TAM	600	110	19	90	47	307	284	356	495	851	696	930	7	83	0.44	47	16	36	35	94	116	98	11%	158	34%	82%	27	63%	15%	6.58	21.9	87	189	$42
11 BOS	506	65	11	56	18	255	261	289	405	694	566	757	4	79	0.22	48	18	34	30	102	104	112	8%	112	23%	75%	23	30%	26%	3.95	-19.7	45	100	$14
12 BOS *	139	26	3	20	6	285	291	310	460	771	856	750	4	82	0.21	54	19	27	33	103	113	95	12%	114	22%	100%	6	50%	33%	5.38	2.5	63	158	$5
13 LA	435	62	6	31	15	283	278	329	407	736	551	796	6	85	0.42	47	23	30	32	104	89	90	5%	120	17%	79%	23	43%	22%	4.75	8.5	60	150	$16
14 LA	343	56	8	46	23	300	286	339	429	767	881	745	4	84	0.29	46	28	26	34	96	85	79	11%	114	31%	79%	22	41%	36%	5.21	13.7	49	132	$22
1st Half	150	21	4	18	9	267	282	293	400	693	616	708	4	87	0.30	45	25	31	29	97	85	78	10%	103	31%	82%	9	56%	22%	4.17	1.9	55	149	$11
2nd Half	193	35	4	28	14	326	289	373	451	823	1090	772	5	82	0.29	47	31	22	38	95	85	81	11%	115	31%	78%	13	31%	46%	6.13	12.5	42	114	$30
15 Proj	**433**	**70**	**10**	**52**	**22**	**289**	**282**	**329**	**435**	**765**	**760**	**766**	**5**	**84**	**0.30**	**48**	**23**	**30**	**33**	**99**	**101**	**87**	**9%**	**118**	**25%**	**80%**				**5.08**	**16.4**	**70**	**185**	**$24**

Crisp,Coco

Age: 35 Bats: B Pos: CF | Ht: 5' 10" Wt: 185
Health B | PT/Exp B | Consist B
LIMA Plan A | Rand Var +1 | MM 2435

PRO: Sustained 2013's power gains in 1H; steady ct% and LD; improved Eye and bb% for third straight year.
CON: Too many day-to-days; three-year SB/SBO slide; power evaporated in 2H. VERDICT: Was party to team-wide infirmity in final months. If healthy, he's still valuable, but forget that 20/20.

Yr Tm	AB	R	HR	RBI	SB	BA	xBA	OBP	SLG	OPS	vL	vR	bb%	ct%	Eye	G	L	F	h%	HctX	PX	xPX	hr/f	Spd	SBO	SB%	#Wk	DOM	DIS	RC/G	RAR	BPV	BPX	R$
10 OAK *	312	55	8	41	33	291	270	356	448	804	949	716	9	83	0.59	47	17	37	33	109	99	98	9%	137	40%	88%	14	57%	14%	6.13	9.2	72	157	$21
11 OAK	531	69	8	54	49	264	273	314	379	693	593	741	7	88	0.63	42	24	34	29	108	75	83	5%	109	41%	84%	26	65%	15%	4.37	-11.2	60	133	$25
12 OAK	455	68	11	46	39	259	274	325	418	742	682	774	9	86	0.70	44	20	36	28	88	95	76	8%	125	36%	91%	26	38%	23%	5.03	2.3	77	193	$22
13 OAK	513	93	22	66	21	261	278	335	444	779	645	857	11	87	0.94	41	20	40	26	91	107	85	12%	108	18%	81%	25	56%	16%	5.27	15.5	91	228	$25
14 OAK	463	68	9	47	19	246	252	336	363	699	640	726	12	86	1.00	39	20	40	27	88	79	76	6%	103	16%	79%	26	54%	23%	4.25	5.0	64	173	$15
1st Half	228	44	6	28	13	289	274	383	447	830	809	836	14	85	1.06	38	22	40	32	109	112	98	8%	96	19%	87%	14	79%	7%	6.47	16.8	87	235	$24
2nd Half	235	24	3	19	6	204	230	289	281	570	533	593	11	87	0.94	41	19	40	22	68	47	56	4%	113	13%	67%	12	25%	42%	2.61	-9.3	43	116	$6
15 Proj	**449**	**68**	**11**	**48**	**18**	**251**	**263**	**329**	**389**	**719**	**647**	**755**	**11**	**86**	**0.89**	**41**	**20**	**39**	**27**	**89**	**90**	**78**	**8%**	**110**	**18%**	**79%**				**4.47**	**8.1**	**76**	**201**	**$17**

Cron,C.J.

Age: 25 Bats: R Pos: 1B DH | Ht: 6' 4" Wt: 235
Health A | PT/Exp D | Consist B
LIMA Plan B | Rand Var 0 | MM 4133

11-37-.256 in 242 AB at LAA. Rookie hit the ball hard and often for first two months, then floundered as he was shuttled between Triple-A and the bigs. PX/xPX authenticate sock, but has to prove 2nd half tank vs. RHP was a fluke and develop plate patience/judgment. Plan on another growth year or two.

Yr Tm	AB	R	HR	RBI	SB	BA	xBA	OBP	SLG	OPS	vL	vR	bb%	ct%	Eye	G	L	F	h%	HctX	PX	xPX	hr/f	Spd	SBO	SB%	#Wk	DOM	DIS	RC/G	RAR	BPV	BPX	R$
10																																		
11																																		
12																																		
13 aa	519	48	11	71	7	242		269	372	641			4	82	0.20				28		93			78	11%	60%				3.29		35	88	$10
14 LAA *	432	46	15	57	1	249	256	283	413	696	751	731	5	75	0.19	35	25	40	30	111	123	122	15%	80	3%	50%	20	45%	45%	3.93	-1.4	32	86	$10
1st Half	244	27	11	38	0	268	287	291	491	782	844	883	3	77	0.15	28	27	45	30	132	161	163	17%	93	0%	0%	10	60%	20%	4.97	6.5	75	203	$15
2nd Half	188	19	4	19	1	225	216	273	311	584	604	583	6	71	0.23	44	23	32	30	84	69	67	12%	73	5%	50%	10	30%	70%	2.75	-7.5	-25	-68	$3
15 Proj	**402**	**40**	**16**	**52**	**3**	**242**	**270**	**276**	**422**	**699**	**721**	**686**	**4**	**77**	**0.19**	**38**	**25**	**38**	**28**	**103**	**131**	**105**	**14%**	**73**	**6%**	**59%**				**3.84**	**-3.9**	**40**	**104**	**$10**

ROB CARROLL

Cruz,Nelson

Age: 35 Bats: R Pos: DH LF
Ht: 6' 2" Wt: 230

Health B | PT/Exp A | Consist A
LIMA Plan B+ | Rand Var 0 | MM 5145

Who needs PEDs? Highly consistent power, ct%, FB% before and after suspension give us reason to believe. Concerns? Sure: advancing age, for one. You're also looking at the only two seasons in his 10-year career with more than 475 MLB AB. He's not going to hit 40 again, but should continue to be a stable power source.

Yr	Tm	AB	R	HR	RBI	SB	BA	xBA	OBP	SLG	OPS	vL	vR	bb%	ct%	Eye	G	L	F	h%	HctX	PX	xPX	hr/f	Spd	SBO	SB%	#Wk	DOM	DIS	RC/G	RAR	BPV	BPX	R$
10	TEX *	429	61	22	81	18	311	293	369	554	924	976	941	9	80	0.46	37	18	45	35	123	163	149	15%	107	19%	82%	21	57%	14%	7.60	20.7	100	217	$27
11	TEX *	497	66	31	90	9	262	278	311	512	823	1096	747	7	76	0.30	41	16	43	28	120	168	144	19%	76	13%	64%	24	71%	17%	5.36	-6.8	78	173	$21
12	TEX	585	86	24	90	8	260	262	319	460	779	944	727	8	76	0.34	41	18	41	30	129	141	151	13%	85	9%	67%	27	48%	19%	4.94	0.9	60	150	$20
13	TEX	413	49	27	76	5	266	264	327	506	833	821	837	8	74	0.32	42	17	41	30	120	162	154	21%	64	6%	83%	20	70%	25%	5.71	14.4	61	153	$18
14	BAL	613	87	40	108	4	271	285	333	525	859	977	823	8	77	0.39	42	17	41	29	119	173	131	20%	89	6%	44%	27	63%	15%	5.91	33.0	92	249	$30
1st Half		310	48	25	66	1	281	288	349	568	916	1156	834	9	77	0.44	41	16	44	29	127	191	159	24%	66	6%	20%	14	64%	7%	6.67	23.3	100	270	$35
2nd Half		303	39	15	42	3	261	280	317	482	799	752	811	7	78	0.34	43	19	38	29	111	155	102	16%	109	6%	75%	13	62%	23%	5.18	10.0	83	224	$24
15	Proj	**549**	**74**	**32**	**94**	**4**	**268**	**277**	**328**	**505**	**833**	**910**	**808**	**8**	**76**	**0.35**	**42**	**17**	**41**	**30**	**120**	**167**	**138**	**19%**	**84**	**6%**	**57%**				**5.62**	**24.9**	**74**	**193**	**$22**

Cruz,Tony

Age: 28 Bats: R Pos: CA
Ht: 5' 11" Wt: 215

Health A | PT/Exp F | Consist B
LIMA Plan D | Rand Var +2 | MM 1001

He could have some truly mad baseball skills that just don't translate to fantasy, but here's what you need to know: He's a backup catcher. Period. With the first-stringer out for two months, the team scoured the waiver wire instead of letting him start. On the flip side, his is routinely the cleanest uniform.

Yr	Tm	AB	R	HR	RBI	SB	BA	xBA	OBP	SLG	OPS	vL	vR	bb%	ct%	Eye	G	L	F	h%	HctX	PX	xPX	hr/f	Spd	SBO	SB%	#Wk	DOM	DIS	RC/G	RAR	BPV	BPX	R$
10	a/a	163	20	5	15	0	231		288	367	655			7	78	0.37				27		97			100	0%	0%				3.51		37	80	$0
11	STL *	214	17	2	23	0	223	206	271	306	577	668	674	6	77	0.28	46	15	38	28	82	64	69	0%	101	4%	0%	15	27%	40%	2.59	-11.7	4	9	-$1
12	STL	126	11	1	11	0	254	237	267	365	632	439	724	2	85	0.16	46	14	40	29	106	79	92	2%	99	4%	0%	25	36%	36%	3.25	-3.8	39	98	-$1
13	STL	123	13	1	13	0	203	241	240	293	533	235	643	3	80	0.16	54	18	28	25	104	67	77	4%	92	0%	0%	21	29%	52%	2.14	-5.9	8	20	-$3
14	STL	135	11	1	17	0	200	222	270	259	530	422	572	9	79	0.46	56	19	25	25	63	50	42	4%	70	9%	0%	25	32%	32%	2.01	-6.2	-1	-3	-$2
1st Half		48	4	0	8	0	250	248	333	292	625	650	613	11	83	0.75	53	25	23	30	62	39	54	0%	74	6%	0%	13	31%	31%	3.04	-0.5	11	30	-$2
2nd Half		87	7	1	9	0	172	213	234	241	475	302	547	7	77	0.35	58	15	27	21	64	56	34	6%	77	11%	0%	12	33%	33%	1.54	-5.4	-7	-19	-$2
15	Proj	**131**	**12**	**1**	**15**	**0**	**214**	**231**	**265**	**287**	**552**	**416**	**610**	**6**	**80**	**0.33**	**53**	**18**	**29**	**26**	**82**	**61**	**61**	**3%**	**82**	**6%**	**0%**				**2.29**	**-4.6**	**0**	**-1**	**$0**

Cuddyer,Michael

Age: 36 Bats: R Pos: RF
Ht: 6' 2" Wt: 220

Health F | PT/Exp C | Consist D
LIMA Plan B+ | Rand Var -1 | MM 5355

Career year, skills-wise, but three DL trips totaling more than three months limited PT. Jump in LD% screams "outlier", so expect BA regression even though he nailed xBA. Home park has amplified his power—with a less-friendly home and continued FB% decline, his value could plummet. DN: .270 BA, 10 HR, even if healthy.

Yr	Tm	AB	R	HR	RBI	SB	BA	xBA	OBP	SLG	OPS	vL	vR	bb%	ct%	Eye	G	L	F	h%	HctX	PX	xPX	hr/f	Spd	SBO	SB%	#Wk	DOM	DIS	RC/G	RAR	BPV	BPX	R$
10	MIN	609	93	14	81	7	271	280	336	417	753	875	700	9	85	0.62	50	17	33	30	114	97	90	8%	116	6%	70%	27	63%	15%	4.85	-5.1	71	154	$18
11	MIN	529	70	20	70	11	284	277	346	459	805	993	728	8	82	0.51	49	18	34	31	105	116	108	14%	99	8%	92%	26	54%	19%	5.71	8.3	69	153	$21
12	COL	358	53	16	58	8	260	296	317	489	806	929	760	8	78	0.41	49	20	31	29	118	155	125	18%	91	14%	73%	19	58%	21%	5.34	2.0	83	208	$13
13	COL	489	74	20	84	10	331	287	389	530	919	815	954	9	80	0.46	50	20	30	38	100	134	101	17%	118	8%	77%	26	65%	23%	7.83	41.7	80	200	$31
14	COL	190	32	10	31	3	332	332	376	579	955	1287	830	7	84	0.47	48	24	27	35	111	165	106	23%	105	6%	100%	10	70%	10%	8.46	21.7	116	314	$12
1st Half		120	16	5	16	3	317	304	366	500	866	1248	735	8	87	0.63	52	21	27	33	122	119	104	14%	101	8%	100%	6	67%	17%	7.08	9.9	90	243	$12
2nd Half		70	16	5	15	0	357	368	392	714	1106	1340	1005	5	80	0.29	41	30	29	39	93	249	110	31%	94	0%	0%	4	75%	0%	11.10	12.5	160	432	$12
15	Proj	**422**	**68**	**19**	**69**	**6**	**315**	**315**	**365**	**546**	**911**	**1066**	**852**	**7**	**81**	**0.42**	**47**	**23**	**29**	**35**	**106**	**163**	**108**	**19%**	**106**	**7%**	**83%**				**7.45**	**39.3**	**101**	**266**	**$26**

Culberson,Charlie

Age: 26 Bats: R Pos: 3B SS 2B
Ht: 6' 0" Wt: 200

Health A | PT/Exp D | Consist C
LIMA Plan D | Rand Var +2 | MM 2311

Those juicy Spd scores are fool's gold; past seasons of double-digit steals came with low SB%. The moderate power he showed in the minors hasn't translated—that and low ct%/bb% will limit OBP, further reducing chances to run. His strong defense, though, allows him to hurt you at multiple positions. So there's that.

Yr	Tm	AB	R	HR	RBI	SB	BA	xBA	OBP	SLG	OPS	vL	vR	bb%	ct%	Eye	G	L	F	h%	HctX	PX	xPX	hr/f	Spd	SBO	SB%	#Wk	DOM	DIS	RC/G	RAR	BPV	BPX	R$
10																																			
11	aa	553	59	8	48	12	237		261	344	605			3	74	0.13				30		88			92	15%	73%				2.98		4	9	$7
12	SF *	498	43	9	41	9	224	257	243	343	587	500	0	3	79	0.12	67	13	20	27	22	79	-11	0%	122	15%	66%	2	0%	100%	2.69	-25.4	22	55	$3
13	COL *	496	49	11	51	13	266	279	286	415	701	668	766	3	79	0.14	55	22	23	32	89	103	86	11%	131	24%	53%	10	40%	50%	3.81	2.1	46	115	$15
14	COL	210	17	3	24	2	195	207	253	290	544	505	559	5	70	0.19	52	14	34	26	73	76	71	6%	125	10%	50%	26	19%	62%	2.13	-8.4	-6	-16	-$2
1st Half		109	8	2	11	2	193	232	241	312	553	525	565	4	73	0.14	58	13	29	24	66	93	65	9%	110	18%	67%	13	31%	62%	2.14	-4.4	10	27	-$2
2nd Half		101	9	1	13	0	198	179	265	267	533	474	553	7	67	0.24	46	16	39	28	81	55	78	4%	133	4%	0%	13	8%	62%	2.08	-4.2	-30	-81	-$1
15	Proj	**134**	**12**	**2**	**14**	**2**	**222**	**234**	**262**	**336**	**598**	**574**	**610**	**4**	**74**	**0.17**	**52**	**18**	**30**	**28**	**80**	**88**	**78**	**8%**	**121**	**14%**	**55%**				**2.70**	**-4.1**	**5**	**12**	**$2**

D Arnaud,Travis

Age: 26 Bats: R Pos: CA
Ht: 6' 2" Wt: 210

Health A | PT/Exp D | Consist D
LIMA Plan B+ | Rand Var +5 | MM 4135

13-41-.242 in 385 AB at NYM. Former top prospect showed his promise with jumps in several key skill measures: xBA, ct%, PX, and xPX. His 2H was especially promising, after a brief demotion to Triple-A. With three major health issues in three years, injury risk is his biggest looming obstacle to... UP: 20 HR, .270 BA.

Yr	Tm	AB	R	HR	RBI	SB	BA	xBA	OBP	SLG	OPS	vL	vR	bb%	ct%	Eye	G	L	F	h%	HctX	PX	xPX	hr/f	Spd	SBO	SB%	#Wk	DOM	DIS	RC/G	RAR	BPV	BPX	R$
10																																			
11	aa	424	61	19	66	3	290		334	504	838			6	74	0.25				35		160			83	6%	61%				5.97		63	140	$18
12	aaa	279	31	12	36	1	287		318	492	810			4	76	0.19				34		139			89	3%	38%				5.51		52	130	$8
13	NYM *	182	18	3	15	0	208	225	315	325	639	298	630	13	74	0.61	47	18	35	26	70	93	74	4%	90	0%	0%	7	29%	43%	3.29	-2.2	28	70	-$2
14	NYM *	448	58	18	53	1	251	285	305	446	751	707	722	7	84	0.49	42	20	39	26	122	129	136	10%	85	1%	100%	23	57%	17%	4.64	15.5	82	222	$11
1st Half		214	22	9	25	1	236	255	300	410	710	688	572	8	83	0.55	43	15	43	25	115	116	116	8%	73	2%	100%	11	45%	27%	4.13	4.8	67	181	$7
2nd Half		234	36	9	28	0	265	304	313	479	792	719	816	6	85	0.43	41	23	36	28	127	141	147	13%	98	0%	0%	12	67%	8%	5.13	11.7	96	259	$16
15	Proj	**444**	**54**	**15**	**51**	**1**	**250**	**270**	**311**	**428**	**739**	**619**	**779**	**8**	**81**	**0.45**	**43**	**19**	**38**	**28**	**101**	**127**	**110**	**11%**	**85**	**1%**	**68%**				**4.51**	**14.7**	**62**	**163**	**$11**

Davis,Chris

Age: 29 Bats: L Pos: 1B 3B
Ht: 6' 3" Wt: 230

Health A | PT/Exp A | Consist F
LIMA Plan B+ | Rand Var +5 | MM 5125

Could say "we told you so", but nobody predicted THIS. Perfect storm: power returned to human levels, FB% regressed, ct% plummeted in 2H, h% went south, plus suspension for amphetamines. Still has elite power, h% history presages a BA rebound. Homework: Compare Mark Reynolds 2009-10 to Davis 2013-14. Discuss.

Yr	Tm	AB	R	HR	RBI	SB	BA	xBA	OBP	SLG	OPS	vL	vR	bb%	ct%	Eye	G	L	F	h%	HctX	PX	xPX	hr/f	Spd	SBO	SB%	#Wk	DOM	DIS	RC/G	RAR	BPV	BPX	R$
10	TEX *	518	56	12	63	5	264	247	320	413	732	411	618	8	70	0.27	42	22	36	36	84	125	75	3%	74	6%	69%	11	9%	36%	4.55	-16.3	18	39	$12
11	2 AL *	398	58	26	71	2	299	278	333	559	892	906	657	5	67	0.16	38	25	37	39	105	202	137	10%	86	2%	100%	16	31%	56%	6.80	12.7	68	151	$20
12	BAL	515	75	33	85	2	270	252	326	501	827	792	836	7	67	0.22	39	23	38	34	102	162	150	25%	75	4%	40%	27	41%	33%	5.46	2.6	36	90	$20
13	BAL	584	103	53	138	4	286	297	370	634	1004	763	1142	11	66	0.36	32	22	46	34	112	266	199	30%	66	3%	80%	27	78%	7%	8.24	59.5	120	300	$38
14	BAL	450	65	26	72	2	196	235	300	404	704	677	716	12	62	0.35	35	25	41	25	96	174	154	23%	65	3%	67%	22	36%	36%	3.71	-6.1	31	84	$8
1st Half		240	35	13	41	2	208	239	329	408	737	690	761	14	64	0.45	34	25	41	26	101	162	158	21%	70	3%	100%	12	33%	25%	4.24	0.6	37	100	$10
2nd Half		210	30	13	31	0	181	231	265	400	665	658	667	9	59	0.24	35	24	41	23	91	190	150	25%	71	3%	0%	10	40%	50%	3.11	-7.2	28	76	$6
15	Proj	**536**	**81**	**33**	**95**	**3**	**240**	**253**	**322**	**474**	**796**	**720**	**829**	**10**	**64**	**0.30**	**35**	**23**	**41**	**31**	**100**	**195**	**159**	**23%**	**67**	**3%**	**62%**				**4.98**	**13.0**	**49**	**128**	**$20**

Davis,Ike

Age: 28 Bats: L Pos: 1B
Ht: 6' 4" Wt: 220

Health C | PT/Exp C | Consist B
LIMA Plan D+ | Rand Var +3 | MM 4023

Stop looking at those 32 HR in 2012. Stop. His hr/f that year is a clear outlier. Marginal ct% limits BA, and historical performance vs. LHP limits PT. His 2H FB% and PX hint at power upside, but with other skills holding him back, he's not hitting .270 or 20 HR without luck. Elite bb% makes him more attractive in OBP leagues.

Yr	Tm	AB	R	HR	RBI	SB	BA	xBA	OBP	SLG	OPS	vL	vR	bb%	ct%	Eye	G	L	F	h%	HctX	PX	xPX	hr/f	Spd	SBO	SB%	#Wk	DOM	DIS	RC/G	RAR	BPV	BPX	R$
10	NYM *	556	79	20	74	3	267	254	358	445	802	805	787	12	74	0.55	43	16	41	33	107	132	129	12%	96	3%	60%	25	60%	20%	5.49	-12.3	58	126	$16
11	NYM	129	20	7	25	0	302	277	383	543	925	493	1142	12	76	0.55	42	17	41	35	119	165	126	17%	109	0%	0%	7	71%	29%	7.61	4.8	94	209	$5
12	NYM	519	66	32	90	0	227	262	308	462	771	560	868	11	73	0.43	39	21	40	25	124	157	166	21%	61	2%	0%	27	48%	30%	4.63	-12.5	58	145	$12
13	NYM *	392	49	13	41	4	207	229	323	358	680	406	727	15	68	0.54	45	20	35	27	77	119	99	12%	80	3%	100%	20	35%	50%	3.77	-9.9	24	60	$3
14	2 NL	360	43	11	51	0	233	255	344	378	722	265	765	15	78	0.81	40	23	37	27	110	107	121	10%	82	3%	0%	27	48%	26%	4.19	0.0	55	149	$6
1st Half		208	28	5	26	0	245	249	360	365	726	258	779	15	79	0.88	42	23	35	29	108	89	107	9%	90	4%	0%	14	43%	29%	4.23	0.4	48	130	$7
2nd Half		152	15	6	25	0	217	265	322	395	717	282	747	14	77	0.71	36	23	41	24	114	131	139	12%	79	2%	0%	13	54%	23%	4.11	-0.3	67	181	$4
15	Proj	**375**	**46**	**13**	**54**	**1**	**228**	**248**	**331**	**385**	**716**	**447**	**770**	**14**	**74**	**0.62**	**41**	**21**	**38**	**27**	**105**	**120**	**126**	**12%**	**77**	**3%**	**33%**				**4.16**	**0.0**	**33**	**86**	**$8**

MATT CEDERHOLM

Davis,Khristopher

Age: 27	Bats: R	Pos: LF	Health	A	LIMA Plan A
Ht: 5' 11"	Wt: 190		PT/Exp	C	Rand Var +3
			Consist	C	MM 5245

Two years of mostly similar skills, with hr/f the main difference. Three reasons there's room to get better: 1) HctX, PX, and xPX all show elite power—he hits the ball hard. 2) Improved contact, especially in 2H, could lead to more HR if hr/f rebounds. 3) BA-xBA variance shows upside. Consider his occasional SB a bonus.

Yr	Tm	AB	R	HR	RBI	SB	BA	xBA	OBP	SLG	OPS	vL	vR	bb%	ct%	Eye	G	L	F	h%	HctX	PX	xPX	hr/f	Spd	SBO	SB%	#Wk	DOM	DIS	RC/G	RAR	BPV	BPX	R$
10																																			
11	aa	124	8	2	12	0	180		228	281	509			6	78	0.29				22		77			94	0%	0%				2.00		17	38	-$4
12	a/a	241	36	11	37	2	305		387	516	903			12	70	0.45				40		160			80	6%	50%				7.13		58	145	$10
13	MIL *	379	51	21	52	7	233	265	294	455	749	1009	918	8	72	0.31	43	20	37	27	141	158	162	29%	96	15%	60%	16	63%	25%	4.30	2.8	61	153	$11
14	MIL	501	70	22	69	4	244	278	299	457	756	777	749	6	76	0.26	39	21	40	28	132	161	158	14%	89	5%	80%	26	54%	23%	4.45	9.9	72	195	$15
1st Half		290	49	14	44	2	259	281	305	490	794	1036	707	5	74	0.21	38	23	39	31	142	174	165	17%	103	6%	67%	14	50%	21%	4.97	10.4	78	211	$21
2nd Half		211	21	8	25	2	223	271	291	412	703	359	802	7	78	0.35	40	20	41	25	118	143	148	12%	76	5%	100%	12	58%	25%	3.80	0.4	66	178	$5
15	Proj	518	68	27	72	5	253	280	323	481	804	802	805	7	75	0.32	41	21	39	29	133	170	158	18%	87	7%	66%				5.01	19.5	73	192	$16

Davis,Rajai

Age: 34	Bats: R	Pos: LF CF	Health	B	LIMA Plan C+
Ht: 5' 9"	Wt: 195		PT/Exp	C	Rand Var -1
			Consist	A	MM 2535

Nice jump in BA, fueled by increased contact. But there are seeds of doubt, too: 1) A year-long drop in Spd; at 34, this could certainly be age related. 2) Decline in SBO, especially in 2H. 3) Continued struggles against RHP could end up limiting PT. Has been a good cheap steals source in the past, but caution is warranted.

Yr	Tm	AB	R	HR	RBI	SB	BA	xBA	OBP	SLG	OPS	vL	vR	bb%	ct%	Eye	G	L	F	h%	HctX	PX	xPX	hr/f	Spd	SBO	SB%	#Wk	DOM	DIS	RC/G	RAR	BPV	BPX	R$
10	OAK	525	66	5	52	50	284	250	320	377	697	784	666	5	85	0.33	48	16	37	33	91	67	58	3%	132	44%	82%	27	37%	22%	4.42	-10.0	45	98	$28
11	TOR	320	44	1	29	34	238	238	273	350	623	829	551	4	80	0.24	44	16	40	29	66	85	50	1%	151	71%	76%	20	35%	45%	3.12	-19.6	46	102	$11
12	TOR	447	64	8	43	46	257	248	309	378	687	783	638	6	77	0.28	45	23	32	32	80	86	75	7%	119	54%	78%	27	26%	44%	3.95	-12.2	28	70	$22
13	TOR	331	49	6	24	45	260	241	312	375	687	857	594	6	80	0.31	39	23	38	31	90	81	84	6%	128	61%	88%	23	26%	30%	4.34	1.0	36	90	$23
14	DET	461	64	8	51	36	282	269	320	401	721	939	617	5	84	0.29	50	19	31	32	73	88	57	7%	105	41%	77%	26	46%	23%	4.46	7.6	48	130	$26
1st Half		225	31	6	27	22	276	258	321	418	739	891	658	5	81	0.28	44	19	37	32	80	101	72	9%	101	51%	79%	14	50%	29%	4.59	4.8	47	127	$27
2nd Half		236	33	2	24	14	288	278	319	386	704	994	581	4	86	0.31	55	19	26	33	67	75	45	4%	104	32%	74%	12	42%	17%	4.32	3.1	47	127	$26
15	Proj	432	61	7	42	34	271	260	313	384	698	884	609	5	82	0.29	47	21	32	32	78	85	66	6%	117	40%	79%				4.19	5.7	50	130	$23

De Aza,Alejandro

Age: 31	Bats: L	Pos: LF	Health	A	LIMA Plan B
Ht: 6' 0"	Wt: 195		PT/Exp	A	Rand Var +1
			Consist	A	MM 3425

Ended string of $20 seasons. Skills remained consistent, so what changed, really? Hr/f dropped to a level more in line with xPX, and PT declined, especially against LHP. Risks remain: no guarantee hr/f returns, especially with xPX below average; poor SB% could put steals at risk. And if stuck in a platoon role, PT will be limited.

Yr	Tm	AB	R	HR	RBI	SB	BA	xBA	OBP	SLG	OPS	vL	vR	bb%	ct%	Eye	G	L	F	h%	HctX	PX	xPX	hr/f	Spd	SBO	SB%	#Wk	DOM	DIS	RC/G	RAR	BPV	BPX	R$
10	CHW *	348	46	4	38	14	252	245	300	362	662	900	692	6	78	0.30	56	12	32	31	94	85	45	0%	122	22%	75%	6	17%	17%	3.70	-12.7	30	65	$9
11	CHW *	537	78	12	51	29	285	266	340	440	780	702	951	8	77	0.36	49	20	31	35	98	115	81	11%	139	33%	61%	10	60%	20%	4.92	0.0	58	129	$24
12	CHW	524	81	9	50	26	281	259	349	410	760	700	779	8	79	0.43	42	26	32	34	99	88	96	7%	123	25%	68%	24	42%	29%	4.79	3.4	43	108	$22
13	CHW	607	84	17	62	20	264	250	323	405	728	816	702	8	76	0.34	41	25	35	32	74	100	81	11%	116	17%	71%	27	37%	44%	4.43	8.0	35	88	$23
14	2 AL	477	56	8	41	17	252	254	314	386	700	400	766	8	75	0.33	42	27	32	32	83	101	84	7%	119	23%	63%	27	33%	41%	3.88	2.7	34	92	$13
1st Half		242	27	5	25	11	223	249	293	347	640	181	749	8	76	0.36	43	24	32	27	70	93	72	8%	100	28%	69%	14	36%	50%	3.17	-4.3	26	70	$12
2nd Half		235	29	3	16	6	281	260	337	426	763	661	783	7	74	0.30	40	29	31	37	97	110	98	6%	131	18%	55%	13	31%	31%	4.73	6.7	40	108	$15
15	Proj	453	59	9	41	16	264	257	325	403	728	607	758	8	76	0.34	42	26	32	33	86	105	87	8%	120	21%	64%				4.29	7.4	42	110	$16

DeJesus,David

Age: 35	Bats: L	Pos: DH	Health	F	LIMA Plan D+
Ht: 5' 11"	Wt: 190		PT/Exp	C	Rand Var +2
			Consist	A	MM 2133

Now THAT's a platoon player, with only 9 PA against LHP. Hand and other nagging injuries cut into 2nd half playing time. Contact and patience still get him on base, but that's about all he has to offer. Even if he manages to rebound to .270 - he always did have a nice BA floor - it will be an empty .270.

Yr	Tm	AB	R	HR	RBI	SB	BA	xBA	OBP	SLG	OPS	vL	vR	bb%	ct%	Eye	G	L	F	h%	HctX	PX	xPX	hr/f	Spd	SBO	SB%	#Wk	DOM	DIS	RC/G	RAR	BPV	BPX	R$
10	KC	352	46	5	37	3	318	282	384	443	827	725	864	9	87	0.72	47	21	32	36	112	86	95	5%	118	5%	50%	16	56%	19%	6.13	2.8	71	154	$13
11	OAK	442	60	10	46	4	240	252	323	376	698	459	787	9	81	0.52	43	20	37	28	98	91	100	8%	111	6%	57%	27	41%	33%	3.85	-26.4	49	109	$7
12	CHC	506	76	9	50	7	263	263	350	403	753	438	826	11	82	0.69	41	24	35	30	127	90	131	6%	122	10%	47%	27	48%	30%	4.56	-4.8	62	155	$12
13	3 TM	391	52	8	38	5	251	257	327	402	729	467	772	9	80	0.49	42	19	39	30	104	111	110	7%	107	8%	63%	22	50%	14%	4.29	-2.4	60	150	$8
14	TAM	238	24	6	19	0	248	272	344	403	748	476	756	11	82	0.70	44	22	35	28	87	111	82	9%	92	5%	0%	16	50%	31%	4.32	1.9	69	186	$2
1st Half		182	18	5	17	0	269	283	367	440	806	629	811	12	82	0.78	42	23	36	30	90	124	94	9%	85	4%	0%	12	58%	25%	5.26	6.4	81	219	$5
2nd Half		56	6	1	2	0	179	238	270	286	556	0	575	8	80	0.45	51	18	31	20	77	65	41	7%	111	8%	0%	4	25%	50%	1.99	-3.8	25	68	-$6
15	Proj	348	42	7	27	2	255	260	339	393	732	479	762	10	81	0.57	45	20	35	30	97	98	88	7%	109	7%	33%				4.19	1.5	48	126	$7

Den Dekker,Matthew

Age: 27	Bats: L	Pos: LF	Health	A	LIMA Plan D+
Ht: 6' 1"	Wt: 210		PT/Exp	C	Rand Var 0
			Consist	A	MM 2203

0-7-.250 with 7 SB in 152 AB at NYM. There are trends here you don't like to see for a 27-year old. Declining power, speed and a SB% that begs the question, "why even consider letting him run?" DOM/DIS shows major inconsistency. Nice pop in contact and patience, especially in 2nd half, but is that enough to grow on?

Yr	Tm	AB	R	HR	RBI	SB	BA	xBA	OBP	SLG	OPS	vL	vR	bb%	ct%	Eye	G	L	F	h%	HctX	PX	xPX	hr/f	Spd	SBO	SB%	#Wk	DOM	DIS	RC/G	RAR	BPV	BPX	R$
10																																			
11	aa	272	35	8	23	9	179		232	314	546			6	62	0.18				25		113			114	30%	59%				2.12		-11	-24	$0
12	a/a	533	63	13	57	16	223		258	361	619			5	65	0.14				32		109			105	26%	60%				2.89		-9	-23	$9
13	NYM *	237	27	5	29	9	213	205	263	319	582	200	572	6	65	0.19	34	29	37	31	92	83	135	8%	104	21%	80%	6	0%	83%	2.76	-9.8	-26	-65	$3
14	NYM *	487	62	5	33	12	239	259	301	348	649	600	673	8	75	0.36	47	27	26	31	116	94	104	0%	99	19%	53%	12	33%	42%	3.31	-7.6	23	62	$8
1st Half		256	27	4	20	3	192	250	235	297	533	0	464	5	72	0.20	44	31	25	25	116	89	126	0%	89	9%	76%	4	0%	75%	2.21	-13.5	-3	-8	$1
2nd Half		231	36	1	13	9	292	274	372	405	777	773	762	11	79	0.60	49	25	26	37	119	100	96	0%	108	25%	48%	8	50%	25%	4.86	6.8	52	141	$16
15	Proj	390	49	3	34	12	245	230	306	332	638	485	652	7	70	0.26	42	28	30	34	107	81	119	3%	93	21%	60%				3.21	-6.3	-5	-14	$9

Denorfia,Chris

Age: 34	Bats: R	Pos: RF LF	Health	A	LIMA Plan D+
Ht: 6' 0"	Wt: 195		PT/Exp	C	Rand Var +4
			Consist	C	MM 1433

PRO: Speed skill still intact, ct% is just below our benchmark, higher xBA in past years. CON: Second year of declines in power, BA, xBA, and ct%; struggled vs. LHP for the first time. VERDICT: He's 34. While two-year trends reverse more often than not, it's less likely at 34. (Upon review, those PROs are really not all that pro.)

Yr	Tm	AB	R	HR	RBI	SB	BA	xBA	OBP	SLG	OPS	vL	vR	bb%	ct%	Eye	G	L	F	h%	HctX	PX	xPX	hr/f	Spd	SBO	SB%	#Wk	DOM	DIS	RC/G	RAR	BPV	BPX	R$
10	SD *	405	52	10	44	13	256	287	316	408	723	763	769	8	81	0.47	59	17	24	29	99	101	68	16%	132	18%	70%	21	33%	29%	4.34	-11.1	63	137	$11
11	SD	307	38	5	19	11	277	263	337	381	718	887	611	8	84	0.57	59	16	25	32	88	70	61	8%	133	18%	65%	23	35%	48%	4.40	-4.7	51	113	$8
12	SD	348	56	8	36	13	293	296	345	451	796	890	697	7	85	0.52	60	18	22	33	109	95	69	13%	146	19%	72%	27	56%	19%	5.51	9.3	76	190	$14
13	SD	473	67	10	47	11	279	271	337	395	732	834	663	8	82	0.50	55	21	24	32	104	79	68	11%	123	8%	100%	27	44%	19%	4.88	12.0	47	118	$17
14	2 TM	330	36	3	21	9	230	251	284	318	602	587	615	7	79	0.36	57	20	23	28	79	64	61	5%	142	15%	75%	26	27%	54%	3.01	-6.8	25	68	$4
1st Half		192	18	1	15	7	250	265	301	344	645	618	658	7	82	0.41	59	18	22	30	82	68	58	3%	141	14%	100%	14	36%	43%	3.72	-0.1	41	111	$6
2nd Half		138	18	2	6	2	203	231	260	283	543	563	507	7	74	0.31	52	23	25	26	75	58	65	8%	120	15%	40%	12	17%	67%	2.19	-6.9	-5	-14	$1
15	Proj	305	40	5	24	8	251	263	306	360	667	702	635	7	80	0.41	56	20	23	30	91	78	65	9%	134	14%	72%				3.75	-2.3	33	87	$8

Descalso,Daniel

Age: 28	Bats: L	Pos: 2B	Health	A	LIMA Plan D
Ht: 5' 10"	Wt: 190		PT/Exp	D	Rand Var -1
			Consist	A	MM 1111

Let's say you're a big fan and want him on your roster. How do you justify it? His 2nd half bb%/ct% was nice, but sample is too small. Spd is below average, and he had difficulty beating out the venerable Mark Ellis and his .466 OPS for playing time. You say you're the champion of the underdog? Do you win many titles?

Yr	Tm	AB	R	HR	RBI	SB	BA	xBA	OBP	SLG	OPS	vL	vR	bb%	ct%	Eye	G	L	F	h%	HctX	PX	xPX	hr/f	Spd	SBO	SB%	#Wk	DOM	DIS	RC/G	RAR	BPV	BPX	R$
10	STL *	502	66	6	53	7	231	276	282	329	611	1000	559	7	88	0.58	61	14	25	25	90	69	30	0%	117	10%	58%	4	25%	75%	3.01	-22.9	57	124	$5
11	STL	326	35	1	28	2	264	241	334	353	687	518	724	9	80	0.51	47	20	33	33	83	72	61	1%	130	4%	50%	27	37%	48%	3.99	-4.9	37	82	$4
12	STL	374	41	4	26	6	227	235	303	324	627	812	564	9	78	0.45	45	23	32	28	103	60	100	4%	144	9%	67%	27	22%	48%	3.14	-11.0	22	55	$2
13	STL	328	43	5	43	6	238	262	290	366	656	529	684	6	83	0.39	48	18	34	27	101	96	85	5%	89	13%	67%	27	41%	30%	3.44	-0.5	50	125	$6
14	STL	161	20	0	10	1	242	220	333	311	644	899	575	11	80	0.61	43	17	39	30	72	68	50	0%	97	8%	25%	26	27%	42%	3.19	-0.4	26	70	$0
1st Half		73	7	0	4	1	192	218	244	247	490	322	520	5	74	0.21	50	20	30	26	58	58	41	0%	93	7%	100%	13	23%	46%	1.87	-3.2	-17	-46	-$3
2nd Half		88	13	0	6	0	284	222	400	364	764	1184	621	15	84	1.14	38	15	47	34	84	74	57	0%	100	9%	0%	13	31%	38%	4.52	3.3	58	157	$2
15	Proj	127	16	1	11	1	234	238	311	325	635	769	600	9	81	0.53	45	19	37	28	86	77	68	2%	101	10%	42%				3.15	-1.0	27	72	$2

MATT CEDERHOLM

Desmond,Ian

Age: 29 Bats: R Pos: SS
Ht: 6' 3" Wt: 215

Health A | PT/Exp A | Consist B
LIMA Plan B | Rand Var -1 | MM 4435

This power/speed profile is highly valuable, but 2nd half h% jump masked some problems: ct% dove into the danger zone. Resulting OBP erosion cuts into SB opps, could even put 20 SB level at risk. Similarly, any further erosion of FB% could threaten HR totals. Rebound to former ct% levels is possible, but there's risk here.

Yr	Tm	AB	R	HR	RBI	SB	BA	xBA	OBP	SLG	OPS	vL	vR	bb%	ct%	Eye	G	L	F	h%	HctX	PX	xPX	hr/f	Spd	SBO	SB%	#Wk	DOM	DIS	RC/G	RAR	BPV	BPX	R$
10	WAS	525	59	10	65	17	269	257	308	392	700	799	664	5	79	0.26	53	16	32	32	85	88	84	8%	126	17%	77%	27	41%	37%	4.19	-4.8	37	80	$16
11	WAS	584	65	8	49	25	253	239	298	358	656	642	659	6	76	0.25	52	18	31	32	84	79	75	6%	133	24%	71%	27	30%	52%	3.56	-16.5	21	47	$15
12	WAS	513	72	25	73	21	292	279	335	511	845	902	828	6	78	0.27	48	18	35	33	112	142	115	18%	117	23%	78%	24	46%	33%	6.06	28.2	74	185	$27
13	WAS	600	77	20	80	21	280	265	331	453	784	766	789	7	76	0.30	43	22	34	34	101	126	100	13%	99	18%	78%	26	50%	31%	5.26	30.2	49	123	$28
14	WAS	593	73	24	91	24	255	247	313	430	743	771	734	7	69	0.25	50	18	32	33	97	136	107	18%	106	20%	83%	27	41%	33%	4.60	22.8	34	92	$26
1st Half		315	32	14	49	9	235	236	288	419	707	693	712	6	68	0.21	50	13	37	30	92	141	107	18%	107	16%	82%	14	36%	36%	3.98	7.0	32	86	$21
2nd Half		278	41	10	42	15	277	258	341	442	783	847	760	8	70	0.30	51	23	27	36	103	131	107	19%	104	23%	83%	13	46%	31%	5.36	17.0	35	95	$32
15	**Proj**	**588**	**76**	**22**	**83**	**24**	**265**	**260**	**318**	**441**	**758**	**785**	**749**	**7**	**73**	**0.26**	**48**	**19**	**32**	**33**	**100**	**134**	**104**	**16%**	**107**	**21%**	**80%**				**4.82**	**27.2**	**49**	**128**	**$25**

Dickerson,Corey

Age: 26 Bats: L Pos: LF
Ht: 6' 1" Wt: 205

Health A | PT/Exp C | Consist B
LIMA Plan A | Rand Var -2 | MM 5255

It's a breakout, yes, though primary change was trading contact for power. It worked, as seen in jump in hr/f (thank you, thin air). Low SB% puts steals at risk, but the skill is there so there's room to grow. If power is sustained and ct% ticks back up, then... UP: 30 HR.

Yr	Tm	AB	R	HR	RBI	SB	BA	xBA	OBP	SLG	OPS	vL	vR	bb%	ct%	Eye	G	L	F	h%	HctX	PX	xPX	hr/f	Spd	SBO	SB%	#Wk	DOM	DIS	RC/G	RAR	BPV	BPX	R$
10																																			
11																																			
12	aa	266	34	13	32	6	274		313	508	821			5	81	0.29				30		143			105	16%	65%				5.42		82	205	$9
13	COL *	509	68	12	47	6	296	287	337	492	829	581	819	6	81	0.33	40	26	34	34	108	124	107	10%	157	16%	29%	14	64%	21%	5.42	19.8	86	215	$19
14	COL	436	74	24	76	8	312	298	364	567	931	724	985	8	77	0.37	37	27	36	36	123	176	135	20%	119	13%	53%	25	60%	24%	7.33	42.6	102	276	$28
1st Half		178	34	10	33	5	343	309	402	618	1020	678	1112	9	75	0.41	34	33	33	41	115	196	130	22%	128	17%	56%	13	69%	15%	9.09	25.4	117	316	$24
2nd Half		258	40	14	43	3	291	289	337	531	868	756	897	7	78	0.33	39	23	39	33	128	162	139	18%	109	10%	50%	12	50%	33%	6.24	18.3	90	243	$31
15	**Proj**	**555**	**84**	**26**	**76**	**6**	**297**	**300**	**342**	**537**	**880**	**673**	**931**	**7**	**79**	**0.34**	**38**	**27**	**35**	**34**	**117**	**163**	**124**	**17%**	**130**	**9%**	**52%**				**6.51**	**42.9**	**94**	**249**	**$28**

Dietrich,Derek

Age: 25 Bats: L Pos: 2B
Ht: 6' 0" Wt: 205

Health B | PT/Exp F | Consist B
LIMA Plan D | Rand Var +1 | MM 4111

5-17-.228 in 158 AB at MIA. Missed almost two months with strained wrist. Ct% trend is a plus, though it's still too low for a player with moderate power, so BA will remain sub-par. Poor defensive rep will keep him in a constant battle for playing time, but could be sneaky power source with enough AB.

Yr	Tm	AB	R	HR	RBI	SB	BA	xBA	OBP	SLG	OPS	vL	vR	bb%	ct%	Eye	G	L	F	h%	HctX	PX	xPX	hr/f	Spd	SBO	SB%	#Wk	DOM	DIS	RC/G	RAR	BPV	BPX	R$
10																																			
11																																			
12	aa	133	18	3	14	0	233		263	358	622			4	69	0.13				31		95			103	4%	0%				3.01		-6	-15	$0
13	MIA *	433	61	17	54	3	226	256	285	414	699	786	644	8	72	0.29	40	25	35	28	89	136	114	16%	114	4%	100%	12	42%	25%	3.93	3.5	46	115	$8
14	MIA *	240	41	9	28	2	235	246	282	398	680	372	762	6	75	0.26	43	19	38	28	99	114	100	11%	105	3%	100%	12	42%	42%	3.77	2.7	38	103	$5
1st Half		204	38	8	27	1	241	251	296	418	714	372	783	7	76	0.32	42	19	39	28	100	120	101	11%	108	2%	100%	12	42%	42%	4.18	4.8	48	130	$8
2nd Half		36	3	1	1	1	197	235	197	289	486	0	0	0	72	0.00	100	0	0	26	0	79	-14		99	13%	100%				1.87	-1.7	-17	-46	-$10
15	**Proj**	**198**	**31**	**7**	**24**	**1**	**239**	**245**	**318**	**405**	**722**	**619**	**744**	**6**	**72**	**0.23**	**41**	**21**	**37**	**30**	**96**	**124**	**106**	**13%**	**104**	**3%**	**53%**				**3.82**	**2.5**	**31**	**80**	**$5**

Dirks,Andy

Age: 29 Bats: L Pos: LF
Ht: 6' 0" Wt: 195

Health F | PT/Exp D | Consist F
LIMA Plan D+ | Rand Var 0 | MM 2321

Missed the entire season recovering from back surgery and a hamstring tear he suffered during rehab. It's possible the back issue was behind his power drop in 2013; it was a chronic problem that he had dealt with since high school. So give him one more chance to make good, but only if he comes to you very cheaply.

Yr	Tm	AB	R	HR	RBI	SB	BA	xBA	OBP	SLG	OPS	vL	vR	bb%	ct%	Eye	G	L	F	h%	HctX	PX	xPX	hr/f	Spd	SBO	SB%	#Wk	DOM	DIS	RC/G	RAR	BPV	BPX	R$
10	a/a	476	60	12	49	17	257		299	395	693			6	83	0.36				29		92			106	19%	79%				4.06		53	115	$14
11	DET *	376	58	13	47	15	265	249	302	423	725	871	675	5	82	0.30	34	19	47	29	79	105	89	8%	96	22%	77%	19	47%	37%	4.42	-5.5	54	120	$14
12	DET *	351	59	9	39	3	307	268	354	470	824	751	889	7	82	0.42	38	24	37	35	100	101	102	8%	141	3%	71%	19	53%	21%	6.10	14.7	68	170	$14
13	DET	438	60	9	37	7	256	251	323	363	686	631	698	9	81	0.50	42	25	33	30	86	72	77	8%	119	6%	88%	27	48%	37%	4.05	0.9	36	90	$10
14																																			
1st Half																																			
2nd Half																																			
15	**Proj**	**229**	**34**	**6**	**24**	**4**	**261**	**257**	**315**	**401**	**715**	**729**	**713**	**7**	**82**	**0.39**	**38**	**22**	**40**	**30**	**87**	**97**	**88**	**8%**	**111**	**9%**	**72%**				**4.26**	**3.5**	**50**	**130**	**$8**

Dominguez,Matt

Age: 25 Bats: R Pos: 3B
Ht: 6' 1" Wt: 215

Health A | PT/Exp B | Consist B
LIMA Plan C | Rand Var 0 | MM 2015

This is not the growth year we hoped for, as almost every skill declined. Ct% history gives us hope of rebound, but what if 2013 PX was an outlier? It continued into 1H, but 2H power drop is frightening, as is overall Eye and xBA. Still young enough to turn it around, but really, 2013 was no great world-beater anyway.

Yr	Tm	AB	R	HR	RBI	SB	BA	xBA	OBP	SLG	OPS	vL	vR	bb%	ct%	Eye	G	L	F	h%	HctX	PX	xPX	hr/f	Spd	SBO	SB%	#Wk	DOM	DIS	RC/G	RAR	BPV	BPX	R$
10	aa	504	51	11	68	0	231		300	368	667			9	78	0.45				27		102			91	2%	0%				3.58		41	89	$4
11	FLA *	385	36	8	42	0	215	250	258	328	586	944	419	5	83	0.34	49	19	32	24	113	79	96	0%	74	1%	0%	4	50%	25%	2.71	-28.3	30	67	$0
12	HOU *	556	47	11	63	0	226	254	263	335	598	655	824	5	86	0.36	54	18	27	24	111	67	89	20%	101	1%	0%	8	38%	25%	2.88	-28.2	39	98	$3
13	HOU	543	56	21	77	0	241	253	286	403	690	627	714	5	82	0.31	42	19	39	26	97	104	96	12%	68	1%	0%	27	56%	30%	3.78	-2.7	45	113	$11
14	HOU	564	51	16	57	0	215	222	256	330	586	677	551	5	78	0.23	44	18	38	25	99	81	97	9%	65	1%	0%	27	22%	41%	2.68	-17.1	7	19	$3
1st Half		308	31	11	37	0	237	234	291	386	677	793	625	7	76	0.30	44	17	38	28	109	108	107	12%	64	1%	0%	14	36%	36%	3.66	-0.3	26	70	$10
2nd Half		256	20	5	20	0	188	208	213	262	474	494	468	3	80	0.13	43	18	38	22	88	49	86	6%	81	0%	0%	13	8%	46%	1.72	-16.1	-11	-30	-$4
15	**Proj**	**532**	**49**	**18**	**60**	**0**	**226**	**243**	**268**	**366**	**634**	**635**	**634**	**5**	**81**	**0.28**	**45**	**18**	**37**	**25**	**99**	**95**	**94**	**11%**	**73**	**1%**	**0%**				**3.17**	**-8.5**	**19**	**49**	**$7**

Donaldson,Josh

Age: 29 Bats: R Pos: 3B
Ht: 6' 0" Wt: 220

Health A | PT/Exp A | Consist F
LIMA Plan B+ | Rand Var 0 | MM 4235

Followed up surprise breakout with surprise non-regression. Sort of. Eye, contact, and power held up; key factors in BA decline were LD drop and H% regression to his previously established level. Given that, this may be the best we'll see from BA. While he pounds LHP, OPS vs. RH isn't cause for concern... yet.

Yr	Tm	AB	R	HR	RBI	SB	BA	xBA	OBP	SLG	OPS	vL	vR	bb%	ct%	Eye	G	L	F	h%	HctX	PX	xPX	hr/f	Spd	SBO	SB%	#Wk	DOM	DIS	RC/G	RAR	BPV	BPX	R$
10	OAK *	326	35	12	48	2	180	199	252	331	583	768	0	9	67	0.29	50	5	45	22	55	115	70	11%	76	5%	62%	6	17%	50%	2.57	-23.5	3	7	-$1
11	aaa	444	52	10	46	8	199		256	317	573			7	72	0.27				25		94			84	15%	64%				2.52		5	11	$1
12	OAK *	483	59	17	62	7	247	257	291	410	701	703	680	6	79	0.29	40	23	38	28	90	107	107	11%	68	10%	68%	17	35%	47%	3.98	-8.1	34	85	$11
13	OAK	579	89	24	93	5	301	282	384	499	883	1042	813	12	81	0.69	44	21	36	34	107	132	97	14%	102	4%	71%	27	48%	19%	6.92	47.4	85	213	$29
14	OAK	608	93	29	98	8	255	264	342	456	798	1007	727	11	79	0.58	45	13	41	28	118	138	126	15%	89	5%	100%	27	56%	30%	5.35	29.8	76	205	$24
1st Half		323	57	18	61	3	248	266	329	464	793	1071	705	11	77	0.51	48	13	39	27	114	144	116	19%	99	3%	100%	14	50%	36%	5.20	14.4	76	205	$28
2nd Half		285	36	11	37	5	263	259	358	446	803	943	753	12	80	0.68	42	14	44	29	122	131	137	11%	84	6%	100%	13	62%	23%	5.51	15.0	77	208	$19
15	**Proj**	**596**	**84**	**25**	**89**	**8**	**260**	**266**	**342**	**446**	**788**	**936**	**730**	**10**	**79**	**0.54**	**44**	**17**	**39**	**29**	**110**	**133**	**114**	**14%**	**89**	**6%**	**82%**				**5.19**	**25.9**	**68**	**178**	**$23**

Doumit,Ryan

Age: 34 Bats: B Pos: LF
Ht: 6' 1" Wt: 220

Health B | PT/Exp C | Consist C
LIMA Plan D | Rand Var +2 | MM 3201

It was a confluence of bad skill and bad luck. Was never a great fit on the Braves roster, ranking about 37th on their depth chart for every position he was qualified to play. Caught just 2 GAMES all year. Bat never got going in the sporadic 6 AB per week they gave him. If his situation changes, there is still draftable skill here.

Yr	Tm	AB	R	HR	RBI	SB	BA	xBA	OBP	SLG	OPS	vL	vR	bb%	ct%	Eye	G	L	F	h%	HctX	PX	xPX	hr/f	Spd	SBO	SB%	#Wk	DOM	DIS	RC/G	RAR	BPV	BPX	R$
10	PIT	406	42	13	45	1	251	246	331	406	738	532	832	9	79	0.47	41	16	43	29	107	108	117	9%	76	1%	100%	26	42%	31%	4.44	0.7	44	96	$7
11	PIT *	244	20	8	32	0	289	272	340	453	793	912	802	7	84	0.47	44	21	36	32	143	106	112	12%	87	1%	0%	19	63%	21%	5.43	7.2	62	138	$6
12	MIN	484	56	18	75	0	275	274	320	461	781	690	823	6	80	0.30	42	22	36	31	113	125	110	13%	66	0%	0%	27	41%	26%	5.12	11.4	52	130	$14
13	MIN	485	49	14	55	1	247	257	314	396	710	753	692	9	80	0.48	47	19	33	28	109	105	110	11%	86	1%	100%	27	44%	26%	4.24	7.7	48	120	$8
14	ATL	157	11	5	17	1	197	203	235	318	553	433	581	4	69	0.14	42	17	40	25	74	93	70	11%	66	3%	100%	27	30%	56%	2.37	-5.3	-19	-51	-$1
1st Half		87	7	3	12	1	218	213	250	345	595	583	596	3	70	0.12	42	19	39	28	93	93	86	13%	71	6%	100%	14	29%	57%	2.80	-1.6	-15	-41	$0
2nd Half		70	4	2	5	0	171	180	216	286	502	333	559	5	67	0.17	43	15	43	22	50	92	49	10%	73	0%	0%	13	31%	54%	1.90	-3.4	-23	-62	-$3
15	**Proj**	**197**	**17**	**6**	**22**	**1**	**240**	**232**	**288**	**382**	**670**	**621**	**687**	**6**	**74**	**0.25**	**43**	**18**	**38**	**29**	**90**	**107**	**87**	**11%**	**70**	**1%**	**93%**				**3.68**	**-0.4**	**6**	**16**	**$4**

MATT CEDERHOLM

Dozier,Brian

Age: 28 Bats: R Pos: 2B | Ht: 5' 11" Wt: 190
Health A | PT/Exp A | Consist C
LIMA Plan A | Rand Var +1 | MM 4435

Did he land at the top of the order because they saw potential for more plate patience, or did he learn to take more pitches once they made him lead off? Either way, result was 100+ runs and solid OBP despite middling BA. xBA, trend vs. RHP, HCtX, PX all say there's room for growth. Could be profit even paying for a 20/20 repeat.

Yr	Tm	AB	R	HR	RBI	SB	BA	xBA	OBP	SLG	OPS	vL	vR	bb%	ct%	Eye	G	L	F	h%	HctX	PX	xPX	hr/f	Spd	SBO	SB%	#Wk	DOM	DIS	RC/G	RAR	BPV	BPX	R$
10																																			
11	aa	311	43	4	25	8	269		314	407	721			6	83	0.39				31		94			124	21%	49%				4.11		59	131	$7
12	MIN *	497	45	7	47	11	223	232	264	318	581	775	547	5	81	0.29	42	21	38	26	77	65	80	6%	108	15%	73%	15	20%	27%	2.74	-21.8	19	48	$4
13	MIN	558	72	18	66	14	244	256	312	414	726	978	649	8	78	0.43	38	21	41	28	89	118	99	10%	124	16%	67%	27	52%	33%	4.19	7.8	64	160	$16
14	MIN	598	112	23	71	21	242	257	345	416	762	804	743	13	78	0.69	37	20	43	27	95	124	97	11%	106	16%	75%	27	44%	19%	4.77	24.9	73	197	$24
1st Half		306	60	15	38	15	235	256	350	422	771	875	733	14	78	0.76	38	19	43	25	87	126	95	15%	103	20%	79%	14	43%	21%	4.90	14.1	75	203	$27
2nd Half		292	52	8	33	6	250	258	340	411	751	744	754	12	79	0.61	36	21	43	29	103	123	100	8%	107	11%	67%	13	46%	15%	4.64	10.8	71	192	$21
15	Proj	593	90	24	76	20	255	264	333	441	774	905	725	10	79	0.53	38	19	43	29	91	131	96	12%	113	17%	72%				4.91	26.7	76	200	$23

Drew,Stephen

Age: 32 Bats: L Pos: SS 2B | Ht: 6' 0" Wt: 190
Health D | PT/Exp C | Consist F
LIMA Plan D+ | Rand Var +5 | MM 3213

Unsigned for first two months. Still has skills hidden in the ugliness, such as return of power in 2H. Hit rate history says BA should be better, but what he really needs is to platoon—skills vs. RHP over past three years (0.56 Eye, 12% bb%, 76% ct%, 124 PX) are quite good. If he gets such a chance, he'll yield some profit.

Yr	Tm	AB	R	HR	RBI	SB	BA	xBA	OBP	SLG	OPS	vL	vR	bb%	ct%	Eye	G	L	F	h%	HctX	PX	xPX	hr/f	Spd	SBO	SB%	#Wk	DOM	DIS	RC/G	RAR	BPV	BPX	R$
10	ARI	565	83	15	61	10	278	271	352	458	810	794	817	10	81	0.57	40	19	41	32	110	117	108	8%	149	9%	67%	26	65%	23%	5.57	22.6	84	183	$18
11	ARI	321	44	5	45	4	252	247	317	396	713	671	728	9	77	0.41	39	21	40	31	97	107	109	5%	114	10%	50%	16	38%	19%	4.12	-0.5	47	104	$6
12	2 TM *	328	42	8	31	1	218	237	306	346	653	563	697	11	74	0.49	32	28	40	27	102	89	122	8%	110	3%	33%	15	33%	40%	3.39	-7.2	25	63	$1
13	BOS	442	57	13	67	6	253	251	333	443	777	585	876	11	72	0.44	33	25	42	32	114	142	156	10%	118	5%	100%	23	52%	26%	5.15	22.3	61	153	$13
14	2 AL	271	18	7	26	1	162	214	237	299	536	371	584	9	72	0.36	31	17	51	20	73	109	98	7%	69	4%	50%	18	33%	50%	2.14	-9.2	17	46	-$5
1st Half		63	1	0	2	1	143	189	169	190	360	143	421	3	70	0.11	53	16	30	20	55	54	44	0%	86	13%	100%	5	20%	60%	1.00	-4.7	-44	-119	-$13
2nd Half		208	17	7	24	0	168	222	255	332	587	435	632	11	73	0.45	25	18	57	19	78	125	114	8%	69	2%	0%	13	38%	46%	2.56	-4.6	36	97	-$2
15	Proj	286	30	7	32	2	233	233	303	379	682	540	734	9	73	0.38	35	21	44	30	89	115	111	8%	93	5%	71%				3.82	5.0	28	73	$5

Duda,Lucas

Age: 29 Bats: L Pos: 1B | Ht: 6' 4" Wt: 255
Health B | PT/Exp C | Consist B
LIMA Plan B+ | Rand Var 0 | MM 4025

Elite power combined with jump in ct% and strong bb% for a solid growth year. Trouble is, all of the growth came vs. RHP, as futility vs. lefties reached new levels. If that is fully exposed, it's quite possible 2014 will have been his peak. Note that his value is much higher in OBP and H2H leagues.

Yr	Tm	AB	R	HR	RBI	SB	BA	xBA	OBP	SLG	OPS	vL	vR	bb%	ct%	Eye	G	L	F	h%	HctX	PX	xPX	hr/f	Spd	SBO	SB%	#Wk	DOM	DIS	RC/G	RAR	BPV	BPX	R$
10	NYM *	509	63	19	75	1	240	267	308	438	746	421	749	9	76	0.41	35	19	46	28	113	145	129	14%	58	1%	100%	6	50%	50%	4.54	-26.0	58	126	$9
11	NYM *	430	55	18	68	1	276	274	352	476	828	705	888	10	79	0.57	34	22	43	31	111	136	116	9%	90	1%	100%	20	60%	30%	5.92	-4.1	76	169	$15
12	NYM *	497	52	17	63	1	233	222	313	374	687	662	745	10	71	0.40	35	23	42	30	118	99	134	13%	50	1%	100%	23	22%	57%	3.90	-22.7	0	0	$7
13	NYM *	380	50	15	38	1	222	221	333	388	721	610	831	14	68	0.52	32	20	48	29	117	130	181	14%	67	3%	16%	18	39%	33%	4.12	-5.4	26	65	$4
14	NYM	514	74	30	92	3	253	263	349	481	830	516	915	12	74	0.51	31	20	49	29	132	165	181	16%	46	4%	60%	27	56%	15%	5.55	20.6	67	181	$20
1st Half		242	30	12	41	2	252	265	345	471	816	490	883	12	75	0.53	34	18	48	29	141	164	179	14%	45	5%	67%	14	50%	14%	5.41	8.9	71	192	$14
2nd Half		272	44	18	51	1	254	261	352	489	841	531	946	12	72	0.49	28	23	50	28	124	166	183	18%	60	3%	50%	13	62%	15%	5.67	12.0	66	178	$26
15	Proj	505	68	25	75	2	243	251	343	445	788	575	860	12	72	0.49	32	21	47	29	124	152	168	15%	54	3%	50%				4.95	11.8	47	124	$16

Dunn,Adam

Age: 35 Bats: L Pos: DH 1B | Ht: 6' 6" Wt: 285
Health | PT/Exp | Consist
LIMA Plan | Rand Var | MM

Has announced his retirement. While he was the poster boy for disappointment in 2011, we honor him as a member of the Three True Outcomes Hall of Fame. Even in the HR era, 8 seasons of 35+ HR is quite an accomplishment, and he was often a top player in OBA leagues before 2011. Enjoy retirement, big man.

Yr	Tm	AB	R	HR	RBI	SB	BA	xBA	OBP	SLG	OPS	vL	vR	bb%	ct%	Eye	G	L	F	h%	HctX	PX	xPX	hr/f	Spd	SBO	SB%	#Wk	DOM	DIS	RC/G	RAR	BPV	BPX	R$
10	WAS	558	85	38	103	0	260	266	356	536	892	719	965	12	64	0.39	33	18	49	33	115	219	195	21%	70	1%	0%	27	59%	30%	6.41	9.2	80	174	$21
11	CHW	415	36	11	42	0	159	180	292	277	569	309	646	15	57	0.42	33	20	48	24	87	113	134	10%	44	1%	0%	27	15%	78%	2.39	-47.2	-33	-73	-$7
12	CHW	539	87	41	96	2	204	238	333	468	800	767	817	16	59	0.47	34	22	44	25	100	207	171	29%	46	2%	67%	27	59%	30%	4.99	1.6	49	123	$13
13	CHW	525	60	34	86	1	219	232	320	442	762	681	786	13	64	0.40	38	19	42	27	105	167	170	24%	55	1%	50%	26	35%	42%	4.56	0.9	33	83	$12
14	2 AL	429	49	22	64	1	219	233	337	415	752	553	783	14	63	0.45	34	23	43	29	88	164	139	19%	47	2%	50%	27	48%	48%	4.44	5.2	27	73	$8
1st Half		228	29	12	33	1	237	234	370	447	817	568	872	17	62	0.55	34	21	45	33	84	184	145	18%	54	3%	50%	14	50%	43%	5.47	9.7	47	127	$11
2nd Half		201	20	10	31	0	199	234	296	378	674	516	689	10	64	0.32	33	26	41	25	92	143	133	19%	48	0%	0%	13	46%	54%	3.39	-4.2	8	22	$6
15	Proj																																		

Duvall,Adam

Age: 26 Bats: R Pos: 1B | Ht: 6' 1" Wt: 205
Health A | PT/Exp D | Consist B
LIMA Plan D | Rand Var +2 | MM 4221

3-5-.192 in 73 AB at SF. A consistent power bat in the minors, he went 27-90-.298 in just 394 AB at AAA (and you can see how the MLEs take a huge chunk out of that). As an older prospect, he'll have a limited window to make any mark. Ct% is actually not horrible for this profile, and low h% indicates possible BA upside.

Yr	Tm	AB	R	HR	RBI	SB	BA	xBA	OBP	SLG	OPS	vL	vR	bb%	ct%	Eye	G	L	F	h%	HctX	PX	xPX	hr/f	Spd	SBO	SB%	#Wk	DOM	DIS	RC/G	RAR	BPV	BPX	R$
10																																			
11																																			
12																																			
13	aa	385	43	11	41	1	203		251	350	601			6	78	0.29				23		102			105	4%	55%				2.78		39	98	$0
14	SF *	432	51	18	63	1	220	246	259	401	659	525	629	5	72	0.18	38	21	42	26	106	135	155	14%	83	2%	100%	11	27%	45%	3.40	-10.3	33	89	$7
1st Half		277	32	14	44	1	220	241	260	421	680	0	667	5	71	0.19	36	18	45	26	84	143	99	20%	103	3%	100%	2	50%	50%	3.60	-4.8	43	116	$12
2nd Half		155	19	4	19	0	220	241	256	365	622	553	609	5	73	0.18	38	21	41	27	113	119	170	12%	76	0%	0%	9	22%	44%	3.06	-5.2	22	59	-$1
15	Proj	113	13	4	14	0	231	253	283	406	688	625	784	5	75	0.23	38	21	40	27	102	130	153	13%	92	2%	65%				3.65	-1.7	33	88	$2

Dyson,Jarrod

Age: 30 Bats: L Pos: CF | Ht: 5' 10" Wt: 160
Health A | PT/Exp D | Consist B
LIMA Plan C | Rand Var -4 | MM 1513

Yeah, we know he has speed, though inflated BA should regress. Plate metrics are solid, and his career OBA vs. RHP is .332, so he could hold his own as a platoon player. Pay for 35 SB, but if there's a way he can sneak into 400+ AB, UP: 50+ SB.

Yr	Tm	AB	R	HR	RBI	SB	BA	xBA	OBP	SLG	OPS	vL	vR	bb%	ct%	Eye	G	L	F	h%	HctX	PX	xPX	hr/f	Spd	SBO	SB%	#Wk	DOM	DIS	RC/G	RAR	BPV	BPX	R$
10	KC *	277	38	2	22	20	219	238	273	302	575	273	783	7	80	0.37	67	5	28	27	68	61	116	9%	138	44%	71%	5	60%	40%	2.64	-21.4	27	59	$6
11	KC *	363	54	2	20	36	221	256	280	275	555	333	544	8	81	0.44	68	16	16	27	64	38	12	0%	160	41%	91%	11	9%	82%	2.89	-24.6	20	44	$10
12	KC *	355	60	0	12	34	261	250	323	332	655	510	689	8	83	0.52	57	19	24	32	89	44	56	0%	203	38%	85%	25	20%	40%	3.99	-9.1	45	113	$14
13	KC *	265	36	2	18	37	231	248	293	324	617	531	741	8	78	0.39	58	17	25	29	74	66	68	5%	154	64%	86%	21	38%	29%	3.52	-5.8	28	70	$14
14	KC	260	33	1	24	36	269	233	324	327	651	604	663	8	80	0.42	63	14	23	33	56	37	39	2%	172	52%	84%	27	19%	48%	4.09	1.5	19	51	$17
1st Half		120	17	1	10	12	292	222	344	350	694	636	705	8	83	0.48	60	12	28	35	52	30	44	4%	188	38%	75%	14	14%	43%	4.39	1.8	28	76	$11
2nd Half		140	16	0	14	24	250	240	307	307	614	583	623	8	78	0.39	65	15	20	32	60	43	35	0%	133	66%	89%	13	23%	54%	3.84	-0.1	4	11	$22
15	Proj	290	39	2	22	37	252	242	311	327	638	521	670	8	80	0.43	61	15	24	31	67	52	56	3%	162	52%	85%				3.83	-0.3	30	80	$17

Eaton,Adam

Age: 26 Bats: L Pos: CF | Ht: 5' 8" Wt: 185
Health D | PT/Exp C | Consist F
LIMA Plan B+ | Rand Var -2 | MM 2545

Missed a month with two DL stints, and had a sore hamstring for most of April. When healthy, 2H jumps in ct%, LD%, and SB% were exciting. Checks off everything on the speedster wish list: lots of GBs, enough BBs, big raw Spd. The poor SB% is the deal-breaker. Just harness those wheels and... UP: 30 SB.

Yr	Tm	AB	R	HR	RBI	SB	BA	xBA	OBP	SLG	OPS	vL	vR	bb%	ct%	Eye	G	L	F	h%	HctX	PX	xPX	hr/f	Spd	SBO	SB%	#Wk	DOM	DIS	RC/G	RAR	BPV	BPX	R$
10																																			
11	aa	212	22	3	20	7	268		333	375	709			9	82	0.54				32		68			130	22%	52%				4.00		40	89	$4
12	ARI *	613	108	7	38	32	312	274	367	440	807	890	737	8	83	0.51	64	12	24	37	108	90	91	13%	139	26%	67%	4	50%	25%	5.76	18.3	64	160	$31
13	ARI *	285	43	4	25	5	235	261	282	341	623	708	665	6	81	0.35	57	19	25	28	89	71	63	6%	131	11%	71%	13	31%	23%	3.19	-7.8	36	90	$4
14	CHW	486	76	1	35	15	300	278	362	401	763	724	778	8	83	0.52	60	20	20	36	87	74	44	1%	155	16%	63%	23	43%	30%	5.05	15.9	56	151	$19
1st Half		251	38	1	22	7	279	261	348	378	726	662	750	9	81	0.50	63	16	21	34	70	69	26	2%	159	16%	58%	12	33%	33%	4.39	3.8	46	124	$17
2nd Half		235	38	0	13	8	323	295	377	426	803	788	808	7	85	0.54	56	25	19	38	105	79	62	0%	140	16%	67%	11	55%	27%	5.85	12.7	62	168	$22
15	Proj	518	79	4	39	19	285	276	349	396	745	771	736	8	83	0.47	59	19	22	34	93	80	60	4%	141	19%	67%				4.67	12.1	53	140	$21

MATT CEDERHOLM

Ellis,A.J.

Age: 34 Bats: R Pos: CA	Health C	LIMA Plan D+	
Ht: 6' 3" Wt: 220	PT/Exp C	Rand Var +3	
	Consist C	MM 1003	

Had knee surgery at the beginning of the season and a sprained ankle in May, and was never quite right. On one hand, you write off the entire year and give him a mulligan. On the other hand, a 34-year-old catcher already coming off of a peak year regression is probably not a great investment anyway.

Yr	Tm	AB	R	HR	RBI	SB	BA	xBA	OBP	SLG	OPS	vL	vR	bb%	ct%	Eye	G	L	F	h%	HctX	PX	xPX	hr/f	Spd	SBO	SB%	#Wk	DOM	DIS	RC/G	RAR	BPV	BPX	R$
10	LA *	169	12	0	20	1	240	215	323	295	617	673	688	11	80	0.60	52	16	32	30	79	49	59	0%	94	1%	100%	22	23%	45%	3.21	-5.8	10	22	$0
11	LA *	269	26	3	25	0	224	224	322	307	628	1069	645	13	82	0.82	49	16	35	26	119	60	99	8%	88	3%	0%	13	46%	31%	3.13	-10.3	31	69	-$1
12	LA	423	44	13	52	0	270	243	373	414	786	702	815	13	75	0.61	45	23	33	33	92	100	102	13%	103	0%	0%	27	48%	37%	5.30	12.2	38	95	$9
13	LA	390	43	10	52	0	238	238	318	364	682	671	684	10	80	0.58	44	19	37	27	120	86	138	9%	90	2%	0%	26	38%	27%	3.79	1.0	38	95	$5
14	LA	283	21	3	25	0	191	197	323	254	577	711	535	16	80	0.93	44	17	39	23	94	50	81	3%	63	0%	0%	21	33%	43%	2.55	-8.0	12	32	-$4
1st Half		90	8	0	4	0	222	213	386	256	642	848	565	20	80	1.22	39	24	38	28	87	33	79	0%	86	0%	0%	8	38%	25%	3.14	-0.7	14	38	-$7
2nd Half		193	13	3	21	0	176	189	291	254	545	630	521	14	80	0.79	47	14	39	21	97	57	82	5%	58	0%	0%	13	31%	54%	2.28	-6.9	12	32	-$2
15	Proj	**361**	**32**	**8**	**38**	**0**	**234**	**227**	**346**	**344**	**690**	**776**	**663**	**14**	**79**	**0.78**	**45**	**19**	**37**	**27**	**100**	**80**	**98**	**8%**	**79**	**1%**	**15%**				**3.89**	**5.4**	**17**	**45**	**$2**

Ellis,Mark

Age: 38 Bats: R Pos: 2B	Health D	LIMA Plan D	
Ht: 5' 10" Wt: 190	PT/Exp C	Rand Var +5	
	Consist C	MM 1311	

Opened the season on the DL with knee tendinitis, then lost time in August with an oblique strain. While these injuries had an impact on 2014, his skills profile has been stable and uninspiring for awhile. At 38, stuff like this does start happening. If only "cagey veteran" was a category.

Yr	Tm	AB	R	HR	RBI	SB	BA	xBA	OBP	SLG	OPS	vL	vR	bb%	ct%	Eye	G	L	F	h%	HctX	PX	xPX	hr/f	Spd	SBO	SB%	#Wk	DOM	DIS	RC/G	RAR	BPV	BPX	R$
10	OAK	436	45	5	49	7	291	258	358	381	739	839	706	8	87	0.71	42	21	37	33	94	65	65	4%	88	9%	54%	24	38%	17%	4.65	-0.8	46	100	$13
11	2 TM	480	55	7	41	14	248	245	288	346	634	693	614	4	84	0.29	46	17	37	28	79	70	66	5%	93	17%	74%	26	35%	42%	3.28	-20.6	32	71	$9
12	LA	415	62	7	31	5	258	260	333	364	697	877	612	9	83	0.57	39	27	34	30	90	72	80	6%	97	4%	100%	21	43%	29%	4.11	-2.8	39	98	$8
13	LA	433	46	6	48	4	270	245	323	351	674	743	644	6	83	0.35	43	24	33	31	92	54	78	5%	117	4%	80%	24	25%	46%	3.84	2.2	23	58	$10
14	STL	178	15	0	12	4	180	215	253	213	466	487	448	7	79	0.37	48	21	31	23	82	34	76	0%	78	13%	80%	22	18%	55%	1.63	-10.0	-17	-46	-$3
1st Half		134	10	0	12	4	194	219	276	239	515	566	477	9	80	0.48	47	19	33	24	96	44	92	0%	76	12%	100%	12	25%	58%	2.14	-5.3	-3	-8	-$2
2nd Half		44	5	0	0	0	136	204	174	136	310	305	316	2	75	0.09	50	25	25	18	38	0	25	0%	94	14%	0%	10	10%	50%	0.52	-4.4	-65	-176	-$6
15	Proj	**164**	**18**	**1**	**15**	**3**	**225**	**243**	**287**	**293**	**580**	**576**	**582**	**6**	**81**	**0.37**	**45**	**23**	**31**	**27**	**76**	**57**	**64**	**3%**	**86**	**10%**	**85%**				**2.70**	**-3.5**	**9**	**25**	**$2**

Ellsbury,Jacoby

Age: 31 Bats: L Pos: CF	Health D	LIMA Plan D+	
Ht: 6' 1" Wt: 195	PT/Exp B	Rand Var +1	
	Consist C	MM 2545	

The only 3 facts you need to know: 1) 5-year avg h% suggests he's a 30% guy. That's a .275 hitter. 2) 2011 was a random HR lightning bolt; multi-year skills point to average power. 3) Per Health grade, two straight healthy years don't erase the long-term injury record. Bottom line: pay for a repeat, nothing more.

Yr	Tm	AB	R	HR	RBI	SB	BA	xBA	OBP	SLG	OPS	vL	vR	bb%	ct%	Eye	G	L	F	h%	HctX	PX	xPX	hr/f	Spd	SBO	SB%	#Wk	DOM	DIS	RC/G	RAR	BPV	BPX	R$
10	BOS *	102	15	0	6	8	239	256	277	297	575	471	488	5	91	0.60	49	16	35	26	49	48	35	0%	103	37%	89%	6	33%	33%	3.00	-6.3	46	100	$2
11	BOS	660	119	32	105	39	321	313	376	552	928	841	965	7	85	0.53	43	23	34	34	114	145	115	17%	109	30%	72%	27	78%	4%	7.42	42.4	106	236	$49
12	BOS	303	43	4	26	14	271	259	313	370	682	648	701	6	86	0.44	47	20	33	30	85	70	91	5%	103	22%	82%	15	53%	20%	4.15	-6.2	44	110	$9
13	BOS	577	92	9	53	52	298	276	355	426	781	641	863	8	84	0.51	51	21	28	34	107	85	78	7%	136	33%	93%	25	56%	20%	5.90	26.6	62	155	$39
14	NYY	575	71	16	70	39	271	276	328	419	747	828	711	8	84	0.53	42	25	34	30	103	98	87	10%	108	28%	89%	25	60%	16%	5.06	19.4	64	173	$31
1st Half		302	39	4	34	22	288	267	358	397	755	878	687	10	82	0.62	41	28	31	34	99	83	79	5%	106	26%	88%	14	50%	21%	5.43	13.4	48	130	$30
2nd Half		273	32	12	36	17	253	287	294	443	737	748	733	5	86	0.39	43	21	36	26	108	114	95	14%	109	32%	89%	11	73%	9%	4.59	5.9	81	219	$32
15	Proj	**574**	**79**	**13**	**62**	**40**	**276**	**276**	**328**	**414**	**742**	**728**	**749**	**7**	**85**	**0.49**	**45**	**22**	**32**	**31**	**100**	**93**	**85**	**8%**	**112**	**29%**	**89%**				**5.00**	**18.8**	**72**	**188**	**$31**

Encarnacion,Edwin

Age: 32 Bats: R Pos: 1B DH	Health C	LIMA Plan A	
Ht: 6' 1" Wt: 230	PT/Exp A	Rand Var +2	
	Consist A	MM 5155	

Was on pace for huge season until quad inury cost him six weeks in 2H. Overall, spotty health history hasn't hurt power—check out trends in HctX and xPX—and xBA shows some BA upside, to boot. Despite age and health score, still a solid power source that might still sneak in another 2012 stat line.

Yr	Tm	AB	R	HR	RBI	SB	BA	xBA	OBP	SLG	OPS	vL	vR	bb%	ct%	Eye	G	L	F	h%	HctX	PX	xPX	hr/f	Spd	SBO	SB%	#Wk	DOM	DIS	RC/G	RAR	BPV	BPX	R$
10	TOR *	364	52	23	58	1	251	281	309	487	796	914	755	8	83	0.48	32	17	51	25	113	143	133	15%	66	1%	100%	21	57%	29%	5.14	-5.3	82	178	$11
11	TOR	481	70	17	55	8	272	275	334	453	787	845	767	8	84	0.56	36	19	44	29	129	124	124	9%	73	8%	80%	27	63%	19%	5.29	-4.8	75	167	$16
12	TOR	542	93	42	110	13	280	285	384	557	941	1086	892	13	83	0.89	33	18	49	27	131	157	153	19%	77	9%	81%	27	81%	7%	7.47	33.5	108	270	$31
13	TOR	530	90	36	104	7	272	311	370	534	904	859	916	13	88	1.32	35	22	43	25	137	150	152	18%	67	5%	88%	25	84%	8%	6.95	35.5	122	305	$28
14	TOR	477	75	34	98	2	268	300	354	547	901	870	909	12	83	0.76	36	16	47	26	137	176	153	18%	75	2%	100%	22	68%	14%	6.75	35.7	119	322	$24
1st Half		313	55	25	65	2	278	316	365	594	959	976	955	12	82	0.73	35	16	48	27	137	201	161	20%	87	2%	100%	14	71%	7%	7.63	30.7	140	378	$34
2nd Half		164	20	9	33	0	250	265	333	457	791	629	825	11	84	0.81	38	17	45	25	136	130	138	14%	56	0%	0%	8	63%	25%	5.21	5.0	82	222	$6
15	Proj	**524**	**81**	**36**	**102**	**5**	**274**	**300**	**362**	**538**	**900**	**889**	**902**	**12**	**84**	**0.87**	**36**	**18**	**46**	**26**	**134**	**164**	**147**	**18%**	**66**	**4%**	**86%**				**6.83**	**39.9**	**113**	**297**	**$28**

Escobar,Alcides

Age: 28 Bats: R Pos: SS	Health A	LIMA Plan B	
Ht: 6' 1" Wt: 185	PT/Exp A	Rand Var -2	
	Consist D	MM 1535	

Year-to-year variation makes him a moving target, though you can count on solid contact, few walks or homers, and 50 RBI. Speed is elite, yes, but fluctuating h% and SBO means unpredictable SB totals. His value is in his legs, so what's a GM to do? Pay for 25+ steals, pray for BA and hope for profit.

Yr	Tm	AB	R	HR	RBI	SB	BA	xBA	OBP	SLG	OPS	vL	vR	bb%	ct%	Eye	G	L	F	h%	HctX	PX	xPX	hr/f	Spd	SBO	SB%	#Wk	DOM	DIS	RC/G	RAR	BPV	BPX	R$
10	MIL	506	57	4	41	10	235	255	288	326	614	614	614	7	86	0.51	44	21	34	27	88	53	77	3%	192	11%	71%	27	41%	19%	3.10	-16.5	60	130	$5
11	KC	548	69	4	46	26	254	262	290	343	633	576	651	4	87	0.34	53	18	29	29	65	58	46	3%	171	27%	74%	27	41%	22%	3.34	-13.7	55	122	$14
12	KC	605	68	5	52	35	293	271	331	390	721	676	739	4	83	0.27	53	23	24	34	76	65	51	4%	143	25%	88%	27	37%	26%	4.73	14.0	39	98	$25
13	KC	607	57	4	52	22	234	250	259	300	559	620	532	3	86	0.23	46	23	31	27	77	45	60	3%	141	17%	100%	26	23%	27%	2.74	-12.5	31	78	$11
14	KC	579	74	3	50	31	285	265	317	377	694	784	663	4	86	0.28	44	24	32	33	83	70	62	2%	138	25%	84%	27	41%	22%	4.31	18.7	50	135	$25
1st Half		288	38	2	28	20	295	274	337	410	746	760	742	5	85	0.36	41	24	35	34	101	91	86	2%	131	30%	91%	14	50%	21%	5.19	15.7	66	178	$28
2nd Half		291	36	1	22	11	275	257	297	344	641	808	582	3	86	0.20	47	24	30	32	64	50	38	1%	146	21%	73%	13	31%	23%	3.53	2.5	35	95	$22
15	Proj	**599**	**69**	**4**	**51**	**28**	**268**	**261**	**301**	**353**	**654**	**708**	**633**	**4**	**86**	**0.28**	**46**	**23**	**30**	**31**	**78**	**62**	**57**	**2%**	**144**	**22%**	**85%**				**3.77**	**9.2**	**42**	**111**	**$21**

Escobar,Eduardo

Age: 26 Bats: B Pos: SS 3B	Health A	LIMA Plan D+	
Ht: 5' 10" Wt: 175	PT/Exp D	Rand Var -3	
	Consist C	MM 2323	

Has graduated from "$1 upside" to "marginally useful" with near-average ct% and decent power. Average HctX held up all year, so BA was not entirely flukey. While still sub-par, OPS trend vs. RHP is a positive. He's an end-gamer who can contribute something beyond positional flexibility.

Yr	Tm	AB	R	HR	RBI	SB	BA	xBA	OBP	SLG	OPS	vL	vR	bb%	ct%	Eye	G	L	F	h%	HctX	PX	xPX	hr/f	Spd	SBO	SB%	#Wk	DOM	DIS	RC/G	RAR	BPV	BPX	R$
10	aa	202	19	3	19	3	241		270	343	613			4	81	0.21				29		68			121	6%	100%				3.18		24	52	$1
11	CHW*	496	46	4	41	11	243	296	279	321	601	667	500	5	76	0.21	67	33	0	31	0	62	2	0%	112	17%	56%	5	0%	40%	2.88	-19.4	0	0	$6
12	2 AL *	269	34	1	17	6	207	227	257	270	526	844	419	6	78	0.30	51	21	28	26	80	41	42	0%	149	11%	84%	19	26%	68%	2.28	-13.6	4	10	-$1
13	MIN *	331	39	6	30	4	251	244	300	383	683	655	619	7	77	0.31	42	21	37	31	81	97	94	6%	135	11%	51%	18	33%	39%	3.76	3.3	42	105	$5
14	MIN	433	52	6	37	1	275	264	315	406	721	877	654	5	79	0.26	41	24	35	34	99	110	93	5%	113	2%	50%	27	41%	26%	4.44	15.6	49	132	$10
1st Half		215	25	2	17	1	274	281	317	409	727	744	720	6	78	0.30	41	27	32	34	101	124	101	4%	104	4%	50%	14	36%	36%	4.52	7.9	57	154	$7
2nd Half		218	27	4	20	0	275	247	312	404	715	979	580	4	79	0.22	41	21	38	33	98	96	85	6%	125	0%	0%	13	46%	15%	4.36	6.9	41	111	$12
15	Proj	**298**	**35**	**4**	**25**	**3**	**256**	**249**	**297**	**372**	**670**	**826**	**606**	**5**	**78**	**0.26**	**43**	**22**	**35**	**32**	**90**	**93**	**85**	**5%**	**123**	**6%**	**63%**				**3.74**	**4.3**	**27**	**70**	**$6**

Escobar,Yunel

Age: 32 Bats: R Pos: SS	Health A	LIMA Plan B	
Ht: 6' 2" Wt: 215	PT/Exp A	Rand Var 0	
	Consist A	MM 1125	

With good plate skills but no power or speed, you need AB to generate counting stats. Problem here is defense was dreadful by any measure. His bat isn't terribly valuable on its own, so teams won't find room for him in the lineup if he's not contributing in the field. Here's where AAA reliability is not a good thing.

Yr	Tm	AB	R	HR	RBI	SB	BA	xBA	OBP	SLG	OPS	vL	vR	bb%	ct%	Eye	G	L	F	h%	HctX	PX	xPX	hr/f	Spd	SBO	SB%	#Wk	DOM	DIS	RC/G	RAR	BPV	BPX	R$
10	2 TM	497	60	4	35	6	256	255	337	318	655	728	634	10	89	0.98	54	18	28	28	109	44	64	3%	85	5%	75%	24	46%	17%	3.62	-8.1	37	80	$7
11	TOR	513	77	11	48	3	290	276	369	413	782	929	740	11	86	0.87	57	18	25	32	91	79	79	10%	130	3%	50%	24	58%	13%	5.35	16.9	71	158	$16
12	TOR	558	58	9	51	5	253	261	300	344	644	644	643	6	87	0.50	56	19	25	28	89	57	69	7%	92	4%	83%	27	44%	22%	3.51	-6.5	37	93	$8
13	TAM	508	61	9	56	4	256	266	332	366	698	750	674	10	86	0.78	53	19	27	28	117	76	98	8%	89	5%	50%	27	59%	19%	4.07	9.6	52	130	$10
14	TAM	476	33	7	39	1	258	244	324	340	664	689	656	8	87	0.72	49	20	31	28	105	57	75	6%	72	1%	50%	25	56%	20%	3.72	7.5	35	95	$6
1st Half		262	13	4	22	0	244	228	322	328	650	885	581	10	88	0.94	49	19	32	27	111	58	82	5%	68	1%	0%	13	62%	23%	3.51	2.1	41	111	$4
2nd Half		214	20	3	17	1	276	253	326	355	681	459	752	6	87	0.46	49	21	29	31	98	56	67	6%	83	2%	100%	12	50%	17%	3.99	4.6	31	84	$9
15	Proj	**495**	**48**	**8**	**45**	**3**	**261**	**258**	**326**	**353**	**678**	**685**	**676**	**8**	**87**	**0.69**	**52**	**20**	**28**	**29**	**104**	**65**	**79**	**6%**	**84**	**3%**	**62%**				**3.89**	**9.4**	**32**	**83**	**$10**

MATT CEDERHOLM

Espinosa,Danny

Age: 28 Bats: B Pos: 2B	Health A	LIMA Plan D	
Ht: 6' 0" Wt: 205	PT/Exp C	Rand Var -1	
	Consist F	MM 3301	

Playing time has dwindled since mid-teens value of 2010-12. Still has some skills (xPX, Spd and vLHP) but terrible plate discipline is overriding them. Until he can improve ct% and abysmal BA, a larger role isn't likely. However, given his secondary skills, there are worse $1 end-gamers.

Yr Tm	AB	R	HR	RBI	SB	BA	xBA	OBP	SLG	OPS	vL	vR	bb%	ct%	Eye	G	L	F	h%	HctX	PX	xPX	hr/f	Spd	SBO	SB%	#Wk	DOM	DIS	RC/G	RAR	BPV	BPX	R$
10 WAS *	584	84	24	73	21	238	232	291	416	707	846	684	7	73	0.28	46	8	46	28	90	120	133	18%	116	27%	60%	6	50%	50%	3.79	-16.6	40	87	$18
11 WAS	573	72	21	66	17	236	241	323	414	737	857	703	9	71	0.34	44	16	40	30	105	132	130	14%	115	17%	74%	27	48%	41%	4.18	-9.4	44	98	$14
12 WAS	594	82	17	56	20	247	234	315	402	717	775	694	7	68	0.24	47	19	34	34	93	123	109	13%	107	19%	77%	27	33%	44%	4.11	-4.1	20	50	$16
13 WAS *	441	33	4	27	6	169	173	199	245	444	529	448	4	63	0.10	51	10	39	26	71	74	95	7%	77	11%	83%	10	40%	50%	1.52	-30.9	-55	-138	-$7
14 WAS	333	31	8	27	8	219	215	283	351	634	859	532	5	63	0.15	44	22	34	32	100	115	134	12%	107	14%	89%	26	27%	54%	3.04	-3.5	-9	-24	$4
1st Half	244	22	6	17	6	217	210	284	348	632	826	560	6	62	0.16	43	22	35	32	108	117	148	13%	105	14%	86%	14	21%	57%	3.03	-2.7	-14	-38	$5
2nd Half	89	9	2	10	2	225	229	281	360	641	917	435	3	67	0.10	47	21	32	31	78	111	99	11%	106	13%	100%	12	33%	50%	3.06	-0.9	-1	-3	-$1
15 Proj	**233**	**24**	**6**	**21**	**5**	**226**	**220**	**284**	**365**	**648**	**847**	**563**	**5**	**66**	**0.15**	**47**	**17**	**36**	**32**	**86**	**119**	**113**	**11%**	**101**	**14%**	**83%**				**3.22**	**-1.3**	**1**	**4**	**$2**

Ethier,Andre

Age: 33 Bats: L Pos: CF	Health A	LIMA Plan D+	
Ht: 6' 2" Wt: 200	PT/Exp B	Rand Var +2	
	Consist B	MM 3233	

Started just 79 games due to an OF logjam and his own poor performance. But could it be a chicken & egg thing? Look: He's posted his best OPS levels when he's gotten the most playing time. Some guys just need a regular spot on the lineup card. But is it correlation or causation? Still tough to bet on him in 2015.

Yr Tm	AB	R	HR	RBI	SB	BA	xBA	OBP	SLG	OPS	vL	vR	bb%	ct%	Eye	G	L	F	h%	HctX	PX	xPX	hr/f	Spd	SBO	SB%	#Wk	DOM	DIS	RC/G	RAR	BPV	BPX	R$
10 LA	517	71	23	82	2	292	286	364	493	857	625	960	10	80	0.58	39	22	40	33	131	135	142	14%	97	2%	67%	25	64%	16%	6.46	24.0	81	176	$21
11 LA	487	67	11	62	0	292	265	368	421	789	563	878	11	79	0.56	44	25	31	35	102	97	80	9%	94	1%	0%	24	46%	25%	5.52	9.9	44	98	$16
12 LA	556	79	20	89	2	284	271	351	460	812	606	945	8	78	0.40	43	24	33	33	109	120	106	14%	94	3%	50%	26	54%	27%	5.57	13.8	53	133	$20
13 LA	482	54	12	52	4	272	268	360	423	783	613	854	11	80	0.64	39	24	37	32	120	109	124	8%	107	5%	57%	25	60%	16%	5.17	14.8	65	163	$13
14 LA	341	29	4	42	2	249	259	322	370	691	567	710	8	78	0.42	52	22	26	31	84	88	63	6%	121	4%	50%	27	44%	30%	3.85	0.2	39	105	$5
1st Half	233	21	4	31	1	249	261	302	373	675	493	709	6	79	0.29	54	20	26	30	90	89	71	8%	110	6%	33%	15	40%	33%	3.57	-2.0	35	95	$7
2nd Half	108	8	0	11	1	250	251	362	361	723	875	710	14	76	0.65	48	24	28	33	72	86	43	0%	130	3%	100%	12	50%	25%	4.38	1.7	41	111	-$2
15 Proj	**376**	**39**	**7**	**46**	**2**	**265**	**266**	**350**	**407**	**757**	**624**	**793**	**10**	**78**	**0.54**	**45**	**23**	**31**	**32**	**98**	**107**	**85**	**8%**	**115**	**4%**	**62%**				**4.79**	**10.1**	**46**	**121**	**$10**

Fielder,Prince

Age: 31 Bats: L Pos: 1B	Health F	LIMA Plan B+	
Ht: 5' 11" Wt: 275	PT/Exp B	Rand Var +3	
	Consist D	MM 4055	

Missed 120 games after mid-May neck surgery; cleared to swing bat in September and is expected to be ready for spring training. PRO: Plate skills as strong as ever. CON: 3-year decline in SLG; uncertainty surrounding injury; body type and age scream "old player skills" decline. Take your chances but this one's a huge risk.

Yr Tm	AB	R	HR	RBI	SB	BA	xBA	OBP	SLG	OPS	vL	vR	bb%	ct%	Eye	G	L	F	h%	HctX	PX	xPX	hr/f	Spd	SBO	SB%	#Wk	DOM	DIS	RC/G	RAR	BPV	BPX	R$
10 MIL	578	94	32	83	1	261	266	401	471	871	668	975	16	76	0.83	42	18	40	29	122	138	134	18%	28	0%	100%	27	56%	22%	6.23	9.9	58	126	$19
11 MIL	569	95	38	120	1	299	306	415	566	981	822	1046	16	81	1.01	43	20	37	31	140	170	145	22%	46	1%	50%	27	74%	15%	8.40	43.2	109	242	$32
12 DET	581	83	30	108	1	313	304	412	528	940	808	1017	13	86	1.01	41	25	33	33	132	126	128	18%	46	0%	100%	27	70%	11%	7.88	40.5	84	210	$30
13 DET	624	82	25	106	1	279	275	362	457	819	819	819	11	81	0.64	41	23	36	31	116	119	128	14%	37	1%	50%	27	56%	11%	5.73	19.8	55	138	$24
14 TEX	150	19	3	16	0	247	251	360	360	720	688	733	14	84	1.04	50	19	31	28	95	83	68	8%	45	0%	0%	7	29%	14%	4.32	0.8	47	127	$1
1st Half	150	19	3	16	0	247	251	360	360	720	688	733	14	84	1.04	50	19	31	28	95	83	68	8%	45	0%	0%	7	29%	14%	4.32	0.7	47	127	$1
2nd Half																																		
15 Proj	**526**	**74**	**23**	**85**	**1**	**279**	**286**	**385**	**467**	**852**	**763**	**901**	**14**	**83**	**0.90**	**40**	**23**	**36**	**30**	**118**	**127**	**113**	**15%**	**39**	**1%**	**67%**				**6.22**	**30.6**	**70**	**185**	**$22**

Flaherty,Ryan

Age: 28 Bats: L Pos: 3B 2B SS	Health A	LIMA Plan D+	
Ht: 6' 3" Wt: 210	PT/Exp F	Rand Var +2	
	Consist A	MM 3213	

Injuries to Manny Machado provided significant playing time boost in April and September. Possesses some pop for a MI, but not enough for a CI. Eye and ct% have slowly improved, but buckets of Ks ensure that low BA. Seems relegated to utilityman role, providing random stretches of value as an injury fill-in.

Yr Tm	AB	R	HR	RBI	SB	BA	xBA	OBP	SLG	OPS	vL	vR	bb%	ct%	Eye	G	L	F	h%	HctX	PX	xPX	hr/f	Spd	SBO	SB%	#Wk	DOM	DIS	RC/G	RAR	BPV	BPX	R$
10 aa	71	7	1	6	1	154		230	210	440			9	81	0.53				18		39			105	5%	100%				1.49		7	15	-$3
11 a/a	475	48	13	57	3	224		275	365	640			7	75	0.28				27		104			89	10%	31%				3.10		26	58	$5
12 BAL *	191	19	8	21	1	224	208	254	380	634	667	613	4	72	0.14	43	13	44	27	80	96	107	13%	123	3%	100%	24	25%	63%	3.20	-7.8	12	30	$1
13 BAL *	280	31	12	31	2	223	240	274	390	665	641	687	7	74	0.28	49	16	36	26	108	116	115	15%	90	3%	100%	24	38%	38%	3.55	-3.3	33	83	$3
14 BAL	281	33	7	32	1	221	244	288	356	644	616	649	7	76	0.32	47	19	34	27	94	104	101	10%	80	2%	100%	26	42%	42%	3.25	-3.6	27	73	$2
1st Half	126	13	3	13	0	206	224	270	317	588	701	565	6	75	0.26	50	17	33	25	78	85	64	10%	66	0%	0%	14	36%	50%	2.59	-4.3	3	8	-$2
2nd Half	155	20	4	19	1	232	257	302	387	689	545	716	8	76	0.38	45	20	35	28	106	120	131	10%	99	3%	100%	12	50%	33%	3.84	0.7	49	132	$5
15 Proj	**295**	**33**	**10**	**33**	**2**	**223**	**242**	**285**	**376**	**661**	**631**	**666**	**6**	**75**	**0.28**	**47**	**17**	**36**	**27**	**97**	**113**	**108**	**12%**	**90**	**3%**	**78%**				**3.38**	**-2.8**	**25**	**65**	**$5**

Flores,Wilmer

Age: 23 Bats: R Pos: SS	Health A	LIMA Plan D+	
Ht: 6' 3" Wt: 205	PT/Exp D	Rand Var +1	
	Consist B	MM 2023	

6-29-.251 in 259 AB at NYM. Struggled in first callup, but made some strides in second tour. Makes enough contact to begin with, and concurrent ct%-and-PX spike in 2H is an attention-grabber. Questions remain about his ability to repeat that trick, as well as about his defense. Age buys him time to provide answers, though.

Yr Tm	AB	R	HR	RBI	SB	BA	xBA	OBP	SLG	OPS	vL	vR	bb%	ct%	Eye	G	L	F	h%	HctX	PX	xPX	hr/f	Spd	SBO	SB%	#Wk	DOM	DIS	RC/G	RAR	BPV	BPX	R$
10																																		
11																																		
12 aa	251	30	7	27	0	274		318	428	746			6	86	0.48				29		95			94	0%	0%				4.78		64	160	$5
13 NYM *	519	53	11	69	1	246	269	276	384	660	447	591	4	81	0.22	51	22	27	28	69	98	47	5%	80	4%	16%	8	50%	50%	3.48	-0.4	36	90	$9
14 NYM *	479	54	14	64	1	247	256	280	390	670	382	739	4	83	0.27	40	20	40	27	101	95	103	7%	110	3%	30%	20	40%	35%	3.62	4.6	54	146	$10
1st Half	215	18	4	25	0	232	233	263	334	597	636	525	4	78	0.19	35	24	41	28	97	75	104	4%	107	3%	0%	9	11%	56%	2.84	-2.6	16	43	$0
2nd Half	264	36	10	39	1	260	279	293	435	729	255	831	5	88	0.39	42	19	40	26	105	109	103	8%	113	4%	46%	11	64%	18%	4.33	8.4	83	224	$18
15 Proj	**367**	**41**	**8**	**48**	**1**	**255**	**258**	**289**	**380**	**669**	**472**	**744**	**5**	**83**	**0.29**	**42**	**21**	**37**	**29**	**89**	**90**	**81**	**7%**	**104**	**3%**	**31%**				**3.71**	**5.0**	**34**	**88**	**$9**

Flowers,Tyler

Age: 29 Bats: R Pos: CA	Health A	LIMA Plan D	
Ht: 6' 4" Wt: 245	PT/Exp D	Rand Var -4	
	Consist C	MM 4003	

2014 looks like a jump into the pool of relevant catchers, but reasons for concern abound. Inflated h% artificially boosted BA; hr/f did same for HR total. xPX, xBA, ct%, GB% all serve as reality checks. Best news here, though, is 2nd half gains vRHP. If those stick, then he'll achieve that relevance. Temper expectations.

Yr Tm	AB	R	HR	RBI	SB	BA	xBA	OBP	SLG	OPS	vL	vR	bb%	ct%	Eye	G	L	F	h%	HctX	PX	xPX	hr/f	Spd	SBO	SB%	#Wk	DOM	DIS	RC/G	RAR	BPV	BPX	R$
10 CHW*	357	34	14	40	1	186	177	283	363	646	0	542	12	59	0.33	33	0	67	27	40	158	119	0%	101	3%	57%	5	0%	80%	3.20	-11.5	19	41	-$1
11 CHW*	332	41	19	41	2	223	210	320	432	752	431	863	13	58	0.34	32	16	51	32	91	179	180	13%	88	3%	61%	10	40%	50%	4.50	3.0	29	64	$6
12 CHW	136	19	7	13	2	213	225	296	412	708	905	586	8	59	0.21	53	18	29	30	64	165	87	30%	81	11%	67%	26	27%	62%	3.64	-2.0	10	25	$1
13 CHW	256	24	10	24	0	195	208	247	355	603	455	661	5	63	0.15	42	17	41	26	86	133	106	15%	73	2%	0%	22	32%	59%	2.62	-8.9	-5	-13	-$1
14 CHW	407	42	15	50	0	241	222	297	396	693	732	679	6	61	0.16	48	24	29	36	82	137	88	21%	74	1%	0%	26	31%	58%	3.74	5.0	-10	-27	$7
1st Half	224	23	5	25	0	237	193	296	326	622	685	600	7	59	0.20	51	25	24	38	73	82	69	16%	79	2%	0%	14	14%	79%	3.13	-1.8	-58	-157	$5
2nd Half	183	19	10	25	0	246	259	298	481	779	787	776	4	63	0.10	44	22	33	33	94	200	109	26%	70	0%	0%	12	50%	33%	4.45	5.7	44	119	$10
15 Proj	**393**	**42**	**14**	**44**	**1**	**222**	**215**	**286**	**374**	**660**	**638**	**669**	**6**	**61**	**0.17**	**47**	**20**	**33**	**33**	**83**	**139**	**104**	**17%**	**72**	**3%**	**45%**				**3.29**	**-1.2**	**-17**	**-45**	**$6**

Forsythe,Logan

Age: 28 Bats: R Pos: 2B DH	Health D	LIMA Plan D	
Ht: 6' 1" Wt: 195	PT/Exp D	Rand Var +1	
	Consist B	MM 2403	

Multi-position utility usually helps secure PT, but here the lack of offensive production caps opportunities and thus value. He's an efficient basestealer, but tepid OBP limits those opps. 624 career AB vs. RHP with a 579 OPS is solid proof that he can't hit RHPs. Tough to generate fantasy relevance from bad-side platoon work.

Yr Tm	AB	R	HR	RBI	SB	BA	xBA	OBP	SLG	OPS	vL	vR	bb%	ct%	Eye	G	L	F	h%	HctX	PX	xPX	hr/f	Spd	SBO	SB%	#Wk	DOM	DIS	RC/G	RAR	BPV	BPX	R$
10 aa	392	56	2	32	14	215		329	283	612			15	71	0.60				29		62			108	15%	72%				3.06		0	0	$3
11 SD *	328	36	4	32	8	226	217	297	326	623	548	577	9	70	0.34	43	20	37	31	91	87	98	0%	99	16%	57%	15	33%	53%	3.06	-16.8	1	2	$3
12 SD *	373	53	7	32	10	263	249	329	383	712	1010	603	9	79	0.46	36	29	35	32	112	77	107	7%	160	11%	83%	18	33%	28%	4.42	0.8	45	113	$9
13 SD *	245	26	7	22	6	221	253	291	360	651	651	593	9	74	0.38	42	28	29	27	98	94	105	13%	113	11%	86%	17	12%	35%	3.49	-1.2	26	65	$2
14 TAM	301	32	6	26	2	223	224	287	329	616	708	536	8	76	0.35	41	19	40	27	83	80	100	6%	108	3%	100%	27	30%	59%	3.08	-2.8	19	51	$2
1st Half	153	16	2	10	0	242	238	293	333	627	730	527	6	81	0.31	43	21	36	29	81	67	83	4%	117	0%	0%	14	43%	50%	3.18	-1.0	26	70	$0
2nd Half	148	16	4	16	2	203	210	281	324	606	683	543	10	72	0.38	38	17	45	25	85	96	121	8%	99	6%	100%	13	15%	69%	2.98	-1.9	15	41	$3
15 Proj	**287**	**33**	**6**	**26**	**5**	**226**	**232**	**301**	**338**	**638**	**729**	**579**	**9**	**75**	**0.40**	**40**	**23**	**37**	**28**	**92**	**85**	**105**	**8%**	**113**	**8%**	**83%**				**3.32**	**-0.6**	**15**	**39**	**$5**

GREG PYRON

Fowler,Dexter

Age: 29	Bats: B	Pos: CF	Health	C	LIMA Plan B
Ht: 6' 4"	Wt: 190		PT/Exp	B	Rand Var -2
			Consist	B	MM 3515

It's an annual tease... He brings his tools into great hitters parks, yet he's broken the $20 barrier only once. Poor SB% undermines elite Spd and very good OBA; meager HctX can't push enough FBs over the fence. Back problems detoured 2014. With health, maybe this is the year. But flat trends argue otherwise.

Yr	Tm	AB	R	HR	RBI	SB	BA	xBA	OBP	SLG	OPS	vL	vR	bb%	ct%	Eye	G	L	F	h%	HctX	PX	xPX	hr/f	Spd	SBO	SB%	#Wk	DOM	DIS	RC/G	RAR	BPV	BPX	R$
10	COL *	545	87	7	44	14	266	261	346	422	768	744	764	11	76	0.50	45	22	33	34	110	107	94	6%	172	14%	63%	24	54%	25%	4.94	2.4	63	137	$15
11	COL *	578	92	6	49	13	251	250	338	406	743	762	807	12	73	0.48	43	21	35	34	103	119	102	4%	161	15%	56%	22	45%	18%	4.48	-5.2	60	133	$12
12	COL	454	72	13	53	12	300	249	389	474	863	857	866	13	72	0.53	39	27	34	39	97	115	125	12%	175	10%	71%	27	33%	33%	6.67	22.9	60	150	$20
13	COL	415	71	12	42	19	263	246	369	407	776	860	741	14	75	0.62	42	23	34	33	80	102	102	11%	135	20%	68%	23	48%	35%	4.99	9.3	50	125	$18
14	HOU	434	61	8	35	11	276	240	375	399	774	887	737	13	75	0.61	44	21	35	35	95	94	107	7%	144	10%	73%	20	45%	35%	5.23	16.6	47	127	$15
1st Half		285	43	6	24	6	270	245	377	396	774	907	721	14	77	0.71	50	19	31	33	103	91	105	9%	146	9%	67%	13	46%	31%	5.12	10.4	54	146	$18
2nd Half		149	18	2	11	5	289	228	371	403	773	823	763	11	72	0.45	31	27	42	39	80	99	112	4%	130	12%	83%	7	43%	43%	5.43	6.6	30	81	$8
15	**Proj**	**490**	**73**	**11**	**44**	**16**	**267**	**244**	**362**	**407**	**769**	**827**	**748**	**13**	**74**	**0.55**	**40**	**24**	**36**	**34**	**90**	**108**	**109**	**8%**	**148**	**14%**	**72%**				**5.05**	**17.0**	**44**	**117**	**$16**

Francisco,Juan

Age: 28	Bats: L	Pos: 3B 1B	Health	A	LIMA Plan D+
Ht: 6' 2"	Wt: 245		PT/Exp	D	Rand Var +1
			Consist	A	MM 5011

16-43-.220 in 287 AB at TOR. There is no doubting his immense power. However, horrific ct% and inability to figure out LHP hold him back from larger role and put a cap on his BA. Extra AB due to TOR injuries amplified his counting stats. Don't count on that happening again in 2015.

Yr	Tm	AB	R	HR	RBI	SB	BA	xBA	OBP	SLG	OPS	vL	vR	bb%	ct%	Eye	G	L	F	h%	HctX	PX	xPX	hr/f	Spd	SBO	SB%	#Wk	DOM	DIS	RC/G	RAR	BPV	BPX	R$
10	CIN *	363	39	16	53	1	258	269	291	477	768	444	753	4	69	0.15	60	11	29	33	97	168	45	10%	101	3%	44%	10	30%	60%	4.72	-3.9	52	113	$9
11	CIN *	393	44	15	52	1	261	278	282	454	736	286	820	3	75	0.11	45	25	30	32	115	142	125	14%	77	1%	100%	8	50%	25%	4.44	-7.4	42	93	$10
12	ATL	192	17	9	32	1	234	240	278	432	710	468	768	5	64	0.16	43	24	33	32	90	158	114	23%	56	6%	50%	25	40%	52%	3.90	-3.7	10	25	$2
13	2 NL	348	36	18	48	0	227	216	296	422	719	425	748	8	60	0.23	45	18	37	32	96	160	143	23%	97	3%	0%	26	31%	54%	3.97	0.2	17	43	$5
14	TOR *	331	47	18	51	0	229	237	296	459	756	390	810	9	62	0.25	39	16	45	31	89	198	156	20%	80	3%	0%	24	63%	29%	4.38	7.1	48	130	$8
1st Half		218	36	14	38	0	247	252	317	505	822	356	899	9	61	0.27	36	20	44	33	94	220	162	27%	74	2%	0%	12	83%	8%	5.32	10.5	65	176	$15
2nd Half		113	11	4	13	0	195	209	256	372	628	431	667	7	62	0.21	42	11	47	27	82	157	148	12%	89	5%	0%	12	42%	50%	2.86	-3.0	17	46	-$5
15	**Proj**	**227**	**26**	**11**	**32**	**0**	**226**	**235**	**284**	**434**	**718**	**418**	**769**	**7**	**63**	**0.21**	**43**	**17**	**40**	**31**	**92**	**179**	**138**	**19%**	**82**	**4%**	**15%**				**3.92**	**1.6**	**27**	**70**	**$5**

Franco,Maikel

Age: 22	Bats: R	Pos: 3B	Health	A	LIMA Plan D+
Ht: 6' 1"	Wt: 180		PT/Exp	F	Rand Var +1
			Consist	F	MM 3233

0-5-.179 in 56 AB at PHI. Solid ct% in the minors, especially for one with a slugger profile, but struggled upon debut. Swings at everything, and MLB pitchers are sure to continue to exploit that weakness. Keep expectations in check for 2015; additional time in the minors would not surprise.

Yr	Tm	AB	R	HR	RBI	SB	BA	xBA	OBP	SLG	OPS	vL	vR	bb%	ct%	Eye	G	L	F	h%	HctX	PX	xPX	hr/f	Spd	SBO	SB%	#Wk	DOM	DIS	RC/G	RAR	BPV	BPX	R$
10																																			
11																																			
12																																			
13	aa	277	36	12	39	1	305		324	492	816			3	87	0.22				31		109			100	4%	26%				5.67		74	185	$11
14	PHI *	577	54	13	65	2	223	240	254	357	611	277	573	4	82	0.24	49	12	40	25	32	96	26	0%	120	3%	68%	5	0%	40%	2.97	-13.1	51	138	$6
1st Half		302	26	4	24	1	183	238	228	276	504			6	81	0.31				21		71			108	1%	100%				1.97		27	73	-$5
2nd Half		275	28	9	42	2	268	264	285	447	732	277	573	2	83	0.14	49	12	40	29	33	123	26	0%	124	5%	59%	5	0%	40%	4.38	5.5	74	200	$17
15	**Proj**	**311**	**34**	**11**	**40**	**2**	**258**	**263**	**278**	**427**	**705**	**510**	**967**	**3**	**80**	**0.17**	**44**	**19**	**38**	**29**	**95**	**118**	**23**	**12%**	**121**	**5%**	**54%**				**4.09**	**3.6**	**43**	**113**	**$9**

Frandsen,Kevin

Age: 33	Bats: R	Pos: LF	Health	A	LIMA Plan D
Ht: 6' 0"	Wt: 190		PT/Exp	D	Rand Var -1
			Consist	A	MM 1121

Due to WAS injuries, he saw more playing time than his skills warranted. Does a fine job of making contact, but with well below average power and high GB%, nothing really happens when he does. At his age with these holes, AB will be tough to come by.

Yr	Tm	AB	R	HR	RBI	SB	BA	xBA	OBP	SLG	OPS	vL	vR	bb%	ct%	Eye	G	L	F	h%	HctX	PX	xPX	hr/f	Spd	SBO	SB%	#Wk	DOM	DIS	RC/G	RAR	BPV	BPX	R$
10	LAA *	359	45	2	24	4	221	266	255	294	549	589	625	4	90	0.43	56	15	28	24	74	55	51	0%	110	8%	78%	16	56%	19%	2.47	-30.7	46	100	$0
11	a/a	288	23	4	28	7	234		256	320	576			3	86	0.20				26		57			98	20%	58%				2.59		25	56	$2
12	PHI *	586	52	3	39	1	271	287	295	360	655	980	762	3	90	0.34	54	24	22	30	104	62	48	5%	102	6%	20%	10	50%	10%	3.55	-20.0	49	123	$8
13	PHI	252	27	5	26	1	234	271	296	341	637	869	536	5	88	0.41	57	18	25	25	94	67	63	9%	106	2%	100%	27	37%	30%	3.08	-7.3	51	128	$1
14	WAS	220	17	1	17	0	259	238	299	309	608	641	592	3	88	0.23	47	21	31	29	91	39	74	2%	83	0%	0%	27	26%	37%	2.97	-5.2	16	43	$1
1st Half		129	10	1	8	0	240	246	300	302	602	560	619	3	88	0.27	52	21	28	27	99	47	75	3%	81	0%	0%	14	29%	29%	2.67	-4.1	23	62	$0
2nd Half		91	7	0	9	0	286	229	298	319	617	718	542	2	88	0.18	41	23	36	33	80	29	73	0%	94	0%	0%	13	23%	46%	3.43	-0.8	9	24	$2
15	**Proj**	**115**	**10**	**1**	**10**	**0**	**256**	**257**	**296**	**330**	**626**	**722**	**577**	**3**	**88**	**0.28**	**51**	**21**	**29**	**28**	**90**	**54**	**65**	**4%**	**95**	**2%**	**54%**				**3.14**	**-2.0**	**20**	**53**	**$2**

Franklin,Nick

Age: 24	Bats: B	Pos: 2B	Health	A	LIMA Plan D+
Ht: 6' 1"	Wt: 195		PT/Exp	C	Rand Var 0
			Consist	B	MM 3303

1-6-.160 in 81 AB at SEA and TAM. xPX/Spd combo, bb% and age make him intriguing, but still plenty of work to do. Contact rate and BA have been in a tailspin since 1st half of 2013 and absent improvement, he may have tough time garnering consistent PT. At 24, there's time; those in keeper leagues should remain patient.

Yr	Tm	AB	R	HR	RBI	SB	BA	xBA	OBP	SLG	OPS	vL	vR	bb%	ct%	Eye	G	L	F	h%	HctX	PX	xPX	hr/f	Spd	SBO	SB%	#Wk	DOM	DIS	RC/G	RAR	BPV	BPX	R$
10																																			
11	aa	83	11	2	5	4	296		338	422	760			6	75	0.26				38		85			128	31%	57%				4.66		22	49	$2
12	a/a	472	53	8	45	10	239		300	373	673			8	74	0.33				31		98			109	13%	69%				3.71		25	63	$7
13	SEA *	511	58	15	59	11	240	239	323	385	709	599	727	11	73	0.46	35	24	41	30	103	111	140	11%	85	9%	92%	19	37%	37%	4.27	8.3	32	80	$12
14	2 AL *	460	52	10	54	11	227	209	309	340	649	369	492	11	70	0.39	41	18	41	30	71	92	103	5%	103	13%	67%	7	14%	71%	3.42	0.4	7	19	$9
1st Half		251	31	7	33	7	244	218	333	384	718	200	396	12	71	0.46	44	15	41	32	68	106	78	0%	112	15%	61%	4	0%	75%	4.19	6.0	27	73	$13
2nd Half		209	21	3	21	4	207	199	278	288	566	571	628	9	69	0.32	38	21	42	29	75	75	131	10%	94	11%	80%	3	33%	67%	2.61	-5.1	-17	-46	$3
15	**Proj**	**346**	**39**	**9**	**38**	**8**	**230**	**228**	**307**	**367**	**674**	**604**	**697**	**10**	**72**	**0.40**	**38**	**21**	**41**	**30**	**84**	**109**	**121**	**9%**	**96**	**11%**	**77%**				**3.77**	**4.0**	**23**	**60**	**$8**

Frazier,Todd

Age: 29	Bats: R	Pos: 3B 1B	Health	A	LIMA Plan B+
Ht: 6' 3"	Wt: 220		PT/Exp	B	Rand Var -1
			Consist	C	MM 4335

Fantastic season overall, but can he repeat? PRO: Stable xPX; HctX growth and improved xBA are positive signs. CON: SBO% looks suspicious; shaky SB% and average Spd puts another 20 SB season in doubt; huge 1st half followed by 2nd half decline. Trust the HR more than the SB.

Yr	Tm	AB	R	HR	RBI	SB	BA	xBA	OBP	SLG	OPS	vL	vR	bb%	ct%	Eye	G	L	F	h%	HctX	PX	xPX	hr/f	Spd	SBO	SB%	#Wk	DOM	DIS	RC/G	RAR	BPV	BPX	R$
10	aaa	480	54	14	50	11	224		277	383	660			7	69	0.24				29		125			106	16%	70%				3.44		25	54	$7
11	CIN *	427	51	18	48	13	221	255	275	396	671	985	654	7	71	0.25	48	21	31	27	105	130	138	23%	93	20%	74%	12	42%	33%	3.53	-20.7	31	69	$8
12	CIN *	461	58	20	72	5	265	258	321	480	801	858	817	8	75	0.32	33	22	45	32	99	143	127	13%	125	7%	72%	25	60%	24%	5.32	9.5	68	170	$15
13	CIN	531	63	19	73	6	234	251	314	407	721	782	696	9	76	0.40	42	18	40	27	102	121	121	12%	98	9%	55%	27	41%	22%	3.95	-0.7	51	128	$12
14	CIN	597	88	29	80	20	273	263	336	459	795	750	807	8	77	0.37	41	22	37	31	114	127	124	17%	93	17%	71%	27	48%	19%	5.24	26.5	54	146	$30
1st Half		310	52	17	46	12	287	277	354	506	860	937	838	9	77	0.40	38	23	39	33	118	151	141	18%	98	20%	71%	14	71%	7%	6.15	21.8	76	205	$36
2nd Half		287	36	12	34	8	258	246	317	408	725	524	775	7	77	0.34	45	20	35	30	109	100	105	15%	87	14%	73%	13	23%	31%	4.35	5.5	29	78	$24
15	**Proj**	**574**	**75**	**26**	**77**	**12**	**264**	**261**	**329**	**452**	**781**	**793**	**777**	**8**	**76**	**0.35**	**41**	**21**	**38**	**31**	**107**	**133**	**123**	**15%**	**101**	**13%**	**67%**				**4.94**	**20.9**	**54**	**142**	**$24**

Freeman,Freddie

Age: 25	Bats: L	Pos: 1B	Health	A	LIMA Plan B+
Ht: 6' 5"	Wt: 225		PT/Exp	A	Rand Var 0
			Consist	D	MM 4145

On the surface, took a step back from 2013, but BPV begs to differ. Improvements in xBA, Eye, LD% and hard-hit balls were the real story. That elite HctX and xPX are waiting for a bit more FB and better ct%. We projected a possible breakout last March; maybe we were a year too early. UP: .320, 30 HR, MVP candidate.

Yr	Tm	AB	R	HR	RBI	SB	BA	xBA	OBP	SLG	OPS	vL	vR	bb%	ct%	Eye	G	L	F	h%	HctX	PX	xPX	hr/f	Spd	SBO	SB%	#Wk	DOM	DIS	RC/G	RAR	BPV	BPX	R$
10	ATL *	485	64	16	74	5	285	272	335	457	792	1667	333	7	79	0.36	44	19	38	33	121	122	120	17%	98	6%	70%	5	20%	40%	5.42	-11.4	59	128	$17
11	ATL	571	67	21	76	4	282	260	346	448	795	707	837	8	75	0.37	42	23	35	34	123	122	138	14%	79	5%	50%	27	37%	33%	5.35	-14.6	41	91	$20
12	ATL	540	91	23	94	2	259	271	340	456	796	714	855	11	76	0.50	37	26	37	30	129	132	137	15%	88	1%	100%	27	52%	30%	5.32	-1.6	60	150	$18
13	ATL	551	89	23	109	1	319	274	396	501	897	764	958	11	78	0.55	38	27	35	38	120	121	151	15%	96	1%	100%	25	60%	16%	7.38	41.0	61	153	$31
14	ATL	607	93	18	78	3	288	283	386	461	847	756	885	13	76	0.62	37	31	32	35	131	134	159	12%	96	4%	43%	27	56%	22%	6.17	33.8	68	184	$24
1st Half		317	55	13	43	0	290	301	385	498	883	941	860	13	79	0.69	33	32	35	33	138	150	161	15%	98	2%	0%	14	79%	14%	6.65	22.1	92	249	$27
2nd Half		290	38	5	35	3	286	263	386	421	807	570	914	13	73	0.56	41	30	29	38	123	114	158	8%	97	5%	60%	13	31%	31%	5.65	12.1	41	111	$21
15	**Proj**	**588**	**90**	**21**	**92**	**3**	**291**	**277**	**377**	**473**	**850**	**730**	**907**	**12**	**76**	**0.55**	**38**	**27**	**35**	**35**	**126**	**136**	**152**	**14%**	**92**	**3%**	**56%**				**6.28**	**34.7**	**59**	**156**	**$27**

GREG PYRON

Freese,David

Age: 32 Bats: R Pos: 3B | Ht: 6' 2" Wt: 225

Health C | PT/Exp B | Consist B | LIMA Plan C+ | Rand Var 0 | MM 3025

2014 stats were so much like '13, it almost looks like a misprint. Unfortunately for those hoping for a bounce-back, that wasn't good news. But there were real signs of life again in the 2H, notably in PX, HctX. FB% is too low to expect 20 HR again, but hard-hit balls are good for plain-old singles and doubles, too. UP: 15-75-.285.

Yr Tm	AB	R	HR	RBI	SB	BA	xBA	OBP	SLG	OPS	vL	vR	bb%	ct%	Eye	G	L	F	h%	HctX	PX	xPX	hr/f	Spd	SBO	SB%	#Wk	DOM	DIS	RC/G	RAR	BPV	BPX	R$
10 STL	240	28	4	36	1	296	248	361	404	765	873	721	8	75	0.36	49	22	29	38	96	83	102	8%	105	3%	50%	13	31%	54%	5.10	1.9	18	39	$7
11 STL	333	41	10	55	1	297	273	350	441	791	900	759	7	77	0.32	52	25	23	36	104	102	121	17%	77	1%	100%	20	30%	50%	5.54	6.7	30	67	$12
12 STL	501	70	20	79	3	293	265	372	467	839	886	824	10	76	0.47	52	22	26	35	119	116	119	20%	93	4%	50%	27	56%	26%	6.06	21.2	46	115	$20
13 STL	462	53	9	60	1	262	253	340	381	721	811	689	9	77	0.44	55	21	24	32	116	91	97	10%	74	2%	33%	25	36%	28%	4.28	4.4	24	60	$10
14 LAA	462	53	10	55	1	260	253	321	383	704	876	656	8	73	0.31	49	26	26	34	124	101	117	11%	76	3%	25%	25	28%	48%	4.07	5.4	13	35	$10
1st Half	210	26	2	21	1	233	219	306	295	602	730	556	8	69	0.29	48	27	25	33	110	57	104	5%	82	3%	50%	12	17%	67%	2.88	-5.2	-35	-95	$3
2nd Half	252	27	8	34	0	282	282	333	456	790	1050	732	7	77	0.32	49	24	26	34	135	134	126	16%	72	3%	0%	13	38%	31%	5.20	10.8	51	138	$16
15 Proj	475	56	12	63	1	270	258	337	405	742	870	703	8	76	0.37	51	23	26	33	119	106	112	13%	78	3%	33%				4.60	12.4	20	52	$12

Freiman,Nathan

Age: 28 Bats: R Pos: 1B | Ht: 6' 8" Wt: 250

Health A | PT/Exp C | Consist C | LIMA Plan D | Rand Var +3 | MM 4021

5-15-.218 in 87 AB at OAK. After a year mostly sitting as a Rule 5 pick, spent most of '14 at Triple-A. While there's not a lot in this skill set about which to get excited, he has shown a little pop and decent splits against LHP, and is about at peak age. A few more AB could earn a small profit for your $1 bid.

Yr Tm	AB	R	HR	RBI	SB	BA	xBA	OBP	SLG	OPS	vL	vR	bb%	ct%	Eye	G	L	F	h%	HctX	PX	xPX	hr/f	Spd	SBO	SB%	#Wk	DOM	DIS	RC/G	RAR	BPV	BPX	R$
10																																		
11																																		
12 aa	516	59	15	77	0	235		287	377	663			7	77	0.31				28		96			79	2%	0%				3.53		23	58	$8
13 OAK	190	10	4	24	0	274	252	327	389	716	805	406	7	84	0.45	38	24	39	31	107	76	92	6%	86	0%	0%	25	32%	44%	4.42	-0.9	37	93	$2
14 OAK *	397	42	14	61	0	212	231	268	372	640	775	523	7	71	0.27	36	19	45	26	87	128	118	17%	90	0%	0%	12	50%	33%	3.23	-11.1	30	81	$4
1st Half	300	29	9	46	0	205	140	263	350	613	1667	0	7	71	0.27	0	0	100	26	102	117	235	33%	83	0%	0%	1	100%	0%	2.95	-11.4	19	51	$6
2nd Half	97	13	5	15	0	233	261	284	443	727	733	549	7	72	0.26	38	20	43	28	87	165	112	15%	95	0%	0%	11	45%	36%	4.19	0.1	64	173	-$2
15 Proj	104	10	4	15	0	244	255	302	414	716	778	505	7	77	0.32	38	21	41	28	95	125	104	12%	92	0%	0%				4.12	-0.1	32	83	$2

Fuld,Sam

Age: 33 Bats: L Pos: CF LF | Ht: 5' 10" Wt: 175

Health D | PT/Exp F | Consist C | LIMA Plan D+ | Rand Var 0 | MM 1521

The latest hard-nosed pepperpot to parlay his spunky grittiness into 350 marginal at-bats. In fairness, his solid walk rate does put him on base, and he clearly knows what to do when he gets there (see SB, SB%). But steals make up his only plus category, and with playing time always at risk, those bags will be tough to count on.

Yr Tm	AB	R	HR	RBI	SB	BA	xBA	OBP	SLG	OPS	vL	vR	bb%	ct%	Eye	G	L	F	h%	HctX	PX	xPX	hr/f	Spd	SBO	SB%	#Wk	DOM	DIS	RC/G	RAR	BPV	BPX	R$
10 CHC *	396	45	3	19	13	200	206	278	277	555	667	374	10	87	0.83	43	9	48	22	92	48	114	0%	150	24%	52%	7	14%	57%	2.28	-32.2	53	115	$0
11 TAM	308	41	3	27	20	240	264	313	360	673	554	710	9	84	0.65	48	19	33	28	87	83	70	4%	129	35%	71%	27	37%	37%	3.71	-13.0	62	138	$8
12 TAM	98	14	0	5	7	255	268	318	327	644	623	656	8	86	0.57	51	26	23	30	67	43	44	0%	142	32%	78%	11	27%	36%	3.56	-3.7	37	93	$1
13 TAM	176	25	2	17	8	199	248	270	267	537	734	417	9	84	0.61	52	23	25	23	65	33	30	5%	168	21%	80%	27	19%	44%	2.37	-10.4	33	83	$1
14 2 AL	351	40	4	36	21	239	256	321	342	663	683	655	11	82	0.68	50	20	30	28	66	74	50	5%	118	24%	84%	22	41%	36%	3.86	-0.2	47	127	$11
1st Half	127	13	1	11	7	213	243	284	339	622	715	594	9	80	0.50	44	16	41	26	70	99	87	2%	98	25%	100%	9	33%	22%	3.41	-1.8	47	127	-$1
2nd Half	224	27	3	25	14	254	264	341	344	685	668	692	12	83	0.81	54	22	24	29	64	60	29	7%	126	24%	78%	13	46%	46%	4.13	1.8	45	122	$17
15 Proj	221	28	2	20	13	242	256	316	334	651	703	627	10	83	0.65	50	21	29	28	68	62	47	4%	129	24%	80%				3.66	-1.3	45	117	$7

Gallo,Joey

Age: 21 Bats: L Pos: 3B | Ht: 6' 5" Wt: 205

Health A | PT/Exp F | Consist F | LIMA Plan D | Rand Var 0 | MM 5301

Let's get this out of the way—he's NOT ready. Fanned 112 times in HALF a Double-A season. That said... he's now led the Carolina League in HR (21) and taken second in the Texas League (21). The fun part? BOTH were in 2014. 42 HR in 439 AB, at age 20. Yes, the Ks are a huge factor. But that PX is pretty huge, too.

Yr Tm	AB	R	HR	RBI	SB	BA	xBA	OBP	SLG	OPS	vL	vR	bb%	ct%	Eye	G	L	F	h%	HctX	PX	xPX	hr/f	Spd	SBO	SB%	#Wk	DOM	DIS	RC/G	RAR	BPV	BPX	R$
10																																		
11																																		
12																																		
13																																		
14 aa	250	36	18	45	2	218		301	478	779			11	52	0.25				32		252			81	3%	100%				4.73		57	154	$7
1st Half	70	12	7	17	0	270		348	641	989			11	49	0.23				43		391			97	0%	0%				7.79		162	438	$2
2nd Half	180	23	11	28	2	198		283	415	698			11	53	0.25				29		203			98	4%	100%				3.78		28	76	$9
15 Proj	156	23	8	30	1	190	202	279	399	678	678	678	11	51	0.25	30	17	53	29		217		20%	95	3%	100%				3.54	-0.8	19	51	$3

Galvis,Freddy

Age: 25 Bats: B Pos: SS | Ht: 5' 10" Wt: 185

Health C | PT/Exp F | Consist A | LIMA Plan D+ | Rand Var +2 | MM 3201

4-12-.176 in 119 AB at PHI. After returning from staph infection (ouch), started the season 2 for 42 (double ouch). Then broke his clavicle in the minors (triple ouch). Showed some pop late, and could hit 10 HR one year with that FB rate. But Eye is awful, and xBA verifies low ceiling. The handful of homers don't offset the rest.

Yr Tm	AB	R	HR	RBI	SB	BA	xBA	OBP	SLG	OPS	vL	vR	bb%	ct%	Eye	G	L	F	h%	HctX	PX	xPX	hr/f	Spd	SBO	SB%	#Wk	DOM	DIS	RC/G	RAR	BPV	BPX	R$
10 aa	501	44	4	36	11	206		240	268	508			4	81	0.24				25		44			117	15%	72%				2.06		5	11	-$1
11 a/a	543	63	7	35	19	250		283	347	630			4	82	0.26				29		70			113	26%	57%				3.10		31	69	$11
12 PHI	190	14	3	24	0	226	265	254	363	617	735	562	4	85	0.24	41	21	38	25	106	95	116	5%	75	0%	0%	10	40%	30%	3.04	-7.5	46	115	-$1
13 PHI *	446	33	8	38	3	221	218	256	340	596	688	662	5	77	0.21	36	19	46	27	95	83	115	8%	125	5%	74%	18	39%	39%	2.85	-11.1	22	55	$1
14 PHI *	254	30	6	23	2	201	218	248	347	596	496	573	6	76	0.27	41	8	51	24	85	112	117	9%	105	7%	60%	12	25%	42%	2.72	-5.3	41	111	$0
1st Half	49	3	0	2	0	58	138	124	75	199	160	155	7	71	0.26	48	6	45	8	59	19	34	0%	97	20%	0%	5	0%	40%	0.20	-5.9	-57	-154	-$16
2nd Half	205	27	6	21	2	235	235	279	413	691	625	851	6	78	0.27	38	9	54	27	97	132	164	13%	112	4%	100%	7	43%	43%	3.88	3.0	64	173	$4
15 Proj	232	21	7	20	3	224	230	266	373	638	628	643	5	78	0.25	40	14	47	26	95	108	114	8%	99	9%	65%				3.21	-0.2	33	88	$3

Garcia,Avisail

Age: 24 Bats: R Pos: RF | Ht: 6' 4" Wt: 240

Health F | PT/Exp F | Consist C | LIMA Plan B | Rand Var 0 | MM 3325

7-29-4-.244 in 172 AB at CHW. April labrum surgery was supposed to end season, but surprised with Aug return. G/F explains why natural power remains mostly untapped, and ct% slide is troubling. Still young, but overall skills point to more growing pains. Even so, he's already the most accomplished Avisail in MLB history.

Yr Tm	AB	R	HR	RBI	SB	BA	xBA	OBP	SLG	OPS	vL	vR	bb%	ct%	Eye	G	L	F	h%	HctX	PX	xPX	hr/f	Spd	SBO	SB%	#Wk	DOM	DIS	RC/G	RAR	BPV	BPX	R$
10																																		
11																																		
12 DET *	262	33	5	21	7	296	292	318	407	725	745	588	3	81	0.17	62	27	11	35	135	67	63	0%	134	20%	54%	6	0%	100%	4.36	-3.6	27	68	$8
13 2 AL *	418	55	13	58	6	309	254	340	453	793	640	770	5	76	0.20	56	18	26	38	107	95	92	15%	141	10%	55%	17	29%	53%	5.49	13.9	34	85	$19
14 CHW *	222	25	8	31	4	253	242	300	406	706	992	620	6	72	0.23	56	15	28	32	81	119	89	19%	77	9%	80%	10	50%	30%	4.17	1.8	19	51	$6
1st Half	30	6	2	4	0	267	262	353	467	820	1500	681	9	77	0.43	57	17	26	29	87	120	105	33%	106	0%	0%	2	50%	50%	5.41	1.2	55	149	-$8
2nd Half	192	19	6	27	4	251	238	294	396	691	928	604	6	71	0.21	56	15	29	33	80	119	86	16%	73	11%	80%	8	50%	25%	3.99	0.0	14	38	$8
15 Proj	435	51	15	50	9	268	259	306	424	731	876	679	5	75	0.19	56	17	27	32	93	112	93	17%	113	15%	61%				4.28	3.5	30	80	$16

Garcia,Leury

Age: 24 Bats: B Pos: 3B | Ht: 5' 8" Wt: 170

Health A | PT/Exp D | Consist C | LIMA Plan F | Rand Var +5 | MM 0501

CHW seems to be collecting uniquely named Garcias. This one's claim to fame is helping them get out from under a year of Alex Rios' contract. Otherwise, must channel his inner 2012 to earn a more lasting legacy. Owns that speedy '12-'13 profile, and age is on his side. But bad plate skills are getting worse.

Yr Tm	AB	R	HR	RBI	SB	BA	xBA	OBP	SLG	OPS	vL	vR	bb%	ct%	Eye	G	L	F	h%	HctX	PX	xPX	hr/f	Spd	SBO	SB%	#Wk	DOM	DIS	RC/G	RAR	BPV	BPX	R$
10																																		
11																																		
12 aa	377	45	2	24	25	280		312	377	690			5	78	0.22				35		60			156	33%	77%				4.19		19	48	$14
13 2 AL *	324	38	4	18	19	227	215	273	314	587	566	445	6	68	0.20	46	25	29	32	44	66	44	0%	158	33%	75%	17	12%	65%	2.84	-8.8	-11	-28	$7
14 CHW	145	13	1	6	11	166	190	192	207	399	368	421	3	67	0.10	62	14	24	24	57	38	25	4%	96	48%	92%	26	12%	73%	1.41	-9.4	-63	-170	-$1
1st Half	72	9	1	2	8	181	225	224	264	488	486	487	5	69	0.18	63	15	23	24	81	75	48	9%	103	69%	89%	14	21%	79%	2.09	-3.1	-19	-51	$1
2nd Half	73	4	0	4	3	151	153	160	151	311	218	365	1	64	0.04	61	13	26	23	33	0	2	0%	100	25%	100%	12	0%	67%	0.84	-6.2	-108	-292	-$2
15 Proj	168	17	1	9	11	203	202	233	255	488	482	492	4	69	0.14	55	18	27	29	49	44	30	2%	119	37%	84%				2.05	-8.7	-36	-96	$3

ROD TRUESDELL

Gardner,Brett

Age: 31	Bats: L	Pos: LF CF	Health	D	LIMA Plan	A
Ht: 5' 10"	Wt: 185		PT/Exp	C	Rand Var	0
			Consist	A	MM	3525

Fascinating profile shift continues. Career HR high, but career-low SBO. Lower abdominal strain nagged at least the entire 2nd half; SB dip is surely related. The newfound power? xPX is skeptical and big 2nd half FB spike cost him his BA. That's a tenuous line he's toeing. The old Gardner had more fantasy value; R$ agrees.

Yr	Tm	AB	R	HR	RBI	SB	BA	xBA	OBP	SLG	OPS	vL	vR	bb%	ct%	Eye	G	L	F	h%	HctX	PX	xPX	hr/f	Spd	SBO	SB%	#Wk	DOM	DIS	RC/G	RAR	BPV	BPX	R$
10	NYY	477	97	5	47	47	277	256	383	379	762	725	776	14	79	0.78	53	19	28	34	58	72	34	5%	157	31%	84%	27	41%	15%	5.41	6.7	50	109	$28
11	NYY	510	87	7	36	49	259	260	345	369	713	616	738	11	82	0.65	52	19	28	30	66	72	48	6%	166	39%	79%	27	44%	30%	4.40	-8.0	58	129	$24
12	NYY	31	7	0	3	2	323	266	417	387	804	2032	426	14	77	0.71	38	38	25	42	122	60	51	0%	99	31%	50%	5	20%	60%	5.24	0.6	17	43	$0
13	NYY	539	81	8	52	24	273	251	344	416	759	744	767	9	76	0.41	41	23	35	34	81	104	70	6%	143	22%	75%	24	42%	29%	4.89	14.3	51	128	$22
14	NYY	555	87	17	58	21	256	254	327	422	749	687	775	9	76	0.42	42	22	37	31	95	117	91	11%	141	18%	81%	27	48%	30%	4.73	17.0	60	162	$22
1st Half		301	49	7	31	15	286	257	357	425	782	749	798	9	76	0.42	45	25	30	35	101	97	90	10%	146	19%	83%	14	43%	36%	5.44	14.5	47	127	$27
2nd Half		254	38	10	27	6	220	254	293	417	710	603	750	9	75	0.41	37	18	45	25	88	142	92	11%	124	15%	75%	13	54%	23%	3.98	1.9	72	195	$16
15	**Proj**	**512**	**82**	**12**	**50**	**22**	**264**	**253**	**340**	**412**	**751**	**698**	**773**	**10**	**77**	**0.47**	**44**	**21**	**35**	**32**	**83**	**107**	**74**	**8%**	**141**	**20%**	**76%**				**4.78**	**15.6**	**59**	**154**	**$19**

Gattis,Evan

Age: 28	Bats: R	Pos: CA	Health	B	LIMA Plan	B+
Ht: 6' 4"	Wt: 260		PT/Exp	D	Rand Var	-2
			Consist	B	MM	5035

Dealt with a crazy mix of health issues—bulging disk, strained wrist, strep throat, kidney stone—but in between again posted terrific power skills. Poor Eye caps BA, but that's not why you'd buy him anyway. AB upside exists, especially if he catches less. If he can avoid, oh, maybe shingles? UP: 30+ HR

Yr	Tm	AB	R	HR	RBI	SB	BA	xBA	OBP	SLG	OPS	vL	vR	bb%	ct%	Eye	G	L	F	h%	HctX	PX	xPX	hr/f	Spd	SBO	SB%	#Wk	DOM	DIS	RC/G	RAR	BPV	BPX	R$
10																																			
11																																			
12	aa	182	19	7	29	1	221		283	430	714			8	81	0.45				24		130			102	6%	40%				3.90		76	190	$1
13	ATL *	375	45	22	66	0	244	264	285	483	768	808	757	5	77	0.24	41	14	45	26	115	163	136	17%	47	0%	0%	24	54%	21%	4.64	10.5	65	163	$11
14	ATL	369	41	22	52	0	263	259	317	493	810	970	773	6	74	0.23	39	17	45	30	124	163	165	18%	72	0%	0%	24	50%	25%	5.19	18.5	60	162	$13
1st Half		224	29	16	39	0	290	277	342	558	900	1155	845	6	76	0.26	38	16	46	32	142	179	187	20%	84	0%	0%	13	62%	15%	6.65	20.3	88	238	$20
2nd Half		145	12	6	13	0	221	229	278	393	672	724	658	5	70	0.18	39	19	42	27	95	136	127	14%	62	0%	0%	11	36%	36%	3.36	-0.1	19	51	$0
15	**Proj**	**429**	**46**	**24**	**63**	**0**	**250**	**265**	**303**	**479**	**782**	**860**	**759**	**6**	**75**	**0.25**	**40**	**16**	**44**	**28**	**115**	**164**	**146**	**17%**	**64**	**1%**	**50%**				**4.76**	**17.2**	**57**	**150**	**$14**

Gennett,Scooter

Age: 25	Bats: L	Pos: 2B	Health	A	LIMA Plan	B
Ht: 5' 10"	Wt: 170		PT/Exp	B	Rand Var	0
			Consist	B	MM	2245

Weeks' weaknesses opened up playing time; lefty bat and a 4-HR, .397 June kept the incumbent at bay. Excels vs. RHP, but small-sample vs LHP (just 39 AB in '14) grades out as "incomplete." Quad issue may have impacted 2nd half. League average pop/speed, but decent underlying skill with a little upside. UP: 15 HR, 15 SB

Yr	Tm	AB	R	HR	RBI	SB	BA	xBA	OBP	SLG	OPS	vL	vR	bb%	ct%	Eye	G	L	F	h%	HctX	PX	xPX	hr/f	Spd	SBO	SB%	#Wk	DOM	DIS	RC/G	RAR	BPV	BPX	R$
10																																			
11																																			
12	aa	533	54	5	36	9	267		299	353	652			4	85	0.30				31		61			96	11%	62%				3.59		28	70	$10
13	MIL *	534	61	8	37	9	275	240	308	381	689	329	946	5	79	0.23	39	24	37	33	115	72	115	10%	152	11%	58%	14	43%	29%	3.99	5.1	32	80	$14
14	MIL	440	55	9	54	6	289	285	320	434	754	253	802	5	85	0.33	41	25	34	32	105	105	92	7%	100	8%	67%	27	52%	15%	4.95	19.3	65	176	$16
1st Half		241	34	6	27	4	311	292	351	485	837	318	912	6	83	0.39	43	23	34	36	110	128	96	9%	113	10%	67%	14	57%	7%	6.27	18.9	83	224	$20
2nd Half		199	21	3	27	2	261	277	280	372	652	0	679	3	87	0.23	40	27	33	29	99	78	89	5%	90	7%	67%	13	46%	23%	3.60	1.2	45	122	$11
15	**Proj**	**455**	**52**	**11**	**44**	**7**	**277**	**273**	**308**	**416**	**724**	**268**	**785**	**4**	**83**	**0.27**	**40**	**25**	**35**	**31**	**108**	**97**	**101**	**8%**	**110**	**10%**	**62%**				**4.43**	**13.6**	**48**	**126**	**$15**

Gentry,Craig

Age: 31	Bats: R	Pos: CF RF	Health	C	LIMA Plan	C
Ht: 6' 2"	Wt: 190		PT/Exp	D	Rand Var	-1
			Consist	C	MM	0513

Headed for career highs in runs and steals, but broke a bone in right hand in July, then suffered season-ending concussion in Sept. But he's been injured before, and weak overall hit tool (see xBA, PX) getting worse. So pencil in 20 SB and 30-40 R, but there's little reason to speculate on more.

Yr	Tm	AB	R	HR	RBI	SB	BA	xBA	OBP	SLG	OPS	vL	vR	bb%	ct%	Eye	G	L	F	h%	HctX	PX	xPX	hr/f	Spd	SBO	SB%	#Wk	DOM	DIS	RC/G	RAR	BPV	BPX	R$
10	TEX *	292	34	3	27	9	249	183	300	323	623	348	633	7	77	0.32	43	9	48	31	82	48	103	0%	185	19%	60%	7	14%	57%	3.16	-17.6	18	39	$5
11	TEX *	243	38	2	19	21	232	248	281	303	585	735	648	6	80	0.35	50	23	27	28	81	52	62	4%	156	37%	94%	21	29%	52%	3.20	-14.4	25	56	$7
12	TEX	240	31	1	26	13	304	245	367	392	759	859	686	6	83	0.34	47	20	33	36	75	61	57	2%	138	28%	65%	27	30%	44%	4.67	-1.2	35	88	$10
13	TEX	246	39	2	22	24	280	253	373	386	759	801	709	11	81	0.63	50	19	31	34	67	74	46	3%	169	34%	89%	24	42%	33%	5.30	7.1	58	145	$14
14	OAK	232	38	0	12	20	254	225	319	289	608	645	564	7	81	0.39	49	21	30	31	59	29	43	0%	161	32%	91%	21	14%	43%	3.38	-3.5	11	30	$9
1st Half		145	28	0	4	15	276	217	335	317	653	670	630	6	77	0.26	47	23	30	36	71	35	57	0%	179	34%	100%	13	8%	54%	4.19	0.8	2	5	$12
2nd Half		87	10	0	8	5	218	235	292	241	533	598	470	8	89	0.80	53	19	28	25	39	20	23	0%	114	28%	71%	8	25%	25%	2.28	-4.7	23	62	$3
15	**Proj**	**239**	**35**	**1**	**19**	**20**	**260**	**240**	**334**	**323**	**657**	**707**	**604**	**8**	**83**	**0.48**	**50**	**20**	**30**	**31**	**62**	**48**	**45**	**1%**	**154**	**34%**	**84%**				**3.78**	**-0.6**	**28**	**74**	**$11**

Gillaspie,Conor

Age: 27	Bats: L	Pos: 3B	Health	A	LIMA Plan	C
Ht: 6' 1"	Wt: 195		PT/Exp	C	Rand Var	-3
			Consist	C	MM	2023

While xBA shows this step up was partly skills-supported, where exactly did he get better? Sure, hit a few more LD in a hot Apr/May. But overall, this is a rather tame and flat skills set. BA may be best chance for more, but 2nd half slide gives no cause for optimism. Won't hurt you, but little upside here.

Yr	Tm	AB	R	HR	RBI	SB	BA	xBA	OBP	SLG	OPS	vL	vR	bb%	ct%	Eye	G	L	F	h%	HctX	PX	xPX	hr/f	Spd	SBO	SB%	#Wk	DOM	DIS	RC/G	RAR	BPV	BPX	R$
10	aa	491	49	7	58	0	268		312	389	701			6	85	0.44				30		78			123	4%	0%				4.06		54	117	$9
11	SF *	447	42	7	41	6	236	201	303	344	647	667	771	9	79	0.45	39	11	50	29	44	75	57	11%	119	14%	35%	6	33%	17%	3.20	-26.2	30	67	$4
12	SF *	433	42	8	35	0	216	284	262	315	577	0	467	6	84	0.40	39	33	28	24	62	62	17	0%	97	0%	0%	2	50%	50%	2.69	-25.5	30	75	$0
13	CHW	408	46	13	40	0	245	243	305	390	695	451	738	8	81	0.47	37	20	42	28	109	91	110	9%	123	1%	0%	27	48%	26%	4.01	0.7	51	128	$6
14	CHW	464	50	7	57	0	282	262	336	416	752	565	805	7	83	0.46	39	22	39	33	105	98	95	5%	116	3%	0%	25	44%	24%	4.76	14.4	62	168	$12
1st Half		221	24	0	27	0	317	281	358	421	779	562	845	7	85	0.48	39	28	33	37	106	88	93	0%	103	2%	0%	13	46%	8%	5.60	11.3	57	154	$11
2nd Half		243	26	7	30	0	251	246	316	412	727	568	769	8	81	0.44	40	16	44	28	103	108	96	8%	128	5%	0%	12	42%	42%	4.09	2.9	68	184	$13
15	**Proj**	**408**	**43**	**9**	**44**	**0**	**260**	**252**	**316**	**395**	**711**	**518**	**757**	**8**	**82**	**0.46**	**39**	**21**	**41**	**30**	**106**	**94**	**101**	**6%**	**117**	**3%**	**9%**				**4.17**	**5.7**	**39**	**102**	**$9**

Goebbert,Jake

Age: 27	Bats: L	Pos: 1B	Health	A	LIMA Plan	D
Ht: 6' 0"	Wt: 205		PT/Exp	C	Rand Var	+3
			Consist	A	MM	2201

1-10-.218 in 101 AB at SD. Hot streak at Triple-A got him a promotion, but it didn't go very well. With marginal power and speed, plus a below average ct% that puts the kibosh on BA, a decent walk rate is all he offers. As a shortstop, this profile might interest us; as a 1B/LF, there are better options.

Yr	Tm	AB	R	HR	RBI	SB	BA	xBA	OBP	SLG	OPS	vL	vR	bb%	ct%	Eye	G	L	F	h%	HctX	PX	xPX	hr/f	Spd	SBO	SB%	#Wk	DOM	DIS	RC/G	RAR	BPV	BPX	R$
10																																			
11	a/a	378	34	6	37	1	257		301	376	677			6	80	0.31				31		89			97	8%	21%				3.65		34	76	$5
12	a/a	398	50	6	37	3	237		310	357	667			10	80	0.54				28		80			110	7%	49%				3.61		40	100	$4
13	a/a	466	48	14	56	4	206		274	351	625			9	74	0.37				25		101			108	8%	54%				3.02		30	75	$3
14	SD *	381	45	9	44	3	211	244	289	347	636	200	668	10	73	0.40	36	29	35	27	92	99	87	4%	115	4%	72%	13	15%	54%	3.24	-11.1	27	73	$3
1st Half		233	24	6	25	1	192	266	261	316	578	0	665	9	74	0.36	44	33	22	23	107	89	13	0%	102	1%	100%	3	33%	67%	2.62	-11.4	16	43	$2
2nd Half		148	21	3	19	2	244	246	333	399	732	200	669	12	72	0.47	35	28	37	32	88	117	98	5%	122	7%	67%	10	10%	50%	4.44	1.2	42	114	$5
15	**Proj**	**127**	**15**	**2**	**14**	**1**	**224**	**220**	**305**	**335**	**639**	**173**	**687**	**10**	**75**	**0.42**	**39**	**19**	**42**	**29**	**79**	**85**	**88**	**4%**	**108**	**6%**	**54%**				**3.22**	**-3.7**	**18**	**46**	**$2**

Goins,Ryan

Age: 27	Bats: L	Pos: 2B	Health	A	LIMA Plan	D
Ht: 5' 10"	Wt: 185		PT/Exp	B	Rand Var	+1
			Consist	B	MM	1111

1-15-.188 in 181 AB at TOR. Probably the most interesting thing about him is his 1111 Mayberry score: there's something pleasingly symmetric in all that sub-mediocrity (2222 would be par mediocrity). And make no mistake, sub-mediocrity is here in abundance, and it's accompanied by smatterings of downright awfulness.

Yr	Tm	AB	R	HR	RBI	SB	BA	xBA	OBP	SLG	OPS	vL	vR	bb%	ct%	Eye	G	L	F	h%	HctX	PX	xPX	hr/f	Spd	SBO	SB%	#Wk	DOM	DIS	RC/G	RAR	BPV	BPX	R$
10																																			
11																																			
12	aa	546	53	6	49	12	260		306	362	668			6	84	0.41				30		70			96	16%	54%				3.63		35	88	$11
13	TOR *	496	43	7	43	2	229	231	264	324	588	576	628	5	74	0.19	56	19	25	30	81	78	53	9%	87	8%	28%	7	14%	43%	2.69	-15.7	-3	-8	$2
14	TOR *	544	42	1	38	3	225	233	262	294	556	395	501	5	78	0.22	55	18	26	29	77	59	51	3%	103	7%	35%	13	23%	62%	2.43	-16.0	2	5	$0
1st Half		290	20	1	17	2	217	212	259	271	530	0	473	5	80	0.29	60	13	28	27	57	43	39	8%	117	6%	40%	4	25%	50%	2.22	-10.5	3	8	-$2
2nd Half		254	22	0	22	2	234	245	264	321	585	484	517	4	76	0.17	53	21	26	31	85	78	58	0%	93	10%	32%	9	22%	67%	2.67	-5.6	4	11	-$3
15	**Proj**	**133**	**11**	**1**	**11**	**1**	**233**	**244**	**269**	**331**	**599**	**537**	**621**	**5**	**77**	**0.22**	**56**	**18**	**26**	**29**	**76**	**79**	**51**	**6%**	**98**	**10%**	**42%**				**2.83**	**-2.3**	**6**	**15**	**$1**

ROD TRUESDELL

Goldschmidt,Paul

Age: 27 Bats: R Pos: 1B	Health B	LIMA Plan C	
Ht: 6' 3" Wt: 245	PT/Exp A	Rand Var -1	
	Consist B	MM 5255	

Was headed for another top-caliber season when felled by a broken left hand. On track to be fully ready for 2015, so we expect another superb year. Overcomes iffy ct% by simply crushing everything he does hit—and HctX actually improved again. All other skills rock-solid, and he's at peak age. UP: MVP

Yr	Tm	AB	R	HR	RBI	SB	BA	xBA	OBP	SLG	OPS	vL	vR	bb%	ct%	Eye	G	L	F	h%	HctX	PX	xPX	hr/f	Spd	SBO	SB%	#Wk	DOM	DIS	RC/G	RAR	BPV	BPX	R$
10																																			
11	ARI *	522	87	30	92	10	260	270	354	498	852	657	855	13	70	0.48	42	21	37	32	126	174	155	21%	90	9%	74%	9	44%	44%	6.04	-3.2	73	162	$23
12	ARI	514	82	20	82	18	286	274	359	490	850	1068	739	10	75	0.46	40	24	36	35	127	149	160	14%	78	15%	86%	27	56%	19%	6.41	14.3	64	160	$25
13	ARI	602	103	36	125	15	302	290	401	551	952	986	941	14	76	0.68	44	21	35	35	131	168	164	23%	92	11%	68%	27	67%	19%	7.94	56.1	96	240	$40
14	ARI	406	75	19	69	9	300	297	396	542	938	1115	894	14	73	0.58	45	22	33	37	139	194	173	19%	95	9%	75%	19	58%	16%	7.78	40.4	105	284	$24
1st Half		314	59	15	53	7	296	291	387	529	916	1000	896	13	72	0.54	45	22	32	37	139	188	165	20%	94	9%	78%	15	60%	7%	7.42	28.5	96	259	$31
2nd Half		92	16	4	16	2	315	318	423	587	1010	1396	887	16	75	0.74	43	23	34	38	139	216	199	17%	91	10%	67%	4	50%	50%	9.06	12.3	133	359	$1
15	Proj	**586**	**101**	**30**	**105**	**14**	**300**	**299**	**396**	**550**	**947**	**1115**	**892**	**14**	**74**	**0.62**	**43**	**22**	**34**	**36**	**134**	**194**	**173**	**20%**	**92**	**11%**	**73%**				**7.88**	**60.5**	**111**	**291**	**$34**

Gomes,Jonny

Age: 34 Bats: R Pos: LF	Health A	LIMA Plan D	
Ht: 6' 1" Wt: 230	PT/Exp D	Rand Var -2	
	Consist C	MM 3201	

Hard contact and power trends show why he's slipping: he just doesn't drive the ball anymore. So with that FB rate, he's basically hitting enough easy cans of corn to fill a grocery shelf. Even his dominance vs lefties has started to crack. Without that, and sans the double-digit HR, he doesn't offer much.

Yr	Tm	AB	R	HR	RBI	SB	BA	xBA	OBP	SLG	OPS	vL	vR	bb%	ct%	Eye	G	L	F	h%	HctX	PX	xPX	hr/f	Spd	SBO	SB%	#Wk	DOM	DIS	RC/G	RAR	BPV	BPX	R$
10	CIN	511	77	18	86	5	266	239	327	431	758	856	709	7	76	0.32	29	21	50	32	105	113	125	9%	113	6%	63%	27	44%	33%	4.70	-3.3	44	96	$17
11	2 NL	311	41	14	43	7	209	219	325	389	714	863	654	13	66	0.46	34	18	48	27	95	138	136	14%	91	12%	70%	27	33%	44%	3.92	-9.8	32	71	$5
12	OAK	279	46	18	47	3	262	225	377	491	868	974	715	14	63	0.42	31	19	50	35	98	171	159	20%	99	4%	75%	28	54%	36%	6.13	12.7	47	118	$10
13	BOS	312	49	13	52	1	247	233	344	426	771	795	745	12	71	0.48	30	20	50	30	89	134	101	11%	73	1%	100%	27	48%	30%	4.90	8.5	41	103	$8
14	2 AL	273	28	6	37	0	234	199	327	330	657	743	510	11	68	0.40	26	24	50	32	84	79	100	6%	82	0%	0%	27	11%	67%	3.53	-1.2	-16	-43	$3
1st Half		166	20	5	27	0	235	208	335	361	696	870	513	12	67	0.42	24	23	52	32	83	104	101	8%	84	0%	0%	14	14%	57%	3.95	1.1	2	5	$6
2nd Half		107	8	1	10	0	234	186	315	280	595	617	499	10	69	0.36	29	25	47	33	86	40	99	3%	78	0%	0%	13	8%	77%	2.90	-2.7	-46	-124	-$2
15	Proj	**217**	**27**	**6**	**31**	**1**	**233**	**207**	**328**	**356**	**685**	**734**	**612**	**11**	**69**	**0.41**	**29**	**22**	**49**	**31**	**89**	**101**	**112**	**9%**	**83**	**2%**	**75%**				**3.80**	**0.4**	**-8**	**-21**	**$5**

Gomes,Yan

Age: 27 Bats: R Pos: CA	Health A	LIMA Plan B	
Ht: 6' 2" Wt: 215	PT/Exp C	Rand Var -1	
	Consist C	MM 4435	

The best sign is that he maintained essentially the same skills over 500 PA that he flashed as a part-timer. That gives us confidence in a repeat, as does strong 2H. Shaky contact means a bit of BA risk, as xBA shows, but he's one of a select group of catchers with this kind of consistent power. Invest.

Yr	Tm	AB	R	HR	RBI	SB	BA	xBA	OBP	SLG	OPS	vL	vR	bb%	ct%	Eye	G	L	F	h%	HctX	PX	xPX	hr/f	Spd	SBO	SB%	#Wk	DOM	DIS	RC/G	RAR	BPV	BPX	R$
10																																			
11	a/a	290	24	10	36	0	206		252	366	618			6	68	0.19				27		130			83	0%	0%				2.96		15	33	$0
12	TOR *	403	38	13	51	3	254	237	292	427	719	701	567	5	71	0.19	48	15	37	33	93	133	127	16%	72	3%	100%	15	27%	47%	4.30	1.9	24	60	$8
13	CLE	293	45	11	38	2	294	261	345	481	826	934	766	6	77	0.27	43	18	39	35	104	131	126	12%	116	3%	100%	26	54%	38%	5.85	17.3	62	155	$11
14	CLE	485	61	21	74	0	278	266	313	472	785	879	745	5	75	0.20	37	24	39	33	101	139	128	14%	101	0%	0%	26	54%	23%	5.21	25.9	54	146	$18
1st Half		250	31	9	28	0	264	242	307	416	723	744	714	6	74	0.23	38	23	39	32	97	109	137	12%	102	0%	0%	14	43%	29%	4.41	7.3	27	73	$13
2nd Half		235	30	12	46	0	294	291	319	532	850	1027	777	4	77	0.16	35	25	40	34	105	170	119	16%	102	0%	0%	12	67%	17%	6.14	17.9	82	222	$24
15	Proj	**498**	**62**	**20**	**72**	**1**	**273**	**263**	**316**	**466**	**782**	**875**	**734**	**5**	**74**	**0.21**	**41**	**21**	**39**	**33**	**101**	**145**	**126**	**14%**	**101**	**1%**	**100%**				**5.10**	**24.2**	**47**	**124**	**$18**

Gomez,Carlos

Age: 29 Bats: R Pos: CF	Health B	LIMA Plan C	
Ht: 6' 3" Wt: 220	PT/Exp B	Rand Var -2	
	Consist B	MM 4535	

Second straight year that a rough July/Aug (mostly injury-related) prevented something truly special. Even so, he's clearly arrived. There are even signs he could take it up another notch: small Eye growth is nice; FB rebound, 1st half xPX shows there's more power upside. With health... UP: 30 HR

Yr	Tm	AB	R	HR	RBI	SB	BA	xBA	OBP	SLG	OPS	vL	vR	bb%	ct%	Eye	G	L	F	h%	HctX	PX	xPX	hr/f	Spd	SBO	SB%	#Wk	DOM	DIS	RC/G	RAR	BPV	BPX	R$
10	MIL *	319	43	5	25	19	246	224	292	347	639	580	694	6	74	0.25	48	16	36	32	59	72	48	7%	142	29%	82%	24	33%	50%	3.54	-11.9	10	22	$9
11	MIL	231	37	8	24	16	225	235	276	403	679	857	566	6	72	0.23	44	12	44	28	107	127	122	11%	144	40%	89%	22	45%	32%	3.79	-7.0	48	107	$7
12	MIL	415	72	19	51	37	260	250	305	463	768	778	762	5	76	0.20	40	17	43	30	108	128	124	14%	128	50%	86%	25	40%	32%	4.85	2.0	57	143	$24
13	MIL	536	80	24	73	40	284	263	338	506	843	993	797	6	73	0.25	40	21	38	35	114	153	137	16%	153	37%	85%	27	48%	30%	6.07	30.1	74	185	$36
14	MIL	574	95	23	73	34	284	262	356	477	833	828	835	8	75	0.33	38	22	41	34	117	142	133	13%	121	31%	74%	26	54%	27%	5.63	29.8	69	186	$36
1st Half		303	52	13	44	13	310	273	375	525	900	820	923	7	75	0.31	33	26	40	38	140	159	161	15%	126	20%	81%	14	57%	21%	7.03	26.3	80	216	$37
2nd Half		271	43	10	29	21	255	248	336	424	760	837	739	8	76	0.36	42	16	42	30	92	123	102	12%	108	45%	70%	12	50%	33%	4.32	3.8	54	146	$34
15	Proj	**568**	**91**	**25**	**75**	**40**	**277**	**264**	**340**	**481**	**820**	**864**	**805**	**7**	**75**	**0.29**	**40**	**20**	**40**	**33**	**109**	**147**	**124**	**15%**	**129**	**36%**	**79%**				**5.51**	**27.3**	**77**	**202**	**$36**

Gonzalez,Adrian

Age: 33 Bats: L Pos: 1B	Health A	LIMA Plan B+	
Ht: 6' 2" Wt: 225	PT/Exp A	Rand Var +2	
	Consist A	MM 4155	

His xPX had been trying to tell us the power was coming back, and it certainly did. 1st half BA dip vs. LHP wasn't fully reflected in skills, and he rebounded to close to normal levels. Still, that's worth watching for signs of decline as he ages. Otherwise, expect more consistent, smooth-swinging goodness.

Yr	Tm	AB	R	HR	RBI	SB	BA	xBA	OBP	SLG	OPS	vL	vR	bb%	ct%	Eye	G	L	F	h%	HctX	PX	xPX	hr/f	Spd	SBO	SB%	#Wk	DOM	DIS	RC/G	RAR	BPV	BPX	R$
10	SD	591	87	31	101	0	298	286	393	511	904	937	887	14	81	0.82	39	21	39	33	124	138	151	16%	63	0%	0%	27	63%	15%	7.30	16.9	81	176	$26
11	BOS	630	108	27	117	1	338	296	410	548	957	787	1046	11	81	0.62	47	21	32	38	129	142	128	16%	79	0%	100%	27	59%	15%	8.61	38.5	85	189	$39
12	2 TM	629	75	18	108	2	299	279	344	463	806	846	783	6	83	0.38	40	24	36	34	121	111	134	10%	62	1%	100%	27	56%	30%	5.79	6.2	52	130	$24
13	LA	583	69	22	100	1	293	272	342	461	803	747	829	7	83	0.48	38	23	39	32	123	110	138	11%	71	1%	100%	27	63%	15%	5.77	19.1	59	148	$24
14	LA	591	83	27	116	1	276	292	335	482	817	588	901	9	81	0.50	38	24	38	30	136	145	145	15%	51	1%	50%	28	68%	11%	5.72	25.7	75	203	$26
1st Half		308	43	13	50	1	256	281	322	445	767	492	877	9	81	0.53	43	21	35	28	138	132	128	15%	56	3%	50%	15	67%	13%	4.90	6.6	66	178	$20
2nd Half		283	40	14	66	0	297	306	349	523	872	711	925	8	81	0.47	33	26	41	32	134	159	163	15%	54	0%	0%	13	69%	8%	6.71	19.9	87	235	$32
15	Proj	**585**	**78**	**24**	**110**	**1**	**290**	**287**	**346**	**481**	**827**	**718**	**873**	**8**	**82**	**0.49**	**38**	**24**	**38**	**32**	**129**	**135**	**143**	**13%**	**59**	**1%**	**72%**				**6.02**	**30.2**	**64**	**169**	**$27**

Gonzalez,Carlos

Age: 29 Bats: L Pos: LF	Health C	LIMA Plan B	
Ht: 6' 1" Wt: 220	PT/Exp C	Rand Var +5	
	Consist F	MM 5335	

An injury-decimated season that ended with patella tendon surgery. When healthy, clearly a skill set to own. But off knee surgery, expect a SB dip—and what if this is chronic? 2010 seems forever away now. Huge risk/reward. UP: 2012. DN: Injuries make even 2014 look good.

Yr	Tm	AB	R	HR	RBI	SB	BA	xBA	OBP	SLG	OPS	vL	vR	bb%	ct%	Eye	G	L	F	h%	HctX	PX	xPX	hr/f	Spd	SBO	SB%	#Wk	DOM	DIS	RC/G	RAR	BPV	BPX	R$
10	COL	587	111	34	117	26	336	302	376	598	974	925	1003	6	77	0.30	43	21	37	39	138	171	140	20%	108	21%	76%	26	54%	19%	8.55	51.2	92	200	$46
11	COL	481	92	26	92	20	295	291	363	526	889	779	943	9	78	0.46	48	18	34	33	119	153	123	21%	100	19%	80%	24	63%	17%	6.84	21.2	85	189	$30
12	COL	518	89	22	85	20	303	285	371	510	881	742	961	10	78	0.49	49	22	29	35	116	134	116	19%	93	16%	80%	26	50%	23%	6.94	31.8	68	170	$30
13	COL	391	72	26	70	21	302	281	367	591	958	875	1004	9	70	0.35	38	22	41	37	112	206	171	24%	122	23%	88%	22	50%	45%	8.09	43.7	102	255	$30
14	COL	260	35	11	38	3	238	256	292	431	723	635	766	7	73	0.27	47	15	38	28	109	146	119	15%	79	6%	100%	15	40%	40%	4.25	3.6	49	132	$6
1st Half		196	27	8	31	2	255	269	307	449	756	740	763	7	77	0.31	50	15	35	29	116	141	105	15%	81	5%	100%	10	40%	40%	4.74	5.7	61	165	$10
2nd Half		64	8	3	7	1	188	218	246	375	621	318	774	7	61	0.20	36	18	46	25	88	166	171	17%	82	9%	100%	5	40%	40%	2.97	-1.6	18	49	-$5
15	Proj	**447**	**70**	**23**	**69**	**9**	**271**	**272**	**335**	**493**	**828**	**688**	**902**	**9**	**73**	**0.35**	**43**	**20**	**37**	**33**	**108**	**166**	**146**	**19%**	**92**	**9%**	**81%**				**5.78**	**26.3**	**74**	**196**	**$21**

Gonzalez,Marwin

Age: 26 Bats: B Pos: SS	Health A	LIMA Plan D+	
Ht: 6' 1" Wt: 205	PT/Exp D	Rand Var -4	
	Consist C	MM 2123	

A nice step up? Only in surface stats. xBA sees a .250 hitter, xPX belies the outward power gains, and most every identifiable skill says this is the same dude as before. He would be overvalued, but most owners have never heard of him, and those that have are probably reading this. UP: He's drafted by someone else in your league.

Yr	Tm	AB	R	HR	RBI	SB	BA	xBA	OBP	SLG	OPS	vL	vR	bb%	ct%	Eye	G	L	F	h%	HctX	PX	xPX	hr/f	Spd	SBO	SB%	#Wk	DOM	DIS	RC/G	RAR	BPV	BPX	R$
10	aa	305	18	3	31	4	220		251	298	549			4	86	0.29				25		51			109	14%	51%				2.34		26	57	$0
11	a/a	413	37	3	27	5	246		286	335	621			5	87	0.43				28		67			95	9%	59%				3.18		43	96	$3
12	HOU *	244	22	3	19	3	241	262	286	342	628	296	713	6	85	0.41	54	20	27	28	90	74	67	4%	83	11%	50%	20	35%	30%	3.17	-5.4	37	93	$1
13	HOU *	376	34	5	25	9	221	240	251	307	559	575	570	4	83	0.24	54	15	30	26	99	62	84	8%	98	16%	74%	20	25%	35%	2.53	-10.4	21	53	$2
14	HOU	285	33	6	23	2	277	253	327	400	727	776	719	6	80	0.29	52	18	30	33	93	92	68	9%	91	8%	33%	26	46%	38%	4.26	8.9	33	89	$7
1st Half		102	13	3	6	1	265	252	324	392	716	563	751	6	81	0.37	60	15	26	30	92	88	74	14%	97	15%	25%	14	50%	29%	3.77	1.6	40	108	$1
2nd Half		183	20	3	17	1	284	252	328	404	733	979	703	5	79	0.26	47	21	33	35	93	94	65	7%	91	4%	50%	12	42%	50%	4.55	6.8	30	81	$10
15	Proj	**266**	**27**	**5**	**20**	**3**	**253**	**255**	**295**	**370**	**664**	**592**	**679**	**5**	**82**	**0.29**	**53**	**17**	**30**	**29**	**94**	**86**	**74**	**8%**	**91**	**11%**	**51%**				**3.52**	**2.2**	**28**	**73**	**$6**

ROD TRUESDELL

Gordon,Alex

Age: 31	Bats: L	Pos: LF	Health A	LIMA Plan B+	
Ht: 6' 1"	Wt: 220		PT/Exp A	Rand Var 0	
			Consist B	MM 4225	

We've seen essentially the same skills for several years now. PX bump not reflected in xPX. BA/xBA decline from 2011-12 to 2013-14 pretty much washed out by overall MLB-wide decline. At 31, odds are for neither a stratospheric spike nor precipitous plummet. Minor blips. Small variances. Consistency is good.

Yr	Tm	AB	R	HR	RBI	SB	BA	xBA	OBP	SLG	OPS	vL	vR	bb%	ct%	Eye	G	L	F	h%	HctX	PX	xPX	hr/f	Spd	SBO	SB%	#Wk	DOM	DIS	RC/G	RAR	BPV	BPX	R$
10	KC *	502	76	17	51	6	239	250	332	405	736	704	660	12	71	0.48	38	23	39	30	106	125	134	11%	82	9%	45%	15	40%	33%	4.31	-9.4	36	78	$10
11	KC	611	101	23	87	17	303	276	376	502	879	829	901	10	77	0.48	40	22	38	36	104	144	117	13%	85	14%	68%	26	65%	27%	6.69	29.9	71	158	$32
12	KC	642	93	14	72	10	294	272	368	455	822	668	908	10	78	0.52	42	25	33	36	96	116	103	8%	86	8%	67%	27	56%	15%	5.95	24.9	54	135	$24
13	KC	633	90	20	81	11	265	247	327	422	749	877	683	8	78	0.37	40	20	39	31	111	104	125	10%	121	8%	79%	26	42%	38%	4.71	13.5	48	120	$22
14	KC	563	87	19	74	12	266	260	351	432	783	787	782	10	78	0.52	43	19	38	31	108	123	118	11%	70	9%	80%	27	48%	26%	5.16	24.0	53	143	$22
1st Half		300	46	9	42	6	273	261	355	440	795	754	812	10	81	0.57	43	15	42	31	113	126	112	9%	65	10%	75%	14	50%	14%	5.32	13.6	65	176	$23
2nd Half		263	41	10	32	6	259	258	348	422	770	824	747	11	74	0.47	42	25	34	31	103	119	125	15%	83	9%	86%	13	46%	38%	4.99	9.6	40	108	$22
15	**Proj**	**600**	**90**	**20**	**75**	**12**	**266**	**259**	**345**	**433**	**779**	**795**	**771**	**10**	**77**	**0.47**	**41**	**20**	**38**	**32**	**106**	**124**	**119**	**11%**	**85**	**9%**	**76%**				**5.10**	**23.6**	**58**	**152**	**$21**

Gordon,Dee

Age: 27	Bats: L	Pos: 2B	Health B	LIMA Plan B	
Ht: 5' 11"	Wt: 170		PT/Exp C	Rand Var -3	
			Consist B	MM 1525	

PRO: Maintained solid SB% and big-time SBO while finally taking on lead role; GB helped propel BA. CON: 2nd half walk rate crash seriously cut into value; 2nd half GB too much of a good thing, as HctX fell. That makes 1st half look like an outlier and spells regression. Fickle OBP will decide whether it'll be 40 SB or... UP: 75 SB

Yr	Tm	AB	R	HR	RBI	SB	BA	xBA	OBP	SLG	OPS	vL	vR	bb%	ct%	Eye	G	L	F	h%	HctX	PX	xPX	hr/f	Spd	SBO	SB%	#Wk	DOM	DIS	RC/G	RAR	BPV	BPX	R$
10	aa	555	65	1	29	40	236		274	291	565			5	82	0.28				29		38			147	45%	64%				2.47		13	28	$14
11	LA *	512	64	0	25	42	277	266	301	329	630	595	727	3	85	0.23	56	23	21	32	37	38	14	0%	161	39%	78%	11	45%	18%	3.56	-17.2	29	64	$20
12	LA *	333	40	1	18	33	226	246	272	276	548	415	632	6	80	0.32	59	21	21	28	52	36	20	2%	142	53%	75%	18	17%	56%	2.51	-19.3	6	15	$9
13	LA *	468	53	1	28	43	234	224	299	295	594	577	623	8	77	0.41	49	21	30	30	52	45	33	5%	164	44%	74%	12	33%	33%	2.98	-10.0	14	35	$18
14	LA	609	92	2	34	64	289	274	326	378	704	719	699	5	82	0.29	60	21	19	35	62	62	27	2%	189	49%	77%	27	37%	19%	4.39	17.7	48	130	$38
1st Half		312	45	2	25	40	292	285	344	410	754	650	784	7	85	0.50	55	23	22	34	77	76	48	4%	174	53%	83%	15	60%	7%	5.32	17.3	68	184	$42
2nd Half		297	47	0	9	24	286	261	306	343	650	798	610	2	80	0.12	65	20	16	36	46	46	4	0%	187	45%	69%	12	8%	33%	3.51	1.0	20	54	$34
15	**Proj**	**576**	**86**	**2**	**31**	**53**	**269**	**257**	**313**	**344**	**657**	**622**	**669**	**5**	**81**	**0.30**	**57**	**21**	**22**	**33**	**54**	**55**	**23**	**2%**	**180**	**45%**	**74%**				**3.67**	**4.8**	**29**	**75**	**$30**

Gose,Anthony

Age: 24	Bats: L	Pos: CF	Health A	LIMA Plan D	
Ht: 6' 1"	Wt: 190		PT/Exp C	Rand Var 0	
			Consist A	MM 1503	

2-13-.226 with 15 SB in 239 AB at TOR. For those looking to accentuate the positive, skills look a bit like Dee Gordon's at a similar age. For you old-timers, there's unfortunately a lot of Esix Snead, too. Atrocious ct% is a BA killer, and it shows no sign of improving. You can't steal first base... still.

Yr	Tm	AB	R	HR	RBI	SB	BA	xBA	OBP	SLG	OPS	vL	vR	bb%	ct%	Eye	G	L	F	h%	HctX	PX	xPX	hr/f	Spd	SBO	SB%	#Wk	DOM	DIS	RC/G	RAR	BPV	BPX	R$
10																																			
11	aa	509	74	15	50	59	239		309	389	698			9	67	0.31				33		115			129	57%	79%				4.09		20	44	$25
12	TOR *	586	85	5	41	39	243	241	302	349	651	710	601	8	71	0.29	60	19	21	33	67	79	51	5%	166	36%	70%	11	18%	73%	3.46	-25.2	14	35	$18
13	TOR *	540	65	5	33	21	227	225	273	330	603	425	788	6	68	0.20	52	22	26	33	83	82	100	7%	172	32%	55%	11	45%	36%	2.71	-26.0	3	8	$9
14	TOR *	444	55	5	33	32	222	221	285	300	585	461	641	8	67	0.26	62	19	19	32	64	67	56	7%	132	40%	70%	21	29%	48%	2.74	-16.1	-21	-57	$13
1st Half		223	24	2	13	12	220	210	307	291	598	610	661	11	68	0.39	66	13	21	32	62	61	70	0%	139	30%	62%	10	20%	60%	2.80	-7.6	-15	-41	$6
2nd Half		221	31	4	20	20	225	228	260	310	570	343	624	5	66	0.14	58	25	17	33	66	72	44	14%	117	53%	75%	11	36%	36%	2.64	-8.5	-34	-92	$20
15	**Proj**	**260**	**34**	**3**	**19**	**18**	**232**	**227**	**296**	**324**	**620**	**462**	**666**	**7**	**68**	**0.24**	**58**	**20**	**22**	**33**	**71**	**78**	**70**	**8%**	**141**	**39%**	**70%**				**3.03**	**-6.8**	**-7**	**-18**	**$9**

Gosewisch,Tuffy

Age: 31	Bats: R	Pos: CA	Health A	LIMA Plan D	
Ht: 5' 11"	Wt: 200		PT/Exp F	Rand Var -2	
			Consist B	MM 1001	

Beat out 42-year-old Henry Blanco to earn a roster spot. That's something of a passing of the torch, since Blanco was a lousy hitter as well. This profile is not remotely draft-worthy, so let's save some ink.

Yr	Tm	AB	R	HR	RBI	SB	BA	xBA	OBP	SLG	OPS	vL	vR	bb%	ct%	Eye	G	L	F	h%	HctX	PX	xPX	hr/f	Spd	SBO	SB%	#Wk	DOM	DIS	RC/G	RAR	BPV	BPX	R$
10	aa	312	31	6	22	0	188		266	308	574			10	74	0.41				23		94			101	0%	0%				2.57		23	50	-$4
11	aa	369	28	9	44	3	190		218	303	522			4	79	0.18				22		80			74	17%	26%				1.88		12	27	-$2
12	aaa	296	18	3	17	0	159		188	250	438			3	75	0.14				20		72			86	3%	0%				1.39		-8	-20	-$8
13	ARI *	295	17	4	21	1	199	241	223	301	524	579	265	3	80	0.15	45	21	34	24	84	79	64	0%	87	4%	29%	9	11%	67%	2.09	-14.9	16	40	-$4
14	ARI	129	6	1	7	0	225	222	242	310	553	509	584	2	81	0.13	53	17	30	27	101	73	58	3%	90	0%	0%	25	32%	36%	2.47	-3.8	18	49	-$2
1st Half		44	2	1	5	0	250	159	267	341	608	733	571	2	86	0.17	57	11	32	27	89	57	60	8%	88	0%	0%	12	17%	33%	3.09	-0.4	24	65	-$2
2nd Half		85	4	0	2	0	212	238	230	294	524	462	594	2	79	0.11	51	21	28	27	107	82	56	0%	96	0%	0%	13	46%	38%	2.19	-3.2	16	43	-$2
15	**Proj**	**135**	**8**	**1**	**8**	**0**	**228**	**229**	**255**	**316**	**571**	**543**	**588**	**4**	**78**	**0.16**	**53**	**17**	**30**	**29**	**100**	**78**	**58**	**3%**	**96**	**3%**	**30%**				**2.61**	**-3.2**	**-7**	**-17**	**$0**

Gosselin,Phil

Age: 26	Bats: R	Pos: 2B	Health A	LIMA Plan D	
Ht: 6' 1"	Wt: 200		PT/Exp C	Rand Var -5	
			Consist B	MM 1311	

1-3-.266 in 128 AB at ATL. At least his BA was better than Dan Uggla's. Nice wheels should be calling card, but poor plate approach, lack of green light put low ceiling on SB. xBA says his one 2014 plus—the BA—will drop. At least he's an RBI machine...*cough*

Yr	Tm	AB	R	HR	RBI	SB	BA	xBA	OBP	SLG	OPS	vL	vR	bb%	ct%	Eye	G	L	F	h%	HctX	PX	xPX	hr/f	Spd	SBO	SB%	#Wk	DOM	DIS	RC/G	RAR	BPV	BPX	R$
10																																			
11																																			
12	aa	484	45	2	38	10	216		273	284	556			7	79	0.36				27		52			96	12%	69%				2.50		1	3	$1
13	ATL *	431	37	2	30	5	220	183	255	271	526	1100	0	4	81	0.24	67	0	33	27	83	39	-15	0%	110	6%	80%	2	0%	100%	2.28	-18.2	-2	-5	$0
14	ATL *	506	58	4	25	6	276	250	301	370	672	653	603	4	79	0.18	58	17	25	34	91	76	61	4%	142	8%	66%	11	9%	36%	3.88	7.1	30	81	$11
1st Half		302	31	2	15	3	262	235	284	350	635			3	79	0.15				32		72			123	5%	100%				3.50		20	54	$10
2nd Half		204	26	2	10	3	296	254	327	401	728	653	603	4	79	0.22	58	17	25	36	91	83	61	4%	138	11%	46%	11	9%	36%	4.50	6.4	36	97	$12
15	**Proj**	**234**	**24**	**2**	**14**	**3**	**250**	**239**	**293**	**325**	**618**	**657**	**590**	**4**	**80**	**0.23**	**58**	**17**	**25**	**31**	**82**	**61**	**55**	**4%**	**129**	**8%**	**68%**				**3.11**	**-2.0**	**3**	**8**	**$4**

Grandal,Yasmani

Age: 26	Bats: B	Pos: CA 1B	Health C	LIMA Plan B	
Ht: 6' 2"	Wt: 225		PT/Exp D	Rand Var +2	
			Consist D	MM 4225	

PRO: Nice step up in PX and FB% while maintaining excellent bb%; great Sept. (.291/.408/.519). CON: Contact rate took a nosedive, crushing BA despite solid HctX; lefties ate him up. With a late start post-ACL surgery, perhaps his slow 1st half was not surprising, and 2nd half surge is encouraging. UP: 20 HR

Yr	Tm	AB	R	HR	RBI	SB	BA	xBA	OBP	SLG	OPS	vL	vR	bb%	ct%	Eye	G	L	F	h%	HctX	PX	xPX	hr/f	Spd	SBO	SB%	#Wk	DOM	DIS	RC/G	RAR	BPV	BPX	R$
10																																			
11	a/a	168	16	3	20	0	267		319	409	728			7	72	0.28				35		124			81	3%	0%				4.41		29	64	$2
12	SD *	386	55	12	60	0	281	248	374	432	806	971	821	13	79	0.69	53	17	30	33	116	102	87	17%	101	0%	0%	15	53%	33%	5.73	3.2	54	135	$12
13	SD *	124	15	1	10	0	221	255	326	327	653	752	635	13	77	0.69	48	24	28	28	117	94	112	5%	86	0%	0%	6	50%	0%	3.49	-4.1	39	98	-$2
14	SD	377	47	15	49	3	225	242	327	401	728	512	781	13	69	0.50	43	19	38	28	108	139	132	15%	74	3%	100%	27	44%	44%	4.38	2.2	40	108	$7
1st Half		161	16	6	17	2	193	227	280	348	628	484	651	11	69	0.40	44	18	38	24	107	124	146	14%	75	5%	100%	14	43%	50%	3.16	-5.2	21	57	-$1
2nd Half		216	31	9	32	1	250	251	360	440	800	524	886	15	70	0.58	42	21	38	32	109	150	122	15%	79	1%	100%	13	46%	38%	5.45	8.1	55	149	$13
15	**Proj**	**428**	**53**	**16**	**52**	**2**	**246**	**254**	**342**	**421**	**763**	**723**	**781**	**13**	**73**	**0.54**	**44**	**20**	**36**	**30**	**112**	**138**	**118**	**14%**	**77**	**2%**	**87%**				**4.88**	**18.8**	**45**	**120**	**$11**

Granderson,Curtis

Age: 34	Bats: L	Pos: RF	Health D	LIMA Plan A	
Ht: 6' 1"	Wt: 200		PT/Exp B	Rand Var +3	
			Consist B	MM 4315	

PRO: Best ct% in years kept improving, maintained xPX; still-solid bb% and SB%; back to full health. CON: didn't rebound at all vR, which was once where he raked; hair-pulling inconsistency (two months sub-.150 BA, two at .300); not running at all anymore. xBA, h% point to minor BA rebound potential.

Yr	Tm	AB	R	HR	RBI	SB	BA	xBA	OBP	SLG	OPS	vL	vR	bb%	ct%	Eye	G	L	F	h%	HctX	PX	xPX	hr/f	Spd	SBO	SB%	#Wk	DOM	DIS	RC/G	RAR	BPV	BPX	R$
10	NYY	466	76	24	67	12	247	258	324	468	792	647	866	10	75	0.46	33	20	47	28	112	142	150	14%	120	12%	86%	24	54%	21%	5.19	-1.0	72	157	$16
11	NYY	583	136	41	119	25	262	272	364	552	916	944	902	13	71	0.50	34	18	48	30	125	198	161	21%	123	22%	71%	27	67%	11%	6.64	23.7	107	238	$36
12	NYY	596	102	43	106	10	232	251	319	492	811	762	839	11	67	0.38	33	23	44	27	91	175	132	24%	99	9%	77%	27	52%	19%	5.17	7.9	63	158	$22
13	NYY *	240	33	8	17	8	238	231	322	411	734	792	695	11	69	0.40	34	23	44	31	95	134	135	11%	144	16%	80%	12	42%	33%	4.48	3.0	49	123	$5
14	NYM	564	73	20	66	8	227	236	326	388	714	742	703	12	75	0.56	34	19	47	27	106	119	132	10%	92	6%	80%	27	56%	26%	4.15	6.2	49	132	$12
1st Half		277	37	11	36	6	231	238	348	400	753	780	742	15	72	0.63	35	20	45	28	106	131	129	12%	100	9%	75%	14	57%	36%	4.66	7.7	54	146	$14
2nd Half		287	36	9	30	2	223	234	302	373	675	703	664	9	78	0.48	34	18	49	26	105	108	135	8%	86	3%	100%	13	54%	15%	3.67	-0.7	45	122	$10
15	**Proj**	**528**	**76**	**21**	**63**	**11**	**233**	**241**	**323**	**412**	**734**	**754**	**726**	**11**	**72**	**0.46**	**34**	**21**	**45**	**28**	**102**	**134**	**135**	**12%**	**108**	**10%**	**79%**				**4.39**	**6.3**	**54**	**142**	**$15**

ROD TRUESDELL

Green,Grant

Age: 27	Bats: R	Pos: LF	Health	B	LIMA Plan	D
Ht: 6' 3"	Wt: 180		PT/Exp	C	Rand Var	0
			Consist	A	MM	2211

1-11-.273 in 99 AB with LAA. Missed a month+ after July back sprain. So we can excuse the poor Sept, but not the rest of these stagnant skills. Swings at everything, is showing no PX growth, and wow, what a bad base stealer. 1st half splits vs. LHP a sample-size fluke. Now 27: it's put up or shut up time.

Yr Tm	AB	R	HR	RBI	SB	BA	xBA	OBP	SLG	OPS	vL	vR	bb%	ct%	Eye	G	L	F	h%	HctX	PX	xPX	hr/f	Spd	SBO	SB%	#Wk	DOM	DIS	RC/G	RAR	BPV	BPX	R$
10																																		
11 aa	530	53	6	43	4	235		273	322	596			5	73	0.20				31		75			88	11%	31%				2.73		-7	-16	$4
12 aaa	524	50	9	52	9	235		268	348	616			4	83	0.26				27		71			102	18%	45%				2.88		30	75	$6
13 2AL *	542	57	7	49	2	245	227	282	348	630	334	804	5	74	0.20	43	21	36	32	81	83	102	3%	135	4%	49%	11	18%	45%	3.27	-7.4	15	38	$6
14 LAA *	297	29	4	35	3	250	250	273	355	628	770	524	3	80	0.15	47	21	32	30	94	83	78	4%	122	16%	33%	16	25%	31%	3.00	-3.5	30	81	$4
1st Half	227	21	3	26	3	259	259	282	357	639	905	606	3	82	0.18	46	24	30	31	107	76	81	5%	121	14%	37%	9	33%	33%	3.20	-1.3	33	89	$7
2nd Half	70	7	1	9	1	223	224	241	350	592	222	368	2	72	0.09	50	11	39	29	52	109	69	0%	120	23%	22%	7	14%	29%	2.40	-2.2	20	54	-$3
15 Proj	**135**	**13**	**2**	**14**	**2**	**248**	**236**	**273**	**358**	**632**	**628**	**634**	**4**	**77**	**0.16**	**46**	**18**	**36**	**31**	**87**	**90**	**85**	**4%**	**128**	**14%**	**37%**				**3.10**	**-2.6**	**11**	**30**	**$0**

Gregorius,Didi

Age: 25	Bats: L	Pos: SS	Health	A	LIMA Plan	D+
Ht: 6' 2"	Wt: 205		PT/Exp	C	Rand Var	0
			Consist	B	MM	2313

6-27-.226 in 270 AB at ARI. PRO: Climb in HctX and xPX with FB tilt could foretell modest power spike; sexy Spd. CON: All those FBs sans elite PX combine with average ct% to kill BA; red-lighted on basepaths. There's power-speed upside here, but it looks like he's at least a year away from turning upside into stats.

Yr Tm	AB	R	HR	RBI	SB	BA	xBA	OBP	SLG	OPS	vL	vR	bb%	ct%	Eye	G	L	F	h%	HctX	PX	xPX	hr/f	Spd	SBO	SB%	#Wk	DOM	DIS	RC/G	RAR	BPV	BPX	R$
10																																		
11 aa	148	12	2	11	2	230		261	322	583			4	81	0.22				27		61			119	13%	48%				2.64		18	40	-$1
12 CIN *	521	60	7	47	3	247	256	293	357	650	1000	556	6	82	0.36	67	13	20	29	0	67	-11	0%	157	7%	28%	4	0%	50%	3.37	-11.4	43	108	$6
13 ARI *	388	51	8	29	1	258	245	324	384	708	512	789	9	83	0.58	37	21	42	29	79	83	87	6%	137	2%	24%	23	52%	30%	4.19	7.8	59	148	$6
14 ARI *	496	62	8	43	5	240	242	292	363	656	424	706	7	83	0.45	37	20	43	27	101	82	106	6%	131	4%	100%	19	42%	26%	3.61	4.7	55	149	$8
1st Half	283	37	4	21	3	247	227	301	368	669	206	921	7	84	0.49	37	14	49	28	116	83	154	10%	137	4%	100%	6	50%	33%	3.81	4.8	60	162	$9
2nd Half	213	25	4	22	2	230	242	283	357	639	543	657	7	83	0.41	38	21	41	26	97	80	95	5%	127	4%	100%	13	38%	23%	3.37	0.8	48	130	$6
15 Proj	**390**	**47**	**9**	**33**	**3**	**251**	**245**	**313**	**391**	**703**	**433**	**796**	**7**	**83**	**0.44**	**37**	**19**	**44**	**28**	**95**	**92**	**107**	**7%**	**133**	**5%**	**64%**				**4.01**	**8.8**	**49**	**130**	**$9**

Grichuk,Randal

Age: 23	Bats: R	Pos: RF	Health	A	LIMA Plan	D
Ht: 6' 1"	Wt: 195		PT/Exp	D	Rand Var	0
			Consist	A	MM	3211

3-8-.245 in 110 AB at STL. We saw a glimpse of his power potential in Aug/Sept (.485 SLG in 66 AB), and FB%, HctX, and xPX are impressive. There's a sample size caution there, though, and poor ct% caps BA and cuts into HR potential. With plate control a work in progress, the power will take time.

Yr Tm	AB	R	HR	RBI	SB	BA	xBA	OBP	SLG	OPS	vL	vR	bb%	ct%	Eye	G	L	F	h%	HctX	PX	xPX	hr/f	Spd	SBO	SB%	#Wk	DOM	DIS	RC/G	RAR	BPV	BPX	R$
10																																		
11																																		
12																																		
13 aa	500	74	18	55	8	231		266	412	678			4	80	0.24				26		117			124	15%	59%				3.51		62	155	$12
14 STL *	546	64	20	59	6	220	228	255	383	638	689	662	4	72	0.17	39	15	46	27	141	124	162	8%	108	14%	43%	11	36%	45%	3.01	-13.8	31	84	$9
1st Half	271	34	9	33	2	215	225	253	380	634	402	557	5	72	0.19	48	7	45	26	126	128	132	8%	112	7%	66%	5	40%	60%	3.10	-6.4	38	103	$7
2nd Half	275	29	11	27	4	226	229	256	385	642	914	720	4	72	0.15	34	20	46	28	149	120	180	9%	104	20%	36%	6	33%	33%	2.93	-8.0	24	65	$11
15 Proj	**134**	**17**	**4**	**15**	**2**	**225**	**235**	**260**	**384**	**643**	**668**	**610**	**4**	**75**	**0.19**	**37**	**18**	**46**	**27**	**140**	**116**	**161**	**9%**	**119**	**15%**	**49%**				**3.12**	**-3.7**	**35**	**93**	**$3**

Grossman,Robert

Age: 25	Bats: B	Pos: LF RF	Health	A	LIMA Plan	D
Ht: 6' 0"	Wt: 195		PT/Exp	B	Rand Var	-1
			Consist	A	MM	2203

6-37-.233 with 9 SB in 360 AB at HOU. It's baffling how some guys don't realize strikeouts DO hurt them. Or maybe he just can't fix it. Without power, but with a decent LD stroke, great bb%, and a bit of speed, he could be a fine leadoff man—if he'd just put it in play. But with this ct%, he's a 4th OF.

Yr Tm	AB	R	HR	RBI	SB	BA	xBA	OBP	SLG	OPS	vL	vR	bb%	ct%	Eye	G	L	F	h%	HctX	PX	xPX	hr/f	Spd	SBO	SB%	#Wk	DOM	DIS	RC/G	RAR	BPV	BPX	R$
10																																		
11																																		
12 aa	485	60	8	35	10	228		311	346	657			11	71	0.42				31		89			115	17%	44%				3.29		14	35	$5
13 HOU *	510	61	6	36	17	254	223	332	339	671	785	669	10	71	0.40	47	23	30	35	85	72	90	7%	118	21%	52%	12	25%	58%	3.56	-6.4	0	0	$13
14 HOU *	535	63	9	47	16	247	231	335	355	690	566	703	12	72	0.46	41	24	35	33	63	92	76	7%	94	17%	56%	21	19%	43%	3.83	2.2	14	38	$13
1st Half	263	27	5	19	6	207	234	292	323	614	415	585	11	72	0.43	45	22	33	27	73	96	85	8%	94	22%	44%	8	25%	38%	2.74	-8.5	17	46	$4
2nd Half	272	36	4	28	10	286	227	376	387	763	657	752	13	71	0.50	40	25	35	39	58	87	72	6%	96	14%	69%	13	15%	46%	5.16	11.0	10	27	$22
15 Proj	**248**	**30**	**4**	**20**	**8**	**251**	**231**	**339**	**359**	**697**	**670**	**707**	**11**	**71**	**0.45**	**44**	**23**	**32**	**34**	**73**	**91**	**82**	**7%**	**106**	**18%**	**55%**				**3.89**	**1.1**	**8**	**21**	**$7**

Guerrero,Alexander

Age: 28	Bats: R	Pos: LF	Health	A	LIMA Plan	D
Ht: 5' 10"	Wt: 205		PT/Exp	F	Rand Var	0
			Consist	F	MM	3401

0-0-.077 in 13 AB at LA. Hear about the Dodgers' new UT? He has no Eye and half an ear. <rimshot> (i.e. 0.08 BB/K ratio, and missed 5 weeks after then-teammate Miguel Olivo bit his ear.) Showed flashes of 20+ HR power displayed in Cuba, but with these plate skills, MLB pitchers will eat him up.

Yr Tm	AB	R	HR	RBI	SB	BA	xBA	OBP	SLG	OPS	vL	vR	bb%	ct%	Eye	G	L	F	h%	HctX	PX	xPX	hr/f	Spd	SBO	SB%	#Wk	DOM	DIS	RC/G	RAR	BPV	BPX	R$
10																																		
11																																		
12																																		
13																																		
14 LA *	256	21	8	27	2	225	286	241	379	620	0	286	2	75	0.08	57	29	14	27	0	110		0%	96	5%	100%	6	0%	83%	3.05	-2.6	23	62	$2
1st Half	118	11	6	16	1	268	272	288	471	759	0	0	3	79	0.13	44	20	36	30	0	132		0%	105	2%	100%	1	0%	100%	4.74	4.6	59	159	$5
2nd Half	138	10	3	11	2	189	263	202	303	504	0	333	2	72	0.05	57	29	14	24	0	90		0%	89	9%	100%	5	0%	80%	1.96	-6.3	-9	-24	$0
15 Proj	**171**	**14**	**5**	**17**	**2**	**233**	**231**	**252**	**373**	**625**	**625**	**625**	**2**	**75**	**0.10**	**38**	**20**	**42**	**29**		**103**		**9%**	**100**	**7%**	**100%**				**3.18**	**-2.9**	**12**	**30**	**$3**

Guyer,Brandon

Age: 29	Bats: R	Pos: LF	Health	F	LIMA Plan	D+
Ht: 6' 2"	Wt: 195		PT/Exp	F	Rand Var	+3
			Consist	A	MM	2533

Was once a nice power/speed prospect, but that was several years and a couple of injuries ago. Now 29, can he tap into some of those owned skills? Best bet is he platoons vs. LHP again, and so won't accumulate many counting stats. But 2011 wasn't THAT long ago. A low-likelihood of... UP: 10 HR, 15 SB.

Yr Tm	AB	R	HR	RBI	SB	BA	xBA	OBP	SLG	OPS	vL	vR	bb%	ct%	Eye	G	L	F	h%	HctX	PX	xPX	hr/f	Spd	SBO	SB%	#Wk	DOM	DIS	RC/G	RAR	BPV	BPX	R$
10 aa	369	55	10	42	22	297		332	493	825			5	84	0.33				33		134			111	31%	86%				6.08		89	193	$19
11 TAM *	429	67	13	50	12	256	263	301	421	722	655	397	6	76	0.27	53	16	31	31	116	120	142	20%	121	20%	64%	7	29%	29%	4.18	-9.5	50	111	$13
12 TAM *	92	9	3	11	2	233	243	274	379	654	714	0	5	79	0.27	83	0	17	26	115	87	114	100%	120	8%	100%	1	100%	0%	3.54	-2.7	34	85	$0
13 aaa	356	55	5	31	17	244		288	368	656			6	78	0.28				30		88			129	25%	82%				3.65		36	90	$11
14 TAM	259	37	3	26	6	266	253	334	367	701	762	656	6	80	0.31	50	20	30	32	98	81	80	5%	124	11%	86%	25	48%	44%	4.01	2.4	35	95	$7
1st Half	105	20	1	11	3	267	259	319	371	690	752	648	5	78	0.22	52	20	28	33	114	93	93	5%	115	17%	75%	12	50%	50%	3.87	0.4	32	86	$5
2nd Half	154	17	2	15	3	266	248	345	364	708	767	661	7	81	0.38	49	20	31	32	87	72	70	6%	128	7%	100%	13	46%	38%	4.10	1.6	36	97	$8
15 Proj	**263**	**39**	**4**	**27**	**9**	**263**	**260**	**332**	**382**	**714**	**783**	**663**	**6**	**79**	**0.31**	**50**	**20**	**30**	**32**	**98**	**93**	**79**	**6%**	**135**	**17%**	**81%**				**4.10**	**2.8**	**43**	**113**	**$9**

Gwynn,Tony

Age: 32	Bats: L	Pos: CF	Health	A	LIMA Plan	D
Ht: 5' 11"	Wt: 193		PT/Exp	D	Rand Var	+5
			Consist	A	MM	0201

0-3-.152 in 105 AB at PHI. Certainly a dismal year for him, on and off the field. His only plus skill—speed—is rapidly dwindling as he moves into his 30s, This playing time projection could well be an "upside." There's no reason to keep him on your radar.

Yr Tm	AB	R	HR	RBI	SB	BA	xBA	OBP	SLG	OPS	vL	vR	bb%	ct%	Eye	G	L	F	h%	HctX	PX	xPX	hr/f	Spd	SBO	SB%	#Wk	DOM	DIS	RC/G	RAR	BPV	BPX	R$
10 SD	289	30	3	20	17	204	240	304	287	591	872	547	12	83	0.82	46	19	35	24	72	54	38	4%	119	25%	81%	23	39%	48%	2.93	-17.0	37	80	$3
11 LA	312	37	2	22	22	256	260	308	353	660	536	696	7	80	0.38	51	23	25	31	64	65	45	3%	137	34%	79%	26	35%	31%	3.79	-9.3	31	69	$9
12 LA *	327	36	0	21	15	232	228	277	292	569	513	598	6	79	0.30	53	19	28	29	80	42	43	0%	129	28%	67%	19	16%	53%	2.62	-20.9	2	5	$4
13 aaa	333	32	1	16	7	215		278	266	543			8	79	0.42				27		37			122	22%	38%				2.11		1	3	$0
14 PHI *	174	19	1	8	4	178	211	272	222	494	125	537	11	78	0.57	49	19	31	23	73	34	54	0%	110	20%	45%	20	25%	45%	1.73	-12.1	-3	-8	-$3
1st Half	89	13	0	3	2	169	211	275	213	488	150	569	13	76	0.62	48	21	32	22	77	35	53	0%	119	8%	100%	13	38%	46%	1.90	-5.7	-3	-8	-$4
2nd Half	85	6	1	5	2	189	201	269	232	501	0	350	10	79	0.52	57	14	29	23	46	33	57	0%	87	32%	31%	7	0%	43%	1.54	-6.7	-10	-27	-$2
15 Proj	**108**	**11**	**0**	**6**	**3**	**202**	**225**	**278**	**255**	**533**	**420**	**565**	**9**	**79**	**0.49**	**50**	**21**	**29**	**25**	**72**	**41**	**46**	**2%**	**106**	**23%**	**49%**				**2.08**	**-6.2**	**-3**	**-8**	**$0**

ROD TRUESDELL

Gyorko,Jedd

Age: 26	Bats: R	Pos: 2B	Health	C	LIMA Plan	C
Ht: 5' 10"	Wt: 210		PT/Exp	B	Rand Var	+4
			Consist	B	MM	4125

10-51-.210 in 400 AB at SD. Sophomore campaign marred by plantar fasciitis in 1H, but there were signs of a 2H recovery: xBA surged thanks to ct% gains, plate patience improved, and PX came back to life. He's already shown great power at a young age, so with a few more FBs and time to heal... UP: Return to 2013 and more

Yr	Tm	AB	R	HR	RBI	SB	BA	xBA	OBP	SLG	OPS	vL	vR	bb%	ct%	Eye	G	L	F	h%	HctX	PX	xPX	hr/f	Spd	SBO	SB%	#Wk	DOM	DIS	RC/G	RAR	BPV	BPX	R$
10																																			
11	aa	236	30	5	29	1	231		291	330	622			8	74	0.33				29		77			86	1%	100%				3.21		3	7	$1
12	a/a	499	58	19	72	4	249		302	409	712			7	77	0.33				29		106			75	7%	43%				4.07		30	75	$12
13	SD	486	62	23	63	1	249	261	301	444	745	829	715	6	75	0.27	38	23	40	29	114	138	140	16%	85	2%	50%	24	54%	29%	4.45	11.3	49	123	$13
14	SD *	424	41	11	54	3	210	239	275	333	608	669	594	8	75	0.36	44	22	35	25	95	93	115	10%	66	5%	60%	20	30%	40%	2.93	-6.1	14	38	$3
1st Half		204	13	5	24	2	162	208	213	270	482	372	509	6	73	0.21	44	17	39	20	83	78	124	8%	82	9%	67%	10	20%	50%	1.69	-11.5	-10	-27	-$4
2nd Half		220	28	6	30	1	254	270	334	391	726	890	689	11	78	0.53	43	27	30	31	106	107	105	11%	64	3%	50%	10	40%	30%	4.42	6.6	39	105	$10
15	Proj	477	54	19	62	3	242	257	306	408	714	800	685	8	75	0.35	41	23	36	28	103	122	124	14%	70	4%	56%				4.09	10.0	32	83	$10

Hairston,Scott

Age: 35	Bats: R	Pos: LF	Health	B	LIMA Plan	D
Ht: 6' 0"	Wt: 200		PT/Exp	F	Rand Var	-2
			Consist	C	MM	3301

Take 2014 results with a grain of salt given the extreme amount of time he spent perfecting his bench demeanor. How often do you see a relatively healthy player get so little PT? Still owns plus power skills, though success vs. LHP remains his only path to playing time. That said, xBA, ct% and Eye trends make retirement an option too.

Yr	Tm	AB	R	HR	RBI	SB	BA	xBA	OBP	SLG	OPS	vL	vR	bb%	ct%	Eye	G	L	F	h%	HctX	PX	xPX	hr/f	Spd	SBO	SB%	#Wk	DOM	DIS	RC/G	RAR	BPV	BPX	R$
10	SD	295	34	10	36	6	210	218	295	346	640	655	633	10	77	0.45	34	15	51	24	75	92	81	9%	96	10%	86%	25	36%	32%	3.24	-18.5	30	65	$3
11	NYM	132	20	7	24	1	235	251	303	470	773	702	886	8	74	0.32	32	13	55	26	103	165	131	13%	105	8%	50%	22	50%	41%	4.48	-3.0	78	173	$2
12	NYM	377	52	20	57	8	263	273	299	504	803	867	739	5	78	0.23	33	21	46	29	110	155	117	15%	92	14%	80%	27	63%	19%	5.19	5.0	75	188	$14
13	2 NL	157	18	10	26	2	191	228	237	414	651	743	276	5	72	0.20	26	14	59	19	77	150	100	14%	79	8%	100%	27	41%	41%	3.12	-4.6	44	110	$1
14	WAS	77	6	1	8	0	208	182	253	299	552	620	412	5	66	0.15	35	16	49	30	94	89	122	4%	92	0%	0%	22	18%	55%	2.37	-3.3	-23	-62	-$2
1st Half		33	4	1	5	0	303	244	324	455	779	787	756	6	79	0.29	25	21	54	36	134	113	146	7%	96	0%	0%	9	22%	33%	5.70	1.8	48	130	$0
2nd Half		44	2	0	3	0	136	134	200	182	382	476	220	4	57	0.11	44	11	44	24	64	63	96	0%	88	0%	0%	13	15%	69%	0.93	-4.2	-85	-230	-$3
15	Proj	98	13	3	16	1	224	217	279	372	651	714	531	7	73	0.26	33	16	51	28	91	116	111	8%	96	8%	77%				3.37	-1.1	25	65	$2

Hamilton,Billy

Age: 24	Bats: B	Pos: CF	Health	A	LIMA Plan	B
Ht: 6' 0"	Wt: 160		PT/Exp	C	Rand Var	0
			Consist	B	MM	1505

Lofty SB total was no surprise given elite wheels and green light on the basepaths. But shaky plate skills continue to magnify BA/OBP risk, and 2nd half xBA plummeted as pitchers made adjustments. A fine one-trick pony, but any slide in batting eye or bad h% luck could mean... DN: 35 SB or less.

Yr	Tm	AB	R	HR	RBI	SB	BA	xBA	OBP	SLG	OPS	vL	vR	bb%	ct%	Eye	G	L	F	h%	HctX	PX	xPX	hr/f	Spd	SBO	SB%	#Wk	DOM	DIS	RC/G	RAR	BPV	BPX	R$
10																																			
11																																			
12	aa	175	29	1	13	45	271		383	360	744			15	73	0.67				37		56			157	89%	73%				4.66		17	43	$16
13	CIN *	523	72	6	36	76	238	276	285	319	604	0	950	6	77	0.29	50	36	14	30	40	59	-15	0%	163	71%	81%	5	20%	40%	3.25	-13.8	19	48	$34
14	CIN	563	72	6	48	56	250	237	292	355	648	669	641	6	79	0.29	42	21	37	31	70	77	55	4%	167	58%	71%	26	46%	38%	3.37	-8.0	42	114	$28
1st Half		281	40	4	28	34	281	256	312	402	714	589	758	4	80	0.24	43	23	34	34	71	90	54	6%	152	67%	74%	14	50%	29%	4.27	3.4	50	135	$35
2nd Half		282	32	2	20	22	220	217	273	309	582	756	528	7	78	0.34	40	20	40	28	69	63	57	2%	173	49%	67%	12	42%	50%	2.60	-11.4	30	81	$22
15	Proj	545	77	4	42	50	246	222	301	333	633	681	618	7	78	0.36	41	21	38	31	70	65	56	3%	174	50%	68%				3.21	-11.0	27	71	$25

Hamilton,Josh

Age: 34	Bats: L	Pos: LF	Health	C	LIMA Plan	B
Ht: 6' 4"	Wt: 240		PT/Exp	B	Rand Var	-2
			Consist	C	MM	4125

Suffered through calf, thumb, and shoulder injuries as production continued to tank. BPV continued its rapid descent as ct% dove further into the danger zone. xBA and h% say he was lucky to hit even .250. Still owns plenty of power, but deteriorating plate skills (and body) suggest a return to $20+ is a reach.

Yr	Tm	AB	R	HR	RBI	SB	BA	xBA	OBP	SLG	OPS	vL	vR	bb%	ct%	Eye	G	L	F	h%	HctX	PX	xPX	hr/f	Spd	SBO	SB%	#Wk	DOM	DIS	RC/G	RAR	BPV	BPX	R$
10	TEX	518	95	32	100	8	359	326	411	633	1044	789	1163	8	82	0.45	42	22	36	39	117	176	135	21%	94	6%	89%	24	79%	0%	10.35	70.7	113	246	$39
11	TEX	487	80	25	94	8	298	297	346	536	882	825	904	7	81	0.42	41	21	38	33	119	154	126	16%	98	7%	89%	22	73%	9%	6.86	26.0	93	207	$26
12	TEX	562	103	43	128	7	285	282	354	577	930	853	965	10	71	0.37	38	21	41	33	115	196	166	26%	78	8%	64%	27	59%	33%	7.15	41.1	86	215	$33
13	LAA	576	73	21	79	4	250	251	307	432	739	596	802	8	73	0.30	39	22	39	31	99	133	128	13%	106	3%	100%	27	48%	30%	4.55	9.6	46	115	$15
14	LAA	338	43	10	44	3	263	238	331	414	745	884	695	9	68	0.30	37	25	39	36	97	132	136	11%	71	7%	50%	17	35%	35%	4.57	8.7	18	49	$10
1st Half		124	15	3	19	3	306	242	381	444	825	1095	707	11	68	0.38	37	29	35	43	115	124	131	10%	85	7%	100%	7	43%	29%	6.40	9.0	19	51	$7
2nd Half		214	28	7	25	0	238	236	302	397	699	732	688	7	68	0.25	37	22	41	32	87	136	138	11%	67	6%	0%	10	30%	40%	3.67	-0.4	18	49	$11
15	Proj	449	61	18	67	4	257	256	322	443	765	767	763	8	71	0.32	38	23	39	33	103	148	138	14%	81	5%	59%				4.80	13.9	42	110	$15

Hanigan,Ryan

Age: 34	Bats: R	Pos: CA	Health	D	LIMA Plan	D+
Ht: 6' 0"	Wt: 210		PT/Exp	D	Rand Var	+3
			Consist	C	MM	1123

Changed things up by trading contact for more power and FBs. Yes, you have to look hard to see the result. Yes, it's there. You might need to borrow my microscope. In the end, a scan of xBA, bb%, even ct% (if you ignore the 1st half), reveals a skill set that has been essentially flat for years. That's not a good thing.

Yr	Tm	AB	R	HR	RBI	SB	BA	xBA	OBP	SLG	OPS	vL	vR	bb%	ct%	Eye	G	L	F	h%	HctX	PX	xPX	hr/f	Spd	SBO	SB%	#Wk	DOM	DIS	RC/G	RAR	BPV	BPX	R$
10	CIN *	249	29	5	41	0	278	271	369	392	761	993	771	13	88	1.24	48	21	31	30	99	75	79	9%	82	0%	0%	21	62%	14%	5.11	5.2	65	141	$6
11	CIN	266	27	6	31	0	267	249	356	357	714	871	685	12	88	1.09	48	22	30	29	89	54	69	9%	78	0%	0%	25	32%	40%	4.37	1.3	44	98	$4
12	CIN	317	25	2	24	0	274	241	365	338	703	840	661	12	88	1.19	53	21	26	31	84	45	48	3%	76	0%	0%	27	44%	22%	4.30	1.5	39	98	$3
13	CIN	222	17	2	21	0	198	243	306	261	567	608	555	12	88	1.07	49	22	29	22	84	44	55	4%	74	2%	0%	22	32%	36%	2.37	-9.4	34	85	-$4
14	TAM	225	18	5	34	1	218	242	318	324	642	602	654	12	83	0.79	38	22	40	24	79	75	86	7%	70	2%	100%	19	53%	32%	3.33	0.0	38	103	$1
1st Half		152	11	4	27	0	230	234	312	355	667	569	692	10	80	0.57	42	20	39	26	84	90	98	9%	69	0%	0%	13	46%	31%	3.62	1.0	36	97	$3
2nd Half		73	7	1	7	1	192	242	330	260	590	649	569	16	88	1.56	30	26	44	21	69	46	65	3%	85	4%	100%	6	67%	33%	2.72	-1.6	47	127	-$3
15	Proj	318	27	5	36	1	240	247	345	322	666	710	653	13	86	1.07	42	22	35	27	81	58	67	5%	73	2%	78%				3.65	2.4	28	74	$5

Hardy,J.J.

Age: 32	Bats: R	Pos: SS	Health	A	LIMA Plan	B+
Ht: 6' 1"	Wt: 190		PT/Exp	A	Rand Var	-4
			Consist	B	MM	2225

Finally rediscovered power skills in 2H, though ct% suggests he had to hack his way back. Collapse in plate approach puts BA at risk once career-high h% falls back to earth. Consistent AB total will prop up value, but fading power trend during post-peak years puts a return to 20+ HR in question.

Yr	Tm	AB	R	HR	RBI	SB	BA	xBA	OBP	SLG	OPS	vL	vR	bb%	ct%	Eye	G	L	F	h%	HctX	PX	xPX	hr/f	Spd	SBO	SB%	#Wk	DOM	DIS	RC/G	RAR	BPV	BPX	R$
10	MIN	340	44	6	38	1	268	264	320	394	714	614	759	8	84	0.52	49	17	34	30	111	85	89	6%	127	2%	50%	23	61%	30%	4.40	2.2	60	130	$7
11	BAL	527	76	30	80	0	269	274	310	491	801	794	803	6	83	0.34	40	16	43	28	123	139	130	16%	84	0%	0%	23	74%	4%	5.32	17.2	80	178	$19
12	BAL	663	85	22	68	0	238	249	282	389	671	767	639	5	84	0.36	43	17	40	25	114	91	109	10%	104	0%	0%	27	56%	19%	3.64	-5.2	53	133	$10
13	BAL	601	66	25	76	2	263	267	306	433	738	783	720	6	88	0.52	45	17	38	26	107	101	99	12%	96	2%	67%	27	63%	19%	4.58	20.0	75	188	$17
14	BAL	529	56	9	52	0	268	234	309	372	682	627	702	5	80	0.28	43	19	38	32	104	81	96	6%	100	0%	0%	27	30%	37%	3.98	12.1	29	78	$11
1st Half		282	27	2	20	0	294	228	321	376	697	677	705	4	84	0.26	44	18	38	35	96	68	72	2%	105	0%	0%	14	29%	29%	4.39	9.0	31	84	$10
2nd Half		247	29	7	32	0	239	240	296	368	664	539	699	6	77	0.29	42	21	37	29	113	97	126	10%	95	0%	0%	13	31%	46%	3.55	2.3	27	73	$13
15	Proj	562	64	16	64	1	252	251	295	389	684	672	688	6	83	0.34	44	18	38	28	109	96	104	9%	99	1%	63%				3.88	10.6	33	86	$13

Harper,Bryce

Age: 22	Bats: L	Pos: LF	Health	D	LIMA Plan	A
Ht: 6' 3"	Wt: 225		PT/Exp	B	Rand Var	-4
			Consist	C	MM	4235

Torn ligament in thumb derailed growth. BA was buoyed by fortunate h%, while ct% tanked and he stopped running. Still just a pup with plus power and promising upside, but injury concerns are mounting. Don't let that upside blind you into paying for numbers he hasn't yet achieved. But, UP: 30 HR, .300. One day. Maybe.

Yr	Tm	AB	R	HR	RBI	SB	BA	xBA	OBP	SLG	OPS	vL	vR	bb%	ct%	Eye	G	L	F	h%	HctX	PX	xPX	hr/f	Spd	SBO	SB%	#Wk	DOM	DIS	RC/G	RAR	BPV	BPX	R$
10																																			
11	aa	129	12	3	10	6	245		311	372	684			9	80	0.48				29		91			101	24%	75%				3.91		42	93	$1
12	WAS *	607	105	23	61	19	265	272	334	459	793	715	869	9	78	0.47	45	23	33	31	103	122	107	16%	139	16%	73%	24	54%	8%	5.27	9.5	72	180	$23
13	WAS	424	71	20	58	11	274	281	368	486	854	648	947	13	78	0.65	47	20	33	31	114	142	118	18%	95	12%	73%	22	64%	27%	6.18	26.0	81	203	$20
14	WAS	352	41	13	32	2	273	234	344	423	768	765	769	10	70	0.37	44	22	35	35	92	110	115	15%	125	4%	50%	18	44%	39%	5.02	12.5	29	78	$10
1st Half		86	9	1	10	1	291	244	358	419	776	1283	596	9	76	0.43	46	21	33	38	121	94	133	5%	122	11%	33%	5	40%	40%	4.98	3.1	35	95	-$4
2nd Half		266	32	12	22	1	267	230	340	425	765	603	825	10	69	0.35	43	22	35	35	83	116	109	19%	114	1%	100%	13	46%	38%	5.03	9.9	24	65	$15
15	Proj	503	67	21	63	7	271	264	348	458	805	757	825	10	75	0.45	45	21	34	32	104	132	117	16%	113	8%	56%				5.40	24.2	54	143	$20

RYAN BLOOMFIELD

Harrison,Josh

Age: 27 Bats: R Pos: 3B LF RF | Ht: 5' 8" Wt: 200

Health A | PT/Exp C | Consist D | LIMA Plan A | Rand Var -5 | MM 3445

Given hit rate, .315 BA won't last; otherwise, lots to like, including lack of platoon split, steady ct% and rising PX. All but two SB came after June 1—may need to improve success rate to keep opportunities coming. Some minor growth, minus a good chunk of the BA, is a reasonable expectation. And, UP: 20 HR

Yr Tm	AB	R	HR	RBI	SB	BA	xBA	OBP	SLG	OPS	vL	vR	bb%	ct%	Eye	G	L	F	h%	HctX	PX	xPX	hr/f	Spd	SBO	SB%	#Wk	DOM	DIS	RC/G	RAR	BPV	BPX	R$
10 aa	520	59	3	59	15	268		302	352	654			5	89	0.46				29		61			100	18%	66%				3.61		48	104	$13
11 PIT *	421	48	5	34	14	269	257	293	381	674	593	685	3	87	0.26	45	17	38	30	82	78	88	2%	112	22%	67%	16	31%	38%	3.78	-16.1	53	118	$11
12 PIT	249	34	3	16	7	233	241	279	345	624	580	647	4	85	0.27	37	22	41	26	101	66	111	3%	153	20%	70%	27	33%	41%	2.96	-12.4	49	123	$2
13 PIT *	356	48	6	40	16	261	276	294	412	705	981	466	4	85	0.31	47	19	35	29	122	103	122	12%	99	34%	66%	18	33%	28%	3.96	-0.3	62	155	$13
14 PIT	520	77	13	52	18	315	284	347	490	837	856	832	4	84	0.27	37	24	39	35	116	121	117	8%	122	20%	72%	27	52%	15%	6.15	34.6	81	219	$29
1st Half	206	30	5	24	7	306	278	345	466	811	784	818	6	84	0.38	40	23	36	34	139	107	140	8%	115	18%	70%	14	43%	21%	5.76	11.8	71	192	$17
2nd Half	314	47	8	28	11	322	288	348	506	854	900	841	3	84	0.20	35	25	40	36	101	130	103	8%	122	21%	73%	13	62%	8%	6.41	23.1	86	232	$36
15 Proj	550	77	15	54	16	285	284	324	460	784	858	752	4	85	0.29	40	22	38	31	112	119	115	8%	122	18%	70%				5.05	21.3	84	222	$22

Hart,Corey

Age: 33 Bats: R Pos: DH | Ht: 6' 6" Wt: 230

Health F | PT/Exp D | Consist F | LIMA Plan D+ | Rand Var +5 | MM 4213

6-21-.203 in 232 AB at SEA. After promising April, lost six weeks to mid-May hamstring strain, then all of August to bruise on surgically-repaired right knee. xPX suggests once-prodigious power is still there, and hr/f regression could reveal it again. Namesake once sang "Never Surrender." Maybe not yet. But have the white flag ready.

Yr Tm	AB	R	HR	RBI	SB	BA	xBA	OBP	SLG	OPS	vL	vR	bb%	ct%	Eye	G	L	F	h%	HctX	PX	xPX	hr/f	Spd	SBO	SB%	#Wk	DOM	DIS	RC/G	RAR	BPV	BPX	R$
10 MIL	558	91	31	102	7	283	279	340	525	865	973	827	7	75	0.32	38	18	44	33	116	166	160	17%	118	10%	54%	27	74%	19%	6.09	7.2	85	185	$26
11 MIL	492	80	26	63	7	285	283	356	510	866	1057	814	9	77	0.45	45	21	35	32	134	150	156	20%	123	10%	54%	23	83%	13%	6.18	7.6	85	189	$22
12 MIL	562	91	30	83	5	270	267	334	507	841	893	825	7	73	0.29	40	19	41	32	122	161	162	18%	107	4%	100%	27	59%	26%	5.79	8.0	70	175	$22
13																																		
14 SEA *	302	22	8	26	2	203	220	253	331	584	568	603	6	75	0.26	40	17	43	24	98	96	138	8%	92	3%	100%	17	29%	41%	2.70	-13.5	17	46	-$1
1st Half	172	13	6	19	2	206	227	256	351	607	638	650	6	75	0.27	39	17	44	24	117	107	170	10%	84	6%	100%	9	33%	33%	2.94	-6.6	25	68	$2
2nd Half	130	9	3	7	0	199	208	248	305	552	473	524	6	74	0.25	42	17	41	25	68	81	84	4%	104	0%	0%	8	25%	50%	2.40	-7.2	7	19	-$4
15 Proj	391	46	15	44	3	239	246	301	409	710	690	719	7	75	0.30	41	18	41	28	106	126	139	12%	99	5%	73%				4.00	-0.6	36	95	$9

Headley,Chase

Age: 31 Bats: B Pos: 3B | Ht: 6' 2" Wt: 220

Health B | PT/Exp A | Consist C | LIMA Plan B+ | Rand Var +2 | MM 4135

Needed strong 2nd half just to post a 2013 repeat. Optimists will pin hopes for improvement to that 2nd half, xPx, and cite that "maybe it was first time healthy since 2012." Pessimists will see slow leak in Eye, PX, and say "best to pretend 2012 never happened." He's probably not done, but 2012 seems equally out of reach.

Yr Tm	AB	R	HR	RBI	SB	BA	xBA	OBP	SLG	OPS	vL	vR	bb%	ct%	Eye	G	L	F	h%	HctX	PX	xPX	hr/f	Spd	SBO	SB%	#Wk	DOM	DIS	RC/G	RAR	BPV	BPX	R$
10 SD	610	77	11	58	17	264	240	327	375	702	589	753	8	77	0.40	46	18	36	33	87	82	85	6%	106	13%	77%	27	33%	30%	4.26	-9.7	25	54	$16
11 SD	381	43	4	44	13	289	249	374	399	773	891	729	12	76	0.57	46	22	32	37	92	95	101	4%	78	12%	87%	21	43%	19%	5.49	7.3	29	64	$13
12 SD	604	95	31	115	17	286	268	376	498	875	801	906	12	74	0.55	48	19	32	34	117	141	134	21%	84	12%	74%	27	56%	37%	6.64	35.8	61	153	$32
13 SD	520	59	13	50	8	250	253	347	400	747	764	740	11	73	0.47	46	23	31	32	104	119	107	11%	85	8%	67%	25	48%	28%	4.52	8.8	36	90	$11
14 2 TM	470	55	13	49	7	243	251	328	372	700	721	693	10	74	0.42	41	27	32	30	114	99	120	12%	70	8%	70%	26	35%	42%	3.95	3.9	18	49	$10
1st Half	214	21	6	23	3	201	238	289	322	612	586	619	9	73	0.39	41	24	34	25	119	93	129	11%	67	8%	75%	13	38%	46%	2.84	-5.8	9	24	$2
2nd Half	256	34	7	26	4	277	262	360	414	774	800	763	10	75	0.45	40	30	30	35	110	104	113	12%	79	8%	67%	13	31%	38%	5.07	10.1	28	76	$17
15 Proj	532	66	18	61	8	258	261	345	418	763	771	760	11	74	0.45	44	24	32	32	109	123	116	14%	77	8%	67%				4.79	17.2	39	103	$17

Hechavarria,Adeiny

Age: 26 Bats: R Pos: SS | Ht: 5' 11" Wt: 185

Health A | PT/Exp B | Consist C | LIMA Plan B+ | Rand Var -2 | MM 1425

Just maybe, things slowly coming together. More frequent contact, and harder, too. Rising GB% might provide opportunities to use elite speed... to get to first, anyway. If he could figure out the basepaths (55% SB% last two seasons), he might be pretty darned intriguing... UP: 20 SB

Yr Tm	AB	R	HR	RBI	SB	BA	xBA	OBP	SLG	OPS	vL	vR	bb%	ct%	Eye	G	L	F	h%	HctX	PX	xPX	hr/f	Spd	SBO	SB%	#Wk	DOM	DIS	RC/G	RAR	BPV	BPX	R$
10 aa	253	28	2	26	5	239		266	314	580			4	82	0.21				28		54			105	14%	58%				2.71		12	26	$2
11 a/a	572	53	6	41	14	229		259	327	586			4	81	0.21				27		70			117	26%	46%				2.51		23	51	$5
12 TOR *	569	64	6	58	5	264	236	300	360	660	590	677	5	77	0.23	48	21	31	33	81	68	98	7%	126	5%	71%	10	30%	50%	3.72	-6.3	13	33	$11
13 MIA	543	30	3	42	11	227	240	267	298	565	589	555	5	82	0.31	52	20	28	27	77	46	55	2%	158	16%	52%	26	31%	50%	2.49	-17.1	26	65	$3
14 MIA	536	53	1	34	7	276	262	308	356	664	742	645	5	84	0.30	54	22	24	33	100	55	73	1%	175	8%	58%	25	40%	44%	3.80	7.8	43	116	$11
1st Half	268	25	0	17	4	272	247	299	332	631	744	605	4	83	0.24	52	21	26	33	112	46	76	0%	147	11%	50%	12	33%	50%	3.35	0.9	24	65	$9
2nd Half	268	28	1	17	3	280	277	316	381	696	740	685	5	85	0.37	56	23	21	33	87	65	70	2%	181	6%	75%	13	46%	38%	4.28	8.0	58	157	$13
15 Proj	574	52	3	43	10	267	255	301	351	652	673	645	5	83	0.29	52	22	26	32	88	59	70	3%	159	11%	60%				3.59	5.8	21	55	$13

Heisey,Chris

Age: 30 Bats: R Pos: LF | Ht: 6' 1" Wt: 210

Health B | PT/Exp D | Consist A | LIMA Plan D+ | Rand Var +3 | MM 4413

Second half reestablished him as an occasional power source best suited for weak side of platoon. But even "resurgence" featured career-low OPS. Given success rate, helpful handful of SB may be sustainable. But so is sub-.250 BA. An end-gamer without much upside at this point.

Yr Tm	AB	R	HR	RBI	SB	BA	xBA	OBP	SLG	OPS	vL	vR	bb%	ct%	Eye	G	L	F	h%	HctX	PX	xPX	hr/f	Spd	SBO	SB%	#Wk	DOM	DIS	RC/G	RAR	BPV	BPX	R$
10 CIN *	280	37	11	30	2	239	234	292	410	702	546	925	7	70	0.25	35	19	45	30	95	127	135	13%	113	7%	55%	23	39%	43%	3.93	-11.2	31	67	$4
11 CIN	279	44	18	50	6	254	249	309	487	797	553	865	6	72	0.24	32	19	49	29	103	157	129	19%	116	11%	86%	24	54%	33%	5.08	-1.5	63	140	$11
12 CIN	347	44	7	31	6	265	234	315	401	715	827	680	5	77	0.22	37	22	41	33	77	90	71	7%	145	11%	67%	27	44%	41%	4.12	-6.0	34	85	$8
13 CIN	224	29	9	23	3	237	245	279	415	694	810	622	4	77	0.18	40	16	44	27	92	121	109	12%	103	7%	100%	19	42%	47%	3.76	-1.9	46	115	$4
14 CIN	275	34	8	22	9	222	235	265	378	643	627	650	5	77	0.23	35	18	47	26	99	115	92	8%	117	22%	82%	27	37%	41%	3.28	-4.2	46	124	$5
1st Half	134	16	2	10	6	216	235	274	343	617	486	672	6	77	0.29	37	19	44	27	104	103	87	4%	92	23%	100%	14	43%	36%	3.18	-2.3	32	86	$3
2nd Half	141	18	6	12	3	227	237	257	411	668	761	628	4	77	0.18	33	16	51	25	95	127	97	11%	132	20%	60%	13	31%	46%	3.36	-1.7	58	157	$7
15 Proj	240	31	8	23	5	235	240	279	401	680	706	668	5	76	0.21	36	18	46	28	94	120	98	10%	118	15%	79%				3.63	-0.8	45	119	$6

Hernandez,Cesar

Age: 25 Bats: B Pos: 3B | Ht: 5' 10" Wt: 166

Health A | PT/Exp C | Consist B | LIMA Plan F | Rand Var +1 | MM 1320

1-4-.237 with 1 SB in 114 AB at PHI. Another year of not establishing himself as major league hitter. BA even took a serious step back in minors, as did SB success rate. "Great Cesar's Ghost"? More like a fanalytic phantom who will haunt your roster should you be foolish enough to draft him.

Yr Tm	AB	R	HR	RBI	SB	BA	xBA	OBP	SLG	OPS	vL	vR	bb%	ct%	Eye	G	L	F	h%	HctX	PX	xPX	hr/f	Spd	SBO	SB%	#Wk	DOM	DIS	RC/G	RAR	BPV	BPX	R$
10																																		
11																																		
12 a/a	532	53	2	48	18	264		299	361	660			5	84	0.30				31		65			117	27%	53%				3.41		34	85	$12
13 PHI *	522	64	2	38	25	278	246	331	344	674	581	722	7	77	0.34	52	26	22	36	73	49	48	0%	164	23%	68%	7	14%	57%	3.92	3.9	13	33	$19
14 PHI *	373	40	3	22	7	244	247	300	315	615	626	551	7	76	0.34	53	26	21	31	64	54	50	6%	132	15%	44%	16	19%	56%	2.95	-5.0	5	14	$5
1st Half	190	17	3	13	2	274	260	333	364	698	781	571	8	78	0.40	55	27	18	34	66	65	66	10%	115	10%	28%	10	20%	70%	3.92	2.9	16	43	$5
2nd Half	183	23	0	9	5	212	221	266	264	530	348	465	7	75	0.29	48	24	29	28	59	42	9	0%	139	22%	53%	6	17%	33%	2.13	-7.4	-9	-24	$4
15 Proj	65	7	0	4	2	256	246	306	325	631	580	656	7	78	0.33	51	25	23	33	66	54	39	3%	127	20%	56%				3.23	-0.9	1	1	$2

Hernandez,Enrique

Age: 23 Bats: R Pos: CF | Ht: 5' 11" Wt: 170

Health A | PT/Exp D | Consist C | LIMA Plan D+ | Rand Var -2 | MM 2221

3-14-.248 in 121 AB at HOU, MIA. In 42 MLB games, managed to play every position but C, 1B. Breakout in minors (.319/.372/.484) intriguing, ct% solid, PX/xPX a nice base from which to build. Running game needs work. Plenty of time to put things together, but may not happen this year.

Yr Tm	AB	R	HR	RBI	SB	BA	xBA	OBP	SLG	OPS	vL	vR	bb%	ct%	Eye	G	L	F	h%	HctX	PX	xPX	hr/f	Spd	SBO	SB%	#Wk	DOM	DIS	RC/G	RAR	BPV	BPX	R$
10																																		
11																																		
12 aa	81	5	1	2	2	216		245	268	513			4	88	0.31				24		33			100	21%	41%				1.92		16	40	-$2
13 aa	437	42	11	36	4	210		256	328	584			6	82	0.35				23		77			101	8%	55%				2.65		34	85	$1
14 2 TM *	497	55	10	45	4	266	263	314	400	714	581	796	7	86	0.52	38	21	41	29	94	91	115	7%	126	9%	39%	9	56%	22%	4.16	5.4	72	195	$12
1st Half	304	36	6	26	4	287	274	322	411	732			5	90	0.49				31	0	84			120	13%	43%	1	100%	0%	4.43		73	197	$17
2nd Half	193	19	4	18	0	233	257	303	384	687	581	796	9	82	0.54	38	21	41	27	88	103	115	7%	137	2%	0%	8	50%	25%	3.77	0.2	70	189	$3
15 Proj	226	23	5	20	2	246	257	308	380	688	558	731	8	85	0.54	38	21	41	27	79	90	104	7%	126	7%	42%				3.78	-0.6	50	131	$4

KRISTOPHER OLSON

Herrera,Dilson

Age: 21 Bats: R Pos: 2B | Ht: 5' 10" Wt: 150
Health: A | PT/Exp: F | Consist: F | LIMA Plan: D+ | Rand Var: -3 | MM: 4521

3-11-.220 in 59 AB at NYM. Made quick jump to majors after showing more power than expected in Double-A. Likely to be a few short-term bumps in the road, perhaps even some time at AAA, as he works to cut down on the strikeouts. But youth, position, and power/speed combo make him an intriguing keeper.

Yr Tm	AB	R	HR	RBI	SB	BA	xBA	OBP	SLG	OPS	vL	vR	bb%	ct%	Eye	G	L	F	h%	HctX	PX	xPX	hr/f	Spd	SBO	SB%	#Wk	DOM	DIS	RC/G	RAR	BPV	BPX	R$
10																																		
11																																		
12																																		
13																																		
14 NYM *	300	45	11	48	7	281	243	345	460	805	539	747	9	74	0.38	36	19	45	35	54	129	81	16%	144	13%	61%	4	50%	50%	5.46	17.8	64	173	$13
1st Half	45	6	1	8	1	310	232	354	421	775			6	74	0.27				40	0	93	-14		115	22%	26%				4.57		21	57	-$12
2nd Half	255	38	10	40	6	276	247	344	467	811	539	747	9	74	0.40	36	19	45	34	54	136	81	16%	150	12%	74%	4	50%	50%	5.62	16.3	72	195	$18
15 Proj	**225**	**30**	**8**	**32**	**5**	**247**	**249**	**308**	**423**	**731**	**655**	**747**	**8**	**77**	**0.38**	**38**	**19**	**43**	**29**	**84**	**122**	**73**	**11%**	**148**	**12%**	**75%**				**4.39**	**6.7**	**56**	**146**	**$5**

Herrera,Elian

Age: 30 Bats: B Pos: RF | Ht: 5' 10" Wt: 195
Health: A | PT/Exp: D | Consist: B | LIMA Plan: D | Rand Var: -3 | MM: 1401

0-5-.274 with 4 SB in 135 AB at MIL. Defensive versatility kept him on big league roster for much of the season, but he did little to secure a job going forward. Above average speed is all he has to offer offensively, and that's negated by his inability to get on base (2 BB all year). At 30, don't expect further growth.

Yr Tm	AB	R	HR	RBI	SB	BA	xBA	OBP	SLG	OPS	vL	vR	bb%	ct%	Eye	G	L	F	h%	HctX	PX	xPX	hr/f	Spd	SBO	SB%	#Wk	DOM	DIS	RC/G	RAR	BPV	BPX	R$
10 a/a	347	33	1	29	20	193		265	241	506			9	72	0.35				26		39			120	37%	61%				1.90		-24	-52	$2
11 aa	378	47	2	24	22	218		290	286	576			9	67	0.31				32		61			121	34%	62%				2.56		-25	-56	$5
12 LA *	460	55	3	40	10	249	255	300	344	644	754	624	7	76	0.30	56	23	20	32	62	72	34	4%	116	19%	49%	14	14%	57%	3.25	-11.9	11	28	$7
13 LA *	416	43	4	27	10	210	230	261	267	528	667	400	7	76	0.29	67	17	17	27	52	42	-15	0%	102	14%	72%	3	0%	67%	2.26	-16.2	-16	-40	$1
14 MIL *	250	28	0	11	7	256	227	281	332	613	484	671	3	76	0.14	45	21	34	34	81	69	65	0%	130	17%	76%	23	13%	61%	3.21	-0.5	5	14	$3
1st Half	176	17	0	7	4	248	224	272	323	595	300	605	3	75	0.13	40	23	37	33	93	70	86	0%	101	16%	62%	10	10%	80%	2.90	-1.8	-6	-16	$3
2nd Half	74	11	0	4	4	277	234	302	355	657	818	751	3	77	0.16	50	19	31	36	67	66	39	0%	139	20%	100%	13	15%	46%	4.08	1.8	12	32	$4
15 Proj	**133**	**16**	**0**	**8**	**5**	**245**	**231**	**286**	**315**	**601**	**606**	**598**	**5**	**75**	**0.22**	**50**	**22**	**28**	**32**	**72**	**61**	**49**	**2%**	**121**	**20%**	**75%**				**3.03**	**-3.9**	**-4**	**-10**	**$3**

Herrera,Jonathan

Age: 30 Bats: B Pos: SS | Ht: 5' 9" Wt: 180
Health: B | PT/Exp: F | Consist: C | LIMA Plan: D | Rand Var: -2 | MM: 1211

0-9-.233 in 90 AB at BOS. Served in his usual utility role until futility at the plate led to July demotion. Then bone chips in his elbow ended his season in August. Putting the ball in play had been his greatest strength, and with that skill now in question, another 200 AB season looks like a longshot.

Yr Tm	AB	R	HR	RBI	SB	BA	xBA	OBP	SLG	OPS	vL	vR	bb%	ct%	Eye	G	L	F	h%	HctX	PX	xPX	hr/f	Spd	SBO	SB%	#Wk	DOM	DIS	RC/G	RAR	BPV	BPX	R$
10 COL *	444	52	2	31	4	245	233	308	298	606	722	680	8	85	0.59	50	18	32	29	70	36	26	2%	130	7%	40%	17	29%	35%	2.98	-20.4	24	52	$3
11 COL	281	28	3	14	4	242	246	313	299	612	615	610	9	86	0.70	49	23	28	27	74	35	48	5%	121	9%	50%	23	22%	39%	3.02	-9.8	28	62	$1
12 COL *	254	31	4	13	4	248	260	293	340	633	638	677	6	84	0.40	52	22	26	28	59	59	39	6%	113	8%	80%	23	30%	30%	3.40	-5.2	32	80	$2
13 COL	195	16	1	16	3	292	255	336	364	701	564	747	7	88	0.58	39	26	35	33	76	47	51	2%	118	8%	60%	26	46%	35%	4.37	5.2	39	98	$3
14 BOS *	145	18	0	12	2	239	220	287	296	583	595	596	6	74	0.26	56	21	24	32	59	40	45	0%	144	15%	28%	13	15%	69%	2.53	-2.8	-14	-38	$0
1st Half	85	9	0	8	1	224	213	295	282	577	513	618	8	73	0.30	58	18	23	31	62	38	48	0%	141	17%	25%	13	15%	69%	2.27	-2.6	-18	-49	-$1
2nd Half	60	9	0	4	1	262	272	294	316	609	1417	0	4	75	0.18	0	67	33	35	0	44	-14		115	12%	35%				2.96	-0.5	-18	-49	$1
15 Proj	**164**	**19**	**1**	**12**	**2**	**259**	**240**	**310**	**334**	**644**	**585**	**668**	**6**	**80**	**0.34**	**51**	**21**	**28**	**32**	**67**	**53**	**44**	**3%**	**128**	**11%**	**47%**				**3.34**	**0.5**	**7**	**19**	**$3**

Heyward,Jason

Age: 25 Bats: L Pos: RF | Ht: 6' 5" Wt: 245
Health: B | PT/Exp: A | Consist: A | LIMA Plan: B+ | Rand Var: -1 | MM: 3335

This was supposed to be a superstar, 2010's #2 prospect behind Strasburg. But after 5 years, rising contact is about the only sign of growth. Power outage is troubling (3 HR in final 348 PA), and success vs LH in '13 looks like a fluke -- just 4 XBH in 159 PA against them in '14. Upside might still be there, but we're losing patience.

Yr Tm	AB	R	HR	RBI	SB	BA	xBA	OBP	SLG	OPS	vL	vR	bb%	ct%	Eye	G	L	F	h%	HctX	PX	xPX	hr/f	Spd	SBO	SB%	#Wk	DOM	DIS	RC/G	RAR	BPV	BPX	R$
10 ATL	520	83	18	72	11	277	278	393	456	849	755	895	15	75	0.71	55	18	27	34	119	126	100	17%	113	9%	65%	25	60%	28%	6.08	13.9	68	148	$20
11 ATL	396	50	14	42	9	227	251	319	389	708	577	754	11	77	0.55	54	13	33	26	109	112	106	14%	92	10%	82%	24	42%	21%	4.09	-12.7	48	107	$7
12 ATL	587	93	27	82	21	269	261	335	479	814	635	934	9	74	0.38	44	19	37	32	112	138	132	17%	110	19%	72%	27	56%	19%	5.51	6.1	60	150	$26
13 ATL	382	67	14	38	2	254	272	349	427	776	801	766	11	81	0.66	44	21	35	28	99	116	95	13%	102	6%	33%	20	65%	25%	4.75	1.5	71	178	$10
14 ATL	573	74	11	58	20	271	251	351	384	735	477	820	10	83	0.68	45	19	36	31	95	80	80	6%	113	13%	83%	26	50%	12%	4.75	10.8	52	141	$21
1st Half	315	40	8	30	9	248	245	344	378	722	451	812	12	81	0.73	44	17	39	28	92	89	78	8%	115	12%	75%	14	43%	14%	4.34	3.2	57	154	$19
2nd Half	258	34	3	28	11	298	257	360	391	752	510	829	9	85	0.62	47	21	32	34	98	69	83	4%	107	14%	92%	12	58%	8%	5.32	9.4	46	124	$24
15 Proj	**551**	**81**	**17**	**70**	**14**	**275**	**265**	**357**	**430**	**788**	**636**	**848**	**11**	**81**	**0.61**	**46**	**19**	**35**	**31**	**101**	**109**	**94**	**11%**	**103**	**11%**	**75%**				**5.32**	**20.9**	**62**	**163**	**$24**

Hicks,Aaron

Age: 25 Bats: B Pos: CF | Ht: 6' 2" Wt: 190
Health: B | PT/Exp: C | Consist: C | LIMA Plan: C+ | Rand Var: 0 | MM: 2305

1-18-.215 with 4 SB in 186 AB at MIN. 1H derailed by concussion, back, and shoulder injuries. Briefly gave up switch-hitting -- OPS splits, career 145 PX vs LH say maybe he should. Improved plate approach, prospect pedigree provide hope for better days ahead, but ceiling looks much lower than it did two years ago.

Yr Tm	AB	R	HR	RBI	SB	BA	xBA	OBP	SLG	OPS	vL	vR	bb%	ct%	Eye	G	L	F	h%	HctX	PX	xPX	hr/f	Spd	SBO	SB%	#Wk	DOM	DIS	RC/G	RAR	BPV	BPX	R$
10																																		
11																																		
12 aa	472	80	10	49	26	258		347	401	748			12	73	0.51				33		96			141	26%	68%				4.63		37	93	$18
13 MIN *	353	42	8	31	10	192	219	258	328	586	713	566	8	70	0.29	45	17	38	25	89	102	104	11%	146	18%	76%	16	44%	44%	2.68	-17.5	22	55	$2
14 MIN *	406	52	5	41	6	234	240	339	327	666	792	512	14	75	0.64	54	20	26	30	78	80	46	3%	110	11%	45%	16	38%	56%	3.52	-4.5	27	73	$6
1st Half	168	22	2	11	2	189	209	327	254	581	825	482	17	70	0.69	55	19	25	26	60	59	40	5%	111	9%	38%	11	36%	64%	2.48	-7.5	-2	-5	-$4
2nd Half	238	30	3	29	4	266	262	348	379	727	729	585	11	78	0.58	52	22	26	33	111	94	56	0%	115	12%	50%	5	40%	40%	4.38	3.6	47	127	$13
15 Proj	**434**	**57**	**5**	**42**	**11**	**247**	**231**	**332**	**350**	**682**	**824**	**616**	**11**	**73**	**0.47**	**50**	**19**	**31**	**33**	**89**	**85**	**71**	**6%**	**129**	**13%**	**62%**				**3.85**	**-0.2**	**16**	**43**	**$11**

Hill,Aaron

Age: 33 Bats: R Pos: 2B | Ht: 5' 11" Wt: 205
Health: C | PT/Exp: B | Consist: D | LIMA Plan: A | Rand Var: +2 | MM: 3135

Year-long struggles, highlighted by career-worst ct%, bb%, led to reduced PT down the stretch. A .290+ BA is unlikely to return, but HctX, xPX indicate that hr/f correction could lead to rebound in power department. But given bb% and ct% trends, just as likely is... DN: Single-digit HR, part-time role.

Yr Tm	AB	R	HR	RBI	SB	BA	xBA	OBP	SLG	OPS	vL	vR	bb%	ct%	Eye	G	L	F	h%	HctX	PX	xPX	hr/f	Spd	SBO	SB%	#Wk	DOM	DIS	RC/G	RAR	BPV	BPX	R$
10 TOR	528	70	26	68	2	205	245	271	394	665	451	729	7	84	0.48	35	11	54	20	106	115	132	11%	80	4%	50%	25	60%	4%	3.26	-24.0	68	148	$5
11 2 TM	520	61	8	61	21	246	250	299	356	655	678	648	6	86	0.49	37	21	42	27	104	75	85	4%	95	22%	75%	25	44%	24%	3.53	-18.5	48	107	$13
12 ARI	609	93	26	85	14	302	286	360	522	882	839	901	8	86	0.60	34	21	45	32	129	132	145	11%	114	12%	74%	27	63%	7%	6.75	40.5	101	253	$30
13 ARI *	351	49	11	44	1	290	275	345	455	800	911	789	8	85	0.57	39	22	40	31	108	108	120	10%	95	5%	20%	18	67%	22%	5.39	17.2	73	183	$12
14 ARI	501	52	10	60	4	244	252	287	367	654	680	645	5	82	0.30	34	25	41	28	114	89	116	6%	86	6%	57%	27	41%	30%	3.45	0.9	36	97	$9
1st Half	302	24	6	40	1	248	251	287	374	661	766	637	5	81	0.26	35	24	42	29	114	92	122	6%	89	3%	50%	15	27%	27%	3.57	1.5	35	95	$10
2nd Half	199	28	4	20	3	236	255	286	357	642	607	660	6	83	0.38	34	26	40	27	113	86	106	6%	84	11%	60%	12	58%	33%	3.29	-0.6	40	108	$7
15 Proj	**523**	**61**	**14**	**63**	**4**	**261**	**264**	**314**	**412**	**726**	**733**	**724**	**7**	**84**	**0.43**	**36**	**22**	**42**	**29**	**114**	**105**	**119**	**8%**	**91**	**7%**	**47%**				**4.29**	**13.7**	**55**	**144**	**$15**

Hoes,LJ

Age: 25 Bats: R Pos: LF | Ht: 6' 0" Wt: 200
Health: A | PT/Exp: C | Consist: C | LIMA Plan: D | Rand Var: +2 | MM: 1221

3-11-.172 in 136 AB at HOU. Not as bad as it appears on the surface, as 20% hit rate in majors dragged down his average. Minor league track record suggests BA/OBP will improve, perhaps significantly. Other upside appears limited, as power is lacking, and horrible SB% will put a cap on much success on the bases.

Yr Tm	AB	R	HR	RBI	SB	BA	xBA	OBP	SLG	OPS	vL	vR	bb%	ct%	Eye	G	L	F	h%	HctX	PX	xPX	hr/f	Spd	SBO	SB%	#Wk	DOM	DIS	RC/G	RAR	BPV	BPX	R$
10																																		
11 aa	344	41	6	48	14	292		361	394	754			10	83	0.64				34		72			87	19%	65%				4.96		37	82	$14
12 BAL *	514	67	5	45	17	267	275	338	357	695	0	0	10	84	0.68	100	0	0	31	0	59	-11	0%	124	19%	57%	1	0%	0%	3.98	-9.0	42	105	$14
13 2 AL *	535	74	4	42	13	277	268	349	363	711	669	710	10	82	0.61	62	20	18	33	72	66	35	4%	110	13%	59%	9	56%	44%	4.32	5.4	35	88	$16
14 HOU *	250	27	4	22	4	210	228	272	304	576	718	275	8	73	0.32	54	19	27	27	60	76	49	12%	74	14%	43%	17	29%	53%	2.50	-9.3	-5	-14	$0
1st Half	177	17	3	17	3	231	240	297	324	621	817	271	9	75	0.38	58	20	22	29	65	76	52	14%	74	16%	38%	10	30%	60%	2.92	-4.5	3	8	$2
2nd Half	73	10	2	5	1	158	199	210	254	465	500	283	6	68	0.21	47	17	37	20	49	76	44	9%	95	5%	100%	7	29%	43%	1.65	-5.0	-23	-62	-$4
15 Proj	**160**	**20**	**3**	**14**	**4**	**253**	**247**	**313**	**351**	**664**	**751**	**587**	**9**	**78**	**0.43**	**55**	**19**	**26**	**31**	**62**	**75**	**42**	**8%**	**94**	**13%**	**59%**				**3.67**	**-0.3**	**17**	**44**	**$4**

BRIAN RUDD

Holaday,Bryan

Age: 27 Bats: R Pos: CA	Health A	LIMA Plan F	
Ht: 6' 0" Wt: 205	PT/Exp F	Rand Var -2	
	Consist A	MM 1201	

When it comes to cherry-picking a catcher for your #2 slot, the mantra is, "at first, do no harm." So, what are the positives we can take out of this table of data? (Scan, scan, scan... 15 minutes later...) Well... his RAR is improving, but that's due to him playing less. So his biggest contribution is that he doesn't play much.

Yr Tm	AB	R	HR	RBI	SB	BA	xBA	OBP	SLG	OPS	vL	vR	bb%	ct%	Eye	G	L	F	h%	HctX	PX	xPX	hr/f	Spd	SBO	SB%	#Wk	DOM	DIS	RC/G	RAR	BPV	BPX	R$
10																																		
11 aa	330	27	5	32	5	207		252	301	553			6	75	0.24				26		76			80	8%	80%				2.46		-1	-2	-$1
12 DET *	262	17	2	19	2	208	282	254	275	530	1250	250	6	81	0.33	60	30	10	25	97	50	39	0%	84	3%	100%	4	25%	50%	2.28	-15.0	4	10	-$3
13 DET *	315	30	4	21	0	228	241	265	325	590	938	690	5	79	0.24	38	25	38	28	72	75	69	11%	111	2%	0%	9	33%	56%	2.79	-8.8	19	48	-$1
14 DET	156	14	0	15	1	231	211	266	276	542	379	686	5	76	0.22	49	20	31	30	61	40	44	0%	115	5%	50%	24	13%	79%	2.41	-4.3	-16	-43	-$1
1st Half	72	9	0	7	1	306	224	338	347	685	539	844	5	76	0.24	48	26	26	40	53	29	26	0%	144	8%	50%	13	15%	77%	4.20	1.6	-16	-43	$1
2nd Half	84	5	0	8	0	167	191	207	214	421	211	575	5	76	0.20	50	15	35	22	67	49	57	0%	84	0%	0%	11	9%	82%	1.34	-5.6	-20	-54	-$3
15 Proj	133	11	1	11	1	220	223	259	291	550	380	698	5	77	0.24	49	19	32	28	61	59	45	3%	104	4%	58%				2.46	-3.8	-13	-34	-$2

Holliday,Matt

Age: 35 Bats: R Pos: LF	Health A	LIMA Plan B+	
Ht: 6' 4" Wt: 250	PT/Exp A	Rand Var +1	
	Consist B	MM 4145	

For second straight year, got off to slow start before finishing with a flourish. 2nd half hr/f returned to typical level, and all plate skills remain intact. Career-worst numbers vs RH lasted all year though, and could be sign of decline. Most folks will pay for a near-repeat, but those risk-averse heed caution... DN: 15 HR, .260

Yr Tm	AB	R	HR	RBI	SB	BA	xBA	OBP	SLG	OPS	vL	vR	bb%	ct%	Eye	G	L	F	h%	HctX	PX	xPX	hr/f	Spd	SBO	SB%	#Wk	DOM	DIS	RC/G	RAR	BPV	BPX	R$
10 STL	596	95	28	103	9	312	298	390	532	922	982	900	10	84	0.74	42	17	41	33	129	142	133	14%	77	8%	64%	27	74%	4%	7.44	35.3	97	211	$32
11 STL	446	83	22	75	2	296	298	388	525	912	883	918	12	79	0.65	46	21	34	33	131	160	128	18%	73	2%	67%	25	64%	12%	7.18	23.6	92	204	$22
12 STL	599	95	27	102	4	295	270	379	497	877	1021	827	11	78	0.57	46	19	35	34	135	132	145	16%	90	4%	50%	27	52%	22%	6.61	31.4	69	173	$27
13 STL	519	103	22	94	6	299	286	388	487	875	799	898	12	83	0.80	46	21	34	32	133	121	126	15%	82	4%	86%	25	68%	0%	6.79	39.1	81	203	$28
14 STL	574	83	20	90	4	272	268	370	441	811	1004	751	11	83	0.74	46	17	38	30	140	119	142	11%	65	3%	80%	26	77%	12%	5.49	27.9	70	189	$22
1st Half	299	40	5	39	2	264	254	369	385	754	796	738	13	83	0.84	47	18	36	30	138	94	125	6%	62	3%	67%	14	64%	21%	4.74	8.7	53	143	$15
2nd Half	275	43	15	51	2	280	282	371	502	873	1282	764	10	82	0.63	44	15	40	29	142	147	161	16%	72	3%	100%	12	92%	0%	6.32	20.0	90	243	$30
15 Proj	559	89	21	90	3	270	275	364	448	812	930	775	11	82	0.71	46	18	36	30	137	125	140	13%	75	3%	64%				5.49	28.1	70	184	$22

Holt,Brock

Age: 27 Bats: L Pos: 3B RF	Health A	LIMA Plan D+	
Ht: 5' 10" Wt: 185	PT/Exp C	Rand Var -2	
	Consist F	MM 1423	

4-29-.281 with 12 SB in 449 AB at BOS. H% fueled hot start and led to everyday work, but regression won out. Hit .207/.267/.257 in last 195 PA before concussion ended season early. Defensive versatility plus speed make him a useful utility player, but lack of other skills may keep him from becoming anything more than that.

Yr Tm	AB	R	HR	RBI	SB	BA	xBA	OBP	SLG	OPS	vL	vR	bb%	ct%	Eye	G	L	F	h%	HctX	PX	xPX	hr/f	Spd	SBO	SB%	#Wk	DOM	DIS	RC/G	RAR	BPV	BPX	R$
10																																		
11 aa	511	50	1	32	14	257		310	341	651			7	83	0.44				31		64			118	19%	57%				3.44		33	73	$8
12 PIT *	542	60	2	44	13	305	275	356	396	751	517	732	7	85	0.54	62	19	19	35	48	64	22	0%	140	17%	47%	6	17%	67%	4.77	2.4	52	130	$18
13 BOS *	350	35	2	29	7	220	221	279	261	540	384	536	8	81	0.44	57	17	26	26	82	31	33	0%	82	11%	67%	8	13%	50%	2.37	-17.1	-7	-18	$1
14 BOS *	557	84	5	34	17	280	272	327	384	711	763	682	7	80	0.35	50	26	23	34	97	80	66	5%	141	13%	84%	19	42%	26%	4.53	13.6	41	111	$19
1st Half	308	44	3	22	10	302	281	346	425	771	902	738	6	82	0.37	48	25	27	36	117	97	86	5%	139	15%	83%	10	50%	10%	5.44	14.9	61	165	$23
2nd Half	249	40	2	12	7	253	259	305	333	638	635	640	7	78	0.32	52	28	20	32	81	59	49	5%	142	12%	88%	9	33%	44%	3.55	-1.1	15	41	$15
15 Proj	260	33	2	18	7	263	259	309	345	654	670	648	7	81	0.40	54	22	23	32	84	64	47	3%	121	13%	71%				3.73	0.2	23	62	$7

Hosmer,Eric

Age: 25 Bats: L Pos: 1B	Health B	LIMA Plan B+	
Ht: 6' 4" Wt: 225	PT/Exp A	Rand Var -2	
	Consist D	MM 3245	

Strong finish to 2013 didn't carry over, as he hit just 1 HR in first 253 AB. Missed August with stress fracture in hand; despite that, rediscovered LD stroke and flashed eye-opening power metrics in 2nd half. Age is on his side, but until we see more FB, a return to .300 BA looks like a better bet than 20 HR.

Yr Tm	AB	R	HR	RBI	SB	BA	xBA	OBP	SLG	OPS	vL	vR	bb%	ct%	Eye	G	L	F	h%	HctX	PX	xPX	hr/f	Spd	SBO	SB%	#Wk	DOM	DIS	RC/G	RAR	BPV	BPX	R$
10 aa	195	30	9	27	2	282		321	514	835			5	85	0.40				29		142			117	8%	68%				5.79		103	224	$7
11 KC *	621	82	21	89	13	309	279	359	471	830	585	886	7	84	0.49	50	19	32	34	115	104	106	13%	88	10%	73%	22	59%	23%	6.18	9.2	62	138	$30
12 KC	535	65	14	60	16	232	262	304	359	663	591	700	9	82	0.59	54	18	28	26	121	80	95	11%	87	12%	94%	26	54%	27%	3.76	-24.6	40	100	$11
13 KC	623	86	17	79	11	302	287	353	448	801	797	803	8	84	0.51	53	22	25	34	128	96	105	13%	102	8%	73%	26	50%	8%	5.77	20.1	60	150	$28
14 KC	503	54	9	58	4	270	259	318	398	716	676	732	7	82	0.38	51	17	32	32	117	99	100	7%	81	5%	67%	23	35%	26%	4.39	3.6	45	122	$13
1st Half	338	36	4	35	2	246	239	288	343	631	567	660	6	82	0.33	53	15	32	29	111	79	81	4%	79	4%	67%	14	29%	29%	3.32	-8.5	28	76	$13
2nd Half	165	18	5	23	2	321	292	379	509	888	949	867	8	81	0.47	47	22	32	38	130	140	139	12%	91	6%	67%	9	44%	22%	7.15	13.2	81	219	$14
15 Proj	557	67	15	70	9	285	279	339	436	775	736	793	8	82	0.46	51	20	29	32	123	109	109	11%	89	7%	76%				5.27	17.4	58	153	$22

Howard,Ryan

Age: 35 Bats: L Pos: 1B	Health F	LIMA Plan C+	
Ht: 6' 4" Wt: 250	PT/Exp C	Rand Var +2	
	Consist C	MM 4015	

Not a misprint: OPS was more than 100 points higher vs. LH than vs RH, but he faced LHers in just 28% of PA. If he can't hit righties, then AB may suffer, though there's $60 million reasons to think otherwise. xPX says power is still there, but HctX isn't as optimistic. Health grade urges caution, too. That's a lot of red flags.

Yr Tm	AB	R	HR	RBI	SB	BA	xBA	OBP	SLG	OPS	vL	vR	bb%	ct%	Eye	G	L	F	h%	HctX	PX	xPX	hr/f	Spd	SBO	SB%	#Wk	DOM	DIS	RC/G	RAR	BPV	BPX	R$
10 PHI	550	87	31	108	1	276	273	353	505	859	826	876	10	71	0.38	40	23	37	33	118	157	153	21%	101	1%	50%	26	46%	31%	6.14	-1.8	63	137	$23
11 PHI	557	81	33	116	1	253	264	346	488	835	634	921	12	69	0.44	40	21	39	31	126	175	175	22%	49	1%	100%	27	48%	41%	5.71	-8.9	57	127	$21
12 PHI	260	28	14	56	0	219	237	295	423	718	604	784	9	62	0.25	43	26	31	29	98	159	143	27%	50	0%	0%	13	38%	54%	3.98	-11.5	9	23	$4
13 PHI	286	34	11	43	0	266	251	319	465	784	539	878	7	67	0.24	39	24	38	36	120	163	160	15%	82	0%	0%	14	36%	43%	5.17	4.8	39	98	$7
14 PHI	569	65	23	95	0	223	225	310	380	690	770	658	11	67	0.35	41	22	37	29	97	123	154	16%	55	0%	0%	27	33%	44%	3.80	-6.6	5	14	$11
1st Half	307	38	14	51	0	238	230	312	410	722	657	744	10	67	0.33	39	22	39	31	96	132	159	17%	73	0%	0%	14	36%	36%	4.28	1.0	17	46	$15
2nd Half	262	27	9	44	0	206	219	308	344	652	869	546	11	66	0.38	43	23	35	27	98	112	147	15%	43	0%	0%	13	31%	54%	3.28	-7.2	-9	-24	$7
15 Proj	412	48	18	71	0	235	240	313	414	727	675	749	10	66	0.31	41	23	36	31	106	146	154	18%	60	0%	67%				4.25	1.1	15	39	$11

Hundley,Nick

Age: 31 Bats: R Pos: CA	Health C	LIMA Plan D	
Ht: 6' 1" Wt: 200	PT/Exp D	Rand Var -3	
	Consist C	MM 3101	

Escaping PETCO for Camden Yards sounded good in theory, but other than slight bump in 2nd half xPX, these are all skills we've seen before. Ongoing OBP issues, futility vs LH led to reduced role following May trade, and deservedly so. Decent pop isn't enough to overcome the other flaws in his game.

Yr Tm	AB	R	HR	RBI	SB	BA	xBA	OBP	SLG	OPS	vL	vR	bb%	ct%	Eye	G	L	F	h%	HctX	PX	xPX	hr/f	Spd	SBO	SB%	#Wk	DOM	DIS	RC/G	RAR	BPV	BPX	R$
10 SD	273	33	8	43	0	249	259	308	418	726	830	692	8	76	0.38	41	19	40	30	102	124	116	10%	107	8%	0%	26	38%	31%	4.09	-0.9	53	115	$4
11 SD *	315	36	10	32	1	272	249	329	449	779	768	839	8	71	0.30	41	21	38	35	99	132	107	12%	145	2%	50%	19	47%	32%	5.14	6.8	52	116	$7
12 SD *	246	16	3	26	0	153	193	209	235	444	306	568	7	72	0.26	39	18	43	20	98	59	100	5%	104	10%	0%	14	14%	79%	1.34	-24.5	-16	-40	-$7
13 SD	373	35	13	44	1	233	240	290	389	679	553	721	7	74	0.27	43	20	37	28	86	115	99	13%	90	1%	100%	27	37%	48%	3.68	-0.4	29	73	$5
14 2 TM	218	18	6	22	1	243	219	273	358	631	570	641	4	71	0.16	37	23	40	32	98	89	109	10%	80	2%	100%	27	22%	52%	3.35	0.2	-9	-24	$2
1st Half	107	6	2	9	0	252	209	274	346	620	340	684	4	73	0.14	40	21	39	33	94	76	92	6%	81	0%	0%	14	36%	50%	3.29	-0.3	-14	-38	$0
2nd Half	111	12	4	13	1	234	223	271	369	641	899	602	5	69	0.18	35	24	41	30	103	102	126	13%	88	4%	100%	13	8%	54%	3.41	0.1	-2	-5	$5
15 Proj	205	18	6	23	1	228	226	273	358	631	533	658	6	72	0.22	39	21	40	29	96	100	107	10%	93	3%	50%				3.18	-1.3	-5	-13	$3

Hunter,Torii

Age: 39 Bats: R Pos: RF	Health A	LIMA Plan B	
Ht: 6' 2" Wt: 225	PT/Exp A	Rand Var +1	
	Consist B	MM 3145	

Numbers were nearly identical to previous two seasons. However, at his age, career-best ct% seems unlikely to repeat. And given that he's refused to take BB since becoming a Tiger, OBP could dip even further. Just 2 HR, 59 xPX in Aug-Sept. Gravity gets stronger as you approach 40, so... DN: 12 HR, .260

Yr Tm	AB	R	HR	RBI	SB	BA	xBA	OBP	SLG	OPS	vL	vR	bb%	ct%	Eye	G	L	F	h%	HctX	PX	xPX	hr/f	Spd	SBO	SB%	#Wk	DOM	DIS	RC/G	RAR	BPV	BPX	R$
10 LAA	573	76	23	90	9	281	283	354	464	819	775	838	10	82	0.58	48	18	34	31	118	123	102	15%	77	13%	43%	27	52%	15%	5.40	3.8	69	150	$22
11 LAA	580	80	23	82	5	262	264	336	429	765	886	715	10	78	0.50	46	21	33	30	128	111	136	15%	91	7%	42%	27	41%	19%	4.76	-6.9	51	113	$18
12 LAA	534	81	16	92	9	313	257	365	451	817	868	798	7	75	0.29	52	23	25	39	108	96	88	16%	84	6%	90%	25	36%	52%	6.08	17.6	18	45	$26
13 DET	606	90	17	84	3	304	276	334	465	800	829	788	4	81	0.23	49	20	31	35	104	110	99	11%	107	3%	60%	26	50%	19%	5.61	22.1	56	140	$26
14 DET	549	71	17	83	4	286	284	319	446	765	799	753	4	84	0.26	48	21	31	32	115	111	97	12%	78	5%	57%	27	44%	15%	4.94	16.1	57	154	$22
1st Half	254	32	9	38	2	252	277	277	413	691	649	706	3	85	0.21	45	20	35	27	118	109	113	12%	67	6%	67%	14	43%	7%	3.84	-1.2	54	146	$14
2nd Half	295	39	8	45	2	315	290	354	475	829	932	792	5	83	0.30	50	23	27	36	113	112	83	12%	87	5%	50%	13	46%	23%	6.03	16.2	60	162	$28
15 Proj	538	74	15	81	3	282	275	323	434	757	794	742	5	81	0.29	49	21	30	32	112	109	97	12%	87	4%	57%				4.86	13.0	46	120	$21

BRIAN RUDD

Iannetta,Chris

Age: 32	Bats: R	Pos: CA	Health: B	LIMA Plan: D+
Ht: 6' 0"	Wt: 230		PT/Exp: D	Rand Var: -2
			Consist: A	MM: 4103

Decent #2 CA target, particularly in OBP leagues, but a few reasons to be wary: Highest BA since 2008 (in COL), and needed career-best h% to get it; mediocre numbers vs RHP puts playing time at risk. FB%, hr/f dip led to just 2 HR in final 213 AB but that should rebound.

Yr Tm	AB	R	HR	RBI	SB	BA	xBA	OBP	SLG	OPS	vL	vR	bb%	ct%	Eye	G	L	F	h%	HctX	PX	xPX	hr/f	Spd	SBO	SB%	#Wk	DOM	DIS	RC/G	RAR	BPV	BPX	R$
10 COL *	251	30	12	39	1	217	251	314	418	732	737	683	12	76	0.60	41	13	45	24	97	134	126	14%	75	2%	100%	22	45%	36%	4.30	-0.5	61	133	$3
11 COL	345	51	14	55	6	238	245	370	414	785	990	718	17	74	0.79	35	20	44	28	96	126	104	12%	73	8%	67%	27	48%	30%	5.04	8.6	55	122	$9
12 LAA *	243	29	9	27	1	235	228	321	385	706	636	756	11	71	0.44	44	20	36	29	98	100	115	16%	85	6%	25%	16	31%	44%	3.94	-1.4	16	40	$3
13 LAA	325	40	11	39	0	225	218	358	372	731	835	663	17	69	0.68	37	19	43	29	95	115	126	11%	70	1%	0%	27	41%	56%	4.34	6.2	27	68	$3
14 LAA	306	41	7	43	3	252	233	373	392	765	880	697	15	70	0.59	38	20	41	34	93	125	100	8%	73	3%	100%	26	46%	35%	4.93	14.4	35	95	$7
1st Half	150	21	5	21	3	253	238	365	413	779	911	666	13	71	0.53	32	22	45	32	100	130	115	10%	71	6%	100%	14	43%	29%	5.11	7.5	39	105	$8
2nd Half	156	20	2	22	0	250	224	379	372	751	829	719	17	69	0.65	44	19	38	35	86	120	86	5%	76	0%	0%	12	50%	42%	4.73	6.1	31	84	$6
15 Proj	**327**	**42**	**9**	**43**	**2**	**240**	**231**	**360**	**385**	**746**	**833**	**701**	**15**	**71**	**0.61**	**39**	**20**	**41**	**31**	**94**	**122**	**109**	**10%**	**72**	**3%**	**65%**				**4.57**	**11.5**	**26**	**69**	**$5**

Ibanez,Raul

Age: 43	Bats: L	Pos: DH LF	Health: A	LIMA Plan: D
Ht: 6' 2"	Wt: 225		PT/Exp: C	Rand Var: +5
			Consist: D	MM: 3111

After hitting 3 HR in first 10 games, he "hit" .159/.258/.256 in 236 PA the rest of the way. He was just 1-for-41 vs LHP on the year, which is legitimately hard to accomplish. With HctX, xPX, and hr/f all collapsing, it's looking like it may be time to hang 'em up.

Yr Tm	AB	R	HR	RBI	SB	BA	xBA	OBP	SLG	OPS	vL	vR	bb%	ct%	Eye	G	L	F	h%	HctX	PX	xPX	hr/f	Spd	SBO	SB%	#Wk	DOM	DIS	RC/G	RAR	BPV	BPX	R$
10 PHI	561	75	16	83	4	275	273	349	444	793	728	822	11	81	0.63	45	18	37	32	118	116	121	9%	91	4%	57%	27	63%	26%	5.44	-6.3	67	146	$17
11 PHI	535	65	20	84	2	245	270	289	419	707	585	747	6	80	0.31	46	19	35	27	112	119	117	13%	64	2%	100%	27	48%	33%	4.10	-27.4	49	109	$12
12 NYY	384	50	19	62	3	240	278	308	453	761	492	812	8	83	0.52	41	19	39	24	114	126	112	15%	79	3%	100%	27	63%	15%	4.65	-2.7	73	183	$9
13 SEA	454	54	29	65	0	242	265	306	487	793	802	790	8	72	0.33	36	21	43	27	103	168	144	21%	68	0%	0%	27	44%	33%	5.02	7.0	61	153	$13
14 2 AL	246	23	5	26	3	167	231	264	285	549	157	627	12	76	0.56	46	19	35	20	79	83	65	8%	93	9%	60%	23	30%	48%	2.28	-14.3	24	65	-$3
1st Half	166	16	3	21	3	157	222	258	265	523	190	593	12	74	0.53	48	17	34	19	75	78	53	7%	97	13%	60%	13	31%	46%	2.04	-11.2	14	38	-$2
2nd Half	80	7	2	5	0	188	250	278	325	603	77	694	11	80	0.63	41	22	38	21	87	92	87	8%	82	0%	0%	10	30%	50%	2.83	-3.1	42	114	-$5
15 Proj	**126**	**14**	**3**	**15**	**1**	**210**	**245**	**289**	**352**	**641**	**457**	**687**	**10**	**77**	**0.48**	**43**	**20**	**37**	**25**	**95**	**101**	**101**	**10%**	**80**	**3%**	**67%**				**3.27**	**-3.1**	**33**	**87**	**$1**

Iglesias,Jose

Age: 25	Bats: R	Pos: SS	Health: F	LIMA Plan: D+
Ht: 5' 11"	Wt: 185		PT/Exp: F	Rand Var: 0
			Consist: C	MM: 1415

Spring shin splints were later determined to be stress fractures in both legs, which cost him the entire 2014 season. Potential for double-digit SB looked like clearest path to fantasy relevance, but we'll have to see how his legs recover. Even still, the need to figure out how to get on base remains the primary challenge.

Yr Tm	AB	R	HR	RBI	SB	BA	xBA	OBP	SLG	OPS	vL	vR	bb%	ct%	Eye	G	L	F	h%	HctX	PX	xPX	hr/f	Spd	SBO	SB%	#Wk	DOM	DIS	RC/G	RAR	BPV	BPX	R$
10 aa	221	22	0	10	4	267		287	335	622			3	77	0.12				35		58			126	11%	64%				3.28		0	0	$2
11 BOS *	363	33	1	27	10	228	285	264	262	526	2000	400	5	83	0.28	75	25	0	27	105	28	2	0%	93	16%	71%	4	0%	50%	2.29	-21.0	-7	-16	$2
12 BOS *	421	44	2	22	11	235	233	281	279	560	536	284	6	85	0.42	59	16	25	27	55	32	23	8%	110	13%	78%	7	0%	43%	2.65	-15.9	11	28	$3
13 2 AL *	469	52	6	41	9	272	250	304	357	661	769	716	4	83	0.27	56	18	26	32	68	59	37	4%	135	11%	63%	22	23%	32%	3.71	3.9	31	78	$12
14																																		
1st Half																																		
2nd Half																																		
15 Proj	**468**	**47**	**6**	**32**	**11**	**248**	**244**	**306**	**324**	**630**	**693**	**590**	**5**	**82**	**0.27**	**57**	**17**	**26**	**29**	**63**	**56**	**31**	**6%**	**128**	**13%**	**70%**				**3.08**	**-2.2**	**10**	**27**	**$10**

Inciarte,Ender

Age: 24	Bats: L	Pos: CF LF	Health: A	LIMA Plan: C
Ht: 5' 10"	Wt: 165		PT/Exp: D	Rand Var: 0
			Consist: A	MM: 1533

4-27-.278 with 19 SB in 418 AB at ARI. After .450 OPS in first 99 PA, hit .299/.344/.398 rest of the way, enabling him to put speed to use. Isn't considered much of a prospect, and still needs to prove himself, but high ct%, GB%, and Spd provide strong BA floor. If he wins full-time job... UP: 35 SB

Yr Tm	AB	R	HR	RBI	SB	BA	xBA	OBP	SLG	OPS	vL	vR	bb%	ct%	Eye	G	L	F	h%	HctX	PX	xPX	hr/f	Spd	SBO	SB%	#Wk	DOM	DIS	RC/G	RAR	BPV	BPX	R$
10																																		
11																																		
12																																		
13 aa	473	59	4	21	37	264		298	341	639			5	89	0.45				29		50			136	37%	81%				3.64		49	123	$20
14 ARI *	527	68	5	35	23	273	271	314	358	672	646	691	6	85	0.40	52	24	25	31	87	60	51	5%	134	20%	81%	23	43%	22%	4.03	-1.0	43	116	$19
1st Half	226	30	1	14	10	248	239	284	308	592	619	508	5	83	0.29	56	17	27	29	72	43	41	0%	132	24%	76%	10	30%	30%	2.99	-6.9	18	49	$9
2nd Half	301	38	4	21	13	292	290	336	395	732	654	771	6	87	0.51	50	26	24	33	94	72	55	7%	130	17%	87%	13	54%	15%	4.94	7.9	59	159	$26
15 Proj	**266**	**34**	**3**	**15**	**14**	**270**	**265**	**308**	**351**	**659**	**648**	**664**	**5**	**87**	**0.42**	**52**	**21**	**27**	**30**	**85**	**57**	**49**	**4%**	**135**	**25%**	**80%**				**3.86**	**0.0**	**43**	**113**	**$10**

Infante,Omar

Age: 33	Bats: R	Pos: 2B	Health: C	LIMA Plan: A
Ht: 5' 11"	Wt: 195		PT/Exp: B	Rand Var: +1
			Consist: D	MM: 1335

BA correction was expected, but not quite to this extent. Lingering shoulder injury, 24% hit rate vs LH likely played some role in his struggles. While that means we can expect mild rebounds in BA and power, Spd trend and age suggest not to bank on more than a handful of SB.

Yr Tm	AB	R	HR	RBI	SB	BA	xBA	OBP	SLG	OPS	vL	vR	bb%	ct%	Eye	G	L	F	h%	HctX	PX	xPX	hr/f	Spd	SBO	SB%	#Wk	DOM	DIS	RC/G	RAR	BPV	BPX	R$
10 ATL	471	65	8	47	7	321	255	359	416	775	665	827	6	87	0.47	47	19	34	36	90	59	65	6%	148	8%	54%	27	41%	26%	5.44	10.7	53	115	$20
11 FLA	579	55	7	49	4	276	263	315	382	696	729	685	6	88	0.51	42	22	36	30	97	66	64	4%	145	4%	67%	26	50%	12%	4.23	-5.9	63	140	$12
12 2 TM	554	69	12	53	17	274	267	300	419	719	872	656	4	88	0.32	41	20	39	29	98	86	97	6%	130	16%	85%	27	52%	22%	4.49	5.1	70	175	$18
13 DET	453	54	10	51	5	318	278	345	450	795	831	778	4	90	0.45	38	24	38	34	100	82	76	6%	120	6%	71%	22	59%	9%	5.81	25.3	73	183	$19
14 KC	528	50	6	66	9	252	247	295	337	632	584	649	6	87	0.49	38	23	39	28	94	59	76	3%	108	9%	75%	25	24%	20%	3.41	0.2	42	114	$11
1st Half	247	28	5	41	3	251	248	297	364	662	576	696	6	87	0.55	35	22	42	27	109	68	92	5%	120	6%	75%	12	25%	8%	3.71	2.3	55	149	$13
2nd Half	281	22	1	25	6	253	246	292	313	606	592	610	5	87	0.43	40	23	36	29	81	51	62	1%	93	11%	75%	13	23%	31%	3.14	-2.1	29	78	$10
15 Proj	**519**	**55**	**10**	**58**	**8**	**276**	**263**	**310**	**391**	**702**	**725**	**692**	**5**	**88**	**0.43**	**39**	**22**	**38**	**30**	**95**	**76**	**77**	**5%**	**116**	**8%**	**73%**				**4.28**	**13.2**	**52**	**138**	**$17**

Izturis,Maicer

Age: 34	Bats: B	Pos: 2B	Health: F	LIMA Plan: D+
Ht: 5' 8"	Wt: 155		PT/Exp: F	Rand Var: -5
			Consist: B	MM: 1321

Tore knee ligament in April and never made it back. Health, age, and '13 numbers indicate speed is a major question mark, and he doesn't have multi-positional eligibility anymore. That means ct% may be all he has going for him, but without SOME power, BA/xBA history shows the parade of easily fielded balls.

Yr Tm	AB	R	HR	RBI	SB	BA	xBA	OBP	SLG	OPS	vL	vR	bb%	ct%	Eye	G	L	F	h%	HctX	PX	xPX	hr/f	Spd	SBO	SB%	#Wk	DOM	DIS	RC/G	RAR	BPV	BPX	R$
10 LAA	212	27	3	27	7	250	261	321	363	684	697	680	9	87	0.78	42	18	40	27	89	78	86	4%	114	18%	70%	15	60%	20%	3.88	-4.5	66	143	$4
11 LAA	449	51	5	38	9	276	267	334	388	722	780	687	7	86	0.51	39	23	38	31	80	87	71	3%	92	13%	60%	27	44%	30%	4.32	-3.5	55	122	$11
12 LAA	289	35	2	20	17	256	252	320	315	634	503	682	8	87	0.66	47	23	30	29	72	42	39	3%	107	22%	89%	26	23%	31%	3.64	-4.4	31	78	$7
13 TOR	365	33	5	32	1	236	261	288	310	597	606	594	7	90	0.71	52	22	26	25	90	48	45	6%	97	6%	17%	21	38%	10%	2.81	-10.2	42	105	$2
14 TOR	35	3	0	1	1	286	207	324	314	639	786	542	5	89	0.50	61	10	29	32	72	25	18	0%	116	9%	100%	3	33%	67%	3.82	0.4	22	59	-$1
1st Half	35	3	0	1	1	286	207	324	314	639	786	542	5	89	0.50	61	10	29	32	72	25	18	0%	116	9%	100%	3	33%	67%	3.82	0.4	22	59	-$1
2nd Half																																		
15 Proj	**207**	**23**	**2**	**18**	**5**	**256**	**258**	**314**	**334**	**648**	**687**	**629**	**7**	**87**	**0.63**	**49**	**20**	**31**	**29**	**79**	**62**	**43**	**3%**	**107**	**13%**	**67%**				**3.51**	**0.7**	**36**	**94**	**$5**

Jackson,Austin

Age: 28	Bats: R	Pos: CF	Health: B	LIMA Plan: B
Ht: 6' 1"	Wt: 185		PT/Exp: A	Rand Var: 0
			Consist: C	MM: 2525

Collapsed down the stretch, with .527 OPS, 0.20 Eye after trade to SEA. Silver lining was 11 SB in those two months (23% SBO), and restoration of SB% says running game may be back in play. However, power skill trends and 2nd half FB% make it difficult to have confidence in return to mid-teens HR.

Yr Tm	AB	R	HR	RBI	SB	BA	xBA	OBP	SLG	OPS	vL	vR	bb%	ct%	Eye	G	L	F	h%	HctX	PX	xPX	hr/f	Spd	SBO	SB%	#Wk	DOM	DIS	RC/G	RAR	BPV	BPX	R$
10 DET	618	103	4	41	27	293	249	345	400	745	600	798	7	72	0.28	48	24	27	40	101	86	94	3%	204	18%	82%	27	33%	41%	5.03	-0.9	36	78	$25
11 DET	591	90	10	45	22	249	218	317	374	690	732	672	9	69	0.31	47	17	36	34	75	94	96	7%	204	17%	81%	27	26%	52%	4.05	-18.2	33	73	$15
12 DET	543	103	16	66	12	300	260	377	479	856	856	856	11	75	0.50	42	24	34	37	112	118	117	11%	179	12%	57%	25	48%	20%	6.33	22.4	73	183	$25
13 DET	552	99	12	49	8	272	263	337	417	754	681	784	9	77	0.40	42	28	31	34	103	103	101	9%	157	8%	67%	22	45%	18%	4.83	9.3	55	138	$18
14 2 AL	597	71	4	47	20	256	238	308	347	655	735	622	7	76	0.33	42	26	33	33	86	75	87	3%	143	16%	77%	27	30%	44%	3.72	-2.9	23	62	$16
1st Half	265	34	3	22	8	242	233	309	355	664	809	615	10	77	0.48	34	24	43	30	94	90	112	3%	150	15%	73%	14	36%	43%	3.77	-0.8	47	127	$10
2nd Half	332	37	1	25	12	268	244	308	340	648	688	628	5	75	0.22	49	27	24	35	79	62	66	2%	132	17%	80%	13	23%	46%	3.68	-1.7	2	5	$20
15 Proj	**579**	**86**	**10**	**50**	**21**	**269**	**252**	**328**	**397**	**725**	**741**	**718**	**8**	**75**	**0.36**	**43**	**25**	**32**	**34**	**94**	**99**	**95**	**7%**	**158**	**17%**	**78%**				**4.57**	**11.9**	**40**	**105**	**$22**

BRIAN RUDD

Jaso,John

Age: 31 Bats: L Pos: CA DH | Ht: 6' 2" Wt: 205

Health D | PT/Exp D | Consist B | LIMA Plan D+ | Rand Var 0 | MM 3343

1st half power surge raised early expectations but that faded quickly. Trying to play through concussion symptoms may have been a factor. Was eventually shut down early for second straight year, fueling speculation that days as CA (and fantasy asset?) may be over.

Yr	Tm	AB	R	HR	RBI	SB	BA	xBA	OBP	SLG	OPS	vL	vR	bb%	ct%	Eye	G	L	F	h%	HctX	PX	xPX	hr/f	Spd	SBO	SB%	#Wk	DOM	DIS	RC/G	RAR	BPV	BPX	R$
10	TAM	339	57	5	44	4	263	266	372	378	750	610	772	15	88	1.51	46	17	37	28	95	75	81	5%	110	3%	100%	25	68%	8%	4.94	7.1	79	172	$8
11	TAM	246	26	5	27	1	224	256	298	354	651	574	662	9	85	0.69	43	18	39	24	98	90	89	6%	80	5%	33%	22	50%	23%	3.33	-6.6	58	129	$0
12	SEA	294	41	10	50	5	276	294	394	456	850	393	927	16	83	1.10	46	25	28	30	108	115	86	14%	92	5%	100%	26	73%	15%	6.41	18.9	84	210	$10
13	OAK	207	31	3	21	2	271	247	387	372	759	442	802	16	78	0.84	40	25	35	33	75	80	58	5%	94	4%	67%	17	35%	35%	4.97	7.5	38	95	$4
14	OAK	307	42	9	40	2	264	273	337	430	767	468	793	8	80	0.47	37	26	38	30	105	117	120	10%	99	3%	100%	21	57%	14%	4.89	13.8	64	173	$8
1st Half		195	29	7	24	2	272	268	356	446	802	411	847	10	76	0.48	39	25	36	32	108	128	127	13%	98	4%	100%	14	57%	21%	5.47	11.6	60	162	$12
2nd Half		112	13	2	16	0	250	283	303	402	705	750	703	5	88	0.43	32	27	40	27	100	100	109	5%	98	0%	0%	7	57%	0%	3.94	1.8	72	195	$2
15	Proj	293	40	7	38	2	263	273	351	411	762	478	792	11	82	0.69	39	25	36	30	96	106	94	8%	95	3%	83%				4.90	12.8	61	161	$7

Jay,Jon

Age: 30 Bats: L Pos: CF RF LF | Ht: 5' 11" Wt: 195

Health A | PT/Exp A | Consist B | LIMA Plan B | Rand Var -3 | MM 1235

Got OBP back up to 2012 level, thanks to elevated h% and league leading 20 HBP. That didn't revive SB totals though, and despite plus Spd, 63% career SB% should quash any thought of that as an asset. Value will continue to be driven by BA, but realize that when 49% h% vs LH drops, playing time could as well.

Yr	Tm	AB	R	HR	RBI	SB	BA	xBA	OBP	SLG	OPS	vL	vR	bb%	ct%	Eye	G	L	F	h%	HctX	PX	xPX	hr/f	Spd	SBO	SB%	#Wk	DOM	DIS	RC/G	RAR	BPV	BPX	R$
10	STL *	452	68	7	49	11	284	275	337	407	743	741	791	7	83	0.47	49	19	32	33	98	91	76	5%	112	12%	73%	21	33%	29%	4.85	0.8	56	122	$15
11	STL	455	56	10	37	6	297	278	344	424	768	727	779	6	82	0.35	54	23	23	34	85	88	69	11%	105	10%	46%	27	48%	30%	4.94	2.0	44	98	$15
12	STL	443	70	4	40	19	305	278	373	400	773	697	804	7	84	0.48	59	22	19	36	95	64	53	6%	127	19%	73%	23	39%	22%	5.15	5.7	41	103	$19
13	STL	548	75	7	67	10	276	270	351	370	721	620	749	9	81	0.50	50	27	23	33	86	70	57	7%	97	9%	67%	27	37%	30%	4.36	4.1	29	73	$18
14	STL	413	52	3	46	6	303	269	372	378	750	859	721	6	81	0.36	52	28	20	37	95	57	64	4%	115	7%	67%	26	19%	50%	4.75	10.5	19	51	$15
1st Half		189	23	1	20	2	296	278	356	381	737	842	711	6	83	0.39	56	26	18	35	110	64	67	4%	110	5%	67%	14	21%	36%	4.68	4.3	29	78	$10
2nd Half		224	29	2	26	4	308	261	385	375	760	869	729	6	80	0.33	48	30	22	38	81	50	60	5%	114	8%	67%	12	17%	67%	4.80	5.8	9	24	$19
15	Proj	424	57	4	46	7	295	271	364	382	746	756	743	7	82	0.40	52	26	21	35	91	66	61	6%	110	8%	62%				4.67	9.6	21	56	$16

Jennings,Desmond

Age: 28 Bats: R Pos: CF | Ht: 6' 2" Wt: 200

Health C | PT/Exp A | Consist B | LIMA Plan A | Rand Var +1 | MM 3525

Bruised knee in late August put an end to his season. Before that, Spd continued its downward trend, and after 11 SB thru May, he stopped running. Even if we cut him slack for injuries, SBO and SB% suggest 20 SB is no longer a lock. And while power has been consistent, that's not why you draft him.

Yr	Tm	AB	R	HR	RBI	SB	BA	xBA	OBP	SLG	OPS	vL	vR	bb%	ct%	Eye	G	L	F	h%	HctX	PX	xPX	hr/f	Spd	SBO	SB%	#Wk	DOM	DIS	RC/G	RAR	BPV	BPX	R$
10	TAM *	420	68	2	30	30	236	229	300	335	636	879	350	8	80	0.47	47	12	41	29	116	72	142	0%	166	35%	82%	6	33%	50%	3.51	-20.2	48	104	$12
11	TAM *	585	96	19	55	33	242	248	318	404	722	791	811	10	74	0.43	47	18	35	30	86	113	100	16%	158	26%	82%	11	64%	18%	4.42	-11.7	56	124	$21
12	TAM	505	85	13	47	31	246	236	314	388	702	735	691	8	76	0.38	42	20	38	30	102	92	99	9%	163	25%	94%	24	54%	33%	4.32	-7.9	46	115	$19
13	TAM	527	82	14	54	20	252	258	334	414	748	857	697	11	78	0.56	47	17	36	30	117	113	110	10%	135	19%	71%	25	72%	20%	4.65	6.4	67	168	$19
14	TAM	479	64	10	36	15	244	252	319	378	697	833	653	9	77	0.44	49	18	34	30	104	105	103	8%	125	17%	71%	22	45%	32%	3.94	0.7	51	138	$12
1st Half		298	40	7	21	12	235	253	330	372	703	844	659	11	77	0.53	50	17	32	29	101	108	96	10%	122	22%	67%	14	50%	29%	3.86	0.0	53	143	$15
2nd Half		181	24	3	15	3	260	250	298	387	685	817	640	5	79	0.26	46	18	36	31	109	100	113	6%	121	7%	100%	8	38%	38%	4.07	1.1	45	122	$7
15	Proj	531	78	13	46	20	249	256	318	398	716	815	679	9	78	0.42	47	18	36	30	106	111	105	9%	137	19%	79%				4.27	6.4	58	152	$18

Jeter,Derek

Age: 41 Bats: R Pos: SS | Ht: 6' 3" Wt: 195

Health | PT/Exp | Consist | LIMA Plan | Rand Var | MM

Farewell tour wasn't always pretty, as reputation, rather than performance, kept his name on lineup card daily. Skills were far cry from his heyday, and faded badly down the stretch. Not how he wanted to go out, but that doesn't take away from a fabulous career. Best to you, Captain.

Yr	Tm	AB	R	HR	RBI	SB	BA	xBA	OBP	SLG	OPS	vL	vR	bb%	ct%	Eye	G	L	F	h%	HctX	PX	xPX	hr/f	Spd	SBO	SB%	#Wk	DOM	DIS	RC/G	RAR	BPV	BPX	R$
10	NYY	663	111	10	67	18	270	282	340	370	710	874	632	9	84	0.59	65	16	18	31	89	68	57	10%	128	12%	78%	27	44%	22%	4.34	3.1	48	104	$21
11	NYY	546	84	6	61	16	297	279	355	388	743	946	666	8	85	0.57	62	19	19	34	86	63	63	7%	138	13%	73%	25	36%	20%	4.93	11.4	50	111	$22
12	NYY	683	99	15	58	9	316	290	362	429	791	941	723	6	87	0.50	62	22	16	35	86	71	44	16%	109	6%	69%	27	30%	15%	5.69	33.0	51	128	$28
13	NYY	63	8	1	7	0	190	255	288	254	542	940	348	11	84	0.80	70	20	9	21	71	39	27	20%	99	0%	0%	4	25%	50%	2.25	-2.3	22	55	-$3
14	NYY	581	47	4	50	10	256	252	304	313	617	592	627	6	85	0.40	62	18	20	30	78	43	47	4%	107	8%	83%	27	26%	30%	3.25	1.3	20	54	$10
1st Half		286	27	2	20	4	273	249	328	329	657	634	669	7	85	0.49	61	18	21	32	79	40	41	4%	126	6%	80%	14	29%	36%	3.75	4.2	25	68	$10
2nd Half		295	20	2	30	6	241	252	279	298	578	529	592	5	85	0.32	62	18	20	28	77	45	53	4%	91	10%	86%	13	23%	23%	2.81	-3.8	15	41	$11
15	Proj																																		

Johnson,Chris

Age: 30 Bats: R Pos: 3B | Ht: 6' 3" Wt: 225

Health A | PT/Exp A | Consist D | LIMA Plan B | Rand Var 0 | MM 3225

Regression was expected, as 2013 h% wasn't sustainable. But he's proven to be able to out-hit his xBA (check out LD history); mid-30s hit rates are the norm. Power decline (HctX, PX, .098 ISO!) is the real concern, particularly vs. RHP. If that goes south for good, playing time will be at risk.

Yr	Tm	AB	R	HR	RBI	SB	BA	xBA	OBP	SLG	OPS	vL	vR	bb%	ct%	Eye	G	L	F	h%	HctX	PX	xPX	hr/f	Spd	SBO	SB%	#Wk	DOM	DIS	RC/G	RAR	BPV	BPX	R$
10	HOU *	490	59	17	76	3	297	274	326	474	800	735	848	4	76	0.18	41	24	35	36	102	127	117	13%	88	3%	100%	18	44%	50%	5.65	7.4	41	89	$19
11	HOU *	459	45	10	53	3	246	248	282	382	664	635	681	5	72	0.18	46	23	31	32	106	108	110	8%	96	6%	46%	23	26%	48%	3.55	-21.1	15	33	$7
12	2 NL	488	48	15	76	5	281	254	326	451	777	672	819	6	73	0.23	39	26	35	36	98	120	112	12%	106	5%	83%	27	33%	44%	5.19	8.0	34	85	$16
13	ATL	514	54	12	68	0	321	268	358	457	816	939	772	5	77	0.25	46	27	28	40	97	104	101	11%	70	0%	0%	26	42%	38%	6.13	29.3	26	65	$21
14	ATL	582	43	10	58	6	263	244	292	361	653	988	570	4	73	0.14	48	27	25	35	83	83	74	9%	71	4%	100%	27	19%	67%	3.69	-0.4	-11	-30	$12
1st Half		313	20	3	24	1	281	242	299	361	660	1055	588	2	74	0.09	48	27	25	37	85	72	67	5%	80	1%	100%	14	14%	71%	3.82	1.1	-16	-43	$9
2nd Half		269	23	7	34	5	242	245	284	361	645	940	546	6	71	0.21	48	26	26	32	80	96	82	14%	68	8%	100%	13	23%	62%	3.54	-1.2	-6	-16	$15
15	Proj	553	50	12	68	5	278	255	315	404	719	877	669	5	74	0.20	46	26	28	36	90	102	91	11%	78	4%	93%				4.51	12.8	8	20	$17

Johnson,Kelly

Age: 33 Bats: L Pos: 3B 1B | Ht: 6' 1" Wt: 200

Health A | PT/Exp C | Consist A | LIMA Plan D | Rand Var +3 | MM 3211

Since strongest asset is power, it should come as no surprise that career-high GB% contributed to poor results, including career-worst HctX and xPX. Won't be relevant again unless he rediscovers power stroke; AB trend (and frequent uniform changes) indicates teams are beginning to lose faith in his ability to do that.

Yr	Tm	AB	R	HR	RBI	SB	BA	xBA	OBP	SLG	OPS	vL	vR	bb%	ct%	Eye	G	L	F	h%	HctX	PX	xPX	hr/f	Spd	SBO	SB%	#Wk	DOM	DIS	RC/G	RAR	BPV	BPX	R$
10	ARI	585	93	26	71	13	284	277	370	496	865	953	825	12	75	0.53	41	21	38	34	114	149	139	16%	115	11%	65%	26	69%	15%	6.38	26.2	78	170	$25
11	2 TM	545	75	21	58	16	222	245	304	413	717	626	750	10	70	0.37	39	20	40	28	106	141	156	14%	115	17%	73%	27	48%	41%	4.01	-13.4	49	109	$12
12	TOR	507	61	16	55	14	225	226	313	365	678	607	705	11	69	0.39	45	21	34	30	94	102	113	14%	93	12%	88%	27	37%	48%	3.80	-11.5	8	20	$9
13	TAM	366	41	16	52	7	235	227	305	410	715	686	723	9	73	0.35	39	15	46	28	85	119	116	13%	107	12%	64%	26	50%	35%	4.03	0.9	39	98	$9
14	3 AL	265	29	7	27	2	215	252	296	362	659	708	653	10	73	0.41	49	21	30	27	81	114	77	12%	93	6%	50%	24	50%	29%	3.37	-2.4	34	92	$1
1st Half		161	14	5	19	2	224	258	300	398	698	798	681	10	72	0.40	53	18	29	28	80	134	88	15%	95	8%	67%	14	50%	36%	3.90	1.0	46	124	$3
2nd Half		104	15	2	8	0	202	246	291	308	598	422	615	10	75	0.42	43	26	31	25	83	86	60	8%	89	4%	0%	10	50%	20%	2.62	-3.5	17	46	-$1
15	Proj	189	23	6	21	3	223	242	305	374	679	671	681	10	73	0.40	44	20	36	28	87	115	96	12%	95	9%	62%				3.62	-0.4	28	73	$4

Johnson,Reed

Age: 38 Bats: R Pos: LF | Ht: 5' 10" Wt: 190

Health B | PT/Exp F | Consist B | LIMA Plan D | Rand Var +5 | MM 2011

One would think that a player with 133 career HBP would know the value of getting on base, and yet he drew just one walk in 201 PA. No longer hits LHP well and had .468 OPS from mid-May on. FB% jump revived xPX, but hr/f says that plan won't work either. Best bet: keep leaning into 'em.

Yr	Tm	AB	R	HR	RBI	SB	BA	xBA	OBP	SLG	OPS	vL	vR	bb%	ct%	Eye	G	L	F	h%	HctX	PX	xPX	hr/f	Spd	SBO	SB%	#Wk	DOM	DIS	RC/G	RAR	BPV	BPX	R$
10	LA	202	24	2	15	2	262	234	291	366	657	790	520	2	75	0.10	43	19	37	34	92	82	75	4%	149	9%	50%	24	33%	58%	3.43	-10.1	18	39	$2
11	CHC	246	33	5	28	2	309	263	348	467	816	797	829	2	74	0.08	43	21	35	40	105	132	89	8%	109	6%	67%	25	40%	44%	5.52	2.5	42	93	$8
12	2 NL	269	30	3	20	2	290	263	337	398	735	798	654	5	77	0.21	57	24	19	37	86	77	58	8%	127	6%	50%	27	48%	37%	4.51	-4.8	20	50	$5
13	ATL	123	13	1	11	0	244	223	311	341	653	673	637	5	74	0.19	56	15	29	32	83	81	70	4%	119	0%	0%	20	15%	55%	3.21	-5.0	8	20	-$1
14	MIA	187	24	2	25	0	235	251	266	348	614	728	548	1	80	0.03	43	20	38	28	105	97	123	4%	74	4%	0%	27	33%	37%	2.69	-7.8	24	65	$1
1st Half		112	13	2	20	0	268	270	297	411	707	714	703	1	82	0.05	39	22	39	31	95	115	108	6%	78	5%	0%	14	50%	29%	3.75	-0.8	48	130	$4
2nd Half		75	11	0	5	0	187	223	222	253	476	751	347	0	77	0.00	48	17	35	24	121	68	148	0%	78	0%	0%	13	15%	46%	1.48	-6.0	-11	-30	-$3
15	Proj	103	13	1	10	0	243	243	286	347	633	743	558	2	77	0.10	49	19	32	31	99	90	100	4%	96	3%	36%				2.99	-2.3	10	25	$1

BRIAN RUDD

Jones,Adam

Age: 29 Bats: R Pos: CF	Health A	LIMA Plan B+	
Ht: 6' 3" Wt: 225	PT/Exp A	Rand Var 0	
	Consist A	MM 4345	

Swing for the fences approach in 2nd half just hurt BA with no benefit to his power. Wasn't much of a factor on the bases, but Spd is intact, and rising SB% could lead to more opportunities to run. Combination of consistency and durability makes him one of the least risky high-dollar investments around.

Yr	Tm	AB	R	HR	RBI	SB	BA	xBA	OBP	SLG	OPS	vL	vR	bb%	ct%	Eye	G	L	F	h%	HctX	PX	xPX	hr/f	Spd	SBO	SB%	#Wk	DOM	DIS	RC/G	RAR	BPV	BPX	R$
10	BAL	581	76	19	69	7	284	260	325	442	767	666	804	4	80	0.19	46	17	37	33	106	103	99	11%	134	10%	50%	27	41%	30%	4.71	-6.2	50	109	$20
11	BAL	567	68	25	83	12	280	273	319	466	785	665	829	5	80	0.26	49	18	33	31	106	120	106	17%	104	12%	75%	27	52%	22%	5.17	1.3	59	131	$23
12	BAL	648	103	32	82	16	287	290	334	505	839	800	852	5	81	0.27	46	21	33	31	125	136	108	19%	109	16%	70%	27	59%	19%	5.70	15.5	76	190	$30
13	BAL	653	100	33	108	14	285	284	318	493	811	732	846	4	79	0.18	48	20	32	32	125	137	127	20%	95	12%	82%	26	62%	19%	5.49	23.0	64	160	$34
14	BAL	644	88	29	96	7	281	270	311	469	780	1003	709	3	79	0.14	47	17	36	32	113	127	119	16%	102	6%	88%	27	52%	30%	5.05	21.0	57	154	$29
1st Half		338	49	15	49	3	305	283	329	500	829	1264	671	3	83	0.17	49	17	33	33	118	127	115	16%	123	4%	100%	14	57%	29%	6.01	19.8	76	205	$32
2nd Half		306	39	14	47	4	255	254	291	435	726	649	747	3	76	0.12	44	18	38	29	109	127	124	16%	72	8%	80%	13	46%	31%	4.11	2.2	34	92	$26
15	**Proj**	**648**	**92**	**30**	**96**	**11**	**280**	**277**	**315**	**475**	**791**	**824**	**779**	**4**	**79**	**0.18**	**47**	**19**	**34**	**31**	**117**	**134**	**118**	**17%**	**98**	**10%**	**78%**				**5.13**	**23.4**	**60**	**158**	**$28**

Jones,Garrett

Age: 34 Bats: L Pos: 1B	Health A	LIMA Plan C	
Ht: 6' 5" Wt: 235	PT/Exp B	Rand Var +1	
	Consist C	MM 4135	

xPX rebounded and HctX was highest since small sample 2007 season. However, recent hr/f slide aligns with similar decline in average FB distance (297, 286, 280). Given his age and mediocre numbers vs RHP the last two years, playing time may be the next shoe to drop.

Yr	Tm	AB	R	HR	RBI	SB	BA	xBA	OBP	SLG	OPS	vL	vR	bb%	ct%	Eye	G	L	F	h%	HctX	PX	xPX	hr/f	Spd	SBO	SB%	#Wk	DOM	DIS	RC/G	RAR	BPV	BPX	R$
10	PIT	592	64	21	86	7	247	261	306	414	720	621	775	8	79	0.43	44	17	39	28	100	115	116	11%	78	7%	70%	27	52%	22%	4.29	-34.5	51	111	$13
11	PIT	423	51	16	58	6	243	258	321	433	753	460	808	10	75	0.46	36	20	45	29	113	141	140	11%	70	9%	67%	27	56%	26%	4.62	-20.7	58	129	$10
12	PIT	475	68	27	86	2	274	277	317	516	832	532	888	6	78	0.32	40	18	42	30	119	152	155	17%	95	2%	100%	27	70%	19%	5.84	5.5	78	195	$19
13	PIT	403	41	15	51	2	233	266	289	419	708	317	730	7	75	0.31	40	24	36	28	101	135	96	14%	74	2%	100%	27	48%	30%	4.04	-6.5	46	115	$6
14	MIA	496	59	15	53	0	246	253	309	411	720	539	749	8	77	0.40	38	20	43	29	124	127	148	9%	84	1%	0%	27	44%	37%	4.27	1.2	52	141	$9
1st Half		277	37	10	36	0	264	253	333	440	774	430	859	10	75	0.44	39	20	42	32	121	135	141	11%	86	1%	0%	14	43%	43%	5.07	7.3	55	149	$15
2nd Half		219	22	5	17	0	224	253	277	374	651	1045	628	6	79	0.33	36	20	44	26	127	117	158	7%	84	0%	0%	13	46%	31%	3.36	-5.3	50	135	$2
15	**Proj**	**421**	**48**	**14**	**51**	**1**	**244**	**259**	**300**	**416**	**716**	**549**	**738**	**7**	**77**	**0.35**	**39**	**20**	**41**	**29**	**116**	**131**	**136**	**10%**	**80**	**2%**	**70%**				**4.21**	**0.5**	**48**	**126**	**$10**

Jones,James

Age: 26 Bats: L Pos: CF	Health A	LIMA Plan D	
Ht: 6' 4" Wt: 200	PT/Exp D	Rand Var 0	
	Consist A	MM 0511	

0-9-.250 with 27 SB in 312 AB at SEA. Got off to hot start that included 17 SB in his first two months. Soon was overmatched and demoted after posting .396 OPS (that's OPS, not OBP) in span of 95 PA. Speed makes him a potential end-game option, but inability to get on base is a major hurdle.

Yr	Tm	AB	R	HR	RBI	SB	BA	xBA	OBP	SLG	OPS	vL	vR	bb%	ct%	Eye	G	L	F	h%	HctX	PX	xPX	hr/f	Spd	SBO	SB%	#Wk	DOM	DIS	RC/G	RAR	BPV	BPX	R$
10																																			
11																																			
12																																			
13	a/a	378	35	4	35	21	233		291	338	629			8	76	0.35				29		73			132	34%	67%				3.14		21	53	$9
14	SEA *	468	61	1	19	32	240	246	271	305	576	586	590	4	77	0.19	54	24	22	31	78	49	52	0%	183	33%	87%	22	18%	45%	2.96	-13.1	14	38	$13
1st Half		274	40	1	11	20	276	266	311	346	656	673	670	5	80	0.26	60	23	17	34	85	51	44	0%	184	33%	81%	10	20%	40%	3.91	0.4	29	78	$20
2nd Half		194	22	0	7	11	189	215	214	248	462	432	460	3	73	0.12	44	25	31	26	67	47	67	0%	146	33%	100%	12	17%	50%	1.88	-12.2	-17	-46	$5
15	**Proj**	**133**	**15**	**0**	**8**	**10**	**236**	**235**	**276**	**299**	**575**	**569**	**578**	**5**	**76**	**0.24**	**50**	**24**	**25**	**31**	**74**	**49**	**58**	**0%**	**144**	**37%**	**83%**				**2.92**	**-3.8**	**3**	**9**	**$4**

Joseph,Caleb

Age: 29 Bats: R Pos: CA	Health A	LIMA Plan D	
Ht: 6' 3" Wt: 180	PT/Exp C	Rand Var +1	
	Consist B	MM 3111	

9-28-.207 in 246 AB at BAL. Showed decent power in big league debut, but as foretold by MLEs, struggled to get on base. That problem was magnified in Sept, when he went 4-for-50. It took him four years to conquer AA, and at his age, we've probably already seen his best work.

Yr	Tm	AB	R	HR	RBI	SB	BA	xBA	OBP	SLG	OPS	vL	vR	bb%	ct%	Eye	G	L	F	h%	HctX	PX	xPX	hr/f	Spd	SBO	SB%	#Wk	DOM	DIS	RC/G	RAR	BPV	BPX	R$
10	aa	378	33	9	39	1	207		255	320	575			6	82	0.35				23		74			95	9%	10%				2.41		28	61	-$1
11	aa	375	34	6	34	4	227		288	316	604			8	82	0.48				26		61			90	7%	64%				2.97		22	49	$2
12	a/a	347	34	10	43	2	224		283	373	657			8	77	0.36				26		102			86	2%	100%				3.50		31	78	$3
13	aa	518	52	17	68	3	243		281	395	676			5	79	0.24				28		104			82	5%	53%				3.68		34	85	$10
14	BAL *	338	27	10	35	0	206	224	248	341	589	643	603	5	72	0.20	33	22	46	26	93	106	138	11%	87	2%	0%	21	24%	57%	2.67	-6.8	10	27	$0
1st Half		177	14	3	15	0	184	209	227	295	522	513	546	5	73	0.21	38	17	45	23	110	94	177	7%	90	0%	0%	9	33%	56%	2.09	-7.4	6	16	-$4
2nd Half		161	13	7	20	0	230	236	273	391	665	765	624	5	70	0.19	29	25	46	28	83	120	116	13%	97	3%	0%	12	17%	58%	3.40	0.0	18	49	$4
15	**Proj**	**165**	**15**	**6**	**19**	**0**	**222**	**240**	**272**	**378**	**650**	**670**	**638**	**6**	**75**	**0.24**	**33**	**22**	**45**	**26**	**94**	**115**	**140**	**11%**	**97**	**3%**	**43%**				**3.25**	**-0.7**	**15**	**41**	**$2**

Joyce,Matt

Age: 30 Bats: L Pos: LF DH	Health A	LIMA Plan C+	
Ht: 6' 2" Wt: 200	PT/Exp B	Rand Var -2	
	Consist A	MM 4115	

Fourth straight year in which he's faded in 2nd half. This time, in addition to his power, ct% nosedived as well. .758 OPS, .130 ISO each marked career lows against RHP, and with each of those levels on a four-year downward trend, playing time could soon be at risk... DN: 300 AB

Yr	Tm	AB	R	HR	RBI	SB	BA	xBA	OBP	SLG	OPS	vL	vR	bb%	ct%	Eye	G	L	F	h%	HctX	PX	xPX	hr/f	Spd	SBO	SB%	#Wk	DOM	DIS	RC/G	RAR	BPV	BPX	R$
10	TAM *	308	43	12	49	3	240	259	358	448	806	263	910	16	74	0.70	33	18	49	29	117	151	179	13%	96	9%	33%	16	69%	19%	5.08	1.4	78	170	$7
11	TAM	462	69	19	75	13	277	269	347	478	825	657	866	10	77	0.46	36	21	42	32	117	144	128	12%	93	11%	93%	27	59%	22%	5.98	13.8	72	160	$20
12	TAM	399	55	17	59	4	241	244	341	429	769	631	810	12	74	0.54	38	19	43	28	106	124	117	13%	99	6%	57%	24	50%	29%	4.71	1.6	53	133	$9
13	TAM	413	61	18	47	7	235	259	328	419	747	499	783	13	79	0.68	37	20	43	26	90	124	91	13%	83	9%	70%	27	44%	41%	4.58	7.6	67	168	$11
14	TAM	418	51	9	52	2	254	232	349	383	732	408	758	13	73	0.56	43	19	38	33	99	104	105	8%	107	5%	29%	26	35%	42%	4.40	8.8	37	100	$9
1st Half		232	30	6	34	1	272	256	355	431	786	360	828	12	77	0.59	38	21	41	33	102	126	119	8%	100	4%	33%	14	43%	36%	5.28	10.3	64	173	$13
2nd Half		186	21	3	18	1	231	202	341	323	663	500	674	14	69	0.53	50	17	34	32	94	75	85	7%	116	6%	25%	12	25%	50%	3.43	-1.8	2	5	$4
15	**Proj**	**397**	**52**	**13**	**50**	**4**	**244**	**244**	**342**	**403**	**745**	**521**	**775**	**13**	**75**	**0.58**	**41**	**19**	**40**	**30**	**99**	**121**	**105**	**11%**	**100**	**7%**	**49%**				**4.52**	**9.2**	**43**	**112**	**$11**

Kawasaki,Munenori

Age: 34 Bats: L Pos: 2B	Health A	LIMA Plan D	
Ht: 5' 11" Wt: 175	PT/Exp F	Rand Var 0	
	Consist B	MM 0323	

0-17-.258 in 240 AB at TOR. Claimed starting job in June, though keeping it was more about his competition than his performance. Spd is primary skill, but after averaging 35 SB per year in Japan in 2009-11, has just 10 in 584 MLB AB. Can someone have negative power? That's the direction his nearly-extinct xPX is headed.

Yr	Tm	AB	R	HR	RBI	SB	BA	xBA	OBP	SLG	OPS	vL	vR	bb%	ct%	Eye	G	L	F	h%	HctX	PX	xPX	hr/f	Spd	SBO	SB%	#Wk	DOM	DIS	RC/G	RAR	BPV	BPX	R$
10	for	602	72	2	52	27	294		333	376	709			5	86	0.43				34		56			127	22%	69%				4.41	-4.1	42	91	$23
11	for	603	69	1	36	28	249		283	319	603			5	87	0.36				29		45			147	26%	72%				3.04	-29.5	39	87	$12
12	SEA	104	13	0	7	2	192	224	257	202	459	255	503	7	83	0.44	61	19	20	23	53	8	30	0%	106	15%	50%	25	16%	52%	1.52	-8.8	-14	-35	-$2
13	TOR *	300	33	1	26	9	222	251	316	285	601	438	681	12	81	0.73	58	22	20	27	65	40	29	3%	163	10%	90%	22	32%	32%	3.08	-5.9	32	80	$2
14	TOR *	356	40	0	23	2	246	271	301	302	602	644	618	7	80	0.39	55	30	15	31	49	50	12	0%	125	3%	58%	17	12%	41%	3.05	-3.6	14	38	$2
1st Half		170	18	0	8	1	233	287	278	314	593	481	706	6	80	0.32	68	25	8	29	47	70	4	0%	139	5%	36%	4	0%	50%	2.83	-2.9	32	86	-$1
2nd Half		186	22	0	15	1	258	259	325	290	616	715	595	8	80	0.46	52	31	17	32	49	32	15	0%	104	2%	100%	13	15%	38%	3.23	-0.9	-4	-11	$5
15	**Proj**	**257**	**29**	**0**	**19**	**4**	**235**	**251**	**306**	**283**	**588**	**488**	**613**	**8**	**81**	**0.48**	**58**	**23**	**19**	**29**	**55**	**38**	**20**	**0%**	**127**	**7%**	**67%**				**2.80**	**-4.6**	**1**	**4**	**$3**

Kelly,Don

Age: 35 Bats: L Pos: 3B 1B	Health A	LIMA Plan D	
Ht: 6' 4" Wt: 190	PT/Exp F	Rand Var -3	
	Consist B	MM 0401	

Lucky surge in h% led to respectable OBP, but he managed just 6 XBH all season. Defensive versatility and decent speed are really all he brings to the table, but he's at an age where those skills decline. Only bb% and ct% are acceptable, but that won't make him draft-worthy.

Yr	Tm	AB	R	HR	RBI	SB	BA	xBA	OBP	SLG	OPS	vL	vR	bb%	ct%	Eye	G	L	F	h%	HctX	PX	xPX	hr/f	Spd	SBO	SB%	#Wk	DOM	DIS	RC/G	RAR	BPV	BPX	R$
10	DET	238	30	9	27	3	244	233	272	374	646	487	663	3	82	0.19	32	19	49	26	86	76	91	9%	109	6%	100%	27	30%	44%	3.45	-10.4	32	70	$4
11	DET	257	35	7	28	2	245	248	291	381	672	381	698	5	88	0.44	29	23	48	26	71	79	72	7%	137	5%	67%	27	48%	22%	3.63	-9.8	67	149	$4
12	DET *	186	20	2	15	5	184	193	270	241	511	298	551	11	77	0.52	40	18	42	23	45	38	44	3%	123	12%	79%	24	21%	50%	2.08	-14.8	0	0	-$2
13	DET	216	33	6	23	2	222	230	309	343	652	574	674	11	87	0.96	39	15	46	23	55	70	44	7%	131	3%	100%	27	44%	26%	3.52	-2.9	68	170	$2
14	DET	163	24	0	7	6	245	226	332	288	620	490	644	11	82	0.69	40	25	35	30	84	35	61	0%	121	13%	86%	27	30%	59%	3.33	-1.6	17	46	$2
1st Half		86	9	0	3	3	233	231	313	291	603	785	578	10	81	0.63	33	29	39	29	111	45	100	0%	125	15%	75%	14	29%	57%	3.06	-1.8	22	59	$0
2nd Half		77	15	0	4	3	260	221	352	286	638	289	724	11	83	0.77	48	21	32	31	55	25	17	0%	102	11%	100%	13	31%	62%	3.65	-0.2	8	22	$4
15	**Proj**	**189**	**28**	**2**	**14**	**5**	**232**	**221**	**312**	**298**	**610**	**462**	**639**	**10**	**83**	**0.66**	**40**	**20**	**40**	**27**	**67**	**47**	**51**	**3%**	**119**	**10%**	**89%**				**3.16**	**-3.0**	**23**	**61**	**$4**

BRIAN RUDD

Kemp,Matt

Age: 30 Bats: R Pos: RF LF CF	Health F	LIMA Plan B+	
Ht: 6' 4" Wt: 215	PT/Exp C	Rand Var 0	
	Consist D	MM 5245	

That 2nd half explosion is going to temp a lot of people to think, "Is this the return to early round relevance?" Truth is, aside from SBs, he potentially could be as productive as he ever was. It's your risk tolerance that will determine how much you ignore the "F" health grade. But, this is real... UP: 40-100-.300

Yr	Tm	AB	R	HR	RBI	SB	BA	xBA	OBP	SLG	OPS	vL	vR	bb%	ct%	Eye	G	L	F	h%	HctX	PX	xPX	hr/f	Spd	SBO	SB%	#Wk	DOM	DIS	RC/G	RAR	BPV	BPX	R$
10	LA	602	82	28	89	19	249	257	310	450	760	809	743	8	72	0.31	41	20	39	30	106	139	146	16%	126	24%	56%	27	56%	26%	4.41	-13.4	54	117	$21
11	LA	602	115	39	126	40	324	284	399	586	986	1142	940	11	74	0.47	36	23	41	39	122	181	164	21%	127	26%	78%	27	74%	19%	8.73	58.7	101	224	$51
12	LA	403	74	23	69	9	303	277	367	538	906	1105	818	9	74	0.39	43	22	35	36	122	155	158	22%	103	11%	69%	21	48%	19%	7.08	21.6	73	183	$23
13	LA	263	35	6	33	9	270	237	328	395	723	853	671	8	71	0.29	40	25	35	36	105	103	142	9%	78	13%	100%	14	29%	50%	4.72	0.8	8	20	$9
14	LA	541	77	25	89	8	287	287	346	506	852	781	879	9	73	0.36	43	26	31	35	128	168	140	20%	89	9%	62%	27	67%	15%	6.18	32.0	73	197	$27
1st Half		266	35	8	31	5	274	281	332	459	791	592	881	8	72	0.32	46	27	26	35	121	151	117	16%	95	14%	56%	14	50%	14%	5.18	9.1	56	151	$17
2nd Half		275	42	17	58	3	298	294	358	553	911	1020	877	9	74	0.39	40	25	36	35	134	184	161	23%	87	5%	75%	13	85%	15%	7.27	24.8	90	243	$36
15	**Proj**	**563**	**84**	**29**	**93**	**9**	**286**	**281**	**346**	**512**	**857**	**913**	**836**	**9**	**73**	**0.34**	**42**	**24**	**35**	**35**	**120**	**170**	**146**	**20%**	**90**	**9%**	**68%**				**6.25**	**35.9**	**73**	**192**	**$27**

Kendrick,Howie

Age: 31 Bats: R Pos: 2B	Health B	LIMA Plan B	
Ht: 5' 10" Wt: 210	PT/Exp A	Rand Var 0	
	Consist A	MM 2345	

As expected, HR jump couldn't last; simply too few FB. Sure, he mustered high hr/f in 2011, too, but that PX/xPX seems to be an outlier. 1st half SBO was intriguing, but with league-average Spd, those opps dried up. Given HctX and decent ct%, BA should hold. But that's about it.

Yr	Tm	AB	R	HR	RBI	SB	BA	xBA	OBP	SLG	OPS	vL	vR	bb%	ct%	Eye	G	L	F	h%	HctX	PX	xPX	hr/f	Spd	SBO	SB%	#Wk	DOM	DIS	RC/G	RAR	BPV	BPX	R$
10	LAA	616	67	10	75	14	279	285	313	407	721	673	741	4	85	0.30	53	19	28	32	109	90	92	7%	94	12%	78%	27	41%	19%	4.48	-2.0	50	109	$19
11	LAA	537	86	18	63	14	285	284	338	464	802	840	782	6	78	0.28	52	22	27	34	112	123	127	17%	114	15%	70%	26	46%	27%	5.30	10.7	58	129	$23
12	LAA	550	57	8	67	14	287	265	325	400	725	797	694	5	79	0.25	59	21	21	35	109	81	87	9%	96	14%	70%	27	33%	37%	4.56	6.1	22	55	$18
13	LAA	478	55	13	54	6	297	289	335	439	775	862	745	5	81	0.26	51	27	21	34	115	93	88	16%	110	7%	67%	23	48%	26%	5.19	19.4	44	110	$18
14	LAA	617	85	7	75	14	293	272	347	397	744	834	714	7	82	0.44	60	19	21	35	133	78	88	7%	102	10%	74%	27	26%	22%	4.92	26.4	38	103	$25
1st Half		312	43	4	32	10	272	277	334	378	713	744	699	7	83	0.46	64	18	19	32	129	76	81	8%	101	16%	71%	14	21%	21%	4.29	8.1	39	105	$21
2nd Half		305	42	3	43	4	315	267	361	416	777	972	728	7	82	0.41	56	20	24	38	137	80	94	5%	103	5%	80%	13	31%	23%	5.64	18.5	37	100	$29
15	**Proj**	**586**	**74**	**9**	**71**	**12**	**294**	**275**	**340**	**409**	**749**	**829**	**720**	**6**	**81**	**0.34**	**56**	**22**	**22**	**35**	**123**	**85**	**90**	**9%**	**103**	**10%**	**72%**				**4.94**	**25.4**	**37**	**98**	**$24**

Kiermaier,Kevin

Age: 25 Bats: L Pos: RF CF	Health A	LIMA Plan C+	
Ht: 6' 1" Wt: 195	PT/Exp D	Rand Var 0	
	Consist B	MM 3533	

10-35-.263 with 5 SB in 331 AB at TAM. When injuries hit, he was the cavalry, supplying divine D and surprising pop. It was no shock that power evaporated, given that 6 HR was his prior high in minors. Spd skills are more legit, but SB% may curtail chances. Could use a platoon mate, though glove may open doors anyway.

Yr	Tm	AB	R	HR	RBI	SB	BA	xBA	OBP	SLG	OPS	vL	vR	bb%	ct%	Eye	G	L	F	h%	HctX	PX	xPX	hr/f	Spd	SBO	SB%	#Wk	DOM	DIS	RC/G	RAR	BPV	BPX	R$
10																																			
11																																			
12																																			
13	TAM *	508	72	5	33	17	263	240	312	381	693	0	0	7	81	0.37	44	20	36	32	0	74	-15	0%	184	23%	56%	1	0%	100%	3.83	-6.1	52	130	$15
14	TAM *	459	58	12	46	14	264	271	314	437	750	507	837	7	79	0.34	53	17	31	31	92	117	82	13%	148	18%	73%	22	45%	32%	4.70	10.8	68	184	$16
1st Half		241	35	9	24	10	292	284	338	500	838	513	1087	7	79	0.33	54	13	33	34	117	143	79	26%	146	22%	77%	9	56%	22%	6.04	14.8	88	238	$22
2nd Half		218	23	3	22	4	234	254	291	367	658	505	703	7	79	0.35	52	18	30	28	79	88	84	6%	147	12%	67%	13	38%	38%	3.45	-2.8	46	124	$9
15	**Proj**	**293**	**38**	**7**	**25**	**10**	**260**	**267**	**315**	**424**	**739**	**485**	**810**	**7**	**79**	**0.36**	**53**	**16**	**31**	**31**	**94**	**109**	**82**	**10%**	**155**	**21%**	**67%**				**4.41**	**3.6**	**60**	**159**	**$10**

Kinsler,Ian

Age: 33 Bats: R Pos: 2B	Health B	LIMA Plan B+	
Ht: 6' 0" Wt: 200	PT/Exp A	Rand Var -1	
	Consist A	MM 2335	

Tough to question a $28 year, however... HctX, PX, xPx call power into question. Spd holding up better, but effect of declining bb% on SB chances raises concerns, too. Tailed in 2nd half... AGAIN. Defense is going to keep him employed so a $20-$25 bid should be safe, but there are no guarantees.

Yr	Tm	AB	R	HR	RBI	SB	BA	xBA	OBP	SLG	OPS	vL	vR	bb%	ct%	Eye	G	L	F	h%	HctX	PX	xPX	hr/f	Spd	SBO	SB%	#Wk	DOM	DIS	RC/G	RAR	BPV	BPX	R$
10	TEX	391	73	9	45	15	286	257	382	412	794	957	743	13	85	0.98	40	18	42	32	106	83	90	7%	111	14%	75%	20	60%	20%	5.54	10.5	68	148	$17
11	TEX	620	121	32	77	30	255	286	355	477	832	880	816	13	89	1.25	35	18	47	24	129	130	125	12%	109	19%	88%	27	85%	0%	5.86	23.0	118	262	$30
12	TEX	655	105	19	72	21	256	268	326	423	749	988	671	8	86	0.67	38	20	42	27	100	103	88	8%	107	19%	70%	27	52%	15%	4.54	7.3	78	195	$22
13	TEX	545	85	13	72	15	277	275	344	413	757	814	733	9	89	0.86	37	24	39	29	124	87	109	7%	102	17%	58%	24	75%	8%	4.71	15.5	76	190	$23
14	DET	684	100	17	92	15	275	267	307	420	727	740	722	4	88	0.37	38	20	43	29	92	96	84	7%	116	12%	79%	27	59%	4%	4.50	21.7	76	205	$28
1st Half		329	55	10	42	9	307	282	344	486	830	759	856	5	89	0.51	35	19	46	32	100	119	99	7%	121	15%	75%	14	79%	0%	6.09	24.4	101	273	$32
2nd Half		355	45	7	50	6	245	253	272	358	630	721	602	3	88	0.25	40	20	40	26	84	74	71	6%	109	9%	86%	13	38%	8%	3.27	-1.3	50	135	$24
15	**Proj**	**624**	**96**	**16**	**81**	**12**	**270**	**270**	**319**	**413**	**732**	**806**	**706**	**6**	**88**	**0.55**	**39**	**21**	**41**	**29**	**103**	**96**	**92**	**7%**	**109**	**11%**	**71%**				**4.49**	**19.8**	**75**	**197**	**$24**

Kipnis,Jason

Age: 28 Bats: L Pos: 2B	Health B	LIMA Plan B+	
Ht: 5' 11" Wt: 190	PT/Exp A	Rand Var +3	
	Consist F	MM 3335	

Off-season weight program to add power backfired. Hit 3 HR in April, just 3 more rest of the way. Admitted that lingering oblique injury affected him all year. There will be a new conditioning program this winter, raising hopes for return of power, better BA, though low FB% limits HR ceiling.

Yr	Tm	AB	R	HR	RBI	SB	BA	xBA	OBP	SLG	OPS	vL	vR	bb%	ct%	Eye	G	L	F	h%	HctX	PX	xPX	hr/f	Spd	SBO	SB%	#Wk	DOM	DIS	RC/G	RAR	BPV	BPX	R$
10	aa	315	49	7	33	5	270		323	417	741			7	78	0.36				33		104			121	8%	83%				4.75		48	104	$8
11	CLE *	479	74	16	61	14	248	262	312	424	736	744	878	8	76	0.38	45	21	34	30	104	121	126	21%	108	13%	93%	8	50%	38%	4.61	0.1	51	113	$15
12	CLE	591	86	14	76	31	257	259	335	379	714	581	787	10	82	0.61	47	23	30	29	97	76	91	10%	106	21%	82%	27	48%	26%	4.44	4.7	41	103	$23
13	CLE	564	86	17	84	30	284	264	366	452	818	850	801	12	75	0.53	43	25	32	35	109	125	128	12%	99	21%	81%	27	48%	44%	6.03	37.0	54	135	$32
14	CLE	500	61	6	41	22	240	249	310	330	640	500	710	9	80	0.50	46	23	31	29	92	72	84	5%	96	18%	88%	23	30%	30%	3.58	2.8	26	70	$13
1st Half		212	24	3	22	8	245	253	326	358	685	614	720	11	79	0.56	46	22	33	30	112	91	110	5%	91	15%	89%	11	45%	36%	4.08	4.4	38	103	$8
2nd Half		288	37	3	19	14	236	245	298	309	607	414	703	8	81	0.45	47	23	30	28	78	58	66	4%	100	21%	88%	12	17%	25%	3.23	-1.4	18	49	$17
15	**Proj**	**568**	**80**	**15**	**72**	**26**	**261**	**265**	**335**	**404**	**739**	**638**	**789**	**10**	**79**	**0.51**	**45**	**23**	**32**	**31**	**98**	**105**	**100**	**11%**	**95**	**19%**	**85%**				**4.77**	**23.0**	**55**	**146**	**$25**

Konerko,Paul

Age: 39 Bats: R Pos: DH 1B	Health	LIMA Plan	
Ht: 6' 2" Wt: 220	PT/Exp	Rand Var	
	Consist	MM	

Perhaps underappreciated at his peak, he saw career come to inglorious end. But hey, he did hit one more HR than Jeter (while starring in far fewer cloying Nike ads). Happy retirement, Paul.

Yr	Tm	AB	R	HR	RBI	SB	BA	xBA	OBP	SLG	OPS	vL	vR	bb%	ct%	Eye	G	L	F	h%	HctX	PX	xPX	hr/f	Spd	SBO	SB%	#Wk	DOM	DIS	RC/G	RAR	BPV	BPX	R$
10	CHW	548	89	39	111	0	312	301	393	584	977	1102	941	12	80	0.65	35	20	45	33	132	170	164	20%	78	1%	0%	27	59%	7%	8.43	38.3	104	226	$31
11	CHW	543	69	31	105	1	300	289	388	517	906	847	924	12	84	0.87	37	22	41	31	125	133	136	16%	52	1%	50%	27	56%	19%	7.26	21.3	83	184	$27
12	CHW	533	66	26	75	0	298	274	371	486	857	846	861	10	84	0.67	41	22	37	31	102	108	96	16%	74	0%	0%	27	63%	15%	6.45	22.8	67	168	$21
13	CHW	467	41	12	54	0	244	252	313	355	669	923	600	9	84	0.61	36	24	39	27	95	71	94	8%	71	0%	0%	25	48%	32%	3.72	-10.7	34	85	$6
14	CHW	208	15	5	22	0	207	230	254	317	572	681	428	5	75	0.20	41	23	36	25	86	84	100	9%	58	0%	0%	26	35%	54%	2.48	-10.1	-1	-3	-$1
1st Half		112	9	4	16	0	214	247	256	366	622	735	489	4	81	0.24	38	19	43	23	114	104	133	10%	67	0%	0%	14	36%	43%	2.94	-3.8	39	105	$1
2nd Half		96	6	1	6	0	198	214	252	260	513	624	346	5	69	0.17	45	27	27	28	54	57	54	6%	65	0%	0%	12	33%	67%	1.97	-6.3	-48	-130	-$3
15	Proj																																		

Kratz,Erik

Age: 35 Bats: R Pos: CA	Health B	LIMA Plan D	
Ht: 6' 4" Wt: 240	PT/Exp F	Rand Var +1	
	Consist A	MM 4021	

5-13-.218 in 110 AB with KC and TOR. Still a threat to go yard; bb% decline, 2nd half ct% decline, 2nd half FB spike suggest increasing desire to make something happen quickly in limited playing time. Leave him be until front-liner ahead of him gets hurt. Even then, beware the BA hit.

Yr	Tm	AB	R	HR	RBI	SB	BA	xBA	OBP	SLG	OPS	vL	vR	bb%	ct%	Eye	G	L	F	h%	HctX	PX	xPX	hr/f	Spd	SBO	SB%	#Wk	DOM	DIS	RC/G	RAR	BPV	BPX	R$
10	PIT *	264	22	6	28	1	194	211	258	327	585	286	284	8	71	0.30	28	16	56	25	58	109	65	0%	78	6%	20%	3	0%	67%	2.55	-15.3	14	30	-$2
11	PHI *	364	40	11	38	1	226	307	280	362	642	0	2500	7	74	0.29	0	60	40	28	150	100	102	0%	74	2%	100%	1	100%	0%	3.36	-11.1	15	33	$3
12	PHI *	265	27	15	48	0	231	264	281	467	748	877	780	7	77	0.31	42	17	41	24	130	154	134	20%	55	0%	0%	16	44%	38%	4.35	0.5	65	163	$5
13	PHI	197	21	9	26	0	213	229	280	386	666	406	729	8	77	0.40	44	14	42	23	107	113	125	14%	68	0%	0%	21	38%	57%	3.49	-1.3	38	95	$1
14	2 AL *	197	21	7	25	0	228	255	267	403	669	647	623	5	77	0.23	41	18	41	26	109	131	122	14%	63	4%	0%	22	41%	50%	3.44	0.7	44	119	$2
1st Half		118	13	5	18	0	223	267	268	398	666	810	472	6	81	0.33	47	17	36	24	102	123	110	14%	64	6%	0%	11	55%	36%	3.32	-0.3	57	154	$3
2nd Half		79	8	3	7	0	236	238	265	410	675	382	864	4	70	0.13	30	20	50	30	122	145	144	13%	75	0%	0%	11	27%	64%	3.62	0.5	30	81	$0
15	**Proj**	**118**	**12**	**5**	**15**	**0**	**225**	**251**	**272**	**415**	**687**	**586**	**743**	**6**	**76**	**0.27**	**40**	**17**	**43**	**25**	**114**	**140**	**129**	**14%**	**69**	**1%**	**13%**				**3.69**	**1.1**	**37**	**98**	**$2**

KRISTOPHER OLSON

Krauss,Marc

Age: 27 Bats: L Pos: 1B	Health A	LIMA Plan F	
Ht: 6' 2" Wt: 245	PT/Exp C	Rand Var 0	
	Consist A	MM 3101	

6-21-.194 in 186 AB at HOU. Older prospect was in the right organization to get a long look but whiffed again, literally. Power even slipped a notch. Harsh reality: most potential employers will have younger, more interesting options. The separation has happened, graduating from prospect to suspect.

Yr Tm	AB	R	HR	RBI	SB	BA	xBA	OBP	SLG	OPS	vL	vR	bb%	ct%	Eye	G	L	F	h%	HctX	PX	xPX	hr/f	Spd	SBO	SB%	#Wk	DOM	DIS	RC/G	RAR	BPV	BPX	R$
10																																		
11 aa	433	48	11	45	1	210		281	366	647			9	68	0.31				28		123			111	5%	29%				3.22		24	53	$1
12 a/a	432	61	14	54	5	217		312	382	694			12	67	0.42				29		129			89	10%	48%				3.74		26	65	$6
13 HOU *	387	38	12	41	4	223	250	309	377	686	333	669	11	72	0.45	42	24	33	28	102	119	119	13%	70	8%	54%	14	29%	43%	3.74	-10.3	28	70	$4
14 HOU *	345	31	9	46	1	208	210	282	334	616	1100	574	9	68	0.33	38	19	43	27	81	106	76	11%	40	1%	100%	18	28%	50%	3.04	-11.7	-8	-22	$2
1st Half	195	19	6	28	0	214	203	300	359	659	1667	551	11	68	0.39	35	15	51	28	75	122	105	11%	46	0%	0%	9	22%	44%	3.50	-4.0	8	22	$3
2nd Half	150	11	3	18	1	200	220	258	303	561	857	610	7	69	0.25	42	25	33	27	89	85	38	11%	56	2%	100%	9	33%	56%	2.51	-7.8	-23	-62	-$1
15 Proj	101	10	3	12	1	212	232	292	357	649	691	645	10	69	0.35	40	22	38	28	91	119	87	12%	67	5%	55%				3.30	-2.7	8	20	-$1

Kubel,Jason

Age: 33 Bats: L Pos: LF	Health B	LIMA Plan D	
Ht: 6' 0" Wt: 220	PT/Exp D	Rand Var -2	
	Consist C	MM 3101	

Return to MIN couldn't pull him out of nose dive. Instead, crashed and burned by June. Pulled rip cord on contract, refused to go to minors. But no one sent search party. Quick scan of ct% tells tale, and it's a horror story. xPX still wants to believe, a bit. But he'd need to rock a spring audition at this point.

Yr Tm	AB	R	HR	RBI	SB	BA	xBA	OBP	SLG	OPS	vL	vR	bb%	ct%	Eye	G	L	F	h%	HctX	PX	xPX	hr/f	Spd	SBO	SB%	#Wk	DOM	DIS	RC/G	RAR	BPV	BPX	R$
10 MIN	518	68	21	92	0	249	256	323	427	750	655	792	10	78	0.48	38	19	43	28	111	117	128	12%	69	1%	0%	27	44%	22%	4.63	-7.1	46	100	$13
11 MIN	366	37	12	58	1	273	250	332	434	766	731	783	8	77	0.37	35	21	43	33	112	117	144	10%	59	2%	50%	19	42%	37%	5.02	-0.8	35	78	$10
12 ARI	506	75	30	90	1	253	265	327	506	833	736	888	10	70	0.38	33	23	44	30	118	176	179	19%	73	2%	50%	27	52%	26%	5.64	14.7	66	165	$17
13 2 TM	259	21	5	32	0	216	203	293	317	610	414	642	10	64	0.32	33	27	41	31	97	85	149	7%	71	1%	0%	22	27%	50%	2.99	-8.1	-30	-75	-$1
14 MIN	156	12	1	13	1	224	199	313	295	607	587	613	11	62	0.32	38	29	33	35	64	71	109	3%	77	2%	100%	10	10%	80%	3.03	-3.3	-47	-127	-$1
1st Half	156	12	1	13	1	224	199	313	295	607	587	613	11	62	0.32	38	29	33	35	64	71	109	3%	77	2%	100%	10	10%	80%	3.03	-3.4	-48	-130	-$1
2nd Half																																		
15 Proj	126	13	3	17	0	240	228	317	377	694	648	711	10	68	0.35	35	25	40	32	96	114	142	10%	73	2%	60%				3.98	0.9	4	10	$3

La Stella,Tommy

Age: 26 Bats: L Pos: 2B	Health A	LIMA Plan D+	
Ht: 5' 11" Wt: 185	PT/Exp F	Rand Var 0	
	Consist F	MM 1233	

1-31-.251 with 2 SB in 319 AB with ATL. A .322 career hitter in minors, he found extra-base hits, and thus BA, harder to come by in first taste of MLB. With experience, near-elite ct%, average HctX, above-average LD should lift average, but no power or speed to be found. Keep expectations modest.

Yr Tm	AB	R	HR	RBI	SB	BA	xBA	OBP	SLG	OPS	vL	vR	bb%	ct%	Eye	G	L	F	h%	HctX	PX	xPX	hr/f	Spd	SBO	SB%	#Wk	DOM	DIS	RC/G	RAR	BPV	BPX	R$
10																																		
11																																		
12																																		
13 aa	283	27	3	35	6	308		378	423	800			10	86	0.80				35		82			92	7%	84%				5.95		59	148	$10
14 ATL *	486	35	2	47	3	247	257	323	308	631	818	603	10	88	0.95	48	23	29	28	104	47	80	1%	80	3%	55%	19	42%	16%	3.34	-0.7	37	100	$4
1st Half	277	22	1	30	3	257	279	334	317	651	824	692	10	90	1.14	49	27	24	28	93	44	51	0%	99	4%	70%	6	50%	0%	3.63	1.9	47	127	$8
2nd Half	209	13	1	17	0	234	235	310	297	607	813	554	10	86	0.76	47	21	32	27	109	51	96	2%	72	2%	0%	13	38%	23%	2.98	-2.6	28	76	$0
15 Proj	378	30	2	40	4	269	265	343	347	690	868	648	10	87	0.86	48	23	29	31	103	61	78	2%	79	5%	74%				4.16	8.3	37	97	$8

Lagares,Juan

Age: 26 Bats: R Pos: CF	Health B	LIMA Plan B+	
Ht: 6' 1" Wt: 215	PT/Exp C	Rand Var -3	
	Consist B	MM 2415	

PRO: Running game took off in 2nd half; success should mean more green lights. Gold Glove-caliber defense should keep him in lineup. Intriguing 2nd half ct% added some lift to xBA. CON: Stagnant bb% is capping OBP, needs to solve RHP, get past season-ending elbow sprain. If contact gains hold... UP: 25 SB

Yr Tm	AB	R	HR	RBI	SB	BA	xBA	OBP	SLG	OPS	vL	vR	bb%	ct%	Eye	G	L	F	h%	HctX	PX	xPX	hr/f	Spd	SBO	SB%	#Wk	DOM	DIS	RC/G	RAR	BPV	BPX	R$
10																																		
11 aa	162	16	2	17	8	302		318	410	728			2	80	0.11				37		79			108	25%	77%				4.75		21	47	$5
12 aa	499	55	3	38	17	240		282	323	605			6	78	0.27				30		62			107	24%	60%				2.90		8	20	$8
13 NYM *	470	43	6	40	7	246	228	281	360	641	657	620	5	76	0.20	49	16	36	31	80	84	81	4%	135	13%	52%	24	21%	42%	3.27	-11.6	22	55	$7
14 NYM	416	46	4	47	13	281	249	321	382	703	875	658	5	79	0.23	46	22	32	35	93	81	89	4%	111	16%	76%	22	41%	36%	4.27	5.2	26	70	$14
1st Half	172	20	2	18	1	285	240	324	407	731	934	667	5	74	0.20	44	20	35	37	80	101	84	4%	117	9%	25%	11	45%	45%	4.34	2.4	25	68	$6
2nd Half	244	26	2	29	12	279	255	318	365	683	820	652	4	82	0.26	47	23	30	33	103	68	92	3%	103	21%	92%	11	36%	27%	4.21	2.4	25	68	$21
15 Proj	549	57	5	55	19	269	245	306	371	676	763	645	4	79	0.22	47	20	33	33	88	81	86	4%	120	19%	76%				3.88	0.4	26	68	$18

Lake,Junior

Age: 25 Bats: R Pos: LF CF	Health A	LIMA Plan D	
Ht: 6' 3" Wt: 215	PT/Exp D	Rand Var 0	
	Consist C	MM 3401	

9-25-.211 with 7 SB in 308 AB at CHC. Sometimes, the worst thing for a youngster is skill-defying success, like his 2013 MLB debut (38% MLB hit rate). But if he thought he didn't need to fix free-swinging approach, 2014 should be a wake-up call, particularly 2nd half. Time to mend ways, but he'll need lots of thread.

Yr Tm	AB	R	HR	RBI	SB	BA	xBA	OBP	SLG	OPS	vL	vR	bb%	ct%	Eye	G	L	F	h%	HctX	PX	xPX	hr/f	Spd	SBO	SB%	#Wk	DOM	DIS	RC/G	RAR	BPV	BPX	R$
10																																		
11 aa	242	31	5	13	14	220		250	326	576			4	73	0.15				28		79			123	34%	87%				2.80		2	4	$3
12 aa	405	46	8	41	17	253		303	385	688			7	71	0.25				34		102			96	31%	57%				3.65		12	30	$11
13 CHC *	392	49	9	30	15	275	258	312	417	729	956	692	5	73	0.20	42	28	30	36	96	112	79	13%	136	26%	61%	12	42%	42%	4.30	2.3	35	88	$14
14 CHC *	373	38	10	30	8	213	204	250	347	598	644	575	5	66	0.15	43	15	42	29	77	109	110	11%	124	18%	67%	25	24%	64%	2.76	-12.4	0	0	$4
1st Half	235	27	9	25	7	230	219	259	404	663	808	621	4	64	0.12	42	16	42	32	85	145	133	15%	116	21%	78%	14	36%	50%	3.49	-2.7	16	43	$10
2nd Half	138	11	1	5	1	185	177	232	250	483	434	313	6	69	0.20	45	14	41	25	44	51	37	0%	128	12%	41%	11	9%	82%	1.71	-9.7	-29	-78	-$8
15 Proj	232	25	5	17	7	229	223	277	354	631	670	608	5	70	0.19	43	20	37	30	75	102	78	9%	124	23%	62%				3.02	-5.2	5	12	$5

Lamb,Jacob

Age: 24 Bats: L Pos: 3B	Health A	LIMA Plan B+	
Ht: 6' 3" Wt: 220	PT/Exp F	Rand Var 0	
	Consist F	MM 4225	

4-11-.230 in 126 AB with ARI. Rose to majors after only 18 Triple-A ABs. No surprise then that MLB pitchers were a bit befuddling (71% ct%, 0.16 Eye). Truth is, ct% issues were there in minors, too, leaving short-term BA in doubt. But his defense is ready, so he should offer decent pop. Watch him grow.

Yr Tm	AB	R	HR	RBI	SB	BA	xBA	OBP	SLG	OPS	vL	vR	bb%	ct%	Eye	G	L	F	h%	HctX	PX	xPX	hr/f	Spd	SBO	SB%	#Wk	DOM	DIS	RC/G	RAR	BPV	BPX	R$
10																																		
11																																		
12																																		
13																																		
14 ARI *	518	59	15	70	2	269	259	324	451	775	364	692	8	70	0.27	52	17	31	36	98	152	105	14%	98	3%	71%	9	33%	44%	5.09	20.5	49	132	$16
1st Half	286	36	9	49	0	285	276	337	502	839			7	72	0.28				37		178			99	0%	0%				6.04		75	203	$19
2nd Half	232	26	7	26	2	266	241	329	424	753	364	692	9	69	0.31	52	17	31	36	97	132	105	14%	95	6%	71%	9	33%	44%	4.83	7.6	30	81	$11
15 Proj	514	60	14	70	3	258	256	317	434	751	416	818	8	70	0.30	52	17	31	34	87	148	95	13%	98	3%	67%				4.74	15.7	43	113	$15

LaRoche,Adam

Age: 35 Bats: L Pos: 1B	Health C	LIMA Plan B+	
Ht: 6' 3" Wt: 205	PT/Exp A	Rand Var 0	
	Consist C	MM 4225	

Some will look at 2nd half and conclude 1st half renaissance was fool's gold. But you know all that really changed was rough turn of h% luck. Yes, he'll hit DL a time or two and should probably sit vs. LHP, but still has plenty of punch. While others grab the "sexy new thing," he's the "ugly old vet" you can win with.

Yr Tm	AB	R	HR	RBI	SB	BA	xBA	OBP	SLG	OPS	vL	vR	bb%	ct%	Eye	G	L	F	h%	HctX	PX	xPX	hr/f	Spd	SBO	SB%	#Wk	DOM	DIS	RC/G	RAR	BPV	BPX	R$
10 ARI	560	75	25	100	0	261	253	320	468	788	758	802	8	69	0.28	38	18	44	33	119	160	172	15%	81	1%	0%	26	50%	38%	5.11	-18.6	47	102	$17
11 WAS	151	15	3	15	1	172	211	288	258	546	395	603	14	75	0.68	43	19	38	21	106	62	119	7%	78	2%	100%	8	13%	38%	2.34	-19.1	5	11	-$3
12 WAS	571	76	33	100	1	271	274	343	510	853	825	864	11	76	0.49	34	22	44	31	124	157	164	17%	77	1%	50%	27	63%	15%	6.18	12.2	75	188	$22
13 WAS	511	70	20	62	4	237	241	332	403	735	566	791	12	74	0.55	37	22	42	28	105	113	134	13%	102	3%	80%	26	50%	31%	4.47	-1.7	45	113	$11
14 WAS	494	73	26	92	3	259	266	362	455	817	620	891	14	78	0.76	37	22	41	28	126	131	162	16%	80	2%	100%	25	52%	16%	5.76	22.5	72	195	$20
1st Half	228	38	12	44	0	307	279	415	509	923	752	977	16	79	0.90	34	25	41	35	131	136	155	16%	92	0%	0%	12	58%	25%	7.85	22.8	85	230	$21
2nd Half	266	35	14	48	3	218	258	315	410	725	525	810	13	78	0.64	39	19	42	23	122	127	168	16%	74	4%	100%	13	46%	8%	4.28	1.0	62	168	$19
15 Proj	488	70	23	84	3	250	258	345	437	783	631	839	13	76	0.62	37	22	42	28	119	131	154	15%	82	2%	88%				5.18	14.6	56	146	$17

KRISTOPHER OLSON

Lawrie,Brett

Age: 25	Bats: R	Pos: 3B 2B	Health	F	LIMA Plan	B+
Ht: 6' 0"	Wt: 210		PT/Exp	C	Rand Var	0
			Consist	A	MM	4335

Perhaps hidden amidst another disappointing, injury-marred season: This is a 25-year-old who just hit 12 HRs in half a season. The power growth is real, given PX/xPX, GB/FB trend. Speed perhaps less so, given poor SB%. The last variable (and a big one) is health. This is still lurking... UP: 25 HR, .275

Yr	Tm	AB	R	HR	RBI	SB	BA	xBA	OBP	SLG	OPS	vL	vR	bb%	ct%	Eye	G	L	F	h%	HctX	PX	xPX	hr/f	Spd	SBO	SB%	#Wk	DOM	DIS	RC/G	RAR	BPV	BPX	R$
10	aa	554	73	7	51	24	263		312	407	719			7	76	0.30				33		103			140	29%	64%				4.16		45	98	$17
11	TOR *	442	67	21	64	15	297	282	345	546	891	786	1022	7	79	0.35	38	17	45	33	122	162	147	17%	137	18%	82%	8	63%	38%	6.86	25.2	103	229	$23
12	TOR	494	73	11	48	13	273	265	324	405	729	813	697	6	83	0.38	50	20	30	31	94	85	78	9%	114	16%	62%	23	43%	35%	4.37	-2.5	47	118	$16
13	TOR *	422	45	12	48	10	252	254	308	393	701	613	742	7	81	0.43	49	17	34	28	105	91	89	10%	121	14%	66%	20	60%	25%	4.04	1.1	52	130	$11
14	TOR	259	27	12	38	0	247	238	301	421	722	595	760	6	81	0.33	47	14	39	26	118	112	122	14%	78	0%	0%	14	43%	29%	4.15	3.6	51	138	$6
1st Half		258	27	12	38	0	244	239	299	419	718	595	755	6	81	0.33	47	14	40	26	118	113	122	14%	76	0%	0%	13	46%	31%	4.07	2.9	51	138	$6
2nd Half		1	0	0	0	0	1000	0	1000	1000	2000	0	2000	0	100	0.00	100	0	0	100	0	0	-14	0%	107	0%	0%	1	0%	0%	0.00	0.0	34	92	-$16
15	**Proj**	**425**	**53**	**17**	**52**	**9**	**263**	**266**	**319**	**445**	**765**	**718**	**781**	**7**	**81**	**0.36**	**47**	**15**	**38**	**29**	**108**	**123**	**104**	**13%**	**114**	**13%**	**68%**				**4.70**	**12.5**	**65**	**170**	**$14**

LeMahieu,DJ

Age: 26	Bats: R	Pos: 2B	Health	A	LIMA Plan	B
Ht: 6' 4"	Wt: 205		PT/Exp	C	Rand Var	-1
			Consist	A	MM	1435

If path to fantasy value is stealing bases, you'd do well to make your chances of success better than a coin flip (or worse, in 2nd half). Sure enough, chances dried up as season wore on. Faltering ct% doesn't bode well, nor does 2nd half give-back of bb% gains. Young enough to refine skills; for now, no sure thing.

Yr	Tm	AB	R	HR	RBI	SB	BA	xBA	OBP	SLG	OPS	vL	vR	bb%	ct%	Eye	G	L	F	h%	HctX	PX	xPX	hr/f	Spd	SBO	SB%	#Wk	DOM	DIS	RC/G	RAR	BPV	BPX	R$
10																																			
11	CHC *	474	40	4	38	6	266	260	294	341	635	667	465	4	86	0.27	65	17	19	30	71	54	38	0%	117	13%	40%	9	11%	56%	3.24	-20.6	30	67	$7
12	COL *	484	46	3	41	9	281	261	318	370	689	681	764	5	85	0.37	56	19	25	33	93	61	72	4%	146	14%	50%	17	41%	35%	3.96	-5.4	44	110	$11
13	COL *	547	59	3	41	23	285	286	316	375	692	652	682	4	84	0.28	55	27	18	34	97	64	64	3%	142	22%	71%	20	30%	30%	4.16	7.8	40	100	$20
14	COL	494	59	5	42	10	267	250	315	348	663	669	660	6	80	0.34	56	21	23	32	97	57	84	5%	146	14%	50%	26	35%	42%	3.58	2.7	26	70	$13
1st Half		255	38	2	23	8	271	263	332	333	665	739	642	8	84	0.55	60	22	18	32	106	46	79	5%	115	16%	62%	14	36%	43%	3.74	2.6	24	65	$16
2nd Half		239	21	3	19	2	264	235	295	364	659	593	680	4	77	0.18	52	19	29	33	87	69	91	6%	163	12%	29%	12	33%	42%	3.39	0.0	22	59	$9
15	**Proj**	**465**	**49**	**4**	**38**	**11**	**273**	**261**	**310**	**358**	**669**	**662**	**671**	**5**	**82**	**0.30**	**56**	**21**	**22**	**33**	**93**	**62**	**74**	**4%**	**144**	**16%**	**55%**				**3.71**	**4.2**	**21**	**54**	**$13**

Lind,Adam

Age: 31	Bats: L	Pos: 1B DH	Health	C	LIMA Plan	B+
Ht: 6' 2"	Wt: 195		PT/Exp	C	Rand Var	-4
			Consist	B	MM	4345

Injuries tamped down AB, while hr/f conspired with always-high GB% to hold back HR. Appears he may have traded a bit of power for contact, but fortunate hit rate helped, too. And just forget about LHP (2-for-33). With health, expect a power rebound, coupled with a BA regression.

Yr	Tm	AB	R	HR	RBI	SB	BA	xBA	OBP	SLG	OPS	vL	vR	bb%	ct%	Eye	G	L	F	h%	HctX	PX	xPX	hr/f	Spd	SBO	SB%	#Wk	DOM	DIS	RC/G	RAR	BPV	BPX	R$
10	TOR	569	57	23	72	0	237	258	287	425	712	341	829	6	75	0.26	41	19	40	28	110	133	135	13%	81	0%	0%	27	48%	22%	4.05	-30.3	44	96	$8
11	TOR	499	56	26	87	1	251	263	295	439	734	639	771	6	79	0.30	40	22	38	27	132	119	135	17%	78	2%	50%	24	54%	38%	4.39	-21.3	47	104	$14
12	TOR *	457	45	17	65	1	274	250	332	445	778	553	795	8	78	0.40	48	17	35	32	98	110	101	12%	101	1%	100%	18	56%	17%	5.21	4.1	49	123	$12
13	TOR	465	67	23	67	1	288	279	357	497	854	573	924	10	78	0.50	46	21	33	33	133	140	141	19%	93	1%	100%	27	52%	15%	6.40	24.5	73	183	$19
14	TOR	290	38	6	40	0	321	283	381	479	860	223	942	9	83	0.58	47	21	33	37	134	119	123	8%	107	0%	0%	21	62%	19%	6.85	21.6	81	219	$12
1st Half		160	30	4	26	0	331	283	406	506	912	259	1033	11	82	0.69	44	20	36	39	149	132	138	9%	115	0%	0%	12	75%	0%	7.83	15.8	92	249	$16
2nd Half		130	8	2	14	0	308	282	348	446	794	111	840	6	85	0.42	50	22	29	35	117	103	105	6%	97	0%	0%	9	44%	44%	5.72	5.9	67	181	$7
15	**Proj**	**424**	**52**	**14**	**60**	**0**	**284**	**279**	**343**	**463**	**805**	**442**	**879**	**8**	**81**	**0.47**	**46**	**20**	**33**	**32**	**125**	**128**	**123**	**13%**	**98**	**0%**	**91%**				**5.67**	**17.8**	**60**	**157**	**$16**

Lindor,Francisco

Age: 21	Bats: B	Pos: SS	Health	A	LIMA Plan	D
Ht: 5' 11"	Wt: 175		PT/Exp	F	Rand Var	0
			Consist	B	MM	1303

Top prospect saw encouraging HR bump, though upper levels also posed some challenges - note a 9/36 BB/K in 165 AB at AAA-Columbus. He was also caught on 7 of 10 SB attempts. Only 21, there's plenty of time for him to smooth out rough edges. Worth repeating - he's 21. That means you don't go bidding $15, even in Cleveland.

Yr	Tm	AB	R	HR	RBI	SB	BA	xBA	OBP	SLG	OPS	vL	vR	bb%	ct%	Eye	G	L	F	h%	HctX	PX	xPX	hr/f	Spd	SBO	SB%	#Wk	DOM	DIS	RC/G	RAR	BPV	BPX	R$
10																																			
11																																			
12																																			
13	aa	76	11	1	6	4	259		351	342	693			12	90	1.40				28		52			118	23%	65%				4.00		63	158	$1
14	a/a	507	61	9	51	23	247		301	340	641			7	79	0.36				30		66			105	29%	57%				3.18		16	43	$16
1st Half		279	39	5	35	16	255		323	355	678			9	80	0.50				30		69			126	28%	67%				3.80		32	86	$22
2nd Half		228	23	4	15	7	239		275	324	599			5	78	0.22				29		64			105	31%	43%				2.54		5	14	$9
15	**Proj**	**262**	**30**	**5**	**23**	**11**	**247**	**221**	**296**	**348**	**644**	**644**	**644**	**7**	**78**	**0.33**	**47**	**15**	**38**	**30**		**71**		**7%**	**116**	**30%**	**52%**				**3.11**	**-1.0**	**14**	**36**	**$8**

Liriano,Rymer

Age: 24	Bats: R	Pos: RF	Health	A	LIMA Plan	C+
Ht: 6' 0"	Wt: 230		PT/Exp	F	Rand Var	0
			Consist	A	MM	3405

1-6-.220 with 4 SB in 109 AB at SD. Piled up steals in A/AA before missing 2013 due to TJS. Earned promotion to majors with 1.182 OPS in 62 Triple-A AB, then big-league pitchers humbled him (64% contact). Still an intriguing power-speed prospect who could blossom with better pitch recognition.

Yr	Tm	AB	R	HR	RBI	SB	BA	xBA	OBP	SLG	OPS	vL	vR	bb%	ct%	Eye	G	L	F	h%	HctX	PX	xPX	hr/f	Spd	SBO	SB%	#Wk	DOM	DIS	RC/G	RAR	BPV	BPX	R$
10																																			
11																																			
12	aa	183	19	2	16	8	219		283	321	604			8	69	0.29				31		81			107	21%	88%				3.10		-8	-20	$1
13																																			
14	SD *	542	62	11	52	18	232	232	284	349	632	543	564	7	67	0.22	49	24	27	33	69	103	93	5%	99	22%	64%	8	0%	75%	3.16	-15.6	-4	-11	$12
1st Half		300	37	10	37	11	224	228	279	375	654			7	67	0.23				30	0	122			94	26%	67%				3.32		10	27	$15
2nd Half		242	30	2	21	8	261	229	316	358	674	543	564	8	68	0.25	49	24	27	38	70	94	93	5%	97	20%	65%	8	0%	75%	3.79	-1.5	-8	-22	$10
15	**Proj**	**419**	**49**	**10**	**40**	**14**	**239**	**228**	**307**	**377**	**684**	**721**	**648**	**8**	**68**	**0.26**	**43**	**21**	**36**	**33**	**63**	**117**	**84**	**10%**	**112**	**20%**	**70%**				**3.71**	**-3.6**	**16**	**43**	**$12**

Lobaton,Jose

Age: 30	Bats: B	Pos: CA	Health	B	LIMA Plan	D
Ht: 6' 0"	Wt: 215		PT/Exp	F	Rand Var	-2
			Consist	C	MM	1001

After a brief flirtation with being one of the shinier objects in the $1 catcher bin in 2013, ct% and PX reverted to BA-killing levels. Loss of patience didn't help, either. This is one of those catchers we warn you about, the one who defies "first, do no harm." Lots of harm here, because of bad stats and in too many ABs.

Yr	Tm	AB	R	HR	RBI	SB	BA	xBA	OBP	SLG	OPS	vL	vR	bb%	ct%	Eye	G	L	F	h%	HctX	PX	xPX	hr/f	Spd	SBO	SB%	#Wk	DOM	DIS	RC/G	RAR	BPV	BPX	R$
10	a/a	265	22	5	27	1	214		279	309	588			8	74	0.35				27		72			91	1%	100%				2.81		0	0	-$1
11	TAM *	218	20	6	23	0	216	237	314	344	658	390	349	12	68	0.44	46	27	27	29	26	102	21	0%	70	0%	0%	7	14%	57%	3.52	-5.7	0	0	-$1
12	TAM *	195	17	2	21	0	201	200	295	291	586	751	584	12	71	0.47	48	16	36	27	80	78	100	5%	67	2%	0%	21	29%	52%	2.68	-9.8	-6	-15	-$3
13	TAM	277	38	7	32	0	249	256	320	394	714	653	745	10	77	0.46	44	23	32	30	88	104	82	10%	99	1%	0%	27	52%	26%	4.25	4.5	41	103	$4
14	WAS	214	18	2	12	0	234	217	287	304	591	483	633	7	71	0.25	49	24	27	32	93	64	95	5%	86	0%	0%	24	21%	58%	2.87	-3.7	-21	-57	-$1
1st Half		135	10	2	10	0	207	211	277	296	573	362	638	8	68	0.28	47	23	30	29	90	81	89	7%	73	0%	0%	14	21%	64%	2.59	-3.4	-22	-59	-$1
2nd Half		79	8	0	2	0	278	228	305	316	621	621	622	4	77	0.17	52	25	23	36	99	39	104	0%	104	0%	0%	10	20%	50%	3.41	0.0	-19	-51	$0
15	**Proj**	**161**	**16**	**2**	**13**	**0**	**239**	**229**	**301**	**326**	**627**	**596**	**642**	**8**	**74**	**0.33**	**48**	**23**	**30**	**31**	**91**	**75**	**93**	**6%**	**89**	**1%**	**10%**				**3.26**	**-0.7**	**-15**	**-39**	**$2**

Lombardozzi,Steve

Age: 26	Bats: B	Pos: 2B	Health	A	LIMA Plan	D
Ht: 6' 0"	Wt: 200		PT/Exp	D	Rand Var	+2
			Consist	B	MM	0221

0-2-.288 in 72 AB at BAL. OK, so he can put the bat on the ball, but there's little oomph behind these swings. Really, those PX/xPX levels reflect amazingly little oomph. They represent lots and lots (solid ct%) of soft grounders to shortstop and easy outfield flies. OBP/bb% make his bat virtually worthless.

Yr	Tm	AB	R	HR	RBI	SB	BA	xBA	OBP	SLG	OPS	vL	vR	bb%	ct%	Eye	G	L	F	h%	HctX	PX	xPX	hr/f	Spd	SBO	SB%	#Wk	DOM	DIS	RC/G	RAR	BPV	BPX	R$
10	aa	105	17	4	10	3	276		341	477	818			9	85	0.65				29		118			131	20%	62%				5.47		93	202	$3
11	WAS *	587	73	7	43	24	273	244	310	371	681	0	459	5	85	0.35	44	19	37	31	48	64	29	0%	125	22%	73%	4	25%	50%	3.99	-12.3	41	91	$18
12	WAS	384	40	3	27	5	273	252	317	354	671	532	715	5	88	0.41	47	20	33	30	75	52	46	3%	118	8%	63%	27	26%	26%	3.77	-4.4	41	103	$7
13	WAS	290	25	2	22	4	259	258	278	338	616	659	601	3	88	0.24	50	20	31	29	76	57	45	3%	102	11%	57%	27	41%	30%	3.15	-4.9	37	93	$3
14	BAL *	343	24	0	22	5	233	247	258	266	524	143	740	3	85	0.22	45	28	28	27	87	26	42	0%	118	12%	52%	6	17%	67%	2.19	-12.5	4	11	$1
1st Half		233	15	0	11	3	232	244	254	258	512	143	740	3	85	0.19	45	28	28	27	87	21	42	0%	123	12%	46%	6	17%	67%	2.06	-9.5	1	3	$0
2nd Half		110	9	0	12	2	235	227	267	283	550			4	85	0.29				28	0	39			99	12%	63%				2.48		11	30	$1
15	**Proj**	**114**	**10**	**1**	**9**	**2**	**250**	**252**	**287**	**316**	**603**	**433**	**653**	**4**	**86**	**0.29**	**47**	**23**	**30**	**29**	**79**	**49**	**44**	**2%**	**111**	**12%**	**59%**				**2.93**	**-1.6**	**18**	**48**	**$2**

KRISTOPHER OLSON

Loney,James

Age: 31 Bats: L Pos: 1B
Ht: 6' 3" Wt: 235
Health A | PT/Exp A | Consist D
LIMA Plan B+ | Rand Var -1 | MM 1145

Power regression not unexpected, but not so severe, either. The outward volatility is all about errant gusts of wind, every year. One-year dalliance with competence vs. LHP came to an end, but otherwise, skills remarkably stable... if unremarkable. Other first basemen are a rock band; he's Muzak.

Yr	Tm	AB	R	HR	RBI	SB	BA	xBA	OBP	SLG	OPS	vL	vR	bb%	ct%	Eye	G	L	F	h%	HctX	PX	xPX	hr/f	Spd	SBO	SB%	#Wk	DOM	DIS	RC/G	RAR	BPV	BPX	R$
10	LA	588	67	10	88	10	267	284	329	395	723	575	785	8	84	0.55	43	25	32	30	92	92	79	6%	70	10%	67%	27	56%	11%	4.43	-20.6	48	104	$16
11	LA	531	56	12	65	4	288	272	339	416	755	561	816	7	87	0.63	41	22	37	31	80	85	79	7%	81	3%	100%	27	48%	15%	5.12	-7.5	58	129	$16
12	2 TM	434	37	6	41	0	249	266	293	336	630	508	662	6	88	0.55	46	25	29	27	93	58	65	5%	55	3%	0%	27	33%	26%	3.26	-26.1	30	75	$4
13	TAM	549	54	13	75	3	299	297	348	430	778	729	797	7	86	0.57	42	30	28	33	102	89	77	10%	60	2%	75%	27	48%	22%	5.48	13.2	50	125	$20
14	TAM	600	59	9	69	4	290	271	336	380	716	601	762	6	87	0.51	42	27	31	32	92	65	78	6%	60	2%	100%	27	48%	26%	4.62	8.0	31	84	$19
1st Half		313	32	4	41	2	278	271	332	377	709	669	725	7	87	0.57	42	25	33	31	101	75	87	4%	59	2%	100%	14	57%	21%	4.43	2.3	40	108	$18
2nd Half		287	27	5	28	2	303	271	341	383	724	527	802	6	87	0.45	43	28	28	34	83	53	68	7%	69	2%	100%	13	38%	31%	4.85	5.3	23	62	$19
15	Proj	**555**	**54**	**8**	**65**	**3**	**286**	**276**	**334**	**382**	**715**	**608**	**755**	**7**	**87**	**0.54**	**43**	**27**	**30**	**32**	**93**	**69**	**75**	**6%**	**60**	**3%**	**76%**				**4.56**	**6.1**	**31**	**81**	**$15**

Longoria,Evan

Age: 29 Bats: R Pos: 3B
Ht: 6' 2" Wt: 210
Health C | PT/Exp B | Consist B
LIMA Plan B+ | Rand Var 0 | MM 4225

Minor jump in ct% came with a drop in HctX. That means that he was hitting the ball more often, but with less authority. That drove across-the-board losses in PX/xPX, xBA. There is some name brand cachet that still boosts his ADP, thanks to memories of 2008-10 debut. This is a different player; there's little profit at $20.

Yr	Tm	AB	R	HR	RBI	SB	BA	xBA	OBP	SLG	OPS	vL	vR	bb%	ct%	Eye	G	L	F	h%	HctX	PX	xPX	hr/f	Spd	SBO	SB%	#Wk	DOM	DIS	RC/G	RAR	BPV	BPX	R$
10	TAM	574	96	22	104	15	294	283	372	507	879	956	845	11	78	0.58	37	20	43	34	116	150	142	11%	123	12%	75%	25	76%	4%	6.80	32.0	95	207	$29
11	TAM	483	78	31	99	3	244	286	355	495	850	943	819	14	81	0.86	37	18	45	24	123	158	137	18%	85	4%	60%	23	70%	17%	5.82	14.6	105	233	$18
12	TAM *	303	39	17	57	2	276	264	357	491	848	1064	842	11	76	0.53	38	22	40	31	126	137	147	20%	84	6%	40%	14	57%	21%	5.99	12.5	64	160	$11
13	TAM	614	91	32	88	1	269	264	343	498	842	950	799	10	74	0.43	37	19	45	32	126	164	173	16%	83	1%	100%	27	63%	33%	5.98	35.8	73	183	$23
14	TAM	624	83	22	91	5	253	249	320	404	724	824	691	8	79	0.43	39	20	41	29	110	105	118	11%	94	3%	100%	27	48%	19%	4.40	13.3	46	124	$19
1st Half		332	45	10	37	3	262	250	331	395	725	915	661	9	78	0.42	43	23	35	31	102	93	103	11%	100	3%	100%	14	43%	21%	4.49	7.6	36	97	$17
2nd Half		292	38	12	54	2	243	249	309	414	723	720	724	8	79	0.43	35	18	47	27	118	119	135	11%	92	3%	100%	13	54%	15%	4.30	5.2	59	159	$21
15	Proj	**600**	**83**	**24**	**94**	**4**	**261**	**254**	**335**	**437**	**772**	**869**	**737**	**10**	**77**	**0.47**	**39**	**20**	**41**	**30**	**118**	**126**	**140**	**13%**	**91**	**3%**	**76%**				**5.01**	**23.0**	**51**	**135**	**$22**

Lough,David

Age: 29 Bats: L Pos: LF
Ht: 5' 11" Wt: 180
Health A | PT/Exp D | Consist C
LIMA Plan D+ | Rand Var 0 | MM 2431

By the time hit-rate pendulum swung in his favor and skills rebounded, playing time had dried up. Healthy SBO indicates team tried, at least, to get him going on basepaths, but no dice. Age 30 is drawing nigh, so chances are that starting gig, healthy SB totals just ain't gonna happen.

Yr	Tm	AB	R	HR	RBI	SB	BA	xBA	OBP	SLG	OPS	vL	vR	bb%	ct%	Eye	G	L	F	h%	HctX	PX	xPX	hr/f	Spd	SBO	SB%	#Wk	DOM	DIS	RC/G	RAR	BPV	BPX	R$
10	aaa	460	48	7	43	10	245		290	367	657			6	83	0.37				28		72			155	14%	64%				3.51		50	109	$7
11	aaa	456	60	6	45	10	269		307	398	705			5	88	0.45				30		79			132	17%	51%				4.00		67	149	$12
12	KC *	550	55	6	48	18	224	229	252	327	579	452	614	4	85	0.24	40	18	42	25	58	60	49	0%	142	21%	79%	6	17%	0%	2.73	-31.0	38	95	$6
13	KC *	469	56	7	46	9	286	258	312	407	719	745	718	4	84	0.24	42	23	35	33	70	79	46	5%	137	14%	52%	21	38%	24%	4.30	4.3	49	123	$15
14	BAL	174	31	4	16	8	247	243	309	385	694	250	749	8	81	0.45	34	23	42	28	83	89	82	7%	147	29%	62%	26	35%	58%	3.75	0.3	57	154	$5
1st Half		115	17	2	8	5	191	197	268	287	555	0	622	9	77	0.41	35	16	49	23	68	67	76	5%	124	26%	71%	14	14%	79%	2.36	-5.1	16	43	$3
2nd Half		59	14	2	8	3	356	322	391	576	967	714	1000	6	90	0.67	33	35	33	37	111	126	91	12%	148	33%	50%	12	58%	33%	7.74	6.4	119	322	$9
15	Proj	**132**	**21**	**3**	**13**	**5**	**261**	**264**	**304**	**405**	**709**	**560**	**734**	**6**	**84**	**0.38**	**38**	**24**	**38**	**29**	**80**	**92**	**66**	**6%**	**141**	**26%**	**58%**				**3.93**	**0.7**	**67**	**177**	**$5**

Lowrie,Jed

Age: 31 Bats: B Pos: SS
Ht: 6' 0" Wt: 190
Health D | PT/Exp B | Consist C
LIMA Plan A | Rand Var +1 | MM 3335

Finger, neck and foot injuries all cost him 2014 time. Chalk up 1st half to h% misfortune, though hr/f, HctX, xPx suggest he was hitting the ball plenty hard. Hit rate returned in the 2nd half, but punch was AWOL. Larger body of work says trust 1st half—but also that he's bound to miss time.

Yr	Tm	AB	R	HR	RBI	SB	BA	xBA	OBP	SLG	OPS	vL	vR	bb%	ct%	Eye	G	L	F	h%	HctX	PX	xPX	hr/f	Spd	SBO	SB%	#Wk	DOM	DIS	RC/G	RAR	BPV	BPX	R$
10	BOS	171	31	9	24	1	287	292	381	526	907	1025	823	13	85	1.00	29	16	54	29	141	153	166	11%	89	4%	50%	12	67%	8%	6.99	13.6	118	257	$6
11	BOS	309	40	6	36	1	252	226	303	382	685	876	582	7	81	0.38	33	18	49	30	107	87	120	5%	126	3%	50%	20	35%	40%	3.92	-2.2	46	102	$5
12	HOU	340	43	16	42	2	244	253	331	438	769	623	819	11	81	0.66	29	19	51	26	125	121	162	11%	93	2%	100%	18	50%	17%	4.90	10.0	73	183	$7
13	OAK	603	80	15	75	1	290	272	344	446	791	772	800	8	85	0.55	33	23	43	32	94	108	99	7%	94	1%	100%	26	69%	8%	5.53	35.3	71	178	$21
14	OAK	502	59	6	50	0	249	250	321	355	676	598	707	9	84	0.65	31	24	44	29	107	79	112	3%	104	0%	0%	25	44%	16%	3.83	9.6	52	141	$7
1st Half		285	40	4	31	0	221	249	316	330	646	618	658	12	84	0.83	30	23	47	25	125	85	144	4%	73	0%	0%	14	43%	14%	3.38	1.2	51	138	$7
2nd Half		217	19	2	19	0	286	253	328	387	715	574	776	6	85	0.39	33	26	41	33	83	70	71	3%	139	0%	0%	11	45%	18%	4.51	7.7	50	135	$6
15	Proj	**511**	**62**	**13**	**56**	**1**	**266**	**262**	**332**	**414**	**746**	**698**	**768**	**9**	**84**	**0.60**	**32**	**23**	**45**	**30**	**105**	**104**	**113**	**7%**	**105**	**1%**	**79%**				**4.76**	**22.3**	**56**	**147**	**$14**

Lucas,Edward

Age: 33 Bats: R Pos: 2B
Ht: 6' 3" Wt: 215
Health B | PT/Exp D | Consist C
LIMA Plan F | Rand Var -4 | MM 1201

1-9-.251 in 179 AB at MIA. Consistent slugger in 2014—in a weird, .277 sort-of way. Defensive versatility may keep him employed (just barely) in the majors, but there's no mistaking that this is an anemic bat. Tough going when xBA, h% regression think this will (and can) get WORSE.

Yr	Tm	AB	R	HR	RBI	SB	BA	xBA	OBP	SLG	OPS	vL	vR	bb%	ct%	Eye	G	L	F	h%	HctX	PX	xPX	hr/f	Spd	SBO	SB%	#Wk	DOM	DIS	RC/G	RAR	BPV	BPX	R$
10	aaa	352	35	8	34	5	243		310	362	672			9	77	0.42				30		87			96	6%	79%				3.80		26	57	$4
11	a/a	421	39	7	38	3	180		234	266	500			7	65	0.20				26		76			86	3%	100%				1.96		-36	-80	-$5
12	aaa	412	35	6	30	3	180		210	263	473			4	73	0.14				23		61			90	12%	35%				1.61		-21	-53	-$5
13	MIA *	532	62	7	38	2	250	241	296	338	634	883	544	6	77	0.28	47	25	29	31	71	69	40	5%	97	3%	52%	19	16%	47%	3.36	-9.9	5	13	$7
14	MIA *	225	22	1	11	1	238	217	277	277	555	749	465	5	73	0.20	55	24	21	32	55	36	37	4%	103	2%	100%	19	16%	58%	2.60	-7.4	-35	-95	$0
1st Half		119	14	1	5	0	244	211	286	277	563	796	442	6	74	0.23	61	22	17	32	57	25	34	7%	109	0%	0%	10	10%	70%	2.67	-3.6	-39	-105	$0
2nd Half		106	8	0	6	1	232	219	268	277	545	688	527	5	72	0.17	42	28	30	32	51	49	44	0%	91	4%	100%	9	22%	44%	2.51	-3.8	-35	-95	$0
15	Proj	**198**	**19**	**1**	**13**	**1**	**230**	**226**	**274**	**290**	**564**	**704**	**474**	**6**	**73**	**0.22**	**49**	**25**	**26**	**31**	**61**	**54**	**40**	**4%**	**97**	**4%**	**67%**				**2.61**	**-4.7**	**-34**	**-88**	**$1**

Lucroy,Jonathan

Age: 29 Bats: R Pos: CA
Ht: 6' 0" Wt: 195
Health B | PT/Exp B | Consist C
LIMA Plan A | Rand Var 0 | MM 3255

Owners may have gotten greedy after monster 1st half, but otherwise hard to quibble with this year of modest growth in ct%, bb%, and continued hitting of the ball on the nose. If this is his "plateau," the view is pretty darn nice. But the potential for hr/f recovery means that he still has... UP: 20 HR.

Yr	Tm	AB	R	HR	RBI	SB	BA	xBA	OBP	SLG	OPS	vL	vR	bb%	ct%	Eye	G	L	F	h%	HctX	PX	xPX	hr/f	Spd	SBO	SB%	#Wk	DOM	DIS	RC/G	RAR	BPV	BPX	R$
10	MIL *	399	36	6	38	4	256	237	298	336	634	735	589	6	84	0.36	44	19	38	29	92	56	79	5%	90	6%	67%	20	30%	30%	3.41	-11.2	20	43	$5
11	MIL	430	45	12	59	2	265	248	313	391	703	869	662	6	77	0.29	42	24	34	32	79	87	82	11%	93	3%	67%	25	36%	40%	4.21	-2.0	20	44	$10
12	MIL	316	46	12	58	4	320	284	368	513	881	1169	782	7	86	0.50	41	21	37	34	131	112	129	12%	123	6%	80%	20	60%	15%	7.00	22.9	86	215	$16
13	MIL	521	59	18	82	9	280	281	340	455	795	859	775	8	87	0.67	39	23	38	29	133	104	135	10%	110	7%	90%	27	48%	7%	5.53	27.0	81	203	$21
14	MIL	585	73	13	69	4	301	298	373	465	837	838	837	10	88	0.93	42	22	36	33	132	119	128	7%	98	5%	50%	27	78%	0%	6.19	44.2	98	265	$23
1st Half		299	39	8	42	3	334	308	403	515	918	954	905	10	89	1.00	42	23	35	36	149	128	131	9%	99	6%	50%	14	79%	0%	7.73	34.4	109	295	$29
2nd Half		286	34	5	27	1	266	287	341	413	753	674	773	10	87	0.86	42	22	36	29	115	110	125	5%	98	3%	50%	13	77%	0%	4.82	11.8	88	238	$16
15	Proj	**525**	**64**	**16**	**71**	**5**	**291**	**290**	**353**	**462**	**815**	**887**	**794**	**9**	**86**	**0.70**	**41**	**22**	**37**	**31**	**126**	**117**	**125**	**9%**	**101**	**5%**	**70%**				**5.81**	**35.5**	**81**	**212**	**$22**

Ludwick,Ryan

Age: 36 Bats: R Pos: LF
Ht: 6' 2" Wt: 215
Health F | PT/Exp D | Consist F
LIMA Plan D | Rand Var 0 | MM 3021

After losing much of 2013 to shoulder injury, question in 2014 was: Would above-average power return? Now that that question has largely been answered "no," he shouldn't see 400+ AB again, especially at his age. Still capable of handling weak side of platoon, if that has value to you.

Yr	Tm	AB	R	HR	RBI	SB	BA	xBA	OBP	SLG	OPS	vL	vR	bb%	ct%	Eye	G	L	F	h%	HctX	PX	xPX	hr/f	Spd	SBO	SB%	#Wk	DOM	DIS	RC/G	RAR	BPV	BPX	R$
10	2 NL	490	63	17	69	0	251	255	325	418	743	609	800	9	75	0.40	32	23	45	30	106	120	126	10%	115	3%	0%	24	42%	42%	4.37	-12.9	52	113	$10
11	2 NL	490	56	13	75	1	237	222	310	363	674	763	644	9	75	0.41	34	19	47	29	101	95	124	7%	72	2%	50%	26	27%	35%	3.73	-22.6	17	38	$8
12	CIN	422	53	26	80	0	275	288	346	531	877	937	853	9	77	0.43	33	24	43	30	107	166	127	18%	68	1%	0%	27	59%	26%	6.30	18.8	81	203	$16
13	CIN *	167	8	3	15	0	209	219	254	295	549	783	577	6	76	0.25	36	24	41	26	59	64	62	5%	71	0%	0%	9	11%	44%	2.42	-8.4	-11	-28	-$3
14	CIN	357	28	9	45	0	244	249	308	375	683	796	645	8	74	0.33	37	26	37	31	99	107	106	9%	79	2%	0%	26	31%	31%	3.76	-0.2	22	59	$5
1st Half		200	15	5	24	0	265	245	326	395	721	725	719	8	73	0.31	39	26	36	34	96	106	100	9%	77	2%	0%	14	36%	36%	4.33	3.4	17	46	$6
2nd Half		157	13	4	21	0	217	252	286	350	636	878	547	8	75	0.35	34	27	39	27	102	107	114	9%	84	3%	0%	12	25%	25%	3.11	-3.1	27	73	$3
15	Proj	**226**	**19**	**6**	**29**	**0**	**236**	**247**	**298**	**373**	**671**	**793**	**631**	**8**	**75**	**0.33**	**35**	**25**	**40**	**29**	**91**	**108**	**101**	**9%**	**77**	**2%**	**3%**				**3.61**	**-0.9**	**9**	**23**	**$4**

KRISTOPHER OLSON

Machado,Manny

Age: 22 Bats: R Pos: 3B	Health C	LIMA Plan A
Ht: 6' 2" Wt: 180	PT/Exp B	Rand Var -2
	Consist A	MM 4345

Another torn ligament, this time in his right knee, cut season short in August. Half-year hr/f trend since '13 (7%, 9%, 14%, 16%) a great sign, but 2nd half ct%, xBA, and SBO all suggest he's not quite ready to break out. Still just 22 with better skills and big future, but the list of obstacles should temper '15 expectations.

Yr	Tm	AB	R	HR	RBI	SB	BA	xBA	OBP	SLG	OPS	vL	vR	bb%	ct%	Eye	G	L	F	h%	HctX	PX	xPX	hr/f	Spd	SBO	SB%	#Wk	DOM	DIS	RC/G	RAR	BPV	BPX	R$
10																																			
11																																			
12	BAL *	593	73	17	74	13	254	251	310	417	727	801	716	8	81	0.44	46	14	40	29	115	103	100	12%	133	12%	75%	9	44%	44%	4.40	-2.4	65	163	$16
13	BAL	667	88	14	71	6	283	277	314	432	746	762	738	4	83	0.26	47	21	32	32	101	107	73	8%	122	9%	46%	26	62%	12%	4.64	13.2	65	163	$22
14	BAL	327	38	12	32	2	278	262	324	431	755	642	802	6	79	0.29	49	20	31	32	100	106	101	15%	112	2%	100%	16	56%	25%	4.91	11.5	49	132	$10
1st Half		213	24	7	17	2	239	262	291	371	662	558	707	7	81	0.37	49	22	28	27	98	88	99	14%	112	4%	100%	10	50%	30%	3.65	-0.3	42	114	$9
2nd Half		114	14	5	15	0	351	257	385	544	929	815	972	4	76	0.19	47	17	36	43	105	142	106	16%	120	0%	0%	6	67%	17%	8.08	12.7	65	176	$11
15	Proj	**511**	**63**	**18**	**57**	**4**	**284**	**275**	**324**	**455**	**779**	**731**	**799**	**5**	**80**	**0.28**	**47**	**20**	**33**	**33**	**104**	**122**	**92**	**13%**	**122**	**5%**	**64%**				**5.16**	**21.1**	**52**	**137**	**$17**

Maldonado,Martin

Age: 28 Bats: R Pos: CA	Health A	LIMA Plan D
Ht: 6' 0" Wt: 230	PT/Exp F	Rand Var -2
	Consist D	MM 3001

It's a bad sign when your BA improves by over 60 points, yet still remains a liability. Gains were the result of h% regression, not an improved plate approach. Power growth suggests double-digit HR could be lurking, but the high FB% and low ct% will likely keep BA mired in the "dude, you're hurting me" category.

Yr	Tm	AB	R	HR	RBI	SB	BA	xBA	OBP	SLG	OPS	vL	vR	bb%	ct%	Eye	G	L	F	h%	HctX	PX	xPX	hr/f	Spd	SBO	SB%	#Wk	DOM	DIS	RC/G	RAR	BPV	BPX	R$
10	a/a	277	21	7	28	1	214		288	337	598			6	70	0.22				28		97			88	7%	18%				2.69		0	0	-$1
11	MIL *	343	33	8	42	1	236	225	288	353	641	0	0	7	73	0.27	44	20	36	30	0	91	2	0%	66	3%	55%	3	0%	100%	3.36	-10.4	-1	-2	$3
12	MIL *	354	30	11	40	1	233	230	281	370	651	612	766	6	72	0.24	43	23	34	29	78	97	78	14%	70	5%	23%	19	37%	53%	3.32	-10.3	0	0	$3
13	MIL	183	13	4	22	0	169	195	236	284	520	446	543	7	71	0.25	42	14	44	21	73	87	101	7%	84	0%	0%	26	27%	65%	1.96	-10.3	-5	-13	-$4
14	MIL	111	14	4	16	0	234	223	320	387	707	721	693	9	71	0.34	36	18	46	29	86	119	107	12%	84	0%	0%	26	31%	54%	3.91	1.5	25	68	$1
1st Half		57	9	2	8	0	263	232	373	421	794	632	859	14	74	0.60	38	18	45	33	76	122	92	11%	93	0%	0%	13	38%	54%	5.30	3.1	50	135	$1
2nd Half		54	5	2	8	0	204	214	259	352	610	788	460	4	69	0.12	34	19	47	26	96	117	126	13%	75	0%	0%	13	23%	54%	2.62	-1.3	-1	-3	$0
15	Proj	**130**	**13**	**4**	**17**	**0**	**229**	**219**	**299**	**374**	**672**	**687**	**665**	**7**	**71**	**0.27**	**39**	**17**	**43**	**29**	**81**	**114**	**103**	**11%**	**78**	**1%**	**28%**				**3.49**	**0.4**	**1**	**2**	**$2**

Marisnick,Jake

Age: 24 Bats: R Pos: RF CF	Health A	LIMA Plan D+
Ht: 6' 4" Wt: 225	PT/Exp D	Rand Var -1
	Consist B	MM 1403

3-19-.249 with 11 SB in 221 AB at MIA/HOU. Finished strong (.280 BA, 2 HR, 5 SB in Sept.), but inability to handle MLB pitching (0.15 Eye, 57 PX in 330 AB) points to more growing pains for this athletic youngster. Short-term value remains tied to SB total, and that's dependent upon playing time he's yet to earn.

Yr	Tm	AB	R	HR	RBI	SB	BA	xBA	OBP	SLG	OPS	vL	vR	bb%	ct%	Eye	G	L	F	h%	HctX	PX	xPX	hr/f	Spd	SBO	SB%	#Wk	DOM	DIS	RC/G	RAR	BPV	BPX	R$
10																																			
11																																			
12	aa	223	21	2	12	12	221		251	319	569			4	79	0.19				27		69			118	37%	73%				2.58		14	35	$2
13	MIA *	374	43	10	45	12	245	244	285	383	668	431	498	5	73	0.21	42	25	33	31	72	98	55	4%	125	24%	62%	9	33%	67%	3.51	-6.1	21	53	$10
14	2 TM *	564	55	9	46	27	237	222	263	333	596	738	568	3	75	0.14	39	22	39	30	74	74	73	5%	124	31%	74%	12	25%	67%	2.89	-15.4	7	19	$15
1st Half		301	28	3	18	17	208	228	235	289	524	222	428	3	77	0.15	46	21	32	26	69	61	39	0%	126	38%	79%	2	0%	100%	2.23	-14.4	1	3	$10
2nd Half		263	27	5	28	10	271	227	295	384	680	847	608	3	74	0.13	37	22	40	35	74	91	81	6%	112	25%	66%	10	30%	60%	3.80	0.5	11	30	$20
15	Proj	**336**	**35**	**3**	**32**	**14**	**242**	**221**	**276**	**327**	**603**	**620**	**597**	**4**	**73**	**0.15**	**41**	**23**	**35**	**32**	**72**	**70**	**60**	**4%**	**124**	**27%**	**69%**				**2.91**	**-11.2**	**-4**	**-10**	**$9**

Markakis,Nick

Age: 31 Bats: L Pos: RF	Health B	LIMA Plan B+
Ht: 6' 1" Wt: 190	PT/Exp A	Rand Var -1
	Consist C	MM 1235

Finally bucked R$ trend thanks to HR boost, but don't get too excited. PX/xPX remained dormant, while xBA failed to rebound as LD% continued its descent. Substantial AB total and plate skills provide a high floor, but there's little room for upside (or profit) as he enters post-peak seasons.

Yr	Tm	AB	R	HR	RBI	SB	BA	xBA	OBP	SLG	OPS	vL	vR	bb%	ct%	Eye	G	L	F	h%	HctX	PX	xPX	hr/f	Spd	SBO	SB%	#Wk	DOM	DIS	RC/G	RAR	BPV	BPX	R$
10	BAL	629	79	12	60	7	297	274	370	436	805	906	762	10	85	0.78	46	18	36	33	93	97	82	6%	129	5%	78%	27	67%	7%	5.86	12.1	80	174	$21
11	BAL	641	72	15	73	12	284	275	351	406	756	628	809	9	88	0.83	43	23	34	30	112	78	96	8%	92	8%	80%	27	59%	15%	5.04	-2.2	63	140	$21
12	BAL	420	59	13	54	1	298	303	363	471	834	877	816	9	88	0.82	42	27	31	31	125	105	111	11%	103	2%	50%	18	78%	6%	6.15	14.9	87	218	$15
13	BAL	634	89	10	59	1	271	259	329	356	685	651	704	8	88	0.72	47	23	31	30	104	56	71	6%	100	2%	33%	27	48%	19%	4.07	-3.9	45	113	$15
14	BAL	642	81	14	50	4	276	258	342	386	729	673	751	9	87	0.74	46	20	34	30	103	74	85	7%	112	3%	67%	27	48%	7%	4.60	12.8	60	162	$18
1st Half		343	40	7	29	4	294	262	356	405	761	702	789	9	87	0.75	45	21	34	32	117	74	100	7%	113	5%	67%	14	57%	7%	5.18	11.3	61	165	$21
2nd Half		299	41	7	21	0	254	249	326	365	691	629	711	9	87	0.73	47	18	35	27	87	74	68	8%	108	0%	0%	13	38%	8%	3.99	-0.1	58	157	$14
15	Proj	**638**	**85**	**14**	**58**	**3**	**277**	**268**	**342**	**392**	**734**	**703**	**748**	**9**	**87**	**0.76**	**45**	**21**	**33**	**30**	**105**	**78**	**84**	**7%**	**107**	**2%**	**63%**				**4.68**	**12.4**	**49**	**129**	**$19**

Marte,Alfredo

Age: 26 Bats: R Pos: LF	Health A	LIMA Plan D
Ht: 5' 11" Wt: 195	PT/Exp D	Rand Var 0
	Consist C	MM 3211

2-9-.170 in 106 AB at ARI. Frequent rider on the Phoenix-Reno shuttle looked overmatched against MLB pitching. Flashed decent power in the minors, but last year's xPX says it failed to translate to the majors. At age 26, he'll have to quickly reverse ct% trend for any hope at meaningful AB, let alone fantasy value. Pass.

Yr	Tm	AB	R	HR	RBI	SB	BA	xBA	OBP	SLG	OPS	vL	vR	bb%	ct%	Eye	G	L	F	h%	HctX	PX	xPX	hr/f	Spd	SBO	SB%	#Wk	DOM	DIS	RC/G	RAR	BPV	BPX	R$
10																																			
11	aa	43	3	1	4	1	205		253	278	532			6	75	0.26				26		53			97	7%	100%				2.34		-14	-31	-$2
12	aa	398	53	16	59	5	268		312	465	778			6	80	0.33				30		125			94	13%	42%				4.77		62	155	$13
13	ARI *	354	27	4	33	1	221	247	257	328	584	549	481	5	76	0.20	48	23	29	28	121	89	146	0%	82	4%	51%	5	0%	60%	2.72	-20.4	11	28	-$1
14	ARI *	376	37	9	37	5	233	237	289	370	658	740	411	7	72	0.28	39	24	38	30	64	107	69	7%	112	5%	100%	14	36%	50%	3.61	-5.4	24	65	$5
1st Half		220	23	5	23	4	273	273	324	413	737	750	556	7	70	0.25	50	33	17	37	75	121	69	0%	103	7%	100%	5	40%	40%	4.82	5.1	22	59	$10
2nd Half		156	13	5	14	1	175	229	240	309	549	739	365	8	76	0.35	37	22	42	20	64	89	69	8%	129	2%	100%	9	33%	56%	2.31	-8.5	30	81	-$2
15	Proj	**98**	**9**	**2**	**10**	**1**	**224**	**237**	**280**	**359**	**640**	**957**	**473**	**6**	**75**	**0.27**	**37**	**22**	**42**	**28**	**58**	**105**	**62**	**7%**	**104**	**6%**	**70%**				**3.21**	**-1.6**	**22**	**57**	**$1**

Marte,Starling

Age: 26 Bats: R Pos: LF CF	Health B	LIMA Plan D+
Ht: 6' 1" Wt: 185	PT/Exp B	Rand Var -2
	Consist B	MM 4535

Almost a full repeat of '13 breakout, but this time with even more promise: 2nd half strides in ct%, FB% hint at new and improved approach; ditto for PX/xPX; and elite speed stayed intact. Already a steady producer as he enters peak years, if he can hold power gains and keep running, we could see... UP: 20 HR, 40 SB, or more.

Yr	Tm	AB	R	HR	RBI	SB	BA	xBA	OBP	SLG	OPS	vL	vR	bb%	ct%	Eye	G	L	F	h%	HctX	PX	xPX	hr/f	Spd	SBO	SB%	#Wk	DOM	DIS	RC/G	RAR	BPV	BPX	R$
10																																			
11	aa	536	74	9	40	19	297		319	436	755			3	80	0.16				36		100			118	26%	59%				4.71		45	100	$21
12	PIT *	555	71	14	68	29	255	262	294	430	723	1042	627	5	73	0.21	57	18	25	32	98	112	83	18%	185	40%	61%	9	33%	44%	3.94	-12.6	51	128	$20
13	PIT	510	83	12	35	41	280	259	343	441	784	1053	724	5	73	0.18	51	22	28	36	100	116	98	12%	194	47%	73%	24	29%	33%	4.73	9.3	54	135	$30
14	PIT	495	73	13	56	30	291	264	356	453	808	781	814	6	74	0.25	47	23	29	37	105	125	114	13%	167	32%	73%	26	50%	35%	5.33	21.2	59	159	$28
1st Half		278	38	5	27	18	259	248	327	385	712	653	722	6	70	0.23	55	22	23	35	100	104	83	12%	165	35%	75%	14	36%	43%	4.02	1.4	27	73	$25
2nd Half		217	35	8	29	12	332	286	393	539	932	892	944	6	78	0.30	38	26	36	40	112	148	148	14%	154	28%	71%	12	67%	25%	7.37	20.6	92	249	$34
15	Proj	**564**	**84**	**17**	**58**	**34**	**289**	**272**	**349**	**468**	**817**	**946**	**785**	**5**	**75**	**0.22**	**48**	**22**	**30**	**36**	**103**	**132**	**108**	**13%**	**175**	**36%**	**70%**				**5.25**	**24.5**	**64**	**168**	**$33**

Martin,Leonys

Age: 27 Bats: L Pos: CF	Health A	LIMA Plan B
Ht: 6' 2" Wt: 190	PT/Exp C	Rand Var -4
	Consist B	MM 1525

Sophomore campaign looked like a decent repeat, though several indicators suggest change is on the way: xBA continued its sharp decline, SBO fell to career low, and he remained futile vs. LHP. 2nd half contact gains offer some hope, and he still owns elite speed, but a third straight year of 30+ SB is far from a lock.

Yr	Tm	AB	R	HR	RBI	SB	BA	xBA	OBP	SLG	OPS	vL	vR	bb%	ct%	Eye	G	L	F	h%	HctX	PX	xPX	hr/f	Spd	SBO	SB%	#Wk	DOM	DIS	RC/G	RAR	BPV	BPX	R$
10																																			
11	TEX *	295	38	3	29	13	262	314	306	364	669	0	875	6	88	0.52	57	29	14	29	127	68	37	0%	122	33%	54%	4	25%	25%	3.45	-14.6	57	127	$8
12	TEX *	277	40	10	35	10	291	294	341	496	837	500	624	7	80	0.37	47	24	29	34	88	135	55	0%	102	30%	49%	12	42%	42%	5.39	4.3	74	185	$12
13	TEX	457	66	8	49	36	260	255	313	385	698	573	749	6	77	0.27	51	21	28	32	80	88	61	8%	140	40%	80%	27	30%	26%	4.09	-1.9	35	88	$23
14	TEX	533	68	7	40	31	274	242	325	364	689	581	725	7	79	0.34	50	22	28	34	88	60	68	6%	159	27%	72%	27	30%	44%	4.08	2.9	26	70	$23
1st Half		261	34	3	22	17	272	243	330	368	698	521	749	8	75	0.34	53	22	25	35	87	73	69	6%	139	31%	71%	14	36%	50%	4.14	2.2	18	49	$21
2nd Half		272	34	4	18	14	276	241	320	360	680	628	700	6	82	0.35	48	22	30	32	90	49	68	6%	171	23%	74%	13	23%	38%	4.02	1.2	32	86	$24
15	Proj	**543**	**73**	**8**	**50**	**32**	**272**	**253**	**324**	**378**	**702**	**590**	**743**	**6**	**79**	**0.33**	**50**	**22**	**28**	**33**	**85**	**76**	**65**	**6%**	**140**	**30%**	**70%**				**4.11**	**4.0**	**34**	**90**	**$24**

RYAN BLOOMFIELD

Martin,Russell

Age: 32	Bats: R	Pos: CA	Health	B	LIMA Plan	B
Ht: 5' 10"	Wt: 215		PT/Exp	B	Rand Var	-5
			Consist	C	MM	3125

Prime example of the difference h% can make. Its likely regression will bring BA back down, but ct% gains say not all the way to '12-'13 levels. A move from PIT (-28% RHB HR; 9 home HR, 17 away since 2013) could provide a boost to flat power skills, so while a $15 repeat is unlikely, he remains a fine catching option.

Yr	Tm	AB	R	HR	RBI	SB	BA	xBA	OBP	SLG	OPS	vL	vR	bb%	ct%	Eye	G	L	F	h%	HctX	PX	xPX	hr/f	Spd	SBO	SB%	#Wk	DOM	DIS	RC/G	RAR	BPV	BPX	R$
10	LA	331	45	5	26	6	248	253	347	332	679	682	678	13	82	0.79	51	21	28	29	89	61	69	6%	79	7%	75%	18	39%	33%	3.89	-4.7	26	57	$5
11	NYY	417	57	18	65	8	237	268	324	408	732	684	750	11	81	0.62	47	19	33	25	110	110	110	16%	62	9%	80%	27	41%	22%	4.37	0.0	52	116	$11
12	NYY	422	50	21	53	6	211	264	311	403	713	880	643	11	77	0.56	48	19	33	22	101	121	107	20%	52	7%	86%	27	52%	22%	3.93	-4.6	47	118	$6
13	PIT	438	51	15	55	9	226	244	327	377	703	610	729	12	75	0.54	51	17	33	27	107	108	104	14%	64	12%	64%	26	38%	35%	3.86	2.2	32	80	$9
14	PIT	379	45	11	67	4	290	255	402	430	832	693	865	13	79	0.76	49	19	32	34	109	102	92	11%	75	6%	50%	23	39%	39%	5.81	25.2	51	138	$16
1st Half		151	19	4	23	3	265	239	407	384	792	407	867	15	75	0.73	52	19	29	33	138	90	101	12%	69	9%	60%	11	27%	55%	4.92	6.7	27	73	$7
2nd Half		228	26	7	44	1	307	264	398	461	858	836	863	12	82	0.78	47	19	34	35	91	110	86	11%	81	4%	33%	12	50%	25%	6.47	19.3	67	181	$22
15	Proj	**429**	**51**	**14**	**65**	**6**	**257**	**256**	**363**	**406**	**768**	**709**	**785**	**12**	**78**	**0.65**	**49**	**19**	**32**	**30**	**107**	**108**	**97**	**13%**	**65**	**7%**	**61%**				**4.79**	**17.7**	**42**	**109**	**$12**

Martinez,J.D.

Age: 27	Bats: R	Pos: LF RF	Health	B	LIMA Plan	B
Ht: 6' 3"	Wt: 220		PT/Exp	C	Rand Var	-5
			Consist	D	MM	4235

23-76-.315 in 441 AB at DET. One of the most profitable spring training cuts of all-time; sorry, HOU fans. Elite HctX trumped a flawed plate approach, while xPX, hr/f growth backed the HR output. Shaky track record should temper expectations, and BA regression a near-given, but 20+ HR likely here to stay.

Yr	Tm	AB	R	HR	RBI	SB	BA	xBA	OBP	SLG	OPS	vL	vR	bb%	ct%	Eye	G	L	F	h%	HctX	PX	xPX	hr/f	Spd	SBO	SB%	#Wk	DOM	DIS	RC/G	RAR	BPV	BPX	R$
10	aa	189	21	3	22	2	281		327	379	706			6	75	0.28				36		75			106	7%	45%				4.24		7	15	$4
11	HOU *	525	66	16	88	1	283	277	339	444	783	1119	620	8	78	0.39	37	28	36	33	114	117	124	10%	78	1%	42%	10	50%	30%	5.31	5.7	48	107	$18
12	HOU *	485	38	11	58	0	230	224	292	349	641	690	683	8	76	0.37	52	17	32	28	87	81	79	12%	97	3%	0%	22	36%	32%	3.28	-18.9	16	40	$3
13	HOU	296	24	7	36	2	250	236	272	378	650	621	664	3	72	0.12	44	22	34	32	102	103	108	9%	84	3%	100%	18	33%	61%	3.57	-3.5	5	13	$4
14	DET *	506	69	30	92	7	307	286	349	567	915	1003	880	6	71	0.22	40	23	37	38	133	195	158	19%	109	9%	71%	24	54%	33%	7.20	48.6	87	235	$31
1st Half		206	30	16	48	3	294	313	333	620	953	487	1135	6	71	0.21	39	21	40	34	144	245	176	21%	102	14%	63%	11	64%	27%	7.26	20.4	126	341	$25
2nd Half		300	39	14	44	4	317	267	362	530	892	1272	764	6	71	0.23	41	24	35	41	127	160	150	18%	116	6%	80%	13	46%	38%	7.11	27.2	61	165	$34
15	Proj	**561**	**63**	**24**	**88**	**5**	**270**	**262**	**312**	**466**	**778**	**808**	**767**	**6**	**71**	**0.21**	**43**	**22**	**35**	**34**	**117**	**153**	**131**	**17%**	**100**	**6%**	**67%**				**5.04**	**21.0**	**42**	**111**	**$22**

Martinez,Victor

Age: 36	Bats: B	Pos: DH 1B	Health	C	LIMA Plan	C
Ht: 6' 2"	Wt: 210		PT/Exp	C	Rand Var	-2
			Consist	F	MM	3155

Led all of MLB in batting eye and BPV en route to impressive career year. Elite ct%, xBA say to expect yet another .300+ BA, and while hr/f spike normally screams regression, xPX fully supported the power gains. Can't ignore health grade at this age, but he's got the skills for another $30 season.

Yr	Tm	AB	R	HR	RBI	SB	BA	xBA	OBP	SLG	OPS	vL	vR	bb%	ct%	Eye	G	L	F	h%	HctX	PX	xPX	hr/f	Spd	SBO	SB%	#Wk	DOM	DIS	RC/G	RAR	BPV	BPX	R$
10	BOS	493	64	20	79	1	302	291	351	493	844	1173	694	8	89	0.77	41	17	42	31	114	116	112	11%	87	1%	100%	23	70%	9%	6.40	7.6	94	204	$20
11	DET	540	76	12	103	1	330	298	380	470	850	823	861	8	91	0.90	43	24	33	35	117	95	94	7%	74	1%	100%	26	62%	8%	6.85	14.4	78	173	$27
12																																			
13	DET	605	68	14	83	0	301	275	355	430	785	735	813	8	90	0.87	42	22	35	32	142	84	126	7%	77	1%	0%	26	62%	8%	5.54	17.2	68	170	$22
14	DET	561	87	32	103	3	335	320	409	565	974	1123	923	11	93	1.67	41	21	38	32	158	135	147	16%	86	3%	60%	26	88%	4%	8.79	69.7	128	346	$38
1st Half		297	43	20	52	2	323	332	384	589	974	1147	913	10	92	1.39	38	22	41	30	164	155	167	18%	79	4%	50%	14	100%	0%	8.47	35.2	138	373	$38
2nd Half		264	44	12	51	1	348	306	435	538	973	1094	933	13	93	2.00	44	21	35	34	151	112	125	14%	95	1%	100%	12	75%	8%	9.10	34.0	116	314	$38
15	Proj	**561**	**79**	**24**	**97**	**2**	**315**	**304**	**382**	**504**	**886**	**951**	**859**	**10**	**91**	**1.25**	**42**	**22**	**37**	**31**	**143**	**118**	**128**	**13%**	**82**	**2%**	**58%**				**7.14**	**46.8**	**92**	**241**	**$31**

Mathis,Jeff

Age: 32	Bats: R	Pos: CA	Health	B	LIMA Plan	F
Ht: 6' 0"	Wt: 205		PT/Exp	F	Rand Var	-2
			Consist	B	MM	2201

Veteran backstop has posted a positive BPV just once in eight seasons. Reasons he'll go 1-for-9? Abysmal ct% dove even further into the abyss, completely overmatched by today's caliber of pitcher. 2012 PX/xPX looks like a pretty clear outlier. It's pretty sad when your career year outlier is an 8-HR, .218 performance.

Yr	Tm	AB	R	HR	RBI	SB	BA	xBA	OBP	SLG	OPS	vL	vR	bb%	ct%	Eye	G	L	F	h%	HctX	PX	xPX	hr/f	Spd	SBO	SB%	#Wk	DOM	DIS	RC/G	RAR	BPV	BPX	R$
10	LAA *	238	23	4	21	3	193	184	221	280	500	580	467	3	70	0.12	39	13	48	26	66	66	72	4%	126	7%	100%	19	11%	68%	2.00	-17.8	-19	-41	-$2
11	LAA	247	18	3	22	1	174	196	225	259	484	469	494	6	70	0.20	39	18	43	24	69	76	81	4%	81	7%	33%	27	26%	59%	1.71	-21.5	-22	-49	-$5
12	TOR	211	25	8	27	1	218	229	249	393	642	660	635	4	68	0.13	36	20	44	28	79	136	118	13%	79	3%	100%	26	38%	46%	3.23	-6.8	14	35	$1
13	MIA	232	14	5	29	0	181	199	251	284	535	698	464	8	67	0.28	43	20	37	25	74	81	87	9%	98	0%	0%	20	25%	60%	2.21	-11.0	-17	-43	-$4
14	MIA	175	12	2	12	0	200	186	263	274	537	675	492	8	63	0.23	42	22	36	30	73	74	101	5%	80	0%	0%	26	19%	62%	2.30	-6.3	-44	-119	-$3
1st Half		90	8	2	6	0	211	193	304	300	604	905	492	12	63	0.36	45	23	32	31	80	76	93	11%	96	0%	0%	14	29%	64%	2.95	-1.2	-32	-86	-$2
2nd Half		85	4	0	6	0	188	180	216	247	463	368	489	3	64	0.10	39	20	41	30	66	73	110	0%	72	0%	0%	12	8%	58%	1.68	-4.6	-57	-154	-$4
15	Proj	**98**	**7**	**2**	**9**	**0**	**195**	**199**	**247**	**293**	**540**	**634**	**504**	**6**	**66**	**0.20**	**41**	**20**	**39**	**28**	**73**	**90**	**99**	**7%**	**83**	**1%**	**79%**				**2.29**	**-3.4**	**-39**	**-103**	**$0**

Mauer,Joe

Age: 32	Bats: L	Pos: 1B	Health	D	LIMA Plan	B
Ht: 6' 5"	Wt: 230		PT/Exp	A	Rand Var	0
			Consist	C	MM	2145

Continued to live up to last year's "D" health grade by missing July with an oblique strain. But here are the harsh realities... He's not too old to have a nice rebound season, assuming he gets healthy. But declining trends temper the heights of that rebound. And without CA eligibility, he's a terrible 1B option.

Yr	Tm	AB	R	HR	RBI	SB	BA	xBA	OBP	SLG	OPS	vL	vR	bb%	ct%	Eye	G	L	F	h%	HctX	PX	xPX	hr/f	Spd	SBO	SB%	#Wk	DOM	DIS	RC/G	RAR	BPV	BPX	R$
10	MIN	510	88	9	75	1	327	310	402	469	871	711	978	11	90	1.23	47	24	29	35	152	98	126	7%	88	3%	20%	27	67%	4%	6.98	18.2	88	191	$23
11	MIN	296	38	3	30	0	287	270	360	368	729	562	829	10	87	0.84	55	23	22	32	92	60	75	5%	93	0%	0%	17	47%	18%	4.70	-7.7	46	102	$6
12	MIN	545	81	10	85	8	319	286	416	446	861	754	918	14	84	1.02	53	25	22	37	137	83	113	10%	95	5%	67%	27	67%	7%	6.89	23.5	61	153	$25
13	MIN	445	62	11	47	0	324	288	404	476	880	882	879	12	80	0.69	47	28	25	39	124	115	113	12%	91	1%	0%	21	57%	24%	7.22	30.9	65	163	$18
14	MIN	455	60	4	55	3	277	269	361	371	732	654	776	12	79	0.63	51	27	22	34	96	79	70	5%	86	2%	100%	22	45%	32%	4.78	8.2	30	81	$12
1st Half		300	38	2	26	3	270	269	342	350	692	537	772	10	79	0.55	53	28	19	33	97	68	62	4%	95	3%	100%	14	43%	29%	4.28	0.9	22	59	$13
2nd Half		155	22	2	29	0	290	270	396	413	809	842	786	14	78	0.76	46	26	27	36	92	101	87	6%	78	0%	0%	8	50%	38%	5.82	7.1	47	127	$10
15	Proj	**491**	**67**	**7**	**65**	**2**	**290**	**280**	**379**	**411**	**789**	**734**	**819**	**12**	**81**	**0.73**	**49**	**26**	**24**	**35**	**111**	**96**	**94**	**8%**	**85**	**2%**	**68%**				**5.57**	**19.2**	**44**	**115**	**$18**

Mayberry,John

Age: 31	Bats: R	Pos: 1B	Health	B	LIMA Plan	D
Ht: 6' 6"	Wt: 230		PT/Exp	D	Rand Var	+5
			Consist	A	MM	4221

7-23-.212 in 146 AB at PHI/TOR. Bad start, he became desperate in 2H, swinging for the fences and tanking BA. PX may say he's a power hitter, but xPX and HctX disagree. That means those hits are dropping for doubles but he's not hitting the ball hard enough for it to be sustainable. Struggles vs. RHP indicates a platooner at best.

Yr	Tm	AB	R	HR	RBI	SB	BA	xBA	OBP	SLG	OPS	vL	vR	bb%	ct%	Eye	G	L	F	h%	HctX	PX	xPX	hr/f	Spd	SBO	SB%	#Wk	DOM	DIS	RC/G	RAR	BPV	BPX	R$
10	PHI *	507	63	14	57	16	226	194	270	353	623	1500	952	6	73	0.23	50	0	50	28	75	94	182	50%	114	19%	78%	5	40%	60%	3.16	-32.8	16	35	$9
11	PHI *	380	49	18	60	9	256	273	310	466	775	953	785	7	78	0.36	42	18	40	28	102	144	109	17%	80	15%	76%	23	52%	22%	4.91	-3.9	68	151	$13
12	PHI	441	53	14	46	1	245	248	301	395	695	811	626	7	75	0.31	52	20	28	30	85	106	74	15%	90	1%	100%	27	33%	48%	4.00	-7.4	28	70	$7
13	PHI	353	47	11	39	5	227	253	286	391	677	756	646	7	75	0.30	43	20	37	27	88	124	81	11%	113	11%	63%	27	44%	33%	3.56	-4.4	47	118	$6
14	2 TM *	179	18	8	26	0	198	245	286	391	677	913	569	11	72	0.45	36	18	46	23	81	151	93	13%	80	0%	0%	22	50%	32%	3.56	-1.2	58	157	$0
1st Half		108	10	5	20	0	222	256	323	426	749	966	581	12	75	0.56	43	19	38	25	84	153	93	16%	79	0%	0%	14	43%	36%	4.43	2.3	72	195	$2
2nd Half		71	8	3	6	0	162	215	236	339	575	807	517	9	69	0.31	16	16	68	19	77	149	90	10%	93	0%	0%	8	63%	25%	2.44	-3.0	41	111	-$3
15	Proj	**192**	**22**	**7**	**23**	**1**	**229**	**248**	**296**	**403**	**700**	**812**	**612**	**9**	**73**	**0.35**	**40**	**18**	**42**	**28**	**85**	**139**	**88**	**12%**	**92**	**4%**	**69%**				**3.93**	**-1.4**	**38**	**100**	**$4**

Maybin,Cameron

Age: 28	Bats: R	Pos: CF	Health	F	LIMA Plan	D+
Ht: 6' 3"	Wt: 205		PT/Exp	D	Rand Var	+1
			Consist	B	MM	1513

1-15-.235 in 251 AB at SD. Biceps injury and amphetamine suspension added to list of lowlights for this once-elite prospect. Excellent speed keeps him clinging to relevance, but subpar plate approach, measly power, and "F" health grade suggest his grip is slipping. A speculative SB flyer, at best.

Yr	Tm	AB	R	HR	RBI	SB	BA	xBA	OBP	SLG	OPS	vL	vR	bb%	ct%	Eye	G	L	F	h%	HctX	PX	xPX	hr/f	Spd	SBO	SB%	#Wk	DOM	DIS	RC/G	RAR	BPV	BPX	R$
10	FLA *	421	62	11	45	13	252	230	308	379	687	584	697	8	71	0.28	53	14	33	33	84	90	100	13%	170	14%	80%	16	31%	56%	4.02	-9.5	25	54	$11
11	SD	516	82	9	40	40	264	251	323	393	716	751	703	8	76	0.35	55	16	29	33	93	93	93	8%	175	35%	83%	25	44%	36%	4.54	-3.7	48	107	$22
12	SD	507	67	8	45	26	243	242	306	349	656	630	666	8	78	0.40	55	16	28	30	107	71	88	7%	139	25%	79%	27	37%	33%	3.62	-16.3	30	75	$14
13	SD *	97	11	4	8	5	176	252	255	304	560	435	481	10	79	0.51	55	19	26	18	76	79	45	9%	102	31%	68%	5	20%	60%	2.33	-5.6	31	78	-$1
14	SD *	304	28	2	18	5	226	243	279	319	599	575	646	7	77	0.32	57	17	26	29	97	73	60	2%	145	11%	60%	20	15%	55%	2.88	-8.8	26	70	$1
1st Half		183	21	2	8	2	248	259	287	376	664	703	718	5	80	0.27	58	13	29	30	104	97	67	3%	155	8%	67%	10	30%	30%	3.63	-1.3	55	149	$2
2nd Half		121	8	0	10	3	194	219	269	233	501	477	505	9	74	0.39	56	23	21	26	87	32	49	0%	117	14%	56%	10	0%	80%	1.92	-7.6	-24	-65	-$1
15	Proj	**322**	**37**	**4**	**27**	**14**	**236**	**239**	**303**	**327**	**630**	**589**	**652**	**8**	**77**	**0.38**	**56**	**18**	**26**	**30**	**91**	**68**	**62**	**6%**	**134**	**22%**	**76%**				**3.28**	**-5.7**	**15**	**40**	**$8**

RYAN BLOOMFIELD

McCann,Brian

Age: 31 Bats: L Pos: CA	Health B	LIMA Plan B+
Ht: 6' 3" Wt: 230	PT/Exp B	Rand Var +4
	Consist C	MM 4035

The prospect of him swinging for Yankee Stadium's short RF porch boosted his ADP, but slow start set an anchor on his production. Low h% still hints at a BA rebound, especially given ct% uptick. Already a stable power option behind the dish, his 2H strides in FB%, xPX - and still, that short porch - hint there's room for... UP: 30 HR

Yr	Tm	AB	R	HR	RBI	SB	BA	xBA	OBP	SLG	OPS	vL	vR	bb%	ct%	Eye	G	L	F	h%	HctX	PX	xPX	hr/f	Spd	SBO	SB%	#Wk	DOM	DIS	RC/G	RAR	BPV	BPX	R$
10	ATL	479	63	21	77	5	269	268	375	453	828	783	845	13	80	0.76	37	20	43	30	127	122	144	13%	69	4%	71%	27	59%	26%	5.79	21.8	65	141	$16
11	ATL	466	51	24	71	3	270	252	351	466	817	794	826	11	81	0.64	38	16	47	29	138	123	162	14%	65	4%	60%	25	56%	28%	5.64	19.2	65	144	$16
12	ATL	439	44	20	67	3	230	252	300	399	698	673	711	9	83	0.58	40	19	41	24	118	98	131	13%	58	3%	100%	27	48%	37%	4.00	-1.7	47	118	$8
13	ATL	356	43	20	57	0	256	273	336	461	796	616	869	10	81	0.59	35	22	42	26	118	125	150	16%	71	1%	0%	21	67%	29%	5.13	14.7	69	173	$11
14	NYY	495	57	23	75	0	232	266	286	406	692	850	633	6	84	0.42	33	22	45	23	114	106	127	12%	64	0%	0%	26	58%	23%	3.76	6.5	56	151	$11
1st Half		263	27	9	36	0	221	256	281	361	642	902	542	7	85	0.48	36	22	42	23	115	87	115	10%	71	0%	0%	14	57%	21%	3.23	-1.3	45	122	$7
2nd Half		232	30	14	39	0	246	277	292	457	749	788	735	5	84	0.35	29	22	48	24	112	127	139	15%	66	0%	0%	12	58%	25%	4.41	7.0	70	189	$16
15	**Proj**	**464**	**54**	**25**	**73**	**1**	**248**	**272**	**313**	**444**	**757**	**765**	**754**	**8**	**83**	**0.51**	**34**	**21**	**44**	**25**	**117**	**123**	**137**	**15%**	**63**	**1%**	**62%**				**4.62**	**16.8**	**57**	**150**	**$13**

McCutchen,Andrew

Age: 28 Bats: R Pos: CF	Health A	LIMA Plan C
Ht: 5' 10" Wt: 190	PT/Exp A	Rand Var -2
	Consist B	MM 4455

It's becoming increasingly difficult to find a hole in his game. Excellent HctX, h% baseline continued to lock in high BA, while PX/xPX inched closer to elite territory. Great wheels say SB can return if he simply runs more. Elite skills, reliable production in peak years cement his status as one of the best.

Yr	Tm	AB	R	HR	RBI	SB	BA	xBA	OBP	SLG	OPS	vL	vR	bb%	ct%	Eye	G	L	F	h%	HctX	PX	xPX	hr/f	Spd	SBO	SB%	#Wk	DOM	DIS	RC/G	RAR	BPV	BPX	R$
10	PIT	570	94	16	56	33	286	279	365	449	814	903	784	11	84	0.79	43	19	38	32	131	106	115	9%	152	24%	77%	27	63%	22%	5.84	17.2	92	200	$28
11	PIT	572	87	23	89	23	259	266	364	456	820	945	779	13	78	0.71	38	20	42	30	135	135	142	12%	113	19%	70%	27	63%	15%	5.52	12.5	83	184	$24
12	PIT	593	107	31	96	20	327	281	400	553	953	1144	900	11	78	0.53	44	22	34	38	126	140	147	19%	139	16%	63%	27	56%	19%	7.99	53.3	88	220	$40
13	PIT	583	97	21	84	27	317	288	404	508	911	1130	864	12	83	0.77	41	24	35	36	137	125	123	12%	129	19%	73%	26	69%	12%	7.44	53.3	95	238	$40
14	PIT	548	89	25	83	18	314	284	410	542	952	912	962	13	79	0.73	40	19	41	36	139	159	155	14%	127	11%	86%	26	65%	12%	8.27	65.9	110	297	$36
1st Half		303	44	12	48	12	314	289	418	525	943	1100	914	15	79	0.86	42	21	37	36	155	154	160	13%	102	11%	100%	14	64%	7%	8.47	37.6	103	278	$37
2nd Half		245	45	13	35	6	314	279	401	563	964	746	1025	11	79	0.58	37	16	47	36	120	166	150	14%	151	12%	67%	12	67%	17%	7.97	27.5	117	316	$34
15	**Proj**	**585**	**99**	**28**	**94**	**20**	**304**	**287**	**394**	**533**	**927**	**972**	**915**	**12**	**80**	**0.68**	**40**	**19**	**40**	**34**	**133**	**156**	**143**	**15%**	**132**	**14%**	**72%**				**7.47**	**58.7**	**105**	**277**	**$38**

McGehee,Casey

Age: 32 Bats: R Pos: 3B	Health A	LIMA Plan B+
Ht: 6' 1" Wt: 220	PT/Exp B	Rand Var -5
	Consist C	MM 1115

Resurrected career after a one-year hiatus in Japan. Career-high Eye says he returned with a much better plate approach, though h% and xBA suggest the BA will come down hard. Despite the power outage, xPX hints there's still life in his bat, and a few more HR might help offset the BA loss.

Yr	Tm	AB	R	HR	RBI	SB	BA	xBA	OBP	SLG	OPS	vL	vR	bb%	ct%	Eye	G	L	F	h%	HctX	PX	xPX	hr/f	Spd	SBO	SB%	#Wk	DOM	DIS	RC/G	RAR	BPV	BPX	R$
10	MIL	610	70	23	104	1	285	276	337	464	801	947	750	8	83	0.49	47	17	36	31	107	117	106	13%	78	1%	50%	27	52%	7%	5.59	8.4	67	146	$21
11	MIL	546	46	13	67	0	223	237	280	346	626	413	689	8	81	0.43	50	16	34	25	104	84	97	9%	85	2%	0%	27	44%	41%	3.13	-32.9	34	76	$3
12	2 TM	318	36	9	41	1	217	240	284	358	643	745	581	8	78	0.41	51	16	33	25	101	95	104	11%	73	3%	50%	25	32%	36%	3.27	-13.1	29	73	$2
13	for	513	76	17	91	2	273		345	429	773			10	78	0.50				32		111			74	3%	35%				5.07	16.1	45	113	$19
14	MIA	616	56	4	76	4	287	235	355	357	712	596	738	10	83	0.66	50	18	31	34	112	57	88	2%	83	3%	67%	27	26%	30%	4.55	14.5	26	70	$17
1st Half		314	29	1	48	1	309	242	376	385	761	594	803	10	83	0.69	49	19	32	37	120	65	91	1%	84	1%	100%	14	36%	21%	5.43	14.8	33	89	$20
2nd Half		302	27	3	28	3	265	226	332	328	660	600	673	9	83	0.62	52	17	31	31	105	48	84	4%	82	5%	60%	13	15%	38%	3.75	0.5	18	49	$14
15	**Proj**	**521**	**57**	**9**	**71**	**3**	**267**	**239**	**333**	**372**	**705**	**680**	**713**	**9**	**81**	**0.54**	**50**	**17**	**33**	**31**	**107**	**79**	**95**	**7%**	**76**	**3%**	**55%**				**4.29**	**8.9**	**22**	**57**	**$14**

McKenry,Michael

Age: 30 Bats: R Pos: CA	Health B	LIMA Plan D
Ht: 5' 10" Wt: 205	PT/Exp F	Rand Var -5
	Consist F	MM 4031

8-22-.315 in 168 AB at COL. Quietly thrived after June call-up, and 2nd half xPX growth indicates it wasn't just because of Coors Field. Subpar contact rate coupled with fluky LD% spike, inflated h% suggest he won't touch that BA again. But the power alone makes him worth a flyer in two-catcher leagues.

Yr	Tm	AB	R	HR	RBI	SB	BA	xBA	OBP	SLG	OPS	vL	vR	bb%	ct%	Eye	G	L	F	h%	HctX	PX	xPX	hr/f	Spd	SBO	SB%	#Wk	DOM	DIS	RC/G	RAR	BPV	BPX	R$
10	COL *	355	26	7	29	1	210	195	252	326	577	1000	0	5	75	0.22	67	0	33	26	0	90	-5	0%	87	3%	34%	4	25%	50%	2.61	-19.5	9	20	-$2
11	PIT *	275	25	4	20	1	229	220	292	337	629	498	629	8	72	0.32	39	20	41	30	79	93	86	4%	89	3%	44%	15	33%	53%	3.22	-9.6	8	18	$0
12	PIT	240	25	12	39	0	233	222	320	442	762	815	746	11	70	0.40	35	14	51	28	97	151	147	14%	69	0%	0%	27	48%	48%	4.64	2.5	43	108	$4
13	PIT	115	9	3	14	0	217	239	262	348	610	475	655	4	79	0.21	37	21	42	25	97	93	101	8%	69	0%	0%	16	25%	56%	2.83	-3.0	22	55	-$2
14	COL *	251	31	10	29	2	290	279	356	463	819	961	891	9	77	0.45	36	29	35	34	105	126	108	18%	78	6%	36%	20	55%	30%	5.68	15.8	53	143	$9
1st Half		137	14	2	11	2	268	257	303	380	683	556	800	5	78	0.23	48	23	30	33	102	95	61	0%	79	12%	46%	8	50%	38%	3.82	1.7	25	68	$5
2nd Half		114	17	8	18	0	316	304	418	561	979	1070	940	14	75	0.68	30	33	37	36	105	164	131	25%	82	2%	0%	12	58%	25%	8.39	15.5	88	238	$14
15	**Proj**	**160**	**17**	**7**	**20**	**1**	**260**	**262**	**328**	**438**	**765**	**754**	**769**	**9**	**76**	**0.39**	**37**	**24**	**39**	**31**	**99**	**131**	**107**	**14%**	**75**	**4%**	**36%**				**4.78**	**6.5**	**36**	**95**	**$5**

McLouth,Nate

Age: 33 Bats: L Pos: LF	Health C	LIMA Plan D
Ht: 5' 10" Wt: 190	PT/Exp C	Rand Var +4
	Consist D	MM 2311

Rode the pine much of the season until torn labrum ended it in August. Small sample warns not to read too much into BPV drop, as he still owns plus power/speed skills with decent plate approach. Inability to hit lefties (76% ct%, .287 OBP since 2012) will likely limit role, but that speed can still add value in part-time duty.

Yr	Tm	AB	R	HR	RBI	SB	BA	xBA	OBP	SLG	OPS	vL	vR	bb%	ct%	Eye	G	L	F	h%	HctX	PX	xPX	hr/f	Spd	SBO	SB%	#Wk	DOM	DIS	RC/G	RAR	BPV	BPX	R$
10	ATL *	370	43	10	37	12	187	226	277	309	586	378	685	11	77	0.55	40	16	44	21	93	83	120	8%	89	15%	86%	18	33%	44%	2.77	-23.9	26	57	$1
11	ATL	267	35	4	16	4	228	237	344	333	677	531	743	14	81	0.85	47	17	36	27	84	74	82	5%	111	7%	67%	15	47%	20%	3.70	-8.8	45	100	$1
12	2 TM *	446	61	15	45	16	225	250	291	380	671	581	731	9	79	0.45	43	20	37	25	95	97	116	9%	94	16%	94%	18	33%	33%	3.78	-12.2	41	103	$10
13	BAL	531	76	12	36	30	258	269	329	399	729	640	753	9	84	0.62	39	25	37	29	95	95	96	7%	115	26%	81%	27	59%	15%	4.55	7.1	66	165	$21
14	WAS	139	10	1	7	4	173	190	280	237	517	530	515	10	75	0.46	52	10	38	22	104	59	137	3%	87	15%	80%	18	28%	56%	1.95	-8.5	-4	-11	-$3
1st Half		122	8	1	7	4	197	192	313	270	583	581	583	12	75	0.53	54	8	38	25	108	66	132	3%	84	15%	80%	14	36%	57%	2.56	-5.0	5	14	-$2
2nd Half		17	2	0	0	0	0	0	0	0	0	0	0	0	71	0.00	33	25	42	0	76	0	173	0%	97	0%	0%	4	0%	50%	0.00	-2.6	-86	-232	-$7
15	**Proj**	**200**	**23**	**4**	**15**	**9**	**220**	**241**	**314**	**332**	**646**	**552**	**673**	**11**	**81**	**0.65**	**46**	**17**	**38**	**25**	**97**	**82**	**112**	**6%**	**93**	**20%**	**86%**				**3.43**	**-1.9**	**45**	**119**	**$4**

Medica,Thomas

Age: 27 Bats: R Pos: 1B LF	Health A	LIMA Plan D
Ht: 6' 3" Wt: 205	PT/Exp F	Rand Var +1
	Consist D	MM 4411

9-27-.233 in 240 AB at SD. The decent power he flashed in the minors translated well, but HctX and xPX remain skeptical he can maintain it. If it slips, his dismal plate skills and poor xBA suggest there's no safety net in place. Too many questions to merit any more than an end-game bid.

Yr	Tm	AB	R	HR	RBI	SB	BA	xBA	OBP	SLG	OPS	vL	vR	bb%	ct%	Eye	G	L	F	h%	HctX	PX	xPX	hr/f	Spd	SBO	SB%	#Wk	DOM	DIS	RC/G	RAR	BPV	BPX	R$
10																																			
11																																			
12																																			
13	SD *	349	48	18	56	3	258	257	321	476	797	599	880	9	70	0.31	39	22	39	32	81	160	116	17%	118	7%	58%	4	50%	25%	5.16	5.8	62	155	$12
14	SD *	329	36	11	38	6	213	234	256	376	633	758	650	5	68	0.18	45	19	36	28	92	130	82	15%	134	12%	86%	24	38%	38%	3.16	-10.4	29	78	$4
1st Half		188	19	6	24	1	214	238	261	387	648	828	759	6	66	0.19	40	24	36	29	81	141	82	17%	156	6%	50%	11	45%	45%	3.22	-5.5	38	103	$4
2nd Half		141	17	5	14	5	213	230	270	362	631	718	561	5	70	0.17	48	15	36	27	101	117	81	14%	95	19%	100%	13	31%	31%	3.09	-4.7	15	41	$5
15	**Proj**	**209**	**26**	**6**	**27**	**4**	**231**	**233**	**288**	**381**	**669**	**623**	**690**	**7**	**69**	**0.23**	**44**	**20**	**36**	**30**	**88**	**122**	**95**	**12%**	**119**	**10%**	**83%**				**3.59**	**-3.6**	**19**	**51**	**$5**

Mercer,Jordy

Age: 28 Bats: R Pos: SS	Health A	LIMA Plan B+
Ht: 6' 3" Wt: 205	PT/Exp C	Rand Var 0
	Consist C	MM 3235

Showed plenty of growth down the stretch as 2nd half ct% spike and PX gains hint of better days ahead. However, HctX suggests the contact has been weak, and his struggles vs. RHP limit overall ceiling. As it stands, his decent BA and double-digit HR make for an acceptable MI option in later rounds.

Yr	Tm	AB	R	HR	RBI	SB	BA	xBA	OBP	SLG	OPS	vL	vR	bb%	ct%	Eye	G	L	F	h%	HctX	PX	xPX	hr/f	Spd	SBO	SB%	#Wk	DOM	DIS	RC/G	RAR	BPV	BPX	R$
10	aa	485	53	2	51	5	246		282	323	605			5	85	0.32				29		61			97	6%	83%				3.11		28	61	$5
11	a/a	491	60	14	52	7	214		254	355	609			5	83	0.31				23		96			91	15%	49%				2.78		47	104	$5
12	PIT *	271	29	4	27	2	236	249	287	356	643	367	690	7	76	0.30	47	22	31	30	61	91	86	7%	93	15%	26%	17	24%	53%	3.07	-8.6	21	53	$2
13	PIT *	429	41	9	41	5	282	269	330	418	748	1152	654	7	81	0.37	47	23	30	33	113	97	117	10%	113	7%	62%	23	52%	26%	4.83	16.1	51	128	$12
14	PIT	506	56	12	55	4	255	264	305	387	693	803	658	6	82	0.39	48	20	32	29	90	94	89	9%	108	4%	80%	27	41%	33%	4.03	10.9	52	141	$11
1st Half		247	30	6	22	1	227	234	261	340	601	871	542	4	80	0.18	52	14	34	26	87	81	80	9%	93	4%	50%	14	43%	36%	2.81	-3.2	22	59	$6
2nd Half		259	26	6	33	3	282	290	346	432	778	765	784	9	85	0.65	43	26	31	31	93	106	97	9%	119	4%	100%	13	38%	31%	5.41	15.9	79	214	$17
15	**Proj**	**523**	**55**	**12**	**55**	**5**	**259**	**270**	**312**	**397**	**709**	**865**	**662**	**7**	**81**	**0.38**	**47**	**22**	**31**	**30**	**94**	**101**	**99**	**9%**	**110**	**7%**	**57%**				**4.13**	**13.6**	**43**	**114**	**$13**

RYAN BLOOMFIELD

Mesoraco,Devin

Age: 27 **Bats:** R **Pos:** CA | **Ht:** 6' 1" **Wt:** 220
Health A | PT/Exp D | Consist D | LIMA Plan B+ | Rand Var -2 | MM 4045

Completely changed plate approach by ditching ct% and swinging for the fences. It worked. HctX says he mashed when he did make contact, and mammoth PX coupled with FB% gains bode well for continued HR production. His BA may not hold (see 2nd half), but power alone makes him a solid CA option.

Yr Tm	AB	R	HR	RBI	SB	BA	xBA	OBP	SLG	OPS	vL	vR	bb%	ct%	Eye	G	L	F	h%	HctX	PX	xPX	hr/f	Spd	SBO	SB%	#Wk	DOM	DIS	RC/G	RAR	BPV	BPX	R$
10 a/a	239	37	14	35	1	255		310	501	811			7	76	0.34				28		161			115	4%	42%				5.23		85	185	$7
11 CIN *	486	50	15	60	1	244	245	304	409	713	625	579	8	78	0.40	40	15	45	28	79	121	83	11%	82	2%	40%	5	60%	20%	4.16	-3.1	53	118	$8
12 CIN	165	17	5	14	1	212	238	288	352	640	803	590	9	80	0.52	45	17	38	24	85	92	80	10%	74	5%	50%	22	45%	32%	3.19	-5.5	36	90	-$1
13 CIN	323	31	9	42	0	238	246	287	362	649	874	576	7	81	0.39	45	21	34	27	89	83	78	10%	62	3%	0%	27	44%	37%	3.43	-2.5	25	63	$4
14 CIN	384	54	25	80	1	273	287	359	534	893	925	883	10	73	0.40	34	23	43	31	123	192	166	20%	63	4%	25%	24	54%	25%	6.25	30.9	86	232	$18
1st Half	168	28	14	40	1	310	318	378	631	1009	938	1030	8	75	0.33	34	24	43	34	141	228	182	26%	83	8%	33%	11	73%	18%	8.10	21.8	125	338	$21
2nd Half	216	26	11	40	0	245	263	345	458	804	910	777	11	72	0.44	34	22	43	29	109	163	152	16%	54	2%	0%	13	38%	31%	5.00	10.4	58	157	$16
15 Proj	447	54	24	72	1	259	273	331	473	805	918	773	9	77	0.41	39	21	40	29	104	154	122	17%	62	4%	27%				5.15	23.0	57	150	$14

Middlebrooks,Will

Age: 26 **Bats:** R **Pos:** 3B | **Ht:** 6' 3" **Wt:** 220
Health F | PT/Exp D | Consist F | LIMA Plan D+ | Rand Var +5 | MM 3203

2-19-.191 in 215 AB at BOS. Disastrous season started with calf, finger injuries, and ended with awful skills down the stretch. Stagnant batting eye indicates the BA risk is going to hand around for awhile, and while xPX says not to worry about the HR dip, that's only good enough to make him a late-round power flyer.

Yr Tm	AB	R	HR	RBI	SB	BA	xBA	OBP	SLG	OPS	vL	vR	bb%	ct%	Eye	G	L	F	h%	HctX	PX	xPX	hr/f	Spd	SBO	SB%	#Wk	DOM	DIS	RC/G	RAR	BPV	BPX	R$
10																																		
11 a/a	427	45	15	68	7	258		288	425	713			4	71	0.15				33		131			78	9%	86%				4.24		23	51	$12
12 BOS *	360	49	22	76	6	293	276	328	530	857	906	798	5	75	0.21	44	22	35	34	120	152	119	21%	78	10%	75%	15	40%	33%	6.22	16.8	57	143	$18
13 BOS *	527	60	24	75	4	228	247	272	409	682	782	656	6	73	0.22	41	20	39	27	116	128	127	17%	70	5%	79%	19	47%	37%	3.68	-4.2	30	75	$11
14 BOS *	319	24	5	25	1	193	209	239	278	517	454	543	6	67	0.19	41	25	34	27	100	74	114	4%	87	3%	50%	14	21%	71%	2.08	-16.1	-31	-84	-$3
1st Half	100	11	2	9	0	191	195	254	281	535	784	562	8	67	0.25	40	21	40	26	84	77	121	11%	81	0%	0%	5	40%	60%	2.25	-4.6	-30	-81	-$5
2nd Half	219	13	3	16	1	193	216	232	277	508	218	535	5	67	0.15	42	27	31	27	108	73	110	0%	97	5%	50%	9	11%	78%	2.00	-11.8	-31	-84	-$3
15 Proj	363	36	10	45	3	222	230	275	354	629	675	610	6	70	0.20	41	23	36	29	108	105	120	11%	80	5%	72%				3.07	-6.9	-3	-7	$5

Miller,Bradley

Age: 25 **Bats:** L **Pos:** SS | **Ht:** 6' 2" **Wt:** 200
Health A | PT/Exp D | Consist C | LIMA Plan B | Rand Var +3 | MM 3325

Broke camp with the full-time gig, but an awful start knocked him to part-time duty. BA felt the wrath of ct% collapse, though 2nd half xBA suggests LD, power may help offset it. Intriguing speed remains an unused weapon, and 2nd half gains at a growth age hint at more upside. Don't give up on him yet.

Yr Tm	AB	R	HR	RBI	SB	BA	xBA	OBP	SLG	OPS	vL	vR	bb%	ct%	Eye	G	L	F	h%	HctX	PX	xPX	hr/f	Spd	SBO	SB%	#Wk	DOM	DIS	RC/G	RAR	BPV	BPX	R$
10																																		
11																																		
12 aa	147	19	3	11	4	284		371	411	782			12	79	0.67				34		82			115	9%	76%				5.45		43	108	$3
13 SEA *	563	82	17	77	10	269	264	329	424	753	674	767	8	81	0.46	46	22	32	31	97	97	79	10%	137	11%	56%	15	53%	13%	4.70	20.9	60	150	$21
14 SEA	367	47	10	36	4	221	236	288	365	653	542	692	8	74	0.36	42	19	39	27	98	105	105	10%	123	7%	67%	27	37%	52%	3.40	2.5	36	97	$4
1st Half	236	30	8	23	3	208	220	277	343	620	460	686	8	73	0.33	43	17	41	25	99	96	102	12%	116	7%	75%	14	29%	57%	3.01	-1.7	22	59	$6
2nd Half	131	17	2	13	1	244	264	308	405	713	766	700	9	76	0.42	42	24	35	31	96	122	109	6%	122	6%	50%	13	46%	46%	4.17	3.7	60	162	$1
15 Proj	414	56	11	45	6	252	254	319	406	725	643	756	9	77	0.43	43	21	36	30	97	110	95	10%	125	9%	62%				4.35	13.6	48	125	$12

Molina,Jose

Age: 40 **Bats:** R **Pos:** CA | **Ht:** 6' 0" **Wt:** 250
Health A | PT/Exp D | Consist B | LIMA Plan F | Rand Var +2 | MM 0101

He was never employed for his bat, but you never want to see a player's production completely flatline either. Meager HctX and LD showed just how weak his contact was, and PX/xPX completely disappeared. Really, a 9 PX!? Did he go to the plate with a tennis racket? Even with an aluminum bat, he'd be far from relevant.

Yr Tm	AB	R	HR	RBI	SB	BA	xBA	OBP	SLG	OPS	vL	vR	bb%	ct%	Eye	G	L	F	h%	HctX	PX	xPX	hr/f	Spd	SBO	SB%	#Wk	DOM	DIS	RC/G	RAR	BPV	BPX	R$
10 TOR	167	13	6	12	1	246	249	304	377	681	464	763	5	78	0.25	43	22	35	28	103	83	123	13%	65	3%	100%	26	31%	50%	3.65	-2.6	12	26	$1
11 TOR	171	19	3	15	2	281	249	342	415	757	754	759	8	74	0.34	43	22	35	36	89	109	90	7%	73	6%	67%	26	35%	46%	4.94	3.6	24	53	$3
12 TAM	251	27	8	32	3	223	239	286	355	640	469	680	7	76	0.33	52	18	29	26	73	87	83	14%	46	7%	75%	27	26%	59%	3.26	-6.6	5	13	$2
13 TAM	283	26	2	18	2	233	231	290	304	594	628	577	7	78	0.35	55	20	26	29	68	60	51	4%	52	4%	67%	27	19%	56%	2.91	-6.9	-8	-20	$0
14 TAM	225	4	0	10	3	178	162	230	187	417	584	366	6	76	0.25	56	12	32	24	65	9	40	0%	60	6%	100%	27	0%	89%	1.36	-14.2	-58	-157	-$6
1st Half	123	1	0	3	1	179	138	215	187	402	633	327	5	75	0.19	58	10	33	24	65	9	48	0%	73	4%	100%	14	0%	93%	1.29	-8.3	-60	-162	-$7
2nd Half	102	3	0	7	2	176	176	248	186	434	519	411	7	76	0.33	54	15	31	23	65	10	30	0%	50	8%	100%	13	0%	85%	1.44	-6.4	-55	-149	-$4
15 Proj	196	12	2	13	2	207	204	265	262	527	584	508	7	76	0.30	53	16	30	26	70	45	54	4%	55	6%	87%				2.22	-7.1	-30	-79	$0

Molina,Yadier

Age: 32 **Bats:** R **Pos:** CA | **Ht:** 5' 11" **Wt:** 220
Health C | PT/Exp B | Consist C | LIMA Plan A | Rand Var 0 | MM 2155

Torn ligament in thumb cost him nearly two months and likely sapped power upon his return. His excellent ct% remained intact, though xBA dip says another .300 BA could be at risk. Pre-injury xPX was in fine shape, so health is likely his biggest obstacle to another $20 season.

Yr Tm	AB	R	HR	RBI	SB	BA	xBA	OBP	SLG	OPS	vL	vR	bb%	ct%	Eye	G	L	F	h%	HctX	PX	xPX	hr/f	Spd	SBO	SB%	#Wk	DOM	DIS	RC/G	RAR	BPV	BPX	R$
10 STL	465	34	6	62	8	262	269	329	342	671	570	714	8	89	0.82	51	21	28	28	97	54	85	5%	63	9%	67%	25	40%	16%	3.79	-7.9	37	80	$9
11 STL	475	55	14	65	4	305	291	349	465	814	842	806	6	91	0.75	45	20	35	31	115	101	101	9%	67	7%	44%	27	67%	7%	5.79	18.5	79	176	$19
12 STL	505	65	22	76	12	315	300	373	501	874	1021	833	8	89	0.82	40	25	35	32	124	107	112	14%	72	10%	80%	27	74%	0%	6.93	36.2	82	205	$26
13 STL	505	68	12	80	3	319	301	359	477	836	883	823	6	89	0.55	42	24	34	34	126	109	111	8%	67	4%	60%	26	65%	23%	6.32	35.5	77	193	$24
14 STL	404	40	7	38	1	282	271	333	386	719	795	695	6	86	0.51	51	23	27	31	115	75	95	7%	64	2%	50%	20	45%	25%	4.48	11.6	40	108	$10
1st Half	275	28	7	28	1	280	277	331	407	738	850	704	7	87	0.56	48	23	30	30	139	86	122	10%	58	1%	100%	14	50%	21%	4.77	10.7	49	132	$14
2nd Half	129	12	0	10	0	287	259	338	341	679	684	678	6	85	0.42	57	23	20	34	63	50	35	0%	78	3%	0%	6	33%	33%	3.87	1.8	18	49	$1
15 Proj	504	58	11	68	4	293	287	344	421	765	813	750	7	88	0.57	48	23	29	32	107	91	89	9%	66	4%	58%				5.10	24.0	52	137	$19

Montero,Jesus

Age: 25 **Bats:** R **Pos:** DH | **Ht:** 6' 3" **Wt:** 235
Health A | PT/Exp D | Consist B | LIMA Plan D | Rand Var 0 | MM 3121

1-2-.235 in 17 AB at SEA. Started the season 40 pounds overweight, ended it on suspension after altercation with a team scout. If that wasn't enough, on-field skills were ominous as Eye continued to erode. Power no longer looks elite enough to compensate for that plate approach. Age, pedigree barely keep him relevant.

Yr Tm	AB	R	HR	RBI	SB	BA	xBA	OBP	SLG	OPS	vL	vR	bb%	ct%	Eye	G	L	F	h%	HctX	PX	xPX	hr/f	Spd	SBO	SB%	#Wk	DOM	DIS	RC/G	RAR	BPV	BPX	R$
10 aaa	453	58	21	66	0	275		336	495	831			8	79	0.43				31		149			96	0%	0%				5.85		82	178	$14
11 NYY *	481	55	22	70	0	281	273	336	469	804	1181	877	8	75	0.33	39	27	34	33	138	130	155	27%	82	0%	0%	5	60%	40%	5.58	-3.4	45	100	$16
12 SEA	515	46	15	62	0	260	253	298	386	685	830	609	5	81	0.29	43	25	33	30	105	80	92	11%	68	2%	0%	28	36%	36%	3.92	-14.5	20	50	$10
13 SEA *	174	14	4	15	0	205	218	261	328	589	531	615	7	72	0.27	42	20	38	27	73	89	87	10%	113	3%	0%	8	25%	50%	2.67	-9.9	8	20	-$2
14 SEA *	381	37	11	51	1	227	244	272	369	641	818	333	6	74	0.24	64	14	21	28	69	112	57	33%	62	1%	100%	3	33%	33%	3.32	-8.3	17	46	$5
1st Half	239	23	6	28	0	216	241	270	347	617	1125	333	7	72	0.27	67	17	17	27	78	107	69	50%	70	0%	0%	2	50%	0%	3.05	-7.4	11	30	$4
2nd Half	142	15	5	23	1	247	201	277	406	683	0	0	4	77	0.17	50	0	50	29	0	118	-14	0%	72	2%	100%	1	0%	100%	3.83	-0.9	33	89	$6
15 Proj	132	13	4	17	0	236	252	285	391	676	813	603	6	74	0.24	41	24	35	29	100	118	115	13%	86	2%	51%				3.65	-1.6	17	44	$3

Montero,Miguel

Age: 31 **Bats:** L **Pos:** CA | **Ht:** 5' 11" **Wt:** 210
Health B | PT/Exp B | Consist C | LIMA Plan D+ | Rand Var +1 | MM 2015

Was on his way back to a 2011-12 repeat until his production cratered in a 2nd half that reeked of a hidden injury. Ct% and xPX rebounds were positive signs. However, his last four half-year BPVs (1, 12, 52, 15) and continued struggles vs. LHP suggest his leash might be getting shorter.

Yr Tm	AB	R	HR	RBI	SB	BA	xBA	OBP	SLG	OPS	vL	vR	bb%	ct%	Eye	G	L	F	h%	HctX	PX	xPX	hr/f	Spd	SBO	SB%	#Wk	DOM	DIS	RC/G	RAR	BPV	BPX	R$
10 ARI	297	36	9	43	0	266	257	332	438	770	661	811	9	76	0.41	38	19	43	32	102	126	134	9%	84	1%	0%	18	39%	39%	4.97	5.1	50	109	$7
11 ARI	493	65	18	86	1	282	281	351	469	820	534	904	9	80	0.48	42	22	36	32	118	131	136	13%	61	2%	50%	27	59%	19%	5.70	18.4	64	142	$18
12 ARI	486	65	15	88	0	286	239	391	438	829	767	859	13	73	0.56	43	21	36	36	99	108	121	12%	99	0%	0%	27	41%	41%	5.94	22.4	37	93	$17
13 ARI	413	44	11	42	0	230	224	318	344	662	492	719	11	73	0.46	47	21	31	29	102	83	106	11%	67	0%	0%	23	22%	48%	3.58	-1.3	4	10	$3
14 ARI	489	40	13	72	0	243	241	329	370	699	563	735	10	80	0.58	46	21	33	28	113	92	124	10%	59	3%	0%	27	41%	33%	3.87	6.0	35	95	$8
1st Half	272	30	11	47	0	265	258	346	430	776	401	889	10	80	0.56	45	20	35	30	127	113	152	14%	66	3%	0%	15	33%	33%	4.92	12.1	52	141	$17
2nd Half	217	10	2	25	0	217	227	306	295	601	820	551	10	81	0.60	48	21	31	26	94	65	89	4%	59	3%	0%	12	50%	33%	2.74	-4.4	15	41	-$2
15 Proj	451	43	12	62	0	246	243	333	378	710	623	738	11	77	0.52	46	21	33	29	105	99	115	11%	66	2%	2%				4.08	9.2	18	46	$9

RYAN BLOOMFIELD

Morales,Kendrys

Age: 32	Bats: B	Pos: DH 1B	Health	D	LIMA Plan	C+		
Ht: 6' 1"	Wt: 225		PT/Exp	B	Rand Var	+5		
			Consist	C	MM	3025		

Unsigned until June, he had to wait until teams no longer had to forfeit a compensation draft pick. Then lived up to that depressed expectation. Continued GB lean, declining post-injury PX means 20 HR is no lock, even in a full year. With marginal hard contact, a h% recovery alone won't be enough to give big boost to BA.

Yr	Tm	AB	R	HR	RBI	SB	BA	xBA	OBP	SLG	OPS	vL	vR	bb%	ct%	Eye	G	L	F	h%	HctX	PX	xPX	hr/f	Spd	SBO	SB%	#Wk	DOM	DIS	RC/G	RAR	BPV	BPX	R$
10	LAA	193	29	11	39	0	290	289	346	487	833	548	1002	6	84	0.39	48	21	31	30	109	113	110	22%	66	2%	0%	8	88%	0%	5.68	-0.8	60	130	$8
11																																			
12	LAA	484	61	22	73	0	273	267	320	467	787	761	791	6	76	0.27	51	20	28	32	118	129	109	21%	67	1%	0%	27	48%	37%	5.14	3.4	42	105	$15
13	SEA	602	64	23	80	0	277	259	336	449	785	794	780	8	81	0.43	49	19	33	31	122	115	134	14%	71	0%	0%	27	56%	30%	5.25	12.7	54	135	$19
14	2 AL	367	28	8	42	0	218	238	274	338	612	661	584	7	81	0.40	49	18	33	25	106	89	102	8%	63	0%	0%	17	41%	41%	2.99	-11.8	32	86	$1
1st Half		79	7	1	9	0	215	242	250	316	566	434	626	5	82	0.29	48	18	33	25	124	82	114	5%	75	0%	0%	4	50%	50%	2.60	-3.5	29	78	-$9
2nd Half		288	21	7	33	0	219	237	281	344	625	712	571	7	81	0.43	49	18	33	25	101	92	98	9%	63	0%	0%	13	38%	38%	3.10	-8.4	34	92	$4
15	**Proj**	**524**	**52**	**17**	**70**	**0**	**248**	**256**	**300**	**399**	**699**	**667**	**715**	**6**	**81**	**0.36**	**49**	**19**	**32**	**28**	**114**	**108**	**113**	**12%**	**64**	**0%**	**0%**				**4.00**	**-0.8**	**31**	**83**	**$10**

Moreland,Mitch

Age: 29	Bats: L	Pos: 1B DH	Health	F	LIMA Plan	B		
Ht: 6' 2"	Wt: 230		PT/Exp	D	Rand Var	0		
			Consist	B	MM	4135		

Mid-season ankle surgery mercifully ended worst MLB season, but a closer look points to sneaky value. Steady surge in xPX muted by fluky hr/f; his power is still legit. Just don't expect .270 BA to return again, as eroding contact seals his fate there. With semi-regular AB, better health... UP: 30 HR, still.

Yr	Tm	AB	R	HR	RBI	SB	BA	xBA	OBP	SLG	OPS	vL	vR	bb%	ct%	Eye	G	L	F	h%	HctX	PX	xPX	hr/f	Spd	SBO	SB%	#Wk	DOM	DIS	RC/G	RAR	BPV	BPX	R$
10	TEX *	498	57	18	72	4	249	273	329	425	754	604	869	11	78	0.55	40	23	38	28	130	121	152	21%	66	5%	67%	11	45%	27%	4.72	-13.4	53	115	$11
11	TEX	464	60	16	51	2	259	250	320	414	733	577	783	8	80	0.42	42	18	40	29	109	104	105	11%	82	3%	50%	27	52%	30%	4.44	-16.2	46	102	$11
12	TEX	327	41	15	50	1	275	262	321	468	789	737	798	7	78	0.32	42	20	38	31	119	125	128	15%	77	3%	50%	22	50%	27%	5.26	-0.1	51	128	$10
13	TEX	462	60	23	60	0	232	255	299	437	736	701	752	9	75	0.38	43	17	39	26	114	143	136	17%	71	0%	0%	26	50%	27%	4.35	-3.5	54	135	$9
14	TEX	167	18	2	23	0	246	235	297	347	644	374	692	7	74	0.28	45	22	33	32	136	86	143	5%	74	0%	0%	10	30%	50%	3.48	-3.2	3	8	$1
1st Half		167	18	2	23	0	246	235	297	347	644	374	692	7	74	0.28	45	22	33	32	136	86	143	5%	74	0%	0%	10	30%	50%	3.48	-3.4	3	8	$1
2nd Half																																			
15	**Proj**	**420**	**51**	**17**	**57**	**1**	**252**	**263**	**310**	**434**	**744**	**607**	**776**	**8**	**77**	**0.36**	**43**	**20**	**37**	**29**	**123**	**132**	**133**	**14%**	**73**	**2%**	**55%**				**4.57**	**4.9**	**45**	**118**	**$12**

Morneau,Justin

Age: 34	Bats: L	Pos: 1B	Health	C	LIMA Plan	B		
Ht: 6' 4"	Wt: 220		PT/Exp	A	Rand Var	-4		
			Consist	C	MM	3045		

First $20+ season since '08, and it wasn't a thin-air production. Both bat-on-ball and hard contact supported power and BA upticks, even if batting crown was aided by friendly 2nd half h%. Just know that deep struggles vs. southpaws and eroding flyball stroke will prevent full return to glory days.

Yr	Tm	AB	R	HR	RBI	SB	BA	xBA	OBP	SLG	OPS	vL	vR	bb%	ct%	Eye	G	L	F	h%	HctX	PX	xPX	hr/f	Spd	SBO	SB%	#Wk	DOM	DIS	RC/G	RAR	BPV	BPX	R$
10	MIN	296	53	18	56	0	345	312	437	618	1055	966	1113	14	79	0.81	33	22	45	39	146	185	187	17%	100	0%	0%	14	93%	7%	10.57	32.8	125	272	$19
11	MIN *	294	25	5	36	0	233	238	281	345	626	401	728	6	84	0.42	35	18	46	26	96	84	97	4%	70	0%	0%	15	40%	33%	3.23	-26.7	39	87	$1
12	MIN	505	63	19	77	1	267	263	333	440	773	569	902	9	80	0.48	41	22	37	30	109	110	115	13%	84	1%	100%	26	42%	23%	5.09	-4.8	52	130	$14
13	2 TM	572	62	17	77	0	259	258	323	411	734	525	819	8	81	0.45	41	21	38	29	99	107	94	10%	85	0%	0%	26	54%	15%	4.50	-1.4	52	130	$13
14	COL	502	62	17	82	0	319	300	364	496	860	665	927	6	88	0.57	44	23	33	34	120	115	109	11%	86	2%	0%	26	69%	8%	6.56	32.0	85	230	$25
1st Half		293	35	13	58	0	314	302	348	519	867	730	924	5	88	0.43	47	20	33	32	123	130	111	15%	74	0%	0%	14	71%	14%	6.70	20.0	90	243	$31
2nd Half		209	27	4	24	0	325	295	385	464	849	532	930	8	88	0.76	40	28	33	36	116	94	106	7%	105	4%	0%	12	67%	0%	6.33	12.2	78	211	$16
15	**Proj**	**484**	**59**	**16**	**77**	**0**	**294**	**284**	**351**	**463**	**815**	**603**	**900**	**8**	**84**	**0.54**	**41**	**23**	**36**	**32**	**113**	**116**	**109**	**11%**	**86**	**2%**	**6%**				**5.74**	**21.2**	**60**	**157**	**$20**

Morrison,Logan

Age: 27	Bats: L	Pos: 1B	Health	F	LIMA Plan	C		
Ht: 6' 3"	Wt: 245		PT/Exp	D	Rand Var	0		
			Consist	A	MM	3133		

11-38-.262 in 336 AB at SEA. 1B/DH types with modest power and poor OBA do just enough to eek out ABs, but this one's good fortune might be on its last legs... unless his 2nd half has its own legs. At 27 and with three years of stagnant skills, that 2nd half better mean something. UP: 20 HR, .275. DN: See 2012

Yr	Tm	AB	R	HR	RBI	SB	BA	xBA	OBP	SLG	OPS	vL	vR	bb%	ct%	Eye	G	L	F	h%	HctX	PX	xPX	hr/f	Spd	SBO	SB%	#Wk	DOM	DIS	RC/G	RAR	BPV	BPX	R$
10	FLA *	482	69	6	51	1	273	277	375	425	800	926	797	14	81	0.84	48	20	32	33	109	108	100	3%	109	3%	18%	11	45%	27%	5.47	-10.9	72	157	$10
11	FLA *	486	56	24	75	2	241	281	318	457	776	723	827	10	79	0.53	47	18	35	26	121	143	129	18%	78	3%	67%	24	71%	13%	4.88	-20.0	75	167	$12
12	MIA	296	30	11	36	1	230	252	308	399	707	659	723	9	80	0.53	41	18	41	25	111	107	117	11%	64	1%	100%	17	47%	29%	4.01	-11.3	47	118	$3
13	MIA *	326	36	7	42	0	233	254	316	364	680	491	778	11	81	0.65	48	20	32	27	110	85	97	8%	103	0%	0%	17	41%	41%	3.82	-7.4	48	120	$3
14	SEA *	401	49	13	43	6	257	272	310	407	717	846	695	7	83	0.44	40	24	36	28	113	104	92	11%	60	8%	76%	20	35%	20%	4.33	2.2	48	130	$11
1st Half		150	17	6	16	3	235	246	307	374	682	652	719	10	80	0.54	38	22	40	26	135	90	131	15%	61	8%	100%	7	29%	29%	3.96	-0.9	33	89	$3
2nd Half		251	32	7	27	3	271	285	319	426	745	895	685	6	84	0.38	40	25	35	30	107	113	80	9%	67	9%	60%	13	38%	15%	4.56	2.9	60	162	$16
15	**Proj**	**312**	**36**	**10**	**36**	**3**	**253**	**267**	**325**	**408**	**732**	**721**	**736**	**9**	**82**	**0.55**	**43**	**21**	**36**	**28**	**115**	**107**	**103**	**11%**	**73**	**4%**	**75%**				**4.46**	**2.7**	**54**	**141**	**$8**

Morse,Michael

Age: 33	Bats: R	Pos: LF 1B	Health	C	LIMA Plan	C+		
Ht: 6' 5"	Wt: 245		PT/Exp	C	Rand Var	-1		
			Consist	F	MM	4033		

Another year removed from his 30-HR breakout, and it's becoming clear it ain't happening again. Good raw power hampered by lack of loft in swing, continued sub-par contact. Free-swinging bats entering their mid-30s won't learn new tricks, so the risk-averse should stop when bidding hits double digits.

Yr	Tm	AB	R	HR	RBI	SB	BA	xBA	OBP	SLG	OPS	vL	vR	bb%	ct%	Eye	G	L	F	h%	HctX	PX	xPX	hr/f	Spd	SBO	SB%	#Wk	DOM	DIS	RC/G	RAR	BPV	BPX	R$
10	WAS *	317	45	17	47	0	276	269	335	495	829	999	806	8	76	0.36	46	16	38	32	122	144	141	19%	118	1%	0%	22	50%	41%	5.75	4.4	71	154	$10
11	WAS	522	73	31	95	2	303	287	360	550	910	892	915	6	76	0.29	44	20	37	35	137	173	154	21%	63	4%	40%	27	59%	22%	6.85	22.8	76	169	$27
12	WAS	406	53	18	62	0	291	263	321	470	791	755	804	4	76	0.16	55	20	25	34	109	116	111	23%	88	1%	0%	19	37%	26%	5.31	6.6	33	83	$15
13	2 AL *	336	36	14	28	0	212	234	261	374	635	667	642	6	72	0.23	45	19	36	25	109	117	115	16%	72	0%	0%	21	33%	57%	3.16	-9.2	17	43	$1
14	SF	438	48	16	61	0	279	269	336	475	811	827	803	7	72	0.26	45	22	33	35	101	156	130	15%	92	0%	0%	24	46%	38%	5.48	20.9	57	154	$14
1st Half		269	32	13	44	0	275	281	328	498	826	721	868	6	74	0.24	46	21	33	33	105	169	132	20%	83	0%	0%	14	57%	29%	5.58	14.0	70	189	$20
2nd Half		169	16	3	17	0	284	250	349	438	787	956	687	8	70	0.27	43	23	33	39	93	135	127	8%	100	0%	0%	10	30%	50%	5.28	7.3	35	95	$5
15	**Proj**	**393**	**44**	**15**	**48**	**0**	**266**	**260**	**321**	**448**	**769**	**805**	**751**	**6**	**73**	**0.25**	**46**	**21**	**33**	**33**	**105**	**142**	**125**	**16%**	**88**	**0%**	**19%**				**4.85**	**12.6**	**33**	**87**	**$12**

Moss,Brandon

Age: 31	Bats: L	Pos: 1B LF RF	Health	A	LIMA Plan	B+		
Ht: 6' 0"	Wt: 210		PT/Exp	B	Rand Var	+1		
			Consist	B	MM	5125		

Consistent 25-30 HR threat with hidden upside for more. Check out yo-yo OPS by half, last two seasons: .772, .989, .876, .637. Steadily climbing bb% an indicator of improved pitch recognition, which may help him smooth out the streakiness. With quick recovery from hip surgery... UP: .265-35-100

Yr	Tm	AB	R	HR	RBI	SB	BA	xBA	OBP	SLG	OPS	vL	vR	bb%	ct%	Eye	G	L	F	h%	HctX	PX	xPX	hr/f	Spd	SBO	SB%	#Wk	DOM	DIS	RC/G	RAR	BPV	BPX	R$
10	PIT *	526	53	15	69	8	208	245	250	347	598	0	392	5	73	0.21	55	15	30	26	119	106	145	0%	89	18%	49%	5	20%	80%	2.64	-43.8	16	35	$4
11	PHI *	442	49	17	60	3	219	196	293	399	693	0	0	9	64	0.29	50	0	50	30	0	154	2	0%	73	10%	29%	2	0%	50%	3.58	-23.2	21	47	$6
12	OAK *	461	68	29	73	4	254	259	314	505	819	770	1006	8	69	0.28	33	21	46	30	111	178	176	26%	72	4%	78%	18	61%	28%	5.42	11.5	59	148	$16
13	OAK	446	73	30	87	4	256	256	337	522	859	649	904	10	69	0.36	30	18	52	30	113	194	174	19%	92	6%	67%	27	70%	15%	5.86	24.7	79	198	$20
14	OAK	500	70	25	81	1	234	242	334	438	772	792	768	12	69	0.44	30	21	49	29	100	156	137	15%	61	1%	100%	27	44%	41%	4.74	15.8	46	124	$14
1st Half		284	39	18	60	1	268	270	355	521	876	816	892	10	74	0.44	31	20	49	30	120	179	157	18%	71	1%	100%	14	64%	14%	6.26	20.6	82	222	$24
2nd Half		216	31	7	21	0	190	208	309	329	637	739	622	14	64	0.44	29	23	48	26	73	121	106	10%	62	0%	0%	13	23%	69%	3.10	-4.4	0	0	$0
15	**Proj**	**450**	**65**	**27**	**75**	**2**	**252**	**254**	**339**	**491**	**830**	**751**	**846**	**11**	**68**	**0.38**	**30**	**20**	**49**	**31**	**102**	**185**	**151**	**18%**	**68**	**3%**	**63%**				**5.50**	**17.7**	**64**	**168**	**$18**

Moustakas,Mike

Age: 26	Bats: L	Pos: 3B	Health	A	LIMA Plan	B+		
Ht: 6' 0"	Wt: 195		PT/Exp	B	Rand Var	+4		
			Consist	A	MM	3135		

15-54-.212 in 457 AB at KC. Former premium prospect finally showing hints of something more, in flashes. Surge in hard contact kept in mothballs due to unfriendly h%; xPX confirms high power ceiling remains. Oct heroics might inflate his value somewhat; be cautious. But with more plate control gains, tweak vs. LH... UP: 30 HR

Yr	Tm	AB	R	HR	RBI	SB	BA	xBA	OBP	SLG	OPS	vL	vR	bb%	ct%	Eye	G	L	F	h%	HctX	PX	xPX	hr/f	Spd	SBO	SB%	#Wk	DOM	DIS	RC/G	RAR	BPV	BPX	R$
10	a/a	484	72	25	95	2	286		322	520	842			5	85	0.36				29		149			83	3%	58%				5.94		97	211	$21
11	KC *	561	54	11	62	3	256	249	301	380	681	494	741	6	82	0.36	38	20	41	29	92	88	83	4%	91	3%	71%	17	35%	24%	3.92	-14.5	41	91	$10
12	KC	563	69	20	73	5	242	236	296	412	708	704	710	6	78	0.31	34	16	50	28	88	115	109	9%	82	6%	71%	27	48%	33%	4.01	-9.0	43	108	$12
13	KC	472	42	12	42	2	233	241	287	364	651	546	682	6	82	0.39	37	19	45	26	84	91	86	7%	73	6%	33%	26	46%	23%	3.30	-9.2	39	98	$4
14	KC *	488	47	16	57	1	217	258	272	365	638	554	653	7	83	0.46	39	20	41	23	115	100	120	9%	69	1%	100%	26	50%	23%	3.25	-6.2	50	135	$5
1st Half		238	22	9	32	0	197	248	262	367	629	607	608	8	82	0.50	35	16	49	20	110	115	137	10%	73	0%	0%	13	54%	15%	3.06	-4.8	62	168	$3
2nd Half		250	25	7	25	1	236	266	288	364	652	527	696	6	84	0.41	41	23	35	25	118	87	106	9%	75	2%	100%	13	46%	31%	3.45	-1.9	44	119	$7
15	**Proj**	**524**	**60**	**19**	**72**	**2**	**245**	**261**	**298**	**409**	**707**	**615**	**735**	**7**	**82**	**0.40**	**38**	**19**	**43**	**27**	**101**	**113**	**105**	**10%**	**71**	**3%**	**59%**				**4.04**	**5.4**	**50**	**131**	**$13**

STEPHEN NICKRAND

Murphy,Daniel	Health	B	LIMA Plan	A
Age: 30 Bats: L Pos: 2B	PT/Exp	A	Rand Var	0
Ht: 6' 1" Wt: 215	Consist	A	MM	2245

In this pitching-heavy period, multi-category bats like this are gold, especially at scarce positions. Solid ability to make hard contact will keep him more than a slap hitter, and steady xBA means you can put a .280 BA in stone. Wheels at risk now that he's in his 30s, but that's quibbling. A LIMA gem.

Yr Tm	AB	R	HR	RBI	SB	BA	xBA	OBP	SLG	OPS	vL	vR	bb%	ct%	Eye	G	L	F	h%	HctX	PX	xPX	hr/f	Spd	SBO	SB%	#Wk	DOM	DIS	RC/G	RAR	BPV	BPX	R$
10 aaa	34	3	1	6	1	238		254	370	624			2	93	0.30				24		87			99	13%	100%				3.24		77	167	-$1
11 NYM	391	49	6	49	5	320	289	362	448	809	755	825	6	89	0.57	47	22	31	35	115	88	95	6%	90	9%	50%	20	45%	10%	5.80	11.5	68	151	$16
12 NYM	571	62	6	65	10	291	285	332	403	735	680	761	6	86	0.44	51	24	25	33	88	79	55	5%	85	8%	83%	27	48%	37%	4.86	8.2	45	113	$17
13 NYM	658	92	13	78	23	286	266	319	415	733	616	790	5	86	0.34	42	21	36	32	112	87	100	6%	100	16%	88%	27	52%	19%	4.84	21.9	53	133	$30
14 NYM	596	79	9	57	13	289	285	332	403	734	695	747	6	86	0.45	42	28	29	33	107	84	89	6%	95	11%	72%	26	50%	23%	4.77	23.1	52	141	$22
1st Half	340	51	6	32	11	303	294	353	418	771	820	756	8	87	0.65	43	29	28	33	114	81	85	7%	95	14%	73%	14	50%	21%	5.41	19.0	60	162	$29
2nd Half	256	28	3	25	2	270	275	303	383	685	541	736	4	83	0.26	42	27	32	31	97	89	95	4%	94	5%	67%	12	50%	25%	3.98	4.3	42	114	$13
15 Proj	583	74	9	63	12	288	280	327	407	734	652	765	5	86	0.40	44	25	31	33	105	88	88	6%	92	10%	75%				4.76	22.4	53	141	$20

Murphy,David	Health	B	LIMA Plan	B
Age: 33 Bats: L Pos: RF	PT/Exp	B	Rand Var	0
Ht: 6' 3" Wt: 210	Consist	F	MM	2135

Once a formidable part-time bat on favorable side of a platoon, but two years of marginal production vs. RHers suggest it's time to re-think profile. Dip in hard contact makes double-digit HR a reach now, and eroding speed, poor SB% mean steals ain't coming back, especially given advancing age.

Yr Tm	AB	R	HR	RBI	SB	BA	xBA	OBP	SLG	OPS	vL	vR	bb%	ct%	Eye	G	L	F	h%	HctX	PX	xPX	hr/f	Spd	SBO	SB%	#Wk	DOM	DIS	RC/G	RAR	BPV	BPX	R$
10 TEX	419	54	12	65	14	291	277	358	449	806	696	847	10	83	0.63	44	19	36	33	112	106	95	9%	100	13%	88%	26	73%	23%	5.94	9.0	69	150	$18
11 TEX	404	46	11	46	11	275	264	328	401	729	507	809	8	85	0.54	54	17	29	30	88	78	82	11%	115	15%	65%	27	52%	37%	4.53	-7.5	54	120	$13
12 TEX	457	65	15	61	10	304	279	380	479	859	845	862	11	84	0.73	43	21	35	34	114	110	109	11%	104	10%	67%	27	59%	15%	6.52	21.0	78	195	$20
13 TEX	436	51	13	45	1	220	271	282	374	656	562	685	8	86	0.63	43	19	38	23	102	100	98	9%	86	5%	20%	26	62%	23%	3.31	-13.1	69	173	$4
14 CLE	416	40	8	58	2	262	259	319	385	703	604	727	8	85	0.59	46	19	35	29	90	89	73	6%	90	5%	40%	24	38%	29%	4.16	3.2	58	157	$9
1st Half	256	27	5	38	2	242	261	311	367	679	644	690	10	85	0.71	48	18	35	27	89	89	78	6%	91	6%	50%	14	29%	29%	3.80	-1.5	60	162	$11
2nd Half	160	13	3	20	0	294	254	331	413	744	435	776	5	86	0.39	44	19	37	33	91	87	65	6%	92	2%	0%	10	50%	30%	4.80	3.6	52	141	$6
15 Proj	419	43	9	51	3	266	263	323	395	719	604	745	8	85	0.58	45	19	36	29	98	93	85	7%	92	5%	42%				4.32	3.9	48	126	$11

Murphy,John	Health	A	LIMA Plan	D
Age: 24 Bats: R Pos: CA	PT/Exp	F	Rand Var	0
Ht: 5' 11" Wt: 195	Consist	B	MM	2121

1-9-.284 in 81 AB at NYY. Bats of young catchers can tease us into speculation, but they often take time to blossom. Those 2013 skills provide a nice foundation, but he has eclipsed .450+ Slg just once in his professional career, so we need to see more. Make him show it again before bidding.

Yr Tm	AB	R	HR	RBI	SB	BA	xBA	OBP	SLG	OPS	vL	vR	bb%	ct%	Eye	G	L	F	h%	HctX	PX	xPX	hr/f	Spd	SBO	SB%	#Wk	DOM	DIS	RC/G	RAR	BPV	BPX	R$
10																																		
11																																		
12 aa	147	19	4	13	0	212		277	372	649			8	77	0.39				25		116			96	0%	0%				3.33		48	120	-$1
13 NYY *	439	55	12	41	1	245	244	311	387	697	641	143	9	80	0.48	38	19	44	28	136	103	126	0%	82	2%	44%	5	0%	60%	4.03	4.0	47	118	$7
14 NYY *	260	20	6	30	0	235	242	274	349	623	686	690	5	74	0.20	36	27	37	30	54	91	53	5%	82	0%	0%	15	40%	53%	3.19	-1.0	4	11	$2
1st Half	123	9	2	13	0	244	243	260	346	606	669	679	2	73	0.08	35	28	37	32	62	89	56	6%	81	0%	0%	10	30%	60%	3.03	-1.3	-4	-11	$0
2nd Half	137	10	4	17	0	227	229	285	352	638	1000	708	8	74	0.31	38	23	38	28	25	92	43	0%	95	0%	0%	5	60%	40%	3.32	-0.3	14	38	$3
15 Proj	130	13	2	14	0	234	248	288	335	624	648	590	7	76	0.32	35	28	37	29	56	85	50	5%	86	1%	50%				3.21	-0.7	1	2	$1

Myers,Wil	Health	C	LIMA Plan	C+
Age: 24 Bats: R Pos: RF	PT/Exp	C	Rand Var	+1
Ht: 6' 3" Wt: 205	Consist	C	MM	3305

6-35-.222 with 6 SB in 325 AB at TAM. Lost season due to mid-year wrist fracture and long path to full health. PRO: bb% surge; bad BA product of wrist-induced lack of hard contact and low h%. CON: GB stroke makes power reliant on high hr/f; contact flat and troubling. A wildcard with an enormous ceiling.

Yr Tm	AB	R	HR	RBI	SB	BA	xBA	OBP	SLG	OPS	vL	vR	bb%	ct%	Eye	G	L	F	h%	HctX	PX	xPX	hr/f	Spd	SBO	SB%	#Wk	DOM	DIS	RC/G	RAR	BPV	BPX	R$
10																																		
11 aa	354	37	5	37	7	225		301	334	636			10	74	0.43				29		90			89	10%	76%				3.33		18	40	$3
12 a/a	522	75	26	83	5	278		337	497	833			8	71	0.31				34		147			106	6%	58%				5.81		52	130	$21
13 TAM *	587	86	24	100	11	275	255	338	463	801	821	834	9	71	0.33	46	20	34	35	117	143	120	15%	96	9%	78%	16	50%	25%	5.50	20.5	45	113	$26
14 TAM *	349	40	8	40	9	221	216	301	329	630	532	649	10	72	0.41	48	16	36	29	99	88	96	7%	105	10%	89%	16	25%	50%	3.33	-6.0	12	32	$6
1st Half	198	26	5	25	3	227	234	313	354	666	538	719	11	74	0.48	47	18	35	28	106	101	104	10%	105	7%	75%	9	44%	33%	3.67	-2.0	32	86	$7
2nd Half	151	14	3	15	6	213	188	283	297	580	523	534	9	69	0.32	50	11	39	29	87	71	83	3%	109	14%	100%	7	0%	71%	2.91	-5.1	-13	-35	$4
15 Proj	590	72	16	78	9	267	229	334	402	736	695	753	9	71	0.36	48	17	36	35	104	109	103	11%	111	6%	80%				4.71	12.2	17	46	$20

Napoli,Mike	Health	B	LIMA Plan	B
Age: 33 Bats: R Pos: 1B	PT/Exp	B	Rand Var	0
Ht: 6' 0" Wt: 220	Consist	B	MM	4115

Exhibit A that guys with chronic nagging injuries don't suddenly become durable, especially as they near their mid-30s. Foot, finger, back were maladies this go-round. Off-season sleep apnea surgery adds another variable. Power still legit, though it's time to lower expectations given dwindling FB% and decline vs RHers. DN: 2H x 2

Yr Tm	AB	R	HR	RBI	SB	BA	xBA	OBP	SLG	OPS	vL	vR	bb%	ct%	Eye	G	L	F	h%	HctX	PX	xPX	hr/f	Spd	SBO	SB%	#Wk	DOM	DIS	RC/G	RAR	BPV	BPX	R$
10 LAA	453	60	26	68	4	238	264	316	468	784	966	700	8	70	0.31	38	20	42	28	105	168	148	19%	59	6%	67%	26	54%	31%	4.71	-12.6	50	109	$12
11 TEX	369	72	30	75	4	320	312	414	631	1046	1049	1044	14	77	0.68	39	20	41	35	136	207	187	25%	75	5%	67%	24	67%	17%	9.66	39.9	125	278	$26
12 TEX	352	53	24	56	1	227	239	343	469	812	706	861	14	64	0.45	40	19	41	28	95	169	157	26%	102	1%	100%	23	43%	48%	5.17	-1.1	53	133	$9
13 BOS	498	79	23	92	1	259	251	360	482	842	899	816	13	62	0.39	37	24	39	37	106	195	156	19%	72	1%	50%	27	56%	41%	5.84	17.8	55	138	$18
14 BOS	415	49	17	55	3	248	235	370	419	789	923	739	16	68	0.59	45	19	36	32	107	139	138	17%	63	3%	60%	23	48%	39%	5.18	12.8	35	95	$11
1st Half	228	27	10	31	2	276	244	393	461	854	890	839	16	69	0.60	43	20	37	36	114	147	134	17%	72	5%	50%	12	50%	42%	6.18	13.2	50	135	$15
2nd Half	187	22	7	24	1	214	223	342	369	711	959	614	16	66	0.57	48	18	34	28	100	128	143	16%	59	2%	100%	11	45%	36%	4.11	-0.3	20	54	$7
15 Proj	432	59	19	66	2	246	243	359	434	794	881	757	14	66	0.50	42	21	37	33	106	157	149	18%	69	3%	66%				5.19	13.1	37	97	$14

Nava,Daniel	Health	B	LIMA Plan	D+
Age: 32 Bats: B Pos: RF LF	PT/Exp	C	Rand Var	-2
Ht: 5' 11" Wt: 200	Consist	D	MM	2113

4-37-.270 in 363 AB at BOS. Streaky hitter takes walks in bunches, but with poor speed and marginal power, he'll continue to struggle to find steady AB. Declining Eye, pessimistic xBA, yada, yada, yada. 2nd straight 2nd half with .300+ BA surge. Essentially, short-term replacement value in deep leagues.

Yr Tm	AB	R	HR	RBI	SB	BA	xBA	OBP	SLG	OPS	vL	vR	bb%	ct%	Eye	G	L	F	h%	HctX	PX	xPX	hr/f	Spd	SBO	SB%	#Wk	DOM	DIS	RC/G	RAR	BPV	BPX	R$
10 BOS *	445	53	8	62	4	245	226	307	374	681	637	727	8	73	0.33	39	16	45	32	90	106	102	2%	86	7%	54%	16	25%	56%	3.80	-15.0	20	43	$7
11 aaa	441	52	7	36	7	226		307	339	646			10	76	0.49				28		89			95	9%	67%				3.41		27	60	$4
12 BOS *	366	53	9	46	4	248	258	337	400	736	613	797	12	78	0.60	38	23	38	30	116	111	104	8%	74	5%	75%	17	47%	35%	4.57	0.0	47	118	$7
13 BOS	458	77	12	66	0	303	263	385	445	831	647	894	10	80	0.55	34	26	40	36	114	103	131	8%	97	1%	0%	26	42%	19%	5.99	25.3	52	130	$19
14 BOS *	446	49	6	47	5	257	229	320	351	671	399	769	8	76	0.38	45	20	35	33	102	79	93	4%	82	7%	62%	24	25%	38%	3.80	1.4	10	27	$9
1st Half	224	20	4	15	3	208	230	283	296	579	254	688	9	73	0.38	40	27	33	27	89	71	89	6%	71	10%	60%	11	27%	55%	2.65	-7.7	-11	-30	$1
2nd Half	222	29	2	32	2	306	235	371	405	776	536	817	8	79	0.39	48	16	36	38	112	87	95	3%	92	4%	67%	13	23%	23%	5.31	9.5	31	84	$17
15 Proj	254	34	4	31	2	263	242	348	374	722	525	775	9	77	0.46	41	22	38	33	106	92	105	5%	86	5%	60%				4.25	1.8	20	54	$7

Navarro Jr,Efren	Health	A	LIMA Plan	D
Age: 29 Bats: L Pos: 1B LF	PT/Exp	C	Rand Var	+1
Ht: 6' 0" Wt: 210	Consist	A	MM	1121

1-14-.245 in 159 AB at LAA. Minor league vet hit first career HR vs. Verlander, but that was high point. When your glove is your only asset and you struggle to hit double-digit HR in hitter-friendly PCL, odds of MLB impact are nil. RotoLab will give you a draft grade of "Ef" if you roster him.

Yr Tm	AB	R	HR	RBI	SB	BA	xBA	OBP	SLG	OPS	vL	vR	bb%	ct%	Eye	G	L	F	h%	HctX	PX	xPX	hr/f	Spd	SBO	SB%	#Wk	DOM	DIS	RC/G	RAR	BPV	BPX	R$
10 aa	453	36	5	39	5	227		265	310	575			5	88	0.43				25		57			97	9%	50%				2.62		39	85	$1
11 LAA *	502	50	8	47	3	244	220	283	357	641	667	536	5	81	0.29	44	11	44	29	82	83	112	0%	94	8%	35%	4	25%	25%	3.25	-25.3	31	69	$5
12 aaa	528	50	4	47	2	220		251	294	545			4	83	0.25				26		55			83	4%	44%				2.37		12	30	$0
13 LAA *	517	49	4	49	6	238	292	294	322	616	0	750	7	75	0.32	67	33	0	31	0	71	-15	0%	82	9%	47%	2	50%	50%	3.05	-14.5	0	0	$5
14 LAA *	432	42	3	42	2	235	255	294	321	615	702	630	8	79	0.40	47	26	27	29	108	71	82	3%	79	6%	33%	18	39%	44%	3.03	-8.6	15	41	$3
1st Half	269	29	2	27	1	230	244	293	324	617	273	987	8	79	0.42	50	20	30	29	114	79	110	0%	86	6%	14%	5	60%	20%	2.99	-6.2	22	59	$4
2nd Half	163	13	1	14	2	242	255	295	316	611	971	540	7	80	0.38	46	27	26	30	107	59	74	4%	82	6%	61%	13	31%	54%	3.10	-3.1	9	24	$0
15 Proj	131	12	1	12	1	234	248	285	308	593	502	615	7	80	0.35	48	24	28	29	110	63	88	2%	81	7%	50%				2.85	-5.2	3	9	$1

STEPHEN NICKRAND

Navarro,Dioner

Age: 31 Bats: B Pos: CA DH	Health A	LIMA Plan B	
Ht: 5' 9" Wt: 205	PT/Exp D	Rand Var -1	
	Consist F	MM 2135	

Prime example of why it's best to target catchers ONCE they enter their 30s. Admirable follow-up to '13 mini-breakout, though erosion of hard contact puts power at risk. Solid contact gives him a good BA floor, which is so important for players who are inconsistent, week-to-week, like him. A H2H killer, but a decent #2 otherwise.

Yr	Tm	AB	R	HR	RBI	SB	BA	xBA	OBP	SLG	OPS	vL	vR	bb%	ct%	Eye	G	L	F	h%	HctX	PX	xPX	hr/f	Spd	SBO	SB%	#Wk	DOM	DIS	RC/G	RAR	BPV	BPX	R$
10	TAM *	265	25	2	23	2	213	223	291	287	579	518	535	10	81	0.58	47	16	37	26	67	58	44	3%	70	5%	69%	18	39%	33%	2.71	-12.2	13	28	-$1
11	LA	176	13	5	17	0	193	221	276	324	600	616	597	10	80	0.57	43	14	43	21	75	85	94	8%	80	0%	0%	18	44%	39%	2.82	-7.6	35	78	-$3
12	CIN *	276	23	6	35	0	262	280	307	380	687	750	754	6	85	0.42	34	31	34	29	119	74	96	10%	58	0%	0%	9	22%	33%	4.03	-1.9	29	73	$4
13	CHC	240	31	13	34	0	300	289	365	492	856	1123	764	9	85	0.64	41	25	34	31	104	110	91	19%	73	1%	0%	26	54%	31%	6.36	17.5	69	173	$9
14	TOR	481	40	12	69	3	274	263	317	395	712	725	707	6	84	0.42	40	24	36	31	97	83	94	8%	58	2%	100%	26	38%	42%	4.48	15.7	35	95	$14
1st Half		241	19	5	34	1	266	259	310	365	675	623	697	7	84	0.44	42	25	33	30	87	69	79	7%	61	1%	100%	14	36%	50%	4.01	4.2	24	65	$11
2nd Half		240	21	7	35	2	283	268	324	425	749	841	717	6	85	0.41	38	23	39	31	107	98	109	9%	63	3%	100%	12	42%	33%	4.98	10.7	49	132	$17
15	**Proj**	**422**	**40**	**13**	**57**	**2**	**273**	**267**	**325**	**405**	**730**	**803**	**704**	**7**	**84**	**0.50**	**40**	**24**	**36**	**30**	**100**	**89**	**93**	**10%**	**62**	**2%**	**75%**				**4.63**	**14.9**	**35**	**93**	**$11**

Negron,Kristopher

Age: 29 Bats: R Pos: 3B	Health A	LIMA Plan D	
Ht: 6' 0" Wt: 195	PT/Exp D	Rand Var -4	
	Consist B	MM 3401	

6-17-5-.271 in 144 AB at CIN. Sneaky power/speed combo in small MLB sample will make him trendy stash, but don't follow suit. Legs won't provide lasting value if he can't reach base or put bat-on-ball. Power has never been his game; we can't bank on that hr/f repeating itself. He'll be overvalued.

Yr	Tm	AB	R	HR	RBI	SB	BA	xBA	OBP	SLG	OPS	vL	vR	bb%	ct%	Eye	G	L	F	h%	HctX	PX	xPX	hr/f	Spd	SBO	SB%	#Wk	DOM	DIS	RC/G	RAR	BPV	BPX	R$
10	a/a	491	61	9	31	26	232		289	342	631			7	76	0.33				29		76			138	30%	72%				3.25		22	48	$11
11	aaa	417	39	7	32	8	178		208	274	482			4	71	0.13				23		72			109	13%	87%				1.81		-15	-33	-$4
12	CIN *	288	27	5	14	12	180	286	225	281	506	2000	250	6	67	0.18	50	50	0	25	0	80	-11	0%	124	31%	78%	2	0%	100%	1.99	-22.0	-16	-40	-$1
13	aaa	334	24	4	23	9	188		234	267	500			6	66	0.18				27		69			92	18%	70%				1.94		-40	-100	-$2
14	CIN *	363	40	8	33	11	231	240	272	373	645	1057	702	5	70	0.19	51	18	31	31	95	119	159	19%	113	18%	81%	13	54%	23%	3.40	0.0	21	57	$7
1st Half		196	19	2	15	5	197	208	225	295	520			3	67	0.11				28	0	88			120	19%	80%				2.13		-17	-46	$1
2nd Half		167	21	6	18	6	270	272	326	463	790	1057	702	8	73	0.31	51	18	31	34	99	154	159	19%	102	17%	81%	13	54%	23%	5.32	9.3	63	170	$14
15	**Proj**	**198**	**20**	**4**	**16**	**6**	**215**	**229**	**265**	**340**	**605**	**757**	**539**	**6**	**69**	**0.20**	**51**	**18**	**31**	**29**	**89**	**106**	**143**	**10%**	**108**	**21%**	**78%**				**2.90**	**-4.9**	**6**	**17**	**$3**

Nieto,Adrian

Age: 25 Bats: B Pos: CA	Health A	LIMA Plan F	
Ht: 6' 0" Wt: 200	PT/Exp F	Rand Var -1	
	Consist F	MM 2001	

2-7-.236 in 106 AB at CHW. After big gains with bat at High-A in '13, found new home via Rule 5 draft. Then showed why he was a Rule 5 guy to begin with. But let's take a step back here. Those big gains in High-A produced a .285/.373/.449 slash line. Decent, but that's High-A. The short-term ceiling here is low.

Yr	Tm	AB	R	HR	RBI	SB	BA	xBA	OBP	SLG	OPS	vL	vR	bb%	ct%	Eye	G	L	F	h%	HctX	PX	xPX	hr/f	Spd	SBO	SB%	#Wk	DOM	DIS	RC/G	RAR	BPV	BPX	R$
10																																			
11																																			
12																																			
13																																			
14	CHW	106	8	2	7	0	236	220	296	340	635	724	611	7	64	0.21	49	26	25	35	82	98	63	12%	104	4%	0%	23	26%	65%	3.14	-0.5	-17	-46	-$1
1st Half		56	5	0	3	0	250	198	333	304	637	1007	544	10	61	0.27	53	26	21	41	53	69	44	0%	116	0%	0%	14	21%	71%	3.33	-0.1	-46	-124	-$2
2nd Half		50	3	2	4	0	220	245	250	380	630	432	686	4	68	0.13	44	26	29	28	115	127	81	20%	90	11%	0%	9	33%	56%	2.80	-0.9	10	27	$0
15	**Proj**	**105**	**8**	**2**	**7**	**0**	**232**	**223**	**286**	**338**	**624**	**652**	**616**	**6**	**65**	**0.20**	**48**	**26**	**26**	**34**	**90**	**98**	**66**	**12%**	**100**	**5%**	**0%**				**2.98**	**-1.3**	**-39**	**-103**	**$1**

Nieuwenhuis,Kirk

Age: 27 Bats: L Pos: LF	Health A	LIMA Plan D+	
Ht: 6' 3" Wt: 225	PT/Exp D	Rand Var +4	
	Consist C	MM 4213	

3-16-.259 in 112 AB at NYM. Given inconsistency, holes in swing, and deep struggles against LHers, would be easy to dismiss as a non-factor. But that surging PX/xPX is now in elite territory, and his poor plate control took a nice step forward in 2nd half. If it holds and LD/FB normalizes... UP: 20 HR

Yr	Tm	AB	R	HR	RBI	SB	BA	xBA	OBP	SLG	OPS	vL	vR	bb%	ct%	Eye	G	L	F	h%	HctX	PX	xPX	hr/f	Spd	SBO	SB%	#Wk	DOM	DIS	RC/G	RAR	BPV	BPX	R$
10	a/a	514	65	12	55	9	228		271	379	650			6	71	0.20				30		124			102	18%	54%				3.23		25	54	$7
11	aaa	188	26	5	11	4	236		324	396	721			12	64	0.36				34		143			114	13%	63%				4.20		30	67	$1
12	NYM	282	40	7	28	4	252	222	315	376	691	515	740	8	65	0.26	51	22	27	36	80	99	90	14%	94	11%	50%	17	18%	71%	3.85	-7.4	-12	-30	$5
13	NYM *	377	45	12	36	6	181	215	252	320	572	111	661	9	65	0.27	46	19	35	24	71	110	100	14%	103	10%	69%	11	27%	64%	2.49	-19.0	0	0	$0
14	NYM *	323	35	9	34	6	209	255	265	381	646	522	855	7	65	0.21	41	31	28	29	113	155	158	14%	73	16%	60%	16	56%	38%	3.15	-6.4	22	59	$3
1st Half		209	20	7	22	1	205	245	236	373	610	500	979	4	63	0.11	25	40	35	29	177	151	285	14%	85	16%	22%	5	80%	0%	2.58	-7.7	8	22	$3
2nd Half		114	14	3	11	5	217	274	312	396	708	533	815	12	69	0.44	46	28	26	29	92	162	110	14%	78	17%	100%	11	45%	55%	4.25	1.8	55	149	$3
15	**Proj**	**301**	**36**	**10**	**37**	**7**	**239**	**245**	**302**	**418**	**720**	**390**	**759**	**9**	**66**	**0.28**	**42**	**23**	**35**	**33**	**100**	**155**	**139**	**15%**	**78**	**13%**	**72%**				**4.24**	**4.5**	**36**	**94**	**$9**

Nieves,Wil

Age: 37 Bats: R Pos: CA	Health B	LIMA Plan D	
Ht: 5' 11" Wt: 190	PT/Exp F	Rand Var -2	
	Consist C	MM 2211	

Speculating on bats of 30-something catchers only goes so far. Fact that this one had ONE walk in 122 AB is reason enough to run for the hills. Scan of PX, HctX validates that there's nothing worth chasing here. xBA says he has risk of becoming batting average killer too. Shouldn't be rostered. Anywhere.

Yr	Tm	AB	R	HR	RBI	SB	BA	xBA	OBP	SLG	OPS	vL	vR	bb%	ct%	Eye	G	L	F	h%	HctX	PX	xPX	hr/f	Spd	SBO	SB%	#Wk	DOM	DIS	RC/G	RAR	BPV	BPX	R$
10	WAS	158	10	3	16	0	203	229	244	310	554	621	537	5	82	0.28	54	15	31	23	92	77	75	8%	77	0%	0%	26	38%	42%	2.39	-9.7	23	50	-$2
11	MIL *	209	10	1	9	1	162	210	201	206	407	343	382	5	80	0.25	71	13	16	19	42	34	8	0%	81	2%	100%	12	17%	67%	1.27	-21.2	-14	-31	-$7
12	2 NL *	194	15	4	17	1	260	256	287	353	640	939	667	4	79	0.17	66	24	10	31	81	62	41	29%	92	6%	19%	15	33%	47%	3.31	-5.5	1	3	$1
13	ARI	195	16	1	22	0	297	233	320	369	690	720	670	4	84	0.25	61	17	21	35	83	59	40	3%	91	0%	0%	27	26%	41%	4.36	3.5	19	48	$3
14	PHI	122	9	1	7	1	254	234	270	344	614	559	632	1	72	0.03	44	25	31	34	69	87	75	4%	75	4%	100%	21	33%	57%	3.10	-1.2	-15	-41	$0
1st Half		54	5	1	4	1	259	270	273	407	680	1000	589	0	74	0.00	50	23	28	33	84	133	85	9%	79	13%	100%	11	45%	36%	3.73	0.5	28	76	$0
2nd Half		68	4	0	3	0	250	208	268	294	562	269	668	1	71	0.05	39	27	35	35	56	49	67	0%	80	0%	0%	10	20%	80%	2.61	-1.6	-50	-135	-$1
15	**Proj**	**137**	**10**	**2**	**10**	**1**	**236**	**245**	**257**	**332**	**589**	**632**	**572**	**2**	**77**	**0.10**	**53**	**22**	**25**	**30**	**73**	**81**	**57**	**7%**	**81**	**3%**	**75%**				**2.81**	**-2.4**	**-10**	**-27**	**$1**

Norris,Derek

Age: 26 Bats: R Pos: CA	Health A	LIMA Plan B	
Ht: 6' 0" Wt: 210	PT/Exp C	Rand Var -4	
	Consist B	MM 4225	

PRO: Elite first half, finally showed progress against RHers, plate control on upswing. CON: 2nd half saw regression vs. RH, heavier GB stroke, spike in Ks. No sure thing, but man, that 1st half is eye-catching. If you want to speculate on a backstop breakout, this is a good place. UP: .280-25-100

Yr	Tm	AB	R	HR	RBI	SB	BA	xBA	OBP	SLG	OPS	vL	vR	bb%	ct%	Eye	G	L	F	h%	HctX	PX	xPX	hr/f	Spd	SBO	SB%	#Wk	DOM	DIS	RC/G	RAR	BPV	BPX	R$
10																																			
11	aa	334	62	17	38	11	190		314	392	706			15	63	0.49				24		164			104	17%	71%				3.85		48	107	$6
12	OAK *	427	47	13	61	9	212	235	274	359	633	618	630	8	74	0.32	40	22	39	26	94	102	93	13%	101	12%	80%	16	31%	63%	3.20	-12.4	24	60	$5
13	OAK	264	41	9	30	5	246	241	345	409	754	990	445	12	73	0.52	36	21	43	30	98	124	95	11%	86	6%	100%	26	46%	38%	4.81	8.5	44	110	$6
14	OAK	385	46	10	55	2	270	243	361	403	763	863	699	12	78	0.63	46	19	35	33	101	99	95	9%	99	3%	50%	26	46%	31%	5.00	18.6	46	124	$11
1st Half		171	25	8	35	2	304	288	406	509	915	1058	805	15	82	0.97	42	21	37	33	102	140	104	15%	98	5%	67%	14	57%	7%	7.54	19.5	101	273	$18
2nd Half		214	21	2	20	0	243	206	322	318	640	674	621	10	74	0.44	50	16	34	32	99	62	86	4%	104	2%	0%	12	33%	58%	3.35	-0.3	0	0	$6
15	**Proj**	**401**	**53**	**14**	**57**	**5**	**251**	**246**	**342**	**412**	**754**	**907**	**626**	**12**	**74**	**0.52**	**41**	**20**	**40**	**31**	**99**	**122**	**94**	**12%**	**95**	**6%**	**75%**				**4.76**	**16.2**	**41**	**109**	**$13**

Nunez,Eduardo

Age: 28 Bats: R Pos: 3B SS	Health C	LIMA Plan D+	
Ht: 6' 0" Wt: 185	PT/Exp F	Rand Var 0	
	Consist B	MM 1521	

4-24-.250 with 9 SB in 204 AB at MIN. With surging Spd that's now in elite territory, there's a path here for fanalytic relevance. Problem is, when you can't consistently reach base 30% of time, it's a wasted talent. Has shown modest plate control in past, so hope not all lost. If he can tap into it again... UP: 30 SB

Yr	Tm	AB	R	HR	RBI	SB	BA	xBA	OBP	SLG	OPS	vL	vR	bb%	ct%	Eye	G	L	F	h%	HctX	PX	xPX	hr/f	Spd	SBO	SB%	#Wk	DOM	DIS	RC/G	RAR	BPV	BPX	R$
10	NYY *	514	59	5	50	25	265	247	307	348	655	692	662	6	87	0.46	65	6	29	30	96	57	52	7%	130	22%	82%	7	29%	0%	3.80	-5.6	45	98	$16
11	NYY	309	38	5	30	22	265	274	313	385	698	742	673	7	88	0.59	45	21	34	29	108	80	70	5%	121	35%	79%	26	54%	8%	4.25	0.6	68	151	$11
12	NYY *	252	28	3	23	23	229	216	262	299	562	860	539	4	83	0.26	44	16	39	27	89	46	90	3%	131	50%	81%	12	33%	50%	2.72	-9.2	17	43	$7
13	NYY	304	38	3	28	10	260	250	307	372	679	652	693	6	83	0.39	41	21	38	30	92	78	81	3%	143	17%	77%	20	45%	35%	3.93	4.5	53	133	$7
14	MIN *	253	32	5	28	10	251	265	274	376	649	586	716	3	83	0.19	56	16	27	29	80	78	43	9%	153	25%	78%	20	45%	40%	3.50	2.4	49	132	$7
1st Half		122	13	3	16	2	283	258	311	402	713	618	896	4	82	0.23	54	19	27	33	106	74	57	12%	132	14%	55%	8	63%	25%	4.23	3.5	37	100	$5
2nd Half		131	19	2	12	8	221	271	239	351	590	569	609	2	84	0.14	57	15	28	25	65	82	34	7%	153	41%	89%	12	33%	50%	2.89	-1.4	54	146	$9
15	**Proj**	**221**	**28**	**4**	**22**	**14**	**248**	**258**	**282**	**367**	**649**	**635**	**660**	**4**	**84**	**0.27**	**50**	**17**	**32**	**28**	**87**	**79**	**61**	**6%**	**141**	**34%**	**83%**				**3.59**	**-0.7**	**53**	**140**	**$9**

STEPHEN NICKRAND

Odor,Rougned

Age: 21 Bats: L Pos: 2B | Health A | LIMA Plan B+
Ht: 5' 11" Wt: 170 | PT/Exp F | Rand Var 0
Consist F | MM 2425

9-48-.259 with 4 SB in 386 AB at TEX. Got call before he had even 300 AB above High-A and didn't disappoint. Plenty of speed to burn, but w/o more walks or better technique, it'll stay under wraps. Low xPX caps HR potential for now. Given age, he's got time to iron out these wrinkles. Keeper gem.

Yr	Tm	AB	R	HR	RBI	SB	BA	xBA	OBP	SLG	OPS	vL	vR	bb%	ct%	Eye	G	L	F	h%	HctX	PX	xPX	hr/f	Spd	SBO	SB%	#Wk	DOM	DIS	RC/G	RAR	BPV	BPX	R$
10																																			
11																																			
12																																			
13	aa	134	18	6	17	4	309		349	529	878			6	82	0.34				34		139			115	19%	69%				6.61		88	220	$5
14	TEX *	515	56	14	62	9	261	250	293	407	700	626	727	4	82	0.24	49	15	36	30	90	91	68	8%	144	16%	47%	22	41%	23%	3.84	6.8	54	146	$16
1st Half		251	31	8	31	7	269	251	294	420	715	550	776	3	82	0.20	44	18	38	30	69	90	63	8%	160	22%	53%	9	33%	33%	3.98	4.4	58	157	$18
2nd Half		264	25	6	31	2	254	248	294	394	688	655	702	5	81	0.29	51	14	35	29	99	93	71	8%	126	10%	33%	13	46%	15%	3.69	2.4	50	135	$13
15	**Proj**	**433**	**51**	**10**	**53**	**11**	**270**	**256**	**312**	**413**	**725**	**644**	**755**	**5**	**82**	**0.28**	**49**	**15**	**35**	**31**	**87**	**96**	**68**	**8%**	**133**	**18%**	**60%**				**4.20**	**10.3**	**51**	**135**	**$14**

Olt,Mike

Age: 26 Bats: R Pos: 3B | Health A | LIMA Plan D
Ht: 6' 2" Wt: 210 | PT/Exp D | Rand Var 0
Consist F | MM 5101

12-33-.160 in 225 AB at CHC. Young bopper owns some of best pop in game. Problem is, it won't matter if his odds of making contact are akin to flipping a coin. At age 26, his window to overhaul approach is starting to close. Even power-starved clubs can't put up with this level of hacking.

Yr	Tm	AB	R	HR	RBI	SB	BA	xBA	OBP	SLG	OPS	vL	vR	bb%	ct%	Eye	G	L	F	h%	HctX	PX	xPX	hr/f	Spd	SBO	SB%	#Wk	DOM	DIS	RC/G	RAR	BPV	BPX	R$
10																																			
11																																			
12	TEX *	387	52	25	69	4	254	255	342	492	834	387	473	12	68	0.42	45	18	36	31	95	166	125	0%	108	5%	80%	8	13%	75%	5.76	13.1	64	160	$14
13	a/a	373	36	11	31	0	169		252	309	561			10	59	0.27				25		128			93	0%	0%				2.39		-10	-25	-$5
14	CHC *	331	34	17	50	1	188	207	257	390	647	681	561	9	58	0.22	38	12	49	26	89	186	162	19%	67	3%	41%	21	43%	48%	3.11	-6.3	19	51	$2
1st Half		162	15	10	25	0	142	193	224	346	570	739	501	9	56	0.23	39	12	49	16	88	177	177	22%	72	4%	0%	14	50%	43%	2.18	-8.3	8	22	-$1
2nd Half		169	19	7	25	1	233	220	294	432	726	595	785	8	59	0.22	36	14	50	35	86	194	124	11%	83	2%	100%	7	29%	57%	4.24	2.8	36	97	$6
15	**Proj**	**127**	**13**	**6**	**17**	**0**	**203**	**209**	**281**	**392**	**673**	**660**	**682**	**9**	**60**	**0.26**	**37**	**13**	**50**	**28**	**87**	**172**	**145**	**15%**	**84**	**2%**	**67%**				**3.48**	**-0.9**	**12**	**31**	**$2**

Ortiz,David

Age: 39 Bats: L Pos: DH | Health C | LIMA Plan A
Ht: 6' 4" Wt: 230 | PT/Exp B | Rand Var +4
Consist D | MM 5055

Only two hitters have 30+ HR last two years: Ortiz and Encarnacion. Other than age, nothing to suggest a decline is imminent; plate control and power are steady and elite. BA dip result of apparently fluky h%... But maybe it's not a fluke at 39. Age is age. Ruling out external forces (ha!), we have to acknowledge reality.

Yr	Tm	AB	R	HR	RBI	SB	BA	xBA	OBP	SLG	OPS	vL	vR	bb%	ct%	Eye	G	L	F	h%	HctX	PX	xPX	hr/f	Spd	SBO	SB%	#Wk	DOM	DIS	RC/G	RAR	BPV	BPX	R$
10	BOS	518	86	32	102	0	270	279	370	529	899	599	1059	14	72	0.57	38	17	45	32	114	188	168	19%	71	1%	0%	27	70%	15%	6.79	14.1	89	193	$21
11	BOS	525	84	29	96	1	309	311	398	554	953	989	934	13	84	0.94	41	21	37	32	164	158	167	17%	73	1%	50%	27	67%	15%	8.10	32.2	113	251	$28
12	BOS	324	65	23	60	0	318	318	415	611	1026	985	1050	15	84	1.10	37	21	42	32	143	175	150	20%	69	1%	0%	17	82%	6%	9.46	39.8	129	323	$19
13	BOS	518	84	30	103	4	309	308	395	564	959	733	1092	13	83	0.86	39	23	39	33	154	162	173	18%	78	2%	100%	25	64%	8%	8.33	53.6	113	283	$31
14	BOS	518	59	35	104	0	263	282	355	517	873	893	863	13	82	0.79	37	18	46	26	159	164	187	18%	47	0%	0%	26	73%	8%	6.37	34.7	99	268	$22
1st Half		296	33	19	52	0	250	271	349	480	829	832	827	13	81	0.77	37	19	44	25	152	145	175	18%	51	0%	0%	14	71%	7%	5.66	14.0	82	222	$21
2nd Half		222	26	16	52	0	279	298	364	568	932	968	913	12	83	0.82	36	16	48	27	168	188	202	18%	56	0%	0%	12	75%	8%	7.38	20.9	125	338	$23
15	**Proj**	**505**	**68**	**28**	**92**	**0**	**268**	**297**	**355**	**506**	**860**	**802**	**892**	**12**	**81**	**0.73**	**40**	**20**	**40**	**28**	**155**	**162**	**178**	**17%**	**61**	**0%**	**6%**				**6.26**	**32.0**	**88**	**233**	**$21**

Overbay,Lyle

Age: 38 Bats: L Pos: 1B | Health A | LIMA Plan D
Ht: 6' 2" Wt: 235 | PT/Exp D | Rand Var +1
Consist A | MM 3221

In his younger days, there was talk that he could be a batting champ given sweet lefty swing. With two .300+ BA seasons in 12 years, days of hoping for something more are long gone. Steep erosion vs. LH, uptick in groundballs confirm end is near, even if he doesn't choose to voluntarily retire.

Yr	Tm	AB	R	HR	RBI	SB	BA	xBA	OBP	SLG	OPS	vL	vR	bb%	ct%	Eye	G	L	F	h%	HctX	PX	xPX	hr/f	Spd	SBO	SB%	#Wk	DOM	DIS	RC/G	RAR	BPV	BPX	R$
10	TOR	534	75	20	67	1	243	264	329	433	762	700	781	11	75	0.51	45	16	39	29	112	138	129	13%	71	1%	100%	27	44%	22%	4.79	-23.2	58	126	$10
11	2 NL	394	43	9	47	2	234	243	310	360	670	651	677	10	78	0.48	46	19	35	28	116	94	120	8%	69	3%	67%	26	35%	38%	3.67	-30.6	28	62	$4
12	2 NL *	138	14	2	12	0	250	266	332	383	716	552	751	11	70	0.40	43	33	24	35	143	119	157	10%	64	0%	0%	20	35%	55%	4.34	-4.3	17	43	$0
13	NYY	445	43	14	59	2	240	251	295	393	688	516	746	7	75	0.32	44	22	35	29	109	112	119	12%	73	2%	100%	27	33%	48%	3.95	-8.4	29	73	$8
14	MIL	258	24	4	35	2	233	237	328	333	661	427	688	12	77	0.60	52	19	29	29	104	83	129	7%	63	3%	100%	27	41%	41%	3.66	-4.0	19	51	$2
1st Half		151	17	3	21	1	245	235	331	351	682	451	719	12	76	0.56	49	20	31	30	114	84	162	8%	75	2%	100%	14	43%	43%	3.99	-0.8	20	54	$4
2nd Half		107	7	1	14	1	215	236	323	308	631	333	647	13	78	0.67	55	18	27	27	89	83	82	5%	55	3%	100%	13	38%	38%	3.23	-3.1	21	57	-$1
15	**Proj**	**156**	**15**	**3**	**20**	**1**	**235**	**247**	**319**	**357**	**676**	**514**	**705**	**11**	**75**	**0.49**	**48**	**21**	**30**	**29**	**110**	**101**	**123**	**9%**	**65**	**2%**	**98%**				**3.82**	**-1.6**	**18**	**48**	**$3**

Owings,Christopher

Age: 23 Bats: R Pos: SS | Health C | LIMA Plan B+
Ht: 5' 10" Wt: 190 | PT/Exp D | Rand Var 0
Consist B | MM 2525

6-26-.261 with 8 SB in 310 AB at ARI. Multi-category bat with more upside than stats show. Shoulder issue torpedoed his 2nd half—check out that 1st half. Wheels firmly elite but won't blossom without more patience, green light. Rising PX puts double-digit HR firmly within reach. If healthy, for now... UP: 15 HR, 20 SB

Yr	Tm	AB	R	HR	RBI	SB	BA	xBA	OBP	SLG	OPS	vL	vR	bb%	ct%	Eye	G	L	F	h%	HctX	PX	xPX	hr/f	Spd	SBO	SB%	#Wk	DOM	DIS	RC/G	RAR	BPV	BPX	R$
10																																			
11																																			
12	aa	297	28	5	23	3	246		267	350	617			3	75	0.12				31		70			116	10%	50%				3.04		0	0	$2
13	ARI *	601	72	8	57	15	282	262	305	397	701	250	932	3	80	0.16	47	24	29	34	66	83	63	0%	121	16%	65%	4	50%	25%	4.17	11.5	31	78	$20
14	ARI *	350	38	6	27	10	255	257	287	386	673	829	672	4	78	0.21	45	24	31	31	90	93	77	8%	159	14%	91%	18	33%	50%	3.90	6.2	45	122	$8
1st Half		238	26	6	21	7	277	278	313	458	771	1012	704	5	79	0.24	44	22	33	33	104	127	94	10%	157	13%	100%	14	43%	36%	5.22	13.4	76	205	$13
2nd Half		112	12	0	6	3	207	222	235	233	467	192	571	3	76	0.15	45	29	25	27	47	17	22	0%	137	15%	74%	4	0%	100%	1.78	-5.2	-33	-89	-$3
15	**Proj**	**575**	**63**	**10**	**45**	**15**	**261**	**252**	**289**	**376**	**665**	**417**	**743**	**3**	**78**	**0.16**	**47**	**24**	**30**	**32**	**69**	**83**	**56**	**7%**	**144**	**15%**	**75%**				**3.70**	**7.7**	**22**	**58**	**$16**

Ozuna,Marcell

Age: 24 Bats: R Pos: CF | Health B | LIMA Plan B+
Ht: 6' 1" Wt: 230 | PT/Exp D | Rand Var -1
Consist A | MM 4425

Mini-breakout for multi-tooled OF. Or was it? Credit hr/f for power spike; all those GBs make it unlikely he'll top 20 HR again without uppercut in swing. What he loses in HR could be made up by SB...if he can get any semblance of a green light. Big holes in swing will keep him a volatile work-in-progress.

Yr	Tm	AB	R	HR	RBI	SB	BA	xBA	OBP	SLG	OPS	vL	vR	bb%	ct%	Eye	G	L	F	h%	HctX	PX	xPX	hr/f	Spd	SBO	SB%	#Wk	DOM	DIS	RC/G	RAR	BPV	BPX	R$
10																																			
11																																			
12																																			
13	MIA *	317	36	7	45	6	270	266	304	426	730	838	647	5	79	0.23	46	21	33	32	104	110	88	4%	117	10%	85%	13	31%	38%	4.56	4.2	50	125	$9
14	MIA	565	72	23	85	3	269	252	317	455	772	728	783	7	71	0.25	49	18	34	34	117	140	133	17%	122	3%	75%	26	42%	38%	5.05	19.7	48	130	$20
1st Half		291	40	14	47	2	265	240	311	454	765	884	734	7	70	0.24	47	16	37	33	120	137	146	18%	122	3%	100%	14	43%	36%	4.98	9.4	41	111	$22
2nd Half		274	32	9	38	1	274	263	323	456	779	543	833	7	72	0.26	51	19	31	35	114	142	119	15%	116	3%	50%	12	42%	42%	5.12	9.9	53	143	$18
15	**Proj**	**592**	**71**	**17**	**86**	**8**	**261**	**256**	**307**	**423**	**730**	**747**	**726**	**6**	**74**	**0.25**	**48**	**19**	**33**	**33**	**112**	**123**	**113**	**11%**	**121**	**8%**	**77%**				**4.46**	**10.3**	**43**	**113**	**$20**

Pacheco,Jordan

Age: 29 Bats: R Pos: CA | Health B | LIMA Plan D
Ht: 6' 1" Wt: 205 | PT/Exp D | Rand Var 0
Consist C | MM 1241

Remember those sexy stats he put up in '12? Neither do we. Production vs. RHers has been waning since then, and he doesn't even hit lefties well enough to be useful in a part-time role. Only potential value here is as a non-BA killing second catcher, but even that is a stretch. Speculate elsewhere.

Yr	Tm	AB	R	HR	RBI	SB	BA	xBA	OBP	SLG	OPS	vL	vR	bb%	ct%	Eye	G	L	F	h%	HctX	PX	xPX	hr/f	Spd	SBO	SB%	#Wk	DOM	DIS	RC/G	RAR	BPV	BPX	R$
10	aa	78	8	1	15	1	303		341	397	738			5	92	0.71				32		65			93	8%	41%				4.72		60	130	$2
11	COL *	447	33	4	39	1	225	277	255	297	552	946	572	4	86	0.28	53	27	20	25	81	51	49	13%	94	4%	29%	4	50%	25%	2.43	-26.6	22	49	$0
12	COL *	542	57	7	60	8	316	283	344	432	776	822	739	4	88	0.36	42	26	31	35	102	78	83	4%	93	6%	79%	23	43%	13%	5.55	18.4	51	128	$20
13	COL *	301	27	2	25	2	240	275	275	324	599	556	614	5	86	0.35	49	25	26	27	81	65	64	2%	88	3%	100%	24	33%	46%	3.02	-6.0	34	85	$1
14	2 NL	153	10	0	16	0	255	261	299	333	632	711	581	6	82	0.33	43	27	31	31	78	69	58	0%	93	0%	0%	23	26%	48%	3.38	-0.3	26	70	$0
1st Half		80	6	0	8	0	250	257	307	363	669	695	657	7	81	0.40	53	17	30	31	85	97	65	0%	111	0%	0%	13	38%	31%	3.73	0.8	52	141	-$1
2nd Half		73	4	0	8	0	260	287	289	301	591	725	475	4	84	0.25	31	38	31	31	70	39	51	0%	74	0%	0%	10	10%	70%	3.01	-0.8	-3	-8	$0
15	**Proj**	**133**	**10**	**1**	**13**	**1**	**258**	**273**	**297**	**344**	**640**	**697**	**604**	**5**	**85**	**0.33**	**44**	**28**	**29**	**30**	**82**	**69**	**62**	**2%**	**89**	**2%**	**80%**				**3.47**	**0.3**	**20**	**53**	**$2**

STEPHEN NICKRAND

Pagan,Angel

Age: 33 Bats: B Pos: CF	Health	F	LIMA Plan	B+	
Ht: 6' 2" Wt: 200	PT/Exp	B	Rand Var	-3	
	Consist	A	MM	1533	

After bad hammy wiped out most of 2013, back issue torpedoed 2014 and sent him under the knife. That 1st half is why he's a legit $20 play when healthy, but health is a BIG if now. While solid contact will keep him a strong BA/SB source, declining Spd tells us days of 30+ swipes are likely gone.

Yr	Tm	AB	R	HR	RBI	SB	BA	xBA	OBP	SLG	OPS	vL	vR	bb%	ct%	Eye	G	L	F	h%	HctX	PX	xPX	hr/f	Spd	SBO	SB%	#Wk	DOM	DIS	RC/G	RAR	BPV	BPX	R$
10	NYM	579	80	11	69	37	290	251	340	425	765	692	788	7	83	0.45	36	20	44	33	95	89	99	5%	139	28%	80%	27	44%	33%	5.27	7.9	62	135	$29
11	NYM	478	68	7	56	32	262	256	322	372	694	672	702	8	87	0.71	35	24	41	29	91	74	93	4%	115	29%	82%	22	55%	9%	4.30	-6.8	61	136	$19
12	SF	605	95	8	56	29	288	270	338	440	778	736	799	7	84	0.49	42	23	35	33	102	95	96	4%	152	22%	81%	27	59%	15%	5.40	12.3	74	185	$26
13	SF	280	44	5	30	9	282	277	334	414	749	807	725	8	87	0.64	43	23	34	31	86	86	77	6%	133	17%	69%	14	79%	0%	4.87	6.1	74	185	$10
14	SF	383	56	3	27	16	300	276	342	389	731	626	790	6	86	0.47	45	27	28	34	86	67	53	3%	123	19%	73%	18	39%	28%	4.82	10.7	49	132	$17
1st Half		242	37	3	19	11	306	285	355	409	764	757	768	7	88	0.63	45	27	29	34	96	75	68	5%	115	19%	79%	11	45%	9%	5.40	10.3	61	165	$21
2nd Half		141	19	0	8	5	291	261	320	355	675	456	835	4	84	0.26	46	27	27	35	69	53	28	0%	122	21%	63%	7	29%	57%	3.91	0.2	24	65	$9
15	Proj	**413**	**61**	**4**	**35**	**17**	**290**	**270**	**334**	**395**	**729**	**644**	**773**	**6**	**86**	**0.47**	**43**	**25**	**32**	**33**	**86**	**77**	**65**	**4%**	**131**	**20%**	**73%**				**4.70**	**9.9**	**56**	**148**	**$16**

Panik,Joe

Age: 24 Bats: L Pos: 2B	Health	A	LIMA Plan	B	
Ht: 6' 1" Wt: 190	PT/Exp	D	Rand Var	-1	
	Consist	C	MM	0435	

1-18-.305 in 269 AB at SF. Easy to glance at absence of HR and SB and move on, but that sexy Spd says not so fast. Reason it wasn't put to use was lack of green light. A flicker there will fix that; he HAS swiped double-digit bags in the minors. xBA says BA will drop some, but good contact gives him solid floor. UP: 15 SB

Yr	Tm	AB	R	HR	RBI	SB	BA	xBA	OBP	SLG	OPS	vL	vR	bb%	ct%	Eye	G	L	F	h%	HctX	PX	xPX	hr/f	Spd	SBO	SB%	#Wk	DOM	DIS	RC/G	RAR	BPV	BPX	R$
10																																			
11																																			
12																																			
13	aa	522	47	3	42	7	217		277	289	566			8	85	0.56				25		53			103	10%	57%				2.55		32	80	$1
14	SF *	562	64	4	48	2	281	263	322	358	680	839	655	6	87	0.47	50	23	27	32	90	53	51	2%	138	3%	46%	17	24%	24%	4.04	10.2	46	124	$13
1st Half		317	33	3	32	2	252	264	297	338	635	1000	360	6	87	0.48	57	19	24	28	161	59	81	0%	106	5%	46%	4	25%	25%	3.34	-0.5	40	108	$12
2nd Half		245	31	1	16	0	318	260	354	384	738	833	692	5	88	0.47	50	23	27	36	84	47	48	2%	147	0%	0%	13	23%	23%	5.10	11.2	45	122	$14
15	Proj	**459**	**49**	**2**	**37**	**8**	**262**	**261**	**307**	**328**	**636**	**701**	**605**	**6**	**87**	**0.50**	**50**	**23**	**27**	**30**	**76**	**50**	**43**	**2%**	**139**	**9%**	**68%**				**3.47**	**1.0**	**29**	**76**	**$10**

Paredes,Jimmy

Age: 26 Bats: B Pos: 3B	Health	A	LIMA Plan	D	
Ht: 6' 3" Wt: 200	PT/Exp	C	Rand Var	-3	
	Consist	A	MM	2411	

2-8-.286 with 4 SB in 63 AB at KC and BAL. Some will be tempted by small sample size power/speed combo, but it's not one worth chasing. That hr/f was the true reason he had any HRs at all. Extreme GB stroke makes any HR a plus. He's a better buy for SB, but dipping Spd tempers that optimism too.

Yr	Tm	AB	R	HR	RBI	SB	BA	xBA	OBP	SLG	OPS	vL	vR	bb%	ct%	Eye	G	L	F	h%	HctX	PX	xPX	hr/f	Spd	SBO	SB%	#Wk	DOM	DIS	RC/G	RAR	BPV	BPX	R$
10																																			
11	HOU *	553	67	10	49	27	250	253	276	371	647	500	773	4	74	0.14	54	21	25	32	101	92	96	7%	131	38%	60%	9	22%	56%	3.19	-27.4	19	42	$16
12	HOU *	581	70	9	43	27	252	224	278	361	639	220	546	4	75	0.15	47	16	36	32	84	77	98	0%	131	31%	68%	6	0%	83%	3.29	-22.0	12	30	$16
13	HOU *	452	45	7	37	16	228	249	271	343	614	282	565	6	72	0.22	60	19	20	30	99	89	73	6%	116	29%	56%	13	0%	69%	2.84	-15.6	9	23	$8
14	2 AL *	464	45	8	48	18	242	244	263	359	622	1100	687	3	69	0.09	57	22	22	33	89	102	89	20%	93	22%	94%	10	40%	50%	3.32	-4.7	-7	-19	$12
1st Half		231	24	4	22	12	256	222	275	370	645	0	444	3	67	0.08	57	14	29	37	83	101	21	0%	115	24%	100%	5	0%	80%	3.75	0.4	-11	-30	$13
2nd Half		233	21	4	26	7	228	253	252	348	600	1222	736	3	71	0.11	56	23	21	30	92	103	101	25%	86	19%	85%	5	80%	20%	2.95	-5.3	-1	-3	$11
15	Proj	**202**	**21**	**3**	**19**	**8**	**239**	**237**	**265**	**349**	**614**	**495**	**648**	**4**	**71**	**0.14**	**54**	**20**	**27**	**32**	**92**	**92**	**94**	**8%**	**108**	**26%**	**74%**				**3.10**	**-3.7**	**4**	**11**	**$5**

Parmelee,Chris

Age: 27 Bats: L Pos: 1B RF LF	Health	A	LIMA Plan	D+	
Ht: 6' 1" Wt: 220	PT/Exp	D	Rand Var	-1	
	Consist	D	MM	3013	

7-28-.256 in 250 AB at MIN. That 2012 power keeps the speculators coming back, but modest pop last two years, consistently subpar HctX reveals it as a mirage. Big 2nd half fade tells us he'll be exposed the more he plays. Steady struggles vs. RH seal fate. Multi-position eligibility is his only value to you.

Yr	Tm	AB	R	HR	RBI	SB	BA	xBA	OBP	SLG	OPS	vL	vR	bb%	ct%	Eye	G	L	F	h%	HctX	PX	xPX	hr/f	Spd	SBO	SB%	#Wk	DOM	DIS	RC/G	RAR	BPV	BPX	R$
10	aa	411	39	4	34	2	246		304	340	644			8	82	0.47				29		72			102	4%	51%				3.44		34	74	$3
11	MIN *	606	64	12	75	0	259	239	328	386	714	935	1069	9	81	0.53	38	19	43	30	97	90	132	15%	102	1%	0%	4	75%	0%	4.32	-14.9	45	100	$11
12	MIN *	420	56	18	61	1	268	250	355	473	828	681	667	12	74	0.51	38	18	44	32	94	141	106	8%	79	2%	43%	20	30%	55%	5.81	11.5	57	143	$13
13	MIN *	467	38	10	40	2	215	231	289	334	623	526	696	9	75	0.42	39	21	40	27	87	92	99	9%	78	2%	63%	19	32%	63%	3.13	-16.6	17	43	$0
14	MIN *	368	37	12	46	0	256	236	308	401	709	859	617	7	75	0.30	36	21	43	31	96	109	106	9%	62	3%	0%	21	33%	52%	4.09	2.1	22	59	$8
1st Half		217	20	9	27	0	264	245	314	431	745	855	685	7	74	0.28	25	24	51	32	112	122	148	11%	73	5%	0%	9	22%	56%	4.41	2.6	32	86	$10
2nd Half		151	17	3	19	0	245	229	305	358	662	862	572	7	76	0.33	43	19	38	30	86	91	80	7%	68	0%	0%	12	42%	50%	3.63	-1.6	15	41	$4
15	Proj	**256**	**26**	**8**	**30**	**0**	**245**	**240**	**314**	**391**	**705**	**765**	**683**	**9**	**76**	**0.38**	**37**	**21**	**42**	**30**	**94**	**111**	**107**	**9%**	**73**	**2%**	**30%**				**4.02**	**-1.1**	**22**	**58**	**$5**

Parra,Gerardo

Age: 28 Bats: L Pos: RF LF	Health	A	LIMA Plan	C+	
Ht: 5' 11" Wt: 200	PT/Exp	B	Rand Var	+1	
	Consist	A	MM	2233	

Surging HctX gave hope for more HR heading into season. Trouble is, all those GBs remove any power upside. Low SB success last two years likely to keep eating into SBO%, so don't put double-digit steals in stone, either. Futility vs. LHP likely seals 4th OF fate, which is all he should be for you.

Yr	Tm	AB	R	HR	RBI	SB	BA	xBA	OBP	SLG	OPS	vL	vR	bb%	ct%	Eye	G	L	F	h%	HctX	PX	xPX	hr/f	Spd	SBO	SB%	#Wk	DOM	DIS	RC/G	RAR	BPV	BPX	R$
10	ARI *	400	36	4	35	3	270	263	311	384	695	701	674	6	80	0.30	51	20	29	33	90	83	92	4%	108	4%	72%	26	38%	42%	4.16	-11.3	31	67	$6
11	ARI	445	55	8	46	15	292	272	357	427	784	790	782	9	82	0.52	50	22	28	34	102	88	84	8%	132	12%	94%	27	44%	26%	5.64	6.1	56	124	$17
12	ARI	385	58	7	36	15	273	267	335	392	727	631	754	8	80	0.43	53	22	24	33	108	83	101	9%	103	22%	63%	27	30%	33%	4.34	-9.1	35	88	$13
13	ARI	601	79	10	48	10	268	283	323	403	726	501	820	7	83	0.48	55	20	25	31	111	97	97	8%	102	13%	50%	27	56%	19%	4.30	-5.4	58	145	$16
14	2 NL	529	64	9	40	9	261	266	308	369	677	554	704	6	81	0.32	54	22	24	31	96	76	85	9%	107	12%	56%	28	25%	43%	3.72	-5.8	31	84	$13
1st Half		333	42	5	24	5	255	270	306	360	667	537	704	6	82	0.36	54	23	22	30	101	74	86	8%	117	11%	56%	15	27%	40%	3.60	-3.9	35	95	$14
2nd Half		196	22	4	16	4	270	258	311	383	694	607	705	5	80	0.26	53	21	26	32	89	80	84	10%	87	14%	57%	13	23%	46%	3.93	-0.4	22	59	$10
15	Proj	**327**	**41**	**6**	**27**	**7**	**268**	**271**	**319**	**388**	**707**	**573**	**742**	**6**	**81**	**0.37**	**54**	**21**	**25**	**32**	**100**	**88**	**91**	**9%**	**100**	**14%**	**59%**				**4.11**	**1.1**	**39**	**101**	**$10**

Pearce,Steve

Age: 32 Bats: R Pos: 1B LF	Health	D	LIMA Plan	B+	
Ht: 5' 11" Wt: 210	PT/Exp	D	Rand Var	-3	
	Consist	C	MM	4235	

Development once stymied by struggles against RHPs. Turnaround last two years should put him back on your radar. While credit for big HR jump should be given to anomalous hr/f, three years of strong xPX were hinting at this kind of a surge. The problem: if he was 5 years younger, we'd be projecting a 30-HR upside. But he's not.

Yr	Tm	AB	R	HR	RBI	SB	BA	xBA	OBP	SLG	OPS	vL	vR	bb%	ct%	Eye	G	L	F	h%	HctX	PX	xPX	hr/f	Spd	SBO	SB%	#Wk	DOM	DIS	RC/G	RAR	BPV	BPX	R$
10	PIT *	158	22	2	16	5	264	266	360	418	777	964	583	13	76	0.63	44	20	36	34	99	121	85	0%	115	16%	67%	4	25%	50%	5.11	-5.3	64	139	$3
11	PIT *	124	12	3	14	0	203	197	246	304	550	589	437	5	75	0.22	43	15	43	25	104	73	98	3%	77	0%	0%	14	21%	64%	2.39	-14.9	-7	-16	-$2
12	3 TM *	351	42	13	47	3	247	240	325	420	745	760	657	10	77	0.49	38	17	45	29	127	117	128	7%	78	7%	49%	15	40%	40%	4.51	-8.1	46	115	$7
13	BAL	119	14	4	13	1	261	243	362	420	782	802	749	11	79	0.60	39	17	44	30	118	112	129	10%	79	3%	100%	19	47%	37%	5.03	1.5	54	135	$1
14	BAL	338	51	21	49	5	293	294	373	556	930	1109	856	11	78	0.53	35	19	46	32	116	188	130	18%	72	5%	100%	26	62%	35%	7.48	31.3	105	284	$18
1st Half		147	18	9	25	2	327	301	385	592	977	1212	858	9	76	0.40	31	24	45	38	112	195	130	18%	64	5%	100%	13	54%	38%	8.74	17.8	99	268	$15
2nd Half		191	33	12	24	3	267	290	365	529	894	1008	854	12	79	0.63	38	16	46	28	119	183	129	17%	84	6%	100%	13	69%	31%	6.63	13.5	112	303	$20
15	Proj	**406**	**55**	**18**	**53**	**5**	**271**	**266**	**357**	**472**	**829**	**884**	**788**	**11**	**78**	**0.53**	**37**	**18**	**45**	**31**	**117**	**148**	**126**	**13%**	**75**	**5%**	**87%**				**5.80**	**19.0**	**72**	**188**	**$16**

Pederson,Joc

Age: 23 Bats: L Pos: CF	Health	A	LIMA Plan	C	
Ht: 6' 1" Wt: 185	PT/Exp	D	Rand Var	-1	
	Consist	C	MM	3203	

0-0-.143 in 28 AB at LA. First 30/30 campaign in PCL history showcased elite power/speed combo. A Three True Outcomes hitter: had a K, BB, or HR in more than 50% of his plate appearances. No L/R splits in minors, so ignore tiny MLB OPS sample vL. He'll hurt your BA, but these are skills to roster.

Yr	Tm	AB	R	HR	RBI	SB	BA	xBA	OBP	SLG	OPS	vL	vR	bb%	ct%	Eye	G	L	F	h%	HctX	PX	xPX	hr/f	Spd	SBO	SB%	#Wk	DOM	DIS	RC/G	RAR	BPV	BPX	R$
10																																			
11																																			
12																																			
13	aa	439	73	20	52	28	260		350	456	806			12	72	0.49				32		142			105	28%	76%				5.48		59	148	$24
14	LA *	473	68	21	49	19	237	214	336	406	742	167	561	13	61	0.38	35	24	41	34	74	141	103	0%	112	23%	56%	5	20%	60%	4.24	6.0	19	51	$17
1st Half		273	37	11	27	13	256	212	341	418	759			11	60	0.32				39		141			120	25%	61%				4.60		12	32	$20
2nd Half		200	31	10	23	6	211	223	329	391	719	167	561	15	64	0.48	35	24	41	28	76	141	103	0%	108	21%	48%	5	20%	60%	3.79	-0.5	31	84	$13
15	Proj	**305**	**47**	**10**	**42**	**13**	**241**	**212**	**339**	**383**	**722**	**480**	**771**	**13**	**66**	**0.43**	**41**	**18**	**41**	**33**	**68**	**117**	**93**	**12%**	**95**	**22%**	**60%**				**4.14**	**2.6**	**14**	**37**	**$12**

STEPHEN NICKRAND

Pedroia,Dustin

Age: 31 Bats: R Pos: 2B	Health C	LIMA Plan A	
Ht: 5' 8" Wt: 165	PT/Exp A	Rand Var 0	
	Consist B	MM 2345	

Wrist plagued him for most of year and lead to Sept. surgery. You'll buy him for a little bit of everything, but there are warts now. Steady declines in PX/xPX put HR rebound in jeopardy, especially with GB tilt. SBs may be done too. xBA had been hinting that he's not a .300 hitter. Don't expect a full bounceback.

Yr	Tm	AB	R	HR	RBI	SB	BA	xBA	OBP	SLG	OPS	vL	vR	bb%	ct%	Eye	G	L	F	h%	HctX	PX	xPX	hr/f	Spd	SBO	SB%	#Wk	DOM	DIS	RC/G	RAR	BPV	BPX	R$
10	BOS	302	53	12	41	9	288	310	367	493	860	700	910	11	87	0.97	39	22	39	30	94	131	97	11%	105	11%	90%	13	69%	15%	6.59	16.9	110	239	$14
11	BOS	635	102	21	91	26	307	288	387	474	861	1010	800	12	87	1.01	48	19	33	33	118	106	115	11%	123	15%	76%	27	70%	15%	6.80	38.6	94	209	$36
12	BOS	563	81	15	65	20	290	288	347	449	797	848	775	8	89	0.80	46	20	35	30	123	98	108	9%	108	17%	77%	26	65%	12%	5.56	22.2	86	215	$24
13	BOS	641	91	9	84	17	301	284	372	415	787	937	722	10	88	0.97	50	22	28	33	116	80	83	6%	124	10%	77%	26	65%	19%	5.67	34.4	77	193	$29
14	BOS	551	72	7	53	6	278	276	337	376	712	727	707	8	86	0.68	48	24	28	31	112	75	89	5%	96	7%	50%	24	54%	13%	4.37	15.4	53	143	$16
1st Half		327	45	4	30	2	272	279	342	379	722	810	688	10	86	0.80	46	25	29	31	111	84	94	5%	96	7%	29%	14	57%	7%	4.36	9.2	62	168	$17
2nd Half		224	27	3	23	4	286	270	328	371	698	600	735	6	87	0.48	51	23	26	32	113	61	81	6%	98	8%	80%	10	50%	20%	4.37	6.1	40	108	$14
15	**Proj**	**575**	**79**	**10**	**65**	**9**	**287**	**281**	**348**	**402**	**750**	**790**	**735**	**9**	**87**	**0.76**	**48**	**22**	**29**	**31**	**114**	**84**	**91**	**7%**	**107**	**7%**	**74%**				**5.01**	**26.3**	**60**	**159**	**$19**

Pena,Brayan

Age: 33 Bats: B Pos: 1B CA	Health A	LIMA Plan D+	
Ht: 5' 9" Wt: 230	PT/Exp D	Rand Var +1	
	Consist C	MM 1033	

Quintessential 2nd CA couldn't duplicate .300 BA, but xBA told us it was a fluke anyway, in spite of premium bat-on-ball ability. Climbing FB, strong 1H HctX give twinge of hope for mid-30s power spike. Problem is, profile as a part-timer is well established now, so don't bid more than a few bucks.

Yr	Tm	AB	R	HR	RBI	SB	BA	xBA	OBP	SLG	OPS	vL	vR	bb%	ct%	Eye	G	L	F	h%	HctX	PX	xPX	hr/f	Spd	SBO	SB%	#Wk	DOM	DIS	RC/G	RAR	BPV	BPX	R$
10	KC	158	11	1	19	2	253	233	306	335	642	509	701	7	83	0.44	45	16	39	30	111	67	93	2%	55	5%	100%	24	25%	54%	3.58	-3.6	18	39	$1
11	KC	222	17	3	24	0	248	262	288	338	625	600	636	5	89	0.50	44	23	33	27	78	62	60	5%	43	0%	0%	25	44%	36%	3.28	-7.1	32	71	$1
12	KC	212	16	2	25	0	236	271	262	321	583	645	554	4	89	0.38	48	25	27	26	111	56	92	4%	50	2%	0%	27	33%	44%	2.79	-9.5	25	63	$0
13	DET	229	19	4	22	0	297	257	315	397	713	608	801	3	89	0.23	52	20	28	32	86	67	38	7%	61	3%	0%	25	40%	32%	4.36	4.2	34	85	$4
14	CIN	348	23	5	26	2	253	268	291	353	645	459	696	5	88	0.48	44	23	33	28	101	71	71	5%	61	6%	40%	26	42%	31%	3.43	-0.2	40	108	$3
1st Half		167	11	3	15	2	251	290	287	377	664	464	726	5	88	0.45	45	26	30	27	123	87	96	7%	57	11%	50%	14	50%	21%	3.58	0.9	51	138	$4
2nd Half		181	12	2	11	0	254	244	295	331	627	453	670	6	88	0.50	43	21	36	28	80	57	48	4%	68	2%	0%	12	33%	42%	3.28	-0.6	31	84	$3
15	**Proj**	**267**	**19**	**5**	**24**	**1**	**261**	**263**	**294**	**368**	**662**	**558**	**707**	**5**	**88**	**0.41**	**46**	**21**	**33**	**28**	**96**	**75**	**65**	**6%**	**57**	**4%**	**30%**				**3.65**	**-4.0**	**32**	**84**	**$5**

Pena,Ramiro

Age: 29 Bats: B Pos: 2B	Health D	LIMA Plan D	
Ht: 5' 11" Wt: 200	PT/Exp F	Rand Var -2	
	Consist D	MM 1121	

When you see negative R$ values—and nothing earned over a buck—you really don't need us to tell you to stay away. But let's do so anyway. Speed has been marginal at best for a while. Occasional flashes of pop never sustained. History of gloomy xBA. And lots of time lost to the DL. Satisfied?

Yr	Tm	AB	R	HR	RBI	SB	BA	xBA	OBP	SLG	OPS	vL	vR	bb%	ct%	Eye	G	L	F	h%	HctX	PX	xPX	hr/f	Spd	SBO	SB%	#Wk	DOM	DIS	RC/G	RAR	BPV	BPX	R$
10	NYY	154	18	0	18	7	227	198	258	247	504	343	545	4	82	0.22	41	19	40	28	51	12	30	0%	126	21%	88%	27	0%	67%	2.22	-13.4	-12	-26	$1
11	NYY *	256	27	5	20	2	215	218	266	313	579	205	403	7	79	0.34	55	10	34	25	75	70	79	10%	93	8%	50%	8	25%	50%	2.63	-19.6	16	36	-$1
12	NYY *	364	30	2	22	1	212	227	263	266	529	0	667	7	76	0.29	50	25	25	28	0	41	-11	0%	100	5%	17%	1	0%	0%	2.17	-27.7	-18	-45	-$3
13	ATL	97	14	3	12	0	278	284	330	443	773	328	869	8	81	0.44	48	25	27	32	104	107	96	14%	100	8%	0%	12	50%	33%	4.79	2.2	59	148	$1
14	ATL	147	9	3	9	1	245	228	304	347	651	679	644	8	74	0.34	42	23	35	31	91	81	84	8%	94	3%	100%	25	28%	56%	3.63	-0.3	8	22	$0
1st Half		92	7	3	8	0	196	205	260	326	586	750	542	8	71	0.30	41	17	42	24	111	100	118	11%	90	0%	0%	14	29%	71%	2.69	-2.9	8	22	$0
2nd Half		55	2	0	1	1	327	263	377	382	759	500	800	8	80	0.45	44	31	24	41	59	54	36	0%	99	5%	100%	11	27%	36%	5.69	2.9	12	32	$0
15	**Proj**	**162**	**14**	**3**	**12**	**1**	**242**	**247**	**296**	**346**	**641**	**436**	**685**	**7**	**78**	**0.36**	**44**	**24**	**31**	**29**	**84**	**79**	**73**	**7%**	**97**	**6%**	**53%**				**3.40**	**0.0**	**8**	**20**	**$2**

Pence,Hunter

Age: 32 Bats: R Pos: RF	Health A	LIMA Plan B+	
Ht: 6' 4" Wt: 220	PT/Exp A	Rand Var 0	
	Consist C	MM 3535	

PRO: $25+ last four of five years; premium health; fine Spd sustains double-digit SB in spite of age. CON: Big dip in HctX and xPX foreshadow power decline, especially with all those GBs; 32 of 47 HR on road last two seasons, so he's close to replacement-level at home. DN: 2nd half x 2

Yr	Tm	AB	R	HR	RBI	SB	BA	xBA	OBP	SLG	OPS	vL	vR	bb%	ct%	Eye	G	L	F	h%	HctX	PX	xPX	hr/f	Spd	SBO	SB%	#Wk	DOM	DIS	RC/G	RAR	BPV	BPX	R$
10	HOU	614	93	25	91	18	282	284	325	461	786	820	776	6	83	0.39	53	15	32	31	106	112	96	15%	123	17%	67%	27	52%	19%	5.19	0.8	73	159	$27
11	2 NL	606	84	22	97	8	314	282	370	502	871	990	836	8	80	0.45	51	18	31	37	114	129	115	15%	130	6%	80%	27	63%	11%	6.93	29.3	79	176	$31
12	2 NL	617	87	24	104	5	253	254	319	425	743	731	748	8	76	0.39	51	17	32	29	101	110	96	16%	117	4%	71%	27	44%	37%	4.55	-10.8	48	120	$18
13	SF	629	91	27	99	22	283	280	339	483	822	976	769	8	82	0.45	47	17	36	31	119	128	112	15%	119	15%	88%	27	52%	11%	5.92	23.2	82	205	$34
14	SF	650	106	20	74	13	277	264	332	445	777	770	779	7	80	0.40	52	14	34	32	97	112	88	11%	163	11%	68%	27	59%	26%	5.11	18.8	75	203	$27
1st Half		329	59	11	31	7	295	276	356	471	827	899	804	8	81	0.48	53	15	32	34	106	118	83	13%	147	9%	78%	14	64%	21%	6.03	18.6	82	222	$28
2nd Half		321	47	9	43	6	259	251	306	417	724	669	750	6	79	0.32	52	13	36	30	88	105	92	10%	170	13%	60%	13	54%	31%	4.26	2.5	65	176	$26
15	**Proj**	**623**	**94**	**19**	**84**	**14**	**275**	**262**	**329**	**436**	**765**	**792**	**754**	**7**	**80**	**0.39**	**51**	**15**	**34**	**32**	**104**	**110**	**97**	**11%**	**142**	**11%**	**74%**				**5.00**	**17.9**	**60**	**159**	**$26**

Pennington,Cliff

Age: 31 Bats: B Pos: SS	Health C	LIMA Plan D	
Ht: 5' 10" Wt: 195	PT/Exp D	Rand Var -2	
	Consist B	MM 1401	

Torn thumb ligament wiped out much of year, a good thing for anyone who owned him. Continues to offer very little when he does play. That combo of Spd and walks is the only thing worth speculating on here, but inconsistent Spd proves its just a tease. xBA gives him wobbly BA floor. No thanks.

Yr	Tm	AB	R	HR	RBI	SB	BA	xBA	OBP	SLG	OPS	vL	vR	bb%	ct%	Eye	G	L	F	h%	HctX	PX	xPX	hr/f	Spd	SBO	SB%	#Wk	DOM	DIS	RC/G	RAR	BPV	BPX	R$
10	OAK	508	64	6	46	29	250	242	319	368	687	655	697	9	81	0.52	36	21	43	30	69	81	70	3%	119	25%	85%	27	48%	41%	4.13	-8.8	45	98	$15
11	OAK	515	57	8	58	14	264	243	319	369	687	670	695	8	80	0.40	36	25	40	32	74	78	76	5%	85	16%	61%	26	38%	42%	3.94	-11.7	24	53	$14
12	OAK	418	50	6	28	15	215	233	278	311	589	420	646	8	78	0.39	41	23	37	26	62	67	63	5%	104	21%	71%	26	27%	54%	2.77	-20.6	16	40	$4
13	ARI	269	25	1	18	2	242	229	310	309	618	637	608	9	80	0.48	42	22	36	30	85	55	68	1%	97	3%	100%	25	40%	48%	3.24	-3.3	12	30	$0
14	ARI	177	21	2	10	6	254	229	340	350	690	797	649	10	80	0.56	42	21	37	31	83	64	91	4%	149	13%	86%	19	32%	42%	4.07	3.5	37	100	$3
1st Half		74	6	0	6	2	243	230	325	324	650	1348	485	9	80	0.47	41	21	38	31	94	67	97	0%	117	15%	67%	10	30%	40%	3.33	-0.1	27	73	-$1
2nd Half		103	15	2	4	4	262	228	350	369	719	578	793	11	80	0.62	42	21	37	31	75	62	87	7%	156	11%	100%	9	33%	44%	4.65	3.7	39	105	$6
15	**Proj**	**127**	**14**	**1**	**8**	**4**	**246**	**232**	**321**	**336**	**658**	**684**	**647**	**9**	**80**	**0.50**	**41**	**22**	**37**	**30**	**79**	**66**	**79**	**3%**	**117**	**12%**	**82%**				**3.66**	**1.6**	**23**	**61**	**$3**

Peralta,David

Age: 27 Bats: L Pos: RF LF	Health A	LIMA Plan B+	
Ht: 6' 2" Wt: 215	PT/Exp F	Rand Var 0	
	Consist F	MM 3345	

8-36-.286 with 6 SB in 329 AB at ARI. Former pitcher quietly has made nice transition to box, making plenty of hard contact and flashing elite wheels late. Excellent plate control in high minors supports better Eye, and there's SB upside with greener light. With some loft in swing too... UP: 15 HR, 30 SB

Yr	Tm	AB	R	HR	RBI	SB	BA	xBA	OBP	SLG	OPS	vL	vR	bb%	ct%	Eye	G	L	F	h%	HctX	PX	xPX	hr/f	Spd	SBO	SB%	#Wk	DOM	DIS	RC/G	RAR	BPV	BPX	R$
10																																			
11																																			
12																																			
13																																			
14	ARI *	531	64	13	69	7	272	282	309	430	740	510	848	5	84	0.34	48	21	31	30	111	103	90	10%	109	8%	71%	17	59%	18%	4.63	12.8	63	170	$17
1st Half		295	36	7	40	3	266	289	303	405	708	513	802	5	86	0.38	64	14	21	29	108	100	71	13%	84	5%	100%	5	60%	20%	4.33	5.0	60	162	$18
2nd Half		236	28	6	29	4	280	274	319	462	781	509	867	5	82	0.30	41	24	35	32	110	108	98	9%	142	12%	57%	12	58%	17%	5.00	8.6	69	186	$17
15	**Proj**	**499**	**60**	**13**	**64**	**10**	**274**	**285**	**311**	**443**	**754**	**504**	**827**	**5**	**83**	**0.32**	**51**	**20**	**29**	**31**	**109**	**108**	**87**	**10%**	**119**	**13%**	**68%**				**4.73**	**10.5**	**69**	**181**	**$19**

Peralta,Jhonny

Age: 33 Bats: R Pos: SS	Health A	LIMA Plan B+	
Ht: 6' 2" Wt: 215	PT/Exp B	Rand Var +2	
	Consist C	MM 4135	

So much for fear that moving to NL would zap power. PX, xPX both validate 20 HR in bat. Volatile BA product of yo-yo h%, so average is a dart throw. Save for 2013 suspension, 500-AB consistency makes him a reliable SS choice. Just cross fingers that lack of range doesn't move him to corner spot soon.

Yr	Tm	AB	R	HR	RBI	SB	BA	xBA	OBP	SLG	OPS	vL	vR	bb%	ct%	Eye	G	L	F	h%	HctX	PX	xPX	hr/f	Spd	SBO	SB%	#Wk	DOM	DIS	RC/G	RAR	BPV	BPX	R$
10	2AL	551	60	15	81	1	249	260	311	392	703	771	677	9	81	0.51	34	22	43	28	97	98	99	8%	96	1%	100%	26	42%	15%	4.20	-5.0	52	113	$10
11	DET	525	68	21	86	0	299	262	345	478	824	765	848	7	82	0.42	36	20	44	33	100	114	116	11%	95	1%	0%	27	48%	30%	5.97	21.2	63	140	$22
12	DET	531	58	13	63	1	239	257	305	384	689	692	688	8	80	0.47	41	22	37	28	107	98	124	8%	83	2%	33%	27	56%	33%	3.85	-4.0	43	108	$7
13	DET	409	50	11	55	3	303	263	358	457	815	964	750	8	76	0.36	39	25	36	38	109	119	136	10%	77	5%	50%	21	57%	24%	5.87	26.7	40	100	$16
14	STL	560	61	21	75	3	263	278	336	443	779	879	751	9	80	0.52	39	23	38	30	117	131	132	12%	69	3%	60%	26	62%	15%	5.04	28.4	66	178	$17
1st Half		282	30	11	36	1	241	278	323	436	759	766	755	10	79	0.52	40	21	39	27	125	146	145	13%	69	3%	50%	14	71%	21%	4.59	11.4	74	200	$13
2nd Half		278	31	10	39	2	284	278	350	450	799	1055	747	9	81	0.52	39	25	36	32	110	116	120	12%	73	4%	67%	12	50%	8%	5.53	18.0	60	162	$21
15	**Proj**	**575**	**65**	**18**	**77**	**3**	**273**	**271**	**338**	**437**	**774**	**872**	**742**	**9**	**79**	**0.46**	**39**	**23**	**38**	**32**	**111**	**123**	**128**	**11%**	**75**	**4%**	**54%**				**5.08**	**30.4**	**48**	**126**	**$19**

STEPHEN NICKRAND

Perez,Juan

Age: 28	Bats: R	Pos: LF	
Ht: 5' 11"	Wt: 185		
Health	A	LIMA Plan	F
PT/Exp	C	Rand Var	+2
Consist	A	MM	2201

1-3-.170 in 100 AB at SF. The definition of a SIXTH outfielder: all glove, no bat at what should be the peak of his career, needs an injury to another player to get a roster spot. A little pop in the second half, but nowhere near enough to overcome his moribund skills. An organizational soldier... DN: Back to the minors.

Yr Tm	AB	R	HR	RBI	SB	BA	xBA	OBP	SLG	OPS	vL	vR	bb%	ct%	Eye	G	L	F	h%	HctX	PX	xPX	hr/f	Spd	SBO	SB%	#Wk	DOM	DIS	RC/G	RAR	BPV	BPX	R$
10																																		
11 aa	457	47	3	32	18	223		258	326	584			5	76	0.20				29		78			127	27%	72%				2.72		15	33	$4
12 aa	483	55	8	45	15	259		286	368	654			4	79	0.18				31		75			101	30%	46%				3.17		16	40	$12
13 SF *	471	41	7	40	13	228	244	253	339	592	523	841	3	76	0.14	52	19	29	29	85	87	79	5%	122	24%	64%	9	33%	56%	2.72	-20.0	18	45	$6
14 SF *	277	33	5	18	4	210	222	247	322	569	477	511	5	76	0.21	43	15	43	26	56	94	59	3%	102	21%	41%	20	20%	60%	2.34	-13.0	22	59	$1
1st Half	113	12	1	7	3	218	212	256	309	566	500	464	5	73	0.19	42	17	42	29	49	87	79	10%	99	30%	46%	12	8%	75%	2.30	-5.6	2	5	-$2
2nd Half	164	21	4	11	1	204	230	240	332	571	450	528	4	78	0.22	43	14	43	24	60	99	49	0%	103	14%	32%	8	38%	38%	2.37	-7.8	34	92	$2
15 Proj	**101**	**11**	**1**	**8**	**2**	**223**	**229**	**261**	**326**	**587**	**527**	**657**	**4**	**77**	**0.18**	**46**	**17**	**37**	**28**	**67**	**86**	**69**	**5%**	**109**	**24%**	**49%**				**2.49**	**-4.0**	**12**	**32**	**-$1**

Perez,Roberto

Age: 26	Bats: R	Pos: CA	
Ht: 5' 11"	Wt: 225		
Health	A	LIMA Plan	F
PT/Exp	D	Rand Var	-5
Consist	D	MM	2001

1-4-.271 in 85 AB at CLE. PRO: A flicker of hope with a little pop, just coming into peak years. CON: An avalanche of despair, from poor plate discipline to lack of minor league cred to lack of any historical support for that 1st half burst. VERDICT: Classic no-hit fifth outfielder. Avoid.

Yr Tm	AB	R	HR	RBI	SB	BA	xBA	OBP	SLG	OPS	vL	vR	bb%	ct%	Eye	G	L	F	h%	HctX	PX	xPX	hr/f	Spd	SBO	SB%	#Wk	DOM	DIS	RC/G	RAR	BPV	BPX	R$
10																																		
11																																		
12 aa	283	28	1	28	0	192		298	265	563			13	73	0.57				26		63			92	1%	0%				2.45		0	0	-$4
13 a/a	280	20	1	26	1	166		271	234	505			13	65	0.41				25		72			80	4%	25%				1.88		-31	-78	-$7
14 CLE *	259	31	7	36	1	256	216	324	393	717	397	786	9	66	0.29	45	17	38	36	85	123	123	5%	77	1%	100%	13	31%	62%	4.39	8.0	5	14	$5
1st Half	157	21	6	30	1	266	227	350	437	788			11	62	0.35				39	0	153			77	2%	100%				5.35		20	54	$10
2nd Half	102	11	1	6	0	241	204	281	328	609	397	786	5	71	0.19	45	17	38	33	91	82	123	5%	83	0%	0%	13	31%	62%	3.10	-0.9	-13	-35	-$2
15 Proj	**126**	**12**	**1**	**13**	**0**	**214**	**200**	**293**	**305**	**599**	**389**	**682**	**10**	**67**	**0.34**	**45**	**17**	**38**	**31**	**82**	**89**	**111**	**4%**	**80**	**2%**	**45%**				**2.88**	**-2.0**	**-23**	**-61**	**$1**

Perez,Salvador

Age: 25	Bats: R	Pos: CA	
Ht: 6' 3"	Wt: 240		
Health	B	LIMA Plan	B+
PT/Exp	B	Rand Var	+1
Consist	B	MM	2145

What happened in 2H? Drew an appalling 4 BB in 299 AB, made less contact, and h% dipped because he was lifting mostly-harmless FBs for three months. Perhaps minor knee/groin issues were hampering him. Seems safe to expect a return to historical performance. In fact, if you double 1st half, there's a sneaky... UP: 20 HR.

Yr Tm	AB	R	HR	RBI	SB	BA	xBA	OBP	SLG	OPS	vL	vR	bb%	ct%	Eye	G	L	F	h%	HctX	PX	xPX	hr/f	Spd	SBO	SB%	#Wk	DOM	DIS	RC/G	RAR	BPV	BPX	R$
10																																		
11 KC *	482	50	10	61	0	280	296	307	401	708	1285	711	4	88	0.33	42	29	29	30	106	79	86	8%	96	1%	0%	8	50%	38%	4.31	1.4	54	120	$12
12 KC *	339	46	11	44	0	301	291	327	450	778	1021	711	4	90	0.41	44	24	32	31	118	87	116	13%	80	0%	0%	16	69%	25%	5.37	11.5	65	163	$12
13 KC	496	48	13	79	0	292	272	323	433	757	867	714	4	87	0.33	47	21	33	31	108	88	96	9%	83	0%	0%	25	52%	28%	5.02	17.8	55	138	$17
14 KC	578	57	17	70	1	260	265	289	403	692	632	710	4	85	0.26	39	21	40	28	115	95	106	9%	70	1%	100%	27	52%	15%	3.99	11.1	48	130	$14
1st Half	279	33	10	29	1	287	291	334	455	790	603	845	6	88	0.53	45	21	33	30	129	111	114	12%	68	1%	100%	14	71%	0%	5.39	15.6	74	200	$16
2nd Half	299	24	7	41	0	234	240	244	355	599	656	581	1	83	0.08	33	22	45	26	103	80	99	6%	84	0%	0%	13	31%	31%	2.88	-4.6	25	68	$11
15 Proj	**536**	**55**	**16**	**72**	**0**	**283**	**275**	**316**	**427**	**743**	**836**	**712**	**4**	**87**	**0.34**	**41**	**22**	**36**	**30**	**112**	**95**	**103**	**9%**	**77**	**0%**	**78%**				**4.78**	**20.9**	**46**	**122**	**$18**

Petit,Gregorio

Age: 30	Bats: R	Pos: SS	
Ht: 5' 10"	Wt: 195		
Health	A	LIMA Plan	D
PT/Exp	C	Rand Var	0
Consist	B	MM	2011

2-9-.278 in 97 AB at HOU. Less than awe-inspiring numbers in minors, so he's not a prospect. Results against lefties are a sample-size quirk (29 AB in MLB), and—stop me if you've heard this before—lack of plate discipline cripples upside. Find other choices in the end game.

Yr Tm	AB	R	HR	RBI	SB	BA	xBA	OBP	SLG	OPS	vL	vR	bb%	ct%	Eye	G	L	F	h%	HctX	PX	xPX	hr/f	Spd	SBO	SB%	#Wk	DOM	DIS	RC/G	RAR	BPV	BPX	R$
10 aaa	471	41	5	37	8	207		252	281	533			6	76	0.25				26		57			99	12%	70%				2.27		-5	-11	-$1
11																																		
12 aaa	377	35	7	31	1	201		241	306	547			5	75	0.21				25		80			81	5%	22%				2.28		0	0	-$2
13 aaa	503	33	2	37	3	205		241	261	502			5	79	0.23				25		44			95	7%	43%				1.96		-7	-18	-$4
14 HOU *	414	43	9	36	1	232	246	257	350	606	1124	551	3	77	0.14	44	22	33	28	107	92	90	8%	92	7%	11%	11	45%	45%	2.81	-4.6	18	49	$4
1st Half	282	24	6	24	1	222	235	252	331	582			4	78	0.19				26	0	81			89	8%	14%				2.55		15	41	$4
2nd Half	132	18	3	12	0	254	254	267	391	658	1124	551	2	74	0.07	44	22	33	33	102	119	90	8%	92	4%	0%	11	45%	45%	3.43	0.8	24	65	$2
15 Proj	**135**	**13**	**3**	**11**	**1**	**224**	**243**	**267**	**336**	**604**	**977**	**439**	**4**	**77**	**0.17**	**44**	**22**	**33**	**27**	**92**	**89**	**81**	**7%**	**95**	**7%**	**33%**				**2.71**	**-2.2**	**5**	**13**	**$1**

Phegley,Joshua

Age: 27	Bats: R	Pos: CA	
Ht: 5' 10"	Wt: 220		
Health	A	LIMA Plan	D+
PT/Exp	C	Rand Var	+5
Consist	A	MM	4131

3-7-.216 in 37 AB at CHW. Newly-emerging power skill makes this Bull Durham prospect worth another look. When he hits the ball, he hits it hard... at least in Triple-A. Age and classic late-blooming catcher profile say he still has time to carry it over to majors. Sneaky double-digit HR potential here makes a nice deep-league flyer.

Yr Tm	AB	R	HR	RBI	SB	BA	xBA	OBP	SLG	OPS	vL	vR	bb%	ct%	Eye	G	L	F	h%	HctX	PX	xPX	hr/f	Spd	SBO	SB%	#Wk	DOM	DIS	RC/G	RAR	BPV	BPX	R$
10 aa	72	6	2	11	0	267		285	399	684			2	66	0.07				38		113			96	0%	0%				3.96		-10	-22	$0
11 a/a	443	43	9	46	1	217		263	332	595			6	80	0.31				25		84			89	3%	27%				2.78		26	58	$1
12 aaa	394	35	6	41	3	245		280	347	627			5	83	0.28				28		71			82	3%	100%				3.32		23	58	$4
13 CHW *	435	44	17	54	3	242	257	272	416	688	668	479	4	80	0.21	39	19	41	27	65	115	72	6%	70	5%	71%	14	21%	57%	3.79	0.9	44	110	$9
14 CHW *	456	48	20	55	0	215	272	251	410	661	1000	622	5	78	0.22	30	26	44	23	163	137	207	25%	69	2%	0%	5	40%	40%	3.29	-0.3	53	143	$6
1st Half	238	22	8	21	0	186	265	235	356	592			6	79	0.30				20	0	124			82	0%	0%				2.63		53	143	-$1
2nd Half	218	26	12	34	0	248	278	269	469	737	1000	622	3	77	0.13	30	26	44	27	161	151	207	25%	71	3%	0%	5	40%	40%	4.15	4.9	58	157	$13
15 Proj	**167**	**17**	**8**	**20**	**1**	**242**	**268**	**270**	**439**	**709**	**884**	**649**	**4**	**79**	**0.22**	**36**	**20**	**43**	**26**	**113**	**137**	**153**	**13%**	**73**	**3%**	**56%**				**4.03**	**3.2**	**52**	**136**	**$4**

Phillips,Brandon

Age: 34	Bats: R	Pos: 2B	
Ht: 6' 0"	Wt: 200		
Health	B	LIMA Plan	B+
PT/Exp	A	Rand Var	0
Consist	B	MM	1235

Thumb ligament injury ended run of high-AB seasons, which were the foundation for his counting stats (and those once reliable 18 HR). xBA and PX tell a mournful tale of gradual, across-the-board decline, typical of the aging veteran. Above average ct% will set a useful BA floor, but limited rebound otherwise caps his value.

Yr Tm	AB	R	HR	RBI	SB	BA	xBA	OBP	SLG	OPS	vL	vR	bb%	ct%	Eye	G	L	F	h%	HctX	PX	xPX	hr/f	Spd	SBO	SB%	#Wk	DOM	DIS	RC/G	RAR	BPV	BPX	R$
10 CIN	626	100	18	59	16	275	283	332	430	762	810	741	7	87	0.55	51	15	33	29	111	96	97	10%	127	17%	57%	27	59%	11%	4.66	-1.0	78	170	$22
11 CIN	610	94	18	82	14	300	282	353	457	810	851	798	7	86	0.52	45	20	35	33	119	104	112	10%	94	14%	61%	27	67%	11%	5.59	14.9	71	158	$28
12 CIN	580	86	18	77	15	281	277	321	429	750	741	754	5	86	0.35	47	21	32	30	99	90	79	11%	92	12%	88%	27	52%	19%	4.87	8.5	56	140	$23
13 CIN	606	80	18	103	5	261	258	310	396	706	746	689	6	84	0.40	46	19	34	29	99	85	92	10%	94	5%	63%	26	58%	23%	4.13	8.2	46	115	$19
14 CIN	462	44	8	51	2	266	258	306	372	678	594	704	5	84	0.31	44	22	34	30	104	79	79	6%	72	4%	40%	22	32%	32%	3.81	5.5	32	86	$10
1st Half	305	29	7	37	1	269	259	301	400	701	673	711	4	82	0.23	44	21	35	31	113	99	91	8%	71	6%	25%	14	29%	29%	4.00	5.4	37	100	$14
2nd Half	157	15	1	14	1	261	257	316	318	634	369	692	6	89	0.56	44	25	31	29	85	44	59	2%	81	2%	100%	8	38%	38%	3.39	0.0	28	76	$2
15 Proj	**529**	**63**	**11**	**66**	**6**	**268**	**264**	**315**	**382**	**697**	**655**	**711**	**5**	**85**	**0.40**	**45**	**21**	**33**	**30**	**99**	**80**	**81**	**7%**	**85**	**6%**	**67%**				**4.07**	**10.4**	**39**	**102**	**$16**

Pierzynski,A.J.

Age: 38	Bats: L	Pos: CA	
Ht: 6' 3"	Wt: 235		
Health	B	LIMA Plan	D+
PT/Exp	B	Rand Var	0
Consist	C	MM	1021

Once-elite ct% has dipped to merely above-average, though that and xPX say he may not be totally finished. Note, however, that the FB lean that drove his 2-year power surge is fading. At 38, you can't hope for much of a rebound. Would have more value if "striking fear in the opposition" were a roto category.

Yr Tm	AB	R	HR	RBI	SB	BA	xBA	OBP	SLG	OPS	vL	vR	bb%	ct%	Eye	G	L	F	h%	HctX	PX	xPX	hr/f	Spd	SBO	SB%	#Wk	DOM	DIS	RC/G	RAR	BPV	BPX	R$
10 CHW	474	43	9	56	3	270	268	300	388	688	642	702	3	92	0.38	49	16	36	28	94	77	80	6%	59	7%	43%	27	56%	15%	3.84	-7.2	54	117	$10
11 CHW	464	38	8	48	0	287	285	323	405	728	808	711	5	93	0.70	51	21	29	30	104	78	72	6%	64	0%	0%	25	52%	8%	4.64	3.4	65	144	$10
12 CHW	479	68	27	77	0	278	289	326	501	827	673	874	6	84	0.36	42	22	36	28	105	125	104	19%	86	0%	0%	27	56%	11%	5.62	18.0	74	185	$18
13 TEX	503	48	17	70	1	272	273	297	425	722	718	724	2	85	0.14	42	22	35	29	107	97	101	11%	63	2%	50%	26	50%	27%	4.26	8.1	42	105	$14
14 2 TM	338	25	5	37	0	251	242	288	337	625	490	677	4	84	0.26	46	21	32	29	97	60	91	5%	69	1%	0%	25	24%	44%	3.19	-2.6	15	41	$4
1st Half	238	17	4	31	0	252	249	281	353	634	462	724	3	84	0.18	51	20	30	29	87	71	81	7%	68	0%	0%	14	29%	43%	3.29	-0.7	21	57	$6
2nd Half	100	8	1	6	0	250	228	306	300	606	697	594	7	84	0.44	36	25	39	29	121	35	113	3%	78	3%	0%	11	18%	45%	2.92	-1.4	3	8	-$3
15 Proj	**201**	**18**	**4**	**23**	**0**	**263**	**256**	**303**	**373**	**676**	**631**	**690**	**4**	**85**	**0.31**	**43**	**22**	**35**	**29**	**106**	**74**	**99**	**7%**	**71**	**2%**	**17%**				**3.75**	**2.1**	**22**	**57**	**$5**

JOSH PALEY

Pillar,Kevin

Age: 26 Bats: R Pos: LF — Ht: 6' 0" Wt: 205
Health: A — PT/Exp: D — Consist: C
LIMA Plan: D+ — Rand Var: 0 — MM: 4331

2-7-.267 in 116 AB at TOR. PRO: Intriguing power in 2H, which got him almost a month of starting time. Owns decent ct% skill, and a power/speed combo supported by BPIs. CON: Poor plate patience; has thus far looked totally overmatched against RHPs. VERDICT: Deep league speculation.

Yr	Tm	AB	R	HR	RBI	SB	BA	xBA	OBP	SLG	OPS	vL	vR	bb%	ct%	Eye	G	L	F	h%	HctX	PX	xPX	hr/f	Spd	SBO	SB%	#Wk	DOM	DIS	RC/G	RAR	BPV	BPX	R$
10																																			
11																																			
12																																			
13	TOR *	607	67	10	56	17	259	237	291	391	682	680	534	4	82	0.25	36	17	47	30	58	96	55	9%	108	26%	52%	8	25%	50%	3.60	-6.9	47	118	$17
14	TOR *	521	65	11	54	23	283	285	310	441	751	783	631	4	84	0.24	51	16	33	32	98	120	82	7%	102	29%	72%	12	17%	42%	4.74	15.7	71	192	$23
1st Half		247	31	2	23	9	278	267	309	411	720	605	357	4	86	0.31	53	10	37	32	87	105	69	0%	108	25%	66%	6	0%	50%	4.32	4.2	69	186	$15
2nd Half		274	34	9	31	14	288	294	312	468	780	1009	698	3	82	0.20	50	19	31	32	103	134	89	11%	90	32%	76%	6	33%	33%	5.13	10.9	72	195	$31
15	Proj	236	28	6	24	8	274	271	308	436	744	853	673	4	83	0.23	45	16	39	31	93	121	70	7%	100	26%	63%				4.39	4.5	68	179	$7

Pinto,Josmil

Age: 26 Bats: R Pos: CA DH — Ht: 5' 11" Wt: 210
Health: A — PT/Exp: D — Consist: B
LIMA Plan: D+ — Rand Var: +1 — MM: 4023

7-18-.219 in 169 AB at MIN. .410 OBP in April was unsustainable, but he fell completely apart, spending most of July and August in AAA. Shaky plate skills (0.14 Eye in MIN) and dubious defense are both obstacles to a larger role. Still, when he makes contact, good things happen. That alone keeps him on the radar. UP: 15 HR.

Yr	Tm	AB	R	HR	RBI	SB	BA	xBA	OBP	SLG	OPS	vL	vR	bb%	ct%	Eye	G	L	F	h%	HctX	PX	xPX	hr/f	Spd	SBO	SB%	#Wk	DOM	DIS	RC/G	RAR	BPV	BPX	R$
10																																			
11																																			
12	aa	47	6	1	7	0	267		315	478	793			7	77	0.30				32		143			105	0%	0%				5.24		67	168	-$1
13	MIN *	532	59	14	68	0	276	262	344	423	767	745	1026	9	78	0.48	43	24	33	33	137	107	143	22%	70	1%	0%	4	75%	25%	5.03	19.9	40	100	$14
14	MIN *	377	44	11	46	0	231	231	318	388	706	663	728	11	76	0.53	47	12	41	28	118	121	143	14%	75	2%	0%	16	44%	50%	4.00	7.7	47	127	$5
1st Half		174	26	8	20	0	227	238	331	411	742	661	760	13	75	0.63	48	13	40	25	120	129	139	18%	81	2%	0%	11	55%	36%	4.37	5.2	58	157	$5
2nd Half		203	18	3	26	0	235	218	307	368	675	667	535	9	76	0.43	43	10	48	30	110	115	164	0%	78	2%	0%	5	20%	80%	3.69	1.8	40	108	$5
15	Proj	252	28	10	36	0	249	256	326	439	765	661	821	10	77	0.49	44	16	40	29	123	141	149	13%	74	2%	0%				4.76	10.2	51	135	$7

Piscotty,Stephen

Age: 24 Bats: R Pos: RF — Ht: 6' 3" Wt: 210
Health: A — PT/Exp: F — Consist: B
LIMA Plan: D — Rand Var: 0 — MM: 1231

2012 compensation pick out of Stanford was ranked #4 STL prospect heading into 2014, but .288/.355/.406 in the PCL doesn't project well, as pedestrian MLEs show. Ct% is a nice building block, but weak bb% and PX say he's not ready to contribute in the bigs. Has time to show more upside, but he's a 4th/5th OF for 2015.

Yr	Tm	AB	R	HR	RBI	SB	BA	xBA	OBP	SLG	OPS	vL	vR	bb%	ct%	Eye	G	L	F	h%	HctX	PX	xPX	hr/f	Spd	SBO	SB%	#Wk	DOM	DIS	RC/G	RAR	BPV	BPX	R$
10																																			
11																																			
12																																			
13	aa	184	13	4	18	5	259		314	371	684			7	89	0.70				27		71			84	17%	62%				3.86		53	133	$3
14	aaa	500	51	6	50	8	241		286	331	617			6	86	0.46				27		69			81	12%	58%				3.09		38	103	$8
1st Half		295	28	3	33	6	262		304	365	669			6	85	0.39				30		83			84	10%	84%				3.88		44	119	$12
2nd Half		205	22	3	17	2	210		260	282	542			6	89	0.59				23		49			97	14%	32%				2.17		37	100	$2
15	Proj	131	12	3	13	3	243	265	293	361	654	654	654	7	88	0.57	46	20	34	26		80		8%	92	15%	55%				3.41	-2.4	45	118	$3

Plouffe,Trevor

Age: 29 Bats: R Pos: 3B — Ht: 6' 2" Wt: 205
Health: B — PT/Exp: B — Consist: A
LIMA Plan: B+ — Rand Var: 0 — MM: 4135

Surface stats say this was the 2013 repeat that in turn makes 2012 the outlier, but... xBA and PX/xPX look more like 2012. The difference? Downturn in hr/f. As always, the truth (and 2015 expectations) lies in the middle, or better: combine the 2nd half ct% with the power upside shown by xPX and... UP: 25 HR, .270 BA.

Yr	Tm	AB	R	HR	RBI	SB	BA	xBA	OBP	SLG	OPS	vL	vR	bb%	ct%	Eye	G	L	F	h%	HctX	PX	xPX	hr/f	Spd	SBO	SB%	#Wk	DOM	DIS	RC/G	RAR	BPV	BPX	R$
10	MIN *	443	46	11	42	4	201	230	237	339	576	400	468	4	75	0.19	50	11	39	24	101	100	173	18%	108	13%	39%	11	18%	55%	2.43	-33.5	22	48	$0
11	MIN *	478	72	18	56	5	248	256	307	433	741	782	665	8	76	0.35	43	17	40	29	115	132	128	10%	123	9%	56%	17	53%	24%	4.41	-5.6	63	140	$12
12	MIN	422	56	24	55	1	235	262	301	455	756	911	691	8	78	0.40	38	18	44	25	112	136	114	17%	92	4%	25%	24	58%	33%	4.36	-2.3	67	168	$9
13	MIN	477	44	14	52	2	254	249	309	392	701	826	663	7	77	0.30	39	25	37	30	103	98	113	10%	104	3%	67%	25	44%	32%	4.05	1.4	31	78	$9
14	MIN	520	69	14	80	2	258	266	328	423	751	783	738	9	79	0.49	38	21	40	30	113	127	133	8%	101	2%	67%	24	58%	17%	4.73	16.0	69	186	$15
1st Half		249	31	5	38	0	241	261	319	398	717	670	734	10	76	0.44	36	23	41	30	104	133	135	6%	101	0%	0%	12	58%	17%	4.21	3.8	60	162	$8
2nd Half		271	38	9	42	2	273	272	337	446	783	872	742	9	82	0.54	40	20	40	30	120	122	132	10%	102	4%	67%	12	58%	17%	5.24	12.0	77	208	$21
15	Proj	508	62	16	68	2	255	261	320	420	739	824	707	8	78	0.41	39	21	40	30	111	123	125	10%	102	3%	55%				4.50	11.9	47	124	$14

Polanco,Gregory

Age: 23 Bats: L Pos: RF — Ht: 6' 4" Wt: 220
Health: A — PT/Exp: F — Consist: B
LIMA Plan: B — Rand Var: 0 — MM: 2335

7-33-.235 with 14 SB in 277 AB at PIT. Big time prospect started hot after call-up, then discovered MLB is challenging. Struggles vs. LHP and lofty GB% are problems that likely won't be cured overnight. Even without an imminent power spike, he's a premium longer-term keeper. Pay for the speed now; be patient for the rest.

Yr	Tm	AB	R	HR	RBI	SB	BA	xBA	OBP	SLG	OPS	vL	vR	bb%	ct%	Eye	G	L	F	h%	HctX	PX	xPX	hr/f	Spd	SBO	SB%	#Wk	DOM	DIS	RC/G	RAR	BPV	BPX	R$
10																																			
11																																			
12																																			
13	a/a	252	30	4	33	11	233		311	344	655			10	85	0.76				26		74			100	27%	60%				3.34		52	130	$6
14	PIT *	551	89	12	72	26	259	253	321	379	701	466	727	8	80	0.45	50	19	31	31	84	86	87	10%	105	25%	69%	17	35%	41%	4.09	-0.1	38	103	$24
1st Half		328	50	7	47	15	297	283	354	430	783	461	860	8	82	0.47	51	25	24	35	67	93	53	13%	110	21%	73%	4	50%	0%	5.45	13.4	51	138	$31
2nd Half		223	39	5	24	11	203	230	274	307	581	468	670	9	77	0.43	49	16	35	24	89	77	101	9%	96	31%	64%	13	31%	54%	2.57	-10.3	18	49	$13
15	Proj	477	72	11	60	22	249	261	316	372	688	476	775	9	81	0.55	50	20	30	28	80	87	82	10%	97	25%	65%				3.86	-2.1	49	128	$19

Pollock IV,A.J.

Age: 27 Bats: R Pos: CF — Ht: 6' 1" Wt: 195
Health: D — PT/Exp: C — Consist: B
LIMA Plan: B+ — Rand Var: 0 — MM: 3545

7-24-.302 with 14 SB in 265 AB at ARI. How surface stats deceive: h% and hr/f say difference between halves was luck. PRO: Elite speed plays nicely with 2H spikes in contact, Eye, and GB%. CON: Inconsistent results vRHP may mean wrong side of platoon. VERDICT: If those 2H spikes are real, then... UP: .290, 30 SB.

Yr	Tm	AB	R	HR	RBI	SB	BA	xBA	OBP	SLG	OPS	vL	vR	bb%	ct%	Eye	G	L	F	h%	HctX	PX	xPX	hr/f	Spd	SBO	SB%	#Wk	DOM	DIS	RC/G	RAR	BPV	BPX	R$
10																																			
11	aa	550	72	6	51	25	266		304	382	686			5	82	0.31				31		87			104	26%	76%				4.02		42	93	$17
12	ARI *	509	47	4	39	14	250	253	289	334	623	808	535	5	86	0.37	50	20	30	29	123	57	110	10%	100	20%	54%	10	40%	20%	3.07	-24.8	30	75	$8
13	ARI	443	64	8	38	12	269	262	322	409	730	811	678	7	81	0.40	48	18	34	31	126	98	112	7%	143	14%	80%	27	48%	22%	4.58	6.1	63	158	$14
14	ARI *	314	43	7	29	14	274	281	318	447	765	953	828	6	84	0.40	52	14	34	31	109	116	97	9%	175	23%	82%	15	73%	13%	5.05	11.0	95	257	$13
1st Half		177	28	6	15	8	316	299	366	554	920	845	941	6	80	0.33	50	13	38	37	109	170	115	11%	171	21%	89%	10	70%	20%	7.59	17.8	120	324	$17
2nd Half		137	15	1	14	6	220	266	263	309	572	1295	621	6	89	0.55	56	17	27	24	104	53	66	5%	164	26%	75%	5	80%	0%	2.67	-5.1	62	168	$6
15	Proj	428	55	9	38	18	269	275	315	418	732	846	679	6	84	0.40	51	17	32	30	116	101	99	7%	158	23%	78%				4.57	8.8	73	193	$17

Posey,Buster

Age: 28 Bats: R Pos: CA 1B — Ht: 6' 1" Wt: 215
Health: B — PT/Exp: A — Consist: D
LIMA Plan: B+ — Rand Var: 0 — MM: 3155

Confirmed 2013's ct% gains, and in 2nd half finally merged those with previously-established power. Elite HctX and xBA say you can nearly ink in a .300 BA. Power growth is still capped by a slight GB% tilt, but he did start to raise that ceiling in 2H. That's enough to make him potentially worthy of a first-round pick.

Yr	Tm	AB	R	HR	RBI	SB	BA	xBA	OBP	SLG	OPS	vL	vR	bb%	ct%	Eye	G	L	F	h%	HctX	PX	xPX	hr/f	Spd	SBO	SB%	#Wk	DOM	DIS	RC/G	RAR	BPV	BPX	R$
10	SF *	578	81	22	90	1	305	291	360	493	853	955	832	8	85	0.57	49	18	33	33	115	119	121	15%	98	2%	19%	20	70%	20%	6.38	31.8	81	176	$24
11	SF	162	17	4	21	3	284	243	368	389	756	681	786	10	81	0.60	53	18	29	33	96	69	84	10%	87	5%	100%	9	44%	33%	5.05	3.1	29	64	$4
12	SF	530	78	24	103	1	336	301	408	549	957	1262	822	12	82	0.72	47	25	29	38	113	137	104	19%	84	1%	50%	27	70%	15%	8.65	60.3	87	218	$30
13	SF	520	61	15	72	2	294	279	371	450	821	891	792	10	87	0.86	47	20	33	32	116	103	116	10%	82	2%	67%	27	56%	7%	5.95	32.6	76	190	$19
14	SF	547	72	22	89	0	311	298	364	490	854	875	844	8	87	0.68	42	24	34	32	131	113	121	13%	81	1%	0%	27	70%	19%	6.57	46.2	82	222	$27
1st Half		264	32	9	40	0	295	292	351	447	798	874	774	8	87	0.69	43	26	31	31	131	99	114	12%	65	1%	0%	14	64%	21%	5.64	16.5	64	173	$20
2nd Half		283	40	13	49	0	325	303	375	530	905	874	922	8	88	0.68	41	23	36	33	131	125	128	14%	99	0%	0%	13	77%	15%	7.53	31.0	99	268	$34
15	Proj	540	70	20	87	1	310	293	374	487	861	932	830	9	86	0.72	45	23	33	33	122	117	116	13%	83	1%	56%				6.69	48.3	72	190	$27

JOSH PALEY

Prado,Martin

Age: 31	Bats: R	Pos: 3B 2B	Health	B	LIMA Plan	A
Ht: 6' 1"	Wt: 190		PT/Exp	A	Rand Var	-1
			Consist	B	MM	2345

A reliable, consistent source of BA and modest, double-digit HR for years—though the underlying BPIs are less clear. Diminished ct% still sets a nice floor for BA, but mounting problems vR are a looming threat to PT. 2nd half surge, driven by fewer GBs and more LDs, restores our confidence in the status quo.

Yr	Tm	AB	R	HR	RBI	SB	BA	xBA	OBP	SLG	OPS	vL	vR	bb%	ct%	Eye	G	L	F	h%	HctX	PX	xPX	hr/f	Spd	SBO	SB%	#Wk	DOM	DIS	RC/G	RAR	BPV	BPX	R$
10	ATL	599	100	15	66	5	307	295	350	459	809	747	834	6	86	0.47	48	21	31	34	108	102	91	9%	126	5%	63%	24	58%	21%	5.86	20.7	76	165	$24
11	ATL *	577	69	13	59	4	255	259	299	374	673	673	692	6	90	0.62	51	15	35	27	87	75	71	8%	120	8%	33%	23	52%	4%	3.63	-18.6	69	153	$11
12	ATL	617	81	10	70	17	301	291	359	438	796	864	760	9	89	0.84	48	23	29	33	110	86	76	6%	125	11%	81%	27	63%	7%	5.82	28.2	81	203	$25
13	ARI	609	70	14	82	3	282	290	333	417	750	852	716	7	91	0.89	48	22	30	29	110	85	89	8%	91	5%	38%	27	67%	4%	4.81	18.7	77	193	$19
14	2 TM	536	62	12	58	3	282	276	321	412	733	979	668	5	85	0.33	49	22	29	31	102	88	78	9%	123	3%	75%	26	46%	27%	4.61	18.4	59	159	$16
1st Half		314	35	3	34	1	268	264	315	363	678	782	655	5	85	0.35	53	21	26	31	102	66	71	4%	133	2%	50%	15	33%	40%	3.82	3.9	44	119	$14
2nd Half		222	27	9	24	2	302	294	330	482	812	1170	687	4	86	0.28	42	24	34	32	101	119	88	14%	109	4%	100%	11	64%	9%	5.85	14.9	80	216	$19
15	Proj	**560**	**68**	**13**	**65**	**3**	**283**	**285**	**327**	**421**	**747**	**909**	**692**	**6**	**88**	**0.50**	**47**	**22**	**31**	**30**	**104**	**93**	**82**	**9%**	**113**	**3%**	**68%**				**4.84**	**18.1**	**60**	**159**	**$17**

Presley,Alex

Age: 29	Bats: L	Pos: LF CF RF	Health	C	LIMA Plan	D
Ht: 5' 10"	Wt: 190		PT/Exp	C	Rand Var	+1
			Consist	A	MM	2321

Bottom line: Hard to get a gig in the majors if you are a LH hitter and RH pitchers own you. (I speak from experience.) Second half was impacted by an oblique injury, but skills already screamed "fifth OF". Plate discipline is consistent, and insufficient. DIS% tells of dry spells that could lead to DN: Minors.

Yr	Tm	AB	R	HR	RBI	SB	BA	xBA	OBP	SLG	OPS	vL	vR	bb%	ct%	Eye	G	L	F	h%	HctX	PX	xPX	hr/f	Spd	SBO	SB%	#Wk	DOM	DIS	RC/G	RAR	BPV	BPX	R$
10	PIT *	541	67	9	64	11	272	261	312	401	712	1500	511	5	83	0.34	64	7	29	31	85	83	13	0%	130	16%	51%	4	25%	75%	4.12	-18.1	51	111	$15
11	PIT *	557	70	10	50	25	285	275	325	419	744	599	893	6	82	0.33	50	23	27	33	98	89	89	8%	135	26%	67%	10	70%	20%	4.66	-9.8	52	116	$22
12	PIT *	499	65	13	42	14	242	270	293	397	690	690	682	7	80	0.35	60	17	23	28	81	91	85	16%	143	20%	61%	22	45%	45%	3.74	-15.0	50	125	$11
13	2 TM *	527	58	6	34	13	250	256	300	344	644	634	705	7	80	0.35	52	23	25	30	81	64	45	9%	144	18%	54%	14	21%	64%	3.30	-11.9	29	73	$10
14	HOU	254	22	6	19	5	244	238	281	346	628	777	613	5	83	0.30	47	18	35	27	92	65	83	8%	96	10%	83%	20	25%	40%	3.32	-2.7	23	62	$4
1st Half		183	16	4	11	3	246	239	289	339	628	874	600	6	84	0.37	46	20	34	28	100	56	92	8%	104	6%	100%	14	29%	50%	3.40	-1.9	24	65	$5
2nd Half		71	6	2	8	2	239	234	260	366	626	400	643	3	80	0.14	47	14	39	27	73	90	60	9%	91	21%	67%	6	17%	17%	3.10	-1.4	28	76	$1
15	Proj	**166**	**17**	**4**	**14**	**4**	**248**	**255**	**290**	**372**	**662**	**623**	**670**	**5**	**81**	**0.29**	**50**	**19**	**31**	**28**	**84**	**84**	**69**	**10%**	**109**	**17%**	**64%**				**3.52**	**-1.1**	**32**	**85**	**$4**

Profar,Jurickson

Age: 22	Bats: B	Pos: 2B	Health	F	LIMA Plan	D+
Ht: 6' 0"	Wt: 165		PT/Exp	D	Rand Var	0
			Consist	D	MM	2321

He was the best prospect in baseball two years ago; now injuries are one of his top skills. A torn shoulder muscle cost him all of 2014. Going into the off-season, his rehab timeline was very much in doubt, with the possibility that he might still be shut down for an extended period of time. Check back in March..

Yr	Tm	AB	R	HR	RBI	SB	BA	xBA	OBP	SLG	OPS	vL	vR	bb%	ct%	Eye	G	L	F	h%	HctX	PX	xPX	hr/f	Spd	SBO	SB%	#Wk	DOM	DIS	RC/G	RAR	BPV	BPX	R$
10																																			
11																																			
12	TEX *	497	66	14	55	14	276	255	349	447	796	0	846	10	83	0.67	54	8	38	31	112	105	123	20%	129	12%	77%	4	25%	75%	5.50	18.9	78	195	$17
13	TEX *	430	52	9	41	7	244	246	313	359	671	541	696	9	80	0.49	41	23	35	29	97	79	88	8%	114	10%	57%	19	26%	26%	3.68	-0.5	36	90	$8
14																																			
1st Half																																			
2nd Half																																			
15	Proj	**209**	**26**	**4**	**21**	**4**	**257**	**257**	**336**	**379**	**715**	**613**	**766**	**9**	**81**	**0.55**	**41**	**23**	**35**	**30**	**87**	**88**	**79**	**7%**	**118**	**11%**	**67%**				**4.20**	**5.0**	**43**	**112**	**$6**

Puig,Yasiel

Age: 24	Bats: R	Pos: RF CF	Health	A	LIMA Plan	A
Ht: 6' 3"	Wt: 235		PT/Exp	C	Rand Var	-1
			Consist	B	MM	4445

Nice follow up, but before we annoint him the next superstar, take a second look. Showed some weakness in 2nd half. Ink in 20 HR and 10 SB on raw talent, but short-term upside is blocked by mediocre ct% and a plethora of GB. He's still young and very raw; there's plenty of time to adjust. But it may not happen quickly.

Yr	Tm	AB	R	HR	RBI	SB	BA	xBA	OBP	SLG	OPS	vL	vR	bb%	ct%	Eye	G	L	F	h%	HctX	PX	xPX	hr/f	Spd	SBO	SB%	#Wk	DOM	DIS	RC/G	RAR	BPV	BPX	R$
10																																			
11																																			
12																																			
13	LA *	529	89	26	74	22	309	284	368	533	900	1001	897	8	76	0.38	50	19	31	37	117	154	106	22%	130	24%	62%	18	61%	28%	6.82	40.3	83	208	$35
14	LA	558	92	16	69	11	296	273	382	480	863	736	901	11	78	0.54	52	15	33	36	116	134	111	11%	143	11%	61%	28	54%	29%	6.29	38.6	85	230	$26
1st Half		296	44	11	45	7	311	279	401	517	917	844	938	12	77	0.58	52	14	33	37	126	148	117	14%	130	15%	50%	15	67%	20%	7.02	26.1	92	249	$31
2nd Half		262	48	5	24	4	279	264	361	439	800	621	857	10	78	0.49	51	15	34	34	106	118	104	7%	149	5%	100%	13	38%	38%	5.51	12.2	73	197	$21
15	Proj	**568**	**93**	**21**	**72**	**15**	**289**	**280**	**372**	**490**	**862**	**819**	**875**	**10**	**77**	**0.47**	**51**	**17**	**32**	**34**	**115**	**146**	**108**	**15%**	**138**	**15%**	**61%**				**6.08**	**33.7**	**81**	**214**	**$29**

Pujols,Albert

Age: 35	Bats: R	Pos: 1B DH	Health	C	LIMA Plan	A
Ht: 6' 3"	Wt: 230		PT/Exp	A	Rand Var	+2
			Consist	B	MM	4155

Observe the flight path of a future Hall of Famer. Skills aren't what they once were, but the new plateau is still highly acceptable. Void of injury, he continues to be a consistent, elite slugger who makes potent contact. xBA even hints at a reprisal of .300 BA. Health and age, though, remind us not to overbid.

Yr	Tm	AB	R	HR	RBI	SB	BA	xBA	OBP	SLG	OPS	vL	vR	bb%	ct%	Eye	G	L	F	h%	HctX	PX	xPX	hr/f	Spd	SBO	SB%	#Wk	DOM	DIS	RC/G	RAR	BPV	BPX	R$
10	STL	587	115	42	118	14	312	323	414	596	1011	1076	983	15	87	1.36	38	17	44	30	150	167	146	18%	72	9%	78%	27	85%	4%	9.14	56.0	135	293	$40
11	STL	579	105	37	99	9	299	311	366	541	906	946	897	10	90	1.05	45	17	38	28	139	137	140	18%	82	6%	90%	26	85%	4%	7.25	25.7	115	256	$33
12	LAA	607	85	30	105	8	285	303	343	516	859	926	836	8	87	0.68	41	19	40	29	128	140	126	14%	61	6%	89%	27	78%	11%	6.32	17.6	98	245	$27
13	LAA	391	49	17	64	1	258	270	330	437	767	690	790	9	86	0.73	38	20	42	26	128	109	135	12%	70	2%	50%	17	59%	12%	4.88	3.1	72	180	$11
14	LAA	633	89	28	105	5	272	299	324	466	790	737	807	7	89	0.68	46	19	35	27	139	122	110	14%	62	4%	83%	27	74%	0%	5.29	20.7	88	238	$26
1st Half		314	44	16	49	3	261	298	315	468	783	725	808	7	89	0.64	46	18	36	25	146	127	126	16%	70	4%	100%	14	71%	0%	5.09	8.4	92	249	$24
2nd Half		319	45	12	56	2	282	298	332	464	796	756	805	7	89	0.71	45	20	34	29	131	116	94	12%	59	4%	67%	13	77%	0%	5.48	11.8	83	224	$29
15	Proj	**578**	**82**	**26**	**98**	**5**	**280**	**295**	**340**	**479**	**819**	**794**	**827**	**8**	**88**	**0.74**	**43**	**19**	**38**	**28**	**134**	**127**	**120**	**14%**	**64**	**4%**	**79%**				**5.76**	**26.0**	**91**	**239**	**$26**

Punto,Nick

Age: 37	Bats: B	Pos: 2B	Health	D	LIMA Plan	D
Ht: 5' 9"	Wt: 195		PT/Exp	F	Rand Var	+1
			Consist	B	MM	1301

Hasn't produced useful fanalytic or real offensive value since 2008—check out all that negative RAR and dollar-store roto value. But one thing that was always worth an end-game buck - his tri-position eligibility. That ends now, along with the rest of his fantasy relevance.

Yr	Tm	AB	R	HR	RBI	SB	BA	xBA	OBP	SLG	OPS	vL	vR	bb%	ct%	Eye	G	L	F	h%	HctX	PX	xPX	hr/f	Spd	SBO	SB%	#Wk	DOM	DIS	RC/G	RAR	BPV	BPX	R$
10	MIN	252	24	1	20	6	238	225	313	302	615	608	618	10	80	0.56	52	15	33	29	61	51	20	2%	89	11%	75%	21	19%	52%	3.20	-10.5	10	22	$2
11	STL *	172	24	1	21	2	260	294	364	375	738	798	814	14	85	1.07	46	31	23	30	64	75	41	4%	114	4%	61%	14	64%	36%	4.65	-0.2	63	140	$2
12	2 TM	160	20	1	10	6	219	222	321	281	602	720	580	14	74	0.60	46	24	30	29	73	54	78	3%	88	12%	100%	27	22%	56%	3.20	-4.7	-5	-13	$0
13	LA	294	34	2	21	3	255	247	328	327	655	723	622	10	77	0.49	40	30	30	32	89	61	75	3%	70	7%	50%	26	27%	50%	3.60	-1.0	1	3	$3
14	OAK	198	21	2	14	3	207	217	296	293	589	607	570	11	72	0.45	45	22	33	28	50	69	35	4%	110	7%	75%	21	19%	52%	2.81	-3.5	0	0	-$1
1st Half		132	16	1	10	2	235	211	336	295	631	591	675	13	69	0.49	44	26	30	33	45	58	24	4%	92	7%	67%	14	7%	64%	3.30	-0.4	-22	-59	$1
2nd Half		66	5	1	4	1	152	230	211	288	499	647	387	7	77	0.33	45	16	39	18	59	89	54	5%	113	10%	100%	7	43%	29%	1.88	-3.3	30	81	-$4
15	Proj	**219**	**23**	**2**	**15**	**4**	**214**	**232**	**295**	**303**	**598**	**653**	**565**	**10**	**76**	**0.48**	**44**	**23**	**33**	**27**	**66**	**70**	**55**	**4%**	**103**	**8%**	**79%**				**2.94**	**-3.1**	**11**	**30**	**$2**

Quentin,Carlos

Age: 32	Bats: R	Pos: LF	Health	F	LIMA Plan	D+
Ht: 6' 1"	Wt: 235		PT/Exp	D	Rand Var	+5
			Consist	D	MM	4021

2007: Hamstring, labrum (45 days on DL). 2009: Shoulder (58). 2011: Shoulder (22). 2012: Knee (54). 2013: Knee (61). 2014: Knee, groin, knee, shoulder, knee (108). Sigh. Scan his metrics and you can only wonder how good he could have been. At 32, he is already showing some skills erosion that probably won't rebound.

Yr	Tm	AB	R	HR	RBI	SB	BA	xBA	OBP	SLG	OPS	vL	vR	bb%	ct%	Eye	G	L	F	h%	HctX	PX	xPX	hr/f	Spd	SBO	SB%	#Wk	DOM	DIS	RC/G	RAR	BPV	BPX	R$
10	CHW	453	73	26	87	2	243	277	342	479	821	764	838	10	82	0.60	37	14	49	24	103	147	125	14%	82	4%	50%	26	73%	0%	5.06	-2.7	91	198	$14
11	CHW	421	53	24	77	1	254	273	340	499	838	943	804	7	80	0.40	32	14	54	27	116	165	143	13%	71	2%	50%	22	64%	23%	5.24	-0.2	90	200	$14
12	SD	284	44	16	46	0	261	290	374	504	877	1018	820	11	86	0.88	35	18	47	28	140	146	165	14%	51	1%	0%	19	74%	16%	5.89	9.6	99	248	$9
13	SD	276	42	13	44	0	275	276	363	493	855	863	852	10	80	0.56	36	20	45	30	123	149	143	13%	72	0%	0%	17	65%	12%	6.04	15.6	83	208	$9
14	SD	130	9	4	18	0	177	201	284	315	599	563	622	12	75	0.52	45	13	43	20	90	105	99	9%	53	0%	0%	11	55%	36%	2.66	-4.6	24	65	-$2
1st Half		88	6	3	10	0	170	190	282	307	588	585	590	10	78	0.53	49	10	41	18	82	94	85	10%	55	0%	0%	8	63%	25%	2.41	-3.8	28	76	-$2
2nd Half		42	3	1	8	0	190	217	288	333	622	521	690	14	67	0.50	35	19	45	26	102	133	130	7%	68	0%	0%	3	33%	67%	3.21	-0.7	24	65	-$2
15	Proj	**221**	**27**	**9**	**34**	**0**	**256**	**258**	**340**	**437**	**777**	**737**	**797**	**10**	**81**	**0.58**	**38**	**17**	**45**	**28**	**110**	**128**	**130**	**11%**	**62**	**1%**	**32%**				**4.93**	**7.6**	**57**	**150**	**$7**

JOSH PALEY

Raburn,Ryan

Age: 34	Bats: R	Pos: RF DH LF	Health B	LIMA Plan D+
			PT/Exp F	Rand Var +4
Ht: 6' 0"	Wt: 185		Consist F	MM 4121

4-22-.200 in 195 AB at CLE. Neck, wrist, and knee injuries wiped out 2014. It is tempting to give him a mulligan, but 2013 was a stupendous outlier even at the time. His calling card has been as a masher of lefties. That will keep him on a roster, but the wrong side of a platoon limits his AB and fanalytic value.

Yr	Tm	AB	R	HR	RBI	SB	BA	xBA	OBP	SLG	OPS	vL	vR	bb%	ct%	Eye	G	L	F	h%	HctX	PX	xPX	hr/f	Spd	SBO	SB%	#Wk	DOM	DIS	RC/G	RAR	BPV	BPX	R$
10	DET *	398	58	15	63	3	285	265	333	478	811	929	753	7	76	0.30	39	18	44	34	105	142	128	12%	113	6%	45%	27	48%	33%	5.52	4.0	67	146	$14
11	DET	387	53	14	49	1	256	238	297	432	729	807	681	5	71	0.18	35	21	45	33	101	135	142	11%	124	2%	50%	27	48%	37%	4.31	-9.6	40	89	$9
12	DET *	265	20	4	20	2	176	201	224	277	500	477	482	6	73	0.23	43	14	43	23	108	82	138	2%	87	6%	63%	19	26%	47%	1.90	-25.4	-1	-3	-$5
13	CLE	243	40	16	55	0	272	282	357	543	901	1020	806	11	72	0.43	45	18	38	31	111	197	145	24%	70	0%	0%	26	62%	27%	6.64	16.4	92	230	$10
14	CLE *	223	21	4	25	0	195	219	244	280	524	596	463	6	74	0.25	41	23	35	24	98	66	103	8%	72	0%	0%	23	26%	61%	2.16	-12.1	-14	-38	-$2
1st Half		138	10	1	15	0	203	205	252	254	505	520	483	7	73	0.27	40	24	36	27	104	45	115	3%	77	0%	0%	14	14%	64%	2.08	-8.3	-33	-89	-$3
2nd Half		85	11	3	10	0	182	244	222	323	545	743	388	5	76	0.21	44	21	35	20	84	101	73	20%	81	0%	0%	9	44%	56%	2.23	-4.8	20	54	-$1
15	Proj	**215**	**26**	**8**	**32**	**0**	**243**	**246**	**302**	**411**	**713**	**771**	**642**	**7**	**74**	**0.29**	**43**	**19**	**38**	**29**	**100**	**128**	**115**	**14%**	**77**	**1%**	**60%**				**4.09**	**0.6**	**24**	**62**	**$3**

Ramirez,Alexei

Age: 33	Bats: R	Pos: SS	Health A	LIMA Plan B+
			PT/Exp A	Rand Var 0
Ht: 6' 2"	Wt: 180		Consist A	MM 1435

Huge 1st half followed by a gentle fade. Which to believe? Contact and speed remain big assets, with huge AB totals helping to maximize their value. But xPX and GB% say that HR were a fluke, and he's reached an age where SB tend to wane. The skinny: Don't pay for more than 10 HR/20 SB.

Yr	Tm	AB	R	HR	RBI	SB	BA	xBA	OBP	SLG	OPS	vL	vR	bb%	ct%	Eye	G	L	F	h%	HctX	PX	xPX	hr/f	Spd	SBO	SB%	#Wk	DOM	DIS	RC/G	RAR	BPV	BPX	R$
10	CHW	585	83	18	70	13	282	281	313	431	744	725	751	4	86	0.33	48	19	33	30	92	93	82	11%	129	15%	62%	27	63%	11%	4.64	7.8	68	148	$22
11	CHW	614	81	15	70	7	269	266	328	399	727	715	731	8	86	0.61	45	19	35	29	95	85	77	8%	115	7%	58%	27	56%	11%	4.43	4.5	65	144	$17
12	CHW	593	59	9	73	20	265	254	287	364	651	724	631	3	87	0.21	46	20	34	29	85	61	69	5%	129	20%	74%	27	37%	33%	3.56	-6.0	43	108	$17
13	CHW	637	68	6	48	30	284	278	313	380	693	701	691	4	89	0.38	49	22	29	31	88	68	51	4%	122	24%	77%	27	52%	15%	4.23	14.7	58	145	$25
14	CHW	622	82	15	74	21	273	278	305	408	713	744	703	4	87	0.30	47	20	33	29	88	92	64	8%	120	18%	84%	26	46%	12%	4.37	21.2	67	181	$26
1st Half		319	40	8	39	13	298	266	329	426	756	655	786	4	87	0.33	49	17	33	32	79	83	60	9%	146	19%	81%	14	43%	14%	5.12	16.7	67	181	$29
2nd Half		303	42	7	35	8	248	290	279	389	668	824	612	3	87	0.26	45	22	33	26	96	102	67	8%	94	16%	89%	12	50%	8%	3.66	3.8	68	184	$23
15	Proj	**614**	**75**	**8**	**66**	**18**	**272**	**268**	**302**	**375**	**678**	**712**	**667**	**4**	**87**	**0.29**	**47**	**21**	**32**	**30**	**89**	**76**	**63**	**5%**	**118**	**16%**	**80%**				**3.96**	**12.7**	**51**	**133**	**$22**

Ramirez,Aramis

Age: 37	Bats: R	Pos: 3B	Health C	LIMA Plan B+
			PT/Exp B	Rand Var -1
Ht: 6' 1"	Wt: 205		Consist C	MM 3245

Hamstring injury, back, and hamstring again followed him through the season and affected his final line. 2nd half fade vR could be sign of things to come. Still hammers lefties, but at his age, those aches, pains and downtime are not going to abate. Still, HctX and xPX indicate he'll remain productive when in the lineup.

Yr	Tm	AB	R	HR	RBI	SB	BA	xBA	OBP	SLG	OPS	vL	vR	bb%	ct%	Eye	G	L	F	h%	HctX	PX	xPX	hr/f	Spd	SBO	SB%	#Wk	DOM	DIS	RC/G	RAR	BPV	BPX	R$
10	CHC	465	61	25	83	0	241	255	294	452	745	816	722	7	81	0.38	27	16	57	25	120	132	147	12%	73	0%	0%	26	54%	27%	4.44	-9.1	66	143	$11
11	CHC	565	80	26	93	1	306	297	361	510	871	824	884	7	88	0.62	34	23	43	31	128	125	129	12%	96	1%	50%	27	74%	7%	6.62	23.4	96	213	$27
12	MIL	570	92	27	105	9	300	299	360	540	901	1049	853	7	86	0.54	39	19	42	31	148	148	164	13%	93	8%	82%	27	74%	7%	6.90	36.1	105	263	$29
13	MIL	304	43	12	49	0	283	265	370	461	831	887	811	11	82	0.65	41	19	39	31	123	118	144	12%	79	1%	0%	19	53%	16%	5.80	15.5	69	173	$10
14	MIL	494	47	15	66	3	285	266	330	427	757	1024	687	4	85	0.28	39	23	39	31	136	94	131	9%	78	2%	100%	24	42%	8%	4.83	15.5	48	130	$17
1st Half		212	27	11	40	3	292	286	345	495	840	1144	745	5	84	0.33	32	24	44	30	156	128	166	14%	74	6%	100%	11	64%	9%	5.94	13.2	74	200	$22
2nd Half		282	20	4	26	0	280	248	318	376	694	906	645	3	85	0.24	44	21	35	32	121	69	105	5%	84	0%	0%	13	23%	8%	4.06	2.9	30	81	$13
15	Proj	**472**	**57**	**16**	**71**	**2**	**286**	**274**	**343**	**449**	**792**	**952**	**746**	**6**	**84**	**0.43**	**39**	**22**	**40**	**31**	**133**	**112**	**139**	**10%**	**82**	**3%**	**79%**				**5.31**	**21.4**	**58**	**152**	**$19**

Ramirez,Hanley

Age: 31	Bats: R	Pos: SS	Health D	LIMA Plan B+
			PT/Exp B	Rand Var 0
Ht: 6' 2"	Wt: 225		Consist F	MM 4355

The good followed by the bad in 2014. 1st half was actually a very worthy followup to 2013's other-wordly outlier of a (half-) year. Second half then showed off his injury skills, as a rash of ailments included everything except an actual rash. Still has 20/20 potential, but bid safely. To ignore his injuries is to wear blinders.

Yr	Tm	AB	R	HR	RBI	SB	BA	xBA	OBP	SLG	OPS	vL	vR	bb%	ct%	Eye	G	L	F	h%	HctX	PX	xPX	hr/f	Spd	SBO	SB%	#Wk	DOM	DIS	RC/G	RAR	BPV	BPX	R$
10	FLA	543	92	21	76	32	300	285	378	475	853	838	858	11	83	0.69	51	16	33	33	126	112	108	14%	120	24%	76%	26	54%	35%	6.44	29.5	80	174	$33
11	FLA	338	55	10	45	20	243	255	333	379	712	994	633	12	80	0.67	51	16	33	27	103	94	96	11%	84	30%	67%	18	33%	22%	4.05	-4.7	47	104	$12
12	2 NL	604	79	24	92	21	257	262	322	437	759	794	745	8	78	0.41	47	18	34	29	114	115	115	15%	95	18%	75%	27	52%	33%	4.73	11.1	52	130	$23
13	LA	304	62	20	57	10	345	326	402	638	1040	1142	1001	8	83	0.52	41	22	37	37	159	186	164	21%	100	14%	83%	18	67%	22%	9.94	50.7	129	323	$25
14	LA	449	64	13	71	14	283	281	369	448	817	869	801	11	81	0.67	45	21	34	32	115	124	115	10%	79	14%	74%	25	56%	16%	5.74	31.3	72	195	$21
1st Half		272	39	11	46	10	272	292	360	471	831	915	806	12	82	0.73	45	20	35	30	127	142	145	14%	71	18%	71%	15	73%	13%	5.80	20.3	88	238	$27
2nd Half		177	25	2	25	4	299	264	383	412	796	797	793	10	80	0.57	46	23	32	36	98	97	68	4%	94	9%	80%	10	30%	20%	5.61	11.6	49	132	$13
15	Proj	**429**	**68**	**15**	**69**	**14**	**296**	**286**	**371**	**481**	**852**	**918**	**830**	**10**	**81**	**0.57**	**45**	**21**	**34**	**34**	**123**	**134**	**118**	**13%**	**91**	**15%**	**76%**				**6.34**	**37.3**	**82**	**215**	**$25**

Ramirez,Jose

Age: 22	Bats: B	Pos: SS	Health A	LIMA Plan D+
			PT/Exp D	Rand Var 0
Ht: 5' 9"	Wt: 165		Consist C	MM 1423

2-17-.262 with 10 SB in 237 AB at CLE. Young player with wheels. Worth our attention? PRO: Monthly upticks in HctX indicates he's making adjustments; has shown elite-level ct% in the past. CON: Minimal power; doesn't walk enough; troublesome SB%. VERDICT: Still a pup, expect SB along with some BA bumps.

Yr	Tm	AB	R	HR	RBI	SB	BA	xBA	OBP	SLG	OPS	vL	vR	bb%	ct%	Eye	G	L	F	h%	HctX	PX	xPX	hr/f	Spd	SBO	SB%	#Wk	DOM	DIS	RC/G	RAR	BPV	BPX	R$
10																																			
11																																			
12																																			
13	CLE *	494	65	2	29	29	240	220	285	302	587	650	1069	6	90	0.66	50	10	40	26	74	39	135	0%	161	37%	61%	4	25%	50%	2.67	-11.7	55	138	$14
14	CLE *	482	57	6	40	25	265	273	312	365	676	676	632	6	86	0.48	47	24	28	30	86	71	71	4%	119	30%	66%	15	47%	27%	3.77	8.5	50	135	$18
1st Half		204	26	4	22	9	259	236	307	372	679	0	211	7	87	0.56	57	5	38	28	52	78	21	0%	99	36%	47%	4	0%	50%	3.34	0.6	57	154	$13
2nd Half		278	31	2	18	16	270	271	315	360	675	730	687	6	84	0.43	46	27	27	31	88	66	77	4%	130	26%	84%	11	64%	18%	4.11	7.0	44	119	$22
15	Proj	**328**	**41**	**2**	**24**	**16**	**249**	**254**	**296**	**329**	**625**	**646**	**616**	**6**	**88**	**0.53**	**50**	**18**	**31**	**28**	**74**	**57**	**55**	**2%**	**130**	**31%**	**61%**				**3.09**	**-1.5**	**45**	**119**	**$10**

Ramos,Wilson

Age: 27	Bats: R	Pos: CA	Health F	LIMA Plan C+
			PT/Exp D	Rand Var 0
Ht: 6' 0"	Wt: 235		Consist A	MM 3033

As in 2013, the context was injury: left hamate surgery, hamstring essentially wiped out a month and a half. When on the field, he provides decent pop that is oddly constructed: an elevated hr/f overrides a heavy GB tilt. Good ct%, improving LD% gives hope—but needs to prove he can stay healthy.

Yr	Tm	AB	R	HR	RBI	SB	BA	xBA	OBP	SLG	OPS	vL	vR	bb%	ct%	Eye	G	L	F	h%	HctX	PX	xPX	hr/f	Spd	SBO	SB%	#Wk	DOM	DIS	RC/G	RAR	BPV	BPX	R$
10	2 TM *	436	38	8	37	1	241	226	265	349	614	1375	544	3	82	0.18	43	13	43	28	110	77	118	3%	78	3%	28%	8	38%	50%	3.04	-17.4	22	48	$3
11	WAS	389	48	15	52	0	267	257	334	445	779	789	776	9	80	0.50	50	15	36	30	106	120	119	13%	72	2%	0%	27	52%	22%	5.04	7.4	59	131	$10
12	WAS	83	11	3	10	0	265	224	354	398	752	762	748	13	77	0.63	66	14	20	31	114	82	96	23%	67	0%	0%	6	33%	33%	4.94	1.5	21	53	$0
13	WAS	287	29	16	59	0	272	279	307	470	777	700	803	5	85	0.36	57	20	24	27	143	114	108	28%	61	1%	0%	18	61%	17%	4.99	10.7	63	158	$10
14	WAS	341	32	11	47	0	267	263	299	399	698	820	661	5	83	0.30	55	22	23	29	99	86	88	17%	49	0%	0%	22	32%	50%	4.18	7.1	28	76	$9
1st Half		106	13	2	13	0	274	276	331	396	727	802	710	9	84	0.59	52	23	25	31	92	93	84	9%	65	0%	0%	9	44%	44%	4.68	3.9	49	132	-$1
2nd Half		235	19	9	34	0	264	252	284	400	684	825	634	3	83	0.18	57	21	22	28	103	84	90	21%	51	0%	0%	13	23%	54%	3.95	3.8	22	59	$13
15	Proj	**324**	**33**	**13**	**51**	**0**	**266**	**271**	**305**	**432**	**737**	**805**	**719**	**6**	**83**	**0.36**	**56**	**19**	**24**	**28**	**113**	**108**	**97**	**20%**	**54**	**1%**	**10%**				**4.57**	**11.0**	**39**	**103**	**$11**

Rasmus,Colby

Age: 28	Bats: L	Pos: CF	Health C	LIMA Plan C+
			PT/Exp B	Rand Var +1
Ht: 6' 2"	Wt: 195		Consist F	MM 5323

18-40-.225 in 346 AB at TOR. 2013 power fully validated in 2014, but so was his feast-or-famine inconsistency (DOM/DIS). HR have value, and LD is on the rise, but declining ct% mars all. Basically, this is an all-or-nothing player at age 28; that label will be tough to shed and tougher to turn into consistent MLB AB.

Yr	Tm	AB	R	HR	RBI	SB	BA	xBA	OBP	SLG	OPS	vL	vR	bb%	ct%	Eye	G	L	F	h%	HctX	PX	xPX	hr/f	Spd	SBO	SB%	#Wk	DOM	DIS	RC/G	RAR	BPV	BPX	R$
10	STL	464	85	23	66	12	276	251	361	498	859	810	875	12	68	0.43	32	19	49	36	100	170	130	15%	122	15%	60%	27	56%	33%	6.12	13.8	71	154	$21
11	2 TM	471	75	14	53	5	225	233	298	391	688	670	695	10	75	0.43	36	16	48	27	124	117	139	8%	122	6%	71%	25	44%	40%	3.84	-18.0	53	118	$7
12	TOR	565	75	23	75	4	223	237	289	400	689	554	740	8	74	0.32	38	20	42	26	114	115	123	13%	112	6%	57%	27	37%	33%	3.66	-20.8	37	93	$10
13	TOR	417	57	22	66	0	276	253	338	501	840	712	893	8	68	0.27	33	22	45	36	109	175	148	17%	101	1%	0%	22	59%	27%	5.85	19.1	59	148	$16
14	TOR *	369	45	18	41	4	218	241	276	427	703	684	752	7	63	0.22	34	23	42	29	111	180	170	19%	87	6%	100%	21	52%	43%	3.89	0.0	40	108	$7
1st Half		200	24	11	27	0	212	236	256	432	688	681	767	6	63	0.16	33	18	49	27	112	187	189	20%	84	0%	0%	10	50%	40%	3.57	-1.8	42	114	$7
2nd Half		169	21	7	14	4	225	246	299	420	720	686	734	10	63	0.29	36	29	36	31	110	171	149	19%	99	11%	100%	11	55%	45%	4.27	2.1	41	111	$6
15	Proj	**352**	**47**	**17**	**44**	**4**	**237**	**249**	**304**	**448**	**752**	**674**	**782**	**8**	**67**	**0.28**	**35**	**23**	**43**	**30**	**111**	**173**	**151**	**17%**	**97**	**6%**	**80%**				**4.53**	**7.0**	**48**	**127**	**$10**

JOSH PALEY

Recker,Anthony

Age: 31 Bats: R Pos: CA	Health A	LIMA Plan D	
Ht: 6' 2" Wt: 240	PT/Exp F	Rand Var 0	
	Consist B	MM 5001	

Plus power and good defense keep him employed, anemic OBP restricts him to a part-time role. How much BA pain can you endure trying to milk a half dozen HR from your second catcher? You need not endure any pain. There are better options.

Yr	Tm	AB	R	HR	RBI	SB	BA	xBA	OBP	SLG	OPS	vL	vR	bb%	ct%	Eye	G	L	F	h%	HctX	PX	xPX	hr/f	Spd	SBO	SB%	#Wk	DOM	DIS	RC/G	RAR	BPV	BPX	R$
10	a/a	288	30	7	30	1	213		263	346	608			6	68	0.21				29		109			100	3%	35%				2.89		3	7	$0
11	OAK *	362	41	9	30	4	209	208	287	341	629	730	450	10	69	0.35	50	10	40	28	70	109	76	0%	85	12%	41%	4	25%	75%	2.98	-16.0	10	22	$1
12	2 TM *	271	25	8	26	2	189	187	262	307	569	417	550	9	64	0.27	38	18	44	26	64	94	99	7%	65	5%	61%	11	27%	45%	2.50	-15.4	-30	-75	-$2
13	NYM	135	17	6	19	0	215	226	280	400	680	783	623	9	64	0.27	38	20	42	29	83	153	124	16%	70	3%	0%	24	46%	46%	3.57	-0.5	18	45	$0
14	NYM	174	18	7	27	1	201	210	246	374	620	282	703	5	63	0.16	28	18	54	27	91	152	155	11%	66	7%	50%	24	38%	63%	2.86	-3.2	7	19	$1
1st Half		110	11	2	10	1	209	189	254	327	582	465	609	5	64	0.15	28	17	55	31	98	118	168	5%	78	10%	50%	13	31%	69%	2.56	-2.9	-15	-41	-$1
2nd Half		64	7	5	17	0	188	247	232	453	685	0	871	6	63	0.17	27	20	54	20	79	211	132	23%	62	0%	0%	11	45%	55%	3.35	-0.1	51	138	$3
15	Proj	**162**	**18**	**8**	**25**	**1**	**201**	**225**	**257**	**395**	**652**	**504**	**705**	**7**	**64**	**0.21**	**31**	**19**	**49**	**26**	**85**	**164**	**138**	**16%**	**65**	**5%**	**41%**				**3.19**	**-1.0**	**14**	**38**	**$0**

Reddick,Josh

Age: 28 Bats: L Pos: RF	Health C	LIMA Plan B+	
Ht: 6' 2" Wt: 180	PT/Exp B	Rand Var -1	
	Consist B	MM 4325	

Started the year horribly, seemingly headed for AAA, then knee/ankle injuries dogged him the rest of the year. But his 2nd half was stellar, with eye-popping ct% gains, circa 2012 PX and a newfound propensity to maul RHP. Though still a platoon guy, he's at right age to maintain those 2H power gains. If so... UP: .270, 20 HR.

Yr	Tm	AB	R	HR	RBI	SB	BA	xBA	OBP	SLG	OPS	vL	vR	bb%	ct%	Eye	G	L	F	h%	HctX	PX	xPX	hr/f	Spd	SBO	SB%	#Wk	DOM	DIS	RC/G	RAR	BPV	BPX	R$
10	BOS *	513	53	15	57	4	241	259	271	408	680	1000	488	4	82	0.23	45	13	43	27	92	113	69	5%	107	13%	36%	9	44%	56%	3.50	-26.0	60	130	$8
11	BOS *	445	71	18	57	4	249	268	319	449	767	766	787	9	79	0.49	31	23	46	28	106	135	121	7%	121	7%	58%	16	56%	25%	4.77	-5.1	81	180	$12
12	OAK	611	85	32	85	11	242	249	305	463	768	751	778	8	75	0.36	29	21	50	27	103	141	131	14%	126	9%	92%	28	64%	21%	4.82	-0.7	70	175	$19
13	OAK	385	54	12	56	9	226	240	307	379	686	667	695	11	78	0.53	36	20	44	26	88	106	110	9%	114	11%	82%	24	58%	25%	3.90	-4.4	53	133	$9
14	OAK	363	53	12	54	1	264	250	316	446	763	533	849	7	83	0.44	33	18	50	29	103	115	118	8%	145	2%	50%	21	62%	14%	4.87	10.2	82	222	$11
1st Half		179	21	4	24	1	229	215	296	358	653	424	764	8	76	0.37	38	18	44	28	85	81	87	7%	161	2%	100%	10	30%	30%	3.49	-2.8	35	95	$4
2nd Half		184	32	8	30	0	299	287	337	533	869	690	921	6	89	0.60	28	17	54	30	120	144	143	9%	130	2%	0%	11	91%	0%	6.47	12.6	125	338	$18
15	Proj	**419**	**61**	**15**	**61**	**4**	**255**	**252**	**313**	**435**	**748**	**644**	**789**	**8**	**81**	**0.45**	**33**	**19**	**48**	**29**	**100**	**121**	**117**	**9%**	**129**	**6%**	**71%**				**4.66**	**8.2**	**70**	**184**	**$14**

Rendon,Anthony

Age: 25 Bats: R Pos: 3B 2B	Health A	LIMA Plan A	
Ht: 6' 1" Wt: 200	PT/Exp C	Rand Var -4	
	Consist D	MM 4445	

Across-the-board skills gain is exciting, and still in growth mode. BPI fully supports five-category value: lots of good, hard contact is his foundation. Plus power with room to expand on it, plenty of speed with knack for stealing bases. Broad base of still-developing skills means lots of paths to value; multi-position elig too. Stud.

Yr	Tm	AB	R	HR	RBI	SB	BA	xBA	OBP	SLG	OPS	vL	vR	bb%	ct%	Eye	G	L	F	h%	HctX	PX	xPX	hr/f	Spd	SBO	SB%	#Wk	DOM	DIS	RC/G	RAR	BPV	BPX	R$
10																																			
11																																			
12	aa	68	11	2	2	0	148		242	320	562			11	76	0.51				15		111			124	0%	0%				2.31		52	130	-$3
13	WAS *	478	55	12	54	2	267	272	343	421	764	830	682	10	79	0.55	41	26	34	32	120	113	115	7%	114	2%	64%	20	45%	20%	5.01	14.0	64	160	$12
14	WAS	613	111	21	83	17	287	279	351	473	824	825	824	9	83	0.56	40	20	40	32	136	126	146	10%	121	12%	85%	27	67%	11%	5.97	38.9	88	238	$32
1st Half		313	53	12	46	6	281	272	338	479	817	963	773	8	82	0.47	39	19	42	31	147	129	167	11%	133	9%	86%	14	71%	7%	5.80	18.7	88	238	$29
2nd Half		300	58	9	37	11	293	286	364	467	831	705	881	9	84	0.66	42	21	37	32	125	123	125	10%	109	15%	85%	13	62%	15%	6.15	20.6	89	241	$35
15	Proj	**603**	**94**	**19**	**78**	**17**	**283**	**276**	**353**	**461**	**814**	**841**	**804**	**9**	**82**	**0.56**	**40**	**21**	**39**	**32**	**129**	**127**	**132**	**10%**	**114**	**12%**	**83%**				**5.80**	**35.9**	**83**	**219**	**$29**

Revere,Ben

Age: 27 Bats: L Pos: CF	Health C	LIMA Plan B	
Ht: 5' 9" Wt: 165	PT/Exp B	Rand Var -1	
	Consist A	MM 0555	

One trick pony, but it's a valuable fantasy trick. High GB% with elite Spd and ct% is a recipe for lots of SBs. It's a pity that hacktastic approach yields poor bb%, as pedestrian OBA caps SB opps. Ankle surgery in October, but should be good to go by spring. Check back then, as his value is all in those wheels.

Yr	Tm	AB	R	HR	RBI	SB	BA	xBA	OBP	SLG	OPS	vL	vR	bb%	ct%	Eye	G	L	F	h%	HctX	PX	xPX	hr/f	Spd	SBO	SB%	#Wk	DOM	DIS	RC/G	RAR	BPV	BPX	R$
10	MIN *	389	35	1	20	28	267	262	316	314	631	368	450	7	88	0.58	68	14	18	30	93	31	40	0%	145	37%	65%	5	20%	80%	3.27	-17.8	34	74	$12
11	MIN *	582	68	1	37	40	267	291	304	311	615	609	624	5	91	0.58	69	20	12	29	52	27	18	0%	156	31%	78%	22	36%	14%	3.38	-24.1	44	98	$20
12	MIN *	605	78	0	37	45	294	278	330	337	667	676	675	5	90	0.53	67	19	15	33	73	26	23	0%	161	30%	80%	24	29%	21%	4.15	-9.1	41	103	$27
13	PHI	315	37	0	17	22	305	277	338	352	691	858	641	5	89	0.44	59	23	17	34	87	32	31	0%	155	30%	73%	15	27%	33%	4.34	2.1	38	95	$15
14	PHI	601	71	2	28	49	306	293	325	361	686	763	653	2	92	0.27	65	21	14	33	64	33	23	3%	175	33%	86%	27	22%	11%	4.51	11.2	52	141	$34
1st Half		280	35	1	9	23	289	292	309	354	663	871	596	3	91	0.31	67	20	14	32	70	36	25	3%	189	33%	88%	14	29%	14%	4.21	2.7	56	151	$25
2nd Half		321	36	1	19	26	321	293	338	368	706	696	711	2	93	0.22	63	22	15	34	59	31	22	2%	143	32%	84%	13	15%	8%	4.78	8.0	44	119	$41
15	Proj	**539**	**63**	**1**	**28**	**41**	**298**	**286**	**327**	**347**	**674**	**736**	**648**	**4**	**91**	**0.41**	**64**	**21**	**15**	**33**	**70**	**33**	**25**	**1%**	**161**	**32%**	**80%**				**4.21**	**5.3**	**39**	**103**	**$28**

Reyes,Jose

Age: 32 Bats: B Pos: SS	Health D	LIMA Plan A	
Ht: 6' 0" Wt: 195	PT/Exp A	Rand Var 0	
	Consist A	MM 2545	

First sign of decline? While he still owns a strong ct%, 2nd half included fewer BB, less hard contact, and a big drop in xPX. Still has excellent speed, but SB% was an outlier on the high side, and he's reaching an age of declining SB. Might have another year at this level, but don't blindly expect another 30 SB.

Yr	Tm	AB	R	HR	RBI	SB	BA	xBA	OBP	SLG	OPS	vL	vR	bb%	ct%	Eye	G	L	F	h%	HctX	PX	xPX	hr/f	Spd	SBO	SB%	#Wk	DOM	DIS	RC/G	RAR	BPV	BPX	R$
10	NYM	563	83	11	54	30	282	274	321	428	749	744	750	5	89	0.49	43	18	40	30	101	88	67	6%	136	29%	75%	25	52%	12%	4.81	10.2	79	172	$24
11	NYM	537	101	7	44	39	337	290	384	493	877	842	888	7	92	1.05	42	21	37	36	110	91	88	4%	180	27%	85%	23	74%	4%	7.53	47.7	113	251	$36
12	MIA	642	86	11	57	40	287	291	347	433	780	753	792	9	91	1.13	46	22	32	30	109	84	83	6%	127	27%	78%	27	74%	4%	5.46	28.5	90	225	$29
13	TOR	382	58	10	37	15	296	275	353	427	780	705	804	8	88	0.72	46	21	33	32	99	84	82	9%	98	18%	71%	17	59%	24%	5.38	21.1	66	165	$18
14	TOR	610	94	9	51	30	287	268	328	398	726	709	732	6	88	0.52	42	23	36	31	89	77	66	5%	131	19%	94%	26	42%	8%	4.93	30.0	67	181	$29
1st Half		280	44	6	23	16	261	270	318	407	725	631	761	8	88	0.66	39	21	40	28	96	98	80	6%	128	24%	94%	13	46%	8%	4.72	12.1	84	227	$23
2nd Half		330	50	3	28	14	309	267	336	391	727	777	708	4	88	0.39	44	24	32	34	84	60	54	3%	123	15%	93%	13	38%	8%	5.12	16.9	50	135	$34
15	Proj	**554**	**84**	**10**	**49**	**26**	**289**	**276**	**336**	**413**	**750**	**721**	**760**	**7**	**89**	**0.65**	**43**	**22**	**35**	**31**	**96**	**83**	**73**	**6%**	**126**	**20%**	**83%**				**5.10**	**29.1**	**76**	**200**	**$27**

Reynolds,Mark

Age: 31 Bats: R Pos: 1B 3B	Health A	LIMA Plan D+	
Ht: 6' 2" Wt: 220	PT/Exp B	Rand Var +5	
	Consist A	MM 4203	

Former poster child for Three True Outcomes, but now doesn't walk enough to claim the title, and his managers are noticing (declining AB). When he hits it in the air, the ball goes far, but he's gotta hit it more to have value. Discount his vLHP splits (just 98 AB), but not his RC/G or R$ trend. Too many "buts" to reconcile.

Yr	Tm	AB	R	HR	RBI	SB	BA	xBA	OBP	SLG	OPS	vL	vR	bb%	ct%	Eye	G	L	F	h%	HctX	PX	xPX	hr/f	Spd	SBO	SB%	#Wk	DOM	DIS	RC/G	RAR	BPV	BPX	R$
10	ARI	499	79	32	85	7	198	218	320	433	753	913	694	14	58	0.39	32	13	55	26	83	196	149	20%	92	8%	64%	26	46%	38%	4.24	-31.8	46	100	$10
11	BAL	534	84	37	86	6	221	248	323	483	806	781	814	12	63	0.38	39	13	48	27	104	209	171	23%	73	8%	60%	27	56%	15%	4.92	-21.9	69	153	$16
12	BAL	457	65	23	69	1	221	236	335	429	763	722	778	14	65	0.46	37	20	42	28	100	161	138	18%	72	3%	25%	25	32%	44%	4.50	-12.9	41	103	$8
13	2 AL	445	55	21	67	3	220	217	306	393	699	725	684	10	65	0.33	39	18	42	29	94	132	125	17%	77	4%	75%	27	44%	48%	3.86	-9.8	13	33	$9
14	MIL	378	47	22	45	5	196	223	287	394	681	573	719	11	68	0.39	38	14	48	22	94	146	155	18%	89	7%	83%	26	46%	38%	3.58	-7.2	38	103	$6
1st Half		239	32	13	31	5	213	220	308	402	710	613	747	12	65	0.38	41	16	44	27	82	146	137	19%	97	9%	83%	14	43%	36%	4.03	-1.0	31	84	$11
2nd Half		139	15	9	14	0	165	220	250	381	631	485	675	10	73	0.39	34	11	55	15	116	146	184	16%	79	0%	0%	12	50%	42%	2.87	-5.9	53	143	-$2
15	Proj	**248**	**32**	**14**	**33**	**2**	**201**	**227**	**297**	**402**	**699**	**656**	**715**	**11**	**67**	**0.39**	**37**	**15**	**47**	**24**	**99**	**154**	**151**	**18%**	**81**	**4%**	**70%**				**3.74**	**-3.3**	**30**	**78**	**$5**

Rios,Alex

Age: 34 Bats: R Pos: RF	Health B	LIMA Plan B+	
Ht: 6' 5" Wt: 210	PT/Exp A	Rand Var -2	
	Consist C	MM 2335	

Ankle injuries in 2nd half; thumb injury ended year in August. xPX, HctX didn't flinch, though HR took the brunt (thank outlying hr/f). Struggles vs. RHP may now beg for future platoon role. Don't rely on speed skill gains; that won't hold up at 34. Won't touch $30 again either, but some profit potential if age scares others away.

Yr	Tm	AB	R	HR	RBI	SB	BA	xBA	OBP	SLG	OPS	vL	vR	bb%	ct%	Eye	G	L	F	h%	HctX	PX	xPX	hr/f	Spd	SBO	SB%	#Wk	DOM	DIS	RC/G	RAR	BPV	BPX	R$
10	CHW	567	89	21	88	34	284	277	334	457	791	717	814	6	84	0.41	45	17	38	31	114	109	107	12%	120	33%	71%	26	58%	19%	5.16	-0.1	72	157	$31
11	CHW	537	64	13	44	11	227	255	265	348	613	704	578	5	87	0.40	42	18	39	24	98	76	76	7%	108	15%	65%	27	48%	26%	2.96	-36.3	54	120	$7
12	CHW	605	93	25	91	23	304	288	334	516	850	857	848	4	85	0.28	40	22	38	33	119	125	111	13%	127	21%	79%	27	59%	19%	6.27	23.6	87	218	$34
13	2 AL	616	83	18	81	42	278	269	324	432	756	889	714	6	82	0.38	44	21	35	31	85	102	83	10%	118	31%	86%	27	52%	26%	5.09	14.3	61	153	$36
14	TEX	492	54	4	54	17	280	260	311	398	709	898	646	4	81	0.25	43	24	34	34	92	89	91	3%	143	22%	65%	23	43%	30%	4.26	5.1	49	132	$18
1st Half		310	34	3	34	13	300	263	332	432	765	1124	660	5	81	0.29	44	24	33	36	91	92	88	4%	171	25%	62%	14	50%	29%	4.99	8.7	61	165	$24
2nd Half		182	20	1	20	4	247	256	274	341	614	602	620	3	81	0.18	42	23	35	30	95	84	96	2%	87	14%	80%	9	33%	33%	3.16	-4.6	27	73	$7
15	Proj	**574**	**72**	**11**	**70**	**14**	**275**	**267**	**309**	**412**	**721**	**805**	**692**	**5**	**82**	**0.28**	**42**	**22**	**35**	**32**	**96**	**100**	**93**	**7%**	**121**	**16%**	**65%**				**4.35**	**5.8**	**54**	**142**	**$21**

JOSH PALEY

Rivera,Rene

Age: 31	Bats: R	Pos: CA	Health A	LIMA Plan D+	
Ht: 5' 10"	Wt: 215		PT/Exp D	Rand Var -3	
			Consist C	MM 3003	

2013 tiny-sample xPX looked like a random outlier in a career lacking any offensive upside. Then he went out and did it again for a half-season. But before you chalk this up as another 30+ catcher power spike, check the platoon splits. Still doesn't have much of a clue vs. RHP. Best case: he repeats this in a platoon role.

Yr	Tm	AB	R	HR	RBI	SB	BA	xBA	OBP	SLG	OPS	vL	vR	bb%	ct%	Eye	G	L	F	h%	HctX	PX	xPX	hr/f	Spd	SBO	SB%	#Wk	DOM	DIS	RC/G	RAR	BPV	BPX	R$
10	a/a	162	12	6	21	0	242		270	421	691			4	75	0.15				29		132			85	0%	0%				3.83		40	87	$1
11	MIN *	253	20	4	22	0	183	180	232	283	515	555	360	6	74	0.24	44	8	48	23	82	81	96	3%	63	0%	0%	15	27%	53%	2.05	-18.8	-5	-11	-$5
12	aaa	288	23	7	25	0	179		239	296	535			7	73	0.30				22		83			87	2%	0%				2.15		2	5	-$4
13	SD *	318	26	3	30	0	242	202	270	325	595	529	618	4	76	0.16	48	13	38	31	124	67	144	0%	77	4%	0%	10	10%	50%	2.84	-8.1	-8	-20	$1
14	SD	294	27	11	44	0	252	252	319	432	751	881	684	8	74	0.36	35	21	44	30	107	138	138	11%	67	0%	0%	27	48%	37%	4.63	10.1	46	124	$6
1st Half		118	7	5	17	0	220	222	276	424	699	846	635	6	73	0.22	31	13	56	26	96	162	171	10%	57	0%	0%	14	50%	36%	3.66	1.0	51	138	$0
2nd Half		176	20	6	27	0	273	262	347	438	784	897	719	10	75	0.45	38	26	36	33	114	122	117	13%	81	0%	0%	13	46%	38%	5.32	9.7	44	119	$11
15	Proj	**300**	**26**	**8**	**37**	**0**	**235**	**227**	**286**	**373**	**659**	**774**	**611**	**7**	**75**	**0.28**	**41**	**16**	**43**	**29**	**109**	**109**	**134**	**8%**	**69**	**1%**	**0%**				**3.51**	**1.1**	**12**	**31**	**$2**

Rizzo,Anthony

Age: 25	Bats: L	Pos: 1B	Health A	LIMA Plan A	
Ht: 6' 3"	Wt: 240		PT/Exp A	Rand Var -2	
			Consist F	MM 5145	

Reached 30-HR level more by minimizing GBs than by improving his power. xPX says he may have outperformed his power skill, actually. But good news abounds: mashes both vL and vR; enough ct% to set a nice BA floor; enough bb% to add value in OBP leagues. A potential new entrant in the first-round conversation.

Yr	Tm	AB	R	HR	RBI	SB	BA	xBA	OBP	SLG	OPS	vL	vR	bb%	ct%	Eye	G	L	F	h%	HctX	PX	xPX	hr/f	Spd	SBO	SB%	#Wk	DOM	DIS	RC/G	RAR	BPV	BPX	R$
10	aa	414	49	14	60	5	242		299	422	722			8	75	0.32				29		138			86	7%	83%				4.27		51	111	$8
11	SD *	484	49	16	72	6	222	228	294	396	690	618	495	9	68	0.32	43	13	44	29	84	146	126	3%	59	14%	44%	11	27%	73%	3.61	-39.9	26	58	$7
12	CHC *	594	80	32	94	4	290	291	340	510	849	599	892	7	79	0.37	45	24	30	32	112	136	119	18%	83	6%	51%	15	60%	20%	6.09	10.9	68	170	$26
13	CHC	606	71	23	80	6	233	269	323	419	742	625	796	11	79	0.60	43	20	38	26	112	130	124	13%	68	7%	55%	27	63%	7%	4.34	-4.5	65	163	$13
14	CHC	524	89	32	78	5	286	286	386	527	913	928	907	12	78	0.63	36	22	42	31	106	164	135	19%	72	6%	56%	25	72%	4%	6.90	40.2	91	246	$28
1st Half		291	53	17	44	1	278	285	389	505	894	932	881	14	79	0.79	40	23	38	30	105	150	128	20%	85	4%	25%	14	64%	7%	6.60	20.3	91	246	$28
2nd Half		233	36	15	34	4	296	288	383	554	937	924	939	9	77	0.44	31	22	47	33	108	181	143	18%	63	8%	80%	11	82%	0%	7.26	20.0	92	249	$27
15	Proj	**594**	**87**	**33**	**91**	**6**	**278**	**283**	**366**	**509**	**875**	**822**	**895**	**11**	**78**	**0.53**	**38**	**21**	**41**	**31**	**107**	**163**	**130**	**17%**	**67**	**6%**	**59%**				**6.25**	**35.5**	**82**	**217**	**$28**

Roberts,Brian

Age: 37	Bats: B	Pos: 2B	Health	LIMA Plan	
Ht: 5' 9"	Wt: 175		PT/Exp	Rand Var	
			Consist	MM	

This skill set is greatly diminished from its once-elite peak, which has finally scrolled off the top of this box. There's still sufficient ct% and speed here, even a hint of power. But none of that matters because health is a skill too, and his lease on that skill expired at age 32. He chose not to renew.

Yr	Tm	AB	R	HR	RBI	SB	BA	xBA	OBP	SLG	OPS	vL	vR	bb%	ct%	Eye	G	L	F	h%	HctX	PX	xPX	hr/f	Spd	SBO	SB%	#Wk	DOM	DIS	RC/G	RAR	BPV	BPX	R$
10	BAL	230	28	4	15	12	278	248	354	391	745	801	726	10	83	0.65	34	22	45	32	93	83	112	5%	103	19%	86%	12	58%	25%	5.04	2.5	50	109	$8
11	BAL	163	18	3	19	6	221	240	273	331	604	583	613	7	87	0.57	29	23	49	24	115	71	121	4%	98	19%	86%	8	50%	13%	3.07	-7.9	50	111	$1
12	BAL *	103	6	1	8	1	186	202	254	248	502	607	370	8	80	0.45	45	16	39	23	43	48	25	0%	84	8%	50%	4	0%	100%	1.92	-7.4	2	5	-$3
13	BAL	265	33	8	39	3	249	262	312	392	704	768	665	9	83	0.59	36	24	39	27	96	92	119	9%	89	6%	75%	15	53%	27%	4.21	4.0	54	135	$6
14	NYY	317	40	5	21	7	237	256	300	360	659	671	655	8	83	0.53	35	25	40	27	109	86	114	5%	134	14%	64%	18	44%	44%	3.51	1.1	60	162	$5
1st Half		237	31	4	17	7	236	254	311	354	665	673	662	10	84	0.64	38	24	38	27	109	79	105	5%	134	17%	64%	14	50%	36%	3.56	1.2	59	159	$8
2nd Half		80	9	1	4	0	238	265	265	375	640	657	634	4	83	0.21	25	29	46	28	108	104	139	3%	110	0%	0%	4	25%	75%	3.32	-0.2	55	149	-$4
15	Proj																																		

Robertson,Daniel T.

Age: 29	Bats: R	Pos: LF CF	Health A	LIMA Plan D	
Ht: 5' 8"	Wt: 170		PT/Exp C	Rand Var -3	
			Consist B	MM 1411	

0-21-.271 in 177 AB at TEX. That he got so many AB shows scope of the injury epidemic in TEX. Owns acceptable contact skills and some wheels, but has had the entirety of his 20s to parlay those into a playable skill set, and it hasn't happened. Only another landslide of injuries will get him another 177-AB opportunity.

Yr	Tm	AB	R	HR	RBI	SB	BA	xBA	OBP	SLG	OPS	vL	vR	bb%	ct%	Eye	G	L	F	h%	HctX	PX	xPX	hr/f	Spd	SBO	SB%	#Wk	DOM	DIS	RC/G	RAR	BPV	BPX	R$
10																																			
11	aa	438	66	3	30	14	215		280	292	572			8	85	0.61				25		54			125	19%	65%				2.60		39	87	$3
12	aaa	490	45	1	24	11	225		272	286	558			6	85	0.41				26		45			108	18%	53%				2.42		20	50	$1
13	aaa	484	56	1	33	14	205		261	271	533			7	82	0.43				25		46			136	19%	65%				2.23		24	60	$2
14	TEX *	227	30	2	26	7	262	252	323	351	675	821	478	8	84	0.56	54	16	29	31	55	67	26	0%	129	17%	64%	21	33%	48%	3.82	-0.4	46	124	$6
1st Half		96	14	2	9	2	223	251	273	341	614	696	361	6	77	0.30	53	19	28	27	61	88	32	0%	120	20%	52%	9	11%	56%	2.87	-3.0	30	81	$1
2nd Half		131	16	0	17	5	290	253	356	359	715	856	525	10	89	0.93	55	16	30	33	55	54	25	0%	124	16%	71%	12	50%	42%	4.60	2.8	56	151	$9
15	Proj	**129**	**16**	**1**	**11**	**4**	**237**	**246**	**295**	**313**	**608**	**740**	**453**	**8**	**84**	**0.51**	**54**	**17**	**29**	**28**	**57**	**57**	**28**	**2%**	**133**	**18%**	**63%**				**3.01**	**-2.9**	**31**	**81**	**$3**

Rodriguez,Sean

Age: 30	Bats: R	Pos: 2B DH	Health A	LIMA Plan D+	
Ht: 6' 0"	Wt: 200		PT/Exp D	Rand Var +4	
			Consist B	MM 4213	

There's always been latent power; so what? Used 1st half hr/f spike to cover up underlying issues: plate skills went from "below average" to "avert your eyes!". Still can't hit RHPs at all, which trumps any optimism about the 2nd half xPX/HctX spikes. But he hasn't hit LHPs in 3 years either, which puts his job in jeopardy.

Yr	Tm	AB	R	HR	RBI	SB	BA	xBA	OBP	SLG	OPS	vL	vR	bb%	ct%	Eye	G	L	F	h%	HctX	PX	xPX	hr/f	Spd	SBO	SB%	#Wk	DOM	DIS	RC/G	RAR	BPV	BPX	R$
10	TAM	343	53	9	40	13	251	239	308	397	705	817	642	6	72	0.22	42	19	39	32	99	112	120	10%	108	21%	81%	27	37%	48%	4.01	-18.5	23	50	$10
11	TAM	373	45	8	36	11	223	235	323	357	679	864	567	9	77	0.44	41	17	41	27	102	98	91	7%	115	20%	61%	27	52%	26%	3.31	-29.4	40	89	$5
12	TAM	301	36	6	32	5	213	220	281	326	607	655	575	8	75	0.36	47	15	38	26	86	82	76	7%	104	7%	100%	25	20%	48%	3.01	-17.4	16	40	$1
13	TAM	195	21	5	23	1	246	227	320	385	704	745	545	8	70	0.29	36	23	41	33	84	110	81	9%	91	8%	25%	27	33%	44%	3.76	-4.3	12	30	$2
14	TAM	237	30	12	41	2	211	262	258	443	701	729	666	4	72	0.15	39	17	44	24	108	170	137	16%	109	9%	67%	27	52%	30%	3.44	-4.4	67	181	$4
1st Half		117	19	7	24	1	205	262	252	453	705	730	669	4	69	0.14	41	15	44	23	99	187	120	20%	98	7%	100%	14	50%	36%	3.49	-2.0	66	178	$6
2nd Half		120	11	5	17	1	217	262	264	433	697	729	663	4	75	0.17	36	19	45	25	117	155	153	12%	114	12%	50%	13	54%	23%	3.39	-2.5	68	184	$3
15	Proj	**263**	**31**	**9**	**37**	**3**	**231**	**245**	**290**	**410**	**700**	**750**	**637**	**6**	**72**	**0.23**	**39**	**19**	**42**	**28**	**99**	**137**	**112**	**12%**	**105**	**10%**	**60%**				**3.68**	**2.3**	**42**	**110**	**$6**

Rollins,Jimmy

Age: 36	Bats: B	Pos: SS	Health B	LIMA Plan A	
Ht: 5' 8"	Wt: 180		PT/Exp A	Rand Var 0	
			Consist B	MM 2425	

2013 hr/f was an outlier to the low side; as it mended, so did HR total. Once-elite ct% skill is fading, with minimal impact on overall value. SB efficiency and that hr/f rebound ensure double-digit HR/SB, albeit with a BA penalty. If you insulate your BA elsewhere, there should be another year of counting stats to enjoy.

Yr	Tm	AB	R	HR	RBI	SB	BA	xBA	OBP	SLG	OPS	vL	vR	bb%	ct%	Eye	G	L	F	h%	HctX	PX	xPX	hr/f	Spd	SBO	SB%	#Wk	DOM	DIS	RC/G	RAR	BPV	BPX	R$
10	PHI	350	48	8	41	17	243	276	320	374	694	773	657	10	91	1.25	46	17	37	25	109	78	82	7%	98	18%	94%	17	71%	6%	4.28	-2.3	78	170	$10
11	PHI	567	87	16	63	30	268	263	338	399	736	609	779	9	90	0.98	39	20	41	28	114	78	94	8%	101	22%	79%	26	62%	12%	4.72	3.6	72	160	$24
12	PHI	632	102	23	68	30	250	266	316	427	743	612	804	9	85	0.65	39	19	42	26	97	106	95	10%	98	22%	86%	27	67%	15%	4.73	11.6	73	183	$24
13	PHI	600	65	6	39	22	252	250	318	348	667	648	674	9	85	0.63	38	23	39	29	81	72	61	3%	94	17%	79%	27	44%	19%	3.84	5.9	44	110	$15
14	PHI	538	78	17	55	28	243	252	323	394	717	679	732	11	81	0.64	40	19	40	27	92	100	101	10%	117	22%	82%	24	50%	29%	4.41	18.0	64	173	$21
1st Half		301	37	8	31	14	249	251	332	385	718	764	703	11	81	0.67	39	22	39	28	96	93	103	8%	110	21%	74%	14	43%	29%	4.35	10.1	56	151	$20
2nd Half		237	41	9	24	14	236	255	312	405	717	598	775	10	82	0.60	42	16	42	25	87	108	97	11%	118	24%	93%	10	60%	30%	4.47	8.8	71	192	$23
15	Proj	**505**	**72**	**13**	**48**	**21**	**247**	**255**	**320**	**385**	**705**	**648**	**728**	**10**	**83**	**0.62**	**41**	**20**	**39**	**28**	**91**	**95**	**88**	**8%**	**106**	**19%**	**82%**				**4.26**	**15.4**	**65**	**171**	**$18**

Romero,Stefen

Age: 26	Bats: R	Pos: RF	Health A	LIMA Plan D	
Ht: 6' 2"	Wt: 220		PT/Exp D	Rand Var +1	
			Consist D	MM 2101	

3-11-.192 in 177 AB at SEA. 1st half split below is the MLB work, where those three HR represent about all that went right for him in SEA. Then he went back to PCL and found conditions much more to his liking (1.055 OPS). Short term, he'll get more chances to build up his travel miles between those two very different worlds.

Yr	Tm	AB	R	HR	RBI	SB	BA	xBA	OBP	SLG	OPS	vL	vR	bb%	ct%	Eye	G	L	F	h%	HctX	PX	xPX	hr/f	Spd	SBO	SB%	#Wk	DOM	DIS	RC/G	RAR	BPV	BPX	R$
10																																			
11																																			
12	aa	216	34	9	45	5	301		341	519	860			6	79	0.29				34		137			100	17%	61%				6.19		70	175	$10
13	aaa	375	34	7	50	5	222		258	341	599			5	72	0.17				29		95			93	14%	53%				2.77		2	5	$3
14	SEA *	328	36	10	35	1	233	232	253	383	636	531	539	3	74	0.11	42	17	41	28	71	107	92	6%	123	14%	8%	21	24%	52%	2.85	-8.5	28	76	$4
1st Half		152	18	3	11	0	191	213	212	316	527	530	615	3	71	0.09	41	17	43	25	72	96	103	7%	133	14%	0%	14	36%	36%	1.87	-9.3	9	24	-$3
2nd Half		176	18	7	24	1	270	257	290	441	731	536	100	3	77	0.13	48	19	33	31	48	115	33	0%	104	14%	12%	7	0%	86%	3.94	1.0	40	108	$10
15	Proj	**101**	**11**	**2**	**13**	**1**	**241**	**228**	**305**	**358**	**663**	**739**	**512**	**4**	**74**	**0.16**	**45**	**18**	**37**	**31**	**58**	**92**	**61**	**7%**	**106**	**14%**	**34%**				**3.01**	**-3.1**	**7**	**19**	**$2**

JOSH PALEY

Rosales,Adam

Age: 32 Bats: R Pos: 1B	Health B	LIMA Plan F
Ht: 6' 1" Wt: 195	PT/Exp D	Rand Var -2
	Consist B	MM 2201

4-19-.262 in 164 AB at TEX. His speed is an asset, though rarely utilized. And he isn't totally lost against LHPs. Sounds like faint praise? Well, when you post a 25% LD% and your xBA still registers under .230, you need to lower standards for what's praise-worthy. Loss of MI eligibility slams the door on his value.

Yr Tm	AB	R	HR	RBI	SB	BA	xBA	OBP	SLG	OPS	vL	vR	bb%	ct%	Eye	G	L	F	h%	HctX	PX	xPX	hr/f	Spd	SBO	SB%	#Wk	DOM	DIS	RC/G	RAR	BPV	BPX	R$
10 OAK	255	31	7	31	2	271	252	321	400	721	794	681	7	75	0.29	38	28	34	34	81	88	68	11%	140	6%	50%	19	37%	37%	4.39	-9.1	26	57	$6
11 OAK *	208	19	4	22	1	166	191	213	244	457	486	184	6	74	0.23	46	14	40	21	52	54	91	10%	104	5%	33%	12	17%	50%	1.55	-27.9	-16	-36	-$4
12 OAK *	374	41	7	38	3	207	236	262	317	579	558	757	7	74	0.28	34	28	38	26	72	85	91	7%	95	7%	49%	16	38%	50%	2.62	-31.3	7	18	$0
13 2AL *	185	17	5	16	1	182	218	231	298	529	721	401	6	77	0.28	48	15	37	21	72	81	87	12%	83	6%	32%	21	33%	33%	2.08	-15.0	11	28	-$3
14 TEX *	436	45	8	44	6	226	223	276	337	612	824	626	6	73	0.25	33	25	42	29	93	89	91	8%	123	8%	74%	14	21%	57%	3.06	-14.3	13	35	$5
1st Half	272	25	4	25	2	204	221	251	312	563			6	71	0.22				27		88			111	3%	100%	1	0%	100%	2.53		3	8	$3
2nd Half	164	20	4	19	4	262	230	328	378	706	824	626	7	74	0.31	33	25	42	33	95	90	91	8%	109	13%	67%	13	23%	54%	4.06	-0.5	19	51	$9
15 Proj	**164**	**17**	**4**	**17**	**2**	**219**	**232**	**276**	**342**	**618**	**664**	**570**	**6**	**74**	**0.27**	**39**	**22**	**39**	**27**	**77**	**94**	**88**	**9%**	**100**	**9%**	**64%**				**2.97**	**-6.1**	**7**	**19**	**$0**

Rosario,Wilin

Age: 26 Bats: R Pos: CA	Health A	LIMA Plan B+
Ht: 5' 11" Wt: 220	PT/Exp C	Rand Var +1
	Consist A	MM 4145

If every opposing pitcher was a lefty, he'd win an MVP. Any hope for solving RHPs? PRO: Ct% and Eye reached career highs, hr/f has room to rebound, wasn't hopeless vR in 2012-13. CON: Too many GBs for a slugger; HctX, xPX trends are troubling. VERDICT: Too young to give up on. Expect some improvement.

Yr Tm	AB	R	HR	RBI	SB	BA	xBA	OBP	SLG	OPS	vL	vR	bb%	ct%	Eye	G	L	F	h%	HctX	PX	xPX	hr/f	Spd	SBO	SB%	#Wk	DOM	DIS	RC/G	RAR	BPV	BPX	R$
10 aa	270	34	17	42	1	275		316	520	837			6	79	0.29				29		155			98	1%	100%				5.81		83	180	$9
11 COL *	459	43	20	42	1	225	251	250	406	656	1089	546	3	75	0.14	40	20	40	26	120	121	137	21%	104	4%	24%	4	50%	25%	3.27	-15.5	38	84	$5
12 COL	396	67	28	71	4	270	278	312	530	843	1140	726	6	75	0.25	46	17	37	29	117	165	142	25%	76	11%	44%	27	67%	15%	5.55	14.6	69	173	$18
13 COL	449	63	21	79	4	292	266	315	486	801	901	760	3	76	0.14	41	23	36	34	111	133	122	17%	82	5%	80%	25	44%	28%	5.50	22.5	42	105	$21
14 COL	382	46	13	54	1	267	275	305	435	739	989	650	6	82	0.33	50	19	31	30	94	120	92	13%	57	1%	100%	23	52%	17%	4.68	13.4	53	143	$11
1st Half	208	24	8	30	1	245	270	279	433	712	956	616	5	79	0.25	50	16	35	28	90	139	101	14%	65	3%	100%	12	50%	25%	4.16	4.7	58	157	$11
2nd Half	174	22	5	24	0	293	282	335	437	772	1034	688	6	85	0.46	51	23	27	32	98	100	82	13%	59	0%	0%	11	55%	9%	5.34	9.4	53	143	$12
15 Proj	**439**	**58**	**19**	**67**	**2**	**271**	**275**	**305**	**461**	**766**	**995**	**680**	**5**	**79**	**0.25**	**44**	**20**	**35**	**30**	**105**	**134**	**110**	**16%**	**67**	**3%**	**65%**				**4.92**	**19.2**	**52**	**138**	**$17**

Ross,Cody

Age: 34 Bats: R Pos: LF RF	Health F	LIMA Plan D
Ht: 5' 10" Wt: 195	PT/Exp D	Rand Var 0
	Consist C	MM 2121

2-15-.252 in 202 AB at ARI. Played hurt all year: missed most of April with hip injury, then calf problem plagued him throughout 2nd half. Destroys lefties when healthy; some marginal value to be extracted here if used that way. Any starts vs. RHP are a clear avoid, though.

Yr Tm	AB	R	HR	RBI	SB	BA	xBA	OBP	SLG	OPS	vL	vR	bb%	ct%	Eye	G	L	F	h%	HctX	PX	xPX	hr/f	Spd	SBO	SB%	#Wk	DOM	DIS	RC/G	RAR	BPV	BPX	R$
10 2 NL	525	71	14	65	9	269	261	322	413	735	883	687	7	77	0.31	46	21	34	33	105	103	94	10%	105	8%	82%	27	33%	37%	4.59	-10.2	37	80	$15
11 SF	405	54	14	52	5	240	241	325	405	730	698	740	11	76	0.51	34	18	48	28	99	122	120	9%	82	7%	71%	22	41%	41%	4.35	-11.1	51	113	$8
12 BOS	476	70	22	81	2	267	262	326	481	807	1010	729	8	73	0.33	36	22	42	32	103	153	118	15%	80	4%	40%	23	57%	30%	5.34	8.4	56	140	$16
13 ARI	317	33	8	38	3	278	264	331	413	745	1012	603	7	84	0.50	43	21	35	31	109	90	103	8%	74	6%	60%	19	37%	26%	4.75	6.3	48	120	$8
14 ARI *	233	16	2	19	0	247	227	294	310	604	639	621	6	78	0.31	46	24	30	31	96	53	69	4%	77	0%	0%	19	32%	42%	3.08	-4.8	-6	-16	$0
1st Half	170	9	1	12	0	214	206	256	260	516	563	521	5	79	0.26	47	21	32	27	84	38	63	3%	79	0%	0%	12	33%	50%	2.16	-8.3	-19	-51	-$1
2nd Half	63	7	1	7	0	333	272	386	444	830	762	882	9	78	0.43	44	30	26	42	121	92	80	8%	83	0%	0%	7	29%	29%	6.65	4.8	29	78	$3
15 Proj	**213**	**23**	**5**	**25**	**1**	**277**	**255**	**332**	**399**	**732**	**813**	**689**	**8**	**79**	**0.39**	**43**	**24**	**33**	**33**	**106**	**94**	**91**	**8%**	**79**	**3%**	**60%**				**4.65**	**5.5**	**20**	**52**	**$6**

Ross,David

Age: 38 Bats: R Pos: CA	Health D	LIMA Plan D
Ht: 6' 2" Wt: 230	PT/Exp F	Rand Var +5
	Consist C	MM 5001

A few certainties amid these small data samples: he'll whiff nearly 40% of the time; DL stints becoming more frequent. Power used to be the counterpoint to those concerns, but xPX/HctX suggest that's starting to fade. Low AB totals minimize the BA pain, but the prospect of any payoff on your $1 investment is just about gone.

Yr Tm	AB	R	HR	RBI	SB	BA	xBA	OBP	SLG	OPS	vL	vR	bb%	ct%	Eye	G	L	F	h%	HctX	PX	xPX	hr/f	Spd	SBO	SB%	#Wk	DOM	DIS	RC/G	RAR	BPV	BPX	R$
10 ATL	121	15	2	28	0	289	281	392	479	871	886	834	14	77	0.71	38	21	41	36	101	150	125	5%	88	3%	0%	26	35%	46%	6.51	7.8	84	183	$3
11 ATL	152	14	6	23	0	263	236	333	428	761	613	833	10	66	0.31	28	26	45	36	98	132	154	14%	71	2%	0%	24	38%	50%	4.80	2.6	14	31	$2
12 ATL	176	18	9	23	1	256	233	321	449	770	712	818	9	66	0.30	34	23	43	34	100	142	152	18%	68	2%	100%	25	44%	48%	5.03	4.6	18	45	$3
13 BOS	102	11	4	10	1	216	199	298	382	681	804	544	10	59	0.26	39	15	46	32	94	151	121	15%	58	4%	100%	16	50%	50%	3.68	0.0	-4	-10	-$1
14 BOS	152	16	7	15	0	184	225	260	368	629	809	518	10	62	0.28	38	21	40	24	75	161	118	18%	80	3%	0%	25	32%	60%	2.92	-1.9	21	57	-$1
1st Half	91	7	4	7	0	176	221	235	363	597	734	492	7	64	0.21	40	16	44	22	81	163	139	16%	83	7%	0%	14	43%	57%	2.49	-2.7	27	73	-$2
2nd Half	61	9	3	8	0	197	229	296	377	673	965	547	13	59	0.36	35	30	35	27	66	158	87	23%	76	0%	0%	11	18%	64%	3.59	0.4	13	35	$0
15 Proj	**126**	**14**	**6**	**15**	**0**	**214**	**227**	**295**	**398**	**693**	**814**	**604**	**10**	**62**	**0.30**	**37**	**22**	**41**	**29**	**84**	**161**	**121**	**18%**	**72**	**3%**	**53%**				**3.78**	**1.5**	**12**	**31**	**$2**

Rua,Ryan

Age: 25 Bats: R Pos: LF	Health A	LIMA Plan D
Ht: 6' 2" Wt: 180	PT/Exp F	Rand Var 0
	Consist C	MM 2221

2-14-.295 in 105 AB at TEX. Nice year at AA led to promotion. bb% was above 10% in minors, but only 2% in majors; that and lack of big-league power confirm he could use more seasoning. He's young enough and versatile enough (didn't qualify, but also plays 1B/3B) to get more chances to make that transition.

Yr Tm	AB	R	HR	RBI	SB	BA	xBA	OBP	SLG	OPS	vL	vR	bb%	ct%	Eye	G	L	F	h%	HctX	PX	xPX	hr/f	Spd	SBO	SB%	#Wk	DOM	DIS	RC/G	RAR	BPV	BPX	R$
10																																		
11																																		
12																																		
13 aa	86	16	3	8	1	218		269	356	625			6	70	0.23				28		94			132	4%	100%				3.17		11	28	-$1
14 TEX *	576	58	16	67	5	270	269	317	414	731	922	664	6	78	0.31	52	23	25	32	97	105	86	9%	105	7%	48%	6	33%	33%	4.45	12.6	42	114	$17
1st Half	269	25	9	30	4	257	245	317	401	718			8	77	0.37				31		103			108	10%	51%				4.21		40	108	$13
2nd Half	307	33	7	37	2	282	275	317	425	742	922	664	5	79	0.25	52	23	25	34	99	107	86	9%	108	5%	43%	6	33%	33%	4.67	8.1	46	124	$21
15 Proj	**184**	**19**	**3**	**21**	**2**	**273**	**259**	**329**	**383**	**712**	**851**	**655**	**6**	**78**	**0.30**	**52**	**23**	**25**	**34**	**89**	**86**	**77**	**8%**	**112**	**7%**	**54%**				**4.18**	**2.3**	**16**	**42**	**$5**

Ruf,Darin

Age: 28 Bats: R Pos: 1B	Health B	LIMA Plan D+
Ht: 6' 3" Wt: 240	PT/Exp C	Rand Var +4
	Consist C	MM 4113

3-8-.235 in 102 AB at PHI. Oblique kept him out until mid-May, then wrist/knee injuries ate another month. Shaky ct% assures ongoing BA issues, but HctX/xPX both confirm that this is a live bat. Minor-league record doesn't indicate much of a platoon split, so may be more than a bad-side platoon play. UP: 20 HR.

Yr Tm	AB	R	HR	RBI	SB	BA	xBA	OBP	SLG	OPS	vL	vR	bb%	ct%	Eye	G	L	F	h%	HctX	PX	xPX	hr/f	Spd	SBO	SB%	#Wk	DOM	DIS	RC/G	RAR	BPV	BPX	R$
10																																		
11																																		
12 PHI *	522	72	32	86	1	267	265	331	514	844	1326	845	9	74	0.37	39	17	43	30	127	163	260	30%	71	1%	100%	4	50%	0%	5.93	7.4	67	168	$19
13 PHI *	556	67	19	63	1	228	213	302	385	687	656	863	10	64	0.29	41	19	41	32	96	133	156	21%	83	2%	23%	13	38%	46%	3.78	-13.6	8	20	$8
14 PHI *	185	17	4	15	1	222	234	270	352	621	916	386	6	72	0.23	44	19	36	29	115	114	135	12%	67	2%	100%	12	42%	42%	3.13	-5.9	12	32	$0
1st Half	44	4	2	2	1	182	245	235	354	589	1133	0	7	74	0.26	83	0	17	21	213	131	110	####	82	10%	100%	2	50%	50%	2.66	-2.1	39	105	-$5
2nd Half	141	13	2	12	0	235	229	281	351	632	897	439	6	71	0.22	41	21	38	32	106	109	137	8%	68	0%	0%	10	40%	40%	3.28	-3.7	6	16	$1
15 Proj	**290**	**34**	**11**	**36**	**0**	**246**	**244**	**324**	**418**	**742**	**824**	**665**	**8**	**70**	**0.29**	**41**	**20**	**39**	**31**	**102**	**141**	**145**	**13%**	**73**	**1%**	**57%**				**4.31**	**1.3**	**24**	**64**	**$7**

Ruggiano,Justin

Age: 33 Bats: R Pos: RF	Health C	LIMA Plan D+
Ht: 6' 1" Wt: 210	PT/Exp D	Rand Var -4
	Consist C	MM 4111

6-28-.281 in 224 AB at CHC. Season in a nutshell: Ankle, hamstring, groin, ankle (w/arthroscopic surgery). That litany of lower-body injuries, combined with age, makes return of double-digit SB unlikely. But plus power and success vL should return, and makes him decent FAAB fodder when he stumbles into a few weeks of regular PT.

Yr Tm	AB	R	HR	RBI	SB	BA	xBA	OBP	SLG	OPS	vL	vR	bb%	ct%	Eye	G	L	F	h%	HctX	PX	xPX	hr/f	Spd	SBO	SB%	#Wk	DOM	DIS	RC/G	RAR	BPV	BPX	R$
10 aaa	457	55	10	50	17	223		271	343	614			6	64	0.18				32		108			90	25%	69%				2.98		-16	-35	$8
11 TAM *	273	31	9	37	9	238	233	285	392	677	576	748	6	70	0.22	53	13	35	31	66	119	108	14%	97	22%	73%	15	27%	53%	3.69	-12.0	20	44	$6
12 MIA *	405	51	16	54	17	291	261	355	499	853	1129	806	9	71	0.34	41	21	38	37	120	157	165	17%	102	27%	59%	17	65%	24%	5.90	8.8	61	153	$19
13 MIA	424	49	18	50	15	222	241	298	396	694	833	631	9	73	0.36	45	17	39	26	108	123	147	15%	85	23%	65%	27	41%	44%	3.63	-12.9	36	90	$11
14 CHC *	245	31	6	28	2	266	226	322	404	726	846	720	8	68	0.26	42	20	38	37	84	119	109	10%	95	9%	33%	17	53%	47%	4.26	1.1	14	38	$6
1st Half	125	17	2	10	0	218	226	301	344	645	848	652	11	71	0.41	45	18	38	29	93	109	127	7%	102	10%	0%	10	70%	30%	3.05	-3.8	24	65	$1
2nd Half	120	14	4	18	2	317	225	341	467	808	844	785	4	66	0.12	39	22	39	45	76	129	92	13%	85	9%	67%	7	29%	71%	5.89	6.2	2	5	$11
15 Proj	**226**	**28**	**8**	**28**	**3**	**256**	**238**	**315**	**421**	**736**	**819**	**690**	**8**	**69**	**0.27**	**43**	**19**	**38**	**34**	**93**	**135**	**125**	**13%**	**91**	**13%**	**45%**				**4.24**	**1.6**	**24**	**63**	**$7**

JOSH PALEY

Ruiz,Carlos

Age: 36 Bats: R Pos: CA	Health D	LIMA Plan D+	
Ht: 5' 10" Wt: 205	PT/Exp C	Rand Var +2	
	Consist D	MM 2133	

After 2012 plantar fasciitis and 2013 hamstring issues, in 2014 he mixed in upper-body injuries: June concussion and post-season shoulder surgery. Still does damage against LHPs (that's where most of his walks come, too), which should allow him to hang on in a platoon role. But ABs against RHPs are pretty much a waste of time.

Yr	Tm	AB	R	HR	RBI	SB	BA	xBA	OBP	SLG	OPS	vL	vR	bb%	ct%	Eye	G	L	F	h%	HctX	PX	xPX	hr/f	Spd	SBO	SB%	#Wk	DOM	DIS	RC/G	RAR	BPV	BPX	R$
10	PHI	371	43	8	53	0	302	279	400	447	847	940	808	13	85	1.02	45	20	35	34	107	102	87	7%	85	1%	0%	25	64%	24%	6.34	20.0	77	167	$12
11	PHI	410	49	6	40	1	283	258	371	383	754	716	766	10	88	1.00	42	21	37	31	120	70	95	4%	72	1%	100%	26	65%	23%	4.89	5.9	54	120	$9
12	PHI	372	56	16	68	4	325	313	394	540	935	906	946	7	87	0.58	43	24	33	34	130	135	131	15%	59	4%	100%	22	82%	14%	7.72	33.8	88	220	$20
13	PHI	310	30	5	37	1	268	254	320	368	688	836	636	5	87	0.46	47	20	34	29	114	69	78	5%	78	1%	100%	19	32%	37%	3.96	2.3	41	103	$5
14	PHI	381	43	6	31	4	252	267	347	370	717	832	681	11	84	0.77	41	23	35	29	85	89	83	5%	86	5%	67%	24	50%	29%	4.17	8.0	57	154	$6
1st Half		230	28	2	14	3	257	267	363	357	719	893	677	12	85	0.89	41	25	34	30	91	79	79	3%	102	6%	75%	13	38%	31%	4.23	5.6	59	159	$7
2nd Half		151	15	4	17	1	245	268	322	391	712	768	688	9	83	0.60	41	21	38	27	76	106	90	8%	63	5%	50%	11	64%	27%	4.06	3.0	58	157	$6
15	Proj	**288**	**32**	**5**	**33**	**2**	**263**	**270**	**341**	**387**	**728**	**807**	**699**	**9**	**86**	**0.66**	**43**	**22**	**35**	**29**	**100**	**92**	**91**	**6%**	**73**	**4%**	**70%**				**4.37**	**8.1**	**51**	**134**	**$5**

Rupp,Cameron

Age: 26 Bats: R Pos: CA	Health A	LIMA Plan F	
Ht: 6' 2" Wt: 250	PT/Exp F	Rand Var 0	
	Consist D	MM 3001	

0-6-.183 in 60 AB at PHI. Unsurprisingly from a guy his size, the ball goes pretty far when he gets ahold of one. But that doesn't happen often enough, and there's little else in the way of promise in this skill set. Owns a career .215 BA in 413 Triple-A AB, which fully justifies this sub-.200 projected BA.

Yr	Tm	AB	R	HR	RBI	SB	BA	xBA	OBP	SLG	OPS	vL	vR	bb%	ct%	Eye	G	L	F	h%	HctX	PX	xPX	hr/f	Spd	SBO	SB%	#Wk	DOM	DIS	RC/G	RAR	BPV	BPX	R$
10																																			
11																																			
12																																			
13	PHI *	338	27	11	35	1	219	199	259	358	617	650	778	5	67	0.17	56	11	33	29	92	112	152	0%	64	3%	38%	2	0%	50%	2.99	-7.3	-11	-28	$1
14	PHI *	254	17	4	19	0	145	156	204	239	443	0	546	7	56	0.17	43	13	45	23	61	101	123	0%	60	0%	0%	6	0%	67%	1.45	-17.0	-59	-159	-$7
1st Half		118	11	4	13	0	141	205	224	290	515	0	556	10	51	0.22	33	33	33	22	74	158	235	0%	68	0%	0%	2	0%	50%	1.93	-5.8	-28	-76	-$5
2nd Half		136	6	0	7	0	148	133	185	194	379	0	544	4	61	0.12	44	9	47	24	62	60	103	0%	66	0%	0%	4	0%	75%	1.08	-10.5	-78	-211	-$10
15	Proj	**132**	**9**	**3**	**11**	**0**	**175**	**164**	**224**	**285**	**510**	**286**	**538**	**6**	**61**	**0.16**	**44**	**8.8**	**47**	**26**	**56**	**106**	**93**	**8%**	**66**	**1%**	**50%**				**1.97**	**-6.1**	**-50**	**-130**	**-$1**

Russell,Addison

Age: 21 Bats: R Pos: SS	Health A	LIMA Plan D+	
Ht: 6' 0" Wt: 195	PT/Exp F	Rand Var 0	
	Consist F	MM 2121	

Torn hamstring delayed start of his season until June, and then he moved from OAK to CHC at the trade deadline. That 2nd-half MLE line, for a 20-year old in Double-A, is a real eye-catcher: ct% is sufficient; power is already evident even before he finishes filling out. He's going to be a gem... but not necessarily in 2015.

Yr	Tm	AB	R	HR	RBI	SB	BA	xBA	OBP	SLG	OPS	vL	vR	bb%	ct%	Eye	G	L	F	h%	HctX	PX	xPX	hr/f	Spd	SBO	SB%	#Wk	DOM	DIS	RC/G	RAR	BPV	BPX	R$
10																																			
11																																			
12																																			
13																																			
14	aa	241	31	10	35	4	278		317	468	785			5	80	0.29				31		130			89	15%	48%				4.93		65	176	$9
1st Half		41	5	1	4	2	270		335	412	748			9	79	0.47				32		98			128	32%	42%				4.07		53	143	-$9
2nd Half		200	25	10	31	2	280		313	479	792			5	81	0.25				31		136			86	10%	52%				5.13		69	186	$13
15	Proj	**201**	**25**	**6**	**30**	**2**	**252**	**249**	**286**	**388**	**674**	**674**	**674**	**5**	**82**	**0.27**	**44**	**17**	**39**	**28**		**96**		**9%**	**87**	**8%**	**50%**				**3.67**	**2.6**	**35**	**92**	**$6**

Rutledge,Josh

Age: 26 Bats: R Pos: SS	Health A	LIMA Plan C+	
Ht: 6' 1" Wt: 190	PT/Exp C	Rand Var -3	
	Consist B	MM 3423	

4-33-.269 in 309 AB at COL. 2014 was to be the tiebreaker between promising 2012 and 2013's follow-up clunker. Surface results say he split the difference, but it wasn't that good. h% propped up BA, ct% plummeted and power is now "average at best." The further 2012 is in the rear view, the longer the odds of return.

Yr	Tm	AB	R	HR	RBI	SB	BA	xBA	OBP	SLG	OPS	vL	vR	bb%	ct%	Eye	G	L	F	h%	HctX	PX	xPX	hr/f	Spd	SBO	SB%	#Wk	DOM	DIS	RC/G	RAR	BPV	BPX	R$
10																																			
11																																			
12	COL *	633	86	21	67	19	291	290	313	492	805	798	766	3	81	0.17	49	20	31	33	90	131	112	12%	132	18%	82%	13	54%	23%	5.56	25.7	75	188	$27
13	COL *	428	59	10	33	13	260	252	308	385	692	533	684	6	80	0.34	49	18	32	31	91	87	91	10%	130	14%	84%	19	32%	53%	4.15	8.1	44	110	$13
14	COL *	363	48	5	36	4	270	239	316	398	714	840	688	6	73	0.25	46	20	34	36	98	100	101	5%	176	11%	37%	24	25%	42%	4.11	8.7	41	111	$9
1st Half		143	21	3	12	2	286	246	338	424	762	1207	688	7	75	0.32	48	18	33	36	106	104	84	9%	144	16%	29%	11	36%	36%	4.55	5.5	45	122	$6
2nd Half		220	27	2	24	2	259	233	310	382	691	701	688	6	72	0.21	45	21	34	35	95	96	108	4%	179	8%	50%	13	15%	46%	3.84	3.9	33	89	$11
15	Proj	**329**	**44**	**7**	**30**	**7**	**269**	**254**	**321**	**413**	**734**	**754**	**725**	**6**	**77**	**0.27**	**47**	**19**	**34**	**33**	**95**	**107**	**98**	**8%**	**154**	**14%**	**63%**				**4.39**	**11.0**	**42**	**111**	**$11**

Saltalamacchia,Jarrod

Age: 30 Bats: B Pos: CA	Health A	LIMA Plan C+	
Ht: 6' 4" Wt: 235	PT/Exp C	Rand Var -2	
	Consist D	MM 4115	

Despite BA dip, 1st half was reasonably in line with historical performance. Missed a couple of weeks in June with a concussion, perhaps that contributed to brutal 2H? Regardless, xBA and h% agree that another foray over .250 BA is unlikely. xPX didn't buy the 2014 PX dip, though, which means he's still capable of... UP: 20 HR.

Yr	Tm	AB	R	HR	RBI	SB	BA	xBA	OBP	SLG	OPS	vL	vR	bb%	ct%	Eye	G	L	F	h%	HctX	PX	xPX	hr/f	Spd	SBO	SB%	#Wk	DOM	DIS	RC/G	RAR	BPV	BPX	R$
10	2 AL *	298	34	9	32	1	217	216	285	381	666	654	573	9	72	0.35	42	5	53	27	31	127	8	0%	95	1%	100%	6	67%	33%	3.55	-7.5	39	85	$1
11	BOS	358	52	16	56	1	235	245	288	450	737	635	786	6	67	0.20	32	21	47	30	113	172	145	14%	85	2%	100%	27	44%	33%	4.25	-1.3	45	100	$8
12	BOS	405	55	25	59	0	222	242	288	454	742	494	779	9	66	0.27	31	23	47	27	95	168	160	20%	79	1%	0%	27	48%	33%	4.26	-0.3	40	100	$8
13	BOS	425	68	14	65	4	273	260	338	466	804	628	873	9	67	0.31	33	29	39	38	109	170	154	13%	69	5%	80%	27	52%	26%	5.56	22.6	46	115	$15
14	MIA	373	43	11	44	0	220	212	320	362	681	600	705	13	62	0.38	37	22	40	32	114	134	163	12%	72	1%	0%	25	32%	52%	3.75	3.3	3	8	$3
1st Half		187	23	7	20	0	241	222	339	412	751	640	784	13	64	0.43	38	19	43	34	125	152	182	13%	83	2%	0%	12	50%	42%	4.64	7.0	32	86	$5
2nd Half		186	20	4	24	0	199	202	300	312	611	557	627	12	59	0.34	37	26	37	31	102	114	142	10%	68	0%	0%	13	15%	62%	2.95	-2.6	-25	-68	$2
15	Proj	**407**	**53**	**14**	**54**	**1**	**242**	**233**	**322**	**410**	**732**	**613**	**768**	**11**	**64**	**0.33**	**35**	**24**	**41**	**34**	**108**	**153**	**156**	**13%**	**71**	**2%**	**57%**				**4.42**	**12.4**	**16**	**42**	**$10**

Sanchez,Carlos

Age: 23 Bats: B Pos: 2B	Health A	LIMA Plan D	
Ht: 5' 11" Wt: 195	PT/Exp C	Rand Var 0	
	Consist D	MM 1313	

0-5-.250 in 100 AB at CHW. Young infielder lived up to scouting reports in his late-season callup, flashing a line-drive approach and plus Spd (despite only 1 SB in MLB). He's still got time for skills growth, but for now subpar bb% and ct% won't support a decent OBP. Short-term, that may relegate him to a utility role.

Yr	Tm	AB	R	HR	RBI	SB	BA	xBA	OBP	SLG	OPS	vL	vR	bb%	ct%	Eye	G	L	F	h%	HctX	PX	xPX	hr/f	Spd	SBO	SB%	#Wk	DOM	DIS	RC/G	RAR	BPV	BPX	R$
10																																			
11																																			
12	a/a	158	18	0	12	6	328		368	407	775			6	81	0.32				41		66			97	23%	54%				5.21		18	45	$5
13	aaa	432	41	0	23	13	218		264	267	531			6	81	0.31				27		43			105	21%	64%				2.24		1	3	$2
14	CHW *	537	48	6	45	12	248	240	289	332	621	867	423	5	77	0.25	42	26	32	31	84	65	87	0%	116	13%	69%	8	25%	75%	3.21	-2.8	9	24	$10
1st Half		313	31	4	26	8	249	224	297	340	637			6	77	0.30				31	0	65			124	13%	69%				3.39		13	35	$13
2nd Half		224	16	2	19	4	247	242	277	321	598	867	423	4	78	0.18	42	26	32	31	84	66	87	0%	95	13%	68%	8	25%	75%	2.97	-2.8	1	3	$6
15	Proj	**265**	**24**	**2**	**19**	**7**	**249**	**245**	**286**	**327**	**613**	**919**	**463**	**5**	**79**	**0.27**	**42**	**26**	**32**	**31**	**76**	**64**	**78**	**3%**	**111**	**17%**	**63%**				**3.11**	**-2.3**	**5**	**14**	**$5**

Sanchez,Gaby

Age: 31 Bats: R Pos: 1B	Health A	LIMA Plan D+	
Ht: 6' 1" Wt: 235	PT/Exp D	Rand Var +2	
	Consist C	MM 3223	

Sign of an organization that "gets it": for first time in his career, had more AB vs. LHP than RHP. Scanning his platoon splits, one can only ask "what took so long?" His year-to-year production vL varies due to sample size; career he's .863 OPS vL, .691 vR. That makes him a very playable option vs. southpaws in daily games.

Yr	Tm	AB	R	HR	RBI	SB	BA	xBA	OBP	SLG	OPS	vL	vR	bb%	ct%	Eye	G	L	F	h%	HctX	PX	xPX	hr/f	Spd	SBO	SB%	#Wk	DOM	DIS	RC/G	RAR	BPV	BPX	R$
10	FLA	572	72	19	85	5	273	265	341	448	788	925	742	9	82	0.56	37	17	46	30	115	117	144	9%	94	3%	100%	27	59%	15%	5.37	-14.4	71	154	$18
11	FLA	572	72	19	78	3	266	261	352	427	779	901	742	11	83	0.76	36	20	45	29	109	109	103	9%	57	2%	75%	27	52%	19%	5.18	-17.7	61	136	$16
12	2 NL *	415	44	10	42	2	222	228	292	348	640	729	566	9	79	0.47	41	17	42	26	101	88	111	7%	71	5%	48%	21	43%	29%	3.27	-27.4	28	70	$2
13	PIT	264	29	7	36	1	254	260	361	402	762	987	619	14	81	0.86	36	23	41	29	118	107	125	8%	73	1%	100%	27	52%	33%	4.97	2.9	61	153	$4
14	PIT	262	31	7	33	2	229	249	293	385	679	746	609	8	78	0.40	38	18	44	27	88	120	108	8%	74	4%	100%	27	41%	41%	3.75	-3.4	48	130	$3
1st Half		132	16	5	15	2	250	270	298	462	760	904	654	6	74	0.24	36	21	43	30	89	166	112	12%	73	8%	100%	14	43%	43%	4.68	2.0	65	176	$5
2nd Half		130	15	2	18	0	208	223	289	308	596	633	543	10	82	0.63	39	17	44	24	87	78	105	4%	74	0%	0%	13	38%	38%	2.87	-5.2	33	89	$2
15	Proj	**252**	**30**	**6**	**34**	**1**	**252**	**249**	**329**	**396**	**725**	**829**	**646**	**10**	**80**	**0.55**	**38**	**19**	**43**	**29**	**100**	**110**	**114**	**7%**	**72**	**2%**	**82%**				**4.44**	**2.0**	**45**	**118**	**$6**

RAY MURPHY

Sanchez,Hector

Age: 25 Bats: B Pos: CA
Ht: 6' 0" Wt: 235

Health	B	LIMA Plan	F
PT/Exp	F	Rand Var	0
Consist	B	MM	2001

Before a July concussion ended his season, there was a tiny flicker of what might have been an emerging power skill: more fly balls, some PX growth, and a big xPX spike. The sample size was tiny, and the rest of the skill set remains a barren wasteland. Tough to snuff a flicker for a 25 y/o, but there's nothing much to invest in here.

Yr	Tm	AB	R	HR	RBI	SB	BA	xBA	OBP	SLG	OPS	vL	vR	bb%	ct%	Eye	G	L	F	h%	HctX	PX	xPX	hr/f	Spd	SBO	SB%	#Wk	DOM	DIS	RC/G	RAR	BPV	BPX	R$
10																																			
11	SF *	184	10	1	18	0	221	197	266	283	550	348	809	6	83	0.37	52	12	36	26	151	53	161	0%	58	3%	0%	7	29%	43%	2.40	-11.1	6	13	-$2
12	SF	218	22	3	34	0	280	237	295	390	685	727	661	2	76	0.10	44	22	34	36	85	88	101	5%	63	0%	0%	25	36%	48%	4.09	-1.2	0	0	$4
13	SF *	214	15	5	26	0	235	247	286	337	623	860	552	7	78	0.33	43	27	31	28	86	71	74	10%	67	0%	0%	19	11%	47%	3.21	-3.0	5	13	$0
14	SF	163	8	3	28	0	196	198	237	301	538	531	540	5	66	0.15	34	21	46	28	95	96	150	6%	59	3%	0%	17	18%	71%	2.16	-6.6	-28	-76	-$2
1st Half		135	7	3	25	0	200	205	233	319	551	595	535	4	65	0.11	30	22	48	28	98	109	159	7%	59	5%	0%	14	21%	71%	2.23	-5.0	-25	-68	-$1
2nd Half		28	1	0	3	0	179	156	258	214	472	333	566	10	71	0.38	50	15	35	25	77	39	110	0%	82	0%	0%	3	0%	67%	1.72	-1.5	-37	-100	-$7
15	Proj	**181**	**13**	**3**	**27**	**0**	**238**	**226**	**275**	**337**	**612**	**652**	**591**	**4**	**74**	**0.17**	**42**	**22**	**36**	**31**	**86**	**85**	**106**	**6%**	**64**	**1%**	**0%**				**3.00**	**-2.1**	**-17**	**-44**	**$0**

Sanchez,Jorge Tony

Age: 27 Bats: R Pos: CA
Ht: 5' 11" Wt: 225

Health	A	LIMA Plan	D
PT/Exp	D	Rand Var	0
Consist	B	MM	4111

2-13-.267 in 75 AB at PIT. Gave back most of the power surge that generated some intrigue a year ago. That leaves him with shaky plate discipline, no speed, a groundball tilt and merely average power. Now approaching peak age, the window for further growth is starting to close. Interest level: waning.

Yr	Tm	AB	R	HR	RBI	SB	BA	xBA	OBP	SLG	OPS	vL	vR	bb%	ct%	Eye	G	L	F	h%	HctX	PX	xPX	hr/f	Spd	SBO	SB%	#Wk	DOM	DIS	RC/G	RAR	BPV	BPX	R$
10																																			
11	aa	402	37	4	35	4	213		279	277	555			8	80	0.46				26		47			92	9%	42%				2.39		5	11	-$1
12	a/a	347	35	6	35	1	220		287	345	632			9	76	0.38				28		97			84	3%	42%				3.20		24	60	$0
13	PIT *	337	37	9	37	0	235	251	286	395	681	765	655	7	75	0.28	45	19	36	29	138	128	139	12%	75	0%	0%	10	40%	30%	3.77	0.7	41	103	$3
14	PIT *	343	24	9	45	0	203	200	265	325	591	148	768	8	67	0.25	53	17	30	28	36	105	60	14%	89	0%	0%	12	8%	58%	2.76	-7.4	-4	-11	$0
1st Half		175	10	5	27	0	199	184	247	311	558	200	768	6	67	0.19	53	18	29	27	38	89	63	15%	96	0%	0%	8	13%	50%	2.44	-5.2	-20	-54	$0
2nd Half		168	14	4	18	0	209	163	285	341	625	0	0	10	67	0.32	50	0	50	29	0	122	-14	0%	65	0%	0%	4	0%	75%	3.12	-1.4	6	16	$0
15	Proj	**161**	**14**	**5**	**18**	**0**	**215**	**238**	**290**	**370**	**660**	**518**	**690**	**8**	**71**	**0.30**	**50**	**18**	**32**	**27**	**78**	**127**	**93**	**14%**	**92**	**2%**	**43%**				**3.31**	**-0.4**	**12**	**33**	**$2**

Sandoval,Pablo

Age: 28 Bats: B Pos: 3B
Ht: 5' 11" Wt: 245

Health	C	LIMA Plan	B+
PT/Exp	B	Rand Var	0
Consist	A	MM	2035

Amid all of the "Fat Panda/Skinny Panda" noise in recent years, these skills and trend lines are straightforward: 2011 is an outlier, power hovers around average levels, LHPs are increasingly shredding him. Home/road splits say these aren't just home-park problems, either. Treat him as a decent BA option on good side of a platoon.

Yr	Tm	AB	R	HR	RBI	SB	BA	xBA	OBP	SLG	OPS	vL	vR	bb%	ct%	Eye	G	L	F	h%	HctX	PX	xPX	hr/f	Spd	SBO	SB%	#Wk	DOM	DIS	RC/G	RAR	BPV	BPX	R$
10	SF	563	61	13	63	3	268	267	323	409	732	589	779	8	86	0.58	44	17	38	29	110	93	106	7%	63	3%	60%	27	56%	22%	4.58	-8.3	53	115	$12
11	SF	426	55	23	70	2	315	301	357	552	909	723	961	7	85	0.51	42	19	39	33	131	145	125	16%	71	5%	33%	21	67%	19%	7.19	24.3	94	209	$22
12	SF	396	59	12	63	1	283	274	342	447	789	745	809	9	85	0.64	43	20	37	31	120	103	117	10%	63	2%	50%	21	48%	24%	5.45	9.4	61	153	$13
13	SF	525	52	14	79	0	278	262	341	417	758	686	786	8	85	0.59	41	21	37	31	102	90	92	8%	54	0%	0%	25	44%	20%	4.97	14.5	47	118	$15
14	SF	588	68	16	73	0	279	263	324	415	739	563	824	6	86	0.46	43	21	37	30	114	89	111	9%	76	0%	0%	27	48%	30%	4.75	17.2	51	138	$18
1st Half		298	38	9	34	0	265	254	316	416	732	592	792	7	82	0.43	42	19	40	30	104	102	111	9%	83	0%	0%	14	50%	36%	4.59	7.7	50	135	$16
2nd Half		290	30	7	39	0	293	273	333	414	747	538	859	5	89	0.52	43	23	34	31	124	77	111	8%	68	0%	0%	13	46%	23%	4.93	9.9	52	141	$20
15	Proj	**521**	**60**	**15**	**72**	**0**	**280**	**268**	**331**	**424**	**755**	**620**	**814**	**7**	**86**	**0.53**	**42**	**21**	**37**	**30**	**114**	**96**	**108**	**9%**	**65**	**1%**	**46%**				**4.94**	**18.4**	**49**	**130**	**$18**

Santana,Carlos

Age: 29 Bats: B Pos: 1B 3B DH
Ht: 5' 11" Wt: 210

Health	A	LIMA Plan	A
PT/Exp	A	Rand Var	+3
Consist	B	MM	4135

Fun with selected endpoints: First 82 AB = .122 BA, 1 HR, 15% h%. Remaining 459 AB = .251 BA, 26 HR, 27% h%. The latter represents his true h% level; xBA agrees. And 2H spikes in HctX, xPX show that he can hit for power and BA at same time. No longer catcher-eligible, but... UP: 30 HR, .270 BA.

Yr	Tm	AB	R	HR	RBI	SB	BA	xBA	OBP	SLG	OPS	vL	vR	bb%	ct%	Eye	G	L	F	h%	HctX	PX	xPX	hr/f	Spd	SBO	SB%	#Wk	DOM	DIS	RC/G	RAR	BPV	BPX	R$
10	CLE *	346	52	15	60	7	263	280	389	469	858	582	1002	17	79	0.96	35	21	44	30	138	144	147	11%	67	6%	100%	9	67%	22%	6.48	8.4	85	185	$12
11	CLE	552	84	27	79	5	239	268	351	457	808	964	732	15	76	0.73	45	15	40	27	120	153	137	16%	67	5%	63%	27	67%	15%	5.35	-4.7	78	173	$15
12	CLE	507	72	18	76	3	252	256	365	420	785	808	772	15	80	0.90	43	19	38	28	107	108	104	12%	84	5%	38%	26	50%	27%	5.10	-2.7	64	160	$13
13	CLE	541	75	20	74	3	268	277	377	455	832	864	815	15	80	0.85	42	22	36	30	106	131	100	13%	72	2%	75%	27	67%	4%	5.95	20.8	76	190	$18
14	CLE	541	68	27	85	5	231	262	365	427	792	864	757	17	77	0.91	40	19	40	25	117	136	125	16%	66	4%	71%	27	56%	22%	5.15	16.4	74	200	$15
1st Half		254	33	12	32	2	205	246	357	390	746	821	708	19	73	0.85	46	17	38	23	104	135	105	17%	76	3%	67%	14	50%	29%	4.39	1.8	63	170	$7
2nd Half		287	35	15	53	3	254	276	373	460	833	905	799	16	80	0.98	36	22	43	27	128	137	140	15%	65	4%	75%	13	62%	15%	5.89	14.5	85	230	$23
15	Proj	**558**	**75**	**25**	**85**	**4**	**251**	**269**	**372**	**442**	**814**	**856**	**793**	**16**	**78**	**0.89**	**41**	**20**	**39**	**28**	**115**	**136**	**118**	**14%**	**69**	**3%**	**62%**				**5.56**	**22.9**	**70**	**185**	**$19**

Santana,Daniel

Age: 24 Bats: B Pos: CF SS
Ht: 5' 11" Wt: 160

Health	A	LIMA Plan	B
PT/Exp	D	Rand Var	-3
Consist	F	MM	3535

7-40-.319 with 20 SB in 405 AB at MIN. Lighty-regarded prospect made most of opportunity, getting on base a ton and providing value with his legs. Warning signs abound, though: lofty h% is unsustainable, swing-at-everything approach likely will be exploited. Amid that regression, SB opps will dwindle.

Yr	Tm	AB	R	HR	RBI	SB	BA	xBA	OBP	SLG	OPS	vL	vR	bb%	ct%	Eye	G	L	F	h%	HctX	PX	xPX	hr/f	Spd	SBO	SB%	#Wk	DOM	DIS	RC/G	RAR	BPV	BPX	R$
10																																			
11																																			
12																																			
13	aa	539	50	1	34	23	263		287	339	625			3	81	0.18				32		53			141	29%	61%				3.15		17	43	$14
14	MIN *	502	82	7	46	23	303	264	335	447	782	786	841	5	74	0.18	46	26	28	40	85	114	63	9%	159	22%	82%	20	50%	35%	5.54	32.8	47	127	$26
1st Half		231	31	2	22	9	291	272	326	404	729	1111	716	5	75	0.20	48	30	21	38	87	98	64	10%	136	19%	81%	8	38%	38%	4.79	10.1	31	84	$16
2nd Half		271	51	5	24	14	314	264	346	483	830	664	912	4	74	0.17	45	24	32	41	84	129	63	8%	169	25%	82%	12	58%	33%	6.22	22.1	60	162	$35
15	Proj	**471**	**64**	**9**	**38**	**17**	**271**	**270**	**304**	**415**	**718**	**710**	**722**	**4**	**77**	**0.18**	**46**	**26**	**28**	**34**	**85**	**107**	**63**	**9%**	**162**	**24%**	**68%**				**4.20**	**4.7**	**47**	**123**	**$18**

Santana,Domingo

Age: 22 Bats: R Pos: LF
Ht: 6' 5" Wt: 225

Health	A	LIMA Plan	F
PT/Exp	D	Rand Var	-1
Consist	A	MM	3301

0-0-.000 in 17 AB at HOU. Small sample size, sure: but 14 K in 18 PA in the majors is a giant flashing neon "NOT READY" sign. Minor-league track record shows legitimate plus power balanced with serious problems making contact. Expect him to be sent back for more seasoning; worth tracking for signs of a refined approach.

Yr	Tm	AB	R	HR	RBI	SB	BA	xBA	OBP	SLG	OPS	vL	vR	bb%	ct%	Eye	G	L	F	h%	HctX	PX	xPX	hr/f	Spd	SBO	SB%	#Wk	DOM	DIS	RC/G	RAR	BPV	BPX	R$
10																																			
11																																			
12																																			
13	aa	416	58	21	51	10	228		292	437	728			8	63	0.24				31		170			98	17%	64%				4.09		35	88	$12
14	HOU *	460	47	12	59	4	246	223	318	384	702	100	0	10	60	0.26	33	33	33	38	86	132	235	0%	91	7%	50%	3	0%	100%	4.02	4.5	-6	-16	$10
1st Half		319	36	10	38	4	263	229	326	422	748			9	64	0.26				38	0	143			92	7%	62%	1	0%	100%	4.69		19	51	$16
2nd Half		141	11	2	21	1	208	175	301	298	599	100	0	12	50	0.26	33	33	33	40	72	102	235	0%	104	7%	25%	2	0%	100%	2.73	-4.5	-63	-170	-$4
15	Proj	**126**	**14**	**2**	**17**	**3**	**229**	**201**	**304**	**330**	**634**	**634**	**634**	**10**	**59**	**0.26**	**53**	**21**	**26**	**37**		**104**		**10%**	**105**	**13%**	**67%**				**3.29**	**-1.8**	**-35**	**-91**	**$3**

Santiago,Ramon

Age: 35 Bats: B Pos: 3B 2B 2B
Ht: 5' 11" Wt: 175

Health	A	LIMA Plan	D
PT/Exp	F	Rand Var	-2
Consist	B	MM	1211

PRO: No serious signs of decline at age 35. CON: It's tough to decline when you're already on the floor. Three years (2012-14) in aggregate: 612 AB, 5 HR, 48 RBI, 3 SB, .224 BA. Three years.

Yr	Tm	AB	R	HR	RBI	SB	BA	xBA	OBP	SLG	OPS	vL	vR	bb%	ct%	Eye	G	L	F	h%	HctX	PX	xPX	hr/f	Spd	SBO	SB%	#Wk	DOM	DIS	RC/G	RAR	BPV	BPX	R$
10	DET	320	38	3	22	2	263	241	337	325	662	763	635	9	83	0.54	49	21	30	31	80	43	30	4%	130	4%	50%	26	27%	42%	3.60	-13.9	22	48	$4
11	DET	258	29	5	30	0	260	262	311	384	695	832	662	6	85	0.45	43	21	35	29	81	79	55	7%	115	0%	0%	26	31%	35%	4.04	-7.9	53	118	$3
12	DET	228	19	2	17	1	206	224	283	272	555	482	580	8	83	0.51	52	17	31	24	71	44	53	4%	107	2%	100%	24	25%	50%	2.38	-15.7	17	43	-$3
13	DET	205	27	1	14	0	224	254	298	288	586	591	584	9	84	0.66	49	24	27	26	56	47	23	2%	110	2%	0%	24	29%	33%	2.75	-7.7	29	73	-$1
14	CIN	179	20	2	17	2	246	239	343	324	667	923	577	12	79	0.63	42	25	34	30	60	64	49	4%	98	5%	67%	26	27%	50%	3.66	-0.2	21	57	$1
1st Half		51	6	0	1	0	216	184	298	235	534	762	461	9	73	0.36	55	18	27	30	24	21	16	0%	115	0%	0%	14	21%	64%	2.19	-2.4	-39	-105	-$7
2nd Half		128	14	2	16	2	258	258	360	359	719	979	624	13	81	0.79	38	27	36	30	74	79	60	5%	89	7%	67%	12	33%	33%	4.34	2.4	43	116	$5
15	Proj	**126**	**14**	**1**	**10**	**1**	**234**	**237**	**318**	**301**	**619**	**748**	**576**	**10**	**81**	**0.58**	**47**	**23**	**31**	**28**	**60**	**54**	**39**	**3%**	**104**	**3%**	**59%**				**3.09**	**-2.3**	**5**	**13**	**$1**

RAY MURPHY

Sardinas,Luis

Age: 22	Bats: B	Pos: 2B		Health	A	LIMA Plan	D
Ht: 6' 1"	Wt: 150			PT/Exp	F	Rand Var	+1
				Consist	A	MM	0431

0-8-.261, 5 SB in 115 AB at TEX. Versatile glove-first prospect relies on good-not-great contact and a moderate running game on offense. Just 5 HR in 1396 minor league AB speak to power shortcomings, and career 6% bb% is an issue. Has time, but will need opportunity and improved SB% to get our attention.

Yr Tm	AB	R	HR	RBI	SB	BA	xBA	OBP	SLG	OPS	vL	vR	bb%	ct%	Eye	G	L	F	h%	HctX	PX	xPX	hr/f	Spd	SBO	SB%	#Wk	DOM	DIS	RC/G	RAR	BPV	BPX	R$
10																																		
11																																		
12																																		
13 aa	135	11	1	13	4	253		273	304	577			3	84	0.17				29		38			92	20%	68%				2.77		2	5	$1
14 TEX *	464	50	1	36	13	256	276	277	324	601	824	552	3	84	0.18	63	21	16	30	41	57	25	0%	126	18%	66%	14	29%	50%	3.01	-5.2	26	70	$10
1st Half	159	17	1	12	2	256	272	280	323	603	833	580	3	84	0.21	67	20	13	30	32	52	18	0%	137	10%	46%	9	22%	56%	2.96	-2.0	26	70	-$1
2nd Half	305	34	0	24	11	256	273	275	325	600	800	518	3	84	0.16	58	23	20	31	53	60	36	0%	116	23%	71%	5	40%	40%	3.03	-3.3	25	68	$15
15 Proj	**170**	**17**	**0**	**14**	**5**	**255**	**265**	**289**	**306**	**594**	**804**	**534**	**3**	**84**	**0.18**	**61**	**22**	**17**	**30**	**45**	**45**	**29**	**0%**	**125**	**17%**	**67%**				**2.83**	**-2.8**	**7**	**18**	**$1**

Saunders,Michael

Age: 28	Bats: L	Pos: RF		Health	C	LIMA Plan	B
Ht: 6' 4"	Wt: 225			PT/Exp	C	Rand Var	-4
				Consist	A	MM	4325

8-34-.273 with 4 SB in 231 AB at SEA. Chain of injuries (knee, shoulder, oblique) from the get-go crippled running game. But power-and-patience remain, as HctX propped up BA. Another sub-.700 OPS vL could result in AB ceiling. But with improved health, he's a good bet for double-digit HR and SB again.

Yr Tm	AB	R	HR	RBI	SB	BA	xBA	OBP	SLG	OPS	vL	vR	bb%	ct%	Eye	G	L	F	h%	HctX	PX	xPX	hr/f	Spd	SBO	SB%	#Wk	DOM	DIS	RC/G	RAR	BPV	BPX	R$
10 SEA *	369	33	10	37	9	201	208	284	325	609	601	686	10	72	0.41	36	16	48	25	77	89	81	11%	96	13%	75%	22	45%	36%	2.96	-25.8	10	22	$1
11 SEA *	397	47	6	31	12	187	167	266	273	540	330	474	10	63	0.29	36	15	50	28	69	76	78	4%	104	18%	68%	14	7%	79%	2.27	-37.3	-33	-73	-$1
12 SEA	507	71	19	57	21	247	259	306	432	738	774	718	8	74	0.33	45	20	35	30	111	130	136	15%	104	22%	84%	28	39%	32%	4.54	-4.7	49	123	$17
13 SEA	406	59	12	46	13	236	241	323	397	720	654	751	12	71	0.46	41	22	37	30	105	123	129	11%	106	16%	72%	25	48%	44%	4.29	0.1	39	98	$11
14 SEA *	286	45	9	40	4	267	246	349	429	778	680	836	11	72	0.45	42	22	36	34	116	121	112	13%	125	10%	44%	18	39%	28%	4.94	8.8	48	130	$10
1st Half	182	31	6	29	2	269	254	322	447	769	612	790	7	74	0.31	35	25	40	33	114	127	117	11%	134	13%	33%	13	38%	23%	4.63	3.4	56	151	$13
2nd Half	104	14	3	10	2	266	222	391	399	789	874	932	17	69	0.66	58	14	28	36	123	110	100	21%	95	7%	67%	5	40%	40%	5.37	4.2	28	76	$4
15 Proj	**433**	**62**	**16**	**50**	**11**	**250**	**250**	**335**	**426**	**761**	**690**	**790**	**12**	**71**	**0.46**	**45**	**19**	**36**	**32**	**110**	**136**	**114**	**14%**	**110**	**13%**	**66%**				**4.79**	**10.2**	**50**	**131**	**$15**

Schafer,Jordan

Age: 28	Bats: L	Pos: LF CF		Health	B	LIMA Plan	C
Ht: 6' 1"	Wt: 190			PT/Exp	D	Rand Var	+1
				Consist	A	MM	1513

Season-long ct% and SBO spikes reaped regular AB following 2H trade. Poor h% hurt 1H BA early, but more GBs and LDs eventually paid off, and elite running game makes his future value PT dependent. Not for the risk averse, but if contact-and-grounders game sticks, UP: 500 AB could mean 50 SB.

Yr Tm	AB	R	HR	RBI	SB	BA	xBA	OBP	SLG	OPS	vL	vR	bb%	ct%	Eye	G	L	F	h%	HctX	PX	xPX	hr/f	Spd	SBO	SB%	#Wk	DOM	DIS	RC/G	RAR	BPV	BPX	R$
10 a/a	252	18	1	10	8	166		220	209	429			6	73	0.26				22		37			114	35%	44%				1.20		-28	-61	-$5
11 2 NL *	486	65	3	31	29	240	237	298	308	606	568	645	8	78	0.37	44	26	30	30	76	53	84	3%	126	28%	77%	16	13%	44%	3.14	-26.4	7	16	$11
12 HOU	313	40	4	23	27	211	196	297	294	591	356	636	10	66	0.34	44	21	35	31	72	66	76	6%	127	42%	75%	23	9%	65%	2.84	-17.3	-21	-53	$7
13 ATL *	263	32	3	22	22	223	220	302	316	618	285	735	10	70	0.38	48	21	30	31	73	73	77	7%	144	39%	79%	21	19%	67%	3.24	-6.6	5	13	$8
14 2 TM	210	26	1	15	30	238	248	310	305	615	400	681	9	77	0.46	53	24	23	30	85	57	69	3%	127	61%	81%	26	23%	58%	3.44	-1.5	13	35	$11
1st Half	65	7	0	2	11	185	244	243	246	489	450	496	7	77	0.33	64	14	21	24	77	63	63	0%	100	85%	100%	14	21%	57%	2.58	-2.4	4	11	-$1
2nd Half	145	19	1	13	19	262	250	340	331	671	386	774	10	77	0.52	48	28	23	33	88	54	71	4%	140	54%	73%	12	25%	58%	3.87	0.6	17	46	$17
15 Proj	**318**	**38**	**3**	**22**	**31**	**239**	**235**	**310**	**318**	**628**	**403**	**683**	**9**	**75**	**0.40**	**50**	**22**	**27**	**31**	**78**	**66**	**73**	**4%**	**128**	**44%**	**78%**				**3.43**	**-3.1**	**12**	**31**	**$14**

Schafer,Logan

Age: 28	Bats: L	Pos: LF		Health	A	LIMA Plan	D
Ht: 6' 1"	Wt: 195			PT/Exp	D	Rand Var	+3
				Consist	A	MM	2311

0-8-.181 in 116 AB at MIL. Profile of a strugging bench player. Contact and BA/xBA fell apart as PX/xPX and patience ticked up. But even in synch, he doesn't offer enough of any skill to be relevant. The good news is that his R$ can't get much worse. The bad news for him is that he's running out of chances to prove it.

Yr Tm	AB	R	HR	RBI	SB	BA	xBA	OBP	SLG	OPS	vL	vR	bb%	ct%	Eye	G	L	F	h%	HctX	PX	xPX	hr/f	Spd	SBO	SB%	#Wk	DOM	DIS	RC/G	RAR	BPV	BPX	R$
10																																		
11 MIL *	362	46	4	30	11	262	269	311	369	679	0	833	7	85	0.48	0	50	50	30	0	73	2	0%	122	21%	53%	4	0%	75%	3.68	-17.2	51	113	$8
12 MIL *	487	58	10	36	12	240	248	276	379	655	250	933	5	81	0.26	29	29	43	28	119	85	143	0%	144	21%	57%	5	40%	20%	3.32	-20.8	48	120	$8
13 MIL	298	29	4	33	7	211	246	279	322	601	497	625	8	80	0.42	46	20	34	25	83	79	82	5%	100	12%	88%	27	33%	37%	2.91	-10.6	30	75	$2
14 MIL *	277	31	2	20	5	202	238	280	325	605	670	538	10	75	0.43	44	18	38	26	87	103	96	0%	116	12%	68%	20	25%	40%	2.88	-7.8	39	105	-$1
1st Half	134	12	0	8	2	171	227	263	269	532	718	543	11	75	0.50	44	16	39	23	87	92	121	0%	104	12%	70%	11	27%	36%	2.18	-6.9	30	81	-$5
2nd Half	143	19	2	12	2	232	252	297	378	675	0	529	8	75	0.36	45	21	34	30	89	114	46	0%	124	11%	66%	9	22%	44%	3.67	-0.3	47	127	$4
15 Proj	**129**	**15**	**1**	**11**	**3**	**219**	**238**	**283**	**318**	**601**	**578**	**604**	**8**	**78**	**0.39**	**45**	**19**	**35**	**27**	**86**	**81**	**79**	**2%**	**107**	**13%**	**67%**				**2.88**	**-3.4**	**27**	**72**	**$1**

Schierholtz,Nate

Age: 31	Bats: L	Pos: RF		Health	B	LIMA Plan	D
Ht: 6' 2"	Wt: 215			PT/Exp	C	Rand Var	+5
				Consist	C	MM	3221

Should have been no surprise that he couldn't build on 2013 career year. Futility vs. LHP caps his AB. Nearly as bad vs. righties last season, as skills plunged across the board. The h% says he'll improve, but who wants to bet on how much and his opportunity? Consistency is a skill, not present here.

Yr Tm	AB	R	HR	RBI	SB	BA	xBA	OBP	SLG	OPS	vL	vR	bb%	ct%	Eye	G	L	F	h%	HctX	PX	xPX	hr/f	Spd	SBO	SB%	#Wk	DOM	DIS	RC/G	RAR	BPV	BPX	R$
10 SF	227	34	3	17	4	242	260	311	366	676	671	678	8	83	0.53	44	18	37	28	94	85	85	4%	124	16%	44%	27	30%	33%	3.48	-11.5	57	124	$2
11 SF	335	42	9	41	7	278	269	326	430	756	562	801	6	82	0.34	40	22	38	32	111	107	114	9%	81	13%	64%	22	50%	23%	4.74	-3.9	51	113	$10
12 2 NL	241	20	6	21	3	257	253	321	407	728	444	826	9	81	0.50	46	20	34	30	80	87	67	9%	121	8%	60%	26	31%	42%	4.41	-5.1	49	123	$3
13 CHC	462	56	21	68	6	251	282	301	470	770	553	799	6	80	0.31	40	20	40	27	104	147	115	14%	85	10%	67%	27	56%	15%	4.66	0.6	75	188	$14
14 2 NL	353	32	7	37	4	195	224	243	309	552	489	566	5	76	0.24	40	20	40	24	91	80	103	6%	102	13%	44%	25	28%	48%	2.21	-21.3	12	32	$0
1st Half	249	23	4	29	3	205	221	256	317	574	525	586	6	76	0.25	38	19	42	25	93	83	106	5%	95	14%	43%	14	29%	50%	2.39	-12.7	12	32	$2
2nd Half	104	9	3	8	1	173	232	209	288	498	369	519	5	77	0.21	45	21	34	19	86	71	98	11%	111	11%	50%	11	27%	45%	1.81	-7.5	9	24	-$6
15 Proj	**99**	**10**	**3**	**10**	**1**	**220**	**250**	**271**	**368**	**639**	**486**	**671**	**6**	**79**	**0.31**	**42**	**20**	**38**	**25**	**93**	**102**	**99**	**10%**	**97**	**11%**	**54%**				**3.13**	**-2.7**	**36**	**95**	**$1**

Schoop,Jonathan

Age: 23	Bats: R	Pos: 2B		Health	A	LIMA Plan	D+
Ht: 6' 2"	Wt: 210			PT/Exp	C	Rand Var	+2
				Consist	A	MM	3115

Rushed prospect flashed power upside, indifferent plate skills and little else in his rookie season. Paired hr/f surge with unfortunate h% as contact deteriorated further in 2nd half. He's young, healthy and athletic enough to improve, and the position helps his value. But... DN: More minor league time.

Yr Tm	AB	R	HR	RBI	SB	BA	xBA	OBP	SLG	OPS	vL	vR	bb%	ct%	Eye	G	L	F	h%	HctX	PX	xPX	hr/f	Spd	SBO	SB%	#Wk	DOM	DIS	RC/G	RAR	BPV	BPX	R$
10																																		
11																																		
12 aa	485	54	12	45	4	226		285	352	637			8	77	0.37				27		86			88	6%	55%				3.24		22	55	$4
13 BAL *	284	30	9	29	1	238	253	268	371	639	1167	750	4	79	0.19	67	17	17	27	135	88	69	50%	89	5%	27%	2	50%	0%	3.22	-4.3	21	53	$3
14 BAL	455	48	16	45	2	209	228	244	354	598	529	625	3	73	0.11	49	14	37	25	83	109	96	13%	84	3%	100%	27	33%	41%	2.65	-10.4	13	35	$4
1st Half	238	26	6	21	0	223	212	266	340	606	523	644	3	76	0.13	53	10	36	27	90	89	101	9%	88	0%	0%	14	21%	36%	2.73	-4.8	11	30	$2
2nd Half	217	22	10	24	2	194	237	219	369	587	537	605	3	70	0.09	45	18	37	23	74	133	89	18%	88	7%	100%	13	46%	46%	2.54	-5.8	19	51	$5
15 Proj	**437**	**46**	**17**	**44**	**2**	**227**	**238**	**268**	**386**	**654**	**594**	**678**	**4**	**75**	**0.17**	**48**	**15**	**37**	**26**	**80**	**115**	**94**	**14%**	**86**	**5%**	**61%**				**3.26**	**-1.8**	**17**	**45**	**$8**

Schumaker,Skip

Age: 35	Bats: L	Pos: LF		Health	C	LIMA Plan	D
Ht: 5' 10"	Wt: 195			PT/Exp	D	Rand Var	+1
				Consist	B	MM	1121

10-yr veteran has parlayed good contact, decent patience and utility into a nice MLB career without ever seeing double-digit HR or SB. But now in his mid-30s, BA/xBA, contact and HctX trends look irreversible; AB and R$ have followed suit. Career-worst 2014 BA is a long way from career .281 mark. The end nears.

Yr Tm	AB	R	HR	RBI	SB	BA	xBA	OBP	SLG	OPS	vL	vR	bb%	ct%	Eye	G	L	F	h%	HctX	PX	xPX	hr/f	Spd	SBO	SB%	#Wk	DOM	DIS	RC/G	RAR	BPV	BPX	R$
10 STL	476	66	5	42	5	265	279	328	338	667	541	691	8	87	0.67	59	22	20	30	90	51	58	6%	92	6%	63%	27	48%	22%	3.78	-20.5	33	72	$9
11 STL	367	34	2	38	0	283	257	333	351	685	714	682	7	86	0.54	52	23	25	32	71	54	51	2%	70	2%	0%	22	36%	41%	4.06	-12.4	25	56	$6
12 STL *	293	40	1	28	2	271	262	338	361	700	496	741	9	82	0.55	54	23	23	33	79	64	52	2%	115	3%	62%	23	43%	43%	4.25	-3.9	33	83	$5
13 LA	319	31	2	30	2	263	271	332	332	665	632	671	8	83	0.52	54	27	18	31	75	56	45	4%	79	4%	50%	27	33%	41%	3.65	-3.7	19	48	$4
14 CIN	247	22	2	22	2	235	242	287	308	595	508	614	7	80	0.36	56	20	24	29	63	62	47	4%	83	5%	67%	19	16%	47%	2.93	-6.3	9	24	$1
1st Half	121	13	1	13	1	240	246	273	314	587	604	584	4	81	0.22	60	18	22	29	72	62	44	5%	87	4%	100%	10	20%	50%	2.88	-3.1	10	27	$1
2nd Half	126	9	1	9	1	230	239	300	302	602	426	643	9	79	0.48	53	22	25	29	54	62	51	4%	82	6%	50%	9	11%	44%	2.96	-3.0	9	24	$0
15 Proj	**162**	**16**	**1**	**15**	**1**	**251**	**256**	**310**	**325**	**635**	**534**	**656**	**8**	**81**	**0.45**	**55**	**23**	**22**	**30**	**69**	**62**	**49**	**4%**	**87**	**4%**	**59%**				**3.37**	**-1.8**	**9**	**23**	**$3**

JOCK THOMPSON

Seager,Kyle

Age: 27 Bats: L Pos: 3B | Ht: 6' 0" Wt: 210
Health A | PT/Exp A | Consist A | LIMA Plan B+ | Rand Var 0 | MM 4135

1st half power and HctX surges pushed HR, RBI and BA to new highs, but the perception is still one of stability, not growth. BPX disagrees, and at 27, we have to think that he has yet to hit his ceiling. Health/consistency combo at a scarce position are valuable. Pay $1 more than perception. UP: 30 HR, .280

Yr Tm	AB	R	HR	RBI	SB	BA	xBA	OBP	SLG	OPS	vL	vR	bb%	ct%	Eye	G	L	F	h%	HctX	PX	xPX	hr/f	Spd	SBO	SB%	#Wk	DOM	DIS	RC/G	RAR	BPV	BPX	R$
10																																		
11 SEA *	554	62	8	51	11	264	261	313	383	697	570	719	7	82	0.40	30	28	42	31	119	91	118	5%	88	14%	57%	12	33%	58%	4.01	-12.9	43	96	$12
12 SEA	594	62	20	86	13	259	259	316	423	738	658	783	7	81	0.42	36	22	42	29	108	106	115	10%	74	13%	72%	28	46%	14%	4.51	-0.6	49	123	$18
13 SEA	615	79	22	69	9	260	252	338	426	764	690	808	10	80	0.56	34	21	45	29	97	111	106	10%	84	7%	75%	27	56%	22%	4.90	17.0	56	140	$19
14 SEA	590	71	25	96	7	268	268	334	454	788	661	862	8	80	0.44	37	22	41	30	131	124	142	13%	84	8%	58%	27	56%	22%	5.07	23.9	63	170	$23
1st Half	296	33	12	55	4	274	279	345	483	828	653	929	8	78	0.42	34	24	42	32	147	150	167	13%	75	10%	57%	14	64%	21%	5.52	15.6	73	197	$23
2nd Half	294	38	13	41	3	262	256	323	425	748	669	794	8	82	0.47	39	21	40	28	115	100	118	13%	96	6%	60%	13	46%	23%	4.62	8.0	54	146	$23
15 Proj	**597**	**72**	**24**	**89**	**8**	**264**	**267**	**329**	**444**	**773**	**674**	**827**	**8**	**81**	**0.46**	**36**	**22**	**42**	**29**	**116**	**123**	**124**	**12%**	**80**	**8%**	**62%**				**4.89**	**20.9**	**62**	**163**	**$20**

Segura,Jean

Age: 25 Bats: R Pos: SS | Ht: 5' 10" Wt: 205
Health A | PT/Exp B | Consist C | LIMA Plan B | Rand Var +3 | MM 1535

Our significant "DOWN" projection warning following huge 2013 wasn't down enough. Plate skills stayed consistent as HctX, h% and power plunges did most of the damage. 2nd half malaise due to nagging injuries and tragic family issue. Expect a bounce; he's better than this. Just not 2013 better.

Yr Tm	AB	R	HR	RBI	SB	BA	xBA	OBP	SLG	OPS	vL	vR	bb%	ct%	Eye	G	L	F	h%	HctX	PX	xPX	hr/f	Spd	SBO	SB%	#Wk	DOM	DIS	RC/G	RAR	BPV	BPX	R$
10																																		
11																																		
12 2 TM *	555	66	7	50	38	274	263	318	365	683	290	756	6	84	0.39	66	15	19	32	82	54	57	0%	156	33%	71%	10	30%	40%	3.98	-2.0	38	95	$23
13 MIL	588	74	12	49	44	294	282	329	423	752	865	716	4	86	0.30	59	18	23	33	100	76	69	10%	174	37%	77%	26	46%	31%	4.91	23.6	66	165	$35
14 MIL	513	61	5	31	20	246	265	289	326	614	511	643	5	86	0.40	59	18	23	28	79	51	52	5%	159	22%	69%	27	33%	41%	3.07	-3.4	46	124	$12
1st Half	303	41	4	22	14	244	270	277	333	610	410	667	4	86	0.27	60	18	22	27	82	54	53	7%	159	31%	64%	14	21%	43%	2.87	-3.4	46	124	$17
2nd Half	210	20	1	9	6	248	258	306	314	620	661	609	7	86	0.59	58	18	23	28	75	47	50	2%	136	12%	86%	13	46%	38%	3.33	0.6	40	108	$5
15 Proj	**564**	**66**	**6**	**40**	**31**	**267**	**269**	**309**	**358**	**667**	**625**	**680**	**5**	**86**	**0.39**	**60**	**18**	**23**	**30**	**86**	**59**	**58**	**6%**	**161**	**27%**	**75%**				**3.79**	**9.2**	**42**	**111**	**$22**

Semien,Marcus

Age: 24 Bats: R Pos: 3B 2B | Ht: 6' 1" Wt: 195
Health A | PT/Exp D | Consist C | LIMA Plan B+ | Rand Var +1 | MM 3425

6-28-.234 with 3 SB in 231 AB at CHW. Versatile prospect shows fine patience, HR pop, running game flashes. But that 8/70 bb%/ct% combo in CHW say skills haven't translated—yet. Aggressive Sept paid off (3 HR, .273 BA, 13/5 K/BB in 66 AB). His BA remains a short-term hazard, but there's potential here.

Yr Tm	AB	R	HR	RBI	SB	BA	xBA	OBP	SLG	OPS	vL	vR	bb%	ct%	Eye	G	L	F	h%	HctX	PX	xPX	hr/f	Spd	SBO	SB%	#Wk	DOM	DIS	RC/G	RAR	BPV	BPX	R$
10																																		
11																																		
12																																		
13 CHW*	587	97	20	61	22	256	249	354	428	782	783	643	13	79	0.71	27	25	48	30	95	118	95	9%	133	16%	74%	5	40%	60%	5.18	25.3	77	193	$24
14 CHW*	534	68	17	62	8	225	245	303	385	688	735	637	10	74	0.42	40	21	39	27	78	120	75	10%	137	8%	77%	15	33%	53%	3.84	7.3	54	146	$10
1st Half	261	31	6	28	4	194	216	267	310	577	714	561	9	70	0.33	42	21	38	25	67	92	59	8%	147	10%	62%	10	10%	70%	2.57	-6.8	16	43	$3
2nd Half	273	37	11	35	4	255	271	337	458	795	778	843	11	78	0.55	38	21	42	29	98	144	108	14%	110	5%	100%	5	80%	20%	5.38	15.8	83	224	$18
15 Proj	**416**	**60**	**12**	**47**	**10**	**241**	**247**	**329**	**394**	**722**	**743**	**712**	**11**	**76**	**0.54**	**36**	**22**	**41**	**29**	**89**	**115**	**91**	**9%**	**133**	**11%**	**76%**				**4.34**	**8.1**	**52**	**137**	**$12**

Sierra,Moises

Age: 26 Bats: R Pos: RF | Ht: 6' 1" Wt: 220
Health A | PT/Exp D | Consist A | LIMA Plan D | Rand Var +1 | MM 3511

2-9-.230, with 3 SB in 161 AB at TOR/CHW. Consistency isn't a good thing when you've had less than 170 MLB AB in each of the last three seasons. Hints of a power/speed combo, but high GB% and low SB% hold him back. Consistently mediocre plate skills make him a bench hand at best, journeyman at worst.

Yr Tm	AB	R	HR	RBI	SB	BA	xBA	OBP	SLG	OPS	vL	vR	bb%	ct%	Eye	G	L	F	h%	HctX	PX	xPX	hr/f	Spd	SBO	SB%	#Wk	DOM	DIS	RC/G	RAR	BPV	BPX	R$
10																																		
11 aa	495	67	16	55	13	252		297	396	693			6	79	0.30				29		95			105	24%	46%				3.60		37	82	$14
12 TOR *	524	56	18	57	6	236	229	282	377	659	815	545	6	73	0.23	53	17	30	29	108	96	134	19%	66	10%	45%	10	40%	50%	3.39	-23.4	1	3	$9
13 TOR *	486	54	10	52	10	240	236	279	382	661	786	845	5	68	0.17	48	20	32	33	89	117	80	4%	123	15%	69%	7	29%	57%	3.52	-11.1	16	40	$10
14 2 AL	161	22	2	9	3	230	236	265	342	606	655	570	5	73	0.19	49	19	31	30	75	90	85	5%	144	12%	75%	24	25%	71%	3.01	-4.3	20	54	$1
1st Half	106	13	2	7	0	208	234	234	302	536	452	588	4	73	0.14	55	22	23	27	81	77	75	11%	99	0%	0%	14	21%	71%	2.30	-5.6	-9	-24	$0
2nd Half	55	9	0	2	3	273	226	322	418	740	956	527	7	75	0.29	38	15	48	37	63	115	104	0%	160	31%	75%	10	30%	70%	4.68	1.1	54	146	$2
15 Proj	**198**	**26**	**3**	**16**	**5**	**244**	**237**	**287**	**375**	**662**	**742**	**610**	**6**	**73**	**0.22**	**47**	**18**	**34**	**32**	**82**	**104**	**94**	**7%**	**143**	**18%**	**66%**				**3.55**	**-2.7**	**27**	**70**	**$5**

Simmons,Andrelton

Age: 25 Bats: R Pos: SS | Ht: 6' 2" Wt: 195
Health B | PT/Exp B | Consist B | LIMA Plan A | Rand Var +1 | MM 1335

Playing through injuries (ankle, hip, shoulder) factored into FB and power decline. PRO: Plus contact, speed still intact; 1H HctX, xPX still positive. CON: No signs of pitch selection or running game (despite good speed). May never fully exploit his physical tools, but improved health should produce a rebound.

Yr Tm	AB	R	HR	RBI	SB	BA	xBA	OBP	SLG	OPS	vL	vR	bb%	ct%	Eye	G	L	F	h%	HctX	PX	xPX	hr/f	Spd	SBO	SB%	#Wk	DOM	DIS	RC/G	RAR	BPV	BPX	R$
10																																		
11																																		
12 ATL *	340	41	5	37	9	278	271	335	396	731	796	726	8	87	0.66	56	17	27	31	85	72	45	8%	127	12%	81%	11	45%	18%	4.74	6.1	62	155	$10
13 ATL	606	76	17	59	6	248	272	296	396	692	692	691	6	91	0.73	42	18	39	25	108	86	89	8%	139	8%	55%	27	59%	7%	3.85	6.3	89	223	$13
14 ATL	540	44	7	46	4	244	250	286	331	617	679	603	6	89	0.53	52	16	31	26	102	56	87	5%	130	7%	44%	26	54%	23%	3.11	-2.9	53	143	$6
1st Half	291	21	5	22	2	247	246	287	351	638	891	587	6	90	0.57	50	15	35	26	115	59	105	5%	162	7%	40%	14	64%	14%	3.31	0.6	68	184	$6
2nd Half	249	23	2	24	2	241	250	284	309	593	481	623	6	88	0.50	56	18	27	27	86	52	66	4%	92	6%	50%	12	42%	33%	2.88	-2.7	34	92	$7
15 Proj	**557**	**58**	**11**	**53**	**6**	**250**	**262**	**298**	**365**	**663**	**694**	**654**	**6**	**89**	**0.63**	**46**	**18**	**36**	**26**	**99**	**73**	**79**	**6%**	**129**	**8%**	**58%**				**3.62**	**6.4**	**54**	**143**	**$12**

Singleton,Jonathan

Age: 23 Bats: L Pos: 1B | Ht: 6' 2" Wt: 255
Health A | PT/Exp C | Consist C | LIMA Plan D+ | Rand Var +5 | MM 5105

13-44-.168 in 310 AB at HOU. Contact struggles weren't surprising given his history, but their extent—57% in HOU—is discouraging. Patience and power metrics are fine; hr/f is potentially scary with more bat-on-ball. He'll adjust, but how much and how quickly? BA-killer could need more Triple-A time.

Yr Tm	AB	R	HR	RBI	SB	BA	xBA	OBP	SLG	OPS	vL	vR	bb%	ct%	Eye	G	L	F	h%	HctX	PX	xPX	hr/f	Spd	SBO	SB%	#Wk	DOM	DIS	RC/G	RAR	BPV	BPX	R$
10																																		
11																																		
12 aa	461	72	17	61	5	252		350	428	777			13	68	0.47				34		131			100	5%	71%				5.08		35	88	$12
13 a/a	283	28	7	31	1	200		307	322	629			13	58	0.37				32		116			92	1%	100%				3.16		-16	-40	-$1
14 HOU *	505	68	23	75	3	190	212	301	375	676	805	559	14	62	0.41	40	14	46	25	78	160	105	16%	61	5%	40%	18	22%	67%	3.47	-10.9	22	59	$6
1st Half	286	37	14	44	2	217	231	316	417	733	989	498	13	60	0.43	46	13	41	27	113	159	119	17%	68	6%	35%	5	20%	80%	4.14	-0.3	40	108	$11
2nd Half	219	31	9	31	1	155	190	283	320	603	685	580	15	55	0.40	36	15	49	22	59	161	99	15%	62	4%	50%	13	23%	62%	2.70	-10.7	1	3	$0
15 Proj	**393**	**50**	**17**	**52**	**2**	**211**	**211**	**321**	**395**	**716**	**973**	**625**	**14**	**60**	**0.40**	**40**	**14**	**46**	**30**	**81**	**165**	**107**	**16%**	**66**	**4%**	**58%**				**4.04**	**-1.5**	**20**	**52**	**$7**

Sizemore,Grady

Age: 32 Bats: L Pos: LF RF CF | Ht: 6' 2" Wt: 200
Health F | PT/Exp F | Consist F | LIMA Plan D+ | Rand Var +2 | MM 3213

5-27-.233 with 6 SB in 347 AB at BOS/PHI. HR and SBs were his game prior to all the surgeries and missed time. FB% now well off its peak, hr/f a shadow of what it was. Can still steal a base but opportunities are unlikely given his brittleness. Won't offer value with his BA. FFF reliability says all you need to know.

Yr Tm	AB	R	HR	RBI	SB	BA	xBA	OBP	SLG	OPS	vL	vR	bb%	ct%	Eye	G	L	F	h%	HctX	PX	xPX	hr/f	Spd	SBO	SB%	#Wk	DOM	DIS	RC/G	RAR	BPV	BPX	R$
10 CLE	128	15	0	13	4	211	207	271	289	560	326	706	7	73	0.26	39	19	42	29	91	65	116	0%	114	21%	67%	7	14%	43%	2.41	-11.0	-7	-15	-$1
11 CLE *	296	35	11	36	0	229	248	280	424	703	582	751	7	69	0.23	40	18	42	29	103	160	137	13%	84	4%	0%	16	44%	31%	3.80	-12.1	45	100	$3
12																																		
13																																		
14 2 TM *	393	38	6	28	6	231	239	296	345	641	491	715	8	78	0.43	42	20	38	28	96	86	102	5%	113	7%	86%	25	40%	32%	3.43	-7.9	35	95	$4
1st Half	198	15	2	15	5	217	233	288	318	606	459	672	9	79	0.46	44	19	37	27	110	78	127	4%	91	10%	100%	12	42%	33%	3.11	-5.4	24	65	$1
2nd Half	195	24	4	13	1	245	244	304	373	677	529	765	8	78	0.39	39	22	39	30	80	94	74	6%	135	4%	50%	13	38%	31%	3.77	-1.3	45	122	$6
15 Proj	**291**	**32**	**5**	**27**	**3**	**229**	**235**	**292**	**360**	**652**	**484**	**720**	**7**	**74**	**0.31**	**40**	**19**	**40**	**29**	**96**	**106**	**113**	**6%**	**102**	**8%**	**64%**				**3.38**	**-3.2**	**26**	**69**	**$4**

JOCK THOMPSON

Smith,Seth

Age: 32 Bats: L Pos: LF RF | Ht: 6' 3" Wt: 210
Health A | LIMA Plan C+ | PT/Exp B | Rand Var +1 | Consist B | MM 4135

Mildly surprising: He hit in SD; reversed skills decline, was able to hold down a defensive position. Not surprising: New manager kept him away from LHP, in line with most of his career. Even though 2nd half seemed rough, plate skills remained, and HctX and PX call for continued pop in 2015.

Yr Tm	AB	R	HR	RBI	SB	BA	xBA	OBP	SLG	OPS	vL	vR	bb%	ct%	Eye	G	L	F	h%	HctX	PX	xPX	hr/f	Spd	SBO	SB%	#Wk	DOM	DIS	RC/G	RAR	BPV	BPX	R$
10 COL	358	55	17	52	2	246	275	314	469	783	393	848	9	81	0.52	36	16	48	26	107	139	132	12%	111	4%	67%	27	63%	30%	4.94	-3.4	89	193	$9
11 COL	476	67	15	59	10	284	276	347	483	830	576	891	9	80	0.49	38	22	40	33	120	133	127	10%	123	10%	83%	27	67%	19%	6.00	9.9	85	189	$18
12 OAK	383	55	14	52	2	240	258	333	420	754	521	805	12	74	0.51	41	23	36	29	107	126	130	14%	84	4%	50%	26	58%	35%	4.56	-1.8	49	123	$8
13 OAK	368	49	8	40	0	253	243	329	391	721	621	748	10	74	0.41	45	20	35	32	88	113	102	8%	87	0%	0%	27	37%	41%	4.33	2.9	36	90	$6
14 SD	443	55	12	48	1	266	281	367	440	807	744	815	13	80	0.79	47	21	32	31	115	126	115	11%	98	1%	50%	27	59%	26%	5.56	22.6	81	219	$11
1st Half	231	30	8	24	1	273	292	376	485	861	726	874	13	80	0.77	50	18	32	31	125	149	116	14%	106	3%	50%	14	71%	21%	6.23	16.5	99	268	$13
2nd Half	212	25	4	24	0	259	272	357	392	749	758	746	13	81	0.83	44	25	31	30	104	101	114	7%	88	0%	0%	13	46%	31%	4.84	6.8	61	165	$10
15 Proj	434	57	12	50	1	258	269	346	422	768	642	792	12	78	0.60	45	21	34	31	106	124	115	10%	94	2%	60%				4.96	15.4	57	149	$9

Smoak,Justin

Age: 28 Bats: B Pos: 1B | Ht: 6' 4" Wt: 230
Health B | LIMA Plan D | PT/Exp C | Rand Var 0 | Consist C | MM 3003

7-30-.202 in 248 AB at SEA. He's not just squandered MLB opps, but also his unique headline potential. The real story—poor ct%, inconsistent SLG despite decent power metrics—is page-3 stuff; nagging injuries, 2nd half demotion limited his AB in 2014. But xPX, HctX and age can't be ignored. Still, end-game material only.

Yr Tm	AB	R	HR	RBI	SB	BA	xBA	OBP	SLG	OPS	vL	vR	bb%	ct%	Eye	G	L	F	h%	HctX	PX	xPX	hr/f	Spd	SBO	SB%	#Wk	DOM	DIS	RC/G	RAR	BPV	BPX	R$
10 2AL *	531	64	19	70	1	222	251	318	376	694	651	691	12	74	0.54	38	23	39	26	124	112	140	13%	57	1%	100%	19	47%	42%	3.93	-27.5	29	63	$6
11 SEA	427	38	15	55	0	234	222	323	396	719	720	719	11	75	0.52	44	14	43	28	106	119	129	11%	71	0%	0%	25	48%	32%	4.24	-17.9	43	96	$5
12 SEA *	549	56	19	54	2	213	224	291	352	643	703	627	10	76	0.46	40	18	42	25	96	90	116	12%	72	1%	100%	26	35%	54%	3.33	-33.1	20	50	$3
13 SEA *	475	54	20	51	0	235	234	326	405	731	548	839	12	74	0.51	35	20	46	28	111	120	152	13%	81	0%	0%	25	44%	40%	4.41	-2.7	41	103	$8
14 SEA *	453	46	11	55	0	225	223	293	350	643	618	611	9	73	0.37	42	18	39	28	116	101	146	10%	60	3%	0%	18	33%	43%	3.26	-12.1	12	32	$4
1st Half	257	29	8	31	0	201	238	269	345	614	626	656	9	73	0.35	41	20	39	24	124	115	156	11%	63	2%	0%	11	45%	36%	2.91	-10.2	22	59	$4
2nd Half	196	17	4	24	0	257	178	326	357	683	539	333	9	74	0.39	50	8	42	33	62	83	82	0%	75	4%	0%	7	14%	57%	3.78	-2.2	5	14	$4
15 Proj	252	26	8	29	0	231	223	310	376	686	674	692	10	74	0.44	42	16	42	28	97	111	125	11%	72	2%	11%				3.77	-3.1	15	38	$4

Smolinski,Jacob

Age: 26 Bats: R Pos: LF | Ht: 5' 11" Wt: 215
Health B | LIMA Plan D | PT/Exp C | Rand Var -1 | Consist B | MM 2221

3-12-.349 in 86 AB at TEX. Quickly established himself as a 2014 Ranger by breaking a bone in his foot after just 36 AB. Lost seven weeks, but impressed in small MLB sample. Minor-league track record (decent plate skills, little power or speed) doesn't indicate it's for real, though.

Yr Tm	AB	R	HR	RBI	SB	BA	xBA	OBP	SLG	OPS	vL	vR	bb%	ct%	Eye	G	L	F	h%	HctX	PX	xPX	hr/f	Spd	SBO	SB%	#Wk	DOM	DIS	RC/G	RAR	BPV	BPX	R$
10																																		
11 aa	396	31	5	27	4	208		290	298	588			10	84	0.73				24		68			85	10%	45%				2.67		39	87	-$2
12 aa	408	57	5	33	7	228		337	333	669			14	78	0.76				28		76			105	9%	62%				3.65		36	90	$4
13 a/a	370	36	6	29	7	219		298	316	614			10	79	0.53				26		69			107	8%	87%				3.13		24	60	$2
14 TEX *	382	47	11	41	4	253	265	305	408	714	1357	757	7	76	0.31	40	26	34	31	122	118	106	14%	92	7%	64%	6	50%	50%	4.21	5.8	43	116	$9
1st Half	277	31	8	24	4	229	258	291	383	674			8	78	0.39				27		113			103	10%	64%				3.63		51	138	$10
2nd Half	105	15	3	16	0	317	259	345	475	820	1357	757	4	72	0.15	40	26	34	42	115	133	106	14%	76	0%	0%	6	50%	50%	6.12	6.7	26	70	$6
15 Proj	160	19	3	16	2	249	253	332	367	699	956	616	8	77	0.40	40	26	34	31	104	94	95	7%	87	6%	69%				3.88	0.7	23	60	$4

Snider,Travis

Age: 27 Bats: L Pos: RF LF | Ht: 6' 0" Wt: 235
Health B | LIMA Plan C+ | PT/Exp D | Rand Var 0 | Consist D | MM 3123

What to ignore: Numerology vs. LHP (42 AB, 42% h%); 2nd half hr/f. What not to ignore: 2nd half skills growth (see BPV splits), and season-long penchant for contact. GB-heavy approach still dogs him, but post-break HctX/xPX tandem rekindles moderate hope for a bit of upside. Flyer-worthy.

Yr Tm	AB	R	HR	RBI	SB	BA	xBA	OBP	SLG	OPS	vL	vR	bb%	ct%	Eye	G	L	F	h%	HctX	PX	xPX	hr/f	Spd	SBO	SB%	#Wk	DOM	DIS	RC/G	RAR	BPV	BPX	R$
10 TOR *	379	47	18	45	8	256	279	298	463	760	702	783	6	73	0.22	41	24	35	31	109	152	129	18%	78	16%	67%	16	38%	19%	4.61	-7.3	50	109	$11
11 TOR *	435	52	6	56	16	247	239	290	367	658	300	708	6	75	0.24	47	17	37	32	94	102	97	6%	73	22%	80%	10	30%	50%	3.65	-20.9	17	38	$11
12 2TM *	373	56	13	55	3	268	259	337	437	774	1110	595	10	74	0.41	56	19	26	33	79	119	74	13%	80	8%	42%	12	25%	58%	4.93	2.2	36	90	$11
13 PIT *	299	32	5	29	3	224	216	290	331	621	291	644	8	72	0.33	52	15	33	30	96	83	78	8%	82	9%	40%	22	32%	59%	3.01	-9.6	-1	-3	$1
14 PIT	322	37	13	38	1	264	268	338	438	776	1054	734	10	79	0.51	49	19	31	30	91	119	90	16%	71	2%	50%	27	48%	33%	5.03	11.6	54	146	$9
1st Half	144	11	4	14	0	229	226	311	340	651	727	645	10	77	0.48	50	19	31	27	78	71	80	12%	98	0%	0%	14	29%	50%	3.45	-1.3	17	46	$0
2nd Half	178	26	9	24	1	292	299	360	517	877	1167	816	9	81	0.53	49	20	32	32	102	157	98	20%	61	4%	50%	13	69%	15%	6.54	13.9	88	238	$16
15 Proj	370	45	12	44	3	255	256	322	411	733	890	707	9	76	0.41	50	18	31	31	92	116	87	14%	71	6%	51%				4.40	4.4	35	93	$11

Sogard,Eric

Age: 29 Bats: L Pos: 2B | Ht: 5' 10" Wt: 190
Health B | LIMA Plan D+ | PT/Exp D | Rand Var +2 | Consist C | MM 1323

Only thing more perplexing than his off-season contest popularity is his profile. Excellent ct%, improving Eye, and outstanding LD history comes with little production. One reason? Persistent weak contact (HctX). Modest SB carry most of his value now, but that "Face of MLB" could soon be planted on the sidewalk.

Yr Tm	AB	R	HR	RBI	SB	BA	xBA	OBP	SLG	OPS	vL	vR	bb%	ct%	Eye	G	L	F	h%	HctX	PX	xPX	hr/f	Spd	SBO	SB%	#Wk	DOM	DIS	RC/G	RAR	BPV	BPX	R$
10 OAK *	521	55	3	44	9	243	362	312	320	632	2000	533	9	84	0.64	50	50	0	28	172	55	78	0%	124	14%	45%	3	33%	33%	3.15	-16.3	39	85	$6
11 OAK *	385	44	5	29	9	229	230	287	318	605	154	652	8	86	0.58	37	19	44	26	76	60	71	8%	100	13%	71%	12	42%	42%	3.01	-13.7	39	87	$3
12 OAK *	259	28	5	22	9	223	256	282	327	609	450	487	8	85	0.56	39	26	35	24	83	60	61	7%	103	20%	72%	14	29%	36%	3.01	-7.1	38	95	$3
13 OAK	368	45	2	35	10	266	256	322	364	686	640	695	7	86	0.53	35	25	40	30	64	73	44	2%	105	16%	67%	27	56%	19%	3.93	5.4	50	125	$9
14 OAK	291	38	1	22	11	223	241	298	268	567	478	581	10	87	0.84	42	24	35	25	65	36	52	1%	89	18%	73%	26	27%	38%	2.66	-4.6	26	70	$4
1st Half	149	18	0	9	6	188	236	261	221	482	296	509	9	88	0.78	44	22	34	21	46	30	31	0%	86	22%	75%	14	21%	43%	1.85	-6.7	21	57	$0
2nd Half	142	20	1	13	5	261	247	338	317	654	633	658	11	87	0.89	39	26	35	30	86	43	75	2%	97	15%	71%	12	33%	33%	3.72	2.0	33	89	$8
15 Proj	287	36	3	24	9	240	249	307	318	626	528	644	9	86	0.71	39	24	37	27	71	57	56	3%	97	17%	70%				3.24	-1.3	40	106	$7

Solano,Donovan

Age: 27 Bats: R Pos: 2B | Ht: 5' 9" Wt: 205
Health A | LIMA Plan D | PT/Exp D | Rand Var 0 | Consist B | MM 1223

3-28-.252 in 310 AB at MIA. Made the Opening Day roster after Ed Lucas was HBP late in spring training, but didn't exactly seize the opportunity. Even in the 2nd half when h% cooperated, too many ground balls, dismal power and no speed resulted in nothing but an empty BA. And that's the best case scenario.

Yr Tm	AB	R	HR	RBI	SB	BA	xBA	OBP	SLG	OPS	vL	vR	bb%	ct%	Eye	G	L	F	h%	HctX	PX	xPX	hr/f	Spd	SBO	SB%	#Wk	DOM	DIS	RC/G	RAR	BPV	BPX	R$
10 aaa	330	29	3	19	1	210		228	268	496			2	88	0.20				23		39			109	4%	55%				1.95		23	50	-$3
11 a/a	330	18	2	22	1	209		244	296	539			4	82	0.26				25		72			83	2%	100%				2.34		22	49	-$4
12 MIA *	426	39	2	38	10	270	248	317	342	659	683	736	6	79	0.32	45	28	27	34	107	53	72	3%	119	8%	100%	20	20%	45%	3.93	-5.1	7	18	$8
13 MIA *	427	39	4	41	3	261	253	304	337	641	544	652	6	84	0.37	50	23	27	30	95	53	52	4%	93	3%	75%	18	17%	44%	3.54	-1.5	18	45	$6
14 MIA *	331	27	3	30	1	240	242	281	309	590	574	638	5	80	0.28	51	24	26	29	95	54	62	5%	82	4%	33%	27	19%	44%	2.85	-5.3	0	0	$2
1st Half	91	6	1	10	0	159	209	194	211	406	458	477	4	78	0.20	48	20	31	19	93	39	64	6%	77	0%	0%	14	0%	43%	1.25	-6.4	-23	-62	-$9
2nd Half	240	21	2	20	1	271	252	320	346	666	628	676	6	80	0.32	52	24	24	33	96	59	61	4%	87	4%	33%	13	38%	46%	3.68	2.0	9	24	$6
15 Proj	298	25	3	27	2	238	247	285	312	597	548	616	5	81	0.30	49	24	27	29	97	56	60	4%	89	4%	68%				2.90	-4.4	-1	-2	$3

Solarte,Yangervis

Age: 27 Bats: B Pos: 3B 2B | Ht: 5' 11" Wt: 195
Health A | LIMA Plan D+ | PT/Exp B | Rand Var 0 | Consist B | MM 1123

Relative unknown popped a .429 Mar BA, a .834 Apr/May OPS and some NYC celebrity before heading to SD in July trade. Overall, improved patience and average HctX provided the tools for his surge. But 2nd half fade, speed-less GB tilt, and below-average power all combine to make a repeat unlikely. Only consider in deep leagues.

Yr Tm	AB	R	HR	RBI	SB	BA	xBA	OBP	SLG	OPS	vL	vR	bb%	ct%	Eye	G	L	F	h%	HctX	PX	xPX	hr/f	Spd	SBO	SB%	#Wk	DOM	DIS	RC/G	RAR	BPV	BPX	R$
10 aa	127	11	2	14	1	240		254	351	605			2	85	0.12				27		82			92	8%	40%				2.88		38	83	$0
11 aa	459	46	4	35	4	278		304	385	689			4	90	0.40				30		75			95	8%	44%				3.99		60	133	$9
12 aaa	518	47	9	37	2	244		283	340	623			5	90	0.56				26		60			84	3%	64%				3.23		47	118	$4
13 aaa	526	47	9	53	2	231		270	334	604			5	85	0.35				26		72			79	2%	100%				3.01		33	83	$4
14 2TM	469	56	10	48	0	260	254	336	369	705	760	673	10	88	0.91	45	19	35	28	99	72	71	7%	85	1%	0%	26	42%	12%	4.23	7.0	56	151	$10
1st Half	235	26	6	30	0	264	261	346	400	746	588	832	11	87	0.90	45	19	36	28	114	94	84	8%	70	0%	0%	14	50%	21%	4.74	7.1	67	181	$10
2nd Half	234	30	4	18	0	256	245	327	338	665	952	520	10	88	0.93	46	20	34	28	85	49	59	6%	112	1%	0%	12	33%	0%	3.73	0.3	48	130	$9
15 Proj	388	41	8	36	1	250	256	307	357	664	772	607	8	87	0.65	46	20	35	27	97	73	69	7%	83	2%	48%				3.69	-0.1	38	99	$7

BRENT HERSHEY

Soler,Jorge

Age: 23 Bats: R Pos: RF
Ht: 6' 4" Wt: 215

Health	B	LIMA Plan	A+
PT/Exp	F	Rand Var	+1
Consist	F	MM	5145

5-20-.292 in 89 AB at CHC. Blasted onto the scene in late Aug. Outside of standard rookie caveat, some caution warranted with his injury history (hamstrings barked in 2014's 1st half; leg sidelined him in 2013), but scouting reports glow with the patience and power that he displayed in this small sample. Keeper gold.

Yr Tm	AB	R	HR	RBI	SB	BA	xBA	OBP	SLG	OPS	vL	vR	bb%	ct%	Eye	G	L	F	h%	HctX	PX	xPX	hr/f	Spd	SBO	SB%	#Wk	DOM	DIS	RC/G	RAR	BPV	BPX	R$
10																																		
11																																		
12																																		
13																																		
14 CHC *	264	38	16	59	1	296	313	365	596	961	701	964	10	74	0.42	52	12	36	35	129	229	131	21%	98	3%	47%	6	67%	33%	7.79	27.0	129	349	$14
1st Half	24	3	0	5	0	299	356	362	566	927			9	77	0.43				39		273			91	0%	0%				7.44		173	468	-$20
2nd Half	240	35	16	54	1	296	309	366	599	965	701	964	10	73	0.42	52	12	36	34	128	224	131	21%	103	4%	47%	6	67%	33%	7.82	25.5	126	341	$17
15 Proj	**522**	**71**	**22**	**91**	**2**	**266**	**280**	**326**	**492**	**819**	**645**	**870**	**9**	**76**	**0.41**	**52**	**12**	**36**	**31**	**115**	**168**	**118**	**16%**	**110**	**3%**	**50%**				**5.62**	**24.5**	**82**	**215**	**$18**

Soriano,Alfonso

Age: 39 Bats: R Pos: RF DH
Ht: 6' 1" Wt: 195

Health	A	LIMA Plan	D
PT/Exp	B	Rand Var	+1
Consist	C	MM	4211

The fall was swift, as his bb% and ct% bottomed out, and the Yankees cut ties in early July. The power skills have eroded, but HctX and xPX are still luminous enough if hr/f would cooperate. That will depend on AB, something that no one was willing to give him in the 2nd half. At 39, this may be the end.

Yr Tm	AB	R	HR	RBI	SB	BA	xBA	OBP	SLG	OPS	vL	vR	bb%	ct%	Eye	G	L	F	h%	HctX	PX	xPX	hr/f	Spd	SBO	SB%	#Wk	DOM	DIS	RC/G	RAR	BPV	BPX	R$
10 CHC	496	67	24	79	5	258	269	322	496	818	944	764	8	75	0.37	29	16	54	30	102	171	159	12%	104	6%	83%	27	67%	11%	5.47	4.4	88	191	$16
11 CHC	475	50	26	88	2	244	263	289	469	759	812	741	5	76	0.24	29	20	51	27	109	154	148	14%	75	3%	67%	26	50%	27%	4.49	-9.4	63	140	$13
12 CHC	561	68	32	108	6	262	262	322	499	821	831	818	7	73	0.29	36	20	44	31	107	161	153	18%	85	6%	75%	27	52%	30%	5.43	6.9	62	155	$21
13 2 TM	581	84	34	101	18	255	267	302	489	791	904	735	6	73	0.23	38	20	42	29	96	164	127	19%	80	23%	67%	26	50%	35%	4.81	6.3	61	153	$28
14 NYY	226	22	6	23	1	221	226	244	367	611	685	563	3	69	0.08	35	20	45	30	93	129	121	8%	78	3%	100%	14	29%	64%	2.92	-7.3	8	22	$1
1st Half	215	21	6	23	1	228	233	251	381	632	716	578	3	70	0.09	36	19	44	30	94	134	118	9%	77	3%	100%	14	29%	64%	3.16	-5.5	17	46	$2
2nd Half	11	1	0	0	0	91	100	91	91	182	0	286	0	45	0.00	0	40	60	20	79	0	185		96	0%	0%				0.23	-1.5	-187	-505	-$11
15 Proj	**165**	**19**	**6**	**26**	**2**	**247**	**242**	**293**	**416**	**708**	**768**	**682**	**6**	**73**	**0.21**	**35**	**20**	**46**	**31**	**101**	**135**	**137**	**10%**	**83**	**8%**	**73%**				**4.05**	**0.2**	**33**	**86**	**$5**

Soto,Geovany

Age: 32 Bats: R Pos: CA
Ht: 6' 1" Wt: 235

Health	F	LIMA Plan	D
PT/Exp	F	Rand Var	0
Consist	D	MM	4011

1-11-.250 in 80 AB at TEX/OAK. Spring training knee surgery wiped out 1st half, groin and back issues took a bite out of 2d half. xPX and HctX show that there's still pop in the bat; improved ct% a good sign, too. But with health history and its related 4-year AB trend, the Risk Meter just blew a fuse.

Yr Tm	AB	R	HR	RBI	SB	BA	xBA	OBP	SLG	OPS	vL	vR	bb%	ct%	Eye	G	L	F	h%	HctX	PX	xPX	hr/f	Spd	SBO	SB%	#Wk	DOM	DIS	RC/G	RAR	BPV	BPX	R$
10 CHC	322	47	17	53	0	280	281	393	497	890	1072	796	16	74	0.75	36	24	40	33	129	153	179	18%	71	1%	0%	22	59%	27%	6.89	24.4	75	163	$11
11 CHC	421	46	17	54	0	228	241	310	411	721	971	643	10	71	0.36	41	19	40	28	111	143	125	14%	64	0%	0%	25	36%	36%	4.11	-1.2	37	82	$6
12 2 TM	324	45	11	39	1	198	237	270	343	613	677	589	8	77	0.39	40	21	40	22	110	94	139	11%	80	1%	100%	23	30%	26%	2.91	-12.5	24	60	$1
13 TEX	163	20	9	22	1	245	240	328	466	794	656	874	11	63	0.33	32	22	46	33	113	181	201	19%	79	7%	33%	25	32%	52%	4.95	6.0	45	113	$3
14 2 AL *	131	12	2	13	0	228	220	275	336	611	677	655	6	70	0.22	44	20	36	31	108	103	161	5%	79	0%	0%	11	45%	36%	3.05	-1.0	1	3	-$1
1st Half																																		
2nd Half	131	12	2	13	0	228	220	275	336	611	677	655	6	70	0.22	44	20	36	31	108	103	161	5%	79	0%	0%	11	45%	36%	3.05	-1.3	1	3	-$1
15 Proj	**223**	**26**	**7**	**27**	**0**	**229**	**239**	**302**	**387**	**689**	**724**	**672**	**9**	**71**	**0.35**	**39**	**21**	**40**	**29**	**112**	**129**	**160**	**12%**	**73**	**2%**	**42%**				**3.81**	**2.8**	**19**	**51**	**$4**

Span,Denard

Age: 31 Bats: L Pos: CF
Ht: 6' 0" Wt: 210

Health	B	LIMA Plan	B+
PT/Exp	A	Rand Var	-2
Consist	B	MM	1555

Overcame early-season concussion to set the franchise record for hits. The .300 BA won't last (see 2nd half h%) but prime ct% and rising HctX ensure a solid floor, even if meager FB% caps the HR. Crossing 30 means the bags become a bit more risky, but he still remains a multi-category asset.

Yr Tm	AB	R	HR	RBI	SB	BA	xBA	OBP	SLG	OPS	vL	vR	bb%	ct%	Eye	G	L	F	h%	HctX	PX	xPX	hr/f	Spd	SBO	SB%	#Wk	DOM	DIS	RC/G	RAR	BPV	BPX	R$
10 MIN	629	85	3	58	26	264	271	331	348	679	696	670	9	88	0.81	54	18	28	30	78	53	48	2%	131	16%	87%	27	59%	11%	4.10	-12.5	54	117	$18
11 MIN *	322	40	2	17	8	253	267	311	339	650	657	698	8	87	0.64	53	21	26	29	80	55	55	3%	131	10%	89%	15	33%	20%	3.70	-10.3	49	109	$4
12 MIN	516	71	4	41	17	283	290	342	395	738	739	737	8	88	0.76	54	21	24	32	80	78	48	4%	110	16%	74%	26	58%	19%	4.81	1.7	66	165	$16
13 WAS	610	75	4	47	20	279	285	327	380	707	539	765	6	87	0.55	54	23	23	31	69	65	41	3%	153	15%	77%	26	46%	12%	4.39	5.0	62	155	$20
14 WAS	610	94	5	37	31	302	288	355	416	771	694	802	8	89	0.77	46	24	30	33	98	80	52	3%	133	21%	82%	27	56%	7%	5.49	28.2	78	211	$30
1st Half	309	47	1	19	13	265	285	312	388	701	682	707	7	90	0.69	44	22	34	29	98	90	61	1%	120	21%	87%	14	57%	14%	4.36	4.5	82	222	$21
2nd Half	301	47	4	18	18	339	291	398	445	843	702	903	9	89	0.85	49	26	25	37	99	70	44	6%	133	21%	78%	13	54%	0%	6.83	23.8	71	192	$40
15 Proj	**549**	**78**	**5**	**38**	**23**	**293**	**288**	**349**	**402**	**750**	**667**	**783**	**8**	**88**	**0.73**	**50**	**23**	**27**	**32**	**86**	**76**	**48**	**4%**	**130**	**18%**	**80%**				**5.10**	**19.1**	**72**	**188**	**$24**

Spangenberg,Cory

Age: 24 Bats: L Pos: 3B
Ht: 6' 0" Wt: 195

Health	A	LIMA Plan	D
PT/Exp	F	Rand Var	-3
Consist	C	MM	1411

2-9-.290 in 62 AB at SD. Today's tip for quickly fitting in: Smack a walk-off HR two days after your call-up. At maturity, though, he's more likely to help your squad with his legs than his bat, but he still needs to work on SB%—and ct%, for that matter. Good candidate for more minor league seasoning.

Yr Tm	AB	R	HR	RBI	SB	BA	xBA	OBP	SLG	OPS	vL	vR	bb%	ct%	Eye	G	L	F	h%	HctX	PX	xPX	hr/f	Spd	SBO	SB%	#Wk	DOM	DIS	RC/G	RAR	BPV	BPX	R$
10																																		
11																																		
12																																		
13 aa	287	30	2	17	16	259		294	325	620			5	75	0.21				34		50			131	37%	57%				2.95		-6	-15	$8
14 SD *	343	38	4	27	15	290	249	318	415	734	667	795	4	74	0.16	45	26	30	38	85	94	113	14%	137	32%	56%	5	20%	40%	4.28	5.7	23	62	$13
1st Half	48	5	0	3	2	235	201	260	305	565			3	71	0.12				33		58			121	45%	52%				2.24		-26	-70	-$14
2nd Half	295	33	4	24	13	299	253	328	433	761	667	795	4	75	0.17	45	26	30	39	86	99	113	14%	136	30%	57%	5	20%	40%	4.70	8.5	29	78	$18
15 Proj	**134**	**14**	**1**	**9**	**6**	**265**	**237**	**295**	**364**	**659**	**608**	**675**	**4**	**74**	**0.16**	**45**	**26**	**30**	**35**	**77**	**76**	**102**	**4%**	**128**	**36%**	**55%**				**3.31**	**-1.6**	**7**	**18**	**$5**

Springer,George

Age: 25 Bats: R Pos: RF
Ht: 6' 3" Wt: 205

Health	C	LIMA Plan	B
PT/Exp	D	Rand Var	0
Consist	F	MM	5405

20-51-.231 with 5 SB in 295 AB at HOU. Before quad injury blew out most of his 2nd half, he produced as advertised - big power numbers with big hole in swing. Team was cautious with SB, but Spd is willing and able. Though BA will be a liability, 20/20 could happen as soon as this year. And then the fun really starts.

Yr Tm	AB	R	HR	RBI	SB	BA	xBA	OBP	SLG	OPS	vL	vR	bb%	ct%	Eye	G	L	F	h%	HctX	PX	xPX	hr/f	Spd	SBO	SB%	#Wk	DOM	DIS	RC/G	RAR	BPV	BPX	R$
10																																		
11																																		
12 aa	73	6	2	4	3	186		233	284	518			6	61	0.16				28		86			97	37%	57%				1.89		-45	-113	-$2
13 a/a	492	81	29	82	34	262		346	501	847			11	61	0.34				36		194			101	32%	79%				5.99		56	140	$33
14 HOU *	346	57	22	57	8	240	241	328	474	802	774	811	12	62	0.34	45	15	39	32	105	191	161	28%	133	11%	80%	14	57%	36%	5.22	13.8	65	176	$14
1st Half	296	50	18	49	6	253	239	343	487	830	736	870	12	62	0.36	41	17	42	34	111	192	167	25%	140	9%	74%	12	50%	42%	5.67	14.6	70	189	$19
2nd Half	50	7	4	8	2	160	239	250	400	650	1167	559	9	60	0.25	70	7	23	15	78	183	135	57%	104	22%	100%	2	100%	0%	3.03	-1.6	38	103	-$13
15 Proj	**512**	**80**	**28**	**84**	**18**	**248**	**224**	**342**	**450**	**793**	**958**	**746**	**11**	**61**	**0.31**	**41**	**18**	**41**	**35**	**91**	**168**	**148**	**22%**	**116**	**16%**	**80%**				**5.04**	**15.9**	**34**	**90**	**$24**

Stanton,Giancarlo

Age: 25 Bats: R Pos: RF
Ht: 6' 6" Wt: 240

Health	B	LIMA Plan	C
PT/Exp	B	Rand Var	-2
Consist	D	MM	5245

A horrific Sept. beaning, yes, but here are three other scary facts: 1) Added double-digit SB in 2014 through efficiency—nothing more. 2) INCREASED his plate patience upon the mass exodus of surrounding lineup talent. 3) He's 25. 25!! Godspeed, Giancarlo. Today's pitching-heavy game needs equalizers like you.

Yr Tm	AB	R	HR	RBI	SB	BA	xBA	OBP	SLG	OPS	vL	vR	bb%	ct%	Eye	G	L	F	h%	HctX	PX	xPX	hr/f	Spd	SBO	SB%	#Wk	DOM	DIS	RC/G	RAR	BPV	BPX	R$
10 FLA *	551	80	39	103	6	269	280	355	551	906	644	889	12	67	0.40	43	16	41	33	114	214	138	23%	112	5%	75%	18	39%	44%	6.79	26.1	96	209	$24
11 FLA	516	79	34	87	5	262	276	356	537	893	1042	849	12	68	0.42	45	16	38	32	136	205	172	25%	109	7%	50%	27	63%	19%	6.31	17.5	94	209	$21
12 MIA	449	75	37	86	6	290	288	361	608	969	1024	950	9	68	0.32	36	22	42	35	132	226	163	29%	84	7%	75%	23	65%	17%	7.72	32.3	99	248	$25
13 MIA	425	62	24	62	1	249	253	365	480	845	1006	789	15	67	0.53	43	18	38	31	108	180	139	22%	84	1%	100%	22	45%	27%	5.90	16.1	69	173	$13
14 MIA	539	89	37	105	13	288	278	395	555	950	1075	920	15	68	0.55	41	20	39	36	120	206	146	26%	82	8%	93%	24	75%	13%	7.94	58.0	95	257	$35
1st Half	310	57	21	60	7	313	290	408	590	999	1214	942	13	71	0.52	39	21	40	38	126	210	141	24%	91	7%	100%	14	79%	7%	9.02	42.0	108	292	$42
2nd Half	229	32	16	45	6	253	258	378	507	884	873	891	17	65	0.59	44	17	38	32	112	200	152	28%	75	9%	86%	10	70%	20%	6.66	18.0	79	214	$25
15 Proj	**572**	**89**	**38**	**103**	**9**	**271**	**273**	**375**	**533**	**908**	**996**	**883**	**14**	**67**	**0.50**	**42**	**19**	**39**	**34**	**118**	**208**	**149**	**25%**	**83**	**6%**	**86%**				**6.99**	**49.2**	**88**	**232**	**$30**

BRENT HERSHEY

Stewart,Chris

Age: 33	Bats: R	Pos: CA	Health	A	LIMA Plan	F
Ht: 6' 4"	Wt: 210		PT/Exp	F	Rand Var	-5
			Consist	C	MM	0111

BA surged over 50 points from previous best, and he posted positive value for the first time, but this is still the same guy. You can't draw any conclusions about a change in skill from 136 AB. His xBA and upcoming LD%, h% regression all say BA will come crashing down, with no power or speed to break the fall in value. Stand back.

Yr	Tm	AB	R	HR	RBI	SB	BA	xBA	OBP	SLG	OPS	vL	vR	bb%	ct%	Eye	G	L	F	h%	HctX	PX	xPX	hr/f	Spd	SBO	SB%	#Wk	DOM	DIS	RC/G	RAR	BPV	BPX	R$
10	SD *	266	21	4	26	1	180	240	242	275	516	0	0	7	81	0.43	44	20	36	21	0	65	-5	0%	118	1%	100%	2	0%	100%	2.08	-19.6	29	63	-$4
11	SF *	257	25	3	16	2	185	215	250	266	515	801	511	8	85	0.57	35	16	49	21	91	59	64	5%	100	5%	57%	19	47%	16%	2.05	-19.1	35	78	-$4
12	NYY	141	15	1	13	2	241	224	292	319	611	579	633	7	85	0.48	34	19	47	28	69	59	43	2%	94	6%	100%	26	27%	46%	3.20	-4.5	31	78	$0
13	NYY	294	28	4	25	4	211	214	293	272	566	503	591	9	83	0.61	42	19	40	24	63	40	62	4%	88	5%	100%	26	27%	38%	2.57	-10.2	12	30	$0
14	PIT	136	9	0	10	0	294	243	362	331	693	1098	555	8	80	0.44	40	30	31	37	65	36	36	0%	80	2%	0%	23	13%	57%	4.08	2.3	-7	-19	$1
1st Half		79	6	0	4	0	241	220	330	253	583	950	469	10	81	0.60	38	28	34	30	64	12	47	0%	96	0%	0%	11	9%	64%	2.70	-1.6	-15	-41	-$1
2nd Half		57	3	0	6	0	368	272	410	439	848	1276	682	5	79	0.25	42	33	26	47	67	70	20	0%	75	5%	0%	12	17%	50%	6.60	4.7	6	16	$3
15	Proj	142	11	1	12	1	245	233	311	302	613	777	546	8	82	0.45	39	24	36	29	68	49	44	2%	82	4%	53%				3.04	-1.5	-6	-15	-$1

Stubbs,Drew

Age: 30	Bats: R	Pos: CF	Health	A	LIMA Plan	C+
Ht: 6' 4"	Wt: 205		PT/Exp	B	Rand Var	-5
			Consist	C	MM	4503

This is why we love Coors Field (.999 OPS home, .616 road). Power surged to new levels in P/T role, and xPX hints he might be able to keep most of it. Elite speed stuck around as well, though BA surge was a fluke as h% spiked and dismal ct% tanked in 2H. Counting stats should stick, but BA regression will prevent R$ repeat.

Yr	Tm	AB	R	HR	RBI	SB	BA	xBA	OBP	SLG	OPS	vL	vR	bb%	ct%	Eye	G	L	F	h%	HctX	PX	xPX	hr/f	Spd	SBO	SB%	#Wk	DOM	DIS	RC/G	RAR	BPV	BPX	R$
10	CIN	514	91	22	77	30	255	237	329	444	773	789	765	10	67	0.33	44	16	40	34	99	138	139	16%	176	26%	83%	27	56%	30%	5.07	4.3	54	117	$24
11	CIN	604	92	15	44	40	243	216	321	364	686	896	636	9	66	0.31	47	20	33	34	92	98	115	11%	168	29%	80%	27	33%	56%	3.96	-15.1	14	31	$21
12	CIN	493	75	14	40	30	213	206	277	333	610	788	541	8	66	0.25	51	15	34	29	77	87	85	13%	146	31%	81%	25	24%	60%	3.05	-25.3	-2	-5	$12
13	CLE	430	59	10	45	17	233	222	305	360	665	718	637	9	67	0.31	47	20	34	32	67	106	88	10%	123	17%	89%	27	33%	52%	3.78	-4.1	11	28	$12
14	COL	388	67	15	43	20	289	246	339	482	821	944	757	7	65	0.22	44	21	35	41	103	163	147	17%	165	23%	87%	27	44%	41%	6.02	23.9	56	151	$22
1st Half		187	33	6	20	9	299	264	340	481	821	1023	695	7	70	0.23	49	22	29	40	110	147	141	15%	147	22%	82%	14	36%	43%	6.10	11.7	57	154	$19
2nd Half		201	34	9	23	11	279	229	338	483	820	851	807	8	60	0.21	39	20	40	42	96	180	153	19%	165	23%	92%	13	54%	38%	5.94	11.9	52	141	$26
15	Proj	398	64	13	42	20	258	232	321	423	743	850	693	8	65	0.26	46	19	35	36	89	138	122	15%	152	23%	86%				4.78	10.8	33	86	$19

Suarez,Eugenio

Age: 23	Bats: R	Pos: SS	Health	A	LIMA Plan	D
Ht: 5' 11"	Wt: 180		PT/Exp	D	Rand Var	-1
			Consist	B	MM	2301

4-23-.242 in 244 AB at DET. Burst onto the scene after June call-up (.279 BA, 3 HR), then posted negative BPV in each month after. Didn't run enough to utilize his decent speed, and PX didn't carry over to majors. Subpar ct% makes him a BA risk and keeps his status stuck as a late-round flyer.

Yr	Tm	AB	R	HR	RBI	SB	BA	xBA	OBP	SLG	OPS	vL	vR	bb%	ct%	Eye	G	L	F	h%	HctX	PX	xPX	hr/f	Spd	SBO	SB%	#Wk	DOM	DIS	RC/G	RAR	BPV	BPX	R$
10																																			
11																																			
12																																			
13	aa	442	43	7	36	7	231		290	347	638			8	77	0.36				29		85			111	18%	38%				3.03		26	65	$4
14	DET *	442	57	10	50	10	246	231	305	379	684	656	650	8	73	0.32	35	22	43	31	87	107	109	5%	111	13%	70%	17	29%	59%	3.87	9.2	30	81	$11
1st Half		266	37	9	35	7	259	245	322	445	767	893	825	9	74	0.36	26	22	52	32	109	145	195	12%	108	16%	68%	5	60%	40%	4.83	12.5	64	173	$18
2nd Half		176	20	1	15	3	227	195	297	278	576	568	580	7	72	0.27	39	21	40	31	78	48	75	2%	108	9%	75%	12	17%	67%	2.59	-3.5	-25	-68	$1
15	Proj	161	18	2	15	3	237	223	306	342	648	658	643	8	75	0.33	37	22	42	30	90	86	123	5%	118	14%	55%				3.25	0.1	10	26	$3

Susac,Andrew

Age: 25	Bats: R	Pos: CA	Health	A	LIMA Plan	D
Ht: 6' 1"	Wt: 215		PT/Exp	F	Rand Var	0
			Consist	A	MM	4311

3-19-.273 in 88 AB at SF. Above average power from minors translated over well in limited sample, and PX/xPX suggest this is his best path to fantasy value. Despite good plate patience, he'll have to clear ct% hurdle against MLB pitching (68%) if he wants to avoid the looming growing pains.

Yr	Tm	AB	R	HR	RBI	SB	BA	xBA	OBP	SLG	OPS	vL	vR	bb%	ct%	Eye	G	L	F	h%	HctX	PX	xPX	hr/f	Spd	SBO	SB%	#Wk	DOM	DIS	RC/G	RAR	BPV	BPX	R$
10																																			
11																																			
12																																			
13	aa	262	24	8	34	1	213		297	359	656			11	71	0.40				27		116			79	1%	100%				3.47		22	55	$1
14	SF *	301	36	9	40	0	229	225	298	368	666	1011	668	9	71	0.34	37	20	43	29	103	113	156	12%	84	0%	0%	12	42%	42%	3.62	1.5	21	57	$4
1st Half		159	16	3	15	0	210	187	281	316	598	2000	0	9	69	0.32	100	0	0	28	0	91	-14	0%	92	0%	0%	1	0%	100%	2.87	-2.6	-5	-14	-$1
2nd Half		142	20	5	25	0	251	250	316	425	742	980	680	9	74	0.38	36	20	44	30	109	135	159	12%	82	0%	0%	11	45%	36%	4.58	5.0	50	135	$9
15	Proj	114	15	4	18	0	226	234	301	380	681	862	574	10	72	0.37	36	20	44	28	98	126	143	10%	84	1%	100%				3.78	1.3	19	50	$2

Suzuki,Ichiro

Age: 41	Bats: L	Pos: RF	Health	A	LIMA Plan	C+
Ht: 5' 11"	Wt: 170		PT/Exp	B	Rand Var	-4
			Consist	B	MM	0533

Career-low BPV, by a wide margin, is a hole that a 41-y/o won't likely climb out of. BA improvement was fueled by h% spike, which masked underlying ct% collapse. Can still run some, but dormant power, fading plate skills at this age suggest pre-retirement tour is more likely than rebound year.

Yr	Tm	AB	R	HR	RBI	SB	BA	xBA	OBP	SLG	OPS	vL	vR	bb%	ct%	Eye	G	L	F	h%	HctX	PX	xPX	hr/f	Spd	SBO	SB%	#Wk	DOM	DIS	RC/G	RAR	BPV	BPX	R$
10	SEA	680	74	6	43	42	315	271	359	394	754	684	789	6	87	0.52	57	17	25	35	78	55	44	4%	141	23%	82%	27	44%	19%	5.39	4.1	50	109	$34
11	SEA	677	80	5	47	40	272	275	310	335	645	648	644	5	90	0.57	60	19	21	30	55	42	29	4%	132	24%	85%	27	37%	11%	3.83	-26.2	45	100	$23
12	2 AL	629	77	9	55	29	283	292	307	390	696	649	724	3	90	0.36	51	25	24	30	70	63	40	7%	133	23%	81%	28	64%	14%	4.31	-9.8	60	150	$24
13	NYY	520	57	7	35	20	262	264	297	342	639	753	590	5	88	0.41	52	21	27	29	62	50	33	6%	140	18%	83%	26	38%	27%	3.59	-10.4	45	113	$15
14	NYY	359	42	1	22	15	284	255	324	340	664	807	632	6	81	0.31	58	22	20	35	67	45	22	2%	136	17%	83%	27	22%	44%	4.03	1.4	14	38	$12
1st Half		158	20	0	10	5	291	247	347	329	676	816	641	8	80	0.42	61	22	17	36	67	31	6	0%	137	13%	71%	14	21%	50%	4.08	0.4	5	14	$8
2nd Half		201	22	1	12	10	279	260	305	348	653	799	624	4	82	0.22	56	22	22	34	66	56	34	3%	124	21%	91%	13	23%	38%	3.97	-0.1	18	49	$15
15	Proj	365	42	2	25	16	279	262	316	343	658	726	636	5	85	0.36	55	22	23	32	66	48	29	3%	133	18%	83%				3.94	-0.7	24	63	$13

Suzuki,Kurt

Age: 31	Bats: R	Pos: CA	Health	A	LIMA Plan	C
Ht: 5' 11"	Wt: 205		PT/Exp	C	Rand Var	-3
			Consist	B	MM	1125

Value was mostly driven by h% boost and fluky RBI spike (.324 BA with RISP). xBA predicts BA will fall a bit, though ct% gains say it should rest above previous levels. Meager PX shows he's still a one-dimensional player, but good health, stable plate skills keep him above the water line in two-catcher leagues.

Yr	Tm	AB	R	HR	RBI	SB	BA	xBA	OBP	SLG	OPS	vL	vR	bb%	ct%	Eye	G	L	F	h%	HctX	PX	xPX	hr/f	Spd	SBO	SB%	#Wk	DOM	DIS	RC/G	RAR	BPV	BPX	R$
10	OAK	495	55	13	71	3	242	259	303	366	669	575	701	6	90	0.67	42	17	41	25	112	72	87	7%	86	4%	60%	24	50%	13%	3.53	-9.9	58	126	$8
11	OAK	460	54	14	44	2	237	262	301	385	686	617	713	8	86	0.59	36	20	44	25	89	97	80	8%	79	4%	50%	27	63%	11%	3.75	-6.3	63	140	$6
12	2 TM	408	36	6	43	2	235	223	276	328	605	628	598	5	82	0.27	41	17	42	27	112	66	102	4%	81	2%	100%	28	21%	46%	2.99	-13.9	17	43	$3
13	2 TM	285	25	5	32	2	232	255	290	337	627	653	619	7	88	0.63	37	23	40	25	104	69	100	5%	89	3%	100%	26	38%	31%	3.24	-4.0	49	123	$2
14	MIN	452	37	3	61	0	288	268	345	383	727	810	695	7	90	0.74	44	22	34	32	101	76	82	2%	70	1%	0%	27	59%	15%	4.58	15.9	57	154	$11
1st Half		234	20	2	32	0	299	268	354	389	743	807	714	7	91	0.86	46	22	32	32	99	68	83	3%	81	0%	0%	14	71%	7%	4.94	10.0	59	159	$12
2nd Half		218	17	1	29	0	275	268	335	376	711	812	675	7	89	0.64	43	21	36	31	102	84	81	1%	61	2%	0%	13	46%	23%	4.22	5.1	55	149	$10
15	Proj	444	39	5	55	1	260	259	316	360	676	729	657	7	88	0.59	41	21	38	29	103	76	90	4%	74	2%	63%				3.82	5.5	39	104	$9

Sweeney,Ryan

Age: 30	Bats: L	Pos: CF RF	Health	F	LIMA Plan	D
Ht: 6' 4"	Wt: 225		PT/Exp	F	Rand Var	+2
			Consist	D	MM	2341

May hamstring strain derailed his 1st half while 2nd half was just a recovery to futility. Measly xPX makes 2012 power outburst look like a clear outlier, and he doesn't hit enough FB anyway. Growing ct% and xBA history are encouraging, but there's little room for growth at 30. His upside is an empty BA, at best.

Yr	Tm	AB	R	HR	RBI	SB	BA	xBA	OBP	SLG	OPS	vL	vR	bb%	ct%	Eye	G	L	F	h%	HctX	PX	xPX	hr/f	Spd	SBO	SB%	#Wk	DOM	DIS	RC/G	RAR	BPV	BPX	R$
10	OAK	303	41	1	36	1	294	274	342	383	725	623	754	7	86	0.59	52	20	28	34	68	68	36	1%	102	2%	50%	15	47%	13%	4.73	-3.4	48	104	$7
11	OAK	264	34	1	25	1	265	241	346	341	687	404	743	11	82	0.69	48	21	31	32	89	55	65	1%	122	2%	50%	25	32%	32%	4.07	-8.2	32	71	$3
12	BOS	204	22	0	16	0	260	264	303	373	675	332	713	6	79	0.28	47	24	29	33	81	94	60	0%	88	0%	0%	15	67%	33%	3.86	-7.5	31	78	$1
13	CHC *	275	27	10	30	2	267	284	323	457	780	824	755	8	82	0.46	48	21	31	29	95	120	90	12%	116	2%	100%	13	69%	15%	5.18	4.5	76	190	$6
14	CHC	207	22	3	20	0	251	270	304	338	642	679	637	7	84	0.45	47	27	26	29	105	64	68	7%	81	0%	0%	17	41%	24%	3.48	-3.7	27	73	$2
1st Half		107	8	0	8	0	206	239	252	243	495	730	476	5	85	0.38	52	23	25	24	111	35	59	0%	79	0%	0%	9	22%	33%	1.93	-6.9	5	14	-$3
2nd Half		100	14	3	12	0	300	300	358	440	798	647	827	8	83	0.53	41	33	27	34	98	97	79	14%	91	0%	0%	8	63%	13%	5.73	4.8	55	149	$7
15	Proj	130	14	2	13	0	265	273	318	381	698	679	702	7	83	0.44	47	25	28	31	95	86	72	7%	92	1%	86%				4.20	1.3	32	85	$3

RYAN BLOOMFIELD

Swisher,Nick

Age: 34 Bats: B Pos: 1B DH
Ht: 6' 0" Wt: 200

Health	C	LIMA Plan	C
PT/Exp	B	Rand Var	+3
Consist	C	MM	4015

Surgery on both knees ended the suffering in August. The effects were disastrous on skills: Already-weak BA plunged thanks to ct% collapse, and xBA trend suggests a full recovery is unlikely. Stable track record, xPX give hope for some rebound, but a pair of bum knees at this age presents considerable risk.

Yr	Tm	AB	R	HR	RBI	SB	BA	xBA	OBP	SLG	OPS	vL	vR	bb%	ct%	Eye	G	L	F	h%	HctX	PX	xPX	hr/f	Spd	SBO	SB%	#Wk	DOM	DIS	RC/G	RAR	BPV	BPX	R$
10	NYY	566	91	29	89	1	288	272	359	511	870	848	879	9	75	0.42	36	20	45	34	134	153	163	15%	90	2%	33%	27	63%	11%	6.40	8.9	72	157	$23
11	NYY	526	81	23	85	2	260	264	374	449	822	957	763	15	76	0.76	39	22	39	30	118	133	133	14%	72	2%	50%	27	63%	26%	5.73	-1.6	66	147	$17
12	NYY	537	75	24	93	2	272	261	364	473	837	769	873	13	74	0.55	39	22	39	33	114	142	127	15%	81	3%	40%	27	48%	30%	5.92	15.8	60	150	$19
13	CLE	549	74	22	63	1	246	255	341	423	763	918	763	12	75	0.56	38	23	39	29	108	124	138	14%	80	1%	100%	26	54%	23%	4.85	5.6	49	123	$13
14	CLE	360	33	8	42	0	208	228	278	331	608	481	658	9	69	0.32	38	24	38	28	98	107	130	8%	65	0%	0%	18	33%	39%	2.98	-11.8	2	5	$0
1st Half		234	20	5	25	0	192	230	283	316	599	505	641	12	70	0.44	35	24	41	25	92	109	130	7%	65	0%	0%	13	38%	38%	2.86	-8.8	12	32	$0
2nd Half		126	13	3	17	0	238	227	267	357	624	422	685	4	67	0.12	44	25	32	33	110	104	129	11%	76	0%	0%	5	20%	40%	3.19	-3.2	-15	-41	$1
15	Proj	505	60	16	67	1	240	245	314	393	707	692	713	10	72	0.38	39	23	38	30	108	124	133	12%	71	1%	52%				4.12	-0.6	18	49	$9

Tabata,Jose

Age: 26 Bats: R Pos: RF
Ht: 5' 11" Wt: 210

Health	B	LIMA Plan	D
PT/Exp	D	Rand Var	+1
Consist	D	MM	1241

0-17-.282 in 174 AB at PIT. A big step back as he enters what should be his peak years. Ct% stayed in great shape, but HctX says he's just slapping. Power once appeared to be on the rise, but xPX never believed. Speed was once a weapon, but he's stopped running. Too many "buts" for any more than an end-game flyer.

Yr	Tm	AB	R	HR	RBI	SB	BA	xBA	OBP	SLG	OPS	vL	vR	bb%	ct%	Eye	G	L	F	h%	HctX	PX	xPX	hr/f	Spd	SBO	SB%	#Wk	DOM	DIS	RC/G	RAR	BPV	BPX	R$
10	PIT *	629	94	6	50	38	290	277	338	389	727	682	767	7	85	0.49	59	16	25	33	105	69	82	5%	146	28%	74%	18	50%	28%	4.69	-8.3	55	120	$28
11	PIT *	367	58	4	23	16	269	270	347	371	718	819	679	11	82	0.67	61	17	22	32	93	79	89	7%	110	22%	63%	18	44%	33%	4.32	-8.9	49	109	$11
12	PIT *	491	60	3	28	12	250	268	303	339	641	706	650	7	84	0.47	62	18	20	29	87	65	52	6%	107	21%	46%	21	29%	29%	3.18	-29.5	35	88	$7
13	PIT *	336	36	6	33	4	271	283	322	408	730	742	778	7	84	0.48	59	18	23	31	95	89	78	10%	137	5%	79%	22	50%	14%	4.61	0.0	65	163	$7
14	PIT *	320	27	0	25	2	256	261	287	310	597	796	594	4	87	0.33	57	22	21	30	90	43	47	0%	116	8%	28%	18	33%	44%	2.89	-11.4	27	73	$3
1st Half		162	13	0	15	1	278	248	311	320	630	814	619	5	84	0.29	57	23	20	33	82	34	44	0%	118	6%	33%	13	31%	54%	3.35	-3.0	8	22	$4
2nd Half		158	14	0	11	1	234	264	263	300	564	765	400	4	90	0.40	57	18	25	26	112	52	57	0%	103	9%	23%	5	40%	20%	2.46	-7.5	43	116	$2
15	Proj	198	20	3	16	3	259	275	308	365	673	737	644	6	86	0.44	59	19	23	29	97	75	62	7%	116	11%	52%				3.65	-2.0	41	108	$4

Taveras,Oscar

Age: 22 Bats: L Pos: RF
Ht: 6' 2" Wt: 200

Health		LIMA Plan	
PT/Exp		Rand Var	
Consist		MM	

Bright future cut short by a car accident that took his life on October 26. Rest in peace.

Yr	Tm	AB	R	HR	RBI	SB	BA	xBA	OBP	SLG	OPS	vL	vR	bb%	ct%	Eye	G	L	F	h%	HctX	PX	xPX	hr/f	Spd	SBO	SB%	#Wk	DOM	DIS	RC/G	RAR	BPV	BPX	R$
10																																			
11																																			
12	aa	477	67	17	76	8	290		338	492	830			7	87	0.58				30		120			96	8%	88%				6.02		90	225	$20
13	aaa	173	20	4	25	4	271		300	397	697			4	86	0.30				30		87			83	13%	78%				4.17		49	123	$4
14	STL *	473	45	8	58	1	256	258	295	363	658	551	599	5	85	0.37	52	20	29	29	113	77	62	5%	91	3%	26%	17	24%	41%	3.60	-6.8	41	111	$9
1st Half		276	30	6	38	1	261	259	302	397	699	633	475	6	85	0.39	48	16	35	29	83	96	34	9%	95	3%	40%	4	50%	25%	4.08	0.7	58	157	$13
2nd Half		197	15	2	20	0	249	237	288	315	603	523	619	5	85	0.33	52	20	28	28	119	49	68	4%	93	2%	0%	13	15%	46%	2.97	-6.0	18	49	$2
15	Proj																																		

Taylor,Chris

Age: 24 Bats: R Pos: SS
Ht: 6' 1" Wt: 190

Health	A	LIMA Plan	D
PT/Exp	F	Rand Var	-4
Consist	B	MM	2503

0-9-.287 with 5 SB in 136 AB at SEA. Held his own after being thrust into starting gig in July. But his BA was buoyed by fortunate h%, which masked a mediocre plate approach. With little power, value is heavily tied to legs, and potential growing pains suggest SB chances may dry up unless he adjusts.

Yr	Tm	AB	R	HR	RBI	SB	BA	xBA	OBP	SLG	OPS	vL	vR	bb%	ct%	Eye	G	L	F	h%	HctX	PX	xPX	hr/f	Spd	SBO	SB%	#Wk	DOM	DIS	RC/G	RAR	BPV	BPX	R$
10																																			
11																																			
12																																			
13	aa	256	42	1	14	16	273		361	353	713			12	76	0.56				36		64			137	22%	83%				4.67		21	53	$10
14	SEA *	438	59	3	34	14	274	220	327	376	703	699	687	7	71	0.26	41	21	38	38	53	93	62	0%	156	20%	62%	11	18%	55%	4.14	12.3	20	54	$14
1st Half		218	31	3	20	7	271	246	326	417	743			8	72	0.29				36		123			133	22%	61%				4.53		44	119	$14
2nd Half		220	27	0	14	7	278	197	327	335	662	699	687	7	69	0.24	41	21	38	40	51	62	62	0%	141	17%	62%	11	18%	55%	3.74	3.2	-16	-43	$13
15	Proj	254	37	1	17	9	243	219	319	335	654	676	637	9	72	0.37	41	21	38	33	46	83	56	2%	165	19%	68%				3.48	1.8	14	37	$6

Taylor,Michael D.

Age: 29 Bats: R Pos: LF
Ht: 6' 5" Wt: 255

Health	A	LIMA Plan	D
PT/Exp	A	Rand Var	0
Consist	A	MM	3201

0-0-.250 in 28 AB at CHW. Fourth straight year that MLB cup of coffee resulted in 30 AB or fewer. BA remained tethered to poor ct%, which puts a firm lid on any future upside. With minimal PX growth over the years, time is running out for a prolonged stay in the majors, let alone any fantasy value.

Yr	Tm	AB	R	HR	RBI	SB	BA	xBA	OBP	SLG	OPS	vL	vR	bb%	ct%	Eye	G	L	F	h%	HctX	PX	xPX	hr/f	Spd	SBO	SB%	#Wk	DOM	DIS	RC/G	RAR	BPV	BPX	R$
10	aaa	464	52	4	51	11	212		265	297	562			7	76	0.30				27		66			112	16%	64%				2.49		7	15	$2
11	OAK *	379	37	11	43	9	207	212	275	324	599	687	490	9	71	0.32	47	16	37	26	75	88	107	14%	81	17%	60%	5	20%	60%	2.77	-28.8	-2	-4	$3
12	OAK *	470	55	7	44	12	214	247	301	314	615	167	556	11	70	0.41	36	36	27	29	139	83	148	0%	72	12%	76%	3	0%	100%	3.09	-25.8	-7	-18	$4
13	OAK *	443	34	11	54	3	199	220	257	316	572	322	0	7	74	0.30	33	22	44	25	0	88	-15	0%	62	6%	56%	4	0%	50%	2.54	-24.4	0	0	$0
14	CHW*	465	48	7	41	5	202	191	274	309	583	564	722	9	69	0.32	53	5	42	27	47	94	104	0%	105	7%	65%	5	20%	80%	2.68	-17.7	4	11	$0
1st Half		254	26	4	21	4	188	217	260	288	549			9	70	0.33				25		88			81	12%	62%				2.31		-5	-14	$0
2nd Half		211	22	3	20	1	220	191	290	334	624	564	722	9	68	0.31	53	5	42	30	47	103	104	0%	107	1%	100%	5	20%	80%	3.18	-5.3	8	22	$1
15	Proj	128	13	3	13	2	206	218	275	330	605	522	676	9	71	0.33	43	17	40	27	42	103	94	8%	96	9%	65%				2.88	-3.5	5	13	$1

Taylor,Michael A.

Age: 24 Bats: R Pos: CF
Ht: 6' 3" Wt: 210

Health	A	LIMA Plan	D
PT/Exp	F	Rand Var	-1
Consist	F	MM	4401

1-5-.205 in 39 AB at WAS. August call-up came after just 13 AB in Triple-A, and he looked overmatched (56% ct%, 0.18 Eye) in the majors. Promising HR/SB totals in minors were supported by PX and Spd, but ability to stick hinges on making more contact, which he hasn't done yet at any level.

Yr	Tm	AB	R	HR	RBI	SB	BA	xBA	OBP	SLG	OPS	vL	vR	bb%	ct%	Eye	G	L	F	h%	HctX	PX	xPX	hr/f	Spd	SBO	SB%	#Wk	DOM	DIS	RC/G	RAR	BPV	BPX	R$
10																																			
11																																			
12																																			
13																																			
14	WAS *	467	65	18	52	27	257	242	320	424	744	1095	553	8	63	0.25	55	23	23	37	49	144	65	20%	116	32%	69%	6	17%	50%	4.49	9.2	19	51	$22
1st Half		299	44	13	38	16	277	225	334	451	785			8	62	0.22				40		147			111	27%	70%				5.13		18	49	$30
2nd Half		168	20	5	13	11	216	237	288	360	648	1095	553	9	63	0.27	55	23	23	31	49	133	65	20%	115	42%	67%	6	17%	50%	3.21	-3.5	12	32	$8
15	Proj	128	17	3	12	6	240	230	319	373	692	1117	612	9	62	0.25	55	23	23	36	44	122	59	18%	115	25%	70%				3.74	-0.5	-1	-2	$4

Teixeira,Mark

Age: 35 Bats: B Pos: 1B
Ht: 6' 3" Wt: 215

Health	F	LIMA Plan	B+
PT/Exp	C	Rand Var	+2
Consist	D	MM	4035

Suffered his way through injuries to seven (!) different body parts, and 2H collapse felt the wrath. His ct% didn't rebound enough to save BA, and h% history suggests this will remain a liability. Fact... his 5-year avg h% before opponents started employing the shift = 32%. In the 5 years since = 25%. Some players don't adjust.

Yr	Tm	AB	R	HR	RBI	SB	BA	xBA	OBP	SLG	OPS	vL	vR	bb%	ct%	Eye	G	L	F	h%	HctX	PX	xPX	hr/f	Spd	SBO	SB%	#Wk	DOM	DIS	RC/G	RAR	BPV	BPX	R$
10	NYY	601	113	33	108	0	256	281	365	481	846	940	804	13	80	0.76	36	19	45	27	122	147	147	15%	73	1%	0%	27	78%	19%	5.83	3.4	87	189	$21
11	NYY	589	90	39	111	4	248	281	341	494	835	967	773	11	81	0.69	35	18	47	24	124	151	133	17%	69	3%	80%	27	63%	19%	5.60	-0.7	92	204	$23
12	NYY	451	66	24	84	2	251	281	332	475	807	865	770	11	82	0.65	41	19	39	26	122	137	120	16%	69	3%	67%	24	67%	21%	5.32	0.4	80	200	$14
13	NYY	53	5	3	12	0	151	239	270	340	609	935	432	13	64	0.42	29	29	43	16	76	139	128	20%	73	0%	0%	3	33%	67%	2.68	-3.3	18	45	-$2
14	NYY	440	56	22	62	1	216	254	313	398	711	691	718	12	75	0.53	41	21	37	24	114	125	119	18%	62	2%	50%	25	36%	40%	3.95	-2.5	45	122	$8
1st Half		215	34	15	41	0	242	274	344	474	818	748	846	12	76	0.58	38	23	39	25	119	151	136	23%	71	2%	0%	12	50%	25%	5.24	6.9	72	195	$16
2nd Half		225	22	7	21	1	191	234	282	324	607	628	599	11	75	0.49	45	20	36	22	109	99	102	12%	65	2%	100%	13	23%	54%	2.89	-9.1	21	57	$1
15	Proj	434	60	23	69	2	231	266	324	434	758	881	701	11	77	0.55	40	20	40	25	106	141	122	17%	59	2%	64%				4.57	5.3	58	154	$13

RYAN BLOOMFIELD

Tejada,Ruben

Age: 25 Bats: R Pos: SS | Ht: 5' 11" Wt: 200

Health	B	LIMA Plan	D
PT/Exp	C	Rand Var	-1
Consist	D	MM	1111

Improved patience fueled a huge OBP spike. His 2nd half plate skills are actually somewhat impressive. Yet still, too little happens after he makes contact. Even with the LD% rebound, zero power and sub-par HctX still leave an uber-soft BA. And the Spd decline keeps his bleak future intact.

Yr	Tm	AB	R	HR	RBI	SB	BA	xBA	OBP	SLG	OPS	vL	vR	bb%	ct%	Eye	G	L	F	h%	HctX	PX	xPX	hr/f	Spd	SBO	SB%	#Wk	DOM	DIS	RC/G	RAR	BPV	BPX	R$
10	NYM *	434	47	2	27	3	228	239	283	290	572	729	541	7	82	0.42	41	23	36	27	70	52	71	2%	86	7%	34%	19	42%	47%	2.59	-25.6	12	26	$0
11	NYM *	535	52	2	53	8	252	255	316	316	632	704	692	9	85	0.61	45	26	30	29	56	47	39	0%	108	7%	72%	18	39%	44%	3.41	-17.3	27	60	$7
12	NYM	464	53	1	25	4	289	264	333	351	685	760	647	5	84	0.37	40	30	30	34	78	51	55	1%	111	6%	50%	21	33%	33%	4.03	-0.9	24	60	$9
13	NYM *	448	44	1	25	3	210	238	249	270	520	719	432	5	86	0.39	47	19	34	24	84	49	62	0%	94	5%	54%	11	45%	18%	2.15	-18.9	25	63	-$3
14	NYM	355	30	5	34	1	237	231	342	310	652	631	658	12	79	0.68	40	24	35	29	81	55	72	5%	79	3%	33%	27	44%	44%	3.37	0.7	12	32	$2
1st Half		208	19	2	17	1	240	232	352	303	655	724	630	14	76	0.66	43	27	30	31	90	52	79	4%	91	3%	50%	14	29%	57%	3.47	1.4	2	5	$3
2nd Half		147	11	3	17	0	231	228	327	320	647	464	695	10	84	0.74	37	21	42	26	69	59	63	6%	77	2%	0%	13	62%	31%	3.21	-0.1	31	84	$2
15	Proj	**211**	**20**	**2**	**17**	**1**	**247**	**238**	**322**	**312**	**634**	**679**	**618**	**9**	**83**	**0.56**	**42**	**23**	**35**	**29**	**78**	**52**	**64**	**3%**	**89**	**4%**	**44%**				**3.24**	**0.0**	**6**	**16**	**$0**

Thole,Josh

Age: 28 Bats: L Pos: CA | Ht: 6' 1" Wt: 205

Health	A	LIMA Plan	D
PT/Exp	F	Rand Var	-3
Consist	A	MM	0001

It was not too long ago that he offered a solid contact rate and workable-enough hard contact index that he could be drafted for a nice BA floor. Both metrics have fallen upon hard times and have been particularly barren since he moved north of the border. At 28, there is still skill upside, but too many other #2 CA options exist.

Yr	Tm	AB	R	HR	RBI	SB	BA	xBA	OBP	SLG	OPS	vL	vR	bb%	ct%	Eye	G	L	F	h%	HctX	PX	xPX	hr/f	Spd	SBO	SB%	#Wk	DOM	DIS	RC/G	RAR	BPV	BPX	R$
10	NYM *	367	32	4	29	1	251	273	325	359	685	343	783	10	85	0.74	44	23	33	28	90	78	73	5%	116	1%	100%	16	38%	6%	4.00	-4.0	60	130	$2
11	NYM	340	22	3	40	0	268	257	345	344	690	525	709	10	86	0.81	49	25	26	30	78	58	55	4%	59	2%	0%	27	52%	41%	3.99	-2.0	31	69	$4
12	NYM	321	24	1	21	0	234	228	294	290	584	562	591	8	84	0.54	58	19	24	27	84	45	58	2%	88	0%	0%	25	28%	32%	2.83	-12.6	18	45	-$1
13	TOR *	269	24	6	31	0	226	229	285	339	624	477	502	8	79	0.40	44	19	37	26	67	73	73	3%	90	2%	0%	17	18%	59%	3.12	-4.9	20	50	$1
14	TOR	133	11	0	7	0	248	214	320	278	598	608	594	10	81	0.56	63	18	20	31	60	29	42	0%	98	7%	0%	27	22%	37%	2.74	-2.3	-1	-3	-$1
1st Half		69	5	0	5	0	261	217	338	290	628	666	613	10	84	0.73	74	14	12	31	38	27	3	0%	99	13%	0%	14	21%	21%	2.82	-1.2	10	27	-$1
2nd Half		64	6	0	2	0	234	212	300	266	566	533	574	9	78	0.43	50	22	28	30	83	31	85	0%	98	0%	0%	13	23%	54%	2.65	-1.4	-14	-38	-$1
15	Proj	**160**	**13**	**0**	**12**	**0**	**240**	**224**	**309**	**288**	**596**	**576**	**602**	**9**	**81**	**0.51**	**54**	**19**	**27**	**29**	**70**	**41**	**59**	**1%**	**94**	**3%**	**1%**				**2.84**	**-2.7**	**-12**	**-31**	**$1**

Tolleson,Steve

Age: 31 Bats: R Pos: 2B 3B | Ht: 5' 11" Wt: 185

Health	A	LIMA Plan	D
PT/Exp	D	Rand Var	-2
Consist	A	MM	2301

3-16-.253 with 3 SB in 170 AB at TOR. Recorded an impressive .332/.412/.503 line (9 HR, 10/2 SB/CS) over 292 Triple-A AB. But that was in 2010. At age 27. In the PCL. Five years later, he's a 31-year-old bench utility guy trying to hang on. Bet against a 2010 repeat.

Yr	Tm	AB	R	HR	RBI	SB	BA	xBA	OBP	SLG	OPS	vL	vR	bb%	ct%	Eye	G	L	F	h%	HctX	PX	xPX	hr/f	Spd	SBO	SB%	#Wk	DOM	DIS	RC/G	RAR	BPV	BPX	R$
10	OAK *	341	38	6	32	5	256	237	312	370	682	1048	459	7	79	0.38	33	23	45	31	128	82	101	6%	140	8%	67%	9	33%	33%	3.92	-8.9	39	85	$6
11	aaa	487	41	4	29	13	181		235	249	484			7	74	0.27				24		56			95	20%	66%				1.79		-16	-36	-$5
12	BAL *	233	16	3	22	3	215	194	283	293	576	596	368	9	76	0.39	53	11	36	27	91	60	59	11%	72	10%	57%	14	43%	43%	2.64	-13.8	-7	-18	-$1
13	aaa	392	33	6	37	10	223		304	330	634			10	69	0.38				31		93			82	16%	60%				3.19		0	0	$4
14	TOR *	242	30	4	22	7	233	211	293	339	632	844	351	8	73	0.31	39	19	42	31	70	80	69	6%	155	15%	76%	23	26%	52%	3.33	-2.4	19	51	$4
1st Half		159	16	3	13	5	211	213	293	340	633	956	331	10	72	0.42	37	17	46	27	82	97	91	7%	142	17%	81%	10	40%	40%	3.27	-2.1	33	89	$3
2nd Half		83	14	1	9	2	277	202	307	337	644	744	382	2	73	0.09	41	21	38	37	59	48	47	4%	124	14%	67%	13	15%	62%	3.43	-0.6	-24	-65	$4
15	Proj	**130**	**15**	**3**	**12**	**3**	**234**	**218**	**294**	**349**	**643**	**757**	**375**	**7**	**73**	**0.29**	**45**	**16**	**39**	**30**	**78**	**90**	**63**	**8%**	**119**	**14%**	**68%**				**3.31**	**-0.3**	**6**	**16**	**$3**

Tomas,Yasmani

Age: 24 Bats: R Pos: RF | Ht: 6' 1" Wt: 229

Health	A	LIMA Plan	B+
PT/Exp	D	Rand Var	0
Consist	B	MM	4145

Cuban national team talent defected in July, should make 2015 MLB debut. MLB power upside is comparable to Jose Abreu, but that kind of success is never a given, especially initially. Tomas is younger, less polished, still pre-peak; i.e. a strikeout/BA risk as he adjusts. That said, we'd still speculate. High-risk, high reward play.

Yr	Tm	AB	R	HR	RBI	SB	BA	xBA	OBP	SLG	OPS	vL	vR	bb%	ct%	Eye	G	L	F	h%	HctX	PX	xPX	hr/f	Spd	SBO	SB%	#Wk	DOM	DIS	RC/G	RAR	BPV	BPX	R$
10	for	91	12	1	11	4	277		324	363	688			7	80	0.36				34		57			129	26%	52%				3.75	-3.7	21	46	$2
11	for	27	4	1	3	0	173		173	357	529			0	72	0.00				22		103			140	45%	0%				1.38	-3.4	14	31	-$2
12	for	272	45	12	49	4	278		310	476	787			5	80	0.24				31		124			93	10%	62%				5.11	0.8	59	148	$10
13	for	277	44	9	59	1	269		335	465	800			9	82	0.56				30		127			113	6%	21%				5.19	6.0	85	213	$10
14	for	241	27	4	35	5	267		317	403	720			7	81	0.38				32		102			101	20%	45%				4.06	0.4	51	138	$6
1st Half																																			
2nd Half																																			
15	Proj	**455**	**63**	**16**	**71**	**4**	**264**	**277**	**317**	**455**	**772**	**772**	**772**	**7**	**79**	**0.37**	**44**	**20**	**36**	**30**		**135**		**12%**	**108**	**8%**	**46%**				**4.85**	**11.3**	**70**	**183**	**$16**

Trout,Mike

Age: 23 Bats: R Pos: CF | Ht: 6' 2" Wt: 230

Health	A	LIMA Plan	C
PT/Exp	A	Rand Var	0
Consist	B	MM	5545

Plate skill and GB plunges don't profile a .320+ hitter. Another SBO nose-dive says his best SB days could be over. But so what? Suddenly scary-elite power hints he's morphing into something else. For where he's headed, he won't need those bags. UP: If you have to ask, you can't afford him.

Yr	Tm	AB	R	HR	RBI	SB	BA	xBA	OBP	SLG	OPS	vL	vR	bb%	ct%	Eye	G	L	F	h%	HctX	PX	xPX	hr/f	Spd	SBO	SB%	#Wk	DOM	DIS	RC/G	RAR	BPV	BPX	R$
10																																			
11	LAA *	476	93	15	50	33	282	253	349	460	808	773	605	9	77	0.44	39	21	40	34	91	119	105	14%	159	32%	76%	11	55%	36%	5.63	7.5	70	156	$26
12	LAA *	636	144	31	92	53	328	276	398	555	953	862	999	10	75	0.47	44	23	33	40	108	144	113	22%	153	28%	90%	24	63%	13%	8.75	66.1	85	213	$54
13	LAA	589	109	27	97	33	323	287	432	557	988	954	1000	16	77	0.81	41	23	36	38	123	159	133	16%	153	18%	83%	27	74%	11%	9.11	77.6	114	285	$47
14	LAA	602	115	36	111	16	287	272	377	561	939	910	948	12	69	0.45	34	19	47	36	115	209	151	18%	146	10%	89%	27	67%	11%	7.61	62.8	115	311	$38
1st Half		287	54	18	59	10	314	293	407	610	1017	1079	990	14	72	0.60	36	20	44	38	124	218	149	19%	143	11%	100%	14	79%	0%	9.62	44.5	136	368	$40
2nd Half		315	61	18	52	6	263	253	349	517	866	675	915	10	67	0.34	32	18	50	34	107	199	153	17%	135	10%	75%	13	54%	23%	6.01	19.7	90	243	$37
15	Proj	**614**	**120**	**37**	**101**	**18**	**298**	**278**	**388**	**568**	**956**	**908**	**973**	**12**	**72**	**0.49**	**36**	**20**	**45**	**36**	**113**	**199**	**136**	**19%**	**151**	**13%**	**78%**				**7.89**	**69.0**	**114**	**300**	**$41**

Trumbo,Mark

Age: 29 Bats: R Pos: 1B LF | Ht: 6' 4" Wt: 235

Health	C	LIMA Plan	B+
PT/Exp	B	Rand Var	+1
Consist	B	MM	4125

April foot injury shelved him until the All-Star break. Despite 2nd half HctX surge, his power was MIA until mid-Sept. Skills set hasn't changed. Mediocre contact and pitch selection kill his BA; stable xPX says 30 HR are still very attainable. With power so rare these days, you can live with the accompanying warts.

Yr	Tm	AB	R	HR	RBI	SB	BA	xBA	OBP	SLG	OPS	vL	vR	bb%	ct%	Eye	G	L	F	h%	HctX	PX	xPX	hr/f	Spd	SBO	SB%	#Wk	DOM	DIS	RC/G	RAR	BPV	BPX	R$
10	LAA *	547	71	24	84	2	237	275	287	421	709	167	200	7	72	0.25	43	29	29	29	42	130	31	0%	101	6%	30%	5	0%	100%	3.91	-38.8	36	78	$11
11	LAA	539	65	29	87	9	254	276	291	477	768	748	778	4	78	0.21	46	16	38	28	116	150	135	18%	78	13%	69%	27	56%	15%	4.61	-26.2	65	144	$19
12	LAA	544	66	32	95	4	268	248	317	491	808	808	808	6	72	0.24	45	16	39	32	114	144	132	21%	92	7%	44%	27	52%	37%	5.20	-3.6	45	113	$21
13	LAA	620	85	34	100	5	234	256	294	453	747	923	685	8	70	0.29	46	17	37	28	104	158	132	21%	83	5%	71%	27	52%	26%	4.43	-2.8	51	128	$19
14	ARI	328	37	14	61	2	235	241	293	415	707	796	679	8	73	0.31	45	15	40	28	111	133	135	14%	85	7%	40%	18	39%	44%	3.94	-2.3	41	111	$8
1st Half		81	12	7	19	0	210	286	264	506	771	1086	675	6	73	0.23	49	15	36	19	91	203	104	33%	76	0%	0%	5	80%	20%	4.18	0.0	90	243	-$2
2nd Half		247	25	7	42	2	243	224	302	385	686	711	678	9	73	0.34	43	15	42	31	118	110	145	9%	92	8%	40%	13	23%	54%	3.82	-2.6	26	70	$11
15	Proj	**506**	**65**	**28**	**91**	**3**	**242**	**257**	**299**	**456**	**755**	**860**	**717**	**7**	**72**	**0.29**	**46**	**16**	**39**	**28**	**108**	**156**	**131**	**19%**	**83**	**6%**	**50%**				**4.48**	**4.7**	**49**	**130**	**$18**

Tulowitzki,Troy

Age: 30 Bats: R Pos: SS | Ht: 6' 3" Wt: 215

Health	F	LIMA Plan	B+
PT/Exp	D	Rand Var	-5
Consist	D	MM	5255

Still injury-plagued, still a force when in the lineup. A 43% h% fueled .417/.497/.748 Coors line and his short-season value, as road numbers (.811 OPS) keep dropping. Chronically-injured players don't suddenly get healthy -- especially on the wrong side of 30. Five-year AB average = 395; set your expectations there.

Yr	Tm	AB	R	HR	RBI	SB	BA	xBA	OBP	SLG	OPS	vL	vR	bb%	ct%	Eye	G	L	F	h%	HctX	PX	xPX	hr/f	Spd	SBO	SB%	#Wk	DOM	DIS	RC/G	RAR	BPV	BPX	R$
10	COL	470	89	27	95	11	315	309	381	568	949	990	930	9	83	0.62	45	15	40	33	137	158	142	17%	114	10%	85%	21	76%	0%	8.05	45.0	115	250	$30
11	COL	537	81	30	105	9	302	307	372	544	916	1049	864	10	85	0.75	42	20	39	31	131	150	126	17%	90	8%	75%	26	81%	19%	7.33	41.8	110	244	$30
12	COL *	208	35	10	31	2	286	268	348	501	849	671	918	9	88	0.76	46	17	37	29	103	118	98	13%	124	7%	50%	9	67%	0%	6.05	11.5	101	253	$8
13	COL	446	72	25	82	1	312	288	391	540	931	906	938	11	81	0.67	42	21	38	34	123	148	147	18%	85	1%	100%	24	75%	17%	7.82	51.9	92	230	$25
14	COL	315	71	21	52	1	340	310	432	603	1035	1348	930	14	82	0.88	38	23	39	36	150	170	164	21%	101	2%	50%	16	75%	13%	9.94	54.4	123	332	$23
1st Half		275	65	18	47	1	353	316	445	618	1064	1269	989	14	83	0.98	38	24	38	38	148	171	153	20%	105	2%	50%	14	79%	14%	10.75	52.7	131	354	$28
2nd Half		40	6	3	5	0	250	268	333	500	833	2292	564	9	75	0.40	33	20	47	26	162	164	243	21%	84	0%	0%	2	50%	0%	5.41	2.6	77	208	-$15
15	Proj	**436**	**81**	**26**	**76**	**4**	**317**	**305**	**398**	**567**	**965**	**1292**	**864**	**11**	**84**	**0.78**	**39**	**20**	**40**	**33**	**138**	**160**	**168**	**18%**	**93**	**4%**	**65%**				**8.23**	**58.7**	**112**	**294**	**$29**

JOCK THOMPSON

Turner,Justin

Age: 30 Bats: R Pos: 3B	Health B	LIMA Plan D+	
Ht: 6' 0" Wt: 210	PT/Exp F	Rand Var -5	
	Consist D	MM 3243	

2014 banner year and likely in-season infield versatility will pique our interest in 2015. Sure, its a h%-fueled unrepeatable BA, and the patience is outlier-ish. But LD/HctX history looks strong, and xPX is supportive of the power surge. Role is an issue, but suddenly he's a defensible end-game flyer.

Yr Tm	AB	R	HR	RBI	SB	BA	xBA	OBP	SLG	OPS	vL	vR	bb%	ct%	Eye	G	L	F	h%	HctX	PX	xPX	hr/f	Spd	SBO	SB%	#Wk	DOM	DIS	RC/G	RAR	BPV	BPX	R$
10 2 TM *	413	49	8	30	5	243	269	286	366	652	143	273	6	84	0.38	57	14	29	27	74	86	84	0%	92	9%	57%	4	50%	50%	3.45	-20.4	46	100	$5
11 NYM *	475	53	4	52	7	257	276	315	355	671	629	715	8	86	0.61	49	23	28	29	68	75	60	4%	87	7%	78%	24	46%	33%	3.86	-17.2	48	107	$8
12 NYM	171	20	2	19	1	269	283	319	392	711	650	768	5	86	0.38	47	24	29	30	92	86	68	5%	93	5%	50%	25	40%	20%	4.10	-2.4	53	133	$2
13 NYM	200	12	2	16	0	280	257	319	385	704	668	735	5	83	0.32	46	22	32	33	120	80	132	4%	92	2%	0%	22	45%	32%	4.24	1.4	36	90	$1
14 LA	288	46	7	43	6	340	283	404	493	897	911	890	9	80	0.48	49	23	28	41	113	117	102	11%	98	7%	86%	26	50%	31%	7.67	29.6	62	168	$17
1st Half	159	21	3	21	2	302	269	358	434	792	718	830	8	81	0.45	49	22	29	36	97	100	85	8%	106	4%	100%	14	43%	29%	5.77	9.0	52	141	$13
2nd Half	129	25	4	22	4	388	298	459	566	1025	1184	958	10	79	0.52	48	25	26	47	134	139	123	15%	87	10%	80%	12	58%	33%	10.56	21.5	75	203	$23
15 Proj	**259**	**33**	**5**	**32**	**4**	**293**	**280**	**352**	**429**	**782**	**761**	**794**	**7**	**82**	**0.44**	**48**	**23**	**29**	**34**	**110**	**106**	**103**	**8%**	**94**	**7%**	**73%**				**5.32**	**11.8**	**52**	**136**	**$8**

Uggla,Dan

Age: 35 Bats: R Pos: 2B	Health A	LIMA Plan D	
Ht: 5' 11" Wt: 210	PT/Exp C	Rand Var +5	
	Consist C	MM 3101	

Patience plunge says he swung at everything in an effort to generate... something. It didn't work, as power followed chronic contact-and-BA woes down a similar hole. HctX and xPX hint at something left, but ATL and SF didn't see it. With his age, neither do we.

Yr Tm	AB	R	HR	RBI	SB	BA	xBA	OBP	SLG	OPS	vL	vR	bb%	ct%	Eye	G	L	F	h%	HctX	PX	xPX	hr/f	Spd	SBO	SB%	#Wk	DOM	DIS	RC/G	RAR	BPV	BPX	R$
10 FLA	589	100	33	105	4	287	269	369	508	877	983	845	12	75	0.52	40	18	43	33	117	152	146	17%	88	3%	80%	27	59%	19%	6.73	34.2	72	157	$27
11 ATL	600	88	36	82	1	233	252	311	453	764	648	808	9	74	0.40	41	15	43	25	109	147	127	19%	98	3%	25%	27	63%	26%	4.51	-2.6	64	142	$16
12 ATL	523	86	19	78	4	220	222	348	384	732	776	710	15	68	0.56	34	20	46	29	95	127	118	11%	78	4%	57%	27	44%	37%	4.21	-0.7	29	73	$10
13 ATL	448	60	22	55	2	179	201	309	362	671	599	692	15	62	0.45	40	13	47	23	81	140	138	17%	117	2%	100%	26	31%	54%	3.38	-4.5	26	65	$2
14 2 NL	141	14	2	10	0	149	170	229	213	442	343	475	7	67	0.24	39	17	45	20	103	54	126	5%	73	0%	0%	17	12%	71%	1.34	-9.6	-48	-130	-$5
1st Half	128	13	2	10	0	164	181	239	234	474	408	491	7	70	0.24	37	18	45	22	110	57	125	5%	74	0%	0%	14	14%	64%	1.57	-7.7	-36	-97	-$4
2nd Half	13	1	0	0	0	0	0	133	0	133	111	167	13	38	0.25	60	0	40	0	33	0	135	0%	81	0%	0%	3	0%	100%	0.00	-1.7	-193	-522	-$7
15 Proj	**155**	**21**	**6**	**19**	**1**	**204**	**217**	**305**	**357**	**662**	**651**	**666**	**11**	**69**	**0.42**	**38**	**17**	**45**	**25**	**101**	**120**	**128**	**12%**	**82**	**2%**	**61%**				**3.35**	**-0.2**	**13**	**35**	**$2**

Upton,B.J.

Age: 30 Bats: R Pos: CF	Health A	LIMA Plan C+	
Ht: 6' 3" Wt: 185	PT/Exp B	Rand Var 0	
	Consist C	MM 3505	

Partial ct% rebound doesn't boost his BA/xBA outlook. Patience and xPX are more hopeful about his power, but previous hr/f has yet to arrive in ATL. Despite SB bounce, his playing time is now at risk. Homework: Compare Adam Dunn 2010-2013 to Upton 2012-2105. Discuss.

Yr Tm	AB	R	HR	RBI	SB	BA	xBA	OBP	SLG	OPS	vL	vR	bb%	ct%	Eye	G	L	F	h%	HctX	PX	xPX	hr/f	Spd	SBO	SB%	#Wk	DOM	DIS	RC/G	RAR	BPV	BPX	R$
10 TAM	536	89	18	62	42	237	247	322	424	745	919	664	11	69	0.41	40	17	44	31	88	149	119	11%	136	38%	82%	27	44%	22%	4.68	-1.7	62	135	$23
11 TAM	560	82	23	81	36	243	244	331	429	759	746	763	11	71	0.44	41	18	41	30	103	136	133	14%	133	31%	75%	27	52%	26%	4.70	-1.5	58	129	$24
12 TAM	573	79	28	78	31	246	246	298	454	752	792	737	7	71	0.27	40	19	41	30	87	145	105	17%	126	29%	84%	25	48%	28%	4.70	0.1	52	130	$24
13 ATL	391	30	9	26	12	184	191	268	289	557	449	598	10	61	0.29	45	19	36	27	82	94	112	10%	98	18%	71%	25	12%	72%	2.40	-21.5	-27	-68	$0
14 ATL	519	67	12	35	20	208	209	287	333	620	566	633	10	67	0.33	43	18	39	29	95	102	129	9%	164	21%	74%	26	31%	31%	3.08	-12.2	19	51	$8
1st Half	302	36	7	24	12	205	214	273	338	611	490	643	9	68	0.30	43	18	39	28	90	105	116	9%	166	22%	80%	14	43%	29%	3.03	-7.9	23	62	$10
2nd Half	217	31	5	11	8	212	204	305	327	632	680	619	11	65	0.37	43	19	39	30	100	98	148	9%	141	20%	67%	12	17%	33%	3.14	-5.0	7	19	$7
15 Proj	**442**	**54**	**12**	**41**	**19**	**212**	**215**	**290**	**347**	**637**	**617**	**643**	**10**	**66**	**0.32**	**43**	**18**	**39**	**29**	**91**	**114**	**124**	**11%**	**130**	**23%**	**75%**				**3.25**	**-8.5**	**12**	**31**	**$10**

Upton,Justin

Age: 27 Bats: R Pos: LF	Health A	LIMA Plan B+	
Ht: 6' 2" Wt: 205	PT/Exp A	Rand Var -1	
	Consist A	MM 5335	

Opened up his swing a bit and PX/xPX took a leap. Given the stability in pretty much the rest of his skill set, this could mean that he's not yet reached his ceiling. Problem is, he's teased us before (2011) so we have no choice but to hedge. Still, at 27, there's this: UP: 35-40 HR.

Yr Tm	AB	R	HR	RBI	SB	BA	xBA	OBP	SLG	OPS	vL	vR	bb%	ct%	Eye	G	L	F	h%	HctX	PX	xPX	hr/f	Spd	SBO	SB%	#Wk	DOM	DIS	RC/G	RAR	BPV	BPX	R$
10 ARI	495	73	17	69	18	273	243	356	442	799	768	808	11	69	0.42	41	19	39	36	116	131	134	12%	125	17%	69%	25	44%	36%	5.42	2.2	45	98	$20
11 ARI	592	105	31	88	21	289	280	369	529	898	929	889	9	79	0.47	37	18	45	32	130	160	142	15%	124	19%	70%	27	81%	15%	6.53	21.3	100	222	$33
12 ARI	554	107	17	67	18	280	250	355	430	785	830	766	10	78	0.52	44	21	36	33	105	96	107	11%	127	15%	69%	27	48%	22%	5.29	8.9	50	125	$24
13 ATL	558	94	27	70	8	263	254	354	464	818	994	762	12	71	0.47	41	22	38	32	88	145	110	18%	109	5%	89%	27	56%	33%	5.69	26.4	59	148	$22
14 ATL	566	77	29	102	8	270	262	342	491	833	981	794	10	70	0.35	40	20	40	34	116	173	159	18%	95	8%	67%	26	62%	19%	5.77	32.3	67	181	$26
1st Half	286	41	16	46	6	276	258	344	503	847	1218	763	9	69	0.31	40	19	42	35	119	176	171	19%	99	9%	86%	14	64%	21%	6.10	19.2	66	178	$26
2nd Half	280	36	13	56	2	264	266	341	479	819	793	827	10	71	0.39	39	22	39	33	112	170	147	16%	93	7%	40%	12	58%	17%	5.44	13.9	69	186	$26
15 Proj	**559**	**86**	**29**	**94**	**10**	**270**	**266**	**348**	**488**	**837**	**945**	**803**	**10**	**72**	**0.41**	**40**	**21**	**39**	**33**	**107**	**165**	**136**	**18%**	**102**	**10%**	**69%**				**5.83**	**33.8**	**69**	**181**	**$27**

Uribe,Juan

Age: 36 Bats: R Pos: 3B	Health D	LIMA Plan C+	
Ht: 6' 0" Wt: 235	PT/Exp D	Rand Var -5	
	Consist D	MM 2123	

Held onto most of his 2013 power and HctX gains. But h% spike fueled his value and first .300+ BA ever. Recent production will attract the 3B needy, but age and return of serious DL time (hamstring) say he's riskier than ever. DN: 250 AB, .250 BA.

Yr Tm	AB	R	HR	RBI	SB	BA	xBA	OBP	SLG	OPS	vL	vR	bb%	ct%	Eye	G	L	F	h%	HctX	PX	xPX	hr/f	Spd	SBO	SB%	#Wk	DOM	DIS	RC/G	RAR	BPV	BPX	R$
10 SF	521	64	24	85	1	248	264	310	440	749	682	766	8	82	0.49	40	15	44	26	115	119	115	12%	77	2%	33%	27	59%	26%	4.51	-8.9	66	143	$13
11 LA	270	21	4	28	2	204	216	264	293	557	485	582	6	78	0.28	42	17	41	25	78	69	76	5%	46	4%	100%	15	13%	47%	2.38	-22.8	-5	-11	-$2
12 LA	162	15	2	17	0	191	218	258	284	542	385	640	7	77	0.35	48	17	35	24	90	72	81	5%	53	3%	0%	20	15%	45%	2.18	-12.5	0	0	-$3
13 LA	388	47	12	50	5	278	259	331	438	769	781	765	7	79	0.37	43	20	37	33	119	111	118	11%	97	5%	100%	27	37%	37%	5.19	13.2	51	128	$13
14 LA	386	36	9	54	0	311	246	337	440	777	733	790	4	80	0.19	47	19	34	37	109	99	87	8%	72	1%	0%	21	33%	38%	5.43	17.9	31	84	$15
1st Half	166	16	4	21	0	289	247	322	428	750	472	823	5	78	0.24	45	19	36	35	118	110	107	9%	69	2%	0%	11	18%	45%	4.87	5.5	32	86	$8
2nd Half	220	20	5	33	0	327	244	348	450	798	908	764	3	82	0.15	48	19	33	38	102	91	72	8%	74	0%	0%	10	50%	30%	5.89	12.7	30	81	$19
15 Proj	**377**	**38**	**9**	**50**	**1**	**277**	**248**	**319**	**408**	**727**	**656**	**751**	**6**	**79**	**0.28**	**45**	**19**	**36**	**33**	**107**	**100**	**94**	**8%**	**72**	**2%**	**61%**				**4.54**	**9.0**	**23**	**61**	**$12**

Utley,Chase

Age: 36 Bats: L Pos: 2B	Health D	LIMA Plan A	
Ht: 6' 1" Wt: 200	PT/Exp B	Rand Var 0	
	Consist B	MM 2335	

Got body in shape for the grind, but was it worth it? Stable plate skills yielded more 2B value, but a great start morphed into just a .245 BA and 7 HR over his final 386 AB. Poor h% from June though Sept was a factor, but that 2nd half PX/xPX is a red flag. If it sticks, DN: Single-digit HR.

Yr Tm	AB	R	HR	RBI	SB	BA	xBA	OBP	SLG	OPS	vL	vR	bb%	ct%	Eye	G	L	F	h%	HctX	PX	xPX	hr/f	Spd	SBO	SB%	#Wk	DOM	DIS	RC/G	RAR	BPV	BPX	R$
10 PHI	425	75	16	65	13	275	279	387	445	832	1003	752	13	85	1.00	41	20	39	29	134	104	127	11%	105	11%	87%	21	48%	5%	5.89	14.2	83	180	$18
11 PHI	398	54	11	44	14	259	258	344	425	769	607	829	9	88	0.83	41	13	46	27	130	100	132	7%	121	13%	100%	19	58%	5%	4.96	2.8	89	198	$12
12 PHI	301	48	11	45	11	256	278	365	429	793	679	869	13	86	1.00	42	21	36	27	129	102	110	12%	92	13%	92%	15	60%	13%	5.29	8.3	79	198	$11
13 PHI	476	73	18	69	8	284	269	348	475	823	754	855	9	83	0.57	38	20	43	31	118	119	126	11%	115	8%	73%	24	67%	21%	5.80	28.9	83	208	$21
14 PHI	589	74	11	78	10	270	276	339	407	746	682	775	8	86	0.62	39	25	36	30	113	95	106	6%	101	7%	91%	27	67%	22%	4.77	23.3	67	181	$19
1st Half	307	45	6	37	2	293	290	353	450	802	767	817	7	86	0.55	38	26	36	33	123	112	132	6%	105	4%	67%	14	71%	14%	5.55	18.5	80	216	$20
2nd Half	282	29	5	41	8	245	261	324	362	686	599	727	9	85	0.71	41	23	36	27	101	77	77	6%	99	10%	100%	13	62%	31%	4.01	5.2	54	146	$18
15 Proj	**508**	**70**	**12**	**71**	**10**	**268**	**271**	**345**	**411**	**757**	**688**	**790**	**9**	**85**	**0.68**	**40**	**23**	**37**	**30**	**117**	**97**	**110**	**7%**	**102**	**8%**	**86%**				**4.87**	**21.7**	**72**	**188**	**$19**

Valaika,Chris

Age: 29 Bats: R Pos: 1B	Health C	LIMA Plan D	
Ht: 5' 11" Wt: 205	PT/Exp D	Rand Var -2	
	Consist B	MM 2101	

3-13-.231 in 121 AB at CHC. Took advantage of injuries to reach career AB, HR and RBI highs off the bench. Sub-par plate skills and power say this is his upside. Versatility may offer him a shot at an MLB pension, but our game is far more demanding.

Yr Tm	AB	R	HR	RBI	SB	BA	xBA	OBP	SLG	OPS	vL	vR	bb%	ct%	Eye	G	L	F	h%	HctX	PX	xPX	hr/f	Spd	SBO	SB%	#Wk	DOM	DIS	RC/G	RAR	BPV	BPX	R$
10 CIN *	462	40	4	42	2	258	249	283	347	629	1104	348	3	79	0.16	41	24	34	32	86	69	64	10%	91	6%	39%	7	14%	57%	3.28	-40.4	9	20	$5
11 CIN *	442	31	5	26	1	216	200	245	292	537	1600	527	4	81	0.21	27	18	55	25	56	55	104	0%	100	1%	100%	6	33%	33%	2.33	-53.3	9	20	-$3
12 aaa	291	21	5	21	1	179		208	277	485			3	73	0.14				23		71			95	11%	28%				1.68		-11	-28	-$5
13 MIA *	194	17	3	17	1	204	221	246	301	546	828	463	5	76	0.23	39	20	41	25	81	77	108	5%	78	5%	38%	5	40%	60%	2.31	-13.8	2	5	-$2
14 CHC *	473	38	10	46	2	218	228	262	322	584	591	635	6	72	0.21	51	21	29	28	90	86	77	12%	77	4%	64%	10	20%	60%	2.74	-21.1	-6	-16	$2
1st Half	257	20	5	27	1	230	228	269	345	613			5	74	0.20				29	0	95			72	4%	34%				3.01		4	11	$3
2nd Half	216	18	4	19	2	203	217	253	296	550	591	635	6	70	0.22	51	21	29	27	88	76	77	12%	83	4%	100%	10	20%	60%	2.44	-11.7	-18	-49	$1
15 Proj	**133**	**11**	**3**	**12**	**1**	**209**	**231**	**257**	**322**	**579**	**651**	**542**	**5**	**74**	**0.20**	**46**	**21**	**34**	**26**	**85**	**90**	**89**	**9%**	**84**	**5%**	**56%**				**2.54**	**-6.7**	**-7**	**-19**	**$1**

JOCK THOMPSON

Valbuena,Luis

Age:	29	Bats:	L	Pos:	3B 2B	Health	A	LIMA Plan	C+
Ht:	5' 10"	Wt:	200			PT/Exp	C	Rand Var	0
						Consist	B	MM	4025

What looked like a growth year actually... was. xPX and HctX are all trended up and vaulted him into double-digit value territory. From here, he's more likely to take a half-step back, and as a platoon player (just 272 AB vs. LHP lifetime), his chances will be capped. Still has some value, though.

Yr	Tm	AB	R	HR	RBI	SB	BA	xBA	OBP	SLG	OPS	vL	vR	bb%	ct%	Eye	G	L	F	h%	HctX	PX	xPX	hr/f	Spd	SBO	SB%	#Wk	DOM	DIS	RC/G	RAR	BPV	BPX	R$
10	CLE *	371	39	6	39	2	209	234	290	312	602	855	467	10	77	0.49	47	18	35	26	76	79	67	3%	66	5%	55%	23	26%	61%	2.89	-25.5	13	28	$0
11	CLE *	463	51	13	56	5	244	205	296	368	664	750	412	7	73	0.28	42	12	45	31	65	93	100	7%	92	8%	60%	9	22%	56%	3.61	-20.5	11	24	$8
12	CHC *	476	52	9	49	1	228	242	309	361	670	624	657	10	75	0.47	43	21	35	28	87	102	82	5%	73	3%	17%	17	35%	24%	3.59	-14.7	28	70	$3
13	CHC	331	34	12	37	1	218	239	331	378	708	647	715	14	81	0.84	40	16	45	23	108	104	131	10%	80	5%	20%	22	64%	27%	3.84	-1.6	61	153	$2
14	CHC	478	68	16	51	1	249	255	341	435	776	610	811	12	76	0.58	31	20	48	30	120	140	155	9%	93	2%	33%	27	56%	19%	4.94	17.3	71	192	$11
1st Half		224	30	5	20	0	268	260	359	442	801	663	822	13	76	0.60	28	24	49	33	132	141	170	6%	101	2%	0%	14	50%	29%	5.44	11.3	75	203	$7
2nd Half		254	38	11	31	1	232	252	324	429	753	580	800	11	76	0.55	35	18	48	26	110	139	142	12%	88	3%	50%	13	62%	8%	4.52	6.3	68	184	$15
15	**Proj**	**463**	**58**	**15**	**51**	**1**	**243**	**251**	**335**	**414**	**749**	**668**	**764**	**12**	**77**	**0.59**	**34**	**20**	**46**	**28**	**107**	**127**	**128**	**9%**	**82**	**4%**	**31%**				**4.53**	**11.6**	**52**	**136**	**$8**

Valdespin,Jordany

Age:	27	Bats:	L	Pos:	2B	Health	A	LIMA Plan	D
Ht:	6' 0"	Wt:	190			PT/Exp	F	Rand Var	+3
						Consist	A	MM	2311

3-10-.214 with 1 SB in 98 AB at MIA. Sadly, trends in ct%, bb%, and Eye are not enough to counter a clear lack of power and low LD rate. Even with decent speed, he doesn't run well, so it will be hard to maintain even his modest SB totals. Has a lot to improve on, and is running out of opportunity and time.

Yr	Tm	AB	R	HR	RBI	SB	BA	xBA	OBP	SLG	OPS	vL	vR	bb%	ct%	Eye	G	L	F	h%	HctX	PX	xPX	hr/f	Spd	SBO	SB%	#Wk	DOM	DIS	RC/G	RAR	BPV	BPX	R$
10	aa	112	6	0	6	3	188		198	247	445			1	77	0.05				25		57			98	32%	55%				1.42		-13	-28	-$3
11	a/a	511	52	13	45	28	229		256	358	614			3	79	0.17				27		90			95	51%	57%				2.63		26	58	$12
12	NYM *	342	44	12	43	17	237	243	274	382	656	573	736	5	79	0.25	49	15	35	27	81	88	64	17%	99	40%	58%	21	33%	48%	3.13	-12.9	29	73	$10
13	NYM *	191	25	6	31	5	239	240	288	386	674	361	599	6	80	0.35	48	13	38	27	69	91	75	11%	132	27%	43%	15	40%	40%	3.26	-2.3	48	120	$4
14	MIA *	320	32	7	28	11	207	227	279	319	598	929	603	9	84	0.62	50	11	39	23	91	71	81	10%	114	29%	47%	11	55%	27%	2.53	-8.9	47	127	$3
1st Half		163	16	2	11	8	200	229	271	272	543			9	82	0.54				23		53			108	43%	43%				1.90		23	62	$1
2nd Half		157	17	6	18	4	215	248	288	368	656	929	603	9	86	0.73	50	11	39	22	93	89	81	10%	118	16%	59%	11	55%	27%	3.31	-0.4	71	192	$6
15	**Proj**	**163**	**18**	**5**	**19**	**6**	**222**	**246**	**283**	**363**	**647**	**605**	**653**	**7**	**82**	**0.42**	**49**	**13**	**37**	**24**	**82**	**92**	**73**	**10%**	**112**	**31%**	**52%**				**2.96**	**-2.3**	**48**	**127**	**$4**

Valencia,Danny

Age:	30	Bats:	R	Pos:	3B 1B	Health	A	LIMA Plan	D
Ht:	6' 2"	Wt:	220			PT/Exp	D	Rand Var	-1
						Consist	D	MM	3021

The hr/f that fueled 2013 deserted him in 2014, and is probably gone for good. But he still hits the ball hard, has average power and makes about average contact. Playing time will continue be the issue, as it's no secret that right-handers give him fits. His most important trend to reverse is AB.

Yr	Tm	AB	R	HR	RBI	SB	BA	xBA	OBP	SLG	OPS	vL	vR	bb%	ct%	Eye	G	L	F	h%	HctX	PX	xPX	hr/f	Spd	SBO	SB%	#Wk	DOM	DIS	RC/G	RAR	BPV	BPX	R$
10	MIN *	484	46	7	57	3	285	253	327	397	723	967	713	6	82	0.36	43	19	38	33	102	84	89	7%	81	3%	100%	19	63%	26%	4.67	-1.8	35	76	$12
11	MIN	564	63	15	72	2	246	252	294	383	677	822	626	7	82	0.39	46	18	36	28	92	93	85	9%	92	6%	25%	27	41%	26%	3.68	-19.0	45	100	$10
12	2 AL *	471	39	9	55	1	210	228	237	326	563	592	448	3	79	0.16	43	18	39	25	118	82	114	6%	77	8%	11%	13	23%	62%	2.34	-32.7	12	30	$0
13	BAL *	423	48	19	59	1	257	278	291	470	761	1031	672	5	78	0.22	38	22	40	29	120	148	142	15%	93	5%	18%	17	47%	35%	4.53	7.2	70	175	$11
14	2 AL	264	20	4	30	1	258	251	296	371	667	835	540	5	77	0.23	45	24	31	32	111	93	106	6%	86	3%	50%	22	36%	50%	3.72	0.3	18	49	$3
1st Half		82	7	1	8	0	280	199	326	366	692	790	554	7	74	0.29	53	15	32	37	109	74	114	5%	101	0%	0%	10	40%	60%	4.27	1.3	3	8	-$2
2nd Half		182	13	3	22	1	247	269	282	374	656	868	535	4	77	0.20	41	28	31	30	112	102	102	7%	77	5%	50%	12	33%	42%	3.47	-1.2	25	68	$6
15	**Proj**	**200**	**18**	**5**	**24**	**1**	**253**	**254**	**288**	**392**	**680**	**841**	**544**	**5**	**78**	**0.23**	**43**	**21**	**35**	**30**	**113**	**108**	**115**	**9%**	**90**	**4%**	**34%**				**3.78**	**0.5**	**23**	**61**	**$4**

Van Slyke,Scott

Age:	28	Bats:	R	Pos:	LF 1B CF	Health	A	LIMA Plan	C+
Ht:	6' 5"	Wt:	220			PT/Exp	D	Rand Var	-5
						Consist	D	MM	5223

Home run potential is tantalizing, though long swing has produced a lot of strikeouts. While MLB platoon split was huge, his minors stat showed no real effect. Near-.300 BA will be impossible to repeat, but his name will come from from HR. Even with straight-platoon AB, UP: 25 HR.

Yr	Tm	AB	R	HR	RBI	SB	BA	xBA	OBP	SLG	OPS	vL	vR	bb%	ct%	Eye	G	L	F	h%	HctX	PX	xPX	hr/f	Spd	SBO	SB%	#Wk	DOM	DIS	RC/G	RAR	BPV	BPX	R$
10	a/a	255	21	3	22	3	188		222	270	491			4	79	0.21				22		58			110	11%	52%				1.82		8	17	-$3
11	aa	457	57	14	65	4	281		345	464	809			9	74	0.37				35		144			85	9%	41%				5.45		55	122	$15
12	LA *	412	45	13	47	4	234	249	285	396	681	538	483	7	77	0.31	44	18	38	27	93	115	85	13%	83	9%	51%	7	43%	14%	3.65	-12.9	40	100	$6
13	LA *	333	49	15	50	6	257	233	356	460	816	764	850	13	66	0.45	36	17	47	35	92	166	147	16%	93	10%	64%	18	44%	44%	5.52	13.9	52	130	$11
14	LA	212	32	11	29	4	297	252	386	524	910	1045	767	12	67	0.39	35	20	45	40	107	185	174	17%	113	9%	67%	28	46%	46%	7.09	19.3	73	197	$10
1st Half		98	18	6	11	2	265	258	424	531	955	1178	668	20	65	0.71	31	19	50	34	102	215	188	19%	113	11%	50%	15	53%	40%	7.20	9.7	108	292	$7
2nd Half		114	14	5	18	2	325	247	347	518	865	901	831	3	68	0.11	38	22	41	44	111	161	162	16%	108	7%	100%	13	38%	54%	6.92	9.2	40	108	$13
15	**Proj**	**252**	**35**	**12**	**34**	**4**	**265**	**253**	**341**	**480**	**821**	**874**	**768**	**10**	**69**	**0.35**	**37**	**19**	**44**	**34**	**100**	**173**	**150**	**16%**	**104**	**10%**	**63%**				**5.51**	**13.0**	**58**	**152**	**$10**

Vargas,Kennys

Age:	24	Bats:	B	Pos:	DH	Health	A	LIMA Plan	C+
Ht:	6' 5"	Wt:	275			PT/Exp	F	Rand Var	0
						Consist	F	MM	3015

9-38-.274 in 215 AB at MIN. Seamless transition to MLB, right? 71% contact in MLB says otherwise; only a 35% h% propped up his BA in MIN. xPX casts serious doubt as to credibility of the big-league power, too. Tempted to pay for the 2nd half line times 2? In the immortal words of Admiral Akbar: "It's a trap!"

Yr	Tm	AB	R	HR	RBI	SB	BA	xBA	OBP	SLG	OPS	vL	vR	bb%	ct%	Eye	G	L	F	h%	HctX	PX	xPX	hr/f	Spd	SBO	SB%	#Wk	DOM	DIS	RC/G	RAR	BPV	BPX	R$
10																																			
11																																			
12																																			
13																																			
14	MIN *	571	65	21	87	0	255	246	310	414	724	602	899	7	76	0.33	47	19	34	30	101	116	109	17%	65	2%	0%	10	40%	50%	4.31	4.4	32	86	$16
1st Half		284	34	10	45	0	266	252	330	414	745			9	81	0.50				30		101			60	1%	0%				4.67		41	111	$16
2nd Half		287	31	11	43	0	244	242	289	415	704	602	899	6	71	0.22	47	19	34	31	94	132	109	17%	71	2%	0%	10	40%	50%	3.97	-0.7	24	65	$15
15	**Proj**	**422**	**46**	**13**	**59**	**0**	**249**	**239**	**306**	**393**	**699**	**572**	**794**	**7**	**75**	**0.31**	**47**	**19**	**34**	**30**	**85**	**109**	**98**	**12%**	**67**	**1%**	**0%**				**3.97**	**-1.0**	**13**	**33**	**$10**

Vazquez,Christian

Age:	24	Bats:	R	Pos:	CA	Health	A	LIMA Plan	D+
Ht:	5' 9"	Wt:	195			PT/Exp	D	Rand Var	-3
						Consist	C	MM	1015

1-20-.240 in 175 AB at BOS. A defensive wizard, but can he hit? 2nd half ct% and Eye were off from his minors numbers, but also showed that he wasn't overmatched in debut. Current secondary skills, though, have a way to go. Too young to write off completely, but don't count on short-term production.

Yr	Tm	AB	R	HR	RBI	SB	BA	xBA	OBP	SLG	OPS	vL	vR	bb%	ct%	Eye	G	L	F	h%	HctX	PX	xPX	hr/f	Spd	SBO	SB%	#Wk	DOM	DIS	RC/G	RAR	BPV	BPX	R$
10																																			
11																																			
12	aa	73	9	0	4	0	199		266	257	523			8	87	0.70				23		48			97	0%	0%				2.18		34	85	-$3
13	a/a	345	37	4	37	5	262		332	355	687			10	86	0.76				30		67			89	11%	49%				3.90		46	115	$7
14	BOS *	419	42	3	36	0	248	229	306	334	640	539	638	8	78	0.39	57	17	26	31	82	76	58	3%	77	1%	0%	12	33%	42%	3.43	1.3	15	41	$4
1st Half		225	27	2	15	0	251	236	297	353	650			6	76	0.27				32		92			88	2%	0%				3.49		20	54	$4
2nd Half		194	16	1	21	0	245	217	317	312	629	539	638	10	81	0.55	57	17	26	30	84	59	58	3%	75	0%	0%	12	33%	42%	3.34	-0.3	14	38	$3
15	**Proj**	**447**	**45**	**3**	**44**	**3**	**252**	**242**	**312**	**334**	**647**	**559**	**671**	**9**	**82**	**0.53**	**57**	**17**	**26**	**30**	**76**	**69**	**52**	**3%**	**79**	**5%**	**42%**				**3.54**	**2.0**	**16**	**43**	**$8**

Venable,Will

Age:	32	Bats:	L	Pos:	CF RF	Health	A	LIMA Plan	C+
Ht:	6' 3"	Wt:	205			PT/Exp	B	Rand Var	+1
						Consist	C	MM	3523

A spring back issue got the season off to a bad start. No one was really expecting a full repeat of 2013, but everything dried up at once. hr/f corrected; PX and xPX plummeted; LD% and HctX ticked down. Even at 32, a previously healthy BPV trend give us reason to expect a mild bounce-back.

Yr	Tm	AB	R	HR	RBI	SB	BA	xBA	OBP	SLG	OPS	vL	vR	bb%	ct%	Eye	G	L	F	h%	HctX	PX	xPX	hr/f	Spd	SBO	SB%	#Wk	DOM	DIS	RC/G	RAR	BPV	BPX	R$
10	SD	392	60	13	51	29	245	218	324	408	732	523	764	10	67	0.35	39	17	44	33	80	116	109	11%	165	33%	81%	25	40%	48%	4.54	-2.9	34	74	$17
11	SD *	428	56	10	50	28	237	241	293	385	678	436	742	7	74	0.31	43	21	36	30	89	101	100	9%	149	30%	90%	26	35%	31%	3.99	-10.2	39	87	$14
12	SD	417	62	9	45	24	264	270	335	429	765	684	780	9	77	0.44	48	22	29	32	106	111	97	10%	133	28%	80%	27	52%	26%	4.96	3.3	59	148	$16
13	SD	481	64	22	53	22	268	277	312	484	796	833	786	6	75	0.25	47	21	32	31	103	142	107	20%	136	26%	79%	27	56%	30%	5.20	15.4	70	175	$23
14	SD	406	47	8	33	11	224	223	288	325	613	506	631	8	74	0.31	48	19	33	29	78	76	76	8%	114	17%	65%	27	22%	48%	2.95	-11.0	7	19	$6
1st Half		228	21	2	14	3	193	208	256	272	528	549	524	7	72	0.27	54	14	32	26	66	69	61	4%	106	13%	50%	14	29%	64%	2.05	-13.3	-8	-22	-$1
2nd Half		178	26	6	19	8	264	239	328	393	721	440	765	8	75	0.36	40	25	35	32	93	85	95	13%	120	21%	73%	13	15%	31%	4.38	2.7	24	65	$16
15	**Proj**	**376**	**50**	**11**	**38**	**16**	**248**	**249**	**308**	**399**	**708**	**632**	**722**	**7**	**75**	**0.32**	**46**	**21**	**33**	**30**	**91**	**108**	**92**	**12%**	**127**	**23%**	**75%**				**4.10**	**2.7**	**42**	**110**	**$14**

MATT CEDERHOLM

Viciedo,Dayan

Age: 26 Bats: R Pos: RF LF	Health	A	LIMA Plan	B+
Ht: 5' 11" Wt: 240	PT/Exp	B	Rand Var	+3
	Consist	A	MM	4025

Surface scan of 2013-14 would suggest that he traded average for power, especially in 2nd half. But that lost BA was really just a fluctuating h%, as stable xBA confirms. In fact, 2nd half HctX is a great sign that he can hit for power without being a significant BA drag. With that FB trend, UP: 30 HR.

Yr Tm	AB	R	HR	RBI	SB	BA	xBA	OBP	SLG	OPS	vL	vR	bb%	ct%	Eye	G	L	F	h%	HctX	PX	xPX	hr/f	Spd	SBO	SB%	#Wk	DOM	DIS	RC/G	RAR	BPV	BPX	R$
10 CHW *	447	50	23	50	2	264	265	282	467	749	960	729	2	75	0.10	42	19	39	30	108	138	124	16%	72	3%	62%	13	38%	46%	4.53	-5.1	39	85	$12
11 CHW *	554	61	20	72	3	271	251	332	433	765	1020	469	8	79	0.43	58	13	29	31	96	112	62	4%	60	2%	71%	5	20%	80%	5.02	1.4	42	93	$16
12 CHW	505	64	25	78	0	255	261	300	444	744	1033	650	5	76	0.23	47	22	31	29	96	118	97	20%	64	2%	0%	27	44%	41%	4.39	-2.5	31	78	$14
13 CHW	441	43	14	56	0	265	253	304	426	731	709	738	5	78	0.24	47	19	34	31	94	111	102	12%	88	0%	0%	25	44%	44%	4.49	6.5	39	98	$10
14 CHW	523	65	21	58	0	231	252	281	405	686	679	689	6	77	0.26	46	17	37	26	110	121	119	14%	80	1%	0%	27	48%	37%	3.67	-0.2	41	111	$9
1st Half	290	38	8	27	0	245	261	299	403	703	745	689	7	78	0.33	48	19	33	29	98	118	96	11%	84	0%	0%	14	57%	21%	4.03	2.5	47	127	$9
2nd Half	233	27	13	31	0	215	241	257	408	665	608	688	5	75	0.19	44	15	41	23	125	125	149	18%	80	2%	0%	13	38%	54%	3.24	-3.6	35	95	$10
15 Proj	**529**	**61**	**22**	**66**	**0**	**250**	**252**	**296**	**423**	**719**	**777**	**697**	**6**	**77**	**0.25**	**45**	**18**	**37**	**29**	**105**	**121**	**113**	**15%**	**76**	**1%**	**19%**				**4.16**	**2.5**	**31**	**82**	**$12**

Victorino,Shane

Age: 34 Bats: R Pos: RF	Health	F	LIMA Plan	B
Ht: 5' 9" Wt: 190	PT/Exp	C	Rand Var	+2
	Consist	D	MM	2543

Lower back strain plus recurring hamstring problems truncated his season. Sketchy 2014 sample size, plus decision to stop switch-hitting mid-2013, call into question the applicability of historical track record. What we do know: chronic leg issues suggest 20-SB level isn't coming back. 500 AB are doubtful, too.

Yr Tm	AB	R	HR	RBI	SB	BA	xBA	OBP	SLG	OPS	vL	vR	bb%	ct%	Eye	G	L	F	h%	HctX	PX	xPX	hr/f	Spd	SBO	SB%	#Wk	DOM	DIS	RC/G	RAR	BPV	BPX	R$
10 PHI	587	84	18	69	34	259	281	327	429	756	921	692	8	87	0.67	45	17	38	27	107	100	86	9%	125	26%	85%	26	62%	12%	4.87	-5.1	82	178	$24
11 PHI	519	95	17	61	19	279	286	355	491	847	1032	789	10	88	0.87	42	16	42	29	98	121	91	9%	147	16%	86%	25	72%	12%	6.16	14.7	114	253	$23
12 2 NL	595	72	11	55	39	255	260	321	383	704	906	627	8	87	0.66	46	18	36	28	89	78	72	6%	127	28%	87%	27	48%	30%	4.35	-8.9	65	163	$22
13 BOS	477	82	15	61	21	294	276	351	451	801	861	769	5	84	0.33	43	22	35	32	101	102	70	11%	104	20%	88%	25	40%	24%	5.48	16.0	62	155	$27
14 BOS *	152	16	2	12	2	238	253	267	336	603	758	650	4	81	0.21	43	25	32	28	74	72	42	6%	92	6%	100%	8	25%	25%	3.07	-3.7	20	54	$0
1st Half	112	11	1	10	2	203	232	231	293	523	693	602	3	79	0.17	41	22	38	25	76	69	46	4%	92	10%	100%	5	20%	20%	2.23	-6.2	9	24	$0
2nd Half	40	5	1	2	0	336	312	368	459	827	867	833	5	87	0.38	50	32	18	37	67	82	30	20%	86	0%	0%	3	33%	33%	6.49	2.6	50	135	$0
15 Proj	**328**	**45**	**8**	**34**	**9**	**252**	**281**	**306**	**399**	**704**	**769**	**670**	**6**	**84**	**0.42**	**45**	**24**	**31**	**28**	**84**	**98**	**55**	**9%**	**126**	**14%**	**82%**				**4.10**	**0.9**	**66**	**175**	**$10**

Villar,Jonathan

Age: 24 Bats: B Pos: SS	Health	A	LIMA Plan	C
Ht: 6' 1" Wt: 205	PT/Exp	C	Rand Var	0
	Consist	B	MM	2503

7-27-.209 with 17 SB in 263 AB at HOU. Sent back to Triple-A after struggling through first half, presumably to work on his plate approach. Drew some bb% after demotion, but no sign of any much-needed ct% gains. Has time to refine approach; combo of Spd/GB/bb% is a starter kit for... UP: 40 SB

Yr Tm	AB	R	HR	RBI	SB	BA	xBA	OBP	SLG	OPS	vL	vR	bb%	ct%	Eye	G	L	F	h%	HctX	PX	xPX	hr/f	Spd	SBO	SB%	#Wk	DOM	DIS	RC/G	RAR	BPV	BPX	R$
10																																		
11 aa	324	40	8	20	11	210		261	341	602			7	67	0.21				29		108			114	26%	63%				2.74		2	4	$2
12 aa	326	41	9	38	30	230		289	339	628			8	70	0.28				30		73			108	45%	77%				3.30		-11	-28	$13
13 HOU *	549	63	8	40	42	246	249	308	361	669	673	627	8	68	0.28	66	20	14	35	84	91	54	6%	142	40%	73%	11	18%	64%	3.70	4.6	6	15	$22
14 HOU *	453	55	9	46	34	213	218	279	325	604	644	608	8	67	0.27	51	19	30	30	85	91	108	13%	103	41%	76%	19	21%	47%	2.97	-3.0	-10	-27	$15
1st Half	225	27	6	22	14	200	239	255	342	597	640	577	6	70	0.22	52	18	30	26	84	113	108	13%	96	43%	78%	14	21%	43%	2.74	-3.6	13	35	$10
2nd Half	228	28	3	24	20	226	207	306	309	615	670	797	10	64	0.32	50	25	25	34	106	68	110	17%	119	40%	75%	5	20%	60%	3.17	-0.5	-32	-86	$19
15 Proj	**373**	**45**	**6**	**35**	**28**	**225**	**229**	**289**	**328**	**617**	**597**	**627**	**8**	**67**	**0.27**	**57**	**21**	**22**	**32**	**92**	**85**	**87**	**11%**	**111**	**40%**	**74%**				**3.11**	**-1.5**	**-2**	**-6**	**$13**

Vogt,Stephen

Age: 30 Bats: L Pos: 1B	Health	A	LIMA Plan	D+
Ht: 6' 0" Wt: 215	PT/Exp	D	Rand Var	-3
	Consist	C	MM	3223

9-35-.279 in 269 AB at OAK. Used a nice ct% spike to extract max value out of an otherwise-average skill set. Heavy FB tilt in 2nd half didn't play well to combo of average power and spacious home park. Return of CA-eligibility in-season will make him a fine do-no-harm backstop, with xPX hinting at more than that.

Yr Tm	AB	R	HR	RBI	SB	BA	xBA	OBP	SLG	OPS	vL	vR	bb%	ct%	Eye	G	L	F	h%	HctX	PX	xPX	hr/f	Spd	SBO	SB%	#Wk	DOM	DIS	RC/G	RAR	BPV	BPX	R$
10																																		
11 a/a	510	48	12	75	3	236		270	381	651			4	80	0.24				27		99			96	5%	54%				3.38		40	89	$7
12 TAM *	374	35	6	31	1	197	168	261	300	561	0	80	8	79	0.40	26	9	65	23	30	68	54	0%	91	1%	100%	9	11%	33%	2.50	-32.7	14	35	-$3
13 OAK *	431	53	11	52	0	242	247	296	386	682	667	698	7	80	0.38	30	24	46	28	98	98	109	8%	102	2%	0%	13	38%	46%	3.75	-10.9	45	113	$6
14 OAK *	357	37	11	46	2	275	254	315	427	742	647	770	6	86	0.42	33	20	47	29	123	97	144	8%	105	2%	100%	17	53%	35%	4.75	6.2	66	178	$11
1st Half	155	17	4	23	2	297	272	327	441	768	0	1005	4	88	0.37	43	20	37	32	108	89	81	9%	107	4%	100%	5	60%	20%	5.30	4.9	65	176	$10
2nd Half	202	20	7	23	0	257	250	306	416	721	891	694	6	85	0.45	29	19	51	27	127	102	166	8%	96	0%	0%	12	50%	42%	4.36	1.2	64	173	$11
15 Proj	**296**	**31**	**9**	**36**	**1**	**250**	**256**	**295**	**406**	**702**	**535**	**729**	**6**	**83**	**0.37**	**33**	**22**	**45**	**27**	**111**	**104**	**122**	**8%**	**101**	**2%**	**70%**				**4.07**	**-0.8**	**48**	**126**	**$7**

Votto,Joey

Age: 31 Bats: L Pos: 1B	Health	F	LIMA Plan	B+
Ht: 6' 2" Wt: 220	PT/Exp	B	Rand Var	+5
	Consist	F	MM	4155

Quad/knee issues started in May and derailed season from there. Production was down even before injury became public, but skills were stable. With health, age and skill set support a return to near-elite performance. But the variable in this projection is AB, and health history warns not to overproject.

Yr Tm	AB	R	HR	RBI	SB	BA	xBA	OBP	SLG	OPS	vL	vR	bb%	ct%	Eye	G	L	F	h%	HctX	PX	xPX	hr/f	Spd	SBO	SB%	#Wk	DOM	DIS	RC/G	RAR	BPV	BPX	R$
10 CIN	547	106	37	113	16	324	313	424	600	1024	863	1115	14	77	0.73	45	20	35	36	126	183	150	25%	90	11%	76%	27	81%	4%	9.44	46.8	112	243	$40
11 CIN	599	101	29	103	8	309	299	416	531	947	987	930	16	78	0.85	39	28	33	35	137	152	145	18%	82	6%	57%	27	70%	15%	7.98	28.3	93	207	$33
12 CIN	374	59	14	56	5	337	311	474	567	1041	887	1109	20	77	1.11	38	30	32	41	134	171	161	15%	74	5%	63%	21	76%	10%	10.12	46.1	110	275	$20
13 CIN	581	101	24	73	6	305	279	435	491	926	824	977	19	76	0.98	44	27	29	37	121	128	128	18%	108	4%	67%	27	67%	0%	7.80	51.2	79	198	$29
14 CIN	220	32	6	23	1	255	276	390	409	799	969	736	18	78	0.96	41	27	33	30	109	122	147	11%	66	2%	50%	11	64%	18%	5.35	7.5	66	178	$4
1st Half	208	32	6	22	1	260	280	398	418	816	985	750	18	78	1.02	41	27	32	31	109	123	147	11%	68	3%	50%	11	64%	18%	5.61	8.8	71	192	$5
2nd Half	12	0	0	1	0	167	215	231	250	481	0	523	8	67	0.25	38	25	38	25	108	98	142		80	0%	0%				1.77	-0.9	-14	-38	-$12
15 Proj	**488**	**81**	**19**	**69**	**6**	**302**	**295**	**429**	**504**	**933**	**909**	**943**	**18**	**78**	**0.97**	**41**	**27**	**32**	**36**	**124**	**153**	**147**	**16%**	**76**	**5%**	**63%**				**7.77**	**48.7**	**89**	**233**	**$25**

Walker,Neil

Age: 29 Bats: B Pos: 2B	Health	B	LIMA Plan	A
Ht: 6' 3" Wt: 210	PT/Exp	B	Rand Var	0
	Consist	B	MM	4145

Took a nice step forward, but two reasons to fear that this is as good as it gets: 1) HR spike, esp. in 2nd half, was driven by hr/f spike rather than any skill gains. 2) Gains vL look like a mirage: still no power vL, 33% hit rate on that side looks fluky. He's a high-teens value, not a $20+ guy.

Yr Tm	AB	R	HR	RBI	SB	BA	xBA	OBP	SLG	OPS	vL	vR	bb%	ct%	Eye	G	L	F	h%	HctX	PX	xPX	hr/f	Spd	SBO	SB%	#Wk	DOM	DIS	RC/G	RAR	BPV	BPX	R$
10 PIT *	594	75	16	85	9	288	275	341	460	801	809	813	7	80	0.40	36	22	41	34	118	122	125	9%	109	9%	69%	20	65%	15%	5.56	14.1	68	148	$22
11 PIT	596	76	12	83	9	273	262	334	408	742	672	767	8	81	0.48	44	21	35	32	127	96	120	7%	96	9%	60%	27	44%	30%	4.68	-0.7	49	109	$18
12 PIT	472	62	14	69	7	280	259	342	426	768	602	824	9	78	0.45	42	24	34	33	104	101	115	11%	86	9%	58%	25	44%	28%	5.08	9.8	39	98	$16
13 PIT *	499	62	16	54	1	252	268	322	415	738	518	805	9	82	0.59	39	23	39	28	114	106	115	11%	101	2%	33%	22	50%	27%	4.50	12.3	65	163	$10
14 PIT	512	74	23	76	2	271	282	342	467	809	727	831	8	83	0.51	38	23	39	29	102	126	106	14%	80	3%	50%	26	65%	12%	5.33	28.5	74	200	$20
1st Half	261	30	11	37	1	272	267	341	433	774	720	786	6	84	0.40	38	22	39	29	112	101	121	13%	66	3%	50%	13	62%	15%	4.74	10.1	51	138	$16
2nd Half	251	44	12	39	1	271	297	343	502	845	732	880	10	82	0.61	39	23	38	29	93	153	90	15%	95	3%	50%	13	69%	8%	5.97	18.6	100	270	$24
15 Proj	**518**	**72**	**20**	**71**	**3**	**269**	**277**	**341**	**449**	**790**	**666**	**823**	**9**	**82**	**0.52**	**39**	**23**	**38**	**30**	**107**	**123**	**109**	**12%**	**88**	**4%**	**53%**				**5.13**	**26.0**	**66**	**175**	**$19**

Walters,Zachary

Age: 25 Bats: B Pos: DH	Health	A	LIMA Plan	C+
Ht: 6' 2" Wt: 210	PT/Exp	D	Rand Var	+2
	Consist	B	MM	4023

10-17-.181 in 127 AB at WAS and CLE. Repeated 2013's power spike across three levels and two organizations. Platoon split is small-sample noise; he had pop from both sides in minors. Plate skills are sketchy, but prospect of multi-position eligibility in-season makes for a great use of your last buck.

Yr Tm	AB	R	HR	RBI	SB	BA	xBA	OBP	SLG	OPS	vL	vR	bb%	ct%	Eye	G	L	F	h%	HctX	PX	xPX	hr/f	Spd	SBO	SB%	#Wk	DOM	DIS	RC/G	RAR	BPV	BPX	R$
10																																		
11																																		
12 a/a	262	26	6	20	1	237		266	377	643			4	73	0.15				30		100			110	2%	100%				3.37		15	38	$1
13 WAS *	495	53	21	58	3	217	272	240	418	658	1333	900	3	70	0.10	50	25	25	26	72	150	110	0%	107	9%	46%	5	20%	20%	3.18	-20.3	40	100	$6
14 2 TM *	395	48	22	59	0	234	265	277	475	752	957	566	6	67	0.19	39	22	39	29	93	190	147	32%	85	3%	0%	16	38%	44%	4.26	2.5	61	165	$10
1st Half	193	23	11	30	0	216	244	256	454	709	1889	269	5	61	0.14	37	21	42	29	70	203	117	38%	99	8%	0%	6	33%	50%	3.55	-3.1	49	132	$7
2nd Half	202	25	11	29	0	251	283	298	496	794	670	676	6	74	0.25	40	22	38	29	106	179	156	30%	83	0%	0%	10	40%	40%	5.03	5.8	77	208	$12
15 Proj	**368**	**47**	**16**	**52**	**1**	**244**	**255**	**282**	**445**	**727**	**759**	**713**	**4**	**70**	**0.15**	**39**	**21**	**40**	**31**	**92**	**159**	**140**	**15%**	**88**	**4%**	**39%**				**4.10**	**0.5**	**40**	**105**	**$10**

RAY MURPHY

Weeks,Rickie

Age: 32 Bats: R Pos: 2B
Ht: 5' 10" Wt: 220

Health	C	LIMA Plan	D+
PT/Exp	C	Rand Var	-4
Consist	C	MM	4223

Injury-marred 2013 and terrible April relegated him to bad side of a platoon. But from May 1 on, he batted .285, and .320 in Aug/Sept. Finally embraced his natural GB lean and leveraged his xPX to boost his BA to an 8-year high. This profile is more sustainable than his power grab. With regular AB ... UP: 12 HR, .280

Yr Tm	AB	R	HR	RBI	SB	BA	xBA	OBP	SLG	OPS	vL	vR	bb%	ct%	Eye	G	L	F	h%	HctX	PX	xPX	hr/f	Spd	SBO	SB%	#Wk	DOM	DIS	RC/G	RAR	BPV	BPX	R$
10 MIL	651	112	29	83	11	269	259	366	464	830	1025	769	10	72	0.41	49	15	36	33	105	140	115	17%	115	8%	73%	27	48%	26%	5.56	15.8	56	122	$24
11 MIL	453	77	20	49	9	269	270	350	468	818	832	814	10	76	0.47	48	17	35	31	116	138	109	16%	102	9%	82%	22	64%	32%	5.61	11.7	68	151	$17
12 MIL	588	85	21	63	16	230	236	328	400	728	740	723	11	71	0.44	45	17	38	29	105	120	114	13%	114	12%	84%	27	41%	33%	4.24	-1.8	40	100	$14
13 MIL	350	40	10	24	7	209	237	306	357	663	705	644	10	70	0.38	49	18	33	27	92	119	99	13%	93	12%	70%	19	42%	47%	3.31	-3.8	26	65	$2
14 MIL	252	36	8	29	3	274	268	357	452	809	865	746	9	71	0.34	57	18	25	36	92	149	108	18%	99	11%	43%	26	42%	42%	5.12	12.7	53	143	$8
1st Half	132	20	3	15	1	265	263	331	409	740	807	636	7	74	0.29	60	17	22	34	89	114	93	14%	110	9%	33%	14	36%	50%	4.25	3.3	37	100	$6
2nd Half	120	16	5	14	2	283	273	383	500	883	951	829	11	68	0.38	52	20	28	38	96	192	126	22%	79	12%	50%	12	50%	33%	6.16	9.6	71	192	$10
15 Proj	252	35	9	26	4	263	258	353	441	794	861	750	10	71	0.38	52	18	30	34	96	146	109	16%	95	11%	60%				5.01	12.0	45	117	$7

Werth,Jayson

Age: 36 Bats: R Pos: RF
Ht: 6' 5" Wt: 240

Health	C	LIMA Plan	B+
PT/Exp	B	Rand Var	-2
Consist	D	MM	4345

Exhibited exactly the same power skills as 2013 (see xPX) but his HR total was cut down by the vagaries of hr/f (see: gusts of wind, errant). Pretty much everything else was the same, within the limits of normal statistical volatility. However, the odds of a three-peat are small at age 36.

Yr Tm	AB	R	HR	RBI	SB	BA	xBA	OBP	SLG	OPS	vL	vR	bb%	ct%	Eye	G	L	F	h%	HctX	PX	xPX	hr/f	Spd	SBO	SB%	#Wk	DOM	DIS	RC/G	RAR	BPV	BPX	R$
10 PHI	554	106	27	85	13	296	278	388	532	921	881	937	13	73	0.56	37	18	45	36	122	176	163	14%	110	9%	81%	27	67%	22%	7.49	36.1	95	207	$29
11 WAS	561	69	20	58	19	232	233	330	389	718	675	730	12	71	0.46	43	17	40	29	96	118	132	12%	89	14%	86%	27	44%	33%	4.25	-15.2	32	71	$13
12 WAS *	321	45	5	34	8	292	249	381	428	809	1037	755	13	80	0.73	42	19	39	35	104	96	88	5%	119	9%	80%	16	69%	13%	5.93	7.0	61	153	$11
13 WAS	462	84	25	82	10	318	281	398	532	931	1092	884	11	78	0.59	36	26	38	36	129	142	142	18%	77	7%	91%	22	64%	14%	8.01	42.1	74	185	$31
14 WAS	534	85	16	82	9	292	262	394	455	849	933	823	13	79	0.73	40	20	40	35	134	123	142	9%	87	5%	90%	26	69%	15%	6.44	34.7	69	186	$25
1st Half	305	43	6	35	5	266	230	349	370	719	796	698	10	80	0.58	40	18	42	31	149	79	166	6%	83	5%	100%	14	50%	21%	4.50	4.4	32	86	$19
2nd Half	229	42	10	47	4	328	301	449	568	1017	1076	995	17	77	0.91	40	22	37	39	113	185	110	15%	88	6%	80%	12	92%	8%	9.58	33.9	119	322	$33
15 Proj	487	81	18	77	10	289	273	387	477	863	967	830	13	78	0.68	39	21	39	34	122	140	130	12%	91	7%	86%				6.60	35.5	80	210	$25

Wieters,Matt

Age: 29 Bats: B Pos: CA
Ht: 6' 5" Wt: 240

Health	D	LIMA Plan	B
PT/Exp	C	Rand Var	-4
Consist	C	MM	4035

After getting off to one of his best starts, Tommy John surgery ended his season in May. Sad, because it looked like he might finally reach the skills level we've been hoping for since 2009; this small-sample power trend is exciting! Follow his health reports. Great breakouts can happen at 29. With health... UP: 30 HR, .300

Yr Tm	AB	R	HR	RBI	SB	BA	xBA	OBP	SLG	OPS	vL	vR	bb%	ct%	Eye	G	L	F	h%	HctX	PX	xPX	hr/f	Spd	SBO	SB%	#Wk	DOM	DIS	RC/G	RAR	BPV	BPX	R$
10 BAL	446	37	11	55	0	249	231	319	377	695	564	741	10	79	0.50	46	15	38	29	93	90	108	8%	76	1%	0%	25	48%	36%	4.06	-1.9	32	70	$6
11 BAL	500	72	22	68	1	262	273	328	450	778	1124	665	9	83	0.57	43	18	39	28	115	122	130	14%	72	1%	100%	27	48%	19%	5.09	12.8	72	160	$15
12 BAL	526	67	23	83	3	249	265	329	435	764	908	715	10	79	0.54	44	20	35	28	110	119	113	16%	65	2%	100%	27	59%	26%	4.85	11.0	52	130	$14
13 BAL	523	59	22	79	2	235	256	287	417	704	872	628	8	80	0.41	39	18	44	25	103	122	124	12%	68	2%	100%	26	62%	27%	4.10	5.9	56	140	$11
14 BAL	104	13	5	18	0	308	292	339	500	839	799	849	5	82	0.32	28	30	43	34	138	127	161	14%	80	4%	0%	6	67%	33%	6.11	8.0	66	178	$4
1st Half	104	13	5	18	0	308	292	339	500	839	799	849	5	82	0.32	28	30	43	34	138	127	161	14%	80	4%	0%	6	67%	33%	6.11	7.8	66	178	$4
2nd Half																																		
15 Proj	452	55	19	70	1	266	270	321	446	767	867	734	8	81	0.44	38	22	40	29	116	124	132	13%	68	2%	44%				4.96	20.4	50	131	$16

Wilkins,Andrew

Age: 26 Bats: L Pos: 1B
Ht: 6' 2" Wt: 225

Health	A	LIMA Plan	D+
PT/Exp	B	Rand Var	+5
Consist	B	MM	4123

0-2-.140 in 43 AB at CHW. You like to see a big power bat with contact rates moving towards 80%. That means, once he's established in the majors, he'll more likely be a 30-HR, .270 guy than a 30-HR, .220 guy. The downside is that, at 26, his window to establish himself is small.

Yr Tm	AB	R	HR	RBI	SB	BA	xBA	OBP	SLG	OPS	vL	vR	bb%	ct%	Eye	G	L	F	h%	HctX	PX	xPX	hr/f	Spd	SBO	SB%	#Wk	DOM	DIS	RC/G	RAR	BPV	BPX	R$
10																																		
11																																		
12 aa	435	52	15	52	5	210		296	375	672			11	75	0.49				25		115			83	9%	50%				3.49		40	100	$4
13 a/a	458	48	15	62	4	240		307	393	700			9	71	0.34				30		118			76	4%	77%				4.05		23	58	$9
14 CHW *	534	52	22	56	0	224	278	259	407	667	667	342	5	75	0.19	38	29	33	26	138	138	140	0%	67	1%	0%	5	20%	80%	3.43	-10.0	40	108	$7
1st Half	284	23	10	25	0	184	238	212	339	551			4	73	0.13				21	0	120			77	0%	0%				2.25		19	51	-$1
2nd Half	250	30	12	32	0	271	299	313	488	801	667	342	6	77	0.27	38	29	33	31	143	159	140	0%	71	2%	0%	5	20%	80%	5.23	8.5	70	189	$16
15 Proj	305	33	12	37	1	234	254	290	418	708	612	713	7	74	0.30	42	19	39	28	129	142	126	14%	68	4%	56%				4.00	-1.5	38	101	$7

Willingham,Josh

Age: 36 Bats: R Pos: LF DH
Ht: 6' 2" Wt: 230

Health	D	LIMA Plan	D+
PT/Exp	C	Rand Var	+1
Consist	C	MM	4301

14-40-.215 in 297 AB at MIN/KC. Early season wrist injury cost him most of April and May, but his power didn't miss a beat upon return (surprising, given that wrist injuries can sap power). That's where he keeps his value. But OPS v. RH is a strong harbinger of likely platoon future. This projection makes that leap.

Yr Tm	AB	R	HR	RBI	SB	BA	xBA	OBP	SLG	OPS	vL	vR	bb%	ct%	Eye	G	L	F	h%	HctX	PX	xPX	hr/f	Spd	SBO	SB%	#Wk	DOM	DIS	RC/G	RAR	BPV	BPX	R$
10 WAS	370	54	16	56	8	268	256	389	459	848	909	828	15	77	0.79	31	20	49	31	132	129	148	11%	92	6%	100%	20	55%	20%	6.23	13.9	72	157	$13
11 OAK	488	69	29	98	4	246	251	332	477	810	783	823	10	69	0.37	35	17	48	29	122	173	161	17%	72	4%	80%	25	56%	32%	5.23	4.3	60	133	$17
12 MIN	519	85	35	110	3	260	272	366	524	890	920	877	13	73	0.54	38	19	43	29	120	176	136	21%	72	3%	60%	26	65%	19%	6.35	26.9	81	203	$22
13 MIN	389	42	14	48	1	208	217	342	368	709	696	714	15	67	0.52	37	18	45	27	95	129	134	12%	76	1%	100%	22	41%	45%	3.84	-1.6	25	63	$2
14 2AL *	324	50	15	42	2	209	214	322	387	709	840	702	14	65	0.48	36	15	49	27	109	142	158	14%	106	2%	100%	20	40%	45%	4.05	3.6	38	103	$5
1st Half	145	21	8	25	0	226	227	347	437	784	910	852	16	68	0.57	30	15	55	28	115	160	182	15%	112	0%	0%	8	50%	38%	5.00	5.5	65	176	$5
2nd Half	179	29	7	17	2	196	202	311	346	658	797	595	13	64	0.42	41	15	45	26	105	126	140	13%	92	4%	100%	12	33%	50%	3.36	-2.1	11	30	$5
15 Proj	211	30	10	30	1	254	229	370	443	813	873	789	14	68	0.50	36	17	47	33	109	151	148	15%	87	2%	90%				5.45	10.5	37	96	$7

Wong,Kolten

Age: 24 Bats: L Pos: 2B
Ht: 5' 9" Wt: 185

Health	A	LIMA Plan	B+
PT/Exp	C	Rand Var	0
Consist	A	MM	1435

12-42-.249 with 20 SB in 402 AB at STL. Shoulder soreness landed him on the DL on June 22, at which point he had 1 HR. He returned on July 6 and then ran off 5 HRs in 7 games. More aggressive bat and FB tilt built that 2nd half power surge. Is it sustainable? PX trend says maybe. Let's see it again.

Yr Tm	AB	R	HR	RBI	SB	BA	xBA	OBP	SLG	OPS	vL	vR	bb%	ct%	Eye	G	L	F	h%	HctX	PX	xPX	hr/f	Spd	SBO	SB%	#Wk	DOM	DIS	RC/G	RAR	BPV	BPX	R$
10																																		
11																																		
12 aa	523	62	7	40	16	251		298	344	642			6	85	0.43				29		59			113	21%	57%				3.29		34	85	$11
13 STL *	471	58	7	35	18	247	272	299	357	656	0	410	7	83	0.44	61	17	22	28	73	72	18	0%	137	16%	94%	8	0%	75%	3.79	1.8	47	118	$12
14 STL *	477	64	14	51	24	257	261	293	394	687	790	656	5	83	0.30	47	19	34	28	93	89	82	11%	105	25%	86%	23	48%	30%	4.08	9.6	46	124	$20
1st Half	222	24	2	23	13	244	262	286	327	613	528	597	5	89	0.52	56	17	28	27	79	54	49	3%	104	25%	93%	10	50%	40%	3.38	-0.1	42	114	$11
2nd Half	255	39	12	28	12	268	263	300	451	751	936	696	4	78	0.21	42	21	38	30	100	124	105	15%	107	26%	80%	13	46%	23%	4.71	9.8	53	143	$28
15 Proj	529	70	10	48	23	261	260	305	373	678	666	680	6	83	0.34	53	18	29	30	84	77	56	8%	114	21%	84%				3.98	9.0	44	117	$20

Wright,David

Age: 32 Bats: R Pos: 3B
Ht: 6' 0" Wt: 205

Health	C	LIMA Plan	B+
PT/Exp	A	Rand Var	0
Consist	D	MM	3335

It all went south in '14—power, patience, contact, ability to hit RHPs, SB opps and success, consistency and luck. The worst part was that he had to experience this without the benefit of any lost DL time. Shoulder woes affected his 2nd half output so there should be some bounce-back. But drop out when bidding hits $18.

Yr Tm	AB	R	HR	RBI	SB	BA	xBA	OBP	SLG	OPS	vL	vR	bb%	ct%	Eye	G	L	F	h%	HctX	PX	xPX	hr/f	Spd	SBO	SB%	#Wk	DOM	DIS	RC/G	RAR	BPV	BPX	R$
10 NYM	587	87	29	103	19	283	267	354	503	856	1066	798	11	73	0.43	38	19	43	35	115	158	147	16%	92	18%	63%	27	59%	30%	6.16	17.9	67	146	$29
11 NYM	389	60	14	61	13	254	252	345	427	771	806	761	12	75	0.54	42	18	40	31	122	126	142	12%	78	13%	87%	19	53%	21%	5.11	0.1	50	111	$14
12 NYM	581	91	21	93	15	306	278	391	492	883	917	867	12	81	0.72	42	22	35	35	116	123	134	13%	93	13%	60%	27	59%	19%	6.83	36.0	76	190	$30
13 NYM	430	63	18	58	17	307	280	390	514	904	1072	836	11	82	0.70	38	23	39	34	122	130	141	13%	146	14%	85%	21	67%	5%	7.40	40.2	99	248	$26
14 NYM	535	54	8	63	8	269	245	324	374	698	921	634	7	79	0.37	40	23	37	33	116	84	114	5%	82	9%	62%	24	38%	46%	4.13	6.4	24	65	$15
1st Half	321	35	6	41	4	277	255	333	396	729	1005	643	7	79	0.38	40	25	36	34	117	95	120	7%	80	9%	50%	14	43%	29%	4.47	7.1	31	84	$19
2nd Half	214	19	2	22	4	257	230	310	341	651	770	621	7	79	0.36	40	22	38	32	115	67	104	3%	86	9%	80%	10	30%	70%	3.65	-0.3	13	35	$8
15 Proj	508	63	13	66	13	282	259	351	429	780	942	726	9	79	0.50	40	22	38	33	118	108	125	9%	100	12%	73%				5.28	23.0	52	137	$22

RON SHANDLER

Yelich,Christian S.

Age: 23 Bats: L Pos: LF	Health A	LIMA Plan B
Ht: 6' 3" Wt: 200	PT/Exp D	Rand Var -1
	Consist A	MM 3545

For an extreme GB hitter to achieve success, he requires combo of hard swings and porous defenses. HctX indicates swing strength has been flat for 2 years. Perhaps some favorable opposition helped boost his 2H hit rate and BA. But this is not a .300 hitter; solid OBP and speed make him a stable SB source, and that's all, for now.

Yr	Tm	AB	R	HR	RBI	SB	BA	xBA	OBP	SLG	OPS	vL	vR	bb%	ct%	Eye	G	L	F	h%	HctX	PX	xPX	hr/f	Spd	SBO	SB%	#Wk	DOM	DIS	RC/G	RAR	BPV	BPX	R$
10																																			
11																																			
12																																			
13	MIA *	433	62	9	41	14	276	276	356	427	782	476	941	11	72	0.44	63	23	14	37	108	114	83	17%	149	15%	73%	10	20%	20%	5.31	15.6	48	120	$16
14	MIA	582	94	9	54	21	284	271	362	402	764	819	747	11	76	0.51	61	21	18	36	113	91	97	12%	133	15%	75%	25	44%	16%	5.16	22.9	42	114	$25
1st Half		255	42	6	24	10	259	283	340	424	764	811	750	11	77	0.54	62	18	20	32	114	114	102	16%	151	15%	91%	12	58%	17%	5.15	10.5	68	184	$17
2nd Half		327	52	3	30	11	303	260	379	385	765	825	744	10	76	0.49	60	23	16	39	113	73	93	8%	110	15%	65%	13	31%	15%	5.16	13.1	19	51	$31
15	Proj	**569**	**88**	**12**	**53**	**20**	**277**	**274**	**356**	**417**	**773**	**652**	**823**	**11**	**75**	**0.47**	**61**	**21**	**18**	**35**	**111**	**108**	**91**	**15%**	**137**	**15%**	**74%**				**5.19**	**23.8**	**46**	**122**	**$22**

Young Jr.,Eric

Age: 30 Bats: B Pos: LF	Health C	LIMA Plan C
Ht: 5' 10" Wt: 195	PT/Exp C	Rand Var +4
	Consist D	MM 1533

Weak hitter with average contact but excellent wheels. The only way that works is if he can maintain a solid OBP; that held its own in the 1st half but then tanked. 2B eligibility would have made him marginally draftable in deep leagues. Assuming he has a job somewhere, he could end up as someone's FAAB target for stray SBs.

Yr	Tm	AB	R	HR	RBI	SB	BA	xBA	OBP	SLG	OPS	vL	vR	bb%	ct%	Eye	G	L	F	h%	HctX	PX	xPX	hr/f	Spd	SBO	SB%	#Wk	DOM	DIS	RC/G	RAR	BPV	BPX	R$
10	COL *	308	41	1	14	24	230	223	293	279	572	552	623	8	78	0.40	54	17	29	29	79	39	55	0%	141	34%	80%	11	27%	45%	2.85	-23.0	2	4	$7
11	COL *	421	64	1	24	35	264	262	335	355	691	618	653	10	81	0.56	58	19	23	32	73	64	69	0%	151	32%	87%	17	18%	35%	4.43	-10.2	41	91	$16
12	COL	174	36	4	15	14	316	257	377	448	825	974	770	7	82	0.42	49	19	32	37	83	81	73	9%	140	29%	88%	20	25%	55%	6.37	7.8	51	128	$10
13	2 NL	539	70	2	32	46	249	260	310	336	645	642	647	8	81	0.46	54	21	25	30	77	64	65	2%	141	40%	81%	27	37%	37%	3.65	-6.5	37	93	$23
14	NYM	280	48	1	17	30	229	261	299	311	610	566	626	8	79	0.40	63	19	18	29	70	60	33	3%	147	50%	83%	24	21%	38%	3.21	-5.0	24	65	$12
1st Half		181	33	1	11	21	238	248	325	320	646	510	696	10	76	0.45	60	18	21	31	74	67	45	4%	135	44%	91%	11	9%	45%	3.84	0.6	19	51	$15
2nd Half		99	15	0	6	9	212	281	248	293	541	669	490	4	84	0.25	67	19	13	25	64	47	16	0%	138	65%	69%	13	31%	31%	2.15	-5.1	24	65	$5
15	Proj	**267**	**43**	**1**	**17**	**22**	**245**	**261**	**306**	**331**	**637**	**663**	**626**	**7**	**81**	**0.40**	**59**	**19**	**22**	**30**	**73**	**61**	**47**	**3%**	**142**	**38%**	**81%**				**3.48**	**-2.1**	**40**	**106**	**$11**

Young,Chris

Age: 31 Bats: R Pos: LF CF	Health B	LIMA Plan D+
Ht: 6' 2" Wt: 200	PT/Exp D	Rand Var +1
	Consist B	MM 4313

11-38-.222 with 8 SB in 325 AB at NYM/NYY. Some precipitous trends... OPS vs LHers, walk rate, PX/xPX combined with a soaring uppercut swing. 48%/48% DOM/DIS is about as far as you can go toward ultimate inconsistency. An impatient, all-or-nothing approach that points to signs of desperation. DN: Done.

Yr	Tm	AB	R	HR	RBI	SB	BA	xBA	OBP	SLG	OPS	vL	vR	bb%	ct%	Eye	G	L	F	h%	HctX	PX	xPX	hr/f	Spd	SBO	SB%	#Wk	DOM	DIS	RC/G	RAR	BPV	BPX	R$
10	ARI	584	94	27	91	28	257	250	341	452	793	826	781	11	75	0.51	34	17	50	30	101	137	135	12%	94	21%	80%	26	69%	8%	5.33	2.7	63	137	$26
11	ARI	567	89	20	71	22	236	247	331	420	751	939	694	12	75	0.58	32	20	49	28	126	135	137	10%	120	20%	71%	27	63%	22%	4.57	-10.3	73	162	$18
12	ARI	325	36	14	41	8	231	259	311	434	745	810	707	10	76	0.46	31	22	47	26	106	143	136	12%	74	15%	73%	24	46%	38%	4.38	-4.6	61	153	$7
13	OAK	335	46	12	40	10	200	231	280	379	659	712	614	10	72	0.39	29	22	50	24	82	131	120	10%	115	19%	77%	26	50%	31%	3.36	-9.7	50	125	$5
14	2 TM *	352	45	13	43	9	229	244	297	403	699	561	720	9	77	0.42	29	20	52	26	94	129	109	8%	103	15%	74%	23	48%	48%	3.93	0.4	62	168	$9
1st Half		209	30	8	26	8	220	236	286	384	669	593	641	8	78	0.42	32	17	51	24	95	115	114	9%	99	22%	72%	13	46%	54%	3.53	-3.1	54	146	$12
2nd Half		143	15	5	16	1	240	258	310	423	733	507	839	9	75	0.41	24	23	53	29	93	148	103	8%	105	3%	100%	10	50%	40%	4.44	1.9	71	192	$4
15	Proj	**285**	**36**	**10**	**35**	**7**	**225**	**245**	**302**	**401**	**703**	**673**	**716**	**9**	**75**	**0.42**	**29**	**21**	**50**	**26**	**95**	**137**	**118**	**9%**	**101**	**15%**	**76%**				**3.93**	**1.6**	**56**	**148**	**$7**

Young,Delmon

Age: 29 Bats: R Pos: DH LF	Health B	LIMA Plan C
Ht: 6' 3" Wt: 240	PT/Exp C	Rand Var -5
	Consist B	MM 3233

In a year when this former #1 prospect should have been completely marginalized, he pulls out a .300 BA and some post-season heroics. It was like he was yelling, "Hey, look here! I'm still only 29!" And while that's true, and his BPIs still show faint signs of life, he remains an end-gamer. With 2010 upside. That sucks for us.

Yr	Tm	AB	R	HR	RBI	SB	BA	xBA	OBP	SLG	OPS	vL	vR	bb%	ct%	Eye	G	L	F	h%	HctX	PX	xPX	hr/f	Spd	SBO	SB%	#Wk	DOM	DIS	RC/G	RAR	BPV	BPX	R$
10	MIN	570	77	21	112	5	298	291	333	493	826	927	781	5	86	0.35	45	15	40	32	111	129	119	11%	68	7%	56%	27	70%	7%	5.81	-0.4	78	170	$25
11	2 AL *	504	58	13	68	1	267	251	300	397	696	759	670	5	82	0.26	47	18	35	30	97	88	88	9%	87	1%	100%	23	35%	30%	4.14	-24.5	35	78	$12
12	DET	574	54	18	74	0	267	255	296	411	707	833	649	3	80	0.18	43	22	35	30	121	93	107	11%	63	2%	0%	27	33%	33%	4.10	-13.1	24	60	$13
13	2 TM *	381	34	12	41	0	253	239	291	389	681	684	724	5	76	0.23	42	22	36	31	113	97	142	12%	76	0%	0%	20	50%	35%	3.87	-7.0	16	40	$6
14	BAL	242	27	7	30	2	302	264	337	442	779	722	809	4	79	0.20	50	21	28	36	102	100	91	13%	100	3%	100%	25	36%	52%	5.37	8.7	36	97	$9
1st Half		110	10	3	11	0	327	269	351	455	805	705	870	3	80	0.14	43	27	30	39	98	92	82	12%	86	0%	0%	14	29%	50%	5.95	5.5	27	73	$5
2nd Half		132	17	4	19	2	280	263	326	432	758	740	766	5	78	0.24	56	17	27	33	105	107	99	14%	107	6%	100%	11	45%	55%	4.94	3.3	42	114	$12
15	Proj	**295**	**31**	**10**	**37**	**1**	**281**	**262**	**318**	**433**	**751**	**745**	**754**	**4**	**79**	**0.22**	**47**	**21**	**32**	**33**	**108**	**109**	**108**	**13%**	**88**	**2%**	**85%**				**4.80**	**6.3**	**28**	**75**	**$10**

Zimmerman,Ryan

Age: 30 Bats: R Pos: LF 3B	Health F	LIMA Plan A
Ht: 6' 3" Wt: 220	PT/Exp B	Rand Var +1
	Consist A	MM 4355

A broken thumb and a Grade 3 hamstring strain leveled his season after two nearly-injury-free campaigns. That makes four years in a row with some time lost. BPIs were fairly stable when he was on the field (though 19 Sept. ABs were a bit weak), which is a good sign. It all comes down to health. Keeper leagues be cautious.

Yr	Tm	AB	R	HR	RBI	SB	BA	xBA	OBP	SLG	OPS	vL	vR	bb%	ct%	Eye	G	L	F	h%	HctX	PX	xPX	hr/f	Spd	SBO	SB%	#Wk	DOM	DIS	RC/G	RAR	BPV	BPX	R$
10	WAS	525	85	25	85	4	307	280	388	510	899	957	879	12	81	0.70	41	18	41	34	133	133	139	14%	91	3%	80%	25	52%	20%	7.28	31.2	84	183	$26
11	WAS	395	52	12	49	3	289	261	355	443	798	919	773	9	82	0.56	50	16	34	33	114	104	114	11%	113	3%	75%	18	56%	17%	5.64	6.0	64	142	$13
12	WAS	578	93	25	95	5	282	274	346	478	824	861	810	9	80	0.49	48	18	33	32	139	126	144	16%	91	4%	71%	25	64%	16%	5.85	20.3	68	170	$24
13	WAS	568	84	26	79	6	275	267	344	465	809	850	794	10	77	0.45	45	21	34	32	128	127	144	18%	105	4%	100%	25	48%	20%	5.69	27.4	61	153	$23
14	WAS	214	26	5	38	0	280	283	342	449	790	779	794	9	83	0.59	44	20	35	32	121	128	115	8%	78	0%	0%	13	69%	15%	5.52	10.9	77	208	$6
1st Half		137	15	3	20	0	248	266	314	409	722	792	704	9	79	0.48	45	19	35	30	127	133	119	8%	65	0%	0%	7	71%	14%	4.41	2.9	62	168	$5
2nd Half		77	11	2	18	0	338	306	391	519	910	762	974	9	90	1.00	42	23	35	36	109	120	109	8%	105	0%	0%	6	67%	17%	8.00	8.6	107	289	$8
15	Proj	**508**	**71**	**20**	**84**	**2**	**292**	**290**	**354**	**491**	**845**	**827**	**851**	**9**	**82**	**0.57**	**45**	**20**	**35**	**32**	**123**	**139**	**127**	**14%**	**94**	**2%**	**86%**				**6.33**	**36.6**	**80**	**211**	**$23**

Zobrist,Ben

Age: 34 Bats: B Pos: 2B LF SS	Health A	LIMA Plan B+
Ht: 6' 3" Wt: 210	PT/Exp A	Rand Var 0
	Consist B	MM 2335

Potentially a better season than it appears. Got off to a torrid start before dislocating his thumb. His bat took a good few months to return and then he had a solid 2nd half. Double his 2nd half and you would not be far from what 2014 could have been. Multi-positions help elevate his value, offset by his age. I'd go $15-$20.

Yr	Tm	AB	R	HR	RBI	SB	BA	xBA	OBP	SLG	OPS	vL	vR	bb%	ct%	Eye	G	L	F	h%	HctX	PX	xPX	hr/f	Spd	SBO	SB%	#Wk	DOM	DIS	RC/G	RAR	BPV	BPX	R$
10	TAM	541	77	10	75	24	238	246	346	353	699	695	700	15	80	0.86	44	18	38	28	96	82	93	6%	100	15%	89%	27	44%	26%	4.32	-4.4	48	104	$15
11	TAM	588	99	20	91	19	269	284	353	469	822	907	783	12	78	0.60	45	20	35	31	117	144	120	12%	97	15%	76%	27	67%	19%	5.77	20.0	82	182	$25
12	TAM	560	88	20	74	14	270	285	377	471	848	879	835	15	82	0.94	43	22	35	30	109	128	114	13%	109	13%	61%	27	67%	19%	6.03	30.5	93	233	$21
13	TAM	612	77	12	71	11	275	260	354	402	756	643	812	11	85	0.79	43	20	37	31	106	87	98	6%	105	7%	79%	27	63%	15%	4.98	21.9	65	163	$20
14	TAM	570	83	10	52	10	272	267	354	395	749	873	703	12	85	0.89	49	18	33	30	103	88	89	6%	111	8%	67%	25	60%	16%	4.88	24.5	70	189	$18
1st Half		272	37	6	18	4	250	263	338	393	731	805	707	12	83	0.80	46	18	36	28	101	99	92	7%	118	7%	67%	13	62%	15%	4.51	9.0	73	197	$10
2nd Half		298	46	4	34	6	292	269	370	396	765	927	699	11	87	1.00	51	19	30	32	106	79	86	5%	102	9%	67%	12	58%	17%	5.25	15.6	67	181	$25
15	Proj	**568**	**85**	**12**	**70**	**12**	**276**	**270**	**361**	**413**	**774**	**813**	**757**	**12**	**84**	**0.85**	**46**	**19**	**34**	**31**	**106**	**99**	**96**	**7%**	**104**	**9%**	**70%**				**5.22**	**29.8**	**70**	**183**	**$22**

Zunino,Mike

Age: 24 Bats: R Pos: CA	Health B	LIMA Plan D+
Ht: 6' 2" Wt: 220	PT/Exp D	Rand Var +3
	Consist F	MM 4003

One of only 7 catchers to hit 20+ HRs, a sub-Mendoza BA seems to come with the territory these days. But it would have been much more encouraging if he didn't plummet in the 2nd half. This skill set could land him on the bench in a hurry -- ct%, HctX, DOM/DIS inconsistency -- so be wary about investing in the power.

Yr	Tm	AB	R	HR	RBI	SB	BA	xBA	OBP	SLG	OPS	vL	vR	bb%	ct%	Eye	G	L	F	h%	HctX	PX	xPX	hr/f	Spd	SBO	SB%	#Wk	DOM	DIS	RC/G	RAR	BPV	BPX	R$
10																																			
11																																			
12	aa	51	6	2	7	0	303		363	520	884			9	84	0.60				32		134			89	0%	0%				6.92		90	225	$0
13	SEA *	376	49	12	44	1	201	219	256	350	606	650	609	7	67	0.22	43	19	39	26	95	117	108	10%	96	1%	100%	12	33%	67%	2.87	-9.9	6	15	$2
14	SEA	438	51	22	60	0	199	226	254	404	658	722	632	4	64	0.11	34	17	49	25	86	170	143	16%	89	5%	0%	27	30%	37%	2.83	-6.8	28	76	$5
1st Half		236	31	12	31	0	225	238	282	441	723	835	669	4	64	0.13	33	20	46	30	83	183	140	17%	95	5%	0%	14	36%	29%	3.60	1.5	40	108	$8
2nd Half		202	20	10	29	0	168	211	221	361	583	561	590	3	64	0.08	35	12	53	20	89	154	147	14%	89	5%	0%	13	23%	46%	2.07	-8.8	15	41	$1
15	Proj	**413**	**54**	**18**	**62**	**0**	**215**	**222**	**272**	**397**	**669**	**711**	**653**	**5**	**65**	**0.14**	**38**	**17**	**46**	**28**	**90**	**150**	**130**	**14%**	**91**	**3%**	**22%**				**3.21**	**-2.4**	**14**	**37**	**$8**

RON SHANDLER

The following section contains player boxes for every pitcher who had significant playing time in 2014 and/or is expected to get fantasy roster-worthy innings in 2015. In most cases, high-end prospects who have yet to make their major league debuts will not appear here; you can find scouting reports for them in the Prospects section.

Snapshot Section

The top band of each player box contains the following information:

Age as of Opening Day 2015.

Throws right (R) or left (L).

Role: Starters (SP) are those projected to face 20+ batters per game; the rest are relievers (RP).

Ht/Wt: Each batter's height and weight.

Type evaluates the extent to which a pitcher allows the ball to be put into play and his ground ball or fly ball tendency. CON (contact) represents pitchers who allow the ball to be put into play a great deal. PWR (power) represents those with high strikeout and/or walk totals who keep the ball out of play. GB are those who have a ground ball rate more than 50%; xGB are those who have a GB rate more than 55%. FB are those who have a fly ball rate more than 40%; xFB are those who have a FB rate more than 45%.

Reliability Grades analyze each pitcher's forecast risk, on an A-F scale. High grades go to those who have accumulated few disabled list days (Health), have a history of substantial and regular major league playing time (PT/Exp) and have displayed consistent performance over the past three years, using xERA (Consist).

LIMA Plan Grade evaluates how well that pitcher would be a good fit for a team using the LIMA Plan draft strategy. Best grades go to pitchers who have excellent base skills and had a 2014 dollar value less than $20. Lowest grades will go to poor skills and values more than $20.

Random Variance Score (Rand Var) measures the impact random variance had on the pitcher's 2014 stats and the probability that his 2015 performance will exceed or fall short of 2014. The variables tracked are those prone to regression—H%, S%, hr/f and xERA to ERA variance. Players are rated on a scale of –5 to +5 with positive scores indicating rebounds and negative scores indicating corrections. Note that this score is computer-generated and the projections will override it on occasion.

Mayberry Method (MM) acknowledges the imprecision of the forecasting process by projecting player performance in broad strokes. The four digits of MM each represent a fantasy-relevant skill—ERA, strikeout rate, saves potential and playing time (IP)—and are all on a scale of 0 to 5.

Commentaries for each pitcher provide a brief analysis of BPIs and the potential impact on performance in 2015. MLB statistics are listed first for those who played only a portion of 2014 at the major league level. Note that these commentaries generally look at performance related issues only. Role and playing time expectations may impact these analyses, so you will have to adjust accordingly. Upside (UP) and downside (DN) statistical potential appears for some players; these are less grounded in hard data and more speculative of skills potential.

Player Stat Section

The past five years' statistics represent the total accumulated in the majors as well as in Triple-A, Double-A ball and various foreign leagues during each year. All non-major league stats have been converted to a major league equivalent (MLE) performance level. Minor league levels below Double-A are not included.

Nearly all baseball publications separate a player's statistical experiences in the major leagues from the minor leagues and outside leagues. While this may be appropriate for official record-keeping purposes, it is not an easy-to-analyze snapshot of a player's complete performance for a given year.

Bill James has proven that minor league statistics (converted to MLEs), at Double-A level or above, provide as accurate a record of a player's performance as Major league statistics. Other researchers have also devised conversion factors for foreign leagues. Since these are adequate barometers, we include them in the pool of historical data for each year.

Team designations: An asterisk (*) appearing with a team name means that Triple-A and/or Double-A numbers are included in that year's stat line. Any stints of less than 10 IP are not included (to screen out most rehab appearances). A designation of "a/a" means the stats were accumulated at both AA and AAA levels that year. "for" represents a foreign or independent league. The designation "2TM" appears whenever a player was on more than one major league team, crossing leagues, in a season. "2AL" and "2NL" represent more than one team in the same league. Players who were cut during the season and finished 2014 as a free agent are designated as FAA (Free agent, AL) and FAN (Free agent, NL).

Stats: Descriptions of all the categories appear in the Encyclopedia.

- The leading decimal point has been suppressed on some categories to conserve space.
- Data for platoons (vL, vR), balls-in-play (G/L/F) and consistency (Wk#, DOM, DIS) are for major league performance only.
- Formulas that use BIP data, like xERA and BPV, are used for years in which G/L/F data is available. Where feasible, older versions of these formulas are used otherwise.

Earned run average is presented alongside skills-based xERA. WHIP appears next, followed by opponents' overall OPS (oOPS). OPS splits vs. left-handed and right-handed batters appear to the right of oOPS. Batters faced per game (BF/G) provide a quick view of a pitcher's role—starters will generally have levels over 20.

Basic pitching skills are measured with Control, or walk rate (Ctl), Dominance, or strikeout rate (Dom), and Command, or strikeout-to-walk rate (Cmd). First-pitch strike rate (FpK) and Swinging strikeout rate (SwK) are also presented with these basic skills. Our research shows that FpK serves as a useful tool for validating Ctl, and SwK serves as a similar check on Dom.

Once the ball leaves the bat, it will either be a (G)round ball, (L)ine drive or (F)ly ball.

Random variance indicators include hit rate (H%)—often referred to as batting average on balls-in-play (BABIP)—which tends to regress to 30%. Normal strand rates (S%) fall within the tolerances of 65% to 80%. The ratio of home runs to fly balls (hr/f) is another sanity check; levels far from 10% are prone to regression.

In looking at consistency for starting pitchers, we track games started (GS), average pitch counts (APC) for all outings (for starters and relievers), the percentage of DOMinating starts (PQS 4 or 5) and DISaster starts (PQS 0 or 1). The larger the variance between DOM and DIS, the greater the consistency.

For relievers, we look at their saves success rate (Sv%) and Leverage Index (LI). A Doug Dennis study showed little correlation between saves success and future opportunity. However, you can increase your odds by prospecting for pitchers who have *both* a high saves percentage (80% or better) *and* high skills. Relievers with LI levels over 1.0 are being used more often by managers to win ballgames.

The final section includes several overall performance measures: runs above replacement (RAR), Base performance value (BPV), Base performance index (BPX, which is BPV indexed to each year's league average) and the Rotisserie value (R$).

2015 Projections

Forecasts are computed from a player's trends over the past five years. Adjustments were made for leading indicators and variances between skill and statistical output. After reviewing the leading indicators, you might opt to make further adjustments.

Although each year's numbers include all playing time at the Double-A level or above, the 2015 forecast only represents potential playing time at the major league level, and again is highly preliminary.

Note that the projected Rotisserie values in this book will not necessarily align with each player's historical actuals. Since we currently have no idea who is going to close games for the White Sox, or whether Noah Syndergaard is going to break camp with the Mets, it is impossible to create a finite pool of playing time, something which is required for valuation. So the projections are roughly based on a 12-team AL/NL league, and include an inflated number of innings, league-wide. This serves to flatten the spread of values and depress individual player dollar projections. In truth, a $25 player in this book might actually be worth $21, or $28. This level of precision is irrelevant in a process that is driven by market forces anyway. So, don't obsess over it.

Be aware of other sources that publish perfectly calibrated Rotisserie values over the winter. They are likely making arbitrary decisions as to where free agents are going to sign and who is going to land jobs in the spring. We do not make those leaps of faith here.

Bottom line… It is far too early to be making definitive projections for 2015, especially on playing time. Focus on the skill levels and trends, then consult BaseballHQ.com for playing time revisions as players change teams and roles become more defined. A free projections update will be available online in March.

Do-it-yourself analysis

Here are some data points you can look at in doing your own player analysis:

- Variance between vLH and vRH opposition OPS
- Variance in 2014 hr/f rate from 10%
- Variance in 2014 hit rate (H%) from 30%
- Variance in 2014 strand rate (S%) to tolerances (65% - 80%)
- Variance between ERA and xERA each year
- Growth or decline in Base Performance Value (BPV)
- Spikes in innings pitched
- Trends in average pitch counts (APC)
- Trends in DOM/DIS splits
- Trends in saves success rate (Sv%)
- Variance between Dom changes and corresponding SwK levels
- Variance between Ctl changes and corresponding FpK levels

Abad,Fernando

Age:	29	Th:	L	Role	RP	Health	D	LIMA Plan	B
Ht:	6' 1"	Wt:	220	Type	FB	PT/Exp	D	Rand Var	-5
						Consist	C	MM	3200

Journeyman reliever recorded career bests in ERA, WHIP, and Dom. Do you believe? PRO: Held 2013 Cmd gains, great SwK trend supports new Dom peak. CON: Elite ERA/WHIP were a H%/S% aberration. xERA tells the truth here: he's a nice bullpen arm, but not an emerging weapon.

Yr Tm	W	L	Sv	IP	K	ERA	xERA	WHIP	oOPS	vL	vR	BF/G	Ctl	Dom	Cmd	FpK	SwK	G	L	F	H%	S%	hr/f	GS	APC	DOM%	DIS%	Sv%	LI	RAR	BPV	BPX	R$
10 HOU *	4	4	0	65	47	2.89	4.84	1.39	636	619	648	6.7	1.8	6.5	3.5	62%	6%	32	8	59	34%	84%	9%	0	14			0	1.29	9.6	77	124	$2
11 HOU *	3	7	0	50	40	6.37	6.43	1.63	946	630	1257	3.8	2.8	7.3	2.6	54%	7%	35	20	45	36%	64%	16%	0	15			0	0.93	-14.8	38	57	-$8
12 HOU *	2	6	2	74	60	4.74	5.74	1.63	892	779	953	6.6	3.2	7.4	2.3	61%	9%	43	21	36	37%	73%	12%	6	22	0%	83%	50	0.67	-6.6	53	68	-$8
13 WAS *	1	3	0	55	41	2.71	4.11	1.37	687	790	619	4.1	2.0	6.7	3.4	64%	10%	39	21	39	35%	81%	6%	0	17			0	0.56	7.8	94	122	-$1
14 OAK	2	4	0	57	51	1.57	3.29	0.85	499	527	475	3.1	2.4	8.0	3.4	61%	11%	41	17	42	21%	87%	7%	0	12			0	1.09	15.4	100	119	$7
1st Half	2	3	0	33	31	2.20	3.19	0.89	506	583	451	3.2	3.0	8.5	2.8	60%	12%	47	14	38	20%	81%	10%	0	12			0	1.01	6.2	97	116	$8
2nd Half	0	1	0	25	20	0.73	3.39	0.81	490	468	515	3.0	1.5	7.3	5.0	63%	9%	33	21	45	23%	95%	3%	0	12			0	1.19	9.2	103	123	$7
15 Proj	2	4	0	58	48	2.96	3.47	1.16	645	657	636	3.8	2.2	7.4	3.3	63%	10%	40	20	40	29%	77%	7%	0						5.6	90	107	$2

Adams,Mike

Age:	36	Th:	R	Role	RP	Health	F	LIMA Plan	C
Ht:	6' 5"	Wt:	210	Type	Pwr	PT/Exp	D	Rand Var	-2
						Consist	A	MM	4410

Came back from 2013 labrum and rotator cuff surgery only to add a sports hernia in the spring and more labrum problems in the summer. Pre-injury version showed closer-worthiness. Amidst 2014 injuries, 1st half micro-sample suggested skills were intact. Needs to establish some health to have any chance at relevance.

Yr Tm	W	L	Sv	IP	K	ERA	xERA	WHIP	oOPS	vL	vR	BF/G	Ctl	Dom	Cmd	FpK	SwK	G	L	F	H%	S%	hr/f	GS	APC	DOM%	DIS%	Sv%	LI	RAR	BPV	BPX	R$
10 SD	4	1	0	67	73	1.76	3.25	1.07	526	540	513	3.8	3.1	9.9	3.2	56%	12%	41	20	39	29%	84%	3%	0	15			0	1.33	19.1	113	182	$9
11 2 TM	5	4	2	74	74	1.47	2.90	0.79	496	538	439	3.7	1.7	9.0	5.3	60%	11%	45	14	41	23%	87%	7%	0	14			40	1.20	22.5	140	210	$15
12 TEX	5	3	1	52	45	3.27	3.96	1.39	718	783	646	3.7	2.9	7.7	2.6	63%	10%	47	21	32	34%	78%	8%	0	14			50	1.32	4.8	85	111	$0
13 PHI	1	4	0	25	23	3.96	3.67	1.36	759	864	697	3.8	4.0	8.3	2.1	56%	9%	55	15	30	27%	79%	24%	0	15			0	1.14	-0.3	75	98	-$3
14 PHI	2	1	0	19	21	2.89	3.18	1.29	660	1117	498	3.6	3.9	10.1	2.6	63%	7%	56	13	31	32%	78%	7%	0	14			0	1.33	2.0	112	134	-$1
1st Half	2	1	0	17	20	2.12	3.01	1.18	612	1078	463	3.7	3.7	10.6	2.9	63%	8%	55	14	31	30%	84%	8%	0	15			0	1.45	3.4	123	147	-$1
2nd Half	0	0	0	2	1	10.80	5.14	2.40	1071	1333	900	2.7	5.4	5.4	1.0	63%	0%	67	0	33	45%	50%	0%	0	12			0	0.61	-1.5	-4	-5	-$7
15 Proj	4	2	3	48	50	3.38	3.22	1.23	635	744	545	3.7	3.7	9.4	2.5	61%	10%	48	16	36	30%	73%	7%	0						2.2	95	113	$2

Affeldt,Jeremy

Age:	36	Th:	L	Role	RP	Health	F	LIMA Plan	B+
Ht:	6' 4"	Wt:	225	Type	xGB	PT/Exp	D	Rand Var	-3
						Consist	C	MM	4100

Displayed a slight reverse LH/RH split in 2014, but it doesn't change who he is or what he does. When healthy, huge GB% and usefulness against hitters from both sides establish his MLB value. But sub-standard Dom, injuries and light usage ensure a marginal fantasy value.

Yr Tm	W	L	Sv	IP	K	ERA	xERA	WHIP	oOPS	vL	vR	BF/G	Ctl	Dom	Cmd	FpK	SwK	G	L	F	H%	S%	hr/f	GS	APC	DOM%	DIS%	Sv%	LI	RAR	BPV	BPX	R$
10 SF	4	3	4	50	44	4.14	3.87	1.60	795	815	784	4.3	4.3	7.9	1.8	58%	8%	56	19	26	35%	75%	11%	0	15			57	1.17	-0.4	60	97	$0
11 SF	3	2	3	62	54	2.63	3.18	1.15	625	406	764	3.9	3.5	7.9	2.3	58%	10%	62	16	22	26%	80%	14%	0	15			50	1.18	10.0	87	131	$5
12 SF	1	2	3	63	57	2.70	3.31	1.26	640	621	656	4.0	3.3	8.1	2.5	61%	8%	60	20	20	32%	77%	3%	0	15			75	1.22	10.3	96	125	$3
13 SF	1	5	0	34	21	3.74	4.22	1.31	642	524	743	3.7	4.5	5.6	1.2	54%	8%	55	25	20	25%	71%	10%	0	13			0	1.35	0.5	11	15	-$3
14 SF	4	2	0	55	41	2.28	2.95	1.10	593	622	562	3.6	2.3	6.7	2.9	56%	11%	67	17	16	29%	78%	4%	0	14			0	0.86	10.0	104	123	$4
1st Half	3	1	0	29	24	1.88	2.61	1.05	569	667	478	3.6	2.2	7.5	3.4	61%	10%	68	19	14	29%	80%	0%	0	13			0	1.08	6.6	122	146	$6
2nd Half	1	1	0	27	17	2.70	3.34	1.16	617	580	660	3.7	2.4	5.7	2.4	52%	11%	65	15	19	28%	77%	6%	0	14			0	0.63	3.4	83	99	$2
15 Proj	2	3	0	51	37	3.22	3.21	1.21	629	593	661	3.6	3.2	6.6	2.1	56%	10%	62	19	19	28%	73%	7%	0						3.2	74	88	$1

Alburquerque,Al

Age:	29	Th:	R	Role	RP	Health	F	LIMA Plan	B+
Ht:	6' 0"	Wt:	195	Type	Pwr	PT/Exp	D	Rand Var	-3
						Consist	B	MM	4510

Fireballer seemed to yield some of his eye-popping Dom in favor of better Ctl, and the result was generally positive. But FpK slide and 2nd half Ctl regression cast doubt as to the sustainability of these gains. That is critical; it's the single variable standing between "UP: 25 saves" and "DN: Unrosterable mop-up fodder."

Yr Tm	W	L	Sv	IP	K	ERA	xERA	WHIP	oOPS	vL	vR	BF/G	Ctl	Dom	Cmd	FpK	SwK	G	L	F	H%	S%	hr/f	GS	APC	DOM%	DIS%	Sv%	LI	RAR	BPV	BPX	R$
10 aa	2	4	3	34	25	6.69	4.90	1.72				6.2	5.2	6.5	1.3						35%	58%								-11.1	52	84	-$5
11 DET	6	1	0	43	67	1.87	2.59	1.15	438	468	412	4.4	6.0	13.9	2.3	52%	16%	57	14	30	28%	82%	0%	0	19			0	1.08	11.1	123	185	$6
12 DET	0	0	0	13	18	0.68	2.75	1.05	420	345	484	6.6	5.4	12.2	2.3	55%	18%	63	11	26	23%	93%	0%	0	29			0	1.55	5.5	114	149	-$1
13 DET	4	3	0	49	70	4.59	3.53	1.49	674	662	683	4.2	6.2	12.9	2.1	57%	16%	40	25	34	33%	71%	13%	0	17			0	0.98	-4.4	81	105	-$3
14 DET	3	1	1	57	63	2.51	3.24	1.17	639	721	551	3.3	3.3	9.9	3.0	51%	14%	45	19	36	28%	85%	13%	0	13			100	1.06	8.7	112	133	$4
1st Half	2	1	1	30	34	3.00	3.05	1.17	653	665	641	3.1	2.7	10.2	3.8	51%	14%	46	20	34	30%	81%	15%	0	13			100	0.99	2.7	135	161	$3
2nd Half	1	0	0	27	29	1.98	3.47	1.17	624	780	442	3.5	4.0	9.5	2.4	50%	14%	43	19	38	26%	90%	12%	0	14			0	1.14	6.0	87	103	$4
15 Proj	4	2	3	58	68	3.30	3.10	1.25	623	680	571	3.7	4.2	10.6	2.5	53%	15%	45	21	34	30%	76%	11%	0						3.1	98	117	$3

Allen,Cody

Age:	26	Th:	R	Role	RP	Health	A	LIMA Plan	C+
Ht:	6' 1"	Wt:	210	Type	Pwr xFB	PT/Exp	C	Rand Var	-5
						Consist	A	MM	5530

Took the closer gig and ran with it. Certainly has the skills to hold the job, and the Dom in particular makes him a sleeper candidate for the 100-K closer club. But xERA cautions that he's not really in the elite closer tier, mostly due to borderline Ctl. A fine mid-tier stopper.

Yr Tm	W	L	Sv	IP	K	ERA	xERA	WHIP	oOPS	vL	vR	BF/G	Ctl	Dom	Cmd	FpK	SwK	G	L	F	H%	S%	hr/f	GS	APC	DOM%	DIS%	Sv%	LI	RAR	BPV	BPX	R$
10																																	
11																																	
12 CLE *	3	3	3	68	65	3.05	3.18	1.19	710	776	654	4.9	3.2	8.5	2.7	53%	10%	39	24	37	28%	78%	6%	0	20			50	0.44	8.2	91	119	$5
13 CLE	6	1	2	70	88	2.43	3.48	1.25	679	691	669	3.9	3.3	11.3	3.4	55%	12%	30	25	45	33%	85%	9%	0	16			50	1.11	12.4	121	158	$7
14 CLE	6	4	24	70	91	2.07	3.08	1.06	601	451	757	3.7	3.4	11.8	3.5	63%	14%	36	15	48	28%	87%	9%	0	15			86	1.43	14.4	135	161	$18
1st Half	3	2	7	35	44	2.60	3.15	1.07	613	320	865	3.5	3.4	11.4	3.4	62%	15%	36	13	51	28%	79%	8%	0	14			88	1.44	4.9	129	154	$13
2nd Half	3	2	17	35	47	1.54	3.02	1.06	591	554	634	3.8	3.3	12.1	3.6	63%	13%	36	18	46	28%	94%	11%	0	16			85	1.42	9.5	142	169	$23
15 Proj	5	3	35	65	81	2.84	3.00	1.15	637	558	713	3.8	3.3	11.1	3.4	60%	13%	34	19	47	30%	79%	9%	0						7.3	123	146	$20

Alvarez,Henderson

Age:	25	Th:	R	Role	SP	Health	F	LIMA Plan	C+
Ht:	6' 0"	Wt:	205	Type	Con GB	PT/Exp	A	Rand Var	-3
						Consist	A	MM	3005

Pushed his Ctl to elite levels in 2014, but flat Dom means he continues to rely on his defenders to record outs. That's a formula that can work, at least to the level of 2013-14 xERA. But SwK doesn't foretell any Dom gains, so he'll continue to walk that tightrope. UP: Another lucky sub-3.00 ERA. DN: 4.00 ERA

Yr Tm	W	L	Sv	IP	K	ERA	xERA	WHIP	oOPS	vL	vR	BF/G	Ctl	Dom	Cmd	FpK	SwK	G	L	F	H%	S%	hr/f	GS	APC	DOM%	DIS%	Sv%	LI	RAR	BPV	BPX	R$
10																																	
11 TOR *	9	7	0	152	99	3.51	3.84	1.20	717	698	738	24.4	1.5	5.9	4.0	65%	7%	53	20	26	30%	74%	15%	10	98	50%	0%			8.1	91	137	$9
12 TOR	9	14	0	187	79	4.85	4.53	1.44	812	885	725	26.0	2.6	3.8	1.5	59%	5%	57	19	24	29%	70%	18%	31	92	32%	19%			-19.3	33	43	-$9
13 MIA	5	6	0	103	57	3.59	3.79	1.14	636	753	524	24.6	2.4	5.0	2.1	61%	7%	53	22	25	27%	66%	3%	17	85	35%	18%			3.4	57	74	$4
14 MIA	12	7	0	187	111	2.65	3.58	1.24	697	678	722	25.7	1.6	5.3	3.4	62%	7%	54	22	24	31%	81%	10%	30	87	47%	13%			25.2	85	102	$13
1st Half	5	3	0	101	64	2.32	3.53	1.28	687	661	719	26.2	1.8	5.7	3.2	60%	8%	54	23	23	32%	82%	5%	16	88	44%	13%			17.7	86	103	$14
2nd Half	7	4	0	86	47	3.03	3.64	1.19	710	697	726	25.2	1.4	4.9	3.6	65%	7%	54	20	26	29%	79%	14%	14	86	50%	14%			7.5	84	100	$12
15 Proj	11	9	0	189	105	3.35	3.54	1.23	704	732	671	24.8	1.9	5.0	2.7	62%	7%	54	21	25	29%	75%	10%	31						9.1	72	85	$10

Anderson,Brett

Age:	27	Th:	L	Role	RP	Health	F	LIMA Plan	C
Ht:	6' 4"	Wt:	225	Type	xGB	PT/Exp	D	Rand Var	-3
						Consist	A	MM	4100

If he coulda been healthy, he woulda been awesome. All the woulda coulda shouldas don't change his horrible health record; he has missed time every year after 2009. Herniated disc surgery ended 2014 season. Given last year's Dom, now he's risky even with a return to health. There are other choices.

Yr Tm	W	L	Sv	IP	K	ERA	xERA	WHIP	oOPS	vL	vR	BF/G	Ctl	Dom	Cmd	FpK	SwK	G	L	F	H%	S%	hr/f	GS	APC	DOM%	DIS%	Sv%	LI	RAR	BPV	BPX	R$
10 OAK	7	6	0	112	75	2.80	3.55	1.19	655	685	646	24.7	1.8	6.0	3.4	56%	7%	55	17	28	30%	77%	6%	19	95	58%	11%			17.7	94	151	$9
11 OAK	3	6	0	83	61	4.00	3.50	1.33	721	761	700	27.4	2.7	6.6	2.4	58%	7%	57	18	25	31%	72%	13%	13	104	54%	31%			-0.6	81	121	-$1
12 OAK *	5	3	0	58	40	3.28	3.47	1.20	565	515	581	21.3	1.8	6.2	3.4	62%	9%	60	24	17	30%	74%	6%	6	88	83%	17%			5.3	91	118	$2
13 OAK	1	4	3	45	46	6.04	3.36	1.61	794	853	774	12.5	4.2	9.3	2.2	58%	9%	63	16	21	37%	63%	18%	5	48	40%	60%	100	0.78	-12.0	94	122	-$7
14 COL	1	3	0	43	29	2.91	3.55	1.32	688	724	675	22.5	2.7	6.0	2.2	62%	9%	61	17	22	32%	77%	3%	8	83	38%	25%			4.5	75	89	-$1
1st Half	0	2	0	15	5	3.60	4.57	1.40	725	375	851	21.7	3.0	3.0	1.0	62%	6%	59	19	22	29%	75%	8%	3	71	33%	33%			0.3	10	12	-$6
2nd Half	1	1	0	28	24	2.54	3.06	1.27	668	904	577	23.0	2.5	7.6	3.0	62%	11%	62	16	22	33%	78%	0%	5	90	40%	20%			4.2	109	130	$2
15 Proj	1	3	0	44	33	3.82	3.32	1.37	717	733	711	18.5	2.9	6.8	2.3	60%	9%	61	18	21	32%	72%	9%	8						-0.4	82	97	-$2

JOSH PALEY

Anderson,Chase

Age: 27	Th: R	Role RP	Health A	LIMA Plan C
Ht: 6' 0"	Wt: 190	Type Pwr	PT/Exp D	Rand Var 0
			Consist D	MM 2203

9-7, 4.01 ERA in 114 IP at ARI. Middling prospect posted surprisingly decent results in MLB debut; 2H skills (all compiled in MLB) are downright interesting. A plus changeup drives the SwK and Dom, though it's possible there's a "second time around the league" correction coming. Nice deep-league speculation.

Yr Tm	W	L	Sv	IP	K	ERA	xERA	WHIP	oOPS	vL	vR	BF/G	Ctl	Dom	Cmd	FpK	SwK	G	L	F	H%	S%	hr/f	GS	APC	DOM%	DIS%	Sv%	LI	RAR	BPV	BPX	R$
10																																	
11																																	
12 aa	5	4	0	104	79	3.70	4.23	1.31				20.5	2.2	6.8	3.0						32%	75%								4.1	76	99	$1
13 aaa	4	7	0	88	63	5.76	5.84	1.67				15.2	3.1	6.4	2.0						36%	66%								-20.6	41	53	-$12
14 ARI *	13	9	0	153	134	3.23	3.79	1.25	779	714	831	23.1	2.7	7.9	2.9	63%	10%	40	24	36	30%	78%	14%	21	90	52%	19%			9.7	82	98	$9
1st Half	9	5	0	84	63	2.37	3.07	1.08	797	610	956	23.3	2.2	6.8	3.1	59%	10%	38	28	34	26%	84%	17%	8	92	38%	25%			14.1	85	101	$19
2nd Half	4	4	0	70	71	4.26	3.69	1.45	768	784	756	23.0	3.4	9.2	2.7	66%	10%	41	22	37	35%	73%	11%	13	89	62%	15%			-4.5	93	112	-$2
15 Proj	**9**	**10**	**0**	**152**	**124**	**4.31**	**3.78**	**1.43**	**798**	**722**	**858**	**19.1**	**2.9**	**7.4**	**2.5**	**63%**	**10%**	**40**	**24**	**36**	**33%**	**72%**	**10%**	**31**						**-10.7**	**72**	**86**	**-$1**

Archer,Chris

Age: 26	Th: R	Role SP	Health A	LIMA Plan B
Ht: 6' 3"	Wt: 190	Type Pwr	PT/Exp B	Rand Var -1
			Consist A	MM 3305

Next point on the ERA trend would be very appealing, but my Magic 8-Ball says "Skills hazy, try again later." PRO: Made big gains against LH batters, regained some lost Dom. CON: Despite recent Ctl progress, Ctl and Cmd aren't (yet) supportive of that next step in ERA. VERDICT: Pay for 3.50 ERA, not 3.00.

Yr Tm	W	L	Sv	IP	K	ERA	xERA	WHIP	oOPS	vL	vR	BF/G	Ctl	Dom	Cmd	FpK	SwK	G	L	F	H%	S%	hr/f	GS	APC	DOM%	DIS%	Sv%	LI	RAR	BPV	BPX	R$
10 aa	8	2	0	70	57	2.02	2.69	1.29				22.1	4.8	7.4	1.5						27%	85%								17.7	81	130	$7
11 a/a	9	7	0	147	112	4.36	4.74	1.63				24.3	4.9	6.9	1.4						33%	73%								-7.7	51	76	-$6
12 TAM *	8	12	0	157	154	4.19	3.21	1.32	624	915	435	21.0	4.2	8.8	2.1	62%	10%	44	18	38	30%	68%	11%	4	82	75%	0%	0	0.99	-3.3	90	118	$3
13 TAM *	14	10	0	179	144	3.64	3.79	1.27	660	801	455	22.1	3.1	7.3	2.4	58%	9%	47	19	34	29%	75%	12%	23	91	43%	35%			5.1	66	87	$10
14 TAM	10	9	0	195	173	3.33	3.68	1.28	650	624	685	25.7	3.3	8.0	2.4	57%	10%	47	22	31	31%	75%	7%	32	99	56%	13%			9.9	79	94	$9
1st Half	4	5	0	100	90	3.24	3.61	1.30	643	562	751	24.9	3.4	8.1	2.4	56%	9%	47	24	29	32%	74%	4%	17	97	65%	18%			6.2	79	94	$7
2nd Half	6	4	0	95	83	3.42	3.75	1.26	658	690	616	26.6	3.2	7.9	2.4	59%	10%	46	21	33	29%	75%	10%	15	101	47%	7%			3.7	78	94	$10
15 Proj	**12**	**10**	**0**	**197**	**171**	**3.53**	**3.55**	**1.30**	**669**	**717**	**604**	**23.4**	**3.5**	**7.8**	**2.2**	**58%**	**9%**	**47**	**21**	**32**	**30%**	**74%**	**8%**	**35**						**5.2**	**70**	**83**	**$10**

Arrieta,Jake

Age: 29	Th: R	Role SP	Health D	LIMA Plan C
Ht: 6' 4"	Wt: 225	Type Pwr	PT/Exp C	Rand Var -1
			Consist B	MM 4405

What changed? Revamped mechanics, with new emphasis on the slider, led to Dom growth supported by SwK. Prospect pedigree always said this was possible; sometimes it just takes a while. Hr/f has to go north, but there's room for a lot of value even with that correction. Use 2nd half as your baseline.

Yr Tm	W	L	Sv	IP	K	ERA	xERA	WHIP	oOPS	vL	vR	BF/G	Ctl	Dom	Cmd	FpK	SwK	G	L	F	H%	S%	hr/f	GS	APC	DOM%	DIS%	Sv%	LI	RAR	BPV	BPX	R$
10 BAL *	12	8	0	173	104	3.67	3.87	1.41	767	898	594	24.5	4.3	5.4	1.3	54%	6%	42	19	39	28%	75%	7%	18	95	17%	33%			8.8	44	71	$5
11 BAL	10	8	0	119	93	5.05	4.45	1.46	791	856	715	23.8	4.4	7.0	1.6	56%	8%	46	16	39	28%	70%	15%	22	95	32%	23%			-16.3	30	45	-$4
12 BAL *	8	13	0	171	151	6.13	4.74	1.47	763	846	664	21.5	3.6	8.0	2.2	56%	8%	44	24	32	33%	58%	15%	18	82	44%	50%	0	0.79	-44.6	62	81	-$15
13 2 TM *	12	9	0	155	120	5.06	4.43	1.49	718	664	775	22.2	4.4	7.0	1.6	60%	7%	40	25	34	31%	67%	12%	14	90	14%	21%			-22.8	50	65	-$7
14 CHC	10	5	0	157	167	2.53	2.79	0.99	535	553	520	24.6	2.4	9.6	4.1	59%	11%	49	22	28	28%	74%	4%	25	97	80%	16%			23.4	136	162	$20
1st Half	5	1	0	65	74	1.81	2.67	1.01	511	513	509	23.2	2.2	10.3	4.6	57%	10%	49	22	29	30%	83%	4%	11	95	73%	27%			15.4	152	182	$19
2nd Half	5	4	0	92	93	3.03	2.87	0.98	552	583	527	25.6	2.4	9.1	3.7	61%	12%	49	23	28	27%	68%	5%	14	98	86%	7%			8.0	125	149	$21
15 Proj	**14**	**8**	**0**	**203**	**198**	**3.23**	**3.15**	**1.21**	**659**	**687**	**632**	**22.9**	**3.0**	**8.8**	**2.9**	**59%**	**9%**	**47**	**21**	**32**	**30%**	**75%**	**8%**	**36**						**12.9**	**101**	**121**	**$18**

Arroyo,Bronson

Age: 38	Th: R	Role SP	Health F	LIMA Plan C
Ht: 6' 3"	Wt: 195	Type Con	PT/Exp A	Rand Var +1
			Consist A	MM 2000

Tommy John Surgery on July 16 ended his season, and puts all of 2015 in doubt. Unless his new elbow ligament came from Walter Johnson himself, there's likely little career value left here. Curt Schilling's nickname for him will remain an all-time classic, though. (For details, use the Google.)

Yr Tm	W	L	Sv	IP	K	ERA	xERA	WHIP	oOPS	vL	vR	BF/G	Ctl	Dom	Cmd	FpK	SwK	G	L	F	H%	S%	hr/f	GS	APC	DOM%	DIS%	Sv%	LI	RAR	BPV	BPX	R$
10 CIN	17	10	0	216	121	3.88	4.31	1.15	679	786	576	26.7	2.5	5.0	2.1	63%	7%	43	16	40	25%	71%	11%	33	99	52%	21%			5.3	45	73	$15
11 CIN	9	12	0	199	108	5.07	4.57	1.37	855	976	745	26.7	2.0	4.9	2.4	62%	6%	39	19	43	29%	71%	16%	32	97	38%	22%			-27.6	50	75	-$6
12 CIN	12	10	0	202	129	3.74	4.19	1.21	721	794	642	26.1	1.6	5.7	3.7	68%	7%	41	21	37	29%	73%	11%	32	92	50%	9%			6.8	80	105	$11
13 CIN	14	12	0	202	124	3.79	3.92	1.15	735	856	607	25.7	1.5	5.5	3.6	65%	6%	44	20	35	27%	74%	14%	32	90	56%	19%			2.0	81	105	$12
14 ARI	7	4	0	86	47	4.08	3.86	1.29	743	640	862	25.5	2.0	4.9	2.5	67%	7%	54	20	27	30%	71%	13%	14	90	29%	29%			-3.6	67	80	$0
1st Half	7	4	0	86	47	4.08	3.86	1.29	743	640	862	25.5	2.0	4.9	2.5	67%	7%	54	20	27	30%	71%	13%	14	90	29%	29%			-3.6	66	79	$0
2nd Half																																	
15 Proj	**3**	**2**	**0**	**44**	**25**	**4.27**	**3.78**	**1.24**	**747**	**784**	**709**	**25.4**	**1.8**	**5.3**	**2.9**	**66%**	**7%**	**45**	**20**	**35**	**28%**	**70%**	**13%**	**7**						**-2.9**	**68**	**81**	**-$2**

Atchison,Scott

Age: 39	Th: R	Role RP	Health F	LIMA Plan B
Ht: 6' 2"	Wt: 200	Type Con GB	PT/Exp D	Rand Var -2
			Consist B	MM 4100

Lack of Dom, lack of save opps, lack of remaining days until his 40th birthday all relegate him to the "irrelevant" bin. But credit to him: for a guy who didn't make his MLB debut until age 30, he's scratched out a nice little living: career 84 BPV, 3.44 ERA, and an MLB pension in his future.

Yr Tm	W	L	Sv	IP	K	ERA	xERA	WHIP	oOPS	vL	vR	BF/G	Ctl	Dom	Cmd	FpK	SwK	G	L	F	H%	S%	hr/f	GS	APC	DOM%	DIS%	Sv%	LI	RAR	BPV	BPX	R$
10 BOS	2	3	0	60	41	4.50	4.24	1.28	736	839	645	5.9	2.9	6.2	2.2	57%	8%	48	11	41	28%	69%	12%	1	23	0%	100%	0	0.95	-3.1	60	97	-$1
11 BOS *	7	2	6	92	69	3.81	3.95	1.28	710	769	669	7.1	1.6	6.8	4.1	55%	8%	46	26	28	33%	71%	0%	0	28			60	0.38	1.5	107	160	$5
12 BOS	2	1	0	51	36	1.58	3.40	0.99	549	485	601	4.8	1.6	6.3	4.0	62%	7%	55	17	28	27%	86%	5%	0	17			0	0.79	15.4	104	136	$6
13 NYM	3	3	0	45	28	4.37	4.16	1.26	647	703	615	3.8	2.4	5.6	2.3	59%	8%	49	21	31	29%	66%	9%	0	15			0	1.08	-2.8	63	82	-$3
14 CLE	6	0	2	72	49	2.75	3.16	1.03	606	723	544	4.0	1.8	6.1	3.5	60%	10%	59	19	23	27%	74%	8%	0	15			29	1.41	8.8	100	119	$7
1st Half	3	0	1	35	24	3.09	2.96	0.91	552	695	484	4.0	1.3	6.2	4.8	61%	9%	62	16	22	25%	67%	9%	0	15			33	0.96	2.8	117	139	$6
2nd Half	3	0	1	37	25	2.43	3.35	1.14	657	745	605	4.0	2.2	6.1	2.8	59%	10%	55	21	24	28%	80%	8%	0	15			25	1.83	6.0	84	100	$7
15 Proj	**3**	**2**	**0**	**53**	**36**	**3.43**	**3.26**	**1.12**	**630**	**693**	**591**	**4.1**	**2.0**	**6.0**	**3.1**	**60%**	**9%**	**54**	**19**	**27**	**28%**	**70%**	**8%**	**0**						**2.0**	**88**	**104**	**$1**

Avilan,Luis

Age: 25	Th: L	Role RP	Health A	LIMA Plan D+
Ht: 6' 2"	Wt: 220	Type xGB	PT/Exp D	Rand Var 0
			Consist A	MM 2000

Extreme ground ball pitcher, which is good because he'll need extreme double plays to offset the free passes he gives hitters. Throws 93mph, maxing at around 95mph, but SwK shows velocity doesn't translate to Dom. Big league hitters do a lot of damage to straight fastballs.

Yr Tm	W	L	Sv	IP	K	ERA	xERA	WHIP	oOPS	vL	vR	BF/G	Ctl	Dom	Cmd	FpK	SwK	G	L	F	H%	S%	hr/f	GS	APC	DOM%	DIS%	Sv%	LI	RAR	BPV	BPX	R$
10																																	
11 aa	4	8	1	105	68	4.82	4.62	1.46				12.5	2.9	5.9	2.0						33%	67%								-11.4	51	77	-$5
12 ATL *	4	6	1	97	81	3.31	3.60	1.31	547	528	559	8.6	3.9	7.5	1.9	55%	11%	47	20	33	28%	77%	3%	0	18			100	0.91	8.5	68	89	$3
13 ATL	5	0	0	65	38	1.52	3.68	0.95	478	383	557	3.4	3.0	5.3	1.7	54%	9%	58	19	24	21%	84%	2%	0	13			0	1.07	18.8	48	63	$9
14 ATL	4	1	0	43	25	4.57	4.41	1.57	764	729	803	3.1	4.4	5.2	1.2	51%	8%	58	19	23	32%	70%	6%	0	11			0	1.16	-4.4	12	14	-$4
1st Half	3	1	0	27	18	4.28	4.22	1.57	714	630	823	2.9	4.3	5.9	1.4	53%	9%	59	19	22	33%	71%	5%	0	10			0	1.40	-1.8	28	34	-$4
2nd Half	1	0	0	16	7	5.06	4.76	1.56	852	943	775	3.6	4.5	3.9	0.9	46%	8%	56	19	25	30%	67%	8%	0	14			0	0.67	-2.6	-17	-20	-$5
15 Proj	**3**	**1**	**0**	**44**	**26**	**4.15**	**4.06**	**1.39**	**712**	**699**	**723**	**3.9**	**4.0**	**5.4**	**1.3**	**51%**	**9%**	**56**	**19**	**25**	**29%**	**69%**	**7%**	**0**						**-2.2**	**22**	**26**	**-$3**

Axford,John

Age: 32	Th: R	Role RP	Health A	LIMA Plan B+
Ht: 6' 5"	Wt: 220	Type Pwr	PT/Exp C	Rand Var +1
			Consist A	MM 3500

Started the season as closer in CLE; supposedly a pitch-tipping problem from 2013 had been corrected. If so, he'll need a new excuse to explain why he's still giving up walks and HR by the bucketful. BPV trend has accelerated from "fade" to "plunge." Save opps aren't likely coming back.

Yr Tm	W	L	Sv	IP	K	ERA	xERA	WHIP	oOPS	vL	vR	BF/G	Ctl	Dom	Cmd	FpK	SwK	G	L	F	H%	S%	hr/f	GS	APC	DOM%	DIS%	Sv%	LI	RAR	BPV	BPX	R$
10 MIL	8	2	24	58	76	2.48	2.86	1.19	588	692	483	4.8	4.2	11.8	2.8	59%	12%	48	19	33	32%	78%	2%	0	20			89	1.37	11.4	125	203	$17
11 MIL	2	2	46	74	86	1.95	3.00	1.14	557	481	621	4.1	3.1	10.5	3.4	61%	10%	50	15	35	31%	85%	6%	0	17			96	1.15	18.1	135	202	$26
12 MIL	5	8	35	69	93	4.67	3.43	1.44	717	671	767	4.1	5.1	12.1	2.4	54%	11%	46	24	30	33%	71%	19%	0	19			80	1.22	-5.6	105	136	$12
13 2 NL	7	7	0	65	65	4.02	3.74	1.52	796	838	761	3.9	3.6	9.0	2.5	53%	10%	45	24	31	35%	79%	17%	0	16			0	1.11	-1.2	88	114	-$2
14 2 TM	2	4	10	55	63	3.95	3.77	1.45	691	630	743	3.9	5.9	10.4	1.8	57%	10%	54	14	33	29%	75%	13%	0	17			77	1.07	-1.4	59	70	$1
1st Half	2	3	9	32	38	3.69	4.10	1.64	737	668	810	4.1	6.8	10.8	1.6	58%	11%	51	16	33	32%	81%	15%	0	17			75	1.18	0.2	39	47	$3
2nd Half	0	1	1	23	25	4.30	3.33	1.17	623	558	664	3.7	4.7	9.8	2.1	56%	9%	57	11	32	25%	64%	11%	0	16			100	0.93	-1.6	84	101	-$1
15 Proj	**3**	**5**	**0**	**58**	**64**	**4.11**	**3.52**	**1.43**	**706**	**684**	**725**	**3.8**	**5.1**	**10.0**	**2.0**	**56%**	**10%**	**48**	**19**	**34**	**30%**	**74%**	**13%**	**0**						**-2.7**	**67**	**80**	**-$2**

JOSH PALEY

Badenhop,Burke

			Health	A	LIMA Plan	B+
Age: 32	Th: R	Role: RP	PT/Exp	C	Rand Var	-5
Ht: 6' 5"	Wt: 220	Type: Con xGB	Consist	A	MM	3001

Rode a super-friendly hr/f to a career-best ERA, but remarkably stagnant xERA track record tells us that sub-3.00 ERAs are not likely a part of his future. Lovely GB% and Ctl set a nice ERA floor, but lack of Dom ensures he'll continue to toil in the relative obscurity of middle relief.

Yr Tm	W	L	Sv	IP	K	ERA	xERA	WHIP	oOPS	vL	vR	BF/G	Ctl	Dom	Cmd	FpK	SwK	G	L	F	H%	S%	hr/f	GS	APC	DOM%	DIS%	Sv%	LI	RAR	BPV	BPX	R$
10 FLA *	2	6	1	84	54	3.87	3.57	1.31	681	700	667	5.3	3.1	5.9	1.9	54%	7%	57	14	29	30%	70%	8%	0	20			33	0.88	2.2	63	101	$1
11 FLA	2	3	1	64	51	4.10	3.48	1.40	689	706	677	5.5	3.4	7.2	2.1	59%	7%	58	21	21	33%	68%	2%	0	20			100	1.03	-1.2	74	112	-$2
12 TAM	3	2	0	62	42	3.03	3.73	1.20	687	844	610	4.0	1.7	6.1	3.5	66%	4%	53	23	25	30%	78%	12%	0	14			0	0.78	7.6	93	122	$2
13 MIL	2	3	1	62	42	3.47	3.56	1.19	694	918	574	4.0	1.7	6.1	3.5	65%	6%	51	22	27	30%	74%	12%	0	15			25	1.01	3.1	91	119	$0
14 BOS	0	3	1	71	40	2.29	3.54	1.26	674	721	646	4.1	2.4	5.1	2.1	62%	4%	61	20	19	30%	81%	2%	0	15			25	1.20	12.6	65	78	$2
1st Half	0	2	1	43	25	1.69	3.34	1.24	708	738	689	4.6	2.1	5.3	2.5	61%	4%	61	20	19	31%	87%	4%	0	17			50	1.32	10.8	77	91	$4
2nd Half	0	1	0	28	15	3.21	3.86	1.29	624	694	584	3.6	2.9	4.8	1.7	63%	3%	62	19	20	30%	72%	0%	0	13			0	1.08	1.8	48	58	-$1
15 Proj	**2**	**2**	**1**	**73**	**45**	**3.27**	**3.43**	**1.25**	**674**	**779**	**614**	**4.0**	**2.3**	**5.6**	**2.4**	**63%**	**5%**	**57**	**20**	**23**	**30%**	**74%**	**7%**	**0**						**4.2**	**73**	**87**	**$1**

Bailey,Homer

			Health	D	LIMA Plan	B
Age: 29	Th: R	Role: SP	PT/Exp	A	Rand Var	+1
Ht: 6' 4"	Wt: 230	Type: Pwr	Consist	A	MM	4203

Investors spent the whole 1st half wondering, "what the heck happened here?" The answer was "nothing." Confluence of unfortunate H%, S% and hr/f inflated his ERA by a full run. The correction was in full bloom in 2nd half when Sept forearm surgery cut the rebound short. This is nearly the same pitcher as 2012-13.

Yr Tm	W	L	Sv	IP	K	ERA	xERA	WHIP	oOPS	vL	vR	BF/G	Ctl	Dom	Cmd	FpK	SwK	G	L	F	H%	S%	hr/f	GS	APC	DOM%	DIS%	Sv%	LI	RAR	BPV	BPX	R$
10 CIN *	6	3	0	128	113	4.22	3.89	1.34	744	677	781	23.2	3.2	7.9	2.5	60%	9%	42	21	37	32%	69%	9%	19	102	58%	21%			-2.2	80	129	$3
11 CIN *	11	8	0	162	124	4.26	4.38	1.32	728	777	687	24.0	2.2	6.9	3.2	62%	10%	39	22	38	32%	71%	12%	22	96	45%	18%			-6.3	76	114	$3
12 CIN	13	10	0	208	168	3.68	3.92	1.24	718	682	747	26.5	2.3	7.3	3.2	66%	10%	45	20	35	30%	75%	12%	33	101	52%	24%			8.6	93	121	$12
13 CIN	11	12	0	209	199	3.49	3.29	1.12	660	746	575	26.5	2.3	8.6	3.7	64%	11%	46	19	34	29%	72%	10%	32	103	66%	9%			9.7	115	150	$16
14 CIN	9	5	0	146	124	3.71	3.46	1.23	703	750	666	26.3	2.8	7.7	2.8	62%	11%	51	21	29	29%	73%	13%	23	99	70%	9%			0.6	92	109	$5
1st Half	8	4	0	105	94	4.39	3.47	1.35	744	849	667	26.2	2.8	8.1	2.9	62%	11%	50	21	29	32%	70%	15%	17	100	71%	12%			-8.3	99	119	$6
2nd Half	1	1	0	41	30	1.98	3.41	0.93	583	488	664	26.3	2.9	6.6	2.3	60%	12%	52	19	30	20%	83%	9%	6	96	67%	0%			8.9	71	85	$4
15 Proj	**10**	**7**	**0**	**180**	**151**	**3.47**	**3.28**	**1.15**	**674**	**683**	**665**	**25.5**	**2.6**	**7.6**	**2.9**	**63%**	**11%**	**48**	**20**	**32**	**28%**	**73%**	**11%**	**28**						**6.0**	**91**	**108**	**$13**

Baker,Scott

			Health	F	LIMA Plan	D+
Age: 33	Th: R	Role: RP	PT/Exp	D	Rand Var	+1
Ht: 6' 4"	Wt: 215	Type: xFB	Consist	A	MM	1101

3-4, 3.87 ERA in 80 IP at TEX. Another chapter in the annals of What Might Have Been If Not For Injuries. Has always had tremendous control, but seems like he left his Dom on the operating table in 2012. Without that, he's a high FB% pitcher without whiffs. xERA shows that to be a terrible proposition.

Yr Tm	W	L	Sv	IP	K	ERA	xERA	WHIP	oOPS	vL	vR	BF/G	Ctl	Dom	Cmd	FpK	SwK	G	L	F	H%	S%	hr/f	GS	APC	DOM%	DIS%	Sv%	LI	RAR	BPV	BPX	R$
10 MIN	12	9	0	170	148	4.49	3.93	1.34	793	830	756	25.0	2.3	7.8	3.4	63%	10%	36	21	43	33%	70%	10%	29	92	48%	28%			-8.7	93	151	$4
11 MIN	8	6	0	135	123	3.14	3.63	1.17	687	743	595	23.8	2.1	8.2	3.8	59%	11%	34	21	45	30%	78%	9%	21	93	48%	10%	0	0.72	13.3	102	154	$11
12																																	
13 CHC	0	0	0	15	6	3.60	5.05	0.87	636	723	581	19.0	2.4	3.6	1.5	65%	9%	28	13	59	14%	70%	11%	3	67	33%	33%			0.5	6	8	-$3
14 TEX *	7	5	0	119	77	5.03	4.77	1.28	790	809	771	15.7	2.0	5.8	2.9	60%	9%	25	25	50	29%	66%	11%	8	48	25%	63%	0	0.60	-18.9	48	57	-$4
1st Half	4	2	0	78	49	4.98	4.80	1.29	764	753	777	18.9	2.1	5.6	2.7	60%	9%	28	26	45	29%	66%	14%	2	53	50%	50%	0	0.32	-12.0	41	49	-$3
2nd Half	3	3	0	40	28	5.13	4.59	1.26	816	864	764	12.0	1.8	6.2	3.5	60%	9%	22	23	55	30%	64%	10%	6	43	17%	67%	0	0.83	-6.9	64	77	-$4
15 Proj	**4**	**5**	**0**	**73**	**50**	**4.30**	**4.08**	**1.28**	**771**	**806**	**730**	**17.6**	**2.3**	**6.2**	**2.7**	**60%**	**10%**	**30**	**23**	**48**	**29%**	**71%**	**10%**	**13**						**-5.0**	**57**	**68**	**-$1**

Balfour,Grant

			Health	B	LIMA Plan	D+
Age: 37	Th: R	Role: RP	PT/Exp	B	Rand Var	0
Ht: 6' 2"	Wt: 200	Type: Pwr	Consist	B	MM	2410

Baltimore voided a contract with him last off-season, based on concerns shown in a physical. Despite lack of DL time or documented injury, the across-the-board plummet of skills suggests that was a good call. Whatever he lost or whatever ailed him, age says it will be hard to walk back this skills decline.

Yr Tm	W	L	Sv	IP	K	ERA	xERA	WHIP	oOPS	vL	vR	BF/G	Ctl	Dom	Cmd	FpK	SwK	G	L	F	H%	S%	hr/f	GS	APC	DOM%	DIS%	Sv%	LI	RAR	BPV	BPX	R$
10 TAM	2	1	0	55	56	2.28	3.67	1.08	619	771	496	3.9	2.8	9.1	3.3	56%	10%	31	20	50	29%	81%	4%	0	17			0	1.25	12.3	98	159	$5
11 OAK	5	2	2	62	59	2.47	3.53	1.03	605	579	630	3.9	2.9	8.6	3.0	60%	7%	38	17	45	24%	84%	11%	0	16			29	1.18	11.3	92	138	$8
12 OAK	3	2	24	75	72	2.53	3.70	0.92	495	476	516	3.9	3.4	8.7	2.6	61%	10%	36	24	41	21%	74%	5%	0	17			92	1.33	13.7	79	103	$19
13 OAK	1	3	38	63	72	2.59	3.54	1.20	610	548	682	4.0	3.9	10.3	2.7	55%	11%	38	23	39	28%	84%	11%	0	18			93	1.23	9.9	97	127	$18
14 TAM	2	6	12	62	57	4.91	4.46	1.44	688	703	672	4.2	5.9	8.2	1.4	54%	8%	44	21	35	28%	64%	5%	0	17			80	1.11	-9.0	10	12	$0
1st Half	0	2	10	32	30	5.34	4.47	1.44	686	720	639	4.4	5.9	8.4	1.4	54%	8%	44	20	37	28%	61%	6%	0	19			83	1.17	-6.3	14	17	-$1
2nd Half	2	4	2	30	27	4.45	4.44	1.45	690	679	698	3.9	5.9	8.0	1.4	55%	8%	44	23	33	28%	67%	4%	0	16			67	1.06	-2.7	6	7	$0
15 Proj	**2**	**4**	**5**	**58**	**57**	**3.98**	**3.70**	**1.27**	**634**	**624**	**645**	**3.9**	**4.7**	**8.9**	**1.9**	**56%**	**9%**	**40**	**22**	**38**	**27%**	**69%**	**7%**	**0**						**-1.7**	**50**	**60**	**$1**

Barrett,Aaron

			Health	A	LIMA Plan	B+
Age: 27	Th: R	Role: RP	PT/Exp	F	Rand Var	-3
Ht: 6' 3"	Wt: 225	Type: Pwr	Consist	A	MM	4510

He has two of the three traits of a closer: Dom (supported by SwK) and high GB%. The missing piece is Ctl. That may or may not come eventually, but FpK is not optimistic. For now, he has some utility as a high-Dom middle reliever, and if he gets the walks under control, then... UP: save opps.

Yr Tm	W	L	Sv	IP	K	ERA	xERA	WHIP	oOPS	vL	vR	BF/G	Ctl	Dom	Cmd	FpK	SwK	G	L	F	H%	S%	hr/f	GS	APC	DOM%	DIS%	Sv%	LI	RAR	BPV	BPX	R$
10																																	
11																																	
12																																	
13 aa	1	1	26	50	54	2.71	3.20	1.26				4.0	2.7	9.7	3.6						34%	79%								7.2	126	164	$11
14 WAS	3	0	0	41	49	2.66	3.24	1.30	605	750	529	3.5	4.4	10.8	2.5	54%	13%	46	25	28	33%	79%	3%	0	14			0	1.07	5.4	100	119	$1
1st Half	3	0	0	28	33	1.93	3.44	1.29	574	712	502	3.8	4.8	10.6	2.2	55%	11%	39	27	33	31%	83%	0%	0	15			0	1.02	6.3	78	93	$3
2nd Half	0	0	0	13	16	4.26	2.79	1.34	664	821	571	3.0	3.6	11.4	3.2	53%	18%	58	22	19	36%	69%	14%	0	12			0	1.15	-0.8	145	173	-$4
15 Proj	**2**	**2**	**3**	**50**	**56**	**3.32**	**3.15**	**1.19**	**527**	**663**	**456**	**3.8**	**4.0**	**10.2**	**2.6**	**55%**	**11%**	**39**	**27**	**33**	**30%**	**70%**	**2%**	**0**						**2.6**	**94**	**112**	**$2**

Bastardo,Antonio

			Health	A	LIMA Plan	B+
Age: 29	Th: L	Role: RP	PT/Exp	D	Rand Var	-1
Ht: 5' 11"	Wt: 200	Type: Pwr xFB	Consist	A	MM	4500

Another middle reliever one skill away from closer-worthiness: brings the big Dom fully backed by SwK. Despite being a southpaw, he handles hitters from both sides of the plate. But this kind of Ctl is intolerable for a would-be closer. Plus it's trending in the wrong direction. Sentenced to more 7th/8th inning work.

Yr Tm	W	L	Sv	IP	K	ERA	xERA	WHIP	oOPS	vL	vR	BF/G	Ctl	Dom	Cmd	FpK	SwK	G	L	F	H%	S%	hr/f	GS	APC	DOM%	DIS%	Sv%	LI	RAR	BPV	BPX	R$
10 PHI *	3	1	3	36	48	3.59	3.31	1.37	669	660	678	3.4	3.9	11.9	3.1	60%	13%	32	15	53	38%	72%	4%	0	14			75	0.60	2.2	134	217	$2
11 PHI	6	1	8	58	70	2.64	3.49	0.93	524	558	506	3.5	4.0	10.9	2.7	60%	16%	25	16	59	19%	77%	8%	0	15			80	1.47	9.3	90	135	$11
12 PHI	2	5	1	52	81	4.33	3.27	1.27	662	569	732	3.4	4.5	14.0	3.1	58%	14%	28	22	50	33%	69%	13%	0	15			20	1.37	-2.0	137	178	$0
13 PHI	3	2	2	43	47	2.32	4.00	1.27	637	598	662	3.7	4.4	9.9	2.2	68%	14%	31	18	50	30%	83%	4%	0	15			40	1.04	8.1	68	88	$2
14 PHI	5	7	0	64	81	3.94	3.76	1.20	614	640	599	4.0	4.8	11.4	2.4	57%	13%	30	17	53	28%	67%	5%	0	17			0	1.00	-1.6	84	100	$2
1st Half	4	3	0	37	45	3.86	4.02	1.21	605	726	547	4.4	5.3	10.8	2.0	53%	12%	32	14	54	26%	67%	4%	0	19			0	1.08	-0.5	62	74	$3
2nd Half	1	4	0	27	36	4.05	3.42	1.20	625	542	677	3.6	4.1	12.2	3.0	64%	14%	27	21	52	31%	67%	6%	0	15			0	0.90	-1.0	115	137	$0
15 Proj	**4**	**5**	**0**	**58**	**74**	**3.52**	**3.30**	**1.22**	**629**	**600**	**647**	**3.6**	**4.4**	**11.5**	**2.6**	**61%**	**14%**	**29**	**19**	**52**	**30%**	**72%**	**6%**	**0**						**1.6**	**95**	**113**	**$2**

Bauer,Trevor

			Health	A	LIMA Plan	B+
Age: 24	Th: R	Role: SP	PT/Exp	C	Rand Var	0
Ht: 6' 1"	Wt: 190	Type: Pwr FB	Consist	D	MM	2305

5-8, 4.18 ERA in 153 IP at CLE. Former top prospect now transitioning into post-hype stage. SwK says a Dom recovery could be taking hold, but the Ctl/FpK picture remains muddier. He's still young; if he takes one more step forward, this will be last year to get him cheap. There is risk here, but also... UP: 3.50 ERA, 200 K

Yr Tm	W	L	Sv	IP	K	ERA	xERA	WHIP	oOPS	vL	vR	BF/G	Ctl	Dom	Cmd	FpK	SwK	G	L	F	H%	S%	hr/f	GS	APC	DOM%	DIS%	Sv%	LI	RAR	BPV	BPX	R$
10																																	
11 aa	1	1	0	17	23	8.11	5.80	1.70				18.9	3.9	12.4	3.2						44%	51%								-8.6	101	152	-$6
12 ARI *	13	4	0	147	154	2.91	3.41	1.32	795	851	729	23.4	4.1	9.4	2.3	64%	7%	45	25	30	31%	80%	15%	4	81	25%	75%			20.0	93	121	$13
13 CLE *	7	9	0	138	104	5.04	5.44	1.72	840	908	778	24.2	5.7	6.8	1.2	57%	7%	35	20	45	32%	73%	13%	4	88	25%	25%			-20.1	30	40	-$14
14 CLE *	9	9	0	199	181	3.76	3.95	1.33	737	729	744	25.0	3.3	8.2	2.5	56%	9%	35	23	41	31%	74%	9%	26	100	46%	27%			-0.5	77	92	$4
1st Half	6	5	0	99	90	3.46	4.30	1.32	815	838	796	25.7	3.0	8.2	2.7	52%	10%	32	26	42	31%	79%	14%	9	102	44%	22%			3.4	71	85	$7
2nd Half	3	4	0	100	91	4.06	4.07	1.33	694	680	710	25.4	3.6	8.2	2.3	58%	9%	37	22	41	31%	70%	6%	17	98	47%	29%			-4.0	65	78	$0
15 Proj	**10**	**9**	**0**	**189**	**167**	**3.93**	**3.84**	**1.34**	**715**	**709**	**720**	**23.7**	**3.6**	**8.0**	**2.2**	**56%**	**9%**	**35**	**24**	**41**	**30%**	**73%**	**9%**	**33**						**-4.3**	**60**	**72**	**$5**

JOSH PALEY

Beachy,Brandon

Age: 28	Th: R	Role SP	Health F	LIMA Plan B+	
Ht: 6' 3"	Wt: 215	Type Pwr FB	PT/Exp D	Rand Var 0	
			Consist A	MM 3301	

2010-11 skills showed real promise, but since then, health has been the dominant theme: 2012 cut short by TJS; returned in 2013 to elbow inflammation. Another TJS followed in March of 2014. Those 2010-11 skills are still part of his profile, but they are now 4+ years and two elbow ligaments ago.

Yr	Tm	W	L	Sv	IP	K	ERA	xERA	WHIP	oOPS	vL	vR	BF/G	Ctl	Dom	Cmd	FpK	SwK	G	L	F	H%	S%	hr/f	GS	APC	DOM%	DIS%	Sv%	LI	RAR	BPV	BPX	R$
10	ATL *	5	3	2	134	140	2.19	2.94	1.19	677	654	704	14.2	2.4	9.4	3.9	51%	10%	36	29	36	33%	82%	0%	3	93	33%	33%			31.3	133	216	$15
11	ATL	7	3	0	142	169	3.68	3.29	1.21	679	707	660	23.6	2.9	10.7	3.7	61%	13%	34	21	45	32%	73%	10%	25	97	60%	12%			4.5	126	190	$9
12	ATL	5	5	0	81	68	2.00	3.96	0.96	507	446	553	24.5	3.2	7.6	2.3	61%	8%	41	18	41	21%	83%	7%	13	102	69%	8%			20.1	68	89	$12
13	ATL *	4	5	0	65	47	4.47	4.44	1.37	705	736	680	20.9	3.5	6.5	1.9	63%	9%	42	17	42	28%	71%	14%	5	90	80%	20%			-4.8	41	54	-$3
14																																		
1st Half																																		
2nd Half																																		
15	Proj	5	4	0	87	83	3.87	3.45	1.20	671	686	660	20.5	3.1	8.6	2.8	61%	10%	38	19	43	29%	71%	9%	17						-1.4	89	106	$3

Beckett,Josh

Age: 35	Th: R	Role	Health	LIMA Plan	
Ht: 6' 5"	Wt: 230	Type	PT/Exp	Rand Var	
			Consist	MM	

Announced his retirement after the Dodgers were eliminated in the 2014 playoffs. Owns two World Series rings, and posted BPVs over 85 eleven times in thirteen seasons. A distinguished career that deserves much respect.

Yr	Tm	W	L	Sv	IP	K	ERA	xERA	WHIP	oOPS	vL	vR	BF/G	Ctl	Dom	Cmd	FpK	SwK	G	L	F	H%	S%	hr/f	GS	APC	DOM%	DIS%	Sv%	LI	RAR	BPV	BPX	R$
10	BOS	6	6	0	128	116	5.78	3.94	1.54	848	940	726	27.5	3.2	8.2	2.6	58%	9%	46	19	35	35%	65%	14%	21	103	43%	19%			-26.8	86	138	-$7
11	BOS	13	7	0	193	175	2.89	3.46	1.03	608	562	671	25.6	2.4	8.2	3.4	61%	11%	40	18	42	25%	77%	10%	30	100	70%	7%			25.0	99	149	$24
12	2 TM	7	14	0	170	132	4.65	4.25	1.33	741	801	672	26.1	2.7	7.0	2.5	61%	9%	43	21	37	31%	67%	11%	28	94	50%	18%			-13.3	72	94	-$2
13	LA	0	5	0	43	41	5.19	4.04	1.50	844	896	790	24.4	3.1	8.5	2.7	63%	12%	39	24	37	34%	70%	16%	8	92	38%	38%			-7.1	86	112	-$7
14	LA	6	6	0	116	107	2.88	3.62	1.17	705	821	578	23.8	3.0	8.3	2.7	61%	11%	43	19	38	26%	83%	14%	20	95	50%	20%			12.3	89	106	$8
1st Half		5	4	0	94	88	2.02	3.29	1.00	614	682	547	24.6	2.7	8.5	3.1	61%	11%	45	19	36	24%	88%	12%	15	99	67%	7%			19.9	103	123	$15
2nd Half		1	2	0	22	19	6.55	5.09	1.86	1030	1232	718	21.2	4.5	7.8	1.7	62%	10%	34	22	45	36%	71%	18%	5	86	0%	60%			-7.6	30	36	-$21
15	Proj																																	

Bedard,Erik

Age: 36	Th: L	Role SP	Health D	LIMA Plan D+	
Ht: 6' 1"	Wt: 200	Type Pwr FB	PT/Exp B	Rand Var +1	
			Consist A	MM 2300	

Way back in 2007, he was 13-5 with 3.16 ERA, 1.09 WHIP, and 221 K. Since then, he has been a mix of injuries and declining skills. The minor bump in his 2014 BPV was driven by better Ctl, but this is more likely a dead cat bounce than a return to rosterability.

Yr	Tm	W	L	Sv	IP	K	ERA	xERA	WHIP	oOPS	vL	vR	BF/G	Ctl	Dom	Cmd	FpK	SwK	G	L	F	H%	S%	hr/f	GS	APC	DOM%	DIS%	Sv%	LI	RAR	BPV	BPX	R$
10																																		
11	2 AL	5	9	0	129	125	3.62	3.65	1.28	681	671	685	22.5	3.3	8.7	2.6	61%	8%	42	20	38	30%	75%	10%	24	93	54%	25%			5.2	86	130	$5
12	PIT	7	14	0	126	118	5.01	4.19	1.47	758	628	786	23.2	4.0	8.5	2.1	62%	8%	43	23	33	33%	67%	11%	24	89	38%	33%			-15.5	65	85	-$6
13	HOU	4	12	1	151	138	4.59	4.52	1.48	773	832	755	20.7	4.5	8.2	1.8	60%	9%	36	18	46	31%	71%	9%	26	84	35%	38%	33	0.81	-13.5	41	54	-$7
14	TAM	4	6	0	76	64	4.76	4.62	1.49	778	827	762	20.1	3.4	7.6	2.2	61%	8%	34	20	46	33%	71%	9%	15	82	40%	47%	0	0.70	-9.5	56	67	-$5
1st Half		4	5	0	73	64	4.21	4.39	1.39	720	837	678	21.5	3.3	7.9	2.4	62%	9%	35	19	46	32%	71%	7%	14	89	43%	43%	0	0.73	-4.2	65	78	-$5
2nd Half		0	1	0	3	0	18.00	11.14	4.00	1711	0	1808	10.0	6.0	0.0	0.0	50%	2%	17	33	50	45%	67%	33%	1	33	0%	100%	0	0.47	-5.3	-167	-200	-$17
15	Proj	3	5	0	58	51	4.48	4.01	1.44	741	753	737	21.4	4.0	8.0	2.0	61%	9%	37	21	42	32%	71%	9%	12						-5.3	52	62	-$3

Bedrosian,Cam

Age: 23	Th: R	Role RP	Health A	LIMA Plan A	
Ht: 6' 0"	Wt: 205	Type Pwr	PT/Exp F	Rand Var +2	
			Consist F	MM 5500	

0-1, 6.52 ERA in 19 IP at LAA. Despite a rough introduction to MLB, he appears to be tracking toward a closer career like his father. Raw Dom is in place, just in need of refinement. 2nd half is a small sample, but a step in the right direction. Closer-in-waiting who can turn a profit in an AL-only league. UP: 80 K, 20 Saves.

Yr	Tm	W	L	Sv	IP	K	ERA	xERA	WHIP	oOPS	vL	vR	BF/G	Ctl	Dom	Cmd	FpK	SwK	G	L	F	H%	S%	hr/f	GS	APC	DOM%	DIS%	Sv%	LI	RAR	BPV	BPX	R$
10																																		
11																																		
12																																		
13																																		
14	LAA *	2	2	17	59	77	3.66	2.07	1.10	801	1055	531	4.2	4.0	11.9	3.0	61%	11%	41	21	38	29%	66%	9%	0	24			81	0.67	0.6	137	163	$8
1st Half		1	1	10	28	35	4.48	1.87	1.07	984	1238	522	4.0	4.8	11.2	2.3	55%	13%	53	16	32	23%	57%	17%	0	24			83	1.10	-2.6	120	143	$7
2nd Half		1	1	7	31	42	3.20	2.51	1.19	715	934	533	4.4	3.5	12.4	3.5	65%	10%	36	24	40	35%	72%	6%	0	24			78	0.44	2.0	150	180	$9
15	Proj	2	2	0	59	72	3.58	2.98	1.20				4.3	4.0	11.1	2.8	62%	10%	42	20	38	30%	72%	9%	0						1.1	111	132	$1

Beimel,Joe

Age: 38	Th: L	Role RP	Health C	LIMA Plan C+	
Ht: 6' 3"	Wt: 205	Type Con	PT/Exp F	Rand Var -5	
			Consist F	MM 1000	

Poor Cmd has plagued him for years and he can't stop righties. 2014 ERA suppressed by unsustainable strand and hit rates—the regression could get ugly. His BPV went up by 60 points, moving him from horrible to subpar. "The only winning move is not to play. How about a nice game of chess?"

Yr	Tm	W	L	Sv	IP	K	ERA	xERA	WHIP	oOPS	vL	vR	BF/G	Ctl	Dom	Cmd	FpK	SwK	G	L	F	H%	S%	hr/f	GS	APC	DOM%	DIS%	Sv%	LI	RAR	BPV	BPX	R$
10	COL	1	2	0	45	21	3.40	4.77	1.36	747	653	862	2.6	3.0	4.2	1.4	63%	10%	43	16	40	28%	79%	8%	0	10			0	1.18	3.8	16	25	-$1
11	PIT	1	1	0	25	17	5.33	4.75	1.70	936	798	1028	3.3	3.2	6.0	1.9	60%	9%	41	18	41	34%	76%	17%	0	12			0	1.16	-4.3	41	62	-$5
12																																		
13	aaa	1	2	0	33	18	5.88	7.35	1.91				5.2	5.0	4.9	1.0						33%	74%								-8.2	-18	-24	-$9
14	SEA	3	1	0	45	25	2.20	4.10	1.18	656	504	791	3.3	2.8	5.0	1.8	65%	8%	50	20	30	26%	86%	10%	0	11			0	1.02	8.6	42	51	$2
1st Half		2	1	0	26	16	1.40	3.89	1.21	625	400	822	3.9	3.2	5.6	1.8	70%	8%	49	23	27	28%	87%	0%	0	13			0	1.15	7.4	43	51	$3
2nd Half		1	0	0	19	9	3.26	4.38	1.14	694	632	750	2.9	2.3	4.2	1.8	60%	9%	50	17	33	22%	83%	18%	0	10			0	0.89	1.2	41	48	$0
15	Proj	2	2	0	44	23	4.28	4.49	1.45	806	684	928	3.6	3.6	4.7	1.3	63%	9%	47	18	35	28%	75%	13%	0						-2.9	13	16	-$4

Belisario,Ronald

Age: 32	Th: R	Role RP	Health A	LIMA Plan C	
Ht: 6' 3"	Wt: 240	Type xGB	PT/Exp C	Rand Var +5	
			Consist A	MM 3100	

Stability of xERA shows that difference between 2013 and 2014 was just strand rate variance. Amid the carnage of 2014, he at least managed to limit the walks; but FpK isn't confident those gains will stick. And unless 2012's Dom magically reappears, BPX column paints the picture of a very average pitcher.

Yr	Tm	W	L	Sv	IP	K	ERA	xERA	WHIP	oOPS	vL	vR	BF/G	Ctl	Dom	Cmd	FpK	SwK	G	L	F	H%	S%	hr/f	GS	APC	DOM%	DIS%	Sv%	LI	RAR	BPV	BPX	R$
10	LA	3	1	2	55	38	5.04	3.55	1.28	702	793	649	3.9	3.1	6.2	2.0	62%	9%	61	17	22	28%	62%	16%	0	15			50	1.08	-6.6	67	108	-$1
11																																		
12	LA	8	1	1	71	69	2.54	2.91	1.07	558	725	440	4.2	3.7	8.7	2.4	61%	11%	64	21	15	25%	77%	11%	0	16			20	1.12	13.0	100	131	$9
13	LA	5	7	1	68	49	3.97	3.74	1.47	725	811	684	3.9	3.7	6.5	1.8	61%	10%	61	21	18	33%	72%	8%	0	14			20	1.45	-0.9	56	73	-$2
14	CHW	4	8	8	66	47	5.56	3.62	1.45	728	817	661	4.7	2.4	6.4	2.6	56%	7%	59	18	23	35%	60%	8%	0	17			67	1.54	-14.9	86	102	-$3
1st Half		3	4	8	37	28	5.54	3.29	1.34	726	751	704	4.7	1.9	6.8	3.5	56%	8%	61	18	22	34%	57%	12%	0	17			67	1.50	-8.3	108	129	$0
2nd Half		1	4	0	29	19	5.59	4.06	1.59	731	909	612	4.7	3.1	5.9	1.9	56%	6%	57	18	25	36%	62%	4%	0	18			0	1.58	-6.6	58	69	-$8
15	Proj	4	6	0	65	48	3.97	3.47	1.42	704	818	631	4.2	3.2	6.7	2.1	59%	8%	60	19	22	32%	72%	8%	0						-1.9	70	83	-$2

Belisle,Matt

Age: 35	Th: R	Role RP	Health A	LIMA Plan C	
Ht: 6' 4"	Wt: 225	Type	PT/Exp C	Rand Var +2	
			Consist B	MM 2101	

Will his ERA go up half a run every year until he retires? Surviving his consistently high H% and line-drive rate was always going to be a difficult task. The collapse of his once-elite Cmd makes it impossible. Next stop on the ERA trend is well within reach. His 2nd half is already foretelling it.

Yr	Tm	W	L	Sv	IP	K	ERA	xERA	WHIP	oOPS	vL	vR	BF/G	Ctl	Dom	Cmd	FpK	SwK	G	L	F	H%	S%	hr/f	GS	APC	DOM%	DIS%	Sv%	LI	RAR	BPV	BPX	R$
10	COL	7	5	1	92	91	2.93	2.93	1.09	646	620	659	4.8	1.6	8.9	5.7	65%	10%	46	20	33	31%	75%	9%	0	19			50	1.03	13.0	142	230	$10
11	COL	10	4	0	72	58	3.25	3.27	1.26	721	656	760	4.1	1.8	7.3	4.1	61%	9%	53	19	28	33%	76%	8%	0	16			0	1.20	6.1	114	172	$5
12	COL	3	8	3	80	69	3.71	3.56	1.36	722	789	672	4.4	2.0	7.8	3.8	65%	9%	51	24	26	35%	73%	8%	0	16			30	1.42	3.0	114	149	$0
13	COL	5	7	0	73	62	4.32	3.27	1.25	707	750	679	4.2	1.8	7.6	4.1	67%	11%	49	26	25	33%	66%	11%	0	16			0	1.16	-4.0	115	149	-$1
14	COL	4	7	0	65	43	4.87	4.13	1.44	757	813	711	4.3	2.6	6.0	2.3	68%	8%	46	25	29	33%	66%	8%	1	16	0%	100%	0	0.82	-9.0	60	72	-$5
1st Half		2	3	0	34	22	4.54	3.70	1.25	706	731	682	4.0	1.9	5.9	3.1	67%	7%	51	21	28	30%	64%	10%	0	14			0	0.57	-3.3	85	101	-$3
2nd Half		2	4	0	31	21	5.23	4.61	1.65	810	918	736	4.5	3.5	6.1	1.8	70%	9%	40	29	31	36%	67%	6%	1	18	0%	100%	0	1.10	-5.7	34	41	-$6
15	Proj	5	7	0	73	53	4.42	3.69	1.43	767	824	726	4.3	2.6	6.6	2.6	67%	9%	46	25	29	34%	70%	9%	0						-6.1	73	87	-$3

JOSH PALEY

Benoit,Joaquin

Age: 37	Th: R	Role RP	Health A	LIMA Plan B
Ht: 6' 3"	Wt: 220	Type Pwr xFB	PT/Exp C	Rand Var -5
			Consist A	MM 5520

For second straight year, turned elite 1st half performance into 2nd half save opps, and converted them successfully. Overall skill set is remarkably stable; historical health concerns have even aged out of his short-term analysis. Worthy of a full-season closer gig if not for September shoulder issues and his age.

Yr Tm	W	L	Sv	IP	K	ERA	xERA	WHIP	oOPS	vL	vR	BF/G	Ctl	Dom	Cmd	FpK	SwK	G	L	F	H%	S%	hr/f	GS	APC	DOM%	DIS%	Sv%	LI	RAR	BPV	BPX	R$
10 TAM	1	2	1	60	75	1.34	2.54	0.68	454	491	419	3.4	1.6	11.2	6.8	54%	15%	39	12	49	20%	91%	9%	0	15			25	1.11	20.4	174	282	$12
11 DET	4	3	2	61	63	2.95	3.26	1.05	581	639	517	3.7	2.5	9.3	3.7	58%	14%	39	18	43	28%	75%	7%	0	15			29	1.26	7.5	117	175	$6
12 DET	5	3	2	71	84	3.68	3.36	1.14	720	721	720	3.9	2.8	10.6	3.8	58%	18%	36	20	44	28%	78%	18%	0	17			33	1.05	3.0	130	170	$5
13 DET	4	1	24	67	73	2.01	3.17	1.03	575	524	645	4.0	3.0	9.8	3.3	63%	15%	42	20	38	27%	84%	8%	0	16			92	1.19	15.3	117	152	$17
14 SD	4	2	11	54	64	1.49	2.98	0.77	459	480	440	3.9	2.3	10.6	4.6	63%	19%	35	15	50	22%	85%	5%	0	15			92	1.25	15.1	141	168	$13
1st Half	3	0	1	35	39	1.30	2.87	0.72	438	450	425	3.7	1.8	10.1	5.6	62%	19%	35	18	48	22%	83%	3%	0	15			100	1.13	10.4	146	174	$14
2nd Half	1	2	10	20	25	1.83	3.18	0.86	495	535	461	4.1	3.2	11.4	3.6	64%	19%	35	9	56	21%	87%	8%	0	16			91	1.47	4.6	132	158	$12
15 Proj	4	3	23	58	68	2.54	2.86	1.00	589	600	577	3.9	2.7	10.5	3.9	62%	17%	37	16	47	27%	79%	8%	0						8.6	132	157	$15

Bergman,Christian

Age: 27	Th: R	Role SP	Health D	LIMA Plan D+
Ht: 6' 1"	Wt: 180	Type Con FB	PT/Exp A	Rand Var 0
			Consist A	MM 1000

3-5, 5.93 ERA in 55 IP at COL. "Few Ks, lots of fly balls" is not a viable approach to pitching at altitude. To be fair, he had a GB tilt in the minors, so there is some chance he will be able to combine more GBs and good Ctl to limit the damage. But "limiting the damage" is the best-case scenario here.

Yr Tm	W	L	Sv	IP	K	ERA	xERA	WHIP	oOPS	vL	vR	BF/G	Ctl	Dom	Cmd	FpK	SwK	G	L	F	H%	S%	hr/f	GS	APC	DOM%	DIS%	Sv%	LI	RAR	BPV	BPX	R$
10																																	
11																																	
12																																	
13 aa	8	7	0	171	84	4.94	5.76	1.38				26.6	1.4	4.4	3.2						30%	72%								-22.7	29	38	-$8
14 COL *	8	11	0	156	79	5.53	5.90	1.53	902	777	994	25.1	2.0	4.6	2.3	69%	7%	33	25	42	33%	67%	10%	10	89	20%	10%			-34.3	24	28	-$15
1st Half	4	6	0	90	45	4.95	5.42	1.39	975	607	1220	25.2	1.6	4.5	2.8	70%	8%	38	28	34	31%	69%	25%	3	84	33%	33%			-13.4	34	40	-$12
2nd Half	4	5	0	66	34	5.75	6.01	1.63	873	840	897	24.5	2.4	4.6	1.9	69%	7%	31	24	45	35%	66%	6%	7	90	14%	0%			-16.4	24	29	-$18
15 Proj	3	3	0	52	26	4.86	4.42	1.47	849	703	955	25.5	1.8	4.5	2.5	69%	7%	34	26	41	32%	72%	12%	9						-7.2	44	52	-$5

Betances,Dellin

Age: 27	Th: R	Role RP	Health A	LIMA Plan B
Ht: 6' 8"	Wt: 260	Type Pwr	PT/Exp D	Rand Var -5
			Consist F	MM 5521

Big-armed, big-bodied SP prospect converted to pen in 2013, and displayed simply preposterous skills in his first full MLB season. Suddenly developed Ctl while Dom grew from "big" to "enormous." Only remaining question is his role: R$ shows his value even without closer gig. If he gets the 9th, then... UP: $30.

Yr Tm	W	L	Sv	IP	K	ERA	xERA	WHIP	oOPS	vL	vR	BF/G	Ctl	Dom	Cmd	FpK	SwK	G	L	F	H%	S%	hr/f	GS	APC	DOM%	DIS%	Sv%	LI	RAR	BPV	BPX	R$
10																																	
11 NYY *	4	9	0	129	121	4.81	4.43	1.57	625	611	571	21.0	5.6	8.4	1.5	6%	1%	14	29	57	31%	70%	0%	1	36	0%	100%	0	0.48	-13.8	61	92	-$7
12 a/a	6	9	0	131	102	8.28	7.13	2.11				24.0	7.1	7.0	1.0						37%	60%								-69.1	18	24	-$41
13 NYY *	6	4	5	89	98	4.16	3.25	1.40	965	1339	804	8.5	5.0	9.9	2.0	65%	9%	36	36	29	32%	69%	25%	0	20			100	0.28	-3.3	98	127	$1
14 NYY	5	0	1	90	135	1.40	2.03	0.78	442	405	482	4.9	2.4	13.5	5.6	66%	13%	47	20	33	26%	85%	7%	0	20			20	1.19	26.0	203	242	$18
1st Half	4	0	0	48	76	1.50	1.89	0.77	409	366	447	5.1	3.0	14.3	4.8	63%	12%	49	20	31	25%	81%	4%	0	22			0	1.02	13.3	203	242	$21
2nd Half	1	0	1	42	59	1.29	2.17	0.79	480	442	525	4.6	1.7	12.6	7.4	70%	14%	44	20	36	27%	90%	9%	0	17			33	1.35	12.7	203	242	$16
15 Proj	5	2	15	87	118	2.41	2.28	1.01	569	526	617	6.7	2.8	12.3	4.4	67%	13%	46	20	34	30%	78%	9%	0						14.3	170	202	$18

Bettis,Chad

Age: 26	Th: R	Role RP	Health A	LIMA Plan D+
Ht: 6' 1"	Wt: 200	Type GB	PT/Exp D	Rand Var +4
			Consist B	MM 1100

0-2, 9.12 ERA in 25 IP at COL. A yo-yo of a season: started year in COL bullpen, got pounded. Went to Triple-A and straightened himself out, then back to COL for more pounding. Shifted to SP role in Triple-A late in season; shoulder problems shut him down. No sign of a path to positive value, at least right now.

Yr Tm	W	L	Sv	IP	K	ERA	xERA	WHIP	oOPS	vL	vR	BF/G	Ctl	Dom	Cmd	FpK	SwK	G	L	F	H%	S%	hr/f	GS	APC	DOM%	DIS%	Sv%	LI	RAR	BPV	BPX	R$
10																																	
11																																	
12																																	
13 COL *	4	7	0	108	82	5.46	5.75	1.54	859	812	906	16.8	2.9	6.9	2.4	61%	8%	47	21	32	34%	69%	12%	8	49	0%	50%	0	0.91	-21.2	38	49	-$11
14 COL *	3	6	3	80	55	5.26	4.78	1.56	1020	901	1138	8.5	3.5	6.1	1.8	50%	6%	46	24	30	34%	65%	14%	0	24			60	0.70	-15.0	53	63	-$8
1st Half	2	3	3	46	31	4.51	3.41	1.28	970	699	1269	6.7	3.3	6.1	1.8	51%	6%	45	21	34	28%	64%	16%	0	22			75	0.47	-4.3	64	76	-$3
2nd Half	1	3	0	34	23	6.27	6.62	1.92	1083	1196	987	12.5	3.7	6.1	1.7	48%	6%	48	29	24	40%	66%	10%	0	27			0	1.09	-10.7	40	48	-$14
15 Proj	2	3	0	44	31	5.51	4.17	1.61	770	722	817	11.4	3.3	6.4	2.0	61%	8%	47	21	32	35%	66%	9%	2						-9.5	52	61	-$7

Billingsley,Chad

Age: 30	Th: R	Role SP	Health F	LIMA Plan C
Ht: 6' 1"	Wt: 240	Type Pwr	PT/Exp D	Rand Var 0
			Consist B	MM 2201

Comeback from 2013 Tommy John surgery was interrupted by a torn flexor tendon in June. Availability for start of 2015 is an open question, though needs to find a team first. By time of his return, he'll have been out for more than two full years. If skills are intact, he's still interesting. But that's a very big IF.

Yr Tm	W	L	Sv	IP	K	ERA	xERA	WHIP	oOPS	vL	vR	BF/G	Ctl	Dom	Cmd	FpK	SwK	G	L	F	H%	S%	hr/f	GS	APC	DOM%	DIS%	Sv%	LI	RAR	BPV	BPX	R$
10 LA	12	11	0	192	171	3.57	3.62	1.28	668	703	629	26.4	3.2	8.0	2.5	59%	9%	50	18	32	31%	71%	4%	31	101	48%	10%			12.1	85	138	$12
11 LA	11	11	0	188	152	4.21	4.18	1.45	729	797	670	25.9	4.0	7.3	1.8	60%	8%	45	21	34	32%	71%	7%	32	101	41%	19%			-6.3	45	68	$0
12 LA	10	9	0	150	128	3.55	3.88	1.29	725	744	703	25.4	2.7	7.7	2.8	60%	9%	45	21	33	32%	74%	7%	25	95	72%	16%			8.6	88	115	$8
13 LA	1	0	0	12	6	3.00	4.68	1.42	766	828	684	24.5	3.8	4.5	1.2	51%	8%	42	25	33	28%	81%	8%	2	91	0%	0%			1.3	0	0	-$3
14																																	
1st Half																																	
2nd Half																																	
15 Proj	5	4	0	73	62	3.97	3.73	1.37	710	749	671	25.3	3.6	7.7	2.1	60%	9%	44	21	35	32%	71%	6%	12						-2.1	63	75	-$1

Black,Victor

Age: 27	Th: R	Role RP	Health A	LIMA Plan B
Ht: 6' 4"	Wt: 210	Type Pwr	PT/Exp D	Rand Var -5
			Consist A	MM 2310

2-3, 2.60 ERA in 35 IP at NYM. Completely lost the Ctl gains he had been making in the upper minors. Reigned that in during tiny 2nd half sample in NY; lost Dom in the process but SwK holding tight. Can't project any higher-leverage role until he re-establishes Cmd. Check back in a year.

Yr Tm	W	L	Sv	IP	K	ERA	xERA	WHIP	oOPS	vL	vR	BF/G	Ctl	Dom	Cmd	FpK	SwK	G	L	F	H%	S%	hr/f	GS	APC	DOM%	DIS%	Sv%	LI	RAR	BPV	BPX	R$
10																																	
11																																	
12 aa	2	3	13	60	67	2.00	2.63	1.25				4.8	4.3	10.0	2.4						30%	84%								14.9	113	147	$10
13 2 NL *	8	3	18	64	64	3.19	2.63	1.21	687	609	741	4.6	3.8	9.0	2.4	61%	10%	30	23	47	29%	73%	4%	0	16			75	1.04	5.3	103	134	$11
14 NYM *	2	4	7	53	47	2.12	2.77	1.35	617	665	580	3.8	5.7	7.9	1.4	49%	11%	46	20	35	26%	85%	6%	0	14			88	1.09	10.7	81	97	$4
1st Half	1	3	7	34	33	1.45	2.69	1.39	585	647	535	4.4	6.5	8.6	1.3	44%	11%	55	18	28	26%	90%	9%	0	18			88	1.03	9.7	88	105	$6
2nd Half	1	1	0	19	14	3.32	4.46	1.26	644	678	619	3.2	4.3	6.6	1.6	53%	12%	38	21	40	26%	74%	5%	0	11			0	1.13	1.0	21	25	-$1
15 Proj	4	3	3	58	54	3.67	3.74	1.34	671	717	637	4.1	4.6	8.4	1.8	49%	11%	45	20	35	29%	74%	8%	0						0.5	51	61	$1

Blevins,Jerry

Age: 31	Th: L	Role RP	Health A	LIMA Plan C
Ht: 6' 6"	Wt: 185	Type Pwr FB	PT/Exp C	Rand Var +4
			Consist A	MM 4400

Looks like this lefty specialist re-established his dominance of LH batters, but in reality it never left. There's a lot of H% noise baked in; his skills were strong on that side all along. Similarly, consistent sub-2.0 Cmd vRHB suggests there's no possibility of a larger role. Should go back to providing $1 ratio insulation.

Yr Tm	W	L	Sv	IP	K	ERA	xERA	WHIP	oOPS	vL	vR	BF/G	Ctl	Dom	Cmd	FpK	SwK	G	L	F	H%	S%	hr/f	GS	APC	DOM%	DIS%	Sv%	LI	RAR	BPV	BPX	R$
10 OAK	2	1	1	49	46	3.70	4.10	1.48	758	598	892	3.5	3.3	8.5	2.6	59%	10%	38	23	39	34%	80%	12%	0	13			50	1.19	2.3	79	128	-$1
11 OAK *	2	0	0	58	53	4.13	3.50	1.28	688	759	636	4.5	3.3	8.2	2.5	59%	9%	38	18	44	30%	69%	6%	0	17			0	0.62	-1.3	86	129	-$1
12 OAK	5	1	1	65	54	2.48	4.10	1.07	637	575	693	4.1	3.4	7.4	2.2	52%	11%	38	18	44	23%	83%	9%	0	16			100	0.92	12.4	57	74	$7
13 OAK	5	0	0	60	52	3.15	4.00	1.07	651	741	581	3.7	2.6	7.8	3.1	58%	10%	31	19	50	25%	75%	8%	0	15			0	0.97	5.3	81	105	$4
14 WAS	2	3	0	57	66	4.87	3.37	1.24	623	419	821	3.8	3.6	10.4	2.9	68%	12%	39	24	37	32%	59%	6%	0	15			0	0.94	-8.0	106	126	-$2
1st Half	2	3	0	30	31	5.16	4.10	1.38	650	414	859	3.6	4.9	9.4	1.9	71%	10%	36	24	40	31%	60%	3%	0	15			0	0.85	-5.2	52	63	-$4
2nd Half	0	0	0	28	35	4.55	2.67	1.08	592	423	775	4.0	2.3	11.4	5.0	65%	14%	42	25	33	33%	57%	9%	0	16			0	1.05	-2.8	163	195	-$1
15 Proj	2	2	0	56	57	3.30	3.28	1.17	636	527	735	3.7	3.1	9.2	2.9	62%	11%	37	22	41	29%	74%	8%	0						3.0	96	114	$1

RAY MURPHY

Bolsinger,Michael

Age: 27	Th: R	Role SP	Health A	LIMA Plan C
Ht: 6' 2"	Wt: 210	Type Pwr xGB	PT/Exp D	Rand Var +3
			Consist A	MM 2201

1-6, 5.50 ERA in 51 IP at ARI. Five years ago, this blend of Ctl/Dom/Cmd plus a GB tilt would have served him well. But as BPX shows, today this is a below-average skill set. Distribution of DOM%/DIS% is poetic: he's 33% great, 33% terrible, and 33% mediocre. That's not a winning mix.

Yr Tm	W	L	Sv	IP	K	ERA	xERA	WHIP	oOPS	vL	vR	BF/G	Ctl	Dom	Cmd	FpK	SwK	G	L	F	H%	S%	hr/f	GS	APC	DOM%	DIS%	Sv%	LI	RAR	BPV	BPX	R$
10																																	
11																																	
12 aa	4	3	0	78	53	4.85	5.62	1.76				23.7	4.5	6.1	1.4						36%	73%								-8.0	38	50	-$10
13 a/a	11	7	0	144	103	4.72	5.10	1.58				24.4	3.3	6.4	1.9						35%	71%								-15.2	49	64	-$8
14 ARI *	9	9	0	144	117	4.61	4.81	1.49	872	906	843	23.0	3.0	7.3	2.5	67%	9%	52	21	26	35%	70%	16%	9	85	33%	33%	0	0.83	-15.4	68	81	-$6
1st Half	6	5	0	96	72	3.61	3.63	1.27	787	793	781	23.2	2.8	6.7	2.4	67%	8%	54	20	26	30%	73%	17%	7	85	43%	29%	0	0.85	1.5	72	86	$2
2nd Half	3	4	0	48	45	6.62	7.19	1.95	1239	1293	1172	22.7	3.3	8.6	2.6	66%	12%	45	26	29	44%	66%	11%	2	82	0%	50%			-16.9	62	74	-$22
15 Proj	4	5	0	74	58	4.37	3.85	1.58	750	781	725	23.1	3.5	7.1	2.0	67%	8%	52	20	27	35%	74%	9%	14						-5.7	64	76	-$5

Boxberger,Brad

Age: 27	Th: R	Role RP	Health A	LIMA Plan B+
Ht: 6' 2"	Wt: 220	Type Pwr FB	PT/Exp D	Rand Var -1
			Consist B	MM 5520

What drove this breakout? Dom has been in place for some time, but pairing it with Ctl/FpK/SwK gains has been a multi-year effort that bore fruit in a big way. Second half was as nasty as any you'll find anywhere. Only question is his role. He's more than qualified to close; even a job share would spike his value.

Yr Tm	W	L	Sv	IP	K	ERA	xERA	WHIP	oOPS	vL	vR	BF/G	Ctl	Dom	Cmd	FpK	SwK	G	L	F	H%	S%	hr/f	GS	APC	DOM%	DIS%	Sv%	LI	RAR	BPV	BPX	R$
10 aa	1	4	0	30	35	9.51	6.96	2.02				6.5	6.5	10.7	1.6						41%	52%								-19.9	50	81	-$10
11 a/a	2	4	11	62	80	2.13	1.63	0.98				4.3	3.8	11.7	3.1						24%	81%								13.9	138	207	$12
12 SD *	2	2	5	71	86	2.43	2.98	1.31	734	820	659	4.8	4.4	11.0	2.5	45%	12%	40	13	46	33%	82%	10%	0	24			71	0.73	13.9	116	152	$6
13 SD *	2	5	6	79	100	3.24	3.28	1.27	760	495	948	5.4	3.4	11.3	3.3	62%	13%	42	17	40	35%	76%	14%	0	22			75	0.66	6.1	125	163	$4
14 TAM	5	2	2	65	104	2.37	2.08	0.84	538	402	659	3.9	2.8	14.5	5.2	67%	15%	41	17	42	24%	82%	19%	0	17			40	1.23	11.0	204	243	$11
1st Half	1	1	0	30	46	2.97	2.41	0.96	618	423	771	4.0	3.6	13.6	3.8	69%	15%	44	14	42	22%	83%	25%	0	17			0	0.76	2.9	171	205	$4
2nd Half	4	1	2	34	58	1.83	1.81	0.73	465	383	547	3.8	2.1	15.2	7.3	65%	15%	39	19	42	27%	82%	13%	0	17			50	1.66	8.1	234	279	$17
15 Proj	4	3	15	66	94	2.55	2.40	1.02	588	443	719	4.3	3.2	12.9	4.0	66%	15%	41	17	42	29%	80%	11%	0						9.7	164	195	$13

Boyer,Blaine

Age: 33	Th: R	Role RP	Health A	LIMA Plan C
Ht: 6' 3"	Wt: 225	Type	PT/Exp F	Rand Var 0
			Consist F	MM 2100

0-1, 3.57 ERA in 40 IP at SD. After no significant work in the majors since his 2008-10 "peak," clawed his way back and posted career-best skills to boot. L/R splits say his best path to sticking around is as a righty specialist. Best case, that places him in the purgatory space between having a job and having relevance.

Yr Tm	W	L	Sv	IP	K	ERA	xERA	WHIP	oOPS	vL	vR	BF/G	Ctl	Dom	Cmd	FpK	SwK	G	L	F	H%	S%	hr/f	GS	APC	DOM%	DIS%	Sv%	LI	RAR	BPV	BPX	R$
10 ARI	3	2	0	57	29	4.26	4.40	1.54	734	895	585	4.6	4.6	4.6	1.0	54%	6%	66	13	21	30%	72%	8%	0	17			0	0.70	-1.3	3	5	-$3
11 NYM *	0	4	1	31	10	14.55	13.57	3.00	1202	946	1438	8.9	6.1	3.1	0.5	67%	8%	55	21	24	45%	51%	29%	0	24			100	0.84	-40.1	-91	-136	-$23
12																																	
13 aaa	0	1	1	15	13	4.24	6.63	1.57				5.1	2.1	7.6	3.6						36%	82%								-0.7	48	63	-$4
14 SD *	1	3	7	69	51	3.27	2.77	1.09	628	813	508	4.8	1.8	6.6	3.7	68%	11%	43	21	37	29%	70%	5%	0	20			78	0.56	4.0	109	130	$4
1st Half	1	2	7	38	27	2.16	2.07	0.96	263	599	0	4.7	1.6	6.2	4.0	74%	8%	56	12	32	26%	79%	0%	0	20			78	0.33	7.5	120	144	$10
2nd Half	0	1	0	31	24	4.65	3.88	1.26	719	875	622	5.0	2.0	7.0	3.4	67%	11%	39	23	38	32%	62%	6%	0	19			0	0.61	-3.5	87	104	-$2
15 Proj	1	3	0	44	33	3.87	3.73	1.42	787	993	636	5.4	3.0	6.7	2.3	61%	9%	50	19	31	32%	75%	11%	0						-0.7	69	82	-$3

Brach,Brad

Age: 29	Th: R	Role RP	Health A	LIMA Plan B+
Ht: 6' 6"	Wt: 215	Type Pwr FB	PT/Exp D	Rand Var 0
			Consist B	MM 3401

7-1, 3.18 ERA in 62 IP at BAL. Sent down on June 8 after an ugly 2 IP/5 BB outing; returned two weeks later with improved Ctl/FpK that mostly held up all season. As a rare multi-IP reliever (12 appearances of 2.0+ IP), the seemingly-outlying IP, K, W totals might repeat. He's like 1.5 RPs crammed into one roster spot.

Yr Tm	W	L	Sv	IP	K	ERA	xERA	WHIP	oOPS	vL	vR	BF/G	Ctl	Dom	Cmd	FpK	SwK	G	L	F	H%	S%	hr/f	GS	APC	DOM%	DIS%	Sv%	LI	RAR	BPV	BPX	R$
10																																	
11 SD *	3	7	34	79	91	2.78	2.59	1.11	747	833	709	4.1	2.1	10.4	5.0	53%	13%	26	53	21	34%	75%	0%	0	17			92	1.06	11.3	165	248	$20
12 SD	2	4	0	67	75	3.78	3.98	1.25	674	718	646	4.2	4.5	10.1	2.3	55%	11%	35	20	45	26%	76%	15%	0	17			0	1.17	1.9	75	98	$1
13 SD *	5	3	3	75	67	2.95	4.72	1.52	819	647	972	5.0	3.9	8.0	2.1	54%	9%	38	23	39	34%	84%	9%	0	19			100	0.62	8.5	63	83	$1
14 BAL *	10	2	1	86	86	3.48	3.64	1.30	640	776	543	5.6	3.3	9.1	2.7	58%	13%	36	19	45	32%	75%	8%	0	23			50	0.82	2.8	94	113	$4
1st Half	4	1	1	48	53	4.15	4.53	1.51	697	976	531	6.7	3.5	10.0	2.9	54%	14%	43	15	43	38%	73%	7%	0	31			50	0.48	-2.4	100	120	$0
2nd Half	6	1	0	38	33	2.63	3.89	1.04	602	663	551	4.7	3.1	7.9	2.5	60%	12%	32	22	46	23%	80%	9%	0	19			0	0.97	5.2	68	81	$10
15 Proj	7	3	0	80	79	3.20	3.56	1.29	690	692	688	4.8	3.4	8.9	2.6	56%	11%	37	21	43	31%	78%	8%	0						5.3	82	98	$4

Bradley,Archie

Age: 22	Th: R	Role SP	Health B	LIMA Plan D+
Ht: 6' 4"	Wt: 225	Type Pwr	PT/Exp F	Rand Var +1
			Consist A	MM 1201

April elbow injury cost him first two months of the season and prevented him from making his MLB debut in 2014. And now some whispers about lack of progress, especially with regard to fastball command and walk rate. But still a pup, and the ceiling remains high. Just don't expect him to get there right away.

Yr Tm	W	L	Sv	IP	K	ERA	xERA	WHIP	oOPS	vL	vR	BF/G	Ctl	Dom	Cmd	FpK	SwK	G	L	F	H%	S%	hr/f	GS	APC	DOM%	DIS%	Sv%	LI	RAR	BPV	BPX	R$
10																																	
11																																	
12																																	
13 aa	12	5	0	123	103	2.60	3.41	1.38				24.7	4.4	7.5	1.7						30%	82%								19.3	74	97	$9
14 a/a	3	7	0	79	59	4.76	3.82	1.53				20.2	5.0	6.7	1.3						31%	66%								-9.9	65	78	-$7
1st Half	1	4	0	28	21	5.11	4.21	1.62				21.0	4.7	6.5	1.4						34%	65%								-4.8	67	80	-$10
2nd Half	2	3	0	51	38	4.57	3.61	1.47				19.8	5.2	6.8	1.3						29%	67%								-5.2	65	77	-$5
15 Proj	6	7	0	102	79	3.94	4.22	1.46				21.7	4.6	7.0	1.5	60%	8%	45	19	36	31%	72%	3%	17						-2.5	25	29	-$1

Breslow,Craig

Age: 34	Th: L	Role RP	Health D	LIMA Plan D+
Ht: 6' 1"	Wt: 190	Type	PT/Exp D	Rand Var +3
			Consist B	MM 1100

If he did, in fact, sell his soul in order to scrape that 1.81 ERA out of a 39 BPV in 2013, the terms apparently called for immediate payment. 2nd half showed some skills recovery, but if he doesn't quickly re-establish some effectiveness against LH batters, he's going to be out of work.

Yr Tm	W	L	Sv	IP	K	ERA	xERA	WHIP	oOPS	vL	vR	BF/G	Ctl	Dom	Cmd	FpK	SwK	G	L	F	H%	S%	hr/f	GS	APC	DOM%	DIS%	Sv%	LI	RAR	BPV	BPX	R$
10 OAK	4	4	5	75	71	3.01	4.13	1.10	620	586	637	4.1	3.5	8.6	2.4	55%	11%	30	15	56	24%	78%	8%	0	16			71	1.03	9.8	68	109	$8
11 OAK	0	2	0	59	44	3.79	4.44	1.52	773	866	714	3.9	3.2	6.7	2.1	58%	10%	38	20	41	35%	76%	5%	0	15			0	0.78	1.1	50	75	-$4
12 2 TM	3	0	0	63	61	2.70	3.66	1.17	645	597	683	4.1	3.1	8.7	2.8	58%	12%	45	19	36	29%	80%	8%	0	17			0	0.83	10.3	95	123	$4
13 BOS	5	2	0	60	33	1.81	4.17	1.12	635	704	581	3.9	2.7	5.0	1.8	58%	9%	45	21	34	25%	86%	5%	0	14			0	1.14	15.1	39	51	$5
14 BOS	2	4	1	54	37	5.96	5.39	1.86	887	838	927	4.3	4.6	6.1	1.3	52%	7%	37	23	40	36%	70%	11%	0	16			50	0.69	-14.9	0	0	-$11
1st Half	2	2	0	28	18	4.23	5.92	1.81	759	733	781	4.7	6.5	5.9	0.9	51%	7%	38	22	40	32%	77%	6%	0	18			0	0.59	-1.7	-54	-65	-$8
2nd Half	0	2	1	27	19	7.76	4.93	1.91	1003	934	1057	4.0	2.7	6.4	2.4	53%	8%	36	24	40	40%	62%	15%	0	15			100	0.78	-13.2	56	67	-$14
15 Proj	3	3	0	58	41	4.37	4.31	1.52	793	778	805	4.0	3.6	6.4	1.8	55%	9%	40	22	39	32%	74%	9%	0						-4.5	36	43	-$4

Britton,Zach

Age: 27	Th: L	Role RP	Health C	LIMA Plan D+
Ht: 6' 3"	Wt: 195	Type xGB	PT/Exp C	Rand Var -5
			Consist F	MM 5230

Seized the closer gig in June and didn't look back. Sustainable? FpK tells us that the Ctl gains might be shaky, but adding 3.5 mph to fastball helped spike SwK and moved GB% to "no, that's not a typo" level. Some regression inevitable, and Dom keeps him out of the elite tier of closers. But he's in the club now.

Yr Tm	W	L	Sv	IP	K	ERA	xERA	WHIP	oOPS	vL	vR	BF/G	Ctl	Dom	Cmd	FpK	SwK	G	L	F	H%	S%	hr/f	GS	APC	DOM%	DIS%	Sv%	LI	RAR	BPV	BPX	R$
10 a/a	10	7	0	153	103	3.28	3.91	1.37				23.8	2.9	6.0	2.1						32%	77%								15.1	65	105	$7
11 BAL *	11	14	0	171	112	4.70	4.44	1.45	735	698	748	22.8	3.4	5.9	1.7	53%	7%	53	19	28	31%	68%	9%	28	90	36%	21%			-16.0	46	70	-$3
12 BAL *	10	5	0	124	92	5.34	4.77	1.53	756	714	778	23.4	4.2	6.7	1.6	51%	10%	61	16	23	32%	66%	14%	11	89	45%	45%	0	0.73	-20.2	45	59	-$9
13 BAL *	8	8	0	143	77	5.48	5.89	1.81	837	849	832	24.6	4.2	4.8	1.1	54%	7%	58	20	22	36%	69%	13%	7	83	14%	43%	0	0.75	-28.5	23	31	-$19
14 BAL	3	2	37	76	62	1.65	2.44	0.90	500	386	559	4.0	2.7	7.3	2.7	55%	13%	75	13	12	22%	85%	17%	0	15			90	1.41	19.7	111	133	$24
1st Half	3	1	10	41	31	1.52	2.47	0.94	513	406	582	4.6	2.8	6.8	2.4	57%	13%	79	12	9	22%	86%	20%	0	17			83	1.42	11.3	102	121	$21
2nd Half	0	1	27	35	31	1.80	2.42	0.86	485	352	535	3.5	2.6	8.0	3.1	53%	14%	71	14	15	21%	82%	15%	0	13			93	1.40	8.4	123	147	$29
15 Proj	3	3	35	70	55	3.02	2.95	1.24	657	593	687	7.1	3.1	7.1	2.3	54%	10%	69	15	16	29%	77%	15%	0						6.2	91	109	$17

RAY MURPHY

Brothers,Rex

Age: 27	Th: L	Role RP	Health A	LIMA Plan C	
Ht: 6' 0"	Wt: 210	Type Pwr	PT/Exp C	Rand Var +4	
			Consist B	MM 3511	

Cherry-picking 4 outings in June, Aug and Sept., he threw 2/3 IP and allowed 13 ER. Remove those and his ERA drops to 3.56. Of course, we can't randomly ignore 4 blow-ups, but it's tough to explain this type of disaster season sans injury. There will be some recovery, but if still in Coors, it will be tougher.

Yr	Tm	W	L	Sv	IP	K	ERA	xERA	WHIP	oOPS	vL	vR	BF/G	Ctl	Dom	Cmd	FpK	SwK	G	L	F	H%	S%	hr/f	GS	APC	DOM%	DIS%	Sv%	LI	RAR	BPV	BPX	R$
10	aa	2	1	4	23	21	5.15	3.96	1.53				4.2	7.2	8.4	1.2						25%	68%								-3.0	57	92	-$1
11	COL *	4	4	1	69	94	2.74	3.69	1.38	644	594	673	4.0	4.3	12.3	2.9	57%	12%	46	16	37	36%	83%	12%	0	15			20	1.01	10.2	118	177	$4
12	COL	8	2	0	68	83	3.86	3.55	1.48	732	587	832	3.9	4.9	11.0	2.2	52%	15%	47	23	30	35%	75%	10%	0	15			0	1.09	1.3	91	118	$0
13	COL	2	1	19	67	76	1.74	3.49	1.29	618	463	686	3.9	4.8	10.2	2.1	58%	13%	49	19	33	29%	90%	9%	0	16			90	1.20	17.7	80	104	$12
14	COL	4	6	0	56	55	5.59	4.83	1.85	825	908	761	3.7	6.2	8.8	1.4	59%	11%	39	30	31	36%	71%	13%	0	15			0	1.20	-12.9	7	8	-$9
1st Half		3	4	0	34	33	4.50	4.30	1.44	697	767	644	3.8	5.6	8.7	1.6	62%	10%	39	27	34	28%	70%	10%	0	15			0	1.12	-3.2	24	29	-$5
2nd Half		1	2	0	22	22	7.25	5.67	2.46	980	1081	903	3.6	7.3	8.9	1.2	56%	12%	39	34	28	45%	73%	18%	0	15			0	1.29	-9.7	-20	-23	-$16
15	**Proj**	**4**	**5**	**5**	**73**	**79**	**3.99**	**3.65**	**1.50**	**707**	**719**	**699**	**3.5**	**5.0**	**9.8**	**2.0**	**57%**	**12%**	**43**	**23**	**34**	**33%**	**76%**	**12%**	**0**						**-2.2**	**62**	**74**	**$0**

Broxton,Jonathan

Age: 31	Th: R	Role RP	Health F	LIMA Plan B	
Ht: 6' 4"	Wt: 295	Type Pwr	PT/Exp C	Rand Var -5	
			Consist A	MM 3210	

A vintage season for this once-elite closer means he's back, right? Not so fast. xERA and H%/S% combo say it was less about skill and more about positive randomness. Strong SwK history shows that the 2H Dom may stick, but health grade reminds us that injury could quickly derail any quest for a closer role.

Yr	Tm	W	L	Sv	IP	K	ERA	xERA	WHIP	oOPS	vL	vR	BF/G	Ctl	Dom	Cmd	FpK	SwK	G	L	F	H%	S%	hr/f	GS	APC	DOM%	DIS%	Sv%	LI	RAR	BPV	BPX	R$
10	LA	5	6	22	62	73	4.04	3.32	1.48	718	626	794	4.2	4.0	10.5	2.6	60%	12%	47	21	32	37%	73%	8%	0	17			76	1.31	0.3	106	171	$9
11	LA	1	2	7	13	10	5.68	5.21	1.89	840	670	951	4.4	6.4	7.1	1.1	48%	9%	42	33	26	34%	73%	18%	0	18			88	1.04	-2.7	-25	-37	-$2
12	2 TM	4	5	27	58	45	2.48	3.55	1.26	676	628	715	4.0	2.6	7.0	2.6	57%	9%	54	22	24	31%	80%	5%	0	16			82	1.33	11.0	86	113	$14
13	CIN	2	2	0	31	25	4.11	4.09	1.27	712	779	656	3.9	3.5	7.3	2.1	53%	13%	46	16	37	27%	71%	12%	0	15			0	1.24	-0.9	61	79	-$3
14	2 NL	4	3	7	59	49	2.30	3.74	1.02	569	564	572	3.7	2.9	7.5	2.6	61%	11%	46	10	44	24%	80%	6%	0	15			47	1.34	10.4	81	96	$8
1st Half		4	0	5	26	18	0.68	4.13	0.80	378	476	319	3.6	3.8	6.2	1.6	63%	11%	42	8	50	15%	90%	0%	0	14			71	1.41	9.9	30	35	$14
2nd Half		0	3	2	32	31	3.62	3.43	1.21	699	619	749	3.8	2.2	8.6	3.9	60%	11%	48	12	40	31%	74%	11%	0	15			25	1.28	0.5	122	145	$3
15	**Proj**	**4**	**4**	**3**	**58**	**50**	**3.03**	**3.45**	**1.18**	**645**	**643**	**646**	**3.8**	**3.1**	**7.8**	**2.5**	**58%**	**11%**	**47**	**15**	**38**	**28%**	**77%**	**8%**	**0**						**5.1**	**81**	**97**	**$4**

Buchanan,David

Age: 26	Th: R	Role SP	Health A	LIMA Plan D+	
Ht: 6' 3"	Wt: 200	Type Con GB	PT/Exp D	Rand Var 0	
			Consist A	MM 2003	

6-8, 3.75 ERA in 118 IP at PHI. Seemingly decent debut, but xERA isn't convinced. Uninspiring FpK suggests 2nd half Ctl gains were a mirage. GB% profile limits some risk, though soft-tossing Dom will cap his upside. Sigh... we're sugar-coating this. He is a 23rd round pick in a deep NL-only league.

Yr	Tm	W	L	Sv	IP	K	ERA	xERA	WHIP	oOPS	vL	vR	BF/G	Ctl	Dom	Cmd	FpK	SwK	G	L	F	H%	S%	hr/f	GS	APC	DOM%	DIS%	Sv%	LI	RAR	BPV	BPX	R$
10																																		
11																																		
12	aa	3	5	0	72	34	4.38	4.72	1.44				25.7	2.8	4.3	1.5						30%	71%								-3.2	27	35	-$5
13	a/a	10	13	0	170	91	5.07	5.06	1.51				26.2	2.8	4.8	1.7						32%	68%								-25.2	30	40	-$11
14	PHI *	12	10	0	175	109	4.04	4.59	1.44	721	592	820	23.2	2.8	5.6	2.0	57%	8%	51	19	30	32%	73%	11%	20	91	50%	20%			-6.5	50	60	-$2
1st Half		9	5	0	87	57	4.78	5.33	1.56	790	697	854	22.4	3.4	5.9	1.7	57%	9%	47	22	31	33%	72%	15%	8	94	25%	13%			-11.1	35	42	-$6
2nd Half		3	5	0	88	52	3.31	3.86	1.32	674	529	795	24.2	2.2	5.4	2.5	56%	8%	53	18	29	31%	75%	7%	12	89	67%	25%			4.7	69	82	$1
15	**Proj**	**9**	**12**	**0**	**167**	**95**	**4.37**	**4.03**	**1.43**	**772**	**642**	**873**	**24.5**	**2.7**	**5.1**	**1.9**	**57%**	**8%**	**51**	**19**	**30**	**31%**	**71%**	**9%**	**29**						**-13.0**	**47**	**56**	**-$3**

Buchholz,Clay

Age: 30	Th: R	Role SP	Health F	LIMA Plan C	
Ht: 6' 3"	Wt: 190	Type	PT/Exp A	Rand Var +4	
			Consist B	MM 3205	

Exhibit A on how swings in luck can wreak havoc on surface stats. ERA tripled from 2013 despite just a minor Dom fade, while other skills held steady. Knee injury in May likely played a role in 1st half struggles, and though that reminds us of health risk, 2nd half xERA, BPV hint at a return to success.

Yr	Tm	W	L	Sv	IP	K	ERA	xERA	WHIP	oOPS	vL	vR	BF/G	Ctl	Dom	Cmd	FpK	SwK	G	L	F	H%	S%	hr/f	GS	APC	DOM%	DIS%	Sv%	LI	RAR	BPV	BPX	R$
10	BOS	17	7	0	174	120	2.33	3.93	1.20	615	651	571	25.4	3.5	6.2	1.8	58%	10%	51	18	32	26%	82%	6%	28	100	43%	21%			37.4	47	76	$21
11	BOS	6	3	0	83	60	3.48	4.16	1.29	706	706	706	25.2	3.4	6.5	1.9	56%	9%	51	11	39	28%	77%	10%	14	97	43%	21%			4.7	55	83	$3
12	BOS	11	8	0	189	129	4.56	4.27	1.33	757	761	751	27.7	3.0	6.1	2.0	63%	9%	48	20	33	29%	69%	13%	29	100	52%	21%			-12.8	54	71	$0
13	BOS	12	1	0	108	96	1.74	3.31	1.02	546	536	560	26.0	3.0	8.0	2.7	60%	10%	48	21	32	25%	84%	5%	16	102	69%	0%			28.3	89	116	$18
14	BOS	8	11	0	170	132	5.34	3.99	1.39	751	793	696	26.3	2.9	7.0	2.4	60%	9%	47	19	34	32%	62%	9%	28	98	57%	21%			-33.5	74	88	-$9
1st Half		3	4	0	57	41	6.75	5.10	1.85	901	859	957	25.0	3.8	6.4	1.7	61%	8%	40	20	40	37%	66%	12%	11	91	36%	45%			-21.3	32	38	-$27
2nd Half		5	7	0	113	91	4.62	3.45	1.15	662	752	549	27.2	2.4	7.2	3.0	60%	9%	51	18	31	29%	59%	7%	17	102	71%	6%			-12.2	95	113	$0
15	**Proj**	**13**	**8**	**0**	**189**	**147**	**3.77**	**3.64**	**1.29**	**704**	**722**	**682**	**25.7**	**3.0**	**7.0**	**2.3**	**60%**	**9%**	**47**	**19**	**34**	**30%**	**73%**	**9%**	**30**						**-0.6**	**70**	**84**	**$8**

Buehrle,Mark

Age: 36	Th: L	Role SP	Health A	LIMA Plan B+	
Ht: 6' 2"	Wt: 240	Type Con	PT/Exp A	Rand Var -2	
			Consist A	MM 2005	

Returned to his normal 13 wins after one-year hiatus, but it was a windy road to get there. Fortunate H%/S% drove 1st half success, and it completely flipped down the stretch. Consistent xERA says not much has changed the past few years, so expect some ERA pullback.

Yr	Tm	W	L	Sv	IP	K	ERA	xERA	WHIP	oOPS	vL	vR	BF/G	Ctl	Dom	Cmd	FpK	SwK	G	L	F	H%	S%	hr/f	GS	APC	DOM%	DIS%	Sv%	LI	RAR	BPV	BPX	R$
10	CHW	13	13	0	210	99	4.28	4.59	1.40	751	749	751	27.2	2.1	4.2	2.0	62%	6%	46	16	38	32%	70%	6%	33	100	33%	15%			-5.2	44	71	$2
11	CHW	13	9	0	205	109	3.59	4.22	1.30	728	683	746	27.7	2.0	4.8	2.4	56%	7%	45	20	35	30%	75%	9%	31	101	45%	10%			8.8	56	84	$8
12	MIA	13	13	0	202	125	3.74	4.19	1.17	710	645	731	26.7	1.8	5.6	3.1	61%	8%	41	22	36	28%	73%	11%	31	99	55%	13%			7.0	71	93	$13
13	TOR	12	10	0	204	139	4.15	4.11	1.35	754	724	764	26.5	2.3	6.1	2.7	59%	7%	45	21	34	31%	72%	11%	33	100	45%	18%			-7.2	73	95	$2
14	TOR	13	10	0	202	119	3.39	4.21	1.36	743	718	752	26.8	2.0	5.3	2.6	59%	6%	44	23	34	32%	76%	7%	32	96	38%	13%			8.8	62	74	$5
1st Half		10	5	0	115	67	2.50	4.16	1.21	690	686	691	27.8	2.3	5.2	2.2	58%	6%	43	23	34	28%	82%	6%	17	102	47%	6%			17.7	52	62	$18
2nd Half		3	5	0	87	52	4.57	4.28	1.55	808	764	822	25.6	1.7	5.4	3.3	60%	7%	45	22	34	37%	71%	7%	15	90	27%	20%			-8.9	75	89	-$13
15	**Proj**	**11**	**10**	**0**	**189**	**115**	**3.86**	**3.86**	**1.33**	**749**	**716**	**760**	**25.9**	**2.0**	**5.5**	**2.7**	**59%**	**7%**	**44**	**21**	**35**	**31%**	**74%**	**9%**	**30**						**-2.8**	**67**	**79**	**$4**

Bueno,Francisley

Age: 34	Th: L	Role RP	Health D	LIMA Plan D+	
Ht: 5' 11"	Wt: 205	Type Con FB	PT/Exp D	Rand Var 0	
			Consist C	MM 1000	

Career minor-leaguer finally got extended look as a situational lefty, but skills cast doubt he can progress beyond that. Pinpoint Ctl was the highlight, though FpK doesn't support such an elite level. Soft-tossing Dom, limited role, and age all point to continued irrelevance.

Yr	Tm	W	L	Sv	IP	K	ERA	xERA	WHIP	oOPS	vL	vR	BF/G	Ctl	Dom	Cmd	FpK	SwK	G	L	F	H%	S%	hr/f	GS	APC	DOM%	DIS%	Sv%	LI	RAR	BPV	BPX	R$
10																																		
11																																		
12	KC *	2	5	6	73	45	2.90	3.32	1.20	568	616	501	5.5	2.2	5.6	2.5	62%	5%	57	16	28	29%	78%	0%	0	12			60	1.13	10.0	72	94	$5
13	KC *	4	3	1	76	44	3.35	4.91	1.58	379	357	393	7.8	3.6	5.3	1.5	48%	10%	52	5	43	33%	80%	0%	0	14			17	1.35	4.8	38	49	-$3
14	KC	0	0	0	32	20	4.18	4.33	1.33	741	505	960	4.7	1.9	5.6	2.9	59%	10%	45	19	37	32%	70%	7%	0	16			0	0.79	-1.7	71	84	-$4
1st Half		0	0	0	7	3	1.29	4.27	1.29	610	444	871	3.3	1.3	3.9	3.0	67%	10%	54	15	31	32%	89%	0%	0	10			0	0.73	2.1	67	79	-$4
2nd Half		0	0	0	25	17	4.97	4.35	1.34	778	529	978	5.3	2.1	6.0	2.8	57%	10%	42	20	38	31%	65%	9%	0	19			0	0.82	-3.9	71	85	-$3
15	**Proj**	**1**	**2**	**0**	**44**	**27**	**4.17**	**4.11**	**1.34**	**685**	**462**	**865**	**5.8**	**2.5**	**5.6**	**2.2**	**57%**	**10%**	**42**	**20**	**38**	**31%**	**70%**	**6%**	**0**						**-2.3**	**53**	**63**	**-$3**

Bumgarner,Madison

Age: 25	Th: L	Role SP	Health A	LIMA Plan C	
Ht: 6' 5"	Wt: 235	Type Pwr	PT/Exp A	Rand Var 0	
			Consist A	MM 5305	

Pushed the envelope even further as SwK continued its steady ascent, which brought Dom to record high. Ctl returned to elite territoy, and FpK gains suggest they will stick. Four straight years of 110+ BPV, 200+ IP as he enters peak makes him Elite. You can have Kershaw, Felix in Rounds 1-2; I'll gladly take him in Round 4.

Yr	Tm	W	L	Sv	IP	K	ERA	xERA	WHIP	oOPS	vL	vR	BF/G	Ctl	Dom	Cmd	FpK	SwK	G	L	F	H%	S%	hr/f	GS	APC	DOM%	DIS%	Sv%	LI	RAR	BPV	BPX	R$
10	SF *	14	7	0	194	137	3.12	4.12	1.33	732	678	751	25.1	2.1	6.4	3.0	60%	8%	45	17	38	32%	79%	8%	18	96	50%	22%			23.0	78	126	$13
11	SF	13	13	0	205	191	3.21	3.25	1.21	670	602	685	25.6	2.0	8.4	4.2	62%	10%	46	21	33	33%	74%	6%	33	97	70%	15%			18.5	121	181	$17
12	SF	16	11	0	208	191	3.37	3.44	1.11	670	581	694	26.5	2.1	8.3	3.9	62%	10%	48	19	33	29%	74%	12%	32	102	66%	13%			16.6	117	153	$23
13	SF	13	9	0	201	199	2.77	3.25	1.03	577	487	602	25.9	2.8	8.9	3.2	60%	11%	47	18	35	26%	76%	8%	31	103	81%	6%			27.2	110	144	$26
14	SF	18	10	0	217	219	2.98	3.08	1.09	653	539	684	26.5	1.8	9.1	5.1	66%	12%	44	20	36	31%	76%	10%	33	102	67%	12%			20.4	137	163	$23
1st Half		9	5	0	109	114	2.90	3.05	1.17	660	587	682	26.4	2.2	9.4	4.4	64%	12%	48	19	33	33%	77%	8%	17	102	65%	12%			11.3	138	164	$22
2nd Half		9	5	0	109	105	3.06	3.11	1.01	645	478	685	26.6	1.4	8.7	6.2	70%	12%	41	20	39	28%	75%	11%	16	102	69%	13%			9.1	137	164	$24
15	**Proj**	**17**	**8**	**0**	**203**	**196**	**2.97**	**2.96**	**1.09**	**641**	**539**	**669**	**25.5**	**2.1**	**8.7**	**4.2**	**64%**	**11%**	**45**	**19**	**36**	**29%**	**76%**	**10%**	**31**						**19.3**	**124**	**148**	**$25**

RYAN BLOOMFIELD

Bundy,Dylan

Age: 22 | Th: R | Role: SP | Ht: 6' 1" | Wt: 195 | Type: Pwr
Health: F | PT/Exp: F | Consist: F
LIMA Plan: D+ | Rand Var: 0 | MM: 2201

Elite prospect will be 21 months removed from Tommy John surgery by Opening Day. His 4.78 ERA and 15/13 K/BB over six starts in High-A suggest the road back will have plenty of obstacles. At 22, still a keeper league gem, but don't expect to see him until later in the season.

Yr	Tm	W	L	Sv	IP	K	ERA	xERA	WHIP	oOPS	vL	vR	BF/G	Ctl	Dom	Cmd	FpK	SwK	G	L	F	H%	S%	hr/f	GS	APC	DOM%	DIS%	Sv%	LI	RAR	BPV	BPX	R$
10																																		
11																																		
12	BAL *	2	0	0	18	11	3.40	3.57	1.37	533	1000	250	15.4	4.3	5.6	1.3	50%	10%	20	0	80	27%	76%	0%	0	15			0	0.40	1.4	51	66	-$3
13																																		
14																																		
1st Half																																		
2nd Half																																		
15	**Proj**	**4**	**2**	**0**	**73**	**60**	**4.10**	**3.92**	**1.42**				**20.5**	**3.5**	**7.4**	**2.1**	**59%**	**9%**	**40**	**22**	**38**	**32%**	**74%**	**10%**	**27**						**-3.2**	**58**	**69**	**-$2**

Burnett,A.J.

Age: 38 | Th: R | Role: SP | Ht: 6' 4" | Wt: 225 | Type: Pwr GB
Health: D | PT/Exp: A | Consist: B
LIMA Plan: C | Rand Var: +1 | MM: 4305

Pitched through an inguinal hernia suffered in April, and skills took a dive. FpK shows he fell behind too often, and once-elite Dom/GB% combo took a hit as well. Off-season surgery will aid recovery, and xERA predicts a mild rebound, but a return to '12-'13 levels at this age is a stretch.

Yr	Tm	W	L	Sv	IP	K	ERA	xERA	WHIP	oOPS	vL	vR	BF/G	Ctl	Dom	Cmd	FpK	SwK	G	L	F	H%	S%	hr/f	GS	APC	DOM%	DIS%	Sv%	LI	RAR	BPV	BPX	R$
10	NYY	10	15	0	187	145	5.26	4.30	1.51	824	820	827	25.1	3.8	7.0	1.9	56%	8%	45	18	37	32%	67%	12%	33	94	45%	33%			-27.1	47	77	-$6
11	NYY	11	11	0	190	173	5.15	3.84	1.43	802	777	831	25.4	3.9	8.2	2.1	57%	10%	49	18	32	30%	68%	17%	32	98	47%	16%	0	0.76	-28.4	68	103	-$5
12	PIT	16	10	0	202	180	3.51	3.38	1.24	668	695	641	27.5	2.8	8.0	2.9	61%	10%	57	19	24	30%	74%	13%	31	98	55%	6%			12.5	105	137	$16
13	PIT	10	11	0	191	209	3.30	2.92	1.21	639	735	547	26.7	3.2	9.8	3.1	62%	11%	57	19	24	32%	73%	9%	30	101	70%	10%			13.4	127	166	$14
14	PHI	8	18	0	214	190	4.59	3.81	1.41	748	785	713	27.5	4.0	8.0	2.0	56%	9%	51	21	29	31%	68%	11%	34	102	59%	9%			-22.4	64	76	-$6
1st Half		5	7	0	111	85	3.89	3.99	1.34	730	837	637	28.0	3.8	6.9	1.8	55%	8%	49	22	29	29%	72%	9%	17	104	47%	6%			-2.1	46	57	$0
2nd Half		3	11	0	103	105	5.35	3.61	1.48	766	733	796	27.0	4.3	9.2	2.1	58%	11%	53	18	28	33%	65%	13%	17	100	71%	12%			-20.3	81	97	-$12
15	**Proj**	**9**	**13**	**0**	**181**	**172**	**3.96**	**3.27**	**1.33**	**696**	**733**	**660**	**25.9**	**3.6**	**8.6**	**2.4**	**59%**	**10%**	**53**	**19**	**27**	**31%**	**71%**	**10%**	**29**						**-4.8**	**87**	**104**	**$5**

Burton,Jared

Age: 34 | Th: R | Role: RP | Ht: 6' 5" | Wt: 225 | Type: Pwr FB
Health: D | PT/Exp: C | Consist: B
LIMA Plan: C | Rand Var: 0 | MM: 2210

Posted career-worst ERA, yet was rewarded with closer role in September. Skills collapse say we may not see him there again; plummeting Dom was the lowlight, which sent Cmd into a tailspin, and xERA took a similar tumble. Health, age, BPV trend all point toward mediocrity.

Yr	Tm	W	L	Sv	IP	K	ERA	xERA	WHIP	oOPS	vL	vR	BF/G	Ctl	Dom	Cmd	FpK	SwK	G	L	F	H%	S%	hr/f	GS	APC	DOM%	DIS%	Sv%	LI	RAR	BPV	BPX	R$
10	CIN *	3	2	4	41	27	3.19	4.09	1.35	0	0	0	4.7	4.0	5.8	1.4	70%	14%	44	11	44	26%	82%	0%	0	11			67	0.47	4.5	37	60	$2
11	CIN	0	0	0	5	3	3.86	5.96	1.93	988	1625	670	3.8	5.8	5.8	1.0	52%	9%	38	19	44	33%	88%	14%	0	16			0	0.46	0.0	-36	-54	-$4
12	MIN	3	2	5	62	55	2.18	3.40	0.92	549	748	421	3.8	2.3	8.0	3.4	64%	14%	49	17	35	23%	81%	9%	0	15			56	1.13	14.1	108	141	$10
13	MIN	2	9	2	66	61	3.82	3.80	1.26	688	713	665	4.0	3.0	8.3	2.8	64%	13%	41	20	39	31%	71%	8%	0	15			29	1.14	0.4	88	114	$0
14	MIN	3	5	3	64	46	4.36	4.45	1.30	681	595	740	4.0	3.5	6.5	1.8	58%	12%	38	21	41	28%	68%	8%	0	15			75	1.12	-4.9	38	45	-$1
1st Half		1	2	1	33	25	5.45	4.93	1.42	751	772	732	4.1	4.1	6.8	1.7	59%	11%	33	18	49	28%	64%	10%	0	15			100	1.00	-7.0	24	28	-$6
2nd Half		2	3	2	31	21	3.19	3.93	1.16	602	382	745	3.8	2.9	6.1	2.1	58%	13%	44	24	32	27%	71%	3%	0	15			67	1.23	2.1	53	64	$4
15	**Proj**	**3**	**6**	**3**	**65**	**51**	**4.07**	**3.85**	**1.28**	**715**	**695**	**729**	**3.9**	**3.2**	**7.1**	**2.2**	**61%**	**13%**	**40**	**20**	**40**	**28%**	**71%**	**10%**	**0**						**-2.7**	**59**	**70**	**$0**

Butler,Eddie

Age: 24 | Th: R | Role: SP | Ht: 6' 2" | Wt: 180 | Type: Con
Health: C | PT/Exp: F | Consist: F
LIMA Plan: D | Rand Var: 0 | MM: 0001

1-1, 6.75 ERA in 16 IP at COL. A considerable step back as shoulder woes cost him two months. Dom collapse was likely related, and it sent Cmd into downward spiral. Plus velocity and GB% make him worth monitoring, but injury concerns, home park suggest you avoid for now.

Yr	Tm	W	L	Sv	IP	K	ERA	xERA	WHIP	oOPS	vL	vR	BF/G	Ctl	Dom	Cmd	FpK	SwK	G	L	F	H%	S%	hr/f	GS	APC	DOM%	DIS%	Sv%	LI	RAR	BPV	BPX	R$
10																																		
11																																		
12																																		
13	aa	1	0	0	28	20	0.90	0.70	0.80				16.7	2.1	6.5	3.2						21%	88%								10.1	127	165	$2
14	COL *	7	11	0	129	56	4.91	5.08	1.50	973	1310	760	25.4	2.9	3.9	1.3	49%	5%	52	25	23	31%	69%	13%	3	86	0%	67%			-18.6	17	20	-$9
1st Half		4	5	0	74	33	3.89	4.52	1.48	1104	1200	1033	26.5	2.8	4.1	1.4	48%	5%	52	26	22	32%	74%	0%	1	87	0%	100%			-1.4	36	43	-$5
2nd Half		3	6	0	55	22	6.73	6.34	1.62	893	1375	593	24.6	3.3	3.6	1.1	49%	5%	51	24	24	31%	61%	20%	2	86	0%	50%			-20.4	-15	-17	-$16
15	**Proj**	**5**	**8**	**0**	**87**	**46**	**5.04**	**5.58**	**1.55**				**25.2**	**3.0**	**4.8**	**1.6**	**0%**	**0%**				**32%**	**70%**		**15**						**-13.9**	**19**	**23**	**-$8**

Cahill,Trevor

Age: 27 | Th: R | Role: RP | Ht: 6' 4" | Wt: 220 | Type: Pwr GB
Health: C | PT/Exp: B | Consist: B
LIMA Plan: D+ | Rand Var: +2 | MM: 2201

3-12, 5.61 ERA in 111 IP at ARI. Dreadful season included bullpen demotion, minor league stint, and career-high ERA. Change in approach didn't help, as once-elite GB% went away. Dom came at the expense of Ctl, which FpK suggests may not recover. Upcoming H%/S% regression won't be enough to save him.

Yr	Tm	W	L	Sv	IP	K	ERA	xERA	WHIP	oOPS	vL	vR	BF/G	Ctl	Dom	Cmd	FpK	SwK	G	L	F	H%	S%	hr/f	GS	APC	DOM%	DIS%	Sv%	LI	RAR	BPV	BPX	R$
10	OAK	18	8	0	197	118	2.97	3.76	1.11	619	630	605	26.1	2.9	5.4	1.9	57%	6%	56	15	29	24%	77%	11%	30	101	47%	10%			26.8	53	86	$22
11	OAK	12	14	0	208	147	4.16	3.88	1.43	738	754	720	26.5	3.6	6.4	1.8	57%	8%	56	19	25	31%	72%	12%	34	100	47%	26%			-5.6	53	79	$1
12	ARI	13	12	0	200	156	3.78	3.60	1.29	706	696	718	26.2	3.3	7.0	2.1	63%	10%	61	16	23	29%	72%	12%	32	99	59%	19%			5.8	75	98	$9
13	ARI *	8	12	0	163	112	4.18	4.16	1.43	745	769	719	23.9	4.0	6.2	1.5	60%	8%	56	20	24	29%	72%	12%	25	91	28%	16%	0	0.85	-6.3	47	61	-$3
14	ARI *	5	14	1	139	126	5.21	4.76	1.58	791	921	662	16.1	4.8	8.2	1.7	57%	11%	48	24	27	33%	67%	10%	17	60	18%	47%	50	0.67	-25.2	60	72	-$11
1st Half		1	7	1	54	55	5.52	5.58	1.67	815	987	684	11.1	5.1	9.1	1.8	54%	10%	48	23	29	35%	69%	12%	4	41	0%	75%	50	0.61	-11.9	51	61	-$15
2nd Half		4	7	0	85	71	5.01	4.23	1.53	777	888	647	23.0	4.6	7.6	1.6	59%	11%	49	25	26	33%	66%	9%	13	88	23%	38%			-13.3	66	79	-$9
15	**Proj**	**5**	**9**	**0**	**103**	**83**	**4.56**	**3.86**	**1.47**	**752**	**819**	**681**	**19.3**	**4.2**	**7.3**	**1.7**	**58%**	**10%**	**50**	**22**	**28**	**31%**	**70%**	**11%**	**21**						**-10.4**	**45**	**53**	**-$4**

Cain,Matt

Age: 30 | Th: R | Role: SP | Ht: 6' 3" | Wt: 230 | Type: Pwr
Health: F | PT/Exp: A | Consist: A
LIMA Plan: C | Rand Var: 0 | MM: 3203

Forgettable season ended with surgeries to ankle and elbow. The effects could be seen in career-low Dom, which makes Ctl erosion look even worse. If, in fact, his elbow woes can be corrected by surgery, there is plenty of upside for a potential rebound. But another 200 IP, sub-3.00 ERA season seems like a long shot.

Yr	Tm	W	L	Sv	IP	K	ERA	xERA	WHIP	oOPS	vL	vR	BF/G	Ctl	Dom	Cmd	FpK	SwK	G	L	F	H%	S%	hr/f	GS	APC	DOM%	DIS%	Sv%	LI	RAR	BPV	BPX	R$
10	SF	13	11	0	223	177	3.14	3.95	1.08	646	663	629	27.2	2.5	7.1	2.9	59%	9%	36	17	47	26%	75%	7%	33	106	67%	6%			25.8	76	123	$23
11	SF	12	11	0	222	179	2.88	3.71	1.08	597	523	674	27.5	2.6	7.3	2.8	61%	10%	42	19	39	27%	73%	4%	33	106	73%	3%			29.0	82	123	$24
12	SF	16	5	0	219	193	2.79	3.71	1.04	635	711	563	27.4	2.1	7.9	3.8	62%	10%	37	21	42	27%	77%	8%	32	105	63%	0%			33.1	101	132	$32
13	SF	8	10	0	184	158	4.00	3.87	1.16	678	644	704	25.3	2.7	7.7	2.9	63%	9%	38	22	40	27%	69%	11%	30	97	53%	13%			-3.1	82	107	$8
14	SF	2	7	0	90	70	4.18	3.96	1.25	725	737	713	24.9	3.2	7.0	2.2	62%	9%	45	19	36	27%	71%	14%	15	96	53%	13%			-4.9	62	74	-$2
1st Half		1	6	0	78	60	4.38	3.96	1.23	718	641	785	24.8	3.1	6.9	2.2	62%	9%	45	18	37	27%	68%	13%	13	95	46%	15%			-6.2	64	76	-$1
2nd Half		1	1	0	12	10	2.92	3.95	1.38	768	1204	105	26.0	3.6	7.3	2.0	64%	9%	44	25	31	29%	87%	18%	2	106	100%	0%			1.3	55	66	-$4
15	**Proj**	**8**	**8**	**0**	**164**	**135**	**3.78**	**3.64**	**1.22**	**701**	**679**	**720**	**25.9**	**2.9**	**7.4**	**2.6**	**62%**	**9%**	**40**	**20**	**40**	**28%**	**72%**	**9%**	**26**						**-0.8**	**73**	**87**	**$7**

Capps,Carter

Age: 24 | Th: R | Role: RP | Ht: 6' 4" | Wt: 230 | Type: Pwr FB
Health: F | PT/Exp: D | Consist: B
LIMA Plan: C+ | Rand Var: +2 | MM: 4500

Elbow strain cost him three months, but was able to avoid Tommy John surgery, for now. In limited sample, fastball velocity returned, and elite Dom remained intact thanks to SwK. xERA offers hope, but injury history will suppress his value. Still a speculative saves flyer, if healthy.

Yr	Tm	W	L	Sv	IP	K	ERA	xERA	WHIP	oOPS	vL	vR	BF/G	Ctl	Dom	Cmd	FpK	SwK	G	L	F	H%	S%	hr/f	GS	APC	DOM%	DIS%	Sv%	LI	RAR	BPV	BPX	R$
10																																		
11																																		
12	SEA *	2	3	19	76	96	2.13	2.58	1.17	667	798	552	5.3	2.6	11.3	4.3	55%	12%	41	28	32	35%	81%	0%	0	26			90	0.50	17.7	160	209	$15
13	SEA	3	3	0	59	66	5.49	3.79	1.63	878	1029	776	5.1	3.5	10.1	2.9	60%	13%	40	24	36	38%	71%	19%	0	20			0	1.05	-11.8	104	136	-$8
14	MIA	0	0	0	20	25	3.98	3.11	1.18	610	836	434	5.1	2.2	11.1	5.0	58%	14%	36	21	43	36%	65%	4%	0	21			0	0.44	-0.6	153	183	-$2
1st Half		0	0	0	12	15	3.00	3.18	1.08	570	830	327	5.4	2.3	11.3	5.0	57%	10%	32	19	48	32%	75%	7%	0	25			0	0.24	1.1	152	181	-$2
2nd Half		0	0	0	8	10	5.40	3.00	1.32	664	845	554	4.6	2.2	10.8	5.0	59%	20%	41	23	36	40%	55%	0%	0	18			0	0.65	-1.7	155	185	-$3
15	**Proj**	**2**	**2**	**0**	**51**	**59**	**3.61**	**3.08**	**1.26**	**591**	**686**	**527**	**4.9**	**3.1**	**10.6**	**3.4**	**60%**	**13%**	**38**	**24**	**38**	**33%**	**74%**	**9%**	**0**						**0.8**	**122**	**145**	**$0**

RYAN BLOOMFIELD

Capuano,Chris

Age: 36	Th: L	Role: RP	Health: C	LIMA Plan: C
Ht: 6' 3"	Wt: 215	Type: Pwr	PT/Exp: B	Rand Var: 0
			Consist: A	MM: 2201

3-4, 4.35 ERA in 97 IP at BOS/NYY. Had brief stints in bullpen and minor leagues before eventual return to rotation. Dom held steady while he gave back GB% gains, and mastery of LHB vanished. 2nd half rebound as SP (3.90 xERA) paired with Ctl, FpK recovery offers hope, but only in the end-game.

Yr Tm	W	L	Sv	IP	K	ERA	xERA	WHIP	oOPS	vL	vR	BF/G	Ctl	Dom	Cmd	FpK	SwK	G	L	F	H%	S%	hr/f	GS	APC	DOM%	DIS%	Sv%	LI	RAR	BPV	BPX	R$
10 MIL *	5	5	0	91	66	3.48	3.92	1.29	755	685	780	13.3	2.5	6.5	2.6	57%	9%	43	17	40	30%	76%	11%	9	44	44%	33%	0	0.65	6.7	70	112	$4
11 NYM	11	12	0	186	168	4.55	3.78	1.35	781	653	818	24.3	2.6	8.1	3.2	64%	11%	43	17	40	32%	70%	12%	31	90	45%	6%	0	0.82	-13.9	98	147	$1
12 LA	12	12	0	198	162	3.72	4.00	1.22	715	602	745	24.8	2.5	7.4	3.0	67%	12%	40	21	39	29%	74%	11%	33	90	55%	18%			7.2	84	110	$12
13 LA	4	7	0	106	81	4.26	3.91	1.41	781	566	858	19.0	2.0	6.9	3.4	61%	10%	46	20	33	34%	72%	10%	20	71	40%	50%	0	0.80	-5.1	93	121	-$4
14 2 AL *	4	4	0	117	98	4.28	4.41	1.39	741	942	665	11.2	3.1	7.6	2.5	61%	9%	39	26	34	32%	72%	10%	12	41	58%	17%	0	1.21	-7.7	68	81	-$3
1st Half	1	1	0	32	29	4.55	4.31	1.55	770	875	685	5.1	4.3	8.2	1.9	58%	6%	36	29	35	34%	72%	9%	0	20			0	1.39	-3.1	47	57	-$11
2nd Half	3	3	0	85	69	4.18	4.29	1.33	727	1020	658	22.1	2.6	7.3	2.8	63%	10%	41	25	34	32%	71%	10%	12	90	58%	17%			-4.6	72	86	$0
15 Proj	**4**	**4**	**0**	**87**	**70**	**4.17**	**3.82**	**1.40**	**759**	**786**	**749**	**15.4**	**3.0**	**7.2**	**2.4**	**62%**	**9%**	**40**	**23**	**36**	**32%**	**73%**	**10%**	**16**						**-4.6**	**67**	**80**	**-$2**

Carpenter,David

Age: 29	Th: R	Role: RP	Health: B	LIMA Plan: A
Ht: 6' 2"	Wt: 230	Type: Pwr	PT/Exp: D	Rand Var: +1
			Consist: D	MM: 4411

ERA jumped by over a full run, but underlying trends point to future success: FpK ascended to elite territory as year went on, which validated Ctl gains, and it didn't come at the expense of Dom, either. 2nd half GB% hints that he could push the envelope further. Saves potential is lurking.

Yr Tm	W	L	Sv	IP	K	ERA	xERA	WHIP	oOPS	vL	vR	BF/G	Ctl	Dom	Cmd	FpK	SwK	G	L	F	H%	S%	hr/f	GS	APC	DOM%	DIS%	Sv%	LI	RAR	BPV	BPX	R$
10																																	
11 HOU *	1	4	15	61	60	2.55	4.40	1.39	809	697	889	3.8	3.3	8.9	2.7	51%	11%	38	24	38	33%	87%	11%	0	14			83	0.95	10.4	78	118	$7
12 2 TM *	1	3	4	59	50	6.01	5.96	1.70	953	1123	842	4.7	3.5	7.7	2.2	62%	13%	42	23	35	38%	65%	13%	0	19			67	0.77	-14.4	51	67	-$10
13 ATL *	5	3	0	81	83	2.31	2.77	1.12	558	643	506	5.2	2.7	9.2	3.4	66%	13%	38	23	39	29%	83%	8%	0	19			0	0.97	15.5	115	150	$8
14 ATL	6	4	3	61	67	3.54	3.33	1.26	663	634	688	4.0	2.4	9.9	4.2	70%	12%	38	24	38	35%	74%	8%	0	15			50	1.45	1.5	130	155	$3
1st Half	4	1	2	28	35	4.23	3.52	1.73	806	786	820	3.9	2.6	11.4	4.4	64%	12%	31	30	39	47%	76%	6%	0	16			50	1.45	-1.7	144	172	-$2
2nd Half	2	3	1	33	32	2.97	3.14	0.87	517	499	533	4.1	2.2	8.6	4.0	76%	12%	44	18	38	23%	69%	9%	0	15			50	1.45	3.2	119	142	$7
15 Proj	**5**	**4**	**5**	**73**	**74**	**3.35**	**3.24**	**1.28**	**682**	**718**	**656**	**4.2**	**2.7**	**9.2**	**3.4**	**67%**	**13%**	**39**	**23**	**38**	**33%**	**76%**	**8%**	**0**						**3.5**	**110**	**131**	**$5**

Carrasco,Carlos

Age: 28	Th: R	Role: RP	Health: F	LIMA Plan: C+
Ht: 6' 3"	Wt: 210	Type: Pwr GB	PT/Exp: C	Rand Var: -1
			Consist: F	MM: 5303

Brutal April (6.46 ERA, but 103 BPV) sent him to the pen, and he returned with a bang in 2nd half. Signs of breakout were all over the place: Dom surge supported by SwK, he maintained elite GB%, and continued to better his Ctl. Health, xERA history give us some pause, but these skills are legit.

Yr Tm	W	L	Sv	IP	K	ERA	xERA	WHIP	oOPS	vL	vR	BF/G	Ctl	Dom	Cmd	FpK	SwK	G	L	F	H%	S%	hr/f	GS	APC	DOM%	DIS%	Sv%	LI	RAR	BPV	BPX	R$
10 CLE *	12	8	0	195	151	3.87	4.04	1.31	816	581	1042	25.2	2.7	6.9	2.6	57%	10%	57	14	29	31%	73%	16%	7	97	57%	0%			5.0	70	114	$9
11 CLE	8	9	0	125	85	4.62	4.08	1.36	754	888	600	25.5	2.9	6.1	2.1	58%	9%	49	17	34	30%	68%	11%	21	94	52%	24%			-10.4	59	89	-$1
12																																	
13 CLE *	4	5	1	118	94	5.15	4.76	1.50	864	980	745	16.5	3.1	7.2	2.3	67%	9%	50	22	28	35%	66%	9%	7	52	14%	86%	100	0.59	-18.8	64	83	-$9
14 CLE	8	7	1	134	140	2.55	2.73	0.99	543	516	566	13.2	1.9	9.4	4.8	63%	14%	53	19	28	29%	75%	7%	14	49	71%	7%	100	0.63	19.6	148	176	$17
1st Half	1	3	1	50	50	4.11	3.20	1.15	648	686	613	10.4	2.7	8.9	3.3	55%	13%	53	12	34	30%	65%	9%	4	40	25%	25%	100	0.62	-2.3	120	143	-$3
2nd Half	7	4	0	84	90	1.61	2.45	0.88	478	411	538	16.1	1.5	9.7	6.4	68%	15%	53	24	24	28%	83%	6%	10	58	90%	0%	0	0.64	22.0	164	196	$28
15 Proj	**11**	**7**	**0**	**169**	**159**	**3.57**	**3.06**	**1.23**	**659**	**685**	**633**	**15.7**	**2.7**	**8.5**	**3.2**	**62%**	**11%**	**51**	**20**	**29**	**31%**	**72%**	**9%**	**25**						**3.5**	**110**	**130**	**$11**

Carroll,Scott

Age: 30	Th: R	Role: RP	Health: A	LIMA Plan: D
Ht: 6' 4"	Wt: 215	Type: Con GB	PT/Exp: D	Rand Var: 0
			Consist: C	MM: 1000

5-10, 4.80 ERA in 129 IP at CHW. Career minor-leaguer finally got a shot, and while ERA improved by 2 runs, he's still on shaky ground. GB% remains his only real weapon, but awful Dom/SwK combo, mediocre Ctl, and DOM/DIS all tell is to drop out when bidding reaches $1. You want him? I don't want him. You can have him.

Yr Tm	W	L	Sv	IP	K	ERA	xERA	WHIP	oOPS	vL	vR	BF/G	Ctl	Dom	Cmd	FpK	SwK	G	L	F	H%	S%	hr/f	GS	APC	DOM%	DIS%	Sv%	LI	RAR	BPV	BPX	R$
10 aa	3	9	0	117	53	4.48	4.74	1.49				25.3	2.5	4.1	1.7						33%	70%								-5.8	38	61	-$4
11 aaa	7	8	0	145	67	6.57	6.92	1.89				27.4	3.1	4.2	1.4						38%	65%								-47.2	10	15	-$26
12 a/a	4	6	0	92	51	6.64	6.82	1.84				12.3	4.6	5.0	1.1						34%	66%								-29.9	-3	-4	-$20
13 aa	0	2	0	25	11	6.35	5.48	1.46				17.8	0.9	3.9	4.1						34%	56%								-7.7	66	86	-$7
14 CHW *	8	11	0	152	74	4.36	4.61	1.48	798	841	733	21.8	3.3	4.4	1.3	60%	6%	53	20	26	31%	71%	11%	19	81	26%	21%	0	0.71	-11.6	29	35	-$7
1st Half	5	5	0	74	34	3.62	4.73	1.54	839	879	773	20.2	3.5	4.1	1.2	63%	6%	50	20	30	31%	77%	9%	6	71	0%	33%	0	0.66	1.1	28	34	-$4
2nd Half	3	6	0	78	40	5.06	4.24	1.42	770	814	709	24.4	3.1	4.6	1.5	59%	6%	56	20	24	30%	65%	13%	13	90	38%	15%	0	0.75	-12.7	33	39	-$9
15 Proj	**3**	**4**	**0**	**58**	**29**	**5.33**	**4.44**	**1.63**	**859**	**905**	**789**	**19.0**	**3.5**	**4.5**	**1.3**	**60%**	**6%**	**53**	**20**	**26**	**33%**	**68%**	**12%**	**12**						**-11.4**	**18**	**21**	**-$8**

Cashner,Andrew

Age: 28	Th: R	Role: SP	Health: F	LIMA Plan: B
Ht: 6' 6"	Wt: 220	Type:	PT/Exp: B	Rand Var: -3
			Consist: A	MM: 4203

Bouts with elbow and shoulder soreness sent him to the DL in May and June. xERA coupled with hr/f, S% luck cast doubt that he can repeat that elite ERA. Pinpoint control and GB% set a high floor, but SwK trend suggests mediocre Dom will limit upside potential, even if he's healthy.

Yr Tm	W	L	Sv	IP	K	ERA	xERA	WHIP	oOPS	vL	vR	BF/G	Ctl	Dom	Cmd	FpK	SwK	G	L	F	H%	S%	hr/f	GS	APC	DOM%	DIS%	Sv%	LI	RAR	BPV	BPX	R$
10 CHC *	8	7	0	111	98	3.54	3.48	1.29	795	904	726	7.2	3.6	8.0	2.2	54%	11%	48	19	33	29%	74%	16%	0	18			0	0.90	7.4	79	127	$6
11 CHC	0	0	0	11	8	1.69	3.29	0.66	351	167	440	5.6	3.4	6.8	2.0	56%	11%	59	7	33	8%	83%	11%	1	21	0%	0%	0	0.56	3.0	67	101	-$1
12 SD *	5	5	0	70	77	3.58	3.15	1.22	688	525	815	7.2	3.1	9.9	3.2	55%	13%	53	23	24	32%	72%	17%	5	24	40%	60%	0	1.25	3.7	116	151	$3
13 SD	10	9	0	175	128	3.09	3.56	1.13	639	703	578	22.8	2.4	6.6	2.7	60%	9%	53	19	29	28%	74%	8%	26	87	65%	12%	0	0.73	16.8	84	110	$14
14 SD	5	7	0	123	93	2.55	3.60	1.13	623	675	573	26.6	2.1	6.8	3.2	63%	8%	48	20	31	29%	79%	6%	19	95	63%	11%			18.1	91	108	$10
1st Half	2	6	0	76	59	2.36	3.54	1.19	612	704	540	26.7	2.6	7.0	2.7	66%	7%	52	22	26	30%	80%	3%	12	95	67%	8%			13.0	85	102	$11
2nd Half	3	1	0	47	34	2.87	3.69	1.02	640	636	646	26.6	1.3	6.5	4.9	59%	11%	42	17	41	27%	77%	9%	7	94	57%	14%			5.0	101	120	$8
15 Proj	**9**	**8**	**0**	**162**	**126**	**3.28**	**3.30**	**1.14**	**635**	**648**	**623**	**24.1**	**2.4**	**7.0**	**3.0**	**59%**	**10%**	**49**	**20**	**31**	**28%**	**73%**	**8%**	**28**						**9.2**	**89**	**106**	**$13**

Casilla,Santiago

Age: 34	Th: R	Role: RP	Health: F	LIMA Plan: C+
Ht: 6' 0"	Wt: 210	Type: Pwr GB	PT/Exp: C	Rand Var: -5
			Consist: B	MM: 4230

Regained closer role in July after sparkling 1st half, and barely slowed down from there. Double-digit SwK indicates 2nd half Dom gains can stick, while GB% will continue to keep firm lid on ERA. Likely Ctl, H% regression will prevent full repeat, but most signs say he can still be an effective closer.

Yr Tm	W	L	Sv	IP	K	ERA	xERA	WHIP	oOPS	vL	vR	BF/G	Ctl	Dom	Cmd	FpK	SwK	G	L	F	H%	S%	hr/f	GS	APC	DOM%	DIS%	Sv%	LI	RAR	BPV	BPX	R$
10 SF	7	2	2	55	56	1.95	3.28	1.19	600	678	564	4.3	4.2	9.1	2.2	54%	11%	51	21	29	28%	84%	5%	0	17			67	1.22	14.5	79	127	$7
11 SF	2	2	6	52	45	1.74	3.60	1.12	534	632	481	4.3	4.4	7.8	1.8	48%	12%	52	20	29	24%	84%	3%	0	17			86	0.95	14.0	54	80	$7
12 SF	7	6	25	63	55	2.84	3.78	1.22	656	727	608	3.7	3.1	7.8	2.5	53%	10%	55	15	30	28%	83%	14%	0	14			81	1.37	9.2	89	116	$15
13 SF	7	2	2	50	38	2.16	4.03	1.28	627	652	611	3.6	4.5	6.8	1.5	54%	10%	54	17	29	26%	84%	5%	0	14			67	1.66	10.5	34	44	$4
14 SF	3	3	19	58	45	1.70	3.07	0.86	493	539	461	4.0	2.3	6.9	3.0	57%	11%	56	15	29	21%	83%	7%	0	16			83	1.37	14.7	96	115	$15
1st Half	1	1	2	32	21	1.11	3.18	0.90	474	628	400	4.2	2.5	5.8	2.3	59%	10%	57	18	25	21%	89%	5%	0	17			40	1.42	10.5	73	87	$11
2nd Half	2	2	17	26	24	2.42	2.94	0.81	515	471	557	3.9	2.1	8.3	4.0	55%	12%	55	10	34	21%	74%	9%	0	14			94	1.32	4.2	127	151	$20
15 Proj	**5**	**3**	**30**	**58**	**48**	**2.72**	**3.31**	**1.18**	**639**	**673**	**615**	**3.9**	**3.1**	**7.4**	**2.3**	**55%**	**11%**	**55**	**15**	**30**	**28%**	**78%**	**7%**	**0**						**7.3**	**81**	**96**	**$16**

Cecil,Brett

Age: 28	Th: L	Role: RP	Health: B	LIMA Plan: A
Ht: 6' 3"	Wt: 220	Type: Pwr	PT/Exp: C	Rand Var: 0
			Consist: C	MM: 5510

Another excellent year in setup role, fully supported by xERA and Dom improved even further. Maintained GB% gains, but poor Ctl remains a hurdle, and FpK says its a big one. With even minor improvement, OPS trend vs. RHB suggests he can thrive in larger role... UP: 25 SV

Yr Tm	W	L	Sv	IP	K	ERA	xERA	WHIP	oOPS	vL	vR	BF/G	Ctl	Dom	Cmd	FpK	SwK	G	L	F	H%	S%	hr/f	GS	APC	DOM%	DIS%	Sv%	LI	RAR	BPV	BPX	R$
10 TOR	15	7	0	173	117	4.22	4.21	1.33	733	597	773	25.9	2.8	6.1	2.2	57%	9%	44	18	38	30%	70%	9%	28	97	50%	18%			-3.0	56	90	$6
11 TOR *	12	13	0	202	139	4.80	4.94	1.37	779	522	876	26.5	2.8	6.2	2.2	59%	9%	38	18	43	29%	70%	13%	20	96	50%	10%			-21.5	36	54	-$2
12 TOR *	6	8	0	144	104	4.50	4.78	1.46	855	603	934	17.1	2.8	6.5	2.4	58%	10%	37	22	41	33%	71%	14%	9	49	44%	22%	0	0.72	-8.5	58	76	-$5
13 TOR	5	1	1	61	70	2.82	2.96	1.10	594	458	736	4.2	3.4	10.4	3.0	58%	12%	51	20	29	28%	76%	9%	0	15			33	0.89	7.8	124	161	$5
14 TOR	2	3	5	53	76	2.70	2.68	1.37	627	714	569	3.5	4.6	12.8	2.8	54%	17%	54	25	22	37%	80%	7%	0	14			71	1.22	6.8	140	167	$3
1st Half	0	3	3	26	36	3.76	3.22	1.71	736	822	676	3.9	5.5	12.3	2.3	52%	16%	53	26	21	43%	76%	0%	0	15			75	1.11	-0.1	105	125	-$3
2nd Half	2	0	2	27	40	1.67	2.19	1.04	504	574	455	3.2	3.7	13.3	3.6	56%	18%	55	22	22	29%	88%	15%	0	13			67	1.32	6.9	174	208	$9
15 Proj	**3**	**2**	**5**	**58**	**69**	**3.08**	**2.86**	**1.28**	**648**	**592**	**682**	**4.5**	**3.7**	**10.6**	**2.8**	**55%**	**14%**	**50**	**22**	**28**	**33%**	**77%**	**10%**	**0**						**4.7**	**118**	**141**	**$4**

RYAN BLOOMFIELD

Chacin,Jhoulys

Age: 27	Th: R	Role SP	Health F	LIMA Plan D+	
Ht: 6' 3"	Wt: 215	Type	PT/Exp C	Rand Var +3	
			Consist B	MM 1001	

Never recovered from preseason shoulder inflammation, which shelved him in April and ultimately ended season in June. BPV took a hit as he gave back Ctl growth, which sent Cmd to a scary level at Coors. xERA and S% predict ERA rebound, but it only matters if health improves.

Yr Tm	W	L	Sv	IP	K	ERA	xERA	WHIP	oOPS	vL	vR	BF/G	Ctl	Dom	Cmd	FpK	SwK	G	L	F	H%	S%	hr/f	GS	APC	DOM%	DIS%	Sv%	LI	RAR	BPV	BPX	R$
10 COL *	12	13	0	173	166	2.92	3.05	1.26	650	705	612	20.2	4.0	8.6	2.2	55%	11%	47	22	32	29%	78%	9%	21	82	57%	10%	0	0.70	24.8	90	146	$16
11 COL	11	14	0	194	150	3.62	3.86	1.31	707	759	654	26.7	4.0	7.0	1.7	55%	9%	56	15	28	27%	75%	12%	31	101	52%	16%			7.7	50	76	$8
12 COL *	4	7	0	92	54	4.66	5.32	1.56	821	910	720	22.3	3.9	5.3	1.4	59%	8%	39	24	37	31%	73%	12%	14	83	29%	50%			-7.3	21	27	-$8
13 COL	14	10	0	197	126	3.47	4.02	1.26	685	722	650	26.3	2.8	5.7	2.1	61%	8%	47	25	29	29%	73%	6%	31	96	48%	13%			9.7	53	69	$10
14 COL	1	7	0	63	42	5.40	4.56	1.44	790	751	821	24.7	4.0	6.0	1.5	63%	9%	43	22	35	29%	64%	12%	11	93	36%	0%			-13.0	21	25	-$7
1st Half	1	7	0	63	42	5.40	4.56	1.44	790	751	821	24.7	4.0	6.0	1.5	63%	9%	43	22	35	29%	64%	12%	11	93	36%	0%			-13.0	21	25	-$7
2nd Half																																	
15 Proj	3	6	0	73	47	4.30	4.19	1.39	744	781	709	23.8	3.7	5.8	1.6	60%	9%	45	22	33	29%	71%	10%	13						-5.0	27	32	-$3

Chamberlain,Joba

Age: 29	Th: R	Role RP	Health F	LIMA Plan B+	
Ht: 6' 2"	Wt: 250	Type Pwr	PT/Exp D	Rand Var 0	
			Consist C	MM 3310	

Could ankle injury in late May have played a bigger role than reported? Had a 155 BPV through May, with a 52 BPV after. GB% spike, return of Ctl drove ERA gains, and he became effective vs. RHB again. 1st half reminds us of what he can do, but health history tells us to exercise caution.

Yr Tm	W	L	Sv	IP	K	ERA	xERA	WHIP	oOPS	vL	vR	BF/G	Ctl	Dom	Cmd	FpK	SwK	G	L	F	H%	S%	hr/f	GS	APC	DOM%	DIS%	Sv%	LI	RAR	BPV	BPX	R$
10 NYY	3	4	3	72	77	4.40	3.36	1.30	693	713	675	4.2	2.8	9.7	3.5	58%	10%	46	17	37	34%	67%	8%	0	16			43	1.02	-2.8	123	200	$2
11 NYY	2	0	0	29	24	2.83	2.84	1.05	628	627	627	4.1	2.2	7.5	3.4	56%	11%	60	16	25	26%	78%	16%	0	16			0	1.08	3.9	114	172	$1
12 NYY	1	0	0	21	22	4.35	3.64	1.55	835	609	962	4.3	2.6	9.6	3.7	54%	12%	45	23	31	39%	76%	15%	0	16			0	1.12	-0.9	125	163	-$5
13 NYY	2	1	1	42	38	4.93	4.80	1.74	825	756	878	4.4	5.6	8.1	1.5	71%	10%	42	25	34	33%	77%	18%	0	17			100	0.61	-5.5	16	21	-$7
14 DET	2	5	2	63	59	3.57	3.27	1.29	647	650	643	3.8	3.4	8.4	2.5	57%	11%	53	23	24	31%	72%	7%	0	15			33	1.25	1.3	90	107	$0
1st Half	1	3	2	34	37	2.94	2.76	1.19	613	663	559	3.7	2.9	9.9	3.4	62%	12%	52	26	22	33%	74%	5%	0	15			50	1.11	3.3	128	153	$3
2nd Half	1	2	0	29	22	4.30	3.90	1.40	685	635	735	3.9	4.0	6.8	1.7	52%	10%	55	20	25	30%	69%	9%	0	15			0	1.41	-2.0	46	55	-$3
15 Proj	3	4	1	65	60	3.85	3.59	1.40	682	659	703	3.9	4.1	8.3	2.0	62%	10%	48	23	29	31%	74%	11%	0						-0.9	64	76	-$1

Chapman,Aroldis

Age: 27	Th: L	Role RP	Health D	LIMA Plan C+	
Ht: 6' 4"	Wt: 205	Type Pwr	PT/Exp A	Rand Var 0	
			Consist A	MM 5530	

Line drive to the head shelved him until early May, but he returned with a vengeance. Blew hitters away as BPV entered Vintage Eck territory. Mediocre Ctl doesn't matter much when you strike this many hitters out. xERA history further proves dominance, and suggests we'll see plenty more of it.

Yr Tm	W	L	Sv	IP	K	ERA	xERA	WHIP	oOPS	vL	vR	BF/G	Ctl	Dom	Cmd	FpK	SwK	G	L	F	H%	S%	hr/f	GS	APC	DOM%	DIS%	Sv%	LI	RAR	BPV	BPX	R$
10 CIN *	11	8	8	109	129	3.84	3.56	1.39	492	368	540	8.5	4.7	10.7	2.3	57%	15%	73	12	15	33%	73%	0%	0	15			80	1.68	3.2	100	162	$9
11 CIN	4	1	1	50	71	3.60	3.17	1.30	534	392	598	3.8	7.4	12.8	1.7	53%	14%	53	16	31	24%	71%	7%	0	16			33	1.13	2.1	62	93	$2
12 CIN	5	5	38	72	122	1.51	2.12	0.81	450	330	501	4.1	2.9	15.3	5.3	53%	18%	37	20	43	28%	85%	7%	0	18			88	1.42	22.2	213	278	$32
13 CIN	4	5	38	64	112	2.54	2.30	1.04	544	379	592	3.8	4.1	15.8	3.9	59%	17%	34	24	42	31%	81%	15%	0	16			88	1.38	10.4	186	243	$23
14 CIN	0	3	36	54	106	2.00	1.52	0.83	406	372	415	3.7	4.0	17.7	4.4	58%	21%	43	22	35	30%	75%	4%	0	17			95	1.44	11.6	231	275	$21
1st Half	0	2	16	24	46	2.66	1.55	0.85	475	192	539	3.9	3.0	17.5	5.8	65%	21%	37	29	34	35%	68%	8%	0	18			89	1.78	3.2	248	296	$16
2nd Half	0	1	20	30	60	1.48	1.48	0.82	348	487	303	3.6	4.7	17.8	3.8	52%	21%	50	15	35	26%	80%	0%	0	17			100	1.19	8.4	220	263	$25
15 Proj	2	4	44	58	105	2.21	1.78	0.93	470	381	498	3.8	4.1	16.3	4.0	57%	19%	42	21	38	30%	78%	9%	0						10.9	202	240	$26

Chatwood,Tyler

Age: 25	Th: R	Role SP	Health F	LIMA Plan D+	
Ht: 6' 0"	Wt: 185	Type GB	PT/Exp D	Rand Var +4	
			Consist C	MM 2000	

Yet another Tommy John casualty, and this was his second time. He didn't go under the knife until July despite last pitching in late April. GB% profile fits well at Coors Field, and xERA trend at this age is enough to keep him on the radar, but not until 2016.

Yr Tm	W	L	Sv	IP	K	ERA	xERA	WHIP	oOPS	vL	vR	BF/G	Ctl	Dom	Cmd	FpK	SwK	G	L	F	H%	S%	hr/f	GS	APC	DOM%	DIS%	Sv%	LI	RAR	BPV	BPX	R$
10 a/a	5	6	0	74	34	4.11	4.36	1.47				24.4	2.9	4.1	1.4						32%	71%								-0.3	38	62	-$2
11 LAA *	7	13	0	158	84	4.73	5.42	1.69	830	862	786	23.0	4.6	4.8	1.0	54%	5%	47	22	31	32%	73%	10%	25	90	20%	44%	0	0.77	-15.4	20	30	-$12
12 COL *	6	9	1	126	83	5.80	5.84	1.72	836	890	774	17.9	4.3	5.9	1.4	54%	6%	56	21	23	34%	67%	19%	12	61	8%	58%	100	0.62	-27.7	27	35	-$18
13 COL *	10	6	0	145	91	3.13	3.90	1.42	711	729	697	23.7	2.9	5.7	1.9	55%	7%	59	21	21	32%	77%	7%	20	89	35%	30%			13.1	64	84	$4
14 COL	1	0	0	24	20	4.50	3.56	1.21	711	472	1015	25.3	3.0	7.5	2.5	50%	10%	46	29	26	26%	68%	22%	4	89	50%	0%			-2.2	78	93	-$3
1st Half	1	0	0	24	20	4.50	3.56	1.21	711	472	1015	25.3	3.0	7.5	2.5	50%	10%	46	29	26	26%	68%	22%	4	89	50%	0%			-2.2	78	93	-$3
2nd Half																																	
15 Proj	2	2	0	33	20	4.55	4.06	1.48	773	730	821	21.9	3.5	5.4	1.5	53%	7%	52	23	24	31%	71%	13%	6						-3.2	32	39	-$4

Chavez,Jesse

Age: 31	Th: R	Role SP	Health A	LIMA Plan B+	
Ht: 6' 2"	Wt: 160	Type Pwr	PT/Exp C	Rand Var 0	
			Consist B	MM 3303	

Rotation debut got off to fast start in 1st half, then 5.20 July ERA resulted in bullpen demotion. Skills indicate he'll be back, as FpK suggests not to worry about 2nd half Ctl, and Dom continued its steady ascent. IP history points to durability concerns as starter, but he's still a useful arm to fill out your staff.

Yr Tm	W	L	Sv	IP	K	ERA	xERA	WHIP	oOPS	vL	vR	BF/G	Ctl	Dom	Cmd	FpK	SwK	G	L	F	H%	S%	hr/f	GS	APC	DOM%	DIS%	Sv%	LI	RAR	BPV	BPX	R$
10 2 TM	5	5	0	63	45	5.89	4.86	1.47	834	884	798	5.5	3.3	6.5	2.0	56%	9%	34	17	48	31%	63%	11%	0	21			0	0.81	-14.0	39	63	-$4
11 KC *	2	4	16	65	47	5.22	6.17	1.69	1112	924	1250	6.0	3.0	6.5	2.2	44%	12%	54	19	27	37%	71%	43%	0	40			76	0.32	-10.3	38	57	-$2
12 2 AL *	9	6	2	130	101	5.37	4.97	1.44	983	1144	888	16.2	2.4	7.0	2.9	62%	11%	36	29	35	34%	64%	26%	2	36	0%	50%	100	0.66	-21.7	65	85	-$6
13 OAK *	4	6	1	87	74	3.64	3.71	1.35	620	630	605	9.1	2.6	7.6	2.9	61%	10%	43	17	39	34%	72%	5%	0	27			50	0.93	2.4	95	124	$0
14 OAK	8	8	0	146	136	3.45	3.72	1.31	692	663	729	19.4	3.0	8.4	2.8	63%	9%	42	23	35	31%	78%	11%	21	75	52%	5%	0	0.66	5.2	89	106	$5
1st Half	6	4	0	98	87	2.94	3.54	1.21	656	706	578	25.6	2.6	8.0	3.1	63%	9%	45	22	33	30%	79%	10%	16	97	56%	6%			9.7	98	116	$11
2nd Half	2	4	0	48	49	4.50	4.09	1.50	762	556	945	13.3	3.9	9.2	2.3	64%	10%	35	23	41	33%	75%	14%	5	53	40%	0%	0	0.55	-4.5	73	87	-$9
15 Proj	9	7	0	162	143	3.86	3.64	1.32	700	655	748	21.4	3.0	8.0	2.6	62%	10%	40	20	40	31%	73%	9%	59						-2.5	80	95	$5

Chen,Wei-Yin

Age: 29	Th: L	Role SP	Health D	LIMA Plan B	
Ht: 6' 0"	Wt: 195	Type	PT/Exp A	Rand Var 0	
			Consist A	MM 2103	

Skills were nearly identical in both halves, and thus highlighted the effect hr/f can have on ERA. Career-high win total propped up R$, but Ctl and GB% gains suggest new approach (more two-seamers) worked well. Mediocre Dom limits upside, but he's a stable cog who's getting better.

Yr Tm	W	L	Sv	IP	K	ERA	xERA	WHIP	oOPS	vL	vR	BF/G	Ctl	Dom	Cmd	FpK	SwK	G	L	F	H%	S%	hr/f	GS	APC	DOM%	DIS%	Sv%	LI	RAR	BPV	BPX	R$
10 for	13	10	0	188	145	3.57	4.46	1.27				26.5	2.9	6.9	2.4						27%	81%								11.9	47	75	$12
11 for	8	10	0	165	89	3.32	3.18	1.13				26.1	2.1	4.9	2.3						26%	73%								12.7	60	90	$11
12 BAL	12	11	0	193	154	4.02	4.33	1.26	729	682	747	25.6	2.7	7.2	2.7	60%	10%	37	21	42	29%	73%	12%	32	98	56%	16%			-0.1	73	95	$8
13 BAL	7	7	0	137	104	4.07	4.19	1.32	761	689	783	24.9	2.6	6.8	2.7	59%	8%	34	25	41	31%	73%	10%	23	95	35%	17%			-3.5	66	86	$1
14 BAL	16	6	0	186	136	3.54	3.86	1.23	727	670	746	24.9	1.7	6.6	3.9	61%	8%	41	22	38	30%	76%	10%	31	96	48%	13%			4.6	92	109	$10
1st Half	7	3	0	92	65	4.19	3.94	1.30	797	854	779	24.3	1.6	6.3	4.1	60%	8%	41	21	38	31%	73%	13%	16	96	31%	19%			-5.1	91	109	$3
2nd Half	9	3	0	93	71	2.89	3.80	1.16	658	493	713	25.6	1.8	6.8	3.7	63%	9%	41	22	38	30%	78%	7%	15	96	67%	7%			9.8	92	110	$17
15 Proj	13	8	0	174	129	3.67	3.69	1.25	728	656	751	24.6	2.2	6.7	3.1	60%	9%	38	23	39	30%	75%	10%	29						1.5	78	93	$9

Cingrani,Tony

Age: 25	Th: L	Role SP	Health B	LIMA Plan C	
Ht: 6' 4"	Wt: 215	Type Pwr FB	PT/Exp D	Rand Var +1	
			Consist D	MM 3403	

Shoulder woes shut him down in June, derailed sophomore campaign. Already-shaky Ctl got worse thanks to FpK dip, while FB% continued to create HR risk. Value hinges on regaining elite Dom, so while there's plenty of upside at this age, injury concerns make 2015 breakout an uphill battle.

Yr Tm	W	L	Sv	IP	K	ERA	xERA	WHIP	oOPS	vL	vR	BF/G	Ctl	Dom	Cmd	FpK	SwK	G	L	F	H%	S%	hr/f	GS	APC	DOM%	DIS%	Sv%	LI	RAR	BPV	BPX	R$
10																																	
11																																	
12 CIN *	5	3	0	94	96	2.81	3.47	1.26	623	533	700	20.3	4.1	9.2	2.2	55%	13%	64	0	36	28%	83%	25%	0	34			0	0.86	14.0	81	105	$7
13 CIN *	10	4	0	136	162	2.60	2.46	1.06	649	533	693	18.2	3.6	10.7	3.0	57%	11%	34	21	45	25%	81%	13%	18	79	61%	22%	0	0.93	21.2	113	147	$18
14 CIN	2	8	0	63	61	4.55	4.51	1.53	811	613	862	21.5	5.0	8.7	1.7	54%	9%	35	22	44	30%	76%	15%	11	86	27%	27%	0	0.85	-6.3	35	41	-$5
1st Half	2	8	0	63	61	4.55	4.51	1.53	811	613	862	21.5	5.0	8.7	1.7	54%	9%	35	22	44	30%	76%	15%	11	86	27%	27%	0	0.85	-6.3	35	41	-$5
2nd Half																																	
15 Proj	7	9	0	137	143	3.87	3.66	1.33	708	563	752	20.2	4.1	9.4	2.3	55%	9%	35	21	44	30%	74%	10%	28						-2.2	71	84	$4

RYAN BLOOMFIELD

Cishek,Steve

Age: 29	Th: R	Role RP	Health A	LIMA Plan C+	
Ht: 6' 6"	Wt: 215	Type Pwr	PT/Exp B	Rand Var +1	
			Consist A	MM 5530	

ERA jumped nearly a full run from '13, but blame H%/S%, not skills. BPV climbed to elite status thanks to Dom spike, while FpK growth suggests his control issues are behind him. Highly reliable arm for a closer, but due to his elevated ERA and team, he'll likely come at a discount.

Yr	Tm	W	L	Sv	IP	K	ERA	xERA	WHIP	oOPS	vL	vR	BF/G	Ctl	Dom	Cmd	FpK	SwK	G	L	F	H%	S%	hr/f	GS	APC	DOM%	DIS%	Sv%	LI	RAR	BPV	BPX	R$
10	FLA *	3	1	2	36	33	4.76	3.33	1.37	276	167	333	6.0	3.0	8.4	2.8	80%	10%	45	9	45	35%	61%	0%	0	21			67	0.14	-3.0	110	177	-$1
11	FLA *	3	2	3	78	70	2.57	2.66	1.23	591	661	545	5.2	3.6	8.2	2.3	59%	9%	57	17	26	30%	78%	3%	0	20			100	0.86	13.2	100	150	$6
12	MIA	5	2	15	64	68	2.69	3.55	1.30	663	787	548	4.0	4.1	9.6	2.3	57%	10%	52	16	31	31%	80%	6%	0	16			79	1.20	10.4	92	120	$10
13	MIA	4	6	34	70	74	2.33	2.96	1.08	568	664	459	4.1	2.8	9.6	3.4	63%	10%	53	18	29	29%	79%	6%	0	16			94	1.23	13.2	126	165	$20
14	MIA	4	5	39	65	84	3.17	2.84	1.21	643	586	713	4.1	2.9	11.6	4.0	67%	10%	43	26	31	35%	74%	6%	0	17			91	1.61	4.6	151	180	$18
1st Half		4	3	18	34	43	2.88	2.91	1.14	601	548	678	4.1	2.9	11.3	3.9	61%	10%	38	31	32	33%	74%	4%	0	17			95	1.75	3.6	141	168	$20
2nd Half		0	2	21	31	41	3.48	2.75	1.29	688	633	744	4.2	2.9	11.9	4.1	74%	10%	48	22	30	38%	74%	8%	0	17			88	1.46	1.0	162	193	$16
15	Proj	**4**	**3**	**35**	**68**	**79**	**2.71**	**2.63**	**1.08**	**583**	**605**	**560**	**3.9**	**3.0**	**10.5**	**3.5**	**65%**	**10%**	**49**	**21**	**30**	**29%**	**76%**	**8%**	**0**						**8.6**	**135**	**161**	**$20**

Clippard,Tyler

Age: 30	Th: R	Role RP	Health A	LIMA Plan B+	
Ht: 6' 3"	Wt: 200	Type Pwr xFB	PT/Exp C	Rand Var -5	
			Consist A	MM 4511	

Shut out from closing gig, but LI says he was trusted in high-leverage spots. Elite SwK hints double-digit Dom can stick, and 2nd half FpK surge drove Ctl gains. FB% still presents HR risk, but skills are better now as compared to his 32-save season in 2012. No reason he can't repeat that feat if he gets a shot.

Yr	Tm	W	L	Sv	IP	K	ERA	xERA	WHIP	oOPS	vL	vR	BF/G	Ctl	Dom	Cmd	FpK	SwK	G	L	F	H%	S%	hr/f	GS	APC	DOM%	DIS%	Sv%	LI	RAR	BPV	BPX	R$
10	WAS	11	8	1	91	112	3.07	3.67	1.21	646	708	594	4.8	4.1	11.1	2.7	55%	15%	28	17	56	30%	77%	7%	0	20			9	1.23	11.4	96	155	$10
11	WAS	3	0	0	88	104	1.83	3.20	0.84	535	549	522	4.6	2.6	10.6	4.0	55%	17%	20	20	60	20%	89%	9%	0	19			0	1.49	23.0	117	176	$15
12	WAS	2	6	32	73	84	3.72	4.03	1.16	621	519	725	4.1	3.6	10.4	2.9	62%	12%	30	14	57	28%	70%	7%	0	17			86	1.25	2.7	98	128	$16
13	WAS	6	3	0	71	73	2.41	3.68	0.86	517	507	527	3.8	3.0	9.3	3.0	59%	15%	28	16	56	18%	81%	9%	0	16			0	1.10	12.8	90	118	$10
14	WAS	7	4	1	70	82	2.18	3.26	1.00	541	642	423	3.7	2.9	10.5	3.6	63%	15%	37	14	49	27%	82%	6%	0	15			14	1.34	13.6	124	148	$10
1st Half		5	2	1	36	47	2.00	3.28	1.14	572	638	507	3.7	4.0	11.8	2.9	59%	15%	35	16	49	30%	85%	5%	0	16			33	1.22	7.7	117	139	$11
2nd Half		2	2	0	34	35	2.36	3.24	0.84	508	643	310	3.7	1.8	9.2	5.0	68%	15%	38	12	50	24%	77%	7%	0	14			0	1.47	5.9	132	157	$9
15	Proj	**6**	**4**	**5**	**73**	**81**	**2.64**	**3.21**	**1.08**	**609**	**657**	**555**	**3.8**	**3.0**	**10.1**	**3.4**	**62%**	**15%**	**32**	**15**	**53**	**28%**	**80%**	**7%**	**0**						**9.9**	**111**	**132**	**$10**

Cobb,Alex

Age: 27	Th: R	Role SP	Health F	LIMA Plan B	
Ht: 6' 3"	Wt: 200	Type Pwr xGB	PT/Exp B	Rand Var 0	
			Consist A	MM 5305	

Missed over a month due to an oblique strain, took a few weeks to get the rust off upon his return, but then stormed into the 2nd half. GB% stayed cemented in elite territory and Cmd continued to climb. Health remains a red flag, but two straight years of triple-digit BPV as he enters peak age say we have a budding ace.

Yr	Tm	W	L	Sv	IP	K	ERA	xERA	WHIP	oOPS	vL	vR	BF/G	Ctl	Dom	Cmd	FpK	SwK	G	L	F	H%	S%	hr/f	GS	APC	DOM%	DIS%	Sv%	LI	RAR	BPV	BPX	R$
10	aa	7	5	0	120	111	3.14	4.33	1.44				22.1	2.7	8.3	3.1						36%	79%								13.8	96	155	$5
11	TAM *	8	3	0	120	96	2.69	3.50	1.29	655	683	617	23.5	2.7	7.2	2.6	58%	8%	54	20	26	31%	80%	7%	9	94	22%	22%			18.6	86	129	$9
12	TAM *	12	13	0	178	142	4.19	3.82	1.34	690	735	633	23.8	2.9	7.2	2.5	62%	8%	59	20	21	32%	69%	13%	23	94	48%	26%			-3.8	79	103	$3
13	TAM	11	3	0	143	134	2.76	3.04	1.15	644	677	592	26.3	2.8	8.4	3.0	59%	10%	56	22	23	28%	80%	15%	22	101	59%	14%			19.5	109	142	$15
14	TAM	10	9	0	166	149	2.87	3.16	1.14	619	590	646	25.2	2.5	8.1	3.2	59%	11%	56	16	27	29%	76%	9%	27	97	59%	11%			17.9	110	132	$14
1st Half		3	6	0	64	56	4.20	3.42	1.24	687	599	771	24.5	2.8	7.8	2.8	61%	12%	55	16	29	30%	68%	13%	11	92	55%	18%			-3.6	98	116	-$2
2nd Half		7	3	0	102	93	2.03	3.00	1.07	574	583	566	25.7	2.4	8.2	3.4	58%	11%	57	17	26	29%	82%	5%	16	100	63%	6%			21.5	118	141	$25
15	Proj	**13**	**9**	**0**	**185**	**164**	**3.06**	**3.00**	**1.19**	**649**	**656**	**642**	**24.5**	**2.7**	**8.0**	**3.0**	**60%**	**10%**	**56**	**19**	**25**	**30%**	**76%**	**10%**	**30**						**15.4**	**105**	**125**	**$16**

Coke,Phil

Age: 32	Th: L	Role RP	Health B	LIMA Plan D+	
Ht: 6' 1"	Wt: 210	Type Pwr	PT/Exp D	Rand Var +2	
			Consist B	MM 2100	

ERA got back on track, but where's the track headed? Hopefully nowhere near your fantasy team, as RHB continued to pound him, and xERA says 2nd half success was a mirage. We should give him credit for GB% gains and Ctl recovery, but odds of escaping middle innings at his age are slim.

Yr	Tm	W	L	Sv	IP	K	ERA	xERA	WHIP	oOPS	vL	vR	BF/G	Ctl	Dom	Cmd	FpK	SwK	G	L	F	H%	S%	hr/f	GS	APC	DOM%	DIS%	Sv%	LI	RAR	BPV	BPX	R$
10	DET	7	5	2	65	53	3.76	4.33	1.44	699	681	713	3.8	3.6	7.4	2.0	54%	12%	35	21	43	33%	73%	2%	1	14	0%	100%	50	1.12	2.6	48	78	$2
11	DET	3	9	1	109	69	4.47	4.46	1.45	728	584	806	9.9	3.3	5.7	1.7	57%	9%	43	22	35	32%	68%	4%	14	35	36%	43%	50	1.05	-7.1	34	52	-$4
12	DET	2	3	1	54	51	4.00	3.91	1.65	854	685	1050	3.7	3.0	8.5	2.8	57%	13%	49	21	30	39%	77%	10%	0	14			33	1.25	0.1	99	129	-$5
13	DET	0	5	1	38	30	5.40	4.82	1.67	809	760	860	3.6	4.9	7.0	1.4	59%	12%	45	21	34	34%	67%	7%	0	13			33	1.17	-7.3	17	22	-$8
14	DET	5	2	1	58	41	3.88	3.88	1.53	790	691	871	4.1	3.1	6.4	2.1	55%	11%	56	21	23	34%	76%	11%	0	15			50	0.88	-1.0	65	77	-$3
1st Half		1	1	1	30	21	5.16	3.64	1.48	798	583	972	4.6	2.7	6.4	2.3	55%	10%	59	21	21	34%	66%	15%	0	17			100	0.81	-5.2	78	93	-$7
2nd Half		4	1	0	28	20	2.54	4.12	1.59	781	800	766	3.8	3.5	6.4	1.8	55%	12%	52	22	26	35%	86%	8%	0	14			0	0.94	4.2	50	60	$2
15	Proj	**2**	**2**	**0**	**36**	**28**	**4.16**	**3.89**	**1.53**	**791**	**709**	**864**	**3.9**	**3.6**	**6.9**	**1.9**	**56%**	**12%**	**50**	**21**	**29**	**33%**	**75%**	**12%**	**0**						**-1.9**	**54**	**64**	**-$4**

Cole,A.J.

Age: 23	Th: R	Role SP	Health A	LIMA Plan B+	
Ht: 6' 4"	Wt: 180	Type FB	PT/Exp F	Rand Var 0	
			Consist F	MM 2100	

Top Nationals' prospect's Double-A dominance (61/15 K/BB, 2.92 ERA in 71 IP) led to Triple-A promotion in late June, which didn't go as well (see 2nd half BPV). Dom drop at that level coupled with xERA suggest there's more work to do. The future is bright, but don't bet on immediate returns in 2015.

Yr	Tm	W	L	Sv	IP	K	ERA	xERA	WHIP	oOPS	vL	vR	BF/G	Ctl	Dom	Cmd	FpK	SwK	G	L	F	H%	S%	hr/f	GS	APC	DOM%	DIS%	Sv%	LI	RAR	BPV	BPX	R$
10																																		
11																																		
12																																		
13	aa	4	2	0	45	41	2.57	2.21	0.97				24.6	1.9	8.2	4.4						27%	76%								7.3	135	176	$4
14	a/a	13	3	0	134	93	3.32	4.43	1.39				22.6	1.9	6.2	3.2						34%	77%								6.9	83	99	$4
1st Half		6	3	0	77	55	2.97	4.14	1.40				21.6	1.7	6.5	3.9						36%	78%								7.3	108	129	$5
2nd Half		7	0	0	57	38	3.80	4.82	1.38				24.1	2.2	5.9	2.6						32%	77%								-0.4	53	63	$2
15	Proj	**4**	**1**	**0**	**44**	**32**	**3.91**	**3.85**	**1.27**				**23.8**	**2.3**	**6.5**	**2.8**	**60%**	**8%**	**37**	**20**	**43**	**30%**	**73%**	**10%**	**7**						**-0.9**	**70**	**84**	**-$1**

Cole,Gerrit

Age: 24	Th: R	Role SP	Health D	LIMA Plan C+	
Ht: 6' 4"	Wt: 240	Type Pwr	PT/Exp D	Rand Var 0	
			Consist B	MM 4305	

11-5, 3.65 ERA in 138 IP at PIT. Shoulder, lat injuries cost him two months, but he looked elite after August return. Dom/GB% combo hints at considerable upside, especially given improving Ctl trend. Health a concern, but 2nd half strides, growth age hint that, with full season of IP there's hope for... UP: 3.00 ERA, 200 K.

Yr	Tm	W	L	Sv	IP	K	ERA	xERA	WHIP	oOPS	vL	vR	BF/G	Ctl	Dom	Cmd	FpK	SwK	G	L	F	H%	S%	hr/f	GS	APC	DOM%	DIS%	Sv%	LI	RAR	BPV	BPX	R$
10																																		
11																																		
12	a/a	4	6	0	65	55	3.58	3.68	1.39				21.0	3.1	7.6	2.4						34%	73%								3.5	90	117	-$1
13	PIT *	15	10	0	185	138	3.27	2.80	1.15	638	614	658	23.7	2.7	6.7	2.5	63%	10%	49	25	26	28%	72%	8%	19	91	63%	0%			13.7	86	112	$16
14	PIT *	14	6	0	160	151	3.45	3.35	1.22	693	729	659	24.9	2.5	8.5	3.4	62%	10%	49	19	32	31%	73%	9%	22	100	64%	9%			5.8	107	127	$10
1st Half		6	4	0	81	73	4.02	3.54	1.36	754	770	738	26.7	3.1	8.1	2.6	64%	9%	51	20	29	32%	73%	12%	13	100	46%	15%			-2.7	91	108	$3
2nd Half		8	2	0	80	78	2.88	2.54	1.07	599	664	541	23.8	1.9	8.8	4.6	60%	12%	47	18	36	30%	73%	6%	9	100	89%	0%			8.5	145	174	$18
15	Proj	**16**	**9**	**0**	**189**	**171**	**3.33**	**3.15**	**1.21**	**668**	**687**	**651**	**23.7**	**2.6**	**8.1**	**3.1**	**62%**	**10%**	**49**	**21**	**30**	**31%**	**73%**	**8%**	**32**						**9.6**	**103**	**122**	**$16**

Coleman,Louis

Age: 29	Th: R	Role RP	Health A	LIMA Plan C	
Ht: 6' 4"	Wt: 205	Type Pwr FB	PT/Exp D	Rand Var +1	
			Consist D	MM 2300	

1 SV, 5.56 ERA in 34 IP at KC. Bone bruise in finger caused April DL stint, and may have wreaked havoc on 1st half skills. Nasty hr/f didn't help, but Cmd collapse and xERA say this was deserved. Previous BPV trend, clean health slate offer hope, but not enough to warrant a bid this draft day.

Yr	Tm	W	L	Sv	IP	K	ERA	xERA	WHIP	oOPS	vL	vR	BF/G	Ctl	Dom	Cmd	FpK	SwK	G	L	F	H%	S%	hr/f	GS	APC	DOM%	DIS%	Sv%	LI	RAR	BPV	BPX	R$
10	a/a	7	3	7	92	82	2.44	2.35	1.02				8.4	2.4	8.0	3.4						26%	79%								18.6	113	182	$15
11	KC	1	4	1	60	64	2.87	3.88	1.17	685	803	619	5.1	3.9	9.7	2.5	62%	13%	30	13	57	25%	84%	11%	0	21			50	1.43	7.9	76	114	$3
12	KC *	0	2	3	71	85	3.67	3.75	1.27	762	827	724	5.5	4.3	10.8	2.5	58%	13%	20	23	58	28%	77%	14%	0	23			100	0.53	3.0	87	113	$1
13	KC *	6	2	6	74	71	1.54	2.70	1.20	493	601	440	5.9	3.0	8.6	2.9	66%	18%	41	24	34	31%	88%	4%	0	16			86	1.05	21.4	112	145	$11
14	KC *	3	1	8	74	63	5.02	5.17	1.51	862	629	971	5.4	4.1	7.7	1.9	62%	11%	42	22	36	31%	71%	15%	0	20			80	0.48	-11.6	42	50	-$4
1st Half		2	0	2	32	24	5.21	5.76	1.51	994	504	1305	5.6	3.6	6.7	1.8	69%	11%	36	22	42	30%	72%	18%	0	21			67	0.56	-5.9	19	23	-$6
2nd Half		1	1	6	41	39	4.87	4.71	1.52	663	962	580	5.3	4.5	8.4	1.9	51%	11%	52	20	27	32%	70%	8%	0	18			86	0.36	-5.8	60	71	-$1
15	Proj	**2**	**1**	**0**	**44**	**41**	**3.91**	**3.78**	**1.36**	**736**	**628**	**798**	**5.6**	**3.8**	**8.5**	**2.2**	**64%**	**13%**	**38**	**20**	**43**	**30%**	**75%**	**10%**	**0**						**-0.9**	**66**	**79**	**-$2**

RYAN BLOOMFIELD

Collmenter,Josh				Health	A	LIMA Plan	C+
Age: 29	Th: R	Role	RP	PT/Exp	B	Rand Var	-1
Ht: 6' 4"	Wt: 235	Type	FB	Consist	A	MM	2103

Moved back into the rotation, and with it, a change in approach. Sacrificed dominance for precision, an effort that produced better results in the 2nd half than the 1st. But xERA keeps saying that he's overachieving and that means regression might push back hard. Competent back-of-rotation guy, little more.

Yr	Tm	W	L	Sv	IP	K	ERA	xERA	WHIP	oOPS	vL	vR	BF/G	Ctl	Dom	Cmd	FpK	SwK	G	L	F	H%	S%	hr/f	GS	APC	DOM%	DIS%	Sv%	LI	RAR	BPV	BPX	R$
10	a/a	12	6	0	137	91	4.01	4.15	1.38				26.2	3.1	6.0	1.9						31%	72%								1.1	55	88	$4
11	ARI	10	10	0	154	100	3.38	4.09	1.07	652	708	594	20.0	1.6	5.8	3.6	62%	8%	33	20	47	26%	72%	8%	24	79	58%	21%	0	0.71	10.7	72	108	$13
12	ARI	5	3	0	90	80	3.69	3.97	1.26	742	806	677	13.4	2.2	8.0	3.6	59%	9%	37	19	43	31%	76%	12%	11	54	36%	27%	0	0.66	3.7	99	130	$2
13	ARI	5	5	0	92	85	3.13	4.05	1.22	649	660	642	7.8	3.2	8.3	2.6	60%	11%	33	21	47	29%	77%	7%	0	32			0	1.40	8.3	74	96	$5
14	ARI	11	9	1	179	115	3.46	4.02	1.13	676	741	608	21.8	2.0	5.8	2.9	60%	8%	39	21	40	27%	72%	8%	28	82	54%	18%	100	0.84	6.2	68	81	$11
1st Half		7	4	1	91	56	3.74	4.40	1.24	717	738	698	19.8	2.6	5.5	2.2	60%	7%	39	18	42	28%	73%	8%	14	74	43%	21%	100	0.88	0.0	48	57	$9
2nd Half		4	5	0	88	59	3.17	3.64	1.01	632	744	497	24.5	1.3	6.0	4.5	59%	9%	38	24	37	26%	72%	8%	14	93	64%	14%			6.2	89	106	$14
15	Proj	9	7	0	146	110	3.71	3.72	1.20	695	757	636	14.0	2.3	6.8	3.0	60%	9%	36	21	43	29%	72%	8%	17						0.5	75	89	$7

Colome,Alexander				Health	D	LIMA Plan	C
Age: 26	Th: R	Role	RP	PT/Exp	D	Rand Var	-1
Ht: 6' 2"	Wt: 210	Type	Pwr	Consist	A	MM	2100

2-0, 2.66 ERA in 24 IP at TAM. Lost two months to PEDs. Used to be you could scan down the Cmd line and think, "Under 2.0? Not interested." Now it's "Under 2.5? Not interested." For him, now? "REALLY not interested." His 95mph FB may play in pen, where rumors have him going. Wait on 2.5 before investing.

Yr	Tm	W	L	Sv	IP	K	ERA	xERA	WHIP	oOPS	vL	vR	BF/G	Ctl	Dom	Cmd	FpK	SwK	G	L	F	H%	S%	hr/f	GS	APC	DOM%	DIS%	Sv%	LI	RAR	BPV	BPX	R$
10																																		
11	aa	3	4	0	52	27	4.18	3.39	1.31				23.9	4.4	4.7	1.1						24%	69%								-1.6	38	57	-$2
12	a/a	8	4	0	92	78	3.74	3.56	1.41				22.8	4.0	7.6	1.9						32%	72%								3.1	81	106	$1
13	TAM *	5	7	0	86	73	3.33	4.08	1.43	715	685	739	21.6	3.9	7.6	1.9	61%	12%	43	22	35	32%	79%	12%	3	88	33%	33%			5.7	67	87	$0
14	TAM *	9	6	0	110	73	4.24	4.02	1.46	590	566	612	23.5	3.4	6.0	1.8	67%	9%	38	22	41	33%	69%	3%	3	77	67%	0%	0	0.68	-6.8	65	78	-$3
1st Half		4	1	0	38	25	3.98	3.97	1.43	581	722	471	22.8	3.7	6.1	1.7	68%	9%	40	10	50	31%	72%	7%	1	82	0%	0%	0	0.77	-1.1	58	69	-$4
2nd Half		5	5	0	72	48	4.38	4.04	1.48	595	500	801	23.8	3.2	6.0	1.9	67%	9%	36	30	34	34%	68%	0%	2	74	100%	0%	0	0.63	-5.7	69	83	-$3
15	Proj	4	4	0	58	42	3.93	3.90	1.43				17.9	3.7	6.5	1.8	0%	0%				32%	72%		5						-1.4	65	77	-$2

Colon,Bartolo				Health	D	LIMA Plan	B
Age: 42	Th: R	Role	SP	PT/Exp	A	Rand Var	0
Ht: 5' 11"	Wt: 285	Type	Con	Consist	A	MM	3103

Grizzled vet's latter-day M.O.: Here it is, see what you can do. Low SwK says hitters do *something*, but not enough to knock him from game. The risk is that one day it becomes batting practice, though no huge sign of that just yet. More likely, another year of eating innings (that's not a fat joke, we swear).

Yr	Tm	W	L	Sv	IP	K	ERA	xERA	WHIP	oOPS	vL	vR	BF/G	Ctl	Dom	Cmd	FpK	SwK	G	L	F	H%	S%	hr/f	GS	APC	DOM%	DIS%	Sv%	LI	RAR	BPV	BPX	R$
10																																		
11	NYY	8	10	0	164	135	4.00	3.70	1.29	751	880	621	23.9	2.2	7.4	3.4	65%	6%	44	20	36	31%	73%	11%	26	88	50%	27%	0	0.77	-1.1	96	144	$5
12	OAK	10	9	0	152	91	3.43	4.23	1.21	692	782	587	26.5	1.4	5.4	4.0	67%	5%	46	18	36	30%	75%	9%	24	89	50%	25%			11.1	84	110	$9
13	OAK	18	6	0	190	117	2.65	4.00	1.17	659	681	636	25.6	1.4	5.5	4.0	65%	7%	42	21	38	30%	80%	6%	30	93	43%	13%			28.6	83	108	$21
14	NYM	15	13	0	202	151	4.09	3.82	1.23	716	681	755	27.3	1.3	6.7	5.0	66%	6%	39	22	39	32%	69%	9%	31	97	68%	16%			-8.8	102	121	$6
1st Half		8	6	0	107	79	3.88	3.79	1.16	694	724	661	27.8	1.3	6.7	5.3	66%	6%	41	21	39	30%	70%	9%	16	99	63%	13%			-1.8	105	125	$10
2nd Half		7	7	0	96	72	4.33	3.87	1.30	741	632	858	26.8	1.4	6.8	4.8	65%	6%	38	23	39	33%	68%	8%	15	95	73%	20%			-6.9	100	119	$2
15	Proj	11	11	0	166	111	4.19	3.65	1.25	729	734	724	25.8	1.4	6.0	4.2	66%	6%	41	21	38	31%	69%	9%	26						-9.2	89	106	$4

Cook,Ryan				Health	C	LIMA Plan	B+
Age: 28	Th: R	Role	RP	PT/Exp	C	Rand Var	-3
Ht: 6' 2"	Wt: 215	Type	Pwr	Consist	A	MM	4410

One-time future closer got waylaid by injuries, flagging skills. Cmd, BPV, OPS vs. LHB all headed in wrong direction. Work in 2nd half offers hope, but don't buy that he made Ctl breakthrough, given low FpK. Unless small-sample gains vs. LHB hold, "solid LIMA play" may be floor as well as ceiling.

Yr	Tm	W	L	Sv	IP	K	ERA	xERA	WHIP	oOPS	vL	vR	BF/G	Ctl	Dom	Cmd	FpK	SwK	G	L	F	H%	S%	hr/f	GS	APC	DOM%	DIS%	Sv%	LI	RAR	BPV	BPX	R$
10	a/a	1	1	0	24	14	5.15	4.04	1.43				25.1	4.4	5.4	1.2						28%	64%								-3.1	39	63	-$3
11	ARI *	1	6	19	69	58	2.75	2.51	1.20	797	734	853	4.6	3.6	7.6	2.1	51%	9%	46	19	35	28%	76%	0%	0	14			79	0.44	10.1	93	140	$11
12	OAK	6	2	14	73	80	2.09	3.23	0.94	517	568	473	4.1	3.3	9.8	3.0	49%	12%	47	16	38	23%	80%	6%	0	16			67	1.40	17.4	112	146	$18
13	OAK	6	4	2	67	67	2.54	3.68	1.29	616	730	526	4.1	3.3	9.0	2.7	58%	11%	47	19	34	33%	80%	3%	0	16			22	1.35	11.0	96	125	$5
14	OAK	1	3	1	50	50	3.42	3.47	1.08	585	815	442	3.7	4.0	9.0	2.3	55%	11%	45	21	34	24%	69%	7%	0	14			33	0.87	2.0	78	93	$1
1st Half		0	1	1	23	25	3.91	4.14	1.48	748	1057	552	4.4	5.9	9.8	1.7	55%	12%	46	18	36	29%	77%	14%	0	16			100	0.81	-0.5	42	50	-$4
2nd Half		1	2	0	27	25	3.00	2.93	0.74	425	570	338	3.2	2.3	8.3	3.6	55%	11%	45	23	32	20%	55%	0%	0	12			0	0.92	2.5	110	131	$6
15	Proj	3	4	3	65	65	3.04	3.25	1.18	611	770	498	3.8	3.6	8.9	2.5	55%	11%	46	20	35	29%	74%	5%	0						5.6	88	105	$4

Corbin,Patrick				Health	F	LIMA Plan	B+
Age: 25	Th: L	Role	SP	PT/Exp	C	Rand Var	0
Ht: 6' 2"	Wt: 185	Type		Consist	B	MM	3201

Top youngster missed all of 2014 due to Tommy John surgery. Team reportedly planning to take conservative approach, not bring him back until May or June, then limit innings. Still a bright future, but for 2015, may have more appeal to rebuilding keeper-league owners.

Yr	Tm	W	L	Sv	IP	K	ERA	xERA	WHIP	oOPS	vL	vR	BF/G	Ctl	Dom	Cmd	FpK	SwK	G	L	F	H%	S%	hr/f	GS	APC	DOM%	DIS%	Sv%	LI	RAR	BPV	BPX	R$
10																																		
11	aa	9	8	0	160	121	4.65	4.63	1.40				26.0	2.1	6.8	3.3						34%	68%								-14.1	80	120	-$2
12	ARI *	11	10	1	186	154	3.90	4.26	1.34	783	780	784	22.1	2.2	7.4	3.3	58%	9%	46	23	31	33%	73%	13%	17	73	47%	35%	100	0.77	2.6	88	114	$6
13	ARI	14	8	0	208	178	3.41	3.48	1.17	671	560	703	26.9	2.3	7.7	3.3	70%	11%	47	22	31	29%	73%	10%	32	96	72%	6%			11.6	100	131	$16
14																																		
1st Half																																		
2nd Half																																		
15	Proj	5	4	0	87	70	3.93	3.44	1.29	727	660	744	24.8	2.5	7.3	2.9	65%	10%	46	23	31	31%	71%	10%	14						-2.1	87	104	$1

Corcino,Daniel				Health	A	LIMA Plan	D
Age: 24	Th: R	Role	SP	PT/Exp	D	Rand Var	-1
Ht: 5' 11"	Wt: 210	Type	Pwr xFB	Consist	F	MM	0101

0-2, 4.34 ERA in 19 IP at CIN. Demoted to AA and didn't exactly excel there (113/70 K/BB), yet "earned" late-season promotion. Success in first start short-lived, as Ctl struggles resurfaced. Should spend much of 2015 away from the majors, and your roster, trying to get things together.

Yr	Tm	W	L	Sv	IP	K	ERA	xERA	WHIP	oOPS	vL	vR	BF/G	Ctl	Dom	Cmd	FpK	SwK	G	L	F	H%	S%	hr/f	GS	APC	DOM%	DIS%	Sv%	LI	RAR	BPV	BPX	R$
10																																		
11																																		
12	aa	8	8	0	143	111	4.00	3.91	1.40				23.2	4.2	7.0	1.6						29%	73%								0.3	58	76	$0
13	aaa	7	14	0	129	78	7.57	6.87	1.89				21.7	5.3	5.5	1.0						34%	61%								-59.0	-2	-2	-$30
14	CIN *	10	14	0	167	117	4.71	4.45	1.42	619	564	644	22.2	4.4	6.3	1.4	49%	9%	30	23	47	27%	70%	8%	3	63	33%	33%	0	0.55	-19.9	34	40	-$6
1st Half		7	6	0	90	56	5.28	5.15	1.60				23.4	5.1	5.6	1.1						29%	69%	0%	0						-17.1	21	26	-$10
2nd Half		3	8	0	77	60	4.31	3.88	1.24	619	564	644	20.9	3.8	7.0	1.8	49%	9%	30	23	47	24%	71%	8%	3	63	33%	33%	0	0.55	-5.4	47	56	$0
15	Proj	4	7	0	72	49	4.99	5.01	1.57	765	714	789	22.0	4.7	6.2	1.3	49%	9%	30	23	47	30%	72%	9%	14						-11.1	-7	-8	-$6

Correia,Kevin				Health	B	LIMA Plan	D+
Age: 34	Th: R	Role	SP	PT/Exp	A	Rand Var	+1
Ht: 6' 3"	Wt: 200	Type	Con	Consist	A	MM	1003

"Desperation play." That describes his role for the hobbled Dodgers rotation down the stretch last year AND his place in the fantasy universe now. Consistently subpar BPIs got worse last year, with hopeful signs tough to find. Seriously, three editors reviewed this data and we all came up empty.

Yr	Tm	W	L	Sv	IP	K	ERA	xERA	WHIP	oOPS	vL	vR	BF/G	Ctl	Dom	Cmd	FpK	SwK	G	L	F	H%	S%	hr/f	GS	APC	DOM%	DIS%	Sv%	LI	RAR	BPV	BPX	R$
10	SD	10	10	0	145	115	5.40	4.12	1.49	783	769	795	22.9	4.0	7.1	1.8	60%	8%	49	21	30	31%	66%	15%	26	90	35%	19%	0	0.75	-23.6	48	78	-$5
11	PIT	12	11	0	154	77	4.79	4.47	1.39	791	745	826	24.4	2.3	4.5	2.0	60%	6%	45	18	36	30%	69%	13%	26	87	27%	27%	0	0.73	-16.1	42	64	-$3
12	PIT	12	11	0	171	89	4.21	4.42	1.30	733	735	731	22.8	2.4	4.7	1.9	62%	6%	51	20	29	28%	70%	12%	28	80	36%	18%	0	0.76	-4.1	48	63	$3
13	MIN	9	13	0	185	101	4.18	4.39	1.42	799	806	792	25.5	2.2	4.9	2.2	58%	6%	44	24	32	32%	74%	12%	31	94	35%	16%			-7.1	51	67	-$3
14	2 TM	7	17	0	154	79	5.44	4.79	1.50	818	838	793	21.5	2.3	4.6	2.0	59%	6%	43	19	38	32%	65%	10%	26	79	35%	27%	0	0.85	-32.2	41	49	-$14
1st Half		4	9	0	90	45	5.08	4.73	1.45	795	795	794	24.8	2.0	4.5	2.3	57%	5%	42	19	39	33%	66%	7%	16	92	38%	25%			-14.9	47	56	-$12
2nd Half		3	8	0	64	34	5.94	4.89	1.57	850	892	792	18.2	2.8	4.8	1.7	60%	7%	44	20	36	32%	65%	13%	10	65	30%	30%	0	0.92	-17.2	33	39	-$16
15	Proj	6	12	0	144	75	4.98	4.32	1.45	803	820	785	21.5	2.5	4.7	1.9	59%	6%	43	20	36	31%	68%	11%	29						-22.0	40	47	-$8

KRISTOPHER OLSON

Cosart,Jarred

Age: 25	Th: R	Role SP	Health A	LIMA Plan B
Ht: 6' 3"	Wt: 195	Type GB	PT/Exp C	Rand Var -1
			Consist B	MM 2105

Hot August after trade to MIA (1.64 ERA) attracted some interest, but really, he was same guy with same lackluster Cmd. Mid-90s fastball, GB% are nice building blocks, but rest of package not quite there. Until FpK, SwK improve enough to boost growth in Ctl and Dom, you'll want to temper enthusiasm.

Yr	Tm	W	L	Sv	IP	K	ERA	xERA	WHIP	oOPS	vL	vR	BF/G	Ctl	Dom	Cmd	FpK	SwK	G	L	F	H%	S%	hr/f	GS	APC	DOM%	DIS%	Sv%	LI	RAR	BPV	BPX	R$
10																																		
11	aa	1	2	0	36	20	4.91	3.91	1.29				21.3	3.0	4.8	1.6						27%	63%								-4.3	38	57	-$3
12	a/a	6	7	0	115	82	3.31	3.55	1.40				23.1	3.7	6.4	1.7						31%	75%								10.0	71	93	$2
13	HOU *	8	5	0	153	114	3.00	3.32	1.39	631	489	849	23.0	4.9	6.7	1.4	52%	6%	55	21	24	27%	79%	7%	10	102	20%	10%			16.3	63	82	$6
14	2 TM	13	11	0	180	115	3.69	4.12	1.36	671	684	657	25.5	3.6	5.7	1.6	58%	7%	54	19	26	29%	73%	6%	30	98	47%	13%			1.1	37	44	$3
1st Half		8	5	0	95	62	3.60	3.94	1.31	666	660	673	24.8	3.5	5.9	1.7	58%	7%	56	18	26	28%	73%	8%	16	98	50%	13%			1.7	45	54	$7
2nd Half		5	6	0	85	53	3.80	4.32	1.43	676	712	641	26.4	3.8	5.6	1.5	58%	7%	52	21	27	31%	72%	4%	14	98	43%	14%			-0.6	28	34	-$1
15	Proj	11	10	0	189	125	3.79	3.90	1.39	696	632	769	24.0	3.8	6.0	1.6	56%	7%	54	20	26	29%	73%	8%	33						-1.1	37	43	$3

Cotts,Neal

Age: 35	Th: L	Role RP	Health A	LIMA Plan C
Ht: 6' 1"	Wt: 200	Type Pwr	PT/Exp D	Rand Var 0
			Consist F	MM 3310

As suspected, could not repeat standout 2013. On whole, skills dip not a disaster, but 2nd half loss of Dom, rise in FB and HR a bit alarming. Won't inspire faith as "lefty specialist" getting hit like this, either. Here's a new descriptive term... PRUNE: A player who forever wallows in the free agent pool. Cotts is a prune.

Yr	Tm	W	L	Sv	IP	K	ERA	xERA	WHIP	oOPS	vL	vR	BF/G	Ctl	Dom	Cmd	FpK	SwK	G	L	F	H%	S%	hr/f	GS	APC	DOM%	DIS%	Sv%	LI	RAR	BPV	BPX	R$
10																																		
11																																		
12	aaa	2	1	3	32	29	6.10	6.09	1.85				5.9	4.8	8.3	1.7						39%	67%								-8.1	54	70	-$7
13	TEX *	11	4	3	80	95	1.10	1.68	0.97	499	565	436	4.1	2.7	10.7	4.0	64%	13%	44	22	34	28%	91%	4%	0	16			50	1.14	27.3	153	199	$18
14	TEX	2	9	2	67	63	4.32	3.91	1.34	713	775	680	3.9	3.1	8.5	2.7	66%	11%	35	25	40	32%	69%	8%	0	15			22	1.32	-4.8	82	98	-$2
1st Half		2	4	0	35	41	3.38	3.24	1.30	666	725	627	3.9	3.1	10.6	3.4	65%	12%	37	28	36	36%	73%	3%	0	15			0	1.37	1.6	122	146	$1
2nd Half		0	5	2	32	22	5.34	4.67	1.38	763	844	729	4.0	3.1	6.2	2.0	68%	9%	33	22	45	29%	64%	11%	0	14			50	1.27	-6.3	39	46	-$5
15	Proj	3	4	2	65	60	3.98	3.56	1.29	687	734	655	4.2	3.2	8.3	2.6	65%	11%	38	24	38	31%	70%	7%	0						-1.9	78	93	$0

Crow,Aaron

Age: 28	Th: R	Role RP	Health A	LIMA Plan B
Ht: 6' 3"	Wt: 195	Type Pwr	PT/Exp C	Rand Var -1
			Consist B	MM 2210

Crow? More appropriately, we're looking at a swan dive when it came to his skills (Dom, Cmd, GB%). Ctl evaporated in 2nd half, he became ultra-hittable, and hr/f misfortune (a familiar bugaboo) compounded his misery. Too young to conclude he's a turkey, but wait to see him take flight before swooping in.

Yr	Tm	W	L	Sv	IP	K	ERA	xERA	WHIP	oOPS	vL	vR	BF/G	Ctl	Dom	Cmd	FpK	SwK	G	L	F	H%	S%	hr/f	GS	APC	DOM%	DIS%	Sv%	LI	RAR	BPV	BPX	R$
10	aa	7	7	0	119	72	6.33	5.56	1.70				24.5	4.3	5.4	1.3						34%	62%								-33.1	27	43	-$13
11	KC	4	4	0	62	65	2.76	3.44	1.39	711	919	537	4.7	4.5	9.4	2.1	51%	12%	52	21	27	30%	86%	18%	0	18			0	1.30	9.1	78	118	$2
12	KC	3	1	2	65	65	3.48	3.22	1.18	601	556	626	3.6	3.1	9.0	3.0	53%	13%	53	19	28	30%	71%	8%	0	13			25	1.09	4.3	111	145	$3
13	KC	7	5	1	48	44	3.38	3.91	1.48	776	846	712	3.7	4.1	8.3	2.0	58%	11%	49	20	31	32%	82%	14%	0	14			25	1.78	2.9	64	84	$0
14	KC	6	1	3	59	34	4.12	4.61	1.29	743	805	693	3.6	3.7	5.2	1.4	53%	8%	43	19	38	24%	74%	14%	0	14			50	0.85	-2.7	16	18	$0
1st Half		3	1	1	35	19	2.60	4.02	1.07	618	659	587	3.6	2.3	4.9	2.1	58%	9%	46	20	34	24%	79%	8%	0	13			33	0.92	4.9	50	60	$4
2nd Half		3	0	2	24	15	6.29	5.51	1.60	908	991	839	3.7	5.5	5.5	1.0	47%	7%	39	18	43	24%	69%	21%	0	15			67	0.75	-7.6	-33	-39	-$5
15	Proj	6	2	3	58	45	3.76	3.94	1.38	759	835	698	3.8	3.9	7.0	1.8	53%	9%	46	19	34	28%	79%	15%	0						-0.1	44	53	$1

Cueto,Johnny

Age: 29	Th: R	Role SP	Health F	LIMA Plan D+
Ht: 5' 11"	Wt: 215	Type Pwr	PT/Exp A	Rand Var -4
			Consist A	MM 4305

A few nits to pick: Hit rate probably can't last. S% a bit high, too. Couldn't hold 1st half GB% gains. Health history warns not to expect 244 IP again, and that may be the best reason to pump brakes. But enough with the nits. BPV now places him in elite class. All he needs is to maintain health.

Yr	Tm	W	L	Sv	IP	K	ERA	xERA	WHIP	oOPS	vL	vR	BF/G	Ctl	Dom	Cmd	FpK	SwK	G	L	F	H%	S%	hr/f	GS	APC	DOM%	DIS%	Sv%	LI	RAR	BPV	BPX	R$
10	CIN	12	7	0	186	138	3.64	4.04	1.28	727	710	741	25.2	2.7	6.7	2.5	55%	10%	42	19	39	30%	74%	9%	31	101	58%	13%			10.2	67	109	$11
11	CIN	9	5	0	156	104	2.31	3.64	1.09	593	588	598	26.3	2.7	6.0	2.2	56%	8%	54	16	30	26%	80%	6%	24	100	54%	13%			31.5	67	100	$18
12	CIN	19	9	0	217	170	2.78	3.59	1.17	667	708	620	26.9	2.0	7.1	3.5	63%	9%	49	22	29	30%	78%	8%	33	105	58%	12%			33.1	99	129	$26
13	CIN	5	2	0	61	51	2.82	3.27	1.05	607	561	644	22.0	2.7	7.6	2.8	61%	11%	51	25	24	25%	79%	17%	11	87	64%	27%			7.8	93	121	$5
14	CIN	20	9	0	244	242	2.25	3.07	0.96	574	561	585	28.3	2.4	8.9	3.7	63%	10%	46	19	35	25%	82%	10%	34	108	65%	0%			44.7	120	143	$38
1st Half		8	5	0	124	122	1.88	2.80	0.84	504	491	514	28.1	2.1	8.8	4.2	63%	10%	53	15	31	22%	82%	9%	17	109	65%	0%			28.5	134	160	$44
2nd Half		12	4	0	119	120	2.64	3.33	1.09	644	623	662	28.4	2.7	9.1	3.3	62%	11%	39	23	38	27%	81%	11%	17	106	65%	0%			16.2	107	127	$32
15	Proj	17	7	0	206	184	2.94	3.09	1.10	627	617	635	25.4	2.5	8.1	3.3	62%	10%	47	21	32	28%	76%	9%	32						20.4	103	123	$24

Cumpton,Brandon

Age: 26	Th: R	Role SP	Health A	LIMA Plan D+
Ht: 6' 2"	Wt: 220	Type Con	PT/Exp D	Rand Var -2
			Consist A	MM 1000

3-4, 4.89 ERA in 70 IP with PIT. Did register a PQS-DOM in half of his 10 MLB starts, but hard to see him as anything but a fringe rotation candidate until Dom picks up. Cmd actually better in bigs than at AAA-Indianapolis (37/20 K/BB in 71 IP). Fine to watch from afar a bit longer.

Yr	Tm	W	L	Sv	IP	K	ERA	xERA	WHIP	oOPS	vL	vR	BF/G	Ctl	Dom	Cmd	FpK	SwK	G	L	F	H%	S%	hr/f	GS	APC	DOM%	DIS%	Sv%	LI	RAR	BPV	BPX	R$
10																																		
11																																		
12	aa	12	11	0	152	69	4.64	4.35	1.44				24.0	2.7	4.1	1.5						31%	67%								-11.8	39	51	-$5
13	PIT *	8	9	0	162	97	3.88	3.85	1.40	541	638	452	23.6	3.0	5.4	1.8	62%	7%	54	17	29	32%	71%	4%	5	75	60%	0%	0	0.71	-0.2	59	77	-$1
14	PIT *	8	8	0	141	74	4.16	4.32	1.41	731	783	694	21.4	2.4	4.7	2.0	62%	7%	44	28	28	32%	70%	3%	10	70	50%	30%	0	0.82	-7.3	51	60	-$3
1st Half		7	3	0	93	48	3.29	3.41	1.29	689	747	646	25.4	2.1	4.6	2.2	62%	7%	45	30	25	31%	73%	2%	9	89	56%	22%			5.2	69	82	$4
2nd Half		1	5	0	49	26	5.82	6.05	1.65	852	907	818	16.7	2.9	4.8	1.6	63%	6%	43	22	34	34%	66%	5%	1	45	0%	100%	0	0.88	-12.5	18	22	-$18
15	Proj	3	4	0	58	31	4.44	4.16	1.46	753	813	707	21.2	2.8	4.9	1.8	62%	7%	48	22	30	32%	70%	7%	12						-5.0	39	46	-$4

Danks,John

Age: 30	Th: L	Role SP	Health F	LIMA Plan D+
Ht: 6' 1"	Wt: 210	Type	PT/Exp B	Rand Var 0
			Consist A	MM 1005

The good news: Maintained sufficient health to approach 200 IP. The bad news: Those innings were worse than mediocre. Dom still not back to where it was before 2012 shoulder surgery. Until it reappears, when the draft bidding gets to you, simply say, "Thanks, but no Danks." [ED: Sorry. I tried to cut that. I really did.]

Yr	Tm	W	L	Sv	IP	K	ERA	xERA	WHIP	oOPS	vL	vR	BF/G	Ctl	Dom	Cmd	FpK	SwK	G	L	F	H%	S%	hr/f	GS	APC	DOM%	DIS%	Sv%	LI	RAR	BPV	BPX	R$
10	CHW	15	11	0	213	162	3.72	3.95	1.22	657	694	640	27.4	3.0	6.8	2.3	60%	9%	45	16	39	28%	71%	7%	32	106	63%	9%			9.5	66	107	$15
11	CHW	8	12	0	170	135	4.33	3.84	1.34	752	704	771	27.0	2.4	7.1	2.9	63%	10%	44	20	36	32%	70%	10%	27	102	59%	19%			-8.2	85	127	$1
12	CHW	3	4	0	54	30	5.70	5.23	1.49	790	831	760	26.4	3.9	5.0	1.3	56%	7%	41	22	37	29%	63%	11%	9	93	33%	33%			-11.2	5	7	-$8
13	CHW *	6	14	0	161	101	4.71	5.06	1.36	798	831	785	25.9	2.4	5.6	2.3	62%	9%	41	22	37	29%	71%	17%	22	100	55%	14%			-16.9	30	39	-$5
14	CHW	11	11	0	194	129	4.74	4.62	1.44	785	710	810	26.7	3.4	6.0	1.7	61%	8%	42	19	38	30%	70%	10%	32	103	34%	22%			-23.9	35	42	-$7
1st Half		7	6	0	99	65	4.26	4.73	1.36	759	693	780	26.9	3.5	5.9	1.7	59%	8%	39	18	43	28%	72%	9%	16	105	38%	19%			-6.3	28	33	-$1
2nd Half		4	5	0	94	64	5.25	4.49	1.53	812	725	842	26.5	3.3	6.1	1.8	64%	8%	45	21	33	32%	68%	12%	16	101	31%	25%			-17.5	43	51	-$14
15	Proj	9	13	0	189	123	4.62	4.24	1.43	787	768	794	25.9	3.3	5.9	1.8	61%	8%	41	20	38	30%	71%	12%	31						-20.4	37	44	-$5

Darvish,Yu

Age: 28	Th: R	Role SP	Health D	LIMA Plan B
Ht: 6' 5"	Wt: 215	Type Pwr	PT/Exp A	Rand Var 0
			Consist A	MM 5505

Spring neck issue a false alarm; mid-August elbow injury (which ended season) a genuine cause for panic. In between, improved FpK led to better Ctl. Now, health is top issue, with uptick in FB% a secondary concern. If he avoids DL, should again set MLB strikeout pace, but not without risk.

Yr	Tm	W	L	Sv	IP	K	ERA	xERA	WHIP	oOPS	vL	vR	BF/G	Ctl	Dom	Cmd	FpK	SwK	G	L	F	H%	S%	hr/f	GS	APC	DOM%	DIS%	Sv%	LI	RAR	BPV	BPX	R$
10	for	12	8	0	202	211	2.21	2.56	1.13				30.7	2.6	9.4	3.6						31%	81%								46.5	130	211	$27
11	for	18	6	0	232	262	1.78	1.65	0.91				30.9	1.7	10.2	5.9						29%	82%								61.8	189	283	$46
12	TEX	16	9	0	191	221	3.90	3.48	1.28	659	674	640	28.1	4.2	10.4	2.5	58%	13%	46	22	32	31%	70%	9%	29	109	72%	3%			2.6	98	128	$13
13	TEX	13	9	0	210	277	2.83	2.86	1.07	611	655	543	26.3	3.4	11.9	3.5	57%	13%	41	21	38	27%	80%	14%	32	108	84%	0%			26.7	140	183	$27
14	TEX	10	7	0	144	182	3.06	3.18	1.26	679	721	605	27.5	3.1	11.3	3.7	62%	11%	36	23	41	35%	79%	9%	22	105	64%	14%			12.2	136	162	$10
1st Half		8	4	0	104	128	2.42	3.24	1.18	615	679	515	28.5	3.2	11.0	3.5	61%	11%	34	24	43	32%	82%	6%	15	107	67%	7%			17.1	124	148	$19
2nd Half		2	3	0	40	54	4.73	3.01	1.48	829	807	879	25.3	2.7	12.2	4.5	63%	11%	43	21	36	41%	72%	15%	7	101	57%	29%			-4.9	167	199	-$12
15	Proj	13	10	0	203	256	3.26	2.75	1.17	638	661	600	25.8	3.2	11.4	3.6	60%	12%	41	22	38	32%	75%	10%	31						12.0	138	165	$20

KRISTOPHER OLSON

Davis,Wade

Age: 29 | Th: R | Role: RP | Ht: 6' 5" | Wt: 220 | Type: Pwr
Health: A | PT/Exp: C | Consist: D
LIMA Plan: C+ | Rand Var: -5 | MM: 5511

Now this is how you say, "I'm a reliever, dammit!" Return to pen yielded career-best, elite skills. RHBs should have just stayed in the dugout (.298 OPS!). Dom spike backed by SwK akin to 2012, when he also pitched only in relief. Given improving FpK, Ctl, GB%, could close very effectively if given the chance.

Yr Tm	W	L	Sv	IP	K	ERA	xERA	WHIP	oOPS	vL	vR	BF/G	Ctl	Dom	Cmd	FpK	SwK	G	L	F	H%	S%	hr/f	GS	APC	DOM%	DIS%	Sv%	LI	RAR	BPV	BPX	R$
10 TAM	12	10	0	168	113	4.07	4.59	1.35	756	776	732	24.9	3.3	6.1	1.8	59%	7%	39	17	44	28%	74%	10%	29	96	31%	17%			0.2	36	59	$5
11 TAM	11	10	0	184	105	4.45	4.78	1.38	771	779	765	27.4	3.1	5.1	1.7	59%	6%	36	21	43	29%	70%	9%	29	102	38%	21%			-11.5	23	35	-$1
12 TAM	3	0	0	70	87	2.43	3.31	1.09	570	464	654	5.3	3.7	11.1	3.0	57%	13%	39	22	40	28%	81%	8%	0	23			0	0.85	13.7	117	153	$7
13 KC	8	11	0	135	114	5.32	4.38	1.68	822	910	721	19.9	3.9	7.6	2.0	59%	8%	41	27	32	37%	69%	11%	24	80	38%	33%	0	0.85	-24.3	51	67	-$13
14 KC	9	2	3	72	109	1.00	2.08	0.85	408	513	298	3.9	2.9	13.6	4.7	61%	15%	48	22	30	29%	87%	0%	0	17			50	1.23	24.3	194	231	$17
1st Half	5	2	0	36	56	1.26	2.21	0.87	362	486	237	4.3	4.0	14.1	3.5	60%	14%	47	23	30	25%	84%	0%	0	19			0	1.43	10.9	170	203	$16
2nd Half	4	0	3	36	53	0.74	1.97	0.83	450	537	357	3.6	1.7	13.1	7.6	62%	16%	48	22	30	32%	90%	0%	0	15			75	1.05	13.4	216	257	$19
15 Proj	6	3	7	73	88	2.60	2.74	1.14	587	652	519	5.8	3.2	10.9	3.4	60%	12%	43	23	33	31%	78%	6%	0						10.2	132	157	$10

De Fratus,Justin

Age: 27 | Th: R | Role: RP | Ht: 6' 4" | Wt: 225 | Type: Pwr
Health: F | PT/Exp: D | Consist: B
LIMA Plan: B+ | Rand Var: -1 | MM: 3300

3-1, 2.39 in 53 IP with PHI. Before you conclude "he'll never close," consider: Strong SwK portends MLB Dom may climb to minor-league levels; FpK suggests Ctl gains may hold. Less good: GB% trend and health history. When he does pitch, should be relatively safe, with a bit of upside.

Yr Tm	W	L	Sv	IP	K	ERA	xERA	WHIP	oOPS	vL	vR	BF/G	Ctl	Dom	Cmd	FpK	SwK	G	L	F	H%	S%	hr/f	GS	APC	DOM%	DIS%	Sv%	LI	RAR	BPV	BPX	R$
10 aa	1	0	6	25	23	2.41	2.27	0.95				4.7	1.7	8.6	4.9						27%	79%								5.1	145	234	$3
11 PHI *	7	3	15	79	86	3.52	3.36	1.29	396	700	125	5.8	3.2	9.7	3.0	47%	9%	44	11	44	34%	73%	0%	0	12			88	0.69	4.1	112	168	$10
12 PHI *	0	1	3	32	26	3.32	2.55	1.04	478	646	361	4.2	2.3	7.2	3.2	61%	12%	52	13	35	26%	70%	0%	0	14			100	0.59	2.8	100	131	$0
13 PHI *	6	3	0	66	56	3.42	3.97	1.49	738	684	759	4.0	4.3	7.6	1.8	56%	12%	44	26	30	33%	77%	8%	0	14			0	1.21	3.6	73	95	-$1
14 PHI *	3	1	3	69	59	3.12	3.64	1.25	632	578	658	4.0	2.1	7.8	3.6	65%	13%	39	22	39	32%	77%	7%	0	15			50	1.02	5.2	105	125	$3
1st Half	2	0	3	38	30	3.28	4.14	1.33	613	502	664	4.5	2.2	7.2	3.3	61%	15%	41	19	41	33%	78%	8%	0	17			60	0.71	2.2	88	105	$2
2nd Half	1	1	0	31	29	2.93	3.67	1.14	644	624	654	3.9	2.1	8.5	4.1	67%	12%	38	23	38	31%	76%	6%	0	15			0	1.20	3.0	114	136	$3
15 Proj	3	2	0	58	51	3.25	3.45	1.26	692	630	719	4.1	2.8	8.0	2.9	61%	13%	41	23	36	31%	75%	6%	0						3.5	88	104	$1

de la Rosa,Jorge

Age: 34 | Th: L | Role: SP | Ht: 6' 1" | Wt: 215 | Type: Pwr
Health: F | PT/Exp: B | Consist: C
LIMA Plan: B | Rand Var: 0 | MM: 3205

xERA says this was "payback" for undeserved 2013 ERA. 2nd half piques interest, even as FpK questions Ctl gains. From 6/24 on, no start below PQS-3. Glass half-empty: "F" health. Half-full: TJS farther in rear-view. If Dom stays on march toward past levels, GB gains hold... UP: 3.50 ERA (again, but justified this time)

Yr Tm	W	L	Sv	IP	K	ERA	xERA	WHIP	oOPS	vL	vR	BF/G	Ctl	Dom	Cmd	FpK	SwK	G	L	F	H%	S%	hr/f	GS	APC	DOM%	DIS%	Sv%	LI	RAR	BPV	BPX	R$
10 COL	8	7	0	122	113	4.22	3.56	1.32	737	671	755	25.6	4.1	8.4	2.1	57%	12%	52	19	29	28%	71%	16%	20	101	60%	10%			-2.1	71	114	$4
11 COL	5	2	0	59	52	3.51	3.73	1.19	627	349	684	24.5	3.4	7.9	2.4	49%	12%	43	20	38	28%	71%	7%	10	96	70%	20%			3.2	73	110	$3
12 COL	0	2	0	11	6	9.28	5.98	1.78	1065	250	1219	17.7	1.7	5.1	3.0	62%	13%	34	14	52	33%	57%	22%	3	68	0%	100%			-6.9	58	75	-$8
13 COL	16	6	0	168	112	3.49	4.14	1.38	721	510	770	23.8	3.3	6.0	1.8	60%	10%	47	25	28	31%	76%	8%	30	92	40%	17%			7.8	43	57	$7
14 COL	14	11	0	184	139	4.10	3.79	1.24	707	532	760	24.0	3.3	6.8	2.1	55%	10%	52	18	31	27%	70%	13%	32	96	44%	19%			-8.2	64	76	$6
1st Half	8	6	0	91	67	4.86	4.05	1.33	755	497	835	22.8	3.9	6.7	1.7	55%	10%	53	16	31	27%	66%	14%	17	92	35%	35%			-12.6	46	55	$0
2nd Half	6	5	0	94	72	3.36	3.55	1.14	660	569	686	25.4	2.7	6.9	2.6	55%	11%	51	19	30	27%	73%	11%	15	100	53%	0%			4.4	80	96	$11
15 Proj	15	9	0	189	145	3.80	3.62	1.27	697	523	743	23.7	3.3	6.9	2.1	55%	11%	49	20	31	28%	72%	10%	32						-1.4	62	74	$10

De La Rosa,Rubby

Age: 26 | Th: R | Role: RP | Ht: 6' 1" | Wt: 205 | Type: Pwr
Health: B | PT/Exp: D | Consist: F
LIMA Plan: D+ | Rand Var: 0 | MM: 2203

4-8, 4.43 in 102 IP at BOS. Wowed in debut, but petered out as season wore on; not surprising given workload increase as he comes back from 2011 TJS. Raw tools (velocity, GB tilt) are there, just needs to rein them in, especially vs. LHB. Worth watching—but maybe not owning—this year.

Yr Tm	W	L	Sv	IP	K	ERA	xERA	WHIP	oOPS	vL	vR	BF/G	Ctl	Dom	Cmd	FpK	SwK	G	L	F	H%	S%	hr/f	GS	APC	DOM%	DIS%	Sv%	LI	RAR	BPV	BPX	R$
10 aa	3	1	0	51	35	1.39	2.15	1.11				25.1	3.2	6.1	1.9						26%	88%								16.9	85	138	$5
11 LA *	6	7	0	101	105	3.30	3.28	1.32	722	759	678	19.8	4.3	9.4	2.2	56%	10%	48	22	30	30%	76%	13%	10	79	50%	20%	0	0.85	8.0	93	140	$5
12 LA	0	0	0	1	0	27.00	30.14	3.00	500	500	500	4.0	27.0	0.0	0.0	50%	5%	0	0	100	0%	0%	0%	0	20			0	0.14	-1.9	-751	-980	-$5
13 BOS *	3	5	0	92	68	5.33	4.80	1.56	877	646	994	11.5	5.0	6.7	1.3	64%	11%	48	14	38	30%	67%	13%	0	17			0	0.50	-16.6	36	48	-$10
14 BOS *	6	12	0	162	120	4.47	4.53	1.48	814	832	792	22.4	3.4	6.7	2.0	52%	9%	46	22	32	33%	70%	12%	18	92	22%	33%	0	0.74	-14.6	58	69	-$7
1st Half	4	5	0	86	72	3.44	3.06	1.27	603	495	715	23.4	3.4	7.5	2.2	50%	11%	49	24	26	30%	72%	13%	5	102	40%	0%			3.2	89	107	$4
2nd Half	2	7	0	76	48	5.64	6.19	1.71	899	958	827	21.5	3.4	5.7	1.6	53%	8%	44	22	34	35%	69%	11%	13	89	15%	46%	0	0.73	-17.8	24	28	-$19
15 Proj	6	9	0	144	111	4.36	3.97	1.47	765	784	743	17.8	3.9	6.9	1.8	54%	9%	47	22	31	31%	71%	10%	27						-11.0	44	52	-$4

Deduno,Samuel

Age: 31 | Th: R | Role: RP | Ht: 6' 3" | Wt: 190 | Type: Pwr GB
Health: C | PT/Exp: C | Consist: A
LIMA Plan: D+ | Rand Var: +1 | MM: 2100

Posted back-to-back PQS-5s in May, then crashed to earth, was banished to pen and then waived. Has always been able to induce GB, and did better job with FpK, leading to borderline acceptable Cmd in small 2nd half sample. But at his age, it's likely too little, too late to earn a meaningful role.

Yr Tm	W	L	Sv	IP	K	ERA	xERA	WHIP	oOPS	vL	vR	BF/G	Ctl	Dom	Cmd	FpK	SwK	G	L	F	H%	S%	hr/f	GS	APC	DOM%	DIS%	Sv%	LI	RAR	BPV	BPX	R$
10 COL *	3	1	0	33	24	3.29	3.78	1.35	879	400	1262	13.9	5.0	6.5	1.3	75%	12%	38	25	38	24%	81%	33%	0	13			0	0.37	3.2	42	68	$0
11 SD *	4	6	0	108	72	3.32	3.79	1.53	899	929	875	11.2	4.8	6.0	1.2	53%	12%	70	20	10	31%	77%	0%	0	35			0	0.16	8.3	61	92	-$1
12 MIN *	7	7	0	121	91	3.97	4.21	1.53	759	723	805	21.9	5.9	6.8	1.1	54%	8%	58	21	20	27%	76%	21%	15	89	27%	47%			0.7	45	58	-$3
13 MIN *	8	8	0	125	79	3.79	3.85	1.40	714	584	884	25.1	3.8	5.7	1.5	51%	8%	60	20	20	30%	73%	10%	18	97	50%	17%			1.2	52	68	$0
14 2AL	2	6	0	101	83	4.47	3.88	1.41	724	742	704	12.7	4.1	7.4	1.8	58%	9%	53	20	26	30%	69%	11%	9	49	22%	56%	0	0.63	-9.1	54	64	-$5
1st Half	2	5	0	61	45	4.99	4.24	1.53	739	791	682	17.1	4.4	6.6	1.5	57%	9%	56	17	27	32%	67%	9%	8	68	25%	50%	0	0.78	-9.4	34	40	-$8
2nd Half	0	1	0	39	38	3.66	3.35	1.22	701	663	741	8.9	3.7	8.7	2.4	61%	10%	50	26	24	28%	73%	15%	1	34	0%	100%	0	0.50	0.4	85	102	$0
15 Proj	2	3	0	58	43	4.11	3.85	1.40	719	669	779	13.9	4.3	6.7	1.6	56%	9%	54	22	25	29%	72%	11%	7						-2.6	36	43	-$3

Degrom,Jacob

Age: 27 | Th: R | Role: SP | Ht: 6' 4" | Wt: 180 | Type: Pwr
Health: A | PT/Exp: D | Consist: D
LIMA Plan: C+ | Rand Var: -2 | MM: 4303

9-6, 2.69 ERA in 140 IP with NYM. Major surprise, but with strong skill support, particularly in torrid 2nd half. Didn't show such lofty Dom in minors, but SwK says it could be legit. Closed year with 12 straight dominating starts, despite brief shoulder tendinitis bout. If 2nd half is real... UP: 15 wins, 200 Ks

Yr Tm	W	L	Sv	IP	K	ERA	xERA	WHIP	oOPS	vL	vR	BF/G	Ctl	Dom	Cmd	FpK	SwK	G	L	F	H%	S%	hr/f	GS	APC	DOM%	DIS%	Sv%	LI	RAR	BPV	BPX	R$
10																																	
11																																	
12																																	
13 a/a	6	7	0	136	90	4.52	4.76	1.51				24.5	2.7	6.0	2.2						35%	70%								-10.9	59	77	-$7
14 NYM *	13	6	0	179	168	2.58	2.82	1.16	613	639	594	24.5	2.6	8.5	3.2	63%	12%	45	23	31	30%	79%	6%	22	102	68%	5%			25.5	114	135	$18
1st Half	5	4	0	93	69	3.03	3.74	1.33	737	716	752	24.1	3.2	6.7	2.1	59%	10%	41	26	33	30%	79%	10%	9	98	33%	11%			8.2	69	82	$9
2nd Half	8	2	0	86	99	2.10	2.60	0.98	530	584	491	25.7	2.0	10.4	5.2	65%	14%	49	21	30	31%	78%	3%	13	104	92%	0%			17.3	160	191	$28
15 Proj	11	7	0	174	157	3.13	3.21	1.21	672	695	655	24.2	2.6	8.1	3.1	63%	12%	46	23	31	31%	75%	7%	29						13.0	100	119	$14

Delgado,Randall

Age: 25 | Th: R | Role: RP | Ht: 6' 3" | Wt: 200 | Type: Pwr FB
Health: A | PT/Exp: C | Consist: B
LIMA Plan: C | Rand Var: +1 | MM: 2301

Manager lost faith after two April PQS-0 disasters; had to wait until September to get another brief starting shot. Skill surge in pen is overshadowed by a few bad outings. Changeup, slider yield plenty of swings and misses, and Ctl improved in 2nd half. When next shot comes, he may be ready to roll.

Yr Tm	W	L	Sv	IP	K	ERA	xERA	WHIP	oOPS	vL	vR	BF/G	Ctl	Dom	Cmd	FpK	SwK	G	L	F	H%	S%	hr/f	GS	APC	DOM%	DIS%	Sv%	LI	RAR	BPV	BPX	R$
10 aa	3	5	0	44	38	5.32	3.28	1.33				22.7	3.9	7.9	2.0						30%	58%								-6.7	83	135	-$2
11 ATL *	8	8	0	174	139	3.98	4.33	1.40	655	683	635	23.0	3.6	7.2	2.0	52%	8%	38	20	42	31%	74%	11%	7	89	29%	14%			-0.9	58	87	$2
12 ATL *	8	12	0	137	121	4.40	4.47	1.48	727	744	711	22.6	4.1	8.0	2.0	60%	9%	50	22	28	32%	72%	11%	17	90	35%	29%	0	0.80	-6.6	63	83	-$3
13 ARI *	7	12	0	180	127	4.73	4.73	1.33	793	765	819	22.7	2.7	6.3	2.4	60%	9%	42	20	38	29%	70%	17%	19	91	47%	5%	0	0.75	-19.1	41	53	-$4
14 ARI	4	4	0	78	86	4.87	3.89	1.36	701	690	710	7.2	4.1	10.0	2.5	56%	14%	35	21	44	33%	64%	7%	4	31	0%	75%	0	0.82	-10.8	83	99	-$3
1st Half	1	1	0	36	42	6.31	3.99	1.60	800	707	867	7.2	4.8	10.6	2.2	54%	14%	40	22	39	36%	62%	13%	2	32	0%	100%	0	0.85	-11.3	79	94	-$11
2nd Half	3	3	0	42	44	3.64	3.79	1.17	606	677	526	7.2	3.4	9.4	2.8	59%	15%	31	20	49	30%	67%	2%	2	30	0%	50%	0	0.79	0.5	86	103	$3
15 Proj	5	6	0	94	88	3.90	3.70	1.36	720	718	721	10.6	3.6	8.5	2.3	58%	12%	39	21	40	31%	73%	8%	2						-1.8	71	85	$0

KRISTOPHER OLSON

DeSclafani,Anthony

Age: 25	Th: R	Role SP	Health A	LIMA Plan C	
Ht: 6' 1"	Wt: 190	Type xFB	PT/Exp D	Rand Var +2	
			Consist B	MM 2100	

2-2, 6.27 ERA in 33 IP in MIA. Fernandez injury helped him beat more highly-touted prospects to bigs. Won first start, then things went south, aided by H%, S% misfortune. Still, 5.2 Cmd in majors nothing to sneeze at. More grooming likely on tap, but potentially a rotation factor in the 2nd half.

Yr	Tm	W	L	Sv	IP	K	ERA	xERA	WHIP	oOPS	vL	vR	BF/G	Ctl	Dom	Cmd	FpK	SwK	G	L	F	H%	S%	hr/f	GS	APC	DOM%	DIS%	Sv%	LI	RAR	BPV	BPX	R$
10																																		
11																																		
12																																		
13	aa	5	4	0	75	52	4.25	4.42	1.36				24.1	1.8	6.2	3.5						34%	70%								-3.6	84	109	-$2
14	MIA *	8	9	0	135	105	4.63	3.87	1.32	801	893	710	17.0	2.4	7.0	2.9	66%	9%	36	24	40	33%	64%	9%	5	42	40%	40%	0	0.40	-14.8	86	103	-$2
1st Half		5	7	0	89	65	5.11	4.41	1.35	868	961	755	21.8	2.2	6.6	3.0	65%	7%	31	27	42	33%	63%	11%	5	81	40%	40%			-15.0	74	89	-$4
2nd Half		3	2	0	47	39	3.72	2.84	1.25	597	545	623	11.9	2.7	7.6	2.9	67%	14%	50	17	33	32%	67%	0%	0	18			0	0.18	0.1	110	131	$0
15	Proj	4	3	0	58	44	4.23	3.94	1.32	650	697	593	21.4	2.2	6.8	3.0	65%	7%	31	27	42	33%	68%	4%	14						-3.5	71	85	-$2

Despaigne,Odrisamer

Age: 28	Th: R	Role SP	Health A	LIMA Plan C	
Ht: 6' 0"	Wt: 195	Type Pwr xGB	PT/Exp F	Rand Var 0	
			Consist F	MM 2203	

4-7, 3.36 ERA in 96 IP at SD. Cuban defector burst onto scene after all of 31 IP in minors, but had tougher time making MLB hitters swing and miss. Skills improved even as results got worse, though still needs to solve LHB. Decent GB% could help him be serviceable, but ceiling appears low.

Yr	Tm	W	L	Sv	IP	K	ERA	xERA	WHIP	oOPS	vL	vR	BF/G	Ctl	Dom	Cmd	FpK	SwK	G	L	F	H%	S%	hr/f	GS	APC	DOM%	DIS%	Sv%	LI	RAR	BPV	BPX	R$
10																																		
11																																		
12																																		
13																																		
14	SD *	5	10	0	128	98	4.03	3.98	1.40	638	713	558	23.4	3.5	6.9	2.0	60%	8%	52	19	29	31%	71%	7%	16	97	44%	25%			-4.6	67	80	-$2
1st Half		3	3	0	45	36	4.44	5.01	1.65	510	572	440	22.4	4.3	7.3	1.7	58%	4%	50	21	29	36%	73%	0%	2	94	50%	0%			-3.9	59	70	-$9
2nd Half		2	7	0	83	62	3.81	3.80	1.26	656	734	574	25.3	3.0	6.8	2.2	60%	9%	52	19	29	29%	70%	8%	14	97	43%	29%			-0.7	70	83	$1
15	Proj	7	12	0	160	123	4.05	3.77	1.41	657	734	576	23.3	3.5	6.9	2.0	60%	9%	52	19	29	32%	72%	7%	29						-6.0	60	72	-$1

Detwiler,Ross

Age: 29	Th: L	Role RP	Health F	LIMA Plan D+	
Ht: 6' 5"	Wt: 210	Type Con	PT/Exp B	Rand Var -1	
			Consist A	MM 2000	

After three seasons as a milquetoast SP, pitched exclusively in relief in '14, and performance was just as unexciting, costing him playoff roster spot. RHB lick their chops when they see him, but that may not last, as he looks like LOOGY-in-training. Fantasy translation: You can ignore him.

Yr	Tm	W	L	Sv	IP	K	ERA	xERA	WHIP	oOPS	vL	vR	BF/G	Ctl	Dom	Cmd	FpK	SwK	G	L	F	H%	S%	hr/f	GS	APC	DOM%	DIS%	Sv%	LI	RAR	BPV	BPX	R$
10	WAS *	4	5	0	67	44	3.60	5.40	1.61	826	1024	780	18.6	3.0	5.9	2.0	51%	6%	43	20	37	35%	80%	14%	5	62	0%	60%	0	0.53	4.0	44	72	-$2
11	WAS *	10	11	0	153	91	4.45	4.71	1.50	704	548	742	21.4	3.0	5.3	1.8	55%	7%	43	24	33	33%	71%	11%	10	65	50%	10%	0	0.90	-9.6	45	68	-$4
12	WAS	10	8	0	164	105	3.40	4.24	1.22	681	513	734	20.8	2.8	5.8	2.0	60%	8%	51	16	33	27%	75%	9%	27	77	33%	22%	0	0.83	12.6	56	73	$10
13	WAS	2	7	0	71	39	4.04	4.33	1.49	811	705	849	24.3	1.8	4.9	2.8	56%	7%	46	23	31	35%	73%	6%	13	86	23%	15%			-1.5	65	85	-$5
14	WAS	2	3	1	63	39	4.00	4.34	1.41	734	516	848	5.8	3.0	5.6	1.9	59%	7%	46	20	33	31%	73%	7%	0	22			50	0.61	-2.0	43	52	-$3
1st Half		0	2	1	36	22	4.00	4.81	1.53	780	527	895	7.3	4.3	5.5	1.3	58%	7%	46	19	35	30%	76%	10%	0	27			100	0.49	-1.1	8	9	-$6
2nd Half		2	1	0	27	17	4.00	3.76	1.26	671	504	776	4.6	1.3	5.7	4.3	61%	8%	47	22	30	33%	67%	4%	0	17			0	0.72	-0.9	91	109	$0
15	Proj	2	3	0	44	26	4.13	4.01	1.42	750	572	826	8.5	2.6	5.5	2.1	58%	7%	47	21	32	32%	71%	7%	0						-2.1	52	62	-$3

Diaz,Jose

Age: 31	Th: R	Role RP	Health A	LIMA Plan D+	
Ht: 6' 4"	Wt: 315	Type Pwr	PT/Exp F	Rand Var -3	
			Consist C	MM 2310	

0-1, 3.38 ERA in 35 IP at CIN. Owner of 105 saves in minors finally got called up and worked way into setup role by season's end. Don't look for him in the 9th, though, as LHBs present considerable difficulty. Still, SwK says he should be able to keep up nearly whiff-per-inning pace. Potentially decent value in holds leagues.

Yr	Tm	W	L	Sv	IP	K	ERA	xERA	WHIP	oOPS	vL	vR	BF/G	Ctl	Dom	Cmd	FpK	SwK	G	L	F	H%	S%	hr/f	GS	APC	DOM%	DIS%	Sv%	LI	RAR	BPV	BPX	R$
10	aa	1	0	4	25	19	2.79	3.61	1.39				5.5	4.1	7.0	1.7						30%	81%								4.0	69	111	$0
11	a/a	0	3	23	45	37	3.59	5.47	1.72				4.2	4.7	7.4	1.6						36%	81%								1.9	48	72	$5
12	aaa	1	2	3	45	27	4.87	5.34	1.69				4.9	4.1	5.3	1.3						34%	71%								-4.7	34	44	-$7
13	aaa	3	4	13	54	46	2.44	4.01	1.34				5.1	4.1	7.6	1.8						27%	89%								9.6	54	70	$6
14	CIN *	2	3	18	68	60	2.36	3.20	1.25	668	778	589	4.2	3.3	8.0	2.4	57%	13%	40	31	30	30%	83%	11%	0	16			90	1.22	11.6	89	107	$10
1st Half		2	2	18	36	26	2.19	3.77	1.29	1126	1089	1167	4.5	2.9	6.5	2.2	50%	7%	50	10	40	29%	87%	50%	0	23			95	0.28	6.9	66	79	$15
2nd Half		0	1	0	32	34	2.56	3.28	1.20	616	729	540	3.9	3.7	9.7	2.6	58%	14%	38	33	28	30%	78%	4%	0	16			0	1.30	4.6	90	108	$4
15	Proj	2	3	3	58	51	3.54	3.73	1.38	689	774	631	4.5	3.8	8.0	2.1	58%	14%	38	33	28	31%	76%	9%	0						1.5	56	67	$0

Dickey,R.A.

Age: 40	Th: R	Role SP	Health B	LIMA Plan B	
Ht: 6' 3"	Wt: 215	Type	PT/Exp A	Rand Var 0	
			Consist A	MM 2205	

Got off to rocky, wild start (6.26 ERA, 5.9 Ctl in first 4 starts), but like old pro he is, he refused to knuckle under. Cy Young year now a clear outlier, but as DOM/DIS shows, he generally gives team (and fantasy owner) a shot at a win. Another year at same level a reasonable expectation. Knuckleballers live forever.

Yr	Tm	W	L	Sv	IP	K	ERA	xERA	WHIP	oOPS	vL	vR	BF/G	Ctl	Dom	Cmd	FpK	SwK	G	L	F	H%	S%	hr/f	GS	APC	DOM%	DIS%	Sv%	LI	RAR	BPV	BPX	R$
10	NYM *	15	11	0	235	131	2.79	3.44	1.21	660	614	693	27.0	1.9	5.0	2.6	59%	9%	55	17	28	29%	79%	8%	26	97	50%	4%	0	0.78	37.2	69	112	$21
11	NYM	8	13	0	209	134	3.28	3.89	1.23	690	774	634	26.5	2.3	5.8	2.5	63%	8%	51	16	33	29%	76%	8%	32	95	47%	9%	0	0.79	17.1	70	105	$12
12	NYM	20	6	0	234	230	2.73	3.22	1.05	640	682	605	27.3	2.1	8.9	4.3	62%	13%	46	20	34	28%	79%	11%	33	99	70%	3%	0	0.76	36.9	127	166	$36
13	TOR	14	13	0	225	177	4.21	4.11	1.24	728	777	672	27.7	2.8	7.1	2.5	61%	10%	40	19	40	27%	71%	13%	34	103	59%	15%			-9.4	69	90	$7
14	TOR	14	13	0	216	173	3.71	4.01	1.23	705	665	735	26.9	3.1	7.2	2.3	63%	11%	42	20	38	27%	74%	11%	34	103	65%	9%			0.7	67	79	$9
1st Half		6	7	0	104	88	4.24	4.17	1.38	762	704	811	27.0	3.7	7.6	2.0	63%	11%	44	20	36	29%	74%	14%	17	104	53%	18%			-6.4	58	69	$0
2nd Half		8	6	0	112	85	3.22	3.86	1.09	648	622	667	26.8	2.5	6.9	2.7	62%	11%	40	21	39	26%	73%	8%	17	102	76%	0%			7.1	74	89	$18
15	Proj	14	11	0	203	161	3.94	3.71	1.25	717	724	712	26.5	2.9	7.1	2.5	62%	11%	41	20	39	28%	72%	10%	31						-4.9	69	82	$9

Diekman,Jake

Age: 28	Th: L	Role RP	Health A	LIMA Plan C	
Ht: 6' 4"	Wt: 200	Type Pwr	PT/Exp D	Rand Var +3	
			Consist C	MM 4511	

Intriguing left-handed power arm with an uncommon delivery and a common flaw: an estranged relationship with the strike zone. FpK foretold Ctl struggles, though if you can take the WHIP hit, SwK says Dom is for real. But since RHBs continue to vex him, he's likely to be limited to situational work.

Yr	Tm	W	L	Sv	IP	K	ERA	xERA	WHIP	oOPS	vL	vR	BF/G	Ctl	Dom	Cmd	FpK	SwK	G	L	F	H%	S%	hr/f	GS	APC	DOM%	DIS%	Sv%	LI	RAR	BPV	BPX	R$
10																																		
11	aa	0	1	3	65	70	3.47	3.47	1.49				5.3	6.0	9.6	1.6						31%	77%								3.8	88	132	-$1
12	PHI *	2	2	7	54	65	3.10	3.53	1.53	696	590	774	4.1	5.7	10.9	1.9	53%	13%	52	25	23	35%	78%	6%	0	17			70	1.18	6.1	107	140	$1
13	PHI *	2	4	11	68	71	4.53	4.30	1.65	598	368	765	4.1	5.5	9.3	1.7	59%	14%	51	29	20	36%	71%	5%	0	14			79	0.92	-5.6	84	110	-$2
14	PHI	5	5	0	71	100	3.80	3.00	1.42	692	577	748	4.3	4.4	12.7	2.9	55%	14%	43	26	31	38%	73%	8%	0	18			0	1.14	-0.5	129	154	$0
1st Half		2	2	0	38	51	4.03	2.87	1.26	657	468	760	4.3	3.6	12.1	3.4	56%	14%	46	22	33	34%	70%	13%	0	17			0	1.23	-1.3	145	173	$0
2nd Half		3	3	0	33	49	3.55	3.16	1.61	730	715	736	4.3	5.5	13.4	2.5	54%	14%	41	30	29	43%	75%	0%	0	19			0	1.04	0.8	112	133	$0
15	Proj	4	4	3	73	91	3.56	3.21	1.41	632	473	723	4.1	5.2	11.4	2.2	56%	14%	45	23	32	34%	74%	5%	0						1.6	88	105	$2

Doolittle,Sean

Age: 28	Th: L	Role RP	Health C	LIMA Plan B	
Ht: 6' 3"	Wt: 210	Type Pwr xFB	PT/Exp C	Rand Var 0	
			Consist B	MM 5530	

Authored book "Overcoming Lefty Bias" by simply posting "vintage Eck" skills from port side. Elite Ctl, Dom, SwK. LHBs hopeless against him; RHBs not much better. Couldn't dodge injury bug entirely, but did go right back into 9th after oblique healed. Closer options don't get much stronger.

Yr	Tm	W	L	Sv	IP	K	ERA	xERA	WHIP	oOPS	vL	vR	BF/G	Ctl	Dom	Cmd	FpK	SwK	G	L	F	H%	S%	hr/f	GS	APC	DOM%	DIS%	Sv%	LI	RAR	BPV	BPX	R$
10																																		
11																																		
12	OAK	2	1	1	47	60	3.04	3.17	1.08	611	794	509	4.3	2.1	11.4	5.5	66%	13%	35	15	50	33%	73%	5%	0	18			50	1.38	5.7	162	211	$3
13	OAK	5	5	2	69	60	3.13	3.55	0.96	573	516	603	3.8	1.7	7.8	4.6	65%	12%	33	20	47	27%	68%	5%	0	15			29	1.21	6.3	106	138	$7
14	OAK	2	4	22	63	89	2.73	2.61	0.73	459	276	550	3.9	1.1	12.8	11.1	72%	17%	23	18	59	27%	66%	6%	0	15			85	1.29	7.8	200	238	$17
1st Half		1	3	11	39	57	2.97	2.40	0.69	461	296	561	3.8	0.5	13.0	28.5	74%	17%	25	18	58	29%	58%	6%	0	15			79	1.43	3.7	225	269	$18
2nd Half		1	1	11	23	32	2.31	2.99	0.81	454	227	532	3.9	2.3	12.3	5.3	68%	17%	20	18	62	25%	76%	6%	0	16			92	1.05	4.1	158	188	$14
15	Proj	3	4	41	65	80	2.84	2.65	0.88	522	445	559	3.8	1.7	11.0	6.5	68%	15%	28	18	54	28%	70%	6%	0						7.2	159	189	$24

KRISTOPHER OLSON

Doubront,Felix

Age: 27	Th: L	Role RP	Health D	LIMA Plan D+
Ht: 6' 2"	Wt: 225	Type Pwr	PT/Exp B	Rand Var +1
			Consist B	MM 1201

4-5, 5.54 ERA in 80 IP at BOS/CHC. Skills on the cusp of relevancy in 2012, then the bottom fell out. For second year, big dips in fastball velocity, Dom, Cmd. Threw more FpK as season wore on, but wasn't fooling anyone. CHC can afford to roster arms like this and try to salvage them. You're under no such obligation.

Yr Tm	W	L	Sv	IP	K	ERA	xERA	WHIP	oOPS	vL	vR	BF/G	Ctl	Dom	Cmd	FpK	SwK	G	L	F	H%	S%	hr/f	GS	APC	DOM%	DIS%	Sv%	LI	RAR	BPV	BPX	R$
10 BOS *	10	5	2	105	83	3.58	4.09	1.48	789	576	911	15.6	3.7	7.1	1.9	61%	7%	47	10	42	34%	75%	9%	3	35	0%	67%	67	0.97	6.5	72	117	$4
11 BOS *	3	5	1	86	63	5.22	5.03	1.50	952	1347	632	12.3	3.6	6.7	1.8	58%	6%	44	28	28	32%	68%	11%	0	16			100	0.33	-13.5	40	60	-$6
12 BOS	11	10	0	161	167	4.86	3.91	1.45	775	760	781	24.4	4.0	9.3	2.4	58%	10%	44	23	33	32%	70%	16%	29	99	45%	24%			-16.8	83	108	-$3
13 BOS	11	6	0	162	139	4.32	4.13	1.43	729	648	760	24.3	3.9	7.7	2.0	53%	8%	46	20	34	32%	70%	8%	27	98	52%	22%	0	0.75	-9.2	56	74	-$1
14 2 TM *	4	7	0	108	75	5.46	5.18	1.57	821	858	805	17.5	3.8	6.3	1.7	58%	7%	38	23	39	33%	66%	11%	14	65	29%	36%	0	0.56	-22.9	39	47	-$11
1st Half	2	4	0	66	48	4.64	4.51	1.44	790	733	811	20.1	3.9	6.5	1.7	56%	7%	36	21	43	30%	70%	11%	10	82	30%	40%	0	0.70	-7.3	44	52	-$8
2nd Half	2	3	0	42	27	6.77	6.23	1.79	882	1028	791	14.8	3.6	5.9	1.6	60%	7%	43	24	33	37%	61%	13%	4	46	25%	25%	0	0.40	-15.5	33	40	-$16
15 Proj	**5**	**5**	**0**	**87**	**68**	**5.19**	**4.14**	**1.55**	**788**	**821**	**774**	**18.3**	**3.8**	**7.1**	**1.8**	**57%**	**8%**	**42**	**22**	**35**	**33%**	**67%**	**9%**	**17**						**-15.5**	**44**	**53**	**-$7**

Duensing,Brian

Age: 32	Th: L	Role RP	Health A	LIMA Plan D+
Ht: 6' 0"	Wt: 205	Type	PT/Exp C	Rand Var -2
			Consist B	MM 2100

ERA continued to improve, but this time it was more about fortunate H% and S%, as 2nd half attested. Dashed hopes that bullpen Dom spike could be sustained; instead, 2013 Dom looks like aberration. Did at least regain ability to get LHB out, but RHB struggles suggest he won't be asked to do more.

Yr Tm	W	L	Sv	IP	K	ERA	xERA	WHIP	oOPS	vL	vR	BF/G	Ctl	Dom	Cmd	FpK	SwK	G	L	F	H%	S%	hr/f	GS	APC	DOM%	DIS%	Sv%	LI	RAR	BPV	BPX	R$
10 MIN	10	3	0	131	78	2.62	3.89	1.20	666	457	751	10.1	2.4	5.4	2.2	57%	8%	53	16	31	28%	82%	9%	13	36	54%	8%	0	0.82	23.6	63	101	$12
11 MIN	9	14	0	162	115	5.23	4.26	1.52	833	522	947	22.2	2.9	6.4	2.2	59%	8%	43	21	36	34%	67%	11%	28	83	50%	32%	0	0.71	-25.7	58	87	-$9
12 MIN	4	12	0	109	69	5.12	4.37	1.40	759	678	808	8.6	2.2	5.7	2.6	60%	8%	47	20	33	33%	64%	8%	11	31	27%	45%	0	1.00	-14.8	67	88	-$7
13 MIN	6	2	1	61	56	3.98	3.89	1.48	750	786	713	3.7	3.2	8.3	2.5	62%	11%	41	27	32	36%	73%	7%	0	14			25	1.25	-0.9	80	104	-$1
14 MIN	3	3	0	54	33	3.31	4.43	1.33	725	587	843	3.7	3.3	5.5	1.7	59%	9%	46	19	35	28%	79%	10%	0	14			0	1.13	2.9	33	39	-$1
1st Half	1	2	0	31	17	2.64	4.48	1.27	693	564	780	4.2	3.5	5.0	1.4	57%	8%	48	16	36	26%	83%	9%	0	17			0	0.98	4.2	21	25	-$1
2nd Half	2	1	0	24	16	4.18	4.37	1.39	764	608	938	3.2	3.0	6.1	2.0	62%	10%	42	23	35	30%	73%	11%	0	12			0	1.26	-1.3	48	57	-$1
15 Proj	**4**	**3**	**0**	**58**	**41**	**3.94**	**3.92**	**1.39**	**745**	**653**	**820**	**4.2**	**3.0**	**6.3**	**2.1**	**60%**	**9%**	**45**	**22**	**34**	**31%**	**74%**	**9%**	**0**						**-1.4**	**55**	**65**	**-$2**

Duffy,Danny

Age: 26	Th: L	Role SP	Health F	LIMA Plan C
Ht: 6' 3"	Wt: 205	Type Pwr FB	PT/Exp C	Rand Var -5
			Consist A	MM 2203

If some want to think "breakout," say: "Be my guest." ERA fueled by random swings of H%, S% and hr/f. In time, skills might catch up with results, as more distance from TJS could add to Dom, and FpK trend validates improved Ctl. But for now, smart play is to let bids head up into double digits without you.

Yr Tm	W	L	Sv	IP	K	ERA	xERA	WHIP	oOPS	vL	vR	BF/G	Ctl	Dom	Cmd	FpK	SwK	G	L	F	H%	S%	hr/f	GS	APC	DOM%	DIS%	Sv%	LI	RAR	BPV	BPX	R$
10 aa	5	2	0	40	34	3.17	3.59	1.24				23.0	1.9	7.7	4.1						33%	76%								4.5	116	187	$2
11 KC *	7	9	0	147	126	5.09	4.90	1.49	864	811	882	22.7	3.7	7.7	2.1	52%	8%	38	22	40	33%	68%	11%	20	98	20%	25%			-20.8	54	81	-$7
12 KC	2	2	0	28	28	3.90	4.80	1.59	771	491	859	20.2	5.9	9.1	1.6	52%	10%	35	21	44	32%	76%	6%	6	88	17%	50%			0.4	19	25	-$4
13 KC *	5	2	0	93	90	4.26	4.48	1.54	608	692	571	19.4	4.4	8.7	2.0	54%	11%	32	27	41	34%	73%	0%	5	94	20%	60%			-4.5	72	94	-$4
14 KC	9	12	0	149	113	2.53	4.24	1.11	605	386	670	19.5	3.2	6.8	2.1	59%	8%	36	18	46	25%	81%	6%	25	78	52%	20%	0	0.87	22.3	50	60	$14
1st Half	5	7	0	73	55	2.60	4.48	1.07	571	304	629	17.3	3.6	6.8	1.9	60%	7%	34	20	46	23%	78%	5%	11	69	55%	27%	0	0.96	10.2	38	45	$14
2nd Half	4	5	0	77	58	2.47	4.18	1.15	637	435	713	22.3	2.8	6.8	2.4	58%	8%	37	17	46	26%	83%	7%	14	90	50%	14%			12.1	62	74	$14
15 Proj	**11**	**10**	**0**	**174**	**145**	**3.76**	**3.90**	**1.29**	**698**	**568**	**740**	**20.2**	**3.4**	**7.5**	**2.2**	**56%**	**8%**	**37**	**20**	**44**	**29%**	**73%**	**7%**	**35**						**-0.4**	**57**	**68**	**$7**

Duke,Zach

Age: 32	Th: L	Role RP	Health C	LIMA Plan B+
Ht: 6' 2"	Wt: 210	Type Pwr GB	PT/Exp D	Rand Var 0
			Consist D	MM 5300

Where'd this guy come from? Began throwing cutter, added tick to fastball (but only to 89.7 mph), threw more FpK and voila! A power reliever with elite Dom, GB%, and no platoon splits. Careful, though. If he keeps posting skills like this, someone's could get the crazy idea to let him start again.

Yr Tm	W	L	Sv	IP	K	ERA	xERA	WHIP	oOPS	vL	vR	BF/G	Ctl	Dom	Cmd	FpK	SwK	G	L	F	H%	S%	hr/f	GS	APC	DOM%	DIS%	Sv%	LI	RAR	BPV	BPX	R$
10 PIT	8	15	0	159	96	5.72	4.57	1.65	881	947	864	25.2	2.9	5.4	1.9	58%	8%	48	20	33	35%	68%	14%	29	91	31%	34%			-32.1	46	74	-$13
11 ARI	3	4	1	77	32	4.93	4.51	1.57	820	571	891	16.1	2.2	3.8	1.7	59%	7%	50	22	28	34%	68%	8%	9	58	11%	22%	100	0.48	-9.3	35	53	-$7
12 WAS *	16	5	0	178	76	4.42	5.82	1.61	556	646	520	23.2	2.3	3.8	1.7	54%	11%	40	28	33	34%	75%	0%	0	27			0	0.37	-8.8	18	24	-$9
13 2 NL *	3	2	2	59	44	4.11	4.41	1.38	806	728	854	4.8	2.4	6.7	2.7	56%	10%	50	21	29	32%	72%	9%	1	20	0%	100%	100	1.09	-1.8	68	89	-$2
14 MIL	5	1	0	59	74	2.45	2.32	1.13	578	569	586	3.2	2.6	11.4	4.4	63%	13%	58	22	20	33%	79%	10%	0	13			0	1.11	9.3	170	202	$5
1st Half	4	0	0	32	42	1.42	2.02	0.98	562	603	532	3.3	1.4	11.9	8.4	63%	12%	52	25	23	34%	90%	12%	0	13			0	1.05	9.1	207	246	$10
2nd Half	1	1	0	27	32	3.67	2.70	1.30	596	530	651	3.1	4.0	10.7	2.7	63%	14%	64	19	17	33%	71%	8%	0	13			0	1.16	0.2	126	150	$0
15 Proj	**3**	**2**	**0**	**51**	**49**	**3.61**	**2.94**	**1.27**	**665**	**587**	**710**	**4.5**	**2.7**	**8.7**	**3.2**	**60%**	**11%**	**54**	**21**	**25**	**32%**	**73%**	**11%**	**0**						**0.8**	**115**	**137**	**$0**

Dunn,Mike

Age: 30	Th: L	Role RP	Health A	LIMA Plan B
Ht: 6' 0"	Wt: 210	Type Pwr FB	PT/Exp D	Rand Var -1
			Consist B	MM 4500

Tied with Tony Watson for 2014's top vulture. Largely held onto Ctl gains from 2013 2nd half, and rising FpK should help lock in that lower walk rate. SwK legitimizes increased Dom. FB tilt, left-handedness may discourage use in 9th. Wins are fickle so vultures rarely repeat. But a safe LIMA choice.

Yr Tm	W	L	Sv	IP	K	ERA	xERA	WHIP	oOPS	vL	vR	BF/G	Ctl	Dom	Cmd	FpK	SwK	G	L	F	H%	S%	hr/f	GS	APC	DOM%	DIS%	Sv%	LI	RAR	BPV	BPX	R$
10 ATL *	4	0	7	66	80	1.88	3.09	1.43	659	581	742	4.5	5.9	10.9	1.8	54%	12%	34	18	48	32%	87%	5%	0	15			78	1.04	18.0	107	173	$8
11 FLA	5	6	0	63	68	3.43	3.84	1.30	723	615	809	3.7	4.4	9.7	2.2	56%	12%	39	16	46	28%	79%	12%	0	16			0	1.20	4.0	72	109	$2
12 MIA *	1	4	1	62	67	5.20	5.19	1.78	806	784	828	3.9	5.4	9.8	1.8	54%	8%	34	28	38	39%	69%	6%	0	15			14	1.11	-9.0	79	103	-$10
13 MIA	3	4	2	68	72	2.66	3.73	1.20	604	549	655	3.8	3.7	9.6	2.6	60%	12%	40	18	43	29%	80%	7%	0	16			40	1.26	10.1	90	117	$5
14 MIA	10	6	1	57	67	3.16	3.57	1.21	635	598	671	3.3	3.5	10.6	3.0	64%	14%	34	20	47	31%	75%	6%	0	13			25	1.47	4.1	109	129	$5
1st Half	5	4	0	31	36	3.73	3.79	1.31	722	727	718	3.6	3.7	10.3	2.8	58%	14%	36	15	49	31%	76%	10%	0	15			0	1.37	0.0	99	118	$3
2nd Half	5	2	1	26	31	2.45	3.31	1.09	525	474	590	2.9	3.2	10.9	3.4	72%	15%	31	26	44	31%	75%	0%	0	11			33	1.56	4.1	119	142	$8
15 Proj	**5**	**4**	**1**	**51**	**58**	**3.20**	**3.30**	**1.25**	**640**	**593**	**687**	**3.3**	**3.6**	**10.2**	**2.8**	**62%**	**13%**	**35**	**21**	**44**	**32%**	**75%**	**5%**	**0**						**3.4**	**100**	**119**	**$2**

Dyson,Sam

Age: 27	Th: R	Role RP	Health A	LIMA Plan C
Ht: 6' 1"	Wt: 205	Type xGB	PT/Exp D	Rand Var -4
			Consist B	MM 3100

3-1, 2.14 ERA in 42 IP at MIA. One of baseball's most extreme GB specialists allowed just 1 HR in 42 IP. That will buy you lots of friends. Mediocre Dom in minors, but SwK improvement suggests gains may be for real. Higher-leverage work likely hinges on figuring out LHB. Until that happens, approach with caution.

Yr Tm	W	L	Sv	IP	K	ERA	xERA	WHIP	oOPS	vL	vR	BF/G	Ctl	Dom	Cmd	FpK	SwK	G	L	F	H%	S%	hr/f	GS	APC	DOM%	DIS%	Sv%	LI	RAR	BPV	BPX	R$
10																																	
11																																	
12 TOR *	2	2	9	46	19	3.62	4.23	1.46	1750	2000	1667	5.6	3.4	3.8	1.1	63%	4%	80	20	0	30%	75%	0%	0	13			90	0.17	2.2	31	40	$0
13 MIA *	4	12	0	117	51	3.97	4.16	1.50	959	1014	919	19.5	3.3	3.9	1.2	48%	6%	69	5	26	32%	72%	18%	1	35	0%	100%	0	0.79	-1.5	39	51	-$6
14 MIA *	5	2	1	67	49	2.33	3.21	1.33	653	781	553	6.3	3.3	6.5	2.0	60%	11%	63	19	18	31%	81%	4%	0	22			33	0.68	11.7	80	96	$3
1st Half	3	1	1	27	18	2.45	3.22	1.37	944	1750	400	7.6	3.6	5.8	1.6	44%	12%	67	33	0	31%	80%	0%	0	17			50	1.00	4.3	73	87	$2
2nd Half	2	1	0	40	31	2.25	3.37	1.30	637	733	561	5.9	3.2	7.0	2.2	61%	11%	63	18	19	31%	82%	4%	0	22			0	0.65	7.4	82	97	$5
15 Proj	**3**	**3**	**0**	**58**	**41**	**3.40**	**3.44**	**1.35**	**618**	**729**	**532**	**8.0**	**3.3**	**6.3**	**1.9**	**61%**	**11%**	**63**	**18**	**19**	**31%**	**74%**	**7%**	**0**						**2.4**	**65**	**77**	**$0**

Elias,Roenis

Age: 26	Th: L	Role SP	Health A	LIMA Plan B+
Ht: 6' 1"	Wt: 190	Type Pwr	PT/Exp C	Rand Var 0
			Consist B	MM 3203

Decent, unexciting debut, but is there more here than meets the eye? Near-100 BPV in May-July. Gets plenty of swings and misses with change-up, curve ball. Bunch of GB, too. Ctl got wobbly in 2nd half, then September elbow strain ended season. If he puts injury behind him, gains stamina... UP: 15 wins, 3.50 ERA

Yr Tm	W	L	Sv	IP	K	ERA	xERA	WHIP	oOPS	vL	vR	BF/G	Ctl	Dom	Cmd	FpK	SwK	G	L	F	H%	S%	hr/f	GS	APC	DOM%	DIS%	Sv%	LI	RAR	BPV	BPX	R$
10																																	
11																																	
12																																	
13 aa	6	11	0	130	101	4.51	4.57	1.51				25.6	3.7	7.0	1.9						33%	71%								-10.4	58	75	-$6
14 SEA	10	12	0	164	143	3.85	3.81	1.31	713	655	729	23.9	3.5	7.9	2.2	60%	10%	45	21	34	30%	73%	10%	29	92	48%	17%			-2.2	70	83	$3
1st Half	7	6	0	105	87	3.96	3.70	1.19	690	685	691	25.3	3.1	7.5	2.4	62%	10%	45	20	34	27%	70%	12%	17	96	53%	6%			-2.8	74	89	$8
2nd Half	3	6	0	59	56	3.66	3.99	1.53	752	611	798	21.9	4.3	8.5	2.0	56%	11%	45	22	33	34%	77%	7%	12	86	42%	33%			0.6	62	74	-$5
15 Proj	**10**	**10**	**0**	**160**	**138**	**3.96**	**3.67**	**1.35**	**713**	**624**	**739**	**23.2**	**3.7**	**7.8**	**2.1**	**58%**	**11%**	**45**	**21**	**34**	**31%**	**72%**	**9%**	**29**						**-4.3**	**65**	**77**	**$4**

KRISTOPHER OLSON

Eovaldi,Nathan

Age: 25	Th: R	Role SP	Health D	LIMA Plan C	
Ht: 6' 2"	Wt: 215	Type	PT/Exp B	Rand Var 0	
			Consist A	MM 2103	

While ERA skyrocketed in 2nd half, skills decline wasn't as drastic. Fastball velocity was top-notch again (4th in MLB), though pedestrian SwK and Dom are puzzling. Gains in FpK and Ctl fuel optimism, and it could come together quickly. If he finds a stikeout pitch ... UP: sub-3.50 ERA

Yr Tm	W	L	Sv	IP	K	ERA	xERA	WHIP	oOPS	vL	vR	BF/G	Ctl	Dom	Cmd	FpK	SwK	G	L	F	H%	S%	hr/f	GS	APC	DOM%	DIS%	Sv%	LI	RAR	BPV	BPX	R$
10																																	
11 LA *	7	7	0	138	109	2.84	2.53	1.21	667	735	619	18.5	3.9	7.1	1.8	54%	10%	41	26	34	27%	76%	6%	6	60	33%	17%	0	0.63	18.7	84	127	$11
12 2 NL *	6	15	0	154	104	4.11	4.40	1.46	771	845	665	21.3	3.5	6.1	1.7	58%	8%	46	23	31	32%	73%	8%	22	94	32%	36%			-1.9	52	67	-$4
13 MIA	4	6	0	106	78	3.39	4.21	1.32	681	665	691	25.1	3.4	6.6	2.0	59%	8%	44	22	34	30%	75%	6%	18	94	67%	17%			6.3	49	64	$2
14 MIA	6	14	0	200	142	4.37	3.90	1.33	732	768	688	25.9	1.9	6.4	3.3	63%	9%	45	22	33	33%	67%	7%	33	97	55%	21%			-15.5	86	102	-$3
1st Half	5	3	0	107	79	3.71	3.81	1.24	720	842	541	26.4	1.7	6.7	4.0	65%	9%	44	19	37	32%	71%	6%	17	101	65%	12%			0.4	97	115	$5
2nd Half	1	11	0	93	63	5.13	4.00	1.44	746	670	820	25.4	2.2	6.1	2.7	61%	9%	45	26	29	35%	63%	7%	16	93	44%	31%			-15.9	73	87	-$14
15 Proj	**9**	**10**	**0**	**174**	**129**	**3.87**	**3.72**	**1.35**	**712**	**736**	**687**	**23.5**	**2.8**	**6.7**	**2.4**	**60%**	**9%**	**44**	**23**	**33**	**32%**	**72%**	**7%**	**31**						**-2.9**	**68**	**81**	**$3**

Erlin,Robert

Age: 24	Th: L	Role RP	Health D	LIMA Plan C	
Ht: 6' 0"	Wt: 190	Type	PT/Exp D	Rand Var +2	
			Consist B	MM 2201	

4-5, 4.99 ERA in 61 IP at SD. ERA doesn't show it, but 1st half was promising, as he improved Dom and got more swings and misses before sore elbow cost him four months. Struggled on rehab assignment and upon return in Sept. Minor league stats indicate bigger upside, but for now, the next step is a sub-4.00 ERA.

Yr Tm	W	L	Sv	IP	K	ERA	xERA	WHIP	oOPS	vL	vR	BF/G	Ctl	Dom	Cmd	FpK	SwK	G	L	F	H%	S%	hr/f	GS	APC	DOM%	DIS%	Sv%	LI	RAR	BPV	BPX	R$
10																																	
11 aa	6	2	0	93	84	3.23	3.69	1.17				21.8	1.0	8.2	8.3						34%	75%								8.1	199	300	$6
12 aa	3	1	0	52	65	2.76	3.77	1.26				19.4	2.2	11.1	5.1						37%	81%								8.1	152	198	$2
13 SD *	11	6	0	154	115	4.41	4.66	1.44	698	823	641	21.2	2.6	6.7	2.6	62%	7%	37	25	37	34%	71%	10%	9	82	33%	22%	0	0.63	-10.3	65	84	-$2
14 SD *	4	6	0	82	62	5.27	5.32	1.52	787	755	799	19.9	2.2	6.7	3.0	65%	9%	41	27	32	36%	66%	10%	11	77	45%	36%	0	0.70	-15.5	68	81	-$8
1st Half	3	4	0	48	39	4.53	3.80	1.30	735	609	785	22.3	2.1	7.4	3.5	63%	9%	39	25	36	33%	66%	8%	8	86	50%	25%	0	0.72	-4.6	93	111	-$3
2nd Half	1	2	0	35	23	6.28	7.11	1.83	950	1214	842	17.9	2.4	5.9	2.4	71%	8%	47	33	20	40%	67%	20%	3	59	33%	67%	0	0.63	-10.9	34	40	-$14
15 Proj	**7**	**5**	**0**	**102**	**80**	**4.16**	**3.77**	**1.39**	**768**	**744**	**778**	**19.5**	**2.6**	**7.1**	**2.8**	**62%**	**8%**	**38**	**25**	**37**	**33%**	**72%**	**8%**	**21**						**-5.3**	**75**	**89**	**-$1**

Estrada,Marco

Age: 31	Th: R	Role RP	Health D	LIMA Plan B+	
Ht: 6' 0"	Wt: 200	Type Pwr xFB	PT/Exp B	Rand Var 0	
			Consist A	MM 3201	

This is what happens when an extreme FB pitcher has hr/f misfortune. Surrendered league-leading 29 HR despite modest IP total, and lost rotation spot. In relief, had 2.89 ERA, just 2 HR allowed in 44 IP. With Cmd and velocity trending down, it's doubtful we see a return to peak level, at least as SP.

Yr Tm	W	L	Sv	IP	K	ERA	xERA	WHIP	oOPS	vL	vR	BF/G	Ctl	Dom	Cmd	FpK	SwK	G	L	F	H%	S%	hr/f	GS	APC	DOM%	DIS%	Sv%	LI	RAR	BPV	BPX	R$
10 MIL *	1	2	0	51	40	5.00	3.73	1.31	908	1348	571	15.2	3.1	7.0	2.2	60%	12%	29	14	57	30%	62%	15%	1	34	0%	100%	0	0.60	-5.8	71	115	-$3
11 MIL	4	8	0	93	88	4.08	3.60	1.21	700	661	733	8.9	2.8	8.5	3.0	57%	11%	40	18	43	29%	69%	10%	7	36	86%	0%	0	0.66	-1.6	96	144	$2
12 MIL	5	7	0	138	143	3.64	3.59	1.14	703	728	681	19.4	1.9	9.3	4.9	62%	11%	34	20	45	31%	73%	10%	23	77	48%	26%	0	0.71	6.3	129	168	$9
13 MIL	7	4	0	128	118	3.87	3.60	1.08	670	651	687	24.4	2.0	8.3	4.1	60%	11%	38	18	44	27%	70%	12%	21	95	62%	14%			0.0	110	144	$8
14 MIL	7	6	0	151	127	4.36	4.15	1.20	752	719	781	16.0	2.6	7.6	2.9	61%	11%	33	18	50	27%	71%	13%	18	65	56%	0%	0	0.63	-11.5	77	91	$2
1st Half	7	4	0	96	85	5.06	4.16	1.26	806	725	866	25.1	3.0	8.0	2.7	62%	9%	35	15	50	26%	69%	17%	16	102	63%	0%			-15.6	75	90	$2
2nd Half	0	2	0	55	42	3.13	4.13	1.10	657	709	596	9.7	2.0	6.9	3.5	59%	14%	29	22	49	28%	75%	6%	2	39	0%	0%	0	0.54	4.1	78	93	$1
15 Proj	**3**	**4**	**0**	**87**	**75**	**3.91**	**3.62**	**1.18**	**708**	**704**	**712**	**10.4**	**2.6**	**7.7**	**3.0**	**60%**	**12%**	**35**	**19**	**46**	**28%**	**72%**	**11%**	**1**						**-1.9**	**82**	**98**	**$2**

Familia,Jeurys

Age: 25	Th: R	Role RP	Health F	LIMA Plan B	
Ht: 6' 3"	Wt: 240	Type Pwr xGB	PT/Exp D	Rand Var -5	
			Consist D	MM 4311	

PRO: Improvement in Ctl, SwK; elite GB% that got even better in 2H; completely overpowered RH batters, who had just 3 extra-base hits against him all year. CON: 5.2 Dom, 1.1 Cmd, .821 OPS vs LHB; FpK% not convinced of Ctl gains. Next step: find an out pitch for LH batters.

Yr Tm	W	L	Sv	IP	K	ERA	xERA	WHIP	oOPS	vL	vR	BF/G	Ctl	Dom	Cmd	FpK	SwK	G	L	F	H%	S%	hr/f	GS	APC	DOM%	DIS%	Sv%	LI	RAR	BPV	BPX	R$
10																																	
11 aa	4	4	0	88	80	3.33	3.84	1.31				21.3	3.1	8.3	2.7						31%	77%								6.6	84	127	$3
12 NYM *	9	9	0	149	122	5.10	4.73	1.64	644	751	560	18.5	4.7	7.3	1.6	42%	9%	48	18	33	35%	68%	0%	1	26	0%	100%	0	0.13	-19.9	61	79	-$12
13 NYM	0	0	1	11	8	4.22	5.79	1.97	908	889	918	5.8	7.6	6.8	0.9	52%	7%	52	15	33	31%	84%	18%	0	22			100	0.69	-0.5	-54	-70	-$5
14 NYM	2	5	5	77	73	2.21	3.36	1.18	587	821	377	4.2	3.7	8.5	2.3	53%	13%	57	15	28	28%	82%	5%	0	16			50	1.18	14.6	87	104	$7
1st Half	1	3	1	42	36	2.36	3.58	1.17	573	810	378	4.5	3.4	7.7	2.3	51%	12%	53	17	31	28%	79%	3%	0	16			33	1.05	7.2	77	92	$6
2nd Half	1	2	4	35	37	2.04	3.07	1.19	603	834	375	4.0	4.1	9.4	2.3	55%	13%	64	12	24	28%	85%	9%	0	16			57	1.31	7.4	101	121	$9
15 Proj	**3**	**4**	**8**	**73**	**66**	**3.37**	**3.34**	**1.36**	**685**	**959**	**433**	**6.8**	**4.0**	**8.2**	**2.0**	**53%**	**13%**	**59**	**14**	**27**	**31%**	**75%**	**7%**	**0**						**3.3**	**77**	**91**	**$4**

Farquhar,Daniel

Age: 28	Th: R	Role RP	Health A	LIMA Plan B+	
Ht: 5' 9"	Wt: 185	Type Pwr	PT/Exp D	Rand Var -1	
			Consist A	MM 5510	

Moved back to setup role and continued to thrive, holding most of previous year's increased Dom. Continues to be effective vs both LH and RH batters. 2nd half BPI, particularly gains in FpK and Ctl, are impressive, and show he may not be far from another shot at closing. UP: 35 Saves.

Yr Tm	W	L	Sv	IP	K	ERA	xERA	WHIP	oOPS	vL	vR	BF/G	Ctl	Dom	Cmd	FpK	SwK	G	L	F	H%	S%	hr/f	GS	APC	DOM%	DIS%	Sv%	LI	RAR	BPV	BPX	R$
10 aa	4	3	17	77	69	3.79	2.95	1.24				5.9	4.7	8.1	1.7						24%	71%								2.7	74	120	$10
11 TOR *	4	5	15	62	45	4.05	4.79	1.55	1170	1750	829	4.7	3.0	6.6	2.2	73%	5%	25	50	25	36%	74%	0%	0	14			83	0.01	-0.8	65	97	$3
12 a/a	3	3	9	68	60	2.85	2.42	1.11				6.1	2.8	7.9	2.8						28%	74%								9.7	107	140	$8
13 SEA *	0	4	22	76	104	3.74	2.59	1.18	586	485	695	5.0	3.1	12.3	4.0	55%	14%	42	25	33	35%	67%	5%	0	20			81	1.18	1.2	157	205	$10
14 SEA	3	1	1	71	81	2.66	2.98	1.13	607	641	578	4.4	2.8	10.3	3.7	59%	12%	42	27	31	31%	79%	9%	0	17			33	0.85	9.5	130	154	$5
1st Half	1	1	1	35	38	2.86	3.53	1.24	609	588	625	4.4	3.6	9.9	2.7	53%	11%	38	26	37	31%	78%	6%	0	18			33	0.76	3.8	95	113	$2
2nd Half	2	0	0	36	43	2.48	2.48	1.02	606	690	531	4.4	2.0	10.7	5.4	65%	12%	46	28	26	30%	79%	13%	0	16			0	0.94	5.7	162	194	$8
15 Proj	**2**	**2**	**6**	**65**	**74**	**2.93**	**2.82**	**1.15**	**612**	**591**	**632**	**4.7**	**2.9**	**10.2**	**3.5**	**58%**	**13%**	**42**	**26**	**31**	**31%**	**76%**	**8%**	**0**						**6.6**	**126**	**150**	**$6**

Feldman,Scott

Age: 32	Th: R	Role SP	Health D	LIMA Plan B+	
Ht: 6' 7"	Wt: 230	Type	PT/Exp A	Rand Var 0	
			Consist A	MM 2005	

GB tilt and decent Ctl have limited the disasters, and helped him settle in as league average SP. However, pedestrian (and declining) Dom leaves thin margin for error. Unless he can reclaim lost Ks, most likely outcome is ERA heading north of 4.00... perhaps by wide margin (see: 2010-12).

Yr Tm	W	L	Sv	IP	K	ERA	xERA	WHIP	oOPS	vL	vR	BF/G	Ctl	Dom	Cmd	FpK	SwK	G	L	F	H%	S%	hr/f	GS	APC	DOM%	DIS%	Sv%	LI	RAR	BPV	BPX	R$
10 TEX	7	11	0	141	75	5.48	4.87	1.60	849	790	904	22.1	2.9	4.8	1.7	58%	6%	43	20	37	34%	67%	10%	22	83	27%	36%	0	0.73	-24.4	30	48	-$10
11 TEX *	5	2	0	82	45	4.76	4.63	1.39	614	391	837	16.4	2.4	5.0	2.0	54%	8%	62	13	25	31%	68%	13%	2	46	50%	0%	0	0.39	-8.2	40	60	-$3
12 TEX	6	11	0	124	96	5.09	4.12	1.38	745	752	736	18.5	2.3	7.0	3.0	61%	8%	42	26	32	33%	64%	11%	21	73	38%	33%	0	0.71	-16.5	83	108	-$6
13 2 TM	12	12	0	182	132	3.86	3.85	1.18	671	672	670	25.3	2.8	6.5	2.4	56%	8%	50	19	32	27%	70%	11%	30	100	50%	17%			0.0	71	92	$9
14 HOU	8	12	0	180	107	3.74	4.13	1.30	725	715	737	26.4	2.5	5.3	2.1	61%	7%	47	22	31	30%	73%	9%	29	102	41%	17%			0.0	54	64	$2
1st Half	4	5	0	78	47	3.92	4.15	1.31	743	730	752	24.3	2.4	5.4	2.2	58%	7%	49	19	32	29%	73%	11%	14	95	29%	21%			-1.8	59	70	-$1
2nd Half	4	7	0	102	60	3.61	4.11	1.30	711	706	720	28.3	2.6	5.3	2.1	63%	6%	46	25	30	30%	73%	7%	15	109	53%	13%			1.7	50	59	$4
15 Proj	**10**	**13**	**0**	**189**	**122**	**4.11**	**3.77**	**1.30**	**725**	**709**	**744**	**23.0**	**2.6**	**5.8**	**2.3**	**59%**	**7%**	**47**	**22**	**31**	**30%**	**70%**	**10%**	**34**						**-8.5**	**61**	**73**	**$3**

Feliz,Neftali

Age: 27	Th: R	Role RP	Health F	LIMA Plan C	
Ht: 6' 3"	Wt: 225	Type Pwr xFB	PT/Exp D	Rand Var -5	
			Consist B	MM 2230	

1.99 ERA with 13 Sv in 32 IP at TEX. Rough spring earned him half-year in Triple-A, but was back to closing in TEX by late July. Mediocre Cmd, high FB% belie the shiny ERA, and health history urges caution. But Aug/Sept return of Dom/SwK% combo could foretell a return to ranks of solid closers. A worthy speculation.

Yr Tm	W	L	Sv	IP	K	ERA	xERA	WHIP	oOPS	vL	vR	BF/G	Ctl	Dom	Cmd	FpK	SwK	G	L	F	H%	S%	hr/f	GS	APC	DOM%	DIS%	Sv%	LI	RAR	BPV	BPX	R$
10 TEX	4	3	40	69	71	2.73	3.28	0.88	516	409	616	3.8	2.3	9.2	3.9	57%	12%	37	15	48	23%	71%	6%	0	15			93	1.27	11.6	118	191	$25
11 TEX	2	3	32	62	54	2.74	4.16	1.16	598	561	644	3.9	4.3	7.8	1.8	53%	12%	37	16	46	24%	78%	5%	0	17			84	1.10	9.2	38	58	$16
12 TEX	3	1	0	43	37	3.16	4.62	1.20	623	616	631	21.9	4.9	7.8	1.6	53%	10%	37	15	48	22%	78%	9%	7	92	57%	14%	0	0.74	4.5	24	32	$1
13 TEX	0	0	0	5	4	0.00	4.72	1.50	659	629	665	3.5	3.9	7.7	2.0	38%	9%	21	29	50	35%	100%	0%	0	18			0	0.75	2.2	34	44	-$4
14 TEX *	3	2	20	60	45	2.75	3.25	1.02	586	513	663	4.3	2.9	6.7	2.3	66%	10%	27	22	51	19%	87%	11%	0	16			87	1.44	7.4	52	62	$12
1st Half	1	1	6	28	23	3.72	4.14	1.09				4.7	2.7	7.6	2.8						22%	80%	0%	0						0.1	50	59	$5
2nd Half	2	1	14	33	22	1.93	2.50	0.95	587	513	663	4.0	3.0	6.0	2.0	66%	10%	27	22	51	18%	92%	11%	0	16			93	1.44	7.3	56	66	$18
15 Proj	**4**	**2**	**34**	**65**	**56**	**3.18**	**3.76**	**1.15**	**688**	**631**	**753**	**5.3**	**3.3**	**7.8**	**2.4**	**57%**	**11%**	**34**	**17**	**48**	**25%**	**79%**	**11%**	**0**						**4.5**	**64**	**77**	**$17**

BRIAN RUDD

Fernandez,Jose

Age: 22	Th: R	Role SP	Health F	LIMA Plan B+	
Ht: 6' 2"	Wt: 225	Type Pwr	PT/Exp C	Rand Var 0	
			Consist B	MM 5401	

Sophomore campaign started off well, as he had 8-plus Ks in 6 of 8 starts, and struck out 41% of RH batters he faced. It came to an abrupt end, as he was forced to undergo Tommy John surgery in May. He'll get late start in 2015, but could still make significant impact. Future upside remains immense.

Yr Tm	W	L	Sv	IP	K	ERA	xERA	WHIP	oOPS	vL	vR	BF/G	Ctl	Dom	Cmd	FpK	SwK	G	L	F	H%	S%	hr/f	GS	APC	DOM%	DIS%	Sv%	LI	RAR	BPV	BPX	R$
10																																	
11																																	
12																																	
13 MIA	12	6	0	173	187	2.19	3.06	0.98	522	546	494	24.3	3.0	9.7	3.2	62%	11%	45	22	33	25%	80%	7%	28	93	75%	14%			35.7	117	152	$28
14 MIA	4	2	0	52	70	2.44	2.45	0.95	536	672	393	25.6	2.3	12.2	5.4	65%	15%	49	17	35	30%	78%	10%	8	98	75%	13%			8.3	185	221	$6
1st Half	4	2	0	52	70	2.44	2.45	0.95	536	672	393	25.6	2.3	12.2	5.4	65%	15%	49	17	35	30%	78%	10%	8	98	75%	13%			8.3	185	221	$6
2nd Half																																	
15 Proj	8	4	0	102	106	3.23	2.83	1.06	583	684	473	24.6	2.6	9.4	3.7	63%	13%	47	19	34	28%	71%	8%	16						6.5	126	150	$10

Fields,Joshua

Age: 29	Th: R	Role RP	Health B	LIMA Plan A	
Ht: 6' 0"	Wt: 190	Type Pwr xFB	PT/Exp D	Rand Var +4	
			Consist B	MM 4520	

Began year as part of closer committee, but rocky start led to brief demotion. Upon return, had 2.32 ERA, 5.5 Cmd rest of the way, with 2 SV in Sept prior to oblique injury. Increased use of changeup seems to have worked, and could put him back in mix for saves, but high FB% heightens risk.

Yr Tm	W	L	Sv	IP	K	ERA	xERA	WHIP	oOPS	vL	vR	BF/G	Ctl	Dom	Cmd	FpK	SwK	G	L	F	H%	S%	hr/f	GS	APC	DOM%	DIS%	Sv%	LI	RAR	BPV	BPX	R$
10 aa	1	1	6	29	24	3.47	2.62	1.38				5.7	5.7	7.4	1.3						27%	72%								2.2	85	138	$1
11 a/a	4	2	4	56	50	4.81	4.16	1.63				6.6	7.1	8.0	1.1						28%	71%								-6.1	59	89	-$3
12 a/a	4	3	12	58	60	2.98	3.30	1.23				5.6	3.2	9.3	2.9						30%	79%								7.5	100	131	$8
13 HOU	1	3	5	38	40	4.97	4.11	1.29	783	884	706	3.9	4.3	9.5	2.2	51%	10%	37	11	52	26%	68%	16%	0	16			83	1.11	-5.2	70	92	-$2
14 HOU	4	6	4	55	70	4.45	3.30	1.23	637	665	613	4.3	2.8	11.5	4.1	59%	13%	31	21	48	36%	62%	3%	0	18			50	1.05	-4.7	141	168	$1
1st Half	1	4	2	27	37	5.93	3.23	1.39	714	709	718	4.3	3.3	12.2	3.7	58%	13%	38	18	44	39%	56%	6%	0	17			67	0.73	-7.4	146	175	-$4
2nd Half	3	2	2	27	33	2.96	3.35	1.06	553	620	492	4.3	2.3	10.9	4.7	60%	13%	24	23	53	33%	69%	0%	0	18			40	1.40	2.6	136	162	$7
15 Proj	4	5	13	59	69	3.48	3.30	1.22	656	708	614	4.3	3.6	10.6	2.9	56%	12%	33	17	50	31%	74%	7%	0						1.9	103	123	$7

Fien,Casey

Age: 31	Th: R	Role RP	Health A	LIMA Plan A	
Ht: 6' 2"	Wt: 205	Type xFB	PT/Exp D	Rand Var 0	
			Consist B	MM 3300	

What was a nice little season came totally unglued late, as he allowed 12 ER in final 9 2/3 IP. While full-year ERA held steady, he wasn't able to maintain previous year's gains in Dom, GB%, and mastery of RH. Should continue to be WHIP contributor, but not much else. Use 2014 as your baseline.

Yr Tm	W	L	Sv	IP	K	ERA	xERA	WHIP	oOPS	vL	vR	BF/G	Ctl	Dom	Cmd	FpK	SwK	G	L	F	H%	S%	hr/f	GS	APC	DOM%	DIS%	Sv%	LI	RAR	BPV	BPX	R$
10 DET *	3	3	8	65	33	3.70	4.98	1.32	1364	1400	1333	5.8	1.9	4.6	2.4	58%	4%	36	18	45	29%	80%	40%	0	23			80	0.11	3.0	28	45	$3
11 aaa	2	2	3	24	19	6.01	8.36	1.78				5.3	3.2	6.9	2.1						34%	78%								-6.2	-19	-28	-$4
12 MIN *	4	6	9	81	63	4.40	3.86	1.27	578	491	638	4.9	2.9	7.0	2.4	57%	10%	25	25	51	29%	68%	6%	0	17			75	0.98	-3.8	68	88	$2
13 MIN	5	2	0	62	73	3.92	2.93	1.02	627	750	545	3.3	1.7	10.6	6.1	67%	15%	37	20	42	29%	67%	14%	0	13			0	1.25	-0.4	159	207	$3
14 MIN	5	6	1	63	51	3.98	3.99	1.17	705	694	713	3.6	1.4	7.2	5.1	68%	11%	32	19	49	31%	69%	7%	0	14			20	1.18	-1.9	102	122	$1
1st Half	4	4	1	34	26	2.41	3.82	0.92	574	700	465	3.5	1.6	7.0	4.3	69%	11%	33	18	49	24%	79%	6%	0	13			50	1.25	5.5	93	111	$8
2nd Half	1	2	0	30	25	5.76	4.18	1.45	833	688	951	3.6	1.2	7.6	6.3	66%	11%	31	20	49	37%	62%	8%	0	14			0	1.10	-7.4	113	135	-$6
15 Proj	4	4	0	65	57	3.95	3.42	1.15	700	706	695	3.7	1.6	7.8	4.9	66%	12%	33	20	47	30%	70%	9%	0						-1.7	108	129	$2

Fiers,Mike

Age: 30	Th: R	Role SP	Health A	LIMA Plan C+	
Ht: 6' 2"	Wt: 190	Type Pwr FB	PT/Exp D	Rand Var -1	
			Consist F	MM 3303	

6-5, 2.13 ERA in 72 IP at MIL. He's teased us before. Posted a 3.74 ERA/114 BPV in 128 IP in 2012, only to go 7.25 ERA/57 BPV the next year, earning a demotion. What's different? Mostly just improved control, but it might not be enough. FpK, FB%, S% all warn of another regression, though likely a softer landing.

Yr Tm	W	L	Sv	IP	K	ERA	xERA	WHIP	oOPS	vL	vR	BF/G	Ctl	Dom	Cmd	FpK	SwK	G	L	F	H%	S%	hr/f	GS	APC	DOM%	DIS%	Sv%	LI	RAR	BPV	BPX	R$
10 aa	1	1	1	32	30	4.27	3.87	1.28				13.0	2.7	8.6	3.3						32%	68%								-0.7	95	154	-$1
11 MIL *	13	3	5	128	110	2.08	2.70	1.08	786	1250	533	13.9	2.8	7.7	2.7	70%	14%	40	40	20	25%	86%	0%	0	21			83	0.07	29.5	91	137	$21
12 MIL *	10	13	0	183	174	4.45	4.23	1.34	694	690	698	23.0	2.8	8.6	3.1	60%	9%	33	28	39	33%	69%	9%	22	94	59%	18%	0	0.74	-9.7	87	113	$2
13 MIL *	2	6	0	51	38	4.68	5.82	1.50	972	999	930	13.8	3.4	6.8	2.0	60%	9%	35	26	39	30%	77%	26%	3	37	0%	100%	0	1.02	-5.1	19	25	-$5
14 MIL *	14	10	0	174	175	2.85	2.97	1.06	531	517	542	21.8	1.9	9.0	4.8	58%	10%	33	20	47	29%	78%	8%	10	80	90%	0%	0	0.74	19.2	135	161	$19
1st Half	6	4	0	79	78	3.38	4.02	1.24	710	408	913	20.0	1.8	8.9	4.9	55%	7%	19	24	57	34%	77%	8%	0	31			0	0.67	3.5	127	152	$8
2nd Half	8	6	0	95	97	2.41	2.11	0.92	510	526	497	23.8	2.0	9.2	4.6	58%	10%	35	19	46	25%	79%	8%	10	100	90%	0%			15.7	143	170	$28
15 Proj	12	11	0	173	160	3.53	3.46	1.22	704	718	692	21.6	2.5	8.3	3.3	59%	10%	34	23	43	30%	75%	9%	39						4.6	95	113	$12

Fister,Doug

Age: 31	Th: R	Role SP	Health D	LIMA Plan C	
Ht: 6' 8"	Wt: 210	Type Con GB	PT/Exp A	Rand Var -4	
			Consist A	MM 4105	

Missed first month due to lat strain, but that obviously had no lingering effects on his Ctl. Dom erosion stands out, but was it by design? With stronger infield defense behind him, he threw a lot more sinkers. Whether or not swing and miss stuff returns, he's a good bet for ERA regression.

Yr Tm	W	L	Sv	IP	K	ERA	xERA	WHIP	oOPS	vL	vR	BF/G	Ctl	Dom	Cmd	FpK	SwK	G	L	F	H%	S%	hr/f	GS	APC	DOM%	DIS%	Sv%	LI	RAR	BPV	BPX	R$
10 SEA	6	14	0	171	93	4.11	4.13	1.28	698	710	685	25.7	1.7	4.9	2.9	64%	5%	47	18	35	31%	68%	6%	28	96	39%	18%			-0.6	68	109	$4
11 2AL	11	13	0	216	146	2.83	3.54	1.06	617	642	586	27.3	1.5	6.1	3.9	65%	7%	48	20	32	28%	74%	5%	31	100	65%	3%	0	0.77	29.7	94	141	$23
12 DET	10	10	0	162	137	3.45	3.45	1.19	683	734	611	25.9	2.1	7.6	3.7	63%	8%	51	22	27	31%	74%	12%	26	97	50%	23%			11.2	111	144	$12
13 DET	14	9	0	209	159	3.67	3.38	1.31	710	687	738	26.7	1.9	6.9	3.6	59%	8%	54	21	24	33%	73%	9%	32	102	63%	13%	0	0.80	5.1	104	136	$8
14 WAS	16	6	0	164	98	2.41	3.75	1.08	654	690	618	26.5	1.3	5.4	4.1	65%	6%	49	17	34	27%	84%	10%	25	99	52%	16%			26.8	88	105	$19
1st Half	6	2	0	64	37	2.83	3.77	1.05	682	778	595	25.8	0.8	5.2	6.2	65%	5%	47	16	37	27%	80%	11%	10	99	50%	20%			7.2	97	115	$10
2nd Half	10	4	0	100	61	2.15	3.73	1.10	637	639	634	26.9	1.6	5.5	3.4	65%	7%	50	17	33	27%	86%	10%	15	99	53%	13%			19.7	83	99	$25
15 Proj	15	9	0	189	128	3.23	3.34	1.16	674	696	648	25.6	1.6	6.1	3.8	63%	7%	50	19	31	29%	75%	10%	29						11.9	95	113	$16

Flande,Yohan

Age: 29	Th: L	Role RP	Health A	LIMA Plan D+	
Ht: 6' 2"	Wt: 180	Type xGB	PT/Exp D	Rand Var +5	
			Consist B	MM 1000	

0-6, 5.19 ERA in 59 IP at COL. You may want to avert your eyes. The only thing worse than bad numbers is bad numbers in a ton of innings. Here is a case where MLE-converted minor league stats were an accurate barometer of MLB performance. GB tilt will help a bit in Coors, but that clearly won't be enough.

Yr Tm	W	L	Sv	IP	K	ERA	xERA	WHIP	oOPS	vL	vR	BF/G	Ctl	Dom	Cmd	FpK	SwK	G	L	F	H%	S%	hr/f	GS	APC	DOM%	DIS%	Sv%	LI	RAR	BPV	BPX	R$
10 aa	10	8	0	158	69	4.92	4.99	1.53				25.5	2.4	3.9	1.6						33%	67%								-16.4	33	53	-$6
11 aaa	8	8	1	137	87	5.06	5.59	1.66				18.6	2.7	5.7	2.1						37%	69%								-18.9	49	74	-$10
12 aaa	6	11	0	148	87	5.04	5.20	1.61				22.6	3.5	5.3	1.5						34%	69%								-18.6	37	48	-$14
13 a/a	9	8	1	136	76	5.80	6.04	1.79				19.6	3.5	5.0	1.4						37%	67%								-32.5	28	36	-$19
14 COL *	3	17	0	147	81	6.19	5.79	1.65	711	481	803	19.4	3.1	5.0	1.6	62%	7%	58	20	22	34%	63%	13%	10	56	10%	30%	0	0.66	-44.5	25	30	-$22
1st Half	2	10	0	82	44	5.50	6.16	1.74	872	700	967	23.3	3.3	4.8	1.5	50%	7%	52	21	27	36%	69%	11%	2	92	0%	0%			-17.7	21	25	-$22
2nd Half	1	7	0	66	38	7.06	5.33	1.54	676	415	772	15.9	2.9	5.2	1.8	65%	7%	60	20	21	33%	53%	13%	8	51	13%	38%	0	0.64	-26.9	31	36	-$21
15 Proj	2	4	0	44	24	5.50	4.21	1.68	850	525	971	19.6	3.4	5.1	1.5	65%	7%	58	20	22	35%	68%	11%	10						-9.4	35	42	-$8

Floyd,Gavin

Age: 32	Th: R	Role SP	Health F	LIMA Plan C	
Ht: 6' 4"	Wt: 235	Type Pwr	PT/Exp C	Rand Var -1	
			Consist A	MM 2200	

2-2, 2.65 ERA in 54 IP at ATL. Returned from TJ surgery, made just 9 starts before reinjuring elbow, this time a fracture. Skills were solid, but sample was small, and he's now coming off another major injury. He'll come cheap and may return a profit, but have a backup plan.

Yr Tm	W	L	Sv	IP	K	ERA	xERA	WHIP	oOPS	vL	vR	BF/G	Ctl	Dom	Cmd	FpK	SwK	G	L	F	H%	S%	hr/f	GS	APC	DOM%	DIS%	Sv%	LI	RAR	BPV	BPX	R$
10 CHW	10	13	0	187	151	4.08	3.73	1.37	719	673	775	25.7	2.8	7.3	2.6	60%	9%	50	18	32	33%	71%	8%	31	97	61%	10%			-0.1	83	135	$5
11 CHW	12	13	0	194	151	4.37	3.66	1.16	685	764	572	25.7	2.1	7.0	3.4	65%	9%	44	19	37	29%	65%	10%	30	97	57%	13%	0	0.83	-10.2	92	138	$8
12 CHW	12	11	0	168	144	4.29	4.05	1.36	755	871	633	25.0	3.4	7.7	2.3	60%	10%	47	18	35	30%	72%	13%	29	95	48%	24%			-5.6	73	95	$2
13 CHW	0	4	0	24	25	5.18	3.83	1.60	893	940	836	22.0	4.4	9.2	2.1	68%	11%	50	21	29	35%	71%	20%	5	84	40%	40%			-3.9	75	97	-$6
14 ATL *	3	4	0	78	58	3.47	4.41	1.36	702	773	629	21.8	2.8	6.6	2.4	64%	12%	49	20	31	31%	79%	12%	9	92	44%	0%			2.6	58	69	-$1
1st Half	3	4	0	78	58	3.47	4.41	1.36	702	773	629	21.8	2.8	6.6	2.4	64%	12%	49	20	31	31%	79%	12%	9	92	44%	0%			2.6	58	70	-$1
2nd Half																																	
15 Proj	3	4	0	58	46	4.03	3.71	1.34	727	793	649	24.1	3.1	7.1	2.3	63%	10%	46	20	34	30%	73%	11%	10						-2.1	67	80	-$1

BRIAN RUDD

Foltynewicz,Mike

Age: 23	Th: R	Role RP	Health A	LIMA Plan D+
Ht: 6' 4"	Wt: 220	Type Pwr	PT/Exp D	Rand Var +1
			Consist D	MM 1211

0-1, 5.30 ERA in 19 IP at HOU. Power arm has regularly hit triple digits on the radar, and minor league numbers say GB% should improve. However, Ctl and secondary offerings are works in progress, and it's unclear if future is as a starter or reliever. May still be a year or two away from providing value.

Yr	Tm	W	L	Sv	IP	K	ERA	xERA	WHIP	oOPS	vL	vR	BF/G	Ctl	Dom	Cmd	FpK	SwK	G	L	F	H%	S%	hr/f	GS	APC	DOM%	DIS%	Sv%	LI	RAR	BPV	BPX	R$
10																																		
11																																		
12																																		
13	aa	5	3	3	103	85	3.22	3.19	1.29				18.4	4.4	7.4	1.7						26%	77%								8.3	68	89	$5
14	HOU *	7	8	0	121	103	5.27	4.69	1.51	864	1062	659	14.2	4.2	7.6	1.8	52%	10%	29	21	51	32%	66%	9%	0	20			0	0.38	-22.8	56	67	-$9
1st Half		6	5	0	78	67	4.56	4.05	1.39				20.4	3.9	7.8	2.0						30%	68%	0%	0						-7.8	66	78	-$3
2nd Half		1	3	0	44	36	6.53	5.83	1.74	864	1062	659	9.5	4.6	7.4	1.6	52%	10%	29	21	51	36%	62%	9%	0	20			0	0.38	-15.0	42	50	-$19
15	**Proj**	**3**	**4**	**3**	**73**	**60**	**4.48**	**4.14**	**1.47**	**668**	**801**	**531**	**13.9**	**4.3**	**7.5**	**1.7**	**52%**	**10%**	**43**	**21**	**36**	**31%**	**71%**	**8%**	**9**						**-6.6**	**39**	**46**	**-$3**

Frasor,Jason

Age: 37	Th: R	Role RP	Health C	LIMA Plan B+
Ht: 5' 9"	Wt: 180	Type Pwr	PT/Exp D	Rand Var -3
			Consist A	MM 3400

Though GB% and Dom spiked in 1H, end result was a near carbon copy of previous year's BPIs. But... average fastball velocity down for third straight year, a trend that could put SwK and Dom at further risk; FpK not in sync with Ctl trend. At 37, odds are against another sub-3.00 ERA.

Yr	Tm	W	L	Sv	IP	K	ERA	xERA	WHIP	oOPS	vL	vR	BF/G	Ctl	Dom	Cmd	FpK	SwK	G	L	F	H%	S%	hr/f	GS	APC	DOM%	DIS%	Sv%	LI	RAR	BPV	BPX	R$
10	TOR	3	4	4	64	65	3.68	3.67	1.38	691	718	671	4.0	3.8	9.2	2.4	65%	9%	46	19	35	33%	74%	6%	0	16			50	1.00	3.2	86	140	$2
11	2 AL	3	3	0	60	57	3.60	4.04	1.40	770	841	706	4.1	3.9	8.6	2.2	59%	8%	37	23	40	31%	78%	10%	0	18			0	1.19	2.5	64	96	$0
12	TOR	1	1	0	44	53	4.12	3.78	1.47	799	915	715	3.8	4.5	10.9	2.4	66%	10%	38	23	38	34%	76%	14%	0	16			0	1.06	-0.6	90	118	-$4
13	TEX	4	3	0	49	48	2.57	3.62	1.14	598	427	699	3.3	3.7	8.8	2.4	62%	10%	45	19	36	26%	81%	9%	0	14			0	1.20	7.8	83	108	$3
14	2 AL	4	1	0	47	46	2.66	3.40	1.23	651	668	641	3.2	3.4	8.7	2.6	60%	9%	47	24	29	30%	80%	8%	0	14			0	1.12	6.3	90	107	$2
1st Half		1	1	0	25	27	2.13	3.19	1.14	585	532	623	3.3	3.6	9.6	2.7	64%	9%	50	20	30	29%	82%	5%	0	14			0	1.14	5.0	105	125	$2
2nd Half		3	0	0	22	19	3.27	3.65	1.32	726	867	658	3.2	3.3	7.8	2.4	56%	8%	44	28	28	31%	78%	11%	0	13			0	1.10	1.3	73	87	$2
15	**Proj**	**4**	**2**	**0**	**51**	**50**	**3.21**	**3.37**	**1.27**	**679**	**687**	**673**	**3.3**	**3.7**	**8.8**	**2.4**	**61%**	**9%**	**44**	**23**	**33**	**30%**	**77%**	**10%**	**0**						**3.3**	**81**	**97**	**$1**

Freeman,Sam

Age: 28	Th: L	Role RP	Health A	LIMA Plan C
Ht: 5' 11"	Wt: 165	Type Pwr xGB	PT/Exp D	Rand Var -2
			Consist B	MM 3200

2-0, 2.61 ERA in 38 IP at STL. Improved Dom and GB%, and continues to hold his own vs RH, albeit with help from 24% h%. But too many walks, especially in 2nd half, and owns career 1.9 Cmd vs LH. Sample too small to draw definitive conclusions, but if he can't get LH out, his job could be in danger.

Yr	Tm	W	L	Sv	IP	K	ERA	xERA	WHIP	oOPS	vL	vR	BF/G	Ctl	Dom	Cmd	FpK	SwK	G	L	F	H%	S%	hr/f	GS	APC	DOM%	DIS%	Sv%	LI	RAR	BPV	BPX	R$
10																																		
11	aa	2	2	3	59	43	2.68	3.37	1.32				4.7	3.9	6.5	1.7						28%	81%								9.2	65	97	$3
12	STL *	3	7	1	68	49	3.08	3.38	1.26	654	808	534	4.2	3.5	6.6	1.9	56%	11%	46	15	39	27%	78%	10%	0	14			50	0.63	7.8	64	83	$2
13	STL *	8	2	2	82	60	3.22	3.22	1.30	515	488	536	5.5	3.6	6.6	1.8	54%	11%	39	19	42	29%	75%	0%	0	16			67	0.84	6.5	72	94	$4
14	STL *	2	1	0	58	55	3.05	4.29	1.52	638	818	518	4.2	4.0	8.5	2.1	52%	12%	56	20	24	35%	80%	8%	0	15			0	1.05	5.0	82	97	-$2
1st Half		1	1	0	36	34	2.97	3.56	1.37	415	492	332	4.8	3.1	8.6	2.8	55%	14%	54	22	24	35%	77%	0%	0	16			0	1.10	3.4	105	126	-$1
2nd Half		1	0	0	23	21	3.18	4.20	1.76	761	1087	593	3.8	5.6	8.3	1.5	50%	11%	57	19	24	36%	84%	13%	0	15			0	1.02	1.6	35	42	-$4
15	**Proj**	**3**	**2**	**0**	**58**	**48**	**3.55**	**3.59**	**1.45**	**690**	**899**	**552**	**4.4**	**4.1**	**7.5**	**1.8**	**52%**	**12%**	**56**	**20**	**24**	**32%**	**76%**	**9%**	**0**						**1.4**	**59**	**70**	**-$1**

Frieri,Ernesto

Age: 29	Th: R	Role RP	Health A	LIMA Plan C+
Ht: 6' 2"	Wt: 205	Type Pwr xFB	PT/Exp B	Rand Var +5
			Consist A	MM 3510

About this disaster... Yes, his SwK took a dive but his other BPIs remained strong. Fate intervened with H% and hr/f. Good skills, bad luck, fine. But the kicker... when a closer posts a 54% strand rate (okay, 59% when he WAS the closer) he has nobody to blame but himself. Maybe there is something to "9th inning nerve."

Yr	Tm	W	L	Sv	IP	K	ERA	xERA	WHIP	oOPS	vL	vR	BF/G	Ctl	Dom	Cmd	FpK	SwK	G	L	F	H%	S%	hr/f	GS	APC	DOM%	DIS%	Sv%	LI	RAR	BPV	BPX	R$
10	SD *	4	2	17	69	83	1.58	1.33	0.99	553	731	469	3.9	4.6	10.7	2.4	59%	14%	25	13	62	21%	87%	5%	0	18			89	0.62	21.4	126	203	$18
11	SD	1	2	0	63	76	2.71	3.98	1.35	692	823	596	4.7	4.9	10.9	2.2	56%	11%	24	21	55	32%	80%	4%	0	19			0	0.60	9.5	66	100	$2
12	2 TM	5	2	23	66	98	2.32	3.12	0.98	556	373	706	4.0	4.1	13.4	3.3	56%	15%	26	21	53	23%	86%	13%	0	18			88	1.03	13.8	134	175	$19
13	LAA	2	4	37	69	98	3.80	3.47	1.24	684	572	826	4.4	3.9	12.8	3.3	63%	17%	24	17	59	32%	76%	12%	0	19			90	1.52	0.5	127	166	$16
14	2 TM	1	4	11	42	48	7.34	3.78	1.46	884	879	894	3.8	3.0	10.4	3.4	61%	11%	33	20	48	34%	54%	19%	0	16			79	1.02	-18.5	116	138	-$4
1st Half		0	3	11	32	38	6.19	3.37	1.31	824	776	916	3.9	2.5	10.7	4.2	60%	10%	35	20	44	32%	59%	21%	0	17			79	1.11	-9.7	137	164	-$2
2nd Half		1	1	0	10	10	11.17	5.20	1.97	1060	1258	841	3.7	4.7	9.3	2.0	65%	12%	25	19	56	39%	44%	17%	0	15			0	0.78	-8.9	45	54	-$10
15	**Proj**	**1**	**2**	**8**	**44**	**53**	**3.76**	**3.37**	**1.28**	**728**	**689**	**771**	**4.0**	**3.8**	**11.0**	**2.9**	**59%**	**13%**	**28**	**19**	**53**	**31%**	**77%**	**12%**	**0**						**-0.1**	**103**	**122**	**$2**

Fujikawa,Kyuji

Age: 34	Th: R	Role RP	Health F	LIMA Plan C+
Ht: 6' 0"	Wt: 190	Type Pwr	PT/Exp D	Rand Var +5
			Consist B	MM 5500

Didn't make season debut until August, and small sample results were mixed. While he maintained Dom, Ctl was up and velocity was down. Control is often last thing to return post-TJ-surgery, and should improve. When it does, he still has the goods to be an impact late-inning reliever.

Yr	Tm	W	L	Sv	IP	K	ERA	xERA	WHIP	oOPS	vL	vR	BF/G	Ctl	Dom	Cmd	FpK	SwK	G	L	F	H%	S%	hr/f	GS	APC	DOM%	DIS%	Sv%	LI	RAR	BPV	BPX	R$
10	for	3	4	28	62	77	2.52	3.91	1.21				4.3	3.6	11.1	3.1						28%	91%								12.0	92	148	$17
11	for	3	3	41	51	76	1.53	1.17	0.84				3.3	2.8	13.4	4.7						26%	86%								15.1	185	278	$25
12	for	2	2	24	47	55	1.66	2.43	1.17				3.9	3.6	10.5	3.0						31%	87%								13.7	127	166	$14
13	CHC	1	1	2	12	14	5.25	2.64	1.08	691	671	711	4.2	1.5	10.5	7.0	58%	13%	50	19	31	34%	50%	10%	0	17			67	0.88	-2.0	177	230	-$3
14	CHC	0	0	0	13	17	4.85	3.57	1.85	843	851	836	4.3	4.2	11.8	2.8	61%	14%	44	23	33	45%	77%	15%	0	16			0	0.20	-1.8	122	145	-$5
1st Half																																		
2nd Half		0	0	0	13	17	4.85	3.57	1.85	843	851	836	4.3	4.2	11.8	2.8	61%	14%	44	23	33	45%	77%	15%	0	16			0	0.20	-1.8	121	145	-$5
15	**Proj**	**2**	**3**	**0**	**51**	**65**	**1.98**	**2.61**	**1.10**	**798**	**797**	**799**	**3.9**	**3.4**	**11.5**	**3.4**	**0%**	**0%**	**46**	**20**	**34**	**28%**	**89%**	**14%**	**0**						**11.0**	**138**	**165**	**$5**

Furbush,Charlie

Age: 29	Th: L	Role RP	Health B	LIMA Plan C+
Ht: 6' 5"	Wt: 215	Type Pwr	PT/Exp D	Rand Var +2
			Consist A	MM 5500

Early-season struggles took him out of high leverage role temporarily, but he soon righted the ship. Continues to stifle LHB (.568 career OPS against), and FpK jump fueled much improved Ctl/Cmd. Improving SwK and BPIs are closer-worthy, and at the very least, should continue to provide strong ratios.

Yr	Tm	W	L	Sv	IP	K	ERA	xERA	WHIP	oOPS	vL	vR	BF/G	Ctl	Dom	Cmd	FpK	SwK	G	L	F	H%	S%	hr/f	GS	APC	DOM%	DIS%	Sv%	LI	RAR	BPV	BPX	R$
10	a/a	4	4	0	82	60	6.11	6.21	1.59				25.9	2.8	6.5	2.3						34%	65%								-20.6	29	47	-$8
11	2 AL *	9	13	0	139	115	4.96	4.67	1.34	850	758	886	15.2	3.0	7.4	2.5	58%	9%	42	19	39	29%	68%	15%	12	53	25%	42%	0	0.88	-17.5	52	78	-$2
12	SEA	5	2	0	46	53	2.72	3.13	0.95	529	404	637	3.8	3.1	10.3	3.3	59%	12%	42	22	37	24%	73%	8%	0	16			0	1.16	7.4	121	158	$5
13	SEA	2	6	0	65	80	3.74	3.40	1.18	603	502	688	3.9	4.0	11.1	2.8	59%	13%	40	22	38	29%	69%	8%	0	16			0	1.60	1.0	109	142	$1
14	SEA	1	5	1	42	51	3.61	2.99	1.16	649	594	701	2.6	1.9	10.8	5.7	63%	14%	35	25	39	34%	71%	9%	0	10			100	1.25	0.7	157	186	$0
1st Half		1	4	0	24	24	3.70	3.48	1.23	682	638	723	3.0	1.8	8.9	4.8	63%	12%	30	30	39	34%	71%	7%	0	11			0	1.39	0.1	118	141	-$1
2nd Half		0	1	1	18	27	3.50	2.35	1.06	604	537	669	2.2	2.0	13.5	6.8	64%	17%	44	17	39	35%	71%	13%	0	9			100	1.10	0.5	211	252	$1
15	**Proj**	**2**	**4**	**0**	**51**	**60**	**3.16**	**2.88**	**1.17**	**622**	**539**	**691**	**3.1**	**2.9**	**10.7**	**3.7**	**61%**	**13%**	**40**	**22**	**39**	**32%**	**75%**	**8%**	**0**						**3.7**	**131**	**156**	**$2**

Gallardo,Yovani

Age: 29	Th: R	Role SP	Health B	LIMA Plan B+
Ht: 6' 2"	Wt: 210	Type Pwr	PT/Exp A	Rand Var 0
			Consist A	MM 3205

Doesn't have swing-and-miss stuff he used to, but he's adapted by throwing fewer fastballs, more sinkers. As a result, Dom is down, but both Ctl and GB% have improved. This version comes with more risk, but xERA remains stable. Note that a BPV of 84 represents league average these days. That's where he's at.

Yr	Tm	W	L	Sv	IP	K	ERA	xERA	WHIP	oOPS	vL	vR	BF/G	Ctl	Dom	Cmd	FpK	SwK	G	L	F	H%	S%	hr/f	GS	APC	DOM%	DIS%	Sv%	LI	RAR	BPV	BPX	R$
10	MIL	14	7	0	185	200	3.84	3.50	1.37	693	781	620	25.9	3.6	9.7	2.7	62%	9%	43	24	33	34%	72%	7%	31	103	81%	13%			5.4	98	158	$10
11	MIL	17	10	0	207	207	3.52	3.34	1.22	686	710	663	26.2	2.6	9.0	3.5	63%	10%	47	17	36	31%	76%	13%	33	105	61%	15%			10.9	118	177	$17
12	MIL	16	9	0	204	204	3.66	3.67	1.30	706	759	654	26.1	3.6	9.0	2.5	56%	8%	48	21	31	30%	76%	15%	33	105	64%	9%			8.9	92	119	$13
13	MIL	12	10	0	181	144	4.18	3.85	1.36	720	729	713	24.9	3.3	7.2	2.2	56%	7%	49	23	28	31%	71%	12%	31	98	52%	19%			-7.1	67	88	$2
14	MIL	8	11	0	192	146	3.51	3.72	1.29	698	637	742	25.5	2.5	6.8	2.7	57%	7%	51	20	29	31%	76%	12%	32	101	53%	13%			5.5	84	100	$5
1st Half		5	5	0	103	80	3.51	3.64	1.24	673	609	716	25.4	2.7	7.0	2.6	55%	7%	52	19	29	29%	75%	12%	17	101	59%	6%			3.0	83	99	$8
2nd Half		3	6	0	90	66	3.51	3.81	1.36	726	665	772	25.7	2.3	6.6	2.9	59%	8%	49	21	30	32%	78%	12%	15	100	47%	20%			2.5	84	100	$1
15	**Proj**	**11**	**11**	**0**	**195**	**159**	**3.67**	**3.49**	**1.33**	**708**	**696**	**718**	**24.9**	**3.0**	**7.3**	**2.5**	**57%**	**8%**	**49**	**21**	**30**	**31%**	**75%**	**12%**	**33**						**1.7**	**79**	**95**	**$7**

BRIAN RUDD

Garcia,Jaime

			Health F	LIMA Plan B+
Age: 28	Th: L	Role SP	PT/Exp D	Rand Var +5
Ht: 6' 2"	Wt: 215	Type GB	Consist B	MM 4201

Limited to 7 games started, as shoulder issues led to late start and early end to season. It's a small sample, but BPIs remained intact or better, with Dom, SwK, and fastball velocity all at career highs. BPV history shows what he's capable of, but "F" health grade is well-deserved, and likely to be ongoing issue.

Yr Tm	W	L	Sv	IP	K	ERA	xERA	WHIP	oOPS	vL	vR	BF/G	Ctl	Dom	Cmd	FpK	SwK	G	L	F	H%	S%	hr/f	GS	APC	DOM%	DIS%	Sv%	LI	RAR	BPV	BPX	R$
10 STL	13	8	0	163	132	2.70	3.64	1.32	638	550	660	24.8	3.5	7.3	2.1	54%	11%	56	19	26	30%	81%	7%	28	93	61%	11%			27.8	70	113	$14
11 STL	13	7	0	195	156	3.56	3.47	1.32	711	770	697	25.8	2.3	7.2	3.1	58%	11%	54	18	28	33%	74%	9%	32	93	47%	16%			9.2	99	149	$9
12 STL *	8	8	0	137	113	4.08	4.06	1.34	730	649	750	24.8	2.2	7.4	3.4	63%	12%	54	20	26	34%	70%	7%	20	88	55%	20%			-1.1	96	125	$2
13 STL	5	2	0	55	43	3.58	3.35	1.30	725	905	666	26.0	2.4	7.0	2.9	68%	12%	63	14	23	31%	76%	15%	9	92	44%	11%			2.0	101	132	$0
14 STL	3	1	0	44	39	4.12	2.89	1.05	696	881	631	25.3	1.4	8.0	5.6	60%	13%	55	20	25	28%	65%	19%	7	90	43%	0%			-2.1	139	165	$0
1st Half	3	1	0	44	39	4.12	2.89	1.05	696	881	631	25.3	1.4	8.0	5.6	60%	13%	55	20	25	28%	65%	19%	7	90	43%	0%			-2.1	139	166	$0
2nd Half																																	
15 Proj	6	3	0	90	70	3.77	3.33	1.28	714	797	690	25.0	2.6	7.1	2.8	62%	12%	53	19	27	31%	73%	12%	15						-0.4	89	106	$2

Garza,Matt

			Health F	LIMA Plan B
Age: 31	Th: R	Role SP	PT/Exp B	Rand Var -1
Ht: 6' 4"	Wt: 215	Type	Consist A	MM 3203

Continues to be viable mid-rotation starter, but there are some chinks in the armor. Missed time again, as oblique strain cost him a month, and velocity, Dom, and SwK have dropped three years in row. xERA trend hints that string of eight straight sub-4.00 ERA's may soon come to an end.

Yr Tm	W	L	Sv	IP	K	ERA	xERA	WHIP	oOPS	vL	vR	BF/G	Ctl	Dom	Cmd	FpK	SwK	G	L	F	H%	S%	hr/f	GS	APC	DOM%	DIS%	Sv%	LI	RAR	BPV	BPX	R$
10 TAM	15	10	1	205	150	3.91	4.27	1.25	728	730	726	25.9	2.8	6.6	2.4	58%	8%	36	19	45	28%	73%	10%	32	99	50%	16%	100	0.76	4.2	58	94	$12
11 CHC	10	10	0	198	197	3.32	3.36	1.26	654	634	672	27.1	2.9	9.0	3.1	64%	12%	46	21	33	32%	75%	8%	31	103	68%	10%			15.2	108	162	$13
12 CHC	5	7	0	104	96	3.91	3.54	1.18	693	745	643	23.6	2.8	8.3	3.0	62%	11%	47	19	33	28%	72%	16%	18	94	56%	22%			1.4	100	130	$4
13 2 TM *	11	7	0	171	144	3.63	3.76	1.23	712	733	687	24.7	2.5	7.6	3.1	64%	10%	39	23	38	30%	74%	12%	24	101	58%	21%			5.0	83	108	$9
14 MIL	8	8	0	163	126	3.64	3.90	1.18	644	634	652	25.2	2.8	6.9	2.5	64%	9%	43	21	36	28%	70%	7%	27	94	48%	22%			2.1	72	85	$7
1st Half	5	5	0	108	81	4.10	4.08	1.28	678	708	654	27.1	2.8	6.8	2.4	66%	10%	44	20	36	30%	68%	7%	17	99	53%	12%			-4.7	67	80	$6
2nd Half	3	3	0	56	45	2.75	3.55	0.99	575	482	650	22.0	2.6	7.3	2.8	62%	10%	43	22	36	24%	75%	7%	10	85	40%	40%			6.8	82	98	$9
15 Proj	9	8	0	167	136	3.93	3.51	1.17	659	656	662	24.7	2.8	7.4	2.7	63%	10%	41	22	36	28%	68%	9%	26						-4.0	77	92	$8

Gausman,Kevin

			Health A	LIMA Plan B
Age: 24	Th: R	Role RP	PT/Exp D	Rand Var -1
Ht: 6' 3"	Wt: 190	Type Pwr	Consist A	MM 3303

7-7, 3.57 ERA in 113 IP at BAL. Put up 3.70 ERA in first 13 starts despite 1.7 Cmd, thanks to 4% hr/f. In last 7 starts, 3.35 ERA was fully supported by 8.9 Dom, 4.4 Cmd. He came up as one of game's top prospects, so late surge may be first step towards breakout. Worth the extra buck.

Yr Tm	W	L	Sv	IP	K	ERA	xERA	WHIP	oOPS	vL	vR	BF/G	Ctl	Dom	Cmd	FpK	SwK	G	L	F	H%	S%	hr/f	GS	APC	DOM%	DIS%	Sv%	LI	RAR	BPV	BPX	R$
10																																	
11																																	
12																																	
13 BAL *	6	11	0	130	119	4.71	4.11	1.30	792	811	772	14.8	1.9	8.3	4.4	61%	10%	42	25	33	34%	65%	19%	5	40	20%	40%	0	0.80	-13.4	115	150	-$2
14 BAL *	8	10	0	157	125	3.60	3.93	1.35	685	700	662	21.1	3.2	7.2	2.3	57%	9%	41	23	35	31%	75%	6%	20	98	35%	20%			2.6	71	85	$2
1st Half	4	5	0	71	54	3.75	4.23	1.41	680	679	680	18.9	3.6	6.8	1.9	58%	8%	41	22	37	31%	75%	3%	5	99	40%	40%			-0.1	58	69	-$1
2nd Half	4	5	0	85	71	3.48	3.86	1.30	686	707	654	23.9	2.8	7.5	2.6	56%	9%	42	24	35	31%	74%	7%	15	97	33%	13%			2.7	78	93	$5
15 Proj	11	9	0	174	152	3.53	3.44	1.28	701	711	689	17.9	2.7	7.9	2.9	59%	10%	42	24	35	32%	75%	9%	32						4.4	89	106	$9

Gee,Dillon

			Health F	LIMA Plan B+
Age: 29	Th: R	Role SP	PT/Exp A	Rand Var 0
Ht: 6' 1"	Wt: 205	Type	Consist A	MM 2103

Missed two months due to lat strain, but despite what ERA says, pre- and post-injury skills were consistently mediocre. 2012 Dom looks like an outlier, so while GB%, decent Ctl help limit the disasters, it's difficult to foresee much improvement. Pay for a repeat, nothing more.

Yr Tm	W	L	Sv	IP	K	ERA	xERA	WHIP	oOPS	vL	vR	BF/G	Ctl	Dom	Cmd	FpK	SwK	G	L	F	H%	S%	hr/f	GS	APC	DOM%	DIS%	Sv%	LI	RAR	BPV	BPX	R$
10 NYM *	15	10	0	194	155	4.74	4.62	1.39	631	653	618	24.8	2.5	7.2	2.8	60%	8%	47	10	43	33%	68%	5%	5	98	20%	0%			-15.9	69	112	$3
11 NYM	13	6	0	161	114	4.43	4.29	1.38	739	743	735	23.5	4.0	6.4	1.6	55%	10%	47	19	33	28%	70%	11%	27	87	41%	22%	0	0.77	-9.6	33	49	$1
12 NYM	6	7	0	110	97	4.10	3.54	1.25	697	770	610	27.2	2.4	8.0	3.3	59%	11%	50	20	30	31%	70%	13%	17	103	71%	0%			-1.2	107	140	$2
13 NYM	12	11	0	199	142	3.62	4.07	1.28	738	822	666	26.3	2.1	6.4	3.0	62%	10%	43	20	38	31%	76%	10%	32	93	44%	16%			6.1	79	103	$8
14 NYM	7	8	0	137	94	4.00	4.12	1.25	715	719	711	25.9	2.8	6.2	2.2	60%	8%	44	18	38	27%	72%	12%	22	96	41%	5%			-4.3	57	68	$2
1st Half	3	1	0	53	33	2.73	4.14	1.06	625	673	584	26.4	2.6	5.6	2.2	61%	7%	41	20	40	23%	80%	10%	8	96	63%	13%			6.5	51	61	$6
2nd Half	4	7	0	85	61	4.78	4.10	1.36	769	741	802	25.6	3.0	6.5	2.2	60%	8%	46	18	36	30%	68%	13%	14	96	29%	0%			-10.9	60	72	-$1
15 Proj	10	10	0	174	124	3.96	3.78	1.28	726	762	690	25.4	2.7	6.4	2.3	60%	9%	45	19	37	29%	73%	11%	28						-4.7	65	77	$5

Gibson,Kyle

			Health A	LIMA Plan D+
Age: 27	Th: R	Role SP	PT/Exp C	Rand Var 0
Ht: 6' 6"	Wt: 210	Type GB	Consist A	MM 2005

Heavy GB tilt is nice, as are minor gains in FpK and SwK, and 3.2 Cmd vs RHers. But hidden beneath the surface are major issues vs LHB (1.0 Cmd), which has been masked by 5% hr/f. That's a huge obstacle to overcome, and makes a 4.00 ERA look like a long shot.

Yr Tm	W	L	Sv	IP	K	ERA	xERA	WHIP	oOPS	vL	vR	BF/G	Ctl	Dom	Cmd	FpK	SwK	G	L	F	H%	S%	hr/f	GS	APC	DOM%	DIS%	Sv%	LI	RAR	BPV	BPX	R$
10 a/a	7	5	0	109	70	3.73	3.52	1.29				23.5	2.2	5.8	2.6						32%	70%								4.7	80	129	$4
11 aaa	3	8	0	95	75	5.64	5.60	1.60				23.4	2.6	7.1	2.7						37%	65%								-20.0	62	93	-$10
12																																	
13 MIN *	9	9	0	153	97	4.50	4.44	1.46	874	875	869	24.2	3.2	5.7	1.8	52%	8%	50	21	28	32%	70%	13%	10	90	20%	30%			-12.0	49	64	-$5
14 MIN	13	12	0	179	107	4.47	4.01	1.31	679	705	650	24.4	2.9	5.4	1.9	57%	9%	54	19	27	29%	65%	8%	31	90	42%	19%			-16.0	51	61	-$1
1st Half	7	6	0	93	50	3.77	4.04	1.20	633	680	579	24.0	2.6	4.8	1.9	58%	9%	55	16	29	27%	69%	7%	16	91	44%	19%			-0.4	50	60	$6
2nd Half	6	6	0	86	57	5.21	3.99	1.42	728	731	723	24.9	3.1	5.9	1.9	57%	10%	53	22	24	32%	62%	9%	15	90	40%	20%			-15.7	54	64	-$7
15 Proj	10	13	0	189	118	4.47	3.89	1.40	707	729	679	23.9	3.0	5.6	1.9	55%	9%	52	20	28	31%	68%	8%	33						-16.9	50	59	-$3

Giles,Kenneth

			Health A	LIMA Plan B
Age: 24	Th: R	Role RP	PT/Exp F	Rand Var -3
Ht: 6' 2"	Wt: 205	Type Pwr FB	Consist F	MM 5511

3-1, 1.18 ERA in 46 IP at PHI. Allowed HR to first batter he faced, and that was it. Armed with 100 mph fastball and nasty slider, turned in elite Cmd, SwK, and FpK. Will need to prove his Ctl gains long-term, as struggled to find the plate in the minors. But could quickly emerge as a front-line closer option.

Yr Tm	W	L	Sv	IP	K	ERA	xERA	WHIP	oOPS	vL	vR	BF/G	Ctl	Dom	Cmd	FpK	SwK	G	L	F	H%	S%	hr/f	GS	APC	DOM%	DIS%	Sv%	LI	RAR	BPV	BPX	R$
10																																	
11																																	
12																																	
13																																	
14 PHI *	5	1	13	74	96	1.56	1.22	0.94	450	436	461	4.1	2.9	11.6	4.0	63%	16%	44	15	41	28%	83%	3%	0	16			93	1.15	20.0	169	202	$17
1st Half	2	0	12	36	44	2.00	1.77	1.08	446	644	298	4.5	4.1	11.1	2.7	58%	21%	56	0	44	28%	82%	25%	0	17			92	0.40	7.7	135	161	$16
2nd Half	3	1	1	39	52	1.16	2.29	0.80	450	403	488	3.8	1.9	12.1	6.5	63%	15%	43	16	41	29%	84%	0%	0	16			100	1.30	12.3	189	225	$18
15 Proj	5	1	8	73	91	2.37	2.72	1.02	487	443	520	4.2	3.2	11.3	3.5	61%	15%	43	16	41	29%	75%	1%	0						12.2	138	164	$12

Gomez,Jeanmar

			Health B	LIMA Plan D+
Age: 27	Th: R	Role RP	PT/Exp C	Rand Var -3
Ht: 6' 3"	Wt: 220	Type GB	Consist B	MM 2000

From July '13 through June '14, flashed career-best BPI (6.9 Dom, 2.7 Ctl), so perhaps hidden injury led to 2nd half collapse. But even those peak skills weren't that special for a reliever. He'd have to do that as a starter to be relevant, and with 4.94 ERA, 4.9 Dom in 46 career starts, odds are against it.

Yr Tm	W	L	Sv	IP	K	ERA	xERA	WHIP	oOPS	vL	vR	BF/G	Ctl	Dom	Cmd	FpK	SwK	G	L	F	H%	S%	hr/f	GS	APC	DOM%	DIS%	Sv%	LI	RAR	BPV	BPX	R$
10 CLE *	12	13	0	174	101	5.17	5.36	1.56	841	752	961	24.6	3.2	5.3	1.6	59%	6%	47	20	33	33%	68%	10%	11	91	18%	36%			-23.4	29	46	-$7
11 CLE *	15	10	0	196	122	3.31	4.07	1.38	804	855	756	25.7	2.8	5.6	2.0	61%	6%	53	20	27	31%	77%	10%	10	87	20%	50%	0	0.83	15.3	56	85	$9
12 CLE *	11	13	0	160	92	5.53	4.92	1.44	810	822	800	22.0	2.8	5.2	1.8	56%	8%	48	19	33	31%	63%	15%	17	73	12%	53%	0	0.68	-30.0	32	42	-$10
13 PIT	3	0	0	81	53	3.35	3.83	1.15	617	621	614	9.8	3.1	5.9	1.9	63%	9%	55	19	26	25%	72%	10%	8	36	50%	50%	0	0.69	5.2	55	72	$2
14 PIT	2	2	1	62	38	3.19	4.35	1.50	810	1065	646	6.1	3.3	5.5	1.7	65%	9%	47	25	28	32%	82%	11%	0	22			100	0.62	4.2	34	41	-$2
1st Half	1	2	0	40	30	3.40	3.80	1.31	813	1080	647	6.9	2.5	6.8	2.7	65%	9%	44	23	33	30%	80%	15%	0	25			0	0.71	1.7	77	92	-$1
2nd Half	1	0	1	22	8	2.82	5.48	1.84	805	1039	644	5.2	4.8	3.2	0.7	64%	7%	51	28	22	35%	83%	0%	0	19			100	0.51	2.5	-44	-52	-$4
15 Proj	3	2	0	58	36	3.77	3.97	1.43	753	867	668	7.9	3.1	5.6	1.8	63%	8%	50	22	27	31%	75%	9%	0						-0.2	44	52	-$2

BRIAN RUDD

Gonzales,Marco

Age: 23	Th: L	Role RP	PT/Exp F	Rand Var -1	Health A	LIMA Plan B+		
Ht: 6' 1"	Wt: 195	Type Pwr xFB	Consist F	MM 2301				

4-2, 4.15 ERA in 35 IP at STL. Velocity is below average, so strong Dom in first full season as a pro was pleasant surprise. Nasty changeup is his calling card, and it generated 25% SwK in those 35 MLB innings. Doesn't possess a ton of upside, but could develop into a solid middle-of-the-rotation starter.

Yr Tm	W	L	Sv	IP	K	ERA	xERA	WHIP	oOPS	vL	vR	BF/G	Ctl	Dom	Cmd	FpK	SwK	G	L	F	H%	S%	hr/f	GS	APC	DOM%	DIS%	Sv%	LI	RAR	BPV	BPX	R$
10																																	
11																																	
12																																	
13																																	
14 STL *	11	5	0	119	104	3.32	3.72	1.27	737	397	827	19.5	2.9	7.8	2.7	61%	10%	36	23	41	30%	77%	10%	5	62	40%	40%	0	1.07	6.2	81	97	$6
1st Half	3	2	0	44	42	3.26	3.44	1.24	921	636	1189	22.2	2.4	8.7	3.7	58%	7%	42	26	32	33%	75%	17%	1	82	0%	0%			2.6	115	138	$0
2nd Half	8	3	0	75	61	3.41	3.96	1.30	701	249	784	18.2	3.3	7.3	2.2	62%	11%	35	22	43	29%	78%	8%	4	60	50%	50%	0	1.11	3.1	64	76	$10
15 Proj	**9**	**6**	**0**	**102**	**88**	**3.66**	**3.78**	**1.28**	**648**	**208**	**730**	**19.6**	**2.9**	**7.8**	**2.7**	**62%**	**11%**	**35**	**22**	**43**	**30%**	**74%**	**7%**	**20**						**1.0**	**75**	**89**	**$5**

Gonzalez,Gio

Age: 29	Th: L	Role SP	PT/Exp A	Rand Var 0	Health C	LIMA Plan B		
Ht: 6' 0"	Wt: 205	Type Pwr	Consist A	MM 4405				

After missing a month with an inflamed shoulder, came back strong as ever in 2nd half. Though fastball velocity was down a tick, used changeup more often and more effectively down the stretch. Seven straight PQS-DOM outings to end the season highlights the potential for... UP: sub-3.00 ERA, again

Yr Tm	W	L	Sv	IP	K	ERA	xERA	WHIP	oOPS	vL	vR	BF/G	Ctl	Dom	Cmd	FpK	SwK	G	L	F	H%	S%	hr/f	GS	APC	DOM%	DIS%	Sv%	LI	RAR	BPV	BPX	R$
10 OAK	15	9	0	201	171	3.23	3.98	1.31	644	615	653	25.8	4.1	7.7	1.9	53%	9%	49	15	35	28%	77%	7%	33	102	58%	18%			21.0	54	87	$15
11 OAK	16	12	0	202	197	3.12	3.68	1.32	654	713	636	27.0	4.1	8.8	2.2	53%	10%	47	18	34	30%	79%	9%	32	106	56%	13%			20.5	74	111	$16
12 WAS	21	8	0	199	207	2.89	3.40	1.13	582	659	561	25.7	3.4	9.3	2.7	59%	10%	48	22	30	28%	75%	6%	32	100	78%	13%			27.7	102	132	$28
13 WAS	11	8	0	196	192	3.36	3.60	1.25	668	568	696	25.6	3.5	8.8	2.5	61%	10%	44	23	33	30%	75%	10%	32	104	69%	22%			12.3	87	113	$12
14 WAS	10	10	0	159	162	3.57	3.41	1.20	647	628	653	24.2	3.2	9.2	2.9	58%	11%	45	19	37	30%	71%	7%	27	97	70%	19%			3.3	103	122	$9
1st Half	5	4	0	69	71	3.93	3.72	1.27	692	832	661	23.9	3.8	9.3	2.4	56%	12%	40	18	42	30%	70%	7%	12	98	67%	17%			-1.6	83	99	$3
2nd Half	5	6	0	90	91	3.30	3.17	1.14	613	530	646	24.4	2.7	9.1	3.4	59%	11%	48	19	32	30%	71%	6%	15	97	73%	20%			4.9	117	140	$13
15 Proj	**14**	**8**	**0**	**191**	**192**	**3.27**	**3.19**	**1.20**	**640**	**615**	**647**	**24.2**	**3.3**	**9.0**	**2.8**	**58%**	**11%**	**46**	**20**	**34**	**30%**	**74%**	**7%**	**32**						**11.1**	**98**	**116**	**$17**

Gonzalez,Miguel

Age: 31	Th: R	Role SP	PT/Exp B	Rand Var -3	Health C	LIMA Plan C+		
Ht: 6' 1"	Wt: 170	Type FB	Consist B	MM 2103				

For second straight year, Dom and GB% took turn for the worse in second half, and gap between ERA/xERA shows just how fortunate he was (thank you, strand rate!). As a fly ball pitcher lacking swing-and-miss stuff, he needs luck on his side to retain this type of value. If and when it runs out... DN: 4.50 ERA

Yr Tm	W	L	Sv	IP	K	ERA	xERA	WHIP	oOPS	vL	vR	BF/G	Ctl	Dom	Cmd	FpK	SwK	G	L	F	H%	S%	hr/f	GS	APC	DOM%	DIS%	Sv%	LI	RAR	BPV	BPX	R$
10																																	
11 a/a	0	6	0	52	38	7.70	6.47	1.84				15.0	4.0	6.7	1.7						38%	57%								-23.9	34	51	-$13
12 BAL *	12	6	1	150	117	3.03	3.02	1.13	694	701	685	18.5	2.8	7.0	2.5	66%	9%	35	22	43	26%	77%	10%	15	94	47%	20%	100	0.69	18.2	78	102	$17
13 BAL	11	8	0	171	120	3.78	4.28	1.23	713	689	736	23.7	2.8	6.3	2.3	59%	9%	39	21	40	27%	74%	11%	28	90	54%	14%	0	0.75	1.8	55	72	$7
14 BAL	10	9	0	159	111	3.23	4.36	1.30	751	772	724	24.9	2.9	6.3	2.2	61%	9%	37	21	42	28%	82%	12%	26	95	46%	19%	0	0.75	10.1	50	60	$6
1st Half	4	5	0	73	58	4.56	4.52	1.56	862	842	882	23.3	3.7	7.2	1.9	60%	9%	40	18	42	32%	76%	14%	13	90	54%	31%	0	0.74	-7.4	47	56	-$8
2nd Half	6	4	0	86	53	2.09	4.21	1.07	649	715	558	26.5	2.2	5.5	2.5	63%	8%	35	23	42	24%	90%	11%	13	100	38%	8%			17.5	53	64	$18
15 Proj	**10**	**9**	**0**	**160**	**111**	**3.82**	**4.08**	**1.30**	**740**	**750**	**729**	**21.6**	**3.0**	**6.3**	**2.1**	**61%**	**9%**	**36**	**21**	**42**	**28%**	**75%**	**11%**	**30**						**-1.5**	**47**	**56**	**$5**

Gonzalez,Miguel Alfredo

Age: 28	Th: R	Role RP	PT/Exp F	Rand Var -2	Health F	LIMA Plan D+		
Ht: 6' 3"	Wt: 200	Type Pwr	Consist F	MM 1201				

0-1, 6.75 ERA in 5 IP at PHI. Shoulder issue delayed his season debut, and after three rough starts in the minors, knocked him out again. Came back as a reliever, posting 2.19 ERA, 12.4 Dom across three levels prior to September call-up. Could make an impact if he stays in pen, but future role remains unclear.

Yr Tm	W	L	Sv	IP	K	ERA	xERA	WHIP	oOPS	vL	vR	BF/G	Ctl	Dom	Cmd	FpK	SwK	G	L	F	H%	S%	hr/f	GS	APC	DOM%	DIS%	Sv%	LI	RAR	BPV	BPX	R$
10 for	6	6	0	100	73	3.70	3.65	1.19				25.0	1.8	6.6	3.7						30%	71%								4.7	93	150	$5
11 for	8	5	0	113	70	3.96	4.55	1.37				29.6	2.9	5.6	1.9						30%	75%								-0.2	39	59	$1
12																																	
13																																	
14 PHI *	0	3	7	36	38	3.49	4.29	1.53	952	1000	915	5.4	5.4	9.5	1.8	59%	12%	19	33	48	32%	80%	10%	0	22			88	0.86	1.1	74	88	-$1
1st Half																																	
2nd Half	0	3	7	36	38	3.49	4.29	1.53	952	1000	915	5.4	5.4	9.5	1.8	59%	12%	19	33	48	32%	80%	10%	0	22			88	0.86	1.1	74	88	-$1
15 Proj	**4**	**6**	**0**	**102**	**83**	**4.13**	**4.41**	**1.48**				**11.3**	**4.4**	**7.3**	**1.7**	**59%**	**12%**				**31%**	**74%**		**5**						**-4.9**	**54**	**65**	**-$3**

Gray,Jonathan

Age: 23	Th: R	Role SP	PT/Exp F	Rand Var +3	Health A	LIMA Plan D+		
Ht: 6' 4"	Wt: 235	Type FB	Consist F	MM 1101				

Shoulder fatigue ended season in August, and may have played a role in 2nd half Ctl issues. Remains among top pitching prospects in the game, and could make an impact soon. But Dom was lower than expected in '14, and he hasn't pitched above AA, so may need more seasoning. Oh, and there's that Coors Field thing.

Yr Tm	W	L	Sv	IP	K	ERA	xERA	WHIP	oOPS	vL	vR	BF/G	Ctl	Dom	Cmd	FpK	SwK	G	L	F	H%	S%	hr/f	GS	APC	DOM%	DIS%	Sv%	LI	RAR	BPV	BPX	R$
10																																	
11																																	
12																																	
13																																	
14 aa	10	5	0	124	89	5.35	4.52	1.41				21.9	3.2	6.4	2.0						31%	63%								-24.7	51	61	-$6
1st Half	7	3	0	79	57	5.15	4.63	1.35				22.0	2.7	6.5	2.5						30%	65%								-13.7	53	63	-$4
2nd Half	3	2	0	45	31	5.71	4.32	1.50				21.8	4.0	6.3	1.6						32%	60%								-11.0	54	64	-$11
15 Proj	**6**	**6**	**0**	**102**	**76**	**4.44**	**4.19**	**1.44**				**21.8**	**3.4**	**6.7**	**2.0**	**60%**	**9%**	**38**	**20**	**42**	**31%**	**72%**	**10%**	**20**						**-8.8**	**45**	**53**	**-$3**

Gray,Sonny

Age: 25	Th: R	Role SP	PT/Exp B	Rand Var 0	Health A	LIMA Plan C		
Ht: 5' 11"	Wt: 195	Type Pwr GB	Consist B	MM 4205				

Has just three PQS-DIS in 43 career starts, thanks to combo of high GB% and ability to get both LH and RH batters out. In six September starts, threw a lot more sinkers, and had season bests in Cmd (2.8), SwK (11%), and GB% (63%). Looks like a rock-solid investment, especially in keeper leagues.

Yr Tm	W	L	Sv	IP	K	ERA	xERA	WHIP	oOPS	vL	vR	BF/G	Ctl	Dom	Cmd	FpK	SwK	G	L	F	H%	S%	hr/f	GS	APC	DOM%	DIS%	Sv%	LI	RAR	BPV	BPX	R$
10																																	
11 aa	1	0	0	20	16	0.44	1.87	1.05				15.5	2.5	7.1	2.9						28%	95%								8.6	115	173	$1
12 a/a	6	9	0	152	84	4.43	4.26	1.48				24.2	3.3	5.0	1.5						32%	69%								-7.8	48	62	-$7
13 OAK *	15	10	0	182	165	3.20	3.29	1.28	570	622	499	23.4	2.8	8.1	2.9	60%	10%	53	20	28	32%	75%	8%	10	83	80%	10%	0	0.66	15.1	101	132	$13
14 OAK	14	10	0	219	183	3.08	3.36	1.19	627	639	614	27.2	3.0	7.5	2.5	58%	9%	56	18	26	28%	76%	9%	33	100	55%	6%			17.8	87	104	$16
1st Half	7	3	0	104	90	3.20	3.45	1.22	625	604	652	27.3	3.2	7.8	2.4	57%	9%	55	19	26	29%	74%	8%	16	101	56%	0%			6.9	86	103	$14
2nd Half	7	7	0	115	93	2.97	3.28	1.17	630	675	582	27.2	2.9	7.3	2.5	60%	9%	57	18	25	28%	77%	11%	17	99	53%	12%			10.9	88	105	$18
15 Proj	**15**	**9**	**0**	**203**	**169**	**3.19**	**3.22**	**1.23**	**635**	**663**	**601**	**24.8**	**2.9**	**7.5**	**2.6**	**59%**	**10%**	**55**	**19**	**26**	**30%**	**75%**	**8%**	**33**						**13.8**	**89**	**106**	**$16**

Greene,Shane

Age: 26	Th: R	Role SP	PT/Exp D	Rand Var +2	Health A	LIMA Plan B+		
Ht: 6' 4"	Wt: 200	Type GB	Consist C	MM 2103				

5-4 3.78 ERA in 79 IP at NYY. Exceeded expectations, as GB%/Dom combo were very impressive. He's always kept the ball down, but nothing in his minor league track record suggested he'd show this level of Dom. That's likely to regress, and he'll be hard-pressed to keep ERA under 4.00.

Yr Tm	W	L	Sv	IP	K	ERA	xERA	WHIP	oOPS	vL	vR	BF/G	Ctl	Dom	Cmd	FpK	SwK	G	L	F	H%	S%	hr/f	GS	APC	DOM%	DIS%	Sv%	LI	RAR	BPV	BPX	R$
10																																	
11																																	
12																																	
13 aa	8	4	0	79	55	4.25	6.14	1.72				25.7	2.5	6.3	2.5						39%	77%								-3.8	50	65	-$6
14 NYY *	10	6	0	145	126	4.63	5.13	1.60	715	765	661	21.4	3.5	7.8	2.2	59%	11%	50	22	28	37%	72%	13%	14	90	43%	29%	0	0.70	-15.8	67	80	-$8
1st Half	5	2	0	61	41	6.16	6.40	1.90	600	1000	333	19.1	3.9	6.0	1.5	17%	4%	100	0	0	39%	66%	0%	0	23			0	0.00	-18.1	39	46	-$22
2nd Half	5	4	0	84	86	3.52	4.22	1.39	714	758	665	23.7	3.2	9.1	2.8	59%	11%	50	22	28	34%	77%	13%	14	95	43%	29%			2.3	90	107	$2
15 Proj	**10**	**9**	**0**	**145**	**110**	**4.03**	**3.82**	**1.42**	**664**	**706**	**617**	**22.8**	**3.2**	**6.9**	**2.1**	**59%**	**9%**	**48**	**22**	**30**	**32%**	**73%**	**9%**	**20**						**-5.3**	**62**	**74**	**$1**

BRIAN RUDD

Greenwood,Nick

						Health	A	LIMA Plan	D+
Age:	27	Th:	L	Role	RP	PT/Exp	D	Rand Var	+3
Ht:	6' 1"	Wt:	180	Type	Con xGB	Consist	D	MM	2000

2-1, 4.75 ERA in 36 IP at STL. Soft-tossing RP with mediocre minor league history put up career AAA numbers (3.02 ERA, 37/10 K/BB in 51 IP) before scuffling in MLB debut. Above average FpK and Ctl/GB% combo don't offset sub-par Dom and recent HR struggles. A half season of good stats does not a career make.

Yr Tm	W	L	Sv	IP	K	ERA	xERA	WHIP	oOPS	vL	vR	BF/G	Ctl	Dom	Cmd	FpK	SwK	G	L	F	H%	S%	hr/f	GS	APC	DOM%	DIS%	Sv%	LI	RAR	BPV	BPX	R$
10																																	
11 a/a	2	4	2	79	44	4.20	4.14	1.33				5.5	2.2	5.0	2.2						30%	70%								-2.5	53	80	-$1
12 aaa	4	3	0	78	38	4.85	5.09	1.56				6.9	2.7	4.4	1.6						34%	69%								-8.0	34	45	-$8
13 a/a	5	12	0	95	36	5.57	6.18	1.71				13.1	2.9	3.4	1.2						34%	69%								-19.9	2	3	-$14
14 STL *	6	5	0	87	45	3.91	3.52	1.15	705	611	759	7.5	1.6	4.7	3.0	63%	8%	59	18	23	28%	68%	18%	1	26	0%	100%	0	0.46	-1.8	68	81	$2
1st Half	4	4	0	52	30	2.95	3.02	1.11	638	891	399	7.6	1.7	5.1	2.9	60%	7%	56	14	31	27%	75%	9%	0	35			0	0.73	5.1	79	94	$6
2nd Half	2	1	0	34	16	5.37	4.28	1.20	733	419	879	7.3	1.3	4.2	3.1	64%	8%	60	20	20	28%	57%	24%	1	22	0%	100%	0	0.37	-6.9	53	63	-$4
15 Proj	**3**	**3**	**0**	**45**	**22**	**4.70**	**3.73**	**1.38**	**708**	**419**	**839**	**8.0**	**2.1**	**4.3**	**2.1**	**64%**	**8%**	**60**	**20**	**20**	**31%**	**67%**	**14%**	**0**						**-5.3**	**59**	**70**	**-$4**

Gregerson,Luke

						Health	B	LIMA Plan	B+
Age:	31	Th:	R	Role	RP	PT/Exp	C	Rand Var	-5
Ht:	6' 3"	Wt:	200	Type	GB	Consist	A	MM	5211

So nice to spend your peak years in pitchers' parks. Dependable RP profile, with closing experience that always yields a few saves. Sub-90 mph velocity and Dom trend look a bit tenuous. But elite SwK% is reassuring along with firming GB% and three years of Ctl gains. Superb bottom-end roster support.

Yr Tm	W	L	Sv	IP	K	ERA	xERA	WHIP	oOPS	vL	vR	BF/G	Ctl	Dom	Cmd	FpK	SwK	G	L	F	H%	S%	hr/f	GS	APC	DOM%	DIS%	Sv%	LI	RAR	BPV	BPX	R$
10 SD	4	7	2	78	89	3.22	2.66	0.83	524	540	511	3.7	2.1	10.2	4.9	62%	16%	48	15	37	23%	65%	12%	0	14			29	1.34	8.3	154	250	$11
11 SD	3	3	0	56	34	2.75	4.18	1.37	681	770	622	4.0	3.1	5.5	1.8	55%	12%	49	22	29	31%	80%	4%	0	14			0	1.15	8.2	43	65	$1
12 SD	2	0	9	72	72	2.39	3.30	1.09	612	663	578	3.8	2.6	9.0	3.4	60%	16%	50	18	32	28%	83%	11%	0	14			69	1.19	14.4	120	156	$10
13 SD	6	8	4	66	64	2.71	3.27	1.01	572	624	521	3.7	2.4	8.7	3.6	60%	14%	45	20	35	27%	73%	5%	0	13			44	1.26	9.4	113	148	$8
14 OAK	5	5	3	72	59	2.12	3.24	1.01	604	526	663	3.9	1.9	7.3	3.9	60%	14%	52	15	33	26%	84%	9%	0	14			27	1.31	14.5	112	133	$9
1st Half	2	1	3	44	40	2.27	3.01	1.01	594	589	598	4.0	1.9	8.2	4.4	62%	15%	50	20	30	28%	80%	8%	0	15			33	1.42	7.9	126	150	$10
2nd Half	3	4	0	29	19	1.88	3.59	1.01	620	436	765	3.8	1.9	6.0	3.2	58%	12%	56	8	36	24%	88%	10%	0	13			0	1.15	6.6	90	108	$7
15 Proj	**5**	**6**	**4**	**73**	**62**	**2.97**	**3.05**	**1.04**	**608**	**576**	**631**	**3.7**	**2.2**	**7.8**	**3.5**	**60%**	**14%**	**50**	**16**	**34**	**27%**	**74%**	**8%**	**0**						**6.9**	**109**	**129**	**$8**

Greinke,Zack

						Health	D	LIMA Plan	C
Age:	31	Th:	R	Role	SP	PT/Exp	A	Rand Var	-1
Ht:	6' 2"	Wt:	195	Type	Pwr	Consist	A	MM	5305

A top-tier SP? Freak injuries ding his Health grade, but recent performance and consistency are first-rate. Coming off consecutive sub-3 ERAs, his DOM%, Cmd, and GB% have never looked better. Hand-count SPs with superior BPVs; you'll still have fingers remaining.

Yr Tm	W	L	Sv	IP	K	ERA	xERA	WHIP	oOPS	vL	vR	BF/G	Ctl	Dom	Cmd	FpK	SwK	G	L	F	H%	S%	hr/f	GS	APC	DOM%	DIS%	Sv%	LI	RAR	BPV	BPX	R$
10 KC	10	14	0	220	181	4.17	3.65	1.25	696	774	601	27.8	2.3	7.4	3.3	61%	8%	46	18	36	31%	67%	8%	33	104	55%	9%			-2.5	97	156	$9
11 MIL	16	6	0	172	201	3.83	2.82	1.20	708	738	679	25.5	2.4	10.5	4.5	60%	11%	47	22	31	33%	71%	14%	28	101	71%	11%			2.4	151	227	$14
12 2 TM	15	5	0	212	200	3.48	3.34	1.20	663	691	635	25.5	2.3	8.5	3.7	59%	9%	49	22	29	31%	73%	10%	34	100	65%	12%			14.1	118	154	$18
13 LA	15	4	0	178	148	2.63	3.43	1.11	647	733	568	25.6	2.3	7.5	3.2	58%	11%	46	24	31	28%	79%	9%	28	101	64%	11%			27.0	96	125	$21
14 LA	17	8	0	202	207	2.71	2.93	1.15	660	627	689	25.7	1.9	9.2	4.8	63%	12%	49	23	29	32%	80%	12%	32	100	75%	6%			25.6	141	168	$21
1st Half	10	4	0	104	111	2.78	2.90	1.17	688	665	709	24.9	1.7	9.6	5.6	64%	11%	48	21	31	33%	82%	13%	17	99	82%	6%			12.3	152	182	$23
2nd Half	7	4	0	99	96	2.65	2.96	1.14	630	585	668	26.5	2.1	8.8	4.2	61%	12%	50	25	26	31%	79%	10%	15	101	67%	7%			13.3	129	153	$19
15 Proj	**16**	**7**	**0**	**196**	**187**	**2.93**	**2.92**	**1.15**	**658**	**673**	**644**	**25.2**	**2.1**	**8.6**	**4.0**	**61%**	**11%**	**48**	**23**	**29**	**31%**	**78%**	**10%**	**31**						**19.6**	**123**	**146**	**$21**

Griffin,A.J.

						Health	F	LIMA Plan	B+
Age:	27	Th:	R	Role	SP	PT/Exp	C	Rand Var	0
Ht:	6' 5"	Wt:	230	Type	xFB	Consist	C	MM	2101

Late April Tommy John surgery ended his 2014 season before it began. With 12-18 month recovery, he's looking at a partial 2015 at best. Cmd, DIS% highlighted a credible sophomore season in 2013 despite FB%. But don't pay for a 2015 repeat. Decent keeper league play.

Yr Tm	W	L	Sv	IP	K	ERA	xERA	WHIP	oOPS	vL	vR	BF/G	Ctl	Dom	Cmd	FpK	SwK	G	L	F	H%	S%	hr/f	GS	APC	DOM%	DIS%	Sv%	LI	RAR	BPV	BPX	R$
10																																	
11 a/a	2	4	0	38	24	5.91	5.70	1.56				23.8	2.9	5.7	2.0						33%	64%								-9.2	29	43	-$6
12 OAK *	14	4	0	184	139	3.03	2.92	1.07	630	629	631	22.4	1.8	6.8	3.8	62%	9%	37	24	39	27%	75%	10%	15	95	53%	27%			22.5	105	137	$22
13 OAK	14	10	0	200	171	3.83	4.10	1.13	688	666	713	25.7	2.4	7.7	3.2	60%	9%	32	18	49	26%	74%	13%	32	100	56%	3%			1.0	83	108	$14
14																																	
1st Half																																	
2nd Half																																	
15 Proj	**7**	**8**	**0**	**116**	**86**	**4.23**	**3.93**	**1.28**	**731**	**720**	**743**	**23.7**	**2.4**	**6.7**	**2.7**	**60%**	**9%**	**34**	**20**	**45**	**29%**	**72%**	**11%**	**20**						**-7.0**	**66**	**79**	**$1**

Grilli,Jason

						Health	D	LIMA Plan	A
Age:	38	Th:	R	Role	RP	PT/Exp	C	Rand Var	0
Ht:	6' 4"	Wt:	235	Type	Pwr FB	Consist	B	MM	4510

Dom and SwK% say he's lost some closer stuff since late 2013 shoulder injury. But the return of his Ctl following late June trade to LAA helped turn his season around. 9th inning experience suggests value upside. But health, age and 2014 volatility point to an end-gamer at best.

Yr Tm	W	L	Sv	IP	K	ERA	xERA	WHIP	oOPS	vL	vR	BF/G	Ctl	Dom	Cmd	FpK	SwK	G	L	F	H%	S%	hr/f	GS	APC	DOM%	DIS%	Sv%	LI	RAR	BPV	BPX	R$
10																																	
11 PIT *	6	2	4	65	69	2.63	3.55	1.35	601	766	508	4.9	4.0	9.5	2.4	59%	13%	45	22	33	32%	83%	7%	0	19			100	1.41	10.6	94	141	$6
12 PIT	1	6	2	59	90	2.91	2.88	1.14	635	485	767	3.8	3.4	13.8	4.1	57%	15%	31	24	45	33%	80%	12%	0	16			40	1.20	8.0	166	217	$5
13 PIT	0	2	33	50	74	2.70	2.57	1.06	595	707	496	3.7	2.3	13.3	5.7	62%	15%	33	25	42	35%	78%	9%	0	16			94	1.17	7.2	188	244	$16
14 2 TM	1	5	12	54	57	4.00	3.83	1.33	702	683	711	3.8	3.5	9.5	2.7	61%	11%	32	26	42	33%	71%	6%	0	15			71	1.10	-1.7	87	103	$2
1st Half	0	3	11	22	23	4.57	4.42	1.57	806	518	969	4.2	4.6	9.6	2.1	63%	12%	26	29	45	33%	77%	14%	0	16			73	1.36	-2.2	52	63	$1
2nd Half	1	2	1	32	34	3.62	3.44	1.18	624	783	485	3.6	2.8	9.5	3.4	59%	11%	36	24	40	33%	66%	0%	0	15			50	0.93	0.5	110	131	$3
15 Proj	**1**	**4**	**3**	**58**	**67**	**3.53**	**3.17**	**1.24**	**665**	**674**	**656**	**3.7**	**3.2**	**10.3**	**3.2**	**60%**	**13%**	**33**	**25**	**42**	**32%**	**73%**	**8%**	**0**						**1.5**	**110**	**131**	**$2**

Grimm,Justin

						Health	A	LIMA Plan	B+
Age:	26	Th:	R	Role	RP	PT/Exp	C	Rand Var	0
Ht:	6' 3"	Wt:	210	Type	Pwr	Consist	D	MM	4310

Sleeper alert... Velocity, Dom, SwK and GB% all spiked with move to the pen. Luckless H% and S% hid 2nd half gains. Allowed just 2 BBs over his final 24 IP. With zero track record, he has much to prove but note that 2nd half BPV. In an unsettled pen... UP: Sub-3.00 ERA, 15 saves.

Yr Tm	W	L	Sv	IP	K	ERA	xERA	WHIP	oOPS	vL	vR	BF/G	Ctl	Dom	Cmd	FpK	SwK	G	L	F	H%	S%	hr/f	GS	APC	DOM%	DIS%	Sv%	LI	RAR	BPV	BPX	R$
10																																	
11																																	
12 TEX *	12	7	0	149	96	4.06	4.07	1.36	935	1006	855	20.7	2.1	5.8	2.8	61%	8%	44	29	27	33%	69%	8%	2	50	50%	50%	0	0.33	-0.8	78	102	$2
13 2 TM *	10	12	0	146	113	5.78	5.37	1.61	846	860	830	17.9	3.4	6.9	2.1	58%	8%	43	21	36	35%	64%	13%	17	61	29%	35%	0	0.80	-34.4	49	64	-$14
14 CHC	5	2	0	69	70	3.78	3.49	1.25	632	528	684	4.0	3.5	9.1	2.6	61%	11%	49	16	35	31%	70%	6%	0	16			0	0.87	-0.4	96	115	$1
1st Half	2	2	0	36	34	3.50	4.00	1.36	683	693	677	4.0	4.8	8.5	1.8	62%	10%	51	13	36	28%	78%	11%	0	15			0	0.95	1.1	54	65	-$1
2nd Half	3	0	0	33	36	4.09	2.97	1.12	576	364	693	4.0	2.2	9.8	4.5	60%	11%	47	19	34	34%	59%	0%	0	16			0	0.78	-1.4	143	171	$3
15 Proj	**4**	**3**	**3**	**59**	**54**	**3.49**	**3.31**	**1.22**	**641**	**616**	**659**	**6.3**	**2.9**	**8.3**	**2.8**	**60%**	**9%**	**47**	**18**	**35**	**30%**	**72%**	**7%**	**0**						**1.8**	**94**	**112**	**$3**

Guerra,Javy

						Health	C	LIMA Plan	D+
Age:	29	Th:	R	Role	RP	PT/Exp	D	Rand Var	-4
Ht:	6' 1"	Wt:	190	Type	Pwr	Consist	F	MM	1100

2-4, 2.91 ERA in 46 IP at CHW. Can still dial it up, but not enough to mitigate his issues. Limited repertoire seen in SwK% and Dom; wavering Ctl and skimpy GB% and FpK don't help. Easy ex-closer-in-waiting call after 2011, now he's the ex-closer least likely to regain that role.

Yr Tm	W	L	Sv	IP	K	ERA	xERA	WHIP	oOPS	vL	vR	BF/G	Ctl	Dom	Cmd	FpK	SwK	G	L	F	H%	S%	hr/f	GS	APC	DOM%	DIS%	Sv%	LI	RAR	BPV	BPX	R$
10 aa	2	0	5	27	22	2.46	4.40	1.72				4.4	6.7	7.5	1.1						32%	86%								5.4	62	101	$0
11 LA *	3	2	24	64	50	2.00	2.20	1.08	608	490	698	4.1	3.2	7.1	2.2	47%	9%	43	20	37	25%	83%	4%	0	17			92	1.07	15.2	90	135	$16
12 LA	2	3	8	45	37	2.60	4.36	1.49	685	781	614	4.4	4.6	7.4	1.6	51%	9%	48	22	30	32%	82%	3%	0	17			62	1.12	7.9	35	46	$2
13 LA *	0	4	12	50	40	4.51	6.26	1.74	826	915	752	6.3	3.5	7.1	2.0	49%	13%	39	33	28	37%	77%	10%	0	26			92	0.44	-4.0	39	50	-$3
14 CHW *	3	5	4	66	46	2.86	3.92	1.42	696	630	777	5.0	4.0	6.4	1.6	53%	8%	40	21	38	30%	81%	6%	0	18			40	1.25	7.1	58	69	$1
1st Half	1	1	3	34	24	2.59	4.49	1.50	728	421	924	5.7	4.3	6.4	1.5	58%	8%	41	21	38	31%	86%	13%	0	22			60	0.80	4.9	46	55	$0
2nd Half	2	4	1	31	22	3.16	4.37	1.34	680	693	658	4.4	3.7	6.3	1.7	50%	9%	40	22	38	30%	76%	3%	0	17			20	1.43	2.2	31	37	$2
15 Proj	**2**	**3**	**0**	**44**	**33**	**3.60**	**4.12**	**1.47**	**766**	**721**	**807**	**5.0**	**3.9**	**6.8**	**1.7**	**51%**	**9%**	**44**	**21**	**35**	**32%**	**76%**	**6%**	**0**						**0.8**	**39**	**46**	**-$3**

JOCK THOMPSON

Guthrie,Jeremy

Age: 36	Th: R	Role SP	Health B	LIMA Plan B
Ht: 6' 1"	Wt: 205	Type Con	PT/Exp A	Rand Var 0
			Consist A	MM 2005

Innings-eater does his thing, which doesn't include offering much R$. Decent Ctl keeps performance barely above water, but as he showed in the 2nd half, a H% swing in the wrong direction can hurt. LHBs kill him; Dom and GB% are dug in. He's healthy, consistent, reliable, cheap and painfully mediocre.

Yr Tm	W	L	Sv	IP	K	ERA	xERA	WHIP	oOPS	vL	vR	BF/G	Ctl	Dom	Cmd	FpK	SwK	G	L	F	H%	S%	hr/f	GS	APC	DOM%	DIS%	Sv%	LI	RAR	BPV	BPX	R$
10 BAL	11	14	0	209	119	3.83	4.36	1.16	714	783	643	27.3	2.1	5.1	2.4	53%	6%	42	14	43	26%	71%	9%	32	104	56%	13%			6.5	54	87	$12
11 BAL	9	17	0	208	130	4.33	4.43	1.34	770	767	773	26.1	2.9	5.6	2.0	59%	7%	40	21	40	29%	71%	10%	32	98	38%	13%	0	0.73	-9.9	42	63	$1
12 2 TM	8	12	0	182	101	4.76	4.76	1.41	822	868	775	23.9	2.5	5.0	2.0	59%	7%	41	23	36	30%	71%	14%	29	89	34%	21%	0	0.74	-16.6	42	55	-$7
13 KC	15	12	0	212	111	4.04	4.55	1.39	784	905	623	27.4	2.5	4.7	1.9	62%	6%	43	22	35	30%	75%	12%	33	102	39%	12%			-4.5	38	50	$1
14 KC	13	11	0	203	124	4.13	4.23	1.30	728	828	601	27.0	2.2	5.5	2.5	63%	8%	44	20	37	30%	71%	9%	32	101	53%	19%			-9.7	62	74	$2
1st Half	5	6	0	112	68	3.77	4.26	1.23	721	794	623	27.6	2.2	5.4	2.5	64%	8%	41	19	40	28%	75%	11%	17	104	53%	12%			-0.3	58	70	$5
2nd Half	8	5	0	90	56	4.58	4.20	1.39	737	869	576	26.3	2.2	5.6	2.5	62%	8%	47	20	33	33%	67%	7%	15	98	53%	27%			-9.4	66	79	-$2
15 Proj	**12**	**13**	**0**	**203**	**118**	**4.26**	**4.05**	**1.35**	**759**	**854**	**642**	**25.7**	**2.3**	**5.2**	**2.2**	**61%**	**7%**	**43**	**21**	**36**	**30%**	**72%**	**10%**	**33**						**-13.0**	**52**	**62**	**$1**

Gutierrez,Juan

Age: 31	Th: R	Role RP	Health D	LIMA Plan D+
Ht: 6' 3"	Wt: 245	Type FB	PT/Exp D	Rand Var -1
			Consist F	MM 2100

Diminished velocity and more secondary pitches produce similar in-season volatility and mediocre results. 2nd half collapse again due to Ctl and H% spikes; SwK says he's now losing dominance. Well-traveled already, the name-change to "J.C." didn't help.

Yr Tm	W	L	Sv	IP	K	ERA	xERA	WHIP	oOPS	vL	vR	BF/G	Ctl	Dom	Cmd	FpK	SwK	G	L	F	H%	S%	hr/f	GS	APC	DOM%	DIS%	Sv%	LI	RAR	BPV	BPX	R$
10 ARI	0	6	15	57	47	5.08	4.52	1.38	806	927	715	4.3	3.7	7.5	2.0	56%	11%	35	14	51	27%	71%	15%	0	16			88	1.15	-7.0	49	79	$2
11 ARI	0	0	0	18	23	5.40	3.67	1.69	793	1009	608	4.5	4.4	11.3	2.6	51%	13%	46	23	32	40%	71%	17%	0	17			0	0.56	-3.3	108	162	-$5
12 a/a	0	1	3	16	9	10.61	8.87	1.99				5.1	3.1	4.9	1.6						38%	47%								-13.0	-28	-37	-$9
13 2 AL	1	5	0	55	45	4.23	4.12	1.37	697	779	609	4.5	3.3	7.3	2.3	61%	10%	43	21	37	31%	70%	8%	0	17			0	0.72	-2.5	65	85	-$4
14 SF	1	2	0	64	44	3.96	4.29	1.19	731	744	724	4.4	2.3	6.2	2.8	62%	9%	37	20	43	28%	70%	8%	0	16			0	0.60	-1.7	66	78	-$1
1st Half	1	2	0	36	28	3.22	3.64	0.91	586	594	583	4.2	1.5	6.9	4.7	65%	10%	38	18	44	24%	67%	7%	0	15			0	0.70	2.3	101	120	$3
2nd Half	0	0	0	27	16	4.94	5.21	1.57	897	879	909	4.7	3.3	5.3	1.6	57%	8%	35	22	43	32%	72%	10%	0	16			0	0.47	-4.0	19	23	-$7
15 Proj	**1**	**3**	**0**	**58**	**43**	**4.37**	**4.01**	**1.34**	**757**	**806**	**720**	**4.3**	**3.0**	**6.6**	**2.2**	**60%**	**9%**	**38**	**20**	**42**	**30%**	**70%**	**10%**	**0**						**-4.5**	**56**	**67**	**-$3**

Hahn,Jesse

Age: 25	Th: R	Role RP	Health C	LIMA Plan B
Ht: 6' 5"	Wt: 190	Type Pwr	PT/Exp F	Rand Var -1
			Consist F	MM 3201

7-4, 3.07 ERA in 73 IP at SD. 1st season with 100+ professional IP following slow recovery from 2010 TJS. Excited us with 88% DOM% in first 8 MLB starts before wilting in August. Health and IP limits cap his immediate upside, but BPIs say he has the goods for... UP: 160 IP, 12 Wins, 3.00 ERA.

Yr Tm	W	L	Sv	IP	K	ERA	xERA	WHIP	oOPS	vL	vR	BF/G	Ctl	Dom	Cmd	FpK	SwK	G	L	F	H%	S%	hr/f	GS	APC	DOM%	DIS%	Sv%	LI	RAR	BPV	BPX	R$
10																																	
11																																	
12																																	
13																																	
14 SD *	9	5	0	116	102	2.75	2.87	1.24	623	656	583	17.4	3.7	8.0	2.2	60%	11%	50	22	27	29%	78%	8%	12	84	58%	8%	0	0.89	14.1	91	109	$8
1st Half	6	2	0	66	64	2.23	3.03	1.24	537	489	591	16.8	3.3	8.7	2.7	57%	12%	47	26	27	31%	83%	12%	5	90	80%	20%			12.3	103	123	$13
2nd Half	3	3	0	50	38	3.44	2.65	1.23	674	771	578	18.3	4.2	6.9	1.7	61%	10%	52	21	27	26%	71%	6%	7	81	43%	0%	0	0.95	1.8	78	93	$2
15 Proj	**7**	**5**	**0**	**102**	**86**	**3.38**	**3.50**	**1.26**	**642**	**666**	**612**	**17.8**	**3.8**	**7.6**	**2.0**	**60%**	**11%**	**50**	**23**	**27**	**29%**	**73%**	**5%**	**18**						**4.5**	**62**	**74**	**$5**

Hale,David

Age: 27	Th: R	Role RP	Health A	LIMA Plan D+
Ht: 6' 2"	Wt: 210	Type xGB	PT/Exp D	Rand Var -3
			Consist B	MM 1000

Minor league SP survived early on solid GB% and fortunate H% in swingman role. Spotty control and 2nd half regression chipped away as league hitters began to catch on. Light Dom will require better Ctl for long-term survival. FpK isn't immediately optimistic.

Yr Tm	W	L	Sv	IP	K	ERA	xERA	WHIP	oOPS	vL	vR	BF/G	Ctl	Dom	Cmd	FpK	SwK	G	L	F	H%	S%	hr/f	GS	APC	DOM%	DIS%	Sv%	LI	RAR	BPV	BPX	R$
10																																	
11																																	
12 aa	8	4	0	146	104	4.96	4.46	1.52				23.4	4.5	6.4	1.4						31%	68%								-16.9	47	61	-$9
13 ATL *	7	9	0	126	77	3.73	5.10	1.58	572	683	480	23.1	2.8	5.5	2.0	61%	14%	63	23	13	35%	77%	0%	2	85	100%	0%			2.1	48	63	-$4
14 ATL	4	5	0	87	44	3.30	4.58	1.47	714	769	667	8.5	4.0	4.5	1.1	52%	9%	56	19	25	29%	78%	7%	6	31	67%	33%	0	0.83	4.8	7	8	-$2
1st Half	3	2	0	54	25	3.02	4.55	1.30	637	699	581	9.5	3.9	4.2	1.1	55%	9%	55	19	27	26%	76%	4%	5	36	80%	20%	0	0.84	4.8	4	5	$1
2nd Half	1	3	0	34	19	3.74	4.61	1.72	828	877	789	7.3	4.3	5.1	1.2	49%	10%	58	18	23	34%	80%	11%	1	27	0%	100%	0	0.82	0.0	12	15	-$7
15 Proj	**3**	**4**	**0**	**58**	**34**	**3.93**	**4.15**	**1.56**	**775**	**828**	**732**	**11.8**	**3.7**	**5.3**	**1.4**	**51%**	**10%**	**57**	**18**	**25**	**32%**	**76%**	**9%**	**4**						**-1.3**	**30**	**35**	**-$4**

Hamels,Cole

Age: 31	Th: L	Role SP	Health C	LIMA Plan C+
Ht: 6' 3"	Wt: 195	Type Pwr	PT/Exp A	Rand Var -3
			Consist A	MM 5305

Spring shoulder woes terrified his owners. But he beat return ETA and recorded vintage 200 IP performance despite missing most of April. Ctl was a little rusty early on, but nothing here suggests he's losing anything, other than wins. BPV column is a thing of beauty. Pay full value.

Yr Tm	W	L	Sv	IP	K	ERA	xERA	WHIP	oOPS	vL	vR	BF/G	Ctl	Dom	Cmd	FpK	SwK	G	L	F	H%	S%	hr/f	GS	APC	DOM%	DIS%	Sv%	LI	RAR	BPV	BPX	R$
10 PHI	12	11	0	209	211	3.06	3.29	1.18	692	645	703	25.9	2.6	9.1	3.5	59%	13%	45	17	38	30%	80%	12%	33	102	61%	12%			26.2	116	187	$21
11 PHI	14	9	0	216	194	2.79	3.02	0.99	596	662	577	26.6	1.8	8.1	4.4	62%	12%	52	15	33	27%	75%	10%	31	98	77%	10%	0	0.76	30.7	126	189	$29
12 PHI	17	6	0	215	216	3.05	3.32	1.12	661	629	673	28.0	2.2	9.0	4.2	63%	14%	43	22	35	30%	78%	12%	31	107	77%	0%			25.6	125	163	$27
13 PHI	8	14	0	221	202	3.59	3.45	1.16	699	712	695	27.4	2.0	8.2	4.0	63%	13%	42	21	36	30%	71%	9%	33	104	76%	3%			7.5	113	148	$13
14 PHI	9	9	0	205	198	2.46	3.20	1.15	641	636	641	27.6	2.6	8.7	3.4	61%	13%	46	22	31	30%	81%	8%	30	105	83%	3%			32.3	111	132	$20
1st Half	2	4	0	89	91	2.84	3.16	1.18	665	628	674	27.8	2.9	9.2	3.1	60%	12%	48	21	31	30%	79%	10%	13	106	85%	8%			9.8	113	135	$10
2nd Half	7	5	0	116	107	2.17	3.23	1.12	622	641	616	27.5	2.3	8.3	3.6	63%	13%	45	24	31	30%	83%	7%	17	103	82%	0%			22.4	110	131	$27
15 Proj	**13**	**9**	**0**	**208**	**199**	**2.87**	**3.04**	**1.14**	**658**	**657**	**658**	**26.8**	**2.3**	**8.6**	**3.7**	**62%**	**13%**	**45**	**21**	**33**	**30%**	**78%**	**9%**	**31**						**22.4**	**115**	**137**	**$22**

Hammel,Jason

Age: 32	Th: R	Role SP	Health D	LIMA Plan C+
Ht: 6' 6"	Wt: 225	Type	PT/Exp A	Rand Var 0
			Consist C	MM 3203

BPIs bounce around year-to-year and even half-to-half, but overall trend is one of improvement. Posted best Ctl of his career in 1st half, but it was 2nd half gopheritis that hurt him. Volatility and R$ history point to risk and FpK doesn't support Ctl gains. It's the old "believe in an even, odd year beware."

Yr Tm	W	L	Sv	IP	K	ERA	xERA	WHIP	oOPS	vL	vR	BF/G	Ctl	Dom	Cmd	FpK	SwK	G	L	F	H%	S%	hr/f	GS	APC	DOM%	DIS%	Sv%	LI	RAR	BPV	BPX	R$
10 COL	10	9	0	178	141	4.81	3.80	1.40	755	761	750	25.7	2.4	7.1	3.0	60%	8%	47	20	33	34%	67%	10%	30	95	47%	20%			-16.1	89	144	$0
11 COL	7	13	1	170	94	4.76	4.66	1.43	778	808	752	23.1	3.6	5.0	1.4	59%	7%	44	21	35	29%	69%	11%	27	85	41%	26%	100	0.78	-17.1	14	22	-$5
12 BAL	8	6	0	118	113	3.43	3.48	1.24	637	586	692	24.7	3.2	8.6	2.7	57%	11%	53	19	28	30%	74%	10%	20	97	50%	15%			8.5	100	130	$7
13 BAL	7	8	1	139	96	4.97	4.52	1.46	813	881	716	23.5	3.1	6.2	2.0	56%	8%	40	22	38	31%	70%	13%	23	89	22%	17%	100	0.77	-19.0	46	60	-$7
14 2 TM	10	11	0	176	158	3.47	3.53	1.12	680	691	670	23.8	2.2	8.1	3.6	57%	10%	40	22	38	28%	74%	12%	29	93	72%	17%	0	0.75	5.9	103	122	$12
1st Half	7	5	0	103	97	2.98	3.20	1.01	618	693	569	25.3	1.8	8.5	4.6	58%	11%	41	23	37	28%	74%	9%	16	100	94%	0%			9.6	122	145	$21
2nd Half	3	6	0	74	61	4.15	4.00	1.28	761	688	839	22.1	2.8	7.5	2.7	56%	8%	39	21	40	28%	75%	16%	13	85	46%	38%	0	0.74	-3.8	75	89	-$1
15 Proj	**9**	**11**	**0**	**174**	**143**	**4.03**	**3.59**	**1.28**	**729**	**740**	**718**	**23.0**	**2.8**	**7.4**	**2.7**	**57%**	**9%**	**42**	**21**	**37**	**29%**	**73%**	**13%**	**31**						**-6.1**	**78**	**93**	**$5**

Hand,Brad

Age: 25	Th: L	Role RP	Health C	LIMA Plan D+
Ht: 6' 3"	Wt: 220	Type Pwr FB	PT/Exp D	Rand Var 0
			Consist A	MM 1101

3-8, 4.38 ERA in 111 IP at MIA. Held his own in the rotation despite 2nd half Dom collapse, thanks to BB and FB reductions. But a long history of poor Ctl and GB% volatility say he has much to prove. Any future success will be limited if the Ks don't return, and SwK is doubtful of that.

Yr Tm	W	L	Sv	IP	K	ERA	xERA	WHIP	oOPS	vL	vR	BF/G	Ctl	Dom	Cmd	FpK	SwK	G	L	F	H%	S%	hr/f	GS	APC	DOM%	DIS%	Sv%	LI	RAR	BPV	BPX	R$
10																																	
11 FLA *	12	12	0	169	100	3.75	3.92	1.37	789	812	783	22.8	4.4	5.3	1.2	54%	7%	29	17	54	25%	76%	10%	12	90	8%	33%			4.0	34	51	$5
12 MIA *	11	8	0	152	133	4.96	4.62	1.55	1169	1850	962	23.7	5.1	7.9	1.6	43%	3%	50	0	50	31%	69%	14%	1	96	0%	100%			-17.6	54	71	-$8
13 MIA *	4	6	0	102	83	4.03	3.96	1.46	553	530	564	19.9	4.9	7.3	1.5	52%	9%	42	20	37	29%	74%	9%	2	43	0%	0%	0	0.73	-2.1	58	76	-$3
14 MIA *	5	8	1	133	85	4.21	4.00	1.34	732	594	789	15.4	3.2	5.8	1.8	59%	7%	50	18	32	29%	70%	9%	16	56	31%	31%	100	0.58	-7.6	50	60	-$2
1st Half	2	1	1	46	38	4.92	4.92	1.54	930	739	1020	10.0	4.8	7.4	1.5	54%	7%	39	16	45	30%	71%	12%	2	29	0%	100%	100	0.40	-6.7	42	51	-$9
2nd Half	3	7	0	87	47	3.83	4.00	1.24	674	547	724	22.6	2.4	4.9	2.0	60%	7%	53	18	29	28%	70%	8%	14	83	36%	21%	0	0.76	-0.9	55	65	$2
15 Proj	**5**	**7**	**0**	**116**	**84**	**4.26**	**4.37**	**1.41**	**742**	**659**	**773**	**17.5**	**4.1**	**6.5**	**1.6**	**56%**	**7%**	**40**	**17**	**43**	**29%**	**71%**	**7%**	**21**						**-7.4**	**24**	**28**	**-$2**

JOCK THOMPSON

Happ,J.A.

Age: 32	Th: L	Role	SP	Health	F	LIMA Plan	B+
Ht: 6' 5"	Wt: 205	Type	Pwr FB	PT/Exp	B	Rand Var	0
				Consist	B	MM	2203

PRO: Rising velocity; 2nd half Cmd spike; Ctl growth with partial support from 3-yr FpK; 100+ BPV and 64% DOM% in 11 Aug/Sept starts. CON: Too many FBs and HRs, and health are skeptical of a late-career step-up. But he's at least worth watching this spring.

Yr Tm	W	L	Sv	IP	K	ERA	xERA	WHIP	oOPS	vL	vR	BF/G	Ctl	Dom	Cmd	FpK	SwK	G	L	F	H%	S%	hr/f	GS	APC	DOM%	DIS%	Sv%	LI	RAR	BPV	BPX	R$
10 2 NL *	7	5	0	122	94	4.68	5.12	1.61	688	551	724	22.5	5.0	6.9	1.4	55%	9%	39	18	43	31%	74%	7%	16	99	56%	19%			-9.0	37	60	-$5
11 HOU *	7	15	0	174	146	5.00	4.60	1.51	806	751	819	24.4	4.8	7.5	1.6	56%	8%	33	23	44	30%	69%	10%	28	106	29%	21%			-22.7	49	74	-$8
12 2 TM	10	11	0	145	144	4.79	3.98	1.40	787	730	807	22.4	3.5	9.0	2.6	64%	10%	44	17	39	33%	68%	12%	24	91	54%	17%	0	0.73	-13.8	89	116	-$2
13 TOR	5	7	0	93	77	4.56	4.83	1.47	734	802	708	23.1	4.4	7.5	1.7	60%	8%	36	18	46	31%	71%	8%	18	96	39%	44%			-8.0	31	40	-$5
14 TOR	11	11	0	158	133	4.22	4.03	1.34	770	874	743	22.4	2.9	7.6	2.6	62%	8%	41	20	40	31%	72%	12%	26	90	50%	27%	0	0.82	-9.2	77	92	$1
1st Half	7	4	0	65	57	4.29	4.32	1.54	799	827	791	20.5	4.2	7.9	1.9	64%	7%	42	21	38	33%	76%	12%	11	83	36%	27%	0	0.76	-4.4	50	59	-$3
2nd Half	4	7	0	93	76	4.16	3.84	1.19	748	911	710	24.1	2.0	7.4	3.6	61%	8%	40	19	41	29%	69%	11%	15	97	60%	27%	0	0.87	-4.8	95	114	$4
15 Proj	**9**	**10**	**0**	**145**	**124**	**4.14**	**3.81**	**1.37**	**761**	**809**	**747**	**21.9**	**3.2**	**7.7**	**2.4**	**61%**	**8%**	**40**	**19**	**41**	**31%**	**73%**	**10%**	**28**						**-7.1**	**69**	**82**	**$2**

Harang,Aaron

Age: 37	Th: R	Role	SP	Health	C	LIMA Plan	B
Ht: 6' 7"	Wt: 260	Type	FB	PT/Exp	A	Rand Var	-1
				Consist	A	MM	2103

Entered June with a 3.29 ERA, 9.8 Dom, 11% SwK and a 3.7 Cmd before mediocrity kicked back in. If you didn't cash your gains then, you're not paying attention, and you got off cheaply. At his age, the increasing risk trumps any low-ceiling upside.

Yr Tm	W	L	Sv	IP	K	ERA	xERA	WHIP	oOPS	vL	vR	BF/G	Ctl	Dom	Cmd	FpK	SwK	G	L	F	H%	S%	hr/f	GS	APC	DOM%	DIS%	Sv%	LI	RAR	BPV	BPX	R$
10 CIN	6	7	0	112	82	5.32	4.60	1.59	841	800	873	22.9	3.1	6.6	2.2	58%	8%	37	22	41	35%	69%	10%	20	94	40%	45%	0	0.70	-17.1	51	83	-$7
11 SD	14	7	0	171	124	3.64	4.22	1.37	758	787	732	25.7	3.1	6.5	2.1	62%	9%	41	18	41	30%	77%	9%	28	98	46%	18%			6.4	54	81	$7
12 LA	10	10	0	180	131	3.61	4.96	1.40	711	761	662	25.4	4.3	6.6	1.5	56%	8%	39	20	41	29%	76%	6%	31	100	32%	23%			9.0	20	26	$4
13 2 TM	5	12	0	143	113	5.40	4.37	1.35	795	800	789	24.1	2.5	7.1	2.8	58%	8%	36	20	44	30%	64%	13%	26	94	46%	27%			-27.1	74	96	-$8
14 ATL	12	12	0	204	161	3.57	4.18	1.40	723	747	702	26.5	3.1	7.1	2.3	59%	9%	39	23	38	33%	76%	6%	33	103	52%	9%			4.4	60	72	$3
1st Half	7	6	0	102	92	3.69	4.03	1.41	729	804	668	25.8	3.4	8.1	2.4	58%	10%	38	22	40	33%	74%	6%	17	103	65%	6%			0.6	69	82	$4
2nd Half	5	6	0	102	69	3.44	4.34	1.39	717	696	738	27.3	2.8	6.1	2.2	60%	7%	41	23	36	32%	77%	7%	16	103	38%	13%			3.8	52	62	$2
15 Proj	**8**	**9**	**0**	**145**	**111**	**4.11**	**4.00**	**1.39**	**747**	**763**	**732**	**24.8**	**3.1**	**6.9**	**2.2**	**59%**	**8%**	**38**	**21**	**40**	**31%**	**73%**	**9%**	**25**						**-6.6**	**56**	**67**	**$0**

Hardy,Blaine

Age: 28	Th: L	Role	RP	Health	A	LIMA Plan	D+
Ht: 6' 2"	Wt: 195	Type	Pwr GB	PT/Exp	D	Rand Var	-2
				Consist	C	MM	2100

2-1, 2.54 ERA in 39 IP at DET. Used GB% to harness LHBs in credible MLB debut. Dominance faded with exposure as Ctl became an issue; 2nd half S% and HR avoidance kept him afloat. Soft-tosser has little margin for error, or any immediate fantasy value.

Yr Tm	W	L	Sv	IP	K	ERA	xERA	WHIP	oOPS	vL	vR	BF/G	Ctl	Dom	Cmd	FpK	SwK	G	L	F	H%	S%	hr/f	GS	APC	DOM%	DIS%	Sv%	LI	RAR	BPV	BPX	R$
10 a/a	4	4	7	93	52	3.01	3.35	1.20				9.3	2.7	5.0	1.9						27%	78%								12.3	53	85	$8
11 a/a	4	4	8	69	51	4.35	4.95	1.57				7.2	4.5	6.7	1.5						31%	75%								-3.4	40	60	-$1
12 a/a	4	3	4	75	46	3.99	6.01	1.72				8.6	3.7	5.5	1.5						35%	80%								0.3	24	31	-$6
13 a/a	8	3	1	92	60	2.21	3.31	1.21				12.3	3.3	5.9	1.8						25%	87%								18.7	54	71	$9
14 DET *	5	3	0	86	71	3.09	3.22	1.31	611	553	657	6.1	3.6	7.4	2.1	54%	8%	52	19	28	30%	76%	3%	0	17			0	1.04	6.9	83	99	$2
1st Half	4	3	0	56	49	3.45	3.02	1.20	548	521	566	8.1	2.9	7.8	2.7	50%	9%	64	18	18	29%	72%	25%	0	17			0	1.00	2.0	94	112	$5
2nd Half	1	0	0	30	22	2.43	4.50	1.52	628	561	680	4.4	4.9	6.7	1.4	56%	8%	49	20	31	32%	82%	0%	0	17			0	1.06	4.8	17	20	-$2
15 Proj	**2**	**1**	**0**	**36**	**26**	**3.92**	**3.99**	**1.39**	**605**	**553**	**645**	**6.8**	**3.8**	**6.5**	**1.7**	**56%**	**8%**	**49**	**20**	**31**	**30%**	**72%**	**6%**	**0**						**-0.8**	**42**	**50**	**-$2**

Haren,Dan

Age: 34	Th: R	Role	SP	Health	C	LIMA Plan	B
Ht: 6' 5"	Wt: 215	Type	FB	PT/Exp	A	Rand Var	0
				Consist	A	MM	3203

PRO: Exquisite Ctl and Dom are intact, BPV remains in a stable and attractive range. CON: Couldn't sustain 1st half GB% spike; SwK and FpK are wavering. Combo of Cmd and hr/f demonstrate that he pays dearly for his mistakes. Declining velocity, advancing age say things only get tougher from here.

Yr Tm	W	L	Sv	IP	K	ERA	xERA	WHIP	oOPS	vL	vR	BF/G	Ctl	Dom	Cmd	FpK	SwK	G	L	F	H%	S%	hr/f	GS	APC	DOM%	DIS%	Sv%	LI	RAR	BPV	BPX	R$
10 2 TM	12	12	0	235	216	3.91	3.66	1.27	736	761	715	28.4	2.1	8.3	4.0	64%	11%	40	19	41	32%	74%	11%	35	107	60%	6%			5.0	111	180	$13
11 LAA	16	10	0	238	192	3.17	3.39	1.02	630	617	648	27.2	1.2	7.3	5.8	64%	10%	43	20	38	28%	71%	8%	34	108	71%	9%	0	0.82	22.6	118	177	$27
12 LAA	12	13	0	177	142	4.33	4.08	1.29	775	731	825	24.9	1.9	7.2	3.7	64%	9%	40	21	40	31%	72%	13%	30	95	53%	17%			-6.9	96	125	$4
13 WAS	10	14	1	170	151	4.67	3.75	1.24	760	722	792	23.1	1.6	8.0	4.9	65%	10%	36	22	42	32%	67%	13%	30	90	40%	20%	100	0.83	-16.8	114	148	$2
14 LA	13	11	0	186	145	4.02	3.81	1.18	718	665	771	24.3	1.7	7.0	4.0	62%	8%	41	20	39	29%	71%	12%	32	97	53%	16%			-6.3	98	117	$7
1st Half	8	4	0	103	69	3.57	3.82	1.21	740	671	802	25.4	1.7	6.0	3.6	64%	7%	47	19	33	29%	77%	14%	17	100	47%	6%			2.2	89	106	$11
2nd Half	5	7	0	83	76	4.57	3.80	1.14	690	658	728	23.0	1.9	8.3	4.5	58%	8%	33	20	47	30%	63%	10%	15	93	60%	27%			-8.5	110	132	$4
15 Proj	**11**	**12**	**0**	**174**	**143**	**4.20**	**3.48**	**1.21**	**741**	**701**	**781**	**23.3**	**1.9**	**7.4**	**4.0**	**63%**	**9%**	**38**	**21**	**41**	**30%**	**71%**	**13%**	**30**						**-9.9**	**99**	**117**	**$7**

Harrison,Matt

Age: 29	Th: L	Role	SP	Health	F	LIMA Plan	D+
Ht: 6' 4"	Wt: 240	Type		PT/Exp	C	Rand Var	-3
				Consist	A	MM	1000

1-1, 4.15 ERA in 17 IP at TEX. Returned throwing GBs while struggling with Ctl before another back surgery ended his season again. Durability—not rust—is the immediate question. With just 6 MLB starts over the past two years, his MLB career is in jeopardy.

Yr Tm	W	L	Sv	IP	K	ERA	xERA	WHIP	oOPS	vL	vR	BF/G	Ctl	Dom	Cmd	FpK	SwK	G	L	F	H%	S%	hr/f	GS	APC	DOM%	DIS%	Sv%	LI	RAR	BPV	BPX	R$
10 TEX	3	2	2	78	46	4.71	4.97	1.52	757	723	770	9.6	4.5	5.3	1.2	54%	8%	47	21	33	29%	72%	12%	6	38	33%	17%	67	0.89	-6.1	-1	-1	-$3
11 TEX	14	9	0	186	126	3.39	3.92	1.28	685	729	667	24.9	2.8	6.1	2.2	56%	8%	47	20	32	30%	75%	7%	30	97	43%	13%	0	0.75	12.6	60	91	$11
12 TEX	18	11	0	213	133	3.29	4.15	1.26	714	571	764	27.4	2.5	5.6	2.3	62%	8%	49	20	31	29%	77%	11%	32	101	50%	13%			19.1	61	79	$16
13 TEX	0	2	0	11	12	8.44	4.34	1.97	970	432	1149	25.5	5.9	10.1	1.7	57%	14%	45	23	32	40%	58%	20%	2	98	0%	50%			-6.0	46	60	-$7
14 TEX *	2	1	0	33	17	3.34	4.36	1.59	783	593	824	21.0	4.5	4.7	1.0	55%	7%	48	25	27	31%	78%	6%	4	86	25%	50%			1.7	41	49	-$3
1st Half	2	1	0	33	17	3.34	4.36	1.59	783	593	824	21.0	4.5	4.7	1.0	55%	7%	48	25	27	31%	78%	6%	4	86	25%	50%			1.7	41	49	-$3
2nd Half																																	
15 Proj	**2**	**3**	**0**	**47**	**28**	**3.72**	**4.16**	**1.40**	**725**	**658**	**746**	**21.0**	**3.5**	**5.4**	**1.5**	**56%**	**8%**	**48**	**22**	**30**	**29%**	**76%**	**10%**	**10**						**0.1**	**29**	**34**	**-$2**

Harvey,Matt

Age: 26	Th: R	Role	SP	Health	F	LIMA Plan	B
Ht: 6' 4"	Wt: 215	Type	Pwr	PT/Exp	C	Rand Var	0
				Consist	B	MM	4403

Spent 2014 recovering from Tommy John surgery, which he'll be almost 18 months past on Opening Day. Hitting 95 mph in September bullpen sessions says he's ahead of schedule. Even with an innings limit, that elite rookie season is worth chasing. He might not be vintage until 2016, but he's still keeper league gold.

Yr Tm	W	L	Sv	IP	K	ERA	xERA	WHIP	oOPS	vL	vR	BF/G	Ctl	Dom	Cmd	FpK	SwK	G	L	F	H%	S%	hr/f	GS	APC	DOM%	DIS%	Sv%	LI	RAR	BPV	BPX	R$
10																																	
11 aa	5	3	0	60	54	4.33	3.57	1.32				20.6	2.9	8.1	2.7						33%	66%								-2.9	94	141	-$1
12 NYM *	10	10	0	169	168	3.50	3.41	1.29	631	662	592	23.2	3.8	8.9	2.4	60%	13%	38	24	37	30%	75%	10%	10	98	70%	0%			10.8	89	115	$10
13 NYM	9	5	0	178	191	2.27	2.73	0.93	530	456	603	26.5	1.6	9.6	6.2	64%	13%	48	20	33	29%	76%	5%	26	104	85%	0%			35.1	157	205	$28
14																																	
1st Half																																	
2nd Half																																	
15 Proj	**11**	**7**	**0**	**151**	**149**	**3.30**	**3.11**	**1.18**	**647**	**615**	**681**	**22.7**	**2.7**	**8.9**	**3.3**	**63%**	**13%**	**44**	**22**	**34**	**31%**	**72%**	**6%**	**27**						**8.2**	**109**	**129**	**$13**

Hatcher,Chris

Age: 30	Th: R	Role	RP	Health	A	LIMA Plan	C
Ht: 6' 1"	Wt: 205	Type	Pwr	PT/Exp	D	Rand Var	0
				Consist	F	MM	3300

0-3, 3.38 ERA in 56 IP at MIA. Apart from rising velocity, little in his history hinted at this. But impressive across-the-board gains survived all season. Finished with four straight months of 100+ BPV. New skills need early confirmation, but he's worth watching.

Yr Tm	W	L	Sv	IP	K	ERA	xERA	WHIP	oOPS	vL	vR	BF/G	Ctl	Dom	Cmd	FpK	SwK	G	L	F	H%	S%	hr/f	GS	APC	DOM%	DIS%	Sv%	LI	RAR	BPV	BPX	R$
10																																	
11 FLA *	2	2	6	58	53	3.02	3.34	1.30	960	618	1237	4.5	3.8	8.3	2.2	45%	5%	53	11	36	30%	78%	15%	0	18			67	0.36	6.6	86	129	$4
12 MIA *	1	0	11	62	47	1.78	3.59	1.32	889	1134	669	5.3	3.5	6.9	2.0	53%	5%	37	22	41	30%	90%	15%	0	27			92	0.16	17.0	70	92	$7
13 MIA *	4	4	33	76	56	5.88	6.43	1.84	961	1130	876	5.3	4.3	6.6	1.5	66%	7%	35	29	35	37%	69%	9%	0	26			92	0.62	-18.9	28	36	$0
14 MIA *	1	5	5	78	78	3.07	3.28	1.18	666	641	687	4.7	2.1	9.0	4.3	66%	11%	47	20	33	32%	76%	8%	0	18			50	0.99	6.5	128	153	$4
1st Half	1	3	5	42	41	2.96	3.62	1.16	746	737	753	5.4	1.8	8.9	4.9	58%	11%	44	19	37	32%	80%	15%	0	19			63	1.09	4.0	130	156	$6
2nd Half	0	2	0	37	37	3.19	3.21	1.20	623	581	655	4.3	2.5	9.1	3.7	69%	10%	49	20	31	33%	72%	3%	0	17			0	0.94	2.5	124	148	$2
15 Proj	**2**	**2**	**0**	**58**	**52**	**3.60**	**3.50**	**1.38**	**722**	**705**	**736**	**4.8**	**3.1**	**8.0**	**2.6**	**65%**	**11%**	**47**	**20**	**33**	**33%**	**75%**	**8%**	**0**						**1.0**	**86**	**103**	**-$1**

JOCK THOMPSON

Hawkins,LaTroy

Age: 42	Th: R	Role RP	Health D	LIMA Plan B	
Ht: 6' 5"	Wt: 220	Type Con	PT/Exp C	Rand Var -2	
			Consist B	MM 3020	

Solid Ctl and fortunate hr/f helped him hold down closer role despite early Dom struggles, then the strikeouts came back in 2nd half. But year-long volatility and advanced age raise questions about the immediate future. Sub-50 BPV for 4 months; 100+ only in Aug. 2nd half GB% is a red flag. Thin ice here.

Yr Tm	W	L	Sv	IP	K	ERA	xERA	WHIP	oOPS	vL	vR	BF/G	Ctl	Dom	Cmd	FpK	SwK	G	L	F	H%	S%	hr/f	GS	APC	DOM%	DIS%	Sv%	LI	RAR	BPV	BPX	R$
10 MIL	0	3	0	16	18	8.44	3.45	1.69	890	783	957	4.1	3.4	10.1	3.0	61%	10%	47	21	32	41%	48%	13%	0	18			0	0.84	-8.6	116	188	-$5
11 MIL	3	1	0	48	28	2.42	3.55	1.24	627	584	661	3.9	1.9	5.2	2.8	62%	6%	62	16	22	31%	80%	3%	0	14			0	0.81	9.1	84	126	$2
12 LAA	2	3	1	42	23	3.64	4.27	1.38	735	576	906	3.7	2.8	4.9	1.8	49%	6%	57	17	26	30%	77%	14%	0	15			25	0.80	1.9	49	63	-$3
13 NYM	3	2	13	71	55	2.93	3.31	1.15	656	670	646	4.0	1.3	7.0	5.5	67%	9%	48	24	28	31%	77%	10%	0	14			81	1.11	8.2	118	153	$8
14 COL	4	3	23	54	32	3.31	4.07	1.20	653	712	597	4.0	2.2	5.3	2.5	67%	7%	47	22	31	29%	73%	5%	0	15			88	1.03	2.9	62	74	$10
1st Half	2	1	14	28	11	2.57	4.50	1.14	628	630	626	3.9	2.3	3.5	1.6	66%	6%	49	19	32	25%	80%	6%	0	14			93	1.02	4.0	30	36	$11
2nd Half	2	2	9	26	21	4.10	3.63	1.25	679	804	568	4.1	2.1	7.2	3.5	67%	7%	44	26	30	33%	66%	4%	0	15			82	1.04	-1.2	96	114	$8
15 Proj	**3**	**2**	**18**	**49**	**32**	**3.82**	**3.61**	**1.24**	**669**	**683**	**657**	**3.8**	**2.2**	**5.9**	**2.7**	**64%**	**7%**	**48**	**22**	**30**	**30%**	**70%**	**7%**	**0**						**-0.5**	**73**	**87**	**$6**

Heaney,Andrew

Age: 24	Th: L	Role SP	Health A	LIMA Plan B+	
Ht: 6' 2"	Wt: 185	Type GB	PT/Exp D	Rand Var +3	
			Consist A	MM 3101	

0-3, 5.83 ERA in 29 IP at MIA. Promising prospect was rushed to MIA after 100 innings at Double/Triple-A. GB% declined with his ascent, and he was victimized by gopheritis in initial MLB exposure. Command pitcher may need some time, but his BPIs remain optimistic.

Yr Tm	W	L	Sv	IP	K	ERA	xERA	WHIP	oOPS	vL	vR	BF/G	Ctl	Dom	Cmd	FpK	SwK	G	L	F	H%	S%	hr/f	GS	APC	DOM%	DIS%	Sv%	LI	RAR	BPV	BPX	R$
10																																	
11																																	
12																																	
13 aa	4	1	0	34	20	3.65	3.83	1.34				23.3	2.5	5.3	2.1						31%	73%								0.9	61	79	-$2
14 MIA *	9	9	0	167	140	3.89	3.60	1.22	847	611	944	21.7	2.3	7.6	3.3	60%	10%	45	19	35	31%	70%	18%	5	68	60%	40%	0	0.66	-3.1	95	113	$5
1st Half	7	5	0	94	78	3.10	3.15	1.15	743	655	790	23.3	1.7	7.5	4.5	61%	11%	52	14	34	31%	74%	18%	3	88	100%	0%			7.4	127	152	$14
2nd Half	2	4	0	73	62	4.91	4.17	1.31	974	523	1097	20.1	3.0	7.6	2.5	59%	8%	37	26	37	30%	65%	19%	2	54	0%	100%	0	0.58	-10.5	67	80	-$6
15 Proj	**8**	**5**	**0**	**109**	**81**	**3.99**	**3.67**	**1.28**	**659**	**667**	**655**	**22.0**	**2.4**	**6.7**	**2.8**	**61%**	**11%**	**47**	**17**	**36**	**31%**	**70%**	**7%**	**20**						**-3.4**	**81**	**96**	**$3**

Hellickson,Jeremy

Age: 28	Th: R	Role SP	Health F	LIMA Plan B+	
Ht: 6' 1"	Wt: 190	Type FB	PT/Exp B	Rand Var +2	
			Consist C	MM 2203	

1-5, 4.52 ERA in 64 IP at TAM. Missed entire 1st half after arthroscopic elbow surgery, struggled upon his return. Cmd was fine; ridiculously poor H% says a rebound is likely. But declining velocity and inability to generate GBs sets a low ceiling. DIS% history is troublesome.

Yr Tm	W	L	Sv	IP	K	ERA	xERA	WHIP	oOPS	vL	vR	BF/G	Ctl	Dom	Cmd	FpK	SwK	G	L	F	H%	S%	hr/f	GS	APC	DOM%	DIS%	Sv%	LI	RAR	BPV	BPX	R$
10 TAM *	16	3	0	154	139	2.90	3.30	1.22	666	906	391	20.1	2.5	8.1	3.3	64%	13%	37	13	50	32%	78%	10%	4	59	100%	0%	0	0.86	22.4	105	170	$16
11 TAM	13	10	0	189	117	2.95	4.58	1.15	660	726	585	26.7	3.4	5.6	1.6	60%	10%	35	20	45	23%	79%	8%	29	102	45%	7%			23.1	21	31	$17
12 TAM	10	11	0	177	124	3.10	4.39	1.25	710	703	717	23.9	3.0	6.3	2.1	60%	9%	42	21	37	27%	82%	12%	31	97	42%	23%			19.9	52	68	$12
13 TAM	12	10	0	174	135	5.17	4.16	1.35	775	785	763	23.0	2.6	7.0	2.7	60%	10%	40	20	40	31%	64%	11%	31	90	35%	26%	0	1.04	-28.0	74	96	-$4
14 TAM *	2	9	0	88	75	5.29	6.06	1.70	759	585	966	21.0	2.7	7.7	2.9	63%	10%	36	23	41	40%	70%	10%	13	91	46%	54%			-16.9	67	80	-$12
1st Half	0	4	0	13	10	11.67	14.03	3.22				19.6	2.2	6.6	2.9						58%	61%	0%	0						-12.7	30	36	-$28
2nd Half	2	5	0	75	66	4.27	4.75	1.44	759	585	966	21.4	2.8	7.9	2.9	63%	10%	36	23	41	35%	72%	10%	13	91	46%	54%			-4.9	76	91	-$9
15 Proj	**10**	**10**	**0**	**176**	**136**	**4.09**	**3.86**	**1.31**	**723**	**702**	**749**	**22.5**	**2.9**	**7.0**	**2.5**	**61%**	**10%**	**38**	**20**	**41**	**30%**	**72%**	**9%**	**32**						**-7.6**	**65**	**77**	**$4**

Henderson,Jim

Age: 32	Th: R	Role RP	Health F	LIMA Plan D+	
Ht: 6' 5"	Wt: 220	Type Pwr FB	PT/Exp D	Rand Var +5	
			Consist A	MM 2410	

Shaky March cost him closer job before shoulder woes and eventual surgery ended his season. Dom and SwK speak to his electric stuff. FpK speaks to his wavering Ctl. hr/f speaks to his FB-and-LD issues. But the only conversation that matters now is with his doctors. Consult before shouting his name at the draft.

Yr Tm	W	L	Sv	IP	K	ERA	xERA	WHIP	oOPS	vL	vR	BF/G	Ctl	Dom	Cmd	FpK	SwK	G	L	F	H%	S%	hr/f	GS	APC	DOM%	DIS%	Sv%	LI	RAR	BPV	BPX	R$
10 aa	4	5	7	61	48	6.73	5.21	1.62				6.0	5.7	7.1	1.2						29%	60%								-20.0	30	49	-$5
11 a/a	7	2	5	61	53	5.20	4.59	1.47				6.2	5.0	7.8	1.5						28%	68%								-9.5	44	66	-$1
12 MIL *	5	6	18	79	87	2.88	3.80	1.46	609	734	497	4.7	4.6	10.0	2.2	66%	16%	42	23	35	35%	81%	4%	0	15			78	1.13	11.1	96	126	$9
13 MIL	5	5	28	60	75	2.70	3.37	1.13	625	786	475	4.0	3.6	11.3	3.1	47%	14%	28	28	44	28%	83%	13%	0	17			88	1.23	8.6	111	145	$16
14 MIL	2	1	0	11	17	7.15	2.91	1.59	945	1315	765	3.6	3.2	13.5	4.3	58%	16%	33	26	41	42%	60%	27%	0	13			0	1.11	-4.8	168	200	-$4
1st Half	2	1	0	11	17	7.15	2.91	1.59	945	1315	765	3.6	3.2	13.5	4.3	58%	16%	33	26	41	42%	60%	27%	0	13			0	1.11	-4.8	169	201	-$4
2nd Half																																	
15 Proj	**4**	**3**	**3**	**44**	**44**	**3.79**	**3.84**	**1.39**	**712**	**884**	**555**	**5.0**	**4.6**	**9.2**	**2.0**	**55%**	**15%**	**33**	**26**	**41**	**30%**	**77%**	**11%**	**0**						**-0.3**	**52**	**62**	**$0**

Hendricks,Kyle

Age: 25	Th: R	Role SP	Health A	LIMA Plan B	
Ht: 6' 3"	Wt: 190	Type Con GB	PT/Exp D	Rand Var -1	
			Consist A	MM 3103	

7-2, 2.46 in 80 IP at CHC. Featured fine Ctl, decent GB% and just enough Dom in small-sample MLB debut. Command and HR avoidance history is encouraging, but BPIs aren't worthy of that sub-3 ERA. Back-of-the-rotation upside, but let someone else bid for 2014 performance.

Yr Tm	W	L	Sv	IP	K	ERA	xERA	WHIP	oOPS	vL	vR	BF/G	Ctl	Dom	Cmd	FpK	SwK	G	L	F	H%	S%	hr/f	GS	APC	DOM%	DIS%	Sv%	LI	RAR	BPV	BPX	R$
10																																	
11																																	
12																																	
13 a/a	13	4	0	166	106	2.46	3.17	1.22				24.9	1.9	5.7	2.9						31%	80%								28.9	90	117	$16
14 CHC *	17	7	0	183	126	3.52	3.49	1.24	610	584	633	24.8	1.9	6.2	3.2	64%	8%	48	19	33	31%	71%	5%	13	89	62%	15%			4.9	92	109	$10
1st Half	9	5	0	95	70	4.26	3.85	1.34				26.3	2.3	6.6	2.9						33%	67%	0%	0						-6.0	87	103	$5
2nd Half	8	2	0	88	56	2.73	3.09	1.13	610	584	633	23.3	1.5	5.7	3.7	64%	8%	48	19	33	29%	77%	5%	13	89	62%	15%			11.0	101	121	$15
15 Proj	**9**	**9**	**0**	**178**	**118**	**3.61**	**3.61**	**1.22**	**640**	**606**	**670**	**24.6**	**1.9**	**6.0**	**3.2**	**64%**	**8%**	**48**	**19**	**33**	**30%**	**72%**	**7%**	**29**						**2.8**	**82**	**98**	**$9**

Hernandez,Felix

Age: 29	Th: R	Role SP	Health A	LIMA Plan D+	
Ht: 6' 3"	Wt: 225	Type Pwr GB	PT/Exp A	Rand Var -3	
			Consist A	MM 5405	

Established career-best ERA and WHIP. Ditto Dom and Ctl, now with hellacious change-up driving SwK spike. GB% is vintage, while DOM% surge speaks to his consistent domination. Ten MLB seasons, still not 30, plenty of bullets left. It's unfair.

Yr Tm	W	L	Sv	IP	K	ERA	xERA	WHIP	oOPS	vL	vR	BF/G	Ctl	Dom	Cmd	FpK	SwK	G	L	F	H%	S%	hr/f	GS	APC	DOM%	DIS%	Sv%	LI	RAR	BPV	BPX	R$
10 SEA	13	12	0	250	232	2.27	3.09	1.06	585	593	576	29.4	2.5	8.4	3.3	61%	10%	54	16	30	27%	81%	8%	34	110	76%	6%			55.7	114	185	$35
11 SEA	14	14	0	234	222	3.47	3.20	1.22	660	662	656	29.2	2.6	8.6	3.3	63%	10%	50	19	31	31%	73%	10%	33	109	70%	6%			13.7	112	169	$17
12 SEA	13	9	0	232	223	3.06	3.19	1.14	629	643	608	28.5	2.2	8.7	4.0	63%	11%	49	22	29	31%	74%	8%	33	104	70%	9%			27.2	124	162	$25
13 SEA	12	10	0	204	216	3.04	2.83	1.13	643	671	610	26.5	2.0	9.5	4.7	62%	11%	51	21	27	32%	75%	10%	31	102	74%	10%			20.8	146	190	$20
14 SEA	15	6	0	236	248	2.14	2.54	0.92	546	519	584	26.8	1.8	9.5	5.4	65%	13%	56	18	26	27%	80%	10%	34	101	88%	6%			46.7	157	187	$38
1st Half	10	2	0	128	137	2.10	2.48	0.92	524	512	541	27.6	1.5	9.6	6.2	64%	13%	54	21	25	29%	77%	5%	18	102	94%	0%			25.9	163	195	$44
2nd Half	5	4	0	108	111	2.17	2.62	0.91	573	527	632	26.0	2.0	9.3	4.6	66%	12%	59	13	28	24%	84%	16%	16	99	81%	13%			20.8	150	179	$31
15 Proj	**16**	**7**	**0**	**232**	**238**	**2.58**	**2.56**	**1.02**	**595**	**588**	**604**	**26.4**	**2.0**	**9.2**	**4.6**	**63%**	**12%**	**54**	**19**	**27**	**29%**	**78%**	**10%**	**34**						**33.3**	**144**	**171**	**$33**

Hernandez,Roberto

Age: 34	Th: R	Role SP	Health B	LIMA Plan D+	
Ht: 6' 4"	Wt: 230	Type GB	PT/Exp B	Rand Var 0	
			Consist C	MM 2003	

Innings-eating GBer curbed a lethal hr/f habit, only to have Cmd plunge create new issues. FpK slid all year despite 2nd half Ctl rebound. Dom skid was concurrent with decline in fastball velocity. ERA gains are fleeting; you don't want him anywhere near your roster. (Always think: Fausto Carmona 2011, if you're ever tempted.)

Yr Tm	W	L	Sv	IP	K	ERA	xERA	WHIP	oOPS	vL	vR	BF/G	Ctl	Dom	Cmd	FpK	SwK	G	L	F	H%	S%	hr/f	GS	APC	DOM%	DIS%	Sv%	LI	RAR	BPV	BPX	R$
10 CLE	13	14	0	210	124	3.77	4.07	1.31	703	722	681	26.7	3.1	5.3	1.7	55%	7%	56	14	31	28%	72%	8%	33	100	39%	15%			8.1	46	75	$9
11 CLE	7	15	0	189	109	5.25	4.10	1.40	776	801	748	26.0	2.9	5.2	1.8	59%	8%	55	19	27	30%	64%	13%	32	94	34%	22%			-30.4	49	74	-$9
12 CLE	0	3	0	14	2	7.53	5.33	1.40	964	1072	805	20.7	1.9	1.3	0.7	59%	3%	51	18	31	25%	50%	24%	3	77	0%	67%			-6.2	1	1	-$7
13 TAM	6	13	1	151	113	4.89	3.53	1.34	797	905	668	20.1	2.3	6.7	3.0	61%	8%	53	22	24	31%	67%	21%	24	75	46%	25%	100	0.84	-19.0	91	119	-$4
14 2 NL	8	11	0	165	105	4.10	4.45	1.39	742	745	738	22.6	4.0	5.7	1.4	56%	9%	50	20	30	28%	73%	12%	29	86	31%	34%	0	0.87	-7.3	24	28	-$2
1st Half	3	7	0	87	64	4.26	4.35	1.45	752	706	784	21.7	4.7	6.6	1.4	58%	9%	53	20	27	28%	73%	14%	15	83	33%	20%	0	0.91	-5.5	24	29	-$5
2nd Half	5	4	0	78	41	3.92	4.55	1.32	730	782	678	23.7	3.2	4.7	1.5	54%	8%	47	21	33	27%	73%	11%	14	88	29%	50%			-1.8	23	27	$1
15 Proj	**8**	**11**	**0**	**160**	**102**	**4.41**	**3.88**	**1.36**	**756**	**800**	**711**	**22.1**	**3.2**	**5.7**	**1.8**	**57%**	**8%**	**52**	**20**	**28**	**29%**	**70%**	**14%**	**30**						**-13.2**	**46**	**55**	**-$2**

JOCK THOMPSON

Herrera,Kelvin

Age: 25	Th: R	Role	RP	Health	A	LIMA Plan	B
Ht: 5' 10"	Wt: 200	Type	Pwr	PT/Exp	C	Rand Var	-5
				Consist	A	MM	5400

All but abandoned his secondary pitches in favor of fastballs, producing fewer Ks but fewer FBs as well. Complete HR avoidance drove ERA plunge, but you know that's an unrepeatable feat. SwK says there's a Dom rebound coming; FpK says there will be no Ctl improvement. All of this will push his ERA back towards 3.00.

Yr Tm	W	L	Sv	IP	K	ERA	xERA	WHIP	oOPS	vL	vR	BF/G	Ctl	Dom	Cmd	FpK	SwK	G	L	F	H%	S%	hr/f	GS	APC	DOM%	DIS%	Sv%	LI	RAR	BPV	BPX	R$
10																																	
11 KC *	5	1	13	55	49	2.38	2.09	0.91	1232	2500	733	5.3	2.0	7.9	4.0	56%	0%	29	14	57	24%	79%	25%	0	16			81	1.25	10.6	122	184	$12
12 KC	4	3	3	84	77	2.35	3.16	1.19	643	742	580	4.5	2.2	8.2	3.7	59%	12%	56	20	25	32%	81%	7%	0	17			75	1.20	17.3	121	158	$9
13 KC *	5	8	4	76	96	3.23	2.90	1.09	701	738	661	4.2	3.2	11.3	3.5	56%	15%	48	18	34	28%	76%	18%	0	17			67	1.19	6.0	121	157	$8
14 KC	4	3	0	70	59	1.41	3.43	1.14	561	617	508	4.1	3.3	7.6	2.3	55%	13%	49	27	24	28%	86%	0%	0	16			0	1.14	20.1	73	87	$7
1st Half	1	2	0	36	31	2.23	3.73	1.24	610	662	565	4.1	3.5	7.7	2.2	53%	13%	46	23	31	30%	80%	0%	0	16			0	1.10	6.8	69	82	$3
2nd Half	3	1	0	34	28	0.53	3.10	1.04	505	570	437	4.1	3.2	7.5	2.3	57%	13%	53	31	16	26%	94%	0%	0	16			0	1.19	13.3	79	94	$12
15 Proj	**4**	**3**	**0**	**65**	**65**	**2.83**	**3.04**	**1.16**	**608**	**664**	**555**	**4.3**	**3.3**	**8.9**	**2.7**	**56%**	**13%**	**48**	**24**	**27**	**29%**	**76%**	**7%**	**0**						**7.4**	**99**	**117**	**$4**

Hochevar,Luke

Age: 31	Th: R	Role	RP	Health	F	LIMA Plan	C
Ht: 6' 5"	Wt: 225	Type	Pwr	PT/Exp	C	Rand Var	0
				Consist	C	MM	3200

Missed all of 2014 after Tommy John surgery in March. Was superb following 2013 bullpen move, as his average velocity spiked into the mid-90s and Cmd turned elite. Pen role may hasten the standard 12-18 month recovery time, though nothing is certain. Worth noting where this free agent lands.

Yr Tm	W	L	Sv	IP	K	ERA	xERA	WHIP	oOPS	vL	vR	BF/G	Ctl	Dom	Cmd	FpK	SwK	G	L	F	H%	S%	hr/f	GS	APC	DOM%	DIS%	Sv%	LI	RAR	BPV	BPX	R$
10 KC	6	6	0	103	76	4.81	4.16	1.43	754	796	712	25.0	3.2	6.6	2.1	54%	10%	46	21	33	32%	67%	8%	17	91	41%	18%	0	0.73	-9.2	56	91	-$2
11 KC	11	11	0	198	128	4.68	4.00	1.28	742	766	714	26.9	2.8	5.8	2.1	57%	8%	50	18	32	28%	65%	12%	31	101	45%	16%			-18.1	57	85	$1
12 KC	8	16	0	185	144	5.73	4.23	1.42	818	877	749	25.0	3.0	7.0	2.4	59%	9%	43	22	35	32%	61%	14%	32	94	44%	31%			-39.2	67	87	-$13
13 KC	5	2	2	70	82	1.92	2.89	0.82	533	607	452	4.5	2.2	10.5	4.8	69%	14%	35	19	46	22%	86%	11%	0	18			40	0.92	16.9	143	187	$12
14																																	
1st Half																																	
2nd Half																																	
15 Proj	**3**	**2**	**0**	**44**	**37**	**3.46**	**3.50**	**1.24**	**708**	**761**	**648**	**11.2**	**2.7**	**7.6**	**2.8**	**60%**	**10%**	**43**	**20**	**37**	**30%**	**75%**	**9%**	**2**						**1.5**	**85**	**101**	**$0**

Holland,Derek

Age: 28	Th: L	Role	SP	Health	F	LIMA Plan	B
Ht: 6' 2"	Wt: 210	Type		PT/Exp	B	Rand Var	-5
				Consist	B	MM	3205

2-1, 1.46 ERA in 37 IP at TEX. Off-season accident and subsequent knee surgery shelved him until September. Shook off rust after minor league rehab to post 96 BPV and five PQS-DOMs in five MLB starts. Expect low-ceiling value, with recent FpK, SwK hopeful of more.

Yr Tm	W	L	Sv	IP	K	ERA	xERA	WHIP	oOPS	vL	vR	BF/G	Ctl	Dom	Cmd	FpK	SwK	G	L	F	H%	S%	hr/f	GS	APC	DOM%	DIS%	Sv%	LI	RAR	BPV	BPX	R$
10 TEX *	9	6	0	120	95	3.12	3.78	1.30	727	362	818	19.8	3.2	7.2	2.2	56%	9%	42	15	43	29%	79%	8%	10	76	40%	50%	0	0.74	14.2	68	110	$8
11 TEX	16	5	0	198	162	3.95	3.80	1.35	724	601	765	26.3	3.0	7.4	2.4	58%	8%	46	20	34	31%	74%	11%	32	100	47%	22%			-0.3	74	112	$7
12 TEX	12	7	0	175	145	4.67	4.08	1.22	745	656	770	25.2	2.7	7.4	2.8	59%	8%	43	17	40	27%	68%	15%	27	95	63%	15%	0	0.81	-14.2	83	108	$4
13 TEX	10	9	0	213	189	3.42	3.78	1.29	711	671	722	27.1	2.7	8.0	3.0	63%	10%	41	23	36	32%	76%	9%	33	99	58%	15%			11.6	90	117	$10
14 TEX *	4	1	0	57	45	2.98	4.55	1.38	601	618	596	20.1	2.6	7.1	2.8	66%	10%	41	17	41	33%	83%	0%	5	95	100%	0%	0	0.66	5.4	69	83	$0
1st Half																																	
2nd Half	4	1	0	57	45	2.98	4.55	1.38	601	618	596	20.1	2.6	7.1	2.8	66%	10%	41	17	41	33%	83%	0%	5	95	100%	0%	0	0.66	5.4	69	83	$0
15 Proj	**14**	**7**	**0**	**203**	**167**	**3.66**	**3.66**	**1.31**	**749**	**650**	**778**	**22.9**	**2.7**	**7.4**	**2.7**	**62%**	**9%**	**43**	**18**	**39**	**31%**	**76%**	**10%**	**37**						**2.2**	**80**	**95**	**$9**

Holland,Greg

Age: 29	Th: R	Role	RP	Health	A	LIMA Plan	C+
Ht: 5' 10"	Wt: 205	Type	Pwr	PT/Exp	A	Rand Var	-5
				Consist	B	MM	5530

Untouchable in the 2nd half and didn't play favorites, as seen in sub-.400 OPS vL and vR. GB% surge held up all season. Cmd and SwK are still first-rate despite declines. After two straight seasons of sub-1.50 ERA and sub-1.00 WHIP, he sits atop the AL closer list.

Yr Tm	W	L	Sv	IP	K	ERA	xERA	WHIP	oOPS	vL	vR	BF/G	Ctl	Dom	Cmd	FpK	SwK	G	L	F	H%	S%	hr/f	GS	APC	DOM%	DIS%	Sv%	LI	RAR	BPV	BPX	R$
10 KC *	3	4	3	75	70	5.03	3.85	1.42	835	838	832	6.3	4.5	8.3	1.8	61%	12%	35	24	42	31%	64%	13%	0	21			60	0.68	-8.8	73	119	-$1
11 KC *	7	1	6	82	95	1.96	1.77	1.01	521	522	519	5.3	3.3	10.4	3.1	60%	17%	45	16	39	26%	82%	6%	0	21			67	1.38	20.0	133	201	$15
12 KC	7	4	16	67	91	2.96	3.31	1.37	653	577	712	4.3	4.6	12.2	2.7	50%	13%	45	18	36	36%	78%	3%	0	17			80	1.41	8.8	120	156	$10
13 KC	2	1	47	67	103	1.21	2.10	0.87	479	512	439	3.8	2.4	13.8	5.7	58%	17%	39	27	33	30%	89%	7%	0	16			94	1.34	22.0	201	262	$31
14 KC	1	3	46	62	90	1.44	2.29	0.91	472	494	444	3.7	2.9	13.0	4.5	57%	15%	48	17	35	28%	87%	7%	0	15			96	1.21	17.7	182	217	$26
1st Half	1	2	23	32	49	1.99	2.13	1.04	566	647	475	3.8	2.6	13.9	5.4	54%	16%	49	16	34	34%	87%	13%	0	16			96	1.35	6.8	209	249	$24
2nd Half	0	1	23	31	41	0.88	2.46	0.78	367	348	392	3.6	3.2	12.0	3.7	60%	15%	47	18	35	22%	88%	0%	0	14			96	1.07	10.8	154	184	$29
15 Proj	**2**	**3**	**45**	**65**	**92**	**1.76**	**2.29**	**0.99**	**510**	**507**	**513**	**3.8**	**3.2**	**12.6**	**4.0**	**57%**	**16%**	**45**	**20**	**35**	**30%**	**84%**	**6%**	**0**						**16.0**	**165**	**196**	**$27**

Hollands,Mario

Age: 26	Th: L	Role	RP	Health	B	LIMA Plan	D+
Ht: 6' 5"	Wt: 220	Type		PT/Exp	D	Rand Var	0
				Consist	D	MM	2100

Hard-throwing lefty with little else to offer. GB% was never all that until MLB debut, ditto his effectiveness vs. LHBs. H% and S% helped him navigate 1st half, before luck turned. September elbow injury ended his season and now threatens his 2015. Avoid.

Yr Tm	W	L	Sv	IP	K	ERA	xERA	WHIP	oOPS	vL	vR	BF/G	Ctl	Dom	Cmd	FpK	SwK	G	L	F	H%	S%	hr/f	GS	APC	DOM%	DIS%	Sv%	LI	RAR	BPV	BPX	R$
10																																	
11																																	
12 a/a	3	7	0	60	32	6.96	7.29	1.93				23.8	4.2	4.8	1.1						36%	65%								-21.8	-3	-3	-$17
13 aa	3	2	0	63	44	4.95	5.49	1.61				21.3	2.9	6.3	2.2						36%	70%								-8.4	47	61	-$7
14 PHI	2	2	0	47	35	4.40	4.12	1.40	693	623	748	4.1	4.0	6.7	1.7	59%	9%	52	20	28	30%	68%	8%	0	15			0	0.73	-3.8	42	50	-$4
1st Half	1	1	0	30	23	2.10	3.64	1.10	592	458	690	3.8	3.0	6.9	2.3	58%	8%	49	20	31	25%	84%	8%	0	15			0	0.87	6.1	71	84	$1
2nd Half	1	1	0	17	12	8.47	5.04	1.94	843	847	839	4.7	5.8	6.4	1.1	61%	9%	55	20	25	37%	53%	7%	0	17			0	0.49	-9.9	-10	-11	-$11
15 Proj	**1**	**2**	**0**	**29**	**20**	**4.78**	**4.03**	**1.45**	**738**	**679**	**786**	**6.7**	**3.7**	**6.2**	**1.7**	**60%**	**9%**	**49**	**21**	**30**	**31%**	**68%**	**10%**	**0**						**-3.8**	**40**	**47**	**-$4**

Holmberg,David

Age: 23	Th: L	Role	SP	Health	A	LIMA Plan	D+
Ht: 6' 3"	Wt: 225	Type	xFB	PT/Exp	D	Rand Var	+3
				Consist	C	MM	0001

2-2, 4.80 ERA in 30 IP at CIN. One-time GB-thrower who turns into an extreme FBer during his rise through the minors is a scary proposition. Now giving up bombs in CIN, and hasn't shown much Dom for a while. Ctl heading in the wrong direction, fully supported by meager FpK. Very little upside here.

Yr Tm	W	L	Sv	IP	K	ERA	xERA	WHIP	oOPS	vL	vR	BF/G	Ctl	Dom	Cmd	FpK	SwK	G	L	F	H%	S%	hr/f	GS	APC	DOM%	DIS%	Sv%	LI	RAR	BPV	BPX	R$
10																																	
11																																	
12 aa	5	5	0	95	58	4.34	5.03	1.47				27.2	2.1	5.5	2.6						34%	72%								-3.8	56	74	-$5
13 ARI *	5	8	0	161	99	3.74	4.29	1.40	950	1100	900	25.2	3.0	5.5	1.8	55%	5%	25	25	50	31%	75%	0%	1	80	0%	100%			2.5	47	61	-$1
14 CIN *	4	8	0	123	67	4.88	5.59	1.65	849	958	817	21.9	3.5	4.9	1.4	55%	9%	38	17	45	34%	71%	19%	5	74	40%	40%	0	0.62	-17.2	25	30	-$13
1st Half	0	4	0	41	23	6.05	6.95	1.99				21.8	4.4	5.0	1.1						39%	69%	0%	0						-11.6	18	21	-$23
2nd Half	4	4	0	82	44	4.30	4.91	1.48	849	958	817	22.0	3.0	4.8	1.6	55%	9%	38	17	45	31%	73%	19%	5	74	40%	40%	0	0.62	-5.6	30	36	-$7
15 Proj	**3**	**5**	**0**	**87**	**51**	**4.75**	**4.76**	**1.55**	**836**	**934**	**806**	**23.6**	**3.1**	**5.2**	**1.7**	**55%**	**9%**	**38**	**17**	**45**	**31%**	**75%**	**11%**	**16**						**-10.9**	**25**	**30**	**-$7**

Hoover,J.J.

Age: 27	Th: R	Role	RP	Health	A	LIMA Plan	C
Ht: 6' 3"	Wt: 230	Type	Pwr xFB	PT/Exp	D	Rand Var	+3
				Consist	C	MM	3500

Could only avoid HRs for so long, and they finally bit him, hard. 1st half Ctl spike added to the pain. Tattooed by the same LHBs that he dominated for two seasons. BPIs are riddled with volatility, even the Dom that makes him watchable. Should recover some, but high FB% keeps him risky.

Yr Tm	W	L	Sv	IP	K	ERA	xERA	WHIP	oOPS	vL	vR	BF/G	Ctl	Dom	Cmd	FpK	SwK	G	L	F	H%	S%	hr/f	GS	APC	DOM%	DIS%	Sv%	LI	RAR	BPV	BPX	R$
10 aa	3	1	0	21	29	4.11	3.67	1.56				22.6	6.6	12.8	1.9						36%	73%								-0.1	113	184	-$1
11 a/a	3	6	2	106	100	3.06	2.82	1.21				9.9	3.4	8.5	2.5						29%	75%								11.5	99	149	$7
12 CIN *	5	0	14	68	77	1.75	1.16	0.89	512	427	589	4.3	3.4	10.2	3.0	59%	11%	24	20	57	22%	83%	5%	0	19			88	0.70	18.9	135	176	$18
13 CIN	5	5	3	66	67	2.86	3.86	1.11	627	477	722	3.9	3.5	9.1	2.6	61%	10%	31	21	48	26%	78%	7%	0	17			60	1.29	8.2	78	101	$6
14 CIN	1	10	0	63	75	4.88	4.07	1.39	785	948	660	5.1	4.5	10.8	2.4	61%	11%	28	19	53	30%	72%	15%	0	21			0	0.87	-8.8	80	95	-$4
1st Half	1	5	0	33	36	5.13	4.84	1.50	802	992	667	5.2	5.4	9.7	1.8	59%	11%	25	17	58	28%	72%	13%	0	21			0	0.87	-5.7	32	38	-$6
2nd Half	0	5	0	29	39	4.60	3.26	1.26	765	901	651	5.0	3.4	12.0	3.5	64%	12%	33	21	47	31%	71%	18%	0	22			0	0.88	-3.1	135	161	-$2
15 Proj	**2**	**5**	**0**	**44**	**49**	**3.69**	**3.45**	**1.21**	**685**	**711**	**666**	**4.7**	**3.8**	**10.2**	**2.7**	**61%**	**11%**	**29**	**20**	**51**	**28%**	**75%**	**11%**	**0**						**0.3**	**88**	**105**	**$0**

JOCK THOMPSON

House,T.J.

House,T.J.			Health	A	LIMA Plan	B+
Age: 25	Th: L	Role: SP	PT/Exp	D	Rand Var	+2
Ht: 6' 1"	Wt: 205	Type: GB	Consist	B	MM	3103

5-3, 3.35 ERA in 102 IP at CLE. A legitimate step up? Rookie GBer scuffled early, sizzled down the stretch with a 2.25 ERA, 48/8 K/BB over his final 52 IP. Credited mechanical tweak for late Ctl gain as SwK spiked in August and September. If he confirms that stretch run, he'll surpass the projection.

Yr Tm	W	L	Sv	IP	K	ERA	xERA	WHIP	oOPS	vL	vR	BF/G	Ctl	Dom	Cmd	FpK	SwK	G	L	F	H%	S%	hr/f	GS	APC	DOM%	DIS%	Sv%	LI	RAR	BPV	BPX	R$
10																																	
11																																	
12 aa	8	5	0	124	77	5.34	4.46	1.48				23.3	3.3	5.6	1.7						32%	63%								-20.4	49	64	-$9
13 a/a	9	11	0	164	116	4.82	5.19	1.61				26.0	3.1	6.4	2.1						36%	70%								-19.3	55	71	-$11
14 CLE *	6	7	0	159	115	3.72	4.27	1.35	749	608	808	22.9	2.1	6.5	3.0	61%	10%	61	21	18	33%	74%	18%	18	83	39%	28%	0	0.72	0.4	79	94	$0
1st Half	1	5	0	84	55	3.93	4.49	1.40	832	787	858	22.2	2.5	5.9	2.3	63%	10%	61	22	17	32%	74%	26%	6	77	33%	33%	0	0.66	-1.9	57	68	-$5
2nd Half	5	2	0	75	60	3.49	4.02	1.31	706	466	787	23.7	1.7	7.2	4.3	59%	10%	61	21	18	34%	74%	14%	12	87	42%	25%			2.3	113	135	$6
15 Proj	7	7	0	145	104	3.84	3.37	1.28	683	567	734	23.1	2.5	6.5	2.6	61%	10%	55	21	25	31%	70%	9%	26						-1.7	83	98	$4

Howell,J.P.

Howell,J.P.			Health	D	LIMA Plan	B+
Age: 32	Th: L	Role: RP	PT/Exp	D	Rand Var	-5
Ht: 6' 0"	Wt: 185	Type: Pwr xGB	Consist	A	MM	3300

PRO: Sustained elite GB% tilt all season; held HR in check until September. CON: Dom gain was offset by wavering Ctl, while September downtime cost him IP and R$. He still offers just moderate bullpen value, as health and walks keep that low ceiling intact.

Yr Tm	W	L	Sv	IP	K	ERA	xERA	WHIP	oOPS	vL	vR	BF/G	Ctl	Dom	Cmd	FpK	SwK	G	L	F	H%	S%	hr/f	GS	APC	DOM%	DIS%	Sv%	LI	RAR	BPV	BPX	R$
10																																	
11 TAM	2	3	1	31	26	6.16	4.22	1.57	770	581	978	3.0	5.3	7.6	1.4	59%	8%	53	19	29	29%	63%	19%	0	12			50	1.04	-8.4	26	39	-$5
12 TAM	1	0	0	50	42	3.04	3.84	1.21	706	612	795	3.7	3.9	7.5	1.9	58%	8%	49	20	31	24%	81%	17%	0	15			0	0.71	6.1	56	73	$0
13 LA	4	1	0	62	54	2.18	3.31	1.05	531	452	608	3.7	3.3	7.8	2.3	57%	10%	57	15	28	25%	79%	4%	0	14			0	0.93	12.9	86	112	$6
14 LA	3	3	0	49	48	2.39	3.31	1.14	547	512	585	2.9	4.6	8.8	1.9	55%	10%	58	18	25	24%	80%	7%	0	12			0	1.30	8.2	70	83	$3
1st Half	1	3	0	28	32	1.59	3.04	1.09	489	464	513	3.0	4.8	10.2	2.1	54%	11%	58	15	26	25%	84%	0%	0	13			0	1.31	7.5	91	108	$4
2nd Half	2	0	0	21	16	3.48	3.70	1.21	624	566	701	2.8	4.4	7.0	1.6	58%	10%	56	20	24	24%	74%	15%	0	11			0	1.29	0.7	42	50	$1
15 Proj	3	2	0	51	45	3.16	3.35	1.18	603	529	683	3.1	4.2	8.0	1.9	57%	10%	56	18	27	25%	75%	10%	0						3.7	63	75	$2

Hudson,Daniel

Hudson,Daniel			Health	F	LIMA Plan	C
Age: 28	Th: R	Role: SP	PT/Exp	F	Rand Var	+5
Ht: 6' 3"	Wt: 225	Type: Pwr FB	Consist	A	MM	2201

Promise of 2011 is a distant memory after consecutive July TJS surgeries in 2012-13. Returned briefly in August to toss 6 Triple-A IP and make three MLB appearances before being shut down in September. Now a long-shot who needs to reclaim skills and health.

Yr Tm	W	L	Sv	IP	K	ERA	xERA	WHIP	oOPS	vL	vR	BF/G	Ctl	Dom	Cmd	FpK	SwK	G	L	F	H%	S%	hr/f	GS	APC	DOM%	DIS%	Sv%	LI	RAR	BPV	BPX	R$
10 2TM *	19	6	0	189	178	3.32	3.50	1.18	579	571	586	24.3	2.9	8.5	2.9	59%	13%	35	19	45	28%	77%	7%	14	103	79%	7%			17.6	86	139	$20
11 ARI	16	12	0	222	169	3.49	3.80	1.20	694	698	691	27.9	2.0	6.9	3.4	60%	10%	42	19	39	30%	72%	6%	33	104	67%	6%			12.5	89	133	$16
12 ARI	3	2	0	45	37	7.35	4.34	1.63	910	994	807	22.4	2.4	7.3	3.1	56%	10%	37	27	36	37%	57%	17%	9	89	22%	44%			-18.6	83	108	-$11
13																																	
14 ARI	0	1	0	3	2	13.50	4.22	1.50	769	500	1200	4.3	0.0	6.8	0.0	54%	8%	45	18	36	42%	0%	0%	0	16			0	0.68	-3.2	145	172	-$4
1st Half																																	
2nd Half	0	1	0	3	2	13.50	4.22	1.50	769	500	1200	4.3	0.0	6.8	0.0	54%	8%	45	18	36	42%	0%	0%	0	16			0	0.68	-3.2	145	173	-$4
15 Proj	8	4	0	93	76	4.20	3.78	1.34	752	800	706	24.2	2.8	7.4	2.6	58%	11%	38	22	41	31%	72%	10%	16						-5.2	73	87	$0

Hudson,Tim

Hudson,Tim			Health	D	LIMA Plan	B
Age: 39	Th: R	Role: SP	PT/Exp	A	Rand Var	0
Ht: 6' 1"	Wt: 175	Type: Con GB	Consist	A	MM	3005

Old man river with late-season hints of skill erosion even as pinpoint control and GBs kept him relevant. Are 2nd half FpK, GB% and xERA early warning signs? Still has value, but his ceiling is lower. And at his age, the risk is growing. DN: 4.00+ ERA.

Yr Tm	W	L	Sv	IP	K	ERA	xERA	WHIP	oOPS	vL	vR	BF/G	Ctl	Dom	Cmd	FpK	SwK	G	L	F	H%	S%	hr/f	GS	APC	DOM%	DIS%	Sv%	LI	RAR	BPV	BPX	R$
10 ATL	17	9	0	229	139	2.83	3.49	1.15	641	667	616	27.1	2.9	5.5	1.9	54%	8%	64	14	22	25%	79%	13%	34	98	50%	9%			35.1	62	100	$24
11 ATL	16	10	0	215	158	3.22	3.32	1.14	627	692	571	26.8	2.3	6.6	2.8	62%	10%	57	19	25	28%	73%	9%	33	97	55%	9%			19.1	91	136	$20
12 ATL	16	7	0	179	102	3.62	4.03	1.21	666	668	663	26.8	2.4	5.1	2.1	62%	8%	55	19	25	28%	71%	8%	28	94	39%	11%			8.7	60	78	$12
13 ATL	8	7	0	131	95	3.97	3.52	1.19	662	661	662	25.4	2.5	6.5	2.6	65%	10%	56	18	27	29%	67%	10%	21	96	57%	19%			-1.8	85	110	$4
14 SF	9	13	0	189	120	3.57	3.61	1.23	713	755	667	25.5	1.6	5.7	3.5	63%	9%	53	21	26	31%	72%	9%	31	90	45%	19%			4.1	90	107	$6
1st Half	7	5	0	108	70	2.59	3.26	1.08	648	742	549	27.2	1.3	5.9	4.4	65%	10%	58	19	23	29%	77%	8%	16	93	56%	13%			15.3	105	125	$19
2nd Half	2	8	0	82	50	4.85	4.07	1.43	792	770	815	23.6	2.0	5.5	2.8	61%	9%	48	23	29	33%	68%	11%	15	86	33%	27%			-11.2	71	85	-$11
15 Proj	11	12	0	189	120	3.76	3.50	1.24	699	716	681	24.9	2.2	5.7	2.7	62%	9%	53	20	27	30%	71%	9%	31						-0.5	76	91	$8

Huff,David

Huff,David			Health	C	LIMA Plan	D+
Age: 30	Th: L	Role: RP	PT/Exp	D	Rand Var	-2
Ht: 6' 2"	Wt: 215	Type:	Consist	C	MM	1000

Rising GB% and hr/f reversal hints that ex-starter might be learning new tricks as long-man out of the pen. But Ctl took a step backward and injuries (shoulder in February, quad in April) cut into his appearances. Volatile BPIs and R$ history warn us to stay away.

Yr Tm	W	L	Sv	IP	K	ERA	xERA	WHIP	oOPS	vL	vR	BF/G	Ctl	Dom	Cmd	FpK	SwK	G	L	F	H%	S%	hr/f	GS	APC	DOM%	DIS%	Sv%	LI	RAR	BPV	BPX	R$
10 CLE *	10	13	0	154	78	5.60	5.94	1.65	917	1040	880	25.5	3.2	4.6	1.4	59%	6%	36	21	43	33%	68%	11%	15	93	20%	53%			-28.8	12	19	-$11
11 CLE *	11	9	0	158	87	4.47	5.01	1.50	757	778	749	23.5	2.8	5.0	1.8	65%	7%	32	20	48	32%	72%	7%	10	84	60%	30%	0	1.15	-10.3	35	53	-$4
12 CLE *	10	7	0	165	82	6.01	7.07	1.67	792	942	716	23.8	2.4	4.5	1.9	67%	9%	38	17	45	34%	69%	13%	4	72	25%	50%	0	0.63	-40.5	-7	-8	-$23
13 2AL *	7	8	1	130	99	5.85	5.77	1.57	733	854	667	15.8	2.5	6.9	2.7	70%	11%	40	24	36	36%	65%	18%	2	40	50%	50%	100	0.67	-31.8	50	66	-$13
14 2TM	4	1	0	59	39	3.36	4.36	1.42	688	614	748	5.6	3.5	5.9	1.7	62%	8%	47	23	30	31%	78%	9%	0	21			0	0.69	2.8	37	44	-$1
1st Half	2	0	0	30	18	5.16	4.55	1.69	790	684	873	6.5	3.6	5.5	1.5	64%	7%	52	21	26	35%	70%	11%	0	25			0	0.55	-5.2	30	36	-$8
2nd Half	2	1	0	29	21	1.53	4.18	1.16	574	538	604	4.8	3.4	6.4	1.9	60%	9%	41	24	35	25%	91%	6%	0	18			0	0.80	8.0	44	52	$5
15 Proj	3	2	0	44	28	4.35	4.21	1.48	794	776	805	8.4	3.0	5.9	1.9	64%	8%	41	22	36	32%	74%	10%	0						-3.3	44	52	-$4

Hughes,Jared

Hughes,Jared			Health	D	LIMA Plan	B
Age: 29	Th: R	Role: RP	PT/Exp	D	Rand Var	-5
Ht: 6' 7"	Wt: 245	Type: xGB	Consist	B	MM	3000

GB% continues to help him out-pitch his other BPIs. But it was year-long H% luck and a positive tick in historically volatile Ctl that produced a career-year to date, in the face of a Dom swoon. Track record warns against expecting ERA, WHIP repeats.

Yr Tm	W	L	Sv	IP	K	ERA	xERA	WHIP	oOPS	vL	vR	BF/G	Ctl	Dom	Cmd	FpK	SwK	G	L	F	H%	S%	hr/f	GS	APC	DOM%	DIS%	Sv%	LI	RAR	BPV	BPX	R$
10 aa	12	8	0	151	93	5.42	5.55	1.58				22.1	2.5	5.5	2.2						35%	66%								-25.0	43	69	-$7
11 PIT *	6	6	0	115	68	4.08	4.05	1.45	630	782	546	8.2	3.2	5.3	1.7	59%	7%	66	21	14	32%	70%	25%	0	16			0	0.72	-2.0	56	85	-$2
12 PIT	2	2	2	76	50	2.85	3.73	1.15	677	734	629	4.8	2.6	5.9	2.3	53%	11%	60	17	23	26%	79%	13%	0	18			50	0.96	10.8	74	97	$5
13 PIT *	3	3	2	55	39	2.99	4.11	1.51	786	967	664	5.0	3.8	6.4	1.7	58%	12%	56	20	23	33%	80%	8%	0	18			100	0.70	5.9	63	82	-$1
14 PIT	7	5	0	64	36	1.96	3.34	1.09	609	592	622	4.1	2.7	5.0	1.9	60%	11%	65	19	17	24%	85%	13%	0	14			0	1.09	14.1	62	74	$7
1st Half	4	2	0	31	15	2.35	3.69	1.17	647	603	684	4.4	2.6	4.4	1.7	58%	11%	62	18	20	26%	82%	11%	0	16			0	1.02	5.3	48	57	$4
2nd Half	3	3	0	34	21	1.60	3.03	1.01	574	578	568	3.8	2.7	5.6	2.1	62%	11%	67	19	14	23%	88%	15%	0	13			0	1.15	8.9	74	89	$9
15 Proj	4	4	0	58	36	3.06	3.48	1.29	691	757	642	4.7	2.9	5.6	1.9	58%	11%	61	19	20	29%	77%	10%	0						4.9	60	72	$1

Hughes,Phil

Hughes,Phil			Health	C	LIMA Plan	C+
Age: 29	Th: R	Role: SP	PT/Exp	A	Rand Var	0
Ht: 6' 5"	Wt: 240	Type: FB	Consist	B	MM	4205

2014 poster boy for why context matters. Dom, GB% upticks helped, but note the improvement vL. Biggest gains were 1) fleeing Yankee Stadium for a HR-supressing home venue, and 2) other-worldly Ctl (check out that FpK!). Should be decent again, but expect some regression.

Yr Tm	W	L	Sv	IP	K	ERA	xERA	WHIP	oOPS	vL	vR	BF/G	Ctl	Dom	Cmd	FpK	SwK	G	L	F	H%	S%	hr/f	GS	APC	DOM%	DIS%	Sv%	LI	RAR	BPV	BPX	R$
10 NYY	18	8	0	176	146	4.19	4.16	1.25	702	728	674	23.5	3.0	7.5	2.5	63%	9%	36	16	47	28%	71%	10%	29	97	55%	14%	0	0.89	-2.3	68	110	$11
11 NYY	5	5	0	75	47	5.79	4.93	1.49	799	841	729	19.6	3.3	5.7	1.7	68%	7%	32	23	45	31%	62%	8%	14	76	29%	43%	0	0.86	-17.0	24	36	-$7
12 NYY	16	13	0	191	165	4.23	4.30	1.26	765	610	928	25.5	2.2	7.8	3.6	66%	9%	32	20	48	30%	73%	12%	32	101	53%	22%			-5.2	91	119	$8
13 NYY	4	14	0	146	121	5.19	4.44	1.46	832	863	793	21.4	2.6	7.5	2.9	71%	9%	31	23	46	34%	68%	11%	29	85	38%	52%	0	0.76	-23.8	74	96	-$10
14 MIN	16	10	0	210	186	3.52	3.39	1.13	674	619	733	26.7	0.7	8.0	11.6	73%	9%	37	23	40	34%	70%	6%	32	95	66%	3%			5.7	140	167	$15
1st Half	8	4	0	103	88	3.58	3.50	1.17	684	557	798	26.3	0.9	7.7	8.8	71%	10%	37	23	40	34%	70%	5%	16	97	56%	0%			2.0	130	155	$13
2nd Half	8	6	0	107	98	3.46	3.29	1.10	664	668	658	27.2	0.5	8.3	16.3	74%	9%	36	24	40	33%	70%	7%	16	94	75%	6%			3.7	149	178	$17
15 Proj	14	11	0	203	174	3.65	3.33	1.15	679	652	711	23.0	1.4	7.7	5.5	71%	9%	34	22	43	31%	71%	8%	35						2.2	113	135	$15

JOCK THOMPSON

Hunter,Tommy

Age: 28	Th: R	Role RP	Health	D	LIMA Plan	B
Ht: 6' 3"	Wt: 260	Type Con	PT/Exp	C	Rand Var	0
			Consist	C	MM	4110

Back-to-back blown saves in May cost him closer role, and spent 3 weeks on the DL (groin) shortly after. Injury may have been behind it all, as 2H skills were superb. Progress vLH batters adds to his resume. Not your typical closer skills, but if 2H and health hold up, he could find himself back in a higher leverage role.

Yr Tm	W	L	Sv	IP	K	ERA	xERA	WHIP	oOPS	vL	vR	BF/G	Ctl	Dom	Cmd	FpK	SwK	G	L	F	H%	S%	hr/f	GS	APC	DOM%	DIS%	Sv%	LI	RAR	BPV	BPX	R$
10 TEX *	14	6	0	155	79	3.92	4.50	1.31	739	763	708	22.0	2.6	4.6	1.8	63%	6%	42	18	40	27%	75%	12%	22	83	18%	23%	0	0.77	3.0	26	42	$7
11 2 AL *	6	6	1	115	61	5.01	5.34	1.44	782	864	686	16.9	1.5	4.8	3.2	66%	6%	41	21	38	33%	68%	11%	11	65	18%	18%	50	0.95	-15.2	52	78	-$5
12 BAL *	10	9	1	163	93	5.24	5.58	1.37	864	840	891	18.0	1.9	5.1	2.7	60%	7%	45	20	35	30%	68%	20%	20	63	25%	25%	50	0.87	-24.6	27	35	-$7
13 BAL	6	5	4	86	68	2.81	3.55	0.98	617	857	344	4.9	1.5	7.1	4.9	64%	11%	39	21	40	25%	78%	11%	0	19			67	1.09	11.2	105	137	$10
14 BAL	3	2	11	61	45	2.97	3.27	1.10	643	639	647	4.0	1.8	6.7	3.8	65%	8%	51	24	25	29%	75%	9%	0	14			65	1.16	5.8	101	120	$7
1st Half	2	1	11	26	19	4.78	4.03	1.48	815	711	909	4.1	2.7	6.5	2.4	66%	8%	47	24	29	34%	69%	12%	0	15			79	1.27	-3.4	68	81	$3
2nd Half	1	1	0	34	26	1.57	2.71	0.82	491	579	404	3.9	1.0	6.8	6.5	65%	8%	54	23	22	25%	81%	5%	0	14			0	1.06	9.2	127	151	$10
15 Proj	**4**	**3**	**3**	**69**	**49**	**3.36**	**3.34**	**1.13**	**676**	**742**	**607**	**5.3**	**1.7**	**6.4**	**3.7**	**64%**	**8%**	**46**	**22**	**32**	**28%**	**74%**	**11%**	**0**						**3.2**	**93**	**110**	**$4**

Hutchison,Drew

Age: 24	Th: R	Role SP	Health	F	LIMA Plan	B+
Ht: 6' 3"	Wt: 195	Type Pwr	PT/Exp	C	Rand Var	0
			Consist	F	MM	3305

Back after prolonged recovery from TJS (2012), with strong overall skill set masked by some S% issues. But optimism for further progress dampended by FB tilt and significant problems vL. Solve one of those, and sub-4.00 ERA is in play. Solve both, and this gets really exciting. He's got time.

Yr Tm	W	L	Sv	IP	K	ERA	xERA	WHIP	oOPS	vL	vR	BF/G	Ctl	Dom	Cmd	FpK	SwK	G	L	F	H%	S%	hr/f	GS	APC	DOM%	DIS%	Sv%	LI	RAR	BPV	BPX	R$
10																																	
11 aa	3	0	0	15	19	1.46	1.39	0.89				18.6	1.2	11.2	9.4						33%	82%								4.6	278	418	$1
12 TOR *	7	4	0	75	59	4.18	4.31	1.33	756	750	763	22.4	2.7	7.1	2.6	54%	9%	45	25	30	31%	72%	15%	11	90	36%	27%			-1.5	65	85	$0
13 a/a	0	4	0	27	26	7.16	6.09	1.75				17.4	2.7	8.7	3.3						42%	57%								-10.8	85	111	-$9
14 TOR	11	13	0	185	184	4.48	3.84	1.26	723	811	615	24.6	2.9	9.0	3.1	59%	11%	36	19	45	31%	67%	10%	32	95	53%	28%			-16.9	96	115	$2
1st Half	5	6	0	92	79	4.00	4.03	1.27	735	761	701	24.3	2.8	7.7	2.7	58%	10%	37	21	42	30%	72%	9%	16	95	50%	31%			-2.9	77	92	$3
2nd Half	6	7	0	92	105	4.97	3.65	1.26	710	864	539	24.8	3.0	10.2	3.4	61%	13%	36	16	48	32%	63%	10%	16	96	56%	25%			-14.0	116	139	$2
15 Proj	**13**	**13**	**0**	**189**	**174**	**4.27**	**3.50**	**1.29**	**734**	**790**	**669**	**23.1**	**2.9**	**8.3**	**2.9**	**57%**	**10%**	**39**	**21**	**40**	**31%**	**70%**	**11%**	**34**						**-12.3**	**90**	**107**	**$6**

Iwakuma,Hisashi

Age: 34	Th: R	Role SP	Health	C	LIMA Plan	C+
Ht: 6' 3"	Wt: 210	Type	PT/Exp	A	Rand Var	+1
			Consist	A	MM	5205

Missed the first five weeks with a strained tendon in his finger. Let's hope his ERA jump scares away potential bidders, as xERA actually improved, thanks to eye-popping Ctl/Cmd growth. FpK supports the elite Ctl; even if that slips a bit, there's still ace-level upside here at a mid-rotation price.

Yr Tm	W	L	Sv	IP	K	ERA	xERA	WHIP	oOPS	vL	vR	BF/G	Ctl	Dom	Cmd	FpK	SwK	G	L	F	H%	S%	hr/f	GS	APC	DOM%	DIS%	Sv%	LI	RAR	BPV	BPX	R$
10 for	10	9	0	201	145	3.50	3.59	1.20				28.9	2.0	6.5	3.2						30%	73%								14.3	86	139	$13
11 for	6	7	0	119	85	3.03	3.35	1.16				27.9	1.8	6.4	3.5						29%	77%								13.5	95	142	$9
12 SEA	9	5	2	125	101	3.16	3.74	1.28	718	716	720	17.3	3.1	7.3	2.3	60%	10%	52	20	27	28%	81%	17%	16	64	44%	13%	100	0.59	13.2	77	101	$9
13 SEA	14	6	0	220	185	2.66	3.29	1.01	630	599	667	26.2	1.7	7.6	4.4	63%	11%	49	18	34	26%	80%	12%	33	94	58%	3%			32.6	117	152	$29
14 SEA	15	9	0	179	154	3.52	3.00	1.05	642	702	573	25.3	1.1	7.7	7.3	66%	10%	50	21	29	30%	70%	13%	28	91	64%	18%			4.9	139	165	$16
1st Half	5	4	0	75	55	3.48	3.01	1.08	681	764	592	26.4	1.0	6.6	6.9	67%	9%	55	20	25	29%	73%	18%	11	93	64%	9%			2.4	126	150	$7
2nd Half	10	5	0	104	99	3.55	2.99	1.03	614	661	559	24.6	1.1	8.6	7.6	66%	10%	47	22	31	30%	68%	11%	17	89	65%	24%			2.5	149	177	$21
15 Proj	**16**	**9**	**0**	**210**	**176**	**3.23**	**2.97**	**1.09**	**655**	**674**	**634**	**23.5**	**1.6**	**7.5**	**4.7**	**64%**	**10%**	**50**	**20**	**30**	**29%**	**75%**	**13%**	**35**						**13.4**	**120**	**142**	**$22**

Jackson,Edwin

Age: 31	Th: R	Role SP	Health	C	LIMA Plan	D+
Ht: 6' 3"	Wt: 210	Type Pwr	PT/Exp	A	Rand Var	+5
			Consist	A	MM	2203

Perhaps the most revealing trend is one not shown here... the pct. of hard-hit balls he's allowed over the past 4 years = 27%, 30%, 32%, 36%. That also helps explain the LD spike. Essentially, opposing batters are just killing his pitches, and nothing good can ever come of that. I will not draft this pitcher.

Yr Tm	W	L	Sv	IP	K	ERA	xERA	WHIP	oOPS	vL	vR	BF/G	Ctl	Dom	Cmd	FpK	SwK	G	L	F	H%	S%	hr/f	GS	APC	DOM%	DIS%	Sv%	LI	RAR	BPV	BPX	R$
10 2 TM	10	12	0	209	181	4.47	3.77	1.39	735	742	725	28.2	3.4	7.8	2.3	57%	11%	49	19	32	32%	69%	11%	32	105	53%	9%			-10.1	77	124	$2
11 2 TM	12	9	0	200	148	3.79	3.96	1.44	768	800	736	26.9	2.8	6.7	2.4	58%	10%	44	25	31	33%	75%	8%	31	101	52%	10%	0	0.76	3.8	67	100	$3
12 WAS	10	11	0	190	168	4.03	3.80	1.22	719	758	677	25.5	2.8	8.0	2.9	62%	13%	47	17	36	29%	70%	12%	31	96	48%	16%			-0.4	94	123	$9
13 CHC	8	18	0	175	135	4.98	3.98	1.46	775	816	741	25.1	3.0	6.9	2.3	56%	9%	51	20	28	33%	66%	10%	31	95	42%	26%			-24.1	72	94	-$9
14 CHC	6	15	0	141	123	6.33	4.32	1.64	869	930	816	22.6	4.0	7.9	2.0	55%	11%	39	26	35	35%	62%	12%	27	89	30%	33%	0	0.77	-45.0	50	59	-$19
1st Half	5	8	0	90	85	5.22	3.93	1.52	804	895	725	24.5	3.9	8.5	2.2	56%	12%	40	27	33	34%	66%	11%	16	96	38%	25%			-16.3	66	78	-$13
2nd Half	1	7	0	51	38	8.29	5.02	1.86	975	987	961	20.1	4.2	6.7	1.6	55%	10%	39	23	38	37%	56%	14%	11	80	18%	45%	0	0.76	-28.6	23	28	-$30
15 Proj	**7**	**16**	**0**	**160**	**130**	**4.67**	**3.90**	**1.44**	**756**	**796**	**721**	**22.3**	**3.6**	**7.3**	**2.0**	**57%**	**11%**	**43**	**22**	**35**	**32%**	**69%**	**9%**	**30**						**-18.2**	**54**	**65**	**-$5**

Jaime,Juan

Age: 27	Th: R	Role RP	Health	A	LIMA Plan	D
Ht: 6' 2"	Wt: 250	Type Pwr	PT/Exp	F	Rand Var	+2
			Consist	A	MM	1500

0-0, 5.84 ERA in 12 IP at ATL. In seven minor-league seasons, had an impressive 12.9 Dom and an equally unimpressive 6.1 Ctl. Sure, he can throw 100+ mph, but right now, he's the Ricky Vaughn at the beginning of "Major League." And new glasses won't be enough to make him rosterable.

Yr Tm	W	L	Sv	IP	K	ERA	xERA	WHIP	oOPS	vL	vR	BF/G	Ctl	Dom	Cmd	FpK	SwK	G	L	F	H%	S%	hr/f	GS	APC	DOM%	DIS%	Sv%	LI	RAR	BPV	BPX	R$
10																																	
11																																	
12																																	
13 aa	2	5	0	42	57	5.53	3.86	1.65				5.4	6.7	12.3	1.8						37%	64%								-8.6	111	145	-$7
14 ATL *	1	0	18	53	68	4.49	4.12	1.73	800	842	767	4.1	7.9	11.5	1.5	56%	12%	38	31	31	35%	73%	10%	0	17			95	0.57	-4.9	98	117	$0
1st Half	1	0	13	31	40	2.63	2.53	1.30	451	200	556	4.0	6.3	11.4	1.8	64%	17%	17	33	50	26%	82%	33%	0	16			100	0.71	4.3	109	131	$8
2nd Half	0	0	5	22	29	7.15	6.39	2.36	911	994	840	4.2	10.1	11.7	1.2	54%	11%	42	31	27	45%	66%	0%	0	18			83	0.52	-9.2	89	106	-$10
15 Proj	**1**	**2**	**0**	**36**	**44**	**4.81**	**4.32**	**1.65**				**4.4**	**7.8**	**10.9**	**1.4**	**55%**	**10%**	**39**	**22**	**39**	**32%**	**69%**	**3%**	**0**						**-4.8**	**2**	**3**	**-$5**

Jansen,Kenley

Age: 27	Th: R	Role RP	Health	B	LIMA Plan	C+
Ht: 6' 5"	Wt: 265	Type Pwr FB	PT/Exp	A	Rand Var	+2
			Consist	A	MM	5530

A crazy first-half H% (mostly vs. LHB) gave owners fits, but otherwise, it was his second straight stellar season. With his Dom, he generates as many Ks as some starters, with 40+ saves to boot. FpK suggests Ctl may come back down, and Dom is rock solid. Expect more eliteness.

Yr Tm	W	L	Sv	IP	K	ERA	xERA	WHIP	oOPS	vL	vR	BF/G	Ctl	Dom	Cmd	FpK	SwK	G	L	F	H%	S%	hr/f	GS	APC	DOM%	DIS%	Sv%	LI	RAR	BPV	BPX	R$
10 LA *	5	0	12	54	84	1.18	1.06	1.05	422	586	273	4.4	5.0	14.0	2.8	53%	15%	34	16	50	28%	88%	0%	0	19			100	0.83	19.3	168	272	$14
11 LA	2	1	5	54	96	2.85	2.38	1.04	494	494	493	4.3	4.4	16.1	3.7	60%	17%	27	24	49	33%	74%	7%	0	19			83	0.88	7.2	177	266	$7
12 LA	5	3	25	65	99	2.35	2.63	0.85	504	518	490	3.9	3.0	13.7	4.5	61%	15%	33	19	48	24%	78%	10%	0	16			78	1.31	13.3	175	229	$22
13 LA	4	3	28	77	111	1.88	2.29	0.86	509	531	494	3.9	2.1	13.0	6.2	64%	16%	37	24	39	29%	83%	10%	0	17			88	1.33	18.8	192	251	$24
14 LA	2	3	44	65	101	2.76	2.43	1.13	610	710	521	3.9	2.6	13.9	5.3	67%	17%	35	28	37	38%	78%	9%	0	16			90	1.27	7.9	193	230	$21
1st Half	0	3	25	35	56	3.89	2.44	1.30	687	756	626	3.9	2.9	14.5	5.1	67%	18%	33	34	34	43%	71%	11%	0	16			89	1.28	-0.7	195	233	$18
2nd Half	2	0	19	31	45	1.47	2.42	0.95	519	657	387	4.0	2.3	13.2	5.6	68%	16%	38	20	42	31%	89%	7%	0	15			90	1.25	8.6	191	228	$25
15 Proj	**3**	**2**	**43**	**65**	**99**	**2.24**	**2.19**	**0.99**	**545**	**610**	**488**	**3.8**	**2.7**	**13.7**	**5.0**	**65%**	**16%**	**35**	**24**	**41**	**32%**	**81%**	**9%**	**0**						**12.1**	**186**	**221**	**$26**

Janssen,Casey

Age: 33	Th: R	Role RP	Health	D	LIMA Plan	B+
Ht: 6' 4"	Wt: 205	Type	PT/Exp	B	Rand Var	0
			Consist	B	MM	4230

Missed six weeks with a bad back, and essentially shared closer role in September. A July bout of food poisoning seemed to trigger 2H Dom decline—1H was as solid as ever—though that doesn't explain uptick in FB. Don't discount the "D" health grade, especially at his age, but he's only hit the DL twice in five years.

Yr Tm	W	L	Sv	IP	K	ERA	xERA	WHIP	oOPS	vL	vR	BF/G	Ctl	Dom	Cmd	FpK	SwK	G	L	F	H%	S%	hr/f	GS	APC	DOM%	DIS%	Sv%	LI	RAR	BPV	BPX	R$
10 TOR	5	2	0	69	63	3.67	3.57	1.38	748	798	709	5.3	2.8	8.3	3.0	64%	9%	47	22	31	34%	77%	12%	0	21			0	0.48	3.5	99	161	$1
11 TOR	6	0	2	56	53	2.26	3.08	1.10	594	539	659	4.1	2.3	8.6	3.8	64%	9%	47	21	31	30%	80%	4%	0	16			50	0.85	11.5	118	178	$7
12 TOR	1	1	22	64	67	2.54	2.92	0.86	564	467	666	3.9	1.6	9.5	6.1	62%	10%	43	21	36	25%	77%	12%	0	15			88	1.03	11.5	149	195	$17
13 TOR	4	1	34	53	50	2.56	3.10	0.99	558	619	458	3.8	2.2	8.5	3.8	64%	8%	48	23	30	27%	76%	7%	0	15			94	1.39	8.5	120	156	$18
14 TOR	3	3	25	46	28	3.94	4.32	1.18	697	733	669	3.8	1.4	5.5	4.0	68%	8%	34	22	44	29%	71%	9%	0	14			83	0.96	-1.1	74	88	$9
1st Half	2	0	12	17	13	1.06	3.26	0.94	519	631	379	3.7	0.5	6.9	13.0	67%	10%	41	24	35	30%	88%	0%	0	14			86	0.98	5.6	129	154	$12
2nd Half	1	3	13	29	15	5.65	4.98	1.33	795	823	780	3.9	1.9	4.7	2.5	69%	7%	31	21	48	28%	63%	13%	0	14			81	0.95	-6.8	43	51	$7
15 Proj	**4**	**2**	**33**	**58**	**46**	**3.23**	**3.28**	**1.09**	**638**	**650**	**626**	**3.7**	**1.7**	**7.2**	**4.2**	**66%**	**8%**	**41**	**22**	**37**	**28%**	**74%**	**9%**	**0**						**3.7**	**102**	**121**	**$16**

MATT CEDERHOLM

Jeffress,Jeremy

Age: 27	Th: R	Role RP	Health A	LIMA Plan C	
Ht: 6' 1"	Wt: 205	Type Pwr xGB	PT/Exp D	Rand Var -3	
			Consist B	MM 4200	

1-1, 2.81 ERA in 32 IP at TOR/MIL. He's still only 27 so there's room to get better. High GB%, 3.6 Cmd after July promotion and league average FpK suggest Ctl improvement. A 46% H% vs. LHB mostly explains the huge L/R split. With a correction and continued development, he could solidify his role.

Yr Tm	W	L	Sv	IP	K	ERA	xERA	WHIP	oOPS	vL	vR	BF/G	Ctl	Dom	Cmd	FpK	SwK	G	L	F	H%	S%	hr/f	GS	APC	DOM%	DIS%	Sv%	LI	RAR	BPV	BPX	R$
10 MIL	1	0	0	10	8	2.70	4.24	1.40	676	792	619	4.2	5.4	7.2	1.3	45%	7%	54	14	32	28%	79%	0%	0	18			0	0.41	1.7	16	26	-$2
11 KC *	4	7	4	71	48	5.78	5.48	1.80	706	790	619	8.4	6.3	6.1	1.0	43%	8%	56	12	32	32%	68%	8%	0	22			67	1.11	-16.1	28	42	-$9
12 KC *	5	4	3	73	63	5.80	4.59	1.62	838	594	1029	6.3	4.8	7.9	1.6	53%	9%	48	26	26	35%	62%	0%	0	22			43	0.64	-16.0	66	87	-$9
13 TOR *	2	0	7	38	35	1.78	3.43	1.43	592	284	829	4.6	4.5	8.3	1.8	60%	12%	69	23	8	32%	88%	50%	0	19			88	0.67	9.7	86	113	$3
14 2 TM *	5	2	5	74	65	2.29	3.62	1.43	709	967	509	5.0	3.7	7.9	2.2	60%	7%	59	26	16	34%	83%	7%	0	16			63	0.85	13.2	91	109	$4
1st Half	4	1	1	37	35	3.14	4.07	1.59	1219	1208	1238	6.2	4.5	8.6	1.9	71%	8%	42	33	25	37%	78%	0%	0	28			33	0.04	2.7	91	109	$1
2nd Half	1	1	4	37	30	1.46	3.17	1.27	624	914	415	4.2	2.8	7.2	2.6	58%	7%	62	24	14	32%	89%	9%	0	15			80	0.94	10.4	95	114	$8
15 Proj	3	2	0	58	50	3.11	3.23	1.45	635	918	430	5.2	3.9	7.8	2.0	58%	7%	62	24	14	33%	78%	7%	0						4.5	75	89	$0

Jennings,Dan

Age: 28	Th: L	Role RP	Health B	LIMA Plan C	
Ht: 6' 3"	Wt: 210	Type Pwr	PT/Exp C	Rand Var -5	
			Consist B	MM 3200	

Concussion and two brief demotions cost him PT. A 95% strand rate explains huge ERA-xERA gap, but SwK hints at continued Dom growth. That's a positive. But Ctl is a major obstacle to sustained success. Just can't get ahead of hitters - those are POOR FpK rates - so odds are his ERA will spike.

Yr Tm	W	L	Sv	IP	K	ERA	xERA	WHIP	oOPS	vL	vR	BF/G	Ctl	Dom	Cmd	FpK	SwK	G	L	F	H%	S%	hr/f	GS	APC	DOM%	DIS%	Sv%	LI	RAR	BPV	BPX	R$
10 aa	4	2	0	53	40	3.16	4.13	1.62				6.3	4.8	6.8	1.4						34%	78%								6.0	70	113	-$1
11 a/a	5	4	4	56	46	5.50	4.89	1.65				5.6	4.5	7.4	1.7						35%	65%								-10.8	60	90	-$4
12 MIA *	2	3	2	71	50	3.34	4.23	1.47	771	788	753	4.7	3.7	6.3	1.7	48%	7%	45	20	35	32%	78%	9%	0	15			50	0.62	5.9	58	76	-$1
13 MIA *	6	6	1	66	58	3.24	3.42	1.39	714	745	675	4.2	3.9	7.9	2.0	53%	11%	49	20	32	32%	76%	3%	0	14			25	1.24	5.0	86	112	$1
14 MIA	0	2	0	40	38	1.34	3.92	1.54	738	753	724	3.9	3.8	8.5	2.2	52%	12%	49	20	32	36%	95%	8%	0	15			0	0.75	12.0	77	92	-$1
1st Half	0	1	0	23	23	0.79	3.94	1.54	729	612	827	4.3	4.4	9.1	2.1	54%	13%	49	18	33	35%	100%	9%	0	17			0	1.11	8.2	74	88	-$1
2nd Half	0	1	0	18	15	2.04	3.88	1.53	751	915	572	3.4	3.1	7.6	2.5	50%	11%	48	21	30	36%	88%	6%	0	14			0	0.38	3.7	81	97	-$1
15 Proj	2	3	0	50	43	3.59	3.66	1.40	694	735	651	4.0	3.8	7.8	2.1	52%	11%	49	20	31	32%	74%	6%	0						0.9	65	77	-$2

Jepsen,Kevin

Age: 30	Th: R	Role RP	Health D	LIMA Plan A	
Ht: 6' 3"	Wt: 235	Type Pwr	PT/Exp D	Rand Var -1	
			Consist C	MM 4410	

Good health likely drove this rebound, and Dom found a new level. Huge FpK jump makes us think 2nd half Ctl can stand, and prior years support 2nd half GB. Health history highlights risk, but these are the skills of an elite reliever, with saves upside... if he can repeat these levels.

Yr Tm	W	L	Sv	IP	K	ERA	xERA	WHIP	oOPS	vL	vR	BF/G	Ctl	Dom	Cmd	FpK	SwK	G	L	F	H%	S%	hr/f	GS	APC	DOM%	DIS%	Sv%	LI	RAR	BPV	BPX	R$
10 LAA	2	4	0	59	61	3.97	3.36	1.41	665	669	661	3.7	4.4	9.3	2.1	62%	11%	56	18	26	33%	70%	5%	0	15			0	1.22	0.8	82	133	-$1
11 LAA *	2	5	7	41	22	5.42	6.33	1.75	981	894	1068	4.7	3.6	4.7	1.3	54%	7%	55	16	29	35%	71%	13%	0	14			64	1.32	-7.6	10	14	-$4
12 LAA *	5	4	4	70	65	3.08	2.72	1.14	647	744	552	3.8	2.6	8.4	3.2	52%	9%	35	23	42	30%	73%	6%	0	14			67	1.16	8.0	112	146	$7
13 LAA	1	3	0	36	36	4.50	4.10	1.53	769	865	679	3.6	3.5	9.0	2.6	53%	9%	40	20	39	37%	71%	7%	0	15			0	1.12	-2.8	86	111	-$5
14 LAA	0	2	2	65	75	2.63	2.93	1.05	547	628	470	3.5	3.2	10.4	3.3	65%	13%	48	20	33	27%	77%	8%	0	14			50	1.04	8.9	127	151	$5
1st Half	0	0	0	32	39	2.53	3.11	1.13	601	732	459	3.4	4.2	11.0	2.6	66%	15%	44	18	38	26%	82%	11%	0	13			0	0.89	4.8	106	126	$3
2nd Half	0	2	2	33	36	2.73	2.77	0.97	496	518	478	3.6	2.2	9.8	4.5	65%	11%	51	21	29	29%	71%	4%	0	15			100	1.19	4.1	146	175	$7
15 Proj	1	4	3	65	68	3.38	3.14	1.23	641	718	567	3.6	3.2	9.4	3.0	60%	11%	45	20	35	31%	73%	7%	0						2.9	106	126	$2

Jimenez,Ubaldo

Age: 31	Th: R	Role SP	Health C	LIMA Plan D+	
Ht: 6' 5"	Wt: 210	Type Pwr FB	PT/Exp A	Rand Var 0	
			Consist C	MM 1403	

Rediscovered poor control in spectacular fashion. Missed time with a bad ankle, but skills were off all year: FB was 2 mph slower, SwK trend is all down, and FpK is a mess. That's now three "disaster" seasons in four years—even if 2010 were a possible prize, it's not a lottery ticket worth scratching.

Yr Tm	W	L	Sv	IP	K	ERA	xERA	WHIP	oOPS	vL	vR	BF/G	Ctl	Dom	Cmd	FpK	SwK	G	L	F	H%	S%	hr/f	GS	APC	DOM%	DIS%	Sv%	LI	RAR	BPV	BPX	R$
10 COL	19	8	0	222	214	2.88	3.42	1.15	610	582	638	27.1	3.7	8.7	2.3	56%	10%	49	16	35	27%	75%	5%	33	109	82%	6%			32.7	83	134	$26
11 2 TM	10	13	0	188	180	4.68	3.72	1.40	752	710	791	25.7	3.7	8.6	2.3	53%	8%	47	20	33	32%	67%	9%	32	102	44%	22%			-17.2	79	119	-$1
12 CLE	9	17	0	177	143	5.40	5.03	1.61	817	854	778	26.0	4.8	7.3	1.5	52%	8%	38	23	38	32%	69%	12%	31	101	35%	19%			-30.2	16	21	-$16
13 CLE	13	9	0	183	194	3.30	3.66	1.33	684	661	708	24.3	3.9	9.6	2.4	58%	9%	44	20	36	31%	78%	9%	32	99	56%	19%			12.7	88	114	$11
14 BAL	6	9	0	125	116	4.81	4.47	1.52	737	779	683	22.1	5.5	8.3	1.5	55%	7%	41	22	37	29%	70%	11%	22	92	32%	36%	0	0.74	-16.5	20	23	-$7
1st Half	3	8	0	96	84	4.31	4.23	1.48	727	765	682	24.5	5.1	7.9	1.6	56%	7%	46	22	32	29%	73%	12%	17	102	35%	35%			-6.8	29	35	-$6
2nd Half	3	1	0	29	32	6.44	5.23	1.64	772	813	681	17.0	7.1	9.8	1.4	53%	7%	24	23	53	29%	61%	10%	5	71	20%	40%	0	0.71	-9.8	-12	-14	-$11
15 Proj	8	11	0	145	143	4.62	4.09	1.49	740	762	711	23.2	5.2	8.9	1.7	55%	8%	38	21	41	30%	71%	10%	25						-15.8	35	41	-$4

Johnson,Jim

Age: 32	Th: R	Role RP	Health A	LIMA Plan C	
Ht: 6' 6"	Wt: 240	Type Pwr xGB	PT/Exp A	Rand Var +5	
			Consist B	MM 3210	

While H%/S% and xERA say "bad luck," Ctl skyrocketed—despite FpK increase. There's no injury or velocity drop to explain it; looks like an outlier. Skills were near closer-worthy for 4 years prior, and managers love guys with 9th inning experience. A recovery is plausible, so more saves might be just an injury away.

Yr Tm	W	L	Sv	IP	K	ERA	xERA	WHIP	oOPS	vL	vR	BF/G	Ctl	Dom	Cmd	FpK	SwK	G	L	F	H%	S%	hr/f	GS	APC	DOM%	DIS%	Sv%	LI	RAR	BPV	BPX	R$
10 BAL	1	1	1	26	22	3.42	3.40	1.41	722	668	773	4.5	1.7	7.5	4.4	64%	10%	51	24	24	36%	77%	10%	0	16			17	1.53	2.1	118	191	-$1
11 BAL	6	5	9	91	58	2.67	3.32	1.11	628	567	690	5.3	2.1	5.7	2.8	64%	10%	61	15	24	27%	77%	8%	0	18			64	1.11	14.3	86	130	$12
12 BAL	2	1	51	69	41	2.49	3.41	1.02	556	581	526	3.8	2.0	5.4	2.7	57%	7%	62	16	21	25%	76%	7%	0	14			94	1.29	12.9	84	109	$27
13 BAL	3	8	50	70	56	2.94	3.17	1.28	699	740	653	3.9	2.3	7.2	3.1	61%	9%	58	20	21	32%	79%	11%	0	15			85	1.39	8.0	103	134	$22
14 2 AL	5	2	2	53	42	7.09	4.66	1.95	861	941	776	4.9	5.9	7.1	1.2	63%	8%	58	20	22	37%	63%	14%	0	18			67	0.60	-22.0	4	5	-$12
1st Half	4	2	2	35	26	5.14	4.67	1.94	824	887	748	5.4	5.4	6.7	1.2	63%	8%	56	22	21	38%	74%	12%	0	20			67	0.70	-6.1	9	11	-$10
2nd Half	1	0	0	18	16	10.80	4.61	1.96	936	1070	823	4.1	6.9	7.9	1.1	63%	6%	62	16	22	36%	41%	17%	0	16			0	0.44	-16.0	-4	-5	-$15
15 Proj	2	2	6	36	29	3.66	3.38	1.37	708	759	656	4.0	3.5	7.1	2.0	62%	8%	60	18	22	31%	75%	12%	0						0.4	72	86	$1

Johnson,Josh

Age: 31	Th: R	Role SP	Health F	LIMA Plan C	
Ht: 6' 7"	Wt: 245	Type Pwr	PT/Exp C	Rand Var 0	
			Consist A	MM 4300	

Missed the season with Tommy John surgery (April). If you're counting, that's 400+ days on the DL in four years. Skills are very good, but he's reached 200 IP once (and 180 IP three times) in his 10-year career. Only consider after several months of proving his worth. Even then, have a contingency plan.

Yr Tm	W	L	Sv	IP	K	ERA	xERA	WHIP	oOPS	vL	vR	BF/G	Ctl	Dom	Cmd	FpK	SwK	G	L	F	H%	S%	hr/f	GS	APC	DOM%	DIS%	Sv%	LI	RAR	BPV	BPX	R$
10 FLA	11	6	0	184	186	2.30	3.11	1.11	607	612	602	26.6	2.4	9.1	3.9	64%	12%	46	21	34	31%	80%	4%	28	107	71%	4%			40.2	125	202	$24
11 FLA	3	1	0	60	56	1.64	3.18	0.98	509	579	422	26.0	3.0	8.4	2.8	55%	9%	51	15	34	24%	84%	4%	9	104	67%	0%			17.1	99	149	$8
12 MIA	8	14	0	191	165	3.81	3.79	1.28	678	691	661	25.7	3.1	7.8	2.5	58%	10%	46	24	30	31%	71%	8%	31	101	65%	13%			4.8	81	106	$7
13 TOR	2	8	0	81	83	6.20	3.89	1.66	852	727	1032	24.0	3.3	9.2	2.8	61%	10%	45	24	31	38%	66%	19%	16	92	44%	25%			-23.4	99	129	-$13
14																																	
1st Half																																	
2nd Half																																	
15 Proj	2	2	0	44	41	3.54	3.33	1.29	675	663	690	24.7	3.2	8.4	2.6	59%	10%	47	20	32	31%	74%	10%	7						1.1	90	107	-$1

Kahnle,Thomas

Age: 25	Th: R	Role RP	Health B	LIMA Plan D+	
Ht: 6' 1"	Wt: 230	Type Pwr	PT/Exp D	Rand Var 0	
			Consist A	MM 2401	

Interesting juxtaposition: A first half of poor skills/good results, then reversed completely in the second half. We'll take the skills growth, as terrible H%/S% is all that stood between him and a solid 2nd half ERA. Is he closer material? 24 IP of closer-worthy stats are interesting but 45% FpK says there's a ways to go..

Yr Tm	W	L	Sv	IP	K	ERA	xERA	WHIP	oOPS	vL	vR	BF/G	Ctl	Dom	Cmd	FpK	SwK	G	L	F	H%	S%	hr/f	GS	APC	DOM%	DIS%	Sv%	LI	RAR	BPV	BPX	R$
10																																	
11																																	
12																																	
13 aa	1	3	15	60	61	3.73	3.89	1.58				5.7	7.3	9.2	1.3						27%	78%								1.0	70	91	$2
14 COL	2	1	0	69	63	4.19	3.82	1.19	628	570	683	5.3	4.1	8.3	2.0	50%	11%	47	17	36	25%	67%	10%	0	20			0	0.83	-3.8	64	76	-$1
1st Half	2	1	0	44	34	2.44	4.06	1.06	570	544	591	5.6	4.3	6.9	1.6	53%	11%	47	15	38	19%	81%	9%	0	21			0	0.59	7.1	34	40	$4
2nd Half	0	0	0	24	29	7.40	3.38	1.44	719	604	856	4.8	3.7	10.7	2.9	45%	13%	48	20	32	36%	47%	14%	0	20			0	1.15	-11.0	119	142	-$10
15 Proj	1	2	0	73	74	3.83	3.81	1.47	673	577	771	5.3	5.3	9.1	1.7	48%	12%	47	18	34	31%	75%	8%	0						-0.8	47	56	-$3

MATT CEDERHOLM

Kaneko,Chihiro

Age: 31	Th: R	Role SP	Health A	LIMA Plan D+	
Ht: 0' 0"	Wt: 0	Type Pwr	PT/Exp A	Rand Var 0	
			Consist B	MM 3203	

One of Japan's best pitchers, but not in the same class as Yu Darvish or Masahiro Tanaka. A few years older, he relies more on pitch mix and deception than velocity. Technically, he won't be a free agent until after the 2015 season so the timing of his debut is a question. Think contributor, not game-changer.

Yr	Tm	W	L	Sv	IP	K	ERA	xERA	WHIP	oOPS	vL	vR	BF/G	Ctl	Dom	Cmd	FpK	SwK	G	L	F	H%	S%	hr/f	GS	APC	DOM%	DIS%	Sv%	LI	RAR	BPV	BPX	R$
10	for	17	8	0	204	180	4.11	4.02	1.24				27.6	2.4	8.0	3.3						30%	71%								-0.8	84	135	$13
11	for	10	4	0	155	117	3.03	3.26	1.18				31.0	2.7	6.8	2.5						27%	78%								17.5	74	112	$13
12	for	4	3	0	64	53	2.97	3.99	1.38				29.9	2.6	7.5	2.9						34%	79%								8.3	90	117	$1
13	for	15	8	0	223	190	2.51	2.71	1.12				30.3	2.9	7.7	2.6						27%	81%								37.4	92	120	$27
14	for	15	5	0	184	184	2.37	2.86	1.14				29.1	2.5	9.0	3.6						31%	81%								31.1	121	144	$21
1st Half																																		
2nd Half																																		
15	Proj	12	8	0	174	142	3.74	3.61	1.28				24.5	2.9	7.4	2.5	62%	8%	44	20	36	29%	76%	14%	23						0.1	75	90	$8

Karns,Nathan

Age: 27	Th: R	Role SP	Health A	LIMA Plan D+	
Ht: 6' 3"	Wt: 230	Type Pwr	PT/Exp D	Rand Var +5	
			Consist B	MM 0301	

1-1, 4.50 ERA in 12 IP at TAM. Lofty minor-league Dom totals came down to Earth at higher levels, but scouts still like his potential. Control is the key. It's better than it was (2013 and 2H), but needs more improvement and consistency. As it is, there are few signs of growth—expect struggles.

Yr	Tm	W	L	Sv	IP	K	ERA	xERA	WHIP	oOPS	vL	vR	BF/G	Ctl	Dom	Cmd	FpK	SwK	G	L	F	H%	S%	hr/f	GS	APC	DOM%	DIS%	Sv%	LI	RAR	BPV	BPX	R$
10																																		
11																																		
12																																		
13	WAS *	10	7	0	145	130	4.48	4.73	1.43	1060	1266	845	23.6	3.5	8.1	2.3	64%	10%	36	31	33	32%	73%	36%	3	82	0%	100%			-10.9	59	77	-$2
14	TAM *	10	10	0	157	134	6.43	5.52	1.62	661	384	859	24.1	4.1	7.7	1.9	49%	10%	43	13	43	34%	61%	23%	2	103	50%	0%			-52.1	46	55	-$19
1st Half		4	5	0	80	69	7.88	6.09	1.74				22.8	4.9	7.8	1.6						35%	55%	0%	0						-40.8	33	40	-$30
2nd Half		6	5	0	77	65	4.93	4.94	1.50	661	384	859	25.7	3.2	7.6	2.4	49%	10%	43	13	43	34%	69%	23%	2	103	50%	0%			-11.3	62	74	-$8
15	Proj	8	7	0	116	101	5.47	5.17	1.53				24.1	3.7	7.8	2.1	0%	0%				33%	66%		21						-24.8	52	62	-$8

Kazmir,Scott

Age: 31	Th: L	Role SP	Health F	LIMA Plan C+	
Ht: 6' 0"	Wt: 185	Type Pwr	PT/Exp B	Rand Var 0	
			Consist A	MM 3305	

Do you believe now? Sure, home park helped, but second year of solid skills confirms 2013 breakout. Dom decline is a minor concern, but improved Ctl kept Cmd solid, and G/F is now a positive. Still owns poor health grade, but it's three years since a significant injury. The odds to repeat are in his favor.

Yr	Tm	W	L	Sv	IP	K	ERA	xERA	WHIP	oOPS	vL	vR	BF/G	Ctl	Dom	Cmd	FpK	SwK	G	L	F	H%	S%	hr/f	GS	APC	DOM%	DIS%	Sv%	LI	RAR	BPV	BPX	R$
10	LAA	9	15	0	150	93	5.94	5.30	1.58	841	790	855	24.4	4.7	5.6	1.2	57%	8%	39	17	44	29%	65%	12%	28	98	18%	46%			-34.4	-11	-17	-$11
11	LAA *	0	5	0	17	11	17.90	9.61	2.94	1643	2667	1214	16.3	11.1	5.8	0.5	36%	3%	30	10	60	43%	33%	17%	1	63	0%	100%			-29.3	9	14	-$16
12																																		
13	CLE	10	9	0	158	162	4.04	3.53	1.32	735	573	794	23.2	2.7	9.2	3.4	61%	11%	41	23	36	34%	73%	12%	29	95	52%	21%			-3.5	113	147	$4
14	OAK	15	9	0	190	164	3.55	3.60	1.16	648	673	641	24.3	2.4	7.8	3.3	62%	10%	44	19	37	29%	71%	8%	32	93	66%	19%			4.6	98	116	$13
1st Half		9	3	0	103	91	2.61	3.30	1.03	609	697	583	24.1	2.1	7.9	3.8	59%	11%	48	16	36	26%	79%	10%	17	93	71%	12%			14.4	113	134	$24
2nd Half		6	6	0	87	73	4.66	3.96	1.32	693	650	709	24.5	2.7	7.6	2.8	66%	9%	39	23	39	33%	64%	6%	15	94	60%	27%			-9.8	80	95	-$1
15	Proj	13	11	0	181	159	3.73	3.50	1.25	675	612	695	23.0	2.9	7.9	2.8	61%	10%	41	21	38	30%	72%	8%	32						0.3	84	101	$10

Kelley,Shawn

Age: 31	Th: R	Role RP	Health F	LIMA Plan A	
Ht: 6' 2"	Wt: 220	Type Pwr xFB	PT/Exp D	Rand Var +4	
			Consist A	MM 4510	

Luck has got to turn soon. Strong skills highlighted by jump in Dom, with SwK to match. FpK suggests small-sample 2H Ctl gains could stick. FB profile leaves him vulnerable to hr/f variation, but path to saves will be deterred only by the quality of the competition for save opportunities. Sneaky end-gamer.

Yr	Tm	W	L	Sv	IP	K	ERA	xERA	WHIP	oOPS	vL	vR	BF/G	Ctl	Dom	Cmd	FpK	SwK	G	L	F	H%	S%	hr/f	GS	APC	DOM%	DIS%	Sv%	LI	RAR	BPV	BPX	R$
10	SEA	3	1	0	25	26	3.96	4.63	1.52	841	696	968	5.1	4.3	9.4	2.2	60%	12%	23	16	61	32%	82%	12%	0	20			0	0.88	0.4	53	85	-$2
11	SEA *	1	1	0	30	25	0.92	2.69	1.08	417	683	226	4.7	2.7	7.3	2.7	62%	12%	38	6	56	26%	99%	0%	0	17			0	0.56	11.3	89	134	$2
12	SEA *	4	4	6	64	65	2.52	2.83	1.12	717	747	701	4.2	2.7	9.1	3.4	60%	12%	29	20	51	29%	81%	8%	0	16			67	1.00	11.8	115	150	$8
13	NYY	4	2	0	53	71	4.39	3.42	1.31	729	760	707	4.0	3.9	12.0	3.1	65%	12%	33	21	46	33%	71%	13%	0	17			0	1.33	-3.4	122	159	-$1
14	NYY	3	6	4	52	67	4.53	3.30	1.26	663	612	709	3.7	3.5	11.7	3.4	61%	15%	34	23	44	34%	65%	9%	0	15			57	1.33	-5.0	128	152	$0
1st Half		1	2	4	22	25	4.43	4.06	1.43	697	660	740	4.0	4.4	10.1	2.3	58%	12%	31	24	46	34%	68%	4%	0	16			80	1.09	-1.9	70	84	-$2
2nd Half		2	4	0	29	42	4.60	2.77	1.13	635	567	686	3.6	2.8	12.9	4.7	64%	18%	36	22	42	33%	62%	14%	0	15			0	1.50	-3.1	172	205	$2
15	Proj	4	5	2	58	71	3.83	3.15	1.21	652	638	661	3.8	3.5	11.0	3.1	63%	14%	32	21	47	31%	71%	9%	0						-0.6	113	134	$2

Kelly,Casey

Age: 25	Th: R	Role SP	Health F	LIMA Plan C	
Ht: 6' 3"	Wt: 210	Type	PT/Exp F	Rand Var 0	
			Consist F	MM 1200	

Missed his second straight season following Tommy John surgery in April 2013; developed elbow soreness in May and didn't pitch again. He's only 25, and was pitching well in rehab, with a 17:1 K:BB in 20 IP. The long-term potential is still there, as long as he suffers no more setbacks.

Yr	Tm	W	L	Sv	IP	K	ERA	xERA	WHIP	oOPS	vL	vR	BF/G	Ctl	Dom	Cmd	FpK	SwK	G	L	F	H%	S%	hr/f	GS	APC	DOM%	DIS%	Sv%	LI	RAR	BPV	BPX	R$
10	aa	3	5	0	95	69	5.78	5.84	1.69				20.4	3.1	6.6	2.1						37%	66%								-19.9	47	76	-$10
11	aa	11	6	0	142	95	3.72	3.88	1.38				22.1	2.7	6.0	2.2						32%	72%								3.9	71	106	$4
12	SD *	2	4	0	58	54	4.52	4.11	1.29	896	892	900	21.6	2.0	8.5	4.3	52%	10%	56	17	27	34%	66%	19%	6	84	33%	50%			-3.6	114	148	-$3
13																																		
14																																		
1st Half																																		
2nd Half																																		
15	Proj	2	2	0	41	32	4.39	4.26	1.38				20.7	2.6	7.1	2.7	0%	0%				33%	69%		8						-3.3	75	89	-$3

Kelly,Joe

Age: 27	Th: R	Role SP	Health D	LIMA Plan D+	
Ht: 6' 1"	Wt: 175	Type GB	PT/Exp C	Rand Var 0	
			Consist A	MM 2003	

Missed 12 weeks with a bad hamstring. Doesn't generate much swing-and-miss for a guy who throws in the mid-90s. While Dom trend is up, it's been at the expense of Ctl, making for an ugly Cmd trend. His penchant for winning more games than deserved isn't really a skill. Let his xERA be your guide.

Yr	Tm	W	L	Sv	IP	K	ERA	xERA	WHIP	oOPS	vL	vR	BF/G	Ctl	Dom	Cmd	FpK	SwK	G	L	F	H%	S%	hr/f	GS	APC	DOM%	DIS%	Sv%	LI	RAR	BPV	BPX	R$
10																																		
11	aa	6	4	0	59	43	4.33	4.78	1.53				23.4	3.4	6.5	1.9						34%	72%								-2.9	54	81	-$2
12	STL *	7	12	0	179	112	3.35	4.17	1.40	740	917	607	21.0	2.8	5.6	2.0	60%	8%	52	21	27	32%	77%	11%	16	71	44%	6%	0	0.78	14.6	57	74	$3
13	STL	10	5	0	124	79	2.69	4.17	1.35	694	691	696	14.4	3.2	5.7	1.8	55%	8%	51	21	28	30%	83%	9%	15	53	33%	13%	0	0.87	18.1	46	60	$7
14	2 TM	6	4	0	96	66	4.20	4.00	1.35	693	689	695	24.4	3.9	6.2	1.6	57%	7%	55	21	24	28%	70%	11%	17	93	41%	24%			-5.5	38	45	-$2
1st Half		1	1	0	15	9	0.59	3.61	1.24	584	705	448	21.7	2.3	5.3	2.3	57%	8%	58	24	18	30%	95%	0%	3	80	33%	33%			6.0	68	81	-$4
2nd Half		5	3	0	81	57	4.89	4.08	1.37	714	687	743	25.0	4.2	6.3	1.5	57%	7%	54	21	25	27%	65%	13%	14	96	43%	21%			-11.5	32	39	-$1
15	Proj	11	8	0	160	104	3.88	3.96	1.39	707	746	669	22.7	3.6	5.9	1.6	57%	8%	52	20	28	30%	73%	9%	28						-2.7	39	46	$2

Kendrick,Kyle

Age: 30	Th: R	Role SP	Health A	LIMA Plan D+	
Ht: 6' 3"	Wt: 210	Type Con	PT/Exp A	Rand Var 0	
			Consist A	MM 2005	

Certainly deserves his "A" consistency grade—even DOM/DIS shows a great amount of stability. The only thing that's really fluctuated is H%/S%, while xERA is a flat line of mediocrity. His results as a full-time starter are not encouraging, and low-strikeout innings-eaters have limited value at the draft table.

Yr	Tm	W	L	Sv	IP	K	ERA	xERA	WHIP	oOPS	vL	vR	BF/G	Ctl	Dom	Cmd	FpK	SwK	G	L	F	H%	S%	hr/f	GS	APC	DOM%	DIS%	Sv%	LI	RAR	BPV	BPX	R$
10	PHI	11	10	0	181	84	4.73	4.68	1.37	807	902	713	23.4	2.4	4.2	1.7	60%	5%	45	17	38	29%	69%	11%	31	86	32%	32%	0	0.74	-14.6	32	52	-$1
11	PHI	8	6	0	115	59	3.22	4.27	1.22	734	766	708	14.1	2.4	4.6	2.0	60%	6%	45	19	36	27%	79%	11%	15	51	47%	40%	0	0.87	10.2	43	64	$6
12	PHI	11	12	0	159	116	3.90	4.21	1.27	731	701	760	18.2	2.8	6.6	2.4	63%	10%	47	18	36	29%	73%	11%	25	68	52%	28%	0	1.06	2.3	68	89	$6
13	PHI	10	13	0	182	110	4.70	4.24	1.40	751	679	812	26.7	2.3	5.4	2.3	63%	7%	49	20	31	32%	67%	10%	30	96	47%	23%			-18.7	62	81	-$5
14	PHI	10	13	0	199	121	4.61	4.35	1.36	769	826	725	27.0	2.6	5.5	2.1	63%	8%	45	21	35	30%	69%	11%	32	97	56%	16%			-21.4	52	62	-$5
1st Half		3	8	0	102	65	4.22	4.32	1.35	741	923	611	27.9	2.6	5.7	2.2	66%	8%	45	20	35	30%	71%	9%	16	101	56%	13%			-6.1	55	66	-$5
2nd Half		7	5	0	97	56	5.03	4.38	1.38	798	731	854	26.2	2.5	5.2	2.1	60%	7%	44	22	34	30%	66%	13%	16	93	56%	19%			-15.3	48	57	-$5
15	Proj	11	12	0	181	110	4.51	4.04	1.36	768	765	770	23.1	2.6	5.4	2.1	62%	8%	45	20	35	30%	70%	11%	33						-17.2	50	60	-$1

MATT CEDERHOLM

Kennedy,Ian

Age: 30	Th: R	Role: SP	Health: A	LIMA Plan: B
Ht: 6' 0"	Wt: 190	Type: Pwr	PT/Exp: A	Rand Var: 0
			Consist: A	MM: 3305

Can't completely trust Dom jump, as 1st half was out of line with SwK, history. 2nd half FpK points to continued Ctl improvement, and AAA Reliability and DOM/DIS speak to his stability despite ERA variance. Might not hit 200 K again, but a repeat is within reach.

Yr Tm	W	L	Sv	IP	K	ERA	xERA	WHIP	oOPS	vL	vR	BF/G	Ctl	Dom	Cmd	FpK	SwK	G	L	F	H%	S%	hr/f	GS	APC	DOM%	DIS%	Sv%	LI	RAR	BPV	BPX	R$
10 ARI	9	10	0	194	168	3.80	4.01	1.20	696	674	716	25.3	3.2	7.8	2.4	63%	9%	37	19	44	27%	73%	11%	32	99	63%	13%			6.6	68	109	$12
11 ARI	21	4	0	222	198	2.88	3.50	1.09	641	656	626	27.3	2.2	8.0	3.6	64%	9%	39	22	40	28%	77%	8%	33	104	70%	6%			29.1	101	152	$28
12 ARI	15	12	0	208	187	4.02	4.06	1.30	775	790	759	27.2	2.4	8.1	3.4	65%	11%	37	21	42	32%	73%	11%	33	102	58%	9%			-0.1	96	126	$9
13 2 NL	7	10	0	181	163	4.91	4.14	1.40	781	828	736	25.6	3.6	8.1	2.2	62%	10%	38	23	39	31%	68%	13%	31	100	48%	19%			-23.4	64	83	-$6
14 SD	13	13	0	201	207	3.63	3.56	1.29	698	689	706	25.6	3.1	9.3	3.0	64%	11%	40	23	38	32%	73%	8%	33	103	70%	3%			2.8	100	119	$9
1st Half	5	9	0	103	111	4.01	3.28	1.23	718	685	744	25.3	2.4	9.7	4.1	60%	10%	41	21	38	34%	69%	8%	17	104	82%	0%			-3.4	129	154	$7
2nd Half	8	4	0	98	96	3.23	3.87	1.35	677	692	662	26.0	4.0	8.8	2.2	68%	11%	38	25	37	31%	78%	7%	16	102	56%	6%			6.2	69	82	$10
15 Proj	**12**	**11**	**0**	**196**	**182**	**3.75**	**3.58**	**1.31**	**726**	**739**	**714**	**25.1**	**3.2**	**8.4**	**2.6**	**64%**	**10%**	**39**	**21**	**40**	**31%**	**74%**	**9%**	**32**						**-0.2**	**81**	**97**	**$9**

Kershaw,Clayton

Age: 27	Th: L	Role: SP	Health: B	LIMA Plan: C
Ht: 6' 3"	Wt: 225	Type: Pwr	PT/Exp: A	Rand Var: -3
			Consist: A	MM: 5505

As if he needed to improve his skills—now they've gone from "ridiculous" to "ludicrous." Every stat here is completely supported by pure skill, and at superhuman levels. Missed 5 weeks with an inflamed Teres Major (upper back), but he's been durable despite 16,000+ pitches in 5 years. What comes after "ludricrous"?

Yr Tm	W	L	Sv	IP	K	ERA	xERA	WHIP	oOPS	vL	vR	BF/G	Ctl	Dom	Cmd	FpK	SwK	G	L	F	H%	S%	hr/f	GS	APC	DOM%	DIS%	Sv%	LI	RAR	BPV	BPX	R$
10 LA	13	10	0	204	212	2.91	3.61	1.18	615	673	599	26.5	3.6	9.3	2.6	60%	11%	40	18	42	29%	77%	6%	32	106	81%	13%			29.5	90	145	$22
11 LA	21	5	0	233	248	2.28	2.95	0.98	554	512	563	27.6	2.1	9.6	4.6	64%	12%	43	18	39	28%	79%	7%	33	105	88%	3%			48.0	137	206	$40
12 LA	14	9	0	228	229	2.53	3.23	1.02	593	570	599	27.3	2.5	9.1	3.6	65%	11%	47	19	34	27%	78%	8%	33	105	82%	6%			41.7	121	157	$36
13 LA	16	9	0	236	232	1.83	2.93	0.92	521	477	532	27.5	2.0	8.8	4.5	65%	12%	46	23	31	26%	82%	6%	33	104	88%	3%			59.2	130	169	$44
14 LA	21	3	0	198	239	1.77	2.27	0.86	521	477	531	27.7	1.4	10.8	7.7	69%	15%	52	19	29	29%	81%	7%	27	101	93%	4%			48.2	187	223	$40
1st Half	9	2	0	79	107	2.04	1.91	0.92	559	419	595	25.7	1.2	12.1	9.7	71%	15%	60	17	23	33%	80%	9%	12	95	92%	8%			16.6	223	266	$28
2nd Half	12	1	0	119	132	1.59	2.51	0.82	493	524	487	29.4	1.5	10.0	6.6	67%	14%	46	20	33	26%	83%	5%	15	106	93%	0%			31.6	163	195	$49
15 Proj	**18**	**5**	**0**	**203**	**224**	**2.07**	**2.44**	**0.92**	**538**	**504**	**547**	**26.8**	**1.9**	**9.9**	**5.4**	**66%**	**13%**	**49**	**20**	**32**	**28%**	**79%**	**7%**	**28**						**41.8**	**155**	**185**	**$38**

Keuchel,Dallas

Age: 27	Th: L	Role: SP	Health: A	LIMA Plan: C+
Ht: 6' 3"	Wt: 210	Type: xGB	PT/Exp: A	Rand Var: 0
			Consist: B	MM: 4105

Big step forward foretold by xERA, with fortune now in his favor. Don't overlook skills growth: Elite GB spiked and Ctl/Cmd followed FpK bump. Lower Dom in 2nd half is a minor injury-related blemish, but other skills held up. Declining DIS and overall reliability make him a safe choice, and there's still some room for growth.

Yr Tm	W	L	Sv	IP	K	ERA	xERA	WHIP	oOPS	vL	vR	BF/G	Ctl	Dom	Cmd	FpK	SwK	G	L	F	H%	S%	hr/f	GS	APC	DOM%	DIS%	Sv%	LI	RAR	BPV	BPX	R$
10 aa	2	6	0	54	32	5.97	4.77	1.50				25.7	1.9	5.3	2.8						36%	57%								-12.5	72	116	-$6
11 a/a	10	7	0	164	79	4.53	4.37	1.36				25.3	2.1	4.3	2.1						31%	67%								-11.8	43	65	-$1
12 HOU *	9	12	0	178	81	4.56	4.48	1.40	823	750	844	23.4	2.9	4.1	1.4	55%	6%	52	17	31	29%	69%	16%	16	87	19%	38%			-12.0	25	33	-$5
13 HOU	6	10	0	154	123	5.15	3.72	1.54	812	750	832	22.0	3.0	7.2	2.4	63%	9%	56	21	23	35%	69%	17%	22	81	36%	18%	0	0.90	-24.4	81	106	-$11
14 HOU	12	9	0	200	146	2.93	3.07	1.18	655	595	674	27.9	2.2	6.6	3.0	65%	9%	64	17	19	30%	76%	10%	29	104	59%	3%			20.1	102	121	$15
1st Half	8	5	0	104	83	2.78	2.91	1.10	622	564	642	27.4	2.3	7.2	3.2	65%	11%	63	16	20	28%	75%	8%	15	103	67%	0%			12.3	110	132	$21
2nd Half	4	4	0	96	63	3.08	3.24	1.26	689	632	705	28.4	2.1	5.9	2.9	65%	7%	64	18	18	31%	77%	11%	14	106	50%	7%			7.8	92	110	$8
15 Proj	**13**	**9**	**0**	**203**	**148**	**3.54**	**3.23**	**1.29**	**690**	**629**	**709**	**24.7**	**2.3**	**6.6**	**2.8**	**63%**	**9%**	**59**	**19**	**22**	**32%**	**73%**	**8%**	**34**						**5.1**	**92**	**110**	**$10**

Kimbrel,Craig

Age: 27	Th: R	Role: RP	Health: A	LIMA Plan: C+
Ht: 5' 11"	Wt: 220	Type: Pwr	PT/Exp: A	Rand Var: -5
			Consist: A	MM: 5530

If he were an ordinary pitcher, we'd say something like "skills declined, as jump in Ctl and lower GB rate led to worst xERA of his career." But Dom this good can cover a lot of deficiencies, and his 3.7 Cmd is still very strong. Yes, we should heed the trends, but for now, I'm still in at $25.

Yr Tm	W	L	Sv	IP	K	ERA	xERA	WHIP	oOPS	vL	vR	BF/G	Ctl	Dom	Cmd	FpK	SwK	G	L	F	H%	S%	hr/f	GS	APC	DOM%	DIS%	Sv%	LI	RAR	BPV	BPX	R$
10 ATL *	7	2	24	76	113	1.48	1.85	1.19	437	523	361	4.4	6.0	13.3	2.2	43%	14%	28	22	50	27%	89%	0%	0	18			89	0.53	24.4	139	226	$21
11 ATL	4	3	46	77	127	2.10	2.21	1.04	499	442	549	3.9	3.7	14.8	4.0	55%	16%	45	15	40	33%	81%	5%	0	17			85	1.32	17.5	189	284	$29
12 ATL	3	1	42	63	116	1.01	1.43	0.65	358	331	387	3.7	2.0	16.7	8.3	71%	20%	49	19	32	28%	89%	10%	0	15			93	1.29	23.3	273	356	$34
13 ATL	4	3	50	67	98	1.21	2.12	0.88	487	574	393	3.8	2.7	13.2	4.9	56%	14%	47	24	29	28%	91%	10%	0	15			93	1.30	22.0	189	247	$32
14 ATL	0	3	47	62	95	1.61	2.36	0.91	430	425	436	3.9	3.8	13.9	3.7	58%	17%	41	23	35	26%	83%	5%	0	17			92	1.44	16.2	166	198	$26
1st Half	0	1	25	33	56	2.16	2.32	0.99	464	462	465	3.9	4.1	15.1	3.7	58%	16%	41	22	38	31%	78%	4%	0	17			86	1.46	6.5	181	217	$26
2nd Half	0	2	22	28	39	0.95	2.40	0.81	386	382	391	3.8	3.5	12.4	3.5	58%	19%	42	25	33	21%	91%	6%	0	16			100	1.41	9.7	149	178	$27
15 Proj	**2**	**3**	**48**	**66**	**98**	**2.04**	**2.04**	**0.87**	**436**	**444**	**426**	**3.7**	**3.3**	**13.5**	**4.1**	**59%**	**17%**	**44**	**22**	**33**	**26%**	**78%**	**7%**	**0**						**13.7**	**176**	**210**	**$29**

Kintzler,Brandon

Age: 30	Th: R	Role: RP	Health: F	LIMA Plan: C
Ht: 5' 10"	Wt: 190	Type: Con xGB	PT/Exp: D	Rand Var: 0
			Consist: C	MM: 3000

Had surgery at end of season for knee issue that had apparently been bothering him for two years. That may explain the drop in skills, though Dom and Cmd have been here before, making 2013 feel like an outlier. Strong GB limits the damage, and good health may lead to skills rebound, but it's not worth speculating.

Yr Tm	W	L	Sv	IP	K	ERA	xERA	WHIP	oOPS	vL	vR	BF/G	Ctl	Dom	Cmd	FpK	SwK	G	L	F	H%	S%	hr/f	GS	APC	DOM%	DIS%	Sv%	LI	RAR	BPV	BPX	R$
10 MIL *	4	1	16	56	45	2.45	2.28	1.00	1045	964	1087	4.4	1.8	7.2	4.0	52%	17%	68	11	21	27%	77%	50%	0	18			80	0.54	11.3	123	199	$13
11 MIL	1	1	0	15	15	3.68	2.86	1.16	725	678	742	6.8	1.8	9.2	5.0	64%	9%	60	9	30	29%	79%	23%	0	25			0	0.57	0.5	154	231	-$2
12 MIL *	3	3	9	64	38	3.94	4.46	1.53	732	744	717	5.3	3.3	5.4	1.6	70%	10%	51	27	22	34%	73%	9%	0	21			90	0.64	0.6	53	69	-$1
13 MIL	3	3	0	77	58	2.69	3.03	1.06	567	540	586	4.3	1.9	6.8	3.6	60%	9%	57	24	18	29%	74%	5%	0	15			0	1.05	11.2	107	139	$5
14 MIL	3	3	0	58	31	3.24	3.87	1.34	781	648	859	3.7	2.5	4.8	1.9	60%	7%	57	18	25	29%	81%	17%	0	14			0	1.04	3.6	54	65	-$1
1st Half	1	3	0	31	15	3.82	4.21	1.53	871	653	981	4.1	2.3	4.4	1.9	64%	5%	57	19	24	32%	81%	19%	0	14			0	0.95	-0.3	51	61	-$5
2nd Half	2	0	0	28	16	2.60	3.50	1.12	667	643	683	3.4	2.6	5.2	2.0	54%	9%	57	18	25	24%	82%	15%	0	13			0	1.14	3.9	58	70	$4
15 Proj	**3**	**2**	**0**	**58**	**36**	**3.51**	**3.42**	**1.24**	**690**	**613**	**739**	**4.1**	**2.4**	**5.7**	**2.4**	**59%**	**8%**	**57**	**21**	**22**	**29%**	**73%**	**12%**	**0**						**1.6**	**72**	**86**	**$0**

Kluber,Corey

Age: 29	Th: R	Role: SP	Health: B	LIMA Plan: D+
Ht: 6' 4"	Wt: 215	Type: Pwr	PT/Exp: A	Rand Var: -2
			Consist: C	MM: 5405

Expected breakout exceeded expectations. A bit of hr/f luck, but skills confirm results, especially Dom and SwK. Skills took off in 2nd half (see DOM/DIS and BPV). Another sub-3.00 ERA is possible, though be prepared for some regression after 3 years of growth. Slot him near the back of the top starting pitcher tier.

Yr Tm	W	L	Sv	IP	K	ERA	xERA	WHIP	oOPS	vL	vR	BF/G	Ctl	Dom	Cmd	FpK	SwK	G	L	F	H%	S%	hr/f	GS	APC	DOM%	DIS%	Sv%	LI	RAR	BPV	BPX	R$
10 a/a	9	9	0	160	137	3.84	4.51	1.52				24.0	3.1	7.7	2.5						36%	74%								4.8	82	132	$2
11 CLE *	7	11	0	155	121	6.46	5.45	1.64	740	900	286	23.1	4.2	7.0	1.7	68%	12%	27	47	27	34%	61%	0%	0	30			0	0.15	-48.0	41	61	-$19
12 CLE *	13	12	0	188	157	4.53	4.91	1.52	834	860	801	24.7	3.2	7.5	2.3	57%	12%	45	22	33	35%	71%	13%	12	90	33%	25%			-12.1	64	84	-$5
13 CLE	11	5	0	147	136	3.85	3.25	1.26	729	751	704	23.4	2.0	8.3	4.1	60%	11%	46	26	29	33%	72%	12%	24	88	42%	17%	0	0.73	0.3	119	155	$6
14 CLE	18	9	0	236	269	2.44	2.74	1.09	624	687	553	28.0	1.9	10.3	5.3	64%	12%	48	21	31	33%	80%	7%	34	103	82%	9%			37.7	158	189	$30
1st Half	7	6	0	117	127	2.99	3.00	1.22	676	760	589	27.0	2.2	9.7	4.4	63%	11%	48	21	31	34%	77%	8%	18	101	72%	11%			10.8	141	168	$19
2nd Half	11	3	0	118	142	1.90	2.49	0.97	571	619	512	29.1	1.7	10.8	6.5	65%	13%	48	21	30	31%	83%	7%	16	106	94%	6%			26.9	176	210	$41
15 Proj	**16**	**9**	**0**	**218**	**221**	**3.33**	**2.94**	**1.24**	**691**	**734**	**640**	**25.3**	**2.3**	**9.1**	**4.0**	**61%**	**12%**	**47**	**23**	**30**	**33%**	**75%**	**9%**	**35**						**11.2**	**127**	**151**	**$18**

Koehler,Tom

Age: 29	Th: R	Role: SP	Health: A	LIMA Plan: B
Ht: 6' 2"	Wt: 235	Type: Pwr	PT/Exp: B	Rand Var: -1
			Consist: B	MM: 2103

ERA says "a little better," while xERA says "not so much." While he benefitted from improvements on both sides of the command equation, it was mostly shifting winds (hr/f) that lifted him. Is DOM/DIS a sign that he's working his way out of mediocrity? It's a positive, yes—but we're not biting yet.

Yr Tm	W	L	Sv	IP	K	ERA	xERA	WHIP	oOPS	vL	vR	BF/G	Ctl	Dom	Cmd	FpK	SwK	G	L	F	H%	S%	hr/f	GS	APC	DOM%	DIS%	Sv%	LI	RAR	BPV	BPX	R$
10 aa	16	2	0	159	129	3.28	4.05	1.37				23.7	2.9	7.3	2.5						33%	78%								15.5	77	125	$11
11 aaa	12	7	0	150	94	5.09	4.72	1.56				23.5	4.7	5.6	1.2						30%	68%								-21.4	33	50	-$8
12 MIA *	12	12	0	164	130	5.28	5.74	1.67	896	818	941	19.9	4.0	7.1	1.8	61%	5%	24	27	49	35%	70%	20%	1	26	0%	0%	0	0.70	-25.6	41	53	-$15
13 MIA *	5	12	0	166	106	4.31	3.99	1.37	754	706	796	21.1	3.7	5.7	1.6	59%	8%	48	22	30	28%	70%	10%	23	78	39%	30%	0	0.72	-9.2	45	59	-$4
14 MIA	10	10	0	191	153	3.81	4.06	1.30	691	649	737	25.1	3.3	7.2	2.2	59%	9%	43	18	39	29%	72%	7%	32	92	56%	9%			-1.6	60	72	$4
1st Half	5	6	0	97	75	3.70	4.06	1.22	665	561	769	25.3	3.5	6.9	2.0	58%	10%	43	19	38	27%	72%	9%	16	94	63%	13%			0.5	51	61	$6
2nd Half	5	4	0	94	78	3.93	4.06	1.37	717	728	703	24.9	3.2	7.5	2.4	60%	8%	43	17	40	32%	72%	6%	16	89	50%	6%			-2.1	70	84	$2
15 Proj	**9**	**10**	**0**	**174**	**131**	**4.21**	**3.97**	**1.40**	**749**	**708**	**791**	**22.7**	**3.5**	**6.8**	**1.9**	**59%**	**8%**	**45**	**19**	**36**	**31%**	**71%**	**8%**	**32**						**-10.0**	**49**	**59**	**$0**

MATT CEDERHOLM

Kontos,George

Age: 30	Th: R	Role: RP	Health: A	LIMA Plan: B+
Ht: 6' 3"	Wt: 215	Type:	PT/Exp: D	Rand Var: -2
			Consist: D	MM: 3200

4-0, 2.78 ERA in 32 IP at SF. While skills rebounded from 2013 and led to sexy surface numbers, there are red flags. Acceptable 2.5 Ctl masks FpK collapse; 3% hr/f masks rising FB rate. LI and frequent trips to minors show lack of managerial faith, so he's likely stuck in low-leverage role, even if he can repeat ERA.

Yr Tm	W	L	Sv	IP	K	ERA	xERA	WHIP	oOPS	vL	vR	BF/G	Ctl	Dom	Cmd	FpK	SwK	G	L	F	H%	S%	hr/f	GS	APC	DOM%	DIS%	Sv%	LI	RAR	BPV	BPX	R$
10 a/a	0	3	0	35	24	5.14	5.60	1.62				8.1	3.4	6.3	1.8						35%	70%								-4.6	37	60	-$5
11 NYY *	4	4	2	95	78	3.74	5.06	1.37	625	400	691	8.5	3.1	7.3	2.3	52%	18%	20	7	73	29%	82%	9%	0	13			67	0.37	2.4	40	60	$1
12 SF *	4	1	1	75	64	2.14	2.33	1.04	591	468	653	4.3	2.2	7.7	3.5	60%	13%	51	15	34	28%	81%	8%	0	15			50	0.62	17.4	116	152	$9
13 SF *	5	4	4	79	67	4.38	4.14	1.30	788	1024	689	4.6	2.4	7.6	3.2	65%	11%	38	25	37	32%	69%	11%	0	17			67	1.01	-5.0	82	106	$1
14 SF *	7	3	4	80	70	2.87	2.89	1.16	587	498	635	5.9	2.5	7.9	3.2	56%	10%	39	18	43	30%	76%	3%	0	20			67	0.56	8.6	107	128	$7
1st Half	3	3	3	47	46	3.96	4.06	1.33	637	632	633	6.4	1.9	8.8	4.6	53%	12%	37	17	46	36%	71%	0%	0	20			60	0.51	-1.2	128	153	$4
2nd Half	4	0	1	33	24	1.35	1.26	0.92	547	364	637	5.2	3.2	6.6	2.0	59%	8%	40	19	40	20%	87%	5%	0	19			100	0.60	9.8	96	114	$12
15 Proj	**3**	**1**	**0**	**44**	**36**	**3.28**	**3.48**	**1.22**	**677**	**598**	**714**	**5.4**	**2.6**	**7.5**	**2.8**	**61%**	**11%**	**44**	**19**	**37**	**30%**	**75%**	**7%**	**0**						**2.5**	**86**	**102**	**$1**

Krol,Ian

Age: 24	Th: L	Role: RP	Health: B	LIMA Plan: C
Ht: 6' 1"	Wt: 210	Type: Pwr FB	PT/Exp: F	Rand Var: +5
			Consist: C	MM: 2200

Sore shoulder, ineffectiveness relegated him to AAA by August, where he sat on the bench. Big minor-league strikeout totals haven't translated to the major leagues—fastball averaged 92 mph, and FpK/SwK aren't in his favor—so expect struggles. Until he can handle RHB in the majors, he'll have little value.

Yr Tm	W	L	Sv	IP	K	ERA	xERA	WHIP	oOPS	vL	vR	BF/G	Ctl	Dom	Cmd	FpK	SwK	G	L	F	H%	S%	hr/f	GS	APC	DOM%	DIS%	Sv%	LI	RAR	BPV	BPX	R$
10																																	
11																																	
12																																	
13 WAS *	3	2	1	57	52	2.61	2.85	1.07	785	593	957	3.8	2.4	8.2	3.4	57%	7%	39	20	41	27%	81%	14%	0	15			20	1.18	8.8	103	134	$4
14 DET	0	0	1	33	28	4.96	4.34	1.68	906	764	1048	3.4	3.6	7.7	2.2	53%	8%	40	29	31	36%	76%	18%	0	14			25	1.24	-4.9	60	72	-$6
1st Half	0	0	1	25	20	4.32	4.26	1.52	913	714	1120	3.2	2.9	7.2	2.5	50%	7%	37	28	35	32%	81%	21%	0	13			50	1.12	-1.8	66	79	-$6
2nd Half	0	0	0	8	8	7.04	4.55	2.22	887	918	856	4.1	5.9	9.4	1.6	61%	10%	50	32	18	47%	65%	0%	0	17			0	1.68	-3.1	39	46	-$7
15 Proj	**2**	**3**	**0**	**55**	**44**	**4.16**	**3.93**	**1.38**	**716**	**595**	**843**	**3.4**	**3.0**	**7.3**	**2.4**	**50%**	**7%**	**37**	**24**	**39**	**31%**	**75%**	**11%**	**0**						**-2.8**	**64**	**77**	**-$3**

Kuroda,Hiroki

Age: 40	Th: R	Role: SP	Health: B	LIMA Plan: C+
Ht: 6' 1"	Wt: 205	Type:	PT/Exp: A	Rand Var: 0
			Consist: A	MM: 3105

Defied the aging trend with another consistent season. Still, there's some risk—league average FpK makes his elite Ctl look vulnerable, Dom is now barely average, DISaster outings are more frequent. But GB%, WHIP, xERA are all assets, even as he passes 40. A set-and-forget mid-rotation arm.

Yr Tm	W	L	Sv	IP	K	ERA	xERA	WHIP	oOPS	vL	vR	BF/G	Ctl	Dom	Cmd	FpK	SwK	G	L	F	H%	S%	hr/f	GS	APC	DOM%	DIS%	Sv%	LI	RAR	BPV	BPX	R$
10 LA	11	13	0	196	159	3.39	3.47	1.16	642	664	623	26.1	2.2	7.3	3.3	59%	11%	51	17	32	29%	72%	8%	31	98	68%	13%			16.6	101	163	$16
11 LA	13	16	0	202	161	3.07	3.65	1.21	716	767	667	26.2	2.2	7.2	3.3	61%	11%	43	22	35	30%	80%	11%	32	100	56%	13%			21.6	91	137	$17
12 NYY	16	11	0	220	167	3.32	3.59	1.17	705	734	665	27.0	2.1	6.8	3.3	59%	10%	52	18	30	28%	76%	13%	33	101	61%	9%			18.9	97	126	$20
13 NYY	11	13	0	201	150	3.31	3.64	1.16	683	742	602	25.8	1.9	6.7	3.5	61%	10%	47	22	31	29%	75%	10%	32	100	50%	6%			13.8	94	122	$14
14 NYY	11	9	0	199	146	3.71	3.59	1.14	668	707	622	25.6	1.6	6.6	4.2	60%	10%	47	21	32	29%	70%	10%	32	97	53%	25%			0.8	101	120	$10
1st Half	5	5	0	96	67	4.23	3.87	1.24	722	748	686	25.1	1.9	6.3	3.4	59%	9%	46	19	34	30%	69%	10%	16	97	44%	25%			-5.8	87	104	$3
2nd Half	6	4	0	103	79	3.22	3.32	1.04	616	662	570	26.1	1.3	6.9	5.3	61%	11%	47	23	30	28%	71%	10%	16	97	63%	25%			6.6	114	136	$17
15 Proj	**11**	**10**	**0**	**189**	**138**	**3.46**	**3.45**	**1.20**	**695**	**740**	**640**	**25.5**	**2.0**	**6.6**	**3.3**	**60%**	**10%**	**46**	**21**	**33**	**30%**	**74%**	**10%**	**30**						**6.5**	**88**	**105**	**$12**

Lackey,John

Age: 36	Th: R	Role: SP	Health: F	LIMA Plan: B
Ht: 6' 6"	Wt: 235	Type:	PT/Exp: B	Rand Var: 0
			Consist: A	MM: 3205

Is that 2nd half a warning? FpK supports elite Ctl, making 2nd half Ctl spike look like an anomaly, and he repeated strong Cmd and overall skills. However, "dead arm" in September reinforces risky health history and FB velocity was down in 2nd half. Expect another league average performance but risk level is up.

Yr Tm	W	L	Sv	IP	K	ERA	xERA	WHIP	oOPS	vL	vR	BF/G	Ctl	Dom	Cmd	FpK	SwK	G	L	F	H%	S%	hr/f	GS	APC	DOM%	DIS%	Sv%	LI	RAR	BPV	BPX	R$
10 BOS	14	11	0	215	156	4.35	4.16	1.42	765	802	719	28.2	3.0	6.5	2.2	63%	7%	46	18	36	32%	70%	7%	33	109	55%	12%			-7.3	60	97	$3
11 BOS	12	12	0	160	108	6.41	4.63	1.62	852	915	778	26.5	3.2	6.1	1.9	61%	7%	40	22	37	35%	61%	10%	28	102	29%	32%			-48.7	42	64	-$17
12																																	
13 BOS	10	13	0	189	161	3.52	3.50	1.16	703	657	760	26.8	1.9	7.7	4.0	64%	10%	47	18	35	29%	75%	13%	29	99	66%	10%			8.1	111	145	$12
14 2 TM	14	10	0	198	164	3.82	3.67	1.28	730	719	742	26.9	2.1	7.5	3.5	68%	10%	44	22	34	32%	74%	12%	31	99	65%	13%			-1.9	99	117	$6
1st Half	9	5	0	112	95	3.62	3.40	1.21	701	712	684	27.2	1.8	7.6	4.3	64%	10%	47	22	31	32%	73%	10%	17	101	65%	12%			1.7	114	137	$13
2nd Half	5	5	0	86	69	4.08	4.03	1.37	767	731	790	26.5	2.6	7.2	2.8	72%	11%	41	21	37	32%	75%	13%	14	97	64%	14%			-3.6	79	94	-$2
15 Proj	**13**	**12**	**0**	**195**	**155**	**3.90**	**3.55**	**1.30**	**740**	**735**	**747**	**25.9**	**2.4**	**7.2**	**3.0**	**66%**	**10%**	**44**	**21**	**35**	**31%**	**74%**	**12%**	**31**						**-3.9**	**87**	**103**	**$7**

Latos,Mat

Age: 27	Th: R	Role: SP	Health: D	LIMA Plan: C+
Ht: 6' 6"	Wt: 245	Type:	PT/Exp: A	Rand Var: -1
			Consist: A	MM: 3205

5-5 with 3.25 ERA in 102 IP at CIN. Elbow (x2), knee, and back cost 13 weeks—which likely caused both skills (4.02 xERA in MLB) and fastball velocity to slip despite strong results. Had more elbow work in off-season, so watch closely. But at his age with his history, a good bet to rebound if health cooperates.

Yr Tm	W	L	Sv	IP	K	ERA	xERA	WHIP	oOPS	vL	vR	BF/G	Ctl	Dom	Cmd	FpK	SwK	G	L	F	H%	S%	hr/f	GS	APC	DOM%	DIS%	Sv%	LI	RAR	BPV	BPX	R$
10 SD	14	10	0	185	189	2.92	3.29	1.08	601	580	623	24.1	2.4	9.2	3.8	62%	12%	45	15	40	29%	76%	8%	31	96	65%	13%			26.3	123	199	$23
11 SD	9	14	0	194	185	3.47	3.57	1.18	655	697	607	25.8	2.9	8.6	3.0	60%	11%	43	16	41	30%	72%	7%	31	102	71%	3%			11.2	98	147	$14
12 CIN	14	4	0	209	185	3.48	3.75	1.16	681	753	608	26.0	2.8	8.0	2.9	62%	11%	46	18	36	28%	74%	12%	33	99	52%	12%			13.7	93	121	$19
13 CIN	14	7	0	211	187	3.16	3.56	1.21	668	699	642	27.5	2.5	8.0	3.2	64%	11%	45	21	34	31%	75%	7%	32	101	66%	6%			18.3	100	130	$17
14 CIN *	7	5	0	126	87	3.34	3.65	1.24	652	609	691	24.3	2.5	6.2	2.4	59%	8%	38	22	40	29%	76%	7%	16	96	63%	6%			6.3	68	81	$4
1st Half	3	1	0	49	28	3.04	3.33	1.21	483	461	506	21.9	2.5	5.1	2.1	58%	9%	39	23	38	28%	77%	3%	4	95	75%	25%			4.2	60	72	$2
2nd Half	4	4	0	77	59	3.52	4.10	1.27	704	662	740	26.9	2.6	6.9	2.7	59%	8%	37	22	41	30%	75%	9%	12	96	58%	0%			2.1	70	84	$6
15 Proj	**11**	**7**	**0**	**189**	**150**	**3.31**	**3.56**	**1.21**	**681**	**680**	**683**	**24.9**	**2.5**	**7.2**	**2.8**	**61%**	**10%**	**41**	**21**	**38**	**29%**	**75%**	**8%**	**30**						**9.9**	**80**	**95**	**$13**

League,Brandon

Age: 32	Th: R	Role: RP	Health: A	LIMA Plan: D+
Ht: 6' 2"	Wt: 215	Type: xGB	PT/Exp: C	Rand Var: -5
			Consist: A	MM: 2000

Even when you throw this many ground balls, 0 HR in 63 IP is an abberration. And that's about all he's got—Ctl/Cmd is ugly, Dom has disappeared, and as LI shows, he's not being used in a role that will generate any additional value. Even if he rebounds from his awful 2nd half, the trends are not in his favor.

Yr Tm	W	L	Sv	IP	K	ERA	xERA	WHIP	oOPS	vL	vR	BF/G	Ctl	Dom	Cmd	FpK	SwK	G	L	F	H%	S%	hr/f	GS	APC	DOM%	DIS%	Sv%	LI	RAR	BPV	BPX	R$
10 SEA	9	7	6	79	56	3.42	3.40	1.19	630	714	556	4.7	3.1	6.4	2.1	50%	11%	63	16	21	26%	74%	14%	0	16			50	1.37	6.4	73	118	$8
11 SEA	1	5	37	61	45	2.79	3.14	1.08	601	658	543	3.8	1.5	6.6	4.5	56%	11%	57	19	24	29%	75%	7%	0	14			88	1.20	8.7	114	172	$18
12 2 TM	2	6	15	72	54	3.13	4.08	1.36	628	755	519	4.1	4.1	6.8	1.6	52%	11%	50	27	23	30%	75%	2%	0	15			71	1.09	7.9	38	50	$6
13 LA	6	4	14	54	28	5.30	4.21	1.55	818	905	758	4.3	2.5	4.6	1.9	55%	10%	60	19	21	33%	68%	19%	0	16			74	0.88	-9.6	54	71	$0
14 LA	2	3	0	63	38	2.57	3.79	1.46	683	754	645	4.3	3.9	5.4	1.4	50%	8%	68	15	18	32%	80%	0%	0	15			0	0.94	9.1	40	47	-$1
1st Half	1	2	0	39	23	2.06	3.17	1.22	587	627	564	4.7	3.0	5.3	1.8	52%	9%	75	14	12	28%	81%	0%	0	16			0	0.79	8.2	67	80	$2
2nd Half	1	1	0	24	15	3.42	4.86	1.86	826	962	759	3.9	5.3	5.7	1.1	46%	8%	57	16	27	37%	80%	0%	0	14			0	1.10	0.9	-6	-7	-$5
15 Proj	**4**	**4**	**0**	**65**	**39**	**3.68**	**3.95**	**1.51**	**732**	**823**	**674**	**4.1**	**3.7**	**5.4**	**1.5**	**51%**	**9%**	**59**	**18**	**22**	**32%**	**75%**	**6%**	**0**						**0.5**	**37**	**44**	**-$3**

Leake,Mike

Age: 27	Th: R	Role: SP	Health: A	LIMA Plan: B
Ht: 5' 10"	Wt: 190	Type: GB	PT/Exp: A	Rand Var: +1
			Consist: A	MM: 3105

Fantasy and reality converge—he's an average mid-rotation starter in both worlds. Signs he's still growing: GB jump due to more sinkers, Dom followed small uptick in SwK, and declining DIS rate shows improved consistency. Control artists walk a fine line at times, but he's a cheap option to eat innings.

Yr Tm	W	L	Sv	IP	K	ERA	xERA	WHIP	oOPS	vL	vR	BF/G	Ctl	Dom	Cmd	FpK	SwK	G	L	F	H%	S%	hr/f	GS	APC	DOM%	DIS%	Sv%	LI	RAR	BPV	BPX	R$
10 CIN	8	4	0	138	91	4.23	4.24	1.50	804	832	779	25.2	3.2	5.9	1.9	59%	8%	50	18	32	32%	76%	13%	22	89	41%	14%	0	0.75	-2.6	48	78	-$1
11 CIN	12	9	0	168	118	3.86	3.64	1.17	714	743	688	23.9	2.0	6.3	3.1	58%	8%	48	21	32	28%	72%	14%	26	88	50%	12%	0	0.81	1.6	85	128	$10
12 CIN	8	9	0	179	116	4.58	4.00	1.35	805	806	803	25.2	2.1	5.8	2.8	63%	7%	49	25	27	31%	70%	17%	30	90	40%	27%			-12.4	76	100	-$3
13 CIN	14	7	0	192	122	3.37	3.93	1.25	719	717	721	25.8	2.2	5.7	2.5	59%	7%	49	21	30	29%	77%	12%	31	94	42%	10%			11.8	69	90	$11
14 CIN	11	13	0	214	164	3.70	3.45	1.25	730	801	674	27.3	2.1	6.9	3.3	60%	8%	53	20	26	31%	73%	13%	33	97	58%	3%			1.2	98	117	$7
1st Half	6	6	0	108	84	3.41	3.27	1.14	678	753	621	27.6	1.9	7.0	3.7	61%	8%	54	20	26	29%	73%	13%	16	98	50%	0%			4.5	106	127	$13
2nd Half	5	7	0	106	80	3.99	3.64	1.35	781	847	727	27.1	2.3	6.8	3.0	60%	7%	53	20	27	32%	73%	13%	17	97	65%	6%			-3.3	91	108	$2
15 Proj	**11**	**10**	**0**	**196**	**136**	**3.81**	**3.52**	**1.30**	**755**	**792**	**722**	**25.7**	**2.2**	**6.3**	**2.8**	**60%**	**7%**	**51**	**20**	**29**	**31%**	**74%**	**13%**	**31**						**-1.7**	**81**	**96**	**$6**

MATT CEDERHOLM

Lecure,Sam

Age: 31	Th: R	Role RP	Health B	LIMA Plan C
Ht: 6' 0"	Wt: 205	Type Pwr	PT/Exp D	Rand Var 0
			Consist A	MM 3300

After three consistent years, took a step back as he missed fewer bats and walks continued to tick upward. 39% H% vs. RHB didn't help, but plummeting FpK rate must be reversed to recapture his relevance. Likely to rebound a bit—less likely to be useful unless BPV gets back into triple digits.

Yr Tm	W	L	Sv	IP	K	ERA	xERA	WHIP	oOPS	vL	vR	BF/G	Ctl	Dom	Cmd	FpK	SwK	G	L	F	H%	S%	hr/f	GS	APC	DOM%	DIS%	Sv%	LI	RAR	BPV	BPX	R$
10 CIN *	10	8	0	146	108	4.55	4.93	1.49	800	928	720	21.0	3.1	6.6	2.2	61%	7%	46	20	34	33%	71%	12%	6	57	17%	17%	0	0.68	-8.5	53	85	-$1
11 CIN	2	1	0	78	73	3.71	3.25	1.00	645	661	635	7.1	2.4	8.5	3.5	63%	9%	46	14	40	24%	68%	13%	4	28	50%	50%	0	0.83	2.2	111	166	$4
12 CIN	3	3	0	57	61	3.14	3.44	1.20	627	613	640	4.9	3.6	9.6	2.7	66%	9%	48	21	31	30%	74%	7%	0	20			0	1.09	6.2	101	132	$2
13 CIN	2	1	1	61	66	2.66	3.37	1.21	624	446	756	4.0	3.5	9.7	2.8	62%	11%	43	23	34	30%	80%	7%	0	16			33	1.32	9.1	101	131	$3
14 CIN	1	4	0	57	48	3.81	4.15	1.52	787	701	852	4.0	3.8	7.6	2.0	54%	8%	44	22	34	33%	78%	10%	0	16			0	1.01	-0.5	56	67	-$4
1st Half	1	1	0	31	27	3.73	4.27	1.53	771	810	743	4.3	4.0	7.8	1.9	54%	8%	44	20	36	34%	78%	9%	0	17			0	1.02	0.0	53	63	-$4
2nd Half	0	3	0	25	21	3.91	4.00	1.50	807	580	1006	3.7	3.6	7.5	2.1	54%	8%	44	25	31	33%	77%	13%	0	14			0	0.99	-0.5	60	72	-$4
15 Proj	2	3	0	58	54	3.47	3.53	1.37	722	617	802	4.3	3.6	8.4	2.4	59%	9%	44	22	33	32%	77%	10%	0						2.0	77	92	-$1

Lee,Cliff

Age: 36	Th: L	Role SP	Health F	LIMA Plan C+
Ht: 6' 3"	Wt: 205	Type	PT/Exp A	Rand Var +3
			Consist A	MM 5303

Felled by elbow injury in mid-May, then beat-up in his July return as team attempted to showcase him before his body was fully healed. Still, maintained amazing BPI through it all; elite Ctl, Cmd, BPV, and consistent ace-level history provide hope. You like high risk/high reward for 2015? Look no further.

Yr Tm	W	L	Sv	IP	K	ERA	xERA	WHIP	oOPS	vL	vR	BF/G	Ctl	Dom	Cmd	FpK	SwK	G	L	F	H%	S%	hr/f	GS	APC	DOM%	DIS%	Sv%	LI	RAR	BPV	BPX	R$
10 2 AL	12	9	0	212	185	3.18	3.26	1.00	618	706	591	30.1	0.8	7.8	10.3	70%	9%	42	18	40	30%	70%	6%	28	106	64%	4%			23.6	141	227	$25
11 PHI	17	8	0	233	238	2.40	2.83	1.03	607	518	634	28.8	1.6	9.2	5.7	65%	10%	46	21	32	30%	80%	9%	32	106	81%	9%			44.3	146	219	$35
12 PHI	6	9	0	211	207	3.16	3.23	1.11	690	626	707	28.2	1.2	8.8	7.4	71%	9%	45	18	37	32%	77%	12%	30	103	80%	3%			22.3	150	195	$20
13 PHI	14	8	0	223	222	2.87	2.94	1.01	631	537	659	28.3	1.3	9.0	6.9	68%	10%	44	22	33	30%	76%	11%	31	105	77%	0%			27.4	149	194	$29
14 PHI	4	5	0	81	72	3.65	3.36	1.38	762	536	815	27.1	1.3	8.0	6.0	65%	8%	48	22	30	37%	75%	9%	13	98	46%	15%			0.9	134	159	-$1
1st Half	4	4	0	68	61	3.18	3.24	1.28	722	509	772	28.9	1.2	8.1	6.8	67%	8%	49	21	30	36%	77%	8%	10	107	60%	10%			4.7	140	167	$2
2nd Half	0	1	0	13	11	6.08	3.97	1.88	953	664	1014	21.0	2.0	7.4	3.7	60%	7%	46	24	30	43%	70%	14%	3	69	0%	33%			-3.8	103	122	-$14
15 Proj	7	6	0	138	131	3.19	2.82	1.12	669	567	698	27.9	1.2	8.6	7.0	68%	9%	46	20	34	32%	74%	10%	19						9.4	145	173	$12

Leone,Dominic

Age: 23	Th: R	Role RP	Health A	LIMA Plan B+
Ht: 5' 11"	Wt: 210	Type Pwr xGB	PT/Exp D	Rand Var -3
			Consist A	MM 5400

Rookie showed he belonged with a year-long strikeout-and-GB profile. Ctl is the next frontier, and FpK shows he's not yet mastered the art of "strike one." Still needs to gain managerial confidence to be trusted in important situations, but it shouldn't take long for an arm like this to get noticed. Solid repeat potential.

Yr Tm	W	L	Sv	IP	K	ERA	xERA	WHIP	oOPS	vL	vR	BF/G	Ctl	Dom	Cmd	FpK	SwK	G	L	F	H%	S%	hr/f	GS	APC	DOM%	DIS%	Sv%	LI	RAR	BPV	BPX	R$
10																																	
11																																	
12																																	
13 aa	1	2	4	18	15	3.33	3.04	1.08				4.4	2.5	7.6	3.0						25%	74%								1.2	85	110	-$1
14 SEA	8	2	0	66	70	2.17	2.98	1.16	624	800	511	4.8	3.4	9.5	2.8	56%	14%	55	21	25	29%	84%	10%	0	19			0	0.98	12.8	112	134	$7
1st Half	2	1	0	33	36	2.18	2.91	1.18	646	645	646	4.7	3.3	9.8	3.0	57%	12%	52	25	23	30%	84%	11%	0	19			0	1.14	6.3	118	141	$4
2nd Half	6	1	0	33	34	2.16	3.05	1.14	602	980	390	4.9	3.5	9.2	2.6	55%	16%	57	16	26	28%	83%	9%	0	19			0	0.81	6.5	106	126	$10
15 Proj	6	3	0	65	68	2.44	2.82	1.16	620	832	486	4.6	3.4	9.4	2.8	56%	14%	55	20	25	29%	81%	9%	0						10.4	111	132	$6

Lester,Jon

Age: 31	Th: L	Role SP	Health A	LIMA Plan C
Ht: 6' 4"	Wt: 240	Type Pwr	PT/Exp A	Rand Var -3
			Consist A	MM 4305

Can't blame him for the OAK summer swoon; metrics actually improved in 2nd half. Got more SwK on his curve ball, which helped pump up his Ks; his improved Ctl sent Cmd to new heights. Prime age, high reliability—lots to like. Plus, years in BOS will come in handy for the impending mega-contract scrutiny.

Yr Tm	W	L	Sv	IP	K	ERA	xERA	WHIP	oOPS	vL	vR	BF/G	Ctl	Dom	Cmd	FpK	SwK	G	L	F	H%	S%	hr/f	GS	APC	DOM%	DIS%	Sv%	LI	RAR	BPV	BPX	R$
10 BOS	19	9	0	208	225	3.25	3.08	1.20	628	651	620	26.9	3.6	9.7	2.7	59%	11%	54	17	30	30%	74%	9%	32	105	69%	6%			21.4	110	178	$22
11 BOS	15	9	0	192	182	3.47	3.46	1.26	690	580	728	25.8	3.5	8.5	2.4	58%	9%	50	16	34	29%	76%	11%	31	103	61%	16%			11.1	87	130	$14
12 BOS	9	14	0	205	166	4.82	3.92	1.38	773	738	785	26.5	3.0	7.3	2.4	58%	9%	49	22	29	32%	67%	14%	33	104	52%	18%			-20.4	77	101	-$4
13 BOS	15	8	0	213	177	3.75	3.88	1.29	702	670	711	27.4	2.8	7.5	2.6	61%	9%	45	20	35	31%	73%	8%	33	108	61%	9%			2.9	81	106	$9
14 2 AL	16	11	0	220	220	2.46	3.19	1.10	635	697	617	27.7	2.0	9.0	4.6	61%	10%	42	21	37	31%	81%	7%	32	109	81%	9%			34.8	129	154	$26
1st Half	9	7	0	114	115	2.92	3.34	1.18	673	701	663	27.5	2.3	9.1	4.0	59%	10%	40	22	38	32%	77%	7%	17	109	76%	18%			11.5	119	143	$23
2nd Half	7	4	0	106	105	1.96	3.04	1.01	595	691	567	27.9	1.6	8.9	5.5	64%	11%	45	19	36	29%	85%	8%	15	109	87%	0%			23.2	140	168	$29
15 Proj	15	10	0	203	189	3.17	3.18	1.19	672	688	667	26.6	2.5	8.4	3.4	61%	10%	45	20	35	31%	76%	9%	31						14.3	108	128	$18

Lewis,Colby

Age: 35	Th: R	Role SP	Health F	LIMA Plan C
Ht: 6' 4"	Wt: 240	Type xFB	PT/Exp C	Rand Var +3
			Consist F	MM 2203

Had his hip "resurfaced" in Aug 2013, but was declared as a "full go" in mid-February, though ERA/WHIP argued otherwise. Ctl and Dom actually passable—but when hitters connected, chaos ensued (oOPS, LD%, FB%). Sure, he's due some H%/S% correction, but with his age and health, the upside is miniscule.

Yr Tm	W	L	Sv	IP	K	ERA	xERA	WHIP	oOPS	vL	vR	BF/G	Ctl	Dom	Cmd	FpK	SwK	G	L	F	H%	S%	hr/f	GS	APC	DOM%	DIS%	Sv%	LI	RAR	BPV	BPX	R$
10 TEX	12	13	0	201	196	3.72	3.78	1.19	660	693	627	26.4	2.9	8.8	3.0	63%	10%	38	17	45	29%	72%	8%	32	103	66%	3%			9.0	95	154	$15
11 TEX	14	10	0	200	169	4.40	4.07	1.21	738	829	616	26.2	2.5	7.6	3.0	66%	9%	34	17	49	28%	70%	12%	32	100	59%	19%			-11.4	81	121	$8
12 TEX	6	6	0	105	93	3.43	3.77	1.08	715	771	641	26.7	1.2	8.0	6.6	69%	9%	33	21	46	29%	75%	11%	16	102	69%	6%			7.6	122	159	$9
13 a/a	0	2	0	24	14	11.14	10.50	2.30				17.5	3.7	5.1	1.4						41%	53%								-21.5	-48	-63	-$15
14 TEX	10	14	0	170	133	5.18	4.48	1.52	840	853	823	26.3	2.5	7.0	2.8	66%	8%	33	23	44	35%	69%	10%	29	97	31%	10%			-30.2	69	82	-$11
1st Half	5	5	0	76	65	5.71	4.60	1.74	897	984	797	25.0	3.1	7.7	2.5	64%	8%	31	24	45	40%	68%	8%	14	96	14%	14%			-18.4	65	77	-$18
2nd Half	5	9	0	95	68	4.75	4.38	1.34	793	752	847	27.5	2.1	6.5	3.1	68%	8%	35	22	44	31%	69%	12%	15	98	47%	7%			-11.8	72	86	-$5
15 Proj	10	11	0	160	129	4.46	3.91	1.35	780	816	735	25.7	2.5	7.3	2.9	66%	8%	33	21	46	32%	71%	10%	26						-14.1	74	88	$0

Lincecum,Tim

Age: 31	Th: R	Role RP	Health A	LIMA Plan C
Ht: 5' 11"	Wt: 170	Type Pwr	PT/Exp A	Rand Var +2
			Consist A	MM 3201

After year #3 of sub-replacement level value, is this the new reality? Dom trend tracking lock-step with loss in velocity; SwK cracking; PQS-DIS piling up; relief appearances more frequent. Retains moderate GB lean and xERA still stubbornly average, but the chance of a mid-career u-turn back to profit borders on freakish.

Yr Tm	W	L	Sv	IP	K	ERA	xERA	WHIP	oOPS	vL	vR	BF/G	Ctl	Dom	Cmd	FpK	SwK	G	L	F	H%	S%	hr/f	GS	APC	DOM%	DIS%	Sv%	LI	RAR	BPV	BPX	R$
10 SF	15	10	0	206	224	3.53	3.22	1.28	681	736	616	27.3	3.2	9.8	3.0	57%	12%	49	19	32	32%	74%	10%	32	104	63%	19%			13.9	116	187	$16
11 SF	13	14	0	217	220	2.74	3.35	1.21	646	628	663	27.3	3.6	9.1	2.6	53%	12%	48	19	33	29%	79%	8%	33	109	73%	6%			32.3	94	141	$22
12 SF	10	15	0	186	190	5.18	3.97	1.47	767	722	813	25.0	4.4	9.2	2.1	55%	12%	46	24	30	32%	66%	15%	33	100	48%	24%			-26.7	72	94	-$8
13 SF	10	14	0	198	193	4.37	3.60	1.32	711	664	755	26.3	3.5	8.8	2.5	56%	12%	45	23	32	31%	69%	12%	32	103	56%	13%			-12.3	88	114	$2
14 SF	12	9	1	156	134	4.74	3.86	1.39	772	750	791	20.4	3.6	7.7	2.1	54%	10%	47	23	30	31%	68%	14%	26	81	54%	35%	100	0.78	-19.2	66	79	-$3
1st Half	6	5	0	92	83	4.42	3.72	1.34	729	764	697	24.3	3.5	8.1	2.3	53%	10%	47	22	31	30%	69%	12%	16	98	56%	25%			-7.7	76	91	$0
2nd Half	6	4	1	64	51	5.20	4.06	1.47	834	732	928	16.7	3.8	7.2	1.9	56%	10%	48	24	28	31%	67%	16%	10	64	50%	50%	100	0.74	-11.5	52	62	-$6
15 Proj	7	7	0	102	88	4.45	3.67	1.38	756	715	794	14.2	3.7	7.8	2.1	55%	10%	46	23	31	30%	70%	13%	13						-8.9	64	76	-$1

Lindstrom,Matt

Age: 35	Th: R	Role RP	Health F	LIMA Plan D+
Ht: 6' 3"	Wt: 215	Type GB	PT/Exp D	Rand Var +2
			Consist B	MM 2110

Mgr awarded him the closer's role due to "experience"—you know, that stellar 2010 campaign. Somehow notched 6 saves with a 1.2 Cmd before ankle surgery in May. Was the same pitcher upon August return—strong GB% but not enough juice to trust at the end of games. Seek better, younger, healthier RPs.

Yr Tm	W	L	Sv	IP	K	ERA	xERA	WHIP	oOPS	vL	vR	BF/G	Ctl	Dom	Cmd	FpK	SwK	G	L	F	H%	S%	hr/f	GS	APC	DOM%	DIS%	Sv%	LI	RAR	BPV	BPX	R$
10 HOU	2	5	23	53	43	4.39	4.20	1.65	792	769	809	4.2	3.4	7.3	2.2	59%	10%	49	19	32	37%	75%	9%	0	16			79	0.97	-2.0	66	108	$5
11 COL	2	2	2	54	36	3.00	3.82	1.22	661	698	636	3.6	2.3	6.0	2.6	58%	9%	47	21	31	30%	76%	6%	0	13			40	1.23	6.3	70	105	$2
12 2 TM	1	0	0	47	40	2.68	3.61	1.26	642	737	573	4.3	2.7	7.7	2.9	60%	10%	51	22	27	32%	79%	5%	0	17			0	0.77	7.7	94	123	$0
13 CHW	2	4	0	61	46	3.12	3.87	1.43	683	778	629	3.4	3.4	6.8	2.0	65%	10%	56	17	27	33%	78%	4%	0	12			0	1.27	5.6	65	84	-$2
14 CHW	2	2	6	34	18	5.03	4.74	1.74	893	857	937	4.5	3.2	4.8	1.5	56%	8%	51	20	28	36%	71%	9%	0	16			60	0.93	-5.4	29	35	-$4
1st Half	2	1	6	19	11	3.32	4.72	1.47	768	769	767	4.4	4.3	5.2	1.2	54%	9%	52	15	33	29%	81%	10%	0	16			67	1.16	1.0	9	11	$1
2nd Half	0	1	0	15	7	7.20	4.78	2.07	1027	952	1113	4.7	1.8	4.2	2.3	57%	7%	50	26	24	43%	63%	7%	0	16			0	0.65	-6.4	55	66	-$10
15 Proj	3	3	3	58	39	4.11	3.86	1.39	700	727	676	3.9	3.3	6.0	1.8	59%	9%	52	20	28	31%	71%	8%	0						-2.6	48	57	-$1

BRENT HERSHEY

Liriano,Francisco

Age: 31	Th: L	Role: SP	Health: D	LIMA Plan: B
			PT/Exp: B	Rand Var: 0
Ht: 6' 2"	Wt: 215	Type: Pwr GB	Consist: B	MM: 4403

A ratio repeat of 2013, but is he an all-in candidate for 2015? A strikeout per inning is standard, and his GB% is likewise elite. But FpK volatility equals a bunch of free passes, and the injury risk (hasn't made 30 starts in four years) puts a cap on his impact. Which makes almost any double-digit bid too risky.

Yr Tm	W	L	Sv	IP	K	ERA	xERA	WHIP	oOPS	vL	vR	BF/G	Ctl	Dom	Cmd	FpK	SwK	G	L	F	H%	S%	hr/f	GS	APC	DOM%	DIS%	Sv%	LI	RAR	BPV	BPX	R$
10 MIN	14	10	0	192	201	3.62	2.99	1.26	670	517	713	26.0	2.7	9.4	3.5	61%	13%	54	19	27	34%	71%	6%	31	97	65%	13%			11.0	128	208	$14
11 MIN	9	10	0	134	112	5.09	4.35	1.49	726	669	744	22.7	5.0	7.5	1.5	49%	12%	49	15	36	29%	67%	10%	24	88	46%	29%	0	0.75	-19.0	26	40	-$5
12 2AL	6	12	0	157	167	5.34	4.12	1.47	741	603	784	20.4	5.0	9.6	1.9	54%	13%	44	21	35	31%	65%	13%	28	80	50%	32%	0	0.83	-25.7	60	78	-$9
13 PIT *	18	9	0	180	182	3.36	3.15	1.26	611	321	689	24.4	3.4	9.1	2.7	58%	14%	50	24	25	31%	74%	8%	26	96	65%	15%			11.1	102	133	$15
14 PIT	7	10	0	162	175	3.38	3.33	1.30	644	735	622	23.8	4.5	9.7	2.2	56%	14%	54	19	27	29%	76%	12%	29	94	62%	17%			7.2	85	102	$6
1st Half	1	6	0	72	77	4.60	3.50	1.45	728	913	682	22.9	4.5	9.6	2.1	58%	14%	54	20	27	32%	70%	15%	14	90	50%	21%			-7.7	83	99	-$8
2nd Half	6	4	0	90	98	2.40	3.19	1.18	570	568	571	24.7	4.5	9.8	2.2	54%	14%	55	18	27	26%	81%	8%	15	97	73%	13%			14.9	88	105	$18
15 Proj	**12**	**10**	**0**	**175**	**183**	**3.61**	**3.22**	**1.32**	**660**	**590**	**678**	**23.4**	**4.2**	**9.4**	**2.2**	**56%**	**14%**	**52**	**20**	**28**	**30%**	**74%**	**11%**	**28**						**2.8**	**85**	**101**	**$9**

Lobstein,Kyle

Age: 25	Th: L	Role: SP	Health: A	LIMA Plan: D+
			PT/Exp: D	Rand Var: 0
Ht: 6' 3"	Wt: 200	Type: FB	Consist: B	MM: 1101

1-2, 4.35 ERA in 39 IP at DET. One case in which skills MLEs pretty much nailed it. True to his name, he's a finesse lefty who relies on changing speeds; his 10-K game in his second start was an abberation. To stick, he'll need to maintain his GB lean and throw strikes. It's a tough gig in this mid-90s culture.

Yr Tm	W	L	Sv	IP	K	ERA	xERA	WHIP	oOPS	vL	vR	BF/G	Ctl	Dom	Cmd	FpK	SwK	G	L	F	H%	S%	hr/f	GS	APC	DOM%	DIS%	Sv%	LI	RAR	BPV	BPX	R$
10																																	
11																																	
12 aa	8	7	0	144	111	4.40	4.48	1.51				23.1	4.1	7.0	1.7						32%	71%								-6.8	57	74	-$5
13 a/a	13	7	0	168	118	4.15	4.49	1.50				25.8	2.9	6.3	2.2						35%	72%								-5.9	65	85	-$2
14 DET *	10	13	0	185	126	4.99	5.51	1.63	665	620	686	25.0	2.8	6.1	2.2	53%	9%	45	17	38	37%	69%	7%	6	90	33%	17%	0	0.70	-28.6	52	62	-$15
1st Half	6	7	0	95	62	4.45	5.85	1.67				25.1	2.8	5.9	2.1						37%	75%	0%	0						-8.3	44	52	-$13
2nd Half	4	6	0	90	64	5.56	5.14	1.60	666	620	686	25.0	2.9	6.3	2.2	53%	9%	45	17	38	37%	64%	7%	6	90	33%	17%	0	0.70	-20.3	61	73	-$18
15 Proj	**6**	**5**	**0**	**106**	**73**	**4.67**	**4.30**	**1.55**	**761**	**706**	**786**	**24.9**	**3.1**	**6.2**	**2.0**	**53%**	**9%**	**44**	**17**	**39**	**34%**	**70%**	**6%**	**16**						**-12.1**	**49**	**58**	**-$6**

Locke,Jeff

Age: 27	Th: L	Role: SP	Health: A	LIMA Plan: D+
			PT/Exp: B	Rand Var: 0
Ht: 6' 0"	Wt: 185	Type:	Consist: A	MM: 2103

7-6, 3.91 ERA in 131 IP at PIT. March oblique injury pinged him early; mediocrity afterwards led to up-and-down season. DOM% improved as GB% solidified, but flaky Ctl and sub-par strikeout rate give little hope of future improvement. A stark reminder that a sub-4.00 ERA isn't what it used to be.

Yr Tm	W	L	Sv	IP	K	ERA	xERA	WHIP	oOPS	vL	vR	BF/G	Ctl	Dom	Cmd	FpK	SwK	G	L	F	H%	S%	hr/f	GS	APC	DOM%	DIS%	Sv%	LI	RAR	BPV	BPX	R$
10 aa	3	2	0	58	45	4.22	4.26	1.33				23.9	1.8	7.0	3.8						34%	69%								-1.0	97	157	-$1
11 PIT *	8	13	0	170	113	4.62	4.46	1.47	954	917	961	22.8	3.4	6.0	1.8	42%	6%	34	28	38	32%	69%	14%	4	74	0%	75%			-14.2	51	77	-$5
12 PIT *	11	8	0	176	135	3.60	4.22	1.38	749	836	716	23.1	2.8	6.9	2.5	62%	9%	49	15	36	32%	76%	17%	6	70	33%	33%	0	0.64	9.1	70	92	$5
13 PIT	10	7	0	166	125	3.52	4.11	1.38	686	748	667	23.7	4.5	6.8	1.5	58%	9%	53	21	26	28%	75%	9%	30	91	30%	23%			7.2	30	39	$4
14 PIT *	10	7	0	181	116	4.16	4.38	1.37	722	521	776	25.4	3.1	5.8	1.9	58%	10%	51	20	30	30%	72%	13%	21	93	48%	19%			-9.3	44	53	-$2
1st Half	4	2	0	84	50	4.38	4.20	1.38	627	515	637	25.1	2.8	5.4	1.9	63%	11%	51	17	32	31%	69%	6%	5	86	60%	0%			-6.6	51	61	-$5
2nd Half	6	5	0	98	66	3.96	4.08	1.37	752	522	832	26.1	3.3	6.1	1.8	57%	9%	50	21	29	29%	76%	16%	16	96	44%	25%			-2.7	48	57	$1
15 Proj	**8**	**10**	**0**	**174**	**120**	**4.03**	**4.01**	**1.45**	**761**	**724**	**771**	**24.7**	**3.5**	**6.2**	**1.8**	**59%**	**9%**	**49**	**19**	**31**	**31%**	**74%**	**9%**	**30**						**-6.2**	**44**	**52**	**-$1**

Lohse,Kyle

Age: 36	Th: R	Role: SP	Health: B	LIMA Plan: C+
			PT/Exp: A	Rand Var: 0
Ht: 6' 2"	Wt: 210	Type: Con	Consist: A	MM: 2105

"Steady" both describes his output over the past few seasons as well as the demeanor his fantasy owners need to have. As in, not over-reacting to his 9-2, 3.08 ERA 1st half, nor his walk "binge" in the 2nd half. xERA, BPV, Cmd all stable. Given how cheaply he'll come, there's low-level profit potential here without much risk.

Yr Tm	W	L	Sv	IP	K	ERA	xERA	WHIP	oOPS	vL	vR	BF/G	Ctl	Dom	Cmd	FpK	SwK	G	L	F	H%	S%	hr/f	GS	APC	DOM%	DIS%	Sv%	LI	RAR	BPV	BPX	R$
10 STL *	5	9	0	111	67	6.40	6.17	1.73	905	985	846	23.0	3.0	5.4	1.8	56%	5%	43	19	38	37%	63%	7%	18	90	22%	39%			-31.7	30	49	-$14
11 STL	14	8	0	188	111	3.39	4.09	1.17	680	696	667	25.8	2.0	5.3	2.6	67%	6%	41	22	37	28%	73%	7%	30	93	47%	10%			12.8	60	91	$14
12 STL	16	3	0	211	143	2.86	4.02	1.09	642	664	623	26.2	1.6	6.1	3.8	69%	7%	41	24	36	28%	77%	8%	33	95	67%	0%			30.1	85	111	$26
13 MIL	11	10	0	199	125	3.35	4.03	1.17	700	727	676	25.2	1.6	5.7	3.5	66%	8%	40	21	38	28%	77%	11%	32	94	53%	6%			12.6	76	99	$13
14 MIL	13	9	0	198	141	3.54	3.99	1.15	682	725	643	26.4	2.0	6.4	3.1	64%	9%	40	19	41	28%	73%	9%	31	97	52%	16%			4.9	78	93	$12
1st Half	9	2	0	114	79	3.08	3.81	1.08	630	599	654	27.3	1.7	6.2	3.6	64%	8%	43	19	38	27%	74%	8%	17	99	59%	6%			9.3	87	103	$20
2nd Half	4	7	0	84	62	4.16	4.22	1.25	751	866	627	25.2	2.5	6.6	2.7	64%	9%	36	20	44	28%	71%	11%	14	94	43%	29%			-4.4	67	80	$0
15 Proj	**12**	**9**	**0**	**189**	**128**	**3.62**	**3.72**	**1.19**	**703**	**751**	**660**	**24.9**	**2.0**	**6.1**	**3.1**	**65%**	**8%**	**40**	**21**	**40**	**28%**	**73%**	**9%**	**30**						**2.8**	**74**	**88**	**$11**

Lopez,Javier

Age: 37	Th: L	Role: RP	Health: A	LIMA Plan: D+
			PT/Exp: D	Rand Var: -4
Ht: 6' 4"	Wt: 220	Type: xGB	Consist: C	MM: 3000

Took 65 appearances to tally those 38 IP; third straight injury-free season of less than 40 frames. At 37, he compensated for a plunging Cmd by getting two-thirds of batted balls to go into the turf. But an aging southpaw with disappearing BPIs and teeny IP is not roster-worthy, even in deep leagues.

Yr Tm	W	L	Sv	IP	K	ERA	xERA	WHIP	oOPS	vL	vR	BF/G	Ctl	Dom	Cmd	FpK	SwK	G	L	F	H%	S%	hr/f	GS	APC	DOM%	DIS%	Sv%	LI	RAR	BPV	BPX	R$
10 2 NL	4	2	0	58	38	2.34	3.53	1.21	636	492	766	3.1	3.1	5.9	1.9	66%	9%	62	16	23	28%	81%	5%	0	11			0	0.94	12.4	62	101	$4
11 SF	5	2	1	53	40	2.72	3.63	1.28	603	430	761	3.2	4.4	6.8	1.5	65%	11%	63	15	22	28%	76%	0%	0	12			33	1.52	8.0	44	66	$3
12 SF	3	0	7	36	28	2.50	3.74	1.42	700	543	979	2.2	3.5	7.0	2.0	61%	11%	60	19	21	33%	82%	4%	0	8			78	1.85	6.7	70	91	$2
13 SF	4	2	1	39	37	1.83	2.99	1.07	573	431	805	2.3	2.7	8.5	3.1	58%	12%	61	16	23	28%	83%	4%	0	9			100	1.40	9.9	117	153	$4
14 SF	1	1	0	38	22	3.11	4.24	1.33	629	538	783	2.6	4.5	5.3	1.2	65%	9%	66	13	22	26%	77%	8%	0	9			0	0.98	2.9	16	19	-$2
1st Half	1	1	0	16	7	3.31	4.95	1.35	697	663	742	2.3	5.0	3.9	0.8	63%	8%	62	13	25	22%	80%	14%	0	8			0	1.25	0.9	-25	-29	-$3
2nd Half	0	0	0	21	15	2.95	3.72	1.31	576	452	818	2.8	4.2	6.3	1.5	66%	9%	69	12	18	28%	75%	0%	0	10			0	0.73	2.1	47	56	-$1
15 Proj	**1**	**2**	**0**	**38**	**24**	**3.83**	**3.55**	**1.24**	**619**	**500**	**811**	**2.4**	**3.6**	**5.8**	**1.6**	**63%**	**10%**	**64**	**15**	**22**	**27%**	**68%**	**6%**	**0**						**-0.4**	**48**	**57**	**-$2**

Loup,Aaron

Age: 27	Th: L	Role: RP	Health: A	LIMA Plan: B+
			PT/Exp: C	Rand Var: -2
Ht: 5' 11"	Wt: 205	Type: Pwr GB	Consist: B	MM: 3211

Twelve MLB saves in three years and a growing LI piques our interest: A manager's fave or potential late-inning weapon? BPI argues for the former—though a GB machine, he couldn't find the plate in 2014 and his ERA benefitted from H% luck. Still has time at 27, but Cmd improvement must come first.

Yr Tm	W	L	Sv	IP	K	ERA	xERA	WHIP	oOPS	vL	vR	BF/G	Ctl	Dom	Cmd	FpK	SwK	G	L	F	H%	S%	hr/f	GS	APC	DOM%	DIS%	Sv%	LI	RAR	BPV	BPX	R$
10																																	
11																																	
12 TOR *	0	5	3	76	56	3.26	3.94	1.31	547	462	638	4.5	2.0	6.6	3.4	58%	6%	55	17	27	33%	76%	0%	0	13			60	1.16	7.1	91	119	$1
13 TOR	4	6	2	69	53	2.47	3.06	1.14	670	506	777	4.4	1.7	6.9	4.1	59%	9%	60	17	23	30%	81%	11%	0	16			67	0.96	12.0	116	152	$6
14 TOR	4	4	4	69	56	3.15	3.58	1.17	647	559	695	4.0	3.9	7.3	1.9	56%	10%	54	20	26	25%	74%	9%	0	15			50	1.25	5.0	58	69	$4
1st Half	2	1	2	38	31	3.29	3.72	1.15	561	453	622	4.2	4.5	7.3	1.6	57%	10%	52	23	25	24%	68%	0%	0	16			50	1.49	2.1	40	48	$4
2nd Half	2	3	2	30	25	2.97	3.40	1.19	752	706	776	3.7	3.3	7.4	2.3	56%	10%	57	17	26	26%	81%	18%	0	14			50	1.00	2.9	81	96	$5
15 Proj	**4**	**5**	**5**	**73**	**56**	**3.39**	**3.43**	**1.24**	**697**	**572**	**777**	**4.1**	**3.3**	**7.0**	**2.1**	**57%**	**9%**	**55**	**18**	**27**	**28%**	**74%**	**9%**	**0**						**3.2**	**70**	**83**	**$4**

Lyles,Jordan

Age: 24	Th: R	Role: SP	Health: D	LIMA Plan: C
			PT/Exp: C	Rand Var: +1
Ht: 6' 4"	Wt: 215	Type:	Consist: B	MM: 2103

Broken left hand cost him two months, and first-pass BPI scan is unimpressive. But if you squint, there are some rays: heavy GBer; keeps team in the game (declining DIS%); youth and pedigree on his side. Pummelled by lefties, though, and Ctl trend a concern. Watchable—but not draftable—for now.

Yr Tm	W	L	Sv	IP	K	ERA	xERA	WHIP	oOPS	vL	vR	BF/G	Ctl	Dom	Cmd	FpK	SwK	G	L	F	H%	S%	hr/f	GS	APC	DOM%	DIS%	Sv%	LI	RAR	BPV	BPX	R$
10 a/a	7	12	0	159	124	4.03	4.97	1.51				25.5	2.5	7.1	2.9						36%	74%								0.9	75	121	$0
11 HOU *	5	11	0	156	104	4.79	4.66	1.39	817	795	834	20.6	2.4	6.0	2.5	62%	9%	41	21	38	32%	67%	12%	15	79	40%	13%	0	0.80	-16.4	55	82	-$5
12 HOU *	10	12	0	182	128	4.72	4.60	1.37	772	886	683	23.9	2.4	6.3	2.6	61%	7%	54	17	29	32%	68%	15%	25	95	36%	32%			-15.8	59	77	-$3
13 HOU *	9	11	1	165	103	5.64	5.11	1.53	801	751	859	21.8	3.0	5.6	1.9	56%	7%	48	21	30	33%	64%	12%	25	91	36%	28%	50	1.01	-36.3	39	50	-$14
14 COL	7	4	0	127	90	4.33	3.90	1.37	750	844	654	24.8	3.3	6.4	2.0	57%	8%	52	23	26	30%	70%	12%	22	95	55%	9%			-9.3	57	68	-$2
1st Half	5	1	0	69	49	3.52	3.73	1.30	709	737	680	24.3	3.4	6.4	1.9	54%	7%	53	25	21	29%	74%	11%	12	94	58%	17%			1.9	55	65	$3
2nd Half	2	3	0	58	41	5.31	4.11	1.44	798	968	624	25.5	3.1	6.4	2.1	60%	9%	50	19	31	32%	64%	12%	10	97	50%	0%			-11.1	59	70	-$9
15 Proj	**9**	**9**	**0**	**174**	**123**	**4.08**	**3.77**	**1.41**	**767**	**822**	**712**	**23.3**	**3.0**	**6.4**	**2.1**	**58%**	**8%**	**50**	**21**	**29**	**32%**	**73%**	**11%**	**32**						**-7.3**	**62**	**74**	**$0**

BRENT HERSHEY

Lynn,Lance

Age: 28	Th: R	Role SP	Health B	LIMA Plan C	
Ht: 6' 5"	Wt: 240	Type Pwr	PT/Exp A	Rand Var -4	
			Consist A	MM 3305	

ERA and R$ portray a breakout, but xERA and BPV are flat. In fact, Dom, SwK say he wasn't quite as imposing, with ERA gains primarily a function of S%. BPX even says his skills dipped below average in today's pitching-rich game. Stability and durability have value, but don't pay for another sub-3.00 ERA.

Yr	Tm	W	L	Sv	IP	K	ERA	xERA	WHIP	oOPS	vL	vR	BF/G	Ctl	Dom	Cmd	FpK	SwK	G	L	F	H%	S%	hr/f	GS	APC	DOM%	DIS%	Sv%	LI	RAR	BPV	BPX	R$
10	aaa	13	10	0	164	118	4.75	4.39	1.40				23.9	3.2	6.5	2.0						31%	67%								-13.6	54	87	$1
11	STL *	8	4	1	110	93	3.67	3.51	1.32	591	723	504	15.1	2.9	7.6	2.6	57%	10%	57	11	32	33%	71%	12%	2	31	50%	0%	50	0.94	3.7	92	138	$4
12	STL	18	7	0	176	180	3.78	3.58	1.32	728	841	624	21.3	3.3	9.2	2.8	61%	10%	44	24	32	32%	73%	10%	29	86	59%	14%	0	0.83	5.0	99	130	$11
13	STL	15	10	0	202	198	3.97	3.63	1.31	701	765	652	25.9	3.4	8.8	2.6	63%	10%	43	23	34	32%	70%	7%	33	102	64%	15%			-2.6	88	115	$8
14	STL	15	10	0	204	181	2.74	3.81	1.26	662	697	635	26.2	3.2	8.0	2.5	60%	9%	44	20	36	30%	80%	6%	33	105	67%	9%			25.2	80	95	$16
1st Half		8	6	0	101	91	3.38	3.83	1.32	675	733	625	25.6	3.3	8.1	2.5	59%	10%	45	20	35	32%	75%	6%	17	101	59%	18%			4.6	80	95	$11
2nd Half		7	4	0	102	90	2.11	3.80	1.20	650	658	644	26.9	3.1	7.9	2.6	61%	9%	44	19	37	29%	85%	6%	16	108	75%	0%			20.6	81	97	$21
15	**Proj**	**16**	**10**	**0**	**203**	**187**	**3.69**	**3.50**	**1.30**	**691**	**754**	**642**	**23.7**	**3.3**	**8.3**	**2.5**	**61%**	**10%**	**43**	**21**	**36**	**31%**	**72%**	**7%**	**35**						**1.2**	**81**	**96**	**$11**

Lyons,Tyler

Age: 27	Th: L	Role SP	Health C	LIMA Plan C	
Ht: 6' 4"	Wt: 200	Type	PT/Exp D	Rand Var +1	
			Consist C	MM 2100	

0-4, 4.42 ERA in 37 IP at STL. Choppy season of comings, goings, starting and relieving, punctuated by shoulder strain. Showed flashes of dominance as RP (9.8 Dom, 4.0 Cmd) against whom LHB had no shot (3 hits in 33 AB). It's probably too early to call LOOGY, but there are far worse vocations.

Yr	Tm	W	L	Sv	IP	K	ERA	xERA	WHIP	oOPS	vL	vR	BF/G	Ctl	Dom	Cmd	FpK	SwK	G	L	F	H%	S%	hr/f	GS	APC	DOM%	DIS%	Sv%	LI	RAR	BPV	BPX	R$
10																																		
11																																		
12	a/a	9	13	0	153	117	4.50	4.45	1.38				23.7	2.2	6.9	3.2						34%	68%								-9.2	82	107	-$2
13	STL *	9	6	0	153	112	4.08	3.21	1.18	725	630	762	21.1	2.1	6.6	3.2	59%	9%	47	19	33	30%	65%	10%	8	66	50%	25%	0	0.97	-4.0	93	121	$6
14	STL *	8	6	0	120	97	4.80	4.91	1.45	682	280	806	19.7	2.2	7.3	3.3	62%	11%	43	16	40	35%	68%	10%	4	49	75%	25%	0	0.54	-15.7	81	96	-$5
1st Half		2	3	0	56	50	5.94	5.22	1.52	743	333	842	18.8	2.9	7.9	2.7	61%	10%	45	14	41	36%	61%	13%	4	61	75%	25%	0	0.66	-15.3	68	81	-$13
2nd Half		6	3	0	64	48	3.79	4.63	1.38	536	205	697	20.6	1.6	6.7	4.3	64%	13%	39	21	39	35%	74%	0%	0	34			0	0.40	-0.4	102	121	$2
15	**Proj**	**4**	**3**	**0**	**58**	**43**	**4.11**	**3.80**	**1.37**	**779**	**510**	**858**	**20.9**	**2.4**	**6.7**	**2.8**	**60%**	**10%**	**44**	**17**	**39**	**32%**	**72%**	**9%**	**12**						**-2.6**	**77**	**92**	**-$2**

Machi,Jean

Age: 33	Th: R	Role RP	Health A	LIMA Plan B	
Ht: 6' 0"	Wt: 255	Type GB	PT/Exp D	Rand Var -3	
			Consist F	MM 4210	

Didn't have the charm of anonymity in his favor in 2014. But despite Dom drop, he was still a force in 1st half before wobbly Ctl, S% dive, and three-HR September caught up with him in the 2nd half. SwK suggests Dom hasn't disappeared, and GB% remains hearty. But you can only sneak up on people once.

Yr	Tm	W	L	Sv	IP	K	ERA	xERA	WHIP	oOPS	vL	vR	BF/G	Ctl	Dom	Cmd	FpK	SwK	G	L	F	H%	S%	hr/f	GS	APC	DOM%	DIS%	Sv%	LI	RAR	BPV	BPX	R$
10	aaa	5	5	23	60	43	4.72	4.77	1.58				4.5	5.0	6.5	1.3						30%	72%								-4.7	40	64	$6
11																																		
12	SF *	2	1	15	63	37	4.40	5.79	1.61	804	286	1352	4.6	2.5	5.2	2.0	61%	13%	41	14	45	35%	75%	20%	0	13			83	0.39	-3.0	33	43	-$1
13	SF *	6	2	2	71	65	2.04	2.34	1.07	586	642	552	4.1	1.9	8.2	4.3	60%	11%	54	20	26	30%	81%	5%	0	15			50	1.16	16.1	140	183	$9
14	SF	7	1	2	66	51	2.58	3.18	0.95	602	686	551	3.5	2.4	6.9	2.8	60%	13%	52	20	28	23%	76%	10%	0	13			40	1.26	9.5	89	106	$8
1st Half		5	0	2	33	25	1.36	2.88	0.91	565	377	645	3.5	1.9	6.8	3.6	63%	13%	57	20	23	24%	86%	5%	0	13			100	1.62	9.7	107	127	$13
2nd Half		2	1	0	33	26	3.78	3.48	0.99	638	893	435	3.5	3.0	7.0	2.4	57%	13%	47	20	34	21%	66%	14%	0	13			0	0.92	-0.2	71	84	$4
15	**Proj**	**5**	**2**	**1**	**58**	**45**	**3.04**	**3.27**	**1.14**	**671**	**773**	**608**	**3.9**	**2.6**	**7.0**	**2.6**	**60%**	**12%**	**52**	**20**	**28**	**27%**	**76%**	**10%**	**0**						**5.0**	**85**	**101**	**$4**

Maeda,Kenta

Age: 27	Th: R	Role SP	Health A	LIMA Plan C+	
Ht: 6' 0"	Wt: 154	Type	PT/Exp A	Rand Var -1	
			Consist B	MM 3203	

One of Japan's finest hurlers, it's not known if he'll be made available to US teams in time for the 2015 season. Eight-year BPIs are nice (1.05 WHIP, 7.3 Dom, 1.9 Ctl, and 3.8 Cmd) even as scouts agree that his repertoire isn't on the Darvish/Tanaka level. But on draft day, preconceptions often trump prudence.

Yr	Tm	W	L	Sv	IP	K	ERA	xERA	WHIP	oOPS	vL	vR	BF/G	Ctl	Dom	Cmd	FpK	SwK	G	L	F	H%	S%	hr/f	GS	APC	DOM%	DIS%	Sv%	LI	RAR	BPV	BPX	R$
10	for	15	8	0	216	165	2.74	3.08	1.09				30.2	2.4	6.9	2.9						26%	81%								35.6	81	130	$26
11	for	10	12	0	216	182	3.05	3.26	1.13				27.5	2.2	7.6	3.4						28%	77%								23.7	95	143	$20
12	for	14	7	0	206	162	1.90	2.59	1.10				27.9	2.4	7.1	3.0						28%	85%								53.8	101	132	$33
13	for	15	7	0	176	150	2.60	2.95	1.07				26.3	2.5	7.7	3.0						25%	82%								27.4	88	114	$23
14	for	11	8	0	171	137	3.20	3.59	1.21				27.6	2.6	7.2	2.8						29%	77%								11.3	78	93	$10
1st Half																																		
2nd Half																																		
15	**Proj**	**10**	**7**	**0**	**158**	**130**	**4.06**	**3.48**	**1.28**				**25.8**	**2.4**	**7.4**	**3.1**	**62%**	**9%**	**44**	**20**	**36**	**31%**	**70%**	**9%**	**27**						**-6.2**	**91**	**108**	**$5**

Maholm,Paul

Age: 33	Th: L	Role RP	Health F	LIMA Plan D+	
Ht: 6' 2"	Wt: 245	Type Con GB	PT/Exp B	Rand Var +1	
			Consist A	MM 1000	

Last seen tearing his ACL on August 1. It was perhaps a merciful end to washout season for starter-turned-reliever who was ineffective in both roles. 55% FpK is anathema to a control pitcher, his Dom and Ctl are on a collision course. GB% continues to be one of his few defenses against hr/f. It's not looking good.

Yr	Tm	W	L	Sv	IP	K	ERA	xERA	WHIP	oOPS	vL	vR	BF/G	Ctl	Dom	Cmd	FpK	SwK	G	L	F	H%	S%	hr/f	GS	APC	DOM%	DIS%	Sv%	LI	RAR	BPV	BPX	R$
10	PIT	9	15	0	185	102	5.10	4.52	1.56	812	645	842	26.3	3.0	5.0	1.6	61%	6%	51	19	30	34%	67%	8%	32	96	34%	31%			-23.3	37	60	-$9
11	PIT	6	14	0	162	97	3.66	4.00	1.29	711	697	714	26.4	2.8	5.4	1.9	60%	6%	50	22	28	29%	72%	8%	26	94	35%	23%			5.7	50	75	$4
12	2 NL	13	11	0	189	140	3.67	3.76	1.22	714	703	718	24.6	2.5	6.7	2.6	63%	8%	51	21	27	29%	73%	13%	31	93	65%	19%	0	0.77	8.1	81	105	$12
13	ATL	10	11	0	153	105	4.41	3.93	1.41	773	559	845	25.8	2.8	6.2	2.2	64%	7%	51	24	25	32%	71%	14%	26	96	35%	19%			-10.3	66	85	-$3
14	LA	1	5	0	71	34	4.84	4.57	1.56	816	745	847	10.4	3.6	4.3	1.2	55%	6%	54	20	26	31%	71%	13%	8	39	25%	50%	0	0.40	-9.6	14	16	-$8
1st Half		1	4	0	52	25	4.85	4.78	1.62	848	720	899	11.1	4.0	4.3	1.1	52%	6%	55	18	27	30%	74%	16%	7	43	14%	57%	0	0.47	-7.1	3	4	-$9
2nd Half		0	1	0	19	9	4.82	4.00	1.39	722	807	676	8.7	2.4	4.3	1.8	64%	5%	53	25	22	32%	62%	0%	1	29	100%	0%	0	0.26	-2.5	44	53	-$5
15	**Proj**	**1**	**3**	**0**	**38**	**21**	**4.51**	**4.13**	**1.47**	**772**	**717**	**793**	**13.9**	**3.4**	**5.0**	**1.5**	**61%**	**6%**	**53**	**22**	**25**	**31%**	**70%**	**10%**	**5**						**-3.6**	**30**	**36**	**-$4**

Maness,Michael

Age: 26	Th: R	Role RP	Health A	LIMA Plan B+	
Ht: 6' 0"	Wt: 190	Type Con xGB	PT/Exp D	Rand Var 0	
			Consist B	MM 5001	

Soft tosser has little margin for error, and in his two seasons he's made few. Low-3.00 xERA, GB% around 60%, Ctl around 1.5—corroborate to keep the opposition at bay. Control artists are susceptible to volatility and there is work to do vLHB, but winning teams seem to have at least one of these guys.

Yr	Tm	W	L	Sv	IP	K	ERA	xERA	WHIP	oOPS	vL	vR	BF/G	Ctl	Dom	Cmd	FpK	SwK	G	L	F	H%	S%	hr/f	GS	APC	DOM%	DIS%	Sv%	LI	RAR	BPV	BPX	R$
10																																		
11																																		
12	aa	11	3	0	124	68	3.62	3.91	1.17				24.7	0.7	5.0	7.6						31%	72%								6.0	162	211	$7
13	STL *	7	4	1	87	49	3.05	4.34	1.37	725	726	724	5.2	1.7	5.1	3.1	67%	7%	68	19	12	33%	79%	17%	0	13			33	1.16	8.8	73	95	$2
14	STL	6	4	3	80	55	2.91	3.17	1.10	668	852	565	4.3	1.2	6.2	5.0	67%	9%	56	19	25	29%	77%	11%	0	15			100	1.14	8.2	112	133	$7
1st Half		3	2	1	37	24	2.65	3.58	1.37	744	777	723	5.0	1.4	5.8	4.0	64%	7%	54	22	24	35%	82%	7%	0	18			100	0.73	5.0	97	116	$2
2nd Half		3	2	2	43	31	3.14	2.82	0.86	593	940	422	3.9	1.0	6.5	6.2	70%	11%	58	16	26	23%	69%	16%	0	13			100	1.47	3.2	125	149	$10
15	**Proj**	**6**	**3**	**0**	**73**	**45**	**3.07**	**3.06**	**1.19**	**722**	**848**	**656**	**5.3**	**1.3**	**5.6**	**4.4**	**68%**	**8%**	**61**	**19**	**20**	**30%**	**77%**	**13%**	**0**						**6.0**	**106**	**126**	**$4**

Marshall,Evan

Age: 25	Th: R	Role RP	Health A	LIMA Plan C	
Ht: 6' 2"	Wt: 220	Type Pwr xGB	PT/Exp F	Rand Var -2	
			Consist C	MM 4300	

4-4, 2.74 ERA in 49 IP at ARI. Rookie became bullpen mainstay upon May arrival and kicked into higher gear in the 2nd half. Small sample size caveat and borderline Ctl warn us not to go all in, but high Dom/GB% profile always makes analysts salivate. In the never-ending search for cheap saves, here's a target.

Yr	Tm	W	L	Sv	IP	K	ERA	xERA	WHIP	oOPS	vL	vR	BF/G	Ctl	Dom	Cmd	FpK	SwK	G	L	F	H%	S%	hr/f	GS	APC	DOM%	DIS%	Sv%	LI	RAR	BPV	BPX	R$
10																																		
11																																		
12	aa	6	3	16	49	23	4.27	5.12	1.61				5.1	2.9	4.3	1.5						35%	73%								-1.6	37	48	$2
13	aaa	3	6	3	58	49	4.11	5.34	1.77				4.9	4.1	7.7	1.9						40%	76%								-1.7	69	89	-$5
14	ARI *	4	5	1	66	70	2.18	3.12	1.24	709	781	666	3.8	2.9	9.5	3.2	62%	15%	61	17	22	33%	84%	10%	0	14			50	1.26	12.7	118	141	$5
1st Half		2	3	1	37	36	2.41	2.78	1.16	771	816	747	4.1	2.8	8.6	3.1	64%	14%	56	17	27	30%	81%	13%	0	16			100	1.25	6.1	111	132	$5
2nd Half		2	2	0	29	34	1.88	2.51	1.36	664	759	604	3.4	3.1	10.7	3.4	60%	15%	64	17	18	37%	87%	7%	0	14			0	1.27	6.6	150	179	$4
15	**Proj**	**4**	**5**	**0**	**58**	**53**	**3.10**	**3.20**	**1.50**	**753**	**834**	**704**	**4.3**	**3.4**	**8.2**	**2.4**	**62%**	**15%**	**61**	**17**	**22**	**36%**	**79%**	**6%**	**0**						**4.6**	**96**	**114**	**-$1**

ROB CARROLL

Martinez,Carlos

Age: 23	Th: R	Role RP	Health	A	LIMA Plan	C
Ht: 6' 0"	Wt: 185	Type Pwr	PT/Exp	D	Rand Var	+1
			Consist	A	MM	3301

Killer SwK and strong Dom showed 'em what 2013's late-season fuss was all about. But while he held RHB to .301 Slg, 0.9 Cmd vL says there is work to do. Initially stymied by lack of clear role, he shook off several PQS-0 starts to shine in 2nd half relief. This may be the last time you'll get him this cheap.

Yr Tm	W	L	Sv	IP	K	ERA	xERA	WHIP	oOPS	vL	vR	BF/G	Ctl	Dom	Cmd	FpK	SwK	G	L	F	H%	S%	hr/f	GS	APC	DOM%	DIS%	Sv%	LI	RAR	BPV	BPX	R$
10																																	
11																																	
12 aa	4	3	0	71	50	3.05	3.32	1.21				19.2	2.6	6.3	2.4						29%	77%								8.5	74	97	$3
13 STL *	8	4	1	108	86	3.16	3.09	1.25	704	764	661	11.9	2.9	7.1	2.4	62%	10%	52	19	29	30%	74%	4%	1	23	0%	100%	100	0.75	9.5	88	115	$6
14 STL	2	4	1	89	84	4.03	3.54	1.41	713	849	609	6.8	3.6	8.5	2.3	58%	14%	51	22	27	34%	70%	6%	7	24	29%	57%	17	1.34	-3.2	83	99	-$3
1st Half	1	3	0	48	40	4.13	3.69	1.33	669	885	482	6.2	4.1	7.5	1.8	56%	13%	56	19	26	30%	68%	6%	3	22	33%	67%	0	1.61	-2.3	57	68	-$3
2nd Half	1	1	1	41	44	3.92	3.36	1.50	760	804	730	7.6	3.0	9.6	3.1	60%	14%	46	25	29	39%	73%	6%	4	27	25%	50%	100	0.96	-0.9	114	136	-$2
15 Proj	**5**	**4**	**0**	**102**	**88**	**3.56**	**3.38**	**1.34**	**690**	**799**	**610**	**9.0**	**3.2**	**7.8**	**2.5**	**58%**	**14%**	**50**	**22**	**28**	**33%**	**73%**	**6%**	**0**						**2.2**	**84**	**100**	**$2**

Martinez,Nicholas

Age: 24	Th: R	Role SP	Health	A	LIMA Plan	D+
Ht: 6' 1"	Wt: 175	Type Con xFB	PT/Exp	D	Rand Var	-1
			Consist	F	MM	1000

Given his less-than-pedestrian BPI, former college middle infielder wasn't horrible in rookie season, at least as long as you only look at the ERA. But with an xERA that starts with a "5", single-digit BPV (and BPX!), and a minus sign in front of a two-digit RAR, well, "not horrible" might actually be soft-pedaling this.

Yr Tm	W	L	Sv	IP	K	ERA	xERA	WHIP	oOPS	vL	vR	BF/G	Ctl	Dom	Cmd	FpK	SwK	G	L	F	H%	S%	hr/f	GS	APC	DOM%	DIS%	Sv%	LI	RAR	BPV	BPX	R$
10																																	
11																																	
12																																	
13 aa	2	0	0	32	19	1.54	0.32	0.66				22.3	2.2	5.4	2.5						15%	79%								9.2	102	133	$4
14 TEX	5	12	0	140	77	4.55	5.24	1.46	795	832	746	21.0	3.5	4.9	1.4	53%	7%	33	20	47	29%	72%	8%	24	83	29%	33%	0	0.84	-14.1	5	6	-$8
1st Half	1	5	0	62	28	4.65	5.99	1.69	865	972	736	18.7	4.4	4.1	0.9	54%	6%	32	20	48	31%	76%	8%	10	73	10%	50%	0	0.88	-6.9	-35	-42	-$16
2nd Half	4	7	0	78	49	4.48	4.68	1.28	736	722	755	23.5	2.9	5.6	2.0	52%	8%	34	19	46	28%	67%	8%	14	93	43%	21%			-7.1	36	43	-$1
15 Proj	**2**	**3**	**0**	**51**	**29**	**4.36**	**4.30**	**1.13**	**625**	**653**	**588**	**21.3**	**3.0**	**5.1**	**1.7**	**53%**	**7%**	**33**	**20**	**47**	**24%**	**62%**	**6%**	**9**						**-3.8**	**22**	**27**	**-$1**

Masterson,Justin

Age: 30	Th: R	Role SP	Health	B	LIMA Plan	C
Ht: 6' 6"	Wt: 250	Type Pwr xGB	PT/Exp	A	Rand Var	+5
			Consist	B	MM	3305

Scattershot BPIs weren't much of a surprise, but everything fell apart at once. Theories why: mid-season knee injury; losing 2-3 mph on his pitches; H% and S% misfortune; unreal 2nd half hr/f. But Dom was still strong and core strength—inducing GB—remained intact. If a bounceback occurs, it will start there.

Yr Tm	W	L	Sv	IP	K	ERA	xERA	WHIP	oOPS	vL	vR	BF/G	Ctl	Dom	Cmd	FpK	SwK	G	L	F	H%	S%	hr/f	GS	APC	DOM%	DIS%	Sv%	LI	RAR	BPV	BPX	R$
10 CLE	6	13	0	180	140	4.70	3.78	1.50	738	784	681	23.6	3.7	7.0	1.9	55%	9%	60	15	25	33%	69%	10%	29	91	41%	28%	0	0.85	-13.8	65	106	-$4
11 CLE	12	10	0	216	158	3.21	3.56	1.28	667	746	560	26.7	2.7	6.6	2.4	57%	8%	55	18	27	31%	75%	6%	33	102	55%	12%	0	0.75	19.6	78	118	$14
12 CLE	11	15	0	206	159	4.93	4.08	1.45	736	825	613	26.6	3.8	6.9	1.8	58%	9%	56	19	25	31%	66%	11%	34	101	47%	26%			-23.3	55	72	-$7
13 CLE	14	10	0	193	195	3.45	3.08	1.20	624	698	507	25.1	3.5	9.1	2.6	58%	10%	58	18	24	29%	72%	11%	29	94	79%	10%	0	0.72	9.9	104	136	$15
14 2 TM	7	9	0	129	116	5.88	3.83	1.63	826	910	729	21.1	4.8	8.1	1.7	55%	10%	58	20	22	34%	64%	15%	25	80	40%	48%	0	0.71	-33.9	52	62	-$14
1st Half	4	5	0	93	85	5.03	3.67	1.54	763	879	619	24.6	4.8	8.2	1.7	57%	10%	60	20	21	33%	66%	9%	17	93	47%	41%			-14.8	55	66	-$12
2nd Half	3	4	0	36	31	8.07	4.23	1.88	978	996	961	15.8	4.8	7.8	1.6	51%	9%	54	22	24	37%	58%	26%	8	61	25%	63%	0	0.64	-19.1	44	52	-$20
15 Proj	**12**	**14**	**0**	**189**	**164**	**3.99**	**3.50**	**1.37**	**688**	**737**	**628**	**23.7**	**4.2**	**7.8**	**1.9**	**55%**	**9%**	**56**	**20**	**25**	**30%**	**72%**	**11%**	**32**						**-5.9**	**61**	**72**	**$4**

Matsuzaka,Daisuke

Age: 34	Th: R	Role RP	Health	F	LIMA Plan	D+
Ht: 6' 0"	Wt: 205	Type Pwr FB	PT/Exp	D	Rand Var	-1
			Consist	D	MM	1201

3-3, 3.89 ERA in 83 IP at NYM. PRO: Logged career bests in Dom and GB%; most MLB IP since 2010; sniffed 2.0 Cmd in 2nd half. CON: Chronically poor walk rate was especially abysmal; elbow troubles stirred memories of TJS. VERDICT: Too much went right in 2014. Ctl, mileage, and health concerns are strong deterrents.

Yr Tm	W	L	Sv	IP	K	ERA	xERA	WHIP	oOPS	vL	vR	BF/G	Ctl	Dom	Cmd	FpK	SwK	G	L	F	H%	S%	hr/f	GS	APC	DOM%	DIS%	Sv%	LI	RAR	BPV	BPX	R$
10 BOS *	11	6	0	170	142	4.46	3.61	1.33	706	770	626	25.3	4.0	7.5	1.9	57%	8%	33	22	45	29%	67%	7%	25	105	48%	16%			-8.0	69	112	$4
11 BOS	3	3	0	37	26	5.30	5.62	1.47	664	777	491	20.9	5.5	6.3	1.1	56%	7%	32	13	56	26%	65%	6%	7	82	43%	57%	0	0.90	-6.3	-27	-40	-$4
12 BOS *	2	10	0	101	76	6.38	6.08	1.63	938	1056	815	19.6	3.8	6.7	1.8	54%	8%	40	18	42	33%	64%	17%	11	77	27%	45%			-29.6	21	28	-$17
13 NYM *	8	11	0	142	104	5.31	4.97	1.53	689	679	700	23.8	3.9	6.6	1.7	61%	8%	28	22	50	32%	67%	8%	7	95	57%	29%			-25.4	41	53	-$11
14 NYM *	4	3	1	101	89	3.56	2.81	1.28	693	778	639	11.2	5.0	7.9	1.6	56%	9%	41	20	39	26%	72%	7%	9	43	44%	22%	50	0.63	2.3	79	95	$2
1st Half	3	2	1	65	58	3.01	2.23	1.25	637	729	575	10.6	5.6	8.1	1.4	53%	8%	41	21	38	24%	75%	4%	6	41	50%	33%	50	0.76	5.9	89	106	$6
2nd Half	1	1	0	36	31	4.46	3.77	1.30	782	866	735	12.5	3.7	7.8	2.1	62%	10%	41	18	41	29%	68%	12%	3	47	33%	0%	0	0.36	-3.2	68	81	-$4
15 Proj	**4**	**5**	**0**	**87**	**70**	**4.41**	**4.26**	**1.41**	**755**	**819**	**700**	**15.4**	**4.3**	**7.3**	**1.7**	**58%**	**9%**	**37**	**19**	**44**	**29%**	**71%**	**8%**	**13**						**-7.2**	**30**	**36**	**-$3**

Matusz,Brian

Age: 28	Th: L	Role RP	Health	B	LIMA Plan	C
Ht: 6' 4"	Wt: 200	Type Pwr xFB	PT/Exp	D	Rand Var	-1
			Consist	C	MM	3400

BPI and BPV corroborate in a near-rerun of 2013. Not much went right in 1st half, but 2nd half was pure alchemy as SwK, Dom, Ctl, hr/f and Cmd coalesced. Continuing trials vR have interfered with his making the next step, but power lefties rarely find themselves unemployed in real life, or in fantasy.

Yr Tm	W	L	Sv	IP	K	ERA	xERA	WHIP	oOPS	vL	vR	BF/G	Ctl	Dom	Cmd	FpK	SwK	G	L	F	H%	S%	hr/f	GS	APC	DOM%	DIS%	Sv%	LI	RAR	BPV	BPX	R$
10 BAL	10	12	0	176	143	4.30	4.33	1.34	718	581	755	23.8	3.2	7.3	2.3	57%	8%	36	19	45	30%	70%	8%	32	94	44%	25%			-4.9	59	95	$4
11 BAL *	3	12	0	110	72	7.02	6.81	1.73	1121	1058	1141	22.8	3.6	5.9	1.6	58%	6%	28	22	50	34%	62%	20%	12	79	0%	75%			-41.8	4	6	-$19
12 BAL *	8	11	1	145	107	5.28	5.24	1.56	818	528	933	14.4	3.6	6.6	1.8	60%	8%	41	20	40	33%	68%	12%	16	50	19%	38%	50	1.34	-22.7	42	54	-$11
13 BAL	2	1	0	51	50	3.53	3.54	1.16	616	502	747	3.2	2.8	8.8	3.1	59%	13%	39	21	40	30%	70%	6%	0	13			0	1.04	2.1	100	130	$0
14 BAL	2	3	0	52	53	3.48	4.02	1.32	750	626	876	3.6	3.0	9.2	3.1	58%	10%	35	15	50	32%	79%	9%	0	15			0	1.42	1.6	99	118	-$1
1st Half	2	2	0	30	24	5.16	5.00	1.69	920	706	1084	3.9	3.9	7.3	1.8	53%	9%	39	13	48	34%	75%	13%	0	15			0	1.56	-5.2	42	50	-$6
2nd Half	0	1	0	22	29	1.23	2.87	0.82	483	535	402	3.2	1.6	11.9	7.3	66%	12%	27	19	54	28%	88%	4%	0	14			0	1.23	6.8	174	208	$6
15 Proj	**2**	**2**	**0**	**44**	**43**	**3.64**	**3.50**	**1.26**	**694**	**566**	**804**	**4.1**	**2.9**	**8.9**	**3.1**	**60%**	**11%**	**35**	**19**	**46**	**31%**	**74%**	**8%**	**0**						**0.5**	**95**	**113**	**-$1**

Matzek,Tyler

Age: 24	Th: L	Role SP	Health	A	LIMA Plan	D+
Ht: 6' 3"	Wt: 210	Type Pwr	PT/Exp	D	Rand Var	-1
			Consist	D	MM	1103

6-11, 4.05 in 118 IP at COL. Guess who had the lowest ERA and highest Dom among Colorado starting pitchers? Yeah, it's the Rockies, but that doesn't discount the rookie's 2nd half advances (Dom, GB, ERA/xERA, DIS%). Wildness remains his nemesis, so the extent of buy-in hinges on your tolerance for it.

Yr Tm	W	L	Sv	IP	K	ERA	xERA	WHIP	oOPS	vL	vR	BF/G	Ctl	Dom	Cmd	FpK	SwK	G	L	F	H%	S%	hr/f	GS	APC	DOM%	DIS%	Sv%	LI	RAR	BPV	BPX	R$
10																																	
11																																	
12																																	
13 aa	8	9	0	142	75	5.34	6.36	1.86				25.6	5.2	4.7	0.9						33%	73%								-25.9	4	5	-$20
14 COL *	11	15	0	184	138	4.23	4.63	1.48	749	434	848	24.8	3.6	6.7	1.9	58%	9%	50	20	30	32%	73%	8%	19	88	47%	16%	0	0.86	-11.2	52	62	-$5
1st Half	6	6	0	90	59	4.47	5.27	1.58	720	800	705	24.7	3.6	5.9	1.6	58%	7%	43	23	35	33%	74%	4%	4	88	50%	50%			-8.1	35	42	-$9
2nd Half	5	9	0	94	79	4.01	3.77	1.39	756	378	890	25.2	3.6	7.5	2.1	58%	9%	52	19	29	31%	72%	10%	15	88	47%	7%	0	0.89	-3.1	68	81	$0
15 Proj	**9**	**12**	**0**	**160**	**111**	**4.37**	**4.25**	**1.57**	**824**	**552**	**899**	**24.8**	**4.0**	**6.2**	**1.6**	**58%**	**8%**	**48**	**21**	**31**	**32%**	**74%**	**11%**	**28**						**-12.4**	**30**	**36**	**-$6**

Maurer,Brandon

Age: 24	Th: R	Role RP	Health	A	LIMA Plan	B+
Ht: 6' 5"	Wt: 220	Type Pwr FB	PT/Exp	D	Rand Var	0
			Consist	C	MM	3201

1-4, 4.65 ERA in 70 IP at SEA. 2014 line was skewered by five PQS-0 starts prior to May demotion. Returned in 2nd half as a reliever in attack mode (note FpK, SwK) and owned it: 9.2 Dom, 7.6 Cmd, 0.96 WHIP in 37 IP. Heed the usual sample-size caution, but ample skills appear to be consolidating. One to watch.

Yr Tm	W	L	Sv	IP	K	ERA	xERA	WHIP	oOPS	vL	vR	BF/G	Ctl	Dom	Cmd	FpK	SwK	G	L	F	H%	S%	hr/f	GS	APC	DOM%	DIS%	Sv%	LI	RAR	BPV	BPX	R$
10																																	
11																																	
12 aa	9	2	0	138	106	3.71	3.89	1.43				24.4	3.2	6.9	2.2						34%	73%								5.2	80	104	$1
13 SEA *	8	12	0	137	111	5.95	5.38	1.57	883	919	835	18.8	3.3	7.3	2.2	59%	10%	44	19	37	35%	63%	15%	14	70	29%	36%	0	0.74	-35.2	50	65	-$14
14 SEA *	2	4	3	89	75	4.25	4.08	1.34	705	631	759	7.4	2.7	7.6	2.9	63%	10%	39	18	43	33%	69%	6%	7	30	0%	86%	75	0.72	-5.6	84	100	-$2
1st Half	2	4	3	55	43	5.44	5.20	1.54	835	797	866	11.4	3.5	7.2	2.0	60%	7%	40	18	42	34%	66%	10%	7	67	0%	86%	100	0.64	-11.5	50	59	-$6
2nd Half	0	0	0	34	32	2.36	3.46	1.02	560	415	653	4.8	1.3	8.4	6.4	68%	13%	39	18	43	31%	76%	2%	0	18			0	0.74	5.9	133	158	$5
15 Proj	**3**	**3**	**0**	**72**	**62**	**3.55**	**3.49**	**1.24**	**664**	**651**	**675**	**9.3**	**2.5**	**7.8**	**3.2**	**62%**	**10%**	**41**	**18**	**40**	**31%**	**73%**	**7%**	**0**						**1.7**	**93**	**111**	**$1**

ROB CARROLL

May,Trevor

Age: 25	Th: R	Role: SP	Health: A	LIMA Plan: D+
Ht: 6' 5"	Wt: 215	Type: Pwr xFB	PT/Exp: D	Rand Var: +2
			Consist: A	MM: 1203

3-6, 7.88 ERA in 46 IP at MIN. Horrible MLB debut (2 IP, 4 ER, 7 BB) kicked off two months of struggle. Allowed 83 baserunners (.900 OPS against) in half as many IP with shoddy Ctl that plagued him throughout minors. Did finish well by whiffing 20 in final 17 IP, but for now he's a very risky play.

Yr Tm	W	L	Sv	IP	K	ERA	xERA	WHIP	oOPS	vL	vR	BF/G	Ctl	Dom	Cmd	FpK	SwK	G	L	F	H%	S%	hr/f	GS	APC	DOM%	DIS%	Sv%	LI	RAR	BPV	BPX	R$
10																																	
11																																	
12 aa	10	13	0	150	129	5.53	5.19	1.55				23.4	4.6	7.8	1.7						31%	67%								-27.9	40	52	-$12
13 aa	9	9	0	152	129	5.18	4.74	1.55				24.6	3.9	7.7	2.0						34%	67%								-24.6	61	80	-$10
14 MIN *	11	12	0	144	119	4.98	4.34	1.48	900	892	907	22.1	3.9	7.4	1.9	62%	10%	36	23	41	33%	66%	12%	9	84	22%	44%	0	0.70	-22.0	64	76	-$7
1st Half	8	4	0	80	64	3.76	3.32	1.31				23.5	3.7	7.3	2.0						30%	71%	0%	0						-0.2	77	92	$4
2nd Half	3	8	0	64	54	6.49	5.62	1.69	900	892	907	20.7	4.3	7.6	1.8	62%	10%	36	23	41	36%	61%	12%	9	84	22%	44%	0	0.70	-21.8	48	58	-$19
15 Proj	**10**	**13**	**0**	**168**	**141**	**4.67**	**4.27**	**1.49**	**693**	**692**	**693**	**22.6**	**4.1**	**7.6**	**1.9**	**62%**	**10%**	**36**	**23**	**41**	**32%**	**70%**	**8%**	**30**						**-19.3**	**40**	**47**	**-$5**

McAllister,Zach

Age: 27	Th: R	Role: RP	Health: D	LIMA Plan: C
Ht: 6' 6"	Wt: 240	Type:	PT/Exp: C	Rand Var: 0
			Consist: A	MM: 2100

4-7, 5.23 ERA in 86 IP at CLE. He's the most exasperating species of SP. Owns distinctly league-average Dom and Cmd, is equally humdrum vL and vR, his DIS%-DOM% is in a dead heat. But in Sept, mostly in RP role, he went out and hung up a 164 BPV in 19 IP. That's just enough to pique our curiousity for a buck.

Yr Tm	W	L	Sv	IP	K	ERA	xERA	WHIP	oOPS	vL	vR	BF/G	Ctl	Dom	Cmd	FpK	SwK	G	L	F	H%	S%	hr/f	GS	APC	DOM%	DIS%	Sv%	LI	RAR	BPV	BPX	R$
10 aaa	9	12	0	150	84	5.82	5.94	1.63				24.7	2.6	5.0	1.9						35%	65%								-32.1	28	45	-$12
11 CLE *	12	4	0	172	120	3.99	4.31	1.38	860	1069	659	25.0	1.9	6.3	3.2	51%	7%	43	27	30	34%	71%	5%	4	85	0%	50%			-0.9	84	126	$3
12 CLE *	11	10	0	189	153	3.97	4.53	1.37	767	724	820	23.9	2.7	7.3	2.7	61%	9%	41	19	40	32%	75%	12%	22	96	50%	18%			1.1	66	86	$4
13 CLE	9	9	0	134	101	3.75	4.46	1.36	739	737	741	24.1	3.3	6.8	2.1	61%	7%	37	22	41	30%	75%	8%	24	96	38%	25%			1.9	48	63	$2
14 CLE *	11	8	0	155	121	4.02	3.93	1.34	750	789	715	19.5	2.5	7.0	2.8	62%	8%	42	21	37	33%	70%	7%	15	66	47%	47%	0	0.91	-5.4	84	101	$2
1st Half	6	4	0	72	59	4.50	4.36	1.40	796	857	737	21.6	3.0	7.4	2.4	62%	7%	40	21	39	32%	69%	9%	10	85	50%	50%			-6.7	69	83	-$2
2nd Half	5	4	0	83	62	3.62	3.56	1.28	692	693	689	18.0	2.0	6.7	3.4	61%	10%	44	20	35	33%	71%	5%	5	51	40%	40%	0	1.01	1.3	102	121	$5
15 Proj	**4**	**3**	**0**	**58**	**44**	**4.00**	**3.83**	**1.36**	**729**	**736**	**722**	**6.2**	**2.6**	**6.8**	**2.6**	**61%**	**8%**	**40**	**21**	**39**	**32%**	**72%**	**7%**	**0**						**-1.8**	**70**	**84**	**-$1**

McCarthy,Brandon

Age: 31	Th: R	Role: SP	Health: F	LIMA Plan: A
Ht: 6' 7"	Wt: 200	Type: Con	PT/Exp: A	Rand Var: +5
			Consist: B	MM: 4105

Convergence of health and 2nd half change of scenery yielded plenty of highlights. Ctl remained perfect while Cmd, Dom, GB% blew by previous bests. Served up lots of HR that fed into ERA/xERA gap, but that's an outlier. Even if he can't quite echo that 2nd half—health permitting, there is still short-term upside.

Yr Tm	W	L	Sv	IP	K	ERA	xERA	WHIP	oOPS	vL	vR	BF/G	Ctl	Dom	Cmd	FpK	SwK	G	L	F	H%	S%	hr/f	GS	APC	DOM%	DIS%	Sv%	LI	RAR	BPV	BPX	R$
10 aaa	4	2	0	56	34	4.29	5.06	1.33				21.3	1.9	5.4	2.8						30%	74%								-1.4	40	65	-$1
11 OAK	9	9	0	171	123	3.32	3.47	1.13	659	675	640	27.6	1.3	6.5	4.9	61%	8%	47	21	32	30%	71%	6%	25	100	64%	4%			13.1	106	160	$13
12 OAK	8	6	0	111	73	3.24	4.23	1.25	706	769	636	26.1	1.9	5.9	3.0	67%	7%	41	24	35	30%	77%	8%	18	92	39%	17%			10.6	73	95	$6
13 ARI	5	11	0	135	76	4.53	3.95	1.35	759	716	807	26.2	1.4	5.1	3.6	68%	6%	48	25	27	33%	67%	10%	22	91	32%	18%			-11.1	79	103	-$4
14 2 TM	10	15	0	200	175	4.05	3.11	1.28	746	751	741	26.1	1.5	7.9	5.3	67%	9%	53	23	25	34%	72%	16%	32	95	56%	6%			-7.6	133	158	$2
1st Half	2	10	0	104	87	5.11	3.15	1.36	795	828	760	26.0	1.6	7.5	4.8	65%	9%	56	22	22	34%	65%	20%	17	90	41%	12%			-17.5	127	152	-$8
2nd Half	8	5	0	96	88	2.91	3.06	1.19	692	669	718	26.3	1.4	8.3	5.9	69%	10%	49	24	27	33%	80%	13%	15	101	73%	0%			9.9	138	164	$16
15 Proj	**13**	**10**	**0**	**189**	**141**	**3.89**	**3.29**	**1.29**	**739**	**737**	**740**	**25.4**	**1.6**	**6.7**	**4.1**	**67%**	**8%**	**49**	**23**	**28**	**32%**	**73%**	**12%**	**30**						**-3.6**	**104**	**123**	**$7**

McFarland,T.J.

Age: 26	Th: L	Role: RP	Health: A	LIMA Plan: C
Ht: 6' 3"	Wt: 220	Type: xGB	PT/Exp: D	Rand Var: 0
			Consist: B	MM: 2001

4-2, 2.76 ERA in 59 IP at BAL. Reliever pitched OK in choppy season marked by multiple recalls and demotions. Inducing GB is his forte, including 13 in five IP during a spot start. He'll need to keep that up because strikeouts were few and xERA says ERA is due for a correction. Roster filler.

Yr Tm	W	L	Sv	IP	K	ERA	xERA	WHIP	oOPS	vL	vR	BF/G	Ctl	Dom	Cmd	FpK	SwK	G	L	F	H%	S%	hr/f	GS	APC	DOM%	DIS%	Sv%	LI	RAR	BPV	BPX	R$
10																																	
11 aa	9	9	0	137	89	4.57	4.59	1.51				23.8	3.2	5.8	1.8						33%	69%								-10.7	52	78	-$4
12 a/a	16	8	0	163	82	4.89	4.81	1.50				26.1	2.5	4.5	1.8						33%	67%								-17.5	42	55	-$7
13 BAL	4	1	0	75	58	4.22	3.85	1.49	737	761	718	8.7	3.4	7.0	2.1	59%	9%	58	18	24	33%	73%	12%	1	32	0%	100%	0	0.81	-3.3	71	92	-$4
14 BAL *	4	3	0	83	54	3.22	3.95	1.39	739	683	776	8.3	2.3	5.9	2.6	60%	8%	62	19	19	34%	76%	5%	1	23	0%	0%	0	0.96	5.3	80	95	-$1
1st Half	0	2	0	51	36	3.48	3.59	1.37	732	752	719	11.2	2.9	6.4	2.2	61%	8%	54	20	26	33%	73%	4%	0	28			0	1.13	1.7	81	97	-$2
2nd Half	4	1	0	32	18	2.81	3.25	1.44	744	629	824	6.0	1.4	5.1	3.6	58%	9%	68	19	13	36%	80%	7%	1	21	0%	0%	0	0.86	3.7	99	119	$3
15 Proj	**5**	**3**	**0**	**73**	**46**	**3.80**	**3.70**	**1.48**	**742**	**716**	**761**	**9.3**	**2.8**	**5.7**	**2.0**	**59%**	**9%**	**59**	**19**	**23**	**34%**	**74%**	**7%**	**0**						**-0.5**	**64**	**76**	**-$2**

McGee,Jake

Age: 28	Th: L	Role: RP	Health: A	LIMA Plan: B
Ht: 6' 3"	Wt: 235	Type: Pwr FB	PT/Exp: C	Rand Var: -4
			Consist: B	MM: 5530

In June, he finally got his chance to close and ran with it. (We'd been lobbying for years.) After that, his 9th innings were thus: 33 IP, 21 H, 5 BB, 50 K. High FB rate does leave him susceptible to HR, but we'll let him iron that one out. For 2015, double his 2nd half save total and act like you knew it all along.

Yr Tm	W	L	Sv	IP	K	ERA	xERA	WHIP	oOPS	vL	vR	BF/G	Ctl	Dom	Cmd	FpK	SwK	G	L	F	H%	S%	hr/f	GS	APC	DOM%	DIS%	Sv%	LI	RAR	BPV	BPX	R$
10 TAM *	4	8	1	111	113	3.52	3.22	1.31	426	697	111	12.0	3.2	9.2	2.9	50%	10%	55	18	27	34%	72%	0%	0	10			100	0.31	7.6	112	182	$5
11 TAM *	9	4	9	61	58	3.75	4.67	1.38	801	510	1143	4.2	2.9	8.6	2.9	56%	10%	33	18	49	33%	78%	13%	0	14			90	1.10	1.5	74	111	$5
12 TAM	5	2	0	55	73	1.95	2.49	0.80	452	665	291	3.1	1.8	11.9	6.6	62%	14%	44	19	37	27%	78%	7%	0	13			0	1.39	14.1	187	244	$10
13 TAM	5	3	1	63	75	4.02	3.20	1.18	659	678	648	3.7	3.2	10.8	3.4	63%	12%	43	19	39	30%	70%	13%	0	16			20	1.16	-1.2	130	169	$2
14 TAM	5	2	19	71	90	1.89	2.68	0.90	486	572	452	3.8	2.0	11.4	5.6	65%	14%	38	19	43	29%	79%	3%	0	16			83	1.38	16.3	166	198	$18
1st Half	3	0	3	36	43	1.24	2.73	0.83	422	568	355	3.5	2.2	10.7	4.8	69%	13%	40	18	41	26%	83%	0%	0	14			75	1.39	11.2	150	179	$16
2nd Half	2	2	16	35	47	2.57	2.64	0.97	548	576	538	4.1	1.8	12.1	6.7	60%	14%	36	20	44	33%	75%	6%	0	17			84	1.37	5.0	183	218	$20
15 Proj	**5**	**3**	**35**	**69**	**85**	**2.55**	**2.58**	**1.01**	**556**	**640**	**516**	**3.7**	**2.4**	**11.1**	**4.7**	**63%**	**13%**	**40**	**19**	**41**	**30%**	**77%**	**7%**	**0**						**10.1**	**155**	**184**	**$22**

McGowan,Dustin

Age: 33	Th: R	Role: RP	Health: F	LIMA Plan: D+
Ht: 6' 3"	Wt: 240	Type: Pwr xFB	PT/Exp: D	Rand Var: 0
			Consist: B	MM: 1201

That he's pitching at all is a testament to his fortitude and commitment as well as the Jays' constancy. Was hit hard as SP but less so after moving to bullpen (1.16 WHIP, 7.5 Dom as RP). SwK, LD% still impressive, but difficult to fully assess BPI sprinkled among 890 DL days. Safer to root for him from afar.

Yr Tm	W	L	Sv	IP	K	ERA	xERA	WHIP	oOPS	vL	vR	BF/G	Ctl	Dom	Cmd	FpK	SwK	G	L	F	H%	S%	hr/f	GS	APC	DOM%	DIS%	Sv%	LI	RAR	BPV	BPX	R$
10																																	
11 TOR *	0	4	0	41	34	5.22	5.50	1.60	823	977	645	18.0	4.7	7.4	1.6	51%	9%	50	16	34	32%	71%	19%	4	75	50%	50%	0	0.60	-6.4	32	49	-$6
12																																	
13 TOR	0	0	0	26	26	2.45	3.99	1.21	609	674	550	4.6	4.2	9.1	2.2	65%	12%	47	14	40	27%	83%	7%	0	18			0	0.79	4.5	75	98	-$2
14 TOR	5	3	1	82	61	4.17	4.64	1.38	768	782	755	6.7	3.6	6.7	1.8	59%	11%	38	15	46	28%	75%	11%	8	26	25%	63%	20	1.14	-4.3	39	46	-$2
1st Half	4	3	1	57	37	4.11	4.74	1.37	763	766	757	9.8	3.2	5.8	1.9	63%	10%	37	16	46	29%	74%	9%	8	38	25%	63%	33	1.18	-2.6	35	42	-$1
2nd Half	1	0	0	25	24	4.32	4.39	1.40	779	837	748	3.9	4.7	8.6	1.8	52%	12%	42	13	46	27%	77%	15%	0	16			0	1.11	-1.8	49	58	-$4
15 Proj	**2**	**4**	**0**	**72**	**60**	**4.29**	**4.19**	**1.44**	**778**	**810**	**755**	**7.1**	**4.0**	**7.5**	**1.9**	**56%**	**11%**	**40**	**14**	**46**	**30%**	**75%**	**11%**	**0**						**-4.9**	**44**	**52**	**-$3**

McHugh,Collin

Age: 28	Th: R	Role: SP	Health: B	LIMA Plan: C+
Ht: 6' 2"	Wt: 195	Type:	PT/Exp: C	Rand Var: 0
			Consist: F	MM: 3205

11-9, 2.73 ERA in 155 IP at HOU. With a name right out of a British whodunit, he wrote his own storyline: Retread shatters every BPI previously held at any level. But lofty heights can make for spectacular falls, so while we'll say "pursue McHugh," you simply can't expect 2015 to be a page-turner like the original.

Yr Tm	W	L	Sv	IP	K	ERA	xERA	WHIP	oOPS	vL	vR	BF/G	Ctl	Dom	Cmd	FpK	SwK	G	L	F	H%	S%	hr/f	GS	APC	DOM%	DIS%	Sv%	LI	RAR	BPV	BPX	R$
10																																	
11 aa	8	2	2	93	80	2.79	2.58	1.17				20.7	2.7	7.8	2.8						30%	75%								13.2	109	164	$9
12 NYM *	7	13	0	170	130	3.81	3.94	1.30	1044	1192	937	21.2	2.8	6.9	2.4	60%	9%	33	28	39	30%	73%	19%	4	50	25%	75%	0	1.17	4.2	68	88	$5
13 2 NL *	6	9	0	139	85	5.41	5.62	1.60	1053	1252	914	22.8	2.2	5.5	2.5	54%	9%	40	28	32	36%	67%	18%	5	62	0%	40%	0	0.56	-26.5	49	64	-$15
14 HOU *	11	9	0	174	167	2.90	2.49	1.05	588	609	556	22.4	2.4	8.7	3.5	58%	11%	42	24	34	27%	74%	9%	25	99	68%	12%			18.0	118	141	$18
1st Half	4	7	0	92	95	3.50	2.69	1.13	607	603	612	21.4	3.5	9.3	2.6	61%	12%	39	22	39	27%	71%	11%	13	101	69%	15%			2.8	101	121	$13
2nd Half	7	2	0	81	72	2.23	2.26	0.95	567	613	486	23.6	1.2	8.0	6.5	56%	11%	45	27	29	28%	79%	8%	12	98	67%	8%			15.2	178	213	$24
15 Proj	**11**	**10**	**0**	**189**	**158**	**3.58**	**3.38**	**1.22**	**689**	**722**	**638**	**22.2**	**2.3**	**7.6**	**3.3**	**58%**	**11%**	**43**	**23**	**35**	**31%**	**72%**	**8%**	**32**						**3.8**	**94**	**112**	**$11**

ROB CARROLL

Medina,Yoervis

Age: 26 | Th: R | Role: RP | Ht: 6' 3" | Wt: 245 | Type: Pwr GB
Health: A | PT/Exp: D | Consist: B
LIMA Plan: B+ | Rand Var: -3 | MM: 4400

Rising Dom and GB tilt help him outpitch his deficiencies. But poor Ctl and substandard command leave him too prone to walks and periodic HRs, capping his R$. Still, age and nasty mid-90s stuff are on his side. Big K-per-inning Dom, success vs hitters from both sides are enough to land him on your watch list, at least.

Yr	Tm	W	L	Sv	IP	K	ERA	xERA	WHIP	oOPS	vL	vR	BF/G	Ctl	Dom	Cmd	FpK	SwK	G	L	F	H%	S%	hr/f	GS	APC	DOM%	DIS%	Sv%	LI	RAR	BPV	BPX	R$
10																																		
11	aa	0	1	0	25	15	5.17	4.94	1.37				26.2	3.2	5.4	1.7						27%	67%								-3.8	19	28	-$4
12	aa	5	5	5	69	67	3.92	4.57	1.59				6.6	4.8	8.7	1.8						35%	76%								0.8	72	94	-$1
13	SEA	4	6	1	68	71	2.91	3.63	1.31	629	644	617	4.6	5.3	9.4	1.8	52%	10%	54	19	27	27%	80%	11%	0	18			25	1.57	8.0	58	76	$3
14	SEA	5	3	0	57	60	2.68	3.38	1.33	642	563	691	3.7	4.4	9.5	2.1	54%	10%	53	22	25	31%	81%	8%	0	14			0	0.95	7.4	82	98	$2
1st Half		4	1	0	30	30	2.43	3.26	1.11	559	510	583	3.7	4.2	9.1	2.1	51%	10%	52	22	26	24%	81%	11%	0	13			0	1.03	4.8	79	95	$5
2nd Half		1	2	0	27	30	2.96	3.50	1.57	724	616	791	3.8	4.6	9.9	2.1	57%	10%	54	22	24	37%	81%	5%	0	14			0	0.87	2.6	86	102	-$1
15	**Proj**	**5**	**5**	**0**	**65**	**68**	**3.25**	**3.34**	**1.39**	**668**	**622**	**699**	**4.2**	**4.8**	**9.4**	**2.0**	**54%**	**10%**	**54**	**21**	**26**	**31%**	**77%**	**9%**	**0**						**3.9**	**71**	**84**	**$1**

Medlen,Kris

Age: 29 | Th: R | Role: RP | Ht: 5' 10" | Wt: 190 | Type:
Health: F | PT/Exp: B | Consist: B
LIMA Plan: B+ | Rand Var: 0 | MM: 4201

Second TJS ended his 2014 in March, and now raises questions about his future. If there's a silver lining, he was terrific following his 2010 surgery. But erring on the side of caution is likely, suggesting a partial season at best. He's a shot in the dark for 2015.

Yr	Tm	W	L	Sv	IP	K	ERA	xERA	WHIP	oOPS	vL	vR	BF/G	Ctl	Dom	Cmd	FpK	SwK	G	L	F	H%	S%	hr/f	GS	APC	DOM%	DIS%	Sv%	LI	RAR	BPV	BPX	R$
10	ATL	6	2	0	108	83	3.68	3.57	1.20	725	765	693	14.1	1.8	6.9	4.0	64%	10%	43	22	35	30%	73%	12%	14	51	50%	21%	0	0.84	5.3	98	159	$6
11	ATL	0	0	0	2	2	0.00	2.87	0.43	250	0	500	4.0	0.0	7.7	0.0	75%	4%	33	17	50	18%	0%	0%	0	12			0	3.05	1.1	150	225	-$3
12	ATL	10	1	1	138	120	1.57	2.97	0.91	529	519	539	10.4	1.5	7.8	5.2	66%	10%	53	19	28	26%	85%	6%	12	38	92%	0%	50	0.81	41.7	131	171	$29
13	ATL	15	12	0	197	157	3.11	3.60	1.22	706	730	680	25.6	2.1	7.2	3.3	65%	11%	45	24	31	31%	78%	10%	31	95	71%	13%	0	0.82	18.4	94	123	$16
14																																		
1st Half																																		
2nd Half																																		
15	**Proj**	**6**	**3**	**0**	**87**	**70**	**2.95**	**3.18**	**1.14**	**671**	**690**	**653**	**15.1**	**1.8**	**7.2**	**4.0**	**65%**	**11%**	**46**	**22**	**32**	**29%**	**77%**	**10%**	**12**						**8.5**	**105**	**125**	**$7**

Mejia,Jenrry

Age: 25 | Th: R | Role: RP | Ht: 6' 0" | Wt: 205 | Type: Pwr GB
Health: F | PT/Exp: C | Consist: D
LIMA Plan: B | Rand Var: +1 | MM: 4431

Struggled early in rotation, but ran with closer job (2.72 ERA, 90% S%) after injuries gave him a shot. Recent H% and hr/f history are troublesome, but durability is the key. You don't often see short relievers posting 90+ innings, so keep an eye on his usage. With sustained health... UP: More skills growth, 40 saves.

Yr	Tm	W	L	Sv	IP	K	ERA	xERA	WHIP	oOPS	vL	vR	BF/G	Ctl	Dom	Cmd	FpK	SwK	G	L	F	H%	S%	hr/f	GS	APC	DOM%	DIS%	Sv%	LI	RAR	BPV	BPX	R$
10	NYM *	2	4	0	74	53	3.01	3.66	1.40	770	590	877	7.8	4.1	6.4	1.6	51%	8%	61	13	26	30%	79%	8%	3	22	0%	100%	0	0.79	9.8	62	100	$1
11	aaa	1	2	0	28	18	2.90	1.62	1.03				21.8	4.0	5.6	1.4						20%	71%								3.6	75	112	$0
12	NYM *	4	6	0	98	49	4.29	4.74	1.52	897	822	964	12.8	3.2	4.5	1.4	54%	7%	67	11	22	32%	72%	17%	3	60	33%	33%	0	0.57	-3.4	34	44	-$6
13	NYM	1	2	0	27	27	2.30	2.65	1.17	641	683	609	22.4	1.3	8.9	6.8	60%	13%	58	22	20	34%	83%	13%	5	87	80%	20%			5.3	160	209	-$1
14	NYM	6	6	28	94	98	3.65	3.59	1.48	723	647	792	6.6	3.9	9.4	2.4	59%	12%	50	20	30	35%	78%	11%	7	25	29%	43%	90	1.25	1.0	91	109	$10
1st Half		4	3	8	58	59	4.17	3.77	1.47	721	583	842	9.7	4.3	9.1	2.1	61%	11%	49	21	30	33%	74%	12%	7	36	29%	43%	89	1.03	-3.1	74	89	$7
2nd Half		2	3	20	35	39	2.80	3.32	1.50	726	745	708	4.3	3.3	9.9	3.0	55%	13%	51	18	30	38%	84%	10%	0	16			91	1.42	4.1	119	142	$15
15	**Proj**	**4**	**5**	**26**	**73**	**71**	**3.40**	**3.17**	**1.31**	**633**	**554**	**694**	**6.9**	**3.6**	**8.8**	**2.5**	**55%**	**10%**	**55**	**17**	**28**	**31%**	**76%**	**10%**	**0**						**3.1**	**95**	**113**	**$12**

Melancon,Mark

Age: 30 | Th: R | Role: RP | Ht: 6' 2" | Wt: 215 | Type: Pwr xGB
Health: A | PT/Exp: C | Consist: B
LIMA Plan: C+ | Rand Var: -3 | MM: 5431

Retained superb control while taking everything else up to near-untouchable levels in the 2nd half. Fortunate H% helped, but SwK, FpK and 2nd half GB spike scream "Stud!" Health and two straight sub-2 ERAs confirm elite tag. Could be the first season he opens as the 9th inning guy and keeps the tag all year.

Yr	Tm	W	L	Sv	IP	K	ERA	xERA	WHIP	oOPS	vL	vR	BF/G	Ctl	Dom	Cmd	FpK	SwK	G	L	F	H%	S%	hr/f	GS	APC	DOM%	DIS%	Sv%	LI	RAR	BPV	BPX	R$
10	2 TM *	9	1	7	82	72	3.97	5.26	1.66	674	457	805	5.7	4.4	7.9	1.8	56%	12%	46	17	37	36%	78%	9%	0	16			70	1.17	1.1	57	92	$2
11	HOU	8	4	20	74	66	2.78	3.16	1.22	631	704	581	4.4	3.1	8.0	2.5	61%	10%	57	22	21	29%	79%	11%	0	16			80	1.12	10.6	94	141	$14
12	BOS *	0	2	12	67	62	4.59	3.82	1.21	754	875	655	4.3	2.1	8.3	4.0	62%	10%	50	24	26	31%	64%	22%	0	18			92	0.62	-4.7	105	137	$2
13	PIT	3	2	16	71	70	1.39	2.33	0.96	511	357	638	3.9	1.0	8.9	8.8	65%	12%	60	24	16	31%	85%	3%	0	14			76	1.31	21.6	170	222	$16
14	PIT	3	5	33	71	71	1.90	2.50	0.87	473	415	524	3.8	1.4	9.0	6.5	69%	14%	57	20	23	27%	78%	5%	0	14			89	1.37	16.1	159	190	$22
1st Half		1	2	15	39	33	2.33	2.88	0.88	469	415	518	3.7	1.4	7.7	5.5	64%	13%	54	20	26	26%	73%	4%	0	13			83	1.45	6.7	133	158	$20
2nd Half		2	3	18	32	38	1.39	2.05	0.87	478	414	531	4.0	1.4	10.6	7.6	75%	16%	62	19	19	29%	85%	7%	0	14			95	1.27	9.4	193	230	$25
15	**Proj**	**3**	**4**	**45**	**73**	**72**	**2.26**	**2.37**	**1.00**	**544**	**497**	**583**	**3.9**	**1.6**	**9.0**	**5.5**	**67%**	**13%**	**58**	**21**	**21**	**30%**	**78%**	**8%**	**0**						**13.3**	**153**	**182**	**$26**

Meyer,Alex

Age: 25 | Th: R | Role: SP | Ht: 6' 9" | Wt: 220 | Type: Pwr
Health: C | PT/Exp: F | Consist: C
LIMA Plan: D+ | Rand Var: +1 | MM: 2300

Top-shelf SP prospect with unhittable stuff when he's right. But ascent has been slowed by erratic control and durability issues. Missed 10 weeks with strained shoulder in 2013, left final 2014 start with shoulder inflammation. A 2015 lottery ticket, if healthy.

Yr	Tm	W	L	Sv	IP	K	ERA	xERA	WHIP	oOPS	vL	vR	BF/G	Ctl	Dom	Cmd	FpK	SwK	G	L	F	H%	S%	hr/f	GS	APC	DOM%	DIS%	Sv%	LI	RAR	BPV	BPX	R$
10																																		
11																																		
12																																		
13	aa	4	3	0	70	70	3.62	3.40	1.35				22.5	3.6	9.0	2.5						33%	72%								2.2	100	130	$0
14	aaa	7	7	0	130	124	4.42	4.60	1.56				21.2	4.5	8.6	1.9						34%	72%								-10.9	70	83	-$6
1st Half		4	4	0	77	70	4.52	4.56	1.51				20.9	4.2	8.1	1.9						33%	71%								-7.5	65	77	-$6
2nd Half		3	3	0	53	54	4.26	4.66	1.64				21.5	5.1	9.2	1.8						36%	74%								-3.4	78	93	-$7
15	**Proj**	**3**	**3**	**0**	**58**	**55**	**4.06**	**3.74**	**1.43**				**21.4**	**4.6**	**8.5**	**1.9**	**59%**	**9%**	**48**	**18**	**34**	**31%**	**73%**	**10%**	**12**						**-2.3**	**56**	**67**	**-$2**

Mikolas,Miles

Age: 26 | Th: R | Role: RP | Ht: 6' 5" | Wt: 220 | Type: Con
Health: C | PT/Exp: D | Consist: B
LIMA Plan: D+ | Rand Var: +3 | MM: 1000

2-5, 6.44 ERA in 57 IP at TEX. Minor league reliever turned starter in the wake of TEX rotation woes. Slight GB tilt gives him a shot at a career out of the pen, but erratic, pedestrian stuff was exposed in the rotation. Light Dom and BPI volatility say he's not worthy.

Yr	Tm	W	L	Sv	IP	K	ERA	xERA	WHIP	oOPS	vL	vR	BF/G	Ctl	Dom	Cmd	FpK	SwK	G	L	F	H%	S%	hr/f	GS	APC	DOM%	DIS%	Sv%	LI	RAR	BPV	BPX	R$
10																																		
11	aa	1	0	9	32	24	1.59	2.36	1.09				4.5	1.6	6.7	4.2						31%	84%								9.4	134	202	$5
12	SD *	5	3	4	64	47	3.23	4.30	1.45	761	664	829	5.1	3.5	6.6	1.9	56%	7%	53	20	27	32%	79%	14%	0	21			44	0.66	6.2	59	77	$1
13	SD *	4	2	26	63	35	2.96	3.83	1.29	286	333	250	4.6	2.4	5.0	2.1	71%	13%	0	25	75	29%	80%	0%	0	15			87	0.15	7.0	54	71	$11
14	TEX *	7	6	2	102	68	5.23	5.04	1.44	769	732	815	16.7	1.9	6.0	3.2	62%	8%	40	23	37	34%	65%	11%	10	93	30%	30%			-18.8	67	80	-$6
1st Half		5	1	2	45	30	3.69	5.14	1.44				11.9	0.6	6.0	9.5						38%	76%	0%	0						0.3	205	245	$1
2nd Half		2	5	0	57	38	6.44	4.51	1.43	769	732	815	25.5	2.8	6.0	2.1	62%	8%	40	23	37	31%	55%	11%	10	93	30%	30%			-19.1	49	59	-$11
15	**Proj**	**2**	**3**	**0**	**58**	**36**	**4.37**	**4.13**	**1.42**	**744**	**700**	**788**	**7.6**	**2.7**	**5.6**	**2.1**	**60%**	**8%**	**42**	**21**	**36**	**32%**	**70%**	**7%**	**0**						**-4.5**	**48**	**57**	**-$4**

Miley,Wade

Age: 28 | Th: L | Role: SP | Ht: 6' 0" | Wt: 220 | Type: Pwr GB
Health: A | PT/Exp: A | Consist: A
LIMA Plan: C | Rand Var: +2 | MM: 3205

From 2012 to 2014, his ERA eroded while his xERA improved. What do you believe? Skills, of course. FpK gives hope that Ctl will rebound. 1st half woes were caused by poor S% and hr/f, which corrected in the 2nd half and should stabilize. In the end, this is a league-average pitcher. No more, no less.

Yr	Tm	W	L	Sv	IP	K	ERA	xERA	WHIP	oOPS	vL	vR	BF/G	Ctl	Dom	Cmd	FpK	SwK	G	L	F	H%	S%	hr/f	GS	APC	DOM%	DIS%	Sv%	LI	RAR	BPV	BPX	R$
10	aa	5	2	0	73	51	2.72	4.26	1.43				23.8	3.7	6.3	1.7						31%	84%								12.2	52	84	$3
11	ARI *	12	5	0	170	107	4.42	4.47	1.44	873	808	885	24.1	3.1	5.7	1.8	60%	9%	46	24	30	31%	70%	15%	7	82	43%	29%	0	0.73	-9.9	47	71	-$1
12	ARI	16	11	0	195	144	3.33	3.89	1.18	685	544	723	25.2	1.7	6.7	3.9	60%	9%	43	23	34	31%	73%	7%	29	94	59%	14%	0	0.82	16.5	95	123	$17
13	ARI	10	10	0	203	147	3.55	3.79	1.32	727	704	732	25.7	2.9	6.5	2.2	59%	8%	52	21	27	30%	76%	13%	33	98	52%	18%			7.8	68	89	$7
14	ARI	8	12	0	201	183	4.34	3.59	1.40	746	727	752	26.2	3.4	8.2	2.4	63%	10%	51	21	28	32%	71%	14%	33	97	48%	15%			-14.8	86	102	-$3
1st Half		3	6	0	105	96	4.78	3.57	1.33	778	753	784	26.4	2.9	8.2	2.8	64%	10%	48	21	31	31%	68%	18%	17	99	53%	12%			-13.6	95	114	-$5
2nd Half		5	6	0	96	87	3.84	3.60	1.48	711	707	713	26.1	3.8	8.2	2.1	63%	10%	54	21	24	34%	74%	9%	16	96	44%	19%			-1.2	76	90	-$1
15	**Proj**	**11**	**11**	**0**	**203**	**165**	**3.63**	**3.51**	**1.36**	**728**	**686**	**740**	**25.3**	**3.1**	**7.3**	**2.4**	**61%**	**9%**	**50**	**21**	**28**	**31%**	**76%**	**11%**	**34**						**2.7**	**77**	**92**	**$6**

JOCK THOMPSON

Miller,Andrew

Age: 30	Th: L	Role RP	Health D	LIMA Plan B+
Ht: 6' 7"	Wt: 210	Type Pwr	PT/Exp D	Rand Var 0
			Consist B	MM 5500

Ctl breakthrough came from out of nowhere, but it combined with awe-inspiring Dom to produce monster season. Recent gains vRHBs are at least partly due to H% luck, and 2nd half FpK says Ctl regression to mere mortal status is likely. But the Ks should keep him plenty good enough.

Yr Tm	W	L	Sv	IP	K	ERA	xERA	WHIP	oOPS	vL	vR	BF/G	Ctl	Dom	Cmd	FpK	SwK	G	L	F	H%	S%	hr/f	GS	APC	DOM%	DIS%	Sv%	LI	RAR	BPV	BPX	R$
10 FLA *	2	13	0	118	85	7.95	7.59	2.24	1054	1262	975	22.1	7.2	6.5	0.9	49%	6%	38	28	34	39%	64%	16%	7	72	0%	71%	0	0.60	-56.4	16	26	-$30
11 BOS *	9	6	0	131	98	4.52	4.59	1.62	857	812	874	19.3	5.5	6.7	1.2	58%	8%	45	23	31	31%	72%	12%	12	72	17%	42%	0	0.61	-9.4	47	71	-$6
12 BOS	3	2	0	40	51	3.35	3.32	1.19	588	429	829	3.2	4.5	11.4	2.6	54%	10%	43	23	34	28%	73%	9%	0	13			0	1.17	3.3	105	137	$1
13 BOS	1	2	0	31	48	2.64	2.47	1.37	624	725	526	3.6	5.0	14.1	2.8	59%	14%	56	21	23	36%	85%	20%	0	15			0	0.81	4.6	153	199	-$1
14 2 AL	5	5	1	62	103	2.02	1.80	0.80	456	467	446	3.3	2.5	14.9	6.1	59%	15%	47	22	31	29%	77%	9%	0	14			50	1.54	13.2	226	270	$11
1st Half	2	5	0	32	53	2.53	2.06	0.97	497	450	527	3.5	2.8	14.9	5.3	63%	14%	44	23	33	35%	73%	5%	0	14			0	1.55	4.8	214	256	$8
2nd Half	3	0	1	30	50	1.48	1.51	0.63	407	485	342	3.1	2.1	14.8	7.1	55%	17%	51	20	29	22%	82%	14%	0	13			50	1.52	8.4	240	286	$15
15 Proj	**4**	**4**	**0**	**65**	**97**	**2.74**	**2.21**	**1.10**	**561**	**562**	**558**	**3.5**	**3.7**	**13.3**	**3.6**	**57%**	**13%**	**49**	**22**	**29**	**31%**	**77%**	**12%**	**0**						**8.1**	**166**	**197**	**$7**

Miller,Shelby

Age: 24	Th: R	Role SP	Health A	LIMA Plan B+
Ht: 6' 3"	Wt: 215	Type Pwr FB	PT/Exp B	Rand Var -2
			Consist B	MM 2205

The struggles from 2nd half of 2013 carried over to this year. Dom plunge and 1st half Ctl were only slightly mitigated by favorable H%. SwK isn't hopeful. But reasons for optimism include age, stable velocity, 2nd half Ctl gains, and fine September fueled by 7.7 Dom rebound. Call it growing pains and expect a bounce.

Yr Tm	W	L	Sv	IP	K	ERA	xERA	WHIP	oOPS	vL	vR	BF/G	Ctl	Dom	Cmd	FpK	SwK	G	L	F	H%	S%	hr/f	GS	APC	DOM%	DIS%	Sv%	LI	RAR	BPV	BPX	R$
10																																	
11 aa	9	3	0	87	77	2.27	2.19	1.12				21.3	3.0	8.0	2.7						29%	79%								17.9	112	168	$11
12 STL *	12	10	0	150	153	4.58	4.54	1.37	463	485	445	19.1	3.1	9.1	3.0	57%	13%	42	15	42	33%	70%	0%	1	33	100%	0%	0	0.88	-10.5	81	106	$1
13 STL	15	9	0	173	169	3.06	3.73	1.21	670	761	588	23.3	3.0	8.8	3.0	62%	10%	38	20	41	29%	79%	10%	31	96	55%	13%			17.2	94	123	$16
14 STL	10	9	0	183	127	3.74	4.44	1.27	697	707	690	23.9	3.6	6.2	1.7	60%	7%	40	19	41	26%	74%	10%	31	89	42%	13%	0	0.75	0.1	33	40	$5
1st Half	7	7	0	99	70	4.10	4.67	1.43	734	811	670	25.0	4.5	6.4	1.4	59%	7%	41	21	38	28%	74%	11%	17	92	35%	18%			-4.4	13	16	$1
2nd Half	3	2	0	84	57	3.31	4.20	1.09	652	579	712	22.6	2.6	6.1	2.4	62%	8%	39	17	44	24%	74%	9%	14	87	50%	7%	0	0.74	4.5	57	68	$8
15 Proj	**13**	**9**	**0**	**189**	**156**	**3.69**	**3.75**	**1.26**	**695**	**728**	**667**	**22.2**	**3.2**	**7.5**	**2.4**	**61%**	**9%**	**39**	**19**	**42**	**29%**	**74%**	**9%**	**32**						**1.2**	**67**	**79**	**$10**

Milone,Tommy

Age: 28	Th: L	Role SP	Health B	LIMA Plan C
Ht: 6' 0"	Wt: 205	Type	PT/Exp B	Rand Var 0
			Consist B	MM 1103

6-4, 4.19 ERA in 118 IP at OAK/MIN. Talked his way into mid-season trade following undeserved Triple-A demotion, but couldn't take advantage of new opportunity. Soft-tossing FBer requires excellent control for marginal success, and he ain't got it. Ctl, FpK and xERA trends look ominous.

Yr Tm	W	L	Sv	IP	K	ERA	xERA	WHIP	oOPS	vL	vR	BF/G	Ctl	Dom	Cmd	FpK	SwK	G	L	F	H%	S%	hr/f	GS	APC	DOM%	DIS%	Sv%	LI	RAR	BPV	BPX	R$
10 aa	12	5	0	158	129	3.65	4.42	1.36				24.5	1.3	7.3	5.5						36%	74%								8.3	135	218	$8
11 WAS *	13	6	0	174	140	3.84	3.57	1.18	742	1164	695	24.1	1.0	7.2	7.2	71%	8%	31	20	49	33%	68%	5%	5	82	20%	40%			2.1	176	264	$11
12 OAK	13	10	0	190	137	3.74	4.10	1.28	738	749	734	25.5	1.7	6.5	3.8	68%	9%	38	25	37	31%	75%	11%	31	98	52%	16%			6.4	87	113	$9
13 OAK	12	9	0	156	126	4.14	4.22	1.27	738	790	724	23.8	2.2	7.3	3.2	67%	9%	35	20	45	30%	73%	11%	26	93	46%	23%	0	0.75	-5.4	83	108	$4
14 2 AL *	7	6	0	146	90	4.71	5.38	1.51	763	729	771	23.4	3.0	5.6	1.8	63%	8%	39	21	39	32%	72%	10%	21	88	24%	24%	0	0.75	-17.4	28	34	-$9
1st Half	6	3	0	90	55	3.79	4.47	1.24	724	787	708	25.4	2.5	5.5	2.2	64%	8%	38	20	41	27%	74%	10%	15	93	27%	7%			-0.5	48	57	$1
2nd Half	1	3	0	56	35	6.21	7.60	1.94	871	551	945	22.1	3.9	5.7	1.5	58%	8%	43	23	34	38%	71%	11%	6	76	17%	67%	0	0.70	-16.9	4	4	-$25
15 Proj	**10**	**8**	**0**	**174**	**122**	**4.57**	**4.09**	**1.47**	**788**	**719**	**806**	**23.3**	**2.6**	**6.3**	**2.4**	**64%**	**8%**	**39**	**22**	**40**	**33%**	**73%**	**11%**	**32**						**-17.8**	**60**	**71**	**-$5**

Minor,Mike

Age: 27	Th: L	Role SP	Health C	LIMA Plan B
Ht: 6' 4"	Wt: 220	Type Pwr	PT/Exp A	Rand Var 0
			Consist C	MM 3203

6-12, 4.77 ERA in 145 IP at ATL. Pre-season shoulder woes shelved him until early May. Maintained average velocity, but apart from his GB%, the skill decline was across the board. He still owns 2013, but health and historical inconsistency warn not to bet the farm on a full rebound.

Yr Tm	W	L	Sv	IP	K	ERA	xERA	WHIP	oOPS	vL	vR	BF/G	Ctl	Dom	Cmd	FpK	SwK	G	L	F	H%	S%	hr/f	GS	APC	DOM%	DIS%	Sv%	LI	RAR	BPV	BPX	R$
10 ATL *	9	9	0	161	169	4.55	3.97	1.34	880	795	907	22.3	3.2	9.4	2.9	58%	12%	35	17	48	33%	67%	10%	8	85	50%	25%	0	0.71	-9.3	96	155	$4
11 ATL *	9	8	0	183	162	3.99	4.60	1.42	785	835	774	25.1	2.9	7.9	2.8	64%	9%	37	27	35	34%	75%	8%	15	92	27%	20%			-1.1	75	113	$2
12 ATL	11	10	0	179	145	4.12	4.18	1.15	702	724	694	24.3	2.8	7.3	2.6	59%	8%	35	21	44	26%	69%	12%	30	95	50%	17%			-2.2	68	89	$10
13 ATL	13	9	0	205	181	3.21	3.68	1.09	657	583	680	25.6	2.0	8.0	3.9	64%	10%	35	22	43	28%	75%	9%	32	98	75%	3%			16.5	102	132	$20
14 ATL *	8	14	0	163	132	5.00	5.34	1.45	798	887	774	23.9	2.6	7.3	2.8	61%	8%	41	23	36	33%	70%	13%	25	97	52%	28%			-25.3	54	64	-$8
1st Half	4	7	0	83	77	5.01	5.94	1.49	829	910	807	23.9	2.5	8.3	3.3	65%	8%	40	26	35	35%	73%	16%	11	102	64%	18%			-13.1	58	69	-$9
2nd Half	4	7	0	79	55	4.99	4.28	1.40	772	868	744	24.5	2.7	6.2	2.3	57%	7%	41	22	37	31%	66%	11%	14	93	43%	36%			-12.2	58	69	-$7
15 Proj	**11**	**11**	**0**	**174**	**145**	**3.87**	**3.66**	**1.29**	**727**	**752**	**719**	**24.0**	**2.7**	**7.5**	**2.8**	**61%**	**9%**	**38**	**23**	**39**	**30%**	**73%**	**10%**	**30**						**-2.8**	**78**	**93**	**$6**

Montero,Rafael

Age: 24	Th: R	Role SP	Health A	LIMA Plan B+
Ht: 6' 0"	Wt: 185	Type Pwr FB	PT/Exp D	Rand Var 0
			Consist C	MM 3301

1-3, 4.06 in 44 IP at NYM. Polished prospect handled Triple-A in hostile PCL venue despite atypical Ctl. Dom held up in uneven MLB debut plagued by walks and unprecedented gopheritis. 2nd half shows he's ready for an opportunity, and there's legitimate long-term upside here.

Yr Tm	W	L	Sv	IP	K	ERA	xERA	WHIP	oOPS	vL	vR	BF/G	Ctl	Dom	Cmd	FpK	SwK	G	L	F	H%	S%	hr/f	GS	APC	DOM%	DIS%	Sv%	LI	RAR	BPV	BPX	R$
10																																	
11																																	
12																																	
13 a/a	12	7	0	155	132	2.60	2.52	1.09				22.5	1.8	7.6	4.3						30%	76%								24.3	133	173	$18
14 NYM *	7	7	0	124	111	3.33	3.55	1.30	825	923	711	19.7	3.7	8.0	2.2	60%	9%	34	22	44	29%	77%	15%	8	84	25%	25%	0	0.60	6.4	77	91	$4
1st Half	4	4	0	70	59	3.72	3.75	1.32	866	1065	652	19.4	4.0	7.6	1.9	59%	8%	33	23	44	28%	75%	19%	4	100	25%	50%			0.2	65	77	$3
2nd Half	3	3	0	54	52	2.82	3.30	1.26	788	804	769	20.0	3.4	8.6	2.5	61%	10%	35	21	44	30%	80%	11%	4	73	25%	0%	0	0.51	6.1	93	111	$6
15 Proj	**5**	**4**	**0**	**73**	**64**	**3.83**	**3.67**	**1.25**	**717**	**802**	**619**	**23.0**	**2.9**	**8.0**	**2.8**	**60%**	**9%**	**34**	**22**	**44**	**30%**	**73%**	**9%**	**14**						**-0.8**	**78**	**93**	**$1**

Moore,Matt

Age: 26	Th: L	Role SP	Health F	LIMA Plan D+
Ht: 6' 3"	Wt: 200	Type Pwr FB	PT/Exp B	Rand Var -5
			Consist A	MM 2301

Velocity plunge, volatile Ctl and elbow pain that shelved him in Aug 2013 were tip-offs. Subsequent TJS in April torpedoed 2014, and will likely delay the start of his 2015. Whenever he returns, if this was a long-term injury-in-process (and Cmd trend hints at that), 2011 MLEs illustrate his speculative upside.

Yr Tm	W	L	Sv	IP	K	ERA	xERA	WHIP	oOPS	vL	vR	BF/G	Ctl	Dom	Cmd	FpK	SwK	G	L	F	H%	S%	hr/f	GS	APC	DOM%	DIS%	Sv%	LI	RAR	BPV	BPX	R$
10																																	
11 TAM *	13	3	0	164	200	2.05	2.05	0.98	651	697	633	20.8	2.5	11.0	4.4	60%	16%	43	19	38	29%	83%	13%	1	56	100%	0%	0	0.79	38.3	155	233	$29
12 TAM	11	11	0	177	175	3.81	4.24	1.35	706	685	712	24.5	4.1	8.9	2.2	60%	12%	37	20	43	30%	74%	9%	31	98	45%	23%			4.6	64	83	$7
13 TAM	17	4	0	150	143	3.29	4.23	1.30	655	617	672	23.8	4.5	8.6	1.9	51%	10%	39	18	42	27%	77%	8%	27	97	41%	22%			10.6	48	63	$12
14 TAM	0	2	0	10	6	2.70	4.75	1.50	777	1010	703	22.0	4.5	5.4	1.2	44%	7%	45	27	27	29%	86%	11%	2	92	0%	50%			1.3	-1	-2	-$3
1st Half	0	2	0	10	6	2.70	4.75	1.50	777	1010	703	22.0	4.5	5.4	1.2	44%	7%	45	27	27	29%	86%	11%	2	92	0%	50%			1.3	-1	-1	-$3
2nd Half																																	
15 Proj	**9**	**3**	**0**	**102**	**96**	**3.80**	**3.80**	**1.30**	**683**	**648**	**697**	**22.9**	**4.1**	**8.5**	**2.1**	**55%**	**11%**	**37**	**21**	**43**	**28%**	**73%**	**9%**	**18**						**-0.8**	**57**	**67**	**$4**

Morales,Franklin

Age: 29	Th: L	Role RP	Health F	LIMA Plan D+
Ht: 6' 1"	Wt: 210	Type Pwr	PT/Exp C	Rand Var +3
			Consist A	MM 1200

Health, wavering control and declining Dom were already a concern for long-term FBer. GB trend hints at new tricks, but they aren't working yet. Coors not responsible for HR barrage; he was worse on the road. Another year of .900+ OPS vRHBs and that DIS% says to stay far away.

Yr Tm	W	L	Sv	IP	K	ERA	xERA	WHIP	oOPS	vL	vR	BF/G	Ctl	Dom	Cmd	FpK	SwK	G	L	F	H%	S%	hr/f	GS	APC	DOM%	DIS%	Sv%	LI	RAR	BPV	BPX	R$
10 COL *	3	4	4	59	53	4.49	4.48	1.55	823	652	900	4.4	6.3	8.2	1.3	54%	7%	39	14	47	27%	74%	13%	0	16			44	0.91	-3.0	47	77	-$1
11 2 TM	1	2	0	46	42	3.69	4.22	1.27	757	789	725	3.9	3.7	8.2	2.2	60%	10%	30	16	54	28%	75%	9%	0	15			0	0.94	1.4	55	83	-$1
12 BOS	3	4	1	76	76	3.77	3.98	1.23	685	490	788	8.8	3.5	9.0	2.5	57%	11%	40	19	41	28%	75%	13%	9	36	44%	33%	100	1.14	2.3	84	109	$2
13 BOS *	3	3	0	45	36	4.48	4.28	1.42	737	446	925	6.8	4.1	7.2	1.7	57%	10%	39	24	38	29%	71%	7%	1	22	0%	0%	0	1.12	-3.4	51	66	-$3
14 COL	6	9	0	142	100	5.37	4.66	1.62	859	699	923	17.0	4.1	6.3	1.5	56%	9%	43	25	33	32%	71%	16%	22	64	36%	41%	0	0.87	-28.7	24	28	-$15
1st Half	4	4	0	77	52	5.75	4.55	1.57	889	770	939	17.2	3.6	6.1	1.7	57%	9%	44	23	33	30%	69%	20%	11	63	36%	45%	0	0.97	-19.0	33	40	-$15
2nd Half	2	5	0	66	48	4.93	4.81	1.69	825	609	905	16.8	4.7	6.6	1.4	55%	9%	41	27	32	34%	72%	10%	11	65	36%	36%	0	0.76	-9.7	12	14	-$14
15 Proj	**2**	**3**	**0**	**44**	**35**	**4.71**	**4.23**	**1.50**	**794**	**647**	**867**	**9.2**	**4.2**	**7.2**	**1.7**	**57%**	**10%**	**40**	**22**	**39**	**31%**	**72%**	**12%**	**0**						**-5.2**	**34**	**41**	**-$4**

JOCK THOMPSON

Morin,Michael

Age: 24	Th: R	Role RP	Health B	LIMA Plan A
Ht: 6' 4"	Wt: 220	Type Pwr	PT/Exp D	Rand Var -2
			Consist B	MM 4300

Got results despite not being the prototypical reliever. An outstanding change-up is his most effective pitch (25% SwK) while his 92 mph four-seamer generates very few swings and misses. FpK and SwK hint at future Cmd gains. Solid LIMA play.

Yr	Tm	W	L	Sv	IP	K	ERA	xERA	WHIP	oOPS	vL	vR	BF/G	Ctl	Dom	Cmd	FpK	SwK	G	L	F	H%	S%	hr/f	GS	APC	DOM%	DIS%	Sv%	LI	RAR	BPV	BPX	R$
10																																		
11																																		
12																																		
13	aa	0	2	10	31	29	2.39	2.95	1.10				4.7	1.4	8.4	6.0						32%	81%								5.7	164	214	$3
14	LAA	4	4	0	59	54	2.90	3.67	1.19	629	737	511	4.1	2.9	8.2	2.8	63%	12%	44	17	39	30%	76%	5%	0	15			0	1.07	6.1	92	110	$3
1st Half		2	1	0	28	25	1.91	3.44	0.99	573	694	427	4.3	2.5	7.9	3.1	63%	12%	42	19	38	25%	85%	7%	0	16			0	0.75	6.4	95	113	$5
2nd Half		2	3	0	31	29	3.82	3.87	1.37	676	775	573	3.9	3.2	8.5	2.6	62%	13%	45	15	40	34%	71%	3%	0	15			0	1.31	-0.3	89	106	$1
15	Proj	3	4	0	65	60	3.15	3.23	1.17	640	743	528	4.2	2.3	8.3	3.6	63%	12%	44	17	39	31%	73%	5%	0						4.7	109	129	$3

Morris,Bryan

Age: 28	Th: R	Role RP	Health A	LIMA Plan B
Ht: 6' 3"	Wt: 225	Type xGB	PT/Exp D	Rand Var -5
			Consist A	MM 4111

Pitched better after June 1 PIT-MIA trade (0.66 ERA, 2.7 Ctl, 8.0 Dom in 40.2 IP). Best asset is xGB profile, but displayed uptick in velocity to 96mph and signs of improving skills. FpK and SwK, along with 2nd half gains suggest there could be additional growth to come. Even with S% regression, could have some value.

Yr	Tm	W	L	Sv	IP	K	ERA	xERA	WHIP	oOPS	vL	vR	BF/G	Ctl	Dom	Cmd	FpK	SwK	G	L	F	H%	S%	hr/f	GS	APC	DOM%	DIS%	Sv%	LI	RAR	BPV	BPX	R$
10	aa	6	4	0	89	68	5.00	4.66	1.45				20.0	3.1	6.8	2.2						33%	66%								-10.1	59	95	-$2
11	aa	3	4	3	78	50	4.07	4.04	1.50				9.6	3.8	5.8	1.5						33%	71%								-1.2	59	89	-$2
12	PIT *	2	2	5	86	67	3.28	4.18	1.31	375	125	533	7.0	2.0	7.0	3.5	65%	20%	73	0	27	33%	78%	0%	0	15			83	0.16	7.8	89	116	$3
13	PIT	5	7	0	65	37	3.46	4.18	1.31	705	745	674	4.9	3.9	5.1	1.3	58%	12%	58	18	25	25%	78%	16%	0	17			0	1.18	3.2	23	29	$0
14	2 NL	8	1	0	64	50	1.82	3.47	1.27	684	726	652	4.5	3.4	7.0	2.1	64%	14%	59	19	21	28%	91%	15%	0	16			0	1.34	15.3	72	86	$6
1st Half		5	0	0	40	29	2.23	3.52	1.41	718	875	617	5.1	3.8	6.5	1.7	64%	13%	67	17	16	30%	89%	20%	0	18			0	1.12	7.5	59	70	$5
2nd Half		3	1	0	24	21	1.13	3.38	1.04	621	476	718	3.8	2.6	7.9	3.0	62%	16%	45	23	31	26%	96%	10%	0	13			0	1.63	7.7	94	112	$7
15	Proj	6	4	3	73	55	3.21	3.33	1.24	682	687	676	4.9	2.9	6.9	2.4	61%	14%	56	19	25	29%	76%	11%	0						4.8	79	94	$4

Morrow,Brandon

Age: 30	Th: R	Role SP	Health F	LIMA Plan D+
Ht: 6' 3"	Wt: 210	Type Pwr	PT/Exp C	Rand Var +4
			Consist B	MM 2201

Injury struck again (torn tendon sheath in right hand). There are some who will continue to cling to the memory of 2012's ERA and speculate, but a scan of pretty much every important trend -- Dom, Cmd, FpK, SwK, xERA, BPV/BPX -- shows that it wasn't real. Even if healthy, he can be safely ignored.

Yr	Tm	W	L	Sv	IP	K	ERA	xERA	WHIP	oOPS	vL	vR	BF/G	Ctl	Dom	Cmd	FpK	SwK	G	L	F	H%	S%	hr/f	GS	APC	DOM%	DIS%	Sv%	LI	RAR	BPV	BPX	R$
10	TOR	10	7	0	146	178	4.49	3.44	1.38	725	739	704	24.2	4.1	10.9	2.7	53%	11%	40	18	42	35%	68%	7%	26	97	58%	23%			-7.4	105	171	$4
11	TOR	11	11	0	179	203	4.72	3.55	1.29	705	641	790	25.9	3.5	10.2	2.9	61%	12%	36	22	42	32%	65%	10%	30	104	67%	23%			-17.1	104	156	$4
12	TOR	10	7	0	125	108	2.96	3.94	1.11	635	561	724	24.0	3.0	7.8	2.6	60%	9%	41	19	40	26%	77%	9%	21	94	48%	29%			16.2	79	104	$14
13	TOR	2	3	0	54	42	5.63	4.58	1.49	880	1014	706	24.2	3.0	7.0	2.3	52%	9%	37	20	43	31%	68%	16%	10	91	30%	30%			-11.8	60	78	-$7
14	TOR	1	3	0	33	30	5.67	4.15	1.65	832	948	708	11.4	4.9	8.1	1.7	52%	9%	51	19	30	35%	64%	7%	6	48	33%	33%	0	0.68	-7.9	44	52	-$6
1st Half		1	2	0	27	26	5.93	4.19	1.72	852	955	737	20.5	5.6	8.6	1.5	54%	9%	53	18	29	35%	64%	9%	6	89	33%	33%			-7.4	34	41	-$7
2nd Half		0	1	0	6	4	4.50	3.96	1.33	737	909	593	3.6	1.5	6.0	4.0	44%	9%	40	25	35	35%	63%	0%	0	12			0	0.58	-0.6	86	102	-$3
15	Proj	5	5	0	87	74	4.49	4.01	1.45	776	808	736	22.7	4.1	7.7	1.9	56%	10%	42	19	39	31%	71%	10%	16						-8.0	47	56	-$3

Morton,Charlie

Age: 31	Th: R	Role SP	Health F	LIMA Plan B+
Ht: 6' 5"	Wt: 235	Type xGB	PT/Exp C	Rand Var 0
			Consist A	MM 3103

Slow-start candidate due to late September hip surgery. While stellar GB% remains his best asset, improved oOPS vLHB, DIS% and career-best Dom were noteworthy. FpK suggests potential Ctl gains—and therein lies the key (better Cmd) to another step forward. But at 31, odds are probably 50-50.

Yr	Tm	W	L	Sv	IP	K	ERA	xERA	WHIP	oOPS	vL	vR	BF/G	Ctl	Dom	Cmd	FpK	SwK	G	L	F	H%	S%	hr/f	GS	APC	DOM%	DIS%	Sv%	LI	RAR	BPV	BPX	R$
10	PIT *	6	16	0	160	98	6.08	6.08	1.68	908	936	887	23.2	3.2	5.5	1.7	56%	8%	47	24	29	35%	65%	18%	17	84	41%	41%			-39.4	25	40	-$16
11	PIT	10	10	0	172	110	3.83	4.02	1.53	737	960	567	26.5	4.0	5.8	1.4	55%	8%	59	23	19	32%	74%	6%	29	94	31%	24%			2.4	32	48	-$1
12	PIT	2	6	0	50	25	4.65	4.25	1.45	812	740	886	24.8	2.0	4.5	2.3	61%	7%	57	21	23	33%	69%	13%	9	88	33%	22%			-3.9	61	80	-$6
13	PIT *	8	6	0	154	101	3.46	3.47	1.30	683	844	552	22.6	3.1	5.9	1.9	59%	9%	63	18	19	29%	74%	9%	20	86	50%	15%			7.7	63	83	$5
14	PIT	6	12	0	157	126	3.72	3.45	1.27	682	664	698	25.6	3.3	7.2	2.2	61%	8%	56	21	23	30%	71%	9%	26	96	50%	8%			0.4	76	90	$3
1st Half		4	9	0	100	84	3.41	3.41	1.23	665	628	702	26.8	3.1	7.5	2.4	61%	9%	55	21	25	29%	73%	9%	16	101	44%	0%			4.1	84	100	$8
2nd Half		2	3	0	57	42	4.26	3.52	1.35	711	730	689	23.7	3.5	6.6	1.9	60%	7%	57	23	20	30%	68%	9%	10	90	60%	20%			-3.7	61	73	-$5
15	Proj	8	11	0	174	120	3.76	3.50	1.32	703	738	670	23.7	3.1	6.2	2.0	60%	8%	58	21	21	30%	72%	10%	30						-0.4	63	75	$4

Motte,Jason

Age: 33	Th: R	Role RP	Health F	LIMA Plan C
Ht: 6' 0"	Wt: 205	Type Pwr FB	PT/Exp C	Rand Var +1
			Consist D	MM 3200

May 2013 Tommy John surgery and a lower back strain sidelined him for 74 games. Fastball velocity dipped 3 mph from pre-TJS; at 33, will it return? SwK, Dom and Ctl didn't make it back to where he had left off. Health/consistency combo urge caution; just too many unknowns.

Yr	Tm	W	L	Sv	IP	K	ERA	xERA	WHIP	oOPS	vL	vR	BF/G	Ctl	Dom	Cmd	FpK	SwK	G	L	F	H%	S%	hr/f	GS	APC	DOM%	DIS%	Sv%	LI	RAR	BPV	BPX	R$
10	STL	4	2	2	52	54	2.24	3.50	1.13	618	789	531	3.7	3.1	9.3	3.0	62%	12%	40	13	47	28%	85%	8%	0	15			67	1.20	11.9	102	164	$6
11	STL	5	2	9	68	63	2.25	3.21	0.96	558	738	454	3.4	2.1	8.3	3.9	61%	12%	44	18	39	27%	76%	3%	0	14			69	1.35	14.2	115	173	$12
12	STL	4	5	42	72	86	2.75	2.91	0.92	576	381	756	4.2	2.1	10.8	5.1	71%	14%	41	20	40	25%	77%	13%	0	17			86	1.43	11.2	155	202	$27
13																																		
14	STL	1	0	0	25	17	4.68	4.75	1.52	891	733	989	3.8	3.2	6.1	1.9	63%	10%	37	21	42	29%	81%	20%	0	14			0	0.49	-2.9	38	45	-$4
1st Half		0	0	0	11	11	3.97	4.04	1.68	931	950	920	3.7	3.2	8.7	2.8	69%	12%	41	24	35	36%	88%	23%	0	14			0	0.54	-0.3	90	107	-$6
2nd Half		1	0	0	14	6	5.27	5.35	1.39	856	555	1054	3.9	3.3	4.0	1.2	57%	8%	34	19	47	24%	73%	18%	0	14			0	0.43	-2.6	-6	-7	-$3
15	Proj	3	2	0	44	36	3.87	3.68	1.19	663	682	649	3.9	3.1	7.5	2.4	65%	13%	41	17	42	28%	69%	7%	0						-0.7	69	82	$0

Mujica,Edward

Age: 31	Th: R	Role RP	Health B	LIMA Plan B+
Ht: 6' 3"	Wt: 225	Type Con	PT/Exp B	Rand Var 0
			Consist A	MM 3110

2012-13 xERA hinted at the 2014 ERA jump; was hit much harder (see LD% and oOPS). His combo of Ctl and Dom means plenty of balls put in play so it's crucial that he induce more soft contact (GB% was his lowest since 2009). Still, a H% correction is all it would take to move that ERA back closer to 3.00 again.

Yr	Tm	W	L	Sv	IP	K	ERA	xERA	WHIP	oOPS	vL	vR	BF/G	Ctl	Dom	Cmd	FpK	SwK	G	L	F	H%	S%	hr/f	GS	APC	DOM%	DIS%	Sv%	LI	RAR	BPV	BPX	R$
10	SD	2	1	0	70	72	3.62	2.86	0.93	684	625	727	4.5	0.8	9.3	12.0	65%	14%	45	13	42	27%	73%	18%	0	17			0	0.66	4.0	169	274	$6
11	FLA	9	6	0	76	63	2.96	3.16	1.03	638	570	700	4.4	1.7	7.5	4.5	61%	11%	48	18	34	27%	75%	10%	0	17			0	1.12	9.2	116	174	$9
12	2 NL	0	3	2	65	47	3.03	3.62	1.04	643	669	620	3.7	1.7	6.5	3.9	70%	11%	51	16	33	26%	75%	11%	0	13			25	1.21	7.9	101	132	$4
13	STL	2	1	37	65	46	2.78	3.52	1.01	674	659	687	3.9	0.7	6.4	9.2	72%	13%	45	16	39	27%	80%	12%	0	14			90	1.29	8.6	119	156	$19
14	BOS	2	4	8	60	43	3.90	3.99	1.38	790	904	694	4.0	2.1	6.5	3.1	69%	11%	43	21	36	33%	74%	9%	0	15			89	0.95	-1.2	80	96	$0
1st Half		2	3	2	29	23	5.65	3.89	1.43	825	920	758	4.1	2.5	7.2	2.9	67%	10%	43	23	33	33%	64%	17%	0	16			67	0.97	-6.8	83	100	-$4
2nd Half		0	1	6	31	20	2.30	4.08	1.34	759	892	626	3.8	1.7	5.7	3.3	70%	11%	43	19	38	34%	83%	3%	0	14			100	0.93	5.6	78	93	$4
15	Proj	2	3	8	58	42	3.30	3.42	1.19	726	780	679	3.9	1.6	6.6	4.2	69%	11%	45	19	36	30%	76%	10%	0						3.2	99	118	$4

Nathan,Joe

Age: 40	Th: R	Role RP	Health D	LIMA Plan B
Ht: 6' 4"	Wt: 230	Type Pwr	PT/Exp A	Rand Var +1
			Consist B	MM 3420

No matter what few positives you can find here, this is not someone who should be closing games anymore. Declines in Ctl, Dom, FpK, SwK and even S% are all on him. Decrease in fastball SwK (14% in 2013; 6% in 2014) especially concerning. Though he's still "the closer" as of now, can't see fit to project many saves.

Yr	Tm	W	L	Sv	IP	K	ERA	xERA	WHIP	oOPS	vL	vR	BF/G	Ctl	Dom	Cmd	FpK	SwK	G	L	F	H%	S%	hr/f	GS	APC	DOM%	DIS%	Sv%	LI	RAR	BPV	BPX	R$
10																																		
11	MIN	2	1	14	45	43	4.84	3.88	1.16	705	620	791	4.0	2.8	8.7	3.1	59%	9%	35	18	47	27%	62%	11%	0	17			82	1.14	-4.9	93	140	$4
12	TEX	3	5	37	64	78	2.80	2.76	1.06	631	617	650	3.9	1.8	10.9	6.0	65%	13%	45	21	33	32%	79%	13%	0	16			93	1.10	9.7	170	222	$21
13	TEX	6	2	43	65	73	1.39	3.25	0.90	464	515	407	3.7	3.1	10.2	3.3	63%	12%	32	23	45	24%	86%	3%	0	15			93	1.43	19.7	110	144	$29
14	DET	5	4	35	58	54	4.81	4.27	1.53	721	755	672	4.2	4.5	8.4	1.9	60%	10%	42	23	36	33%	69%	8%	0	17			83	1.30	-7.6	49	59	$9
1st Half		4	2	17	30	30	6.37	4.09	1.58	795	902	658	4.3	3.9	9.1	2.3	60%	9%	40	24	36	35%	62%	15%	0	17			77	1.26	-9.6	76	90	$7
2nd Half		1	2	18	28	24	3.18	4.46	1.48	637	604	689	4.1	5.1	7.6	1.5	60%	10%	43	21	36	32%	76%	0%	0	17			90	1.34	2.0	21	25	$12
15	Proj	4	3	10	51	50	4.01	3.56	1.28	641	656	621	3.9	3.8	8.8	2.3	61%	10%	39	22	39	30%	69%	7%	0						-1.7	73	87	$4

GREG PYRON

Nelson,Jimmy

Age: 26	Th: R	Role SP	Health A	LIMA Plan B+	
Ht: 6' 6"	Wt: 245	Type Pwr GB	PT/Exp D	Rand Var 0	
			Consist B	MM 3201	

2-9, 4.93 ERA in 69 IP at MIL. MLB surface stats weren't pretty, but there are four reasons for optimism: BPV growth; refined Ctl is supported by FpK; SwK hints more Ks could be on the way; strong GB%. Needs to translate minors success to The Show and make some strides vLHB, but future looks bright.

Yr Tm	W	L	Sv	IP	K	ERA	xERA	WHIP	oOPS	vL	vR	BF/G	Ctl	Dom	Cmd	FpK	SwK	G	L	F	H%	S%	hr/f	GS	APC	DOM%	DIS%	Sv%	LI	RAR	BPV	BPX	R$
10																																	
11																																	
12 aa	2	4	0	46	37	4.88	4.28	1.72				20.9	7.6	7.2	0.9						29%	71%								-4.9	55	72	-$8
13 MIL *	10	10	0	162	147	3.67	3.79	1.43	286	473	63	22.3	4.0	8.2	2.0	49%	11%	42	33	25	33%	74%	0%	1	36	0%	0%	0	0.28	4.0	81	105	$3
14 MIL *	12	11	0	180	152	2.97	3.08	1.20	793	804	782	23.4	2.6	7.6	2.9	63%	10%	48	20	32	30%	76%	8%	12	79	58%	17%	0	0.83	17.1	98	117	$13
1st Half	10	2	0	103	94	1.89	2.20	1.08	547	200	757	25.1	2.9	8.2	2.8	64%	12%	40	7	53	27%	83%	0%	1	107	100%	0%			23.6	111	132	$28
2nd Half	2	9	0	77	59	4.42	4.26	1.37	814	842	784	21.6	2.2	6.8	3.1	63%	10%	49	21	30	34%	68%	10%	11	77	55%	18%	0	0.83	-6.5	82	98	-$7
15 Proj	6	7	0	102	86	3.64	3.52	1.30	646	674	616	21.8	3.3	7.6	2.3	63%	10%	49	21	30	30%	74%	9%	19						1.3	76	90	$3

Neshek,Pat

Age: 34	Th: R	Role RP	Health B	LIMA Plan C+	
Ht: 6' 3"	Wt: 210	Type xFB	PT/Exp D	Rand Var -5	
			Consist C	MM 3310	

I often wonder how a veteran player suddenly has a breakout season at an age when most others have already peaked or are fading. Can an old dog really learn new tricks? Was it a small sample size fluke? Did he have outside help? This is an impressive season. Likely unrepeatable, but impressive nonetheless.

Yr Tm	W	L	Sv	IP	K	ERA	xERA	WHIP	oOPS	vL	vR	BF/G	Ctl	Dom	Cmd	FpK	SwK	G	L	F	H%	S%	hr/f	GS	APC	DOM%	DIS%	Sv%	LI	RAR	BPV	BPX	R$
10 MIN *	5	2	1	48	27	4.94	5.42	1.67	696	730	686	5.3	4.3	5.0	1.2	44%	10%	32	20	48	33%	71%	8%	0	16			33	1.11	-5.1	23	37	-$4
11 SD *	2	3	3	51	30	3.80	5.05	1.60	742	661	819	4.6	5.6	5.3	0.9	54%	9%	30	19	51	27%	81%	12%	0	19			50	0.70	0.9	15	23	-$3
12 OAK *	5	3	11	64	52	3.39	4.08	1.33	530	1108	369	4.5	2.1	7.3	3.5	63%	13%	35	17	48	34%	76%	12%	0	14			69	1.21	4.9	96	125	$5
13 OAK	2	1	0	40	29	3.35	4.90	1.36	738	922	644	3.9	3.3	6.5	1.9	54%	11%	33	19	48	29%	82%	10%	0	15			0	0.39	2.6	37	48	-$2
14 STL	7	2	6	67	68	1.87	3.21	0.79	480	541	442	3.6	1.2	9.1	7.6	67%	13%	35	11	54	25%	80%	4%	0	14			60	1.38	15.5	144	172	$14
1st Half	2	0	2	33	32	0.83	3.06	0.55	335	243	379	3.2	1.1	8.8	8.0	65%	14%	34	9	57	18%	88%	2%	0	13			50	1.28	11.7	141	168	$15
2nd Half	5	2	4	35	36	2.86	3.35	1.01	604	734	505	4.1	1.3	9.3	7.2	69%	13%	35	13	52	30%	75%	6%	0	15			67	1.50	3.8	147	175	$13
15 Proj	6	2	5	65	57	3.09	3.57	1.12	633	746	567	3.8	2.3	7.8	3.5	62%	12%	34	14	51	28%	76%	6%	0						5.2	92	109	$7

Nicasio,Juan

Age: 28	Th: R	Role RP	Health F	LIMA Plan D+	
Ht: 6' 3"	Wt: 210	Type Pwr	PT/Exp C	Rand Var +1	
			Consist B	MM 2100	

6-6, 5.38 ERA in 94 IP at COL. Struggles as starter forced mid-June demotion to AAA. He returned in August as a reliever (3.48 ERA, 5 BB and 17 K in 20.2 IP) which fits his two-pitch profile. Still has issues vLHB, but if smaller workload helps reduce health risk, the role switch might be a winner.

Yr Tm	W	L	Sv	IP	K	ERA	xERA	WHIP	oOPS	vL	vR	BF/G	Ctl	Dom	Cmd	FpK	SwK	G	L	F	H%	S%	hr/f	GS	APC	DOM%	DIS%	Sv%	LI	RAR	BPV	BPX	R$
10																																	
11 COL *	9	5	0	128	106	3.53	3.75	1.24	735	859	595	23.7	2.0	7.4	3.7	58%	9%	46	22	32	32%	74%	11%	13	89	38%	23%			6.5	100	151	$7
12 COL	2	3	0	58	54	5.28	4.19	1.62	861	902	825	23.4	3.4	8.4	2.5	60%	8%	40	25	36	37%	69%	11%	11	93	45%	27%			-9.0	77	100	-$8
13 COL	9	9	0	158	119	5.14	4.40	1.47	782	737	820	22.6	3.7	6.8	1.9	57%	8%	45	21	34	32%	66%	10%	31	92	29%	26%			-24.7	47	61	-$8
14 COL *	9	8	1	129	88	5.43	6.00	1.58	860	900	827	13.2	3.3	6.2	1.9	59%	8%	46	20	34	33%	70%	18%	14	49	36%	36%	100	0.76	-27.0	21	25	-$11
1st Half	6	6	0	84	53	6.17	6.51	1.69	907	984	836	23.8	3.2	5.7	1.8	60%	8%	46	21	33	34%	66%	19%	14	92	36%	36%			-25.2	14	16	-$16
2nd Half	3	2	1	45	35	4.05	5.03	1.37	675	442	799	7.0	3.3	7.1	2.1	54%	11%	45	16	40	28%	79%	17%	0	17			100	0.77	-1.7	35	42	-$1
15 Proj	4	3	0	58	44	4.40	4.05	1.47	789	777	799	5.8	3.6	6.8	1.9	57%	9%	44	20	35	31%	73%	12%	-3						-4.7	47	56	-$3

Niese,Jon

Age: 28	Th: L	Role SP	Health D	LIMA Plan B	
Ht: 6' 3"	Wt: 220	Type	PT/Exp A	Rand Var 0	
			Consist A	MM 3103	

Battled injuries again (elbow and shoulder), but improved upon a tough 2013. Given his below average Dom and average SwK, the rebound in Ctl is big. With his GB lean, plus Cmd and history of sub-4.00 xERA, there is value if his health cooperates.

Yr Tm	W	L	Sv	IP	K	ERA	xERA	WHIP	oOPS	vL	vR	BF/G	Ctl	Dom	Cmd	FpK	SwK	G	L	F	H%	S%	hr/f	GS	APC	DOM%	DIS%	Sv%	LI	RAR	BPV	BPX	R$
10 NYM	9	10	0	174	148	4.20	3.88	1.46	783	831	772	25.7	3.2	7.7	2.4	60%	9%	48	21	32	33%	74%	12%	30	98	40%	23%			-2.5	77	125	$1
11 NYM	11	11	0	157	138	4.40	3.49	1.41	754	664	781	25.7	2.5	7.9	3.1	59%	9%	51	21	28	35%	70%	10%	26	92	42%	15%	0	0.76	-9.0	103	155	$1
12 NYM	13	9	0	190	155	3.40	3.70	1.17	663	665	663	26.3	2.3	7.3	3.2	63%	8%	48	21	31	28%	75%	13%	30	101	70%	7%			14.3	95	124	$16
13 NYM	8	8	0	143	105	3.71	3.93	1.44	739	660	765	25.9	3.0	6.6	2.2	61%	8%	52	21	27	33%	75%	8%	24	98	50%	17%			2.7	67	88	$0
14 NYM	9	11	0	188	138	3.40	3.68	1.27	722	656	742	26.2	2.2	6.6	3.1	63%	8%	48	23	30	31%	76%	10%	30	93	57%	10%			7.8	87	103	$7
1st Half	5	4	0	103	74	2.88	3.74	1.19	660	565	687	26.6	2.4	6.5	2.6	59%	6%	48	21	31	29%	78%	7%	16	96	56%	6%			10.9	76	91	$12
2nd Half	4	7	0	85	64	4.04	3.61	1.36	794	748	809	25.7	1.8	6.8	3.8	67%	10%	47	24	29	33%	73%	13%	14	90	57%	14%			-3.1	99	118	-$1
15 Proj	10	9	0	174	130	3.66	3.56	1.32	726	673	742	25.3	2.5	6.7	2.7	63%	8%	48	22	30	31%	75%	10%	28						1.8	78	93	$6

Noesi,Hector

Age: 28	Th: R	Role SP	Health A	LIMA Plan D+	
Ht: 6' 3"	Wt: 205	Type FB	PT/Exp C	Rand Var +1	
			Consist C	MM 1103	

Despite improvement in xERA, little reason for excitement. oOPS shows he wasn't as hittable as in the past, but subpar Cmd, heavy FB% profile and gopheritis remained problematic. SwK suggests some K upside, but it has yet to materialize. Without a surge in strikeouts, any fantasy relevance is a longshot.

Yr Tm	W	L	Sv	IP	K	ERA	xERA	WHIP	oOPS	vL	vR	BF/G	Ctl	Dom	Cmd	FpK	SwK	G	L	F	H%	S%	hr/f	GS	APC	DOM%	DIS%	Sv%	LI	RAR	BPV	BPX	R$
10 a/a	9	5	0	117	84	4.28	4.34	1.33				24.4	1.8	6.4	3.6						33%	69%								-2.9	87	141	$3
11 NYY *	3	3	0	81	59	4.50	5.05	1.60	785	806	766	10.0	3.6	6.6	1.8	63%	10%	41	26	34	35%	72%	10%	2	32	0%	100%	0	0.80	-5.6	53	80	-$6
12 SEA *	4	18	0	171	115	5.70	5.16	1.47	826	865	782	22.2	3.1	6.0	1.9	64%	10%	37	18	45	31%	63%	14%	18	78	39%	33%	0	0.64	-35.5	33	43	-$15
13 SEA *	4	4	0	105	71	6.30	6.23	1.66	935	938	931	16.2	2.5	6.1	2.4	58%	9%	36	27	36	36%	64%	8%	1	41	0%	100%	0	0.40	-31.4	36	47	-$16
14 3AL	8	12	0	172	123	4.75	4.37	1.37	774	728	834	22.2	2.9	6.4	2.2	62%	10%	38	21	41	30%	70%	13%	27	83	48%	15%	0	0.79	-21.5	53	63	-$5
1st Half	2	5	0	71	54	5.07	4.44	1.49	807	736	887	18.5	2.9	6.8	2.3	61%	10%	38	22	40	34%	68%	10%	11	71	36%	18%	0	0.82	-11.6	60	72	-$13
2nd Half	6	7	0	101	69	4.53	4.31	1.28	749	723	788	26.2	2.9	6.1	2.1	62%	10%	38	21	41	26%	71%	15%	16	97	56%	13%			-9.9	47	57	$0
15 Proj	7	11	0	174	120	4.82	4.20	1.45	818	807	831	22.5	2.9	6.2	2.1	63%	10%	38	21	41	31%	70%	11%	29						-23.1	48	58	-$7

Nolasco,Ricky

Age: 32	Th: R	Role SP	Health D	LIMA Plan C	
Ht: 6' 2"	Wt: 235	Type	PT/Exp A	Rand Var +4	
			Consist B	MM 2105	

Move to MIN couldn't hide the fact that he allows far too much hard contact, as oOPS and LD% show. FB%, SwK and Dom took a turn for the worse and hr/f sprung back to pre-2011 levels. FpK trend points to Ctl downside. Given his propensity to get hit hard, the last thing he needs is more walks. Stay clear.

Yr Tm	W	L	Sv	IP	K	ERA	xERA	WHIP	oOPS	vL	vR	BF/G	Ctl	Dom	Cmd	FpK	SwK	G	L	F	H%	S%	hr/f	GS	APC	DOM%	DIS%	Sv%	LI	RAR	BPV	BPX	R$
10 FLA	14	9	0	158	147	4.51	3.60	1.28	766	758	772	25.6	1.9	8.4	4.5	66%	11%	40	19	41	33%	69%	12%	26	95	54%	23%			-8.4	118	191	$7
11 FLA	10	12	0	206	148	4.67	3.82	1.40	770	835	708	27.0	1.9	6.5	3.4	65%	9%	45	24	31	34%	68%	10%	33	97	48%	15%			-18.6	87	132	-$3
12 MIA	12	13	0	191	125	4.48	4.27	1.37	755	809	696	26.8	2.2	5.9	2.7	63%	9%	47	22	32	32%	68%	9%	31	96	39%	23%			-10.9	71	93	-$1
13 2 NL	13	11	0	199	165	3.70	3.62	1.21	693	721	660	24.5	2.1	7.4	3.6	60%	11%	43	24	33	31%	71%	9%	33	94	42%	12%	0	0.75	4.0	99	129	$11
14 MIN	6	12	0	159	115	5.38	4.13	1.52	861	906	816	25.7	2.2	6.5	3.0	58%	9%	42	22	36	35%	67%	12%	27	98	41%	22%			-32.1	79	94	-$13
1st Half	4	6	0	96	69	5.74	4.29	1.59	901	921	881	26.3	2.5	6.5	2.6	59%	9%	42	22	36	35%	66%	13%	16	101	38%	19%			-23.6	68	82	-$17
2nd Half	2	6	0	63	46	4.83	3.88	1.41	801	885	713	24.9	1.6	6.5	4.2	56%	9%	41	24	35	35%	67%	10%	11	93	45%	27%			-8.5	95	113	-$8
15 Proj	10	14	0	203	151	4.48	3.75	1.40	799	846	749	25.0	2.2	6.7	3.1	59%	10%	42	22	36	33%	71%	11%	29						-18.4	81	97	-$2

Norris,Bud

Age: 30	Th: R	Role SP	Health B	LIMA Plan B	
Ht: 6' 0"	Wt: 220	Type Pwr	PT/Exp A	Rand Var 0	
			Consist A	MM 3303	

Note that 2011 and 2014 were nearly identical from a skills perspective. 2011 was 20% above league average; 2014 was 5% below. But as stagnant as this career has been for a 30-year-old, there is something more here. 2nd half hints at that further upside. Tuck him away; go an extra buck.

Yr Tm	W	L	Sv	IP	K	ERA	xERA	WHIP	oOPS	vL	vR	BF/G	Ctl	Dom	Cmd	FpK	SwK	G	L	F	H%	S%	hr/f	GS	APC	DOM%	DIS%	Sv%	LI	RAR	BPV	BPX	R$
10 HOU	9	10	0	154	158	4.92	4.00	1.48	758	799	721	25.3	4.5	9.3	2.1	54%	11%	43	18	39	33%	69%	11%	27	101	52%	30%			-15.9	66	106	-$2
11 HOU	6	11	0	186	176	3.77	3.81	1.33	732	811	650	25.6	3.4	8.5	2.5	59%	11%	40	21	39	31%	76%	12%	31	102	55%	13%			3.9	80	120	$6
12 HOU	7	13	0	168	165	4.65	4.10	1.37	751	782	720	25.3	3.5	8.8	2.5	58%	11%	39	21	40	31%	69%	12%	29	97	59%	21%			-13.2	81	105	-$2
13 2 AL	10	12	0	177	147	4.18	4.27	1.49	779	889	629	24.2	3.4	7.5	2.2	61%	10%	40	21	38	34%	74%	8%	30	94	47%	27%	0	0.88	-6.8	61	79	-$3
14 BAL	15	8	0	165	139	3.65	3.77	1.22	710	753	659	24.5	2.8	7.6	2.7	60%	8%	42	21	37	28%	74%	11%	28	98	46%	7%			1.9	80	95	$9
1st Half	7	5	0	87	60	3.62	4.05	1.16	690	696	682	25.4	2.9	6.2	2.1	60%	8%	41	21	38	25%	73%	10%	14	102	50%	0%			1.3	53	63	$9
2nd Half	8	3	0	78	79	3.68	3.46	1.28	731	809	632	23.6	2.8	9.1	3.3	60%	9%	43	20	36	32%	76%	12%	14	94	43%	14%			0.6	110	131	$9
15 Proj	13	9	0	174	152	3.75	3.53	1.25	698	760	625	23.4	2.9	7.8	2.7	60%	9%	41	21	38	30%	73%	10%	30						-0.1	81	97	$10

GREG PYRON

Norris,Daniel

Age: 22	Th: L	Role	RP	Health	C	LIMA Plan	D+
Ht: 6' 2"	Wt: 180	Type	Pwr FB	PT/Exp	F	Rand Var	+2
				Consist	F	MM	2400

0-0, 5.40 ERA in 7 IP at TOR. Breakout season for 2011 2nd-rounder as he climbed from High-A to MLB in same season. That ascent makes him more risky than most young SP, with just 65 IP above AA. Went under knife in Oct to clean out elbow, adding to that risk. A growth stock worth monitoring from a distance.

Yr Tm	W	L	Sv	IP	K	ERA	xERA	WHIP	oOPS	vL	vR	BF/G	Ctl	Dom	Cmd	FpK	SwK	G	L	F	H%	S%	hr/f	GS	APC	DOM%	DIS%	Sv%	LI	RAR	BPV	BPX	R$
10																																	
11																																	
12																																	
13																																	
14 TOR *	6	2	0	65	81	4.98	4.12	1.35	667	594	719	15.0	4.1	11.3	2.7	43%	7%	35	20	45	32%	66%	11%	1	28	0%	100%	0	0.85	-10.0	93	111	-$2
1st Half	1	0	0	16	22	4.02	2.88	1.06				21.1	3.3	12.3	3.8						27%	67%	0%	0						-0.6	129	154	-$4
2nd Half	5	2	0	49	59	5.29	4.53	1.44	667	594	719	13.8	4.4	10.9	2.5	43%	7%	35	20	45	33%	66%	11%	1	28	0%	100%	0	0.85	-9.3	84	100	-$1
15 Proj	**4**	**2**	**0**	**50**	**53**	**4.76**	**3.81**	**1.38**				**16.3**	**4.9**	**9.6**	**2.0**	**56%**	**9%**	**36**	**20**	**44**	**29%**	**68%**	**12%**	**8**						**-6.3**	**55**	**65**	**-$2**

Nova,Ivan

Age: 28	Th: R	Role	SP	Health	F	LIMA Plan	C
Ht: 6' 4"	Wt: 225	Type		PT/Exp	C	Rand Var	+5
				Consist	B	MM	3101

Another SP bitten by early 2014 TJS bug. Concurrent xERA, SwK improvements heading into year made him a solid mid-3s ERA arm with Dom upside. That 2014 blowup was induced by S% and hr/f, so ignore it. However, likely not to regain arm strength until 2nd half, so don't view him as anything more than a stash.

Yr Tm	W	L	Sv	IP	K	ERA	xERA	WHIP	oOPS	vL	vR	BF/G	Ctl	Dom	Cmd	FpK	SwK	G	L	F	H%	S%	hr/f	GS	APC	DOM%	DIS%	Sv%	LI	RAR	BPV	BPX	R$
10 NYY *	13	5	0	187	122	3.93	4.64	1.47	729	747	703	24.3	3.3	5.9	1.8	60%	7%	51	18	30	32%	75%	10%	7	67	43%	43%	0	0.91	3.5	46	74	$3
11 NYY *	17	6	0	181	113	3.79	4.03	1.34	706	681	730	24.3	2.9	5.6	1.9	60%	7%	53	18	29	29%	74%	8%	27	92	37%	19%	0	0.82	3.5	50	75	$8
12 NYY	12	8	0	170	153	5.02	3.95	1.47	860	848	872	26.7	3.0	8.1	2.7	58%	9%	45	22	32	34%	70%	17%	28	96	46%	21%			-21.1	89	116	-$6
13 NYY *	11	6	0	157	130	3.08	3.57	1.29	678	676	680	24.8	2.8	7.4	2.7	54%	10%	54	20	26	31%	78%	8%	20	91	50%	20%	0	0.77	15.2	86	112	$10
14 NYY	2	2	0	21	12	8.27	4.53	1.84	1033	764	1444	24.0	2.6	5.2	2.0	64%	5%	49	20	31	36%	59%	26%	4	82	0%	75%			-11.6	51	60	-$7
1st Half	2	2	0	21	12	8.27	4.53	1.84	1033	764	1444	24.0	2.6	5.2	2.0	64%	5%	49	20	31	36%	59%	26%	4	82	0%	75%			-11.6	51	61	-$7
2nd Half																																	
15 Proj	**7**	**5**	**0**	**87**	**63**	**3.76**	**3.67**	**1.35**	**707**	**651**	**775**	**23.8**	**2.9**	**6.5**	**2.3**	**60%**	**8%**	**50**	**20**	**30**	**31%**	**74%**	**9%**	**15**						**-0.3**	**68**	**81**	**$1**

Nuno,Vidal

Age: 27	Th: L	Role	SP	Health	B	LIMA Plan	C
Ht: 5' 11"	Wt: 195	Type	FB	PT/Exp	C	Rand Var	+1
				Consist	F	MM	2103

Soft-tosser easy to overlook given ERA spike. However, sweeping skill gains in 2nd half came with full support from jumps in FpK and SwK. Slight FB tilt will keep ERA volatility an issue; 5+ ERA at cozy home parks was due to gopheritis. If GB uptick holds, he's a 3.50-ERA pitcher you can probably get for a few bucks.

Yr Tm	W	L	Sv	IP	K	ERA	xERA	WHIP	oOPS	vL	vR	BF/G	Ctl	Dom	Cmd	FpK	SwK	G	L	F	H%	S%	hr/f	GS	APC	DOM%	DIS%	Sv%	LI	RAR	BPV	BPX	R$
10																																	
11																																	
12 aa	9	5	0	114	80	3.19	4.88	1.42				24.2	2.3	6.3	2.8						33%	82%								11.6	61	79	$3
13 NYY *	3	2	0	45	33	2.15	2.47	0.94	654	691	643	16.9	1.7	6.6	3.9	66%	4%	35	18	47	24%	85%	6%	3	63	33%	0%	0	1.03	9.5	105	137	$4
14 2 TM	2	12	0	162	129	4.56	4.08	1.26	745	582	793	21.9	2.6	7.2	2.8	67%	9%	38	19	43	29%	68%	12%	28	83	43%	25%	0	0.71	-16.4	76	91	-$3
1st Half	2	4	0	73	55	5.42	4.42	1.40	820	740	843	19.7	3.0	6.8	2.3	64%	7%	38	19	43	29%	67%	15%	13	76	38%	38%	0	0.67	-15.2	58	70	-$10
2nd Half	0	8	0	89	74	3.86	3.81	1.14	681	444	751	24.3	2.2	7.5	3.4	69%	10%	38	19	43	28%	69%	9%	15	92	47%	13%			-1.3	91	108	$3
15 Proj	**6**	**10**	**0**	**160**	**122**	**3.71**	**3.79**	**1.27**	**739**	**566**	**790**	**20.6**	**2.4**	**6.9**	**2.8**	**67%**	**9%**	**38**	**19**	**43**	**30%**	**75%**	**10%**	**32**						**0.6**	**74**	**88**	**$5**

O Day,Darren

Age: 32	Th: R	Role	RP	Health	C	LIMA Plan	B
Ht: 6' 4"	Wt: 220	Type	Pwr FB	PT/Exp	C	Rand Var	-5
				Consist	A	MM	5410

Seemed to debunk stereotype as good middle-man susceptible to blowups vs. LHB... or did he? Alternating years of misery vLHB make us skeptical these gains will stick. Tiny ERA fueled by friendly H%/S%; xERA confirms he's a 3-ish guy. Surging SwK gives him closer's stuff—but his mgr won't trust him vLHB, either.

Yr Tm	W	L	Sv	IP	K	ERA	xERA	WHIP	oOPS	vL	vR	BF/G	Ctl	Dom	Cmd	FpK	SwK	G	L	F	H%	S%	hr/f	GS	APC	DOM%	DIS%	Sv%	LI	RAR	BPV	BPX	R$
10 TEX	6	2	0	62	45	2.03	3.62	0.89	548	561	542	3.3	1.7	6.5	3.8	60%	10%	37	21	42	23%	82%	7%	0	12			0	1.15	15.7	86	138	$9
11 TEX *	1	1	1	38	37	4.21	5.50	1.27	929	900	938	4.6	2.3	8.8	3.9	68%	11%	35	17	48	28%	82%	30%	0	17			100	0.47	-1.3	59	88	-$2
12 BAL	7	1	0	67	69	2.28	3.34	0.94	613	664	584	3.8	1.9	9.3	4.9	65%	12%	34	23	43	26%	81%	8%	0	15			0	1.10	14.3	128	167	$10
13 BAL	5	3	2	62	59	2.18	3.38	1.00	617	922	443	3.6	2.2	8.6	3.9	63%	12%	37	22	41	26%	85%	10%	0	14			33	1.22	12.9	110	144	$8
14 BAL	5	2	4	69	73	1.70	2.99	0.89	550	633	497	4.0	2.5	9.6	3.8	59%	14%	45	17	38	23%	87%	10%	0	16			50	1.33	17.3	128	152	$12
1st Half	2	1	2	33	30	1.36	3.25	1.12	656	709	627	4.0	2.2	8.2	3.8	62%	13%	47	19	34	30%	91%	7%	0	16			40	1.43	9.7	113	135	$8
2nd Half	3	1	2	36	43	2.02	2.76	0.67	446	573	346	4.0	2.8	10.9	3.9	55%	14%	42	15	42	14%	80%	12%	0	16			67	1.23	7.6	141	168	$16
15 Proj	**5**	**2**	**3**	**65**	**67**	**2.77**	**2.99**	**1.05**	**653**	**801**	**563**	**3.8**	**2.3**	**9.2**	**4.0**	**61%**	**13%**	**40**	**20**	**40**	**28%**	**79%**	**10%**	**0**						**7.8**	**121**	**144**	**$7**

O Flaherty,Eric

Age: 30	Th: L	Role	RP	Health	F	LIMA Plan	B+
Ht: 6' 2"	Wt: 220	Type	xGB	PT/Exp	D	Rand Var	-5
				Consist	A	MM	5200

Slow road back in recovery from 2013 TJS. PRO: Historically decent vR, so may be more than LOOGY; xGBer. CON: xERA reveals those sub-2.50 ERAs to be flukes; recent Ctl gains not supported by FpK. Has never shown elite K ability, so will be confined to middle work. Only value to you is as a deep-league LIMA arm.

Yr Tm	W	L	Sv	IP	K	ERA	xERA	WHIP	oOPS	vL	vR	BF/G	Ctl	Dom	Cmd	FpK	SwK	G	L	F	H%	S%	hr/f	GS	APC	DOM%	DIS%	Sv%	LI	RAR	BPV	BPX	R$
10 ATL	3	2	0	44	36	2.45	3.43	1.25	647	598	690	3.2	3.7	7.4	2.0	58%	10%	57	20	23	28%	81%	7%	0	12			0	1.15	8.8	68	110	$2
11 ATL	2	4	0	74	67	0.98	3.03	1.09	572	512	599	3.9	2.6	8.2	3.2	64%	11%	56	19	26	29%	92%	4%	0	15			0	1.23	26.9	112	168	$10
12 ATL	3	0	0	57	46	1.73	3.14	1.15	602	305	759	3.6	3.0	7.2	2.4	60%	11%	66	16	18	28%	87%	11%	0	13			0	1.24	16.2	93	122	$5
13 ATL	3	0	0	18	11	2.50	3.62	0.94	555	420	620	3.7	2.5	5.5	2.2	59%	9%	58	13	29	20%	80%	13%	0	13			0	1.23	3.0	68	88	$0
14 OAK	1	0	1	20	15	2.25	3.21	0.95	608	536	658	3.8	1.8	6.8	3.8	60%	9%	54	18	28	22%	88%	19%	0	15			50	0.61	3.7	105	125	$0
1st Half																																	
2nd Half	1	0	1	20	15	2.25	3.21	0.95	608	536	658	3.8	1.8	6.8	3.8	60%	9%	54	18	28	22%	88%	19%	0	15			50	0.61	3.7	105	126	$0
15 Proj	**3**	**1**	**0**	**58**	**48**	**2.51**	**3.05**	**1.17**	**646**	**541**	**709**	**3.6**	**2.6**	**7.4**	**2.9**	**61%**	**10%**	**58**	**18**	**24**	**29%**	**81%**	**10%**	**0**						**8.8**	**100**	**119**	**$3**

Oberholtzer,Brett

Age: 26	Th: L	Role	SP	Health	A	LIMA Plan	C
Ht: 6' 1"	Wt: 225	Type	Con FB	PT/Exp	D	Rand Var	0
				Consist	C	MM	2103

5-13, 4.39 ERA in 144 IP at HOU. Some will note big jump in Cmd and make him $1 end-gamer. You'll see that it was driven by Ctl gains w/o support of FpK and be skeptical. As a FB soft-tosser w/change-up as only true K pitch, value is linked heavily with friendly hr/f, which we can't bet on. Very little profit potential here.

Yr Tm	W	L	Sv	IP	K	ERA	xERA	WHIP	oOPS	vL	vR	BF/G	Ctl	Dom	Cmd	FpK	SwK	G	L	F	H%	S%	hr/f	GS	APC	DOM%	DIS%	Sv%	LI	RAR	BPV	BPX	R$
10																																	
11 aa	11	12	0	155	107	4.22	3.69	1.32				23.8	2.8	6.2	2.2						31%	68%								-5.3	70	105	$3
12 a/a	10	10	0	167	119	4.48	5.10	1.42				25.2	2.0	6.4	3.1						33%	72%								-9.6	63	82	-$3
13 HOU *	10	11	0	152	106	3.94	3.92	1.26	654	745	617	21.4	2.3	6.3	2.8	66%	9%	36	22	42	30%	71%	7%	10	85	70%	10%	0	0.69	-1.4	69	90	$4
14 HOU *	6	15	0	175	120	4.50	4.87	1.37	752	726	760	25.3	1.6	6.2	3.9	61%	8%	37	20	43	33%	70%	6%	24	94	46%	25%			-16.3	81	97	-$5
1st Half	3	8	0	88	70	4.61	5.08	1.36	739	561	792	24.6	1.7	7.1	4.1	58%	8%	38	20	42	33%	71%	6%	10	92	60%	30%			-9.5	82	98	-$5
2nd Half	3	7	0	86	50	4.38	4.55	1.39	760	828	738	26.8	1.5	5.2	3.6	63%	8%	37	21	43	34%	69%	5%	14	95	36%	21%			-6.8	69	82	-$6
15 Proj	**6**	**10**	**0**	**131**	**88**	**4.32**	**4.00**	**1.36**	**764**	**783**	**757**	**24.2**	**2.1**	**6.1**	**2.9**	**62%**	**8%**	**37**	**21**	**42**	**32%**	**71%**	**8%**	**23**						**-9.3**	**68**	**81**	**-$1**

Odorizzi,Jake

Age: 25	Th: R	Role	SP	Health	A	LIMA Plan	B+
Ht: 6' 2"	Wt: 185	Type	Pwr xFB	PT/Exp	C	Rand Var	0
				Consist	A	MM	2303

On surface, a so-so young SP. But four reasons to support breakout: 1) Dom, SwK, BPV all surging; 2) Big gains against lefties; 3) 15% SwK% on split-change borrowed from Alex Cobb in spring; 4) FpK trend—especially jump in 2nd half—support Ctl reduction. With just a few fewer FB... UP: 3.25 ERA, 200 K

Yr Tm	W	L	Sv	IP	K	ERA	xERA	WHIP	oOPS	vL	vR	BF/G	Ctl	Dom	Cmd	FpK	SwK	G	L	F	H%	S%	hr/f	GS	APC	DOM%	DIS%	Sv%	LI	RAR	BPV	BPX	R$
10																																	
11 aa	5	3	0	69	45	4.97	4.56	1.32				23.7	2.7	5.9	2.2						28%	66%								-8.7	41	61	-$2
12 KC *	15	6	0	153	117	3.36	3.89	1.32	820	899	400	22.6	3.0	6.9	2.3	56%	7%	27	27	46	30%	77%	8%	2	76	0%	50%			12.3	69	89	$10
13 TAM *	9	7	1	154	129	3.83	3.46	1.22	744	846	627	21.5	2.7	7.5	2.8	57%	8%	32	26	42	29%	71%	8%	4	76	25%	25%	100	0.80	0.7	83	108	$7
14 TAM	11	13	0	168	174	4.13	3.96	1.28	692	663	726	23.2	3.2	9.3	2.9	61%	10%	30	21	49	31%	71%	9%	31	98	52%	29%			-8.0	90	108	$4
1st Half	3	7	0	83	97	4.14	3.63	1.33	685	673	702	22.3	3.7	10.6	2.9	60%	11%	36	21	43	34%	70%	7%	16	97	44%	31%			-4.0	104	124	$0
2nd Half	8	6	0	85	77	4.11	4.27	1.23	699	651	744	24.1	2.6	8.1	3.1	63%	10%	25	22	53	29%	72%	10%	15	98	60%	27%			-3.9	78	93	$8
15 Proj	**13**	**11**	**0**	**178**	**159**	**3.81**	**3.80**	**1.27**	**692**	**659**	**728**	**22.3**	**2.9**	**8.1**	**2.7**	**62%**	**10%**	**29**	**21**	**49**	**30%**	**73%**	**8%**	**33**						**-1.5**	**73**	**87**	**$9**

STEPHEN NICKRAND

Ogando,Alexi

Age:	31	Th:	R	Role	RP	Health	F	LIMA Plan	C
Ht:	6' 4"	Wt:	200	Type	Pwr FB	PT/Exp	D	Rand Var	+5
						Consist	B	MM	2300

Continues to be bitten by injury bug. This time it was elbow. Hoping rest will do the trick, but health history deters any optimism. Follow BF/G to see which role he belongs in; 100+ BPV in seasons used as RP before this injury-shortened one. oOPS vR, xERA trends cement it: he's got no upside as a SP now.

Yr Tm	W	L	Sv	IP	K	ERA	xERA	WHIP	oOPS	vL	vR	BF/G	Ctl	Dom	Cmd	FpK	SwK	G	L	F	H%	S%	hr/f	GS	APC	DOM%	DIS%	Sv%	LI	RAR	BPV	BPX	R$
10 TEX *	4	1	1	72	71	1.93	2.02	1.07	554	678	492	4.5	3.5	8.8	2.5	63%	11%	44	18	38	25%	84%	5%	0	16			20	1.02	19.2	109	177	$9
11 TEX	13	8	0	169	126	3.51	3.90	1.14	649	709	560	22.4	2.3	6.7	2.9	58%	10%	36	24	40	28%	72%	8%	29	88	62%	21%	0	0.74	8.9	73	110	$14
12 TEX	2	0	3	66	66	3.27	3.52	1.00	615	637	598	4.5	2.3	9.0	3.9	59%	14%	38	21	41	25%	74%	12%	1	18	0%	100%	50	1.20	6.0	115	151	$6
13 TEX *	8	5	0	123	78	3.60	3.92	1.26	678	620	753	18.6	3.3	5.7	1.7	55%	8%	41	18	41	25%	77%	9%	18	74	50%	17%	0	0.73	4.0	37	48	$4
14 TEX	2	3	1	25	22	6.84	5.36	1.92	795	732	848	4.5	5.4	7.9	1.5	58%	10%	35	19	46	40%	62%	3%	0	18			50	0.80	-9.6	10	12	-$7
1st Half	2	3	1	25	22	6.84	5.36	1.92	795	732	848	4.5	5.4	7.9	1.5	58%	10%	35	19	46	40%	62%	3%	0	18			50	0.80	-9.6	10	12	-$7
2nd Half																																	
15 Proj	**3**	**2**	**0**	**45**	**39**	**3.70**	**3.68**	**1.29**	**684**	**679**	**687**	**5.9**	**3.0**	**7.9**	**2.6**	**58%**	**10%**	**38**	**20**	**42**	**31%**	**73%**	**8%**	**0**						**0.2**	**77**	**92**	**-$1**

Ondrusek,Logan

Age:	30	Th:	R	Role	RP	Health	C	LIMA Plan	C
Ht:	6' 8"	Wt:	230	Type	Pwr	PT/Exp	D	Rand Var	+5
						Consist	C	MM	3300

When you're a low-leverage middleman that can't return positive value, your fanalytic value is nil. But there are seeds of hope here, if you squint. Increasing Ks supported by good SwK, elite Dom vs. LH last two years. Tiny-sample 2nd half skills worth tucking away. Stashable arm, but only in very deep leagues.

Yr Tm	W	L	Sv	IP	K	ERA	xERA	WHIP	oOPS	vL	vR	BF/G	Ctl	Dom	Cmd	FpK	SwK	G	L	F	H%	S%	hr/f	GS	APC	DOM%	DIS%	Sv%	LI	RAR	BPV	BPX	R$
10 CIN *	5	1	1	78	51	4.02	3.56	1.24	669	561	725	4.3	2.7	5.8	2.2	57%	11%	48	14	38	28%	69%	10%	0	15			25	1.06	0.6	62	100	$2
11 CIN	5	5	0	61	41	3.23	4.45	1.35	676	635	698	4.1	4.1	6.0	1.5	57%	9%	49	17	34	27%	79%	9%	0	15			0	1.26	5.4	24	37	$1
12 CIN	5	2	2	55	39	3.46	5.22	1.50	752	643	828	3.9	5.1	6.4	1.3	57%	10%	43	15	42	27%	82%	12%	0	15			50	1.46	3.8	-1	-2	-$1
13 CIN	3	1	0	55	53	4.09	3.55	1.25	730	854	633	4.5	2.6	8.7	3.3	59%	12%	46	19	36	31%	72%	14%	0	17			0	0.72	-1.5	109	143	-$1
14 CIN	3	3	0	41	42	5.49	4.00	1.61	802	817	791	4.7	3.5	9.2	2.6	57%	12%	45	17	38	38%	67%	10%	0	17			0	0.83	-8.8	94	112	-$6
1st Half	2	2	0	28	25	3.86	4.27	1.57	738	668	777	4.9	3.9	8.0	2.1	52%	12%	44	19	36	36%	74%	3%	0	18			0	1.02	-0.4	63	75	-$5
2nd Half	1	1	0	13	17	9.00	3.47	1.69	932	1107	820	4.4	2.8	11.8	4.3	66%	12%	45	13	43	42%	50%	24%	0	16			0	0.47	-8.4	160	191	-$8
15 Proj	**3**	**2**	**0**	**44**	**39**	**3.73**	**3.58**	**1.31**	**686**	**654**	**706**	**4.1**	**3.4**	**8.1**	**2.4**	**56%**	**11%**	**45**	**17**	**37**	**30%**	**74%**	**9%**	**0**						**0.1**	**76**	**91**	**-$1**

Otero,Dan

Age:	30	Th:	R	Role	RP	Health	A	LIMA Plan	B
Ht:	6' 3"	Wt:	215	Type	Con xGB	PT/Exp	D	Rand Var	-4
						Consist	F	MM	4000

Strike-throwing GB specialist now one of most trusted in his bullpen. Pinpoint Ctl and GBs are calling cards, and with near-elite FpK and steady GB tilt, it's one he can continue to ride. Only managed 10%+ SwK% with one pitch—90-mph FB—so limited arsenal will prevent role expansion. But did I mention all those GBs?

Yr Tm	W	L	Sv	IP	K	ERA	xERA	WHIP	oOPS	vL	vR	BF/G	Ctl	Dom	Cmd	FpK	SwK	G	L	F	H%	S%	hr/f	GS	APC	DOM%	DIS%	Sv%	LI	RAR	BPV	BPX	R$
10																																	
11 a/a	4	4	13	74	61	2.52	3.63	1.24				5.4	1.3	7.4	5.8						35%	81%								12.9	151	227	$10
12 SF *	5	5	0	74	43	3.35	4.47	1.41	894	950	864	5.2	1.2	5.2	4.6	63%	8%	67	22	11	36%	76%	0%	0	16			0	0.29	6.1	109	142	-$1
13 OAK *	3	0	15	66	44	1.27	1.97	0.99	613	613	613	4.5	1.0	5.9	6.2	63%	6%	56	20	24	29%	86%	0%	0	18			94	0.75	21.3	173	226	$15
14 OAK	8	2	1	87	45	2.28	3.50	1.10	607	698	539	4.8	1.6	4.7	3.0	69%	7%	56	24	20	28%	80%	7%	0	17			25	1.26	15.6	76	91	$9
1st Half	6	1	1	51	25	2.10	3.40	0.99	565	643	503	5.2	1.2	4.4	3.6	71%	5%	58	23	20	26%	80%	6%	0	17			25	1.40	10.4	81	97	$13
2nd Half	2	1	0	35	20	2.55	3.66	1.25	669	780	588	4.4	2.0	5.1	2.5	66%	8%	54	25	20	30%	81%	9%	0	16			0	1.10	5.2	69	82	$2
15 Proj	**4**	**2**	**0**	**65**	**39**	**2.94**	**3.20**	**1.15**	**620**	**670**	**577**	**4.7**	**1.4**	**5.4**	**3.8**	**66%**	**7%**	**56**	**23**	**22**	**30%**	**74%**	**5%**	**0**						**6.4**	**93**	**111**	**$3**

Ottavino,Adam

Age:	29	Th:	R	Role	RP	Health	A	LIMA Plan	C+
Ht:	6' 5"	Wt:	230	Type	Pwr	PT/Exp	C	Rand Var	+2
						Consist	B	MM	4410

PRO: Bad first half driven by a fluky H%; surging BPV now elite; posted 3.0+ Cmd vs. both LH and RH.
CON: Ctl gains not supported by FpK; increasing shift from LD to FB raises HR risk if 2nd half GB doesn't stick.
If control vs. LH holds, he's legit closer material. UP: 30 SV

Yr Tm	W	L	Sv	IP	K	ERA	xERA	WHIP	oOPS	vL	vR	BF/G	Ctl	Dom	Cmd	FpK	SwK	G	L	F	H%	S%	hr/f	GS	APC	DOM%	DIS%	Sv%	LI	RAR	BPV	BPX	R$
10 STL *	5	5	0	70	47	5.50	5.27	1.49	1072	1213	973	21.6	2.7	6.0	2.3	57%	6%	36	32	32	33%	65%	18%	3	84	0%	33%	0	0.53	-12.3	42	69	-$4
11 aaa	7	8	0	141	94	5.18	5.52	1.73				24.7	4.6	6.0	1.3						35%	70%								-21.5	35	52	-$13
12 COL *	5	1	0	99	99	4.43	4.60	1.46	717	745	698	6.4	3.8	9.1	2.4	59%	12%	48	26	26	34%	72%	16%	0	25			0	0.64	-5.0	74	97	-$4
13 COL	1	3	0	78	78	2.64	3.62	1.33	672	853	544	6.6	3.6	9.0	2.5	61%	12%	46	22	33	32%	82%	7%	0	25			0	1.01	11.8	89	116	$2
14 COL	1	4	1	65	70	3.60	3.09	1.28	735	943	645	3.6	2.2	9.7	4.4	61%	12%	47	19	34	35%	74%	10%	0	14			17	1.31	1.1	140	166	$0
1st Half	0	3	0	37	38	4.66	3.25	1.34	804	1103	685	3.8	1.5	9.3	6.3	62%	12%	44	18	39	37%	67%	10%	0	15			0	1.30	-4.2	150	179	-$4
2nd Half	1	1	1	28	32	2.22	2.88	1.20	641	751	587	3.4	3.2	10.2	3.2	60%	10%	51	22	26	31%	84%	11%	0	14			25	1.33	5.3	127	151	$5
15 Proj	**2**	**3**	**8**	**68**	**68**	**3.33**	**3.11**	**1.27**	**684**	**832**	**601**	**4.7**	**3.1**	**9.1**	**3.0**	**61%**	**12%**	**47**	**22**	**31**	**32%**	**76%**	**10%**	**0**						**3.4**	**107**	**127**	**$4**

Owens,Henry

Age:	22	Th:	L	Role	SP	Health	A	LIMA Plan	B
Ht:	6' 6"	Wt:	205	Type	Pwr FB	PT/Exp	F	Rand Var	0
						Consist	B	MM	2300

Has mowed down batters at every stop in Boston system. Missing piece was control, but he paired high Ks and low BBs in AAA debut (44/12 K/BB in 38 IP). Ability to handcuff both LH/RH bats will ease transition to MLB. Young starting pitchers without MLB experience are risky, but he's worth taking if you can stash on bench.

Yr Tm	W	L	Sv	IP	K	ERA	xERA	WHIP	oOPS	vL	vR	BF/G	Ctl	Dom	Cmd	FpK	SwK	G	L	F	H%	S%	hr/f	GS	APC	DOM%	DIS%	Sv%	LI	RAR	BPV	BPX	R$
10																																	
11																																	
12																																	
13 aa	3	1	0	30	40	2.08	2.58	1.14				20.0	4.3	11.8	2.8						27%	87%								6.7	118	154	$1
14 a/a	17	5	0	159	145	3.67	3.25	1.25				24.9	3.3	8.2	2.5						30%	71%								1.5	90	108	$9
1st Half	10	3	0	92	81	2.81	2.54	1.15				24.3	3.6	7.9	2.2						26%	77%								10.5	91	109	$18
2nd Half	7	2	0	67	64	4.85	4.24	1.40				25.7	2.9	8.6	2.9						35%	65%								-9.2	91	109	-$3
15 Proj	**7**	**2**	**0**	**65**	**57**	**3.92**	**3.75**	**1.27**				**23.1**	**3.6**	**7.9**	**2.2**	**60%**	**9%**	**40**	**18**	**42**	**29%**	**70%**	**7%**	**12**						**-1.5**	**64**	**76**	**$1**

Papelbon,Jonathan

Age:	34	Th:	R	Role	RP	Health	A	LIMA Plan	C
Ht:	6' 4"	Wt:	215	Type	Pwr FB	PT/Exp	A	Rand Var	-5
						Consist	B	MM	5430

Another dominant year, at least on surface. While late surge saved skills, it masked growing warts. BPV continued muli-year decline, Dom no longer elite. SwK says it can rebound, but FB velocity (from 95 to 91 mph from 2011-14) leaves little margin for error. Risk-averse should stop when bidding hits $20.

Yr Tm	W	L	Sv	IP	K	ERA	xERA	WHIP	oOPS	vL	vR	BF/G	Ctl	Dom	Cmd	FpK	SwK	G	L	F	H%	S%	hr/f	GS	APC	DOM%	DIS%	Sv%	LI	RAR	BPV	BPX	R$
10 BOS	5	7	37	67	76	3.90	3.63	1.27	674	717	619	4.4	3.8	10.2	2.7	63%	13%	38	18	44	31%	72%	9%	0	18			82	1.37	1.5	98	159	$18
11 BOS	4	1	31	64	87	2.94	2.47	0.93	546	428	663	4.0	1.4	12.2	8.7	68%	18%	38	21	41	33%	68%	5%	0	16			91	1.27	8.0	197	297	$20
12 PHI	5	6	38	70	92	2.44	2.84	1.06	621	627	616	4.1	2.3	11.8	5.1	62%	13%	41	18	40	31%	83%	12%	0	16			90	1.24	13.6	169	221	$24
13 PHI	5	1	29	62	57	2.92	3.58	1.14	631	644	618	4.2	1.6	8.3	5.2	64%	11%	40	17	43	31%	78%	8%	0	16			81	1.18	7.2	124	162	$15
14 PHI	2	3	39	66	63	2.04	3.25	0.90	500	462	539	3.9	2.0	8.5	4.2	64%	13%	42	16	42	26%	78%	3%	0	15			91	1.42	14.0	119	142	$23
1st Half	2	1	18	32	28	1.39	3.72	0.93	464	452	474	3.8	2.5	7.8	3.1	70%	13%	35	16	49	25%	83%	0%	0	16			90	1.29	9.4	86	102	$22
2nd Half	0	2	21	34	35	2.65	2.81	0.88	533	470	603	4.0	1.6	9.3	5.8	58%	12%	49	15	36	27%	71%	6%	0	15			91	1.54	4.6	151	180	$23
15 Proj	**3**	**3**	**35**	**63**	**65**	**2.94**	**2.87**	**1.00**	**567**	**546**	**588**	**3.9**	**2.0**	**9.3**	**4.7**	**63%**	**13%**	**42**	**17**	**42**	**29%**	**72%**	**6%**	**0**						**6.2**	**134**	**159**	**$19**

Parker,Jarrod

Age:	26	Th:	R	Role	SP	Health	F	LIMA Plan	B
Ht:	6' 1"	Wt:	195	Type		PT/Exp	C	Rand Var	0
						Consist	B	MM	2101

Spring TJ surgery—his second—wiped out entire season. Former 1st-rd pick has yet to live up to hype. Sub-4 ERAs have never been validated by skills. On plus side, owns elite changeup (24% SwK% on it last two yrs), and he's still young enough to develop rest of arsenal. But list of successful SPs with 2nd TJS is very short.

Yr Tm	W	L	Sv	IP	K	ERA	xERA	WHIP	oOPS	vL	vR	BF/G	Ctl	Dom	Cmd	FpK	SwK	G	L	F	H%	S%	hr/f	GS	APC	DOM%	DIS%	Sv%	LI	RAR	BPV	BPX	R$
10																																	
11 ARI *	11	8	0	136	95	4.10	3.50	1.33	513	286	641	21.0	3.5	6.3	1.8	55%	7%	35	6	59	30%	69%	0%	1	73	0%	0%			-2.6	65	98	$3
12 OAK *	14	8	0	202	157	3.35	3.43	1.28	670	685	654	25.1	3.1	7.0	2.3	55%	10%	44	26	30	30%	75%	7%	29	98	62%	10%			16.6	78	102	$13
13 OAK	12	8	0	197	134	3.97	4.28	1.22	695	725	654	25.6	2.9	6.1	2.1	60%	10%	41	19	40	27%	71%	10%	32	94	56%	16%			-2.6	51	67	$7
14																																	
1st Half																																	
2nd Half																																	
15 Proj	**7**	**5**	**0**	**101**	**71**	**3.95**	**3.92**	**1.30**	**702**	**727**	**671**	**23.3**	**3.2**	**6.4**	**2.0**	**58%**	**10%**	**42**	**22**	**36**	**29%**	**71%**	**8%**	**18**						**-2.6**	**50**	**59**	**$2**

STEPHEN NICKRAND

Parnell,Bobby

Age: 30	Th: R	Role: RP	Health: F
PT/Exp: C	Rand Var: +5	LIMA Plan: C+	
Ht: 6' 3"	Wt: 205	Type: Pwr GB	Consist: F
MM: 5320			

Entered year with firm hold on closer job due to elite skills driven by surging Cmd. But that ended after going under knife for TJ surgery in April. Rising FpK means once-shaky Ctl now is a strength. Combo of Cmd plsu GBs gives him very closer-worthy profile. Just temper expectations until the 2nd half.

Yr Tm	W	L	Sv	IP	K	ERA	xERA	WHIP	oOPS	vL	vR	BF/G	Ctl	Dom	Cmd	FpK	SwK	G	L	F	H%	S%	hr/f	GS	APC	DOM%	DIS%	Sv%	LI	RAR	BPV	BPX	R$
10 NYM *	1	2	4	76	67	3.78	3.99	1.41	686	806	614	5.0	3.0	7.9	2.6	58%	11%	56	26	18	34%	73%	5%	0	14			50	0.69	2.8	89	144	$1
11 NYM	4	6	6	59	64	3.64	3.57	1.47	679	685	672	4.5	4.1	9.7	2.4	57%	11%	51	17	32	35%	76%	8%	0	18			50	1.10	2.2	93	140	$2
12 NYM	5	4	7	69	61	2.49	3.23	1.24	648	626	666	3.9	2.6	8.0	3.1	59%	10%	62	17	22	32%	81%	9%	0	15			58	1.13	12.9	113	148	$8
13 NYM	5	5	22	50	44	2.16	3.09	1.00	555	606	519	4.0	2.2	7.9	3.7	65%	10%	52	22	26	28%	78%	3%	0	16			85	1.66	10.5	114	149	$14
14 NYM	0	0	0	1	1	9.00	7.71	3.00	1100	1667	667	6.0	9.0	9.0	1.0	100%	4%	25	25	50	52%	67%	0%	0	25			0	1.74	-0.6	-78	-93	-$4
1st Half	0	0	0	1	1	9.00	7.71	3.00	1100	1667	667	6.0	9.0	9.0	1.0	100%	4%	25	25	50	52%	67%	0%	0	25			0	1.74	-0.6	-78	-93	-$4
2nd Half																																	
15 Proj	**2**	**2**	**16**	**41**	**39**	**2.99**	**3.06**	**1.27**	**637**	**668**	**615**	**4.1**	**3.0**	**8.6**	**2.8**	**60%**	**10%**	**54**	**20**	**26**	**32%**	**77%**	**7%**	**0**						**3.8**	**104**	**123**	**$6**

Parra,Manny

Age: 32	Th: L	Role: RP	Health: F
PT/Exp: D	Rand Var: +4	LIMA Plan: D+	
Ht: 6' 3"	Wt: 215	Type: Pwr	Consist: C
MM: 2300			

Proof that an established arm with long history of bad control is who he is. Dandy 2013 Ctl came and went, and even with improved FpK, we can't bank on a sub-3 Ctl again. hr/f regression would help, but it seems untimely HRs are engrained in his DNA. Worsening health cements it: Pass.

Yr Tm	W	L	Sv	IP	K	ERA	xERA	WHIP	oOPS	vL	vR	BF/G	Ctl	Dom	Cmd	FpK	SwK	G	L	F	H%	S%	hr/f	GS	APC	DOM%	DIS%	Sv%	LI	RAR	BPV	BPX	R$
10 MIL	3	10	0	122	129	5.02	3.96	1.62	816	983	752	13.3	4.6	9.5	2.0	58%	12%	47	18	34	35%	72%	15%	16	51	19%	19%	0	0.60	-14.1	71	115	-$7
11																																	
12 MIL	2	3	0	59	61	5.06	4.22	1.65	738	635	827	4.4	5.4	9.4	1.7	53%	10%	49	24	27	36%	68%	7%	0	17			0	0.79	-7.6	50	66	-$8
13 CIN	2	3	0	46	56	3.33	2.93	1.20	684	475	893	3.3	2.9	11.0	3.7	69%	15%	44	22	34	32%	76%	13%	0	13			0	1.06	3.1	140	182	$0
14 CIN	0	3	1	37	34	4.66	3.84	1.55	781	676	923	3.1	4.4	8.3	1.9	64%	14%	51	22	26	34%	72%	15%	0	12			50	1.50	-4.2	60	71	-$5
1st Half	0	0	1	22	24	4.43	3.65	1.52	781	739	838	3.0	4.4	9.7	2.2	66%	16%	46	25	29	34%	74%	18%	0	11			50	1.37	-1.9	78	93	-$5
2nd Half	0	3	0	14	10	5.02	4.17	1.60	781	572	1048	3.3	4.4	6.3	1.4	61%	10%	59	18	23	33%	68%	10%	0	13			0	1.71	-2.3	31	38	-$5
15 Proj	**1**	**3**	**0**	**58**	**56**	**4.52**	**3.70**	**1.43**	**705**	**628**	**776**	**3.8**	**4.6**	**8.7**	**1.9**	**61%**	**13%**	**46**	**23**	**31**	**31%**	**70%**	**12%**	**0**						**-5.6**	**55**	**65**	**-$4**

Paxton,James

Age: 26	Th: L	Role: SP	Health: F
PT/Exp: D	Rand Var: -1	LIMA Plan: B+	
Ht: 6' 4"	Wt: 220	Type: Pwr xGB	Consist: A
MM: 3203			

Promising young hurler sidelined for much of season due to shoulder inflammation. No command upon return in September, but chalk that up to rust. He's got the goods to emerge: three swing-and-miss pitches, mid-90s heat, GB lean. Next step is piecing together healthy season. It's a big step.

Yr Tm	W	L	Sv	IP	K	ERA	xERA	WHIP	oOPS	vL	vR	BF/G	Ctl	Dom	Cmd	FpK	SwK	G	L	F	H%	S%	hr/f	GS	APC	DOM%	DIS%	Sv%	LI	RAR	BPV	BPX	R$
10																																	
11 aa	3	0	0	39	45	2.04	2.47	1.12				22.0	3.0	10.5	3.5						31%	83%								9.1	134	202	$3
12 aa	9	4	0	106	96	3.68	4.34	1.58				22.3	4.8	8.1	1.7						34%	76%								4.4	72	95	-$2
13 SEA *	11	11	0	170	131	4.25	4.35	1.48	533	790	475	22.8	3.2	6.9	2.1	54%	10%	59	17	24	34%	71%	13%	4	96	75%	0%			-8.1	67	88	-$3
14 SEA	6	4	0	74	59	3.04	3.50	1.20	612	527	629	23.3	3.5	7.2	2.0	54%	8%	55	23	23	28%	74%	6%	13	91	38%	23%			6.4	67	80	$4
1st Half	2	0	0	12	13	2.25	2.23	0.67	528	333	637	21.5	1.5	9.8	6.5	64%	14%	56	19	26	16%	83%	29%	2	80	50%	0%			2.2	169	201	-$2
2nd Half	4	4	0	62	46	3.19	3.78	1.31	626	613	627	23.6	3.9	6.7	1.7	53%	7%	55	23	22	29%	74%	3%	11	93	36%	27%			4.2	47	56	$5
15 Proj	**11**	**7**	**0**	**156**	**135**	**3.57**	**3.49**	**1.41**	**649**	**610**	**655**	**22.6**	**4.0**	**7.8**	**2.0**	**53%**	**7%**	**55**	**23**	**22**	**32%**	**74%**	**7%**	**26**						**3.4**	**66**	**79**	**$5**

Peacock,Brad

Age: 27	Th: R	Role: SP	Health: A
PT/Exp: C	Rand Var: 0	LIMA Plan: D+	
Ht: 6' 1"	Wt: 210	Type: Pwr FB	Consist: B
MM: 1303			

Owner of one of the most risky profiles you can find: lots of walks and a flyball tilt. It's a combination that means tons of blowup risk. With low FpK and long-absent GBs, we can't bet on improvement, so what he does offer in strikeouts just isn't worth his downside. Speculate elsewhere.

Yr Tm	W	L	Sv	IP	K	ERA	xERA	WHIP	oOPS	vL	vR	BF/G	Ctl	Dom	Cmd	FpK	SwK	G	L	F	H%	S%	hr/f	GS	APC	DOM%	DIS%	Sv%	LI	RAR	BPV	BPX	R$
10 aa	2	2	0	39	25	5.85	4.99	1.56				24.2	5.1	5.9	1.2						28%	64%								-8.4	24	38	-$5
11 WAS *	17	3	0	159	149	2.68	2.35	1.07	438	355	568	22.0	2.9	8.5	2.9	60%	5%	32	8	61	27%	77%	0%	2	67	0%	0%	0	1.30	24.7	109	164	$22
12 aaa	12	9	0	135	115	6.17	5.28	1.65				21.5	4.3	7.7	1.8						35%	62%								-35.7	54	70	-$16
13 HOU *	11	8	0	162	141	4.21	4.23	1.31	779	919	594	21.0	3.3	7.8	2.4	56%	8%	37	19	45	29%	73%	14%	14	83	43%	36%	0	0.79	-7.0	60	78	$3
14 HOU	4	9	0	132	119	4.72	4.59	1.56	801	793	811	21.0	4.8	8.1	1.7	57%	9%	37	21	42	31%	74%	12%	24	85	29%	29%	0	0.81	-15.8	32	38	-$9
1st Half	2	4	0	73	63	4.21	4.49	1.51	740	669	820	21.1	5.0	7.8	1.6	57%	9%	41	21	38	30%	75%	10%	11	82	36%	18%	0	0.82	-4.2	26	31	-$7
2nd Half	2	5	0	59	56	5.34	4.71	1.63	872	906	794	20.9	4.6	8.5	1.9	57%	9%	32	22	46	33%	73%	14%	13	88	23%	38%			-11.6	40	48	-$11
15 Proj	**6**	**9**	**0**	**131**	**115**	**4.84**	**4.18**	**1.50**	**791**	**849**	**704**	**21.0**	**4.2**	**7.9**	**1.9**	**56%**	**8%**	**36**	**20**	**44**	**31%**	**71%**	**11%**	**27**						**-17.8**	**43**	**51**	**-$6**

Peavy,Jake

Age: 34	Th: R	Role: SP	Health: D
PT/Exp: A	Rand Var: 0	LIMA Plan: B+	
Ht: 6' 1"	Wt: 195	Type: FB	Consist: A
MM: 2203			

Yo-yo ERA symbolizes how much he has bounced around over last two years. Still tempting to bid on a repeat of 2012, but it ain't coming back. Three years of eroding skills—as shown in xERA and BPV trends—confirm consistent sub-4.00 ERA days are behind him. Limited profit above $5 now.

Yr Tm	W	L	Sv	IP	K	ERA	xERA	WHIP	oOPS	vL	vR	BF/G	Ctl	Dom	Cmd	FpK	SwK	G	L	F	H%	S%	hr/f	GS	APC	DOM%	DIS%	Sv%	LI	RAR	BPV	BPX	R$
10 CHW	7	6	0	107	93	4.63	3.87	1.23	696	729	663	26.4	2.9	7.8	2.7	62%	9%	41	18	42	29%	65%	10%	17	101	59%	18%			-7.2	83	134	$3
11 CHW *	8	8	0	141	118	5.12	4.32	1.31	701	669	740	23.2	1.7	7.5	4.4	63%	10%	39	23	39	34%	62%	8%	18	98	67%	17%	0	0.81	-20.4	108	163	-$2
12 CHW	11	12	0	219	194	3.37	3.82	1.10	671	714	614	27.6	2.0	8.0	4.0	63%	10%	37	19	44	28%	74%	10%	32	109	75%	0%			17.4	104	136	$22
13 2AL	12	5	0	145	121	4.17	4.00	1.15	697	731	659	25.7	2.2	7.5	3.4	66%	9%	33	21	47	28%	68%	10%	23	103	74%	13%			-5.4	86	112	$7
14 2TM	7	13	0	203	158	3.73	4.12	1.28	742	766	719	26.6	2.8	7.0	2.5	64%	10%	38	20	42	29%	74%	9%	32	101	56%	9%			0.3	67	80	$4
1st Half	1	7	0	105	81	4.82	4.42	1.44	813	825	800	26.7	3.4	7.0	2.0	63%	9%	39	19	42	31%	71%	13%	17	103	53%	12%			-13.9	50	59	-$10
2nd Half	6	6	0	98	77	2.57	3.80	1.10	661	685	641	26.5	2.1	7.1	3.3	66%	11%	38	20	42	28%	78%	5%	15	98	60%	7%			14.1	86	102	$19
15 Proj	**10**	**9**	**0**	**174**	**139**	**3.87**	**3.76**	**1.24**	**727**	**754**	**699**	**25.9**	**2.6**	**7.2**	**2.8**	**65%**	**10%**	**36**	**20**	**44**	**29%**	**72%**	**9%**	**27**						**-2.8**	**74**	**88**	**$7**

Pelfrey,Mike

Age: 31	Th: R	Role: SP	Health: F
PT/Exp: C	Rand Var: +5	LIMA Plan: D	
Ht: 6' 7"	Wt: 250	Type:	Consist: D
MM: 0000			

Former ninth overall pick in 2005 draft has returned positive value in only TWO of nine seasons. Other fun facts: 1) Has posted a 2.0+ Cmd just once in his career; 2) Zero years with a Dom over 6.0; 3) Has averaged just 120 IP per season. Thank goodness for #3.

Yr Tm	W	L	Sv	IP	K	ERA	xERA	WHIP	oOPS	vL	vR	BF/G	Ctl	Dom	Cmd	FpK	SwK	G	L	F	H%	S%	hr/f	GS	APC	DOM%	DIS%	Sv%	LI	RAR	BPV	BPX	R$
10 NYM	15	9	1	204	113	3.66	4.34	1.38	735	776	690	25.6	3.0	5.0	1.7	62%	6%	48	20	32	30%	74%	6%	33	100	45%	24%	100	0.82	10.5	35	56	$8
11 NYM	7	13	0	194	105	4.74	4.63	1.47	777	776	778	25.3	3.0	4.9	1.6	64%	6%	46	20	35	31%	69%	9%	33	95	30%	24%	0	0.75	-19.1	30	46	-$8
12 NYM	0	0	0	20	13	2.29	3.77	1.42	683	672	697	28.3	1.8	5.9	3.3	64%	9%	53	27	20	36%	82%	0%	3	102	33%	0%			4.2	89	116	-$3
13 MIN	5	13	0	153	101	5.19	4.59	1.55	789	762	821	23.4	3.1	6.0	1.9	55%	6%	43	21	36	34%	67%	7%	29	94	21%	34%			-24.9	44	57	-$13
14 MIN	0	3	0	24	10	7.99	6.83	1.99	924	648	1315	23.8	6.8	3.8	0.6	50%	5%	44	18	38	30%	62%	15%	5	91	0%	100%			-12.4	-94	-112	-$9
1st Half	0	3	0	24	10	7.99	6.83	1.99	924	648	1315	23.8	6.8	3.8	0.6	50%	5%	44	18	38	30%	62%	15%	5	91	0%	100%			-12.4	-95	-113	-$9
2nd Half																																	
15 Proj	**1**	**4**	**0**	**44**	**23**	**5.64**	**4.85**	**1.63**	**820**	**730**	**922**	**23.7**	**4.2**	**4.8**	**1.1**	**57%**	**6%**	**45**	**20**	**36**	**31%**	**67%**	**10%**	**8**						**-10.2**	**-4**	**-5**	**-$8**

Peralta,Joel

Age: 39	Th: R	Role: RP	Health: C
PT/Exp: C	Rand Var: +2	LIMA Plan: A	
Ht: 5' 11"	Wt: 210	Type: Pwr xFB	Consist: B
MM: 4510			

Tough to dismiss a +1 ERA jump as fluky, but that was the case here. Doomed by early hr/f, late H%/S% anomalies. Even as he nears 40, history of elite Cmd makes return to 2012-2013 likely. In spite of no longer being in saves mix, he's still a premium LIMA arm to stash in your bullpen.

Yr Tm	W	L	Sv	IP	K	ERA	xERA	WHIP	oOPS	vL	vR	BF/G	Ctl	Dom	Cmd	FpK	SwK	G	L	F	H%	S%	hr/f	GS	APC	DOM%	DIS%	Sv%	LI	RAR	BPV	BPX	R$
10 WAS *	3	0	20	82	76	1.83	2.25	0.97	521	596	474	4.7	1.9	8.3	4.5	61%	12%	26	18	56	27%	86%	7%	0	19			91	0.85	22.8	136	219	$19
11 TAM	3	4	6	68	61	2.93	3.73	0.92	586	435	718	3.6	2.4	8.1	3.4	55%	11%	27	16	57	22%	73%	7%	0	15			75	1.20	8.5	86	130	$9
12 TAM	2	6	2	67	84	3.63	3.23	0.99	629	556	708	3.4	2.3	11.3	4.9	60%	13%	30	18	52	28%	68%	11%	0	14			40	1.15	3.2	149	195	$6
13 TAM	3	8	1	71	74	3.41	4.16	1.14	586	556	627	3.6	4.3	9.3	2.2	59%	11%	27	19	54	24%	73%	7%	0	15			25	1.38	4.0	57	75	$3
14 TAM	3	4	1	63	74	4.41	3.35	1.18	708	670	763	3.8	2.1	10.5	4.9	64%	12%	33	20	47	33%	67%	11%	0	16			14	1.08	-5.2	143	170	$0
1st Half	2	3	1	35	39	4.11	3.48	1.20	720	719	721	3.9	2.8	10.0	3.5	63%	12%	37	19	44	29%	74%	17%	0	17			20	1.14	-1.6	119	142	$1
2nd Half	1	1	0	28	35	4.76	3.19	1.16	693	611	815	3.8	1.3	11.1	8.8	65%	13%	29	21	51	38%	58%	5%	0	15			0	1.02	-3.6	172	206	-$1
15 Proj	**3**	**4**	**2**	**58**	**66**	**3.42**	**3.14**	**1.12**	**653**	**609**	**711**	**3.6**	**2.6**	**10.2**	**4.0**	**62%**	**12%**	**30**	**19**	**51**	**30%**	**73%**	**9%**	**0**						**2.3**	**122**	**145**	**$4**

STEPHEN NICKRAND

Peralta,Wily

Age: 26	Th: R	Role SP	Health A	LIMA Plan B	
Ht: 6' 1"	Wt: 245	Type Pwr GB	PT/Exp A	Rand Var 0	
			Consist B	MM 3205	

Young power arm took a nice step forward. The timing for full breakout is murky, since all-in look is mixed bag. PRO: Mid-90s heat; induces GBs; Cmd jump. CON: So-so FpK and SwK don't hint at further command gains; LH hitting him harder. There's a 3.00 ERA in his arm, but he's got more work to do.

Yr Tm	W	L	Sv	IP	K	ERA	xERA	WHIP	oOPS	vL	vR	BF/G	Ctl	Dom	Cmd	FpK	SwK	G	L	F	H%	S%	hr/f	GS	APC	DOM%	DIS%	Sv%	LI	RAR	BPV	BPX	R$
10 aa	2	3	0	42	26	3.88	5.24	1.64				23.6	4.9	5.6	1.1						31%	80%								1.0	24	39	-$3
11 a/a	11	7	0	151	140	3.31	3.23	1.27				23.7	3.3	8.3	2.5						31%	75%								11.8	93	140	$10
12 MIL *	9	12	0	176	146	5.34	5.17	1.71	601	639	564	23.4	4.8	7.5	1.6	61%	9%	55	21	24	36%	68%	0%	5	76	60%	20%	0	0.66	-28.7	56	72	-$18
13 MIL	11	15	0	183	129	4.37	4.17	1.42	722	753	692	25.1	3.6	6.3	1.8	58%	9%	51	21	28	30%	71%	12%	32	93	41%	22%			-11.4	46	60	-$2
14 MIL	17	11	0	199	154	3.53	3.62	1.30	714	820	606	26.2	2.8	7.0	2.5	58%	9%	54	19	28	30%	77%	14%	32	100	59%	13%			5.1	83	99	$9
1st Half	9	5	0	101	76	3.20	3.51	1.25	697	806	588	26.4	2.2	6.8	3.0	59%	9%	53	20	27	30%	79%	14%	16	100	69%	0%			6.8	93	111	$12
2nd Half	8	6	0	97	78	3.88	3.72	1.36	732	834	625	25.9	3.3	7.2	2.2	58%	9%	54	18	29	30%	74%	13%	16	100	50%	25%			-1.7	72	86	$5
15 Proj	**13**	**12**	**0**	**189**	**149**	**3.67**	**3.51**	**1.32**	**685**	**756**	**615**	**24.1**	**3.2**	**7.1**	**2.2**	**58%**	**9%**	**53**	**20**	**28**	**30%**	**74%**	**11%**	**32**						**1.7**	**71**	**85**	**$8**

Perez,Chris

Age: 30	Th: R	Role RP	Health D	LIMA Plan D+	
Ht: 6' 4"	Wt: 230	Type Pwr FB	PT/Exp B	Rand Var -1	
			Consist A	MM 1300	

Embattled closer now far removed from 9th inning. Even favor from H% gods couldn't stop this disaster. Has never generated enough whiffs to be lockdown guy, and without sturdy Ctl, he's a late-inning liability. Abysmal FpK says it's not likely coming back. Speculate elsewhere.

Yr Tm	W	L	Sv	IP	K	ERA	xERA	WHIP	oOPS	vL	vR	BF/G	Ctl	Dom	Cmd	FpK	SwK	G	L	F	H%	S%	hr/f	GS	APC	DOM%	DIS%	Sv%	LI	RAR	BPV	BPX	R$
10 CLE	2	2	23	63	61	1.71	3.90	1.08	583	752	445	4.1	4.0	8.7	2.2	61%	8%	34	20	46	24%	88%	5%	0	17			85	1.53	18.4	61	98	$16
11 CLE	4	7	36	60	39	3.32	4.80	1.21	648	598	702	3.9	3.9	5.9	1.5	55%	6%	28	21	50	24%	75%	6%	0	15			90	1.68	4.6	6	9	$16
12 CLE	0	4	39	58	59	3.59	3.67	1.13	652	538	780	4.0	2.5	9.2	3.7	60%	10%	41	19	40	29%	71%	9%	0	16			91	1.23	3.0	117	153	$17
13 CLE	5	3	25	54	54	4.33	3.86	1.43	847	916	765	4.5	3.5	9.0	2.6	61%	8%	42	23	35	31%	77%	20%	0	17			83	1.24	-3.1	88	114	$8
14 LA	1	3	1	46	39	4.27	4.53	1.36	755	752	756	4.1	4.9	7.6	1.6	51%	9%	38	19	43	26%	72%	11%	0	17			50	0.67	-3.0	21	25	-$3
1st Half	0	3	1	28	26	5.20	4.39	1.45	859	939	816	3.9	4.6	8.5	1.9	53%	9%	32	22	45	29%	69%	14%	0	16			50	0.87	-5.0	40	47	-$5
2nd Half	1	0	0	19	13	2.89	4.73	1.23	589	573	609	4.3	5.3	6.3	1.2	49%	8%	45	15	40	22%	77%	5%	0	19			0	0.32	2.0	-7	-8	$1
15 Proj	**3**	**3**	**0**	**58**	**51**	**4.25**	**4.09**	**1.40**	**765**	**766**	**765**	**4.1**	**4.5**	**7.9**	**1.8**	**55%**	**9%**	**39**	**19**	**43**	**29%**	**73%**	**10%**	**0**						**-3.6**	**39**	**47**	**-$3**

Perez,Martin

Age: 24	Th: L	Role SP	Health F	LIMA Plan D+	
Ht: 6' 0"	Wt: 190	Type GB	PT/Exp C	Rand Var -1	
			Consist A	MM 2101	

Partially-torn UCL led to TJ surgery in May. Never has been able to sustain upside beyond tiny bursts. Needs a true whiff pitch; won't be able to push the needle on mediocre Dom without better SwK. Does own a 15% SwK% on both change and slider, so growth potential is there... for 2016.

Yr Tm	W	L	Sv	IP	K	ERA	xERA	WHIP	oOPS	vL	vR	BF/G	Ctl	Dom	Cmd	FpK	SwK	G	L	F	H%	S%	hr/f	GS	APC	DOM%	DIS%	Sv%	LI	RAR	BPV	BPX	R$
10 aa	5	8	0	100	90	7.35	6.52	1.82				19.3	4.5	8.1	1.8						38%	60%								-40.2	38	61	-$16
11 a/a	8	6	0	137	102	4.69	4.93	1.56				22.3	3.5	6.7	1.9						35%	70%								-12.6	55	83	-$6
12 TEX *	8	10	0	165	83	4.95	4.68	1.51	819	596	924	21.0	3.7	4.5	1.2	60%	7%	49	21	30	30%	68%	8%	6	55	0%	50%	0	0.75	-19.0	28	36	-$11
13 TEX *	15	8	0	168	109	3.77	4.27	1.35	728	759	718	25.0	2.5	5.9	2.3	61%	10%	48	21	31	31%	75%	12%	20	93	55%	25%			2.0	56	72	$5
14 TEX	4	3	0	51	35	4.38	3.73	1.34	743	707	753	25.9	3.3	6.1	1.8	60%	8%	53	23	25	30%	67%	8%	8	97	13%	38%			-4.1	52	61	-$2
1st Half	4	3	0	51	35	4.38	3.73	1.34	743	707	753	25.9	3.3	6.1	1.8	60%	8%	53	23	25	30%	67%	8%	8	97	13%	38%			-4.1	51	61	-$2
2nd Half																																	
15 Proj	**5**	**4**	**0**	**74**	**49**	**4.14**	**3.90**	**1.36**	**724**	**619**	**763**	**22.6**	**3.4**	**6.0**	**1.8**	**60%**	**8%**	**50**	**22**	**28**	**29%**	**71%**	**10%**	**14**						**-3.7**	**43**	**52**	**-$1**

Perez,Oliver

Age: 33	Th: L	Role RP	Health B	LIMA Plan A	
Ht: 6' 3"	Wt: 220	Type Pwr FB	PT/Exp D	Rand Var 0	
			Consist B	MM 4510	

Not the first repeatedly-failing rotation arm to find new life in the pen. Three years of improving xERA confirms it's no fluke, as does double-digit Dom against both LH and RH bats. Surging Cmd, otherworldly BPIs in 2nd half give hope for more. Closer-worthy skills, though age, left-handedness will likely block save opps.

Yr Tm	W	L	Sv	IP	K	ERA	xERA	WHIP	oOPS	vL	vR	BF/G	Ctl	Dom	Cmd	FpK	SwK	G	L	F	H%	S%	hr/f	GS	APC	DOM%	DIS%	Sv%	LI	RAR	BPV	BPX	R$
10 NYM	0	5	0	46	37	6.80	6.44	2.07	935	863	956	13.8	8.2	7.2	0.9	54%	7%	35	19	46	32%	70%	13%	7	56	14%	43%	0	0.96	-15.5	-78	-126	-$11
11 aa	3	5	0	76	41	4.27	6.66	1.76				21.7	3.5	4.9	1.4						34%	81%								-3.1	3	5	-$7
12 SEA *	3	5	1	61	56	3.55	4.59	1.57	628	679	575	4.8	4.4	8.4	1.9	63%	11%	33	23	44	35%	78%	3%	0	14			25	1.24	3.5	70	91	-$3
13 SEA	3	3	2	53	74	3.74	3.47	1.43	731	645	786	3.8	4.4	12.6	2.8	61%	13%	31	20	49	37%	77%	10%	0	16			67	1.50	0.8	116	151	-$1
14 ARI	3	4	0	59	76	2.91	3.03	1.26	679	780	602	3.8	3.7	11.7	3.2	62%	13%	44	22	34	33%	80%	10%	0	15			0	1.09	6.0	132	158	$2
1st Half	0	1	0	32	32	2.27	3.61	1.20	621	669	581	3.9	3.7	9.1	2.5	60%	11%	42	21	36	30%	81%	3%	0	15			0	1.04	5.7	84	101	$1
2nd Half	3	3	0	27	44	3.67	2.38	1.33	744	918	624	3.7	3.7	14.7	4.0	64%	16%	47	22	31	40%	78%	22%	0	15			0	1.15	0.2	190	227	$3
15 Proj	**3**	**4**	**2**	**58**	**72**	**2.96**	**3.07**	**1.22**	**624**	**631**	**620**	**3.9**	**4.2**	**11.2**	**2.7**	**61%**	**12%**	**39**	**21**	**41**	**30%**	**79%**	**10%**	**0**						**5.6**	**105**	**125**	**$4**

Perkins,Glen

Age: 32	Th: L	Role RP	Health B	LIMA Plan B	
Ht: 6' 0"	Wt: 205	Type Pwr	PT/Exp B	Rand Var +1	
			Consist B	MM 5430	

2nd-tier stopper? Maybe not. H% surge explains the 3.00+ ERA. Three seasons of elite skills and 80%+ Sv% confirm he's a premium closer; four straight years of improving Cmd suggest he'll maintain these levels. Needs to confirm he's okay after September forearm injury (non-surgical). If so, there's hidden profit here.

Yr Tm	W	L	Sv	IP	K	ERA	xERA	WHIP	oOPS	vL	vR	BF/G	Ctl	Dom	Cmd	FpK	SwK	G	L	F	H%	S%	hr/f	GS	APC	DOM%	DIS%	Sv%	LI	RAR	BPV	BPX	R$
10 MIN *	5	10	0	146	87	6.78	6.71	1.82	938	657	1080	17.3	2.7	5.4	2.0	58%	8%	50	22	28	39%	62%	14%	1	26	0%	100%	0	0.64	-48.5	30	48	-$22
11 MIN	4	4	2	62	65	2.48	3.04	1.23	644	589	681	3.9	3.1	9.5	3.1	65%	12%	50	21	29	33%	80%	4%	0	14			40	1.22	11.1	116	174	$5
12 MIN	3	1	16	70	78	2.56	3.12	1.04	631	488	721	4.0	2.0	10.0	4.9	63%	14%	42	19	39	29%	82%	12%	0	15			80	0.92	12.6	144	188	$14
13 MIN	2	0	36	63	77	2.30	2.67	0.93	562	544	568	3.9	2.2	11.1	5.1	70%	14%	36	26	38	28%	79%	9%	0	15			90	1.16	12.1	155	202	$21
14 MIN	4	3	34	62	66	3.65	3.34	1.18	720	772	700	4.1	1.6	9.6	6.0	65%	12%	35	23	42	34%	73%	9%	0	15			83	1.13	0.7	143	170	$15
1st Half	3	0	20	33	45	3.24	2.78	1.11	664	758	632	4.2	1.6	12.2	7.5	63%	13%	40	18	42	37%	71%	5%	0	16			87	1.24	2.1	193	230	$19
2nd Half	1	3	14	28	21	4.13	4.06	1.27	786	780	788	4.0	1.6	6.7	4.2	68%	11%	31	28	41	31%	74%	14%	0	14			78	1.01	-1.4	86	103	$9
15 Proj	**3**	**3**	**37**	**65**	**68**	**2.90**	**2.90**	**1.08**	**646**	**630**	**653**	**4.0**	**1.9**	**9.4**	**4.9**	**66%**	**13%**	**38**	**23**	**39**	**30%**	**77%**	**9%**	**0**						**6.8**	**133**	**159**	**$20**

Pestano,Vinnie

Age: 30	Th: R	Role RP	Health A	LIMA Plan B+	
Ht: 6' 0"	Wt: 200	Type Pwr FB	PT/Exp D	Rand Var -4	
			Consist C	MM 3500	

Profile as RH-dominator put into question after 2013 blowup. Now 2013 is looking like an anomaly, as 3.0 Cmd is back. But flyball lean, chronic struggles vs. LHB, and fastball that barely hits 90 now all give him uphill climb to get into saves mix again. Good LIMA stash; anything more is gravy.

Yr Tm	W	L	Sv	IP	K	ERA	xERA	WHIP	oOPS	vL	vR	BF/G	Ctl	Dom	Cmd	FpK	SwK	G	L	F	H%	S%	hr/f	GS	APC	DOM%	DIS%	Sv%	LI	RAR	BPV	BPX	R$
10 CLE *	2	3	18	65	71	2.15	2.80	1.22	614	875	408	4.2	3.0	9.8	3.3	48%	18%	30	20	50	33%	82%	0%	0	20			90	0.39	15.4	128	207	$13
11 CLE	1	2	2	62	84	2.32	2.82	1.05	577	812	410	3.7	3.5	12.2	3.5	59%	17%	39	19	42	28%	82%	9%	0	15			33	1.22	12.4	142	214	$7
12 CLE	3	3	2	70	76	2.57	3.55	1.10	631	752	487	4.1	3.1	9.8	3.2	61%	11%	41	17	43	27%	81%	9%	0	17			40	1.54	12.5	112	146	$7
13 CLE	1	2	6	35	37	4.08	4.53	1.64	838	878	792	4.3	5.3	9.4	1.8	57%	12%	35	21	44	33%	81%	14%	0	18			67	0.81	-0.9	38	50	-$3
14 2 AL *	3	6	6	57	63	2.13	3.17	1.23	725	1200	482	3.7	3.1	9.9	3.2	56%	14%	34	13	53	32%	85%	12%	0	13			86	0.80	11.4	116	138	$6
1st Half	2	3	6	30	30	2.63	3.05	1.21	1162	1333	1049	3.7	2.3	9.1	4.0	52%	8%	31	19	50	34%	78%	13%	0	12			86	0.42	4.1	135	161	$7
2nd Half	1	3	0	27	33	1.58	3.31	1.25	536	1125	268	3.6	4.0	10.8	2.7	58%	17%	35	10	55	30%	94%	12%	0	13			0	0.95	7.3	104	124	$5
15 Proj	**2**	**4**	**0**	**56**	**62**	**3.31**	**3.36**	**1.30**	**701**	**842**	**567**	**3.8**	**3.7**	**10.0**	**2.7**	**59%**	**14%**	**38**	**19**	**43**	**31%**	**78%**	**9%**	**0**						**2.9**	**95**	**114**	**$1**

Petit,Yusmeiro

Age: 30	Th: R	Role SP	Health A	LIMA Plan B+	
Ht: 6' 1"	Wt: 250	Type Pwr FB	PT/Exp C	Rand Var +1	
			Consist B	MM 4403	

Late bloomer now showing why he was top-50 prospect... 10 yrs ago. Elite FpK, SwK support awesome Cmd. Crazy 29% SwK% on curve gives him one of best punchout pitches in game. Next step is handling a full-season rotation workload. With opportunity, durability... UP: 3.00 ERA, 180 K

Yr Tm	W	L	Sv	IP	K	ERA	xERA	WHIP	oOPS	vL	vR	BF/G	Ctl	Dom	Cmd	FpK	SwK	G	L	F	H%	S%	hr/f	GS	APC	DOM%	DIS%	Sv%	LI	RAR	BPV	BPX	R$
10 aaa	4	2	0	59	45	5.35	4.40	1.31				10.2	2.5	6.9	2.8						30%	61%								-9.3	64	103	-$2
11																																	
12 SF *	7	7	0	171	118	3.48	4.47	1.42	936	885	1100	25.0	2.0	6.2	3.1	70%	2%	38	25	38	35%	76%	0%	1	94	0%	100%			11.3	80	105	$2
13 SF *	9	7	0	136	115	4.36	4.47	1.30	660	562	717	24.3	1.6	7.6	4.7	69%	13%	30	26	44	33%	70%	7%	7	91	57%	14%	0	0.73	-8.3	108	141	$1
14 SF	5	5	0	117	133	3.69	3.03	1.02	635	777	510	11.8	1.7	10.2	6.0	69%	13%	36	21	43	30%	66%	9%	12	43	50%	17%	0	0.52	0.7	152	182	$8
1st Half	3	3	0	57	54	4.11	3.63	1.16	680	848	544	10.5	2.2	8.5	3.9	71%	12%	34	22	44	30%	67%	8%	5	38	40%	20%	0	0.59	-2.6	106	127	$3
2nd Half	2	2	0	60	79	3.30	2.50	0.88	591	713	473	13.5	1.2	11.9	9.9	67%	15%	37	20	43	30%	66%	10%	7	50	57%	14%	0	0.42	3.3	196	234	$13
15 Proj	**7**	**6**	**0**	**140**	**137**	**3.51**	**3.16**	**1.13**	**681**	**738**	**638**	**21.6**	**1.8**	**8.8**	**5.0**	**69%**	**13%**	**34**	**23**	**44**	**31%**	**72%**	**9%**	**23**						**4.0**	**122**	**146**	**$10**

STEPHEN NICKRAND

Petricka,Jacob

Age: 27	Th: R	Role	RP	Health	A	LIMA Plan	B
Ht: 6' 5"	Wt: 205	Type	Pwr xGB	PT/Exp	D	Rand Var	-2
				Consist	D	MM	2120

PRO: Extreme GB tilt keeps ball in park (3 HR in 73 IP); FpK spike could mean Ctl dip; incumbent closer. CON: Shaky Cmd, mediocre SwK, skills overall not closer-worthy; xERA points to ERA spike; LH batters devouring him. Overall profile puts saves VERY much at risk. DN: Less than 10 saves

Yr	Tm	W	L	Sv	IP	K	ERA	xERA	WHIP	oOPS	vL	vR	BF/G	Ctl	Dom	Cmd	FpK	SwK	G	L	F	H%	S%	hr/f	GS	APC	DOM%	DIS%	Sv%	LI	RAR	BPV	BPX	R$
10																																		
11																																		
12	aa	3	3	0	58	23	6.94	7.15	2.01				27.8	6.3	3.6	0.6						32%	67%								-20.8	-19	-25	-$17
13	CHW *	6	1	1	74	58	2.63	3.92	1.56	688	775	644	6.9	4.8	7.1	1.5	51%	9%	63	21	16	33%	82%	0%	0	20			50	0.94	11.3	70	92	$1
14	CHW	1	6	14	73	55	2.96	3.57	1.37	671	830	549	4.6	4.1	6.8	1.7	61%	8%	63	17	19	30%	78%	7%	0	18			78	1.52	7.0	53	63	$5
1st Half		0	2	2	44	33	2.03	3.62	1.26	578	673	504	5.3	4.5	6.7	1.5	63%	8%	64	17	18	26%	84%	4%	0	21			67	1.34	9.4	42	50	$5
2nd Half		1	4	12	29	22	4.40	3.51	1.53	807	1061	614	3.8	3.5	6.9	2.0	58%	8%	62	17	21	35%	71%	11%	0	14			80	1.72	-2.3	71	85	$5
15	**Proj**	**3**	**4**	**19**	**68**	**48**	**3.69**	**3.86**	**1.56**	**762**	**960**	**610**	**5.9**	**4.6**	**6.4**	**1.4**	**60%**	**8%**	**63**	**17**	**20**	**32%**	**76%**	**9%**	**0**						**0.4**	**33**	**39**	**$4**

Phelps,David

Age: 28	Th: R	Role	RP	Health	F	LIMA Plan	C
Ht: 6' 2"	Wt: 200	Type	Pwr	PT/Exp	B	Rand Var	0
				Consist	A	MM	2301

Sore elbow cost him over a month in 2nd half, and he was awful after returning late. Throw that out, and he was pretty much the same guy: decent Cmd, low SwK, and slightly-below-league-average skills. His versatility is much more valuable to his MLB team than to you. Deep-league filler, at best.

Yr	Tm	W	L	Sv	IP	K	ERA	xERA	WHIP	oOPS	vL	vR	BF/G	Ctl	Dom	Cmd	FpK	SwK	G	L	F	H%	S%	hr/f	GS	APC	DOM%	DIS%	Sv%	LI	RAR	BPV	BPX	R$
10	a/a	10	2	0	159	117	3.23	3.70	1.30				25.1	2.2	6.6	3.0						33%	75%								16.7	89	145	$10
11	aaa	6	6	0	107	72	4.51	6.23	1.64				26.6	2.5	6.1	2.4						36%	77%								-7.6	36	55	-$7
12	NYY	4	4	0	100	96	3.34	3.82	1.19	682	786	597	12.5	3.4	8.7	2.5	62%	7%	43	19	38	27%	78%	14%	11	51	45%	45%	0	0.83	8.3	84	110	$6
13	NYY	6	5	0	87	79	4.98	3.97	1.42	749	756	738	17.1	3.6	8.2	2.3	59%	7%	42	22	36	33%	65%	9%	12	68	58%	17%	0	0.92	-12.0	70	91	-$4
14	NYY	5	5	1	113	92	4.38	4.21	1.42	751	699	805	15.5	3.7	7.3	2.0	62%	6%	41	24	35	31%	72%	11%	17	60	35%	12%	100	0.86	-8.9	52	62	-$4
1st Half		3	4	1	76	68	4.26	4.09	1.41	765	720	810	16.7	3.7	8.1	2.2	61%	5%	40	23	38	31%	72%	11%	11	65	36%	9%	100	1.07	-4.9	64	76	-$2
2nd Half		2	1	0	37	24	4.62	4.48	1.46	724	657	794	13.7	3.6	5.8	1.6	64%	6%	44	26	30	30%	70%	11%	6	51	33%	17%	0	0.50	-4.0	28	34	-$7
15	**Proj**	**5**	**4**	**0**	**102**	**90**	**4.11**	**3.75**	**1.37**	**715**	**705**	**728**	**15.0**	**3.7**	**8.0**	**2.2**	**62%**	**6%**	**41**	**22**	**37**	**31%**	**72%**	**9%**	**14**						**-4.6**	**64**	**76**	**$0**

Pimentel,Stolmy

Age: 25	Th: R	Role	RP	Health	D	LIMA Plan	D+
Ht: 6' 3"	Wt: 230	Type	Pwr xFB	PT/Exp	D	Rand Var	+4
				Consist	C	MM	1200

Power arm played well in relief, as Dom spike shows. FpK, pre-2014 Ctl trend says walks will regress to manageable level. Biggest issues now are iffy health and extreme flyball lean—allowed 5 HR in 32 IP despite elite SwK. Regardless, if he settles in relief, 1st half hints at upside.

Yr	Tm	W	L	Sv	IP	K	ERA	xERA	WHIP	oOPS	vL	vR	BF/G	Ctl	Dom	Cmd	FpK	SwK	G	L	F	H%	S%	hr/f	GS	APC	DOM%	DIS%	Sv%	LI	RAR	BPV	BPX	R$
10																																		
11	aa	0	9	0	50	26	10.06	7.92	2.04				16.3	3.8	4.6	1.2						39%	49%								-38.0	-6	-9	-$19
12	aa	6	7	0	116	74	6.08	5.06	1.56				23.1	3.4	5.7	1.7						33%	60%								-29.5	41	54	-$15
13	PIT *	6	9	0	179	108	3.71	3.58	1.28	411	214	530	22.9	2.8	5.4	2.0	55%	14%	41	19	41	29%	72%	0%	0	29			0	0.34	3.3	58	75	$3
14	PIT	2	1	0	33	38	5.23	4.19	1.53	790	775	796	7.4	4.4	10.5	2.4	62%	14%	28	22	50	35%	69%	11%	0	30			0	0.54	-6.0	75	90	-$4
1st Half		2	1	0	21	25	3.80	3.69	1.41	749	700	781	10.4	3.4	10.5	3.1	65%	14%	33	22	45	35%	78%	12%	0	42			0	0.93	-0.1	109	131	-$3
2nd Half		0	0	0	11	13	7.94	5.18	1.76	866	893	829	4.9	6.4	10.3	1.6	57%	14%	19	22	59	35%	56%	11%	0	20			0	0.22	-5.9	11	13	-$8
15	**Proj**	**2**	**3**	**0**	**44**	**34**	**4.48**	**4.29**	**1.44**	**708**	**654**	**745**	**15.6**	**3.3**	**7.0**	**2.1**	**65%**	**14%**	**33**	**22**	**45**	**31%**	**73%**	**10%**	**7**						**-3.9**	**46**	**55**	**-$3**

Pineda,Michael

Age: 26	Th: R	Role	SP	Health	F	LIMA Plan	B
Ht: 6' 7"	Wt: 265	Type	xFB	PT/Exp	D	Rand Var	-5
				Consist	B	MM	4301

Fascinating season, from the pine tar episode to a sparkling sprint to the finish. Stunning Ctl fueled the latter—which will regress. But late-year SwK spike means Dom upside, too. Sub-2.00 ERA won't repeat, but 2nd half xERA is attainable. Durability is the big "if" here, not skills.

Yr	Tm	W	L	Sv	IP	K	ERA	xERA	WHIP	oOPS	vL	vR	BF/G	Ctl	Dom	Cmd	FpK	SwK	G	L	F	H%	S%	hr/f	GS	APC	DOM%	DIS%	Sv%	LI	RAR	BPV	BPX	R$
10	a/a	11	4	0	139	140	3.41	2.92	1.13				22.0	2.0	9.0	4.4						32%	70%								11.5	137	222	$13
11	SEA	9	10	0	171	173	3.74	3.53	1.10	621	653	587	24.9	2.9	9.1	3.1	64%	12%	36	19	45	27%	69%	9%	28	96	75%	11%			4.3	100	150	$13
12																																		
13	a/a	2	1	0	32	28	5.23	4.30	1.32				16.7	3.7	7.8	2.1						28%	64%								-5.5	52	68	-$4
14	NYY	5	5	0	76	59	1.89	3.39	0.83	526	533	518	22.3	0.8	7.0	8.4	67%	12%	39	19	42	25%	81%	5%	13	88	77%	8%			17.5	120	143	$11
1st Half		2	2	0	20	15	1.83	4.09	1.02	647	712	528	19.3	1.4	6.9	5.0	62%	10%	25	18	58	28%	84%	3%	4	77	75%	25%			4.6	89	106	-$2
2nd Half		3	3	0	57	44	1.91	3.14	0.76	483	450	515	23.7	0.6	7.0	11.0	69%	12%	44	19	37	23%	79%	7%	9	93	78%	0%			12.8	131	156	$16
15	**Proj**	**8**	**7**	**0**	**124**	**110**	**3.38**	**3.33**	**1.08**	**651**	**678**	**619**	**20.3**	**2.0**	**8.0**	**4.0**	**65%**	**12%**	**36**	**19**	**45**	**28%**	**72%**	**8%**	**21**						**5.5**	**103**	**123**	**$11**

Pino,Yohan

Age: 31	Th: R	Role	RP	Health	A	LIMA Plan	D+
Ht: 6' 3"	Wt: 158	Type	xFB	PT/Exp	D	Rand Var	0
				Consist	B	MM	1101

2-5, 5.07 ERA in 60 IP at MIN. Extreme FB ways, marginal SwK add up to a volatile mix—and 8 HR in 60 IP. Solid Cmd helps, but without second pitch to make batters miss, Dom is likely maxed out. So there's more downside than up in these skills... and they aren't that great to begin with.

Yr	Tm	W	L	Sv	IP	K	ERA	xERA	WHIP	oOPS	vL	vR	BF/G	Ctl	Dom	Cmd	FpK	SwK	G	L	F	H%	S%	hr/f	GS	APC	DOM%	DIS%	Sv%	LI	RAR	BPV	BPX	R$
10	aaa	10	9	0	146	89	6.65	6.77	1.75				25.6	3.1	5.5	1.8						36%	64%								-46.2	14	23	-$17
11	a/a	4	8	0	99	82	4.89	4.94	1.31				10.4	1.5	7.5	5.0						33%	67%								-11.6	100	150	-$2
12	a/a	10	10	0	143	88	6.20	6.13	1.59				22.6	2.2	5.5	2.5						35%	63%								-38.6	34	45	-$18
13	a/a	5	7	6	132	89	4.57	4.91	1.51				16.4	2.5	6.1	2.4						35%	70%								-11.4	59	77	-$5
14	MIN *	12	7	0	133	102	4.21	4.18	1.28	759	754	767	20.3	2.8	6.9	2.4	60%	8%	29	23	48	29%	71%	9%	11	92	36%	18%			-7.7	58	70	$2
1st Half		9	3	0	77	56	3.45	3.92	1.25	780	931	671	18.3	2.5	6.6	2.6	69%	9%	27	27	46	29%	77%	4%	3	87	33%	33%			2.7	65	78	$9
2nd Half		3	4	0	57	46	5.23	4.52	1.33	752	711	818	23.5	3.2	7.3	2.3	58%	7%	29	22	49	29%	64%	10%	8	94	38%	13%			-10.4	50	60	-$7
15	**Proj**	**5**	**6**	**0**	**87**	**63**	**4.59**	**4.32**	**1.44**	**791**	**806**	**772**	**19.2**	**2.9**	**6.5**	**2.3**	**62%**	**8%**	**28**	**24**	**48**	**32%**	**71%**	**9%**	**18**						**-9.2**	**46**	**55**	**-$4**

Pomeranz,Drew

Age: 26	Th: L	Role	RP	Health	D	LIMA Plan	B+
Ht: 6' 5"	Wt: 240	Type	Pwr	PT/Exp	D	Rand Var	-2
				Consist	C	MM	3301

5-4, 2.35 ERA in 69 IP at OAK. Star of the action thriller, "Escape from Colorado." As xERA shows, gains were mostly skills-supported. There's a "but" here, though: poor FpK shows he's unlikely to maintain Ctl. So he'll give a bunch of those ERA gains back. No breakout until he can start getting ahead of hitters more.

Yr	Tm	W	L	Sv	IP	K	ERA	xERA	WHIP	oOPS	vL	vR	BF/G	Ctl	Dom	Cmd	FpK	SwK	G	L	F	H%	S%	hr/f	GS	APC	DOM%	DIS%	Sv%	LI	RAR	BPV	BPX	R$
10																																		
11	COL *	3	2	0	42	32	3.35	2.06	1.03	700	522	727	18.1	2.3	6.8	2.9	57%	5%	47	26	26	27%	66%	0%	4	67	25%	25%			3.1	107	160	$2
12	COL *	6	13	0	147	122	4.31	5.15	1.59	775	464	864	20.3	4.2	7.5	1.8	56%	10%	44	20	36	34%	75%	14%	22	77	18%	64%			-5.3	49	64	-$7
13	COL *	8	6	0	113	95	5.86	5.64	1.69	951	405	1150	21.2	4.3	7.6	1.8	54%	8%	51	17	32	35%	66%	19%	4	52	0%	100%	0	0.78	-27.7	43	57	-$13
14	OAK *	8	5	0	115	107	2.90	3.47	1.23	586	664	563	16.7	3.3	8.3	2.5	52%	9%	46	18	36	29%	81%	10%	10	57	50%	20%	0	0.75	12.0	83	99	$7
1st Half		5	4	0	56	48	2.91	3.81	1.24	647	782	611	13.4	3.7	7.8	2.1	52%	8%	47	19	35	26%	82%	13%	8	55	38%	25%	0	0.80	5.7	64	76	$7
2nd Half		3	1	0	60	59	2.89	3.38	1.23	310	277	323	22.0	2.9	8.9	3.0	50%	12%	40	17	43	31%	79%	0%	2	66	100%	0%	0	0.51	6.3	101	120	$8
15	**Proj**	**7**	**6**	**0**	**116**	**102**	**3.96**	**3.66**	**1.38**	**712**	**661**	**726**	**18.8**	**3.5**	**7.9**	**2.2**	**54%**	**9%**	**46**	**19**	**35**	**31%**	**73%**	**10%**	**23**						**-3.1**	**71**	**84**	**$1**

Porcello,Rick

Age: 26	Th: R	Role	SP	Health	A	LIMA Plan	C+
Ht: 6' 5"	Wt: 200	Type	Con GB	PT/Exp	A	Rand Var	0
				Consist	B	MM	3105

Step up we anticipated after 2013 skills breakout did materialize, but BPIs actually regressed a bit. Still, this was pretty good. Gave up all of 2013's strikeout gains for more attacking approach (see FpK); career-high IP was the result, so it's a decent trade. Solid, if unspectacular, going forward.

Yr	Tm	W	L	Sv	IP	K	ERA	xERA	WHIP	oOPS	vL	vR	BF/G	Ctl	Dom	Cmd	FpK	SwK	G	L	F	H%	S%	hr/f	GS	APC	DOM%	DIS%	Sv%	LI	RAR	BPV	BPX	R$
10	DET *	11	14	0	191	100	4.76	4.47	1.38	752	784	717	25.8	2.2	4.7	2.1	57%	6%	50	18	32	31%	66%	10%	27	96	30%	19%			-16.0	45	72	-$1
11	DET	14	9	0	182	104	4.75	4.05	1.41	774	857	650	25.3	2.3	5.1	2.3	61%	7%	51	19	30	32%	67%	10%	31	92	29%	23%			-18.1	60	90	-$2
12	DET	10	12	0	176	107	4.59	4.15	1.53	808	883	725	25.3	2.2	5.5	2.4	63%	8%	53	24	23	35%	71%	12%	31	91	32%	26%			-12.6	69	90	-$9
13	DET	13	8	0	177	142	4.32	3.32	1.28	709	808	602	23.0	2.1	7.2	3.4	60%	9%	55	21	24	32%	68%	14%	29	89	48%	17%	0	0.84	-10.0	105	137	$4
14	DET	15	13	0	205	129	3.43	3.74	1.23	712	732	686	26.3	1.8	5.7	3.1	64%	8%	49	22	29	30%	74%	9%	31	95	55%	13%	0	0.83	7.9	80	96	$10
1st Half		10	4	0	98	62	3.41	3.76	1.19	696	692	700	26.1	2.2	5.7	2.6	61%	8%	46	25	29	28%	74%	10%	15	100	60%	0%			4.0	67	81	$14
2nd Half		5	9	0	107	67	3.45	3.72	1.27	726	766	674	26.4	1.4	5.6	3.9	68%	8%	51	20	29	32%	75%	9%	16	91	50%	25%	0	0.89	3.9	92	110	$7
15	**Proj**	**13**	**12**	**0**	**189**	**125**	**3.72**	**3.49**	**1.31**	**728**	**780**	**665**	**24.8**	**2.0**	**6.0**	**3.0**	**63%**	**8%**	**52**	**22**	**27**	**32%**	**73%**	**10%**	**31**						**0.4**	**83**	**99**	**$7**

ROD TRUESDELL

Price,David

Age: 29	Th: L	Role SP	Health	C	LIMA Plan	C		
Ht: 6' 6"	Wt: 220	Type Pwr	PT/Exp	A	Rand Var	0		
			Consist	A	MM	5405		

Not his best surface stats, but these were among his best skills. Slightly elevated 1st half H% and hr/f, or he'd have been in the Cy Young talk again. Now at peak age, only a career-high workload, 2013 triceps strain loom as cautions. UP: 2012 again. That's still in play.

Yr	Tm	W	L	Sv	IP	K	ERA	xERA	WHIP	oOPS	vL	vR	BF/G	Ctl	Dom	Cmd	FpK	SwK	G	L	F	H%	S%	hr/f	GS	APC	DOM%	DIS%	Sv%	LI	RAR	BPV	BPX	R$
10	TAM	19	6	0	209	188	2.72	3.78	1.19	637	569	656	26.9	3.4	8.1	2.4	62%	10%	44	17	40	28%	79%	7%	31	105	68%	3%	0	0.77	35.0	76	123	$24
11	TAM	12	13	0	224	218	3.49	3.32	1.14	659	508	709	27.0	2.5	8.7	3.5	60%	9%	44	19	37	29%	72%	10%	34	109	62%	12%			12.5	111	167	$19
12	TAM	20	5	0	211	205	2.56	3.10	1.10	602	520	626	27.0	2.5	8.7	3.5	63%	9%	53	20	27	29%	80%	11%	31	107	74%	13%			37.9	120	157	$32
13	TAM	10	8	0	187	151	3.33	3.34	1.10	661	489	712	27.4	1.3	7.3	5.6	68%	8%	45	22	33	30%	72%	9%	27	100	78%	7%			12.4	119	155	$15
14	2 AL	15	12	0	248	271	3.26	3.00	1.08	647	657	644	29.7	1.4	9.8	7.1	70%	11%	41	21	38	32%	73%	10%	34	110	82%	3%			14.7	159	189	$23
1st Half		6	7	0	124	144	3.63	2.81	1.09	681	705	672	29.8	1.0	10.5	10.3	71%	12%	43	19	38	34%	72%	13%	17	111	82%	0%			1.7	182	217	$20
2nd Half		9	5	0	124	127	2.90	3.19	1.07	613	601	617	29.5	1.7	9.2	5.3	69%	10%	40	22	38	31%	74%	6%	17	109	82%	6%			13.0	136	163	$27
15	**Proj**	**17**	**7**	**0**	**225**	**223**	**3.04**	**2.93**	**1.09**	**634**	**574**	**653**	**27.6**	**1.8**	**8.9**	**4.8**	**69%**	**10%**	**42**	**21**	**37**	**30%**	**75%**	**9%**	**32**						**19.4**	**131**	**156**	**$26**

Putnam,Zach

Age: 27	Th: R	Role RP	Health	F	LIMA Plan	B		
Ht: 6' 2"	Wt: 225	Type Pwr	PT/Exp	D	Rand Var	-5		
			Consist	D	MM	3320		

PRO: Elite SwK means Dom upside; recent GB tilt; generally a strike-thrower. CON: Won't likely have 25% H% again to artificially suppress ERA; odd 2nd half tumbles in FpK, GB% cause for concern; checkered injury past. Was in mix for saves at year's end, and if the skills he's shown align... UP: 30 saves

Yr	Tm	W	L	Sv	IP	K	ERA	xERA	WHIP	oOPS	vL	vR	BF/G	Ctl	Dom	Cmd	FpK	SwK	G	L	F	H%	S%	hr/f	GS	APC	DOM%	DIS%	Sv%	LI	RAR	BPV	BPX	R$
10	a/a	4	2	3	76	55	3.97	3.91	1.33				8.5	1.9	6.5	3.5						34%	69%								1.0	99	160	$2
11	CLE *	7	4	9	76	65	4.31	3.99	1.32	915	692	1060	6.1	2.6	7.7	2.9	53%	14%	30	43	26	32%	68%	17%	0	14			64	0.58	-3.5	85	127	$4
12	COL *	3	4	12	63	37	4.69	6.41	1.84	929	500	1417	5.7	4.0	5.4	1.3	67%	17%	43	14	43	37%	76%	0%	0	15			71	0.05	-5.2	22	28	-$5
13	CHC *	1	1	4	23	21	6.33	5.85	1.77	1251	1625	1000	4.7	2.6	8.5	3.2	68%	11%	53	27	20	43%	62%	33%	0	14			80	0.18	-6.9	94	122	-$5
14	CHW	5	3	6	55	46	1.98	3.41	1.08	551	623	468	4.3	3.3	7.6	2.3	61%	14%	53	15	32	25%	82%	4%	0	18			86	1.47	11.9	78	93	$8
1st Half		2	1	1	31	25	2.30	3.24	1.09	572	605	538	4.7	3.2	7.2	2.3	66%	15%	61	12	27	25%	81%	9%	0	18			100	1.17	5.6	83	99	$6
2nd Half		3	2	5	23	21	1.54	3.61	1.07	523	644	358	4.0	3.5	8.1	2.3	53%	14%	42	20	38	26%	84%	0%	0	17			83	1.80	6.3	72	86	$10
15	**Proj**	**4**	**3**	**15**	**65**	**58**	**3.57**	**3.35**	**1.25**	**680**	**785**	**554**	**5.0**	**3.0**	**8.0**	**2.7**	**61%**	**14%**	**49**	**17**	**34**	**31%**	**72%**	**6%**	**0**						**1.4**	**90**	**108**	**$7**

Quackenbush,Kevin

Age: 26	Th: R	Role RP	Health	A	LIMA Plan	B		
Ht: 6' 4"	Wt: 220	Type Pwr	PT/Exp	D	Rand Var	-3		
			Consist	B	MM	4410		

Fared well in September closer audition. While xERA shows sparkly 2nd half ERA was a bit fortunate, his skills still show closer potential. Issues: Ctl, LD both higher than we'd like, but FpK is optimistic for future Ctl gains. At minimum, well worth a LIMA bid. And surely he'll get nicknamed "The Doctor," which would be awesome.

Yr	Tm	W	L	Sv	IP	K	ERA	xERA	WHIP	oOPS	vL	vR	BF/G	Ctl	Dom	Cmd	FpK	SwK	G	L	F	H%	S%	hr/f	GS	APC	DOM%	DIS%	Sv%	LI	RAR	BPV	BPX	R$
10																																		
11																																		
12																																		
13	a/a	10	2	17	65	72	1.74	2.60	1.25				4.6	3.9	9.9	2.6						32%	86%								17.0	119	155	$15
14	SD	3	3	6	54	56	2.48	3.40	1.10	568	512	633	4.0	3.0	9.3	3.1	64%	9%	37	27	36	29%	78%	4%	0	16			86	1.17	8.4	101	121	$6
1st Half		1	1	0	22	20	2.91	3.27	0.78	503	468	539	3.7	2.5	8.3	3.3	61%	8%	38	21	42	20%	63%	5%	0	15			0	0.74	2.2	98	117	$2
2nd Half		2	2	6	33	36	2.20	3.47	1.32	606	535	691	4.1	3.3	9.9	3.0	66%	10%	37	30	33	35%	83%	3%	0	17			86	1.45	6.2	104	124	$9
15	**Proj**	**5**	**3**	**5**	**58**	**61**	**2.99**	**3.18**	**1.16**	**578**	**519**	**645**	**4.1**	**3.3**	**9.5**	**2.9**	**64%**	**9%**	**37**	**26**	**37**	**30%**	**73%**	**3%**	**0**						**5.3**	**97**	**115**	**$6**

Qualls,Chad

Age: 36	Th: R	Role RP	Health	B	LIMA Plan	B+		
Ht: 6' 4"	Wt: 240	Type xGB	PT/Exp	C	Rand Var	+1		
			Consist	B	MM	5230		

Took "old mechanics" he re-discovered prior to 2013 up another notch, with career-best Cmd. FpK says it's almost sustainable. Even oOPS vL was driven by an aberrant H%. Despite age, he could stay at this level for a while. Likely a bargain too, because anyone with a long-term memory is not going to draft Chad Qualls..

Yr	Tm	W	L	Sv	IP	K	ERA	xERA	WHIP	oOPS	vL	vR	BF/G	Ctl	Dom	Cmd	FpK	SwK	G	L	F	H%	S%	hr/f	GS	APC	DOM%	DIS%	Sv%	LI	RAR	BPV	BPX	R$
10	2 TM	3	4	12	59	49	7.32	4.04	1.80	894	1031	766	4.0	3.2	7.5	2.3	63%	9%	55	17	28	40%	59%	12%	0	15			63	1.01	-23.6	81	131	-$5
11	SD	6	8	0	74	43	3.51	3.76	1.25	689	881	537	4.0	2.4	5.2	2.2	64%	9%	57	17	26	28%	74%	11%	0	14			0	1.22	4.0	63	95	$2
12	3 TM	2	1	0	52	27	5.33	4.44	1.47	809	988	679	3.9	2.4	4.6	1.9	59%	8%	55	19	26	32%	66%	15%	0	14			0	0.81	-8.5	52	67	-$7
13	MIA	5	2	0	62	49	2.61	3.14	1.23	658	600	698	3.8	2.8	7.1	2.6	65%	11%	63	17	20	30%	81%	11%	0	13			0	1.41	9.6	95	123	$3
14	HOU	1	5	19	51	43	3.33	2.97	1.15	667	828	512	3.7	0.9	7.5	8.6	66%	11%	57	18	25	33%	74%	13%	0	12			76	1.15	2.6	147	175	$7
1st Half		1	1	9	28	27	1.91	2.76	1.02	600	951	361	3.7	1.0	8.6	9.0	63%	12%	53	20	27	31%	85%	9%	0	12			82	1.09	6.4	160	191	$10
2nd Half		0	4	10	23	16	5.09	3.23	1.30	745	729	769	3.7	0.8	6.3	8.0	70%	10%	62	15	23	34%	63%	17%	0	12			71	1.21	-3.8	131	156	$4
15	**Proj**	**2**	**5**	**30**	**58**	**46**	**3.59**	**2.92**	**1.17**	**647**	**727**	**576**	**3.6**	**1.8**	**7.2**	**4.1**	**65%**	**10%**	**59**	**17**	**24**	**31%**	**71%**	**12%**	**0**						**1.1**	**118**	**141**	**$13**

Quintana,Jose

Age: 26	Th: L	Role SP	Health	A	LIMA Plan	B		
Ht: 6' 1"	Wt: 220	Type	PT/Exp	A	Rand Var	-1		
			Consist	A	MM	3205		

Another fine growth season. The issue in maintaining the growth is his SwK. It's currently capped at an average level, so Dom is likely maxed. Without refining a bat-missing pitch, further upside appears limited. That's not meant to diminish his current solid level—just frame it.

Yr	Tm	W	L	Sv	IP	K	ERA	xERA	WHIP	oOPS	vL	vR	BF/G	Ctl	Dom	Cmd	FpK	SwK	G	L	F	H%	S%	hr/f	GS	APC	DOM%	DIS%	Sv%	LI	RAR	BPV	BPX	R$
10																																		
11																																		
12	CHW *	7	9	0	185	117	3.68	4.06	1.35	754	700	775	22.7	2.8	5.7	2.0	61%	8%	47	22	31	30%	74%	11%	22	87	32%	32%	0	0.73	7.6	55	72	$3
13	CHW	9	7	0	200	164	3.51	3.85	1.22	695	717	687	25.2	2.5	7.4	2.9	66%	9%	43	20	37	29%	75%	10%	33	101	55%	12%			8.8	86	112	$10
14	CHW	9	11	0	200	178	3.32	3.51	1.24	662	686	653	25.9	2.3	8.0	3.4	66%	9%	45	22	33	33%	73%	5%	32	105	66%	6%			10.3	104	124	$9
1st Half		5	7	0	105	90	3.44	3.58	1.28	673	650	680	25.7	2.7	7.7	2.9	64%	8%	46	23	30	32%	73%	6%	17	105	65%	12%			3.9	92	109	$8
2nd Half		4	4	0	96	88	3.20	3.42	1.20	649	716	618	26.2	2.0	8.3	4.2	69%	9%	43	21	36	33%	73%	4%	15	104	67%	0%			6.4	117	139	$11
15	**Proj**	**10**	**10**	**0**	**203**	**168**	**3.43**	**3.43**	**1.25**	**683**	**700**	**676**	**24.7**	**2.4**	**7.5**	**3.1**	**66%**	**9%**	**44**	**21**	**35**	**31%**	**74%**	**7%**	**33**						**7.8**	**91**	**108**	**$11**

Ramirez,Erasmo

Age: 25	Th: R	Role SP	Health	C	LIMA Plan	C		
Ht: 5' 11"	Wt: 200	Type	PT/Exp	D	Rand Var	0		
			Consist	B	MM	2101		

1-6, 5.26 ERA in 75 IP at SEA. On the surface, another step back, and let's face it, he wasn't good. But the seeds for better are STILL here—notably sterling Ctl, fine SwK. Gopheritis is the problem, and FB rate went the wrong way. Regression to pre-2014 FB% could mean sub-4.00 ERA.

Yr	Tm	W	L	Sv	IP	K	ERA	xERA	WHIP	oOPS	vL	vR	BF/G	Ctl	Dom	Cmd	FpK	SwK	G	L	F	H%	S%	hr/f	GS	APC	DOM%	DIS%	Sv%	LI	RAR	BPV	BPX	R$
10																																		
11	a/a	10	8	0	153	106	4.45	4.24	1.34				24.4	1.7	6.3	3.7						34%	67%								-9.6	93	140	$0
12	SEA *	7	6	0	136	101	3.35	3.11	1.14	616	612	622	17.4	1.8	6.6	3.6	64%	12%	40	24	36	29%	72%	10%	8	55	50%	25%	0	0.76	11.1	102	133	$10
13	SEA *	8	6	0	121	96	4.36	4.71	1.42	772	791	742	23.3	3.1	7.2	2.3	59%	9%	42	21	36	32%	73%	14%	13	91	54%	31%	0	0.74	-7.3	56	73	-$2
14	SEA *	7	11	0	162	117	4.42	4.72	1.40	815	790	848	21.3	2.5	6.5	2.6	61%	11%	38	19	43	32%	71%	13%	14	76	29%	50%	0	0.63	-13.6	58	69	-$4
1st Half		2	7	0	83	61	4.59	5.44	1.54	815	789	849	22.5	3.8	6.6	1.7	55%	11%	40	18	42	31%	75%	14%	11	85	27%	45%			-8.7	30	36	-$10
2nd Half		5	4	0	79	56	4.24	3.97	1.24	814	794	843	20.1	1.2	6.4	5.4	73%	13%	32	23	45	33%	66%	9%	3	60	33%	67%	0	0.40	-4.9	129	153	$2
15	**Proj**	**4**	**4**	**0**	**73**	**54**	**4.23**	**3.83**	**1.34**	**731**	**732**	**729**	**21.2**	**2.3**	**6.7**	**2.9**	**63%**	**11%**	**39**	**21**	**40**	**32%**	**70%**	**8%**	**14**						**-4.4**	**74**	**88**	**-$2**

Ramirez,Neil

Age: 26	Th: R	Role RP	Health	A	LIMA Plan	B		
Ht: 6' 4"	Wt: 190	Type Pwr xFB	PT/Exp	D	Rand Var	-5		
			Consist	C	MM	3410		

3-3, 1.44 ERA with 3 Sv in 44 IP at CHC. Conversion to short relief went swimmingly. High S%, fortunate hr/f helped, and xERA is a better guide than ERA—but hey, that's still pretty good. Has elite SwK and Dom that managers love in closers, but as long as Ctl and FpK are mediocre, keep him away from 9th innings.

Yr	Tm	W	L	Sv	IP	K	ERA	xERA	WHIP	oOPS	vL	vR	BF/G	Ctl	Dom	Cmd	FpK	SwK	G	L	F	H%	S%	hr/f	GS	APC	DOM%	DIS%	Sv%	LI	RAR	BPV	BPX	R$
10																																		
11	a/a	5	3	0	93	91	3.66	3.63	1.34				16.2	4.0	8.8	2.2						30%	74%								3.3	82	123	$2
12	a/a	8	13	0	123	89	7.77	5.87	1.57				19.3	3.5	6.5	1.9						32%	51%								-57.1	24	31	-$22
13	aa	9	3	0	108	109	4.53	3.33	1.29				20.1	3.9	9.1	2.3						30%	65%								-8.8	90	117	$1
14	CHC	3	3	3	44	53	1.44	3.44	1.05	550	591	522	3.5	3.5	10.9	3.1	58%	14%	26	24	50	28%	89%	4%	0	15			60	0.97	12.4	106	126	$6
1st Half		1	1	3	21	30	1.27	2.85	0.80	468	539	430	3.4	3.4	12.7	3.8	60%	15%	24	20	56	19%	93%	9%	0	15			100	0.71	6.5	139	166	$7
2nd Half		2	2	0	22	23	1.61	4.05	1.30	619	623	615	3.7	3.6	9.3	2.6	56%	13%	27	27	46	33%	86%	0%	0	15			0	1.22	5.9	74	88	$5
15	**Proj**	**4**	**4**	**3**	**58**	**61**	**3.39**	**3.64**	**1.24**	**663**	**669**	**656**	**5.9**	**3.7**	**9.4**	**2.6**	**57%**	**14%**	**26**	**24**	**50**	**30%**	**74%**	**6%**	**0**						**2.5**	**75**	**89**	**$3**

ROD TRUESDELL

Ramos,A.J.				Health	B	LIMA Plan	C+
Age: 28	Th: R	Role	RP	PT/Exp	D	Rand Var	-5
Ht: 5' 10"	Wt: 205	Type	Pwr FB	Consist	B	MM	3501

Which is wilder, his arm or his luck? Saved by miniscule hit, hr/f rates despite walking one of every six batters faced. No doubt about his swing-and-miss stuff, but if control trend continues, even that won't save him. 2nd half was better, but not remotely good enough. Don't speculate wildly.

Yr	Tm	W	L	Sv	IP	K	ERA	xERA	WHIP	oOPS	vL	vR	BF/G	Ctl	Dom	Cmd	FpK	SwK	G	L	F	H%	S%	hr/f	GS	APC	DOM%	DIS%	Sv%	LI	RAR	BPV	BPX	R$
10																																		
11																																		
12	MIA *	3	3	21	78	89	2.11	2.13	1.04	754	436	1056	4.6	3.3	10.2	3.1	65%	18%	32	23	45	26%	83%	20%	0	14			81	0.94	18.3	124	162	$19
13	MIA	3	4	0	80	86	3.15	3.97	1.26	603	740	484	5.0	4.8	9.7	2.0	61%	12%	39	19	43	28%	75%	5%	0	20			0	0.98	7.1	61	79	$3
14	MIA	7	0	0	64	73	2.11	3.89	1.23	543	522	555	4.0	6.0	10.3	1.7	57%	14%	42	19	39	25%	82%	2%	0	16			0	1.36	12.9	42	49	$6
1st Half		4	0	0	37	42	2.17	4.20	1.39	605	564	630	4.2	7.0	10.1	1.4	56%	14%	42	23	35	26%	84%	3%	0	17			0	1.62	7.2	13	16	$5
2nd Half		3	0	0	27	31	2.03	3.51	1.01	453	462	444	3.7	4.7	10.5	2.2	59%	14%	43	13	44	23%	78%	0%	0	15			0	1.00	5.6	81	97	$7
15	**Proj**	**3**	**4**	**0**	**73**	**80**	**3.57**	**3.67**	**1.32**	**619**	**681**	**572**	**4.3**	**5.2**	**10.0**	**1.9**	**59%**	**13%**	**40**	**18**	**42**	**29%**	**72%**	**3%**	**0**						**1.5**	**56**	**66**	**$1**

Ramos,Cesar				Health	A	LIMA Plan	D+
Age: 31	Th: L	Role	RP	PT/Exp	C	Rand Var	-1
Ht: 6' 2"	Wt: 200	Type	Pwr	Consist	A	MM	2201

Middling early results as SP not too surprising given past skills, but shaky Ctl was. Still didn't find it fully even after relegation to bullpen—which is a problem when other skills are rather pedestrian. Given age and history, don't bet on another shot at starting, or any high-leverage role.

Yr	Tm	W	L	Sv	IP	K	ERA	xERA	WHIP	oOPS	vL	vR	BF/G	Ctl	Dom	Cmd	FpK	SwK	G	L	F	H%	S%	hr/f	GS	APC	DOM%	DIS%	Sv%	LI	RAR	BPV	BPX	R$
10	SD *	6	8	0	104	62	4.12	4.77	1.59	1049	697	1330	10.5	4.2	5.3	1.3	59%	13%	44	21	35	32%	74%	8%	0	14			0	0.71	-0.5	38	62	-$3
11	TAM	0	1	0	44	31	3.92	4.62	1.40	670	639	705	3.3	5.2	6.4	1.2	49%	9%	49	16	35	26%	74%	9%	0	12			0	0.82	0.1	3	4	-$3
12	TAM *	6	5	1	92	65	3.79	4.13	1.27	490	510	470	9.0	2.6	6.3	2.4	63%	10%	54	20	25	28%	75%	10%	1	25	0%	100%	33	0.26	2.6	55	72	$2
13	TAM	2	2	1	67	53	4.14	4.09	1.31	687	693	682	6.0	2.9	7.1	2.4	65%	10%	41	24	35	30%	70%	8%	0	21			100	0.84	-2.3	67	87	-$2
14	TAM	2	6	0	83	66	3.70	4.39	1.35	675	650	689	8.4	4.2	7.2	1.7	58%	8%	44	19	37	28%	75%	9%	7	30	29%	43%	0	0.59	0.4	37	44	-$2
1st Half		2	3	0	57	44	4.13	4.58	1.39	694	615	744	9.9	4.4	7.0	1.6	57%	7%	42	20	38	28%	73%	9%	7	36	29%	43%	0	0.60	-2.7	26	31	-$2
2nd Half		0	3	0	26	22	2.77	4.00	1.27	633	749	580	6.2	3.8	7.6	2.0	60%	8%	48	17	35	28%	81%	8%	0	24			0	0.56	3.1	60	72	-$1
15	**Proj**	**2**	**5**	**0**	**73**	**56**	**4.04**	**3.98**	**1.40**	**711**	**724**	**702**	**6.7**	**3.8**	**7.0**	**1.9**	**60%**	**9%**	**44**	**20**	**36**	**30%**	**73%**	**9%**	**0**						**-2.7**	**47**	**56**	**-$2**

Ranaudo,Anthony				Health	A	LIMA Plan	D
Age: 25	Th: R	Role	SP	PT/Exp	D	Rand Var	0
Ht: 6' 7"	Wt: 230	Type	xFB	Consist	F	MM	0001

4-3, 4.81 ERA in 39 IP at BOS. Towering righty can throw hard, and LOOKS like a strikeout guy. But SwK shows he's earned that mediocre K/9 rate. Add shaky Ctl and a serious FB lean, and it makes for a volatile cocktail—and says "not ready." Avoid until he starts missing more bats.

Yr	Tm	W	L	Sv	IP	K	ERA	xERA	WHIP	oOPS	vL	vR	BF/G	Ctl	Dom	Cmd	FpK	SwK	G	L	F	H%	S%	hr/f	GS	APC	DOM%	DIS%	Sv%	LI	RAR	BPV	BPX	R$
10																																		
11																																		
12	aa	1	3	0	38	23	9.05	7.06	2.09				20.5	6.8	5.4	0.8						35%	55%								-23.4	6	8	-$17
13	a/a	11	5	0	140	104	3.66	3.53	1.28				23.0	3.1	6.7	2.2						29%	73%								3.5	70	92	$6
14	BOS *	18	7	0	177	104	3.75	4.38	1.41	837	870	800	24.2	3.7	5.3	1.4	58%	6%	34	14	52	28%	77%	14%	7	91	29%	57%			-0.1	33	40	$3
1st Half		9	4	0	96	65	3.10	3.37	1.35				23.5	4.2	6.1	1.5						28%	77%	0%	0						7.5	62	74	$9
2nd Half		9	3	0	82	39	4.50	5.58	1.48	837	870	800	25.1	3.2	4.3	1.4	58%	6%	34	14	52	28%	76%	14%	7	91	29%	57%			-7.6	0	0	-$4
15	**Proj**	**7**	**6**	**0**	**112**	**71**	**4.38**	**4.77**	**1.43**	**704**	**734**	**672**	**23.0**	**3.5**	**5.7**	**1.6**	**58%**	**6%**	**34**	**14**	**52**	**29%**	**73%**	**7%**	**21**						**-8.8**	**20**	**23**	**-$3**

Rasmus,Cory				Health	A	LIMA Plan	B+
Age: 27	Th: R	Role	RP	PT/Exp	D	Rand Var	-1
Ht: 6' 0"	Wt: 200	Type	Pwr xFB	Consist	B	MM	2301

3-2, 2.57 ERA in 56 IP at LAA. Finally healthy the last couple years, and this season began to overcome his biggest hurdle, those walks. That's the metric to watch: With an 8-plus Dom, a sub-4 Ctl makes him a legit sleeper. If he keeps that & gets a rotation shot... UP: 170 IP, 10+ wins

Yr	Tm	W	L	Sv	IP	K	ERA	xERA	WHIP	oOPS	vL	vR	BF/G	Ctl	Dom	Cmd	FpK	SwK	G	L	F	H%	S%	hr/f	GS	APC	DOM%	DIS%	Sv%	LI	RAR	BPV	BPX	R$
10																																		
11																																		
12	aa	3	5	7	59	52	4.84	4.03	1.53				5.1	5.3	8.0	1.5						31%	67%								-6.0	68	89	-$3
13	2 TM *	5	3	17	68	65	2.94	3.31	1.29	910	1145	683	4.3	4.9	8.6	1.8	52%	13%	30	19	51	26%	82%	17%	0	21			85	0.57	7.8	71	93	$10
14	LAA *	5	3	2	84	76	2.96	2.81	1.15	578	647	520	6.4	3.3	8.1	2.4	58%	13%	38	19	43	27%	77%	8%	6	29	0%	100%	100	0.82	8.1	91	108	$6
1st Half		4	1	2	40	29	3.73	3.35	1.35	701	656	745	5.2	3.9	6.5	1.7	65%	13%	40	18	43	30%	71%	0%	0	20			100	0.49	0.0	70	83	$2
2nd Half		1	2	0	44	47	2.25	2.32	0.98	539	643	457	8.3	2.8	9.6	3.4	56%	13%	38	19	43	24%	84%	10%	6	35	0%	100%	0	1.02	8.1	115	137	$9
15	**Proj**	**6**	**5**	**0**	**102**	**96**	**3.46**	**3.76**	**1.27**	**606**	**717**	**519**	**5.4**	**3.9**	**8.5**	**2.2**	**56%**	**13%**	**40**	**19**	**41**	**28%**	**77%**	**9%**	**0**						**3.5**	**64**	**76**	**$4**

Redmond,Todd				Health	A	LIMA Plan	D+
Age: 30	Th: R	Role	RP	PT/Exp	D	Rand Var	-3
Ht: 6' 3"	Wt: 200	Type	xFB	Consist	B	MM	1201

Ridden hard in July (17 relief IP), and it showed up in lost Ctl, with at least 2 walks per outing from 7/31–8/15. Otherwise, basically the same guy in relief as starting. Fortuitous hr/f helped ERA, which is almost certain to spike. There are dozens like him, most with far less blowup risk.

Yr	Tm	W	L	Sv	IP	K	ERA	xERA	WHIP	oOPS	vL	vR	BF/G	Ctl	Dom	Cmd	FpK	SwK	G	L	F	H%	S%	hr/f	GS	APC	DOM%	DIS%	Sv%	LI	RAR	BPV	BPX	R$
10	aaa	9	10	0	163	118	5.25	5.00	1.42				24.7	2.6	6.5	2.5						32%	66%								-23.5	52	83	-$4
11	aaa	10	8	0	170	116	3.77	4.66	1.40				25.6	2.7	6.2	2.3						31%	77%								3.7	51	76	$3
12	CIN *	8	12	0	152	110	4.82	5.99	1.58	1193	1199	1167	24.8	2.8	6.5	2.3	59%	14%	33	27	40	35%	74%	17%	1	91	0%	100%			-15.1	35	46	-$10
13	TOR *	7	4	0	104	98	4.97	4.44	1.31	757	724	794	18.6	2.5	8.5	3.4	60%	11%	30	19	50	32%	65%	12%	14	76	36%	36%	0	0.80	-14.2	84	110	-$2
14	TOR	1	4	1	75	60	3.24	4.39	1.33	726	822	657	7.5	3.2	7.2	2.2	62%	9%	33	19	48	31%	77%	5%	0	29			100	0.53	4.6	53	63	$0
1st Half		0	4	1	42	32	2.98	4.24	1.35	742	859	639	8.9	2.3	6.8	2.9	66%	8%	34	20	47	33%	78%	3%	0	32			100	0.64	4.0	71	85	-$1
2nd Half		1	0	0	33	28	3.58	4.61	1.32	706	759	677	6.2	4.4	7.7	1.8	58%	9%	32	17	51	27%	75%	6%	0	25			0	0.42	0.6	29	35	$0
15	**Proj**	**3**	**3**	**0**	**73**	**57**	**4.33**	**4.17**	**1.37**	**822**	**859**	**791**	**10.6**	**3.1**	**7.0**	**2.3**	**61%**	**9%**	**32**	**19**	**50**	**30%**	**73%**	**10%**	**2**						**-5.2**	**53**	**63**	**-$3**

Reed,Addison				Health	A	LIMA Plan	B
Age: 26	Th: R	Role	RP	PT/Exp	A	Rand Var	+2
Ht: 6' 4"	Wt: 220	Type	Pwr xFB	Consist	A	MM	4530

Ah, the life of a flyball-prone closer. Errant wind gusts mean gopheritis is always a risk. But look closer: elite skills here, notably Dom/SwK, with solid control. Has always thrown in hitters parks, which hurts his rep, but regardless, when 1st half hr/f and 2nd half H% normalize, stats will finally match the gaudy save totals.

Yr	Tm	W	L	Sv	IP	K	ERA	xERA	WHIP	oOPS	vL	vR	BF/G	Ctl	Dom	Cmd	FpK	SwK	G	L	F	H%	S%	hr/f	GS	APC	DOM%	DIS%	Sv%	LI	RAR	BPV	BPX	R$
10																																		
11	CHW *	0	1	4	49	66	1.70	1.59	0.86	802	875	728	6.1	2.0	12.0	5.8	61%	18%	20	35	45	27%	85%	11%	0	23			67	0.13	13.6	193	290	$8
12	CHW	3	2	29	55	54	4.75	4.13	1.36	753	773	737	3.8	2.9	8.8	3.0	66%	10%	33	24	43	34%	67%	9%	0	15			88	1.53	-5.0	91	118	$8
13	CHW	5	4	40	71	72	3.79	3.75	1.11	603	608	597	4.3	2.9	9.1	3.1	65%	12%	33	22	45	28%	67%	7%	0	17			83	1.19	0.7	96	125	$19
14	ARI	1	7	32	59	69	4.25	3.51	1.21	740	610	863	4.1	2.3	10.5	4.6	66%	14%	29	23	48	32%	72%	14%	0	16			84	1.25	-3.7	134	160	$11
1st Half		1	3	19	34	40	3.93	3.31	1.14	744	681	799	4.1	1.8	10.5	5.7	65%	14%	32	23	45	30%	77%	19%	0	16			86	1.19	-0.8	149	178	$14
2nd Half		0	4	13	25	29	4.68	3.79	1.32	733	519	950	4.0	2.9	10.4	3.6	67%	14%	24	24	51	35%	67%	8%	0	16			81	1.33	-2.9	112	134	$7
15	**Proj**	**2**	**5**	**38**	**58**	**64**	**3.39**	**3.22**	**1.19**	**685**	**608**	**764**	**4.0**	**2.6**	**9.9**	**3.8**	**66%**	**13%**	**31**	**21**	**48**	**31%**	**77%**	**10%**	**0**						**2.5**	**117**	**139**	**$16**

Reed,Evan				Health	A	LIMA Plan	D+
Age: 29	Th: R	Role	RP	PT/Exp	D	Rand Var	+2
Ht: 6' 4"	Wt: 255	Type	Pwr xGB	Consist	C	MM	2100

0-1, 4.18 ERA in 32 IP at DET. Here's a safe bet: he'll do better than a 39% H%. Beyond that, well, there are some decent groundball skills here, and if Cmd gains hold, he MIGHT carve out a middle relief role. So if 1 vultured win and 0 saves floats your boat, go nuts.

Yr	Tm	W	L	Sv	IP	K	ERA	xERA	WHIP	oOPS	vL	vR	BF/G	Ctl	Dom	Cmd	FpK	SwK	G	L	F	H%	S%	hr/f	GS	APC	DOM%	DIS%	Sv%	LI	RAR	BPV	BPX	R$
10	a/a	2	1	5	43	33	2.00	3.44	1.35				5.6	3.2	6.9	2.2						32%	85%								11.0	84	135	$4
11																																		
12	a/a	5	4	13	67	60	5.99	5.08	1.68				6.1	4.2	8.0	1.9						38%	62%								-16.4	69	90	-$5
13	DET *	1	5	1	73	54	3.75	4.02	1.47	775	760	782	6.5	3.7	6.6	1.8	58%	9%	53	22	26	33%	74%	10%	0	24			100	0.36	1.1	65	85	-$3
14	DET *	0	2	0	56	45	4.84	5.04	1.62	776	870	696	5.0	2.8	7.3	2.6	57%	11%	56	20	24	39%	68%	8%	0	18			0	0.55	-7.5	79	95	-$8
1st Half		0	1	0	29	25	5.14	5.54	1.69	813	933	716	4.6	3.5	8.0	2.3	56%	11%	56	22	23	39%	69%	10%	0	19			0	0.55	-4.9	69	83	-$9
2nd Half		0	1	0	27	20	4.52	4.52	1.54	535	522	550	5.6	2.2	6.5	3.0	60%	12%	56	13	31	38%	67%	0%	0	15			0	0.57	-2.6	93	111	-$6
15	**Proj**	**1**	**2**	**0**	**36**	**27**	**4.42**	**3.98**	**1.45**	**664**	**788**	**564**	**5.5**	**3.7**	**6.6**	**1.8**	**56%**	**11%**	**50**	**20**	**30**	**31%**	**70%**	**9%**	**0**						**-3.0**	**46**	**55**	**-$4**

ROD TRUESDELL

Richards,Garrett

Age: 27 | Th: R | Role: RP | Ht: 6' 3" | Wt: 210 | Type: Pwr GB
Health: D | PT/Exp: B | Consist: B | LIMA Plan: D+ | Rand Var: -2 | MM: 4203

Torn patellar tendon ended year in August. Even with the injury, we can still call this a massive breakout, even a bit better than we forecasted a year ago. Now, with a 6- to 9-month recovery time, he'll be late to the '15 party. With these skills, he's worth inviting, even for a partial season.

Yr Tm	W	L	Sv	IP	K	ERA	xERA	WHIP	oOPS	vL	vR	BF/G	Ctl	Dom	Cmd	FpK	SwK	G	L	F	H%	S%	hr/f	GS	APC	DOM%	DIS%	Sv%	LI	RAR	BPV	BPX	R$
10																																	
11 LAA *	12	4	0	157	96	3.94	3.89	1.30	989	1140	813	22.3	2.7	5.5	2.1	66%	9%	43	28	28	29%	71%	31%	3	36	0%	67%	0	0.64	0.1	54	81	$5
12 LAA *	11	6	1	148	102	4.23	4.65	1.54	793	900	682	14.7	3.9	6.2	1.6	55%	11%	45	22	33	33%	73%	9%	9	40	22%	22%	33	0.95	-3.9	50	65	-$4
13 LAA	7	8	1	145	101	4.16	3.70	1.34	699	751	626	13.2	2.7	6.3	2.3	54%	9%	58	19	23	31%	70%	11%	17	50	59%	18%	50	0.78	-5.2	75	98	$0
14 LAA	13	4	0	169	164	2.61	3.08	1.04	529	519	542	26.1	2.7	8.8	3.2	55%	11%	51	21	28	28%	74%	4%	26	101	81%	8%			23.4	113	135	$21
1st Half	8	2	0	101	99	2.76	3.33	1.12	548	550	545	25.8	3.4	8.8	2.6	52%	11%	48	22	30	28%	75%	4%	16	101	75%	6%			12.2	94	112	$23
2nd Half	5	2	0	68	65	2.39	2.72	0.92	500	453	540	26.5	1.7	8.6	5.0	60%	11%	55	20	25	27%	73%	4%	10	101	90%	10%			11.2	142	169	$17
15 Proj	**10**	**5**	**0**	**145**	**125**	**3.34**	**3.12**	**1.20**	**624**	**653**	**590**	**18.2**	**2.7**	**7.8**	**2.8**	**56%**	**11%**	**53**	**20**	**27**	**30%**	**72%**	**7%**	**26**						**7.1**	**97**	**116**	**$10**

Rienzo,Andre

Age: 27 | Th: R | Role: RP | Ht: 6' 3" | Wt: 190 | Type: Pwr
Health: A | PT/Exp: D | Consist: C | LIMA Plan: D | Rand Var: +3 | MM: 1200

4-5, 6.82 ERA in 65 IP at CHW. That's two years in a row where his stuff simply hasn't played up to the higher levels. Awful control, and when he did get something over, it was pounded mercilessly. He's a bit better than this debacle, but let those positive skills germinate in the free agent pool this year.

Yr Tm	W	L	Sv	IP	K	ERA	xERA	WHIP	oOPS	vL	vR	BF/G	Ctl	Dom	Cmd	FpK	SwK	G	L	F	H%	S%	hr/f	GS	APC	DOM%	DIS%	Sv%	LI	RAR	BPV	BPX	R$
10																																	
11																																	
12 a/a	4	3	0	78	70	4.05	3.81	1.50				24.2	4.8	8.0	1.7						32%	72%								-0.4	77	101	-$3
13 CHW *	10	9	0	169	132	5.16	5.01	1.57	794	780	821	24.8	4.4	7.1	1.6	48%	7%	48	19	33	32%	69%	18%	10	94	50%	30%			-26.9	43	56	-$12
14 CHW *	5	9	0	111	86	5.83	5.94	1.72	898	920	871	18.0	4.8	7.0	1.5	51%	9%	45	22	33	34%	68%	17%	11	70	18%	36%	0	0.54	-28.7	28	33	-$15
1st Half	4	7	0	73	52	5.76	5.58	1.64	823	832	810	20.3	4.4	6.5	1.5	51%	9%	44	22	34	32%	67%	13%	11	87	18%	36%	0	0.73	-18.2	29	35	-$15
2nd Half	1	2	0	38	34	5.96	6.65	1.87	1519	1768	1289	15.0	5.5	7.9	1.4	56%	7%	52	26	22	36%	71%	60%	0	27			0	0.04	-10.5	26	31	-$15
15 Proj	**2**	**3**	**0**	**44**	**34**	**5.33**	**4.43**	**1.67**	**817**	**810**	**829**	**19.8**	**4.8**	**7.1**	**1.5**	**50%**	**8%**	**45**	**21**	**35**	**33%**	**70%**	**11%**	**10**						**-8.5**	**21**	**25**	**-$7**

Roark,Tanner

Age: 28 | Th: R | Role: SP | Ht: 6' 2" | Wt: 230 | Type: Con
Health: A | PT/Exp: B | Consist: F | LIMA Plan: C | Rand Var: -2 | MM: 3105

Why his ERA will go up: Troubling fly ball trend, H%/S% likely to normalize. Why it won't be a disaster: Elite Ctl, growing SwK keeps baserunners—and bad starts—to a minimum. 2014 xERA showed he wasn't a true sub-3.00 ERA starting pitcher. Last year's bargain will be overvalued this time around.

Yr Tm	W	L	Sv	IP	K	ERA	xERA	WHIP	oOPS	vL	vR	BF/G	Ctl	Dom	Cmd	FpK	SwK	G	L	F	H%	S%	hr/f	GS	APC	DOM%	DIS%	Sv%	LI	RAR	BPV	BPX	R$
10 aa	11	6	0	141	88	4.93	5.47	1.58				22.2	2.8	5.6	2.0						35%	70%								-14.8	40	64	-$5
11 aa	9	9	0	117	72	5.87	5.47	1.61				24.7	3.0	5.6	1.9						35%	63%								-27.7	39	58	-$11
12 aaa	6	17	0	148	100	5.47	5.74	1.63				23.5	2.8	6.1	2.1						36%	67%								-26.5	43	57	-$17
13 WAS *	16	4	2	159	103	3.04	2.60	1.08	476	634	358	13.2	1.8	5.8	3.3	71%	7%	50	24	26	28%	72%	3%	5	54	80%	0%	100	0.95	16.3	99	129	$18
14 WAS	15	10	0	199	138	2.85	3.80	1.09	632	672	591	25.7	1.8	6.3	3.5	65%	9%	41	21	38	28%	77%	7%	31	97	71%	6%			21.7	84	100	$19
1st Half	7	5	0	100	74	2.98	3.76	1.15	642	650	634	25.6	2.2	6.7	3.1	66%	8%	47	17	37	29%	76%	6%	16	96	63%	13%			9.4	86	103	$17
2nd Half	8	5	0	99	64	2.73	3.83	1.03	623	693	546	25.9	1.4	5.8	4.3	64%	9%	36	24	39	27%	77%	8%	15	97	80%	0%			12.4	82	98	$22
15 Proj	**15**	**10**	**0**	**189**	**126**	**3.54**	**3.60**	**1.21**	**684**	**793**	**584**	**24.3**	**2.0**	**6.0**	**3.0**	**67%**	**8%**	**44**	**22**	**33**	**30%**	**72%**	**8%**	**32**						**4.8**	**77**	**91**	**$12**

Robertson,David

Age: 30 | Th: R | Role: RP | Ht: 5' 11" | Wt: 195 | Type: Pwr
Health: C | PT/Exp: C | Consist: A | LIMA Plan: C+ | Rand Var: +3 | MM: 5530

No pressure HERE, he merely replaced Superman in Metropolis. And he held up remarkably well: 89% Sv% equalled Mo's career average. Well supported with surge in Dom and SwK, and if Ctl spike normalizes to past 2-year levels, we're talking Eck-territory BPV. Newest elite closer in town.

Yr Tm	W	L	Sv	IP	K	ERA	xERA	WHIP	oOPS	vL	vR	BF/G	Ctl	Dom	Cmd	FpK	SwK	G	L	F	H%	S%	hr/f	GS	APC	DOM%	DIS%	Sv%	LI	RAR	BPV	BPX	R$
10 NYY	4	5	1	61	71	3.82	3.74	1.50	724	759	697	4.3	4.8	10.4	2.2	55%	8%	40	25	36	35%	76%	9%	0	18			33	1.12	2.0	75	121	$0
11 NYY	4	0	1	67	100	1.08	2.57	1.13	506	466	549	3.9	4.7	13.5	2.9	61%	11%	46	22	32	31%	91%	2%	0	17			25	1.38	23.5	139	210	$11
12 NYY	2	7	2	61	81	2.67	2.84	1.17	638	575	710	3.8	2.8	12.0	4.3	65%	10%	45	20	35	34%	80%	10%	0	15			40	1.15	10.1	163	213	$5
13 NYY	5	1	3	66	77	2.04	2.66	1.04	584	484	695	3.7	2.4	10.4	4.3	59%	10%	51	20	29	29%	84%	11%	0	15			60	1.19	15.0	151	197	$9
14 NYY	4	5	39	64	96	3.08	2.38	1.06	588	437	765	4.1	3.2	13.4	4.2	61%	13%	44	23	33	31%	75%	16%	0	17			89	1.67	5.3	177	211	$20
1st Half	0	2	18	28	48	2.93	1.76	1.01	588	428	807	4.1	2.9	15.6	5.3	57%	14%	53	19	28	35%	76%	20%	0	18			90	1.78	2.8	233	278	$15
2nd Half	4	3	21	37	48	3.19	2.88	1.09	588	445	738	4.1	3.4	11.8	3.4	64%	12%	39	26	35	28%	75%	13%	0	16			88	1.58	2.5	136	162	$24
15 Proj	**4**	**4**	**43**	**65**	**89**	**2.70**	**2.39**	**1.10**	**598**	**485**	**723**	**3.8**	**3.1**	**12.3**	**3.9**	**61%**	**11%**	**46**	**22**	**32**	**31%**	**79%**	**13%**	**0**						**8.4**	**160**	**191**	**$23**

Rodney,Fernando

Age: 38 | Th: R | Role: RP | Ht: 5' 11" | Wt: 220 | Type: Pwr GB
Health: B | PT/Exp: A | Consist: A | LIMA Plan: C | Rand Var: -1 | MM: 5530

A Colon-like late-career surge, with three best skills seasons starting at age 35. 2nd half Ctl spike mostly driven by one September meltdown vs. OAK, when he walked 4. All signs point to another solid year, and another big save total. But how far do you push the bidding for a 38-year-old? You don't. I'll go $15.

Yr Tm	W	L	Sv	IP	K	ERA	xERA	WHIP	oOPS	vL	vR	BF/G	Ctl	Dom	Cmd	FpK	SwK	G	L	F	H%	S%	hr/f	GS	APC	DOM%	DIS%	Sv%	LI	RAR	BPV	BPX	R$
10 LAA	4	3	14	68	53	4.24	4.32	1.54	739	728	750	4.3	4.6	7.0	1.5	52%	10%	50	20	30	32%	72%	6%	0	18			67	1.10	-1.3	29	47	$3
11 LAA	3	5	3	32	26	4.50	4.87	1.69	672	766	588	3.8	7.9	7.3	0.9	62%	9%	58	19	22	28%	72%	5%	0	16			43	1.69	-2.2	-45	-68	-$3
12 TAM	2	2	48	75	76	0.60	2.58	0.78	417	435	394	3.7	1.8	9.2	5.1	61%	13%	58	17	25	23%	95%	4%	0	15			96	1.24	31.4	152	198	$37
13 TAM	5	4	37	67	82	3.38	3.24	1.34	634	716	538	4.3	4.9	11.1	2.3	56%	13%	51	25	25	32%	74%	7%	0	18			82	1.34	4.0	97	126	$17
14 SEA	1	6	48	66	76	2.85	3.19	1.34	646	726	530	4.1	3.8	10.3	2.7	60%	11%	49	24	27	34%	79%	6%	0	16			94	1.36	7.3	110	131	$19
1st Half	1	3	23	32	37	2.23	2.87	1.24	608	758	393	4.0	3.1	10.3	3.4	58%	11%	49	27	24	34%	82%	5%	0	16			92	1.42	6.0	130	155	$20
2nd Half	0	3	25	34	39	3.44	3.51	1.44	682	697	657	4.3	4.5	10.3	2.3	62%	11%	48	22	30	35%	77%	7%	0	17			96	1.30	1.3	90	108	$18
15 Proj	**3**	**4**	**38**	**65**	**73**	**3.12**	**3.02**	**1.29**	**622**	**684**	**543**	**4.0**	**4.1**	**10.0**	**2.5**	**59%**	**12%**	**51**	**23**	**26**	**32%**	**76%**	**6%**	**0**						**5.0**	**99**	**118**	**$17**

Rodon,Carlos

Age: 22 | Th: L | Role: SP | Ht: 6' 3" | Wt: 234 | Type: Pwr
Health: A | PT/Exp: F | Consist: F | LIMA Plan: C | Rand Var: 0 | MM: 3300

2014 first rounder out of NC State appears to be on a Sale-esque fast track to CHW. Often compared to David Price, the hard-throwing lefty with a malevolent slider posted a 2.92 ERA and 38/13 K/BB in 25 IP in minors, including a 3-start stint in Triple-A. Keeper league must-own.

Yr Tm	W	L	Sv	IP	K	ERA	xERA	WHIP	oOPS	vL	vR	BF/G	Ctl	Dom	Cmd	FpK	SwK	G	L	F	H%	S%	hr/f	GS	APC	DOM%	DIS%	Sv%	LI	RAR	BPV	BPX	R$
10																																	
11																																	
12																																	
13																																	
14																																	
1st Half																																	
2nd Half																																	
15 Proj	**4**	**3**	**0**	**56**	**53**	**3.86**	**3.65**	**1.36**				**21.6**	**4.2**	**8.5**	**2.0**	**59%**	**9%**	**45**	**20**	**35**	**30%**	**73%**	**9%**	**24**						**-0.8**	**64**	**76**	**-$1**

Rodriguez,Fernando

Age: 31 | Th: R | Role: RP | Ht: 6' 3" | Wt: 235 | Type: Pwr FB
Health: F | PT/Exp: D | Consist: C | LIMA Plan: C | Rand Var: -5 | MM: 2300

1-0, 1.00 ERA in 9 IP at OAK. Another TJS success story? Started a nice little comeback after missing all of 2013. Skills play better in relief, 2nd half Dom growth bodes well post-surgery. xFB ways an issue in smaller parks, though. Likely won't see high-leverage use, but watch Dom for upside.

Yr Tm	W	L	Sv	IP	K	ERA	xERA	WHIP	oOPS	vL	vR	BF/G	Ctl	Dom	Cmd	FpK	SwK	G	L	F	H%	S%	hr/f	GS	APC	DOM%	DIS%	Sv%	LI	RAR	BPV	BPX	R$
10 aaa	4	6	0	97	66	6.15	7.05	1.92				14.9	3.6	6.1	1.7						40%	69%								-24.8	26	42	-$14
11 HOU *	4	6	2	76	83	3.29	4.21	1.47	781	755	796	5.2	4.9	9.8	2.0	54%	9%	35	22	43	32%	81%	11%	0	20			100	0.97	6.2	77	116	$2
12 HOU	2	10	0	70	78	5.37	4.25	1.45	764	710	792	4.4	4.4	10.0	2.3	59%	11%	35	18	46	33%	65%	11%	0	18			0	1.28	-11.8	75	98	-$7
13																																	
14 OAK *	4	0	0	55	43	1.96	3.16	1.28	343	413	300	5.0	3.1	7.1	2.3	58%	7%	33	11	56	31%	85%	0%	0	17			0	0.57	12.0	87	103	$3
1st Half	2	0	0	31	21	2.21	2.38	1.19	379	413	353	5.1	3.4	6.1	1.8	60%	8%	33	13	54	28%	79%	0%	0	19			0	0.65	5.8	85	101	$3
2nd Half	2	0	0	24	22	1.63	4.17	1.38	0	0	0	4.8	2.8	8.3	3.0	33%	0%	33	0	67	35%	92%	0%	0	7			0	0.09	6.2	92	110	$3
15 Proj	**3**	**3**	**0**	**51**	**47**	**3.37**	**3.82**	**1.32**	**692**	**645**	**718**	**5.0**	**3.6**	**8.3**	**2.3**	**57%**	**10%**	**35**	**20**	**45**	**30%**	**77%**	**7%**	**0**						**2.3**	**65**	**77**	**$0**

ROD TRUESDELL

Rodriguez,Francisco

			Health: B	LIMA Plan: C
Age: 33	Th: R	Role: RP	PT/Exp: B	Rand Var: -1
Ht: 6' 0"	Wt: 195	Type: Pwr	Consist: A	MM: 5430

Rode 2013 skills rebound to another full-time stopper shot, and boy did it go well. The key was his changeup - 30% SwK%, its highest since 2011. Best Cmd of his career too. Likely regressions of H% and hr/f should offset each other. With elite skills in last 4 of 5 years, he's got the goods to ride this secondary wave.

Yr	Tm	W	L	Sv	IP	K	ERA	xERA	WHIP	oOPS	vL	vR	BF/G	Ctl	Dom	Cmd	FpK	SwK	G	L	F	H%	S%	hr/f	GS	APC	DOM%	DIS%	Sv%	LI	RAR	BPV	BPX	R$
10	NYM	4	2	25	57	67	2.20	3.19	1.15	597	680	531	4.5	3.3	10.5	3.2	60%	12%	42	19	39	31%	83%	5%	0	18			83	1.22	13.3	120	195	$16
11	2 NL	6	2	23	72	79	2.64	3.17	1.30	663	776	515	4.2	3.3	9.9	3.0	57%	13%	52	17	31	34%	81%	6%	0	16			79	1.37	11.5	120	181	$14
12	MIL	2	7	3	72	72	4.38	3.87	1.33	708	723	684	3.9	3.9	9.0	2.3	61%	8%	42	26	33	30%	69%	12%	0	16			30	1.15	-3.2	77	101	-$1
13	2 TM	3	2	10	47	54	2.70	3.22	1.20	734	513	1003	4.0	2.7	10.4	3.9	60%	11%	36	25	39	31%	86%	15%	0	16			100	0.91	6.7	129	168	$6
14	MIL	5	5	44	68	73	3.04	2.99	0.99	648	526	772	3.9	2.4	9.7	4.1	59%	12%	44	21	35	23%	83%	23%	0	15			90	1.19	5.8	132	157	$23
1st Half		3	2	27	42	49	2.34	2.65	0.87	571	522	617	3.8	1.9	10.4	5.4	60%	12%	41	24	35	24%	84%	17%	0	15			90	1.23	7.3	155	185	$29
2nd Half		2	3	17	26	24	4.21	3.58	1.17	768	531	1032	4.0	3.2	8.4	2.7	57%	11%	48	18	34	21%	82%	32%	0	15			89	1.12	-1.5	92	110	$13
15	Proj	**4**	**5**	**39**	**65**	**69**	**3.30**	**3.01**	**1.15**	**699**	**575**	**835**	**3.8**	**2.9**	**9.6**	**3.3**	**59%**	**11%**	**43**	**22**	**35**	**27%**	**81%**	**20%**	**0**						**3.5**	**114**	**136**	**$19**

Rodriguez,Wandy

			Health: F	LIMA Plan: C
Age: 36	Th: L	Role: SP	PT/Exp: C	Rand Var: +5
Ht: 5' 10"	Wt: 195	Type:	Consist: B	MM: 2101

Miserable year resulted in May release, then knee surgery ended it in June. Even with good health, prior mid-3.00s ERA baseline is probably history. Worsening DOM/DIS% underscores volatility. Plus, that 2013 Ctl is clearly an anomaly, and with marginal Dom, room for error is tiny. Risk far greater than reward now.

Yr	Tm	W	L	Sv	IP	K	ERA	xERA	WHIP	oOPS	vL	vR	BF/G	Ctl	Dom	Cmd	FpK	SwK	G	L	F	H%	S%	hr/f	GS	APC	DOM%	DIS%	Sv%	LI	RAR	BPV	BPX	R$
10	HOU	11	12	0	195	178	3.60	3.53	1.29	700	642	715	25.7	3.1	8.2	2.6	60%	9%	48	20	32	31%	74%	9%	32	100	66%	16%			11.5	89	144	$12
11	HOU	11	11	0	191	166	3.49	3.75	1.31	739	628	768	26.9	3.3	7.8	2.4	62%	9%	45	20	35	30%	78%	13%	30	105	57%	7%			10.7	76	114	$10
12	2 NL	12	13	0	206	139	3.76	4.19	1.27	695	689	697	25.7	2.5	6.1	2.5	66%	8%	48	20	32	29%	73%	10%	33	94	52%	15%	0	0.83	6.4	69	90	$9
13	PIT	6	4	0	63	46	3.59	3.87	1.12	707	785	681	21.7	1.7	6.6	3.8	62%	7%	42	19	39	27%	75%	13%	12	86	50%	25%			2.1	92	120	$3
14	PIT	0	2	0	27	20	6.75	4.68	1.69	1059	898	1087	20.8	2.7	6.8	2.5	62%	8%	42	15	42	33%	71%	26%	6	76	17%	50%			-9.9	69	82	-$7
1st Half		0	2	0	27	20	6.75	4.68	1.69	1059	898	1087	20.8	2.7	6.8	2.5	62%	8%	42	15	42	33%	71%	26%	6	76	17%	50%			-9.9	69	82	-$7
2nd Half																																		
15	Proj	**5**	**6**	**0**	**95**	**72**	**4.57**	**3.74**	**1.37**	**822**	**750**	**839**	**22.4**	**2.6**	**6.9**	**2.7**	**63%**	**8%**	**45**	**18**	**37**	**30%**	**74%**	**17%**	**18**						**-9.6**	**77**	**92**	**-$3**

Rogers,Esmil

			Health: C	LIMA Plan: D+
Age: 29	Th: R	Role: RP	PT/Exp: C	Rand Var: +2
Ht: 6' 3"	Wt: 200	Type: Pwr	Consist: B	MM: 2200

2-0, 5.72 ERA in 46 IP at TOR/NYY. Talented arm has never been able to put raw tools to use, but they're still there. Few are better against RHB (9.4 Dom, 6.8 Cmd). But lefties murder him, so somebody needs to stick him in short relief and let him develop there. Keep on radar but avoid until role is better defined.

Yr	Tm	W	L	Sv	IP	K	ERA	xERA	WHIP	oOPS	vL	vR	BF/G	Ctl	Dom	Cmd	FpK	SwK	G	L	F	H%	S%	hr/f	GS	APC	DOM%	DIS%	Sv%	LI	RAR	BPV	BPX	R$
10	COL *	5	6	0	133	106	6.14	5.08	1.55	835	919	772	14.5	3.0	7.2	2.4	51%	10%	52	21	27	36%	59%	8%	8	45	13%	50%	0	0.85	-33.9	65	105	-$11
11	COL *	7	9	0	110	76	6.80	7.13	1.90	919	991	860	21.6	4.3	6.2	1.4	59%	8%	42	22	35	37%	66%	14%	13	84	46%	38%	0	0.63	-38.8	10	15	-$20
12	2 TM	3	3	0	79	83	4.69	3.63	1.44	749	676	817	5.2	3.4	9.5	2.8	59%	10%	47	23	30	35%	68%	10%	0	22			0	0.77	-6.6	103	135	-$4
13	TOR	5	9	0	138	96	4.77	4.12	1.42	799	854	731	13.6	2.9	6.3	2.2	56%	7%	47	23	30	31%	70%	16%	20	51	35%	35%	0	0.67	-15.4	60	79	-$7
14	2 AL *	4	2	0	94	75	5.14	5.06	1.54	809	959	677	8.9	3.6	7.2	2.0	60%	9%	38	20	43	33%	68%	14%	1	25	100%	0%	0	0.88	-16.3	51	61	-$8
1st Half		2	1	0	50	44	5.55	5.89	1.67	932	1165	692	8.9	3.6	7.9	2.2	63%	10%	41	15	44	37%	68%	17%	0	26			0	0.38	-11.1	52	62	-$12
2nd Half		2	1	0	45	31	4.68	4.13	1.39	694	729	665	8.9	3.7	6.3	1.7	58%	9%	34	24	41	29%	67%	10%	1	24	100%	0%	0	1.32	-5.2	51	61	-$4
15	Proj	**3**	**2**	**0**	**64**	**50**	**4.07**	**3.87**	**1.37**	**722**	**793**	**653**	**8.8**	**3.4**	**7.1**	**2.1**	**58%**	**9%**	**42**	**22**	**36**	**30%**	**73%**	**11%**	**0**						**-2.5**	**56**	**67**	**-$2**

Romo,Sergio

			Health: A	LIMA Plan: B
Age: 32	Th: R	Role: RP	PT/Exp: B	Rand Var: 0
Ht: 5' 10"	Wt: 185	Type: Pwr FB	Consist: A	MM: 5530

Early bouts of gopheritis cost him closer job. Chronically cranky elbow, declining Dom heading into year foreshadowed problems, but it was hr/f and S% that teamed to torpedo him. Dom, BPV spikes in 2nd half confirm that he's still made of closer stock, as does elite FpK and SwK combo. There's profit here now.

Yr	Tm	W	L	Sv	IP	K	ERA	xERA	WHIP	oOPS	vL	vR	BF/G	Ctl	Dom	Cmd	FpK	SwK	G	L	F	H%	S%	hr/f	GS	APC	DOM%	DIS%	Sv%	LI	RAR	BPV	BPX	R$
10	SF	5	3	0	62	70	2.18	3.20	0.97	599	652	570	3.6	2.0	10.2	5.0	69%	14%	35	14	51	28%	83%	8%	0	13			0	1.28	14.5	141	228	$9
11	SF	3	1	1	48	70	1.50	2.03	0.71	458	599	402	2.7	0.9	13.1	14.0	72%	17%	34	24	42	29%	81%	5%	0	10			50	1.39	14.5	223	335	$10
12	SF	4	2	14	55	63	1.79	2.64	0.85	525	491	537	3.1	1.6	10.2	6.3	67%	16%	49	21	30	26%	86%	12%	0	12			93	1.43	15.2	168	219	$15
13	SF	5	8	38	60	58	2.54	3.39	1.08	614	745	511	3.8	1.8	8.7	4.8	69%	14%	41	24	36	30%	80%	8%	0	15			88	1.58	9.9	126	165	$21
14	SF	6	4	23	58	59	3.72	3.27	0.95	622	777	528	3.6	1.9	9.2	4.9	69%	15%	37	18	45	25%	67%	13%	0	14			82	1.26	0.1	130	154	$13
1st Half		3	3	22	32	27	5.01	3.55	1.02	680	826	586	3.9	1.9	7.5	3.9	75%	14%	41	19	41	24%	56%	16%	0	15			81	1.45	-5.1	101	121	$16
2nd Half		3	1	1	26	32	2.10	2.95	0.86	547	706	452	3.3	1.8	11.2	6.4	62%	15%	31	16	52	26%	84%	9%	0	12			100	1.05	5.2	164	195	$10
15	Proj	**5**	**4**	**25**	**58**	**63**	**2.72**	**2.73**	**0.94**	**587**	**714**	**511**	**3.3**	**1.8**	**9.7**	**5.5**	**68%**	**15%**	**38**	**20**	**42**	**27%**	**77%**	**11%**	**0**						**7.3**	**144**	**172**	**$17**

Rondon,Bruce

			Health: F	LIMA Plan: A
Age: 24	Th: R	Role: RP	PT/Exp: F	Rand Var: 0
Ht: 6' 3"	Wt: 275	Type: Pwr	Consist: A	MM: 4510

High-octane arm fell victim to TJS in March. 120 BPV flashed in 2nd half of 2013 proof he could enter late-game mix soon. Missing piece is command vs. LH (1.3 Cmd in 2013). Lethal vs. RHers (10.2 Dom, 6.7 Cmd), 100-mph fastball, 27% SwK% on slider give him all the tools. Great stash. UP: 30 saves

Yr	Tm	W	L	Sv	IP	K	ERA	xERA	WHIP	oOPS	vL	vR	BF/G	Ctl	Dom	Cmd	FpK	SwK	G	L	F	H%	S%	hr/f	GS	APC	DOM%	DIS%	Sv%	LI	RAR	BPV	BPX	R$
10																																		
11																																		
12	a/a	1	1	14	30	26	1.45	3.03	1.28				4.1	4.6	8.0	1.7						26%	93%								9.4	77	100	$6
13	DET *	2	3	15	58	63	2.68	2.58	1.18	720	873	608	3.9	3.8	9.6	2.6	47%	15%	47	24	29	29%	78%	9%	0	15			79	0.93	8.5	110	143	$9
14																																		
1st Half																																		
2nd Half																																		
15	Proj	**2**	**2**	**3**	**42**	**50**	**2.89**	**3.16**	**1.30**				**3.6**	**4.1**	**10.7**	**2.6**	**0%**	**0%**				**33%**	**79%**		**0**						**4.5**	**113**	**134**	**$1**

Rondon,Hector

			Health: A	LIMA Plan: C
Age: 27	Th: R	Role: RP	PT/Exp: C	Rand Var: -2
Ht: 6' 3"	Wt: 180	Type: Pwr	Consist: C	MM: 4330

Turned from toiling middleman to reliable closer by adding two mph to fastball and plenty of control. Those Ctl gains came with full FpK support, so they can stick. Skills got even better as season went along, and that 2nd half LI shows it was in even higher leverage situations. Solid, 2nd tier saves option.

Yr	Tm	W	L	Sv	IP	K	ERA	xERA	WHIP	oOPS	vL	vR	BF/G	Ctl	Dom	Cmd	FpK	SwK	G	L	F	H%	S%	hr/f	GS	APC	DOM%	DIS%	Sv%	LI	RAR	BPV	BPX	R$
10	aaa	1	3	0	32	29	8.88	9.02	1.91				21.4	2.7	8.1	3.0						40%	58%								-18.8	6	10	-$9
11																																		
12																																		
13	CHC	2	1	0	55	44	4.77	4.39	1.41	737	546	908	5.4	4.1	7.2	1.8	54%	11%	43	22	35	29%	68%	10%	0	21			0	0.65	-6.1	40	52	-$5
14	CHC	4	4	29	63	63	2.42	2.99	1.06	526	616	454	4.0	2.1	9.0	4.2	65%	12%	49	23	28	30%	77%	4%	0	16			88	1.16	10.4	131	156	$17
1st Half		1	2	10	31	36	3.73	3.05	1.31	602	622	586	4.3	3.4	10.3	3.0	67%	13%	51	21	27	35%	70%	4%	0	17			83	0.94	0.0	122	146	$7
2nd Half		3	2	19	32	27	1.13	2.91	0.81	447	607	316	3.7	0.8	7.6	9.0	63%	10%	47	25	28	26%	88%	4%	0	14			90	1.36	10.3	139	166	$26
15	Proj	**3**	**3**	**33**	**58**	**52**	**3.15**	**3.15**	**1.16**	**609**	**589**	**626**	**4.8**	**2.6**	**8.1**	**3.1**	**60%**	**11%**	**47**	**23**	**31**	**30%**	**74%**	**8%**	**0**						**4.3**	**100**	**119**	**$16**

Rosenthal,Trevor

			Health: A	LIMA Plan: C+
Age: 25	Th: R	Role: RP	PT/Exp: B	Rand Var: -1
Ht: 6' 2"	Wt: 220	Type: Pwr	Consist: B	MM: 5531

Drafted as 1st tier closer after superb 2013. In spite of sexy saves total, this was a mess. Bad Ctl result of inability to get strike one (FpK), then H% gods cursed him late. High Sv%, LI reflect manager's faith, ability to work out of jams, so he's got role security for now. But too risky to be your #1 stopper.

Yr	Tm	W	L	Sv	IP	K	ERA	xERA	WHIP	oOPS	vL	vR	BF/G	Ctl	Dom	Cmd	FpK	SwK	G	L	F	H%	S%	hr/f	GS	APC	DOM%	DIS%	Sv%	LI	RAR	BPV	BPX	R$
10																																		
11																																		
12	STL *	8	8	0	132	114	3.06	2.40	1.09	513	395	597	13.2	3.2	7.8	2.4	58%	13%	54	13	33	26%	73%	11%	0	19			0	0.63	15.6	94	123	$14
13	STL	2	4	3	75	108	2.63	2.47	1.10	608	586	626	4.2	2.4	12.9	5.4	63%	15%	44	19	36	36%	77%	6%	0	17			38	1.21	11.5	190	247	$7
14	STL	2	6	45	70	87	3.20	3.69	1.41	641	523	738	4.3	5.4	11.1	2.1	56%	13%	38	25	37	33%	76%	3%	0	18			88	1.42	4.7	71	85	$17
1st Half		0	3	24	38	49	3.05	3.44	1.28	589	517	659	4.4	5.4	11.5	2.1	56%	13%	38	28	34	30%	75%	3%	0	18			89	1.49	3.3	78	93	$18
2nd Half		2	3	21	32	38	3.38	3.99	1.56	700	530	813	4.1	5.3	10.7	2.0	57%	13%	38	22	40	36%	78%	3%	0	17			88	1.34	1.4	64	76	$16
15	Proj	**3**	**5**	**32**	**73**	**90**	**3.38**	**3.04**	**1.25**	**607**	**521**	**676**	**4.5**	**4.2**	**11.2**	**2.6**	**59%**	**14%**	**41**	**23**	**37**	**32%**	**72%**	**5%**	**0**						**3.3**	**105**	**125**	**$15**

STEPHEN NICKRAND

Ross,Robbie

Age: 26 | Th: L | Role: RP | Ht: 5' 11" | Wt: 215 | Type: GB
Health: A | PT/Exp: C | Consist: C
LIMA Plan: C | Rand Var: +2 | MM: 3101

3-6, 6.20 ERA in 78 IP at TEX. To say re-conversion to a starting role didn't go well would be an understatement. Right-handed bats killed him. Has fared better against them in the past, so there's a glimmer of hope for a rebound—if he ends up back in the pen. Avoid if he's a starter.

Yr	Tm	W	L	Sv	IP	K	ERA	xERA	WHIP	oOPS	vL	vR	BF/G	Ctl	Dom	Cmd	FpK	SwK	G	L	F	H%	S%	hr/f	GS	APC	DOM%	DIS%	Sv%	LI	RAR	BPV	BPX	R$
10																																		
11	aa	1	1	0	38	30	3.14	4.01	1.12				25.0	1.2	7.1	5.9						29%	81%								3.8	125	189	$0
12	TEX	6	0	0	65	47	2.22	3.52	1.20	624	613	632	4.6	3.2	6.5	2.0	58%	8%	62	18	20	28%	83%	8%	0	18			0	0.97	14.4	71	93	$6
13	TEX	4	2	0	62	58	3.03	3.43	1.32	684	950	523	4.1	2.7	8.4	3.1	68%	11%	45	28	26	33%	78%	8%	0	15			0	1.18	6.4	100	130	$1
14	TEX *	8	10	0	139	85	5.61	5.72	1.62	851	766	892	15.8	3.0	5.5	1.8	67%	7%	54	19	27	34%	66%	12%	12	50	17%	42%	0	0.75	-32.0	32	38	-$15
1st Half		3	4	0	67	41	5.53	5.62	1.61	858	797	890	14.9	3.2	5.5	1.7	67%	8%	54	21	25	34%	67%	13%	9	57	22%	33%	0	0.74	-14.8	30	36	-$16
2nd Half		5	6	0	71	44	5.69	5.82	1.62	827	633	900	16.7	2.8	5.6	2.0	66%	6%	50	14	36	35%	66%	10%	3	38	0%	67%	0	0.76	-17.1	34	40	-$14
15	Proj	5	3	0	73	53	3.83	3.59	1.35	717	743	703	5.0	2.8	6.5	2.4	66%	8%	51	21	28	31%	74%	11%	0						-0.8	72	86	$0

Ross,Tyson

Age: 28 | Th: R | Role: RP | Ht: 6' 5" | Wt: 225 | Type: Pwr GB
Health: C | PT/Exp: B | Consist: B
LIMA Plan: C | Rand Var: 0 | MM: 4305

Sub-3.00 ERA breakout came with solid skill support. Dom uptick supported by elite SwK—200 Ks are well within reach. But with slider as his only whiff pitch, he's riding fine line there. Subpar FpK also, so 4.0 Ctl baseline could catch up to him. Cmd risk makes further growth iffy, but should repeat.

Yr	Tm	W	L	Sv	IP	K	ERA	xERA	WHIP	oOPS	vL	vR	BF/G	Ctl	Dom	Cmd	FpK	SwK	G	L	F	H%	S%	hr/f	GS	APC	DOM%	DIS%	Sv%	LI	RAR	BPV	BPX	R$
10	OAK *	3	5	1	65	58	4.69	3.97	1.44	754	674	819	8.6	4.4	8.0	1.8	54%	10%	53	18	29	31%	67%	12%	2	27	0%	100%	50	0.58	-4.9	71	114	-$2
11	OAK *	6	5	0	73	53	5.23	5.24	1.68	617	617	616	18.2	4.2	6.5	1.6	57%	8%	48	22	30	35%	68%	3%	6	60	50%	33%	0	0.76	-11.6	47	71	-$7
12	OAK *	8	13	0	152	98	4.76	4.73	1.56	870	974	759	20.2	3.9	5.8	1.5	55%	7%	50	23	27	33%	69%	10%	13	72	23%	38%	0	0.97	-13.9	45	59	-$10
13	SD	3	8	0	125	119	3.17	3.20	1.15	627	709	548	14.4	3.2	8.6	2.7	54%	12%	55	15	30	28%	74%	8%	16	57	81%	19%	0	1.09	10.8	102	133	$7
14	SD	13	14	0	196	195	2.81	3.02	1.21	634	635	632	26.2	3.3	9.0	2.7	58%	13%	57	21	22	30%	79%	11%	31	101	68%	10%			22.6	107	127	$16
1st Half		6	8	0	108	102	3.18	3.17	1.27	664	598	730	26.6	3.5	8.5	2.4	55%	13%	60	18	22	30%	77%	14%	17	99	65%	12%			7.5	97	115	$13
2nd Half		7	6	0	88	93	2.35	2.84	1.14	596	682	510	25.6	3.1	9.5	3.1	61%	14%	53	25	22	30%	80%	8%	14	102	71%	7%			15.1	119	143	$20
15	Proj	13	12	0	196	181	3.11	3.10	1.22	643	688	599	18.5	3.2	8.3	2.6	57%	12%	54	20	25	30%	76%	9%	36						15.2	95	113	$16

Russell,James

Age: 29 | Th: L | Role: RP | Ht: 6' 4" | Wt: 200 | Type: FB
Health: A | PT/Exp: C | Consist: A
LIMA Plan: B | Rand Var: -4 | MM: 2100

These days, you can't walk 10 feet without stepping on a high-skilled, high-upside bullpen arm worth speculating on. So this one is easy to step over. As a flyball pitcher who can't strike guys out, he's reliant on friendly H% and hr/f to have value. Consistent 4.00+ xERAs show his downside. Pass.

Yr	Tm	W	L	Sv	IP	K	ERA	xERA	WHIP	oOPS	vL	vR	BF/G	Ctl	Dom	Cmd	FpK	SwK	G	L	F	H%	S%	hr/f	GS	APC	DOM%	DIS%	Sv%	LI	RAR	BPV	BPX	R$
10	CHC	1	1	0	49	42	4.96	4.27	1.35	822	726	887	3.8	2.0	7.7	3.8	63%	12%	31	20	49	31%	71%	14%	0	15			0	0.94	-5.3	93	151	-$3
11	CHC	1	6	0	68	43	4.12	4.50	1.33	812	685	902	4.6	1.9	5.7	3.1	63%	10%	38	14	48	30%	76%	11%	5	17	0%	100%	0	0.89	-1.5	69	103	-$2
12	CHC	7	1	2	69	55	3.25	4.36	1.30	732	727	735	3.8	3.0	7.1	2.4	61%	10%	37	21	41	31%	76%	6%	0	15			40	0.98	6.6	63	82	$3
13	CHC	1	6	0	53	37	3.59	4.54	1.22	746	543	1033	2.9	3.1	6.3	2.1	62%	10%	33	16	51	26%	75%	9%	0	11			0	1.38	1.8	42	54	-$1
14	2 NL	0	2	1	58	42	2.97	4.12	1.13	582	805	421	3.6	3.1	6.6	2.1	65%	8%	39	24	37	26%	74%	5%	1	14	0%	100%	33	0.91	5.5	51	60	$1
1st Half		0	1	1	23	19	1.96	4.21	1.04	566	719	402	2.8	3.9	7.4	1.9	64%	9%	39	13	48	21%	86%	7%	0	12			33	1.15	5.1	46	54	$2
2nd Half		0	1	0	35	23	3.63	4.06	1.18	593	882	429	4.4	2.6	6.0	2.3	65%	7%	39	30	31	29%	68%	3%	1	16	0%	100%	0	0.66	0.5	54	65	$1
15	Proj	1	3	0	51	37	3.85	4.02	1.31	732	766	703	3.5	3.0	6.6	2.2	63%	9%	37	21	43	30%	72%	7%	0						-0.7	53	64	-$2

Ryu,Hyun-Jin

Age: 28 | Th: L | Role: SP | Ht: 6' 2" | Wt: 255 | Type: Pwr
Health: C | PT/Exp: A | Consist: A
LIMA Plan: B | Rand Var: 0 | MM: 5303

Second season even better than first, save for late shoulder issue. Blame uptick in ERA on H% jump. That 2nd half SwK/Dom combo keeps him firmly in 3.00 ERA territory, or better. Ability to sustain pinpoint control more in doubt, as FpK more solid than great. Still, if shoulder is okay, he's a $15 pitcher.

Yr	Tm	W	L	Sv	IP	K	ERA	xERA	WHIP	oOPS	vL	vR	BF/G	Ctl	Dom	Cmd	FpK	SwK	G	L	F	H%	S%	hr/f	GS	APC	DOM%	DIS%	Sv%	LI	RAR	BPV	BPX	R$
10	for	16	4	0	193	177	2.26	2.97	1.12				30.4	2.6	8.3	3.2						28%	85%								43.3	100	162	$27
11	for	11	7	0	126	121	4.17	3.88	1.23				21.3	3.4	8.7	2.6						27%	72%								-3.5	72	108	$6
12	for	9	9	0	183	199	3.30	2.96	1.21				27.3	2.8	9.8	3.5						33%	72%								16.2	127	165	$15
13	LA	14	8	0	192	154	3.00	3.51	1.20	660	738	633	26.1	2.3	7.2	3.1	59%	9%	51	19	31	30%	77%	9%	30	102	60%	7%			20.5	97	126	$16
14	LA	14	7	0	152	139	3.38	3.23	1.19	658	665	656	24.3	1.7	8.2	4.8	62%	9%	47	22	30	33%	72%	6%	26	94	73%	12%			6.9	127	151	$11
1st Half		9	4	0	89	73	3.12	3.62	1.21	667	689	659	24.8	1.9	7.4	3.8	62%	8%	45	20	35	32%	75%	6%	15	96	73%	7%			6.8	104	124	$14
2nd Half		5	3	0	63	66	3.73	2.67	1.16	645	619	652	23.5	1.4	9.5	6.6	62%	11%	51	26	23	36%	66%	5%	11	91	73%	18%			0.1	161	192	$5
15	Proj	12	7	0	160	149	3.31	2.95	1.19	651	682	641	24.5	2.1	8.4	4.0	61%	9%	49	22	29	32%	73%	8%	26						8.5	122	146	$13

Rzepczynski,Marc

Age: 29 | Th: L | Role: RP | Ht: 6' 2" | Wt: 220 | Type: Pwr xGB
Health: A | PT/Exp: D | Consist: B
LIMA Plan: C | Rand Var: -3 | MM: 5300

Sub-3.00 ERA will put this power GBer on many end-game radars again. That stat is product of his club being smart enough to know when to use him—he's plain horrible against RHers. Strong 4.4 Cmd, 67% GB% vLHB confirms where his value lies. Bottom line - just not enough innings to have much of an impact.

Yr	Tm	W	L	Sv	IP	K	ERA	xERA	WHIP	oOPS	vL	vR	BF/G	Ctl	Dom	Cmd	FpK	SwK	G	L	F	H%	S%	hr/f	GS	APC	DOM%	DIS%	Sv%	LI	RAR	BPV	BPX	R$
10	TOR *	9	9	0	131	108	5.13	5.34	1.59	840	671	895	22.1	3.7	7.4	2.0	60%	10%	51	16	32	34%	70%	13%	12	77	33%	42%	0	0.83	-16.9	49	80	-$5
11	2 TM	2	6	0	62	61	3.34	2.90	1.23	623	478	748	3.6	3.8	8.9	2.3	53%	12%	65	15	20	29%	73%	9%	0	13			0	1.28	4.6	100	151	$2
12	STL	1	3	0	47	33	4.24	3.78	1.35	729	682	781	2.8	3.3	6.4	1.9	46%	10%	59	22	19	28%	73%	25%	0	11			0	1.31	-1.3	63	82	-$4
13	2 TM *	1	2	0	75	52	3.49	4.03	1.47	674	480	859	4.6	3.5	6.3	1.8	49%	13%	56	17	27	33%	76%	9%	0	12			0	0.71	3.4	64	84	-$3
14	CLE	0	3	0	46	46	2.74	3.12	1.33	656	441	944	2.7	3.7	9.0	2.4	53%	16%	60	19	22	33%	78%	4%	0	10			0	1.18	5.7	100	119	-$1
1st Half		0	2	0	29	25	3.99	3.88	1.53	719	476	1025	3.2	4.6	7.7	1.7	55%	14%	57	19	24	33%	73%	5%	0	12			0	0.94	-0.9	49	58	-$4
2nd Half		0	1	0	17	21	0.54	1.95	0.96	533	377	768	2.1	2.2	11.3	5.3	48%	19%	66	18	16	32%	94%	0%	0	8			0	1.48	6.6	190	226	$5
15	Proj	2	2	0	51	47	2.89	3.05	1.30	681	502	879	3.0	3.3	8.3	2.5	50%	14%	60	18	22	32%	78%	8%	0						5.3	97	116	$0

Sabathia,CC

Age: 34 | Th: L | Role: SP | Ht: 6' 7" | Wt: 285 | Type: Pwr
Health: F | PT/Exp: A | Consist: B
LIMA Plan: C+ | Rand Var: +5 | MM: 5301

Season-ending knee surgery in July ended this 5.00+ ERA disaster. Blame crazy H%, hr/f for it; skills were firmly elite, as xERA shows. Risk isn't lack of skill, it's health. Prior durability now fully in question, as years of putting near-300 lbs on legs may not be fixed by one surgery. A risk/reward play now.

Yr	Tm	W	L	Sv	IP	K	ERA	xERA	WHIP	oOPS	vL	vR	BF/G	Ctl	Dom	Cmd	FpK	SwK	G	L	F	H%	S%	hr/f	GS	APC	DOM%	DIS%	Sv%	LI	RAR	BPV	BPX	R$
10	NYY	21	7	0	238	197	3.18	3.55	1.19	656	678	649	28.5	2.8	7.5	2.7	58%	10%	51	15	34	29%	76%	9%	34	106	56%	3%			26.3	88	142	$24
11	NYY	19	8	0	237	230	3.00	3.17	1.23	666	554	709	29.8	2.3	8.7	3.8	63%	12%	47	23	30	33%	77%	8%	33	109	79%	0%			27.7	120	180	$23
12	NYY	15	6	0	200	197	3.38	3.29	1.14	666	667	665	29.8	2.0	8.9	4.5	63%	12%	48	21	31	31%	74%	13%	28	108	75%	4%			15.8	132	172	$21
13	NYY	14	13	0	211	175	4.78	3.89	1.37	770	662	804	28.4	2.8	7.5	2.7	65%	10%	45	22	33	32%	68%	13%	32	104	44%	6%			-23.7	83	108	-$2
14	NYY	3	4	0	46	48	5.28	3.29	1.48	875	570	921	26.1	2.0	9.4	4.8	70%	11%	48	22	30	37%	71%	23%	8	100	50%	13%			-8.7	142	169	-$5
1st Half		3	4	0	46	48	5.28	3.29	1.48	875	570	921	26.1	2.0	9.4	4.8	70%	11%	48	22	30	37%	71%	23%	8	100	50%	13%			-8.7	142	170	-$5
2nd Half																																		
15	Proj	8	6	0	116	111	3.76	3.05	1.24	719	600	750	26.6	2.3	8.6	3.8	65%	11%	48	21	31	31%	75%	16%	18						-0.3	119	142	$6

Salas,Fernando

Age: 30 | Th: R | Role: RP | Ht: 6' 2" | Wt: 210 | Type: Pwr FB
Health: D | PT/Exp: D | Consist: B
LIMA Plan: A | Rand Var: 0 | MM: 4410

Year removed from being in saves discussion, many will pass now. Don't follow suit. Excellent Cmd came with full FpK and SwK support. Ignore vR oOPS; had a 35/3 K/BB in 27 IP against them. Exorcised inconsistency demons too: 100+ BPV in all but April. Flyball lean could prevent save opps, but a LIMA gem nonetheless.

Yr	Tm	W	L	Sv	IP	K	ERA	xERA	WHIP	oOPS	vL	vR	BF/G	Ctl	Dom	Cmd	FpK	SwK	G	L	F	H%	S%	hr/f	GS	APC	DOM%	DIS%	Sv%	LI	RAR	BPV	BPX	R$
10	STL *	1	0	19	66	64	3.74	3.19	1.21	748	866	665	4.4	3.2	8.7	2.7	56%	12%	33	18	48	29%	71%	10%	0	21			95	0.48	2.8	95	153	$9
11	STL	5	6	24	75	75	2.28	3.52	0.95	566	649	502	4.3	2.5	9.0	3.6	59%	11%	34	14	52	24%	81%	7%	0	17			80	1.45	15.4	106	159	$20
12	STL	1	4	0	59	60	4.30	4.13	1.41	720	681	747	3.9	4.1	9.2	2.2	67%	13%	38	24	38	33%	71%	8%	0	16			0	1.18	-2.0	70	91	-$4
13	STL *	1	5	12	52	38	3.48	2.88	1.09	715	829	645	4.1	2.0	6.6	3.3	69%	10%	32	15	53	28%	70%	7%	0	17			80	1.05	2.4	96	125	$5
14	LAA	5	0	0	59	61	3.38	3.41	1.09	637	510	771	4.2	2.1	9.4	4.4	64%	13%	29	30	42	30%	71%	8%	0	17			0	1.00	2.6	117	140	$3
1st Half		4	0	0	27	28	2.96	3.93	1.32	705	578	854	4.2	3.6	9.2	2.5	63%	13%	29	31	40	31%	82%	10%	0	16			0	1.10	2.6	75	89	$3
2nd Half		1	0	0	31	33	3.73	2.99	0.89	574	438	703	4.2	0.9	9.5	11.0	64%	13%	29	28	43	29%	58%	6%	0	17			0	0.90	0.0	155	185	$4
15	Proj	3	2	1	58	58	3.22	3.20	1.12	644	583	696	4.0	2.4	9.1	3.8	63%	13%	34	23	44	30%	74%	7%	0						3.7	111	132	$3

STEPHEN NICKRAND

Salazar,Danny

Salazar,Danny				Health	A	LIMA Plan	B+
Age: 25	Th: R	Role	SP	PT/Exp	D	Rand Var	+1
Ht: 6' 0"	Wt: 190	Type	Pwr FB	Consist	B	MM	4403

6-8, 4.25 in 110 IP in CLE. That 1st half implosion fueled by soaring H%, Ctl spike and gopheritis led to mid-May demotion. Steadied after 2nd half recall until an uneven September. Terrific Dom, 2nd half Ctl rebound point to huge upside. But DIS% hints at the risk; he could use a GB pitch.

Yr Tm	W	L	Sv	IP	K	ERA	xERA	WHIP	oOPS	vL	vR	BF/G	Ctl	Dom	Cmd	FpK	SwK	G	L	F	H%	S%	hr/f	GS	APC	DOM%	DIS%	Sv%	LI	RAR	BPV	BPX	R$
10																																	
11																																	
12 aa	4	0	0	34	20	2.44	2.62	1.12				22.3	2.2	5.3	2.5						27%	78%								6.6	82	107	$1
13 CLE *	8	8	1	145	176	3.08	2.86	1.11	655	588	733	18.4	2.4	10.9	4.6	67%	15%	34	26	40	32%	75%	14%	10	82	50%	40%			14.0	150	195	$14
14 CLE *	10	14	0	171	184	4.23	4.60	1.43	751	696	786	23.4	3.3	9.7	3.0	59%	12%	34	23	42	35%	73%	10%	20	93	40%	35%			-10.4	89	106	-$1
1st Half	3	9	0	77	84	5.46	6.30	1.67	886	744	998	22.9	3.6	9.9	2.8	57%	12%	33	21	46	39%	71%	15%	8	94	25%	50%			-16.2	61	73	-$16
2nd Half	7	5	0	94	100	3.23	3.22	1.24	668	659	673	23.8	3.0	9.6	3.2	61%	12%	35	25	40	32%	75%	7%	12	93	50%	25%			5.9	113	135	$11
15 Proj	12	10	0	174	183	3.60	3.34	1.29	692	632	742	21.5	2.9	9.5	3.2	62%	13%	34	24	41	33%	75%	9%	30						3.0	103	123	$10

Sale,Chris

Sale,Chris				Health	C	LIMA Plan	C
Age: 26	Th: L	Role	RP	PT/Exp	A	Rand Var	-3
Ht: 6' 6"	Wt: 180	Type	Pwr	Consist	A	MM	5505

More elbow woes shelved him for a month early on, but you'd never know it. FpK/SwK surge fueled his dominance, as he stepped things up vRHB. GB trend could be healthier and that hr/f won't survive, but it seems like only physical injuries can derail him right now.

Yr Tm	W	L	Sv	IP	K	ERA	xERA	WHIP	oOPS	vL	vR	BF/G	Ctl	Dom	Cmd	FpK	SwK	G	L	F	H%	S%	hr/f	GS	APC	DOM%	DIS%	Sv%	LI	RAR	BPV	BPX	R$
10 CHW	2	1	4	23	32	1.93	2.61	1.07	546	694	454	4.4	3.9	12.3	3.2	55%	10%	51	12	37	28%	87%	11%	0	19			100	1.65	6.2	147	238	$3
11 CHW	2	2	8	71	79	2.79	3.00	1.11	612	558	660	5.0	3.4	10.0	2.9	60%	12%	50	18	32	28%	78%	11%	0	19			80	1.25	10.1	116	174	$9
12 CHW	17	8	0	192	192	3.05	3.27	1.14	660	601	682	25.7	2.4	9.0	3.8	57%	11%	45	23	32	30%	77%	12%	29	101	72%	7%	0	0.87	22.9	120	157	$24
13 CHW	11	14	0	214	226	3.07	2.94	1.07	636	360	699	28.9	1.9	9.5	4.9	63%	11%	47	21	32	30%	76%	13%	30	108	77%	3%			21.2	144	187	$23
14 CHW	12	4	0	174	208	2.17	2.81	0.97	567	393	608	26.3	2.0	10.8	5.3	67%	14%	41	18	41	29%	81%	8%	26	106	81%	4%			33.7	158	188	$27
1st Half	7	1	0	78	84	2.30	2.84	0.89	528	285	576	25.1	1.8	9.7	5.3	67%	13%	45	16	38	26%	78%	8%	12	103	75%	8%			13.9	147	176	$25
2nd Half	5	3	0	96	124	2.07	2.78	1.02	597	458	634	27.4	2.2	11.7	5.4	67%	14%	37	20	43	32%	84%	7%	14	109	86%	0%			19.7	166	199	$28
15 Proj	13	8	0	203	229	2.58	2.68	1.04	605	460	648	18.0	2.2	10.2	4.6	64%	12%	43	20	37	29%	79%	10%	35						29.0	145	172	$28

Samardzija,Jeff

Samardzija,Jeff				Health	A	LIMA Plan	C+
Age: 30	Th: R	Role	SP	PT/Exp	A	Rand Var	-2
Ht: 6' 5"	Wt: 225	Type	Pwr	Consist	A	MM	5305

Rebounded from "poor" 2013 and then some. Confirmed morph from FBer to GBer as Ctl turned elite. BPV and xERA trends keep on keepin' on. Gopheritis hurts and he could use some run support. But with that support, more Ctl preeminence and a little luck... UP: 16 wins, $25.

Yr Tm	W	L	Sv	IP	K	ERA	xERA	WHIP	oOPS	vL	vR	BF/G	Ctl	Dom	Cmd	FpK	SwK	G	L	F	H%	S%	hr/f	GS	APC	DOM%	DIS%	Sv%	LI	RAR	BPV	BPX	R$
10 CHC *	13	5	0	131	91	5.45	4.47	1.57	930	470	1202	13.7	6.0	6.3	1.0	56%	6%	30	17	52	27%	66%	11%	3	53	0%	67%	0	0.57	-22.0	37	60	-$5
11 CHC	8	4	0	88	87	2.97	4.11	1.30	613	660	581	5.1	5.1	8.9	1.7	56%	11%	41	18	41	27%	78%	5%	0	20			0	0.85	10.6	41	62	$6
12 CHC	9	13	0	175	180	3.81	3.45	1.22	698	759	636	25.8	2.9	9.3	3.2	60%	13%	45	22	33	30%	72%	13%	28	99	64%	11%			4.4	112	146	$10
13 CHC	8	13	0	214	214	4.34	3.49	1.35	736	783	695	27.7	3.3	9.0	2.7	60%	11%	48	20	31	32%	70%	13%	33	105	70%	9%			-12.5	100	130	$1
14 2 TM	7	13	0	220	202	2.99	3.05	1.07	646	662	631	26.6	1.8	8.3	4.7	65%	12%	50	19	31	29%	75%	11%	33	101	73%	6%			20.3	129	154	$19
1st Half	2	7	0	108	103	2.83	3.14	1.20	672	738	622	26.4	2.6	8.6	3.3	67%	11%	52	20	27	31%	78%	9%	17	99	65%	6%			12.1	115	138	$14
2nd Half	5	6	0	112	99	3.14	2.95	0.93	619	596	641	26.9	1.0	8.0	8.3	64%	12%	48	18	34	27%	71%	12%	16	103	81%	6%			8.2	143	171	$24
15 Proj	13	9	0	210	201	3.29	3.05	1.17	662	693	634	20.4	2.5	8.6	3.5	62%	12%	48	20	33	30%	74%	9%	41						11.8	113	135	$18

Sanchez,Aaron

Sanchez,Aaron				Health	A	LIMA Plan	B+
Age: 23	Th: R	Role	RP	PT/Exp	F	Rand Var	0
Ht: 6' 4"	Wt: 200	Type	Pwr xGB	Consist	F	MM	4201

2-2, 1.09 ERA and 3 Sv in 33 IP at TOR. Elite SP prospect has struggled to harness his control—until MLB debut out of the pen. Posted sample 3.0 Cmd and 110 BPV as RP, but age, 8.8 career Dom and GB tilt say a rotation shot is still in his future. Could be a work-in-progress.

Yr Tm	W	L	Sv	IP	K	ERA	xERA	WHIP	oOPS	vL	vR	BF/G	Ctl	Dom	Cmd	FpK	SwK	G	L	F	H%	S%	hr/f	GS	APC	DOM%	DIS%	Sv%	LI	RAR	BPV	BPX	R$
10																																	
11																																	
12																																	
13																																	
14 TOR *	5	9	3	133	101	3.96	3.46	1.37	367	469	306	12.1	4.5	6.8	1.5	53%	7%	66	15	20	28%	71%	6%	0	19			100	1.17	-3.6	64	76	$0
1st Half	3	5	0	86	63	4.92	4.10	1.58				21.1	5.5	6.6	1.2						31%	67%	0%	0						-12.6	57	68	-$7
2nd Half	2	4	3	47	38	2.19	2.29	0.97	367	469	306	6.4	2.5	7.2	2.9	53%	7%	66	15	20	23%	83%	6%	0	19			100	1.17	9.0	93	111	$13
15 Proj	4	3	0	80	66	3.56	3.24	1.25	628	820	515	9.2	3.4	7.4	2.2	53%	7%	60	16	23	29%	73%	10%	0						1.8	81	97	$2

Sanchez,Anibal

Sanchez,Anibal				Health	D	LIMA Plan	B
Age: 31	Th: R	Role	SP	PT/Exp	A	Rand Var	-2
Ht: 6' 0"	Wt: 205	Type	Pwr	Consist	B	MM	4305

ERA regressed as gyrating SwK makes 2013 Dom looks outlier-ish. Despite a 2nd half-killing H%/S%, Ctl and GB% remain solid. Health is a concern; shoulder and finger woes slowed him down before pectoral injury shelved him for the final seven weeks. Pass when the bidding hits $12.

Yr Tm	W	L	Sv	IP	K	ERA	xERA	WHIP	oOPS	vL	vR	BF/G	Ctl	Dom	Cmd	FpK	SwK	G	L	F	H%	S%	hr/f	GS	APC	DOM%	DIS%	Sv%	LI	RAR	BPV	BPX	R$
10 FLA	13	12	0	195	157	3.55	4.06	1.34	680	686	674	26.3	3.2	7.2	2.2	58%	10%	45	17	38	32%	73%	5%	32	101	59%	16%			12.6	66	107	$10
11 FLA	8	9	0	196	202	3.67	3.38	1.28	711	671	751	25.9	2.9	9.3	3.2	63%	12%	44	20	36	32%	74%	10%	32	101	66%	16%			6.7	109	165	$10
12 2 TM	9	13	0	196	167	3.86	3.70	1.27	716	645	797	26.5	2.2	7.7	3.5	66%	10%	46	21	32	32%	72%	11%	31	99	68%	13%			3.6	103	134	$8
13 DET	14	8	0	182	202	2.57	3.08	1.15	616	673	548	25.7	2.7	10.0	3.7	62%	13%	45	22	33	32%	79%	6%	29	103	72%	7%			29.1	131	170	$22
14 DET	8	5	0	126	102	3.43	3.58	1.10	597	562	648	23.4	2.1	7.3	3.4	60%	10%	46	19	35	29%	67%	3%	21	95	48%	19%	0	0.75	4.9	97	116	$8
1st Half	5	2	0	82	66	2.63	3.58	0.98	552	498	638	23.4	2.3	7.2	3.1	60%	9%	42	22	36	26%	72%	2%	14	98	50%	14%			11.2	88	106	$16
2nd Half	3	3	0	44	36	4.91	3.56	1.32	676	684	664	23.4	1.8	7.4	4.0	60%	11%	51	15	33	35%	61%	4%	7	90	43%	29%	0	0.69	-6.3	112	134	-$6
15 Proj	12	10	0	189	166	3.54	3.28	1.19	637	628	648	23.8	2.4	7.9	3.3	61%	11%	45	20	36	31%	70%	5%	32						4.8	100	120	$13

Santana,Ervin

Santana,Ervin				Health	A	LIMA Plan	B
Age: 32	Th: R	Role	SP	PT/Exp	A	Rand Var	0
Ht: 6' 2"	Wt: 185	Type	Pwr	Consist	A	MM	3205

Ctl regression was neutralized by Dom spike but 1st half struggles vLHB hurt. His skills trade within a narrow range, his seasonal R$ depending on the swings and occasional abberations like the 2013 Ctl or the 2012 hr/f. Still a viable third tier option; pay the projected value and hope for more.

Yr Tm	W	L	Sv	IP	K	ERA	xERA	WHIP	oOPS	vL	vR	BF/G	Ctl	Dom	Cmd	FpK	SwK	G	L	F	H%	S%	hr/f	GS	APC	DOM%	DIS%	Sv%	LI	RAR	BPV	BPX	R$
10 LAA	17	10	0	223	169	3.92	4.29	1.32	744	793	687	28.9	3.0	6.8	2.3	63%	9%	35	22	43	30%	74%	9%	33	108	55%	6%			4.3	56	91	$11
11 LAA	11	12	0	229	178	3.38	3.87	1.22	693	703	681	28.8	2.8	7.0	2.5	63%	9%	44	19	38	28%	76%	10%	33	105	58%	6%			15.7	72	108	$15
12 LAA	9	13	0	178	133	5.16	4.38	1.27	774	867	664	25.5	3.1	6.7	2.2	62%	9%	43	20	37	25%	66%	19%	30	95	47%	23%			-25.1	59	77	-$2
13 KC	9	10	0	211	161	3.24	3.66	1.14	668	675	659	26.8	2.2	6.9	3.2	66%	10%	46	21	33	27%	77%	12%	32	100	66%	6%			16.2	89	116	$15
14 ATL	14	10	0	196	179	3.95	3.57	1.31	724	763	676	26.4	2.9	8.2	2.8	63%	12%	43	25	33	32%	71%	9%	31	96	68%	3%			-5.0	91	108	$5
1st Half	6	5	0	96	86	4.05	3.39	1.30	745	924	555	26.3	2.6	8.1	3.1	64%	13%	46	26	28	32%	70%	10%	15	96	67%	7%			-3.6	98	117	$3
2nd Half	8	5	0	100	93	3.86	3.75	1.32	704	626	806	26.4	3.1	8.3	2.7	62%	12%	40	23	37	32%	72%	8%	16	97	69%	0%			-1.4	83	99	$7
15 Proj	12	11	0	196	164	3.87	3.50	1.26	707	735	673	26.0	2.8	7.5	2.7	63%	11%	43	22	35	30%	72%	10%	31						-3.1	82	98	$9

Santiago,Hector

Santiago,Hector				Health	A	LIMA Plan	B
Age: 27	Th: L	Role	RP	PT/Exp	B	Rand Var	-1
Ht: 6' 0"	Wt: 210	Type	Pwr xFB	Consist	A	MM	1301

Skills consistency and another sub-4.00 ERA, but the good news ends there. Dom trend and unexciting SwK with more velocity decline are red flags. Sub-par Ctl paired with rising FB% is disconcerting. Now with role uncertainty, he offers more risk than reward. DOWN: 4.50 ERA.

Yr Tm	W	L	Sv	IP	K	ERA	xERA	WHIP	oOPS	vL	vR	BF/G	Ctl	Dom	Cmd	FpK	SwK	G	L	F	H%	S%	hr/f	GS	APC	DOM%	DIS%	Sv%	LI	RAR	BPV	BPX	R$
10																																	
11 CHW *	7	5	0	89	66	4.34	4.06	1.50	170	0	311	22.5	4.7	6.7	1.4	56%	6%	60	13	27	31%	71%	0%	0	33			0	0.43	-4.4	57	86	-$2
12 CHW	4	1	4	70	79	3.33	4.11	1.34	680	592	744	7.3	5.1	10.1	2.0	56%	9%	38	20	42	27%	81%	14%	4	32	50%	50%	67	0.83	6.0	60	78	$3
13 CHW	4	9	0	149	137	3.56	4.38	1.40	739	686	762	19.3	4.3	8.3	1.9	57%	9%	36	20	44	30%	78%	9%	23	79	52%	17%	0	0.88	5.5	46	59	$1
14 LAA	6	9	0	127	108	3.75	4.53	1.36	698	606	762	18.1	3.7	7.6	2.0	56%	8%	31	19	50	29%	76%	8%	24	76	29%	25%	0	0.80	-0.1	45	54	$0
1st Half	0	7	0	53	47	4.08	4.35	1.32	680	732	660	17.4	3.6	8.0	2.2	50%	7%	32	19	49	30%	72%	8%	10	72	30%	40%	0	0.70	-2.2	58	69	-$6
2nd Half	6	2	0	74	61	3.51	4.66	1.39	711	510	781	18.7	3.9	7.4	1.9	60%	8%	30	20	50	29%	79%	8%	14	79	29%	14%	0	0.87	2.1	36	43	$5
15 Proj	5	6	0	111	96	3.94	4.18	1.41	723	646	756	17.9	4.2	7.8	1.9	56%	8%	34	20	46	30%	75%	9%	25						-2.7	39	47	$0

JOCK THOMPSON

Scheppers,Tanner

Age: 28 | Th: R | Role: RP | Ht: 6' 4" | Wt: 200 | Type: Pwr
Health: F | PT/Exp: D | Consist: D | LIMA Plan: C | Rand Var: +5 | MM: 3210

Hit the DL with elbow issues after just four April starts, and then out for good following four June relief appearances. A 9.00 ERA can be traced to small-sample H%, S% and hr/9 luck. But underlying skills were off too. Velocity was down and the Dom trend isn't good. A surgery waiting to happen? Avoid for now.

Yr Tm	W	L	Sv	IP	K	ERA	xERA	WHIP	oOPS	vL	vR	BF/G	Ctl	Dom	Cmd	FpK	SwK	G	L	F	H%	S%	hr/f	GS	APC	DOM%	DIS%	Sv%	LI	RAR	BPV	BPX	R$
10 a/a	1	3	6	80	75	6.01	5.36	1.63				9.9	3.5	8.4	2.4						38%	63%								-19.1	70	113	-$6
11 a/a	4	1	2	44	35	4.31	4.17	1.56				6.8	4.4	7.2	1.7						34%	71%								-2.0	70	106	-$2
12 TEX *	2	3	12	63	54	4.34	5.57	1.51	908	949	881	4.2	1.9	7.7	4.2	53%	9%	43	20	37	37%	75%	15%	0	14			80	0.95	-2.6	89	116	$0
13 TEX	6	2	1	77	59	1.88	3.48	1.07	605	599	610	4.0	2.8	6.9	2.5	60%	10%	50	19	31	25%	87%	9%	0	14			33	1.26	18.8	77	100	$10
14 TEX	0	1	0	23	17	9.00	4.50	1.78	922	925	916	13.9	3.9	6.7	1.7	56%	7%	56	14	31	34%	51%	24%	4	52	25%	50%	0	0.76	-14.9	48	57	-$9
1st Half	0	1	0	23	17	9.00	4.50	1.78	922	925	916	13.9	3.9	6.7	1.7	56%	7%	56	14	31	34%	51%	24%	4	52	25%	50%	0	0.76	-14.9	48	57	-$9
2nd Half																																	
15 Proj	**2**	**2**	**8**	**45**	**36**	**4.03**	**3.64**	**1.34**	**665**	**674**	**655**	**5.9**	**3.2**	**7.2**	**2.3**	**56%**	**9%**	**49**	**18**	**33**	**31%**	**72%**	**10%**	**0**						**-1.6**	**71**	**84**	**$1**

Scherzer,Max

Age: 30 | Th: R | Role: SP | Ht: 6' 3" | Wt: 220 | Type: Pwr FB
Health: A | PT/Exp: A | Consist: A | LIMA Plan: C | Rand Var: 0 | MM: 5505

"Regressed" right on schedule, as projected here. Of course, you can count the consecutive $30+ R$ repeats from the last decade not named Kershaw on one hand. Note that his only foray below 3.00 ERA was driven by H% fortune, so don't expect a return to those levels. Still, bushels of strikeouts keep him in the top tier.

Yr Tm	W	L	Sv	IP	K	ERA	xERA	WHIP	oOPS	vL	vR	BF/G	Ctl	Dom	Cmd	FpK	SwK	G	L	F	H%	S%	hr/f	GS	APC	DOM%	DIS%	Sv%	LI	RAR	BPV	BPX	R$
10 DET *	14	11	0	211	197	3.30	3.22	1.19	700	666	737	25.6	3.1	8.4	2.7	59%	10%	40	20	40	29%	75%	10%	31	106	65%	13%			20.2	91	147	$19
11 DET	15	9	0	195	174	4.43	3.78	1.35	780	840	706	25.2	2.6	8.0	3.1	62%	10%	40	20	39	32%	71%	13%	33	101	52%	9%			-11.7	93	139	$4
12 DET	16	7	0	188	231	3.74	3.35	1.27	721	831	588	24.6	2.9	11.1	3.9	61%	13%	36	22	41	34%	75%	12%	32	102	63%	19%			6.3	136	177	$14
13 DET	21	3	0	214	240	2.90	3.16	0.97	583	645	494	26.1	2.4	10.1	4.3	64%	13%	36	19	45	27%	73%	8%	32	106	88%	3%			25.6	132	172	$33
14 DET	18	5	0	220	252	3.15	3.24	1.18	663	685	629	27.4	2.6	10.3	4.0	63%	12%	37	22	42	33%	76%	8%	33	110	82%	6%			16.2	131	156	$20
1st Half	9	3	0	111	132	3.64	3.27	1.25	707	737	665	27.3	2.6	10.7	4.1	61%	13%	36	21	43	35%	73%	9%	17	110	94%	6%			1.4	136	163	$15
2nd Half	9	2	0	109	120	2.64	3.21	1.10	615	631	588	27.5	2.6	9.9	3.9	66%	12%	37	23	40	30%	78%	6%	16	111	69%	6%			14.8	125	149	$25
15 Proj	**19**	**6**	**0**	**218**	**244**	**3.19**	**2.98**	**1.14**	**654**	**696**	**595**	**25.8**	**2.6**	**10.1**	**3.9**	**63%**	**12%**	**37**	**21**	**42**	**31%**	**75%**	**8%**	**33**						**14.7**	**127**	**151**	**$24**

Schlitter,Brian

Age: 29 | Th: R | Role: RP | Ht: 6' 5" | Wt: 235 | Type: xGB
Health: C | PT/Exp: D | Consist: B | LIMA Plan: D+ | Rand Var: 0 | MM: 2000

The GBs remained consistent throughout. But 1st half Ctl that helped fuel fine start collapsed as shoulder woes sidelined him for a month. Decent minor league track record, but he has yet to show anything resembling his pre-MLB strikeouts. At 29, he can be ignored unless that changes.

Yr Tm	W	L	Sv	IP	K	ERA	xERA	WHIP	oOPS	vL	vR	BF/G	Ctl	Dom	Cmd	FpK	SwK	G	L	F	H%	S%	hr/f	GS	APC	DOM%	DIS%	Sv%	LI	RAR	BPV	BPX	R$
10 CHC *	2	2	13	54	41	4.88	5.80	1.75	1167	1478	906	5.6	4.4	6.8	1.6	57%	8%	31	26	43	36%	73%	13%	0	26			81	0.89	-5.3	40	65	$0
11																																	
12 aa	3	4	6	42	35	3.93	5.05	1.58				6.4	2.7	7.4	2.8						38%	75%								0.4	80	104	-$2
13 a/a	1	6	22	63	44	3.23	4.97	1.53				5.1	2.5	6.3	2.5						36%	81%								4.9	63	83	$5
14 CHC	2	3	0	56	31	4.15	3.91	1.37	682	819	611	4.0	3.0	5.0	1.6	57%	6%	60	21	19	30%	68%	6%	0	15			0	1.18	-2.9	45	54	-$3
1st Half	2	2	0	37	20	2.70	3.49	0.90	512	645	446	3.9	2.2	4.9	2.2	55%	4%	58	20	22	21%	71%	8%	0	15			0	1.39	4.7	65	77	$2
2nd Half	0	1	0	20	11	6.86	4.73	2.24	935	1067	863	4.1	4.6	5.0	1.1	59%	7%	63	23	15	43%	66%	0%	0	15			0	0.85	-7.6	8	9	-$14
15 Proj	**1**	**3**	**0**	**44**	**26**	**4.07**	**3.83**	**1.43**	**687**	**845**	**603**	**4.4**	**3.4**	**5.5**	**1.6**	**58%**	**6%**	**58**	**21**	**21**	**31%**	**71%**	**7%**	**0**						**-1.8**	**41**	**49**	**-$4**

Shaw,Bryan

Age: 27 | Th: R | Role: RP | Ht: 6' 1" | Wt: 210 | Type: Pwr
Health: A | PT/Exp: C | Consist: A | LIMA Plan: B | Rand Var: -4 | MM: 3210

Another workhorse season from an effective reliever whose multi-inning stints and high-leverage appearances resulted in a handful of wins and saves. Does most things reasonably well, though Dom and inconsistency vLHB cap his ceiling. He's a defensible deep league end-gamer.

Yr Tm	W	L	Sv	IP	K	ERA	xERA	WHIP	oOPS	vL	vR	BF/G	Ctl	Dom	Cmd	FpK	SwK	G	L	F	H%	S%	hr/f	GS	APC	DOM%	DIS%	Sv%	LI	RAR	BPV	BPX	R$
10 aa	4	9	2	101	62	5.72	5.06	1.67				13.8	4.0	5.5	1.4						35%	64%								-20.6	43	70	-$9
11 ARI *	5	1	16	67	49	2.56	3.44	1.19	699	587	776	4.2	2.5	6.6	2.6	56%	11%	60	22	18	28%	83%	13%	0	15			94	0.58	11.3	73	110	$11
12 ARI	1	6	2	59	41	3.49	4.03	1.42	747	863	630	3.9	3.6	6.2	1.7	57%	9%	56	21	23	31%	76%	10%	0	15			50	0.78	3.9	48	62	-$2
13 CLE	7	3	1	75	73	3.24	3.58	1.17	586	678	506	4.5	3.4	8.8	2.6	57%	11%	43	25	33	29%	73%	6%	0	18			20	0.99	5.8	88	115	$5
14 CLE	5	5	2	76	64	2.59	3.62	1.09	602	776	493	3.9	2.6	7.5	2.9	59%	11%	46	18	36	27%	79%	8%	0	16			22	1.37	10.8	90	107	$7
1st Half	2	1	2	36	30	2.75	3.80	1.14	629	966	436	3.9	2.5	7.5	3.0	62%	12%	41	20	39	29%	77%	5%	0	16			50	1.47	4.4	87	103	$5
2nd Half	3	4	0	40	34	2.45	3.47	1.04	578	621	548	3.9	2.7	7.6	2.8	56%	10%	50	17	33	25%	82%	11%	0	16			0	1.28	6.4	92	110	$9
15 Proj	**4**	**4**	**5**	**65**	**54**	**3.03**	**3.42**	**1.19**	**632**	**762**	**533**	**4.1**	**3.0**	**7.5**	**2.5**	**58%**	**11%**	**47**	**21**	**33**	**28%**	**76%**	**8%**	**0**						**5.7**	**78**	**93**	**$5**

Shields,James

Age: 33 | Th: R | Role: SP | Ht: 6' 3" | Wt: 215 | Type:
Health: A | PT/Exp: A | Consist: A | LIMA Plan: C | Rand Var: 0 | MM: 3205

Dependable BPIs and IP history suggest little is amiss. Dom erosion concurrent with splitter use—in place of that once-vaunted change-up—introduces some uncertainty, but his Ctl is in peak form. Price him for stability, not any sort of performance improvement, and you should be OK.

Yr Tm	W	L	Sv	IP	K	ERA	xERA	WHIP	oOPS	vL	vR	BF/G	Ctl	Dom	Cmd	FpK	SwK	G	L	F	H%	S%	hr/f	GS	APC	DOM%	DIS%	Sv%	LI	RAR	BPV	BPX	R$
10 TAM	13	15	0	203	187	5.18	3.81	1.46	828	796	866	26.4	2.3	8.3	3.7	62%	10%	41	20	38	35%	68%	14%	33	99	48%	18%	0	0.81	-27.6	107	173	-$2
11 TAM	16	12	0	249	225	2.82	3.21	1.04	623	602	648	29.5	2.3	8.1	3.5	63%	11%	46	18	35	26%	78%	11%	33	108	67%	9%			34.7	107	161	$32
12 TAM	15	10	0	228	223	3.52	3.23	1.17	678	706	645	28.6	2.3	8.8	3.8	61%	11%	52	19	29	30%	73%	13%	33	110	70%	6%			13.9	127	165	$21
13 KC	13	9	0	229	196	3.15	3.72	1.24	678	614	753	27.8	2.7	7.7	2.9	58%	10%	42	23	35	30%	77%	9%	34	108	71%	9%			20.2	87	113	$16
14 KC	14	8	0	227	180	3.21	3.56	1.18	702	698	706	27.6	1.7	7.1	4.1	63%	10%	45	21	34	30%	76%	10%	34	107	65%	9%			14.8	104	124	$15
1st Half	8	3	0	112	87	3.79	3.71	1.29	771	801	737	28.0	1.9	7.0	3.6	61%	9%	46	21	34	32%	75%	13%	17	106	53%	12%			-0.6	98	117	$9
2nd Half	6	5	0	115	93	2.65	3.42	1.08	632	595	674	27.2	1.6	7.3	4.7	64%	11%	45	21	35	29%	78%	7%	17	108	76%	6%			15.5	111	133	$22
15 Proj	**14**	**8**	**0**	**218**	**179**	**3.39**	**3.36**	**1.21**	**692**	**673**	**714**	**27.1**	**2.2**	**7.4**	**3.4**	**61%**	**10%**	**44**	**21**	**35**	**30%**	**75%**	**9%**	**32**						**9.4**	**97**	**115**	**$16**

Shoemaker,Matthew

Age: 28 | Th: R | Role: SP | Ht: 6' 2" | Wt: 225 | Type:
Health: A | PT/Exp: C | Consist: C | LIMA Plan: B | Rand Var: 0 | MM: 3205

16-4, 3.04 ERA in 136 IP at LAA. Rookie stunner, with his minor league numbers explaining why. His new splitter was huge, but 5-pitch command and 2nd half H%/S% were critical to success. GB%, history and sub-par velocity say HR will be an issue. Expect some regression... DOWN: 4.00+ ERA.

Yr Tm	W	L	Sv	IP	K	ERA	xERA	WHIP	oOPS	vL	vR	BF/G	Ctl	Dom	Cmd	FpK	SwK	G	L	F	H%	S%	hr/f	GS	APC	DOM%	DIS%	Sv%	LI	RAR	BPV	BPX	R$
10 aaa	2	1	0	15	7	5.84	5.51	1.84				23.8	4.2	4.3	1.0						37%	65%								-3.3	37	60	-$4
11 a/a	12	7	0	177	114	3.39	3.93	1.26				26.8	2.3	5.8	2.5						29%	77%								12.0	61	92	$10
12 aaa	11	10	0	177	100	5.43	5.79	1.59				26.9	2.0	5.1	2.5						36%	67%								-30.8	44	57	-$17
13 LAA *	11	13	0	189	131	4.25	4.70	1.35	328	490	0	26.3	1.3	6.2	4.6	53%	10%	42	25	33	34%	71%	0%	1	93	100%	0%			-9.1	99	128	$0
14 LAA *	17	4	0	162	144	3.47	3.55	1.18	658	702	610	20.2	1.8	8.0	4.5	63%	11%	41	20	39	31%	73%	9%	20	78	65%	10%	0	0.81	5.3	120	143	$12
1st Half	6	2	0	80	73	4.90	4.94	1.43	774	791	751	18.8	2.3	8.2	3.6	64%	12%	43	20	37	36%	68%	14%	8	65	63%	13%	0	0.72	-11.4	89	107	-$3
2nd Half	11	2	0	82	71	2.09	3.24	0.93	576	627	526	22.5	1.3	7.8	5.9	62%	11%	40	19	41	27%	81%	7%	12	90	67%	8%	0	0.89	16.7	123	147	$27
15 Proj	**12**	**9**	**0**	**203**	**157**	**3.81**	**3.58**	**1.29**	**773**	**823**	**717**	**23.3**	**1.9**	**7.0**	**3.7**	**63%**	**11%**	**41**	**20**	**39**	**32%**	**74%**	**10%**	**36**						**-1.8**	**94**	**112**	**$8**

Siegrist,Kevin

Age: 25 | Th: L | Role: RP | Ht: 6' 5" | Wt: 215 | Type: Pwr FB
Health: D | PT/Exp: D | Consist: F | LIMA Plan: C | Rand Var: +5 | MM: 4500

Shelved by May forearm strain and ineffective afterward, but velocity was off all season. October MRI revealed inflammation and torn hand muscles in need of rehab. Clearly he's not 2013 good, but the 2nd half Ctl and Dom struggles look injury-related. Health is critical to any upside from here.

Yr Tm	W	L	Sv	IP	K	ERA	xERA	WHIP	oOPS	vL	vR	BF/G	Ctl	Dom	Cmd	FpK	SwK	G	L	F	H%	S%	hr/f	GS	APC	DOM%	DIS%	Sv%	LI	RAR	BPV	BPX	R$
10																																	
11																																	
12 aa	1	2	0	32	23	3.92	3.37	1.15				16.0	2.4	6.3	2.6						26%	69%								0.4	69	90	-$2
13 STL *	5	2	1	67	86	1.14	0.74	0.84	432	388	479	3.9	3.7	11.5	3.1	61%	10%	39	24	37	20%	89%	3%	0	15			100	0.84	22.7	151	197	$14
14 STL	1	4	0	30	37	6.82	4.17	1.58	818	827	811	3.8	4.7	11.0	2.3	65%	10%	30	20	49	36%	58%	12%	0	16			0	1.32	-11.5	77	92	-$7
1st Half	1	1	0	20	27	3.60	3.20	1.25	647	761	563	3.7	3.6	12.2	3.4	65%	11%	31	25	44	35%	71%	5%	0	15			0	1.46	0.3	131	156	-$3
2nd Half	0	3	0	10	10	13.06	6.33	2.23	1089	1017	1109	3.9	7.0	8.7	1.3	65%	10%	29	14	57	36%	42%	20%	0	16			0	1.08	-11.9	-25	-30	-$13
15 Proj	**2**	**2**	**0**	**44**	**47**	**3.09**	**3.16**	**1.11**	**624**	**626**	**618**	**5.3**	**3.2**	**9.7**	**3.0**	**63%**	**10%**	**34**	**25**	**41**	**28%**	**74%**	**8%**	**0**						**3.5**	**100**	**120**	**$2**

JOCK THOMPSON

Simmons,Shae

Age: 24	Th: R	Role: RP	Health: D	LIMA Plan: A
Ht: 5' 11"	Wt: 175	Type: Pwr GB	PT/Exp: F	Rand Var: 0
			Consist: F	MM: 5510

1-2, 2.91 ERA, 1 Sv in 22 IP at ATL. 2012 draft pick dominated in brief minor league career that includes a 1.76 ERA, 13.1 Dom and zero HR allowed over 102 IP. Didn't miss a beat in ATL until July shoulder strain sapped his velocity and ended his season. Premium relief upside if healthy.

Yr Tm	W	L	Sv	IP	K	ERA	xERA	WHIP	oOPS	vL	vR	BF/G	Ctl	Dom	Cmd	FpK	SwK	G	L	F	H%	S%	hr/f	GS	APC	DOM%	DIS%	Sv%	LI	RAR	BPV	BPX	R$
10																																	
11																																	
12																																	
13																																	
14 ATL *	1	3	15	46	49	2.73	2.40	1.19	598	489	730	3.8	3.7	9.8	2.6	63%	12%	53	25	23	30%	76%	8%	0	14			100	1.36	5.7	119	142	$7
1st Half	0	0	15	36	39	1.10	1.66	0.99	549	160	980	3.8	2.0	9.7	4.7	61%	12%	53	29	18	30%	88%	0%	0	12			100	1.29	11.7	170	203	$12
2nd Half	1	3	0	10	11	8.91	5.41	2.01	659	905	327	3.9	10.2	10.1	1.0	65%	13%	53	16	32	31%	53%	17%	0	18			0	1.47	-6.2	61	73	-$12
15 Proj	3	1	1	44	50	3.17	2.65	1.16				4.6	3.0	10.3	3.4	62%	11%	52	21	27	31%	74%	10%	0						3.1	134	159	$2

Simon,Alfredo

Age: 34	Th: R	Role: SP	Health: B	LIMA Plan: C+
Ht: 6' 6"	Wt: 265	Type:	PT/Exp: B	Rand Var: 0
			Consist: A	MM: 2105

Journeyman reliever surprised in a starting role. 1st half was fueled by terrific Ctl and more H% magic before he fell back to earth in the 2nd half, both in terms of skill and luck. Skills range remains consistent; his bottom line depends on swings in H%, S% and hr/f. More roster-worthy out of the pen.

Yr Tm	W	L	Sv	IP	K	ERA	xERA	WHIP	oOPS	vL	vR	BF/G	Ctl	Dom	Cmd	FpK	SwK	G	L	F	H%	S%	hr/f	GS	APC	DOM%	DIS%	Sv%	LI	RAR	BPV	BPX	R$
10 BAL *	5	3	17	66	47	4.23	5.45	1.53	825	684	953	5.4	3.7	6.4	1.7	53%	11%	47	19	34	31%	78%	18%	0	17			81	1.16	-1.2	26	43	$5
11 BAL *	5	9	0	134	97	4.85	4.86	1.47	834	808	862	21.2	3.2	6.6	2.1	57%	9%	43	20	37	32%	69%	11%	16	83	44%	38%	0	0.84	-15.0	48	72	-$6
12 CIN	3	2	1	61	52	2.66	3.77	1.43	747	745	748	7.5	3.2	7.7	2.4	63%	9%	54	21	25	34%	81%	4%	0	28			100	0.61	10.2	82	108	$1
13 CIN	6	4	1	88	63	2.87	3.90	1.07	625	729	543	5.7	2.7	6.5	2.4	58%	10%	45	18	36	25%	77%	9%	0	21			33	0.73	10.7	67	88	$8
14 CIN	15	10	0	196	127	3.44	3.93	1.21	690	715	665	25.6	2.6	5.8	2.3	62%	9%	48	21	31	27%	75%	12%	32	94	53%	16%			7.3	61	73	$11
1st Half	10	3	0	103	64	2.81	3.75	1.05	641	685	596	25.9	2.1	5.6	2.7	62%	9%	48	21	31	24%	79%	12%	16	93	56%	13%			11.9	70	84	$22
2nd Half	5	7	0	94	63	4.13	4.12	1.38	741	748	734	25.3	3.1	6.1	2.0	62%	8%	48	22	30	30%	72%	11%	16	95	50%	19%			-4.5	52	62	-$1
15 Proj	11	10	0	189	133	3.75	3.71	1.30	724	751	699	21.9	2.8	6.4	2.2	61%	9%	48	20	32	29%	73%	10%	36						-0.3	64	76	$7

Sipp,Tony

Age: 31	Th: L	Role: RP	Health: A	LIMA Plan: B
Ht: 6' 0"	Wt: 190	Type: Pwr xFB	PT/Exp: D	Rand Var: -1
			Consist: C	MM: 3510

Dom is once again elite, and he's somehow kept RHers and the long-ball in check for the past two years. But his R$ is still hostage to the control issues that reappeared in the 2nd half. Talented but volatile—and those big HR seasons still make this xFBer a scary proposition.

Yr Tm	W	L	Sv	IP	K	ERA	xERA	WHIP	oOPS	vL	vR	BF/G	Ctl	Dom	Cmd	FpK	SwK	G	L	F	H%	S%	hr/f	GS	APC	DOM%	DIS%	Sv%	LI	RAR	BPV	BPX	R$
10 CLE	2	2	1	63	69	4.14	4.32	1.38	770	805	742	3.8	5.6	9.9	1.8	57%	12%	31	14	55	25%	77%	14%	0	16			33	1.15	-0.5	36	58	$0
11 CLE	6	3	0	62	57	3.03	4.24	1.11	664	664	665	3.6	3.5	8.2	2.4	56%	13%	26	14	60	23%	81%	10%	0	15			0	1.25	7.0	59	88	$5
12 CLE	1	2	1	55	51	4.42	4.29	1.27	739	663	823	3.7	3.8	8.3	2.2	52%	10%	33	25	42	27%	70%	14%	0	15			50	0.91	-2.7	60	78	-$2
13 ARI	3	2	0	38	42	4.78	4.80	1.51	780	859	701	3.1	5.3	10.0	1.9	61%	12%	26	16	58	31%	73%	10%	0	13			0	1.00	-4.2	43	56	-$4
14 HOU	4	3	4	51	63	3.38	3.06	0.89	517	503	531	3.5	3.0	11.2	3.7	62%	14%	31	21	47	22%	65%	9%	0	15			67	1.60	2.3	129	154	$6
1st Half	1	0	1	22	29	1.61	2.41	0.63	416	283	545	3.8	1.2	11.7	9.7	66%	16%	31	25	44	21%	83%	10%	0	15			100	1.31	5.9	187	223	$6
2nd Half	3	3	3	28	34	4.76	3.62	1.09	592	666	520	3.4	4.4	10.8	2.4	58%	13%	31	19	50	23%	57%	9%	0	15			60	1.79	-3.6	84	100	$5
15 Proj	4	3	1	51	58	3.79	3.48	1.25	713	725	701	3.4	3.9	10.2	2.6	59%	13%	30	20	50	28%	75%	12%	0						-0.3	87	103	$1

Skaggs,Tyler

Age: 23	Th: L	Role: SP	Health: D	LIMA Plan: B+
Ht: 6' 4"	Wt: 215	Type:	PT/Exp: C	Rand Var: +1
			Consist: A	MM: 3200

Dom downtick and S% issues were minor blemishes on a nice step forward that began in March with the return of his velocity. Unfortunately it all ended in mid-August with Tommy John surgery, which gives him zero value for 2015. With his youth, a decent 2016 stash for keeper league rebuilders.

Yr Tm	W	L	Sv	IP	K	ERA	xERA	WHIP	oOPS	vL	vR	BF/G	Ctl	Dom	Cmd	FpK	SwK	G	L	F	H%	S%	hr/f	GS	APC	DOM%	DIS%	Sv%	LI	RAR	BPV	BPX	R$
10																																	
11 aa	4	1	0	58	64	2.68	2.59	1.06				22.4	2.1	10.0	4.8						31%	77%								9.0	151	227	$5
12 ARI *	10	9	0	152	122	3.53	3.99	1.28	785	333	863	22.2	2.7	7.3	2.7	52%	10%	34	18	48	30%	76%	13%	6	87	33%	50%			9.0	71	93	$8
13 ARI *	8	13	0	143	127	4.48	4.16	1.40	780	710	799	23.2	3.1	8.0	2.6	62%	9%	45	20	35	34%	68%	17%	7	94	29%	43%			-10.9	82	107	-$2
14 LAA	5	5	0	113	86	4.30	3.59	1.21	674	742	655	25.8	2.4	6.8	2.9	64%	9%	50	19	31	30%	65%	9%	18	95	61%	11%			-7.8	87	103	$0
1st Half	4	4	0	77	58	4.34	3.67	1.24	672	794	639	26.6	2.8	6.8	2.4	61%	8%	52	19	29	29%	65%	9%	12	95	67%	8%			-5.7	77	92	$2
2nd Half	1	1	0	36	28	4.21	3.43	1.16	678	636	691	24.2	1.5	6.9	4.7	70%	10%	46	19	35	31%	64%	8%	6	95	50%	17%			-2.1	109	130	-$3
15 Proj	1	1	0	15	12	4.05	3.35	1.24	690	680	692	23.7	2.4	7.5	3.1	64%	9%	47	19	34	31%	68%	8%	2						-0.6	96	114	-$3

Smith,Carson

Age: 25	Th: R	Role: RP	Health: A	LIMA Plan: A
Ht: 6' 6"	Wt: 215	Type: Pwr GB	PT/Exp: F	Rand Var: -3
			Consist: B	MM: 5400

1-0, 0.00 ERA in 8 IP at SEA. Another terrific SEA bullpen prospect. Hard sinking stuff led to 11.2 Dom and huge GB totals in the minors, as well as closer roles at three different levels. Obviously we need more than a small MLB sample, but he's a late-inning candidate to watch.

Yr Tm	W	L	Sv	IP	K	ERA	xERA	WHIP	oOPS	vL	vR	BF/G	Ctl	Dom	Cmd	FpK	SwK	G	L	F	H%	S%	hr/f	GS	APC	DOM%	DIS%	Sv%	LI	RAR	BPV	BPX	R$
10																																	
11																																	
12																																	
13 aa	1	3	15	50	61	2.50	2.48	1.18				4.6	3.2	10.9	3.4						33%	78%								8.4	140	182	$8
14 SEA *	2	3	10	51	48	2.54	3.09	1.26	249	83	369	4.4	2.6	8.4	3.2	64%	10%	81	6	13	34%	79%	0%	0	13			77	0.62	7.6	116	138	$5
1st Half	0	2	4	23	16	4.10	5.07	1.62				4.6	2.9	6.3	2.1						37%	74%	0%	0						-1.0	64	77	-$4
2nd Half	2	1	6	29	32	1.30	1.52	0.98	249	83	369	4.2	2.4	10.0	4.2	64%	10%	81	6	13	29%	85%	0%	0	13			100	0.62	8.6	162	193	$12
15 Proj	2	3	0	58	61	2.91	2.85	1.19				4.4	3.0	9.5	3.1	63%	9%	52	20	28	32%	74%	3%	0						6.0	119	142	$2

Smith,Joe

Age: 31	Th: R	Role: RP	Health: A	LIMA Plan: C+
Ht: 6' 2"	Wt: 205	Type: Pwr xGB	PT/Exp: C	Rand Var: -5
			Consist: B	MM: 5211

Had been serviceable previously, but nothing like this. Eclipsed all of his prior career bests in IP, Dom, Ctl, and ERA, as the wins and brief time as closer drove his R$. That 2nd half H% will get real in 2015, but his GB%, control, and saves-vulturing abilities should keep him valuable.

Yr Tm	W	L	Sv	IP	K	ERA	xERA	WHIP	oOPS	vL	vR	BF/G	Ctl	Dom	Cmd	FpK	SwK	G	L	F	H%	S%	hr/f	GS	APC	DOM%	DIS%	Sv%	LI	RAR	BPV	BPX	R$
10 CLE *	4	3	2	63	47	3.24	3.16	1.33	659	979	538	3.6	4.9	6.7	1.4	56%	8%	56	16	28	26%	77%	13%	0	12			50	1.13	6.5	63	103	$3
11 CLE	3	3	0	67	45	2.01	3.44	1.09	541	460	582	3.8	2.8	6.0	2.1	59%	6%	57	20	23	26%	81%	2%	0	14			0	1.05	15.9	68	102	$6
12 CLE	7	4	0	67	53	2.96	3.68	1.16	594	585	600	3.9	3.4	7.1	2.1	57%	9%	58	17	25	26%	76%	8%	0	15			0	1.22	8.8	73	96	$5
13 CLE	6	2	3	63	54	2.29	3.59	1.22	643	698	592	3.7	3.3	7.7	2.3	59%	9%	49	21	30	28%	85%	10%	0	14			38	1.37	12.3	77	101	$6
14 LAA	7	2	15	75	68	1.81	2.67	0.80	491	584	385	3.8	1.8	8.2	4.5	66%	8%	59	15	26	22%	80%	8%	0	15			79	1.25	17.8	136	162	$18
1st Half	2	0	7	34	39	2.94	2.46	1.10	643	754	497	4.0	2.1	10.4	4.9	71%	10%	58	19	23	32%	76%	15%	0	16			64	1.09	3.3	166	198	$9
2nd Half	5	2	8	41	29	0.88	2.83	0.56	349	401	296	3.6	1.5	6.4	4.1	61%	7%	60	12	28	15%	86%	3%	0	13			100	1.39	14.5	111	132	$26
15 Proj	6	3	8	73	61	2.50	2.92	0.99	549	610	494	3.6	2.6	7.6	2.9	62%	9%	56	17	27	25%	76%	8%	0						11.1	101	121	$11

Smith,Will

Age: 25	Th: L	Role: RP	Health: A	LIMA Plan: C+
Ht: 6' 5"	Wt: 250	Type: Pwr	PT/Exp: C	Rand Var: +3
			Consist: C	MM: 4501

Dom spike puts him in a select circle during his first full MLB season, and that SwK points to his upside. But unexpected control issues plagued him throughout, and gopheritis crushed him in the 2H. More consistency would make him rosterable; volatility is a reason he's in the bullpen.

Yr Tm	W	L	Sv	IP	K	ERA	xERA	WHIP	oOPS	vL	vR	BF/G	Ctl	Dom	Cmd	FpK	SwK	G	L	F	H%	S%	hr/f	GS	APC	DOM%	DIS%	Sv%	LI	RAR	BPV	BPX	R$
10 a/a	3	6	0	72	41	6.18	6.49	1.79				25.4	3.2	5.2	1.6						37%	66%								-18.6	22	35	-$10
11 aa	13	9	0	161	90	4.10	4.31	1.40				25.2	2.4	5.0	2.1						32%	71%								-3.1	53	80	$2
12 KC *	10	13	0	179	120	4.56	5.28	1.54	853	897	835	25.2	2.7	6.0	2.2	57%	7%	42	23	35	35%	72%	11%	16	88	50%	44%			-12.0	48	63	-$8
13 KC *	8	5	4	122	123	3.65	3.77	1.24	631	557	684	10.6	2.3	9.0	3.8	63%	16%	43	16	41	32%	74%	19%	1	26	0%	100%	44	1.72	3.3	109	142	$7
14 MIL	1	3	1	66	86	3.70	3.15	1.42	737	516	872	3.7	4.2	11.8	2.8	53%	13%	44	23	33	36%	76%	11%	0	14			17	1.48	0.3	119	142	-$1
1st Half	1	0	1	40	49	1.36	2.91	1.29	642	368	796	3.8	3.9	11.1	2.9	54%	13%	53	19	28	34%	92%	7%	0	15			20	1.74	11.6	127	151	$4
2nd Half	0	3	0	26	37	7.27	3.48	1.62	874	705	989	3.5	4.8	12.8	2.6	53%	14%	31	28	41	40%	55%	15%	0	13			0	1.15	-11.3	109	130	-$10
15 Proj	3	5	0	73	79	3.58	3.16	1.28	698	564	782	5.4	3.2	9.9	3.0	57%	13%	41	21	37	32%	74%	10%	0						1.5	109	130	$1

JOCK THOMPSON

Smyly,Drew

Age: 26	Th: L	Role SP	Health B	LIMA Plan B	
Ht: 6' 3"	Wt: 190	Type Pwr FB	PT/Exp C	Rand Var -1	
			Consist C	MM 4303	

Took a while to cement a rotation spot, but he excelled in the role from June onward. Ctl rebound and fortunate H% led the way until he was shut down in September to limit IP. He's a lefty killer and there's a lot to like about his BPIs. A caveat: Declining velocity and fly ball tilt hint at some latent risk.

Yr Tm	W	L	Sv	IP	K	ERA	xERA	WHIP	oOPS	vL	vR	BF/G	Ctl	Dom	Cmd	FpK	SwK	G	L	F	H%	S%	hr/f	GS	APC	DOM%	DIS%	Sv%	LI	RAR	BPV	BPX	R$
10																																	
11 aa	4	3	0	46	44	1.35	2.00	1.06				22.2	2.8	8.7	3.1						28%	88%								14.6	124	187	$6
12 DET *	4	5	0	117	114	4.51	4.39	1.36	732	671	759	16.3	3.1	8.8	2.8	58%	9%	40	19	41	32%	70%	10%	18	76	56%	33%	0	0.83	-7.2	78	102	-$3
13 DET	6	0	2	76	81	2.37	3.06	1.04	601	471	699	4.8	2.0	9.6	4.8	59%	11%	43	18	39	30%	79%	5%	0	20			33	1.12	14.0	139	182	$10
14 2 AL	9	10	0	153	133	3.24	3.79	1.16	688	486	763	22.1	2.5	7.8	3.2	62%	10%	37	20	43	28%	77%	10%	25	93	56%	16%	0	0.73	9.5	89	106	$10
1st Half	4	7	0	76	65	3.57	4.12	1.36	746	385	893	20.1	3.1	7.7	2.5	58%	9%	38	20	42	31%	78%	10%	13	86	46%	31%	0	0.71	1.6	71	85	$3
2nd Half	5	3	0	77	68	2.91	3.47	0.97	626	609	631	24.8	1.9	7.9	4.3	67%	11%	35	20	45	25%	75%	9%	12	101	67%	0%			7.9	105	126	$17
15 Proj	11	8	0	174	158	3.26	3.33	1.13	661	517	733	21.2	2.4	8.2	3.4	61%	10%	39	19	42	29%	74%	8%	26						10.4	99	118	$15

Soria,Joakim

Age: 31	Th: R	Role RP	Health F	LIMA Plan B+	
Ht: 6' 3"	Wt: 200	Type Pwr	PT/Exp D	Rand Var 0	
			Consist A	MM 5320	

Almost three years beyond his 2nd TJS, he's still racking up DL days. August oblique strain shelved him for five weeks and impacted his 2nd half effectiveness. Between injuries, his Ctl-fueled skills look vintage and suggest that the only thing standing in his way is health. So don't pay for a workhorse closer.

Yr Tm	W	L	Sv	IP	K	ERA	xERA	WHIP	oOPS	vL	vR	BF/G	Ctl	Dom	Cmd	FpK	SwK	G	L	F	H%	S%	hr/f	GS	APC	DOM%	DIS%	Sv%	LI	RAR	BPV	BPX	R$
10 KC	1	2	43	66	71	1.78	2.99	1.05	568	587	541	4.1	2.2	9.7	4.4	63%	10%	48	17	35	30%	86%	7%	0	17			93	1.28	18.6	142	230	$25
11 KC	5	5	28	60	60	4.03	3.51	1.28	709	631	793	4.3	2.5	9.0	3.5	57%	10%	40	21	39	32%	71%	10%	0	17			80	1.32	-0.6	111	166	$12
12																																	
13 TEX	1	0	0	24	28	3.80	3.43	1.35	624	316	943	3.9	5.3	10.6	2.0	56%	10%	52	18	30	29%	73%	12%	0	17			0	1.04	0.2	78	102	-$3
14 2 AL	2	4	18	44	48	3.25	2.93	0.99	605	675	503	3.8	1.2	9.7	8.0	63%	10%	43	22	35	32%	67%	5%	0	14			90	1.12	2.7	164	195	$9
1st Half	1	3	15	28	39	2.93	2.31	0.80	462	605	252	3.8	1.3	12.7	9.8	64%	13%	41	23	36	32%	59%	0%	0	15			94	1.19	2.8	212	253	$14
2nd Half	1	1	3	17	9	3.78	4.14	1.32	826	783	889	3.8	1.1	4.9	4.5	61%	6%	46	20	34	32%	75%	10%	0	14			75	1.02	-0.1	82	98	$0
15 Proj	3	4	20	53	51	3.23	3.03	1.16	677	669	688	3.8	1.8	8.6	4.8	61%	9%	43	20	36	32%	75%	8%	0						3.4	127	151	$10

Soriano,Rafael

Age: 35	Th: R	Role RP	Health B	LIMA Plan C	
Ht: 6' 4"	Wt: 230	Type Pwr xFB	PT/Exp A	Rand Var -2	
			Consist A	MM 3321	

Another Jekyll-and-Hyde 1H/2H performance. H% and S% reversed in July with return of lofty LD%. SwK fueled Dom rebound, and stable Ctl helps. But aging xFBer with diminshed/inconsistent velocity is no longer in his prime. His biggest saves years are history.

Yr Tm	W	L	Sv	IP	K	ERA	xERA	WHIP	oOPS	vL	vR	BF/G	Ctl	Dom	Cmd	FpK	SwK	G	L	F	H%	S%	hr/f	GS	APC	DOM%	DIS%	Sv%	LI	RAR	BPV	BPX	R$
10 TAM	3	2	45	62	57	1.73	3.51	0.80	509	590	431	3.7	2.0	8.2	4.1	59%	12%	33	16	52	21%	83%	5%	0	14			94	1.44	18.0	105	169	$28
11 NYY	2	3	2	39	36	4.12	4.10	1.30	645	850	477	3.9	4.1	8.2	2.0	58%	12%	35	20	44	28%	70%	8%	0	16			40	1.14	-0.9	50	75	-$1
12 NYY	2	1	42	68	69	2.26	3.78	1.17	639	713	549	4.0	3.2	9.2	2.9	56%	12%	36	24	40	29%	85%	8%	0	16			91	1.27	14.6	93	121	$23
13 WAS	3	3	43	67	51	3.11	4.15	1.23	668	785	584	4.1	2.3	6.9	3.0	55%	9%	34	25	42	30%	79%	8%	0	17			88	1.27	6.3	73	95	$19
14 WAS	4	1	32	62	59	3.19	3.84	1.13	639	614	662	3.9	2.8	8.6	3.1	57%	14%	32	19	49	29%	73%	5%	0	16			82	1.05	4.2	90	107	$15
1st Half	1	0	19	33	31	1.09	3.44	0.82	461	577	360	3.6	2.7	8.5	3.1	57%	13%	34	15	51	20%	88%	3%	0	15			90	1.11	10.8	91	108	$22
2nd Half	3	1	13	29	28	5.59	4.30	1.48	803	647	950	4.3	2.8	8.7	3.1	57%	14%	29	23	48	37%	63%	7%	0	17			72	1.00	-6.6	88	105	$8
15 Proj	4	2	20	73	66	3.43	3.57	1.20	663	684	644	3.9	2.7	8.2	3.0	56%	12%	33	22	46	30%	73%	7%	0						2.8	85	101	$11

Stammen,Craig

Age: 31	Th: R	Role RP	Health A	LIMA Plan C	
Ht: 6' 4"	Wt: 225	Type GB	PT/Exp C	Rand Var 0	
			Consist B	MM 3201	

End-game value play was on his way to more of the same until July. Lost both Dom and GB pitch, as H%, LD% and hr/f spikes fueled 2nd half ineffectiveness. He's clearly not without skills, but the volatility here speaks volumes. It's why he's in the pen and an end-gamer at best.

Yr Tm	W	L	Sv	IP	K	ERA	xERA	WHIP	oOPS	vL	vR	BF/G	Ctl	Dom	Cmd	FpK	SwK	G	L	F	H%	S%	hr/f	GS	APC	DOM%	DIS%	Sv%	LI	RAR	BPV	BPX	R$
10 WAS *	6	4	0	148	93	4.85	4.89	1.47	814	742	871	16.7	2.7	5.6	2.1	58%	10%	51	23	26	33%	68%	12%	19	60	37%	32%	0	0.59	-14.0	46	75	-$4
11 WAS *	11	8	0	152	108	5.72	6.05	1.64	272	192	333	21.2	2.7	6.4	2.4	61%	15%	52	14	33	36%	67%	0%	0	21			0	1.55	-33.4	41	62	-$13
12 WAS	6	1	1	88	87	2.34	3.80	1.20	636	605	655	6.3	3.7	8.9	2.4	59%	14%	45	20	35	28%	84%	8%	0	23			50	0.92	18.2	84	109	$9
13 WAS	7	6	0	82	79	2.76	3.07	1.29	684	761	634	6.2	3.0	8.7	2.9	61%	13%	60	16	24	33%	79%	7%	0	23			0	0.95	11.2	114	149	$5
14 WAS	4	5	0	73	56	3.84	3.49	1.27	708	767	660	6.2	1.7	6.9	4.0	61%	11%	48	23	29	33%	70%	8%	0	23			0	1.05	-0.9	104	124	$0
1st Half	0	3	0	41	34	2.83	3.02	0.97	563	581	546	6.8	1.3	7.4	5.7	65%	12%	53	20	28	29%	69%	3%	0	25			0	0.91	4.6	128	153	$3
2nd Half	4	2	0	31	22	5.17	4.13	1.66	881	1025	780	5.6	2.3	6.3	2.8	56%	10%	43	27	30	38%	71%	13%	0	21			0	1.19	-5.5	73	87	-$4
15 Proj	5	4	0	73	60	3.69	3.35	1.35	735	787	698	6.4	2.5	7.5	3.0	60%	12%	50	21	28	33%	74%	9%	0						0.5	95	113	$1

Stauffer,Tim

Age: 33	Th: R	Role RP	Health F	LIMA Plan B+	
Ht: 6' 1"	Wt: 210	Type Pwr	PT/Exp D	Rand Var +1	
			Consist B	MM 4300	

Dom spike, 2nd half Ctl and PETCO Park (2.10 ERA, 6 wins) helped him overcome GB% plunge and lofty H% -- and produce another credible middle relief performance. It keeps him in MLB, but caps his ceiling in our games. Age and Health say there are better roster-fill ideas.

Yr Tm	W	L	Sv	IP	K	ERA	xERA	WHIP	oOPS	vL	vR	BF/G	Ctl	Dom	Cmd	FpK	SwK	G	L	F	H%	S%	hr/f	GS	APC	DOM%	DIS%	Sv%	LI	RAR	BPV	BPX	R$
10 SD *	6	5	0	100	67	2.41	3.01	1.24	591	529	641	10.7	2.8	6.0	2.1	60%	7%	55	15	31	29%	80%	4%	7	38	57%	29%	0	0.74	20.6	79	127	$8
11 SD	9	12	0	186	128	3.73	3.69	1.25	729	774	683	25.1	2.6	6.2	2.4	57%	7%	52	20	28	29%	73%	13%	31	97	45%	16%			4.8	72	109	$8
12 SD	0	0	0	5	5	5.40	4.40	2.00	893	833	984	24.0	5.4	9.0	1.7	60%	10%	53	20	27	40%	78%	25%	1	91	0%	0%			-0.9	47	62	-$5
13 SD *	5	3	0	112	93	3.57	3.88	1.35	644	529	748	9.2	2.8	7.5	2.7	60%	9%	51	23	26	33%	74%	14%	0	26			0	0.84	4.1	83	108	$1
14 SD	6	2	0	64	67	3.50	3.40	1.40	727	680	775	6.2	3.2	9.4	2.9	61%	11%	42	28	30	36%	76%	7%	3	25	33%	67%	0	0.64	1.9	102	121	$0
1st Half	2	2	0	36	41	3.96	3.53	1.49	727	593	834	7.2	4.5	10.2	2.3	60%	10%	42	29	29	36%	73%	7%	3	31	33%	67%	0	0.65	-1.0	83	99	-$2
2nd Half	4	0	0	28	26	2.89	3.23	1.29	726	767	671	5.2	1.6	8.4	5.2	63%	13%	41	27	32	35%	79%	8%	0	19			0	0.63	2.9	126	151	$4
15 Proj	5	2	0	65	58	3.36	3.34	1.33	720	691	749	7.8	2.7	7.9	2.9	61%	10%	47	24	29	33%	76%	8%	0						3.0	93	111	$1

Storen,Drew

Age: 27	Th: R	Role RP	Health D	LIMA Plan B	
Ht: 6' 1"	Wt: 195	Type	PT/Exp C	Rand Var -5	
			Consist B	MM 4231	

Rebound from 2013 outlier following elbow surgery validates our 'buy low' call. Ended 2014 a perfect 10-for-10 in save opportunities during September closer audition. Dom isn't closer-elite, and both Ctl and GB gains need stabilizing. But with health and some luck... UP: 40 saves.

Yr Tm	W	L	Sv	IP	K	ERA	xERA	WHIP	oOPS	vL	vR	BF/G	Ctl	Dom	Cmd	FpK	SwK	G	L	F	H%	S%	hr/f	GS	APC	DOM%	DIS%	Sv%	LI	RAR	BPV	BPX	R$
10 WAS *	4	4	9	72	64	3.07	2.99	1.21	655	624	674	4.3	3.1	8.1	2.6	57%	10%	40	20	40	30%	75%	5%	0	17			82	1.25	9.0	95	154	$8
11 WAS	6	3	43	75	74	2.75	3.16	1.02	599	541	643	4.2	2.4	8.8	3.7	66%	9%	47	17	35	26%	78%	11%	0	15			90	1.42	11.1	120	180	$25
12 WAS	3	1	4	30	24	2.37	3.31	0.99	496	635	418	3.1	2.4	7.1	3.0	59%	14%	54	18	28	26%	73%	0%	0	11			80	1.21	6.1	96	125	$3
13 WAS	4	2	3	62	58	4.52	3.85	1.36	729	816	668	3.9	2.8	8.5	3.1	59%	10%	41	20	39	33%	69%	10%	0	14			38	1.09	-5.0	96	126	-$2
14 WAS	2	1	11	56	46	1.12	3.23	0.98	540	592	500	3.4	1.8	7.3	4.2	63%	11%	53	15	33	27%	91%	4%	0	12			79	1.21	18.2	116	138	$11
1st Half	2	1	0	26	22	1.03	3.02	0.80	501	487	507	3.2	1.4	7.5	5.5	65%	10%	48	17	35	23%	90%	4%	0	11			0	1.10	8.8	124	148	$9
2nd Half	0	0	11	30	24	1.20	3.41	1.13	573	666	492	3.6	2.1	7.2	3.4	61%	11%	56	12	31	30%	91%	4%	0	14			85	1.31	9.4	107	128	$13
15 Proj	4	2	28	73	62	2.97	3.14	1.10	595	661	547	3.5	2.2	7.7	3.5	61%	11%	49	17	34	29%	74%	6%	0						6.9	105	125	$16

Straily,Dan

Age: 26	Th: R	Role SP	Health A	LIMA Plan D+	
Ht: 6' 2"	Wt: 215	Type Pwr xFB	PT/Exp C	Rand Var +2	
			Consist C	MM 1201	

1-3, 6.75 ERA in 52 IP at OAK/CHC. Wobbly control amid another big velocity plunge was lethal for xFBer. His slider still generates Ks, but he needs more than one plus offering. Safe to ignore until he demonstrates an ability to reverse this Cmd trend.

Yr Tm	W	L	Sv	IP	K	ERA	xERA	WHIP	oOPS	vL	vR	BF/G	Ctl	Dom	Cmd	FpK	SwK	G	L	F	H%	S%	hr/f	GS	APC	DOM%	DIS%	Sv%	LI	RAR	BPV	BPX	R$
10																																	
11																																	
12 OAK *	11	8	0	191	190	3.15	2.94	1.11	803	1047	640	23.5	2.7	8.9	3.3	51%	10%	30	15	55	28%	75%	17%	7	96	29%	43%			20.5	107	139	$21
13 OAK *	13	9	0	184	151	3.48	3.26	1.22	666	711	617	23.2	3.2	7.4	2.3	60%	12%	36	20	44	28%	74%	8%	27	91	37%	30%			8.7	76	99	$12
14 2 TM *	8	11	0	170	145	5.86	5.46	1.55	832	765	906	21.8	3.9	7.7	2.0	47%	12%	35	16	49	32%	65%	13%	8	63	38%	25%	0	0.60	-44.5	41	48	-$16
1st Half	5	5	0	101	87	5.49	4.88	1.39	794	794	794	25.1	3.8	7.7	2.0	48%	13%	36	13	51	28%	65%	16%	7	87	43%	29%			-21.9	41	49	-$12
2nd Half	3	6	0	69	57	6.41	6.30	1.77	917	675	1121	18.6	4.0	7.5	1.9	44%	10%	33	23	44	38%	65%	5%	1	39	0%	0%	0	0.41	-22.6	40	48	-$23
15 Proj	6	6	0	102	87	4.27	4.13	1.40	754	828	684	21.8	3.5	7.7	2.2	52%	11%	34	16	51	31%	73%	8%	20						-6.7	56	66	-$1

JOCK THOMPSON

Strasburg,Stephen

Age: 26	Th: R	Role: SP	Health: D	LIMA Plan: C+
Ht: 6' 4"	Wt: 230	Type: Pwr	PT/Exp: A	Rand Var: +1
			Consist: A	MM: 5505

Last year, we said remaining hurdle to $25 breakout was 200 IP. H% and hr/f ruined the party, but under the surface, he pushed the envelope further. FpK gains sent Ctl to elite territory while he racked up the Ks. Skills already worthy of a sub-3.00 ERA... seems like everyone else is already there wondering where he is.

Yr Tm	W	L	Sv	IP	K	ERA	xERA	WHIP	oOPS	vL	vR	BF/G	Ctl	Dom	Cmd	FpK	SwK	G	L	F	H%	S%	hr/f	GS	APC	DOM%	DIS%	Sv%	LI	RAR	BPV	BPX	R$
10 WAS *	12	5	0	123	147	2.33	2.02	0.99	596	680	533	20.4	2.2	10.7	4.9	60%	13%	48	21	32	30%	78%	10%	12	89	58%	17%			26.6	167	271	$20
11 WAS	1	1	0	24	24	1.50	2.68	0.71	398	296	489	17.6	0.8	9.0	12.0	72%	12%	38	25	38	26%	76%	0%	5	66	60%	40%			7.2	158	237	$2
12 WAS	15	6	0	159	197	3.16	2.96	1.15	649	714	578	23.3	2.7	11.1	4.1	62%	12%	44	23	33	32%	76%	11%	28	93	71%	14%			16.7	149	194	$19
13 WAS	8	9	0	183	191	3.00	2.98	1.05	587	629	550	24.4	2.8	9.4	3.4	59%	11%	52	17	31	27%	74%	11%	30	95	77%	13%			19.5	125	163	$19
14 WAS	14	11	0	215	242	3.14	2.78	1.12	672	653	687	25.5	1.8	10.1	5.6	65%	12%	46	23	31	32%	76%	13%	34	97	79%	12%			16.0	158	188	$20
1st Half	6	6	0	105	123	3.70	2.87	1.28	713	651	760	26.1	2.0	10.6	5.3	65%	12%	46	23	31	37%	73%	11%	17	97	82%	18%			0.6	161	192	$10
2nd Half	8	5	0	110	119	2.61	2.68	0.97	628	655	605	24.9	1.6	9.7	6.0	65%	12%	46	23	32	28%	80%	15%	17	97	76%	6%			15.4	154	184	$29
15 Proj	**16**	**7**	**0**	**200**	**225**	**2.94**	**2.63**	**1.07**	**617**	**640**	**598**	**23.6**	**2.2**	**10.1**	**4.6**	**63%**	**12%**	**46**	**21**	**33**	**30%**	**76%**	**10%**	**33**						**19.9**	**147**	**175**	**$26**

Street,Huston

Age: 31	Th: R	Role: RP	Health: D	LIMA Plan: C
Ht: 6' 0"	Wt: 195	Type: Pwr FB	PT/Exp: B	Rand Var: -5
			Consist: B	MM: 4330

Posted career-best ERA and Sv total, though his absence from the DL was just as surprising. Stable SwK predicted the Dom rebound, but favorable hr/f gods were behind these gains. History shows those gods can turn at any time, especially given his FB%, so while he's an effective closer, don't pay for a repeat.

Yr Tm	W	L	Sv	IP	K	ERA	xERA	WHIP	oOPS	vL	vR	BF/G	Ctl	Dom	Cmd	FpK	SwK	G	L	F	H%	S%	hr/f	GS	APC	DOM%	DIS%	Sv%	LI	RAR	BPV	BPX	R$
10 COL	4	4	20	47	45	3.61	3.48	1.06	648	575	700	4.3	2.1	8.6	4.1	62%	14%	37	16	48	28%	69%	8%	0	16			80	1.22	2.7	113	182	$11
11 COL	1	4	29	58	55	3.86	3.38	1.22	781	811	760	3.9	1.4	8.5	6.1	67%	13%	35	24	41	32%	75%	14%	0	15			88	1.18	0.6	128	193	$11
12 SD	2	1	23	39	47	1.85	2.76	0.72	425	384	461	3.6	2.5	10.8	4.3	63%	14%	42	20	38	19%	77%	6%	0	15			96	1.19	10.4	147	191	$15
13 SD	2	5	33	57	46	2.70	3.93	1.02	691	689	693	3.8	2.2	7.3	3.3	64%	12%	30	22	48	22%	89%	16%	0	15			94	1.22	8.1	79	104	$17
14 2TM	2	2	41	59	57	1.37	3.36	0.94	521	482	561	3.8	2.1	8.6	4.1	64%	13%	36	20	43	26%	90%	6%	0	15			93	1.45	17.4	112	134	$23
1st Half	1	0	22	30	32	0.90	2.79	0.77	452	553	366	3.7	2.1	9.6	4.6	64%	14%	44	18	38	21%	95%	7%	0	15			100	1.46	10.5	138	164	$26
2nd Half	1	2	19	29	25	1.84	3.95	1.13	586	427	780	3.8	2.1	7.7	3.6	65%	12%	30	22	48	29%	87%	5%	0	15			86	1.43	6.9	88	105	$21
15 Proj	**2**	**3**	**35**	**58**	**55**	**2.83**	**3.29**	**1.14**	**670**	**617**	**721**	**3.9**	**2.2**	**8.5**	**3.9**	**64%**	**13%**	**35**	**21**	**44**	**30%**	**80%**	**9%**	**0**						**6.5**	**108**	**128**	**$17**

Stroman,Marcus

Age: 24	Th: R	Role: SP	Health: A	LIMA Plan: B
Ht: 5' 9"	Wt: 185	Type: Pwr GB	PT/Exp: D	Rand Var: 0
			Consist: B	MM: 5303

11-6, 3.65 ERA in 131 IP at TOR. Called up in May, landed rotation gig in June, and didn't look back. Plenty of reasons for optimism: pinpoint Ctl + GB% set a nice value floor; showed no L/R split; and xERA says this could've been even better. At 24 years old, he's a lucrative investment.

Yr Tm	W	L	Sv	IP	K	ERA	xERA	WHIP	oOPS	vL	vR	BF/G	Ctl	Dom	Cmd	FpK	SwK	G	L	F	H%	S%	hr/f	GS	APC	DOM%	DIS%	Sv%	LI	RAR	BPV	BPX	R$
10																																	
11																																	
12																																	
13 aa	9	5	0	112	114	3.70	3.81	1.20				22.5	2.1	9.2	4.4						32%	74%								2.3	117	153	$6
14 TOR *	13	10	1	166	150	3.70	3.23	1.20	633	646	620	20.3	2.0	8.1	4.0	58%	9%	54	18	28	33%	69%	6%	20	80	65%	20%	100	0.84	0.8	123	147	$9
1st Half	6	6	0	78	75	3.95	3.68	1.27	717	761	650	17.8	2.1	8.6	4.1	58%	9%	49	18	34	34%	69%	9%	6	65	83%	17%	0	0.88	-2.0	121	144	$5
2nd Half	7	4	1	88	75	3.48	3.06	1.15	592	573	609	23.7	1.9	7.7	3.9	59%	9%	56	19	25	31%	68%	5%	14	91	57%	21%	100	0.81	2.9	120	143	$13
15 Proj	**14**	**9**	**0**	**174**	**162**	**3.52**	**3.00**	**1.18**	**650**	**676**	**621**	**21.2**	**2.2**	**8.4**	**3.8**	**58%**	**9%**	**50**	**18**	**31**	**31%**	**72%**	**9%**	**33**						**4.7**	**120**	**142**	**$14**

Strop,Pedro

Age: 30	Th: R	Role: RP	Health: C	LIMA Plan: B+
Ht: 6' 1"	Wt: 220	Type: Pwr GB	PT/Exp: C	Rand Var: -2
			Consist: B	MM: 5510

Closer-worthy ERA returned, but unlike 2012, it was backed by skill support. Restored elite GB%, and major SwK surge suggests double-digit Dom can continue. Ctl gains also a great sign, bute FpK casts doubt he'll hold that 2nd half level. At worst, BPV growth makes him an intriguing LIMA target.

Yr Tm	W	L	Sv	IP	K	ERA	xERA	WHIP	oOPS	vL	vR	BF/G	Ctl	Dom	Cmd	FpK	SwK	G	L	F	H%	S%	hr/f	GS	APC	DOM%	DIS%	Sv%	LI	RAR	BPV	BPX	R$
10 TEX *	1	2	13	53	56	3.91	4.25	1.52	1109	1132	1093	4.3	4.4	9.6	2.2	64%	12%	31	28	42	36%	74%	13%	0	16			76	1.22	1.1	88	143	$3
11 2AL *	6	5	11	70	63	3.42	4.33	1.58	519	515	521	4.9	4.4	8.1	1.8	58%	10%	56	20	24	36%	78%	0%	0	16			73	1.12	4.5	77	116	$4
12 BAL	5	2	3	66	58	2.44	3.72	1.34	613	674	556	4.0	5.0	7.9	1.6	53%	11%	64	16	20	28%	82%	6%	0	16			30	1.25	12.9	48	63	$5
13 2TM	2	5	1	57	66	4.55	3.24	1.24	663	653	671	3.8	4.1	10.4	2.5	55%	13%	49	26	26	29%	64%	14%	0	15			25	1.25	-4.9	103	135	-$2
14 CHC	2	4	2	61	71	2.21	2.65	1.07	535	621	478	3.8	3.7	10.5	2.8	56%	16%	55	24	21	27%	79%	7%	0	14			33	1.12	11.5	122	145	$6
1st Half	0	3	2	27	30	3.04	2.99	1.20	569	676	504	3.7	5.1	10.1	2.0	58%	14%	59	23	18	25%	77%	18%	0	14			67	0.86	2.3	83	99	$0
2nd Half	2	1	0	34	41	1.57	2.40	0.96	508	581	456	3.8	2.6	10.7	4.1	55%	18%	52	25	23	29%	82%	0%	0	14			0	1.34	9.2	153	182	$10
15 Proj	**2**	**4**	**3**	**58**	**65**	**3.10**	**2.82**	**1.19**	**604**	**654**	**567**	**3.7**	**4.0**	**10.1**	**2.5**	**55%**	**14%**	**54**	**24**	**22**	**29%**	**74%**	**8%**	**0**						**4.6**	**105**	**125**	**$3**

Stults,Eric

Age: 35	Th: L	Role: SP	Health: C	LIMA Plan: C
Ht: 6' 2"	Wt: 220	Type: Con	PT/Exp: A	Rand Var: 0
			Consist: A	MM: 2003

Production continued down the wrong path, and skills question whether he can right the ship. Lefties started to figure him out and xERA inched upward. As a soft-tosser with decent control, he's barely on our radar, if only as a PETCO streaming option (3.46 ERA at home, 4.18 on road, last three years).

Yr Tm	W	L	Sv	IP	K	ERA	xERA	WHIP	oOPS	vL	vR	BF/G	Ctl	Dom	Cmd	FpK	SwK	G	L	F	H%	S%	hr/f	GS	APC	DOM%	DIS%	Sv%	LI	RAR	BPV	BPX	R$
10																																	
11 COL *	4	4	1	80	55	4.81	5.63	1.45	802	589	943	5.9	2.2	6.1	2.8	58%	9%	28	15	58	32%	73%	17%	0	32			20	0.39	-8.5	39	59	-$4
12 2TM *	9	4	0	134	82	2.86	3.31	1.25	667	482	728	20.3	2.7	5.5	2.0	62%	7%	40	26	34	29%	78%	6%	15	76	60%	0%	0	0.67	19.2	66	86	$10
13 SD	11	13	0	204	131	3.93	4.22	1.27	729	554	780	26.0	1.8	5.8	3.3	62%	8%	40	21	39	31%	71%	7%	33	98	45%	15%			-1.7	74	97	$5
14 SD	8	17	0	176	111	4.30	4.30	1.38	778	780	778	23.8	2.3	5.7	2.5	63%	8%	43	21	36	31%	73%	13%	32	89	38%	22%			-12.0	61	73	-$4
1st Half	2	11	0	87	48	5.36	4.63	1.51	845	778	874	23.1	2.2	4.9	2.3	64%	8%	43	22	35	32%	69%	15%	17	84	29%	29%			-17.4	51	61	-$16
2nd Half	6	6	0	89	63	3.25	3.99	1.24	707	780	684	24.7	2.4	6.4	2.6	61%	8%	44	20	36	29%	78%	10%	15	94	47%	13%			5.4	71	85	$9
15 Proj	**7**	**9**	**0**	**131**	**84**	**3.95**	**3.90**	**1.32**	**753**	**677**	**777**	**24.2**	**2.2**	**5.8**	**2.6**	**62%**	**8%**	**42**	**21**	**37**	**31%**	**74%**	**10%**	**22**						**-3.3**	**64**	**76**	**$1**

Swarzak,Anthony

Age: 29	Th: R	Role: RP	Health: B	LIMA Plan: D+
Ht: 6' 4"	Wt: 210	Type: Con	PT/Exp: C	Rand Var: -1
			Consist: B	MM: 1001

Started the year on the DL (ribs), which likely played a part in 1st half struggles. Miniscule Dom all year prevents us from giving him a pass, though, especially given subpar SwK. Continued struggles vs. LHB, xERA history should keep him in middle innings, and away from your roster.

Yr Tm	W	L	Sv	IP	K	ERA	xERA	WHIP	oOPS	vL	vR	BF/G	Ctl	Dom	Cmd	FpK	SwK	G	L	F	H%	S%	hr/f	GS	APC	DOM%	DIS%	Sv%	LI	RAR	BPV	BPX	R$
10 aaa	5	12	0	112	54	7.11	6.62	1.82				23.6	3.2	4.3	1.4						37%	60%								-41.8	12	19	-$18
11 MIN *	6	8	0	134	75	4.43	4.45	1.39	724	690	766	17.1	2.2	5.0	2.2	60%	6%	38	20	42	32%	69%	6%	11	62	64%	27%	0	0.69	-8.1	50	76	-$2
12 MIN	3	6	0	97	62	5.03	4.58	1.42	798	771	821	9.4	2.9	5.8	2.0	60%	8%	43	21	35	30%	68%	13%	5	33	0%	40%	0	0.77	-12.1	47	61	-$7
13 MIN	3	2	0	96	69	2.91	3.79	1.16	649	772	540	8.1	2.1	6.5	3.1	61%	8%	45	19	36	29%	77%	7%	0	31			0	0.78	11.4	84	109	$5
14 MIN	3	2	0	86	47	4.60	4.74	1.49	752	733	768	7.6	2.9	4.9	1.7	60%	7%	45	20	36	33%	68%	5%	4	28	25%	75%	0	0.82	-9.2	32	39	-$7
1st Half	1	0	0	39	21	3.96	5.05	1.42	687	644	714	6.8	3.7	4.9	1.3	60%	9%	43	17	40	30%	70%	2%	0	25			0	0.88	-1.0	9	10	-$6
2nd Half	2	2	0	47	26	5.13	4.50	1.54	802	783	825	8.4	2.3	4.9	2.2	59%	6%	46	22	33	35%	67%	7%	4	31	25%	75%	0	0.76	-8.1	51	61	-$7
15 Proj	**3**	**3**	**0**	**87**	**52**	**4.39**	**4.13**	**1.41**	**747**	**758**	**736**	**8.4**	**2.6**	**5.4**	**2.0**	**60%**	**7%**	**44**	**20**	**36**	**32%**	**69%**	**7%**	**0**						**-6.9**	**48**	**57**	**-$4**

Syndergaard,Noah

Age: 22	Th: R	Role: SP	Health: A	LIMA Plan: A
Ht: 6' 6"	Wt: 240	Type: Pwr	PT/Exp: F	Rand Var: +1
			Consist: A	MM: 4401

Held his own all season in hitter-friendly Las Vegas, but The Call never came. Continued to show excellent Cmd, and 2nd half surge indicates he has little left to show in the minors at this point. A keeper league gem, but as with most prospects, expect some bumps along the way.

Yr Tm	W	L	Sv	IP	K	ERA	xERA	WHIP	oOPS	vL	vR	BF/G	Ctl	Dom	Cmd	FpK	SwK	G	L	F	H%	S%	hr/f	GS	APC	DOM%	DIS%	Sv%	LI	RAR	BPV	BPX	R$
10																																	
11																																	
12																																	
13 aa	6	1	0	54	63	3.04	3.42	1.09				19.2	1.8	10.4	5.7						31%	79%								5.5	151	197	$4
14 aaa	9	7	0	133	130	3.58	3.84	1.32				21.2	2.3	8.8	3.8						35%	73%								2.6	116	138	$4
1st Half	6	4	0	69	64	4.16	4.18	1.33				20.5	2.4	8.3	3.5						34%	70%								-3.6	96	115	$3
2nd Half	3	3	0	64	66	2.96	3.48	1.31				22.0	2.3	9.3	4.1						37%	76%								6.2	137	164	$5
15 Proj	**7**	**4**	**0**	**93**	**90**	**3.86**	**3.08**	**1.18**				**20.2**	**2.5**	**8.8**	**3.5**	**62%**	**9%**	**47**	**18**	**35**	**31%**	**69%**	**9%**	**16**						**-1.4**	**115**	**137**	**$4**

RYAN BLOOMFIELD

Tanaka,Masahiro

Age: 26	Th: R	Role SP	Health D	LIMA Plan C+
Ht: 6' 2"	Wt: 205	Type	PT/Exp A	Rand Var 0
			Consist A	MM 5303

Lived up to hype until partially torn UCL put season on hold in July. Avoided surgery, and even made it back for two starts in September. Skills are among the best in the game, but elbow issue and splitter-heavy repertoire are scary combo. UP: 2.50 ERA, 200 Ks. DN: Out for season. Yes, the possibilities are that wide.

Yr	Tm	W	L	Sv	IP	K	ERA	xERA	WHIP	oOPS	vL	vR	BF/G	Ctl	Dom	Cmd	FpK	SwK	G	L	F	H%	S%	hr/f	GS	APC	DOM%	DIS%	Sv%	LI	RAR	BPV	BPX	R$
10	for	11	6	0	155	113	3.10	4.34	1.36				32.4	2.3	6.6	2.8						32%	80%								18.7	72	116	$9
11	for	19	5	0	226	229	1.58	2.21	0.96				31.6	1.3	9.1	6.8						29%	87%								65.8	192	289	$44
12	for	10	4	0	173	160	2.33	2.97	1.13				31.1	1.2	8.3	6.8						34%	80%								36.0	185	242	$23
13	for	22	0	1	199	164	1.52	2.41	1.03				29.5	1.7	7.4	4.4						29%	88%								57.7	132	173	$38
14	NYY	13	5	0	136	141	2.77	2.76	1.06	657	632	687	27.1	1.4	9.3	6.7	62%	14%	47	24	29	31%	79%	14%	20	100	80%	5%			16.3	155	185	$16
1st Half		11	3	0	116	127	2.10	2.63	0.95	611	569	657	28.1	1.4	9.9	7.1	62%	14%	45	24	31	28%	86%	14%	16	107	94%	0%			23.4	163	195	$24
2nd Half		2	2	0	21	14	6.53	3.60	1.65	880	869	902	23.0	1.3	6.1	4.7	64%	10%	53	26	22	40%	59%	13%	4	76	25%	25%			-7.1	105	126	-$27
15	**Proj**	**14**	**6**	**0**	**178**	**158**	**3.15**	**2.92**	**1.14**	**658**	**650**	**671**	**26.4**	**1.5**	**8.0**	**5.5**	**63%**	**12%**	**48**	**22**	**30**	**32%**	**75%**	**10%**	**27**						**13.1**	**130**	**155**	**$17**

Tazawa,Junichi

Age: 29	Th: R	Role RP	Health D	LIMA Plan A
Ht: 5' 11"	Wt: 200	Type Pwr	PT/Exp D	Rand Var -2
			Consist A	MM 4400

Elite-level Cmd is well-established by now, and he's proven to be quite durable. High LD% will continue to put elevated H% in play, but that's the only flaw in this skill set. He's a safe bet for strong ratios and holds, and is always a decent target for saves speculation.

Yr	Tm	W	L	Sv	IP	K	ERA	xERA	WHIP	oOPS	vL	vR	BF/G	Ctl	Dom	Cmd	FpK	SwK	G	L	F	H%	S%	hr/f	GS	APC	DOM%	DIS%	Sv%	LI	RAR	BPV	BPX	R$
10																																		
11	BOS *	4	3	0	40	41	5.02	4.68	1.38	974	1500	722	8.9	2.5	9.1	3.6	46%	9%	13	0	88	35%	66%	14%	0	18			0	0.21	-5.4	93	139	-$2
12	BOS *	4	3	5	86	89	2.56	3.10	1.23	558	519	583	5.6	2.5	9.3	3.7	67%	15%	49	24	27	34%	79%	3%	0	18			63	0.82	15.5	126	165	$9
13	BOS	5	4	0	68	72	3.16	3.31	1.20	744	790	704	4.0	1.6	9.5	6.0	62%	13%	34	27	39	34%	79%	12%	0	15			0	1.09	5.9	140	182	$3
14	BOS	4	3	0	63	64	2.86	3.42	1.19	660	615	702	3.7	2.4	9.1	3.8	60%	12%	37	28	36	32%	79%	8%	0	14			0	1.34	6.9	114	136	$3
1st Half		1	1	0	34	35	2.14	3.26	1.10	631	648	615	3.6	2.1	9.4	4.4	61%	13%	33	30	37	30%	85%	9%	0	13			0	1.30	6.7	121	145	$4
2nd Half		3	2	0	29	29	3.68	3.61	1.30	692	577	791	3.7	2.8	8.9	3.2	58%	11%	41	24	35	33%	72%	7%	0	15			0	1.38	0.2	104	124	$2
15	**Proj**	**5**	**4**	**0**	**65**	**66**	**3.23**	**3.21**	**1.26**	**703**	**682**	**720**	**4.2**	**2.5**	**9.1**	**3.6**	**62%**	**13%**	**38**	**26**	**37**	**33%**	**77%**	**9%**	**0**						**4.1**	**111**	**132**	**$3**

Teheran,Julio

Age: 24	Th: R	Role SP	Health A	LIMA Plan D+
Ht: 6' 2"	Wt: 200	Type FB	PT/Exp A	Rand Var -2
			Consist B	MM 3305

A lot to like, in addition to age: mastery of LHB, stellar Ctl, and just 5 PQS-DIS starts in last 2 years. Even flashed further upside with 9.1 Dom over 17-start span, before fading late. But skills haven't supported sub-3.00 ERA. He'll likely be very good, but there's little room for profit in 2015.

Yr	Tm	W	L	Sv	IP	K	ERA	xERA	WHIP	oOPS	vL	vR	BF/G	Ctl	Dom	Cmd	FpK	SwK	G	L	F	H%	S%	hr/f	GS	APC	DOM%	DIS%	Sv%	LI	RAR	BPV	BPX	R$
10	aa	3	2	0	40	35	3.71	2.57	1.17				22.8	3.6	7.9	2.2						27%	68%								1.8	92	150	$1
11	ATL *	16	4	0	164	122	3.19	3.39	1.28	828	968	598	22.5	3.0	6.7	2.2	60%	7%	30	24	46	30%	76%	13%	3	70	0%	67%	0	0.72	15.2	76	115	$13
12	ATL *	7	9	0	137	92	5.55	5.16	1.49	467	250	579	21.1	2.7	6.0	2.2	52%	8%	22	33	44	33%	64%	0%	1	50	0%	100%	0	0.71	-26.0	44	58	-$12
13	ATL	14	8	0	186	170	3.20	3.67	1.17	700	823	580	25.8	2.2	8.2	3.8	65%	11%	38	21	41	30%	78%	10%	30	96	60%	10%			15.3	105	137	$16
14	ATL	14	13	0	221	186	2.89	3.73	1.08	639	687	587	26.8	2.1	7.6	3.6	60%	11%	35	21	44	28%	77%	8%	33	99	73%	6%			23.2	93	111	$22
1st Half		7	5	0	119	103	2.34	3.48	0.95	576	531	619	27.3	1.7	7.8	4.5	61%	12%	38	18	44	25%	80%	8%	17	99	82%	6%			20.5	109	130	$31
2nd Half		7	8	0	102	83	3.53	4.03	1.24	708	841	547	26.3	2.5	7.3	3.0	60%	11%	31	25	43	30%	75%	8%	16	99	63%	6%			2.7	74	89	$11
15	**Proj**	**15**	**10**	**0**	**201**	**174**	**3.33**	**3.46**	**1.18**	**690**	**781**	**595**	**24.3**	**2.2**	**7.8**	**3.6**	**62%**	**11%**	**36**	**22**	**43**	**30%**	**75%**	**8%**	**33**						**10.1**	**95**	**113**	**$17**

Tepesch,Nicholas

Age: 26	Th: R	Role SP	Health D	LIMA Plan D+
Ht: 6' 4"	Wt: 225	Type Con	PT/Exp C	Rand Var 0
			Consist C	MM 2001

5-11, 4.36 ERA in 126 IP at TEX. Posted 7.9 Dom in first three May starts, then Ks disappeared: just 3.3 Dom rest of the season. Reported knee soreness in July; did it linger all year? Age and 2013 BPIs say he can't be dismissed yet, but best left on reserve until we get some answers.

Yr	Tm	W	L	Sv	IP	K	ERA	xERA	WHIP	oOPS	vL	vR	BF/G	Ctl	Dom	Cmd	FpK	SwK	G	L	F	H%	S%	hr/f	GS	APC	DOM%	DIS%	Sv%	LI	RAR	BPV	BPX	R$
10																																		
11																																		
12	aa	6	3	0	90	55	5.78	6.13	1.63				25.1	2.8	5.4	2.0						35%	67%								-19.7	24	31	-$12
13	TEX	4	6	0	93	76	4.84	3.81	1.37	757	841	646	21.4	2.6	7.4	2.8	62%	9%	47	22	30	32%	67%	13%	17	81	29%	35%	0	0.83	-11.2	87	113	-$5
14	TEX *	11	12	0	172	88	3.68	3.91	1.30	774	725	840	23.6	2.8	4.6	1.6	56%	6%	42	24	35	28%	74%	10%	22	88	32%	32%	0	0.84	1.3	40	48	$3
1st Half		9	4	0	90	61	2.71	3.38	1.23	746	711	811	24.3	2.6	6.1	2.3	58%	7%	42	23	35	29%	80%	10%	8	94	50%	38%			11.4	72	86	$15
2nd Half		2	8	0	82	27	4.74	5.03	1.37	789	733	851	23.1	3.0	3.0	1.0	56%	6%	42	24	34	27%	68%	10%	14	85	21%	29%	0	0.88	-10.1	-7	-9	-$9
15	**Proj**	**5**	**7**	**0**	**102**	**62**	**4.52**	**4.04**	**1.38**	**777**	**781**	**772**	**22.5**	**2.7**	**5.5**	**2.0**	**59%**	**7%**	**44**	**23**	**33**	**30%**	**70%**	**11%**	**19**						**-9.8**	**47**	**56**	**-$3**

Thayer,Dale

Age: 34	Th: R	Role RP	Health A	LIMA Plan B+
Ht: 6' 0"	Wt: 210	Type Pwr	PT/Exp C	Rand Var -5
			Consist A	MM 4310

Sure, abnormally high S% aided 1st half ERA, but consistently strong BPIs remained intact. Spike in FpK led to improved Ctl, which included 32 inning span with just 4 walks. Time has probably run out for an extended shot at a closer role, but should continue to provide ratio insulation.

Yr	Tm	W	L	Sv	IP	K	ERA	xERA	WHIP	oOPS	vL	vR	BF/G	Ctl	Dom	Cmd	FpK	SwK	G	L	F	H%	S%	hr/f	GS	APC	DOM%	DIS%	Sv%	LI	RAR	BPV	BPX	R$
10	TAM *	4	1	3	62	43	5.15	6.76	1.97	1385	1000	1556	6.3	4.1	6.3	1.5	54%	6%	50	30	20	40%	74%	50%	0	53			75	0.37	-8.2	36	58	-$7
11	NYM *	4	6	21	81	52	3.22	3.56	1.16	729	1295	474	5.0	1.7	5.8	3.3	60%	6%	44	28	28	28%	76%	0%	0	14			81	0.59	7.3	79	119	$13
12	SD	2	2	7	58	47	3.43	3.82	1.13	627	654	607	3.7	1.9	7.3	3.9	58%	10%	41	21	38	30%	70%	6%	0	15			70	1.15	4.1	100	131	$4
13	SD	3	5	1	65	64	3.32	3.57	1.25	691	770	622	3.9	3.0	8.9	2.9	59%	9%	41	22	37	30%	78%	12%	0	16			25	1.00	4.3	96	125	$1
14	SD	4	5	0	65	62	2.34	3.45	1.06	627	636	619	3.8	2.2	8.5	3.9	64%	10%	39	21	40	26%	87%	13%	0	15			0	0.94	11.3	111	132	$6
1st Half		3	2	0	35	32	1.80	3.69	1.17	636	630	640	3.7	2.6	8.2	3.2	64%	9%	39	21	39	29%	92%	10%	0	15			0	0.94	8.4	96	115	$7
2nd Half		1	3	0	30	30	2.97	3.20	0.92	615	644	594	3.8	1.8	8.9	5.0	64%	10%	39	20	41	23%	78%	15%	0	15			0	0.94	2.9	129	154	$5
15	**Proj**	**3**	**5**	**2**	**65**	**60**	**3.29**	**3.23**	**1.13**	**659**	**700**	**627**	**3.8**	**2.2**	**8.2**	**3.7**	**61%**	**10%**	**40**	**21**	**39**	**29%**	**76%**	**11%**	**0**						**3.7**	**106**	**126**	**$4**

Thielbar,Caleb

Age: 28	Th: L	Role RP	Health A	LIMA Plan D+
Ht: 6' 0"	Wt: 195	Type	PT/Exp D	Rand Var -3
			Consist F	MM 2100

Sample is still fairly small, but he's been more of a fly ball pitcher in majors than in minors. Couple that with 89 mph heater, and margin for error is pretty thin. Drop in Dom and SwK indicates he wasn't fooling anybody, and 2014 xERA shows what might happen with a little hr/f regression.

Yr	Tm	W	L	Sv	IP	K	ERA	xERA	WHIP	oOPS	vL	vR	BF/G	Ctl	Dom	Cmd	FpK	SwK	G	L	F	H%	S%	hr/f	GS	APC	DOM%	DIS%	Sv%	LI	RAR	BPV	BPX	R$
10																																		
11																																		
12	a/a	5	1	5	65	47	3.67	4.54	1.42				6.8	2.8	6.4	2.3						32%	77%								2.8	59	76	$1
13	MIN *	4	3	1	72	65	2.75	2.49	1.08	530	482	575	4.3	2.8	8.1	2.9	55%	12%	27	19	54	27%	77%	6%	0	13			100	0.72	9.9	104	136	$6
14	MIN	2	1	0	48	35	3.40	4.48	1.41	738	760	713	3.8	3.0	6.6	2.2	57%	7%	32	26	42	33%	77%	5%	0	15			0	0.88	2.0	47	56	-$2
1st Half		2	0	0	27	19	3.00	4.19	1.00	666	704	628	3.4	2.3	6.3	2.7	58%	7%	24	23	53	24%	72%	5%	0	14			0	1.20	2.5	53	64	$1
2nd Half		0	1	0	21	16	3.92	4.85	1.94	813	813	810	4.4	3.9	7.0	1.8	56%	8%	39	30	31	42%	79%	4%	0	17			0	0.45	-0.5	37	44	-$7
15	**Proj**	**3**	**2**	**0**	**58**	**43**	**3.91**	**4.01**	**1.39**	**736**	**735**	**735**	**4.3**	**3.2**	**6.7**	**2.1**	**56%**	**9%**	**38**	**24**	**38**	**32%**	**72%**	**6%**	**0**						**-1.2**	**51**	**61**	**-$2**

Thornburg,Tyler

Age: 26	Th: R	Role RP	Health F	LIMA Plan D+
Ht: 5' 11"	Wt: 190	Type Pwr FB	PT/Exp D	Rand Var -3
			Consist A	MM 2301

Take 2014 Ctl with a grain of salt, as elbow soreness ended his season in June. Inability to induce GB is probably larger issue going forward. But he's shown glimpses of promise in the past, and could work his way back into a rotation mix. End-game flyer? Maybe a speculative cautionary deep reserve flyer.

Yr	Tm	W	L	Sv	IP	K	ERA	xERA	WHIP	oOPS	vL	vR	BF/G	Ctl	Dom	Cmd	FpK	SwK	G	L	F	H%	S%	hr/f	GS	APC	DOM%	DIS%	Sv%	LI	RAR	BPV	BPX	R$
10																																		
11																																		
12	MIL *	10	4	0	135	116	4.17	4.45	1.37	922	757	1071	19.5	3.1	7.8	2.5	53%	8%	42	20	38	31%	73%	32%	3	48	0%	100%	0	0.42	-2.5	66	86	$1
13	MIL *	3	10	0	141	121	4.43	4.64	1.50	575	479	684	18.5	3.6	7.7	2.2	60%	7%	36	24	39	34%	72%	1%	7	59	86%	0%	0	0.52	-9.8	64	84	-$7
14	MIL	3	1	0	30	28	4.25	4.91	1.52	670	458	808	4.9	6.4	8.5	1.3	54%	11%	36	19	45	29%	70%	3%	0	19			0	0.94	-1.9	-5	-6	-$3
1st Half		3	1	0	30	28	4.25	4.91	1.52	670	458	808	4.9	6.4	8.5	1.3	54%	11%	36	19	45	29%	70%	3%	0	19			0	0.94	-1.9	-5	-6	-$3
2nd Half																																		
15	**Proj**	**4**	**6**	**0**	**88**	**78**	**4.16**	**3.93**	**1.39**	**744**	**493**	**947**	**9.1**	**3.8**	**8.0**	**2.1**	**56%**	**10%**	**36**	**21**	**43**	**31%**	**71%**	**7%**	**0**						**-4.5**	**57**	**67**	**-$1**

BRIAN RUDD

Thornton,Matt

Thornton,Matt							
Age: 38	Th: L	Role	RP	Health	C	LIMA Plan	B+
Ht: 6' 6"	Wt: 235	Type	GB	PT/Exp	D	Rand Var	-5
				Consist	B	MM	4200

Nifty late-career renaissance. OK, so xERA says not THAT nifty, but halted Dom slide and struggles vs. RHB, which might have saved career. Strong GB rate, and no one took him deep. Good Ctl despite weak FpK: veteran savvy? Naaah. We always search for planetary alignment. That means regression.

Yr Tm	W	L	Sv	IP	K	ERA	xERA	WHIP	oOPS	vL	vR	BF/G	Ctl	Dom	Cmd	FpK	SwK	G	L	F	H%	S%	hr/f	GS	APC	DOM%	DIS%	Sv%	LI	RAR	BPV	BPX	R$
10 CHW	5	4	8	61	81	2.67	2.64	1.01	547	500	584	3.9	3.0	12.0	4.1	60%	16%	40	23	37	30%	74%	6%	0	16			80	1.38	10.5	154	249	$11
11 CHW	2	5	3	60	63	3.32	3.28	1.36	649	619	672	4.2	3.2	9.5	3.0	65%	11%	49	24	27	35%	76%	7%	0	17			43	1.28	4.6	113	169	$2
12 CHW	4	10	3	65	53	3.46	3.42	1.23	685	660	709	3.6	2.4	7.3	3.1	59%	9%	54	20	26	31%	72%	8%	0	14			43	1.43	4.4	101	131	$3
13 2AL	0	4	0	43	30	3.74	4.09	1.43	738	638	827	3.1	3.1	6.2	2.0	66%	8%	51	19	30	32%	76%	10%	0	12			0	1.33	0.7	57	74	-$4
14 2TM	1	3	0	36	28	1.75	3.43	1.14	596	569	634	2.4	2.0	7.0	3.5	54%	9%	56	13	31	31%	83%	0%	0	10			0	1.20	8.8	106	126	$1
1st Half	0	1	0	18	15	2.55	3.54	1.19	576	508	677	2.3	2.5	7.6	3.0	51%	9%	56	15	30	31%	76%	0%	0	11			0	1.21	2.6	102	122	-$2
2nd Half	1	2	0	18	13	0.98	3.31	1.09	615	633	588	2.4	1.5	6.4	4.3	56%	9%	56	11	33	31%	90%	0%	0	9			0	1.19	6.2	109	131	$4
15 Proj	2	5	1	51	40	3.44	3.28	1.23	679	638	725	2.7	2.4	7.2	3.0	59%	9%	53	16	30	30%	73%	8%	0						1.9	96	114	$0

Tillman,Chris

Tillman,Chris							
Age: 27	Th: R	Role	SP	Health	A	LIMA Plan	C+
Ht: 6' 5"	Wt: 210	Type	FB	PT/Exp	A	Rand Var	-1
				Consist	A	MM	2205

On skills front, season turned on a dime. Futzed around with low BPV for three months, then wham! No PQS-DISasters after July 7, second straight closing flourish. H%, S% helped, so don't buy 2nd half ERA. Stagnant SwK, low FpK suggest no quantum leap ahead. This skills set is more likely to see an ERA of 4.00 than 3.00.

Yr Tm	W	L	Sv	IP	K	ERA	xERA	WHIP	oOPS	vL	vR	BF/G	Ctl	Dom	Cmd	FpK	SwK	G	L	F	H%	S%	hr/f	GS	APC	DOM%	DIS%	Sv%	LI	RAR	BPV	BPX	R$
10 BAL *	13	12	0	175	111	4.56	4.61	1.41	828	930	733	23.1	3.1	5.7	1.8	50%	7%	43	22	36	30%	70%	15%	11	87	18%	55%			-10.4	40	65	$1
11 BAL *	6	11	0	138	91	5.94	6.08	1.65	812	797	823	22.1	4.1	5.9	1.4	53%	6%	37	18	45	32%	68%	5%	13	90	31%	54%			-34.1	12	18	-$15
12 BAL *	17	12	0	179	143	4.02	3.95	1.31	639	601	701	23.0	2.9	7.2	2.4	55%	9%	35	21	44	30%	72%	11%	15	96	60%	20%			-0.1	70	91	$8
13 BAL	16	7	0	206	179	3.71	3.87	1.22	730	744	711	25.6	3.0	7.8	2.6	57%	9%	39	22	40	27%	76%	14%	33	105	52%	15%			4.0	77	101	$13
14 BAL	13	6	0	207	150	3.34	4.21	1.23	671	670	672	25.6	2.9	6.5	2.3	58%	8%	41	20	39	28%	76%	8%	34	100	41%	15%			10.2	59	70	$11
1st Half	7	4	0	99	62	4.18	4.82	1.39	733	774	681	25.5	3.6	5.6	1.6	56%	7%	39	21	40	29%	72%	9%	17	99	24%	24%			-5.4	20	24	$0
2nd Half	6	2	0	108	88	2.58	3.68	1.08	611	567	663	25.8	2.2	7.3	3.4	59%	8%	42	19	39	27%	80%	8%	17	101	59%	6%			15.6	93	111	$21
15 Proj	12	10	0	203	156	3.67	3.81	1.26	707	705	711	24.3	2.9	6.9	2.4	57%	8%	39	20	40	28%	75%	10%	34						1.9	63	75	$10

Tolleson,Shawn

Tolleson,Shawn							
Age: 27	Th: R	Role	RP	Health	F	LIMA Plan	B+
Ht: 6' 2"	Wt: 210	Type	Pwr FB	PT/Exp	D	Rand Var	-5
				Consist	F	MM	4400

Quietly solid season amid TEX chaos. New high in IP, but reasons to think ERA won't last. With so many FB, low hr/f really saved him in 2nd half. H%, S% helped, too. And then there's that health history. Still, 2nd half was mildly intriguing as he did get both LHB and RHB out. Worth a buck or two.

Yr Tm	W	L	Sv	IP	K	ERA	xERA	WHIP	oOPS	vL	vR	BF/G	Ctl	Dom	Cmd	FpK	SwK	G	L	F	H%	S%	hr/f	GS	APC	DOM%	DIS%	Sv%	LI	RAR	BPV	BPX	R$
10																																	
11 aa	4	2	12	44	47	1.65	3.22	1.22				4.7	2.0	9.5	4.7						35%	88%								12.6	147	222	$9
12 LA *	3	2	5	60	67	3.75	3.19	1.19	698	988	485	4.1	3.7	10.1	2.7	67%	12%	38	22	40	28%	72%	10%	0	16			100	0.65	1.9	99	129	$3
13 LA	0	0	0	0	0	0.00	0.00	0.00		0	1000	2.0	0.0	0.0	0.0						0%	100%	0%	0	11			0	0.70	0.0	-22	-29	-$5
14 TEX	3	1	0	72	69	2.76	3.80	1.17	659	643	672	4.6	3.5	8.7	2.5	56%	10%	40	18	42	26%	84%	12%	0	18			0	0.75	8.6	79	94	$4
1st Half	2	1	0	39	37	3.43	3.90	1.19	740	724	749	4.9	3.4	8.5	2.5	58%	9%	41	14	45	24%	84%	18%	0	20			0	0.62	1.5	79	94	$2
2nd Half	1	0	0	32	32	1.95	3.69	1.14	559	573	544	4.3	3.6	8.9	2.5	52%	10%	39	23	38	28%	83%	3%	0	16			0	0.89	7.1	80	95	$5
15 Proj	3	2	0	65	68	3.24	3.33	1.22	672	781	587	4.3	3.4	9.3	2.7	60%	11%	39	20	41	29%	77%	10%	0						4.0	93	111	$3

Tomlin,Josh

Tomlin,Josh							
Age: 30	Th: R	Role	RP	Health	F	LIMA Plan	B+
Ht: 6' 1"	Wt: 190	Type		PT/Exp	D	Rand Var	+1
				Consist	F	MM	3101

6-9, 4.76 in 104 IP at CLE. Age 30, so-so results. Nothing to see, right? Not so fast. Elite FpK, rising SwK lifted Dom and made Cmd legit. BPV was 110 in May, then rose in June, July, Aug. Thanks to bad swings in 2nd half H% and S%, most won't give second look. Uncertain role cloaks value, too. $1 bet could pay big.

Yr Tm	W	L	Sv	IP	K	ERA	xERA	WHIP	oOPS	vL	vR	BF/G	Ctl	Dom	Cmd	FpK	SwK	G	L	F	H%	S%	hr/f	GS	APC	DOM%	DIS%	Sv%	LI	RAR	BPV	BPX	R$
10 CLE *	14	8	0	180	107	3.66	3.69	1.22	773	682	881	22.8	2.6	5.3	2.0	60%	8%	28	21	50	27%	74%	9%	12	93	50%	17%			9.4	49	80	$12
11 CLE	12	7	0	165	89	4.25	4.04	1.08	712	753	666	25.5	1.1	4.8	4.2	65%	8%	38	22	40	26%	65%	11%	26	91	42%	4%			-6.2	72	109	$9
12 CLE	5	8	0	103	56	6.36	4.82	1.46	860	945	768	21.5	2.2	4.9	2.2	64%	8%	42	21	37	31%	59%	13%	16	77	25%	31%	0	0.89	-29.9	49	64	-$13
13 CLE *	2	0	0	23	11	2.52	1.91	0.92	500	0	667	14.3	0.0	4.4	0.0	67%	8%	38	0	63	28%	69%	0%	0	36			0	0.23	3.8	0	0	$0
14 CLE *	8	10	0	144	119	4.24	4.52	1.24	781	718	848	18.8	1.6	7.4	4.8	68%	10%	37	27	36	31%	71%	15%	16	69	50%	25%	0	0.94	-8.8	101	120	$2
1st Half	7	6	0	99	79	3.37	3.49	1.10	694	628	771	24.3	1.7	7.2	4.2	65%	10%	36	23	40	28%	75%	13%	10	95	70%	20%	0	0.88	4.5	101	121	$11
2nd Half	1	4	0	45	40	6.16	6.80	1.55	909	865	949	13.0	1.2	8.0	6.5	71%	10%	39	32	29	38%	66%	20%	6	48	17%	33%	0	0.99	-13.3	111	133	-$18
15 Proj	6	7	0	118	88	3.91	3.60	1.27	760	747	773	18.2	1.7	6.7	4.0	66%	9%	39	22	39	31%	75%	12%	17						-2.4	92	110	$2

Torres,Alexander

Torres,Alexander							
Age: 27	Th: L	Role	RP	Health	A	LIMA Plan	D+
Ht: 5' 10"	Wt: 175	Type	Pwr	PT/Exp	D	Rand Var	-3
				Consist	F	MM	2400

On-again, off-again relationship with strike zone hit the rocks, a shame as his SwK stayed strong and GB% improved. FpK, especially unsightly 2nd half, offers little hope of return to 2013 Ctl level, which had been credited to old pitching coach. Is his number still in the Rolodex?

Yr Tm	W	L	Sv	IP	K	ERA	xERA	WHIP	oOPS	vL	vR	BF/G	Ctl	Dom	Cmd	FpK	SwK	G	L	F	H%	S%	hr/f	GS	APC	DOM%	DIS%	Sv%	LI	RAR	BPV	BPX	R$
10 aa	11	6	0	143	129	4.14	4.64	1.59				23.3	4.5	8.2	1.8						35%	74%								-1.1	69	111	$0
11 TAM *	10	8	0	154	141	3.47	4.31	1.60	701	450	897	22.0	5.1	8.2	1.6	46%	7%	59	23	18	34%	78%	0%	0	40			0	0.71	8.9	72	108	$1
12 aaa	3	7	0	69	75	8.35	6.18	2.07				13.0	8.2	9.8	1.2						38%	58%								-36.9	58	76	-$23
13 TAM *	6	4	0	104	111	2.85	2.00	1.10	468	466	470	8.5	3.6	9.6	2.7	56%	13%	42	20	38	28%	73%	2%	0	23			0	1.03	13.1	121	158	$10
14 SD	2	1	0	54	51	3.33	4.19	1.46	645	737	557	3.4	5.5	8.5	1.5	55%	13%	47	23	30	30%	77%	4%	0	14			0	0.74	2.7	30	35	-$2
1st Half	1	0	0	33	31	1.89	3.78	1.26	567	539	584	4.1	5.1	8.4	1.6	60%	14%	51	24	26	26%	85%	5%	0	17			0	0.72	7.6	41	49	$1
2nd Half	1	1	0	21	20	5.66	4.86	1.79	756	981	512	2.8	6.1	8.7	1.4	48%	12%	42	22	36	36%	67%	4%	0	12			0	0.76	-4.9	12	15	-$7
15 Proj	3	3	0	58	58	3.96	3.76	1.40	651	767	553	4.6	5.0	9.0	1.8	54%	13%	44	21	34	30%	71%	5%	0						-1.6	48	58	-$2

Torres,Carlos

Torres,Carlos							
Age: 32	Th: R	Role	RP	Health	A	LIMA Plan	B
Ht: 6' 1"	Wt: 180	Type	Pwr	PT/Exp	C	Rand Var	-2
				Consist	B	MM	3201

Traded a bit of Ctl to add Dom, which took bite out of sterling Cmd of 2013, yet still got results. Fantasy owners may pine to see him start, but scavenger wins are a nice consolation prize. Already strong SwK improved slightly, as did GB%. Buy for skills, hope for a juicier role.

Yr Tm	W	L	Sv	IP	K	ERA	xERA	WHIP	oOPS	vL	vR	BF/G	Ctl	Dom	Cmd	FpK	SwK	G	L	F	H%	S%	hr/f	GS	APC	DOM%	DIS%	Sv%	LI	RAR	BPV	BPX	R$
10 CHW *	9	10	0	174	123	4.93	5.02	1.60	1041	1039	1041	24.0	4.9	6.3	1.3	53%	9%	29	35	37	31%	71%	11%	1	54	0%	0%	0	0.24	-18.3	34	55	-$7
11																																	
12 COL *	10	7	0	114	83	5.20	4.97	1.59	723	660	768	11.2	4.2	6.5	1.5	57%	8%	44	27	29	33%	68%	5%	0	29			0	0.60	-16.6	45	58	-$9
13 NYM *	10	9	0	158	126	3.60	4.02	1.22	701	678	716	14.2	2.0	7.2	3.6	67%	11%	44	20	37	30%	76%	16%	9	40	78%	22%	0	1.04	5.3	84	109	$8
14 NYM	8	6	2	97	96	3.06	3.57	1.31	715	680	734	5.5	3.5	8.9	2.5	61%	12%	47	17	36	31%	81%	12%	1	22	100%	0%	40	1.07	8.1	90	107	$5
1st Half	3	4	2	48	52	3.21	3.35	1.51	761	621	861	5.5	3.6	9.8	2.7	62%	12%	51	20	29	38%	80%	8%	0	22			67	1.16	3.1	109	130	$1
2nd Half	5	2	0	49	44	2.92	3.76	1.11	666	759	615	5.6	3.5	8.0	2.3	60%	12%	43	15	43	23%	83%	15%	1	21	100%	0%	0	0.98	5.0	72	85	$9
15 Proj	6	4	0	73	63	3.44	3.65	1.34	742	720	754	8.0	3.4	7.8	2.3	62%	11%	45	19	36	30%	79%	12%	0						2.7	72	85	$2

Treinen,Blake

Treinen,Blake							
Age: 27	Th: R	Role	SP	Health	A	LIMA Plan	C
Ht: 6' 5"	Wt: 215	Type	Con xGB	PT/Exp	D	Rand Var	-1
				Consist	C	MM	2000

2-3, 2.49 ERA in 51 IP at WAS. Not elite prospect, but held his own in first taste of MLB. Induces GB well. Dom low for now, but don't rule him out due to size (6-5), heat (up to 97 mph). FpK, SwK on right path. Needs to solve LHB, but keep an eye on him.

Yr Tm	W	L	Sv	IP	K	ERA	xERA	WHIP	oOPS	vL	vR	BF/G	Ctl	Dom	Cmd	FpK	SwK	G	L	F	H%	S%	hr/f	GS	APC	DOM%	DIS%	Sv%	LI	RAR	BPV	BPX	R$
10																																	
11																																	
12																																	
13 aa	6	7	0	119	68	4.60	5.14	1.55				24.7	2.5	5.1	2.0						34%	71%								-10.7	43	56	-$8
14 WAS *	10	5	0	131	79	3.41	4.06	1.39	678	798	564	17.8	2.3	5.4	2.4	57%	8%	59	22	19	33%	75%	3%	7	49	43%	14%	0	0.56	5.3	70	83	$2
1st Half	5	3	0	70	44	2.22	3.27	1.29	669	728	608	17.0	2.6	5.6	2.2	52%	8%	60	19	20	31%	82%	4%	5	60	40%	0%	0	0.48	13.2	78	93	$8
2nd Half	5	2	0	61	35	4.78	4.97	1.49	699	983	469	18.8	1.9	5.2	2.7	67%	10%	57	27	16	35%	68%	0%	2	32	50%	50%	0	0.69	-7.9	63	75	-$5
15 Proj	4	3	0	65	38	4.05	3.69	1.48	752	982	548	20.3	2.5	5.3	2.2	61%	9%	56	24	20	34%	73%	9%	14						-2.5	63	75	-$3

KRISTOPHER OLSON

Tropeano,Nicholas

Age: 24	Th: R	Role SP		Health	A	LIMA Plan	B+
Ht: 6' 4"	Wt: 205	Type xFB		PT/Exp	D	Rand Var	-3
				Consist	F	MM	2101

1-3, 4.57 ERA in 22 IP at HOU. A fantastic year in AAA ended in a 4-start look in the majors. Despite good size, he's not overpowering, and will need to tap his above-average Ctl to get MLB hitters out. Those hitters were more discerning than their minor league counterparts (1.4 Cmd) in the tiny sample. Take it slow.

Yr Tm	W	L	Sv	IP	K	ERA	xERA	WHIP	oOPS	vL	vR	BF/G	Ctl	Dom	Cmd	FpK	SwK	G	L	F	H%	S%	hr/f	GS	APC	DOM%	DIS%	Sv%	LI	RAR	BPV	BPX	R$
10																																	
11																																	
12																																	
13 aa	7	10	5	134	113	4.69	4.95	1.46				20.4	2.6	7.6	2.9						35%	70%								-13.6	71	92	-$4
14 HOU *	10	8	0	146	115	3.40	2.66	1.08	626	648	576	21.1	2.5	7.1	2.8	54%	9%	40	13	46	26%	70%	0%	4	92	50%	25%			6.1	93	110	$11
1st Half	6	4	0	87	69	2.51	2.43	1.01				20.8	2.2	7.2	3.3						25%	79%	0%	0						13.2	102	122	$19
2nd Half	4	4	0	59	46	4.71	3.00	1.18	626	648	576	21.6	3.0	7.0	2.4	54%	9%	40	13	46	28%	59%	0%	4	92	50%	25%			-7.1	82	98	-$1
15 Proj	**5**	**6**	**0**	**87**	**66**	**4.15**	**4.04**	**1.29**	**673**	**672**	**675**	**21.1**	**3.0**	**6.9**	**2.3**	**54%**	**9%**	**40**	**13**	**46**	**30%**	**69%**	**6%**	**17**						**-4.4**	**62**	**73**	**$0**

Turner,Jacob

Age: 24	Th: R	Role SP		Health	B	LIMA Plan	D+
Ht: 6' 5"	Wt: 215	Type		PT/Exp	C	Rand Var	+5
				Consist	A	MM	1001

A mid-season buy-low for the Cubs; should you follow suit? PRO: Ctl/FpK improving; throwing more GB overall; ERA has to get better after nasty H%/S%. CON: Dom stuck in neutral; one in three starts a DISaster. VERDICT: Easy for his value to increase from this starting point. Profit, though, will be more difficult.

Yr Tm	W	L	Sv	IP	K	ERA	xERA	WHIP	oOPS	vL	vR	BF/G	Ctl	Dom	Cmd	FpK	SwK	G	L	F	H%	S%	hr/f	GS	APC	DOM%	DIS%	Sv%	LI	RAR	BPV	BPX	R$
10																																	
11 DET *	4	6	0	144	102	4.34	3.82	1.27	904	903	910	25.5	2.3	6.4	2.8	58%	8%	41	20	39	30%	67%	17%	3	80	33%	67%			-7.1	74	112	$1
12 2 TM *	8	7	0	145	88	3.68	3.80	1.32	716	548	853	24.0	3.3	5.5	1.6	57%	10%	45	19	36	28%	74%	14%	10	90	40%	10%			6.1	48	62	$4
13 MIA *	6	12	0	174	107	4.31	4.44	1.45	746	716	770	24.8	3.5	5.5	1.6	54%	9%	46	19	35	30%	72%	9%	20	93	40%	20%			-9.5	39	51	-$6
14 2 NL	6	11	0	113	71	6.13	4.27	1.60	845	812	867	17.9	2.6	5.7	2.2	57%	8%	49	21	30	35%	62%	10%	18	65	22%	33%	0	0.74	-33.3	58	69	-$15
1st Half	2	6	0	57	38	6.44	4.01	1.69	874	868	877	18.6	2.5	6.0	2.4	57%	9%	55	21	24	38%	62%	12%	9	65	22%	33%	0	0.80	-19.1	73	87	-$19
2nd Half	4	5	0	56	33	5.82	4.53	1.51	813	749	856	17.2	2.7	5.3	1.9	57%	8%	43	21	37	33%	62%	9%	9	65	22%	33%	0	0.68	-14.3	42	51	-$10
15 Proj	**5**	**8**	**0**	**102**	**64**	**4.64**	**4.21**	**1.50**	**795**	**737**	**838**	**20.6**	**3.1**	**5.6**	**1.8**	**56%**	**9%**	**46**	**20**	**34**	**32%**	**70%**	**9%**	**21**						**-11.3**	**41**	**49**	**-$6**

Uehara,Koji

Age: 40	Th: R	Role RP		Health	D	LIMA Plan	B
Ht: 6' 2"	Wt: 195	Type Pwr xFB		PT/Exp	C	Rand Var	-1
				Consist	A	MM	5530

Wild 1H/2H swings in ERA were the polar opposite of stability of BPV, Cmd over the same period. As usual, H%/S% were the guilty party, but remember that a closer holds full responsibility for a 70% strand rate. Even at 40, elite Ctl/Dom/Cmd and FpK/SwK all point to a SKILLS rebound. As for ROLE, we must wait.

Yr Tm	W	L	Sv	IP	K	ERA	xERA	WHIP	oOPS	vL	vR	BF/G	Ctl	Dom	Cmd	FpK	SwK	G	L	F	H%	S%	hr/f	GS	APC	DOM%	DIS%	Sv%	LI	RAR	BPV	BPX	R$
10 BAL	1	2	13	44	55	2.86	3.06	0.95	598	747	474	4.1	1.0	11.3	11.0	66%	13%	24	18	58	32%	76%	8%	0	16			87	1.23	6.6	177	286	$9
11 2 AL	2	3	0	65	85	2.35	2.61	0.72	535	472	597	3.7	1.2	11.8	9.4	67%	17%	32	14	53	22%	83%	14%	0	14			0	1.06	12.7	188	283	$10
12 TEX	0	0	1	36	43	1.75	2.74	0.64	466	545	369	3.5	0.8	10.8	14.3	67%	19%	33	17	51	21%	84%	10%	0	14			100	0.66	10.1	184	240	$5
13 BOS	4	1	21	74	101	1.09	2.24	0.57	400	338	466	3.6	1.1	12.2	11.2	70%	20%	40	11	48	20%	89%	7%	0	14			88	1.34	25.5	209	272	$27
14 BOS	6	5	26	64	80	2.52	2.70	0.92	629	613	650	3.9	1.1	11.2	10.0	64%	20%	32	23	45	29%	84%	14%	0	15			84	1.48	9.7	181	216	$18
1st Half	3	1	18	38	48	1.19	2.39	0.72	500	410	612	3.7	1.2	11.5	9.6	64%	20%	35	23	43	23%	100%	15%	0	14			95	1.55	11.8	187	223	$26
2nd Half	3	4	8	27	32	4.39	3.15	1.20	788	857	697	4.1	1.0	10.8	10.7	64%	19%	29	23	48	36%	70%	14%	0	16			67	1.39	-2.1	174	208	$7
15 Proj	**4**	**3**	**35**	**59**	**75**	**2.81**	**2.33**	**0.82**	**573**	**585**	**559**	**3.6**	**1.0**	**11.4**	**10.9**	**66%**	**19%**	**34**	**18**	**48**	**27%**	**74%**	**12%**	**0**						**6.8**	**188**	**224**	**$22**

Vargas,Jason

Age: 32	Th: L	Role SP		Health	D	LIMA Plan	B+
Ht: 6' 0"	Wt: 215	Type Con FB		PT/Exp	A	Rand Var	-1
				Consist	A	MM	2105

Indulge us in an eye test: Scan through his five-year xERA column. And then his five-year BPV/BPX columns. While you thought he was stagnant, here he is, improving every season. Yes, that improvement is within a narrow range of mediocrity but it IS growth. Interested? No?? Eh, we tried.

Yr Tm	W	L	Sv	IP	K	ERA	xERA	WHIP	oOPS	vL	vR	BF/G	Ctl	Dom	Cmd	FpK	SwK	G	L	F	H%	S%	hr/f	GS	APC	DOM%	DIS%	Sv%	LI	RAR	BPV	BPX	R$
10 SEA	9	12	0	193	116	3.78	4.64	1.25	699	550	747	26.2	2.5	5.4	2.1	62%	8%	36	17	47	28%	72%	6%	31	97	39%	13%			7.0	43	70	$9
11 SEA	10	13	0	201	131	4.25	4.48	1.31	712	720	709	26.8	2.6	5.9	2.2	63%	8%	36	20	44	30%	70%	8%	32	102	50%	22%			-7.7	48	73	$3
12 SEA	14	11	0	217	141	3.85	4.37	1.18	714	705	717	26.9	2.3	5.8	2.6	60%	9%	40	19	40	26%	74%	13%	33	102	48%	21%			4.4	62	80	$13
13 LAA	9	8	0	150	109	4.02	4.30	1.39	758	789	747	26.8	2.8	6.5	2.4	61%	9%	40	21	38	32%	74%	9%	24	99	38%	21%			-2.9	61	80	$0
14 KC	11	10	0	187	128	3.71	4.13	1.27	713	661	731	26.3	2.0	6.2	3.1	63%	9%	38	23	39	31%	74%	8%	30	100	53%	23%			0.8	74	88	$5
1st Half	7	3	0	112	74	3.53	4.08	1.25	724	691	735	27.6	2.0	5.9	3.0	64%	9%	41	21	38	29%	76%	10%	17	103	59%	18%			3.0	72	85	$9
2nd Half	4	7	0	75	54	3.98	4.20	1.31	698	612	724	24.7	1.9	6.5	3.4	61%	10%	35	26	40	33%	70%	5%	13	97	46%	31%			-2.2	78	93	-$1
15 Proj	**11**	**11**	**0**	**189**	**125**	**3.88**	**4.00**	**1.33**	**733**	**704**	**743**	**25.7**	**2.4**	**6.0**	**2.5**	**62%**	**9%**	**38**	**21**	**41**	**31%**	**73%**	**8%**	**30**						**-3.3**	**60**	**71**	**$4**

Varvaro,Anthony

Age: 30	Th: R	Role RP		Health	A	LIMA Plan	B+
Ht: 6' 0"	Wt: 190	Type Pwr		PT/Exp	D	Rand Var	-2
				Consist	B	MM	3200

Non-descript reliever who has quietly transformed himself into bullpen asset over past two seasons. In 2013, pitched to contact at Dom expense, but re-added the Ks in 2014. FpK and SwK on board; xERA and WHIP approve, too. Could handle larger role in bullpen if needed.

Yr Tm	W	L	Sv	IP	K	ERA	xERA	WHIP	oOPS	vL	vR	BF/G	Ctl	Dom	Cmd	FpK	SwK	G	L	F	H%	S%	hr/f	GS	APC	DOM%	DIS%	Sv%	LI	RAR	BPV	BPX	R$
10 SEA *	1	4	9	69	64	4.87	4.10	1.54	1167	1300	1115	5.6	5.4	8.4	1.5	38%	5%	46	31	23	31%	68%	67%	0	24			69	0.35	-6.7	69	112	-$1
11 ATL *	2	10	1	83	78	3.48	3.16	1.34	594	627	566	6.2	5.4	8.5	1.6	57%	11%	33	20	47	26%	76%	11%	0	22			33	0.69	4.8	76	114	$1
12 ATL *	1	3	6	61	58	3.51	4.50	1.63	766	869	656	6.0	5.2	8.5	1.7	59%	11%	42	16	42	35%	79%	11%	0	27			75	0.48	3.8	73	95	-$2
13 ATL	3	1	1	73	43	2.82	4.24	1.27	644	548	717	4.9	3.1	5.3	1.7	63%	8%	47	24	29	28%	78%	4%	0	18			33	0.57	9.4	37	48	$2
14 ATL	3	3	0	55	50	2.63	3.21	1.08	632	481	720	3.6	2.1	8.2	3.8	63%	10%	50	18	33	28%	80%	10%	0	15			0	0.96	7.5	118	141	$3
1st Half	3	1	0	32	34	2.25	2.87	1.13	613	648	597	3.8	2.3	9.6	4.3	65%	11%	54	17	29	32%	82%	8%	0	15			0	0.92	5.9	143	171	$6
2nd Half	0	2	0	23	16	3.18	3.68	1.01	661	297	947	3.3	2.0	6.4	3.2	60%	9%	44	18	38	24%	75%	12%	0	14			0	1.01	1.6	83	99	$0
15 Proj	**2**	**3**	**0**	**51**	**41**	**3.05**	**3.51**	**1.23**	**663**	**497**	**777**	**4.2**	**3.1**	**7.3**	**2.3**	**62%**	**9%**	**48**	**20**	**32**	**29%**	**77%**	**8%**	**0**						**4.3**	**72**	**86**	**$1**

Ventura,Yordano

Age: 24	Th: R	Role SP		Health	B	LIMA Plan	C+
Ht: 6' 0"	Wt: 180	Type Pwr		PT/Exp	C	Rand Var	-1
				Consist	A	MM	3303

Most figured that May's elbow scare would end on the operating table; instead, he compiled 30 starts and the post-season spotlight. Opp OPS gives indication of how difficult he is to square up; that high-90s heat will continue to produce SwK. Calming his walk rate is job #1; staying healthy #1a. A bright future.

Yr Tm	W	L	Sv	IP	K	ERA	xERA	WHIP	oOPS	vL	vR	BF/G	Ctl	Dom	Cmd	FpK	SwK	G	L	F	H%	S%	hr/f	GS	APC	DOM%	DIS%	Sv%	LI	RAR	BPV	BPX	R$
10																																	
11																																	
12 aa	1	2	0	29	21	5.20	2.98	1.28				20.1	3.8	6.5	1.7						28%	56%								-4.3	74	97	-$4
13 KC *	8	7	0	150	140	3.71	3.76	1.37	693	687	700	21.7	3.5	8.4	2.4	53%	8%	49	15	36	33%	74%	18%	3	81	33%	33%			2.9	86	112	$3
14 KC	14	10	0	183	159	3.20	3.78	1.30	669	642	705	25.2	3.4	7.8	2.3	61%	11%	48	21	31	30%	77%	8%	30	96	60%	17%	0	0.77	12.3	75	89	$10
1st Half	5	7	0	88	76	3.26	3.46	1.27	688	636	757	24.8	2.5	7.7	3.0	63%	11%	52	19	29	32%	76%	9%	15	94	53%	20%			5.2	101	120	$7
2nd Half	9	3	0	95	83	3.14	4.08	1.32	650	648	652	25.6	4.2	7.9	1.9	59%	10%	43	23	34	29%	78%	8%	15	99	67%	13%	0	0.77	7.0	50	60	$13
15 Proj	**12**	**9**	**0**	**174**	**156**	**3.40**	**3.51**	**1.33**	**679**	**656**	**710**	**23.2**	**3.5**	**8.1**	**2.3**	**61%**	**11%**	**47**	**22**	**32**	**31%**	**76%**	**8%**	**31**						**7.3**	**75**	**89**	**$9**

Veras,Jose

Age: 34	Th: R	Role RP		Health	B	LIMA Plan	C
Ht: 6' 6"	Wt: 240	Type Pwr		PT/Exp	C	Rand Var	+2
				Consist	A	MM	3410

From the Sometimes Things Don't Work Out dept.: As CHC closer, allowed 5 ER in first four games with 7 walks to 3 Ks. Oblique injury and two outings later he was DFA'd. Regained "form" with HOU in 2nd half: lots of Ks; lots of walks. At 34, unlikely to get saves chances, which seriously dings his fantasy value.

Yr Tm	W	L	Sv	IP	K	ERA	xERA	WHIP	oOPS	vL	vR	BF/G	Ctl	Dom	Cmd	FpK	SwK	G	L	F	H%	S%	hr/f	GS	APC	DOM%	DIS%	Sv%	LI	RAR	BPV	BPX	R$
10 FLA *	4	4	2	77	83	4.53	4.47	1.57	622	555	686	4.7	5.4	9.7	1.8	49%	10%	40	23	37	33%	72%	12%	0	17			50	1.22	-4.3	74	120	-$2
11 PIT	2	4	1	71	79	3.80	3.78	1.24	636	690	600	3.9	4.3	10.0	2.3	53%	9%	37	18	45	28%	71%	7%	0	16			13	1.26	1.2	79	119	$2
12 MIL	5	4	1	67	79	3.63	3.94	1.51	694	724	665	4.2	5.4	10.6	2.0	53%	9%	44	25	31	34%	77%	9%	0	18			50	0.91	3.2	68	89	-$1
13 2 AL	0	5	21	63	60	3.02	3.67	1.07	605	684	520	3.8	3.2	8.6	2.7	61%	10%	42	15	44	25%	75%	8%	0	15			84	1.15	6.6	90	117	$11
14 2 TM	4	1	1	46	50	4.50	3.90	1.39	704	772	665	4.4	5.3	9.8	1.9	53%	9%	44	22	34	28%	71%	15%	0	18			17	1.07	-4.3	55	66	-$2
1st Half	0	1	0	15	14	8.22	4.99	1.76	840	869	819	5.0	7.6	8.2	1.1	49%	6%	52	19	29	29%	52%	17%	0	21			0	0.65	-8.5	-28	-33	-$14
2nd Half	4	0	1	31	36	2.64	3.43	1.21	631	713	585	4.1	4.1	10.6	2.6	55%	11%	40	23	37	27%	85%	14%	0	17			33	1.27	4.2	97	116	$4
15 Proj	**4**	**3**	**5**	**65**	**69**	**3.88**	**3.52**	**1.36**	**697**	**737**	**667**	**4.1**	**4.4**	**9.5**	**2.2**	**54%**	**9%**	**43**	**20**	**37**	**31%**	**73%**	**10%**	**0**						**-1.1**	**73**	**87**	**$2**

BRENT HERSHEY

Verlander,Justin

Age: 32	Th: R	Role SP	Health A	LIMA Plan C
Ht: 6' 5"	Wt: 225	Type Pwr FB	PT/Exp A	Rand Var 0
			Consist A	MM 3305

Velocity dropped for 5th year in row and worsened in 2nd half, while SwK/Cmd were lowest since 2008. Shoulder issue a factor, but with all those innings (avg nearly 220 IP/yr for 9 straight years), may never again be 100% healthy and effective. Disturbing xERA, BPV trends indicate days as top-tier SP probably over.

Yr	Tm	W	L	Sv	IP	K	ERA	xERA	WHIP	oOPS	vL	vR	BF/G	Ctl	Dom	Cmd	FpK	SwK	G	L	F	H%	S%	hr/f	GS	APC	DOM%	DIS%	Sv%	LI	RAR	BPV	BPX	R$
10	DET	18	9	0	224	219	3.37	3.55	1.16	630	635	622	28.0	2.8	8.8	3.1	63%	10%	41	19	40	30%	72%	6%	33	114	70%	3%			19.6	100	162	$23
11	DET	24	5	0	251	250	2.40	3.14	0.92	555	504	617	28.5	2.0	9.0	4.4	61%	11%	40	18	42	25%	79%	9%	34	116	88%	0%			47.7	124	187	$45
12	DET	17	8	0	238	239	2.64	3.35	1.06	601	608	593	29.0	2.3	9.0	4.0	61%	12%	42	22	36	29%	78%	8%	33	114	79%	3%			40.3	121	158	$36
13	DET	13	12	0	218	217	3.46	3.75	1.31	691	658	739	27.2	3.1	8.9	2.9	65%	11%	38	23	39	33%	76%	8%	34	109	65%	9%			10.9	94	122	$11
14	DET	15	12	0	206	159	4.54	4.27	1.40	756	686	849	27.9	2.8	6.9	2.4	62%	9%	40	20	41	33%	68%	7%	32	107	56%	9%			-20.4	66	79	-$3
1st Half		6	7	0	111	85	4.80	4.44	1.49	771	680	899	28.8	3.5	6.9	2.0	61%	10%	42	18	40	33%	68%	7%	17	111	47%	12%			-14.4	50	60	-$8
2nd Half		9	5	0	95	74	4.25	4.08	1.29	738	693	795	26.9	2.1	7.0	3.4	63%	8%	36	22	42	32%	68%	7%	15	102	67%	7%			-6.0	84	100	$4
15	Proj	**13**	**11**	**0**	**210**	**183**	**3.78**	**3.63**	**1.30**	**703**	**662**	**758**	**27.1**	**2.9**	**7.9**	**2.8**	**63%**	**10%**	**38**	**21**	**41**	**31%**	**72%**	**7%**	**32**						**-1.1**	**81**	**97**	**$9**

Villanueva,Carlos

Age: 31	Th: R	Role RP	Health B	LIMA Plan C
Ht: 6' 2"	Wt: 215	Type Pwr FB	PT/Exp B	Rand Var +2
			Consist A	MM 2300

Once again displayed elite skills out of the bullpen, but his five starts were ratio killers (10.23 ERA, 2.19 WHIP). Hasn't had a sub-4.00 ERA since 2007, so it's not going to cost much to acquire him, and if he remains a reliever throughout the year... UP: 2nd half times two.

Yr	Tm	W	L	Sv	IP	K	ERA	xERA	WHIP	oOPS	vL	vR	BF/G	Ctl	Dom	Cmd	FpK	SwK	G	L	F	H%	S%	hr/f	GS	APC	DOM%	DIS%	Sv%	LI	RAR	BPV	BPX	R$
10	MIL	2	0	1	53	67	4.61	3.35	1.33	702	768	637	4.6	3.8	11.4	3.0	58%	13%	34	27	39	33%	68%	13%	0	18			25	0.98	-3.5	117	189	$0
11	TOR	6	4	0	107	68	4.04	4.46	1.26	696	713	677	13.8	2.7	5.7	2.1	55%	8%	36	22	43	28%	70%	8%	13	53	46%	23%	0	0.75	-1.3	44	67	$2
12	TOR	7	7	0	125	122	4.16	4.02	1.27	758	816	703	13.7	3.3	8.8	2.7	59%	11%	37	19	44	28%	74%	15%	16	53	63%	19%	0	0.79	-2.3	84	109	$3
13	CHC	7	8	0	129	103	4.06	3.91	1.22	726	731	721	11.1	2.8	7.2	2.6	58%	11%	40	21	39	28%	69%	10%	15	42	60%	20%	0	0.85	-3.0	72	94	$3
14	CHC	5	7	2	78	72	4.64	3.79	1.39	754	758	751	8.2	2.2	8.3	3.8	59%	12%	41	20	38	36%	67%	6%	5	31	0%	80%	100	0.96	-8.6	110	131	-$2
1st Half		3	5	1	44	35	5.77	4.37	1.65	824	967	727	9.8	2.3	7.2	3.2	56%	11%	41	22	37	39%	65%	7%	4	37	0%	75%	100	0.83	-10.9	88	105	-$8
2nd Half		2	2	1	34	37	3.18	3.11	1.06	647	413	785	6.5	2.1	9.8	4.6	64%	14%	41	17	41	31%	71%	6%	1	25	0%	100%	100	1.08	2.4	138	165	$5
15	Proj	**4**	**5**	**0**	**68**	**60**	**4.05**	**3.71**	**1.36**	**757**	**747**	**764**	**8.7**	**3.0**	**8.0**	**2.6**	**59%**	**11%**	**39**	**20**	**41**	**32%**	**72%**	**8%**	**2**						**-2.6**	**79**	**94**	**-$1**

Vincent,Nick

Age: 28	Th: R	Role RP	Health C	LIMA Plan A
Ht: 5' 11"	Wt: 180	Type Pwr	PT/Exp D	Rand Var 0
			Consist A	MM 5400

Despite huge difference in 1H/2H ERA, skills were impressive all year long. Rough patch in early June can be blamed on both a sore shoulder that landed him on DL, and an absurdly low S%. RHB can't touch him, and gains in FpK, Cmd indicate he'll continue to be a reliable LIMA option.

Yr	Tm	W	L	Sv	IP	K	ERA	xERA	WHIP	oOPS	vL	vR	BF/G	Ctl	Dom	Cmd	FpK	SwK	G	L	F	H%	S%	hr/f	GS	APC	DOM%	DIS%	Sv%	LI	RAR	BPV	BPX	R$
10																																		
11	aa	8	2	3	79	76	2.25	2.06	0.98				4.6	2.2	8.6	3.8						26%	79%								16.5	129	195	$13
12	SD *	4	1	2	58	56	3.17	3.09	1.20	551	475	598	3.9	2.7	8.8	3.2	56%	13%	37	24	39	31%	75%	8%	0	17			40	1.03	6.0	110	144	$3
13	SD *	10	6	1	72	69	2.61	2.88	1.17	525	781	313	4.1	2.8	8.6	3.1	56%	12%	43	23	34	30%	80%	3%	0	16			50	1.08	11.1	107	140	$8
14	SD	1	2	0	55	62	3.60	3.00	1.00	626	825	507	3.4	1.8	10.1	5.6	61%	12%	33	22	45	30%	66%	8%	0	14			0	1.07	1.0	145	173	$2
1st Half		0	2	0	27	32	5.67	3.15	1.04	735	1049	583	3.6	2.0	10.7	5.3	60%	12%	27	20	53	28%	48%	15%	0	15			0	1.09	-6.4	143	170	-$3
2nd Half		1	0	0	28	30	1.61	2.84	0.96	517	650	420	3.3	1.6	9.6	6.0	62%	13%	40	24	37	31%	81%	0%	0	13			0	1.05	7.4	148	176	$7
15	Proj	**4**	**2**	**0**	**58**	**60**	**3.13**	**2.96**	**1.07**	**627**	**861**	**464**	**3.7**	**2.2**	**9.4**	**4.2**	**59%**	**12%**	**38**	**23**	**40**	**30%**	**72%**	**7%**	**0**						**4.4**	**124**	**148**	**$4**

Vizcaino,Arodys

Age: 24	Th: R	Role RP	Health F	LIMA Plan C
Ht: 6' 0"	Wt: 190	Type Pwr	PT/Exp F	Rand Var +4
			Consist F	MM 1200

0-0, 5.40 ERA in 5 IP at CHC. Former top prospect had missed previous two seasons following TJ surgery. Future role remains unclear, but 100 mph fastball will give him lots of rope. Ctl is a work in progress, so there's likely to be some inconsistency, but he's an intriguing long-term keeper target.

Yr	Tm	W	L	Sv	IP	K	ERA	xERA	WHIP	oOPS	vL	vR	BF/G	Ctl	Dom	Cmd	FpK	SwK	G	L	F	H%	S%	hr/f	GS	APC	DOM%	DIS%	Sv%	LI	RAR	BPV	BPX	R$
10																																		
11	ATL *	4	4	0	74	74	4.04	3.58	1.32	636	696	593	9.0	3.2	9.0	2.8	56%	9%	35	17	48	33%	69%	4%	0	19			0	1.28	-0.9	99	148	$1
12																																		
13																																		
14	CHC *	1	1	1	37	31	5.03	4.97	1.60	837	200	1318	4.5	4.3	7.4	1.7	59%	7%	40	20	40	34%	69%	17%	0	19			50	0.02	-5.9	56	66	-$6
1st Half		1	1	1	17	15	3.75	3.40	1.25				3.8	2.7	7.9	2.9						31%	70%	0%	0						0.0	95	114	-$2
2nd Half		0	0	0	20	16	6.13	6.30	1.90	837	200	1318	5.2	5.6	7.0	1.3	59%	7%	40	20	40	37%	68%	17%	0	19			0	0.02	-5.9	33	39	-$8
15	Proj	**2**	**2**	**0**	**56**	**49**	**4.26**	**4.09**	**1.43**				**5.6**	**3.8**	**7.8**	**2.0**	**59%**	**8%**				**32%**	**71%**		**0**						**-3.6**	**71**	**85**	**-$3**

Vogelsong,Ryan

Age: 37	Th: R	Role SP	Health D	LIMA Plan B
Ht: 6' 4"	Wt: 215	Type	PT/Exp A	Rand Var 0
			Consist B	MM 2103

Velocity, Cmd, and SwK all returned to 2011-12 levels, making 2013 look like a bit of an outlier. Age, GB% decline, and September fade (1.6 Cmd, 31 BPV) show there's still a good deal of risk. But BPX provides the proper perspective; at his 2011-12 peak, he was just league average.

Yr	Tm	W	L	Sv	IP	K	ERA	xERA	WHIP	oOPS	vL	vR	BF/G	Ctl	Dom	Cmd	FpK	SwK	G	L	F	H%	S%	hr/f	GS	APC	DOM%	DIS%	Sv%	LI	RAR	BPV	BPX	R$
10	aaa	3	8	1	95	80	5.41	6.48	1.99				13.9	5.9	7.5	1.3						39%	73%								-15.7	40	64	-$12
11	SF	13	7	0	180	139	2.71	3.85	1.25	671	727	626	25.1	3.1	7.0	2.3	62%	8%	46	20	34	29%	81%	8%	28	98	61%	7%	0	0.75	27.4	67	100	$16
12	SF	14	9	0	190	158	3.37	4.02	1.23	688	722	653	25.4	2.9	7.5	2.5	61%	8%	44	18	38	29%	75%	8%	31	99	61%	13%			15.1	78	101	$15
13	SF	4	6	0	104	67	5.73	4.62	1.56	840	736	928	24.6	3.3	5.8	1.8	60%	6%	41	27	32	33%	65%	13%	19	92	26%	32%			-23.8	35	45	-$12
14	SF	8	13	0	185	151	4.00	3.95	1.28	730	787	675	24.4	2.8	7.4	2.6	62%	8%	38	24	37	30%	71%	9%	32	96	50%	13%			-5.8	72	86	$3
1st Half		5	4	0	91	78	3.96	3.93	1.32	755	793	723	24.1	2.9	7.7	2.7	60%	9%	36	25	39	32%	71%	7%	16	95	50%	13%			-2.4	76	91	$3
2nd Half		3	9	0	94	73	4.04	3.98	1.24	705	782	623	24.7	2.8	7.0	2.5	64%	7%	40	24	36	28%	70%	11%	16	96	50%	13%			-3.4	69	83	$2
15	Proj	**8**	**11**	**0**	**174**	**132**	**4.14**	**3.93**	**1.38**	**758**	**773**	**745**	**23.0**	**3.2**	**6.8**	**2.2**	**62%**	**7%**	**40**	**24**	**37**	**31%**	**72%**	**10%**	**32**						**-8.5**	**55**	**66**	**$0**

Volquez,Edinson

Age: 31	Th: R	Role SP	Health B	LIMA Plan C
Ht: 6' 0"	Wt: 220	Type Pwr	PT/Exp A	Rand Var -3
			Consist A	MM 2205

Spike in FpK led to career-best Ctl -- still nothing to write home about -- but it came at the expense of Dom. Capped season with 1.36 ERA over final 10 starts, a streak that boosted this outwardly solid effort. It wasn't. xERA and BPV tell the true story of stable mediocrity. Use those numbers as your guide.

Yr	Tm	W	L	Sv	IP	K	ERA	xERA	WHIP	oOPS	vL	vR	BF/G	Ctl	Dom	Cmd	FpK	SwK	G	L	F	H%	S%	hr/f	GS	APC	DOM%	DIS%	Sv%	LI	RAR	BPV	BPX	R$
10	CIN *	7	3	0	86	84	3.82	3.55	1.36	739	691	776	22.4	4.6	8.8	1.9	57%	14%	54	15	31	29%	73%	12%	12	92	50%	33%			2.7	79	127	$3
11	CIN *	9	9	0	196	168	4.49	4.64	1.49	833	862	811	25.6	4.4	7.7	1.7	54%	12%	52	18	30	31%	73%	21%	20	98	35%	20%			-13.2	51	77	-$3
12	SD	11	11	0	183	174	4.14	4.14	1.45	706	700	711	25.1	5.2	8.6	1.7	53%	11%	51	21	28	30%	72%	10%	32	101	44%	25%			-2.8	44	57	$1
13	2 NL	9	12	0	170	142	5.71	4.28	1.59	804	836	771	23.5	4.1	7.5	1.8	57%	9%	48	23	30	34%	65%	12%	32	91	25%	28%	0	0.77	-38.7	51	67	-$16
14	PIT	13	7	0	193	140	3.04	3.95	1.23	674	728	634	25.3	3.3	6.5	2.0	60%	9%	50	17	33	27%	78%	9%	31	93	61%	23%	0	0.76	16.7	56	67	$12
1st Half		6	6	0	95	63	4.07	4.12	1.24	703	744	676	23.6	2.9	6.0	2.0	59%	9%	49	17	34	27%	70%	11%	16	86	50%	25%	0	0.75	-3.9	55	65	$5
2nd Half		7	1	0	98	77	2.03	3.78	1.22	645	713	586	27.2	3.7	7.1	1.9	61%	9%	52	16	31	27%	86%	7%	15	101	73%	20%			20.6	58	70	$20
15	Proj	**12**	**9**	**0**	**189**	**153**	**4.03**	**3.86**	**1.40**	**721**	**758**	**690**	**24.2**	**4.2**	**7.3**	**1.8**	**58%**	**10%**	**49**	**19**	**32**	**30%**	**73%**	**10%**	**33**						**-6.7**	**46**	**55**	**$3**

Wacha,Michael

Age: 24	Th: R	Role SP	Health D	LIMA Plan B+
Ht: 6' 6"	Wt: 210	Type Pwr	PT/Exp D	Rand Var -2
			Consist C	MM 3303

First eight starts: 10.8 Dom, 13% SwK; next seven starts: 5.4 Dom, 8% SwK. Then missed 2+ months with shoulder issues. Upon return, velocity was strong as ever. Age, mastery of LHB, high FpK point to big things ahead, and there's likely room for profit this year. UP: 18 Wins, 3.00 ERA

Yr	Tm	W	L	Sv	IP	K	ERA	xERA	WHIP	oOPS	vL	vR	BF/G	Ctl	Dom	Cmd	FpK	SwK	G	L	F	H%	S%	hr/f	GS	APC	DOM%	DIS%	Sv%	LI	RAR	BPV	BPX	R$
10																																		
11																																		
12																																		
13	STL *	9	4	0	150	127	2.79	2.68	1.06	603	493	710	19.3	2.2	7.7	3.5	58%	12%	44	17	39	27%	77%	7%	9	69	33%	22%	0	0.66	19.9	105	137	$16
14	STL	5	6	0	107	94	3.20	3.70	1.20	636	581	687	23.5	2.8	7.9	2.8	64%	11%	42	22	36	30%	74%	5%	19	89	47%	21%			7.2	87	104	$5
1st Half		5	5	0	90	83	2.79	3.43	1.12	603	569	638	24.7	2.6	8.3	3.2	64%	11%	44	22	35	29%	76%	6%	15	93	60%	7%			10.6	101	120	$9
2nd Half		0	1	0	17	11	5.40	5.19	1.62	796	654	867	19.0	3.8	5.9	1.6	66%	9%	33	24	43	35%	65%	4%	4	74	0%	75%			-3.4	16	19	-$17
15	Proj	**10**	**8**	**0**	**174**	**151**	**3.28**	**3.48**	**1.23**	**671**	**554**	**763**	**23.7**	**2.6**	**7.8**	**3.1**	**62%**	**11%**	**40**	**21**	**39**	**31%**	**75%**	**6%**	**32**						**9.9**	**90**	**107**	**$11**

BRIAN RUDD

Wada,Tsuyoshi

Age: 34 Th: L Role SP	Health F	LIMA Plan B+
Ht: 5' 11" Wt: 180 Type xFB	PT/Exp D	Rand Var -3
	Consist F	MM 2203

4-4, 3.25 ERA in 69 IP at CHC. Some will look at nice surface stats, skill spike in 2nd half and speculate on sophomore profit. You'll see so-so FpK, ugly xERA, and know that further gains are unlikely. Combo of high DIS%, flyball tilt, oOPS vR, age reflect risk, holes, lack of upside. Speculate elsewhere.

Yr Tm	W	L	Sv	IP	K	ERA	xERA	WHIP	oOPS	vL	vR	BF/G	Ctl	Dom	Cmd	FpK	SwK	G	L	F	H%	S%	hr/f	GS	APC	DOM%	DIS%	Sv%	LI	RAR	BPV	BPX	R$
10 for	17	8	0	169	160	3.90	3.85	1.32				26.9	3.6	8.5	2.3						30%	73%								3.7	77	125	$11
11 for	16	5	0	184	159	1.88	2.74	1.12				27.9	2.4	7.8	3.2						29%	86%								46.7	106	159	$28
12																																	
13 aaa	5	6	0	103	58	5.81	6.86	1.88				25.4	3.6	5.1	1.4						37%	70%								-24.6	12	15	-$18
14 CHC *	14	10	0	183	145	3.53	4.71	1.39	731	429	799	24.1	2.6	7.1	2.8	59%	9%	36	23	41	33%	79%	8%	13	88	46%	23%			4.7	66	79	$4
1st Half	9	4	0	99	74	3.41	5.21	1.49				26.7	2.7	6.7	2.5						34%	81%	0%	0						4.1	55	66	$4
2nd Half	5	6	0	84	71	3.68	4.11	1.27	731	429	799	21.5	2.4	7.6	3.1	59%	9%	36	23	41	31%	75%	8%	13	88	46%	23%			0.6	80	95	$4
15 Proj	**12**	**9**	**0**	**174**	**134**	**3.99**	**4.00**	**1.36**	**728**	**425**	**797**	**24.2**	**2.8**	**6.9**	**2.5**	**59%**	**9%**	**36**	**23**	**41**	**31%**	**74%**	**8%**	**30**						**-5.3**	**63**	**75**	**$4**

Wainwright,Adam

Age: 33 Th: R Role SP	Health D	LIMA Plan D+
Ht: 6' 7" Wt: 235 Type	PT/Exp A	Rand Var -3
	Consist A	MM 4205

Easy to go all-in on sub-2.50 ERA workhorse, but not so fast. 30% drop in skills hidden by trifecta of H%/S%/hr/f help. FpK is average now, so walks are headed up. And sub-elite SwK means that 2nd half Dom might be more than mirage, especially given late elbow issues. DN: 3.50+ ERA, DL

Yr Tm	W	L	Sv	IP	K	ERA	xERA	WHIP	oOPS	vL	vR	BF/G	Ctl	Dom	Cmd	FpK	SwK	G	L	F	H%	S%	hr/f	GS	APC	DOM%	DIS%	Sv%	LI	RAR	BPV	BPX	R$
10 STL	20	11	0	230	213	2.42	3.04	1.05	604	575	627	27.6	2.2	8.3	3.8	61%	10%	52	18	31	28%	79%	8%	33	102	82%	3%			47.1	121	195	$34
11																																	
12 STL	14	13	0	199	184	3.94	3.36	1.25	701	724	681	26.0	2.4	8.3	3.5	64%	9%	51	23	26	32%	69%	10%	32	97	69%	13%			1.8	115	151	$11
13 STL	19	9	0	242	219	2.94	2.94	1.07	636	631	639	28.1	1.3	8.2	6.3	65%	10%	49	23	28	31%	74%	8%	34	104	82%	6%			27.5	139	181	$29
14 STL	20	9	0	227	179	2.38	3.31	1.03	580	625	542	28.1	2.0	7.1	3.6	61%	9%	46	24	30	27%	78%	5%	32	102	72%	6%			38.1	98	117	$30
1st Half	10	4	0	116	105	2.01	3.06	0.90	525	573	482	27.9	1.7	8.1	4.8	63%	10%	44	22	34	26%	78%	4%	16	102	81%	6%			24.8	122	146	$39
2nd Half	10	5	0	111	74	2.77	3.60	1.17	636	678	600	28.3	2.3	6.0	2.6	58%	9%	48	25	26	29%	77%	7%	16	102	63%	6%			13.3	73	88	$21
15 Proj	**16**	**8**	**0**	**190**	**156**	**3.28**	**3.11**	**1.13**	**647**	**667**	**628**	**27.3**	**2.1**	**7.4**	**3.6**	**62%**	**9%**	**48**	**23**	**28**	**29%**	**72%**	**8%**	**27**						**10.9**	**104**	**124**	**$18**

Walden,Jordan

Age: 27 Th: R Role RP	Health D	LIMA Plan B+
Ht: 6' 5" Wt: 250 Type Pwr	PT/Exp D	Rand Var -2
	Consist A	MM 4510

PRO: Sexy SwK shows he's got the goods to close again; sky-high LI confirms manager's faith. CON: Long history of 4+ Ctl with marginal FpK and funky mechanics make wildness chronic. Add in spotty health history and odds are he won't be counted on for an expanded role. Speculate, but only in deep leagues.

Yr Tm	W	L	Sv	IP	K	ERA	xERA	WHIP	oOPS	vL	vR	BF/G	Ctl	Dom	Cmd	FpK	SwK	G	L	F	H%	S%	hr/f	GS	APC	DOM%	DIS%	Sv%	LI	RAR	BPV	BPX	R$
10 LAA *	1	2	9	65	57	3.33	4.16	1.50	670	527	803	4.7	4.0	7.9	2.0	55%	14%	60	23	17	34%	78%	17%	0	17			64	1.00	6.0	78	126	$3
11 LAA	5	5	32	60	67	2.98	3.38	1.24	642	650	631	4.1	3.9	10.0	2.6	60%	13%	45	18	37	31%	76%	5%	0	18			76	1.70	7.1	98	148	$17
12 LAA	3	2	1	39	48	3.46	3.68	1.36	674	606	743	3.8	4.2	11.1	2.7	60%	14%	40	25	36	34%	76%	8%	0	16			50	0.61	2.7	105	137	-$1
13 ATL	4	3	1	47	54	3.45	3.53	1.13	620	542	690	3.9	2.7	10.3	3.9	62%	15%	31	18	51	31%	71%	6%	0	16			33	1.23	2.4	123	160	$2
14 ATL	0	2	3	50	62	2.88	3.27	1.20	541	599	488	3.5	4.9	11.2	2.3	58%	15%	45	19	36	28%	76%	5%	0	15			60	1.40	5.3	93	110	$2
1st Half	0	0	2	21	28	2.95	3.32	1.27	560	639	464	3.8	5.1	11.8	2.3	65%	16%	45	16	39	30%	77%	5%	0	16			100	1.29	2.1	99	118	$0
2nd Half	0	2	1	29	34	2.83	3.23	1.15	527	559	503	3.4	4.7	10.7	2.3	53%	14%	45	21	33	27%	75%	5%	0	14			33	1.47	3.2	88	106	$3
15 Proj	**2**	**3**	**3**	**58**	**68**	**3.13**	**3.14**	**1.22**	**599**	**597**	**601**	**3.6**	**4.1**	**10.7**	**2.6**	**59%**	**15%**	**41**	**20**	**40**	**30%**	**75%**	**6%**	**0**						**4.3**	**101**	**120**	**$3**

Walker,Taijuan

Age: 22 Th: R Role SP	Health D	LIMA Plan B
Ht: 6' 4" Wt: 230 Type Pwr	PT/Exp D	Rand Var 0
	Consist C	MM 4301

2-3, 2.61 ERA in 38 IP at SEA. Premium prospect derailed by balky shoulder. 95 mph heat, small-sample 8.0 Cmd vRHB at MLB show upside when healthy. Couldn't find plate against lefties; re-worked mechanics as a result of shoulder issues possible reason. If healthy, for now... UP: 3.50 ERA

Yr Tm	W	L	Sv	IP	K	ERA	xERA	WHIP	oOPS	vL	vR	BF/G	Ctl	Dom	Cmd	FpK	SwK	G	L	F	H%	S%	hr/f	GS	APC	DOM%	DIS%	Sv%	LI	RAR	BPV	BPX	R$
10																																	
11																																	
12 aa	7	10	0	127	110	5.27	4.37	1.45				21.6	3.5	7.8	2.3						33%	63%								-19.7	71	93	-$7
13 SEA *	10	10	0	156	156	3.33	3.04	1.22	546	536	563	22.6	3.3	9.0	2.7	57%	10%	38	21	40	30%	74%	0%	3	78	33%	0%			10.3	101	132	$11
14 SEA *	9	7	0	116	109	3.97	3.77	1.27	642	729	501	20.6	3.2	8.4	2.6	61%	10%	47	27	26	30%	72%	7%	5	78	40%	20%	0	0.57	-3.3	81	96	$3
1st Half	4	1	0	42	41	3.76	3.25	1.04	857	1121	647	20.1	2.6	8.8	3.4	50%	10%	53	33	13	24%	72%	100%	1	94	100%	0%			-0.1	91	108	$4
2nd Half	5	6	0	74	68	4.09	4.06	1.40	603	682	461	20.9	3.6	8.2	2.3	63%	10%	45	26	28	33%	72%	0%	4	76	25%	25%	0	0.55	-3.2	78	93	$2
15 Proj	**9**	**8**	**0**	**123**	**117**	**3.78**	**3.33**	**1.27**	**641**	**701**	**535**	**21.4**	**3.2**	**8.6**	**2.6**	**63%**	**10%**	**45**	**24**	**30**	**31%**	**71%**	**9%**	**24**						**-0.6**	**90**	**107**	**$5**

Warren,Adam

Age: 27 Th: R Role RP	Health A	LIMA Plan B
Ht: 6' 1" Wt: 200 Type Pwr	PT/Exp C	Rand Var -1
	Consist C	MM 3201

Trim walks, increase swing-and-miss a notch, shave couple points from hit rate and voilà! Middling middleman gains value. Like many, surge in Ks last two years tied to move to pen, but SwK supports it. LI shows he can handle pressure, and if gains vs. LHB stick... UP: 10 SV

Yr Tm	W	L	Sv	IP	K	ERA	xERA	WHIP	oOPS	vL	vR	BF/G	Ctl	Dom	Cmd	FpK	SwK	G	L	F	H%	S%	hr/f	GS	APC	DOM%	DIS%	Sv%	LI	RAR	BPV	BPX	R$
10 aa	4	2	0	54	49	3.84	3.74	1.35				22.7	2.7	8.2	3.0						34%	71%								1.6	100	162	$0
11 aaa	6	8	0	152	91	5.00	5.36	1.58				24.8	3.5	5.4	1.5						32%	70%								-19.8	27	40	-$10
12 NYY *	7	8	0	155	87	5.19	6.13	1.71	1588	1500	1636	26.0	3.0	5.1	1.7	59%	5%	29	29	43	36%	71%	33%	1	77	0%	100%			-22.5	25	33	-$18
13 NYY	3	2	1	77	64	3.39	4.02	1.43	766	896	625	9.7	3.5	7.5	2.1	56%	11%	45	22	32	31%	81%	13%	2	38	50%	50%	100	0.58	4.5	63	82	-$1
14 NYY	3	6	3	79	76	2.97	3.31	1.11	615	525	690	4.7	2.7	8.7	3.2	58%	12%	45	24	31	29%	73%	6%	0	19			50	1.26	7.4	105	126	$6
1st Half	1	4	2	43	41	2.70	3.39	1.22	654	557	740	4.9	2.7	8.5	3.2	56%	12%	45	25	30	32%	78%	5%	0	20			50	1.31	5.6	104	124	$5
2nd Half	2	2	1	35	35	3.31	3.21	0.96	566	479	631	4.5	2.8	8.9	3.2	59%	12%	46	22	33	25%	66%	7%	0	18			50	1.21	1.9	108	129	$7
15 Proj	**3**	**4**	**0**	**73**	**62**	**3.23**	**3.44**	**1.25**	**693**	**710**	**679**	**6.8**	**3.0**	**7.7**	**2.5**	**57%**	**11%**	**45**	**23**	**32**	**30%**	**77%**	**9%**	**0**						**4.6**	**80**	**95**	**$2**

Watson,Tony

Age: 30 Th: L Role RP	Health A	LIMA Plan B
Ht: 6' 4" Wt: 225 Type Pwr	PT/Exp C	Rand Var -5
	Consist B	MM 5311

Trimmed ERA even further as skills continue to surge. Sure, dandy S% helped, but nice Ctl and Dom came with solid FpK and SwK support, so they could stick. Increasing LI shows manager confidence, and 4+ Cmd vs. LHB and RHB tells us he's no LOOGY. Today a vulture, maybe a closer-in-waiting tomorrow?

Yr Tm	W	L	Sv	IP	K	ERA	xERA	WHIP	oOPS	vL	vR	BF/G	Ctl	Dom	Cmd	FpK	SwK	G	L	F	H%	S%	hr/f	GS	APC	DOM%	DIS%	Sv%	LI	RAR	BPV	BPX	R$
10 aa	6	4	2	111	81	3.27	3.14	1.09				12.8	2.0	6.5	3.3						27%	74%								11.1	88	143	$10
11 PIT *	5	5	0	75	63	3.47	3.42	1.25	711	708	713	4.4	3.7	7.5	2.0	63%	9%	32	24	44	27%	76%	13%	0	15			0	1.28	4.4	68	102	$3
12 PIT	5	2	0	53	53	3.38	3.86	1.13	623	554	691	3.2	3.9	8.9	2.3	64%	12%	40	18	42	25%	73%	9%	0	13			0	1.21	4.2	74	97	$3
13 PIT	3	1	2	72	54	2.39	3.44	0.88	544	483	582	4.2	1.5	6.8	4.5	63%	12%	44	19	37	24%	76%	7%	0	16			50	1.14	13.1	103	135	$9
14 PIT	10	2	2	77	81	1.63	2.76	1.02	613	531	646	3.9	1.7	9.4	5.4	65%	14%	48	21	32	30%	88%	8%	0	15			22	1.34	20.1	149	177	$13
1st Half	5	0	0	38	48	0.96	2.48	1.04	560	563	559	4.0	2.4	11.5	4.8	65%	14%	51	20	30	32%	92%	4%	0	16			0	1.31	12.9	171	203	$14
2nd Half	5	2	2	40	33	2.27	3.02	1.01	666	502	736	3.8	1.1	7.5	6.6	65%	13%	45	21	33	28%	83%	11%	0	15			33	1.37	7.2	128	152	$12
15 Proj	**5**	**3**	**5**	**73**	**67**	**2.31**	**2.99**	**1.01**	**607**	**538**	**645**	**3.9**	**2.1**	**8.3**	**4.0**	**64%**	**12%**	**44**	**20**	**36**	**27%**	**81%**	**8%**	**0**						**12.8**	**115**	**137**	**$10**

Weaver,Jered

Age: 32 Th: R Role SP	Health D	LIMA Plan C+
Ht: 5' 9" Wt: 210 Type xFB	PT/Exp A	Rand Var -1
	Consist A	MM 2205

Writing on the wall finally catching up to him. ERA jump reflective of increasing xERA downside. With below-average skills now, his downside is even worse than that mediocre 2nd half. Avoidance of disaster is his only redeemable skill, and 2nd half DIS% reveals cracks there too. Stop at $10. DN: 4.00+ ERA

Yr Tm	W	L	Sv	IP	K	ERA	xERA	WHIP	oOPS	vL	vR	BF/G	Ctl	Dom	Cmd	FpK	SwK	G	L	F	H%	S%	hr/f	GS	APC	DOM%	DIS%	Sv%	LI	RAR	BPV	BPX	R$
10 LAA	13	12	0	224	233	3.01	3.46	1.07	622	593	653	26.6	2.2	9.3	4.3	62%	12%	36	16	48	29%	76%	8%	34	109	79%	6%			29.6	124	200	$27
11 LAA	18	8	0	236	198	2.41	3.75	1.01	598	578	621	28.1	2.1	7.6	3.5	64%	10%	32	19	49	26%	80%	6%	33	114	79%	6%			44.7	88	133	$35
12 LAA	20	5	0	189	142	2.81	4.01	1.02	605	541	690	24.6	2.1	6.8	3.2	61%	9%	36	21	43	25%	77%	9%	30	95	60%	17%			27.9	78	102	$29
13 LAA	11	8	0	154	117	3.27	4.17	1.14	671	638	725	26.4	2.2	6.8	3.2	60%	10%	31	22	47	28%	75%	8%	24	100	63%	8%			11.4	74	96	$12
14 LAA	18	9	0	213	169	3.59	4.25	1.21	684	723	620	26.1	2.7	7.1	2.6	56%	9%	33	19	48	28%	75%	9%	34	99	47%	9%			4.1	65	78	$13
1st Half	8	6	0	111	86	3.33	4.11	1.14	654	726	514	26.4	2.7	7.0	2.6	54%	9%	36	17	48	26%	76%	9%	17	99	59%	0%			5.6	67	80	$16
2nd Half	10	3	0	103	83	3.86	4.40	1.29	715	719	709	25.9	2.8	7.3	2.6	58%	9%	30	22	48	30%	74%	9%	17	98	35%	18%			-1.5	63	75	$10
15 Proj	**14**	**10**	**0**	**196**	**156**	**3.79**	**3.83**	**1.25**	**713**	**711**	**715**	**25.8**	**2.5**	**7.1**	**2.9**	**59%**	**10%**	**33**	**20**	**47**	**30%**	**73%**	**8%**	**31**						**-1.2**	**73**	**87**	**$10**

STEPHEN NICKRAND

Webb,Daniel

Age: 25	Th: R	Role RP	Health A	LIMA Plan D+	Rand Var 0
Ht: 6' 3"	Wt: 215	Type Pwr GB	PT/Exp D	Consist C	MM 2300

Flopped at chance to gain prominent role in pitching-starved pen. The culprit again was too many walks, and with Ctl history and horrific FpK, it's a chronic one. 18%+ SwK on three pitches does give him a higher ceiling, especially with his GB tilt. But it won't matter if he can't find home plate.

Yr Tm	W	L	Sv	IP	K	ERA	xERA	WHIP	oOPS	vL	vR	BF/G	Ctl	Dom	Cmd	FpK	SwK	G	L	F	H%	S%	hr/f	GS	APC	DOM%	DIS%	Sv%	LI	RAR	BPV	BPX	R$
10																																	
11																																	
12																																	
13 CHW *	1	1	8	59	60	3.19	3.07	1.37	502	553	439	5.8	4.5	9.2	2.0	67%	15%	56	22	22	32%	75%	0%	0	19			89	0.71	4.9	100	130	$2
14 CHW	6	5	0	68	58	3.99	4.33	1.49	736	623	834	5.2	5.6	7.7	1.4	51%	11%	52	18	31	29%	75%	10%	0	21			0	0.99	-2.1	18	21	-$2
1st Half	4	2	0	35	27	3.31	4.92	1.56	703	600	795	5.7	6.6	6.9	1.0	47%	9%	50	17	33	27%	79%	6%	0	23			0	1.32	1.9	-27	-32	-$1
2nd Half	2	3	0	32	31	4.73	3.73	1.42	770	648	871	4.7	4.5	8.6	1.9	55%	13%	53	18	28	30%	69%	15%	0	19			0	0.68	-4.0	66	79	-$3
15 Proj	4	3	0	65	61	3.77	3.72	1.42	706	605	793	5.3	4.9	8.4	1.7	52%	11%	52	18	30	30%	74%	8%	0						-0.2	49	58	-$1

Webb,Ryan

Age: 29	Th: R	Role RP	Health B	LIMA Plan C	Rand Var -1
Ht: 6' 6"	Wt: 245	Type xGB	PT/Exp C	Consist A	MM 3100

Bullpen sinkerballers that don't miss many bats tend to wear out their welcome over time, both on MLB clubs and yours. This one's value is dependent on defense and help from hit, strand, and hr/f rates, none of which we can bank on. Won't hurt you much, but better to spend elsewhere.

Yr Tm	W	L	Sv	IP	K	ERA	xERA	WHIP	oOPS	vL	vR	BF/G	Ctl	Dom	Cmd	FpK	SwK	G	L	F	H%	S%	hr/f	GS	APC	DOM%	DIS%	Sv%	LI	RAR	BPV	BPX	R$
10 SD *	4	1	1	80	64	2.37	3.11	1.26	680	846	566	4.6	2.7	7.2	2.7	64%	9%	62	21	17	32%	81%	3%	0	18			33	0.80	16.8	97	158	$6
11 FLA	2	4	0	51	31	3.20	3.81	1.34	693	771	627	4.0	3.6	5.5	1.6	59%	8%	61	17	22	29%	76%	6%	0	14			0	1.15	4.7	42	63	$0
12 MIA	4	3	0	60	44	4.03	4.03	1.52	749	809	706	4.2	3.0	6.6	2.2	62%	7%	52	27	21	36%	72%	5%	0	16			0	1.03	-0.1	68	88	-$4
13 MIA	2	6	0	80	54	2.91	3.74	1.21	695	714	681	5.0	3.0	6.0	2.0	58%	9%	56	19	25	27%	77%	8%	0	18			0	1.20	9.4	61	80	$2
14 BAL	3	3	0	49	37	3.83	3.64	1.26	637	613	649	4.1	2.2	6.8	3.1	64%	8%	49	23	29	32%	68%	5%	0	14			0	0.96	-0.5	89	106	-$1
1st Half	2	1	0	36	30	2.48	3.08	0.99	535	488	558	4.1	2.0	7.4	3.8	65%	9%	53	20	27	27%	74%	4%	0	14			0	1.03	5.7	111	133	$2
2nd Half	1	2	0	13	7	7.62	5.30	2.00	859	876	850	4.1	2.8	4.8	1.8	60%	7%	41	28	31	41%	60%	6%	0	14			0	0.80	-6.2	31	37	-$11
15 Proj	2	2	0	44	32	3.67	3.39	1.32	710	750	681	4.3	2.7	6.6	2.4	62%	8%	55	21	23	31%	72%	8%	0						0.4	79	94	-$1

Webster,Allen

Age: 25	Th: R	Role SP	Health A	LIMA Plan D+	Rand Var -1
Ht: 6' 2"	Wt: 190	Type Pwr	PT/Exp D	Consist B	MM 2101

Scouts will tell you that his stuff is some of the best in the game. High SwK% reflects velocity, plus changeup. So does consistently mediocre control, since he can't keep his hard, moving stuff over plate. Case-in-point: more BBs than Ks vs. LHBs last two years. Don't speculate without a bench.

Yr Tm	W	L	Sv	IP	K	ERA	xERA	WHIP	oOPS	vL	vR	BF/G	Ctl	Dom	Cmd	FpK	SwK	G	L	F	H%	S%	hr/f	GS	APC	DOM%	DIS%	Sv%	LI	RAR	BPV	BPX	R$
10																																	
11 aa	6	3	0	91	64	4.96	4.50	1.48				21.7	3.1	6.3	2.0						34%	66%								-11.4	60	90	-$4
12 aa	6	9	0	131	110	5.11	4.85	1.70				20.4	4.4	7.6	1.7						38%	67%								-17.7	72	94	-$14
13 BOS *	9	6	0	135	120	5.33	3.85	1.33	926	1253	550	19.4	4.0	8.0	2.0	62%	13%	43	21	36	28%	61%	19%	7	67	29%	57%	0	0.71	-24.5	64	83	-$4
14 BOS *	9	7	1	181	118	4.28	4.15	1.43	736	703	773	24.1	3.7	5.9	1.6	60%	12%	46	21	33	31%	70%	5%	11	87	18%	27%			-11.9	51	61	-$4
1st Half	4	4	0	99	66	3.65	4.18	1.40				24.5	3.3	6.1	1.8						31%	75%	0%	0						1.0	55	65	-$1
2nd Half	5	3	1	82	52	5.02	4.13	1.46	736	703	773	23.5	4.1	5.6	1.4	60%	12%	46	21	33	30%	65%	5%	11	87	18%	27%			-13.0	48	57	-$8
15 Proj	6	5	0	105	78	4.40	4.04	1.40	715	805	612	21.6	3.8	6.7	1.7	61%	12%	45	21	34	30%	69%	7%	17						-8.5	39	47	-$2

Wheeler,Zack

Age: 25	Th: R	Role SP	Health A	LIMA Plan B	Rand Var 0
Ht: 6' 4"	Wt: 195	Type Pwr	PT/Exp C	Consist B	MM 4405

On surface, near carbon copy of MLB debut. But three reasons there's a breakout coming... 1) Dom uptick with SwK support; 2) Ks plus GBs are a premium combo; 3) 142 BPV with good control vs. RH bats. Last hurdle is FpK and Ctl, especially against lefties. And then... UP: 3.00 ERA, 200 K

Yr Tm	W	L	Sv	IP	K	ERA	xERA	WHIP	oOPS	vL	vR	BF/G	Ctl	Dom	Cmd	FpK	SwK	G	L	F	H%	S%	hr/f	GS	APC	DOM%	DIS%	Sv%	LI	RAR	BPV	BPX	R$
10																																	
11																																	
12 a/a	12	8	0	149	132	3.44	2.58	1.19				23.9	3.3	8.0	2.4						29%	69%								10.5	101	132	$12
13 NYM *	11	7	0	169	148	3.38	3.58	1.29	696	766	639	23.1	3.7	7.9	2.2	52%	9%	43	23	33	29%	77%	10%	17	102	59%	12%			10.2	72	94	$9
14 NYM	11	11	0	185	187	3.54	3.37	1.33	678	745	615	24.8	3.8	9.1	2.4	54%	10%	54	19	27	31%	75%	10%	32	103	59%	19%			4.5	92	109	$6
1st Half	3	8	0	95	95	4.25	3.39	1.38	696	808	601	23.8	4.0	9.0	2.3	57%	10%	54	19	27	33%	69%	9%	17	99	53%	24%			-6.0	86	103	-$2
2nd Half	8	3	0	90	92	2.80	3.34	1.27	659	686	631	25.9	3.7	9.2	2.5	51%	11%	54	18	28	30%	81%	12%	15	109	67%	13%			10.4	98	117	$15
15 Proj	14	10	0	196	192	3.24	3.21	1.26	653	712	601	23.6	3.6	8.8	2.5	53%	10%	50	21	30	30%	76%	10%	34						12.0	91	108	$15

Whitley,Chase

Age: 26	Th: R	Role RP	Health A	LIMA Plan C	Rand Var +2
Ht: 6' 3"	Wt: 215	Type Pwr	PT/Exp D	Consist A	MM 3200

4-3, 5.23 ERA in 76 IP at NYY. Scary MLB ERA, lack of prospect pedigree will keep many away. Don't follow suit. Elite skills with NYY torpedoed by crazy H% and hr/f in 2nd half. Premium changeup makes up for lack of velocity, while solid 2.6 Cmd vLHB says not to be swayed by that oOPS. Stash.

Yr Tm	W	L	Sv	IP	K	ERA	xERA	WHIP	oOPS	vL	vR	BF/G	Ctl	Dom	Cmd	FpK	SwK	G	L	F	H%	S%	hr/f	GS	APC	DOM%	DIS%	Sv%	LI	RAR	BPV	BPX	R$
10																																	
11 aa	3	4	1	43	32	4.04	6.15	1.68				10.1	4.1	6.7	1.6						34%	82%								-0.5	21	32	-$3
12 a/a	9	5	2	84	61	3.90	3.41	1.20				7.9	3.0	6.5	2.2						27%	70%								1.2	64	84	$4
13 aaa	3	2	3	68	51	4.21	4.33	1.47				10.0	3.1	6.8	2.2						34%	71%								-2.9	69	89	-$3
14 NYY *	7	5	0	107	90	4.40	4.39	1.37	831	866	792	13.2	2.2	7.6	3.4	62%	11%	45	21	34	34%	69%	12%	12	53	33%	50%	0	0.83	-8.8	90	107	-$2
1st Half	6	4	0	72	55	4.03	3.72	1.31	762	839	645	18.7	2.0	6.8	3.4	63%	11%	44	21	35	34%	68%	6%	9	83	33%	44%			-2.6	100	119	$2
2nd Half	1	1	0	35	35	5.19	5.80	1.48	937	924	946	8.3	2.6	9.1	3.5	60%	13%	48	20	32	35%	71%	24%	3	34	33%	67%	0	0.85	-6.2	69	82	-$9
15 Proj	3	3	0	56	46	3.92	3.51	1.30	696	711	682	9.6	2.8	7.4	2.7	61%	12%	46	21	33	31%	72%	10%	7						-1.3	83	99	-$1

Wilhelmsen,Tom

Age: 31	Th: R	Role RP	Health A	LIMA Plan C+	Rand Var -5
Ht: 6' 6"	Wt: 220	Type Pwr	PT/Exp B	Consist C	MM 3301

It's tempting to add recent former closers to your bullpen, since prior experience in that role does carry MLB weight. But so does skill, and this one hasn't had any in a while. Only reason for sub-3.00 ERA was friendly H% and S%. Waning LI shows lack of manager confidence. Speculate elsewhere.

Yr Tm	W	L	Sv	IP	K	ERA	xERA	WHIP	oOPS	vL	vR	BF/G	Ctl	Dom	Cmd	FpK	SwK	G	L	F	H%	S%	hr/f	GS	APC	DOM%	DIS%	Sv%	LI	RAR	BPV	BPX	R$
10																																	
11 SEA *	6	5	0	93	62	5.55	5.13	1.58	580	508	651	10.5	4.0	6.0	1.5	59%	12%	34	21	45	32%	66%	5%	0	20			0	0.59	-18.5	34	51	-$8
12 SEA	4	3	29	79	87	2.50	3.37	1.11	578	637	519	4.5	3.3	9.9	3.0	57%	12%	48	16	35	28%	80%	7%	0	17			85	1.38	14.9	115	150	$20
13 SEA	0	3	24	59	45	4.12	4.54	1.32	603	743	468	4.3	5.0	6.9	1.4	55%	11%	43	23	34	26%	67%	4%	0	17			83	1.13	-1.8	9	11	$6
14 SEA	3	2	1	79	72	2.27	3.48	1.05	542	505	573	5.6	4.1	8.2	2.0	59%	13%	52	19	29	21%	82%	10%	2	21	0%	100%	33	0.92	14.4	67	80	$8
1st Half	0	1	1	45	38	2.60	3.54	1.16	581	518	643	5.8	4.4	7.6	1.7	56%	13%	57	22	21	23%	80%	12%	0	22			33	0.79	6.3	53	63	$5
2nd Half	3	1	0	34	34	1.83	3.42	0.90	487	484	488	5.2	3.7	8.9	2.4	62%	13%	44	15	41	18%	86%	9%	2	20	0%	100%	0	1.09	8.1	83	99	$12
15 Proj	3	3	0	73	64	3.53	3.66	1.27	642	678	610	5.2	4.1	8.0	1.9	58%	12%	46	19	35	28%	73%	7%	0						1.9	56	67	$1

Williams,Jerome

Age: 33	Th: R	Role RP	Health B	LIMA Plan C	Rand Var +1
Ht: 6' 3"	Wt: 240	Type	PT/Exp A	Consist A	MM 2101

Former 1999 first-rounder and 2014 tri-team hot potato continues to hang on to swingman role for pitching-desperate teams. That pedigree is his only redeeming quality, since skills have been lifeless in all but one of nine MLB seasons. Evaporating swing-and-miss stuff offers no hope for late-career spike.

Yr Tm	W	L	Sv	IP	K	ERA	xERA	WHIP	oOPS	vL	vR	BF/G	Ctl	Dom	Cmd	FpK	SwK	G	L	F	H%	S%	hr/f	GS	APC	DOM%	DIS%	Sv%	LI	RAR	BPV	BPX	R$
10																																	
11 LAA *	11	2	0	118	72	3.95	4.87	1.40	769	628	911	23.7	2.3	5.5	2.4	62%	11%	50	16	34	32%	76%	13%	6	68	50%	17%	0	0.82	-0.1	45	68	$2
12 LAA	6	8	1	138	98	4.58	3.79	1.26	743	747	738	17.9	2.3	6.4	2.8	60%	10%	54	18	28	30%	66%	14%	15	64	40%	20%	100	0.67	-9.5	86	112	$0
13 LAA	9	10	0	169	107	4.57	4.30	1.39	772	818	716	19.7	2.9	5.7	1.9	58%	10%	47	21	32	30%	70%	13%	25	71	28%	32%	0	0.74	-14.7	48	63	-$4
14 3 TM	6	7	0	115	82	4.77	4.10	1.40	756	787	720	13.4	2.8	6.4	2.3	63%	8%	45	23	32	32%	67%	10%	11	50	27%	9%	0	0.67	-14.7	62	74	-$5
1st Half	1	4	0	48	38	6.04	4.16	1.57	836	817	854	8.4	3.0	7.2	2.4	64%	9%	45	24	31	35%	63%	14%	0	31			0	0.63	-13.5	71	85	-$15
2nd Half	5	3	0	67	44	3.88	4.06	1.28	694	765	608	25.3	2.7	5.9	2.2	63%	8%	44	22	34	29%	70%	7%	11	92	27%	9%			-1.1	56	67	$2
15 Proj	5	5	0	87	59	4.60	3.82	1.38	762	778	744	15.8	2.7	6.1	2.3	61%	9%	47	21	32	31%	69%	11%	13						-9.2	62	74	-$3

STEPHEN NICKRAND

Wilson,Brian

Age: 33	Th: R	Role RP	Health	F	LIMA Plan	C		
Ht: 6' 1"	Wt: 205	Type Pwr	PT/Exp	D	Rand Var	+2		
			Consist	F	MM	3500		

Pitchers returning from TJS don't always come back vintage, or better. Threw as hard as ever, but control was way off. With a slowly-eroding, and now below-average FpK, that control may not rebound. Best bet for future value might be as a situational righty-killer. Um, killer is harsh. More like a righty-oppressor.

Yr Tm	W	L	Sv	IP	K	ERA	xERA	WHIP	oOPS	vL	vR	BF/G	Ctl	Dom	Cmd	FpK	SwK	G	L	F	H%	S%	hr/f	GS	APC	DOM%	DIS%	Sv%	LI	RAR	BPV	BPX	R$
10 SF	3	3	48	75	93	1.81	2.97	1.18	597	607	587	4.4	3.1	11.2	3.6	65%	11%	49	13	38	33%	86%	4%	0	19			91	1.50	20.9	144	233	$28
11 SF	6	4	36	55	54	3.11	3.84	1.47	660	599	720	4.3	5.1	8.8	1.7	61%	7%	53	17	30	32%	78%	4%	0	18			88	1.54	5.7	53	80	$16
12 SF	0	0	1	2	2	9.00	7.66	3.00	1100	933	1143	6.0	9.0	9.0	1.0	67%	7%	25	38	38	52%	67%	0%	0	28			100	0.39	-1.2	-78	-102	-$5
13 LA	2	1	0	14	13	0.66	2.66	0.88	467	413	485	2.7	2.6	8.6	3.3	57%	10%	56	19	25	24%	92%	0%	0	12			0	1.00	5.4	117	152	$0
14 LA	2	4	1	48	54	4.66	4.20	1.61	771	914	674	3.7	5.4	10.1	1.9	58%	8%	38	24	38	35%	73%	10%	0	17			20	1.27	-5.4	51	61	-$5
1st Half	1	2	1	29	33	4.66	4.31	1.72	789	901	705	4.0	5.9	10.2	1.7	58%	8%	40	27	34	36%	74%	11%	0	19			50	0.94	-3.3	43	51	-$6
2nd Half	1	2	0	19	21	4.66	4.05	1.45	743	938	629	3.2	4.7	9.8	2.1	58%	10%	35	20	45	32%	69%	9%	0	14			0	1.71	-2.2	64	76	-$3
15 Proj	3	4	0	51	55	4.04	3.56	1.39	680	720	647	3.7	4.8	9.8	2.0	60%	9%	44	19	37	31%	72%	10%	0						-1.9	68	81	-$1

Wilson,C.J.

Age: 34	Th: L	Role SP	Health	C	LIMA Plan	D+		
Ht: 5' 11"	Wt: 210	Type Pwr	PT/Exp	A	Rand Var	+1		
			Consist	A	MM	2305		

Ankle injury landed him on the DL to start the 2nd half and it likely lingered the rest of the way. If we give him a mulligan on that, his excellent 1st half bodes well for 2015. But even if you don't believe in mulligans, xERA shows that 2014 was no worse than 2013. Solid investment as long as you monitor health.

Yr Tm	W	L	Sv	IP	K	ERA	xERA	WHIP	oOPS	vL	vR	BF/G	Ctl	Dom	Cmd	FpK	SwK	G	L	F	H%	S%	hr/f	GS	APC	DOM%	DIS%	Sv%	LI	RAR	BPV	BPX	R$
10 TEX	15	8	0	204	170	3.35	3.88	1.25	622	400	679	25.8	4.1	7.5	1.8	54%	7%	49	17	34	27%	73%	5%	33	104	45%	12%			18.3	51	83	$16
11 TEX	16	7	0	223	206	2.94	3.34	1.19	651	658	650	26.9	3.0	8.3	2.8	59%	9%	49	19	32	29%	77%	8%	34	106	59%	15%			27.6	96	144	$23
12 LAA	13	10	0	202	173	3.83	4.07	1.34	684	590	713	25.4	4.0	7.7	1.9	57%	8%	50	20	30	29%	74%	11%	34	101	47%	12%			4.7	57	75	$8
13 LAA	17	7	0	212	188	3.39	3.94	1.34	684	485	741	27.7	3.6	8.0	2.2	60%	9%	44	22	33	31%	76%	7%	33	111	48%	9%			12.4	68	89	$12
14 LAA	13	10	0	176	151	4.51	3.99	1.45	724	572	774	24.5	4.4	7.7	1.8	59%	8%	48	23	30	31%	70%	11%	31	100	39%	29%			-16.6	48	57	-$3
1st Half	8	6	0	108	100	3.90	3.45	1.26	677	529	732	26.3	3.7	8.3	2.3	57%	9%	51	20	29	28%	71%	13%	17	109	59%	18%			-2.2	80	96	$6
2nd Half	5	4	0	67	51	5.48	4.93	1.75	791	648	832	22.4	5.5	6.8	1.2	61%	6%	43	27	30	34%	69%	9%	14	89	14%	43%			-14.4	-4	-5	-$18
15 Proj	14	9	0	189	166	3.78	3.70	1.39	698	553	742	24.3	4.0	7.9	2.0	59%	8%	47	22	31	31%	74%	9%	33						-0.9	58	69	$6

Wilson,Justin

Age: 27	Th: L	Role RP	Health	A	LIMA Plan	C		
Ht: 6' 2"	Wt: 205	Type Pwr GB	PT/Exp	C	Rand Var	0		
			Consist	A	MM	3300		

xERA and BPX show the consistency of the past three years despite ERA volatility. But there is also growth. Combining elite 9+ Dom with 50%+ GB is the ideal recipe for a low ERA. Solid SwK and growing FpK make this profile even more intriguing. That means... UP: Sub-3.00 ERA, with BPI support this time

Yr Tm	W	L	Sv	IP	K	ERA	xERA	WHIP	oOPS	vL	vR	BF/G	Ctl	Dom	Cmd	FpK	SwK	G	L	F	H%	S%	hr/f	GS	APC	DOM%	DIS%	Sv%	LI	RAR	BPV	BPX	R$
10 aa	11	8	0	143	108	3.64	3.14	1.36				22.1	4.4	6.8	1.6						29%	72%								7.8	74	119	$6
11 aaa	10	8	3	124	73	4.84	5.10	1.64				18.5	4.7	5.3	1.1						31%	71%								-13.7	28	41	-$6
12 PIT *	9	6	0	140	113	4.69	3.58	1.35	1111	1053	1161	15.8	4.5	7.3	1.6	58%	10%	20	53	27	28%	66%	0%	0	13			0	0.43	-11.7	63	82	-$1
13 PIT	6	1	0	74	59	2.08	3.59	1.06	543	501	563	5.1	3.4	7.2	2.1	59%	10%	53	17	30	24%	82%	7%	0	21			0	1.11	16.3	68	89	$8
14 PIT	3	4	0	60	61	4.20	3.68	1.32	643	681	622	3.7	4.5	9.2	2.0	61%	10%	51	14	34	29%	68%	7%	0	15			0	1.05	-3.4	72	86	-$2
1st Half	2	0	0	31	33	4.70	3.88	1.37	602	659	568	3.8	5.0	9.7	1.9	59%	9%	45	18	38	32%	62%	0%	0	16			0	0.96	-3.6	63	75	-$3
2nd Half	1	4	0	29	28	3.68	3.47	1.26	687	705	677	3.5	4.0	8.6	2.2	63%	11%	58	11	31	27%	76%	16%	0	14			0	1.15	0.2	82	98	$0
15 Proj	4	4	0	65	60	3.41	3.35	1.22	631	644	624	4.8	3.8	8.3	2.2	60%	10%	53	15	32	28%	73%	8%	0						2.6	78	93	$2

Withrow,Chris

Age: 26	Th: R	Role RP	Health	F	LIMA Plan	D+		
Ht: 6' 4"	Wt: 215	Type Pwr	PT/Exp	D	Rand Var	-5		
			Consist	C	MM	2400		

Dodgers' first round pick in 2007, he struggled through several years as a starter before he moved to the bullpen in 2012. That's when everything came together. But something was clearly wrong from almost the get-go this spring. We now know why. Season-ending TJ surgery puts 2015 at risk.

Yr Tm	W	L	Sv	IP	K	ERA	xERA	WHIP	oOPS	vL	vR	BF/G	Ctl	Dom	Cmd	FpK	SwK	G	L	F	H%	S%	hr/f	GS	APC	DOM%	DIS%	Sv%	LI	RAR	BPV	BPX	R$
10 aa	4	9	0	130	107	5.86	5.02	1.61				21.3	4.1	7.4	1.8						35%	63%								-28.4	56	91	-$10
11 aa	6	6	0	129	112	4.17	3.53	1.41				21.7	4.6	7.9	1.7						30%	70%								-3.6	75	113	$0
12 aa	3	3	2	60	55	5.35	4.17	1.57				12.0	5.4	8.2	1.5						33%	64%								-9.9	71	92	-$7
13 LA *	7	0	1	61	71	2.20	2.73	1.16	536	533	538	4.8	3.6	10.4	2.9	55%	12%	36	21	44	29%	85%	15%	0	23			33	1.51	12.6	113	148	$7
14 LA	0	0	0	21	28	2.95	3.79	1.31	551	97	813	4.5	7.6	11.8	1.6	47%	14%	47	16	37	22%	78%	6%	0	19			0	1.08	2.1	33	39	-$2
1st Half	0	0	0	21	28	2.95	3.79	1.31	551	97	813	4.5	7.6	11.8	1.6	47%	14%	47	16	37	22%	78%	6%	0	19			0	1.08	2.1	32	38	-$2
2nd Half																																	
15 Proj	1	0	0	15	15	3.89	3.81	1.39	665	351	847	7.1	5.5	9.6	1.8	50%	13%	42	18	40	29%	72%	6%	0						-0.3	46	54	-$3

Wood,Alex

Age: 24	Th: L	Role SP	Health	A	LIMA Plan	C+		
Ht: 6' 4"	Wt: 215	Type Pwr	PT/Exp	C	Rand Var	-1		
			Consist	A	MM	5405		

Excellent follow-up to last year's debut, despite being shuffled in and out of the rotation, and back-and-forth to the minors (though he never got a start there) in the 1st half. Metrics are elite across-the-board, though FpK was a little soft in the 2nd half. Quibbles. This is a 7th rounder who could earn 2nd round value.

Yr Tm	W	L	Sv	IP	K	ERA	xERA	WHIP	oOPS	vL	vR	BF/G	Ctl	Dom	Cmd	FpK	SwK	G	L	F	H%	S%	hr/f	GS	APC	DOM%	DIS%	Sv%	LI	RAR	BPV	BPX	R$
10																																	
11																																	
12																																	
13 ATL *	8	5	0	140	132	2.43	2.83	1.22	670	622	690	13.4	2.8	8.5	3.0	62%	10%	49	24	27	32%	80%	5%	11	42	36%	45%	0	0.60	24.7	113	147	$13
14 ATL	11	11	0	172	170	2.78	3.20	1.14	651	667	645	19.8	2.4	8.9	3.8	62%	10%	46	19	35	30%	79%	10%	24	77	75%	0%	0	0.91	20.4	121	144	$16
1st Half	6	6	0	73	74	3.19	3.14	1.21	689	750	663	15.0	2.1	9.1	4.4	67%	11%	45	23	33	33%	78%	12%	9	57	67%	0%	0	1.02	5.0	130	155	$10
2nd Half	5	5	0	98	96	2.47	3.23	1.09	621	583	633	26.3	2.6	8.8	3.4	58%	10%	47	17	36	28%	81%	9%	15	103	80%	0%			15.4	114	136	$21
15 Proj	13	8	0	181	176	2.99	3.00	1.16	644	629	650	22.5	2.5	8.7	3.6	62%	10%	47	21	32	30%	77%	9%	44						16.8	116	139	$18

Wood,Travis

Age: 28	Th: L	Role SP	Health	A	LIMA Plan	D+		
Ht: 5' 11"	Wt: 175	Type Pwr FB	PT/Exp	A	Rand Var	+1		
			Consist	A	MM	1205		

Those taken in by 2013's low ERA were forewarned. Granted, the 2-run ERA spike was a little excessive, but blame H% and S% for that. This is the same pitcher as 2013. It may seem like a cop-out to split the difference for 2015, but xERA concurs. Sometimes planetary alignment takes two years.

Yr Tm	W	L	Sv	IP	K	ERA	xERA	WHIP	oOPS	vL	vR	BF/G	Ctl	Dom	Cmd	FpK	SwK	G	L	F	H%	S%	hr/f	GS	APC	DOM%	DIS%	Sv%	LI	RAR	BPV	BPX	R$
10 CIN *	10	10	0	203	171	3.54	3.27	1.15	616	446	651	24.4	2.2	7.6	3.4	58%	8%	31	21	48	29%	72%	6%	17	95	59%	12%			13.4	98	158	$16
11 CIN *	8	9	0	158	116	5.26	5.21	1.56	813	807	815	21.7	3.2	6.6	2.0	54%	7%	32	22	45	34%	67%	7%	18	81	33%	22%	0	0.79	-25.7	49	73	-$10
12 CHC *	9	16	0	197	151	4.47	4.25	1.28	745	614	779	24.5	3.0	6.9	2.3	58%	7%	34	22	44	28%	70%	13%	26	96	46%	15%			-11.2	53	69	$2
13 CHC	9	12	0	200	144	3.11	4.34	1.15	643	599	656	25.7	3.0	6.5	2.2	61%	8%	33	22	44	26%	76%	7%	32	97	66%	16%			18.8	47	62	$15
14 CHC	8	13	0	174	146	5.03	4.59	1.53	782	619	837	25.2	3.9	7.6	1.9	57%	7%	34	23	42	33%	69%	9%	31	98	39%	26%			-27.5	42	50	-$11
1st Half	7	6	0	96	77	4.52	4.45	1.40	723	451	811	26.2	3.7	7.2	2.0	60%	7%	38	19	43	31%	69%	7%	16	99	44%	25%			-9.1	48	57	-$3
2nd Half	1	7	0	78	69	5.65	4.76	1.69	850	801	867	24.1	4.3	8.0	1.9	54%	7%	30	28	42	36%	69%	11%	15	97	33%	27%			-18.4	36	42	-$21
15 Proj	8	14	0	189	151	4.49	4.12	1.40	758	654	790	24.2	3.5	7.2	2.1	58%	7%	33	23	44	31%	70%	9%	33						-17.3	47	56	-$2

Workman,Brandon

Age: 26	Th: R	Role RP	Health	A	LIMA Plan	C		
Ht: 6' 5"	Wt: 225	Type Pwr	PT/Exp	D	Rand Var	0		
			Consist	A	MM	2201		

1-10, 5.17 ERA in 87 IP at BOS (and 7-1 in minors). Sox finished 20 gms under .500; he accounted for nearly half of that. But he's better than this. DOM/DIS shows twice as many dominating starts as disasters. 112 BPV in 2H of 2013, solid spring, showed signs of upside. Deep league end-gamer for those with patience.

Yr Tm	W	L	Sv	IP	K	ERA	xERA	WHIP	oOPS	vL	vR	BF/G	Ctl	Dom	Cmd	FpK	SwK	G	L	F	H%	S%	hr/f	GS	APC	DOM%	DIS%	Sv%	LI	RAR	BPV	BPX	R$
10																																	
11																																	
12 aa	3	1	0	25	19	5.47	4.47	1.36				20.9	1.9	6.8	3.5						34%	60%								-4.5	85	111	-$4
13 BOS *	14	5	0	143	134	4.32	4.54	1.39	751	712	801	16.2	2.9	8.4	2.9	63%	10%	39	27	34	33%	72%	13%	3	39	100%	0%	0	1.23	-8.0	77	101	$2
14 BOS *	8	11	0	148	113	5.33	5.17	1.48	746	745	747	21.2	3.3	6.9	2.1	58%	8%	41	22	37	32%	67%	11%	15	75	40%	20%	0	1.01	-29.0	42	50	-$10
1st Half	4	2	0	80	60	5.03	4.59	1.31	593	633	524	20.7	2.8	6.7	2.4	56%	8%	41	22	38	29%	66%	9%	6	70	50%	0%	0	1.08	-12.7	48	57	-$6
2nd Half	4	9	0	68	54	5.68	5.85	1.67	868	844	888	21.9	3.9	7.0	1.8	60%	8%	42	23	36	35%	68%	13%	9	80	33%	33%	0	0.94	-16.3	37	45	-$14
15 Proj	6	6	0	87	73	4.47	3.84	1.47	790	770	817	19.0	3.2	7.6	2.3	60%	9%	40	24	36	33%	73%	12%	18						-7.8	67	79	-$3

RON SHANDLER

Worley,Vance

Worley,Vance		Health	C	LIMA Plan	C
Age: 27	Th: R Role SP	PT/Exp	C	Rand Var	0
Ht: 6' 2"	Wt: 230 Type Con	Consist	F	MM	2101

8-4, 2.85 ERA in 111 IP at PIT. Called up in mid-June and ran off 21 innings of sub-2.00 ERA. It wasn't real. While he does a great job of getting ahead of hitters—hence, his superb Ctl—poor SwK and mediocre Dom left his fate in the hands of the PIT defense. A good thing in 2014, but you can't always count on it.

Yr	Tm	W	L	Sv	IP	K	ERA	xERA	WHIP	oOPS	vL	vR	BF/G	Ctl	Dom	Cmd	FpK	SwK	G	L	F	H%	S%	hr/f	GS	APC	DOM%	DIS%	Sv%	LI	RAR	BPV	BPX	R$
10	PHI *	11	8	0	171	112	3.79	4.40	1.41	512	500	520	22.6	2.6	5.9	2.3	61%	7%	45	15	39	32%	74%	8%	2	41	0%	0%	0	0.40	6.1	58	94	$5
11	PHI *	16	5	0	182	161	2.99	3.39	1.23	673	570	775	21.7	2.9	7.9	2.7	61%	6%	39	24	37	30%	79%	7%	21	87	71%	14%	0	0.80	21.5	88	133	$17
12	PHI	6	9	0	133	107	4.20	4.16	1.51	806	847	764	25.7	3.2	7.2	2.3	61%	6%	46	24	30	35%	74%	10%	23	95	39%	22%			-3.0	68	89	-$5
13	MIN *	7	8	0	107	51	5.81	6.57	1.79	1004	1013	994	25.9	2.7	4.3	1.6	59%	4%	47	22	31	37%	68%	16%	10	92	10%	40%			-25.6	15	19	-$17
14	PIT *	11	6	0	157	111	3.48	3.79	1.24	679	666	691	25.4	1.5	6.4	4.3	63%	6%	49	20	30	32%	73%	9%	17	88	59%	6%	0	0.76	5.0	107	128	$7
1st Half		5	2	0	67	44	3.99	3.71	1.19	605	695	552	26.8	0.9	5.9	6.2	65%	5%	41	17	41	32%	67%	8%	3	95	67%	0%			-2.1	146	174	$2
2nd Half		6	4	0	90	67	3.10	3.54	1.27	695	660	729	25.2	1.9	6.7	3.5	62%	6%	51	21	28	32%	78%	9%	14	86	57%	7%	0	0.76	7.1	99	118	$10
15	Proj	7	5	0	102	68	3.99	3.80	1.42	769	778	760	25.1	2.2	6.1	2.8	61%	5%	46	21	32	34%	73%	8%	17						-3.1	74	88	-$1

Wright,Jamey

Wright,Jamey		Health	B	LIMA Plan	C
Age: 40	Th: R Role RP	PT/Exp	C	Rand Var	0
Ht: 6' 6"	Wt: 240 Type Pwr xGB	Consist	A	MM	3200

Small sample sizes, but the massive swings in hit rate and strand rate are the sole reasons for his 5-run ERA spike in the 2nd half. Note xERA for reality. So, he's 40 now and he's appropriately regressed from 2013's random skills spike. These are okay skills, but the only number that matters, really, is 40.

Yr	Tm	W	L	Sv	IP	K	ERA	xERA	WHIP	oOPS	vL	vR	BF/G	Ctl	Dom	Cmd	FpK	SwK	G	L	F	H%	S%	hr/f	GS	APC	DOM%	DIS%	Sv%	LI	RAR	BPV	BPX	R$
10	2 AL	1	3	0	58	28	4.17	4.31	1.37	705	641	758	5.4	3.9	4.3	1.1	55%	5%	61	14	25	28%	69%	6%	0	20			0	1.02	-0.6	13	20	-$2
11	SEA	2	3	1	68	48	3.16	3.74	1.33	713	700	725	4.8	4.0	6.3	1.6	56%	7%	58	17	24	28%	79%	13%	0	18			20	1.02	6.6	43	65	$1
12	LA	5	3	0	68	54	3.72	3.59	1.51	678	643	703	4.6	4.0	7.2	1.8	55%	10%	67	21	12	34%	74%	8%	0	17			0	0.75	2.4	67	87	-$2
13	TAM	2	2	0	70	65	3.09	3.32	1.20	647	665	620	4.4	3.0	8.4	2.8	59%	10%	51	20	29	30%	75%	7%	1	17	0%	100%	0	0.60	6.7	100	130	$2
14	LA	5	4	1	70	54	4.35	3.75	1.41	683	620	737	5.0	3.5	6.9	2.0	61%	9%	56	20	23	32%	68%	6%	1	18	0%	100%	50	0.71	-5.3	65	78	-$2
1st Half		3	2	1	38	23	2.11	3.70	1.10	558	342	727	5.0	3.1	5.4	1.8	62%	9%	61	16	24	24%	83%	7%	0	18			100	0.67	7.7	53	64	$5
2nd Half		2	2	0	32	31	7.03	3.77	1.78	814	884	748	5.1	3.9	8.7	2.2	60%	9%	51	26	23	41%	57%	4%	1	18	0%	100%	0	0.75	-13.0	80	96	-$11
15	Proj	4	3	0	65	51	4.23	3.59	1.43	697	680	713	4.7	3.7	7.0	1.9	59%	9%	56	21	23	32%	69%	6%	0						-3.9	61	73	-$3

Wright,Wesley

Wright,Wesley		Health	A	LIMA Plan	C
Age: 30	Th: L Role RP	PT/Exp	D	Rand Var	-2
Ht: 5' 11"	Wt: 185 Type Pwr GB	Consist	A	MM	3200

Situational lefty with a skills profile that has been declining for two straight years. LI shows that managerial faith his his abilities have also waned during that time. Yes, he's a hard thrower who keeps the ball on the ground, but marginal control caps his ceiling. Still, he gets those lefties out.

Yr	Tm	W	L	Sv	IP	K	ERA	xERA	WHIP	oOPS	vL	vR	BF/G	Ctl	Dom	Cmd	FpK	SwK	G	L	F	H%	S%	hr/f	GS	APC	DOM%	DIS%	Sv%	LI	RAR	BPV	BPX	R$
10	HOU *	5	3	0	103	63	5.44	5.77	1.65	890	678	967	15.8	4.0	5.5	1.4	56%	10%	44	20	37	33%	69%	16%	4	40	25%	50%	0	0.31	-17.2	19	30	-$8
11	HOU *	3	1	2	77	53	2.32	3.01	1.20	583	205	1352	5.2	3.4	6.2	1.8	55%	8%	57	11	32	26%	84%	11%	0	8			67	1.96	15.5	66	99	$6
12	HOU	2	2	1	52	54	3.27	3.13	1.18	638	538	790	2.9	2.9	9.3	3.2	65%	10%	55	22	24	30%	74%	12%	0	11			50	1.10	4.8	121	158	$1
13	2 AL	0	4	0	54	55	3.69	3.35	1.36	769	753	786	3.3	3.2	9.2	2.9	55%	8%	50	22	28	33%	77%	16%	0	13			0	1.05	1.2	108	141	-$3
14	CHC	0	3	0	48	37	3.17	3.82	1.39	667	594	719	3.6	3.5	6.9	1.9	55%	9%	52	24	24	32%	77%	6%	0	13			0	0.97	3.4	58	70	-$2
1st Half		0	1	0	22	17	2.42	3.55	1.16	590	567	606	3.3	2.4	6.9	2.8	52%	10%	54	19	26	29%	80%	6%	0	13			0	1.19	3.6	90	108	-$1
2nd Half		0	2	0	26	20	3.81	4.08	1.58	733	616	817	3.9	4.5	6.9	1.5	57%	8%	50	28	22	34%	75%	6%	0	14			0	0.76	-0.2	31	37	-$3
15	Proj	0	2	0	36	31	3.67	3.44	1.37	705	628	770	3.5	3.4	7.7	2.2	56%	9%	51	23	26	32%	74%	10%	0						0.3	75	90	-$3

Yates,Kirby

Yates,Kirby		Health	A	LIMA Plan	B+
Age: 28	Th: R Role RP	PT/Exp	D	Rand Var	-2
Ht: 5' 10"	Wt: 195 Type Pwr xFB	Consist	B	MM	3500

0-2, 3.75 ERA in 36 IP at TAM. Dominated AAA before June call-up and had a very nice courtship period. Even sported a 1.24 LI in the earlygoing, earning his manager's confidence. It went south from there, and his September line included a 6.00 ERA, 1.83 WHIP, 7.5 Ctl and -18 BPV. Prospect rating of 7C=low ceiling.

Yr	Tm	W	L	Sv	IP	K	ERA	xERA	WHIP	oOPS	vL	vR	BF/G	Ctl	Dom	Cmd	FpK	SwK	G	L	F	H%	S%	hr/f	GS	APC	DOM%	DIS%	Sv%	LI	RAR	BPV	BPX	R$
10																																		
11																																		
12	aa	4	2	16	68	78	2.99	3.21	1.37				5.7	5.1	10.3	2.0						31%	79%								8.6	100	130	$8
13	aaa	3	2	20	62	75	2.31	2.18	1.12				4.8	3.5	11.0	3.2						31%	80%								11.9	137	178	$13
14	TAM *	1	2	17	61	70	2.40	2.58	1.15	699	844	644	4.2	3.6	10.3	2.8	60%	9%	32	23	45	29%	81%	9%	0	19			94	0.66	10.1	116	139	$10
1st Half		1	0	16	35	40	1.12	1.66	1.02	700	955	588	4.6	3.3	10.3	3.1	61%	9%	26	30	44	27%	90%	8%	0	25			100	0.22	11.2	137	164	$18
2nd Half		0	2	1	26	30	4.10	3.76	1.33	699	795	665	3.9	4.1	10.3	2.5	59%	9%	35	20	45	31%	72%	10%	0	17			50	0.78	-1.2	87	103	-$1
15	Proj	2	2	0	58	64	3.80	3.42	1.23	603	666	580	4.5	3.6	9.9	2.8	59%	9%	35	20	45	30%	71%	7%	0						-0.4	95	113	$0

Young,Chris

Young,Chris		Health	F	LIMA Plan	C
Age: 36	Th: R Role SP	PT/Exp	C	Rand Var	-4
Ht: 6' 10"	Wt: 255 Type xFB	Consist	F	MM	0101

First healthy season since....... 2007. While the odds that he's now a monument of health at 36 are remote, the odds of a repeat 3.65 ERA follow-up are even less likely. Note the 5.06 xERA. Note that a BPV of 18 is about 80% below league average. Only relevant number = 10, as in "foot pole, do not touch with a"

Yr	Tm	W	L	Sv	IP	K	ERA	xERA	WHIP	oOPS	vL	vR	BF/G	Ctl	Dom	Cmd	FpK	SwK	G	L	F	H%	S%	hr/f	GS	APC	DOM%	DIS%	Sv%	LI	RAR	BPV	BPX	R$
10	SD	2	0	0	20	15	0.90	4.93	1.05	459	468	455	20.5	5.0	6.8	1.4	62%	8%	29	16	55	18%	95%	3%	4	77	50%	25%			7.8	-5	-8	$1
11	NYM	1	0	0	24	22	1.88	4.37	0.96	548	378	789	23.8	4.1	8.3	2.0	58%	9%	19	15	66	16%	90%	8%	4	99	50%	25%			6.1	34	51	$1
12	NYM	4	9	0	115	80	4.15	5.20	1.35	784	843	727	24.7	2.8	6.3	2.2	63%	9%	22	20	58	30%	73%	8%	20	92	50%	20%			-1.9	37	48	-$2
13	aaa	1	2	0	32	11	10.08	11.33	2.46				24.1	4.2	3.2	0.8						40%	63%								-24.5	-80	-104	-$18
14	SEA	12	9	0	165	108	3.65	5.06	1.23	733	810	632	22.9	3.3	5.9	1.8	59%	8%	22	19	59	25%	77%	9%	29	91	48%	28%	0	0.78	1.8	18	21	$7
1st Half		7	4	0	91	47	3.15	5.28	1.16	671	681	657	23.4	3.4	4.6	1.3	57%	6%	25	18	57	22%	79%	7%	15	92	47%	27%	0	0.78	6.6	-7	-8	$11
2nd Half		5	5	0	74	61	4.28	4.79	1.32	806	978	606	22.4	3.1	7.5	2.4	61%	10%	19	20	61	28%	75%	10%	14	90	50%	29%			-4.9	49	58	$1
15	Proj	6	7	0	116	77	4.61	5.01	1.56	887	982	779	22.5	3.7	6.0	1.6	61%	8%	22	19	59	31%	75%	9%	23						-12.4	8	10	-$7

Ziegler,Brad

Ziegler,Brad		Health	A	LIMA Plan	B+
Age: 35	Th: R Role RP	PT/Exp	C	Rand Var	+1
Ht: 6' 4"	Wt: 210 Type xGB	Consist	A	MM	4110

Whenever his name was mentioned in 2014, it always came with the reminder "Addison Reed is still the closer." While this Plan B rarely saw 9th innings, his LI shows that he saw MORE IMPORTANT innings (Reed's LI was 1.25). Knee problems hurt 2nd half stats, ending in September surgery. Age urges caution.

Yr	Tm	W	L	Sv	IP	K	ERA	xERA	WHIP	oOPS	vL	vR	BF/G	Ctl	Dom	Cmd	FpK	SwK	G	L	F	H%	S%	hr/f	GS	APC	DOM%	DIS%	Sv%	LI	RAR	BPV	BPX	R$
10	OAK	3	7	0	61	41	3.26	4.08	1.35	694	1034	560	4.0	4.2	6.1	1.5	55%	8%	54	19	27	28%	77%	8%	0	14			0	1.14	6.1	29	47	$1
11	2 TM	3	2	1	58	44	2.16	2.96	1.23	598	889	464	3.6	2.9	6.8	2.3	58%	8%	69	18	13	31%	81%	0%	0	13			50	0.96	12.8	90	135	$4
12	ARI	6	1	0	69	42	2.49	2.92	1.09	578	749	501	3.4	2.8	5.5	2.0	65%	10%	76	17	8	26%	77%	13%	0	12			0	0.93	12.9	79	103	$7
13	ARI	8	1	13	73	44	2.22	3.16	1.14	594	647	550	3.8	2.7	5.4	2.0	63%	10%	70	19	11	26%	81%	13%	0	13			87	1.50	14.8	72	94	$13
14	ARI	5	3	1	67	54	3.49	3.23	1.25	681	596	734	4.1	3.2	7.3	2.3	59%	11%	64	17	19	29%	73%	14%	0	14			11	1.39	2.1	86	102	$2
1st Half		3	1	1	42	36	2.34	2.95	1.04	570	499	610	3.8	3.2	7.7	2.4	58%	12%	67	13	20	24%	80%	13%	0	13			20	1.39	7.3	97	116	$7
2nd Half		2	2	0	25	18	5.47	3.72	1.62	855	729	946	4.7	3.3	6.6	2.0	62%	10%	59	24	18	36%	66%	14%	0	17			0	1.41	-5.3	66	79	-$7
15	Proj	5	2	3	58	41	3.31	3.16	1.27	676	684	670	3.9	3.1	6.3	2.1	61%	10%	66	19	15	29%	74%	12%	0						3.1	75	90	$2

Zimmermann,Jordan

Zimmermann,Jordan		Health	B	LIMA Plan	C
Age: 29	Th: R Role SP	PT/Exp	A	Rand Var	-2
Ht: 6' 2"	Wt: 220 Type	Consist	A	MM	4205

A perfect confluence of nearly all the skills he's displayed over the years, plus a few career highs. 2nd half is interesting, though. Allowed a whopping 15% fewer GB, with 5% going to LD and 10% to FB... all leading to an even better skills profile. Regression says he'll give some of it back but still a solid buy.

Yr	Tm	W	L	Sv	IP	K	ERA	xERA	WHIP	oOPS	vL	vR	BF/G	Ctl	Dom	Cmd	FpK	SwK	G	L	F	H%	S%	hr/f	GS	APC	DOM%	DIS%	Sv%	LI	RAR	BPV	BPX	R$
10	WAS *	2	2	0	53	39	3.13	3.30	1.08	817	812	819	17.1	2.6	6.7	2.6	62%	6%	49	13	38	24%	79%	22%	7	79	43%	57%			6.2	64	104	$3
11	WAS	8	11	0	161	124	3.18	3.75	1.15	671	703	643	25.5	1.7	6.9	4.0	63%	8%	39	19	42	30%	74%	6%	26	95	62%	8%			15.2	95	143	$13
12	WAS	12	8	0	196	153	2.94	3.78	1.17	686	650	723	25.2	2.0	7.0	3.6	69%	9%	43	23	33	30%	78%	9%	32	97	56%	6%			25.9	94	123	$20
13	WAS	19	9	0	213	161	3.25	3.50	1.09	654	702	601	27.0	1.7	6.8	4.0	67%	9%	48	21	31	28%	73%	10%	32	96	66%	6%			16.2	103	134	$22
14	WAS	14	5	0	200	182	2.66	3.22	1.07	631	655	606	25.0	1.3	8.2	6.3	71%	11%	40	24	36	31%	77%	6%	32	91	75%	9%			26.6	130	155	$22
1st Half		6	4	0	104	91	2.95	3.25	1.19	665	657	671	24.9	1.6	7.9	4.8	71%	11%	47	22	31	33%	76%	6%	17	90	71%	12%			10.1	123	146	$17
2nd Half		8	1	0	96	91	2.34	3.19	0.95	593	653	526	25.1	0.9	8.5	9.1	71%	11%	32	27	41	29%	79%	6%	15	93	80%	7%			16.5	139	165	$28
15	Proj	13	6	0	181	152	2.86	3.12	1.08	643	666	618	24.2	1.5	7.6	4.9	69%	10%	42	23	35	30%	76%	8%	29						19.7	115	136	$21

RON SHANDLER

MAJOR LEAGUES • INJURIES

5-Year Injury Log

The following chart details the disabled list stints for all players during the past five years. Use this as a supplement to our health grades in the player profile boxes as well as the "Risk Management" charts that start on page 267. It's also where to turn when you want to check whether, say, Brandon McCarthy's right shoulder pain in spring training should be concerning (answer: very concerning).

For each injury, the number of days the player missed during the season is listed. A few DL stints are for fewer than 15 days; these are cases when a player was placed on the DL prior to Opening Day (only in-season time lost is listed). Abbreviations:

Lt, L = left
Rt, R = right
fx = fractured
R/C = rotator cuff
str = strained
surg = surgery
TJS = Tommy John (ulnar collateral ligament reconstruction) surgery
x 2 = two occurrences of the same injury
x 3 = three occurrences of the same injury

Throughout the spring and all season long, BaseballHQ.com has comprehensive injury coverage.

FIVE-YEAR INJURY LOG

Batters	Yr	Days	Injury
Abreu,Jose	14	15	Lt. ankle tendinitis
Abreu,Tony	13	103	Strained Lt. knee + bursitis
Adams,Matt	13	15	Rt. oblique strain
	14	14	Tightness in Lt. calf
Adduci,James	14	118	Concussion; Fx Lt finger
Adrianza,Ehire	14	82	Strained Rt. hamstring x 2
Almanzar,Michael	14	92	Patella tendinitis in Lt. knee
Almonte,Zoilo	13	51	Sprained Lt. ankle
Alonso,Yonder	13	41	Rt. hand contusion
	14	55	Strained Rt. forearm/Rt. wrist tend
Alvarez,Pedro	11	66	R. quadriceps tightness
Andino,Robert	12	15	Subluxation of L. shoulder
Ankiel,Rick	10	80	Strained R. quadriceps
	11	37	R. wrist sprain
	12	10	Quad injury
Aoki,Norichika	14	20	Strained Lt. groin
Arcia,Oswaldo Celest	14	35	Strained Rt. wrist
Arenado,Nolan	14	40	Fractured Lt. middle finger
Arencibia,JP	12	43	Fractured R. hand
Arias,Joaquin	13	18	Appendicitis
Arruebarrena,Erisbel	14	21	Strained Rt. hip flexor
Asche,Cody	14	26	Strained Lt. hamstring
Avila,Alex	12	15	Strained R. hamstring
	13	31	Lt. forearm bruise; Concussion
	14	5	Concussion
Aybar,Erick	11	17	Strained L. oblique muscle
	12	15	Fractured R. toe
	13	20	Bruised Lt. heel
Baker,Jeff	11	14	L. groin strain
	13	35	Sprained Rt. thumb
Baker,John	10	143	Strained R. elbow
	11	158	Recovery from TJS
Barajas,Rod	10	26	Strained L. oblique muscle
	11	25	Sprained R. ankle
Barmes,Clint	11	29	L. hand fracture
	14	50	Strained Lt. groin
Barney,Darwin	11	15	L. knee sprain
	13	15	Lt. knee laceration
Bartlett,Jason	10	17	Strained R. hamstring
	12	140	Strained R. knee
	14	14	Sprained Lt. ankle
Barton,Daric	11	27	Torn labrum in R. shoulder
	12	4	Sprained R. shoulder
Bautista,Jose	12	77	Inflam R. wrist/Surgery on R. wrist
	13	40	Lt. hip bone bruise
Baxter,Mike	11	126	Torn ligament in L. thumb
	12	58	Displaced R. collarbone
Bay,Jason	10	69	Post concussion syndrome
	11	21	Strained L. rib cage
	12	67	Non-displaced Rib+ Concussionx2
Beckham,Gordon	13	54	Fractured hamate bone, Lt. wrist
	14	25	Strained Lt. oblique
Beckham,Timothy	14	133	Rec. from surgery Rt. Knee- torn ACL
Belt,Brandon	11	44	Hairline L. wrist fracture
	14	81	Concussion x 2/Fx Lt. thumb

FIVE-YEAR INJURY LOG

Batters	Yr	Days	Injury
Beltran,Carlos	10	102	Recovery from surgery - R. knee
	11	15	Strained R. hand
	14	29	Concussion; hyper ext. Rt elbow
Beltre,Adrian	11	40	Strained L. hamstring
	14	12	Strained Lt. quadriceps
Beltre,Engel	14	184	Fractured Rt. tibia
Berkman,Lance	10	32	Sprained ankle;L. knee surg
	12	108	R. knee inflam x2 + L. calf str
	13	56	Lt. hip inflammation
Betancourt,Yuniesky	12	30	Sprained R. ankle
Betemit,Wilson	12	21	Injured R. wrist
	13	148	Rt. PCL tear
Bianchi,Jeff	13	32	Lt. hip bursitis
	14	74	Sprained Rt. elbow
Blackmon,Charlie	11	83	Fractured L. foot
	12	135	Turf toe
Blanco,Henry	12	59	Sprained L. thumb
Blanks,Kyle	10	138	Strained R. elbow
	11	26	Recovery from TJS
	12	173	Labrum tear L. shoulder
	13	80	Lt. Achilles tendinitis
	14	109	Strnd Lt. calf; Lt. Achilles tendinitis
Bloomquist,Willie	11	23	Strained R. hamstring
	12	23	Strained lower back
	13	122	Str. Rt. Intercostal;Lt. hand bruise
	14	67	Bruised Rt. knee
Boesch,Brennan	11	20	Torn ligament in R. thumb
Bogaerts,Xander	14	7	Concussion
Bogusevic,Brian	13	77	Lt. hamstring strain
Bonifacio,Emilio	12	112	Sprained L. thumb x2; spr. R. knee
	14	39	Strained Rt. ribcage
Borbon,Julio	11	20	Inflam - L. hamstring
Bourgeois,Jason	11	50	Strained L. oblique
Bourjos,Peter	11	15	Tight R. hamstring
	12	15	Sore R. wrist
	13	100	Fx Rt wrist; Strained Lt hammy
Bourn,Michael	13	25	Rt. hand laceration
	14	56	Rec from surg: strained Lt. hamstring
Brantley,Michael	11	34	Inflam in R. wrist
Braun,Ryan	13	28	Rt. thumb contusion
	14	10	strained Rt. oblique muscle
Brignac,Reid	14	31	Sprained Lt. ankle
Brown,Domonic	13	13	Concussion
Bruce,Jay	14	16	Rec from meniscus repair on Lt. knee
Buck,John	10	15	Laceration – R. thumb
Buck,Travis	10	100	Strained R. oblique
	12	128	R. Achilles tendinitis
Burriss,Emmanuel	10	82	Fractured - L. foot
Byrd,Marlon	11	40	Facial fractures
Cabrera,Asdrubal	10	63	Fractured L. forearm
	13	22	Rt. quadriceps strain
Cabrera,Everth	10	49	Strained R. hamstring x 2
	13	18	Strained Lt. hamstring
	14	75	Strained Lt. hamstring x 2
Cabrera,Melky	13	82	Strained Lt. knee; Tendinitis
	14	21	Fractured Rt. pinky finger

FIVE-YEAR INJURY LOG

FIVE-YEAR INJURY LOG

Batters	Yr	Days	Injury
Cain,Lorenzo	12	89	Strained L. groin
	13	26	Strained Lt. oblique
	14	18	Strained Lt. groin
Cairo,Miguel	12	22	Strained L. hamstring
Calhoun,Kole	14	35	Sprained Rt. ankle
Callaspo,Alberto	13	20	Rt. calf tightness
	14	15	Strained Rt. hamstring
Carp,Mike	12	91	Strained R. shoulder x2; R. groin
Carpenter,Matt	12	30	R. oblique strain
Carroll,Brett	10	10	Strained L. oblique
Casali,Curtis	14	5	Concussion
Casilla,Alexi	10	51	Bone spur in R. elbow
	11	62	Strained R. hamstring
Castillo,Welington	12	71	MCL sprain in R. knee
	13	5	Surgery - Rt. knee
	14	19	Lt. ribcage inflammation
Castro,Jason	11	182	R. knee surgery
	12	36	R. knee swelling
	13	13	Cyst on Rt. knee
Cedeno,Ronny	11	20	Concussion
	12	46	L. intercostal strain+str R. calf
Cervelli,Francisco	11	50	Fractured L. foot; Concussion
	13	156	Fractured Rt. hand
	14	64	Hamstring injury
Cespedes,Yoenis	12	25	Strained muscle in L. hand
	13	15	Strained muscle, Lt. hand
Chavez,Endy	12	50	Strained intercostal muscle
Chavez,Eric	10	135	Neck spasms
	11	81	Broken L. foot
	12	8	Concussion
	13	44	Hip, knee and oblique
	14	51	Sprained Lt. knee (retired 7/30/14)
Chirinos,Robinson	12	182	Concussion
Chisenhall,Lonnie	12	71	Fractured R. ulna
Choice,Michael	14	14	Strained Lt. hamstring
Choo,Shin-Soo	10	20	Sprained R. thumb
	11	71	Fract. L. thumb; Strain L. oblique
	14	35	Bone spur in Lt. elbow
Christian,Justin	12	15	Sprained L. wrist
Clevenger,Steve	12	33	Strained R. oblique
	13	169	Lt. oblique strain
Coghlan,Chris	10	69	Torn meniscus – L. knee
	11	104	L. knee Inflam
	13	84	Rt. calf irritation
Colon,Christian	14	12	fractured right middle finger
Colvin,Tyler	10	13	Chest puncture wound
Cooper,David	12	42	Strained back
Corporan,Carlos	13	20	Concussion
Cousins,Scott	11	108	Lower back strain
Cowgill,Collin	12	24	Sprained L. ankle
	14	22	Fractured nose
Cozart,Zack	11	67	Hyperextended L. elbow
Craig,Allen	11	78	L. groin strain
	12	43	Surg recovery; L. hamstring strain
	14	16	Sprained Lt. foot

FIVE-YEAR INJURY LOG

Batters	Yr	Days	Injury
Crawford,Carl	11	30	Strained L. hamstring
	12	148	Recovery from L. wrist surgery+ TJS
	13	33	Strained Lt. hamstring
	14	43	Sprained Lt. ankle
Crisp,Coco	10	77	Fx finger; ribcage muscle
	12	18	Infected ear/sinus
	13	15	Strained Lt. hamstring
Crowe,Trevor	11	160	Recov. from surgery - R. shoulder
	13	51	Sprained AC joint in Rt. shoulder
Cruz,Luis	13	24	Sprained Rt. knee
Cruz,Nelson	10	56	Strained R. & L. hammy
	11	34	Strained R. quad; Strained L. ham.
Cruz,Tony	13	17	Stress fracture, Lt. forearm
Cuddyer,Michael	12	61	R. oblique strainx2
	13	15	Bulging disk in neck
	14	112	Strnd L hamstring x 2/strnd L should
d'Arnaud,Travis	14	14	Concussion
d'Arnaud,Chase	11	29	Fractured little finger on R. hand
	13	61	Lt. thumb surgery
Darnell,James	12	139	R. shoulder subluxation
	13	34	Strained Lt. oblique
Davis,Chris	11	22	Strained R. shoulder
	14	14	Strained Lt. oblique
Davis,Ike	11	141	L. ankle sprain and bone bruise
	13	21	Strained Rt. oblique
Davis,Rajai	11	64	Sore R. ankle; Torn L. hamstring
	13	24	Strained oblique
De Aza,Alejandro	12	15	Bruised L. ribs
DeJesus,David	10	72	Torn ligament – R. thumb
	13	39	Rt. shoulder sprain
	14	74	Fractured Lt. hand
Denorfia,Chris	11	35	Strained R. hamstring
DeRosa,Mark	10	147	Neuritis - L. wrist
	11	91	Sore L. wrist
	12	85	L. abdominal strain+ oblique str
Desmond,Ian	12	26	Torn L. oblique
DeWitt,Blake	13	119	Lower back strain
Diaz,Jonathan	14	182	Lt. hamstring injury
Diaz,Matt	10	45	Infected R. thumb
	12	75	R. thumb contusion
	13	134	Lt. knee bone contusion
Dickerson,Chris	10	101	Fractured hamate bone - R. hand
Dietrich,Derek	14	53	Strained Rt. wrist
Dirks,Andy	12	61	Tendinitis in R. Achilles tendon
	14	184	Recovering from surgery on back
Donald,Jason	11	29	Fractured L. hand
Doumit,Ryan	10	16	Concussion
	11	135	L. ankle sprain
	13	8	Concussion
Drew,Stephen	12	83	Recovering from R. ankle surgery
	13	31	Rt. Hamstring tight; Concussion
Duda,Lucas	13	46	Strained Lt. intercostal
Dyson,Jarrod	13	37	Rt. ankle sprain
Eaton,Adam	13	100	Lt. elbow strain
	14	31	Rt oblique muscle; Rt hamstring

FIVE-YEAR INJURY LOG

Batters	Yr	Days	Injury
Ellis,A.J.	13	15	Lt. oblique strain
	14	54	Sprained Rt. ankle/Lt. knee surgery
Ellis,Mark	10	31	Strained L. hamstring
	11	15	Strained R. hamstring
	12	46	Sprained L. leg
	13	22	Strained Rt. quad
	14	29	Strained Lt. oblique/Lt. knee tend
Ellsbury,Jacoby	10	158	Fractured ribs x 3
	12	90	Subluxation of R. shoulder
Elmore,Jake	14	74	Strained Lt. quadriceps
Encarnacion,Edwin	10	48	Sprained R. wrist & shoulder
	13	13	Surgery (cart) - Lt. wrist
	14	39	Strained Rt. quadriceps
Escobar,Yunel	10	15	Strained L. adductor
	11	9	Inflam - L. elbow
	14	16	Sore Rt. shoulder
Espinosa,Danny	13	15	Broken bone in Rt. wrist
Ethier,Andre	10	16	Fractured pinkie finger – R. hand
	12	15	Strained L. oblique
Fielder,Prince	14	129	Herniated disc in neck (surgery)
Fields,Josh	13	57	Rt. forearm strain
Figgins,Chone	11	33	Strained R. hip flexor
	14	52	Strained Lt. quadriceps
Flores,Jesus	10	182	Recov. from surgery - R. shoulder
Flowers,Tyler	13	28	Rt. shoulder surgery
Forsythe,Logan	12	60	L. foot fracture
	13	71	Plantar fasciitis, Rt. foot
Fowler,Dexter	11	40	L. abdominal strain
	13	15	Rt. wrist soreness
	14	43	Strained Rt. intercostal
Francisco,Ben	12	35	Strained L. hamstring
Francisco,Juan	11	31	L. calf strain
Freeman,Freddie	13	15	Strained Rt. oblique
Freese,David	10	97	Sprained R. ankle
	11	56	Broken hamate bone in L. hand
	13	8	Strained lower back
	14	17	Fractured Rt. middle finger
Fukudome,Kosuke	12	122	Strained R. oblique
Fuld,Sam	12	110	Surgery - R. wrist
	14	36	Concussion
Furcal,Rafael	10	58	Strained lower back; L. hammy
	11	70	Broken L. thumb
	12	34	R. elbow strain
	13	183	Rt. elbow surgery
	14	174	Strained Lt. hamstring x 2
Galvis,Freddy	12	119	Fracture of L4-5 veR.ebra
	14	15	Staph infection in Lt. knee
Gamel,Mat	10	61	Torn R. lat muscle
	12	155	Torn R. ACL
	13	183	Torn Rt. ACL
Garcia,Avisail	13	30	Bruised Rt. heel
	14	128	Surgery on Lt. shoulder torn labrum
Gardner,Brett	12	164	Sore R. elbow
Gattis,Evan	13	26	Oblique strain
	14	21	Bulging thoracic disc in back

FIVE-YEAR INJURY LOG

Batters	Yr	Days	Injury
Gentry,Craig	10	34	Fractured R. wrist
	11	14	Concussion
	13	27	Fractured Lt. hand
	14	39	Fx Rt. hand; lower back strain
Getz,Chris	10	15	Tight R. oblique muscle
	12	89	Bruised ribs+str L. leg+fx L. thumb
	13	15	Lt. knee sprain
Giambi,Jason	11	17	Strained L. quadriceps
	12	42	Viral syndrome
	13	11	Lower back strain
	14	118	Lt. knee inflammation;RT calf;fx rib
Gillaspie,Conor	14	11	Sore/bruised Lt. hand
Gillespie,Cole	14	25	Strained oblique muscle
Gimenez,Chris	11	64	Strained L. oblique muscle
Gimenez,Hector	11	173	R. knee surgery
Goldschmidt,Paul	14	58	Fractured Lt. hand
Gomes,Yan	14	7	Concussion
Gomez,Carlos	10	36	Concussion; Strained R. hip
	11	42	Fractured L. clavicle
	12	15	Strained L. hamstring
Gomez,Hector	12	182	Groin strain
Gonzalez,Alex	12	151	R. knee injury
Gonzalez,Carlos	11	37	Strained R. wrist
	13	29	Sprained Rt. middle finger
	14	51	L knee tendinitis/Lt. finger inflam
Gonzalez,Marwin	12	38	Bruised R. heel
Gordon,Alex	10	13	Fractured tip of R. thumb
Gordon,Dee	11	22	Bruised R. shoulder
	12	68	Torn R. thumb ligament
Grandal,Yasmani	12	17	Strained R. oblique
	13	85	Rt. knee sprain
Granderson,Curtis	10	26	Strained L. groin
	13	113	Fx finger Lt hand; Fx Lt finger
Green,Grant	14	39	Lumbar strain
Green,Taylor	13	183	Lt. hip labral injury
Gregorius,Didi	13	23	Concussion; Rt. elbow strain
Guillen,Carlos	10	97	L. hammy; R. calf; L. knee
	11	127	Recov. fr L. knee surg; Sore L. wrist
Gutierrez,Franklin	11	71	Gastritis; Strained L. oblique
	12	128	Concussion + torn R. pec muscle
	13	123	Strained Rt. hamstring x 2
Guyer,Brandon	12	144	Strained L. shoulder
	13	60	Fractured Rt. middle finger
	14	24	Fractured Lt. thumb
Guzman,Jesus	14	16	Back spasms
Gwynn Jr.,Tony	10	25	Fractured hamate bone – R. hand
Gyorko,Jedd	13	32	Strained Rt. groin
	14	52	Plantar fasciitis in Lt. foot
Hafner,Travis	10	17	Sore R. shoulder
	11	50	Strained R. oblique; Strain R. foot
	12	82	Inflamed lower back+sore R. knee
	13	60	Strained Rt. rotator cuff
Hairston Jr.,Jerry	10	15	Sprained R. elbow
	11	18	R. wrist fracture
	12	71	L. hip Inflam+ L. hammy str
	13	21	Strained Lt. groin

FIVE-YEAR INJURY LOG

Batters	Yr	Days	Injury
Hairston,Scott	10	17	Strained L. hamstring
	11	36	L. oblique strain
	14	29	Strained Lt. oblique
Hamilton,Josh	11	40	Fractured R. humerus
	14	55	Surgery on Lt. thumb torn UCL
Hanigan,Ryan	10	41	Fractured L. thumb
	13	50	Sprained Lt. wrist; Lt. oblique
	14	54	Strained Lt. oblique; Rt hamstring
Hannahan,Jack	10	26	Strained R. groin
	12	19	Strained L. calf
	14	119	Rec from surgery on Rt. shoulder
Hardy,J.J.	10	46	Sore L. wrist
	11	30	Strained L. oblique muscle
Harper,Bryce	13	35	Lt. knee bursitis
	14	64	Surgery on Lt. thumb
Hart,Corey	11	27	L. oblique strain
	13	183	Recovery from Rt. knee surgery
	14	75	Bruised Rt. knee; strained LT hammy
Hawpe,Brad	10	15	Strained L. quad muscle
	11	102	Strained R. middle finger
Headley,Chase	11	43	Fractured L. pinkie finger
	13	17	Broken Lt. thumb
	14	15	Strained Rt. calf
Hechavarria,Adeiny	13	15	Bruised Lt. elbow
	14	11	Strained Rt. triceps
Heisey,Chris	11	26	Strained L. oblique
	13	58	Strained Rt. hamstring
Helton,Todd	10	29	Stiff lower back
	12	77	R. hip labrum tear+ hip Inflam
	13	15	Lt. forearm inflammation
Hermida,Jeremy	10	42	Fractured ribs
	12	160	Strained R. hip flexor
Hernandez,Ramon	10	17	Inflam – R. knee
	12	50	L. hand strain
Herrera,Jonathan	11	23	R. index finger fracture
	12	45	Infection in L. wrist+ R. hammy str.
Heyward,Jason	10	18	Bone bruise – L. thumb
	11	23	Sore R. shoulder
	13	55	Fx Rt. jaw; appendectomy
Hicks,Aaron	13	22	Lt. hamstring strain
	14	22	Strained Rt. shoulder;concussion
Hicks,Brandon	10	13	Fractured R. index finger
Hill,Aaron	10	15	Strained R. hamstring
	11	18	Sore R. hamstring
	13	71	Broken Lt. hand
Holliday,Matt	11	15	L. quadriceps strain
	13	15	Strained Rt. hamstring
Holt, Brock	14	23	Concussion
Hosmer,Eric	14	31	Stress fracture in Rt. hand
Howard,Ryan	10	19	Sprained L. ankle
	12	93	Recov. Fr. L. Achilles tendon surg.
	13	86	Lt. knee inflammation
Huff,Aubrey	12	94	Anxiety disorder+R. knee spr x 2
Hundley,Nick	11	71	R. oblique strain
	12	49	Torn meniscus in R. knee
Iannetta,Chris	12	80	Fractured R. wrist

FIVE-YEAR INJURY LOG

Batters	Yr	Days	Injury
Iglesias,Jose	14	184	Stress fracture in both shins
Inciarte,Ender David	14	7	Concussion
Infante,Omar	11	15	Fractured R. middle finger
	13	39	Sprained Lt. ankle
	14	15	Disc irritation in lower back
Inge,Brandon	10	15	Fractured L. hand
	11	22	Mononucleosis
	12	68	Str. R. shouldx2+str groin x2
	13	23	Rt. scapula soreness
Izturis,Cesar	11	136	Irritation, ulnar nerve, R. hand numbness;
	12	27	Strained L. hamstring
Izturis,Maicer	10	85	Inflam R. shouldx2; Str. L. forearm
	13	40	Sprained Lt. ankle
	14	169	Sprained Lt. knee
Jackson,Austin	12	15	Strained abdominal
	13	33	Strained Rt. hamstring
Jackson,Ryan	14	27	Strained Rt. wrist
Janish,Paul	13	40	Recovery from Lt. shoulder surgery
Jaso,John	11	39	Stained R. oblique muscle
	13	67	Concussion
	14	15	Concussion
Jay,Jon	12	38	Sprained R. shoulder
Jennings,Desmond	12	24	Sprained L. knee
	13	39	Fractured Lt. middle finger
	14	30	Bruised Lt. Knee
Jeter,Derek	11	20	Strained R. calf
	13	163	Lt ankle sorenesss; Rt calf; Rt quad
Johnson,Chris	10	20	Strained intercostal muscle
Johnson,Dan	14	33	Strained Lt. hamstring
Johnson,Elliot	11	19	Sprained L. knee
Johnson,Nick	12	98	Sprained R. wrist
Johnson,Reed	10	26	Lower back spasms
	11	15	Lower back spasms
	13	43	Lt. knee tendinitis
Johnson,Rob	12	50	Torn ligament in L. thumb
Joseph,Corban	13	24	Recovery from Rt. shoulder surgery
Joyce,Matt	10	57	Strained R. elbow
	12	27	Tightness in lower back
Kalish,Ryan	11	4	Herniated cervical disc
	13	183	Recovery from Rt. shoulder surgery
Kearns,Austin	12	15	R. hamstring strain
Kemp,Matt	12	58	Strained L. hamstring
	13	97	Str Rt. ham; Sore A/c joint, Lt. ankle
	14	16	Recovering from surgery on Lt. ankle
Kendrick,Howie	11	15	Strained R. hamstring
	13	35	Sprained Lt. knee
Kennedy,Adam	12	38	Strained R. groin
Keppinger,Jeff	10	15	Fractured big to – L. foot
	11	57	L. foot surgery
	12	34	Broken R. big toe
	14	45	Rec from surgery on Rt. shoulder
Kinsler,Ian	10	61	Sprained R. ankle; Stra. L. groin
	13	28	Rt. intercostal strain
Kipnis,Jason	11	23	Strained R. hamstring
	14	26	Strained Rt. oblique
Kobernus,Jeff	14	74	Fractured Lt. hand

FIVE-YEAR INJURY LOG

Batters	Yr	Days	Injury
Konerko,Paul	12	9	Concussion
	13	19	Strained lower back
Kotchman,Casey	13	138	Strained Lt. oblique; hammy
Kotsay,Mark	12	33	Lower back strain+R. calf str
Kouzmanoff,Kevin	14	91	Herniated disc in back
Kratz,Erik	13	35	Lt. knee surgery
Kubel,Jason	11	52	Strained L. foot
	13	15	Strained Lt. quad
Lagares,Juan	14	39	Strnd R intercostal/strnd R hamstring
Laird,Gerald	11	45	R. index finger fracture
	13	16	Kidney stone
LaRoche,Adam	11	130	Torn labrum in L. shoulder
	14	13	Strained Rt. quadriceps
Lavarnway,Ryan	14	76	Strained Lt. wrist
Lawrie,Brett	11	8	Fractured R. middle finger
	12	34	Strained R. oblique
	13	61	Sprained Lt. ankle; Lt. ribcage
	14	95	Strained Lt. oblique; fx Rt finger
Lee,Carlos	12	15	Stained L. hamstring
Lee,Derrek	11	18	Strained L. oblique muscle
Lewis,Fred	10	11	Strain intercostal muscle - L. side
	11	35	Strained R. oblique
Lillibridge,Brent	11	20	Fract. metacarpal bone in R. hand
Lind,Adam	11	27	Soreness - lower back
	12	31	Strained mid-back
	14	52	Fx Rt. foot; lower back tightness
Lobaton,Jose	11	46	Sprained L. knee
	12	45	Sore R. shoulder
Longoria,Evan	11	30	Strained L. oblique muscle
	12	98	Torn L. hamstring
Lowrie,Jed	10	108	Mononucleosis
	11	52	Sore L. shoulder
	12	66	R. ankle + R. thumb sprains
	14	18	Fractured Rt. index finger
Lucas,Edward	14	30	Fractured Lt. hand
Lucroy,Jonathan	11	12	Fractured R. pinkie finger
	12	58	R. hand fracture
Ludwick,Ryan	10	28	Strained L. calf muscle
	11	15	Mid-back muscle spasms
	13	132	Torn cartilage in Rt. shoulder
Machado,Manny	13	5	Torn ligament - Lt. knee
	14	79	Surgery Lt. knee 10/13; Rt knee surgery
Mahoney,Joseph	13	59	Hammy strain; intercostal strain
Maldonado,Carlos	12	127	Strained lower back
Markakis,Nick	12	40	Fractured R. hand
Marrero,Chris	12	184	Torn L. hamstring
Marson,Lou	13	173	Neck strain; Sore Rt. shoulder
Marte,Starling	12	19	Strained R. oblique
	13	19	Rt. hand contusion
	14	13	Concussion
Martin,Russell	10	60	Torn labrum – R. hip
	14	26	Strained Lt. hamstring
Martinez,Fernando	12	9	Concussion
	13	21	Strained Lt. oblique
Martinez,J.D.	13	65	Sprnd Rt. knee; Sprained Lt. wrist
Martinez,Michael	12	65	R. foot fracture

FIVE-YEAR INJURY LOG

Batters	Yr	Days	Injury
Martinez,Victor	10	28	Fractured L. thumb
	11	15	Strained R. groin
	12	183	Recovery from surgery - L. knee
Mastroianni,Darin	13	121	Stress reaction in Lt. ankle
Mathis,Jeff	10	58	Fractured R. wrist
	13	44	Broken Rt. collarbone
Mauer,Joe	11	79	Bilateral leg weakness; Pneumonia
	13	41	Concussion
	14	40	Strained Rt. oblique muscle
Maxwell,Justin	11	28	Recovery from TJS
	12	17	Loose bodies in L. ankle
	13	69	Fractured Lt. hand; Concussion
Mayberry,John	14	40	Lt. wrist inflammation
Maybin,Cameron	11	16	R. knee Inflam
	13	163	Strained Lt. knee; Sore Rt. wrist
	14	29	Ruptured Lt. biceps tendon
McCann,Brian	11	19	Strained L. oblique
	13	36	Recovery from Rt. shoulder surgery
	14	8	Concussion
McCutchen,Andrew	14	15	Fractured Lt. rib
McDonald,Darnell	11	19	Strained L. quad muscle
	12	24	Strained R. oblique
McDonald,John	11	21	Strained R. hamstring
	12	29	Strained L. oblique
	13	26	Lower back discomfort
McKenry,Michael	13	64	Lt. knee surgery
McLouth,Nate	10	41	Post concussion syndrome
	11	89	L. oblique strain
	14	19	Rt. shoulder inflammation
Mesoraco,Devin	12	8	Concussion
	14	20	strnd Lt. hamstring/strnd Lt. oblique
Middlebrooks,Will	12	54	Fractured R. wrist
	13	17	Low back strain
	14	94	Fx Rt index finger; strained Rt calf
Miller,Corky	13	25	Rt. quad contusion
Molina,Yadier	13	15	Sprained Rt. knee
	14	50	Torn ligament in Rt. thumb
Montero,Miguel	10	62	Torn meniscus - R. knee
	13	28	Lower back strain
Moore,Adam	10	40	Sublexed L. fibula
	11	175	Surgery to repair R. meniscus
Moore,Jeremy	12	182	Recovering from L. hip surgery
Morales,Kendrys	11	183	Recovery from surgeries - L. ankle
Morel,Brent	12	75	Strained back
Moreland,Mitch	12	40	Strained L. hamstring
	13	15	Strained Rt. hamstring
	14	111	Surgery on Lt. ankle impingement
Morgan,Nyjer	10	15	Strained R. hip flexor
	11	36	Deep thigh bruise
	14	82	Sprained Rt. knee
Morneau,Justin	10	87	Concussion
	11	80	Strain L. wrist; Post conc. synd.
	12	15	Sore R. wrist
	14	8	Strained neck

FIVE-YEAR INJURY LOG

Batters	Yr	Days	Injury
Morrison,Logan	11	22	L. foot strain
	12	67	R. knee Inflam
	13	70	Recovery from Rt. knee surgery
	14	56	Strained Rt. hamstring
Morse,Michael	10	35	Strained L. calf
	12	58	Strained R. lat
	13	38	Strained Rt. quad
Murphy,Daniel	10	50	Sprained R. knee
	11	52	Torn ligament in L. knee
	14	11	Strained Rt. calf
Murphy,David	14	26	Strained Rt. abdominal
Murphy,Donnie	10	31	Dislocated R. wrist
	11	128	R. wrist Inflam
	12	15	L. hamstring strain
	14	15	Strained neck
Myers,Wil	14	80	Sprained Rt. wrist
Nady,Xavier	11	47	Fractured L. hand
	12	69	R. wrist tendonitis
Nakajima,Hiroyuki	13	53	Strained Lt. hamstring
Napoli,Mike	11	22	Strained L. oblique muscle
	12	35	Strained L. quadriceps
	14	14	Sprained Lt. ring finger
Nava,Daniel	12	40	Sprained L. wristx2
Navarro,Dioner	11	26	R. oblique strain
Neal,Thomas	13	53	Dislocated Rt. shoulder
Negron,Kristopher	12	34	R. knee injury
Nelson,Chris	12	37	Irreg. heaR.beat+ L. wrist Inflam
	13	19	Strained Rt. hamstring
Nieves,Wil	12	31	Turf toe in R. foot
	14	27	Strained Rt. quadriceps
Nishioka,Tsuyoshi	11	85	Fract. L. fibula; Strain R. oblique
Nix,Jayson	11	23	Contusion - L. shin
	13	65	fX Lt. hand; Strained Rt hammy
Nix,Laynce	10	23	Sprained R. ankle
	12	73	Strained R. elbow
Norris,Derek	13	15	Fractured big toe, Lt. foot
Nunez,Eduardo	13	61	Lt. ribcage strain
	14	16	Strained Rt. hamstring
Olivo,Miguel	12	23	Strained R. groin
Ortiz,David	12	78	Strained R. achilles tendonx2
	13	20	Rt. Achilles tendon soreness
Owings,Christopher	14	65	Strained Lt. shoulder
Ozuna,Marcell	13	69	Torn Lt. thumb ligament
Pacheco,Jordan	14	33	Rt. shoulder tendinitis
Pagan,Angel	11	35	Pulled L. oblique
	13	125	Strained Rt. hamstring
	14	43	Strained back
Parrino,Andy	12	24	Injured R. hand
Pastornicky,Tyler	13	46	Torn Lt. ACL
Paulino,Ronny	11	19	Anemia
Pearce,Steve	10	131	Sprained R. ankle
	11	91	R. calf strain
	13	61	Lt. wrist tendinitis x2
Pedroia,Dustin	10	97	Fx L. navicular bone; sore L. foot
	12	15	Sprained R. thumb
	14	29	Lt. thumb/wrist surgery

FIVE-YEAR INJURY LOG

Batters	Yr	Days	Injury
Peguero,Francisco	14	85	Strained Rt. wrist
Pena,Carlos	10	15	Plantar Fasciitis - R. foot
	13	13	Appendectomy
Pena,Ramiro	11	50	Appendicitis
	13	105	Rt. shoulder impingement
Pennington,Cliff	12	18	Tendinitis in L. elbow
	14	64	Sprained ligament in Lt. thumb
Perez,Eury	14	70	Fractured Lt. toe
Perez,Salvador	12	78	Surgery for torn L. meniscus
	13	7	Concussion
Phelps,Cord	13	33	Rt. wrist inflammation
Phillips,Brandon	14	38	Surgery for torn ligament on Lt. thumb
Pie,Felix	10	81	Strained L. shoulder
Pierzynski,A.J.	11	20	Bruised L. wrist
	13	15	Strained Rt. oblique
Pill,Brett	13	15	Recovery from minor knee surgery
Pina,Manuel	12	149	Surgery on R. knee
Plouffe,Trevor	12	23	Bruised R. thumb
	13	23	Concussion; Strained Lt. calf
	14	15	Strained Lt. oblique
Polanco,Placido	10	21	Bone spur –R. elbow
	11	40	Lower back Inflam
	12	57	Lower back Inflamx2
	13	8	Concussion
Pollock IV,A.J.	14	93	Fractured Rt. hand
Posada,Jorge	10	16	Stress fracture – R. foot
Posey,Buster	11	126	Fract. L. fibula and torn ankle lig.
Prado,Martin	10	17	Fractured R. pinky finger
	11	37	Staph infection in R. calf
	14	14	Appendectomy
Presley,Alex	11	33	L. hand contusion
	12	12	Concussion
	14	56	Strained Rt. oblique muscle
Profar,Jurickson	14	183	Torn muscle in Rt. shoulder
Pujols,Albert	11	15	Fractured L. forearm
	13	65	Plantar fasciitis
Punto,Nick	11	99	SpoR.s hernia surgery
	14	37	Strained Rt. hamstring
Quentin,Carlos	11	22	Sprained L. shoulder
	12	54	R. knee surgery
	13	61	Rt. knee strain
	14	108	Sore Lt. knee x 2
Quintero,Humberto	11	39	High R. ankle sprain
Raburn,Ryan	12	52	Sprain R. thumb; Strain R. quad
	13	15	Strained Lt. Achilles
	14	14	Sore Rt. wrist
Ramirez,Aramis	13	64	Sprained Lt. knee x 2
	14	22	Strained Lt. hamstring
Ramirez,Hanley	11	72	L. back strain
	13	60	Str Lt. hamMY; Rt. thumb ligament
	14	14	Strained Rt. oblique
Ramirez,Wilkin	13	109	Head Injury; Fractured Lt. tibia
Ramos,Wilson	12	144	Torn R. knee ligament
	13	64	Strained Lt. hamstring x 2
	14	50	Strained Rt. hamstring/Fx Lt. hand

FIVE-YEAR INJURY LOG

Batters	Yr	Days	Injury
Rasmus,Colby	11	23	Jammed R. wrist
	13	41	Lt. oblique str; contusion - Lt. eye
	14	33	Tightness in Rt. hamstring
Reddick,Josh	13	39	Sprained Rt. wrist x 2
	14	44	Strained Rt. knee;hyper Rt knee
Reimold,Nolan	12	156	Surgery for herniated disk
	13	129	Str Rt hammy; Nerve inflam neck
	14	108	Strnd Lt. calf; cervical spine fusion
Renteria,Edgar	10	57	Strained R. groin; hammy; biceps
Repko,Jason	11	36	Strain R. quad; Bursitis-L. should.
	12	62	Separation of R. shoulder
Revere,Ben	13	78	Broken Rt. foot
Reyes,Jose	10	6	Recovery from hypeR.hyroidism
	11	37	L. hamstring strain
	13	74	Sprained Lt. ankle
	14	19	Tightness in Lt. hamstring
Reynolds,Mark	12	17	Strained L. oblique
Rios, Alex	14	24	Rt. thumb infection
Rivera,Juan	12	148	Torn L. hamstring
Roberts,Brian	10	104	Strained ab muscle; sore back
	11	135	Concussion
	12	162	Surg.-torn R. hip labrum+concuss.
	13	86	Ruptured tendon, Rt. knee
Robinson,Shane	13	15	Strained Rt. shoulder
	14	34	Surgery on Lt. shoulder
Rodriguez,Alex	10	15	Strained L. calf
	11	44	Torn meniscus in R. knee
	12	40	Broken L. hand
	13	127	Lt. hip surgery
Rodriguez,Sean	12	15	Fractured R. hand
Rohlinger,Ryan	10	30	Strained L. hamstring
Rollins,Jimmy	10	65	Strained R. calf x 2
	11	17	R. groin strain
Romine,Austin	12	182	Strained lower back
Rosales,Adam	10	29	Stress fracture – R. ankle
	11	67	Fractured R. foot
	13	25	Strained Lt. intercostal
Rosario,Wilin	14	25	Lt. wrist inflammation/viral infection
Ross,Cody	11	21	R. calf strain
	12	31	Fractured bone in L. foot
	13	62	Lt. calf strain; Dislocated Rt. hip
	14	71	Strained Lt. calf/recovery Rt. hip
Ross,David	13	77	Concussion x 2
	14	18	Plantar fasciitis in Rt. foot
Rowand,Aaron	10	15	Fractured check bone
Ruf,Darin	14	49	Strained Lt. oblique
Ruggiano,Justin	11	22	Bursitis in L. knee
	14	65	Surgery Lt. ankle/strnd Lt. hamstring
Ruiz,Carlos	10	21	Concussion
	11	15	Lower back Inflam
	12	35	Plantar fasciitis in L. foot
	13	29	Strained Rt. hamstring
	14	26	Concussion
Rutledge,Josh	14	11	Viral infection
Ryan,Brendan	11	15	Sprained L. shoulder
	14	36	Pinched nerve in neck

FIVE-YEAR INJURY LOG

Batters	Yr	Days	Injury
Saltalamacchia,Jarro	10	35	Strained upper back; infected leg
	14	17	Concussion
Sanchez,Angel	13	45	Lower back strain
Sanchez,Freddy	10	45	Recov. from surgery - L. shoulder
	12	182	Recov. from surgery - R. shoulder
Sanchez,Hector	12	15	L. knee sprain
	13	15	Strained Rt. shoulder
	14	37	Concussion
Sandoval,Pablo	11	45	Broken hamate bone in R. hand
	12	56	Strained L. hamstring+ Fx R. hand
	13	15	Strained Lt. foot
Sands,Jerry	14	98	Strained Lt. wrist
Santana,Carlos	12	10	Concussion
	14	10	Concussion
Santana,Daniel	14	21	Bone bruise in Lt. knee
Saunders,Michael	13	18	Sprained Rt. shoulder
	14	74	Strained Lt oblique; A/C joint inflam
Schafer,Jordan	10	43	Recovery from surgery - L. wrist
	11	26	Chip fracture in L. middle finger
	12	25	Shoulder
	13	37	Rt. ankle contusion
Schafer,Logan	14	13	Strained Rt. hamstring
Schierholtz,Nate	11	38	Hairline fracture in R. foot
	12	19	Fractured R. great toe
Schneider,Brian	10	15	Strained R. Achilles
	11	43	Straing L. hamstring
	12	77	Strain L. hamstring+ spr R. Ankle
Schumaker,Skip	11	37	R. triceps strain
	12	36	R. hammy strain+torn R. oblique
Scott,Luke	10	18	Strained L. hamstring
	11	86	Bruise-R. knee; Strain R. should.
	12	50	Str R. oblique+back spasms
	13	46	Back spasms; Strained Rt. calf
Scutaro,Marco	11	30	Strained L. oblique muscle
	14	170	Strained lower back x 2
Sellers,Justin	12	134	Bulging disc in lower back
Shoppach,Kelly	10	54	Sprained R. knee
Sierra,Moises	14	15	Strained Lt. oblique
Silverio,Alfredo	13	183	Sprained Rt. elbow
Simmons,Andrelton	12	63	Non-displaced fract. R. hand
Sizemore,Grady	10	139	Bone brse—L. knee;microfrac surg.
	11	77	Recv. L. knee surg.; Bruise R. Knee
	12	183	Recovery from back surgery
Sizemore,Scott	12	182	Recovery from torn ACL surgery
	13	173	Torn Lt. ACL
Smith,Seth	12	18	Strained L. hamstring
Smoak,Justin	11	20	Fracture of the nose
	13	19	Rt. oblique strain
	14	23	Strained Lt. quadriceps
Smolinski,Jacob	14	53	Bone bruise in Lt. foot
Snider,Travis	10	63	Sprained R. wrist
	13	35	Lt. big toe discomfort
Snyder,Brandon	13	24	Ulnar neuritis, Rt. elbow
Snyder,Chris	11	126	Sore lower back
Sogard,Eric	12	58	Strained back/sprained ankle
Solano,Donovan	13	34	Strained Lt. intercostal muscle

FIVE-YEAR INJURY LOG

Batters	Yr	Days	Injury
Solano,Jhonatan	12	78	L. oblique strain
Soriano,Alfonso	11	15	L. quadriceps strain
Soto,Geovany	10	30	Sprain R. shoulder; Shoulder Surg.
	11	18	L. groin strain
	12	30	Torn L. meniscus
	14	126	Strained Rt. groin; surg. Rt knee
Souza,Steven	14	22	Bruised Lt. shoulder
Span,Denard	11	91	Concussion; Migraine headaches
	12	15	Strained R. sternoclavicular joint
	14	7	Concussion
Spilborghs,Ryan	11	45	Plantar fascitis in R. foot
Springer,George	14	68	Lt. quadriceps injury
Stairs,Matt	10	24	Sore R. knee
Stanton,Giancarlo	12	30	AR.hroscopic R. knee surgery
	13	41	Strained Rt. hamstring
Stassi,Max	13	32	Concussion
Stewart,Chris	14	21	Surgery on Rt. knee
Stewart,Ian	10	28	Strained R. oblique
	12	113	Sore L. wrist
	13	33	Strained Lt. quad
	14	39	Bruised Lt. hand
Stubbs,Drew	12	19	Strained L. oblique
Sucre,Jesus	13	72	Lt. wrist sprain
Suzuki,Kurt	10	22	Intercostal strain
Sweeney,Ryan	10	83	Pending surg. for patella tendinitis
	12	93	Concussion+toe+fx L. hand
	13	63	Fractured Lt. rib
	14	74	Strnd L hamstring/strnd R hamstring
Swisher,Nick	14	66	Hyperextend L knee; R knee soreness
Tabata,Jose	11	50	R. hand contusion
	13	39	Strained Lt. oblique
Teagarden,Taylor	12	100	Strained back
	13	37	Dislocated Lt. thumb
	14	37	Strained Lt. hamstring
Teahen,Mark	10	73	Fractured R. middle finger
	11	24	Strained R. oblique muscle
Teixeira,Mark	13	167	Rt wrist surgery; Strained Rt wrist
	14	15	Strained Rt. hamstring
Tejada,Miguel	11	28	Lower abdominal strain
	13	50	Strained Rt. calf
Tejada,Ruben	12	48	Strained R. quadriceps
	13	37	Rt. quad strain
Thames,Marcus	10	21	Strained R. hamstring
	11	34	R. quad strain
Theriot,Ryan	12	15	R. elbow Inflam
Thole,Josh	12	24	Concussion
Thomas,Brad	11	141	R. elbow surgery
Thome,Jim	11	45	Strain L. oblique; Strain L. quad
	12	92	Strained lower back, Back spasms
Tolbert,Matt	10	45	Sprained R. middle finger
Torrealba,Yorvit	13	8	Concussion
Torres,Andres	11	45	Strained L. Achilles Tendon
	12	24	L. calf strain
	13	39	Surgery, Lt. Achilles
Tracy,Chad	12	65	R. adductor strain

FIVE-YEAR INJURY LOG

Batters	Yr	Days	Injury
Treanor,Matt	10	30	Sprained R. knee
	11	32	Concussion
Trumbo,Mark	14	78	Stress fracture in Lt. foot
Tuiasosopo,Matt	13	15	Strained Lt. intercostal
Tulowitzki,Troy	10	39	Fractured L. wrist
	12	126	Strained L. groin muscle
	13	27	Fractured rib, Rt. ribcage
	14	69	Strained Lt. hip flexor
Turner,Justin	12	18	Sprained R. ankle
	13	35	Intercostal strain
	14	19	Strained Lt. hamstring
Uggla,Dan	13	15	Eye surgery
Upton,B.J.	12	15	Soreness in lower back
	13	21	Rt. adductor strain
Uribe,Juan	11	83	L. hip flexor muscle strain
	12	28	L. wrist injury
	14	51	Strained Rt. hamstring x 2
Utley,Chase	10	49	Sprained R. thumb
	11	53	R. knee tendinitis
	12	84	Worn caR.ilage behind L. kneecap
	13	31	Strained Rt. oblique
Valaika,Chris	13	76	Fractured Lt. wrist
Valbuena,Luis	13	29	Rt. oblique strain
Valencia,Danny	14	21	Sprained Lt. hand
Van Slyke,Scott	13	17	Lt. shoulder bursitis
Velez,Eugenio	10	18	Concussion
Venable,Will	10	19	Lower back pain
Viciedo,Dayan	11	6	Fractured R. thumb
	13	21	Strained Lt. oblique
Victorino,Shane	10	15	Strained L. abdominal muscle
	11	30	R. hamstring strain
	13	18	Lt. hamstring strain
	14	139	Lower back; strained Rt. Hammy x2
Votto,Joey	12	50	Torn medial meniscus in L. knee
	14	103	Strained Lt. quadriceps x 2
Walker,Neil	13	32	Strained Rt. oblique; Rt. finger cut
	14	15	Appendectomy
Weeks,Rickie	11	42	Sprained L. ankle
	13	53	Lt. hamstring surgery
Wells,Casper	13	32	Vision complications
Wells,Vernon	11	28	Strained R. groin
	12	67	Torn ligament in R. thumb
Werth,Jayson	12	87	Broken L. wrist
	13	32	Strained Rt. hamstring
Whiteside,Eli	11	7	Concussion
Wieters,Matt	10	15	Strained R. hamstring
	14	94	Strained Rt. Elbow; TJS
Wigginton,Ty	11	16	L. oblique strain
Willingham,Josh	10	48	Surgery – L. knee
	11	19	Strained L. achilles tendon
	13	39	Medial meniscus tear, Lt. knee
	14	43	Fractured Lt. wrist
Willits,Reggie	10	10	Strained R. hamstring
	11	13	Strained L. calf
Wilson,Bobby	10	22	Bruised ankle; concussion
	12	13	Concussion

FIVE-YEAR INJURY LOG

Batters	Yr	Days	Injury
Wilson,Jack	10	101	Fract R. hand; Strain R. hamstring
	11	15	Bruised L. heel
	12	82	Dislocated R. pinky finger
Wise,DeWayne	13	65	Strained Rt. hamstring
Wong,Kolten	14	15	Sore Lt. shoulder
Wood,Brandon	10	22	R. Hip flexor strain
Worth,Danny	13	3	Dislocated Lt. shoulder
Wright,David	11	67	Lower back stress fracture
	13	48	Strained Rt. hamstring
Yelich,Christian S.	14	13	Strained lower back
Youkilis,Kevin	10	61	Sprained R. thumb
	11	16	Sore back; Bursitis R. hip
	12	23	Strained lower back
	13	141	Strained lower back x 2
Young Jr.,Eric	14	21	Strained Rt. hamstring
Young,Chris	12	30	R. shoulder contusion
	14	15	Strained Rt. quadriceps
Young,Delmon	11	39	Strain L. oblique; Sprain R. ankle
	13	30	Recovery from Rt. ankle surgery
Young,Eric	10	77	Stress Fracture; R. tibia
	12	45	L. intercostal muscle strain
Zimmerman,Ryan	11	65	L. abdominal strain
	12	17	Sore R. shoulder
	13	15	Strained Lt. hamstring
	14	110	Fx Rt. thumb/strained Rt. hamstring
Zobrist,Ben	14	15	Dislocated Lt. thumb
Zunino,Mike	13	38	Fractured Lt. hamate bone

FIVE-YEAR INJURY LOG

Pitchers	Yr	Days	Injury
Aardsma,David	11	182	Recov. from surgery-L. hip; TJS
Abad,Fernando	11	88	L. shoulder tendinitis
	12	20	R. intercostal strain
Aceves,Alfredo	10	147	Herniated disk in lower back
Adams,Mike	10	26	Strained L. oblique
	13	117	Back Strain; Rt. biceps tend.
	14	106	Rt. rotator cuff inflammation
Affeldt,Jeremy	10	28	Torn L. oblique muscle
	12	15	Sprained R. knee
	13	71	Strained Lt. groin; Rt. oblique
	14	18	Strained ligament in Rt. knee
Albers,Matt	11	15	Sore R. lat muscle
	14	157	Rt. shoulder tendinitis
Alburquerque,Al	11	39	Inflam - R. elbow; Concussion
	12	141	Recov. fr. surg. - R. elbow
Alvarez,Henderson	13	95	Mild Rt. shoulder inflammation
	14	14	Rt. shoulder inflammation
Anderson,Brett	10	90	L. elbow Inflam x 2
	11	115	Soreness in L. elbow
	12	137	Recovery from TJS
	13	119	Rt. foot stress fracture
	14	144	Strained lower back/fx Lt. finger
Arredondo,Jose	11	60	R. shoulder Inflam
Arrieta,Jake	11	59	Bone spur in R. elbow
	14	34	Tightness in Rt. shoulder
Arroyo,Bronson	14	105	Rt. elbow tendinitis
Atchison,Scott	12	60	Tightness In R. forearm
	13	60	Rt. groin strain; Rt. elbow
Augenstein,Bryan	11	169	R. groin strain
Ayala,Luis	11	28	Strained lat muscle
	13	71	Anxiety disorder
Bailey,Andrew	10	32	R. intercostal strain
	11	59	Strained R. forearm
	12	132	R. thumb surgery
	13	100	Rt biceps soreness; Rt shoulder str
Bailey,Homer	10	83	Inflam – R. shoulder
	11	66	R. shoulder impingement
	14	16	Strained flexor tendon in Rt. elbow
Baker,Scott	11	58	Strained R. flexor muscle
	12	182	TJS - R. elbow
	13	161	Strained Rt. elbow
Balfour,Grant	10	34	Strained intercostal muscle
	11	15	Strained R. oblique muscle
Barnes,Scott	13	32	Sprained Lt. wrist
Bass,Anthony	12	72	R. shoulder Inflam
	14	49	Chest injury/strained Rt. intercostal
Bastardo,Antonio	10	29	Ulnar Neuritis – L. elbow
Batista,Miguel	12	16	Lower back strain
Beachy,Brandon	11	39	L. oblique strain
	12	109	TJS
	13	160	Rt. elbow inflam; Rt. elbow surgery
	14	184	Recovering from Tommy John surgery
Beato,Pedro	11	15	R. elbow tendinitis
	12	92	R. shoulder stiffness
	14	22	Sore Rt. elbow
Beavan,Blake	14	98	Rt. shoulder tendinitis

FIVE-YEAR INJURY LOG

Pitchers	Yr	Days	Injury
Beckett,Josh	10	65	Strained lower back
	12	18	Inflam in R. shoulder
	13	139	Neck & shoulder surgery
	14	87	Lt. hip impinge x 2/sprained Rt. thumb
Bedard,Erik	10	182	Recov. fr. surg. on L. shoulder
	11	31	Sprained L. knee
Beimel,Joe	11	48	Sore L. elbow
Bell,Trevor	14	174	Rt. elbow inflammation
Bergman,Christian	14	60	Fractured Lt. hand/thumb
Betances,Dellin	12	15	R. shoulder Inflam
Betancourt,Rafael	10	15	Strained R. groin
	13	98	Strained Rt. groin; Rt. elbow; Appx
Billings,Bruce	14	18	Strained Rt. forearm
Billingsley,Chad	10	16	Strained R. groin
	12	46	R. elbow pain
	13	177	Rt. elbow surgery; finger bruise
	14	184	Recovering from Tommy John surgery
Black,Victor	14	11	Herniated disc in neck
Blackburn,Nick	11	38	Strained R. forearm
	12	18	Strained L. quad
Blackley,Travis	13	15	Lt. shoulder strain
Blanton,Joe	10	29	Strained L. oblique
	11	127	Impingement in R. elbow
Braddock,Zach	11	32	Sleep disorder
Braden,Dallas	10	27	Sore L. elbow
	11	165	Surg. - torn capsule in L. shoulder
	12	182	Recov. fr. surg. - L. shoulder
Brasier,Ryan	14	184	Strained Rt. elbow
Bray,Bill	12	78	Lumbar strain+ L. groin str
Breslow,Craig	13	36	Lt. shoulder tendinitis
	14	13	Strained Lt. shoulder
Britton,Zach	11	17	Strained L. shoulder
	12	62	L. shoulder impingement
Broxton,Jonathan	11	148	Sore R. elbow
	13	108	Rt. flexor strain x 2
	14	9	Rec from surgery Rt. elbow/forearm
Buchholz,Clay	10	24	Strained L. hamstring
	11	103	Strained lower back
	12	24	Gastro-intestinal problem
	13	93	Neck strain
	14	28	Hyperextended Lt. knee
Buchholz,Taylor	10	129	Sore back; R. elbow
	11	122	R. shoulder fatigue
Bueno,Francisley	14	55	Sprained Lt. middle finger
Burgos,Hiram	13	37	Rt. shoulder impingement
Burnett,A.J.	12	17	Fractured R. orbital bone
	13	28	Strained Rt. calf
Burnett,Sean	13	150	Sore Lt. forearm; Lt. elbow surgery
	14	180	Torn UCL in Lt. elbow; surgery recovery
Burton,Jared	11	135	AR.hroscopic surg-R. shoulder
Butler,Eddie	14	40	Rt. rotator cuff inflammation
Byrdak,Tim	10	20	Strained R. hamstring
	12	62	L. shoulder soreness
Cabral,Cesar	12	182	Fractured L. elbow
	13	75	Lt. elbow pain
Cabrera,Edwar	13	183	Lt. shoulder impingement

FIVE-YEAR INJURY LOG

Pitchers	Yr	Days	Injury
Cahill,Trevor	10	16	Stress reaction - L. scapula
	13	47	Rt. hip contusion
Cain,Matt	13	15	Rt. forearm contusion
	14	93	Rt. elbow inflam/Rt. ham/cut Rt. finger
Camp,Shawn	13	24	Sprained Rt. big toe
Capps,Carter	14	97	Sprained Rt. elbow
Capps,Matt	12	88	Irritation of R. rotator cuff
Capuano,Chris	13	39	Lt. lat strain; Strained Lt. calf
Carignan,Andrew	12	120	TJS - R. elbow
Carlson,Jesse	11	182	Surgery - torn L. rotator cuff
Carp,Mike	14	36	Fractured Rt. foot
Carpenter,Chris	12	171	Nerve irritation in R. shoulder
	12	182	Recov. fr. surg.-bone spur R. elbow
	13	183	Nerve irritation, Rt. shoulder
Carpenter,David	14	15	Strained Rt. biceps
Carrasco,Carlos	11	16	Inflam - R. elbow
	12	183	Recovery from TJS
Cashner,Andrew	11	150	R. rotator cuff strain
	12	59	Strained R. latissimus dorsi
	14	82	Sore Rt. elbow/sore Rt. shoulder
Casilla,Santiago	11	57	Sore R. elbow
	13	53	Cyst on Rt. knee
	14	24	Strained Rt. hamstring
Cassevah,Bobby	12	22	Inflam in R. shoulder
Castillo,Alberto	11	33	L. shoulder tendinitis
Castillo,Lendy	12	87	L. groin strain
Cecil,Brett	13	13	Lt. elbow soreness
	14	16	Strained Lt. groin
Ceda,Jose	12	184	TJS
	13	183	Recovery from Rt. elbow surgery
Chacin,Jhoulys	12	111	R. shoulder Inflam
	13	15	Lt. lower back strain
	14	128	Rt. shoulder inflammation/strain
Chamberlain,Joba	11	115	TJS
	12	117	Dislocated R. ankle
	13	30	Strained Rt. oblique
Chapman,Aroldis	11	39	L. shoulder Inflam
	14	41	Facial fractures, concussion
Chatwood,Tyler	13	31	Rt. elbow inflammation
	14	168	Strnd Rt. elbow/strnd Lt. hamstring
Chen,Bruce	11	49	Strained L. lat muscle
	14	64	Inflamed disc in lower back
Chen,Wei-Yin	13	58	Strained Rt. oblique
Choate,Randy	11	44	L. elbow Inflam
Cingrani,Tony	13	15	Strained lower back
	14	17	Lt. shoulder tendinitis
Cisnero,Jose	14	143	Rt. elbow injury
Cobb,Alex	11	53	Surgery - rib cage
	13	60	Concussion
	14	38	Strained Lt. oblique muscle
Coello,Robert	12	101	Strained R. elbow
	13	98	Rt. shoulder inflammation
Coffey,Todd	10	21	Bruised R. thumb
	11	15	L. calf strain
	12	109	R. knee Inflam+TJS

FIVE-YEAR INJURY LOG

Pitchers	Yr	Days	Injury
Coke,Phil	11	15	Bone bruise in R. foot
	13	15	Lt. groin strain
Cole,Gerrit	14	63	Tightness Rt. lat/Rt. shoulder fatigue
Coleman,Louis	14	14	Bone bruised/sprained R middle finger
Collins,Tim	14	27	Strained flexor in Lt. elbow
Collmenter,Josh	12	22	Ulcers
Colome,Alexander	13	94	Strained Rt. elbow
Colon,Bartolo	11	20	Strained L. hamstring
	12	15	Strained R. oblique
	13	15	Lt. groin strain
Contreras,Jose	11	135	R. elbow strain
	12	136	R. elbow strain
	13	16	Lower back inflammation
Cook,Aaron	10	54	Turf toe; Fx R. fibula
	11	69	Broken finger on R. hand
	12	49	Laceration of L. knee
Cook,Ryan	14	39	Strned Rt. forearm; Rt shoulder inflam
Corbin,Patrick	14	184	Recovering from Tommy John surgery
Cordero,Francisco	12	63	R. foot sesamoiditis
Cortes,Dan	11	15	Bruised L. ankle
Crain,Jesse	12	51	Strained R. shoulder+ L. oblique
	13	85	Sprained Rt. shoulder
	14	183	Recovering from surgery on Rt. biceps
Crotta,Michael	11	141	R. posterior elbow Inflam
Cruz,Juan	11	15	Strained R. groin
	12	22	R. shoulder Inflam
Cruz,Rhiner	12	15	Sprained R. ankle
Cueto,Johnny	11	39	R. biceps/triceps irritation
	13	130	Strained Rt. lat x 2; Rt. shoulder
Daley,Matt	10	87	Inflam – R. shoulder
	11	120	R. shoulder Inflam
Danks,John	11	24	Strained R. oblique muscle
	12	137	Surgery - strained L. shoulder
	13	54	Recovery from Lt. shoulder surgery
Darvish,Yu	13	15	Upper back strain
	14	61	Rt elbow inflam; stiff neck
Davies,Kyle	11	111	Inflam R/C; Impingement R. should.
Davis,Erik	14	183	Sprained Rt. elbow
Davis,Wade	10	18	Strained R. shoulder
	11	15	Strained R. forearm
De Fratus,Justin	12	152	R. elbow sprain
De La Rosa,Dane	14	63	Rt shoulder irritation; Rt forearm
De La Rosa,Jorge	10	74	Torn tendon – L. middle finger
	11	127	TJS
	12	168	TJS
De La Rosa,Rubby	11	59	TJS
De Vries,Cole	12	20	Fractured Rib
	13	48	Rt. forearm strain
Deduno,Samuel	13	31	Rt. shoulder soreness
deGrom,Jacob	14	12	Tendinitis in Rt. rotator cuff
Del Rosario,Enerio	11	27	Strained R. shoulder
Delabar,Steve	13	29	Rt. shoulder inflammation
Demel,Sam	11	38	R. shoulder tendinitis
Dempster,Ryan	12	37	R. quad strain, Tight R. lat.
Detwiler,Ross	10	110	R. hip strain; hip caR.ilage
	13	116	Back strain; x 2

FIVE-YEAR INJURY LOG

Pitchers	Yr	Days	Injury
Devine,Joey	10	182	Recov. fr. surg. - R. elbow
	11	2	Strained rhomboid- R. shoulder
	12	182	TJS - R. elbow
Diamond,Scott	13	13	Recovery from Lt. elbow surgery
Dolis,Rafael	13	126	Strained Rt. forearm
Dominguez,Jose	13	69	Lt. quad strain
Doolittle,Sean	14	36	Strained Rt. intercostal muscle
Dotel,Octavio	11	8	Sore L. hamstring
	12	16	Inflam in R. elbow
	13	163	Rt. elbow inflammation
Doubront,Felix	11	8	Inflam - L. forearm
	12	15	Contusion in R. knee
	14	59	Strained Lt. calf/strained Lt. shoulder
Downs,Darin	13	28	Lt. rotator cuff tendinitis
	14	14	Strained Rt. oblique muscle
Downs,Scott	11	27	Fx L. big toe; Gastrointestinal virus
	12	21	Strained L. shoulder
	14	16	Sprained/stiff neck
Drabek,Kyle	12	112	TJS
	13	95	Recovery from Rt. elbow surgery
Drake,Oliver	12	8	Tendinitis in R. shoulder
Duchscherer,Justin	10	156	L. Hip Inflam x 2
	11	182	Strained L. hip
Duffy,Danny	12	143	TJS
	13	99	Recov Rt elbow surg; Rt flexor strain
Duke,Zach	10	25	Strained L. elbow
	11	58	Broken L. hand
Edgin,Josh	13	62	Ribcage stress fracture
Elbert,Scott	12	62	L. elbow Inflam x2
	13	183	Recovery from Lt. elbow surgery
	14	132	Tommy John surgery
Elias, Roenis	14	7	Strained flexor muscle in Rt. elbow
Eovaldi,Nathan	13	79	Mild Rt. shoulder inflammation
Erlin,Robert	14	88	Sore Lt. elbow
Escalona,Edgmer	11	20	R. rotator cuff strain
	12	27	R. elbow Inflam
	13	22	Rt. elbow inflammation
	14	84	Rt. shoulder impingement
Escalona,Sergio	11	33	L. elbow tendinitis
	12	183	TJS
Estrada,Marco	10	124	R. shoulder fatigue
	12	33	R. quadriceps strain
	13	64	Strained Lt. hamstring
Familia,Jeurys	13	128	Rt. elbow surgery
Farina,Alan	12	183	Recovery from TJS
Farnsworth,Kyle	12	86	Strained R. elbow
Feldman,Scott	10	16	Bone bruise – R. knee
	11	105	Recov. fr. surg. - R. knee
	14	18	Rt. biceps tendinitis
Feliciano,Pedro	11	183	Strained L. rotator cuff
	12	182	Recov. fr. surg. - R. shoulder
Feliz,Neftali	11	15	Inflam - R. shoulder
	12	136	TJS - R. elbow
	13	155	Recovery from Rt. elbow surgery
Fernandez,Jose	14	140	Sprained Rt. elbow
Fields,Joshua	14	19	Sore Rt. forearm

FIVE-YEAR INJURY LOG

Pitchers	Yr	Days	Injury
Fife,Stephen	13	66	Rt. shoulder bursitis x 2
	14	14	Recovery from TJS
Figaro,Alfredo	13	30	Strained Rt. oblique
Figueroa,Pedro	14	159	Lt. elbow inflammation
Fish,Robert	12	183	L. elbow tendinitis
Fister,Doug	10	24	R. shoulder fatigue
	12	47	Strained L. side
	14	41	Strained Rt. lat
Floyd,Gavin	12	31	Strain R. elbow flex+ tend R. Elbow
	13	155	Rt. elbow surgery
	14	143	Recovery from TJS/fx Rt. elbow
Francis,Jeff	10	73	Soreness – L. shoulder x 2
	13	24	Lt. groin strain
Francisco,Frank	10	36	Strained R. lat muscle
	11	19	Sore R. pectoral
	12	42	L. oblique strain
	13	160	Rt. elbow inflammation
Frasor,Jason	12	48	Tightness In R. forearm
Friedrich,Christian	12	67	Stress fract-R. side of lower spine
	13	53	Lower back inflammation
Frieri,Ernesto	11	15	Back problem
Fuentes,Brian	10	178	Mid-back strain
Fujikawa,Kyuji	13	153	Rt. elbow strain; Rt. forearm
	14	129	Recovering from Tommy John surgery
Fulchino,Jeff	10	34	Tendinitis - R. elbow
Furbush,Charlie	12	30	Strained L. triceps muscle
Gallardo,Yovani	10	17	Strained oblique muscle
	13	17	Strained Lt. hamstring
Garcia,Christian	13	183	Strained Rt. forearm tendon
Garcia,Freddy	11	20	Lacerated R. index finger
Garcia,Jaime	12	74	L. shoulder strain
	13	135	Lt. shoulder strain
	14	69	Lt. shoulder inflammation x 2
Garcia,Luis	14	13	Strained Rt. forearm
Garcia,Onelki	14	184	Recovering from surgery on Lt. elbow
Garland,Jon	11	133	L. oblique strain
Garza,Matt	11	13	R. elbow bone contusion
	12	68	R. elbow stress reaction
	13	51	Strained Lt. lat
	14	27	Strained Lt. oblique
Gast,John	13	127	Lt. shoulder tightness
Gaudin,Chad	11	156	R. shoulder Inflam
	13	60	Rt. elbow bruise; sore wrist
Gearrin,Cory	14	184	Sprained Rt. elbow
Gee,Dillon	12	88	Damaged aR.ery in R. shoulder
	14	55	Tightness in Rt. lat
Germen,Gonzalez	14	29	Illness/Flu
Gomes,Brandon	13	146	Strained Rt. lat
Gomez,Jeanmar	13	23	Rt. forearm tightness
Gonzalez,Edgar	13	104	Strained Rt. shoulder
Gonzalez,Gio	14	30	Lt. shoulder inflammation
Gonzalez,Miguel	13	17	Rt. thumb blister
	14	11	Strained Rt. oblique
	14	97	Rt. arm fatigue
Gonzalez,Mike	10	102	Strained L. shoulder

FIVE-YEAR INJURY LOG

Pitchers	Yr	Days	Injury
Gorzelanny,Tom	11	26	L. elbow Inflam
	13	16	Lt. shoulder tendinitis
	14	76	Rec from surgery on Lt. shoulder
Green,Sean	10	126	Strained R. ribcage
Gregerson,Luke	11	28	L. oblique strain
Gregg,Kevin	14	45	Rt. elbow inflammation
Greinke,Zack	11	35	Fractured L. rib
	13	33	Broken Lt. collarbone
Griffin,A.J.	12	27	Strained R. shoulder
	14	184	Strained flexor muscle in Rt. elbow
Grilli,Jason	13	42	Strained Rt. forearm
	14	28	Strained Lt. oblique
Guerra,Javy	12	63	Strained L. oblique+ R. knee Inflam
Guerrier,Matt	12	133	R. elbow tendinitis
	13	53	Rt. elbow soreness
Guthrie,Jeremy	12	22	R. shoulder sprain
Gutierrez,Juan	10	15	Inflam – R. shoulder
	11	127	R. shoulder Inflam
Halladay,Roy	12	50	R. back strain
	13	111	Rt. shoulder surgery
Hamels,Cole	11	16	L. shoulder Inflam
	14	27	Lt. biceps tendinitis
Hammel,Jason	10	18	Strained R. groin
	12	54	Injured R. knee
	13	38	Rt. forearm tenderness
Hand,Brad	14	40	Sprained Rt. ankle
Hanrahan,Joel	10	8	Strained flexor tendon - R. forearm
	13	162	Rt elbow surgery; Sore Rt hamstring
	14	150	Recovering from Tommy John surgery
Hanson,Tommy	11	68	R. shoulder tendinitis
	12	17	Lower back strain
	13	32	Strained Rt. forearm
Happ,J.A.	10	81	Strained L. forearm
	12	30	Fractured R. foot
	13	89	Head contusion
	14	18	Strained back
Harang,Aaron	10	61	Lower back spasms
	11	29	Sore R. foot
Harden,Rich	10	64	Tendinitis R. should.; Strain L. glut.
	11	92	Strained R. shoulder
Haren,Dan	12	18	Stiff lower back
	13	15	Rt. shoulder inflammation
Harrison,Matt	10	22	L. biceps tendinitis
	13	177	Inflamed nerve in lower back
	14	55	Lower back inflam; back surg recovery
Harvey,Matt	13	34	Torn Rt. UCL
	14	183	Recovering from Tommy John surgery
Hawkins,LaTroy	10	136	R. shoulder weakness x 2
	11	22	R. shoulder surgery
	12	33	Fractured R. pinkie finger
Hawksworth,Blake	11	26	Strained R. groin
	12	183	R. elbow surgery
Hefner,Jeremy	13	51	Partially torn ligament, Rt. elbow
Heilman,Aaron	11	20	R. shoulder tendinitis
Hellickson,Jeremy	12	15	Fatigued R. shoulder
	14	99	Recovering from surgery on Rt. elbow

FIVE-YEAR INJURY LOG

Pitchers	Yr	Days	Injury
Henderson,Jim	13	15	Strained Rt. hamstring
	14	150	Rt. shoulder inflammation
Hensley,Clay	10	20	Strained L. neck muscle
	11	62	L. rib contusion
	12	15	R. groin strain
Hernandez,David	10	33	Sprained L. ankle
	14	184	Surgery on Rt. elbow torn ligament
Hernandez,Roberto	11	15	Strained R. quad muscle
Herndon,David	12	157	TJS
Herrmann,Frank	13	182	Rt. elbow surgery
Hill,Rich	11	119	Sprained L. elbow
	12	107	TJS recov.+Soreness in L. forearm
Hochevar,Luke	10	83	Strained R. elbow
	14	184	Tommy John surgery
Holland,Derek	10	62	L. rotator cuff Inflam
	12	31	Fatigued L. shoulder
	14	164	Recovering from surgery on Lt. knee
Holland,Greg	12	21	Stress reaction in L. ribs
Hollands,Mario	14	24	Strained flexor in Lt. elbow
Horst,Jeremy	13	106	Strained Lt. elbow
Howell,J.P.	10	182	Strained L. shoulder
	11	50	Recov. fr. surg. - L. labrum
Hudson,Daniel	12	137	R. shoulder impingement +TJS
	13	183	Recovery from Rt. elbow surgery
	14	155	Recovering from Tommy John surgery
Hudson,Tim	12	25	Recovering from back surgery
	13	67	Fractured Rt. ankle
Huff,David	12	18	Strained R. hamstring
	14	20	Strained Lt. quadriceps
Hughes,Jared	13	57	Rt. shoulder inflammation
Hughes,Phil	11	82	Tired arm
	13	6	Rt. upper back thoracic injury
Humber,Philip	11	15	Facial Contusion
	12	30	Strained R. elbow
Hunter,Tommy	10	24	Strained L. oblique
	11	92	Stained R. groin
	14	17	Strained Lt. groin
Hutchison,Drew	12	110	TJS - R. elbow
	13	131	Recovery from Rt. elbow surgery
Igarashi,Ryota	10	32	Strained L. hamstring
Irwin,Phillip	13	119	Rt. arm fatigue
Iwakuma,Hisashi	14	35	Torn tendon in Rt. middle finger
Jackson,Edwin	14	29	Strained Rt. lat
Jakubauskas,Chris	10	115	Concussion
Jansen,Kenley	11	49	R. shoulder Inflam
Janssen,Casey	11	34	Sore R. forearm
	14	42	Strained lower back
Jenkins,Chad	14	24	Fractured Rt. hand
Jenks,Bobby	11	132	Strain R. biceps; Tightness in back
	12	183	Recov. fr. surg. - back
Jennings,Dan	14	24	Concussion
Jepsen,Kevin	13	82	Rt tricep tightness; Appendectomy
Jimenez,Ubaldo	11	17	Cuticle cut on R. thumb
	14	29	Sprained Rt. ankle
Johnson,Jim	10	91	Small tear in R. elbow

FIVE-YEAR INJURY LOG

Pitchers	Yr	Days	Injury
Johnson,Josh	11	135	R. shoulder Inflam
	13	90	Strnd Rt forearm; Strnd Rt triceps
	14	184	Strained flexor in Rt. forearm
Johnson,Steve	13	86	Strained Rt oblique; Strained Rt lat
Jones,Nate	14	184	Strained Lt. hip;TJS
Jordan,Taylor	13	44	Lower back strain
	14	55	Sore Rt. elbow
Jurrjens,Jair	10	61	Strained L. hamstring
	11	28	Sore R. torso
	12	64	Strained R. groin
Kahnle,Thomas	14	17	Rt. shoulder inflammation
Karstens,Jeff	12	68	Sore R. shoulder
	13	183	Rt. shoulder inflammation
Kazmir,Scott	10	36	Strain R. hammy;Fatigue L. should.
	11	178	Lower back stiffness
	13	18	Strained Rt. rib cage
Kelley,Shawn	10	109	R. elbow Inflam
	11	132	Recov. fr. surg. - R. elbow
	14	29	Strained lumbar spine
Kelly,Casey	13	183	Rt. elbow surgery
	14	184	Recovering from Tommy John surgery
Kelly,Joe	14	85	Strained Lt. hamstring
Kendrick,Kyle	13	8	Inflammation - Rt. shoulder
Kershaw,Clayton	14	38	Back muscle inflam/strnd Lt. shoulder
Kimball,Cole	11	111	R. shoulder Inflam
	12	184	Rehab from R. shoulder surgery
Kinney,Josh	13	89	Stress reaction, Lt. shoulder
Kintzler,Brandon	11	147	R. triceps tendonitis
	12	151	Sore R. forearm
	14	15	Strained Rt. rotator cuff
Kirkman,Michael	13	86	Cutaneous lymphoma in Rt. triceps
Kluber,Corey	13	32	Sprained finger, Rt. hand
Kohn,Michael	12	182	R. forearm strain
Krol,Ian	14	15	Lt. shoulder inflammation
Kuo,Hong-Chih	10	18	Sore L. shoulder
	11	56	L. low back strain
Lackey,John	11	24	Strained R. elbow
	12	182	TJS - R. elbow
	13	176	Rt. biceps strain
Laffey,Aaron	10	42	Fatigued – L. shoulder
Lannan,John	13	106	Strained Lt. quad; Lt. knee tend.
Latos,Mat	10	15	Strained L. oblique
	11	11	Strained R. shoulder
	14	76	Recovering from surgery on Lt. knee
Leake,Mike	10	15	Fatigue – R. shoulder
LeCure,Sam	11	30	R. forearm strain
Lee,Cliff	10	26	Strained R. abdominal muscle
	12	20	L. oblique strain
	14	122	Lt. flexor pronator strain x 2
Leroux,Chris	10	30	Strained R. elbow
	11	25	Strained L. calf
	12	151	Strained R. pectoral muscle
Lester,Jon	11	19	Strained lower L. lat muscle
Lewis,Colby	12	101	Surg. torn tendon R. elbow
	13	185	Recovery from Rt. elbow surgery

FIVE-YEAR INJURY LOG

Pitchers	Yr	Days	Injury
Lidge,Brad	10	47	Inflam R. elbow;R knee; elbow surg.
	11	113	R. posterior rotator cuff strain
	12	46	Abdominal wall strain
Lilly,Ted	10	20	Recov. fr. surg. - L. shoulder
	12	143	L. shoulder inflam.; str neck
	13	85	Neck sprain; Rt. ribcage strain
Lincoln,Brad	11	11	Bruised R. arm
Lindstrom,Matt	10	15	Back spasms
	11	16	Nerve injury in upper R. arm
	12	47	Torn ligament in R. middle finger
	14	84	Lt. ankle injury
Liriano,Francisco	11	36	Inflam L. should.; Strain L. should.
	13	41	Fractured Rt. forearm
	14	32	Strained Lt. oblique
Litsch,Jesse	10	128	TJS recovery; Torn labrum R. hip
	11	60	Impingement in R. shoulder
	12	183	Surgery to repair R. biceps tendon
Locke,Jeff	14	12	Strained Rt. oblique
Logan,Boone	14	86	Diverticulitis/Lt. elbow inflam x 3
Lohse,Kyle	10	84	Exertional compart,R. forearm
Lopez,Wilton	11	19	Irritation-ulnar nerve R. elbow
	12	28	Sprained R. elbow
Loux,Shane	12	62	Neck strain
Lowe,Mark	10	148	Herniated lumbar disc
	12	45	Strained R. intercostal muscle
	13	16	Neck stiffness
Luebke,Cory	12	159	TJS
	13	183	Recovery from Lt. elbow surgery
	14	184	Recovering from Tommy John surgery
Lyles,Jordan	14	62	Fractured Lt. hand
Lynn,Lance	11	50	L. oblique strain
Lyon,Brandon	11	142	PaR.ially rotator cuff tear
Lyons,Tyler	14	36	Strained Lt. shoulder
Madson,Ryan	10	70	Fractured R. toe + surgery
	11	26	R. hand contusion
	12	183	TJS
	13	127	Recovery from Rt. elbow surgery
Maholm,Paul	11	42	L. shoulder strain
	13	32	Bruised Lt. wrist
	14	58	Torn ACL in Rt. knee
Maloney,Matt	11	87	L. oblique strain
Manship,Jeff	14	37	Strained Rt. quadriceps
Marcum,Shaun	10	16	Inflam – R. elbow
	12	70	R. elbow tightness
	13	41	Neck Strain; TOS
Mariot,Michael	14	32	Strained Rt. hamstring
Marmol,Carlos	12	16	Strained R. hamstring
Marquis,Jason	10	111	Debris in R. elbow
	11	44	Fractured R. fibula
	12	43	Fractured L. wrist
	13	72	Strained Rt. elbow
Marshall,Brett	14	82	Strained tendon in Rt. middle finger
Marshall,Sean	13	131	Sprained Lt. shoulder; Tendinitis
	14	127	Strnd Lt. shoulder/Lt. shoulder inflam
Marte,Luis	12	51	Strained L. hamstring
	13	61	Recovery from Rt. shoulder surgery

FIVE-YEAR INJURY LOG

Pitchers	Yr	Days	Injury
Martin,Ethan	14	51	Strained Rt. shoulder
Martinez,Cristhian	13	176	Rt. shoulder strain
Martinez,Nicholas	14	14	Lt. side injury
Masset,Nick	12	182	Sore R. shoulder
	13	183	Recovery from Rt. shoulder surgery
	14	15	Strained patellar tendon in Lt. knee
Masterson,Justin	14	22	Rt. knee inflammation
Mateo,Marcos	11	86	R. elbow soreness
	12	183	Sore R. elbow
Matsuzaka,Daisuke	10	44	Strained neck; R. forearm
	11	135	Sprained R. elbow
	12	121	TJS recovery+trained R. upper trap
	14	33	Rt. elbow inflammation
Mattheus,Ryan	11	25	R. shoulder strain
	12	27	Plantar fascia strain in L. foot
	13	67	Fractured Rt. hand
Matusz,Brian	11	59	Strained L. intecostal muscle
McAllister,Zach	13	50	Sprained Rt. middle finger
	14	27	Strained lower back
McCarthy,Brandon	10	66	Recovery from shoulder surgery
	11	45	Stress reaction in R. scapula
	12	95	Strained R. shoulderx2 + skull Fx
	13	65	Rt. shoulder inflammation
McClellan,Kyle	11	15	L. hip flexor strain
	12	139	R. elbow strain
McCoy,Patrick	14	25	Strained Rt. hamstring
McDonald,James	13	129	Rt. shoulder discomfort
	14	183	Rt. shoulder inflammation
McGowan,Dustin	10	182	Sore R. shoulder
	11	158	Recov. fr. surg. - R. shoulder
	12	183	R. Plant. Fasciitis+R. should. surg.
	13	101	Strnd Rt oblique; Sore Rt shoulder
McHugh,Collin	14	15	Rt. middle finger injury
McPherson,Kyle	13	34	Recovery from Rt. elbow surgery
Medlen,Kris	10	59	Partial tear of UCL- R. elbow
	11	178	Recovery from TJS
	14	184	Recovering from Tommy John surgery
Meek,Evan	11	116	R. shoulder tendinitis
Mejia,Jenry	13	160	Rt. elbow inflamon; discomfort
Mijares,Jose	10	58	Strained L. knee; blured vision
	11	15	Strained L. elbow
Mikolas, Miles	14	30	Sore Rt. shoulder
Miller,Andrew	12	32	Strained L. hamstring
	13	85	Lt. foot surgery
Miller,Justin	13	62	Recovery from Rt. elbow surgery
Millwood,Kevin	10	16	Strained R. forearm
Milone, Tommy	14	23	Neck inflammation
Minor,Mike	14	37	Lt. shoulder tendinitis
Mitre,Sergio	10	49	Strained L. oblique
	11	75	Tendinitis in R. shoulder
Moore,Matt	13	36	Lt. elbow soreness
	14	174	Lt. elbow injury
Morales,Franklin	10	27	L. shoulder weakness
	11	33	Strained L. forearm
	12	41	Fatigue in L. shoulder
	13	106	Strained lower back; Lt. pectoral

FIVE-YEAR INJURY LOG

Pitchers	Yr	Days	Injury
Moran,Brian	14	184	Lt. elbow inflammation
Morin,Michael	14	15	Lacerated Lt. foot
Morrow,Brandon	11	21	Inflam - R. forearm
	12	74	Strained L. oblique
	13	121	Rt. forearm strain
	14	122	Torn tendon sheath in Rt. hand
Mortensen,Clayton	13	15	Rt. hip impingement
Morton,Charlie	10	35	R. shoulder weakness
	12	137	Recovering from R. hip surgery+TJS
	13	74	Recovery from Rt. elbow surgery
	14	35	Rt. hip inflammation
Moscoso,Guillermo	10	4	Blister - R. index finger
Moseley,Dustin	11	60	L. shoulder strain
	12	179	Strained R. shoulder
Mota,Guillermo	10	15	IT band syndrome
Motte,Jason	10	27	Sprained R. shoulder
	13	183	Rt. elbow surgery
	14	77	Recovery TJS/strained lower back
Moylan,Peter	11	143	Back surgery
Mujica,Edward	12	18	Fractured R. pinky toe
Myers,Brett	13	131	Rt. elbow inflammation
Narveson,Chris	11	15	L. thumb laceration
	12	171	L. rotator cuff tear
	13	74	Sprained middle finger
Nathan,Joe	10	182	TJS - R. elbow
	11	31	Strained R. flexor muscle
Neshek,Pat	10	37	Inflamed R. middle finger
Nicasio,Juan	11	54	Neck surgery
	12	123	Strained L. knee
Niemann,Jeff	10	21	Strained R. shoulder
	11	45	Stiff back
	12	109	Fractured R. fibula
	13	183	Rt. shoulder surgery
Niese,Jon	10	19	Strained R. hamstring
	11	36	Intercostal strain of the R. side
	13	51	Partially torn Lt. rotator cuff
	14	30	Strained Lt. shoulder/Lt. elbow inflam
Nolasco,Ricky	10	35	Torn meniscus – R. knee
	14	38	Strained Rt. elbow
Norberto,Jordan	12	68	Str + tendinitis in L. shoulder
Norris,Bud	10	35	Biceps tendinitis – R. shoulder
	12	16	L. knee sprain
	14	11	Strained Rt. groin
Nova,Ivan	12	17	Inflam in R. rotator cuff
	13	27	Rt. triceps inflammation
	14	162	Torn UCL Rt. elbow
Nuno,Vidal	13	23	Strained Lt. groin
O Flaherty,Eric	14	95	Recovering from Tommy John surgery
O'Day,Darren	11	85	Torn labrm R. hip+Inflam R. should.
O'Flaherty,Eric	10	41	Viral infection
	13	135	Lt. elbow surgery
Ogando,Alexi	12	35	Strained R. groin
	13	87	Rt. shoulder inflam x 2; Rt. biceps
	14	117	Rt. elbow inflammation

FIVE-YEAR INJURY LOG

Pitchers	Yr	Days	Injury
Ohlendorf, Ross	10	68	Strained R. lat; sore back
	11	136	R. shoulder strain
	13	20	Rt. shoulder inflammation
	14	184	Sprained Rt. lumbar
Okajima, Hideki	10	22	Strained R. hamstring
Oliver, Darren	13	22	Lt. shoulder strain
Olsen, Scott	10	68	Tightness L. shoulder
	11	182	L. shoulder Inflam
Ondrusek, Logan	11	18	Strained R. forearm
	14	27	Strained Rt. shoulder
Ortiz, Joseph	14	128	Fractured Lt. foot
Ortiz, Ramon	13	119	Rt. elbow strain
Oswalt, Roy	11	63	Lower back Inflam
	13	60	Strained Lt. hamstring
Outman, Josh	10	182	Recov. fr. surg. - L. elbow
	12	37	Strained oblique
Oviedo, Juan	12	73	TJS
	13	183	Recovery from Rt. elbow surgery
	14	22	Recovering from Tommy John surgery
Owings, Micah	12	161	R. elbow surgery
Padilla, Vicente	10	75	Sore R. foreram; herniated disc
	11	161	R. elbow surgery
	12	15	Strained R. bicep
Parker, Blake	12	112	R. elbow stress react+bone bruise
Parker, Jarrod	14	184	Recovering from Tommy John surgery
Parnell, Bobby	11	40	Circulatory issues R. middle finger
	13	61	Neck stiffness
	14	180	Torn MCL in Rt. elbow
Parra, Manny	11	183	Facet joint injury in R. back
	13	30	Strained Lt. pectoral muscle
Patton, Troy	12	39	Sprained R. ankle
	14	80	Sore Lt. shoulder
Paulino, Felipe	10	83	R. shoulder tendinitis
	12	149	TJS - L. elbow
	13	183	Recovery from Rt. elbow surgery
	14	163	Rt. rotator cuff inflammation
Paxton, James	14	115	Strained Lt. lat in back
Peavy, Jake	10	88	Detached lat in R. shoulder
	11	57	Recov.,R. should, Str adductor
	13	44	Fractured rib
Pelfrey, Mike	12	165	TJS
	13	15	Back strain
	14	149	Strained Lt. groin
Pena, Tony	11	124	Tendinitis In R. elbow
Peralta, Joel	14	16	Illness
Perez, Chris	13	31	Rt. shoulder soreness
	14	28	Bone spurs in Rt. ankle
Perez, Juan	13	51	Torn UCL ligament, Lt. elbow
Perez, Luis	12	87	TJS - L. elbow
	13	155	Recovery from Lt. elbow surgery
Perez, Martin	13	43	Cracked ulna bone, Lt. forearm
	14	141	Lt. elbow inflammation
Perez, Rafael	12	161	Strained L. lat/ankle injury
Perkins, Glen	11	26	Strained R. oblique muscle
	14	10	Strained Lt. Forearm

FIVE-YEAR INJURY LOG

Pitchers	Yr	Days	Injury
Perry, Ryan	10	26	Tendinitis upper R. biceps
	11	15	Infected eye
Pestano, Vinnie	13	16	Rt. elbow tendinitis
Pettibone, Jonathan	13	63	Strained Rt. shoulder
Pettitte, Andy	12	83	Fractured fibula in L. ankle
	13	17	Strained Lt. trapezius muscle
Phelps, David	13	71	Rt. forearm strain
	14	56	Rt. elbow inflammation/tendinitis
Pimentel, Stolmy	14	56	Sprained R ankle/ R shoulder inflam
Pineda, Michael	12	182	Surgery torn labrum R. shoulder
	13	98	Recovery from Rt. shoulder surgery
	14	99	Strained muscle in Rt. shoulder
Pomeranz, Drew	13	45	Lt. bicep tendinitis
	14	26	Fractured Rt. hand
Pomeranz, Stuart	12	131	Strained L. oblique
Price, David	13	47	Lt. triceps strain
Pryor, Stephen	13	168	Torn Rt. lat muscle
	14	19	Surgery torn lat muscle Rt. shoulder
Purcey, David	10	19	Strained ligaments – R. foot
Purke, Matt	14	66	Recovering from Tommy John surgery
Putkonen, Luke	14	161	Rt. elbow inflammation
Putnam, Zach	13	110	Rt. elbow soreness
	14	15	Rt. shoulder inflammation
Putz, J.J.	10	15	Tendinitis – R. knee
	11	27	R. elbow tendinitis
	13	75	Strnd Rt. elbow; dislocated finger
	14	35	Tightness in Rt. forearm
Qualls, Chad	12	15	Irritation of L. toe
Ramirez, Erasmo	12	62	Strained R. elbow flexor
Ramirez, Neil	14	12	Sore Rt. triceps
Ramirez, Ramon	12	24	Hamstring strain
Ramos, A.J.	14	17	Rt. shoulder inflammation
Rauch, Jon	11	33	Appendicitis; Torn caR.ilge R. knee
Ray, Chris	10	16	Strained R. ribcage muscle
	11	61	Strained R. shoulder
Resop, Chris	10	49	Strained L. oblique
Reyes, Jo-Jo	10	33	Strained R. knee
Reynolds, Greg	10	70	Bruised R. elbow
Reynolds, Matt	13	112	Strained Lt. elbow
	14	184	Recovering from Tommy John surgery
Rice, Scott	13	21	Sports hernia
Richard, Clayton	11	86	Strained L. shoulder
	13	122	Lt. shoulder surgery; stomach virus
Richards, Garrett	11	21	R. adductor strain
	14	39	Torn patellar tendon in Lt. knee
Richmond, Scott	10	78	Impingement - R. shoulder
Rivera, Mariano	12	153	Torn ACL in R. knee
Robertson, David	12	33	Strained L. oblique
	14	14	Strained Lt. groin
Robles, Maricio	11	74	Recov. fr. surg. - L. shoulder
Rodney, Fernando	11	39	Strained upper back
Rodriguez, Fernando	13	183	Rt. elbow surgery
	14	31	Recovering from Tommy John surgery
Rodriguez, Francisco	11	142	Inflam - R. shoulder
Rodriguez, Henry	11	28	R. arm injury
	12	91	Low back strain+ R. index finger

FIVE-YEAR INJURY LOG

Pitchers	Yr	Days	Injury
Rodriguez,Paco	14	55	Strained Lt. shoulder
Rodriguez,Wandy	11	21	Fluid in L. elbow
	13	116	Lt. forearm tightness
	14	24	Rt. knee inflammation
Rogers,Esmil	11	84	R. lat strain
Rogers,Mark	13	152	Rt. shoulder instability
Romero,J.C.	10	18	Recov. fr. surg. on L. elbow
	11	15	R. calf strain
Romo,Sergio	11	18	R. elbow Inflam
Rondon,Bruce	14	184	Surgery on Rt. elbow
Rosario,Sandy	12	110	R. quad strain
Ross,Robbie	12	20	Sore L. forearm
Ross,Tyson	11	66	Strained L. oblique muscle
	13	17	Lt. shoulder subluxation
Rosscup,Zachary	14	31	Sore Lt. shoulder
Runzler,Dan	10	54	Dislocated L. knee
	12	153	Strained lat muscle
Ryu,Hyun-Jin	14	35	Strained Rt. hip/Lt. shoulder inflam
Rzepczynski,Marc	10	45	Fractured middle finger - L. hand
Sabathia,C.C.	12	15	Sore L. elbow+ strain abductor
	13	5	Strained Lt. hamstring
	14	141	Fluid in Rt. knee
Saito,Takashi	10	18	L. hamstring strain
	11	88	L. hamstring strain
	12	126	Strained L. hamstring+ calf str
Salas,Fernando	13	36	Rt. shoulder irritation
	14	21	Rt. shoulder inflammation
Sale,Chris	14	30	Strained flexor muscle in Rt. elbow
Sanabia,Alex	13	126	Rt. groin discomfort
Sanches,Brian	10	22	Strained R. hamstring
	11	26	R. elbow strain
Sanchez,Anibal	13	20	Strained Rt. shoulder
	14	66	Strnd Rt. pectoral muscle;cut Rt finger
Sanchez,Eduardo	11	92	R. shoulder strain
Sanchez,Jonathan	11	80	L. biceps tendinitis
	12	61	L. bicep tendinitis
	12	36	Tendinitis in L. bicep
Sanit,Amauri	11	110	Inflam - R. elbow
Santana,Johan	11	182	L. sholder surgery
	12	70	Inflam of lower back+ spr R. ankle
	13	183	Lt. shoulder surgery
	14	119	Rec from surgery on Lt. shoulder
Santos,Sergio	12	166	Surgery torn labrum in R. shoulder
	13	109	Rt. triceps strain
	14	34	Strained Rt. elbow/forearm
Saunders,Joe	12	15	L. shoulder strain
	14	51	Bruised Lt. ankle
Savery,Joe	13	45	Lt. elbow stiffness
Scheppers,Tanner	14	158	Rt. elbow inflammation x2
Schlereth,Daniel	12	166	Tendinitis in L. shoulder
Schlitter,Brian	14	14	Rt. shoulder inflammation
Schugel,Andrew	14	111	Rt. hamstring injury
Schumaker,Skip	14	43	Concussion/dislocated Lt. shoulder
Schwimer,Michael	13	39	Rt. shoulder strain
Scribner,Evan	11	27	R. shoulder strain

FIVE-YEAR INJURY LOG

Pitchers	Yr	Days	Injury
Septimo,Leyson	12	18	Inflam in L. biceps
	13	72	Lt. shoulder strain
Sheets,Ben	12	25	R. shoulder Inflam
Sherrill,George	10	15	Back tightness
	11	30	L. elbow Inflam
	12	177	TJS - L. elbow
Shoemaker, Matt	14	13	Strained Lt oblique
Siegrist,Kevin	14	60	Strained Lt. forearm
Simmons,Shae	14	62	Strained Rt. shoulder
Simon,Alfredo	10	21	Strained L. hamstring
	11	16	Strained R. hamstring
Skaggs,Tyler	14	81	Strained Lt. forearm; Rt hammy
Slaten,Doug	11	89	L. elbow ulnar neuritis
Slowey,Kevin	10	15	Strained R. triceps
	11	94	Sore R. biceps; Abdominal strain
	13	66	Rt. forearm discomfort
Smith,Joe	11	15	Abdominal strain
Smith,Jordan	12	182	Sore R. elbow
Smyly,Drew	12	37	Strain R. intercostal+ fing. blister
Sonnanstine,Andy	10	16	Strained L. hamstring
Soria,Joakim	12	182	Recovering from TJS
	13	99	Recovery from Rt. elbow surgery
	14	50	Strained Lt. oblique
Soriano,Rafael	11	76	Inflam - R. elbow
Stauffer,Tim	10	52	Appendectomy
	12	182	R. elbow sprain
Stetter,Mitch	11	137	L. hip injury
Storen,Drew	12	106	Elbow injury
Strasburg,Stephen	10	61	Stiff R. shoulder; TJS surgery 9/10
	11	160	Recovery from TJS
	13	15	Strained Rt. latissimus dorsi
Street,Huston	10	79	Strained R. shoulder
	11	17	R. triceps strain
	12	72	Strained L. calf+ L. lat str
	13	15	Strained Lt. calf
Strop,Pedro	13	15	Lower back strain
	14	23	Strained Lt. groin
Stults,Eric	12	48	Strained L. latissimus dorsi
Stutes,Michael	12	26	R. shoulder Inflam
	13	89	Rt. biceps tendinitis
Surkamp,Eric	12	182	TJS
	13	88	Recovery from Lt. elbow surgery
Swarzak,Anthony	12	33	Strained R. rotator cuff
	13	7	Fractured ribs
Talbot,Mitch	10	15	Strained back
	11	125	Strain R. elbow; Strain lower back
	11	56	Strained R. intercostal muscle
Tanaka,Masahiro	14	74	Rt. elbow inflammation
Taylor,Andrew	13	183	Lt. labrum tear
Tazawa,Junichi	10	182	TJS out for 2010
	11	88	Recovery from TJS
Teaford,Everett	12	25	Strained lower abdominal
Tejeda,Robinson	10	30	Tendinitis – R. biceps
	11	36	Inflam - R. shoulder
Tepesch,Nicholas	13	57	Rt. elbow inflammation
Texeira,Kanekoa	10	27	Strained R. elbow

FIVE-YEAR INJURY LOG

Pitchers	Yr	Days	Injury
Thatcher,Joe	10	18	Strained L. shoulder
	11	125	L. shoulder surgery
	12	37	Mid-back strain
	14	57	Sprained Lt. ankle
Thompson,Rich	10	20	Inflam – R. shoulder
Thornburg,Tyler	14	114	Sore Rt. elbow
Thornton,Matt	10	16	Inflam L. forearm
	13	20	Strained Rt. oblique
Tillman,Chris	13	5	Strained Lt. abdominal
Tobin,Mason	11	162	TJS
Tolleson,Shawn	13	170	Strained lower back
Tomlin,Josh	11	35	Soreness in R. elbow
	12	72	Inflam in R. elbow+R. wrist
	13	146	Recovery from Rt. elbow surgery
Troncoso,Ramon	13	21	Pericarditis
Turner,Jacob	14	24	Strained Rt. shoulder
Uehara,Koji	10	70	Strained L. hammy; R. elbow
	12	77	Strained R. lat
Valdes,Raul	12	62	Torn meniscus R. knee+Str R. hip
Vargas,Jason	13	56	Blood clot, Lt. arm
	14	23	Appendectomy
Venters,Jonny	12	16	L. elbow impingement
	13	183	Sprained Lt. elbow
	14	184	Recovering from Tommy John surgery
Veras,Jose	14	18	Strained Lt. oblique
VerHagen,Drew	14	28	Stress reaction in spine
Villanueva,Carlos	11	27	Strained R. forearm
Vincent,Nick	14	34	Rt. shoulder fatigue
Vizcaino,Arodys	12	183	TJS
	13	183	Recovery from Rt. elbow surgery
Vogelsong,Ryan	12	10	Strained lower back
	13	80	Fractured Rt. hand
Volquez,Edinson	10	104	Recovery from TJS 8/09
Wacha,Michael	14	74	Stress reaction in Rt. shoulder
Wada,Tsuyoshi	12	182	TJS - R. elbow
	13	74	Recovery from Lt. elbow surgery
Wade,Cory	10	88	Surg.-frayed labrum, R/C
Wainwright,Adam	11	182	TJS
Walden,Jordan	12	41	Strained R. bicep
	13	17	Rt. shoulder inflammation
	14	30	Strained Lt. hamstring
Walker,Taijuan	14	73	Rt. shoulder impingement
Walters,PJ	12	79	Inflam in R. shoulder
Wang,Chien-Ming	10	182	Recov. fr. surg. - R. shoulder
	11	121	Recovery from R. shoulder surgery
	12	113	Strained L. hamstring+R. hip str
Wang,Wei-Chung	14	53	Tightness in Lt. shoulder
Weaver,Jered	12	22	Strained lower back
	13	51	Fractured Lt. elbow
Webb,Brandon	10	182	Recovery from 8/09 shoulder surg.
	11	183	Recov. fr. surg. - R. shoulder
Webb,Ryan	11	51	R. shoulder Inflam
Weiland,Kyle	12	162	R. shoulder bursitis
Wells,Randy	11	50	R. forearm strain
Westbrook,Jake	13	51	Sore back; Rt. elbow inflammation
Wheeler,Dan	11	15	Strained L. calf

FIVE-YEAR INJURY LOG

Pitchers	Yr	Days	Injury
White,Alex	11	94	Soreness in R. middle finger
	13	184	Rt. elbow strain
	14	63	Recovering from Tommy John surgery
Wieland,Joe	12	150	TJS
	13	183	Recovery from Rt. elbow surgery
	14	141	Recovering from Tommy John surgery
Williams,Jerome	12	35	Respir. infection+str L. hamstring
Wilson,Alex	13	83	Sprained Rt. thumb
Wilson,Brian	11	35	L. oblique strain
	12	174	TJS
	13	20	Recovery from Rt. elbow surgery
	14	15	Nerve imflammation in Rt. elbow
Wilson,C.J.	14	23	Sprained Rt. ankle
Withrow,Chris	12	32	R. shoulder strain
	14	127	Tommy John surgery
Wojciechowski,Ashe	14	87	Strained Rt. lat muscle
Wolf,Randy	12	11	TJS 10/2012
Wood,Blake	12	182	TJS - R. elbow
	13	103	Recovery from Rt. elbow surgery
Wood,Kerry	10	52	Strained back; R. index finger
	11	22	Blister on R. index finger
	12	19	R. shoulder fatigue
Wood,Tim	13	150	Rt. rotator cuff strain
Worley,Vance	12	54	Loose bodies in R. elbow+ Inflam
Wright,Steven	14	70	Recovering from surgery sports hernia
Wuertz,Michael	10	29	Tendinitis - R. shoulder
	11	53	Strain L. hammy; Tndnts R. thumb
Young,Chris	10	164	Inflam - R. shoulder
	11	165	R. biceps tendinitis
	13	18	Strained Lt. quad
Zambrano,Carlos	11	15	Lower back soreness
Zeid,Josh	14	64	Surgery Lt. foot bilateral sesamoiditis
Zimmermann,Jord.	10	119	Recovery from TJS
Zito,Barry	11	110	R. foot sprain
Zumaya,Joel	10	96	Fract. olecranon process-R. elbow
	11	183	Recov. fr. surg. - R. elbow
	12	173	Recovery from TJS

Top 75 Impact Prospects for 2015

by Rob Gordon and Jeremy Deloney

Looking for a rookie infusion in 2015? Here's the place to start. The following is a list of prospects most likely to contribute and have an impact in the 2015 season. These capsules provide a primer on the strengths and weaknesses of rookie-eligible players, and are ranked in an attempt to balance both raw skill and likelihood of 2015 playing time.

For additional information, including profiles of over 1000 minor-leaguers, statistics, and our overall HQ100 top prospect list, see our sister publication, the *2015 Minor League Baseball Analyst*—as well as the weekly reports on BasebalHQ.com. Happy prospecting!

1. **Kris Bryant (3B, CHC)** established himself as the top offensive prospect in baseball in his first full season as a professional. The 22-year-old torched pitchers at AA/AAA to the tune of .325/.438/.661 with 34 doubles and a minor league leading 43 home runs. The Cubs opted not to give Bryant a September call-up, but he should contend for the starting 3B job in 2015 and has tremendous long-term potential.

2. **Jorge Soler (OF, CHC)** missed more than half of the minor league season with a variety of ailments including a chronic hamstring injury, but he made up for lost time by hitting .340/.432/.707 in 200 minor league AB with excellent plate discipline. Soler played well in his MLB debut and enters spring training with a starting role.

3. **Aaron Sanchez (RHP, TOR)** is one of the Blue Jays best prospects as a starting pitcher, but was moved to the bullpen upon his promotion to the big leagues. He held major league batters to a .128 oppBA in 33 innings with Toronto while also racking up three saves and a 1.09 ERA. He has more value as a starter, but his success as a reliever cannot be ignored.

4. **Archie Bradley (RHP, ARI)** got off to a slow start at Triple-A and was then sidelined for two months with an elbow injury. He was slightly better when he returned to action, but for the year put up fairly pedestrian numbers: 3-7 with a 4.45 ERA. Struggles with control continue to be the primary culprit, but Bradley's raw stuff is too good for him not to have success in 2015.

5. **Dylan Bundy (RHP, BAL)** was somewhat forgotten after missing the entire 2013 season due to Tommy John surgery. He appeared in the majors as a 19-year-old in 2012 and all he needs is to log innings. He pitched 41 innings between short-season and High-A in 2014 and should eventually work his way back to the majors and regain his top prospect status.

6. **Noah Syndergaard (RHP, NYM)** put up surprisingly pedestrian numbers in his first full year at Triple-A, going 9-7 with a 4.60 ERA. Don't read too much into those year-end numbers as his raw stuff remains elite. Syndergaard walked just 43 while striking out 145 in 133 IP and he was unlucky with a .378 BABIP and a 62% strand rate. Look for better results in 2015.

7. **Alex Guerrero (2B, LA)** had an interesting pro debut. A pulled muscle and an ear-biting incident limited him to just 285 AB, and he was stuck in the minors as he watched Dee Gordon establish himself as an All-Star. On the year, Guerrero hit .333/.373/.621 with 19 doubles and 17 home runs. At some point, Guerrero's bat will force the Dodgers to give him playing time, and he has the skills to succeed.

8. **Francisco Lindor (SS, CLE)** has an outside chance at winning the Indians starting shortstop job in spring training after posting respectable numbers between Double-A and Triple-A in 2014. He smashed a career-high 11 HR while featuring his polished all-around game. He can hit, run, and field equally well, and should be a cornerstone player for years to come.

9. **Andrew Heaney (LHP, MIA)** has established himself as the top left-handed pitching prospect in the minors. The 23-year-old has excellent raw stuff that includes a plus mid-90s fastball, a slider, and a good change-up. He locates all three offerings and has some nice deception to keep hitters off-balance. He should be given a chance to win a starting role this spring.

10. **Joc Pederson (OF, LA)** became the first player to put up a 30 HR/30 SB season in the PCL since 1934. He has an exciting package of tools (for the year, hit .303/.435/.582 with 33 HR). Peterson also walked 100 times and plays an above-average centerfield. The current Dodgers OF is crowded, but he appears to be ready for the MLB challenge.

11. **Maikel Franco (3B, PHI)** got off to a slow start at Triple-A Lehigh Valley, but don't be fooled by his year-end slash line (.257/.299/.428). He heated up in the second half, hitting .309/.326/.521 after the break. Franco still whiffs too much and needs to improve on defense, but he has plus raw power and if Ryan Howard continues to struggle, Franco could see action at both corner spots.

12. **Jameson Taillon (RHP, PIT)** missed all of 2014 with Tommy John surgery, but resumed throwing from 75 feet in October. Prior to the injury, Taillon sat in the mid-to-upper 90s with his fastball, a power curve, and a solid change-up. Control is often the last thing to return to form after TJS, but Taillon has the tools to be a #1 starter and has sleeper potential in 2015.

13. **Carlos Rodon (RHP, CHW)** was the third overall pick in the 2014 draft and there was speculation he'd start a game or two with the White Sox at the end of the year. That didn't happen, but there is a very strong chance he'll do so in 2015. With a solid-average fastball and a knockout slider, he can retire batters at any level.

14. **Daniel Norris (LHP, TOR)** pitched on four levels in 2014, including 6 innings with the Blue Jays at the end of the season. He is a strikeout machine who could make a large impact in the starting rotation or bullpen in 2015. He underwent minor elbow surgery in October, but should be ready to make a strong case for a roster spot in spring training.

15. **Taijuan Walker (RHP, SEA)** was limited by shoulder issues throughout most of the first half of 2014 and only pitched 120

innings between four levels of baseball. He looked quite solid with the Mariners, and has the pitch mix, demeanor, and pitchability to be a rotation stud. If he can stay healthy, his upside is as high as any pitching prospect in baseball.

16. Joey Gallo (3B, TEX) crushed 42 HR between High-A and Double-A and his natural, plus-plus power will play anywhere. There are questions about his BA potential as he swings and misses frequently, but his pop is unmatched in the minors. He will draw walks to get on base and his glove, though not polished, is good enough to play at either 3B or 1B.

17. Marco Gonzales (LHP, STL) is a polished, athletic lefty who comes right after hitters with a low-90s fastball, good breaking ball, and a plus change-up. Gonzales held his own when moved up to Triple-A Memphis, going 4-1 with a 3.35 ERA and 9 BB/39 K in 45.2 IP. Gonzales got valuable post-season experience and should get first dibs on any opening in the rotation.

18. Alex Meyer (RHP, MIN) was targeted to reach the majors in 2014 after showcasing his plus arm and dominance in Triple-A, but shoulder inflammation in late August derailed those plans. He has improved his delivery, though still needs to clean up his control in order to be counted on as a #2-type starter. He'll be 25 at the start of the year and should get a long look in spring training.

19. Jose Berrios (RHP, MIN) has arguably the best natural stuff in the Twins system thanks to three above-average to plus offerings. He was dynamite in High-A, posting a 1.96 ERA, 2.2 Ctl, and 10.2 Dom across 16 starts before a promotion to Double-A. He wasn't quite as dominant at that level, but he is tough to make hard contact against and will only be 20 to start 2015.

20. Anthony Ranaudo (RHP, BOS) is one of many Red Sox prospects who will get a long look in the spring. He earned seven starts with Boston after duplicating his success from 2012 with a strong campaign at Triple-A Pawtucket. There are questions about his ability to miss bats at upper levels, but he knows how to pitch and induce weak contact.

21. Jake Lamb (3B, ARI) had a huge breakout season at Double-A Mobile, hitting .318 with 35 doubles and 14 home runs, but looked overmatched in 104 MLB AB. Lamb handled LHP surprisingly well and has always been a solid defender with a plus arm. Lamb's solid glove with likely give him a good chance to win the starting 3B job in Arizona in 2015, but don't expect monster power numbers.

22. Randal Grichuk (OF, STL) continues to be an intriguing prospect. The 23-year-old CF has well above-average power and hit 25 home runs in 436 Triple-A AB, but just 3 in 110 AB with the Cardinals. His aggressive approach at the plate (28 BB/108 K) continues to limit his BA, and he will be in the Cardinals OF mix in 2015.

23. Henry Owens (LHP, BOS) will likely not break camp with the Red Sox in 2015, though he's a strong bet to pitch meaningful innings later in the year. He was the Double-A Eastern League pitcher of the year in 2014 after posting a 2.60 ERA, 3.5 Ctl, and

9.4 Dom in 20 starts. Hitters have a hard time squaring up against the tall lefty as his offerings exhibit plus movement and break.

24. Rafael Montero (RHP, NYM) held his own in his MLB debut, going 1-3 with a 4.06 ERA in 44.1 IP. Montero has some of the best control in the minors and has an advanced feel for pitching that allows his average stuff to play up. The 23-year-old righty should get a chance to win a rotation spot in NY in the spring.

25. Rymer Liriano (OF, SD) had a nice bounce-back season after missing all of 2013 following Tommy John surgery. The 23-year-old OF hit .291 with 31 doubles and 14 home runs in the minors. He struggled to adjust to major league pitching, hitting just .220 in 109 AB with the Padres. Long-term, he had good raw power and should see plenty of action in SD in 2015.

26. Jonathan Gray (RHP, COL) has yet to have the type of breakout season you would expect from the 3rd overall pick in the 2013 draft. In 24 Double-A starts, Gray was 10-5 with a 3.91 ERA. He's shown good command and still has an upper-90s heater, but his change and slider need refinement. The Rockies lack of quality big-league pitching makes an MLB debut likely in 2015, but Gray could be a boom or bust pick.

27. Trevor May (RHP, MIN) has some control issues, but has the ability to miss bats with his power repertoire. He didn't fare very well in nine starts with the Twins in 2014, though he did strike out nearly a batter per inning. The 25-year-old had his best season since 2010, and has a solid chance to be in the starting rotation to begin the year.

28. Matt Barnes (RHP, BOS) has been a steady and consistent performer since signing as a first round pick in 2011. He wasn't as dominant as hoped in Triple-A in 2014, but he continues to exhibit good fastball command and low walk rates. A flyball tendency could hurt him, but he knows how to pitch and has plenty of durability.

29. Robbie Ray (LHP, DET) was obtained from the Nationals in the curious Doug Fister trade in December 2013, and started six games with the Tigers later in 2014. He was knocked around in a few of those appearances, and could use some more innings at Triple-A. At his best, he uses his athletic delivery to pepper the strike zone with quality pitches.

30. Michael Taylor (OF, WAS) had an impressive breakout season, hitting .313 with 17 doubles, 22 home runs, and 34 SB in 384 Double-A AB. The 23-year-old OF got into 17 games with the Nationals, but looked a bit overmatched. But with the right opportunity, Taylor has the potential to be a 20/20 player.

31. Aaron Nola (RHP, PHI) continues to excel despite his relatively small stature. At 6-1, 195, Nola has a good 92-94 mph fastball that he commands to both sides of the plate. He also mixes in an average slider and change-up. The 7th overall pick in the draft fared well at two different levels, going 4-3 with a 2.93 ERA and 10 BB/45 K in 55.1 IP. The Phillies rotation was a mess, in 2014 so Nola could get a shot as early as spring training.

32. Edwin Escobar (LHP, BOS) was relatively unheralded entering the season despite being a top prospect in the Giants organization. The Red Sox acquired him in July 2014 and he pitched well late in the year. He could use more seasoning, but exhibits plenty of durability to go along with his three solid to above average pitches.

33. Blake Swihart (C, BOS) has shown steady improvement each season as a pro and his offensive breakout resulted in a late season promotion to Triple-A. He hit .300 with 12 HR in Double-A and he makes excellent contact. Continued progression behind the plate makes him a very viable option for Boston at some point in 2015, with a possibility of him winning the starting job outright.

34. Addison Russell (SS, CHC) continues to establish himself as one of the best all-around prospects in baseball. The 20-year-old SS came over to the Cubs as part of the Jeff Samardzjia trade. Russell is an above-average defender with good power, nice speed, and an advanced approach at the plate. On the year, Russell hit .295/.350/.508, and the Cubs need to figure out how to get him into their lineup at some point in 2015.

35. Byron Buxton (OF, MIN) missed the majority of the season after a variety of injuries, including a broken finger in the Arizona Fall League. His 2013 campaign between Low-A and High-A elevated him to the top of prospect lists and his plus tools remain despite the missed time. The Twins could use a jolt of excitement, and it might behoove them to insert him in CF during the year.

36. Stephen Piscotty (OF, STL) lacks the flash, but is the kind of player that the Cardinals love and have had success with in the past. Piscotty works hard and gets the most out of his tools. He has moderate power, hits for average, and has an advanced approach at the plate. He spent all of 2014 at Triple-A, but will still have a tough time breaking into the Cardinals starting lineup in 2015.

37. Domingo Santana (OF, HOU) had about as poor a major league debut as one could have—0-17 with 14 strikeouts—but his tools and offensive production trump the small sample size. He has the natural strength to be a middle-of-the-order producer with plenty of pop from the right side. He will always swing and miss due to his long arms, but he fits the ideal RF prototype.

38. Rusney Castillo (OF, BOS) was a high-profile signing from Cuba in August 2014, and he eventually earned 36 AB with the Red Sox in September, batting .333/.400/.528 with 2 HR. Given his ability to play CF, he has a terrific shot to be a starter at the beginning of 2015. He possesses good power and speed and makes excellent contact.

39. Cory Spangenberg (2B, SD) gets the most from his somewhat limited skill set. He has a nice compact stroke, and hit .331 in 281 Double-A AB. Spangenberg is a solid defender, and can play 2B, 3B, and the OF. He held his own in 62 AB with the Padres, and should contend for a starting role in 2015.

40. Nick Kingham (RHP, PIT) continues to make steady progress and profiles as a solid back-end starter. He features a good low-90s fastball, a power curve, a good change-up, and throws plenty of strikes. He'll have to wait for an opening in the Pirates rotation, but could be a decent NL-only endgame option.

41. Mike Foltynewicz (RHP, HOU) did not have the best campaign in Triple-A in 2014, but he still possesses one of the best fastballs in baseball. There is work to be done with his command and control, but he is capable of that. He is at his best when he sits in the mid-90s, adds some movement, and complements the heater with two above-average breaking balls.

42. Kevin Plawecki (C, NYM) had another solid season at the plate, hitting .309 with 24 doubles and a career-high 11 home runs. Plawecki's hit tool is his best asset, and he now owns a career minor league average of .295 with an Eye of 0.78. Defensively he is below-average, but his bat could propel him into the playing time picture in 2015.

43. Miguel Sano (3B, MIN) sat out the entire season after undergoing Tommy John surgery in March. The Twins decided not to give him game action at the end of the campaign, but he remains a premium prospect capable of hitting 30-40 HR on an annual basis. Given his offensive firepower, he could provide production at midseason 2015.

44. D.J. Peterson (3B, SEA) put on a power display in the hitter-friendly environment at High-A High Desert, but continued to showcase his well above-average pop upon a promotion to Double-A. He finished with a combined 31 doubles and 31 HR in 495 AB. Though his swing can get long at times, look for him to make an impact at either 3B or 1B for the Mariners in 2015.

45. Carlos Correa (SS, HOU) was enjoying another terrific season before he underwent surgery in late June to repair a fractured ankle. There are no concerns about his recovery or lasting effects. The 20-year-old has the tools and intangibles to be a superstar, and it won't be long until he makes his presence felt in the middle of the Astros infield.

46. Tim Cooney (RHP, STL) has some of the best control in the minors. He's walked just 77 batters in 368 minor league innings and has as K/BB ratio of 4.0. The 23-year-old Cooney has a good low-90s heater, a curve, and above-average change-up. Cooney is a solid rotation option in 2015 if Marco Gonzalez proves not ready.

47. Eddie Butler (RHP, COL) took a step back in 2014, underwhelming in the minors and then looking over-matched in three starts with the Rockies (1-1 with a 6.75 ERA). Butler's dominance has declined steadily since mid-2013, and the 23-year-old hurler whiffed just 5.3 per nine at Double-A. Shoulder soreness caused him to pull out of the Arizona Fall League, and he will need to prove he is healthy and miss more bats in 2015.

48. Luis Sardinas (SS, TEX) was up and down with the Rangers in 2014, and he may be on the same shuttle for 2015. Though Texas has a nice variety of middle infielders, the 21-year-old has nifty defensive skills along with above-average speed. He won't provide much power—he only has 5 career HR—but he is a solid switch-hitter with BA potential.

49. C.J. Edwards (RHP, CHC) missed more than three months of action with a shoulder injury. He avoided surgery and looked fine in six August starts (0-2, with a 2.30 ERA). Edwards is the Cubs best and most advanced pitching prospect, featuring a mid-90s fastball. He still needs to refine his secondary offerings, and the shoulder injury has slowed his development. The Cubs continue to improve, and Edwards will be a critical piece if they are going to be competitive in 2015.

50. A.J. Cole (RHP, WAS) had another solid season of growth, going 13-3 with a 3.16 ERA while splitting time between Double- and Triple-A. The 23-year-old right-hander has solid above-average offerings and has a career K/BB ratio of 4.2. The pitching-rich Nationals could use Cole in relief in 2015 before moving him into the starting rotation.

51. Chris Reed (LHP, LA) had another up and down season in 2014, going 4-8 with a 3.22 ERA at Double-A, but getting crushed when he moved up to Triple-A—0-3 with a 10.97 ERA in five starts. Reed has solid stuff including a mid-90s sinking fastball, but his secondary stuff remains below average, and he doesn't miss many bats. The back end of the Dodgers rotation was in shambles by the end of season, so Reed could be called upon in 2015.

52. Matt Wisler (RHP, SD) got off to a quick start at Double-A San Antonio, going 1-0 with a 2.10 ERA in 6 starts, earning him an early promotion to Triple-A El Paso. Wisler was bit by the long ball in the PCL, giving up 19 home runs in 116.2 IP en route to a 5.10 ERA. The gopheritis should be correctable, as his best offering is a plus 92-94 mph sinker, and he had given only 11 home runs in his three previous seasons as a pro. Wisler has solid command and is an attractive option pitching in PETCO.

53. Jorge Alfaro (C, TEX) is mostly known for his bat, though has shown some improvement behind the plate and has a cannon arm. He's also seen some action at 1B. His plus natural strength and bat speed lead to well above average-raw power, and he runs fairly well. The Rangers need him to develop with the glove, and if he does, he should be in the lineup soon.

54. Kyle Crick (RHP, SF) has one of the best fastballs in the minors, hitting 98 mph when working in relief. Crick mixes in an above-average curve and a decent change-up, and has a career Dom rate of 11.1. Unfortunately Crick also struggles to find the strike zone consistently, and walked 6.1 per nine in 2015. The Giants don't need him in the rotation right away, and they have a good track record of bringing strong-armed hurlers to the majors to work in relief.

55. Brandon Nimmo (OF, NYM) had his best season as a pro, hitting .278 with 21 doubles, 9 home runs, and 14 SB. The 13th overall pick in 2011 has been slow to develop and struggled when moved up to Double-A (.238 in 240 AB). But the Mets desperately need his bat and all-around athleticism, and could let him learn on the job in 2015.

56. Kyle Zimmer (RHP, KC) did not pitch until September due to a strained lat muscle and general shoulder discomfort, and then left the Arizona Fall League and underwent minor shoulder surgery. His health is a wild card, but he has a clean delivery, plus fastball, and plus-plus slider. When healthy, he is still among the best pitching prospects in baseball.

57. Corey Seager (SS, LA) continues to emerge as an elite prospect. The strong, athletic SS mashed the ball at both Double and Triple-A, hitting .349/.402/.602 with 50 doubles and 20 home runs. At 6-4, 215, it is unlikely that Seager will stick at short over the long term, but his left-handed bat definitely plays at 3B or the OF. Seager would rank higher on this list if not for his limited exposure at Double-A.

58. Kyle Parker (OF, COL) took a step back in 2014, hitting .289 with 30 doubles and 15 home runs at Triple-A. He still has nice offensive potential, but was less selective at the plate, and the Rockies did not give him a ton of action once he was called up to the majors. Still, an injury or trade could create an opening, and Parker's power would play well in Coors Field.

59. Travis Shaw (1B, BOS) enjoyed his best pro season to date and is now on the cusp of reaching the big leagues. He hit a career-high 21 HR while batting .278/.353/.473 between Double-A and Triple-A. He also made good contact and improved his selectivity at the plate. The 24-year-old is relegated to 1B, though he might get a look in the outfield at some point.

60. Steven Moya (OF, DET) was the Double-A Eastern League's MVP after a breakout season that saw him hit .276/.306/.555 with 33 doubles and 35 HR. Sure, he strikes out a lot (161) and rarely draws walks (23), but his power is usable—and playable—at any level. The Tigers could use another left-handed power bat and he could get a shot in 2015.

61. Micah Johnson (2B, CHW) is all about speed and quickness and the top of a lineup. He missed time with a hamstring injury before being shut down in late August. He is a viable challenger to win the starting 2B job outright in spring training. Don't expect much power from the 24-year-old, but he improved enough with the glove to be reliable defensively.

62. Christian Bethancourt (C, ATL) made his MLB debut and logged 113 AB while filling in for the injured Evan Gattis. The 23-year-old backstop held his own, hitting .248/.300/.379. He is never going to provide the power that Gattis brings to the table, but he is an excellent defender and could force Gattis to the OF.

63. Clayton Blackburn (RHP, SF) doesn't have overpowering stuff, relying instead of changing speeds, keeping hitters off balance, and pinpoint control. Blackburn tops out at 92 mph with his fastball, but he has a plus four-pitch mix and a career ERA 2.98, a 1.05 WHIP, and a K/BB ratio of 5.3. While others have better stuff, Blackburn knows how to pitch and profiles as an excellent backend starter.

64. Luis Severino (RHP, NYY) had his breakout campaign in 2014 and pitched on three levels, topping out at Double-A. He was a standout at each level and was tough to make hard contact against. He'll turn 21 in February, and has the natural arm strength and advanced change-up to be effective in the big leagues very quickly.

65. Kyle Schwarber (C, CHC) had an impressive pro debut, hitting .344/.428/.634 at three different levels. The Cubs really want Schwarber to stick behind the plate, so the current plan is to start him back at High-A in the FSL, but if that experiment fails, his advanced bat could see him in the majors in the 2nd half of 2015. Schwarber slugged 18 home runs in just 262 AB and gives the Cubs another blue-chip prospect.

66. Eddie Rosario (2B/OF, MIN) missed the first 50 games of the season due to a "drug of abuse" suspension and didn't perform well upon his return. He is a natural hitter with some power potential and a selective eye at the plate. That wasn't apparent in 2014, as he only hit .237 with 8 HR in Double-A and struggled at CF and 2B. Nevertheless, he has valuable skills for a young team with a new regime.

67. Mark Appel (RHP, HOU) did not live up to the expectation of a number one overall pick from 2013, though reports out of the Arizona Fall League are much more optimistic. The size, velocity, and deep repertoire are all there. He just needs a little more polish before he fronts a major league rotation.

68. Brian Johnson (LHP, BOS) may not have a dominant fastball or a swing-and-miss secondary pitch, but he has outstanding command of a solid-average arsenal and can get hitters to bury the ball into the ground. The Red Sox have a plethora of options in the high minors, but the 24-year-old may be the safest bet to find success at the big league level, probably as a #4-5 starter.

69. James Ramsey (OF, CLE) was acquired by the Indians as part of the Justin Masterson trade in July. Ramsey doesn't have off-the-chart raw tools, but is above-average across the board. Ramsey hit .295/.382/.509 with 23 doubles and 16 home runs in 352 AB. The Indians could use a bit more pop in their OF and Ramsey could make the team as their 4th OF.

70. Eduardo Rodriguez (LHP, BOS) was acquired from the Orioles at the trade deadline and pitched much better in his new organization. He has increased his velocity over the last few years,

which has enhanced the potency of his slider and change-up. Still young at 21, he has the goods to pitch in the majors in 2015 and could be used in relief if needed.

71. Robert Stephenson (RHP, CIN) struggled in his first full season at Double-A, going 7-10 with a 4.74 ERA. Poor command was the primary culprit and the 21-year-old righty walked a career worst 4.9 per nine. On the positive side, he still whiffed 9.2 per nine and limited opposing hitters to a stingy .224 oppBAA in 136.2 innings. Long-term, Stephenson has some of the best raw stuff in the minors, so look for better results in 2015.

72. Robert Refsnyder (2B, NYY) has always been a good hitter, but the 2014 season was particularly fruitful. He slugged a career-high 14 HR while getting on base at a consistent clip and batting .318. If the Yankees still have a hole at 2B, it is entirely possible for the 23-year-old to win the starting job in spring training. The defense needs work, though the all-around game is enticing.

73. James McCann (C, DET) may be the in-house option for the Tigers if Alex Avila cannot overcome his recurring head injuries. He is a solid-average hitter for BA with a hint of power, though he doesn't profile as an offensive behemoth. Given his quality defensive ability, he should get enough playing time to warrant consideration in all fantasy formats.

74. Dalton Pompey (OF, TOR) was the breakout prospect of the year in a season which started in High-A and ended in the majors. He has the talent and work ethic to challenge for a starting outfield job. He is extremely fast and is starting to grow into his long, lean frame. There's plenty to work on, but there is also a lot to dream on as well.

75. Gary Sanchez (C, NYY) is a sturdy backstop with plus power potential and a knack for hitting (.270/.338/.406; 13 HR in 429 AB at Double-A in 2014). Still a pup at 21, his defense is a work in progress, and will determine his fantasy value. Sanchez has a big upside if he remains at catcher; less so if he's forced to move to 1B or become mainly a DH.

Top 75 Impact Prospects for 2015

The chart below lists projected Mayberry scores for the Top 75 Impact Prospects for 2015. Mayberry scores are explained in the Introduction, and here reflect 2015 only, not a player's long-term impact. Batters are dark shaded; pitchers are lighter shaded.

RANK/BATTER/POS, TM	POWER	SPEED	BATAVG	PT '15	RANK/BATTER/POS, TM	POWER	SPEED	BATAVG	PT '15
RANK/PITCHER/POS, TM	ERA	DOM	SAVES	PT '15	RANK/PITCHER/POS, TM	ERA	DOM	SAVES	PT '15
1 Kris Bryant (3B, CHC)	4	1	4	5	39 Cory Spangenberg (2B, SD)	1	2	3	3
2 Jorge Soler (OF, CHC)	3	1	3	5	40 Nick Kingham (RHP, PIT)	3	2	0	1
3 Aaron Sanchez (RHP, TOR)	3	4	0	3	41 Mike Foltynewicz (RHP, HOU)	2	3	0	1
4 Archie Bradley (RHP, ARI)	4	3	0	3	42 Kevin Plawecki (C, NYM)	1	1	3	1
5 Dylan Bundy (RHP, BAL)	3	4	0	3	43 Miguel Sano (3B, MIN)	3	1	2	1
6 Noah Syndergaard (RHP, NYM)	3	4	0	3	44 D.J. Peterson (3B, SEA)	2	1	3	1
7 Alex Guerrero (2B, LA)	3	1	3	3	45 Carlos Correa (SS, HOU)	1	3	3	1
8 Francisco Lindor (SS, CLE)	1	3	3	3	46 Tim Cooney (RHP, STL)	2	2	0	1
9 Andrew Heaney (LHP, MIA)	3	3	0	3	47 Eddie Butler (RHP, COL)	1	2	0	3
10 Joc Pederson (OF, LA)	3	3	3	3	48 Luis Sardinas (SS, TEX)	1	4	3	1
11 Maikel Franco (3B, PHI)	3	1	3	3	49 C.J. Edwards (RHP, CHC)	2	2	0	1
12 Jameson Taillon (RHP, PIT)	3	4	0	3	50 A.J. Cole (RHP, WAS)	2	3	0	1
13 Carlos Rodon (RHP, CHW)	2	3	0	3	51 Chris Reed (LHP, LA)	1	2	0	1
14 Daniel Norris (LHP, TOR)	3	3	0	3	52 Matt Wisler (RHP, SD)	3	1	0	1
15 Taijuan Walker (RHP, SEA)	4	3	0	3	53 Jorge Alfaro (C, TEX)	2	1	1	1
16 Joey Gallo (3B, TEX)	3	1	2	1	54 Kyle Crick (RHP, SF)	1	3	1	0
17 Marco Gonzales (LHP, STL)	3	2	0	3	55 Brandon Nimmo (OF, NYM)	2	2	1	1
18 Alex Meyer (RHP, MIN)	2	2	0	3	56 Kyle Zimmer (RHP, KC)	2	2	0	1
19 Jose Berrios (RHP, MIN)	2	2	0	3	57 Corey Seager (SS, LA)	2	3	3	1
20 Anthony Ranaudo (RHP, BOS)	2	2	0	1	58 Kyle Parker (OF, COL)	2	1	2	3
21 Jake Lamb (3B, ARI)	3	1	2	3	59 Travis Shaw (1B, BOS)	1	1	2	1
22 Randall Grichuk (OF, STL)	3	1	2	3	60 Steven Moya (OF, DET)	3	1	1	3
23 Henry Owens (LHP, BOS)	2	2	0	1	61 Micah Johnson (2B, CHW)	1	4	2	3
24 Rafael Montero (RHP, NYM)	3	2	1	0	62 Christian Bethancourt (C, ATL)	1	1	1	3
25 Rymer Liriano (OF, SD)	2	2	2	3	63 Clayton Blackburn (RHP, SF)	3	1	0	1
26 Jonathan Gray (RHP, COL)	2	3	0	1	64 Luis Severino (RHP, NYY)	1	2	0	1
27 Trevor May (RHP, MIN)	2	2	0	3	65 Kyle Schwarber (C, CHC)	3	1	3	1
28 Matt Barnes (RHP, BOS)	2	1	0	1	66 Eddie Rosario (2B, MIN)	1	2	2	1
29 Robbie Ray (LHP, DET)	2	1	0	3	67 Mark Appel (RHP, HOU)	2	2	0	1
30 Michael Taylor (OF, WAS)	3	3	2	1	68 Brian Johnson (LHP, BOS)	1	1	0	1
31 Aaron Nola (RHP, PHI)	3	2	0	3	69 James Ramsey (OF, CLE)	2	1	2	1
32 Edwin Escobar (LHP, BOS)	1	1	0	1	70 Eduardo Rodriguez (LHP, BOS)	1	1	0	1
33 Blake Swihart (C, BOS)	2	1	2	1	71 Robert Stephenson (RHP, CIN)	2	3	0	1
34 Addison Russell (SS, CHC)	2	2	3	3	72 Robert Refsnyder (2B, NYY)	1	2	2	3
35 Byron Buxton (OF, MIN)	1	3	3	1	73 James McCann (C, DET)	1	1	2	3
36 Stephen Piscotty (OF, STL)	2	2	3	1	74 Dalton Pompey (OF, TOR)	1	4	3	3
37 Domingo Santana (OF, HOU)	3	2	2	1	75 Gary Sanchez (C, NYY)	2	1	3	1
38 Rusney Castillo (OF, BOS)	2	2	2	3					

Top Japanese Players for 2015 and Beyond

by Tom Mulhall

Single-handedly, Masahiro Tanaka almost made 2014 as good a year for Japanese rookies as 2012. With the restrictive posting system possibly showing some cracks, consider stashing away more Japanese prospects if your league has a large reserve or farm roster. As usual, there is no sure ML-level hitting talent on the horizon, but there could easily be a dozen very capable pitchers now ready for MLB.

Yoshio Itoi (OF, Orix Buffaloes) is a good defender with decent BA and speed, somewhat similar to Aoki but with a little more power. Itoi is reminiscent of Kosuke Fukudome in that he doesn't do anything great but he does everything well. He has requested to be posted, but at age 34, his window of opportunity has probably closed. Itoi could be a capable fourth outfielder if he arrives sooner rather than later.
Possible ETA: 2015.

Tatayki Kajitani (OF, Yokohama DeNA Baystars) was an infielder who was moved to the outfield to improve his offense, and responded with 16 HR and 39 SB. Like Itoi, he is similar to Aoki with more power, and he could provide low double-digit HR and higher double digit SB. At age 27 and finishing his eight year as a professional, he is getting close to posting time. Kajitani is a better gamble than Itoi if the lefty can improve his middling BA.
Possible ETA: 2016.

Chihiro Kaneko (RHP, Orix Buffaloes) pushed himself into consideration as Japan's best starting pitcher with an extraordinary season in 2014. Kaneko finished this season with a league-low ERA of 1.98 with almost exactly one strikeout per inning. He is just one year away from international free agency, which is usually when a team will post a player. Kaneko is a notch below Darvish and Tanaka, but he is major league ready right now and could be a solid #3 SP. If not posted in 2015, he will almost certainly be in the ML in 2016.
Probable ETA: 2016.

Yusei Kikuchi (LHP, Seibu Lions) drew interest from several MLB teams when it looked like he might pass up the Japanese draft to sign with the ML in 2009. Instead, the lefty stayed home. After a solid 2013 season, he struggled in 2014 and posted a losing record. Just 23 years old and years away from international free agency, he would have to hope for the posting rules to loosen or a change of heart by his team. He could use more seasoning, so the delay could work in his favor.
Possible ETA: 2016.

Kenta Maeda (RHP, Hiroshima Toyo Carp) is a control pitcher with a solid fastball in the low 90's. In 2010, he became the youngest pitcher in the history of Japanese baseball to win the pitching Triple Crown. He led the Central League in 2013 with a sub 2.00 ERA. His 2014 season was also successful, but not quite good enough to force his team to let him migrate like Tanaka. Maeda is just 27 years old and nearing his peak years, and he has expressed a desire to pitch in the majors. Considered to be one of the best SP in Japan, he projects to be a decent 4th SP or better if he ends up with the right team.
Possible ETA: 2015.

Takeya Nakamura (3B, Seibu Lions) is possibly the premier Japanese power hitter. But his BA is a major concern, and would probably prevent a smooth transition to MLB. With three years remaining on his current contract, he is a long-shot for MLB.
Possible ETA: 2016.

Seung-Hwan Oh (RHP, Hanshin Tigers) came up through the slightly inferior Korean league. He was considered one of the greatest closers in the history of that league. Oh signed a two-year contract with a Japanese team, which expires at the end of 2015. If his 2015 season is as successful as his 2014 season (39 saves with a 1.76 ERA), he may decide to move up another level. Closers have had some success making the switch to the ML, but it's difficult to resist drafting a player nicknamed the "Stone Buddha" for his calm demeanor. Oh is definitely a player to target.
Probable ETA: 2016.

Shohei Otani (RHP, Nippon Ham Fighters), a.k.a. "The Fastball Prince", is too young to be on this list at just age 20. But he might be the top ML pitching prospect if he were not playing in Japan. Otani consistently pitches in the mid 90's and once touched 99 mph…on the final pitch of the game for a strikeout. Otani has the usual complement of supporting pitches, including a splitter and curve. He is near the league lead in ERA and strikeouts, and had just 57 walks in 155.1 IP. Otani is the first player in Japan to have double-figure wins and double-figure HR. That's right, he also plays outfield.
Possible ETA if there is any justice: 2017.

Toshiya Sugiuchi (LHP, Yomiuri Giants) has exceptional command of his pitches and more international experience than almost any player from any country. He had two sub-2.00 ERA seasons in a row, but was something of a disappointment in 2013 and 2014 with an ERA "only" in the low 3's. The former MVP and Sawamura Award winner could be a capable ML pitcher in the right situation, but at age 34 and signed through 2015, his time may have passed.
Possible ETA: 2016.

Young and talented: Unless the posting system completely collapses, these players are years away and should not be rostered except in leagues with very long-term farm systems: Takahiro Norimoto (RHP), Hideto Asamura (IF), and especially Shintaro Fujinami (RHP).

Caveat about pitching stats: Japan instituted a new ball in 2011 which had lower-elasticity rubber surrounding the cork. The new design limited offense and inflated pitching stats. A more hitter-friendly ball was introduced in 2013 and HR increased to pre-2011 levels, but the slightly smaller and lighter ball still favors pitchers. Just in case, continue to be somewhat skeptical when analyzing pitching stats.

Major League Equivalents

In his 1985 *Baseball Abstract*, Bill James introduced the concept of major league equivalencies. His assertion was that, with the proper adjustments, a minor leaguer's statistics could be converted to an equivalent major league level performance with a great deal of accuracy.

Because of wide variations in the level of play among different minor leagues, it is difficult to get a true reading on a player's potential. For instance, a .300 batting average achieved in the high-offense Pacific Coast League is not nearly as much of an accomplishment as a similar level in the Eastern League. MLEs normalize these types of variances, for all statistical categories.

The actual MLEs are not projections. They represent how a player's previous performance might look at the major league level. However, the MLE stat line can be used in forecasting future performance in just the same way as a major league stat line would.

The model we use contains a few variations to James' version and updates all of the minor league and ballpark factors. In addition, we designed a module to convert pitching statistics, which is something James did not originally do.

Players are listed if they spent at least part of 2013 or 2014 in Triple-A or Double-A and had at least 100 AB or 30 IP within those two levels (players who split a season at both levels are indicated as a/a). Major league and Single-A (and lower) stats are excluded. Each player is listed in the organization with which they finished the season. Some players over age 30 with major-league experience have been omitted for space.

These charts also provide the unique perspective of looking at two years' worth of data. These are only short-term trends, for sure. But even here we can find small indications of players improving their skills, or struggling, as they rise through more difficult levels of competition. Since players—especially those with any modicum of talent —are promoted rapidly through major league systems, a two-year scan is often all we get to spot any trends. Five-year trends do appear in the *Minor League Baseball Analyst.*

Used correctly, MLEs are excellent indicators of potential. But, just like we cannot take traditional major league statistics at face value, the same goes for MLEs. The underlying measures of base skill—contact rates, pitching command ratios, BPV, etc.—are far more accurate in evaluating future talent than raw home runs, batting averages or ERAs. This chart format focuses more on those underlying gauges.

Here are some things to look for as you scan these charts:

Target players who...

- had a full season's worth of playing time in AA and then another full year in AAA
- had consistent playing time from one year to the next
- improved their base skills as they were promoted

Raise the warning flag for players who...

- were stuck at the same level both years, or regressed
- displayed marked changes in playing time from one year to the next
- showed large drops in BPIs from one year to the next

BATTER	yr	b	age	pos	lvl	org	ab	hr	sb	ba	bb%	ct%	px	sx	bpv
Abraham,Adam	13	R	26	1B	a/a	CLE	182	1	0	202	7	65	57	41	-65
	14	R	27	3B	a/a	CLE	163	2	1	195	8	81	66	43	8
Abreu,Tony	13	B	29	2B	aaa	SF	65	1	1	248	1	70	129	60	4
	14	B	30	2B	aaa	SF	282	4	2	200	3	85	61	63	14
Adames,Cristhian	13	B	22	SS	aa	COL		3	10	257	7	80	62	86	11
	14	B	23	SS	a/a	COL	475	2	8	258	6	82	54	77	8
Adams,David	13	R	26	3B	aaa	NYY	220	5	0	232	10	77	83	48	11
	14	R	27	2B	a/a	BAL	376	7	3	203	5	78	78	75	9
Adams,Lane	13	R	24	RF	aa	KC	156	4	12	213	8	69	94	150	14
	14	R	25	CF	aa	KC	405	8	29	232	8	76	97	131	40
Adams,Ryan	14	R	27	2B	aa	LA	125	1	0	240	4	74	89	47	-9
Adams,Trever	14	R	26	1B	aa	TEX	482	11	5	237	6	76	112	73	29
Aguilar,Jesus	13	R	23	1B	aa	CLE	499	11	0	233	8	75	90	24	-2
	14	R	24	1B	aaa	CLE	427	14	0	260	10	74	131	24	29
Ahmed,Nick	13	R	23	SS	aa	ARI	487	4	22	223	5	84	59	134	37
	14	R	24	SS	aaa	ARI	407	3	9	257	5	84	69	87	32
Albernaz,Craig	13	R	31	C	aaa	TAM	102	1	2	169	5	72	51	71	-39
	14	R	32	C	aa	DET	205	0	4	131	3	74	23	80	-53
Alberto,Hanser	13	R	21	SS	aa	TEX	356	4	11	205	4	88	39	115	28
	14	R	22	SS	aa	TEX	178	2	6	255	3	90	47	92	32
Albitz,Vance	13	R	25	2B	a/a	STL	226	2	4	209	2	86	36	74	0
	14	R	26	2B	a/a	LAA	293	2	3	231	3	87	79	87	44
Alcantara,Arismendy	13	B	22	SS	aa	CHC	494	12	25	245	9	72	121	116	42
	14	B	23	2B	aaa	CHC	335	8	16	272	5	72	143	154	62
Aldridge,Cory	14	L	35	RF	a/a	TOR	138	5	0	200	5	65	96	26	-42
Aliotti,Anthony	13	L	26	1B	a/a	OAK	494	9	2	257	11	69	96	41	-13
	14	L	27	1B	a/a	OAK	409	5	1	203	9	58	107	43	-50
Allen,Brandon	13	L	27	1B	aaa	SD	423	11	4	196	8	73	98	96	16
	14	L	28	1B	aaa	NYM	320	7	1	180	8	72	72	63	-19
Allie,Stetson	14	R	23	1B	aa	PIT	407	14	7	204	11	67	110	52	-6
Almanzar,Michael	13	R	23	3B	aa	BOS	507	12	10	244	6	78	99	92	34
	14	R	24	3B	a/a	BAL	183	5	1	223	5	73	94	39	-10
Almonte,Abraham	13	B	24	CF	a/a	SEA	440	11	20	258	10	75	101	119	38
	14	B	25	CF	aaa	SEA	277	4	5	211	6	71	66	88	-23
Almonte,Zoilo	13	B	24	LF	aaa	NYY	259	6	3	269	9	80	78	58	18
	14	B	25	LF	aaa	NYY	421	14	4	218	5	71	107	49	-4
Almora,Albert	14	R	20	CF	aa	CHC	142	2	0	212	1	84	72	94	24
Alonso,Carlos	14	R	26	3B	aa	PHI	467	8	6	222	8	82	69	76	24
Altherr,Aaron	14	R	23	CF	aa	PHI	449	11	9	204	4	72	109	86	12
Alvarez,Dariel	13	R	25	RF	aa	BAL	31	1	0	163	2	67	51	6	-83
	14	R	26	CF	a/a	BAL	532	12	6	251	3	86	89	70	44
Anderson,Bryan	13	L	27	C	aaa	CHW	210	6	1	183	8	65	123	62	-5
	14	L	28	C	a/a	OAK	253	6	0	242	8	75	110	57	22
Anderson,Lars	13	L	26	1B	aaa	CHW	227	2	1	160	11	62	47	31	-83
	14	L	27	1B	a/a	CHC	211	4	0	244	8	78	101	31	21
Andino,Robert	13	R	29	SS	aaa	PIT	249	2	1	198	4	72	60	51	-38
	14	R	30	SS	aaa	PIT	424	4	1	159	4	76	48	55	-34
Andreoli,John	13	R	23	LF	aa	CHC	201	2	13	257	8	79	72	127	29
	14	R	24	LF	aa	CHC	209	0	20	178	11	73	25	150	-18
Angelini,Carmen	13	R	25	SS	aa	NYY	236	4	6	190	7	75	73	76	-4
	14	R	26	SS	a/a	NYY	354	3	1	172	4	75	59	44	-29
Angle,Matt	13	L	28	CF	aaa	LA	400	5	14	208	7	67	78	124	-18
	14	L	29	RF	aaa	MIA	239	0	2	153	5	67	37	52	-75
Anna,Dean	13	L	27	2B	aaa	SD	498	6	2	245	7	83	74	63	25
	14	L	28	SS	aaa	PIT	198	1	1	158	10	85	47	73	22
Aplin,Andrew	14	L	23	CF	a/a	HOU	452	5	19	226	12	82	46	87	15
Arcia,Francisco	13	L	24	C	aa	NYY	68	2	0	156	5	71	63	5	-55
	14	L	25	C	a/a	NYY	225	1	0	231	3	78	50	30	-30
Arencibia,J.P.	14	R	28	C	aaa	TEX	190	9	1	215	3	66	141	37	-5
Argo,Willie	14	R	25	LF	aa	TAM	384	3	18	167	11	67	49	108	-39
Arruebarrena,Erisbel	14	R	24	SS	a/a	LA	180	1	1	209	5	63	64	67	-67
Asencio,Yeison	13	R	24	RF	aa	SD	291	2	2	222	4	88	52	72	25
	14	R	25	RF	a/a	SD	536	10	5	226	3	84	67	65	20
Ashley,Nevin	13	R	29	C	aaa	CIN	238	5	3	189	9	68	93	68	-13
	14	R	30	C	aaa	PIT	203	1	0	182	6	75	60	32	-27
Austin,Jamal	14	R	24	CF	aa	SEA	244	1	14	223	2	86	50	123	25
Austin,Tyler	13	R	22	RF	aa	NYY	319	6	3	236	10	73	84	70	3
	14	R	23	RF	aa	NYY	396	8	2	244	7	78	89	78	20
Avery,Xavier	13	L	23	CF	a/a	SEA	467	3	24	233	8	71	67	120	-8
	14	L	24	LF	aaa	SEA	400	6	21	223	6	73	82	109	4
Baez,Javier	13	R	21	SS	aa	CHC	218	16	6	268	7	66	224	73	79
	14	R	22	SS	aaa	CHC	388	18	12	231	6	63	174	99	37
Bandy,Jett	13	R	23	C	aa	LAA	245	3	0	213	4	82	83	56	23
	14	R	24	C	aa	LAA	312	11	2	219	8	77	95	36	13
Barfield,Jeremy	13	R	25	RF	a/a	OAK	216	8	1	167	9	74	87	45	-2
	14	R	26	RF	aa	OAK	142	2	0	211	13	66	85	61	-23
Barnes,Austin	13	R	24	C	aa	MIA	62	1	0	307	14	82	73	75	39
	14	R	25	2B	aa	MIA	284	7	6	245	12	85	104	99	79
Barnhart,Tucker	13	B	22	C	aa	CIN	339	3	1	245	11	81	66	40	14
	14	B	23	C	aaa	CIN	256	1	0	207	7	85	40	40	-1
Barton,Daric	13	L	28	1B	aaa	OAK	391	4	1	220	13	81	71	41	22
	14	L	29	DH	aaa	OAK	313	5	0	185	9	83	67	37	18
Baxter,Mike	13	L	29	LF	aaa	NYM	187	4	2	196	7	80	88	104	37
	14	L	30	RF	aaa	LA	412	4	6	195	5	71	72	97	-15
Belnome,Vince	13	L	25	1B	aaa	TAM	444	6	0	253	13	71	103	55	10
	14	L	26	1B	aaa	TAM	413	8	2	203	12	63	107	57	-20
Belza,Thomas	14	L	25	LF	aa	ARI	413	1	8	268	8	75	64	99	1

BATTER	yr	b	age	pos	lvl	org	ab	hr	sb	ba	bb%	ct%	px	sx	bpv
Benson,Joe	14	R	26	RF	a/a	MIA	424	6	10	208	9	72	82	101	4
Beresford,James	13	L	24	2B	a/a	MIN	356	0	7	264	6	84	29	87	-1
	14	L	25	2B	aaa	MIN	507	1	6	240	5	83	54	75	11
Bermudez,Ronald	13	R	25	CF	a/a	BOS	234	1	1	228	4	78	52	65	-17
	14	R	26	RF	aa	BAL	357	2	1	239	3	80	61	40	-12
Bernier,Douglas	13	B	33	SS	aaa	MIN	302	2	3	225	6	69	67	97	-27
	14	B	34	SS	aaa	MIN	404	4	4	219	7	76	73	64	-4
Berry,Quintin	13	L	29	CF	aaa	BOS	319	2	20	152	9	69	45	108	-36
	14	L	30	LF	aaa	BAL	365	2	16	213	9	70	56	85	-28
Berset,Chris	13	B	25	C	aa	CIN	55	0	0	159	8	87	69	29	32
	14	B	26	C	a/a	CIN	142	0	0	145	8	75	12	29	-63
Berti,Jonathon	14	R	24	2B	aa	TOR	541	6	32	240	5	83	65	131	33
Betemit,Wilson	13	B	32	DH	a/a	BAL	29	0	0	185	10	61	33	10	-105
	14	B	33	DH	aaa	TAM	396	13	1	165	8	53	133	40	-52
Bethancourt,Christian	13	R	22	C	aa	ATL	358	10	10	256	4	82	97	70	37
	14	R	23	C	aaa	ATL	343	6	5	241	3	79	74	67	4
Betts,Mookie	14	R	22	2B	a/a	BOS	399	9	27	330	11	87	116	132	103
Bianucci,Michael	13	R	27	DH	aaa	TEX	196	9	0	231	7	74	143	27	35
	14	R	28	DH	aa	LAA	241	9	1	220	3	72	137	68	25
Bixler,Brian	13	R	31	CF	aaa	NYM	309	3	4	171	4	60	66	72	-75
	14	R	32	SS	a/a	SD	307	1	4	141	5	65	26	66	-88
Black,Daniel	13	B	26	1B	aa	CHW	449	15	5	246	15	73	116	55	35
	13	L	25	SS	aa	MIA	315	1	6	174	8	73	34	124	-23
Black,Daniel	14	L	26	2B	a/a	MIA	331	2	6	171	9	71	53	109	-23
	14	B	27	DH	a/a	CHW	334	8	2	204	8	71	95	34	-10
Blanco,Andres	14	B	30	SS	aaa	PHI	137	0	2	179	6	76	35	58	-37
Blanks,Kyle	13	R	27	1B	aaa	SD	38	1	0	169	9	66	96	48	-26
	14	R	28	1B	aaa	OAK	104	6	0	215	9	67	163	19	22
Blash,Jabari	13	R	24	RF	aa	SEA	97	7	1	279	15	67	188	22	55
	14	R	25	RF	a/a	SEA	289	12	4	177	9	62	148	74	8
Bloxom,Justin	13	B	25	1B	aa	WAS	460	6	4	215	11	73	69	56	-15
	14	B	26	1B	aa	WAS	111	1	1	200	6	68	80	36	-40
Bocock,Brian	13	R	28	SS	aaa	PIT	143	2	2	135	5	76	63	53	-19
	14	R	29	3B	a/a	KC	365	1	3	210	5	75	56	68	-22
Boesch,Brennan	13	L	28	RF	aaa	NYY	30	0	0	163	16	67	60	47	-35
	14	L	29	RF	aaa	LAA	374	13	5	227	4	69	131	93	17
Boggs,Brandon	13	B	30	RF	aaa	ATL	411	5	3	180	9	60	78	71	-56
	14	B	31	RF	aaa	ATL	297	4	3	189	5	70	84	82	-16
Bogusevic,Brian	13	L	29	RF	aaa	CHC	265	7	11	248	10	72	100	116	25
	14	L	30	LF	aaa	MIA	265	3	3	187	7	73	75	91	-6
Bonifacio,Jorge	13	R	20	RF	aa	KC	93	2	2	283	9	75	102	59	19
	14	R	21	RF	aa	KC	505	3	7	213	7	74	59	87	-13
Bonilla,Leury	13	R	28	3B	a/a	SEA	228	1	4	193	7	72	34	52	-52
	14	R	29	3B	aaa	SEA	278	1	3	169	4	70	60	62	-44
Borbon,Julio	13	L	27	LF	aaa	CHC	73	0	4	210	11	75	57	76	-8
	14	L	28	CF	aaa	BAL	466	4	22	223	5	81	33	108	-7
Borenstein,Zachary	14	L	24	LF	a/a	ARI	461	11	6	220	6	69	111	86	6
Boscan,J.C.	13	R	34	C	aaa	CHC	233	0	1	176	6	76	30	29	-50
	14	R	35	C	aa	LA	131	1	1	118	6	68	47	40	-62
Bour,Justin	13	L	25	1B	aa	CHC	317	14	0	200	8	77	118	30	30
	14	L	26	1B	aaa	MIA	385	10	2	239	6	82	97	43	33
Bourgeois,Jason	13	R	31	LF	aaa	TAM	348	1	16	222	6	86	41	119	25
	14	R	32	CF	aaa	CIN	550	3	15	203	4	88	45	87	23
Boyd,Jayce	14	R	24	1B	aa	NYM	413	6	1	235	8	80	68	51	9
Boyer,Brad	13	L	30	3B	aa	MIN	41	0	1	184	9	79	36	66	-18
	14	L	31	SS	aa	MIN	256	0	10	191	3	84	29	105	-1
Brady,Patrick	13	R	25	2B	aa	SEA	32	1	1	309	10	63	160	46	15
	14	R	26	2B	a/a	SEA	160	4	2	181	2	68	75	76	-37
Brantly,Rob	13	L	24	C	aaa	MIA	70	1	0	162	3	87	48	54	13
	14	L	25	C	aaa	MIA	364	2	0	203	4	80	47	39	-20
Brenly,Michael	14	R	28	C	aa	BOS	143	1	1	140	6	69	76	55	-32
Brentz,Bryce	13	R	25	RF	aaa	BOS	326	12	1	229	4	70	124	38	1
	14	R	26	LF	aaa	BOS	230	9	1	210	9	71	132	74	32
Brett,Ryan	13	R	22	2B	aa	TAM	105	2	3	211	6	85	87	132	64
	14	R	23	2B	aa	TAM	422	6	22	265	4	80	88	140	43
Brignac,Reid	13	L	27	3B	aaa	COL	165	1	1	175	6	77	50	51	-21
	14	L	28	2B	aaa	PHI	128	4	2	207	8	69	118	88	16
Britton,Buck	13	L	27	2B	a/a	BAL	467	10	4	224	5	83	74	70	25
	14	L	28	3B	a/a	BAL	457	11	2	226	5	85	82	57	34
Brown,Andrew	13	R	29	RF	aaa	NYM	153	4	0	239	8	69	145	91	36
	14	R	30	RF	aaa	NYM	386	12	1	185	7	68	110	44	-10
Brown,Corey	13	L	28	CF	aaa	WAS	389	13	8	198	6	59	142	81	-11
	14	L	29	CF	aaa	BOS	325	11	4	186	6	60	142	70	-13
Brown,Gary	13	R	25	CF	aaa	SF	558	7	11	181	4	72	77	105	-11
	14	R	26	CF	aaa	SF	536	6	23	207	4	73	65	119	-10
Brown,Jordan	13	L	30	1B	aaa	MIA	291	1	0	226	6	85	61	26	11
	14	L	31	1B	a/a	TEX	113	3	0	161	5	78	77	32	-5
Brown,Kelson	13	R	26	1B	aa	PIT	104	0	3	156	8	83	22	81	-10
	14	R	27	2B	aa	PIT	129	0	2	230	2	84	22	55	-25
Broxton,Keon	13	R	23	CF	aa	ARI	334	7	5	217	7	63	102	103	-21
	14	R	24	CF	aa	PIT	407	10	18	227	9	67	119	133	24
Bruno,Stephen	14	R	24	2B	aa	CHC	384	2	4	236	5	77	80	95	13
Bryant,Kris	14	R	22	3B	a/a	CHC	492	34	12	291	12	64	228	85	89
Buck,John	14	R	34	C	aaa	LAA	119	1	0	197	5	75	63	16	-33
Buck,Travis	13	L	30	LF	aaa	SD	125	3	0	174	3	78	97	36	8
	14	L	31	LF	aaa	SD	142	2	0	190	5	70	57	36	-51
Burg,Alex	13	R	26	3B	a/a	MIA	78	1	1	182	5	64	61	38	-71
	14	R	27	3B	aa	MIA	227	4	1	209	9	65	82	59	-36

BATTER	yr	b	age	pos	lvl	org	ab	hr	sb	ba	bb%	ct%	px	sx	bpv
Burgamy,Brian	14	B	33	3B	aa	NYM	450	15	4	195	9	69	124	59	14
Burns,Andrew	13	R	23	3B	aa	TOR	265	6	9	223	6	76	108	106	38
	14	R	24	3B	aa	TOR	495	13	14	228	6	77	117	111	50
Burns,Billy	13	B	24	CF	aa	WAS	114	0	16	288	12	84	29	124	20
	14	B	25	CF	a/a	OAK	473	1	37	187	7	79	44	144	12
Burriss,Emmanuel	13	B	28	SS	aaa	CIN	369	1	13	196	4	86	15	72	-12
	14	B	29	SS	aaa	WAS	444	4	15	231	6	89	51	113	44
Buschini,Adam	13	R	26	2B	aa	SD	285	6	10	196	5	77	70	122	14
	14	R	27	3B	aa	SD	358	7	8	169	8	74	64	97	-7
Buss,Nicholas	13	L	27	RF	aaa	LA	459	11	14	229	5	75	102	136	36
	14	L	28	RF	aaa	OAK	542	3	9	219	6	79	42	87	-9
Butler,Daniel	13	R	27	C	aaa	BOS	282	10	1	219	8	75	123	24	24
	14	R	28	C	aaa	BOS	286	3	0	201	7	70	87	28	-26
Cabrera,Ramon	13	B	24	DH	a/a	DET	461	1	3	251	9	87	60	71	37
	14	B	25	C	aa	PIT	440	4	1	221	5	89	50	30	18
Calixte,Orlando	13	R	21	SS	aa	KC	484	6	11	231	7	72	82	96	-2
	14	R	22	SS	aa	KC	374	8	7	216	6	74	83	74	-1
Campana,Tony	13	L	27	CF	aaa	ARI	351	1	18	223	5	73	41	139	-21
	14	L	28	CF	aaa	LAA	365	0	9	192	4	76	29	102	-32
Campbell,Eric	13	R	26	RF	aaa	NYM	341	5	7	228	10	77	81	83	21
	14	R	27	1B	aaa	NYM	141	2	2	249	7	81	93	73	36
Canha,Mark	13	R	24	1B	aa	MIA	425	9	5	241	10	73	114	85	31
	14	R	25	LF	aaa	MIA	465	11	2	240	8	71	106	68	8
Canham,Mitchell	13	L	29	C	a/a	KC	306	1	8	211	10	77	75	99	19
	14	L	30	C	aa	WAS	103	1	2	148	5	78	23	87	-31
Cantwell,Patrick	14	R	24	C	aa	TEX	276	1	1	238	5	77	59	66	-13
Canzler,Russ	13	R	27	DH	aaa	PIT	452	8	1	202	9	74	64	46	-18
	14	R	28	DH	aaa	PHI	388	9	2	216	8	68	131	66	14
Carlin,Luke	13	B	33	C	aaa	LAA	244	2	3	154	8	71	39	62	-48
	14	B	34	C	aaa	CLE	183	3	0	163	9	73	93	22	-7
Carrera,Ezequiel	13	L	26	CF	aaa	CLE	416	4	35	209	7	75	58	139	3
	14	L	27	CF	aaa	DET	374	4	31	255	9	80	64	139	31
Carrillo,Xorge	13	R	24	C	aa	NYM	108	0	0	242	5	76	44	26	-39
	14	R	25	C	a/a	NYM	207	1	0	213	4	80	42	36	-27
Carrithers,Alden	13	L	29	3B	a/a	ATL	278	2	12	224	10	85	50	87	25
	14	L	30	3B	aaa	OAK	387	1	8	200	8	85	31	86	7
Carson,Matt	13	R	32	RF	aaa	CLE	436	10	10	196	6	65	85	92	-32
	14	R	33	CF	aaa	CLE	274	7	7	194	6	59	107	102	-33
Carter,Kes	14	L	24	CF	aa	TAM	199	2	6	204	8	73	94	105	18
Cartwright,Albert	13	R	26	2B	aa	PHI	489	5	18	204	4	72	54	123	-20
	14	R	27	2B	aa	PHI	445	2	19	192	4	69	53	108	-38
Casali,Curtis	13	R	25	C	aa	TAM	120	4	0	324	12	82	123	30	61
	14	R	26	C	a/a	TAM	226	3	0	213	13	65	95	8	-35
Casilla,Alexi	14	B	30	2B	aaa	BAL	197	1	6	197	4	82	35	77	-11
Casteel,Ryan	14	R	23	1B	aa	COL	436	14	2	261	6	78	107	49	27
Castellanos,Alex	13	R	27	RF	aaa	LA	385	12	12	193	6	64	105	120	-11
	14	R	28	3B	aaa	SD	360	5	4	188	5	61	97	104	-36
Castillo,Ali	13	R	24	SS	aa	NYY	156	0	3	191	6	79	33	103	-12
	14	R	25	SS	aa	NYY	410	2	13	215	6	87	44	93	27
Castro,Daniel	14	R	22	SS	aa	ATL	173	3	2	250	2	88	75	75	42
Castro,Erik	13	L	26	1B	aa	HOU	410	14	1	231	9	69	126	32	5
	14	L	27	1B	a/a	ATL	138	2	0	148	9	63	67	40	-61
Castro,Leandro	13	R	24	RF	aaa	PHI	438	6	15	218	3	80	70	90	8
	14	R	25	CF	aaa	PHI	425	5	5	215	4	80	64	86	10
Cavazos-Galvez,Bria	13	R	26	LF	aa	LA	377	6	12	223	3	84	58	83	14
	14	R	27	RF	a/a	LA	242	2	2	178	2	78	62	62	-12
Cave,Andrew	14	L	22	CF	aa	NYY	176	4	2	247	8	73	114	97	29
Cecchini,Garin	13	L	22	3B	aa	BOS	240	2	6	276	14	77	80	98	31
	14	L	23	3B	aaa	NYM	407	4	7	196	6	71	64	72	-31
Ceciliani,Darrell	13	L	23	CF	aa	NYM	418	5	24	223	5	70	67	142	-10
	14	L	24	CF	aa	NYM	395	5	11	231	4	73	68	106	-14
Cedeno,Ronny	14	R	31	2B	aaa	ARI	281	2	3	228	4	78	66	69	-5
Centeno,Juan	13	L	24	C	a/a	NYM	236	0	1	236	3	85	38	67	-1
	14	L	25	C	a/a	NYM	256	1	1	217	5	82	32	37	-24
Chambers,Adron	13	L	27	RF	aaa	STL	333	5	11	197	8	73	68	117	-2
	14	L	28	LF	aaa	TOR	180	4	1	233	7	78	79	38	2
Chang,Ray	13	R	30	2B	a/a	CIN	261	3	0	214	7	78	49	29	-27
	14	R	31	2B	a/a	CIN	150	0	0	171	5	80	48	40	-19
Chapman,Ethan	14	L	24	LF	aa	KC	298	1	9	208	8	73	34	87	-36
Chavez,Endy	13	L	35	CF	aaa	SEA	28	0	0	320	6	85	25	75	-3
	14	L	36	DH	aaa	SEA	114	0	0	194	6	80	13	43	-43
Chen,Pin-Chieh	14	L	23	LF	aa	CHC	155	0	4	201	11	88	45	81	35
Chester,David	14	R	25	DH	aa	BOS	212	5	0	204	6	64	105	23	-40
Chiang,Chih-Hsien	13	L	25	RF	aa	TEX	476	10	0	235	4	79	102	49	23
	14	L	26	RF	aa	BAL	201	2	0	178	4	84	67	43	11
Choi,Ji-Man	13	L	22	1B	a/a	SEA	243	8	2	234	10	84	103	59	58
	14	L	23	1B	a/a	SEA	248	4	1	238	10	79	62	67	9
Choice,Michael	13	R	24	LF	aaa	OAK	510	9	1	245	9	74	81	41	-9
	14	R	25	LF	aaa	TEX	150	5	1	218	9	64	125	45	-10
Christian,Justin	13	R	33	LF	aaa	STL	374	2	9	201	5	85	40	85	10
	14	R	34	LF	aaa	TAM	461	7	12	210	6	80	95	111	44
Chung,Derrick	14	R	26	C	aa	TOR	171	0	0	202	3	90	28	31	0
Ciriaco,Audy	13	R	26	SS	a/a	MIA	260	4	5	191	6	80	54	104	9
	14	R	27	1B	aaa	CLE	373	10	1	202	5	72	118	50	12
Ciriaco,Juan	13	R	30	SS	a/a	SF	144	1	2	174	4	79	37	48	-29
	14	R	31	LF	aaa	SF	149	3	8	214	4	85	68	116	39
Ciriaco,Pedro	13	R	28	SS	aaa	KC	160	1	3	230	3	84	49	87	8
	14	R	29	SS	aaa	KC	205	1	4	231	2	79	84	109	21

BATTER	yr	b	age	pos	lvl	org	ab	hr	sb	ba	bb%	ct%	px	sx	bpv
Clark,Matthew	14	L	28	1B	a/a	MIL	414	20	0	244	6	70	146	20	18
Cleary,Delta	13	B	24	CF	aa	COL	397	2	14	190	6	76	36	108	-21
	14	B	25	CF	a/a	COL	406	2	17	215	7	74	46	110	-18
Clevenger,Steve	13	L	27	C	aaa	BAL	123	4	0	272	10	84	94	35	46
	14	L	28	C	aaa	BAL	226	1	1	237	6	83	52	35	0
Cokinos,M.P.	14	R	24	DH	aa	HOU	203	1	1	229	3	87	33	37	-8
Colabello,Chris	13	R	30	1B	aaa	MIN	338	15	1	267	8	66	154	35	16
	14	R	31	1B	aaa	MIN	213	7	0	207	7	68	120	23	-11
Coleman,Dustin	13	R	26	SS	a/a	OAK	505	2	12	203	7	62	93	123	-24
	14	R	27	SS	aa	OAK	489	12	11	174	7	50	141	111	-39
Collier,Zachary	13	L	23	CF	aa	PHI	446	6	13	190	7	67	74	125	-18
	14	L	24	CF	aa	PHI	267	7	4	204	6	64	109	100	-12
Collins,Tyler	13	L	23	LF	aa	DET	466	17	3	212	8	72	123	46	19
	14	L	24	LF	aaa	DET	468	14	9	230	7	73	95	80	9
Colon,Christian	13	R	24	2B	aaa	KC	512	9	12	242	6	88	49	98	34
	14	R	25	SS	a/a	KC	352	5	12	261	6	90	64	81	50
Colvin,Tyler	13	L	28	CF	aaa	COL	229	5	3	211	8	68	96	110	1
	14	L	29	RF	aaa	SF	163	1	1	161	4	66	70	81	-46
Conrad,Brooks	14	B	34	2B	aaa	SD	295	10	0	183	6	62	124	41	-27
Constanza,Jose	13	L	30	LF	aaa	ATL	341	0	15	212	6	81	20	98	-17
	14	L	31	LF	aaa	ATL	447	0	19	218	5	85	18	96	-3
Cooper,David	13	L	26	1B	aaa	CLE	26	0	0	161	6	91	0	8	-21
	14	L	27	DH	aaa	CLE	143	0	0	177	9	88	36	20	6
Costanzo,Mike	13	L	30	1B	a/a	CIN	382	12	2	194	10	62	132	64	-7
	14	L	31	1B	aaa	CIN	129	3	0	141	7	52	90	14	-100
Court,Ryan	13	R	25	3B	aa	ARI	178	1	2	233	13	65	97	38	-25
	14	R	26	1B	aa	ARI	136	2	3	208	9	66	125	91	11
Cowart,Kaleb	13	B	21	3B	aa	LAA	498	5	12	201	6	73	57	80	-24
	14	B	22	3B	aa	LAA	435	5	23	204	8	75	68	121	9
Cox,Zack	13	L	24	3B	a/a	MIA	288	2	2	234	10	74	68	68	-8
	14	L	25	3B	aaa	MIA	312	4	1	224	6	76	83	67	2
Coyle,Robert	13	L	24	LF	aa	LA	111	0	0	150	7	66	25	50	-83
	14	L	25	LF	aa	LA	142	3	0	231	3	81	95	36	17
Coyle,Sean	14	R	22	2B	aa	BOS	336	13	11	279	8	70	158	99	54
Cron,C.J.	13	R	23	1B	aa	LAA	519	11	7	242	4	82	93	65	31
	14	R	24	1B	aaa	LAA	190	4	1	240	5	74	101	54	7
Crouse,Michael	14	R	24	LF	aa	TOR	346	8	12	217	8	66	119	128	14
Crowe,Trevor	13	B	30	LF	aaa	HOU	237	2	11	231	6	81	41	107	2
	14	B	31	DH	aaa	DET	258	3	6	185	5	81	65	62	6
Crumbliss,Conner	13	L	26	LF	a/a	OAK	406	8	9	203	12	77	80	94	29
	14	L	27	2B	aa	OAK	439	7	9	198	10	82	76	101	40
Cuevas,Noel	14	R	23	CF	aa	LA	425	5	4	189	5	75	57	94	-13
Cunningham,Aaron	13	R	27	LF	aaa	TEX	421	8	8	202	8	76	95	90	26
	14	R	28	LF	aaa	ARI	243	0	1	191	6	76	62	76	-7
Cunningham,Jarek	13	R	24	2B	aa	PIT	468	13	9	181	5	71	94	96	-2
	14	R	25	3B	aa	PIT	309	5	2	198	6	75	83	85	6
Cunningham,Todd	13	B	24	CF	aaa	ATL	427	2	16	229	7	83	38	117	14
	14	B	25	CF	aaa	ATL	470	6	13	235	5	80	72	81	12
Curley,Chris	14	R	27	3B	aa	CHW	504	4	5	225	4	82	64	75	10
Curry,Matthew	13	L	25	1B	aa	PIT	105	3	2	205	3	63	93	52	-49
	14	L	26	DH	a/a	PIT	206	2	1	184	6	68	64	56	-45
Curtis,Jermaine	13	R	26	3B	aaa	STL	370	3	7	206	9	83	50	70	14
	14	R	27	3B	aaa	STL	225	0	3	194	11	88	25	58	14
Cuthbert,Cheslor	13	R	21	3B	aa	KC	237	4	4	196	6	78	93	63	20
	14	R	22	3B	a/a	KC	446	8	8	244	7	81	82	63	26
Cutler,Charles	13	L	27	DH	aa	PIT	255	2	2	240	10	83	66	73	29
	14	L	28	C	aa	CHC	284	3	1	243	10	85	56	39	18
D Arnaud,Chase	13	R	26	SS	a/a	PIT	254	3	13	187	5	81	52	140	18
	14	R	27	CF	aaa	PIT	376	1	21	196	5	75	58	151	2
Danks,Jordan	13	L	27	CF	aaa	CHW	208	5	2	229	9	66	96	82	-15
	14	L	28	CF	aaa	CHW	348	11	1	202	8	62	120	35	-29
Darvill,Wesley	14	L	23	SS	aa	CHC	121	1	1	200	5	79	46	73	-13
Davidson,Matthew	13	R	22	3B	aaa	ARI	443	11	1	235	6	67	128	51	-2
	14	R	23	3B	aaa	CHW	478	15	0	164	7	61	112	21	-46
Davis,Blake	13	L	30	SS	aaa	MIL	332	1	3	191	4	72	57	82	-34
	14	L	31	2B	aaa	PIT	233	1	2	181	3	81	41	53	-21
Davis,Kentrail	13	L	25	RF	a/a	MIL	500	6	19	227	9	70	81	117	1
	14	L	26	RF	aa	MIL	359	2	10	203	11	75	70	86	4
Davis,Lars	13	L	28	C	aaa	COL	298	2	1	192	4	67	67	52	-54
	14	L	29	C	a/a	PHI	101	1	0	141	6	77	51	7	-36
Davis,Taylor	14	R	25	C	aa	CHC	138	3	0	268	6	88	99	42	58
Dayleg,Terrence	14	R	27	3B	aa	MIA	199	1	1	191	3	71	80	54	-28
De Jesus,Ivan	13	R	26	2B	aaa	PIT	304	2	4	266	7	76	94	77	16
	14	R	27	SS	aaa	BOS	417	4	1	239	8	76	69	69	-2
De la Cruz,Keury	14	L	23	LF	aa	BOS	258	5	2	273	4	77	99	45	10
Decker,Cody	13	R	26	1B	a/a	SD	359	14	0	205	8	61	157	62	4
	14	R	27	1B	aaa	SD	449	15	0	182	6	56	144	46	-34
Decker,Jaff	13	L	23	CF	aaa	SD	350	7	3	227	10	67	97	57	-14
	14	L	24	LF	aaa	PIT	350	4	5	215	9	77	89	58	19
Delarosa,Anderson	13	R	29	C	a/a	MIL	242	2	2	210	4	71	77	46	-30
	14	R	30	C	a/a	LAA	184	1	0	149	2	67	76	35	-56
Den Dekker,Matthew	13	L	26	CF	aaa	NYM	179	4	5	216	6	67	90	121	-10
	14	L	27	CF	aaa	NYM	335	5	5	234	6	74	104	100	23
Dent,Ryan	13	R	24	2B	a/a	BOS	219	2	8	214	6	73	51	82	-29
	14	R	25	SS	a/a	BOS	122	1	0	213	4	70	92	71	-18
Deshields Jr.,Delino	14	R	22	CF	aa	HOU	411	9	41	207	10	69	81	133	5
Diaz,Aledmys	14	R	24	SS	aa	STL	117	2	5	246	1	77	99	106	22

BATTER	yr	b	age	pos	lvl	org	ab	hr	sb	ba	bb%	ct%	px	sx	bpv
Diaz,Argenis	14	R	27	SS	a/a	ARI	363	1	2	212	4	76	53	53	-25
Diaz,Elias	14	R	24	C	a/a	PIT	359	4	2	261	6	83	66	38	8
Diaz,Jonathan	13	B	28	2B	aaa	BOS	332	1	7	207	9	76	41	83	-21
	14	B	29	SS	aaa	TOR	244	1	3	165	10	78	61	95	9
Diaz,Juan	13	B	25	SS	aaa	CLE	442	6	2	209	8	66	82	38	-42
	14	B	26	SS	aaa	MIA	464	6	3	215	3	70	82	56	-31
Diaz,Robinzon	13	R	30	C	a/a	MIL	351	5	1	232	3	89	66	42	29
	14	R	31	C	a/a	MIL	292	2	1	201	3	86	44	33	-2
Dickerson,Alex	13	L	23	RF	aa	PIT	451	12	8	251	4	79	118	84	46
	14	L	24	RF	aa	SD	137	2	0	273	5	75	113	79	27
Dickerson,Chris	13	L	31	RF	aaa	BAL	136	2	1	189	10	68	77	92	-19
	14	L	32	CF	aaa	PIT	236	4	8	230	8	66	101	98	-8
Dickson,O'Koyea	14	R	24	1B	aa	LA	461	12	3	218	5	83	106	66	49
Dominguez,Chris	13	R	27	3B	aaa	SF	466	8	3	223	3	70	85	65	-24
	14	R	28	RF	aaa	SF	496	11	13	199	3	63	97	92	-35
Donald,Jason	13	R	29	2B	aaa	CIN	251	2	1	174	4	64	76	74	-50
	14	R	30	2B	aaa	TEX	222	3	2	172	5	64	69	82	-55
Dorn,Daniel	13	L	29	RF	aaa	DET	496	18	6	205	8	68	112	71	1
	14	L	30	RF	aaa	ARI	247	7	1	223	7	70	119	83	15
Douglas,Brandon	13	R	28	2B	a/a	DET	354	4	9	227	5	79	61	101	9
	14	R	29	2B	aaa	DET	263	3	3	178	6	80	62	78	8
Dowd,Michael	13	R	23	C	aa	SEA	112	1	0	182	3	80	46	41	-23
	14	R	24	C	aa	SEA	182	1	1	175	5	77	35	47	-39
Dozier,Hunter	14	R	23	3B	aa	KC	234	3	2	186	9	68	79	60	-24
Drury,Brandon	14	R	22	3B	aa	ARI	105	3	0	274	5	81	118	16	33
Duffy,Matt	14	R	23	SS	aa	SF	367	2	16	296	9	80	78	114	35
Duffy,Matthew	13	R	24	DH	aa	HOU	89	4	1	212	3	71	124	49	5
	14	R	25	1B	a/a	HOU	517	13	1	237	4	75	89	53	-3
Dugan,Kelly	13	L	23	RF	aa	PHI	212	8	0	228	2	71	126	43	3
	14	L	24	RF	aa	PHI	253	4	1	253	8	74	98	57	9
Dugas,Taylor	14	L	25	LF	a/a	NYY	351	1	5	251	9	80	51	82	7
Duran,Edgar	13	B	22	SS	aa	PHI	405	3	9	195	4	75	60	81	-18
	14	B	23	SS	a/a	PHI	376	3	5	187	5	80	44	68	-14
Duran,Juan	14	R	23	RF	aa	CIN	338	15	1	214	5	56	181	59	-1
Duvall,Adam	13	R	25	3B	aa	SF	385	11	1	203	6	78	102	78	31
	14	R	26	3B	aaa	SF	359	15	1	226	5	72	140	75	34
Dykstra,Allan	13	L	26	1B	aa	NYM	372	16	0	216	16	59	154	13	-4
	14	L	27	1B	aaa	NYM	343	9	0	194	12	63	121	41	-15
Dykstra,Cutter	14	R	25	2B	aa	WAS	358	4	7	223	7	74	71	77	-9
Earley,Michael	13	R	25	LF	a/a	CHW	319	4	3	222	6	79	72	72	8
	14	R	26	LF	aa	CHW	354	2	3	201	4	78	51	59	-19
Easley,Edward	13	R	28	C	aaa	ARI	293	4	1	249	5	78	79	41	1
	14	R	29	C	aaa	STL	277	6	0	217	5	79	85	44	7
Eibner,Brett	13	R	25	CF	aa	KC	441	13	5	210	8	63	126	118	6
	14	R	26	CF	aaa	KC	274	4	3	193	7	67	84	89	-21
Elmore,Jake	13	R	26	2B	aaa	HOU	268	4	12	246	8	83	69	117	40
	14	R	27	2B	aaa	CIN	267	0	8	216	9	80	48	75	3
Erickson,Gorman	13	B	25	C	aa	LA	181	8	0	171	12	67	140	36	16
	14	B	26	C	aaa	LA	155	4	1	218	7	75	101	36	7
Evans,Nick	13	R	27	1B	aa	ARI	454	15	2	230	10	71	116	47	14
	14	R	28	3B	aaa	ARI	198	7	0	270	6	82	133	53	65
Exposito,Luis	13	R	26	C	aaa	BAL	206	3	0	188	6	71	86	27	-24
	14	R	27	C	aaa	OAK	162	2	0	167	7	66	77	21	-53
Falu,Irving	13	B	30	3B	aaa	KC	508	1	14	203	6	88	38	95	24
	14	B	31	2B	aaa	MIL	247	1	6	222	6	88	34	64	12
Farrell,Jeremy	14	R	28	3B	aa	CHW	243	2	1	189	6	64	77	67	-47
Farris,Eric	13	R	27	2B	a/a	MIN	406	2	16	199	5	84	34	100	6
	14	R	28	CF	aaa	MIN	483	3	12	227	4	86	47	78	14
Featherston,Taylor	14	R	25	2B	aa	COL	497	13	10	234	5	76	120	94	40
Federowicz,Tim	13	R	26	C	aaa	LA	79	5	0	333	10	58	269	55	88
	14	R	27	C	aaa	LA	299	8	1	238	5	71	121	36	5
Fedroff,Tim	13	L	26	CF	aaa	CLE	513	5	18	204	10	72	41	80	-32
	14	L	27	LF	a/a	CLE	342	1	4	189	11	66	63	51	-45
Fellhauer,Joshua	13	L	25	RF	a/a	CIN	270	4	2	235	10	72	70	48	-20
	14	L	26	CF	a/a	MIL	262	0	1	218	9	69	68	76	-27
Fermin,Andy	14	L	25	3B	aa	TOR	126	4	0	228	5	91	88	27	53
Field,Tommy	13	R	26	SS	aaa	LAA	314	6	4	224	8	73	88	73	1
	14	R	27	SS	aaa	PIT	339	4	3	225	6	76	78	96	11
Fields,Daniel	13	L	22	CF	aa	DET	457	8	19	261	7	70	105	131	21
	14	L	23	CF	a/a	DET	302	4	7	197	5	71	84	116	-3
Fields,Matthew	13	R	28	1B	aa	KC	454	20	4	175	9	53	158	63	-24
	14	R	29	1B	aaa	KC	465	16	1	195	5	59	149	53	-19
Figueroa,Cole	13	L	26	3B	aaa	TAM	461	2	8	237	8	92	42	97	50
	14	L	27	3B	aaa	TAM	262	2	3	232	10	86	60	82	41
Fiorito,Dan	13	R	23	3B	a/a	NYY	32	0	2	169	3	79	26	76	-31
	14	R	24	3B	a/a	NYY	378	3	1	198	5	78	65	58	-5
Fisher,Ryan	13	L	25	3B	aa	MIA	145	3	2	188	8	65	113	66	-13
	14	L	26	3B	aa	MIA	111	3	0	163	6	65	75	36	-55
Fletcher,Scott	13	R	25	LF	a/a	KC	315	12	5	250	4	74	111	87	21
	14	R	26	DH	a/a	KC	183	5	3	233	5	64	87	69	-39
Flores,Jesus	13	R	29	C	aaa	TAM	253	1	0	131	3	70	46	15	-72
	14	R	30	C	aaa	KC	137	3	0	182	5	71	70	26	-41
Flores,Jorge	14	R	23	SS	aa	TOR	205	0	4	265	4	85	39	66	2
Flores,Luis	13	R	27	C	aaa	CHC	191	4	0	164	8	80	63	14	-8
	14	R	28	C	a/a	CHC	194	3	0	197	13	76	65	30	-6
Flores,Ramon	13	L	21	LF	aa	NYY	534	6	6	241	11	80	65	80	22
	14	L	22	RF	aaa	NYY	235	6	2	217	10	79	117	80	55

BATTER	yr	b	age	pos	lvl	org	ab	hr	sb	ba	bb%	ct%	px	sx	bpv
Flores,Wilmer	14	R	23	SS	aaa	NYM	220	8	0	248	4	78	108	56	26
Florimon Jr.,Pedro	14	B	28	SS	aaa	MIN	280	3	9	210	7	65	96	124	-10
Fontana,Nolan	14	L	23	2B	aa	HOU	229	1	4	225	17	62	113	57	-10
Fontenot,Mike	13	L	33	2B	aaa	TAM	417	3	4	200	6	73	77	81	-10
	14	L	34	2B	aaa	TAM	398	2	4	213	7	72	63	53	-29
Ford,Darren	13	R	28	LF	aaa	PIT	239	1	21	181	7	73	40	134	-21
	14	R	29	LF	aaa	SF	321	2	21	205	5	69	41	106	-49
Forsythe,Blake	13	R	24	C	aa	NYM	307	8	2	155	7	61	116	77	-24
	14	R	25	C	aa	OAK	232	3	0	183	8	61	93	49	-47
Fox,Jake	13	R	31	LF	aaa	ARI	34	0	0	102	3	59	54	20	-107
	14	R	32	DH	aa	PHI	286	16	0	234	4	77	138	14	35
Franco,Angel	13	B	23	2B	aa	KC	282	3	6	266	5	85	63	78	24
	14	B	24	2B	aa	KC	338	1	6	206	6	84	34	82	2
Franco,Maikel	13	R	21	3B	aa	PHI	277	12	1	305	3	87	109	59	62
	14	R	22	3B	aaa	PHI	521	13	2	228	4	83	102	68	43
Francoeur,Jeff	14	R	30	RF	aaa	SD	456	8	6	192	2	70	73	73	-31
Franklin,Nick	13	B	22	2B	aaa	SEA	142	3	5	279	13	84	82	76	51
	14	B	23	2B	aaa	TAM	379	9	9	241	11	72	95	75	11
Freeman,Michael	13	L	26	2B	aa	ARI	454	1	23	216	10	79	42	88	-3
	14	L	27	CF	a/a	ARI	414	4	8	213	6	81	70	133	33
Freiman,Nathan	14	R	27	1B	aaa	OAK	310	9	0	210	8	71	116	33	2
Freitas,David	13	R	24	C	a/a	OAK	321	7	0	187	7	81	67	36	4
	14	R	25	C	a/a	BAL	190	5	0	219	8	84	90	18	31
Frey,Evan	13	L	27	CF	a/a	TAM	293	0	13	202	10	76	30	104	-20
	14	L	28	LF	aaa	COL	161	1	1	162	7	79	50	64	-11
Fryer,Eric	13	R	28	C	aaa	MIN	200	3	5	167	10	72	83	115	10
	14	R	29	C	aaa	MIN	111	0	4	201	7	68	68	103	-27
Fuentes,Reymond	13	L	22	RF	a/a	SD	400	5	27	282	9	76	75	113	18
	14	L	23	CF	a/a	SD	327	4	18	239	7	76	68	137	16
Gale,Rocky	13	R	25	C	a/a	SD	227	1	0	191	3	89	22	23	-13
	14	R	26	C	aaa	SD	228	0	1	216	2	81	35	31	-32
Gallas,Anthony	14	R	27	LF	aa	CLE	280	11	0	235	5	68	141	41	11
Gallo,Joey	14	L	21	3B	aa	TEX	250	18	2	218	11	52	252	46	47
Galloway,Isaac	13	R	24	CF	aa	MIA	139	1	4	152	4	62	69	105	-56
	14	R	25	CF	aa	MIA	314	2	6	181	3	60	77	132	-49
Galvez,Jonathan	13	R	22	2B	aaa	SD	410	4	15	225	5	70	70	102	-21
	14	R	23	LF	aaa	SD	343	6	2	212	7	72	94	57	-3
Galvis,Freddy	13	B	24	SS	aaa	PHI	241	2	2	209	3	75	74	78	-7
	14	B	25	SS	aaa	PHI	135	2	1	222	6	78	124	78	48
Gamache,Dan	14	L	24	2B	aa	PIT	138	4	0	226	5	75	123	42	22
Gamel,Benjamin	13	L	21	RF	aa	NYY	67	1	1	221	5	71	84	39	-24
	14	L	22	LF	aa	NYY	544	2	11	235	5	82	57	84	13
Garcia,Adonis	13	R	28	CF	aaa	NYY	199	3	3	211	4	87	54	58	19
	14	R	29	CF	aaa	NYY	342	7	7	244	3	81	81	98	26
Garcia,Drew	13	B	27	2B	aaa	COL	216	1	2	177	3	66	75	67	-46
	14	B	28	SS	aaa	COL	304	3	3	182	4	62	84	67	-56
Garcia,Edwin	14	B	23	SS	aa	TEX	102	0	1	185	6	78	36	64	-27
Garcia,Greg	13	L	24	SS	aaa	STL	354	2	10	228	9	78	71	107	20
	14	L	25	2B	a/a	STL	397	5	6	221	7	71	63	83	-25
Garcia,Rene	13	R	23	C	a/a	HOU	368	4	2	256	4	84	62	48	12
	14	R	24	C	aa	HOU	270	4	4	206	2	86	63	69	22
Garcia,Willy	14	R	22	RF	aa	PIT	439	12	6	232	4	65	133	93	5
Garneau,Dustin	13	R	26	C	aa	COL	326	11	3	209	5	81	101	54	34
	14	R	27	C	a/a	COL	263	5	3	197	6	83	86	62	34
Gaynor,Wade	13	R	25	3B	aa	DET	477	9	9	192	5	65	108	105	-11
	14	R	26	3B	a/a	DET	381	9	8	193	6	61	148	118	12
Geiger,Dustin	14	R	23	1B	aa	CHC	399	9	1	194	8	70	106	40	-4
Giansanti,Anthony	13	R	25	RF	a/a	CHC	130	0	1	229	3	76	72	82	-5
	14	R	26	LF	aa	CHC	221	2	2	195	5	81	41	67	-11
Giavotella,Johnny	13	R	26	2B	aaa	KC	370	5	6	242	9	82	73	54	23
	14	R	27	2B	aaa	KC	441	4	13	244	7	90	70	93	60
Gibbs,Micah	14	B	26	C	aa	KC	161	1	2	182	8	76	71	35	-13
Gibson,Derrik	13	R	24	2B	aa	BOS	260	1	9	224	9	74	75	95	5
	14	R	25	CF	a/a	BOS	369	3	8	259	8	79	70	100	19
Gillespie,Cole	13	R	29	LF	aaa	SF	235	5	4	199	8	71	80	87	-8
	14	R	30	LF	aaa	TOR	140	5	4	288	11	79	133	104	75
Gillies,Tyson	13	L	25	CF	a/a	PHI	390	8	12	200	5	71	82	123	1
	14	L	26	CF	aaa	PHI	159	2	2	172	3	67	56	54	-65
Gimenez,Chris	13	R	31	C	aaa	TAM	308	2	1	168	11	73	52	40	-28
	14	R	32	C	aaa	TEX	134	4	0	211	8	72	90	57	-7
Gimenez,Hector	14	B	32	LF	a/a	MIL	261	8	0	167	5	69	113	16	-17
Gimenez,Wilfredo	14	R	24	C	aa	MIA	148	1	1	206	2	86	50	42	3
Gindl,Caleb	13	L	25	CF	aaa	MIL	312	9	1	246	6	72	117	45	11
	14	L	26	RF	aaa	MIL	362	6	1	186	8	70	88	45	-17
Glaesmann,Todd	13	R	23	LF	aa	TAM	487	9	5	208	4	74	87	82	2
	14	R	24	RF	aa	ARI	166	1	4	186	4	66	70	80	-47
Glenn,Brad	13	R	26	RF	a/a	TOR	485	17	1	219	7	71	125	51	15
	14	R	27	RF	a/a	TOR	403	12	2	228	7	68	125	62	4
Goebbert,Jake	13	L	26	LF	a/a	OAK	466	14	4	206	9	74	101	81	22
	14	L	27	LF	aaa	SD	280	8	1	209	10	75	110	71	29
Goedert,Jared	13	R	28	3B	aaa	PIT	464	7	3	189	7	72	89	72	-3
	14	R	29	3B	aaa	TOR	344	8	2	201	9	71	85	63	-10
Goins,Ryan	13	L	25	SS	aaa	TOR	377	5	2	221	5	73	80	50	-14
	14	L	26	SS	aaa	TOR	363	0	3	244	6	79	57	57	-8
Gomez,Hector	13	R	25	SS	aa	MIL	368	2	5	168	4	75	41	65	-37
	14	R	26	SS	aaa	MIL	408	12	4	235	4	76	118	90	35
Gomez,Raywilly	13	B	23	C	aa	ARI	224	0	1	255	10	88	49	28	23
	14	B	24	C	aa	PHI	221	3	0	214	7	87	51	17	10

BATTER	yr	b	age	pos	lvl	org	ab	hr	sb	ba	bb%	ct%	px	sx	bpv
Gonzales,Michael	14	L	26	1B	aa	MIN	106	2	0	219	6	72	100	28	-12
Gonzalez,Erik	14	R	23	SS	aa	CLE	129	1	5	315	4	79	68	127	20
Gonzalez,Maikol	14	R	28	LF	aa	LAA	319	1	24	221	11	80	38	132	13
Gonzalez,Miguel	13	R	23	C	a/a	CHW	169	2	2	227	8	76	65	65	-8
	14	R	24	C	a/a	CHW	146	2	0	202	4	84	74	42	18
Goodwin,Brian	13	L	23	CF	aa	WAS	457	8	15	227	10	72	91	136	22
	14	L	24	CF	aaa	WAS	275	3	4	186	11	62	76	90	-39
Goris,Diego	14	R	24	SS	aa	SD	146	3	1	207	1	79	65	59	-8
Gose,Anthony	13	L	23	CF	aaa	TOR	393	3	17	215	7	65	75	143	-20
	14	L	24	CF	aaa	TOR	205	3	17	218	6	64	75	142	-28
Gosselin,Phil	13	R	25	2B	a/a	ATL	425	2	5	218	4	81	39	79	-12
	14	R	26	3B	aaa	ATL	378	3	4	279	3	79	87	94	25
Gotay,Ruben	13	B	31	3B	aa	STL	498	10	10	204	9	75	80	63	4
	14	B	32	2B	aaa	CIN	518	12	2	187	7	67	84	49	-34
Graham,Tyler	14	R	30	CF	aa	SF	412	2	27	194	4	78	33	111	-19
Graterol,Juan	13	R	24	C	aa	KC	182	2	2	250	2	87	44	51	5
	14	R	25	C	a/a	KC	266	3	0	233	2	86	66	9	7
Grayson,Christopher	14	L	25	CF	aa	TEX	158	2	2	208	8	69	72	52	-33
Green,Dean	14	L	25	DH	aa	DET	409	7	0	255	4	78	85	33	0
Green,Grant	13	R	26	2B	aaa	LAA	402	6	2	243	4	76	83	66	0
	14	R	27	SS	aaa	LAA	198	3	2	239	3	80	91	89	27
Green,Taylor	14	L	28	3B	a/a	MIL	179	2	0	185	4	81	61	19	-13
Greene,Brodie	13	R	26	2B	aa	CIN	304	3	3	197	6	85	42	55	3
	14	R	27	SS	aa	CIN	362	2	7	180	7	82	44	76	3
Greene,Tyler	13	R	30	RF	aaa	ATL	250	3	7	196	5	61	83	107	-44
	14	R	31	SS	aaa	SD	473	5	4	197	3	58	92	79	-63
Gregor,Conrad	14	L	22	1B	aa	HOU	109	2	0	210	8	78	78	59	12
Gregorius,Didi	13	L	23	DH	aaa	ARI	31	1	1	324	4	96	103	55	94
	14	L	24	2B	aaa	ARI	226	2	2	256	6	87	75	100	51
Grichuk,Randal	13	R	22	RF	aa	LAA	500	18	8	231	4	80	117	122	61
	14	R	23	LF	aaa	STL	436	17	6	214	4	72	124	85	24
Grider,Casio	14	R	27	2B	a/a	LA	142	2	5	148	5	51	79	119	-84
Griffin,Jonathan	13	R	24	1B	aa	ARI	220	3	0	213	5	65	65	51	-60
	14	R	25	1B	aa	ARI	353	12	0	188	6	64	115	24	-29
Grossman,Robert	13	B	24	CF	aaa	HOU	253	2	11	239	13	69	59	100	-19
	14	B	25	CF	aaa	HOU	175	3	7	275	8	73	111	69	21
Guerrero,Alexander	14	R	28	2B	aaa	LA	243	8	2	233	2	76	114	81	26
Guevara,Hector	13	R	22	3B	aa	TAM	113	0	2	202	8	83	28	52	-11
	14	R	23	2B	aa	TAM	102	1	0	183	6	89	79	15	37
Guez,Ben	13	R	26	RF	aaa	DET	425	14	6	206	10	64	117	78	-5
	14	R	27	RF	aaa	DET	404	12	5	188	6	63	131	89	-1
Ha,Jae-Hoon	13	R	23	CF	a/a	CHC	323	5	12	224	6	77	74	87	9
	14	R	24	CF	a/a	CHC	462	4	4	194	4	81	51	46	-12
Hager,Jake	14	R	21	SS	aa	TAM	447	3	3	242	5	77	76	71	4
Hagerty,Jason	13	B	26	C	aaa	SD	25	0	0	117	11	85	0	16	-31
	14	B	27	1B	aa	SD	350	8	3	209	10	74	91	56	6
Hague,Matt	13	R	28	1B	aaa	PIT	536	5	3	226	8	79	72	50	7
	14	R	29	3B	aaa	TOR	383	12	1	228	8	75	113	42	20
Hague,Rick	13	R	25	2B	aa	WAS	437	6	2	211	5	74	70	76	-12
	14	R	26	3B	aa	WAS	321	3	6	182	5	73	71	60	-20
Halton,Sean	13	R	26	RF	aaa	MIL	352	8	4	221	7	68	126	78	11
	14	R	27	LF	aaa	MIL	416	6	0	238	5	73	96	54	-4
Hamilton,Mark	13	L	29	DH	aaa	BOS	283	8	1	210	10	62	139	40	-8
	14	L	30	1B	aaa	ATL	257	4	0	171	9	60	92	51	-52
Haniger,Mitch	14	R	24	RF	aa	ARI	267	8	3	233	6	81	88	88	35
Hanson,Alen	13	B	21	SS	aa	PIT	137	1	5	231	4	81	59	123	17
	14	B	22	SS	aa	PIT	482	7	19	242	4	81	80	128	36
Hanson,Nate	13	R	26	3B	a/a	MIN	431	6	1	197	6	80	71	59	11
	14	R	27	DH	a/a	MIN	450	4	1	210	6	82	75	49	16
Harris,Devin	14	R	26	LF	aa	SF	394	9	2	211	5	64	124	71	-12
Hassan,Alexander	13	R	25	RF	aaa	BOS	187	3	0	283	12	69	109	21	-2
	14	R	26	RF	aaa	BOS	408	6	2	251	10	69	114	52	5
Hazelbaker,Jeremy	13	L	26	LF	aaa	BOS	428	8	27	218	6	64	75	120	-33
	14	L	27	RF	a/a	LA	361	5	13	177	5	66	72	121	-29
Head,Miles	13	R	22	3B	aa	OAK	148	1	0	168	6	69	44	32	-65
	14	R	23	DH	aa	OAK	210	5	1	186	4	72	81	55	-19
Hebert,Brock	14	R	23	2B	a/a	SEA	123	0	2	148	6	64	18	66	-97
Hedges,Austin	13	R	21	C	aa	SD	67	0	3	198	7	85	34	58	0
	14	R	22	C	aa	SD	427	5	1	195	4	76	64	40	-22
Heid,Andrew	13	L	26	LF	a/a	LAA	347	4	5	240	9	70	83	79	-9
	14	L	27	RF	a/a	LAA	352	1	5	187	6	77	35	97	-21
Heineman,Tyler	14	B	23	C	aa	HOU	265	1	2	208	6	84	59	85	23
Henry,Justin	13	L	28	2B	aaa	BOS	357	1	6	172	7	81	50	82	4
	14	L	29	2B	aaa	BOS	215	1	4	205	9	78	54	98	3
Henson,Tyler	13	R	26	3B	a/a	PHI	353	6	9	227	7	60	122	104	-16
	14	R	27	2B	aaa	PHI	426	7	13	217	6	62	109	103	-20
Heras,Leonardo	13	L	23	LF	aa	HOU	39	1	1	181	14	68	112	114	25
	14	L	24	LF	aa	HOU	313	4	14	201	11	78	71	125	32
Hermida,Jeremy	13	L	29	DH	aaa	CLE	474	12	1	194	12	60	113	44	-32
	14	L	30	RF	aaa	MIL	340	12	0	196	11	65	128	21	-7
Hernandez,Brian	14	R	26	1B	aa	LAA	458	5	4	261	6	78	68	43	-7
Hernandez,Cesar	13	B	23	2B	a/a	PHI	401	2	25	274	7	76	52	141	7
	14	B	24	SS	a/a	PHI	259	2	6	247	8	79	61	95	9
Hernandez,Enrique	13	R	22	2B	aa	HOU	437	11	4	210	6	82	77	69	24
	14	R	23	2B	a/a	MIA	376	7	4	272	6	88	85	65	52
Hernandez,Gorkys	13	R	26	CF	aaa	KC	430	4	19	225	5	67	69	130	-25
	14	R	27	CF	aaa	CHW	189	0	5	174	5	69	45	73	-54
Herrera,Dilson	14	R	20	2B	aa	NYM	241	8	7	296	8	75	132	106	57

BATTER	yr	b	age	pos	lvl	org	ab	hr	sb	ba	bb%	ct%	px	sx	bpv
Herrera,Elian	13	B	28	2B	aaa	LA	408	4	10	209	7	76	43	87	-20
	14	B	29	CF	aaa	MIL	115	0	3	236	5	78	74	123	20
Herrera,Odubel	13	L	22	2B	aa	TEX	389	2	13	246	4	82	50	123	14
	14	L	23	2B	aa	TEX	368	2	10	293	6	79	57	92	5
Herrmann,Chris	13	L	26	C	aaa	MIN	247	1	2	186	6	71	52	91	-31
	14	L	27	C	aaa	MIN	204	3	3	255	7	74	129	112	49
Hessman,Mike	13	R	35	1B	aaa	CIN	420	21	0	193	8	59	189	21	11
	14	R	36	3B	aaa	DET	420	19	3	191	8	66	139	67	14
Hester,John	13	R	30	C	aaa	LAA	253	4	2	159	5	61	81	68	-60
	14	R	31	C	aaa	LAA	241	3	2	173	5	61	87	57	-58
Hewitt,Anthony	13	R	24	RF	aa	PHI	386	12	15	205	5	60	125	113	-16
	14	R	25	DH	aa	PHI	100	1	2	114	1	54	31	86	-128
Hicks,Aaron	13	B	24	CF	aaa	MIN	72	0	1	193	9	68	79	93	-17
	14	B	25	CF	a/a	MIN	220	4	2	250	11	79	96	66	39
Hicks,Brandon	13	R	28	SS	aaa	NYM	318	7	5	197	5	53	96	104	-68
	14	R	29	2B	aaa	SF	133	3	0	152	6	53	151	27	-47
Hicks,John	13	R	24	C	aa	SEA	296	3	11	215	6	76	67	108	4
	14	R	25	C	a/a	SEA	290	3	5	235	6	72	67	87	-17
Hill,Koyie	13	B	34	C	aaa	MIA	190	1	0	185	5	75	66	25	-27
	14	B	35	C	aaa	PHI	176	2	0	170	10	67	85	39	-33
Hissey,Peter	13	L	23	RF	aa	BOS	262	2	13	237	6	74	80	119	9
	14	L	24	LF	a/a	BOS	183	0	4	259	6	73	56	99	-21
Hobson,KC	14	L	24	1B	aa	TOR	177	4	1	190	6	74	90	38	-8
Hoes,LJ	13	R	23	RF	aaa	BAL	365	3	6	274	11	83	69	66	32
	14	R	24	CF	aaa	HOU	128	1	4	246	8	72	64	65	-23
Holt,Brock	13	L	25	2B	aaa	BOS	291	2	6	223	7	79	32	63	-24
	14	L	26	SS	aaa	BOS	108	1	5	277	5	87	88	139	73
Holt,Tyler	13	R	24	CF	aa	CLE	521	1	20	221	7	80	52	127	15
	14	R	25	CF	a/a	CLE	351	1	24	256	12	76	58	115	11
Hood,Destin	13	R	23	RF	aa	WAS	392	3	4	201	5	68	72	91	-29
	14	R	24	LF	a/a	WAS	382	8	7	255	4	76	99	81	17
Hopkins,Gregory	14	R	26	2B	aa	MIL	209	5	4	171	8	76	74	78	7
Howard,Justin	13	L	26	1B	aa	PIT	283	5	5	258	9	75	81	61	3
	14	L	27	DH	aa	PIT	159	2	1	179	6	70	78	42	-31
Hoying,Jared	13	L	24	RF	a/a	TEX	341	11	5	231	4	66	128	119	14
	14	L	25	CF	aaa	TEX	509	18	13	223	5	68	145	113	35
Hudson,Kyle	13	L	26	LF	aa	BAL	353	0	19	241	10	81	17	97	-10
	14	L	27	CF	aa	LAA	197	0	9	202	10	76	21	101	-27
Humphries,Brian	14	L	24	LF	aa	COL	402	3	7	254	2	81	67	91	11
Hunt,Bridger	14	R	29	3B	aa	SD	140	1	1	161	3	82	28	68	-21
Hunter,Cedric	13	L	25	LF	a/a	CLE	330	10	3	236	5	82	118	75	59
	14	L	26	LF	aa	ATL	399	10	11	246	10	84	108	93	72
Ibarra,Walter	13	B	26	SS	a/a	NYY	199	3	2	237	4	63	68	75	-62
	14	B	27	2B	a/a	LA	365	3	4	196	3	74	43	43	-49
Inciarte,Ender David	13	L	23	CF	aa	ARI	473	4	37	264	5	89	50	136	49
	14	L	24	CF	aaa	ARI	109	1	4	258	5	78	68	130	17
Iribarren,Hernan	13	L	29	2B	aaa	COL	253	1	5	232	5	79	50	80	-7
	14	L	30	LF	aaa	CIN	249	1	1	169	6	76	37	60	-34
Ishikawa,Travis	13	L	30	1B	aaa	CHW	297	7	1	225	10	67	113	57	-2
	14	L	31	1B	aaa	SF	240	6	0	189	6	66	82	24	-51
Jackson,Brett	13	L	25	CF	a/a	CHC	310	4	7	183	8	58	89	105	-49
	14	L	26	RF	aaa	ARI	240	4	3	163	6	49	105	95	-75
Jacobo,Gabriel	13	R	26	1B	aa	TOR	123	5	1	306	5	80	126	37	45
	14	R	27	1B	aa	TOR	137	3	1	121	3	67	84	16	-50
Jacobs,Mike	13	L	33	1B	aaa	ARI	329	10	0	217	5	73	96	21	-14
	14	L	34	1B	aaa	ARI	501	11	0	217	6	69	108	22	-18
Jamieson,Sean	14	R	25	SS	aa	ARI	329	4	5	262	7	79	85	100	29
Janish,Paul	13	R	31	SS	aaa	ATL	135	0	0	157	6	69	31	22	-78
	14	R	32	SS	aaa	KC	362	2	1	199	5	82	52	39	-8
Jankowski,Travis	14	L	23	CF	aa	SD	100	0	8	206	6	84	39	138	21
Jensen,Kyle	13	R	25	RF	a/a	MIA	447	19	5	197	8	63	163	68	22
	14	R	26	RF	aaa	MIA	497	15	1	197	6	64	120	34	-22
Jeroloman,Brian	13	L	28	C	a/a	WAS	179	0	0	181	9	65	41	45	-74
	14	L	29	C	aa	WAS	234	4	0	137	7	69	52	23	-59
Jimenez,Antonio	13	R	23	C	a/a	TOR	233	2	1	240	5	81	78	38	10
	14	R	24	C	a/a	TOR	313	3	2	223	5	81	78	55	14
Jimenez,Luis	13	R	25	3B	aaa	LAA	197	2	7	215	3	84	54	101	18
	14	R	26	3B	aaa	LAA	469	11	7	206	3	80	96	78	27
Johnson,Dan	13	L	34	1B	aaa	BAL	472	16	1	196	12	77	100	23	23
	14	L	35	1B	aaa	TOR	362	14	0	185	14	71	123	24	21
Johnson,Elliot	14	B	30	LF	aaa	CLE	314	3	7	176	8	66	76	118	-22
Johnson,Jamie	13	L	26	RF	aa	DET	406	1	20	230	15	79	44	107	18
	14	L	27	CF	aa	DET	446	3	7	203	8	86	52	90	33
Johnson,Joshua	13	B	27	SS	a/a	WAS	249	6	7	239	10	81	83	99	40
	14	B	28	2B	aaa	WAS	258	0	4	185	10	80	26	69	-14
Johnson,Kyle	14	R	25	LF	aa	NYM	359	3	8	200	7	72	80	102	1
Johnson,Micah	13	L	23	2B	aa	CHW	21	0	1	212	0	78	0	74	-62
	14	L	24	2B	a/a	CHW	419	4	15	242	6	80	61	94	13
Jones,Corey	13	L	26	2B	a/a	DET	78	0	1	161	7	77	32	49	-36
	14	L	27	3B	aa	DET	415	3	3	239	4	79	76	50	2
Jones,James	13	L	25	RF	a/a	SEA	378	4	21	233	8	76	73	131	21
	14	L	26	CF	aaa	SEA	156	1	5	219	5	75	58	111	-8
Jones,Jonathan	14	R	25	CF	aa	TOR	172	1	5	202	7	82	53	108	20
Jones,Mycal	13	R	26	CF	aa	ATL	345	3	23	223	8	78	59	107	9
	14	R	27	CF	a/a	ATL	381	2	15	202	7	76	61	100	0
Joseph,Corban	13	L	25	2B	aaa	NYY	188	6	2	212	9	76	92	62	17
	14	L	26	DH	aaa	NYY	235	3	0	217	5	84	65	49	17
Kalish,Ryan	14	L	26	CF	aaa	CHC	287	6	8	205	7	69	94	99	-2

BATTER	yr	b	age	pos	lvl	org	ab	hr	sb	ba	bb%	ct%	px	sx	bpv
Kang,Kyeong	13	L	25	LF	aa	TAM	346	11	2	212	10	65	133	103	21
	14	L	26	DH	aa	BAL	376	9	1	232	6	73	103	56	5
Kawasaki,Munenori	13	L	32	SS	aaa	TOR	60	0	2	191	14	74	0	63	-56
	14	L	33	SS	aaa	TOR	116	0	1	221	5	81	84	66	23
Kazmar,Sean	13	R	29	SS	aaa	ATL	272	1	6	175	4	81	52	78	-1
	14	R	30	3B	aaa	ATL	232	3	1	221	5	84	75	57	24
Kelly,Tyler	13	B	25	2B	a/a	SEA	480	3	5	252	13	77	63	62	8
	14	B	26	2B	aaa	SEA	456	9	7	203	10	74	76	75	1
Kemp,Anthony	14	L	23	2B	aa	HOU	233	3	10	254	8	84	73	125	51
Kennelly,Matt	13	R	24	C	a/a	CIN	88	1	1	194	5	80	47	64	-10
	14	R	25	C	aa	ATL	252	0	1	225	6	82	36	50	-15
Keyes,Kevin	14	R	25	RF	aa	WAS	402	13	1	190	6	71	100	36	-12
Keys,Brent	13	L	23	RF	aa	MIA	32	0	1	255	12	90	0	41	-3
	14	L	24	RF	aa	MIA	293	0	5	206	12	87	27	71	17
Kiermaier,Kevin	13	L	23	CF	a/a	TAM	508	5	17	263	7	81	74	138	38
	14	L	24	CF	aaa	TAM	128	2	9	268	7	79	95	166	59
Kieschnick,Roger	13	L	26	RF	aaa	SF	374	7	3	212	6	67	122	99	10
	14	L	27	RF	aaa	ARI	369	9	3	199	4	71	112	78	7
Kivlehan,Patrick	14	R	25	3B	aa	SEA	377	8	7	250	8	75	105	99	31
Kleinknecht,Barrett	13	R	25	1B	aa	ATL	235	6	0	207	6	78	79	34	1
	14	R	26	1B	aa	ATL	293	7	2	232	4	79	101	76	28
Knudson,Kyle	13	R	26	C	aa	MIN	88	0	0	243	7	83	44	16	-12
	14	R	27	C	aa	MIN	247	0	0	174	4	73	58	16	-48
Kobernus,Jeff	13	R	25	LF	aaa	WAS	371	1	31	268	5	82	47	124	14
	14	R	26	LF	a/a	WAS	230	1	12	210	7	76	65	101	1
Koch,Matthew	14	R	26	C	aa	MIN	217	1	1	175	8	69	53	46	-48
Komatsu,Erik	13	L	26	RF	a/a	WAS	54	0	0	137	7	73	16	46	-66
	14	L	27	LF	a/a	MIL	259	5	5	155	9	69	72	64	-29
Kozma,Pete	14	R	26	SS	aaa	STL	379	5	7	193	7	81	69	69	15
Kral,Robert	13	L	24	DH	aa	SD	65	2	0	130	16	75	79	7	-3
	14	L	25	C	aa	SD	193	4	1	147	12	66	80	33	-35
Krauss,Marc	13	L	26	LF	aaa	HOU	253	8	2	230	13	75	110	61	34
	14	L	27	1B	aaa	HOU	159	3	1	224	8	66	116	34	-16
Krill,Brett	13	R	24	RF	aa	SF	225	1	2	213	3	72	50	59	-46
	14	R	25	RF	a/a	SF	128	0	1	165	5	75	39	104	-28
Krizan,Jason	14	L	25	LF	aa	DET	464	5	10	241	7	89	68	80	49
Kubitza,Kyle	14	L	24	3B	aa	ATL	440	6	16	258	12	65	128	132	27
Kvasnicka,Michael	14	B	26	RF	aa	MIN	370	7	4	213	5	75	90	44	-3
La Stella,Tommy	13	L	24	2B	aa	ATL	283	3	6	308	10	86	82	77	55
	14	L	25	2B	aaa	ATL	167	1	1	241	10	90	36	44	23
Ladendorf,Tyler	13	R	25	3B	a/a	OAK	294	4	1	199	7	81	68	54	10
	14	R	26	SS	aaa	OAK	273	1	2	227	8	75	70	77	-4
LaHair,Bryan	14	L	32	1B	a/a	CLE	399	3	1	167	8	67	64	46	-50
Laird,Brandon	13	R	26	3B	aaa	HOU	470	12	1	225	4	77	100	48	14
	14	R	27	3B	aaa	WAS	463	12	0	241	5	75	109	31	10
Lalli,Blake	13	L	30	C	aaa	MIL	284	8	0	211	5	68	95	19	-35
	14	L	31	C	aaa	ARI	284	2	0	198	5	74	62	32	-33
Lamb,Jacob	14	L	24	3B	a/a	ARI	392	11	1	282	8	70	167	79	57
Lambo,Andrew	13	L	25	LF	a/a	PIT	444	22	5	234	7	68	157	92	41
	14	L	26	1B	aaa	PIT	238	7	2	264	6	77	126	76	47
Landoni,Emerson	13	B	24	2B	aa	ATL	40	1	0	291	4	83	75	77	23
	14	B	25	2B	aa	ATL	181	1	4	229	8	81	35	62	-12
Landry,Leon	13	L	24	LF	aa	SEA	422	5	19	196	5	81	55	111	12
	14	L	25	CF	aa	SEA	422	1	18	233	3	86	57	131	37
Langfels,Jayson	13	R	25	3B	aa	COL	376	12	10	197	6	63	101	69	-31
	14	R	26	3B	aa	COL	307	3	11	243	9	64	63	106	-42
Lara,Jordy	14	R	23	RF	aa	SEA	126	3	0	250	4	83	135	19	55
LaRoche,Andy	13	R	30	3B	aaa	TOR	365	9	3	212	6	80	86	49	20
	14	R	31	3B	aaa	TOR	202	4	0	197	5	79	96	28	14
Latimore,Quincy	13	R	24	LF	aa	CLE	295	4	4	190	6	74	75	67	-10
	14	R	25	LF	aa	WAS	303	7	10	225	7	72	81	92	-4
LaTorre,Tyler	13	L	30	C	a/a	SF	89	1	0	94	8	54	37	15	-131
	14	L	31	C	a/a	SF	190	1	1	197	7	68	47	49	-60
Lavarnway,Ryan	13	R	26	C	aaa	BOS	180	2	0	214	9	84	61	24	12
	14	R	27	1B	a/a	BOS	230	3	0	240	10	76	65	15	-17
Lavin,Peter	14	L	27	LF	aa	PHI	251	4	4	226	4	85	83	101	45
Lavisky,Alex	13	R	22	C	aa	CLE	21	0	0	163	7	89	36	29	10
	14	R	23	C	aa	CLE	241	3	1	243	4	79	63	38	-12
Lawley,Dustin	13	R	24	LF	aaa	NYM	20	1	0	227	0	88	113	30	52
	14	R	25	3B	aa	NYM	447	14	3	182	5	63	133	55	-12
Lee,Hak-Ju	13	L	23	SS	aaa	TAM	45	1	5	380	17	77	110	147	75
	14	L	24	SS	aaa	TAM	315	3	10	176	9	69	52	94	-36
Lemmerman,Jacob	13	R	24	SS	aa	STL	308	5	8	189	12	67	85	89	-11
	14	R	25	3B	a/a	SD	218	3	1	134	8	65	80	69	-37
Lemon,Marcus	13	L	25	2B	aa	DET	294	1	2	210	6	76	49	105	-10
	14	L	26	2B	a/a	DET	212	2	1	180	6	76	62	62	-13
Lennerton,Jordan	13	L	27	1B	aaa	DET	514	13	0	232	11	70	93	26	-13
	14	L	28	1B	aaa	DET	410	7	0	199	11	67	100	43	-14
Leon,Sandy	13	B	24	C	aa	WAS	310	2	0	155	10	80	47	40	-8
	14	B	25	C	aaa	WAS	170	4	1	191	9	76	84	48	6
Leonard,Joe	13	R	25	3B	aaa	ATL	418	0	1	194	4	74	51	51	-38
	14	R	26	3B	a/a	ATL	247	1	1	214	6	73	53	54	-35
Leonida,Cole	14	R	26	C	aa	WAS	106	0	0	186	8	68	87	36	-29
Lerud,Steven	13	L	29	C	aaa	PHI	180	2	1	165	12	64	65	32	-56
	14	L	30	C	aaa	ATL	164	2	1	184	10	65	86	58	-32
Liddi,Alex	13	R	25	3B	aaa	BAL	425	13	8	212	5	61	124	122	-6
	14	R	26	3B	a/a	LA	338	7	2	153	6	54	96	60	-74
Lillibridge,Brent	14	R	31	2B	aaa	TEX	312	6	9	173	5	62	96	107	-33
Lindor,Francisco	13	B	20	SS	aa	CLE	76	1	4	259	12	90	52	105	60
	14	B	21	SS	a/a	CLE	507	9	23	247	7	79	66	104	15
Lindsey,Taylor	13	L	22	2B	aa	LAA	508	14	3	248	7	80	90	77	33
	14	L	23	2B	aaa	SD	441	6	4	180	5	84	59	87	21
Linton,Ollie	14	L	28	CF	aa	CLE	150	1	9	198	7	71	59	127	-13
Lipka,Matthew	14	R	22	CF	aa	ATL	106	0	8	168	6	84	48	112	24
Liriano,Rymer	14	R	23	LF	a/a	SD	433	10	14	235	7	68	117	99	9
Lisson,Mario	14	R	30	3B	aa	SF	379	11	8	201	9	68	112	71	5
Lohman,Devin	13	R	24	SS	aa	CIN	484	8	14	214	6	80	66	65	6
	14	R	25	SS	aa	CIN	330	4	6	205	6	73	72	78	-13
Lollis,Ryan	13	L	27	CF	aa	SF	469	5	4	207	7	84	55	61	14
	14	L	28	LF	aa	SF	203	1	1	172	6	83	31	88	-3
Loman,Seth	13	L	28	1B	a/a	BAL	316	11	0	198	7	59	137	29	-30
	14	L	29	1B	aa	ATL	318	8	3	201	5	68	109	65	-7
Lombardozzi,Steve	14	B	26	2B	aaa	BAL	270	0	4	218	4	86	26	61	-7
Long,Matt	13	L	26	LF	a/a	LAA	488	9	14	230	8	72	93	123	17
	14	L	27	CF	a/a	LAA	416	6	16	185	8	65	75	126	-24
Lopez,Alfredo	14	R	25	2B	aa	MIA	213	0	8	179	7	77	41	75	-19
Lopez,Rafael	13	L	26	C	aa	CHC	316	6	0	204	10	75	92	28	5
	14	L	27	C	a/a	CHC	355	3	1	233	10	73	63	32	-25
Lopez,Roberto	13	R	28	LF	aaa	LAA	432	5	6	205	4	78	67	81	-1
	14	R	29	LF	aaa	LAA	400	6	2	198	3	76	64	47	-21
Lowery,Jake	13	L	23	C	aa	CLE	236	4	0	234	9	68	126	21	-1
	14	L	24	C	aa	CLE	219	4	1	169	10	63	83	77	-37
Lozada,Jose	13	B	28	SS	aa	WAS	201	1	2	164	6	69	33	53	-70
	14	B	29	RF	a/a	WAS	165	1	3	211	5	74	27	56	-56
Lutz,Donald	13	L	24	LF	aa	CIN	229	7	3	225	7	72	120	120	35
	14	L	25	LF	a/a	CIN	284	10	4	229	6	64	141	102	13
Lutz,Zach	13	R	27	3B	aaa	NYM	399	8	0	208	7	66	99	45	-26
	14	R	28	3B	aaa	NYM	227	4	1	197	6	70	75	60	-27
Machado,Dixon	14	R	22	SS	aa	DET	292	4	6	267	9	87	85	68	56
Maggi,Andrew	13	R	24	SS	aa	PIT	264	1	14	217	7	80	53	117	13
	14	R	25	3B	aa	PIT	347	2	26	227	9	81	37	95	3
Mahtook,Mikie	13	R	24	RF	aa	TAM	511	5	20	218	6	77	80	135	26
	14	R	25	CF	aaa	TAM	489	9	15	251	7	67	121	113	14
Maile,Luke	14	R	23	C	aa	TAM	351	4	2	232	7	75	77	69	0
Malm,Jeffrey	14	L	24	LF	aa	TAM	326	4	2	217	5	74	71	50	-19
Marder,Jack	13	R	23	2B	aa	SEA	275	3	7	202	7	76	62	98	-1
	14	R	24	2B	aa	SEA	238	3	1	235	8	80	71	73	17
Marisnick,Jake	13	R	22	CF	aa	MIA	265	9	9	271	5	72	121	125	36
	14	R	23	CF	aaa	MIA	343	6	16	229	3	79	78	126	25
Marrero,Chris	13	R	25	1B	aaa	WAS	408	8	0	225	6	81	67	39	5
	14	R	26	1B	a/a	BAL	355	10	0	193	5	75	95	41	2
Marrero,Christian	13	L	27	1B	aa	ATL	399	6	5	193	14	78	81	75	29
	14	L	28	DH	aa	CHW	161	5	3	232	12	73	119	50	27
Marrero,Deven	13	R	23	SS	aa	BOS	72	0	5	211	9	76	0	76	-53
	14	R	24	SS	a/a	BOS	454	5	13	235	7	77	89	92	24
Marte,Alfredo	13	R	24	RF	aaa	ARI	311	4	1	225	4	77	91	46	3
	14	R	25	LF	aaa	ARI	270	7	4	257	8	74	108	88	26
Marte,Andy	13	R	30	3B	aaa	LAA	94	3	0	252	4	77	74	41	-12
	14	R	31	3B	aaa	ARI	471	11	1	240	5	83	93	49	33
Marte,Jefry	13	R	22	3B	aa	OAK	245	1	6	243	8	78	73	92	15
	14	R	23	3B	aa	OAK	405	7	7	219	8	81	66	62	13
Marte,Ketel	14	B	21	SS	a/a	SEA	523	3	22	267	4	83	70	117	33
Martin,Dustin	13	L	29	RF	aa	ARI	217	6	9	247	9	72	125	132	46
	14	L	30	RF	a/a	ARI	273	6	4	209	8	72	98	59	2
Martinez,Francisco	13	R	23	CF	aa	SEA	126	0	6	192	4	62	58	86	-71
	14	R	24	3B	aa	DET	317	1	15	185	4	75	37	97	-31
Martinez,Jose	13	R	27	2B	a/a	HOU	338	4	3	240	4	88	62	55	30
	14	R	28	3B	aaa	OAK	446	4	1	200	6	85	45	33	-1
Martinez,Luis	13	R	28	C	a/a	BAL	214	1	0	204	6	76	65	29	-22
	14	R	29	C	aaa	OAK	231	2	0	170	5	76	68	24	-23
Martinez,Michael	13	B	31	SS	aaa	PHI	243	2	4	229	5	80	55	86	1
	14	B	32	2B	aaa	PIT	315	1	5	181	5	82	28	91	-9
Martinez,Osvaldo	13	R	25	3B	a/a	LA	296	3	4	203	6	84	55	53	8
	14	R	26	SS	a/a	ATL	351	1	4	206	6	83	41	79	1
Martinez,Teodoro	13	R	21	LF	aa	TEX	443	14	18	239	3	84	73	93	32
	14	R	22	LF	aa	TEX	311	3	2	253	4	81	61	38	-6
Martinson,Jason	13	R	25	SS	aa	WAS	173	3	2	159	8	64	69	99	-41
	14	R	26	SS	aa	WAS	466	6	15	187	6	68	69	113	-24
Marzilli,Evan	14	L	23	CF	aa	ARI	285	2	6	225	7	74	79	112	12
Massey,Joseph	14	L	25	RF	aa	COL	469	7	21	234	5	79	71	126	24
Mastroianni,Darin	13	R	28	CF	aaa	MIN	50	0	3	187	12	73	17	85	-42
	14	R	29	CF	aaa	TOR	364	4	15	223	7	75	71	98	3
Mateo,Luis	13	R	23	SS	a/a	STL	360	3	11	202	4	82	44	91	2
	14	R	24	SS	a/a	STL	302	2	2	206	3	80	57	51	-11
Mattair,Travis	13	R	25	1B	aa	CIN	475	13	2	217	7	74	79	51	-10
	14	R	26	1B	aa	CIN	474	11	2	195	6	66	105	60	-22
Matthes,Kent	13	R	26	RF	a/a	COL	431	15	11	235	4	73	128	92	32
	14	R	27	LF	a/a	OAK	396	10	5	175	5	64	117	84	-12
Mattison,Kevin	13	L	28	CF	aaa	MIA	334	4	13	176	8	50	121	152	-40
	14	L	29	CF	aaa	MIL	217	5	9	164	6	52	136	130	-28
Maxwell,Justin	13	R	30	RF	a/a	HOU	49	1	1	91	5	63	29	82	-88
	14	R	31	RF	aaa	KC	207	5	2	211	6	55	118	70	-52
Mayora,Daniel	14	R	29	3B	aa	LA	494	6	4	221	5	83	61	62	12
McBride,Matt	13	R	28	C	aaa	COL	180	9	0	251	3	86	146	28	78
	14	R	29	RF	aaa	COL	187	4	0	231	3	88	81	42	38

BATTER	yr	b	age	pos	lvl	org	ab	hr	sb	ba	bb%	ct%	px	sx	bpv
McCann,James	13	R	23	C	aa	DET	441	6	2	246	5	79	84	51	12
	14	R	24	C	aaa	DET	417	5	7	258	4	76	98	66	15
McCoy,Mike	13	R	32	2B	aaa	TOR	355	3	20	190	10	75	52	100	-6
	14	R	33	SS	aaa	BOS	259	1	5	146	10	74	56	69	-19
McDade,Michael	13	B	24	DH	aaa	CHW	428	9	1	218	7	67	91	26	-34
	14	B	25	1B	a/a	TOR	298	6	0	210	5	76	72	14	-23
McElroy,Casey	14	L	25	2B	aa	SD	347	7	1	204	10	82	62	52	16
McGuiness,Christoph	13	L	25	1B	aaa	TEX	362	9	1	210	12	73	117	43	26
	14	L	26	1B	aaa	PIT	420	6	0	211	9	80	86	36	22
Mejia,Alejandro	14	R	23	SS	aa	STL	163	2	2	233	6	86	40	48	6
Mejias-Brean,Seth	14	R	23	3B	aa	CIN	226	3	1	204	10	75	56	52	-19
Melendres,Nathan	14	R	24	2B	aa	SEA	148	1	4	206	4	78	60	90	-4
Melker,Adam	13	L	25	RF	aa	STL	318	5	5	208	6	73	80	73	-10
	14	L	26	CF	aa	LAA	275	4	10	218	5	78	46	86	-13
Meneses,Heiker	13	R	22	SS	a/a	BOS	376	2	10	235	5	73	65	109	-13
	14	R	23	SS	a/a	BOS	364	1	7	182	5	82	38	88	-5
Meredith,Brandon	14	R	25	DH	aa	HOU	127	6	3	195	12	67	151	58	33
Merrifield,Whit	13	R	24	LF	aa	KC	322	2	13	240	5	81	76	115	31
	14	R	25	LF	a/a	KC	483	5	12	271	6	82	96	95	45
Mesa,Melky	13	R	26	CF	aaa	NYY	314	12	11	227	3	58	145	120	-7
	14	R	27	CF	a/a	TOR	215	7	2	223	3	64	144	71	-1
Meyer,Jonathan	13	R	23	3B	aa	HOU	484	12	2	227	6	74	89	40	-6
	14	R	24	3B	a/a	HOU	447	3	1	178	5	76	41	58	-36
Miclat,Gregory	13	B	26	2B	a/a	TEX	290	0	7	199	9	78	32	63	-25
	14	B	27	2B	a/a	STL	155	0	7	134	10	72	17	80	-55
Middlebrooks,Will	13	R	25	3B	aaa	BOS	179	7	1	231	6	76	97	37	6
	14	R	26	3B	aaa	BOS	104	3	0	197	4	67	77	60	-44
Mier,Jiovanni	13	R	23	SS	aa	HOU	355	4	7	168	9	69	48	64	-46
	14	R	24	SS	a/a	HOU	355	3	4	186	7	71	58	61	-37
Minicozzi,Mark	13	R	30	3B	aa	SF	443	6	2	228	8	64	88	47	-43
	14	R	31	1B	aaa	SF	315	6	1	210	8	65	92	37	-36
Mitchell,Derrick	13	R	26	LF	a/a	PHI	329	10	9	198	7	68	121	90	14
	14	R	27	RF	a/a	ATL	134	3	3	170	12	74	76	67	4
Mitchell,Jared	13	L	25	CF	a/a	CHW	300	4	13	142	13	52	77	100	-74
	14	L	26	LF	a/a	CHW	426	14	10	204	10	56	125	89	-26
Moncrief,Carlos	13	L	25	RF	aa	CLE	489	12	11	231	7	76	95	100	26
	14	L	26	RF	aaa	CLE	480	8	6	220	5	67	110	83	-6
Monell,Johnny	13	L	27	C	aaa	SF	415	11	4	206	8	69	111	69	2
	14	L	28	C	aaa	LA	206	2	2	164	4	75	64	61	-20
Montero,Jesus	13	R	24	1B	aaa	SEA	73	1	0	201	7	61	126	90	-13
	14	R	25	DH	aaa	SEA	364	10	1	227	6	73	112	41	10
Montilla,Gerson	14	R	25	2B	aa	ARI	336	5	1	236	6	78	66	59	-4
Moore,Adam	13	R	29	C	aaa	KC	131	5	0	146	8	52	136	34	-54
	14	R	30	C	aaa	SD	312	7	1	197	5	64	96	34	-43
Moore,Jeremy	13	L	26	LF	a/a	LA	240	5	4	166	6	59	96	72	-53
	14	L	27	LF	a/a	TAM	315	13	1	185	7	64	126	43	-13
Moore,Logan	14	L	24	C	aa	PHI	190	3	0	187	7	71	97	22	-16
Moore,Scott	13	L	30	3B	aaa	SD	424	8	0	185	7	65	100	31	-36
	14	L	31	3B	aaa	STL	416	9	1	168	6	71	82	39	-25
Moore,Tyler	13	R	26	LF	aaa	WAS	173	7	1	261	8	74	146	47	44
	14	R	27	1B	aaa	WAS	302	7	0	212	9	70	108	27	-5
Moran,Colin	14	L	22	3B	aa	HOU	112	2	0	268	6	77	75	25	-12
Morban,Julio	13	L	21	RF	aa	SEA	295	6	7	283	8	65	138	123	24
	14	L	22	RF	a/a	SEA	214	1	0	213	6	64	61	52	-64
Morel,Brent	13	R	26	3B	aaa	CHW	395	5	11	221	9	68	101	98	2
	14	R	27	3B	aaa	PIT	336	2	5	213	6	77	64	86	-1
Morin,Parker	14	L	23	C	a/a	KC	192	2	0	175	5	67	60	20	-67
Morris,Hunter	13	L	25	1B	aaa	MIL	497	19	2	206	6	71	121	57	10
	14	L	26	1B	a/a	MIL	356	9	0	231	4	73	103	38	-3
Mota,Jonathan	13	R	26	1B	aa	CHC	301	5	1	229	7	76	77	61	0
	14	R	27	1B	a/a	CHC	317	3	3	201	3	73	57	70	-33
Motter,Taylor	14	R	25	RF	aa	TAM	452	12	11	230	5	81	83	90	31
Moya,Steven	14	L	23	RF	aa	DET	515	25	11	235	3	66	172	104	42
Muncy,Max	13	L	23	1B	aa	OAK	172	3	0	214	10	78	96	61	28
	14	L	24	1B	aa	OAK	435	5	5	223	14	76	73	73	12
Muno,Daniel	13	B	24	2B	aa	NYM	449	7	11	202	13	74	79	82	13
	14	B	25	2B	aaa	NYM	359	8	5	187	9	71	75	69	-15
Murphy,James	13	R	28	1B	aa	PHI	505	16	1	212	7	70	104	33	-10
	14	R	29	1B	aaa	PHI	396	8	1	182	8	65	100	37	-32
Murphy,John	13	R	22	C	a/a	NYY	413	12	1	250	9	81	106	39	40
	13	B	25	C	a/a	TOR	205	2	0	187	5	78	74	41	-6
Murphy,John	14	B	26	C	a/a	TOR	163	5	0	189	9	73	99	27	-2
	14	R	23	C	aaa	NYY	179	5	0	213	5	74	98	13	-10
Myers,D'Arby	13	R	25	CF	aa	OAK	485	3	15	235	2	83	61	113	22
	14	R	26	LF	aa	OAK	213	1	7	249	6	79	73	105	17
Myles,Bryson	14	R	25	LF	aa	CLE	300	4	9	220	6	66	90	102	-21
Nakajima,Hiroyuki	13	R	31	3B	aaa	OAK	346	2	2	202	4	68	52	45	-61
	14	R	32	2B	aaa	OAK	295	3	3	177	6	71	50	44	-49
Naquin,Tyler	13	L	22	CF	aa	CLE	80	1	1	193	4	69	54	60	-51
	14	L	23	CF	aa	CLE	304	3	11	274	7	73	69	127	2
Nash,Telvin	14	R	23	1B	aa	HOU	273	17	1	197	9	53	182	37	-12
Navarro Jr,Efren	13	L	27	1B	aaa	LAA	513	4	5	238	7	75	72	63	-7
	14	L	28	1B	aaa	LAA	273	2	1	228	8	77	68	59	-2
Navarro,Reynaldo	13	B	24	3B	aa	KC	446	9	5	249	3	87	73	81	38
	14	B	25	SS	a/a	CIN	485	10	4	235	6	86	87	48	41
Neal,Thomas	13	R	26	RF	aaa	NYY	265	2	2	281	7	76	66	47	-12
	14	R	27	1B	aaa	CIN	364	3	1	197	6	76	56	48	-24

BATTER	yr	b	age	pos	lvl	org	ab	hr	sb	ba	bb%	ct%	px	sx	bpv
Negron,Kristopher	14	R	28	SS	aaa	CIN	219	2	6	204	4	68	89	114	-13
Nelson,Brad	13	L	31	1B	aaa	CHC	428	14	1	208	7	73	98	45	0
	14	L	32	1B	aaa	MIN	227	3	0	178	8	76	66	31	-14
Nelson,Chris	13	R	28	3B	aaa	LAA	134	3	2	234	3	77	99	59	15
	14	R	29	3B	aaa	SD	319	3	0	186	6	70	56	33	-51
Newman,Matthew	14	L	26	RF	aa	TOR	298	5	1	208	4	68	123	69	-1
Ngoepe,Gift	13	B	23	SS	aa	PIT	220	2	8	152	9	61	78	124	-37
	14	B	24	2B	aa	PIT	437	6	9	196	7	66	82	111	-19
Nicholas,Brett	13	L	25	1B	aa	TEX	506	18	2	259	7	73	117	58	18
	14	L	26	C	aaa	TEX	452	7	3	219	4	71	71	40	-38
Nickeas,Mike	13	R	30	C	aaa	TOR	175	1	0	129	6	71	68	29	-40
	14	R	31	C	aaa	TOR	150	2	1	162	8	74	40	32	-44
Nicol,Sean	13	R	27	3B	aa	WAS	277	1	4	209	9	83	46	69	8
	14	R	28	3B	a/a	WAS	117	0	3	191	5	78	54	91	-4
Nieuwenhuis,Kirk	13	L	26	CF	aaa	NYM	282	9	4	179	8	65	110	89	-9
	14	L	27	LF	aaa	NYM	211	6	2	183	4	65	121	83	-9
Nimmo,Brandon	14	L	21	CF	aa	NYM	240	5	4	198	10	74	90	103	22
Nina,Angelys	13	R	25	2B	aa	COL	446	9	14	255	5	87	78	99	50
	14	R	26	2B	aaa	COL	390	5	4	226	3	82	63	63	5
Nix,Jayson	14	R	32	2B	aaa	TAM	191	2	1	210	7	75	88	70	9
Noel,Rico	13	B	24	CF	aa	SD	496	0	48	227	8	71	49	147	-14
	14	B	25	CF	aaa	SD	333	1	19	187	7	69	35	106	-48
Nola,Austin	14	R	25	SS	aa	MIA	499	1	6	217	10	78	47	83	-2
Nolan,Kevin	13	R	26	SS	aa	TOR	451	7	4	216	6	83	71	68	22
	14	R	27	SS	a/a	TOR	425	4	7	213	5	84	64	80	22
Noonan,Nick	13	L	24	2B	aaa	SF	165	0	1	206	6	69	76	64	-28
	14	L	25	SS	aaa	SF	379	2	4	184	3	69	47	51	-61
Noriega,Gabriel	13	B	23	SS	aa	SEA	371	2	6	238	3	78	54	95	-7
	14	R	24	3B	a/a	SEA	389	2	2	229	2	72	69	49	-36
Nunez,Gustavo	13	B	25	2B	aaa	DET	186	0	5	167	5	73	19	57	-62
	14	B	26	SS	aa	ATL	306	1	8	251	6	77	44	96	-14
O Malley,Shawn	13	B	26	SS	aa	TAM	321	2	18	216	7	77	57	159	19
	14	B	27	SS	a/a	LAA	350	2	9	243	8	81	65	123	31
O Neill,Mike	13	L	25	LF	a/a	STL	471	1	14	259	12	91	30	87	40
	14	L	26	LF	a/a	STL	417	1	4	223	8	88	40	71	24
Oberacker,Chad	13	L	24	RF	aa	OAK	448	4	13	201	7	74	88	143	26
	14	L	25	LF	aa	OAK	291	1	6	179	6	79	53	108	5
O'Brien,Christopher	14	B	25	C	aa	LA	354	5	2	210	7	78	103	59	28
O'Brien,Peter	14	R	24	1B	aa	ARI	287	19	0	223	4	68	191	44	49
Odor,Rougned	13	L	19	2B	aa	TEX	134	6	4	309	6	82	139	110	86
	14	L	20	2B	aa	TEX	129	5	5	268	4	82	91	104	45
O'Dowd,Chris	14	B	24	C	aa	COL	134	0	5	244	8	77	50	65	-16
Ohlman,Michael	14	R	24	C	aa	BAL	403	2	0	199	7	76	63	27	-21
Olmedo,Ray	13	B	32	3B	aaa	MIN	312	1	7	176	7	81	36	87	-5
	14	B	33	3B	aaa	TAM	362	0	7	173	5	72	33	91	-47
Olt,Mike	13	R	25	3B	a/a	CHC	373	11	0	169	10	59	128	34	-28
	14	R	26	1B	aaa	CHC	106	5	1	248	5	63	193	38	29
Orlando,Paulo	13	R	28	CF	aaa	KC	293	3	6	226	5	77	53	100	-6
	14	R	29	CF	aaa	KC	501	3	21	230	5	79	58	119	9
Oropesa,Ricky	13	L	24	1B	aa	SF	241	4	0	169	4	65	56	16	-80
	14	L	25	1B	aa	SF	349	3	0	202	7	70	63	19	-45
Orr,Lee	13	R	25	RF	aa	SD	62	1	1	185	5	53	105	82	-68
	14	R	26	1B	aa	SD	222	6	5	136	4	45	132	81	-81
Orr,Pete	13	L	34	2B	aaa	PHI	325	3	6	196	3	75	68	104	-4
	14	L	35	2B	aaa	MIL	359	3	5	231	2	72	76	108	-13
Ortega,Rafael	13	L	22	CF	aa	COL	158	1	7	220	9	84	43	119	24
	14	L	23	CF	a/a	STL	379	5	13	210	9	82	46	102	14
Ortiz,Danny	13	L	23	LF	aa	MIN	484	8	1	225	4	80	82	62	15
	14	L	24	LF	a/a	MIN	424	9	2	252	2	78	110	93	34
Ortiz,Ryan	13	R	26	C	aaa	OAK	115	2	0	209	6	75	83	59	-3
	14	R	27	C	aaa	OAK	247	1	0	158	12	67	48	47	-56
Overbeck,Cody	13	R	27	1B	aaa	PHI	440	14	1	205	4	61	138	35	-26
	14	R	28	1B	aa	SD	251	10	0	182	3	66	108	44	-29
Pagnozzi,Matt	13	R	31	C	aaa	ATL	290	4	0	159	5	71	56	39	-48
	14	R	32	C	aaa	MIL	228	8	1	164	6	64	97	37	-43
Panik,Joe	13	L	23	2B	aa	SF	522	3	7	217	8	85	53	80	25
	14	L	24	2B	aaa	SF	293	3	2	259	6	87	60	81	33
Paolini,Daniel	13	R	24	1B	aa	SEA	103	0	1	150	13	73	55	58	-17
	14	R	25	1B	aa	SEA	410	9	2	223	9	78	114	48	37
Paredes,Jimmy	13	B	25	RF	aaa	HOU	327	6	12	242	6	75	101	128	35
	14	B	26	3B	aaa	BAL	401	6	14	235	3	68	98	121	-7
Parker,Jarrett	13	L	24	RF	aa	SF	444	11	9	202	9	58	113	102	-26
	14	L	25	RF	a/a	SF	442	9	8	224	8	66	111	98	2
Parker,Kyle	13	R	24	LF	aa	COL	480	20	5	267	6	79	120	68	45
	14	R	25	RF	aaa	COL	502	10	2	239	4	78	94	60	14
Parmelee,Chris	13	L	25	1B	aaa	MIN	173	2	1	193	8	79	85	66	23
	14	L	26	1B	aaa	MIN	118	5	0	257	8	76	130	8	31
Parrino,Andy	13	B	28	SS	aaa	OAK	367	2	2	154	7	65	57	75	-55
	14	B	29	SS	aaa	OAK	427	4	4	194	6	67	66	76	-43
Pastornicky,Tyler	13	R	24	2B	aaa	ATL	288	3	7	253	7	81	59	96	15
	14	R	25	2B	aaa	ATL	176	1	5	238	4	84	32	69	-7
Paul,Xavier	14	L	29	DH	aaa	ARI	299	7	1	182	5	65	92	58	-39
Paulino,Carlos	13	R	24	C	a/a	PIT	334	0	4	190	6	84	29	77	-3
	14	R	25	C	a/a	PIT	100	1	0	220	3	69	51	31	-68
Paulsen,Benjamin	13	L	26	1B	aaa	COL	459	12	1	234	4	69	127	79	11
	14	L	27	1B	aaa	COL	435	13	2	235	7	69	140	71	25
Pederson,Joc	13	L	21	CF	aa	LA	439	20	28	260	12	72	142	121	64
	14	L	22	CF	aaa	LA	445	21	19	243	12	61	150	96	20

BATTER	yr	b	age	pos	lvl	org	ab	hr	sb	ba	bb%	ct%	px	sx	bpv
Pedroza,Jaime	13	B	27	SS	aa	ATL	370	3	5	236	8	78	49	73	-10
	14	B	28	SS	aa	CLE	356	5	3	195	5	78	69	91	4
Peguero,Carlos	13	L	26	RF	aaa	SEA	454	12	7	203	6	57	131	76	-30
	14	L	27	LF	aaa	KC	368	18	7	205	7	56	177	80	5
Peguero,Francisco	13	R	25	RF	aaa	SF	272	2	2	252	3	78	51	76	-18
	14	R	26	RF	aaa	BAL	304	2	3	220	2	73	62	71	-30
Pena,Francisco	13	R	24	C	a/a	NYM	287	6	1	198	4	81	89	36	17
	14	R	25	C	aaa	KC	342	17	0	191	3	79	118	36	28
Peralta,David	14	L	27	LF	aa	ARI	202	5	1	249	6	88	105	70	69
Peraza,Jose	14	R	20	2B	aa	ATL	185	1	21	315	3	91	49	159	60
Perdomo,Carlos	14	R	24	SS	aa	HOU	195	2	2	207	8	83	30	53	-12
Perez,Audry	13	R	25	C	a/a	STL	305	4	0	169	1	82	58	28	-15
	14	R	26	C	aaa	STL	236	4	0	229	1	83	65	30	-4
Perez,Carlos	13	R	23	C	a/a	HOU	317	2	1	236	7	82	58	34	-1
	14	R	24	C	aaa	HOU	301	4	2	214	6	79	74	66	9
Perez,Eury	13	R	23	CF	aaa	WAS	403	5	17	263	2	83	65	120	25
	14	R	24	RF	aaa	WAS	212	1	15	268	4	82	64	127	26
Perez,Felix	13	L	29	LF	aaa	CIN	462	9	3	210	5	75	76	55	-13
	14	L	30	RF	aaa	CIN	460	8	0	206	4	75	97	43	1
Perez,Hernan	13	R	22	2B	a/a	DET	429	3	24	277	3	87	74	110	47
	14	R	23	SS	aaa	DET	547	5	17	259	5	87	72	116	54
Perez,Juan	13	R	27	RF	aaa	SF	382	6	11	221	2	76	89	113	14
	14	R	28	RF	aaa	SF	177	4	4	232	5	77	96	74	17
Perez,Roberto	13	R	25	C	a/a	CLE	280	1	1	166	13	65	72	27	-48
	14	R	26	C	aaa	CLE	174	6	1	249	11	64	140	54	8
Perez,Rossmel	13	L	24	C	aa	ARI	237	2	3	223	7	93	24	35	17
	14	L	25	C	a/a	CIN	280	3	1	267	6	90	66	47	39
Perkins,Cameron	14	R	24	LF	a/a	PHI	451	4	6	230	5	80	75	66	11
Petersen,Bryan	13	L	27	RF	aaa	MIA	506	5	9	229	9	72	86	92	5
	14	L	28	RF	aaa	TEX	452	9	4	193	6	59	118	77	-34
Peterson,Brock	13	R	30	1B	aaa	STL	456	15	1	219	6	68	123	38	-5
	14	R	31	1B	aaa	LA	419	8	1	204	6	66	93	46	-36
Peterson,D.J.	14	R	22	3B	aa	SEA	222	9	1	229	7	74	115	37	15
Peterson,Jace	14	L	24	SS	a/a	SD	322	2	11	245	10	77	83	112	31
Peterson,Shane	13	L	25	CF	aaa	OAK	463	7	12	196	10	68	81	90	-15
	14	L	26	CF	aaa	OAK	543	6	7	236	7	69	97	97	-2
Petit,Gregorio	13	R	29	SS	aaa	SD	503	2	3	205	5	79	44	55	-20
	14	R	30	SS	aaa	HOU	317	7	1	218	4	78	83	46	1
Pham,Thomas	13	R	25	CF	a/a	STL	269	5	6	234	7	71	90	109	4
	14	R	26	CF	aaa	STL	346	6	14	256	7	72	87	128	11
Phegley,Joshua	13	R	25	C	aaa	CHW	231	13	1	275	5	80	159	48	76
	14	R	26	C	aaa	CHW	419	17	0	215	5	79	130	49	45
Phelps,Cord	13	B	26	2B	aaa	CLE	255	7	3	226	8	77	104	57	25
	14	B	27	2B	aaa	BAL	343	5	1	205	9	79	64	73	9
Pillar,Kevin	13	R	24	CF	a/a	TOR	505	7	17	269	4	84	96	110	56
	14	R	25	LF	aaa	TOR	405	9	22	287	4	86	122	116	87
Pina,Manny	13	R	26	C	a/a	KC	298	5	1	190	4	85	71	32	16
	14	R	27	C	a/a	DET	213	3	1	214	6	84	58	52	12
Pinto,Josmil	13	R	24	C	a/a	MIN	456	10	0	265	10	79	98	30	27
	14	R	25	C	aaa	MIN	208	4	0	241	10	80	112	36	43
Pirela,Jose	13	R	24	2B	a/a	NYY	482	9	16	244	9	85	80	116	60
	14	R	25	2B	aaa	NYY	535	8	11	254	5	84	67	108	33
Piscotty,Stephen	13	R	22	RF	aa	STL	184	4	5	259	7	89	71	50	43
	14	R	23	RF	aaa	STL	500	6	8	241	6	86	69	63	33
Pizzano,Dario	14	L	23	LF	aa	SEA	272	6	1	195	11	84	89	66	51
Plawecki,Kevin Jeffre	14	R	23	C	a/a	NYM	376	8	0	243	5	84	79	28	22
Polanco,Gregory	13	L	22	CF	a/a	PIT	252	4	11	233	10	85	74	100	52
	14	L	23	RF	aaa	PIT	274	5	12	283	7	81	96	128	54
Polanco,Jorge	14	B	21	SS	aa	MIN	146	1	6	258	5	80	47	65	-12
Pompey,Dalton	14	B	22	CF	a/a	TOR	165	3	12	296	8	81	101	153	70
Popkins,David	14	B	25	RF	aa	STL	276	3	3	200	7	71	67	60	-30
Poythress,Richard	13	R	26	1B	a/a	SEA	379	10	2	208	9	75	108	51	20
	14	R	27	1B	aa	ATL	251	4	1	209	6	82	57	38	-2
Price,Robby	13	L	25	2B	aa	TAM	420	4	2	187	8	88	30	31	3
	14	L	26	LF	aaa	TAM	213	2	1	179	9	85	43	59	13
Pridie,Jason	13	L	30	CF	aaa	BAL	479	12	6	211	6	68	97	89	-8
	14	L	31	CF	aaa	COL	418	7	15	209	5	79	72	114	19
Prince,Joshua	13	R	25	CF	aaa	MIL	418	9	17	195	9	70	81	103	-4
	14	R	26	LF	aa	MIL	345	4	27	203	11	74	61	100	-1
Puello,Cesar	13	R	22	RF	aa	NYM	331	13	19	282	6	71	135	119	43
	14	R	23	LF	aaa	NYM	318	4	8	187	5	73	79	111	0
Quintanilla,Omar	13	L	32	SS	aaa	NYM	126	1	1	225	8	72	74	75	-13
	14	L	33	SS	aaa	NYM	155	2	1	149	2	81	62	71	2
Quintero,Humberto	13	R	34	C	aaa	PHI	24	1	0	224	10	73	142	53	42
	14	R	35	C	aaa	SEA	259	2	1	209	2	74	75	61	-19
Quiroz,Guillermo	13	R	32	C	aaa	SF	34	0	0	211	10	73	45	4	-50
	14	R	33	C	aaa	SF	240	2	0	188	2	69	60	30	-60
Rahl,Christopher	13	R	30	RF	aaa	WAS	399	5	9	222	2	69	77	106	-24
	14	R	31	LF	aaa	MIN	332	5	6	202	1	69	77	85	-31
Ramirez,Jose	13	B	21	2B	aa	CLE	482	2	29	237	6	91	38	129	45
	14	B	22	2B	aaa	CLE	245	4	15	268	7	86	82	107	59
Ramirez,Max	13	R	29	DH	aaa	KC	411	6	0	207	7	70	67	18	-46
	14	R	30	1B	a/a	KC	179	2	0	182	10	67	51	36	-58
Ramirez,Nick	14	L	25	1B	aa	MIL	490	16	1	197	8	63	126	62	-11
Ramirez,Wilkin	13	R	28	DH	aa	MIN	29	0	1	133	4	75	28	73	-44
	14	R	29	RF	aaa	MIN	386	3	6	208	4	67	79	94	-32
Ramos,Henry	14	B	22	RF	aa	BOS	181	2	2	310	5	78	78	77	7
Ramsey,Caleb	14	L	26	RF	aa	WAS	473	1	13	194	5	82	31	81	-12

BATTER	yr	b	age	pos	lvl	org	ab	hr	sb	ba	bb%	ct%	px	sx	bpv
Ramsey,James	13	L	24	CF	a/a	STL	350	10	6	205	10	65	95	87	-17
	14	L	25	CF	a/a	CLE	352	12	4	247	9	66	141	77	19
Ravelo,Rangel	14	R	22	1B	aa	CHW	476	10	8	272	9	82	105	75	53
Realmuto,Jacob	13	R	22	C	aa	MIA	368	4	8	221	8	80	75	100	29
	14	R	23	C	aa	MIA	375	5	14	259	8	83	91	129	59
Refsnyder,Rob	14	R	23	2B	a/a	NYY	515	12	7	279	8	77	115	76	41
Renfroe,Hunter	14	R	22	LF	aa	SD	224	4	2	201	8	73	83	32	-14
Reyes,Elmer	14	R	24	SS	a/a	ATL	417	4	4	252	2	74	93	80	-1
Reynolds,Matt	14	R	24	SS	a/a	NYM	478	4	13	267	6	74	60	105	-12
Rhymes,Will	13	L	30	2B	aaa	WAS	453	2	5	207	8	92	33	63	32
	14	L	31	2B	aaa	WAS	392	3	3	193	5	83	62	86	19
Richardson,Antoan	13	B	30	CF	a/a	MIN	421	0	26	219	10	72	54	151	-3
	14	B	31	CF	aaa	NYY	258	2	17	204	8	72	47	137	-16
Richardson,D' Vontre	14	R	26	CF	aa	MIL	289	4	11	198	5	79	67	127	22
Richmond,Joshua	14	R	25	RF	a/a	CHW	389	8	6	197	6	71	94	101	3
Rickard,Joey	14	R	23	CF	aa	TAM	206	1	7	208	10	78	40	84	-8
Rieger,Ryan	14	L	24	1B	aa	MIA	100	1	0	214	4	76	101	47	11
Riggins,Harold	14	R	24	1B	aa	COL	179	6	2	242	8	54	160	76	-14
Rincon,Edinson	13	R	23	DH	aa	KC	52	0	0	136	1	76	17	28	-70
	14	R	24	DH	aa	KC	224	1	0	207	7	75	51	19	-36
Rivera,T.J.	14	R	26	SS	aa	NYM	201	1	1	278	4	83	53	41	-5
Rivera,Yadiel	14	R	22	SS	aa	MIL	183	2	4	239	4	78	89	137	35
Rivero,Carlos	13	R	25	3B	a/a	WAS	396	4	1	205	5	73	59	29	-38
	14	R	26	3B	a/a	BOS	390	5	0	230	6	73	82	41	-16
Rivers,Kevin	14	L	26	RF	aa	SEA	320	2	1	188	8	73	86	65	-3
Roberts,Ryan	13	R	33	2B	aaa	TAM	124	1	2	157	11	68	44	51	-52
	14	R	34	2B	aaa	BOS	274	5	1	224	5	76	108	56	19
Robinson,Clint	13	L	28	1B	a/a	TOR	397	10	1	203	9	74	97	44	6
	14	L	29	1B	aaa	LA	429	10	0	215	7	74	101	45	5
Robinson,Drew	14	L	22	RF	a/a	TEX	354	10	7	177	8	61	132	107	-1
Robinson,Shane	14	R	30	CF	aaa	STL	191	1	3	221	7	83	54	62	9
Robinson,Trayvon	13	B	26	CF	a/a	BAL	376	9	15	206	8	64	102	102	-12
	14	B	27	LF	aaa	LA	400	3	6	166	5	65	70	72	-53
Rodriguez,Guilder	13	B	30	3B	a/a	TEX	348	1	12	194	8	85	22	83	0
	14	B	31	SS	a/a	TEX	335	0	6	197	7	81	20	64	-23
Rodriguez,Jonathan	14	R	25	1B	aa	STL	406	8	7	220	9	73	82	71	-2
Rodriguez,Josh	13	R	29	3B	aa	NYM	441	4	3	198	10	71	72	67	-16
	14	R	30	3B	aaa	MIA	424	5	4	185	6	66	75	68	-42
Rodriguez,Reynaldo	13	R	27	1B	aa	MIN	415	13	3	184	7	69	141	95	33
	14	R	28	RF	a/a	MIN	493	15	4	223	6	79	117	76	46
Rodriguez,Ronny	13	R	21	SS	aa	CLE	468	4	9	231	3	82	65	110	20
	14	R	22	2B	aa	CLE	413	4	3	202	5	75	75	60	-10
Rodriguez,Starlin	13	B	24	2B	aa	STL	248	4	6	210	4	72	78	87	-15
	14	B	25	CF	aa	STL	100	1	1	215	6	76	77	45	-7
Rodriguez,Steven	14	L	24	C	aa	ARI	105	0	0	237	10	72	87	44	-6
Rodriguez,Yorman	13	R	21	RF	aa	CIN	262	4	4	256	8	68	98	86	-5
	14	R	22	CF	aa	CIN	450	8	9	234	8	71	88	103	1
Rogers,Jason	13	R	25	1B	aa	MIL	481	19	5	236	9	79	114	70	48
	14	R	26	3B	a/a	MIL	493	15	4	248	7	77	113	84	39
Rohlfing,Danny	13	R	24	C	a/a	MIN	375	2	0	228	9	71	52	47	-39
	14	R	25	C	aaa	MIN	219	1	0	177	9	71	88	41	-12
Rohlinger,Ryan	13	R	30	3B	aaa	CLE	319	4	2	208	8	72	66	52	-27
	14	R	31	2B	aaa	CLE	292	3	0	174	5	78	62	25	-17
Rohm,David	14	R	24	RF	aa	ATL	364	0	2	221	4	71	63	76	-34
Rojas Jr.,Mel	13	B	23	CF	aa	PIT	446	4	11	239	6	76	84	117	21
	14	B	24	CF	a/a	PIT	437	7	8	240	8	76	74	82	6
Rojas,Miguel	13	R	24	SS	aa	LA	420	4	9	206	7	87	40	78	19
	14	R	25	SS	aaa	LA	159	2	4	227	3	84	65	74	18
Roller,Kyle	13	L	25	1B	aa	NYY	443	15	0	220	9	63	128	32	-17
	14	L	26	1B	a/a	NYY	456	21	1	250	9	62	176	54	24
Romak,Jamie	13	R	28	RF	aaa	STL	458	14	4	184	7	69	119	70	8
	14	R	29	3B	aaa	LA	418	13	2	191	4	66	127	61	-7
Romero,Deibinson	13	R	27	3B	a/a	MIN	335	8	3	219	10	71	94	60	-3
	14	R	28	3B	aaa	MIN	419	5	0	215	9	75	93	38	5
Romero,Niuman	13	B	28	SS	a/a	BAL	419	3	6	213	10	80	53	61	1
	14	B	29	3B	aa	BAL	482	4	5	246	10	83	59	61	22
Romero,Stefen	13	R	25	LF	aaa	SEA	375	7	5	222	5	72	95	85	0
	14	R	26	RF	aaa	SEA	151	7	1	280	3	76	135	61	40
Romine,Austin	13	R	25	C	aaa	NYY	42	1	0	297	7	67	44	18	-74
	14	R	26	C	aaa	NYY	285	5	1	196	6	77	77	38	-4
Roof,Jonathan	14	R	25	RF	aa	BOS	188	2	1	228	7	72	94	71	2
Rosa,Garabez	13	R	24	RF	aa	BAL	460	5	6	237	1	81	56	82	-2
	14	R	25	SS	aa	BAL	465	9	5	236	2	76	85	68	0
Rosales,Adam	13	R	30	SS	aaa	OAK	38	0	1	148	5	76	37	69	-34
	14	R	31	3B	aaa	TEX	272	4	2	204	6	71	88	77	-7
Rosario,Eddie	13	L	22	2B	aa	MIN	289	3	5	254	5	75	87	97	12
	14	L	23	CF	aa	MIN	316	6	6	211	4	77	101	106	29
Rua,Ryan	13	R	23	3B	aa	TEX	86	3	1	218	6	70	94	123	8
	14	R	24	3B	a/a	TEX	471	14	4	265	7	77	108	59	28
Ruettiger,Johnny	13	L	24	RF	aa	BAL	53	0	1	243	12	72	34	43	-44
	14	L	25	LF	aa	BAL	149	0	6	236	5	83	36	101	3
Rupp,Cameron	13	R	25	C	a/a	PHI	325	11	1	215	5	67	113	27	-22
	14	R	26	C	aaa	PHI	194	4	0	133	7	53	110	21	-77
Russell,Addison	14	R	20	SS	aa	CHC	241	10	4	278	5	80	130	72	60
Saladino,Tyler	13	R	24	SS	aa	CHW	424	5	23	200	10	76	56	103	3
	14	R	25	SS	aaa	CHW	294	7	5	248	6	79	90	82	27
Salcedo,Edward	13	R	22	3B	aa	ATL	468	10	18	222	8	74	88	91	10
	14	R	23	RF	aaa	ATL	364	7	9	178	7	69	97	90	-1

BATTER	yr	b	age	pos	lvl	org	ab	hr	sb	ba	bb%	ct%	px	sx	bpv
Samson,Nathan	13	R	26	2B	aa	CHC	35	0	0	213	13	76	48	44	-15
	14	R	27	SS	aa	ARI	117	3	4	229	8	75	103	104	31
Sanchez,Adrian	14	R	24	3B	aa	WAS	269	2	5	183	5	83	30	69	-12
Sanchez,Angel	13	R	30	3B	aaa	CHW	148	1	0	144	6	78	34	52	-32
	14	R	31	SS	aa	LA	183	1	0	180	4	81	39	44	-24
Sanchez,Carlos	13	B	21	2B	aaa	CHW	432	0	13	218	6	81	43	98	-1
	14	B	22	2B	aaa	CHW	437	6	11	248	6	78	68	102	10
Sanchez,Gary	13	R	21	C	aa	NYY	92	2	0	232	11	81	89	24	28
	14	R	22	C	aa	NYY	429	12	1	246	8	77	89	26	4
Sanchez,Jorge Tony	13	R	25	C	a/a	PIT	277	7	0	236	7	75	129	25	26
	14	R	26	C	aaa	PIT	268	7	0	186	9	68	113	16	-14
Sanchez,Yeral	13	R	28	RF	aa	NYY	110	2	0	146	5	59	70	32	-87
	14	R	29	RF	aa	NYY	102	1	0	128	5	62	64	50	-75
Sandoval,Rylan	13	R	26	2B	aaa	NYM	110	3	2	240	5	69	101	67	-11
	14	R	27	SS	a/a	NYM	113	1	1	182	6	62	51	48	-84
Sands,Jerry	13	R	26	RF	aaa	PIT	343	5	0	169	10	66	80	46	-38
	14	R	27	RF	aaa	TAM	190	7	1	218	10	66	137	48	7
Santana,Domingo	13	R	21	RF	aa	HOU	416	21	10	228	8	63	170	97	35
	14	R	22	RF	aaa	HOU	443	12	4	256	10	61	134	62	-7
Sardinas,Luis	13	B	20	SS	aa	TEX	135	1	4	253	3	84	37	68	-6
	14	B	21	SS	a/a	TEX	349	1	8	254	2	84	59	104	23
Satin,Josh	13	R	29	1B	aaa	NYM	220	5	0	207	10	72	89	34	-11
	14	R	30	3B	aaa	NYM	374	5	1	188	8	70	79	27	-30
Schafer,Logan	14	L	28	CF	aaa	MIL	161	2	3	218	8	74	114	117	41
Schebler,Scott	14	L	24	LF	aa	LA	489	20	7	227	6	74	132	110	47
Schimpf,Ryan	13	L	25	3B	aa	TOR	442	18	2	178	11	63	139	64	8
	14	L	26	2B	a/a	TOR	397	20	2	196	9	66	172	71	41
Schlehuber,Braeden	13	R	25	C	aa	ATL	176	3	2	172	4	78	50	62	-19
	14	R	26	C	aa	ATL	239	2	1	190	7	85	50	49	10
Schlehuber,Jared	14	R	26	1B	aa	KC	158	1	0	147	7	67	49	10	-75
Schoop,Sharlon	14	R	27	SS	aa	BAL	267	2	0	172	6	75	56	32	-32
Schroder,Myles	14	B	27	3B	aa	SF	362	3	8	206	4	75	66	123	-2
Sclafani,Joe	14	B	24	2B	a/a	HOU	336	2	7	267	7	86	46	98	26
Scruggs,Xavier	13	R	26	1B	aa	STL	448	19	8	194	11	53	151	60	-24
	14	R	27	1B	aaa	STL	472	13	2	219	7	70	111	57	3
Seager,Corey	14	L	20	SS	aa	LA	148	2	1	304	5	71	140	96	35
Segedin,Robert	13	R	25	3B	aa	NYY	71	3	0	294	6	71	200	60	75
	14	R	26	3B	a/a	NYY	402	7	1	210	9	78	80	40	9
Segovia,Alejandro	14	R	24	DH	aa	TAM	295	7	2	185	9	73	94	51	3
Seitzer,Cameron	13	L	23	1B	aa	TAM	489	5	1	232	12	77	62	39	-5
	14	L	24	1B	aa	TAM	450	10	2	203	8	77	93	46	15
Sellers,Justin	13	R	27	SS	aaa	LA	326	4	3	203	5	79	83	76	17
	14	R	28	SS	aaa	CLE	355	2	2	197	5	83	50	47	-3
Selsky,Steve	13	R	24	RF	aa	CIN	83	0	0	162	9	72	23	25	-64
	14	R	25	LF	a/a	CIN	287	2	1	226	11	63	69	42	-58
Semien,Marcus	13	R	23	SS	a/a	CHW	518	18	20	256	14	80	117	121	82
	14	R	24	SS	aaa	CHW	303	11	5	218	11	77	127	80	57
Seratelli,Anthony	13	B	30	RF	aaa	KC	400	7	17	214	12	75	72	115	19
	14	B	31	2B	aaa	NYM	244	3	4	182	8	63	66	89	-50
Serna,Casey	14	R	25	SS	aa	PHI	165	2	1	227	2	83	54	64	-1
Shaffer,Richie	14	R	23	3B	aa	TAM	427	14	3	191	9	68	142	88	34
Shaw,Nicholas	13	L	25	2B	aa	MIL	450	2	6	218	10	81	28	67	-10
	14	L	26	SS	aa	MIL	356	0	4	223	12	76	41	66	-19
Shaw,Travis	13	L	23	1B	aa	BOS	444	12	5	200	12	71	107	76	19
	14	L	24	1B	a/a	BOS	490	16	6	252	8	78	121	74	48
Shoemaker,Brady	14	R	27	LF	aa	MIA	413	7	1	215	10	74	90	57	6
Shuck,J.B.	14	L	27	CF	aaa	LAA	406	3	5	230	5	90	47	81	37
Silva,Rubi	13	L	24	RF	aa	CHC	468	12	10	248	3	76	114	111	36
	14	L	25	RF	aa	CHC	301	4	5	205	4	72	78	84	-16
Silverio,Alfredo	14	R	27	RF	a/a	MIA	319	2	1	156	2	71	41	45	-65
Silverio,Juan	14	R	23	3B	a/a	CIN	344	9	1	228	3	76	99	63	8
Simon,Jared	14	R	25	RF	aa	COL	293	9	4	198	7	68	113	49	-6
Simunic,Andrew	13	R	28	RF	aaa	HOU	144	0	6	216	7	75	16	87	-46
	14	R	29	RF	aaa	ATL	107	1	1	195	6	68	53	43	-60
Singleton,Jonathan	13	L	22	1B	a/a	HOU	283	7	1	200	13	58	116	48	-30
	14	L	23	1B	aaa	HOU	195	10	1	226	13	69	160	54	49
Sizemore,Scott	14	R	29	3B	aaa	NYY	289	5	0	202	6	62	108	53	-38
Skipworth,Kyle	13	L	23	C	aaa	MIA	239	8	0	165	4	63	138	58	-11
	14	L	24	C	aaa	MIA	204	6	1	170	5	58	108	58	-52
Skole,Jake	14	L	22	CF	aa	TEX	342	5	5	200	9	68	87	86	-12
Skole,Matt	14	L	25	1B	aa	WAS	461	9	2	194	10	69	101	43	-10
Smalling,Tim	13	R	26	3B	aa	COL	114	1	0	208	5	77	67	69	-5
	14	R	27	LF	a/a	COL	265	3	5	218	6	78	93	95	27
Smith,Bryson	13	R	25	RF	aa	CIN	207	5	2	246	8	81	81	66	27
	14	R	26	RF	aa	CIN	132	1	1	185	4	83	28	23	-27
Smith,Curt	13	R	27	DH	aa	MIN	147	3	0	183	5	64	89	26	-54
	14	R	28	1B	aa	STL	390	7	2	202	6	79	67	54	0
Smith,Jordan	14	L	24	RF	aa	CLE	459	1	7	212	5	79	57	81	-1
Smith,Kevan	14	R	26	C	aa	CHW	389	8	1	235	8	78	84	44	13
Smoak,Justin	13	B	27	1B	aaa	SEA	21	0	0	183	0	70	83	32	-42
	14	B	28	1B	aaa	SEA	205	4	0	253	9	74	92	20	-7
Smolinski,Jacob	13	R	24	LF	a/a	MIA	370	6	7	219	10	79	69	88	18
	14	R	25	LF	a/a	TEX	296	8	4	226	8	77	115	89	46
Snyder,Brad	13	L	31	CF	aaa	ARI	411	7	4	225	5	62	109	85	-26
	14	L	32	RF	aaa	TEX	232	12	2	212	6	55	179	69	-2
Snyder,Brandon	13	R	27	1B	aaa	BOS	249	7	2	219	5	67	124	72	2
	14	R	28	1B	aaa	BOS	126	6	1	169	6	52	182	30	-23
Snyder,Michael	14	R	24	1B	aa	LAA	166	2	1	184	6	63	91	43	-49
Solano,Jhonatan	13	R	28	C	aaa	WAS	140	0	0	166	2	85	39	34	-10
	14	R	29	C	aaa	WAS	343	7	1	189	4	82	66	48	7
Soler,Jorge	14	R	22	RF	a/a	CHC	175	11	0	298	12	74	236	62	129
Solis,Ali	13	R	26	C	a/a	PIT	84	0	1	145	4	72	31	78	-53
	14	R	27	C	aaa	TAM	251	2	0	166	2	63	56	65	-76
Sosa,Ruben	13	B	23	LF	aaa	HOU	125	1	6	238	7	68	64	133	-22
	14	B	24	LF	a/a	HOU	236	3	18	225	8	67	99	160	11
Soto,Elliot	13	R	24	SS	aa	CHC	121	2	1	163	8	76	36	43	-38
	14	R	25	SS	a/a	CHC	242	1	3	202	8	80	47	56	-8
Soto,Neftali	13	R	24	3B	aaa	CIN	461	14	2	244	4	74	96	45	-2
	14	R	25	3B	aaa	CIN	278	2	0	244	5	82	74	15	3
Souza,Steven	13	R	24	RF	aa	WAS	273	12	16	265	10	69	168	111	68
	14	R	25	RF	aaa	WAS	346	13	19	293	10	75	138	97	62
Spangenberg,Cory	13	L	22	2B	aa	SD	287	2	16	259	5	75	49	118	-12
	14	L	23	2B	aa	SD	281	2	11	290	4	73	91	128	15
Spears,Nate	13	L	28	2B	a/a	CLE	214	3	4	171	10	69	65	87	-24
	14	L	29	2B	aaa	PHI	144	1	3	228	6	61	88	101	-42
Spring,Matthew	13	R	29	C	aa	BOS	185	6	0	176	3	57	156	20	-32
	14	R	30	C	a/a	BOS	137	5	0	194	6	57	201	38	15
Stamets,Eric	14	R	23	SS	aa	LAA	344	3	10	211	6	80	52	107	7
Stanley,Cody	13	L	25	C	aa	STL	272	3	3	202	4	77	50	61	-24
	14	L	26	C	aa	STL	385	8	10	230	6	79	74	86	16
Stassi,Brock	14	L	25	1B	aa	PHI	440	6	2	192	6	87	47	61	17
Stassi,Max	13	R	22	C	aa	HOU	289	14	1	248	5	73	154	50	44
	14	R	23	C	aaa	HOU	392	7	1	208	4	70	86	57	-26
Statia,Hainley	13	B	27	2B	aaa	MIL	291	4	4	189	11	80	47	48	-4
	14	B	28	3B	a/a	MIL	222	4	4	218	12	82	71	63	30
Stevenson,Casey	13	L	25	3B	a/a	NYY	214	5	2	208	8	75	81	41	-4
	14	L	26	2B	aa	NYY	162	1	1	167	7	81	47	62	-3
Stewart,Ian	13	L	28	3B	aaa	LA	199	4	0	123	9	49	129	53	-65
	14	L	29	1B	aaa	LAA	121	2	1	131	7	55	75	53	-90
Story,Trevor	14	R	22	SS	aa	COL	205	8	2	191	10	60	144	79	2
Strausborger,Ryan	13	R	25	CF	aa	TEX	461	9	22	195	6	75	81	121	17
	14	R	26	LF	a/a	TEX	361	4	15	227	5	80	74	142	36
Stromsmoe,Skyler	13	B	29	SS	aa	SF	118	1	1	196	5	84	54	82	15
	14	B	30	2B	aa	SF	296	0	8	178	12	76	43	93	-8
Suarez,Eugenio	13	R	22	SS	aa	DET	442	7	7	231	8	77	85	82	18
	14	R	23	SS	a/a	DET	198	6	7	251	7	74	145	100	60
Sucre,Jesus	13	R	25	C	aaa	SEA	87	0	1	240	5	86	26	43	-11
	14	R	26	C	aaa	SEA	175	1	0	213	1	79	48	31	-30
Susac,Andrew	13	R	23	C	aa	SF	262	8	1	213	11	71	116	29	7
	14	R	24	C	aaa	SF	213	6	0	211	10	73	89	24	-10
Susdorf,Stephen	13	L	27	RF	aaa	PHI	310	2	8	252	8	79	61	72	4
	14	L	28	DH	aaa	PHI	272	1	5	214	6	75	65	73	-13
Swanner,William	14	R	23	1B	aa	COL	104	3	1	260	3	66	125	40	-17
Sweeney,Darnell	14	B	23	2B	aa	LA	490	10	11	239	10	73	108	81	22
Swift,James	13	R	26	SS	a/a	LAA	406	4	4	211	3	70	71	68	-36
	14	R	27	SS	a/a	LAA	172	2	0	156	2	71	50	39	-60
Swihart,Blake	14	B	22	C	a/a	BOS	416	10	7	278	6	80	116	95	53
Szczur,Matthew	13	R	24	CF	aa	CHC	512	2	17	245	7	83	55	100	24
	14	R	25	CF	aaa	CHC	414	1	22	218	5	78	38	100	-15
Tabata,Jose	13	R	25	RF	aaa	PIT	28	0	1	149	7	73	32	38	-55
	14	R	26	RF	aaa	PIT	146	0	1	226	4	89	50	47	21
Taijeron,Travis	13	R	24	RF	aa	NYM	232	11	0	201	7	60	180	22	8
	14	R	25	RF	aa	NYM	330	11	1	193	9	60	165	40	4
Tanaka,Kensuke	13	L	32	2B	aaa	SF	343	1	13	239	7	86	34	93	15
	14	L	33	2B	aaa	TEX	213	3	7	191	7	83	52	94	19
Tartamella,Travis	13	R	26	C	a/a	STL	199	2	0	179	5	64	44	17	-90
	14	R	27	C	a/a	STL	224	1	0	133	4	70	29	14	-83
Taveras,Oscar	13	L	21	CF	aaa	STL	173	4	4	271	4	86	87	72	46
	14	L	22	LF	aaa	STL	239	5	1	272	6	86	100	49	50
Taylor,Beau	13	L	23	C	aa	OAK	267	2	1	161	9	70	53	31	-47
	14	L	24	C	aa	OAK	209	2	1	200	8	67	93	37	-30
Taylor,Chris	13	R	23	SS	aa	SEA	256	1	16	273	12	76	64	139	22
	14	R	24	SS	aaa	SEA	302	3	9	269	7	70	106	123	19
Taylor,Michael	13	R	28	RF	aaa	OAK	420	11	3	207	7	73	93	52	0
	14	R	23	CF	a/a	WAS	428	17	27	262	9	63	142	121	22
Taylor,Michael	14	R	29	RF	aaa	CHW	437	7	5	199	9	69	98	75	-2
Teagarden,Taylor	14	R	31	C	aaa	NYM	178	8	0	202	8	53	149	16	-45
Tekotte,Blake	13	L	26	CF	aaa	CHW	296	3	9	196	8	70	111	98	15
	14	L	27	RF	aaa	ARI	301	7	1	190	5	64	118	50	-22
Telis,Tomas	13	B	22	C	aa	TEX	348	4	7	251	2	86	62	67	21
	14	B	23	C	a/a	TEX	406	4	6	281	4	89	67	83	44
Terdoslavich,Joseph	13	B	25	RF	aaa	ATL	321	14	2	270	5	76	140	49	42
	14	B	26	1B	aaa	ATL	507	10	1	204	8	74	69	29	-22
Thomas,Anthony	13	R	27	LF	a/a	BOS	478	7	13	192	5	68	108	135	10
	14	R	28	2B	aa	MIN	453	8	10	192	5	62	117	130	-5
Thomas,Clete	13	L	30	CF	aaa	MIN	125	6	4	222	9	64	149	55	12
	14	L	31	CF	aaa	PHI	174	1	6	185	8	65	78	77	-35
Thomas,Mark	13	R	25	C	aa	TAM	186	3	1	125	3	64	79	100	-42
	14	R	26	C	aa	ARI	204	7	0	163	5	63	127	65	-14
Thompson,Trayce	13	R	22	CF	aa	CHW	507	14	21	210	10	70	108	123	23
	14	R	23	CF	aa	CHW	518	13	15	203	9	66	128	116	24
Threlkeld,Mark	14	R	24	1B	aa	KC	301	6	1	215	6	72	87	52	-15
Tilson,Charlie	14	L	22	CF	aa	STL	139	1	2	208	3	78	49	89	-13
Tolbert,Matt	13	B	31	2B	a/a	PHI	91	0	1	197	4	87	13	72	-11
	14	B	32	3B	a/a	PHI	101	0	1	154	4	90	13	40	-8

BATTER	yr	b	age	pos	lvl	org	ab	hr	sb	ba	bb%	ct%	px	sx	bpv
Tomlinson,Kelby	14	R	24	2B	aa	SF	433	1	39	233	7	79	33	146	1
Toole,Justin	13	R	27	2B	a/a	CLE	177	0	1	232	5	86	29	43	-8
	14	R	28	3B	a/a	CLE	236	1	2	216	4	83	45	59	-5
Torreyes,Ronald	13	R	21	2B	aa	HOU	375	2	4	244	6	91	57	103	55
	14	R	22	2B	aaa	HOU	460	2	9	258	4	94	43	90	45
Torrez,Riccio	13	R	24	3B	aa	TAM	299	4	2	210	4	78	71	76	3
	14	R	25	3B	aa	TAM	106	1	1	149	2	68	59	151	-29
Tovar,Wilfredo	13	R	22	SS	aa	NYM	441	3	9	224	6	87	39	102	24
	14	R	23	SS	aa	NYM	255	2	6	230	6	90	33	70	20
Trapp,Justin	14	R	24	2B	aa	KC	364	3	9	210	6	76	40	84	-24
Travis,Devon	14	R	23	2B	aa	DET	396	7	11	258	6	84	85	121	53
Triunfel,Carlos	13	R	23	SS	aaa	SEA	383	3	4	236	3	77	69	83	-5
	14	R	24	SS	aaa	LA	300	2	1	167	2	75	84	60	-21
Tucker,Preston	13	L	23	LF	aa	HOU	237	8	0	229	8	78	112	47	33
	14	L	24	LF	a/a	HOU	536	18	4	236	7	73	122	45	21
Tuiasosopo,Matt	14	R	28	LF	aaa	CHW	409	9	1	178	10	62	89	28	-50
Urrutia,Henry	13	L	26	RF	a/a	BAL	314	7	1	293	7	81	93	44	27
	14	L	27	RF	aaa	BAL	204	0	1	212	2	70	55	52	-54
Urshela,Giovanny	13	R	22	3B	aa	CLE	445	6	1	233	2	88	62	41	20
	14	R	23	3B	a/a	CLE	486	14	1	244	5	84	116	67	62
Valaika,Chris	13	R	28	2B	aaa	MIA	130	2	1	197	6	77	63	53	-14
	14	R	29	1B	aaa	CHC	352	7	1	213	6	72	87	36	-17
Valdespin,Jordany	13	L	26	2B	aaa	NYM	58	2	1	357	8	84	117	106	78
	14	L	27	2B	aaa	MIA	222	4	10	204	9	84	67	97	39
Valdez,Jeudy	13	R	24	SS	aa	SD	443	8	13	213	5	71	101	107	10
	14	R	25	SS	aaa	CHC	182	2	2	187	6	76	54	76	-17
Valera,Breyvic	14	B	22	2B	aa	STL	227	0	3	254	5	89	33	79	20
Valle,Sebastian	13	R	23	C	aa	PHI	354	9	1	174	4	72	91	54	-14
	14	R	24	C	a/a	PHI	240	4	0	201	3	75	72	19	-30
Vargas,Kennys	14	B	24	1B	aa	MIN	356	12	0	243	9	79	103	22	23
Vasquez,Andy	13	B	26	LF	aa	PIT	262	3	9	203	4	69	48	114	-40
	14	L	27	LF	aa	PIT	272	7	11	207	3	74	104	100	17
Vaughn,Cory	13	R	24	LF	aa	NYM	262	8	7	220	6	64	96	96	-23
	14	R	25	RF	a/a	NYM	371	7	7	155	6	65	79	86	-37
Vazquez,Christian	13	R	23	C	a/a	BOS	345	4	5	262	10	86	67	62	38
	14	R	24	C	aaa	BOS	244	2	0	254	6	76	89	36	2
Velez,Eugenio	13	B	31	2B	aaa	MIL	373	6	19	237	9	77	80	113	27
	14	B	32	LF	aaa	MIL	404	5	18	237	5	78	77	103	15
Vettleson,Drew	14	L	23	RF	aaa	WAS	248	6	2	207	4	67	112	72	-13
Villalona,Angel	13	R	23	1B	aa	SF	196	5	0	195	3	66	109	29	-34
	14	R	24	1B	aa	SF	365	7	1	195	5	71	95	69	-8
Villanueva,Christian	13	R	22	3B	aa	CHC	490	15	4	236	5	74	137	58	36
	14	R	23	3B	a/a	CHC	457	8	1	199	6	74	108	40	10
Villar,Jonathan	13	B	22	SS	aaa	HOU	339	7	24	248	7	69	103	151	20
	14	B	23	SS	aaa	HOU	190	2	17	219	11	63	51	149	-40
Vitters,Josh	13	R	24	3B	aaa	CHC	88	4	1	256	9	75	117	40	27
	14	R	25	LF	aaa	CHC	375	8	3	177	4	67	81	45	-43
Vucinich,Shea	13	R	25	3B	aa	MIL	222	2	3	170	13	64	67	54	-45
	14	R	26	SS	aa	MIL	183	2	5	158	10	66	78	109	-20
Wagner,Daniel	13	L	25	3B	aa	CHW	296	1	18	235	5	87	27	91	8
	14	L	26	2B	a/a	CHW	261	2	4	155	3	82	42	77	-6
Waldrop,Kyle	14	L	23	RF	aa	CIN	232	7	2	278	5	78	127	66	46
Walker,Christian	13	R	22	1B	aa	BAL	62	0	0	214	7	83	65	28	7
	14	R	23	1B	a/a	BAL	532	21	1	252	7	72	123	41	17
Walker,Keenyn	13	B	23	RF	aa	CHW	462	3	31	179	12	63	59	139	-35
	14	B	24	C	aa	CHW	110	2	8	128	7	42	72	151	-112
Wallace,Brett	13	L	27	1B	aaa	HOU	233	8	1	263	7	63	148	65	4
	14	L	28	1B	aaa	TOR	472	14	0	232	6	65	99	23	-38
Walsh,Colin	13	B	24	2B	aa	STL	118	1	2	181	9	77	54	62	-10
	14	B	25	2B	a/a	OAK	249	2	1	221	8	70	49	38	-53
Walters,Zachary	13	B	24	SS	aaa	WAS	487	21	3	214	3	70	151	83	32
	14	B	25	2B	aaa	CLE	268	12	0	258	5	70	184	69	60
Ward,Brian	13	R	28	C	a/a	BAL	154	2	1	207	7	78	62	52	-8
	14	R	29	C	a/a	BAL	211	1	1	183	9	72	36	44	-50

BATTER	yr	b	age	pos	lvl	org	ab	hr	sb	ba	bb%	ct%	px	sx	bpv
Waring,Brandon	13	R	27	3B	a/a	BAL	383	20	0	176	9	54	169	12	-24
	14	R	28	3B	aa	MIN	345	9	1	166	8	48	181	44	-35
Wates,Austin	13	R	25	LF	aa	HOU	136	1	11	261	8	81	54	143	30
	14	R	26	CF	aaa	MIA	392	1	24	224	8	80	49	123	12
Watkins,Logan	13	L	24	2B	aaa	CHC	412	6	8	210	9	73	80	95	5
	14	L	25	2B	aaa	CHC	324	3	16	214	7	72	80	120	5
Weber,Garrett	13	R	24	3B	aa	ARI	320	3	4	259	6	79	79	71	13
	14	R	25	2B	a/a	ARI	396	6	0	267	4	76	88	61	4
Weeks,Jemile	13	B	26	2B	aaa	OAK	520	2	11	212	9	77	50	128	7
	14	R	27	2B	aaa	BAL	207	1	5	221	11	82	60	95	30
Weisenburger,Adam	13	R	25	C	aa	MIL	175	4	0	219	10	68	99	45	-15
	14	R	26	C	a/a	MIL	239	2	1	211	10	78	64	48	-2
Welch,Stefan	13	L	25	1B	aa	PIT	74	1	0	122	9	76	38	21	-38
	14	L	26	1B	aa	BOS	333	6	1	194	10	66	100	72	-14
Wendle,Joey	14	L	24	2B	aa	CLE	336	6	3	216	6	81	91	91	36
Westlake,Aaron	14	L	26	1B	aa	DET	419	10	5	188	5	67	96	67	-23
Wheeler,Ryan	13	L	25	3B	aaa	COL	438	8	2	248	4	77	88	65	8
	14	L	26	3B	aaa	LAA	302	3	0	193	4	74	45	20	-50
Wheeler,Timothy	13	L	25	RF	aaa	COL	397	3	7	210	5	76	53	82	-18
	14	L	26	LF	aaa	COL	416	7	5	188	5	71	95	69	-7
Wheeler,Zelous	13	R	26	3B	a/a	BAL	408	9	4	230	7	80	80	54	17
	14	R	27	3B	aaa	NYY	304	7	1	236	6	75	109	43	16
Whitaker,Josh	13	R	24	RF	aa	OAK	125	2	2	200	6	68	130	104	22
	14	R	25	RF	a/a	OAK	281	8	3	236	5	73	105	55	4
Whiteside,Eli	13	R	34	C	aaa	TEX	225	4	0	143	5	66	55	23	-73
	14	R	35	C	aaa	CHC	206	4	0	160	5	69	93	6	-35
Wickens,Stephen	14	R	25	3B	aa	MIN	161	0	4	184	4	80	32	81	-20
Wilkerson,Shannon	13	R	25	CF	aa	BOS	465	3	17	207	8	75	68	125	11
	14	R	26	CF	a/a	BOS	461	1	9	228	5	78	65	100	4
Wilkins,Andrew	13	L	25	1B	a/a	CHW	458	15	4	240	9	71	118	50	15
	14	L	26	1B	aaa	CHW	491	22	0	231	5	77	142	29	41
Williams,Jackson	13	R	27	C	aaa	SF	261	3	0	172	5	77	63	47	-14
	14	R	28	C	aaa	COL	242	3	2	196	8	73	73	31	-24
Williams,Mason	13	L	22	CF	aa	NYY	72	1	0	139	1	73	72	88	-19
	14	L	23	CF	aa	NYY	507	4	17	196	7	85	47	108	27
Williams,Matthew	13	R	24	2B	aa	STL	28	0	1	87	2	88	0	59	-23
	14	R	25	SS	aa	STL	304	1	10	207	10	76	37	85	-18
Wilson,Bobby	13	R	30	C	aaa	NYY	216	6	0	166	10	78	88	25	12
	14	R	31	C	aaa	ARI	270	2	0	191	4	78	42	23	-35
Wilson,Jacob	14	R	24	2B	aa	STL	131	4	2	259	6	80	131	50	54
Wilson,Josh	13	R	32	2B	aaa	ARI	192	2	1	153	3	71	54	33	-56
	14	R	33	SS	aaa	TEX	305	3	1	181	3	64	58	48	-76
Wilson,Kenneth	13	R	23	CF	aa	TOR	216	2	12	208	6	71	89	110	1
	14	R	24	CF	a/a	OAK	447	1	22	202	5	71	55	133	-19
Wimberly,Corey	13	B	30	2B	a/a	CIN	254	1	7	200	4	85	41	89	8
	14	B	31	CF	aa	MIN	246	0	12	197	4	81	55	146	23
Wisdom,Patrick	14	R	23	3B	aa	STL	452	10	4	183	6	64	100	82	-26
Wise,Jeremy	13	R	27	1B	aa	LA	278	6	0	203	10	62	123	21	-27
	14	R	28	DH	aa	TEX	142	8	0	252	6	66	205	24	47
Wiswall,Maguire	14	L	26	1B	aa	SEA	166	3	0	174	3	65	73	21	-66
Wolters,Tony	14	L	22	C	aa	CLE	341	1	2	221	8	76	50	61	-21
Wong,Joey	13	L	25	SS	aa	COL	279	2	2	217	5	79	67	52	-3
	14	L	26	3B	aa	COL	257	1	4	194	6	77	59	90	-2
Workman,Andrew	14	R	26	RF	aa	LAA	117	2	2	157	9	70	58	59	-38
Worth,Danny	13	R	28	2B	aaa	DET	305	1	7	182	8	65	71	92	-38
	14	R	29	2B	aaa	DET	223	1	6	164	8	53	92	94	-69
Wren,Kyle	14	L	23	CF	aa	ATL	205	0	10	252	6	78	64	135	16
Wright,Ryan	14	R	25	2B	aa	CIN	219	2	1	170	3	72	63	58	-35
Yarbrough,Alex	13	B	23	2B	aa	LAA	544	4	5	256	5	74	86	75	1
Yastrzemski,Mike	14	L	24	CF	aa	BAL	184	2	1	213	5	79	96	85	32
Ynoa,Rafael	13	B	26	2B	aa	LA	484	5	13	226	8	83	65	71	23
	14	B	27	SS	aaa	COL	427	3	4	236	5	79	77	67	10
Zambrano,Eliezer	14	B	28	C	aa	SF	194	1	1	212	4	83	21	31	-31
Zarraga,Shawn	13	B	24	C	aa	MIL	168	1	0	257	6	79	55	22	-18

PITCHER	yr	t	age	lvl	org	ip	era	whip	bf/g	ctl	dom	cmd	hr/9	h%	s%	bpv
Achter,A.J.	13	R	25	a/a	MIN	60	2.97	1.41	6.2	4.9	6.6	1.3	1.0	27	83	46
	14	R	26	a/a	MIN	79	2.79	1.07	7.1	3.0	7.1	2.3	0.5	25	75	91
Adam,Jason	13	R	22	aa	KC	144	6.10	1.57	24.3	3.3	6.5	2.0	0.7	35	60	54
	14	R	23	a/a	MIN	121	5.66	1.58	18.3	2.7	6.4	2.4	0.7	36	63	60
Adams,Austin	13	R	27	aa	CLE	55	2.99	1.46	5.2	4.8	9.9	2.1	0.5	34	80	93
	14	R	28	aaa	CLE	54	3.08	1.31	5.3	2.8	6.7	2.4	0.7	31	79	72
Additon,Nicholas	13	L	26	aaa	STL	132	4.70	1.33	22.7	2.7	6.3	2.4	1.0	30	66	59
	14	L	27	a/a	BAL	119	4.74	1.66	16.7	3.9	5.4	1.4	0.6	34	71	38
Adleman,Timothy	14	R	27	aa	CIN	79	3.57	1.36	11.0	2.4	6.4	2.6	1.0	31	77	61
Alderson,Tim	13	R	25	a/a	BAL	89	4.85	1.38	8.5	2.3	6.6	2.8	1.2	32	67	62
	14	R	26	aaa	BAL	50	7.23	1.78	8.2	3.5	5.2	1.5	1.3	36	60	13
Alexander,Scott	13	L	24	aa	KC	33	6.34	1.91	6.5	5.0	8.7	1.7	0.0	42	63	79
	14	L	25	a/a	KC	68	5.33	1.51	6.4	3.5	5.1	1.4	0.9	31	65	31
Alvarez,R.J.	14	R	23	aa	SD	43	1.37	1.03	4.4	2.6	11.3	4.3	0.0	32	85	172
Ambriz,Hector	13	R	29	aaa	HOU	17	6.89	1.95	5.7	1.8	5.0	2.7	2.0	40	68	7
	14	R	30	aaa	SD	55	3.62	1.49	4.6	2.8	5.4	1.9	0.7	33	77	48
Anderson,Chase	13	R	26	aaa	ARI	88	5.76	1.67	15.2	3.1	6.4	2.0	1.1	36	66	41
	14	R	27	aa	ARI	39	0.93	0.88	24.1	1.5	6.7	4.5	0.3	25	92	140
Anderson,Cody	14	R	24	aa	CLE	126	6.27	1.63	22.4	3.1	4.9	1.6	1.2	33	62	18
Anderson,John	14	L	26	aa	TOR	69	6.12	1.54	11.1	4.5	7.6	1.7	1.2	31	61	47
Anderson,Matthew	14	R	23	aa	SEA	66	5.77	1.54	22.2	1.8	5.3	3.0	0.6	36	61	66
Anderson,Tyler	14	L	25	aa	COL	118	2.82	1.35	21.4	3.4	6.1	1.8	0.3	30	79	68
Andriese,Matt	13	R	24	aa	SD	135	3.36	1.28	20.4	1.8	6.1	3.4	0.3	33	73	97
	14	R	25	aaa	TAM	162	4.68	1.43	24.6	2.8	5.9	2.2	1.1	32	69	46
Antigua,Jeffry	13	L	23	a/a	CHC	53	5.48	1.49	10.9	3.7	6.0	1.6	1.1	31	64	36
	14	L	24	a/a	CHC	55	4.60	1.56	11.0	3.4	4.6	1.4	0.7	32	71	31
Antolin,Dustin	13	R	24	aa	TOR	32	13.32	2.42	6.5	7.7	7.3	0.9	1.3	41	41	9
	14	R	25	aa	TOR	43	4.41	1.58	5.1	3.4	9.1	2.7	0.0	40	69	106
Appel,Mark Stewart	14	R	23	aa	HOU	39	4.07	1.31	23.0	2.9	7.6	2.6	0.5	32	68	89
Arenas,Orangel	13	R	24	aaa	LAA	25	5.80	1.85	19.2	4.3	2.4	0.6	1.1	33	70	-17
	14	R	25	aa	LAA	114	4.97	1.60	19.4	3.6	3.3	0.9	0.6	32	68	16
Arguelles,Noel	13	L	23	aa	KC	71	7.11	1.92	13.5	6.7	4.5	0.7	0.8	32	62	15
	14	L	24	aa	KC	62	8.83	2.07	7.2	6.6	5.1	0.8	1.4	34	57	-3
Arias,Gabriel	14	R	25	a/a	CLE	149	4.29	1.43	23.5	2.5	4.5	1.8	0.8	32	71	38
Armstrong,Shawn	13	R	23	aa	CLE	33	4.29	1.63	4.9	5.3	10.1	1.9	0.5	37	73	87
	14	R	24	a/a	CLE	56	2.75	1.25	4.7	3.4	9.8	2.8	0.6	32	80	107
Arrowood,Ryan	14	R	24	aa	COL	88	5.31	1.61	9.7	3.8	3.6	1.0	0.9	31	67	11
Asher,Alec	14	R	23	aa	TEX	154	4.84	1.29	22.6	2.0	5.9	3.0	1.3	30	66	58
Atkins,Mitch	13	R	28	aa	ATL	96	4.93	1.76	25.9	3.8	5.6	1.5	0.7	36	72	34
	14	R	29	a/a	ATL	141	4.79	1.47	21.7	2.6	5.4	2.1	1.0	33	69	42
Augenstein,Bryan	14	R	28	a/a	DET	47	6.59	1.60	6.9	2.9	6.0	2.1	0.9	35	58	46
Augliera,Mike	14	R	24	aa	BOS	148	5.94	1.54	25.8	1.3	3.8	3.0	0.8	35	61	50
Aumont,Phillippe	13	R	24	aaa	PHI	36	4.76	2.02	5.4	9.8	9.0	0.9	0.0	34	74	78
	14	R	25	aaa	PHI	55	4.62	1.74	7.2	6.6	8.8	1.3	0.4	35	72	72
Avila,Nick	14	R	26	aa	DET	34	7.08	2.04	10.2	3.8	4.1	1.1	2.8	36	72	-54
Axelrod,Dylan	14	R	29	aaa	CIN	130	4.80	1.55	23.7	3.2	5.7	1.8	1.0	33	71	36
Baez,Angel	14	R	23	aa	KC	62	5.62	1.55	7.7	4.3	8.4	2.0	1.3	33	66	52
Baez,Pedro	13	R	25	aa	LA	23	5.47	1.71	6.6	3.2	7.3	2.3	1.4	37	71	41
	14	R	26	a/a	LA	42	3.70	1.34	4.4	2.5	6.5	2.6	0.8	32	74	72
Ballew,Travis	14	R	23	aa	HOU	51	6.77	1.91	6.6	5.6	6.3	1.1	0.9	36	64	26
Banuelos,Manuel	14	L	23	a/a	NYY	64	5.16	1.43	12.9	4.2	6.8	1.6	1.7	27	69	28
Banwart,Travis	13	R	27	aaa	OAK	131	4.99	1.68	20.3	3.8	6.7	1.8	1.2	35	73	33
	14	R	28	aaa	CLE	89	3.85	1.39	23.5	3.5	6.1	1.7	0.9	30	74	49
Barbato,John	14	R	22	aa	SD	31	3.10	1.20	4.7	2.7	8.6	3.2	0.9	30	77	99
Barnes,Jacob	14	R	24	aa	MIL	106	5.10	1.41	19.4	3.4	5.5	1.6	0.9	30	65	40
Barnes,Matt	13	R	23	a/a	BOS	113	5.01	1.59	20.0	3.8	9.4	2.5	0.9	38	70	78
	14	R	24	aaa	BOS	128	5.10	1.50	24.0	3.4	6.0	1.8	0.6	33	65	52
Barnes,Scott	13	L	26	aaa	CLE	28	10.23	2.11	5.9	6.9	9.2	1.3	1.5	40	50	29
	14	L	27	aaa	CLE	32	4.46	1.36	5.3	4.7	7.9	1.7	0.9	27	69	65
Barreda,Manuel	14	R	26	aa	MIL	73	3.70	1.66	7.0	5.4	7.9	1.5	1.3	32	82	41
Barrett,Jake	13	R	22	aa	ARI	25	0.49	1.00	3.9	1.1	6.9	6.1	0.9	27	105	150
	14	R	23	a/a	ARI	55	3.38	1.39	4.2	4.1	6.4	1.5	0.5	29	76	61
Bassitt,Chris	13	R	24	aa	CHW	48	2.99	1.31	24.6	3.8	6.0	1.6	0.5	28	78	60
	14	R	25	aa	CHW	35	1.85	1.33	24.0	4.1	7.8	1.9	0.6	29	89	75
Bates,Colin	14	R	26	aa	WAS	87	4.20	1.50	9.7	1.5	4.0	2.7	0.4	35	71	59
Batista,Frank	13	R	24	aa	CHC	62	3.20	1.51	5.6	4.3	6.2	1.5	0.3	32	78	59
	14	R	25	a/a	CHC	46	2.37	1.28	4.7	2.7	5.4	2.0	1.1	28	88	45
Bauer,Trevor	13	R	22	aaa	CLE	121	5.01	1.71	25.0	5.3	6.9	1.3	1.1	33	73	34
	14	R	23	aaa	CLE	46	2.38	1.15	26.1	2.6	7.4	2.9	0.9	28	85	84
Baumann,George	13	L	26	a/a	KC	53	3.29	1.67	7.4	4.6	9.3	2.0	0.9	37	83	68
	14	L	27	aaa	KC	90	3.69	1.46	9.7	3.2	5.1	1.6	0.6	32	75	45
Bawcom,Logan	13	R	25	aaa	SEA	65	3.08	1.29	5.2	3.1	7.4	2.4	0.5	31	77	84
	14	R	26	aaa	SEA	46	5.20	1.69	5.15	4.7	5.2	1.1	1.1	32	71	19
Beato,Pedro	13	R	27	aaa	BOS	51	3.96	1.64	6.73	4.6	6.1	1.3	1.4	31	81	20
	14	R	28	aaa	ATL	48	4.87	1.45	4.91	3.4	6.6	1.9	1.4	31	70	39
Beavan,Blake	13	R	24	aaa	SEA	94	5.75	1.60	26	2.0	3.8	1.9	1.3	34	66	15
	14	R	25	aaa	SEA	39	3.82	1.39	8.65	3.0	6.0	2.0	1.4	30	78	36
Beck,Chris	13	R	23	aa	CHW	28	3.73	1.23	22.7	1.1	6.2	5.6	0.0	34	66	153
	14	R	24	a/a	CHW	150	3.92	1.44	23.7	2.8	4.4	1.5	0.6	31	73	40
Beckman,Ryan	13	R	23	aa	PIT	19	2.67	1.46	5.42	3.1	5.7	1.8	0.0	34	80	71
	14	R	24	aa	PIT	55	2.77	1.22	4.94	3.2	3.6	1.1	0.3	26	77	45
Bedrosian,Cam	14	R	23	a/a	LAA	39	2.25	0.76	3.7	3.2	13.1	4.0	0.2	22	69	188
Beeler,Dallas	13	R	24	aa	CHC	55	3.85	1.26	24.8	3.0	4.8	1.6	0.6	27	69	51
	14	R	25	aaa	CHC	124	4.12	1.34	25.8	2.5	4.9	2.0	0.6	30	69	52
Belfiore,Michael	13	L	25	aaa	BAL	76	4.15	1.70	9.33	3.7	7.8	2.1	1.2	37	79	46
	14	L	26	aaa	DET	91	4.22	1.66	11.7	3.8	4.5	1.2	1.2	32	78	11
Beliveau,Jeff	13	L	26	a/a	TAM	49	2.90	1.51	5.14	4.4	12.1	2.8	0.2	41	80	127
	14	L	27	aaa	TAM	36	1.95	1.08	4.68	3.8	10.1	2.7	0.0	28	80	134

PITCHER	yr	t	age	lvl	org	ip	era	whip	bf/g	ctl	dom	f	hr/9	h%	s%	bpv
Bellatti,Andrew	13	R	22	aa	TAM	27	7.79	1.70	8.6	3.5	5.4	1.5	1.9	33	56	-2
	14	R	23	aa	TAM	71	4.05	1.37	6.5	2.7	8.8	3.3	0.7	35	71	100
Below,Duane	13	L	28	aaa	MIA	100	3.40	1.50	25.3	2.6	4.6	1.8	0.4	34	77	48
	14	L	29	aaa	DET	117	5.14	1.80	24.5	3.6	3.4	0.9	1.1	34	73	-3
Benedict,Matt	14	R	25	aa	PIT	53	6.23	1.75	8.1	4.0	4.6	1.1	0.3	35	62	34
Berg,Jeremy	13	R	27	a/a	LAA	78	3.14	1.29	5.9	2.1	6.5	3.1	0.7	32	77	84
	14	R	28	a/a	STL	69	6.55	1.71	5.8	2.8	7.0	2.6	0.6	39	60	65
Bergman,Christian	13	R	25	aa	COL	171	4.94	1.38	26.6	1.4	4.4	3.2	2.0	30	72	29
	14	R	26	a/a	COL	101	5.31	1.51	25.8	2.2	4.3	2.0	1.4	32	68	17
Berken,Jason	13	R	30	aaa	CHW	161	5.51	1.81	27.6	3.4	4.9	1.5	1.3	36	72	10
	14	R	31	aaa	SF	132	4.85	1.72	25.0	3.0	4.5	1.5	0.7	36	72	25
Berrios,Jose	14	R	20	a/a	MIN	44	5.20	1.33	20.1	2.9	5.6	1.9	0.4	30	58	64
Berry,Timothy	14	L	23	aa	BAL	133	4.02	1.36	24.2	3.0	6.1	2.0	0.9	30	73	53
Bettis,Chad	13	R	24	aa	COL	63	5.34	1.44	22.3	2.0	7.5	3.7	1.9	33	69	60
	14	R	25	aaa	COL	55	3.54	1.31	11.4	3.4	6.8	2.0	0.2	31	71	82
Bibens-Dirkx,Austin	13	R	28	aa	TOR	66	2.44	1.17	21.9	2.5	6.1	2.4	0.5	28	81	78
	14	R	29	a/a	TOR	113	4.93	1.51	14.4	2.1	5.5	2.6	1.7	33	73	30
Biddle,Jesse	13	L	22	aa	PHI	138	3.94	1.38	21.5	5.1	8.8	1.7	0.7	29	72	79
	14	L	23	aa	PHI	82	5.82	1.58	22.7	4.7	7.5	1.6	1.3	32	65	40
Billings,Bruce	13	R	28	aaa	OAK	148	4.78	1.46	22.7	3.2	6.2	1.9	1.0	32	69	48
	14	R	29	a/a	LA	96	5.40	1.73	20.7	3.2	4.9	1.6	1.0	36	70	23
Binford,Christian	14	R	22	a/a	KC	58	3.95	1.33	20.1	1.6	6.0	3.7	1.2	32	74	77
Bischoff,Matthew	13	R	26	aa	BAL	51	5.47	1.57	8.9	4.1	6.9	1.7	1.1	33	66	42
	14	R	27	a/a	BAL	70	6.13	1.89	13.8	3.8	5.7	1.5	1.8	37	71	0
Blach,Ty	14	L	24	aa	SF	141	3.56	1.41	23.9	2.5	4.8	2.0	0.5	32	75	53
Black,Corey	14	R	23	aa	CHC	124	3.99	1.48	20.6	5.2	7.3	1.4	1.0	28	76	50
Blackburn,Clayton	14	R	21	aa	SF	93	3.56	1.29	21.2	1.8	7.2	3.9	0.1	35	70	123
Blair,Aaron	14	R	22	aa	ARI	46	2.36	1.08	22.6	3.0	7.6	2.5	0.9	25	83	85
Blair,Seth	13	R	24	aa	STL	130	5.41	1.62	24.0	3.2	6.7	2.1	1.1	35	68	43
	14	R	25	a/a	STL	79	6.60	1.90	11.7	6.5	4.7	0.7	1.0	32	65	9
Blazek,Michael	13	R	24	a/a	STL	46	2.13	1.23	5.1	5.0	8.4	1.7	0.2	26	82	97
	14	R	25	aaa	MIL	102	4.96	1.63	12.3	3.7	6.4	1.7	1.0	34	71	40
Bleich,Jeremy	13	L	26	aa	NYY	65	3.77	1.78	11.1	6.1	6.2	1.0	0.2	34	77	52
	14	L	27	a/a	NYY	111	5.56	1.72	19.3	4.4	5.8	1.3	1.1	34	69	25
Bleier,Richard	13	L	26	a/a	TEX	81	4.56	1.59	8.5	2.5	4.2	1.7	0.9	34	73	25
	14	L	27	a/a	TOR	87	5.45	1.67	11.1	1.3	3.7	2.9	2.0	35	73	9
Blough,Bryan	14	R	25	aa	CHW	62	5.00	1.58	15.2	3.8	4.2	1.1	0.7	32	68	24
Bochy,Brett	13	R	26	aaa	SF	56	3.97	1.25	5.1	2.4	7.2	3.0	0.3	32	66	102
	14	R	27	aaa	SF	54	3.79	1.54	6.7	4.3	6.1	1.4	1.0	31	79	35
Boggs,Mitchell	13	R	29	aaa	COL	46	8.23	2.38	7.0	4.9	3.2	0.7	1.1	41	65	-23
	14	R	30	aaa	SF	49	9.04	2.42	7.3	4.4	3.0	0.7	0.8	43	61	-17
Bolsinger,Michael	13	R	25	a/a	ARI	144	4.72	1.58	24.4	3.3	6.4	1.9	0.8	35	71	49
	14	R	26	aaa	ARI	92	4.10	1.44	23.0	3.0	6.8	2.3	0.6	34	72	70
Bonilla,Lisalberto	13	R	23	a/a	TEX	73	6.17	1.58	6.9	4.3	10.8	2.5	1.3	37	62	78
	14	R	24	aaa	TEX	75	4.49	1.42	8.1	3.0	9.0	3.0	1.2	34	71	82
Boone,Randy	13	R	29	aa	TOR	62	4.51	1.66	8.5	2.6	5.4	2.1	0.9	36	74	38
	14	R	30	a/a	TOR	58	4.08	1.52	5.6	3.3	6.4	1.9	0.7	34	74	56
Boscan,Wilfredo	13	R	24	a/a	SD	62	6.11	1.68	14.7	2.3	4.2	1.8	1.7	34	67	1
	14	R	25	a/a	BOS	66	4.86	1.67	13.5	2.4	5.2	2.1	0.9	37	72	37
Boshers,Jeffrey	13	L	25	a/a	LAA	48	3.51	1.34	4.6	4.3	9.3	2.1	0.3	32	73	99
	14	L	26	a/a	LAA	74	3.45	1.36	7.7	4.6	8.0	1.7	0.2	30	73	87
Bowman,Matthew	14	R	23	a/a	NYM	135	2.82	1.25	22.8	2.1	7.3	3.5	0.5	33	78	106
Boyd,Matt	14	L	23	aa	TOR	43	8.72	1.82	19.8	2.8	8.0	2.9	1.3	42	51	55
Brach,Brett	13	R	25	a/a	CLE	142	5.38	1.45	20.9	2.3	4.4	1.9	0.9	32	63	34
	14	R	26	a/a	WAS	38	6.24	2.06	20.6	1.8	4.4	2.4	0.5	44	68	37
Bradford,Chasen	13	R	24	aa	NYM	25	0.76	1.12	5.0	2.7	5.5	2.0	0.4	26	96	75
	14	R	25	a/a	NYM	73	2.72	1.25	5.2	1.1	6.9	6.2	0.7	34	81	150
Bradley,Archie	13	R	21	aa	ARI	123	2.60	1.38	24.7	4.4	7.5	1.7	0.5	30	82	74
	14	R	22	a/a	ARI	79	4.76	1.53	20.2	5.0	6.7	1.3	0.2	31	66	65
Bradley,Jed	14	L	24	aa	MIL	87	5.45	1.85	23.9	3.9	6.3	1.6	1.0	38	72	29
Brady,Michael	13	R	26	aa	MIA	53	2.06	1.19	4.3	1.7	7.3	4.3	0.3	32	83	126
	14	R	27	a/a	LAA	68	4.83	1.51	6.5	2.9	6.5	2.2	0.5	35	67	67
Branham,Matthew	13	R	26	a/a	SD	34	3.97	1.38	6.2	4.4	8.4	1.9	0.8	30	73	74
	14	R	27	a/a	SD	91	4.18	1.53	10.5	2.8	6.1	2.2	0.8	35	74	53
Brazis,Matt	14	R	25	aa	SEA	33	1.91	1.00	7.4	2.7	7.8	2.9	0.3	26	81	114
Brewer,Charles	13	R	25	aaa	ARI	140	4.82	1.48	24.0	2.5	5.5	2.2	0.8	34	68	51
	14	R	26	a/a	ARI	170	5.19	1.54	25.5	2.6	5.8	2.3	0.8	35	66	53
Brigham,Jacob	13	R	25	a/a	TEX	127	5.41	1.73	17.6	4.2	5.3	1.3	0.7	35	68	32
	14	R	26	aaa	PIT	92	4.88	1.45	21.9	2.7	5.2	1.9	1.1	31	68	36
Britton,Drake	13	L	24	a/a	BOS	103	4.67	1.56	25.0	3.3	6.1	1.9	0.5	35	69	57
	14	L	25	aaa	BOS	58	7.74	2.31	6.7	6.2	4.6	0.7	1.4	39	67	-18
Bromberg,David	13	R	26	a/a	PIT	147	4.24	1.45	22.4	3.4	6.3	1.8	0.7	32	71	56
	14	R	27	aaa	ATL	37	5.28	1.61	20.5	4.0	7.2	1.8	0.8	35	67	53
Brooks,Aaron	13	R	23	aa	KC	104	5.00	1.36	27.1	1.0	4.7	4.9	1.1	33	65	91
	14	R	24	aaa	KC	139	4.21	1.37	23.3	1.6	5.0	3.2	0.8	33	71	68
Brown,Brooks	13	R	28	aaa	PIT	91	6.08	1.59	10.8	2.5	4.9	2.0	1.1	34	62	28
	14	R	29	aaa	COL	47	5.24	1.71	5.8	3.5	6.0	1.7	1.0	36	71	34
Brummett,Tyson	13	R	29	a/a	TOR	88	7.72	1.81	11.9	3.9	6.0	1.5	1.1	37	56	25
	14	R	30	aa	LA	71	3.16	1.47	21.7	2.7	5.4	2.0	0.3	34	78	62
Bucciferro,Tony	14	R	25	aa	CHW	36	5.94	1.65	26.8	1.7	4.4	2.6	0.9	37	64	40
Buchanan,David	13	R	24	a/a	PHI	170	5.07	1.51	26.2	2.8	4.8	1.7	1.0	32	68	30
	14	R	25	aaa	PHI	57	4.64	1.74	21.7	3.4	6.0	1.8	0.5	38	73	47
Buchanan,Jake	13	R	24	a/a	HOU	158	3.41	1.23	21.4	1.3	4.8	3.8	0.6	31	73	89
	14	R	25	aaa	HOU	88	4.18	1.37	23.2	1.6	3.9	2.4	0.7	32	70	48
Buchter,Ryan	13	L	26	aaa	ATL	62	3.44	1.58	5.35	7.9	12.2	1.5	0.8	30	80	97
	14	L	27	aaa	ATL	63	3.82	1.62	5.71	6.0	7.2	1.2	0.7	30	78	51
Buckner,Billy	13	R	30	aaa	LAA	94	4.85	1.71	23.7	4.6	5.4	1.2	0.6	34	71	36
	14	R	31	aaa	MIL	76	7.73	2.17	19.9	5.0	5.3	1.1	1.8	39	66	-17

PITCHER	yr	t	age	lvl	org	ip	era	whip	bf/g	ctl	dom	cmd	hr/9	h%	s%	bpv
Burawa,Daniel	13	R	25	aa	NYY	66	3.47	1.59	6.32	6.3	7.3	1.2	0.2	30	77	70
	14	R	26	a/a	NYY	59	5.93	1.78	6.5	4.9	8.8	1.8	0.6	39	65	67
Burns,Cory	13	R	26	aaa	TEX	38	2.79	1.72	4.5	3.9	8.9	2.3	0.0	41	82	94
	14	R	27	a/a	TAM	64	6.17	1.82	6.87	2.4	6.5	2.7	1.2	40	67	43
Buschmann,Matthev	13	R	29	a/a	TAM	161	3.68	1.56	24.3	4.1	7.1	1.7	0.6	34	77	58
	14	R	30	aaa	OAK	133	4.93	1.64	25.8	3.5	6.1	1.8	0.9	35	71	39
Butler,Eddie	13	R	22	aa	COL	28	0.90	0.80	16.7	2.1	6.5	3.2	0.0	21	88	127
	14	R	23	a/a	COL	113	4.65	1.45	25.4	2.8	4.2	1.5	1.0	30	70	24
Cabral,Cesar	13	L	24	a/a	NYY	30	8.15	1.93	5.63	4.7	9.6	2.1	0.8	43	56	64
	14	L	25	a/a	NYY	39	7.76	2.04	5.88	8.4	8.3	1.0	0.9	35	61	43
Cabrera,Alberto	13	R	25	a/a	CHC	133	4.75	1.57	17.7	3.7	6.9	1.9	1.1	33	72	45
	14	R	26	aaa	CHC	66	4.07	1.34	6.83	4.5	6.6	1.5	1.4	25	75	38
Cabrera,Edwar	14	L	27	a/a	TEX	146	4.29	1.63	21.7	2.9	5.4	1.9	0.8	35	75	40
Cain,Colton	14	L	23	aa	HOU	39	6.93	2.11	13.6	5.9	6.7	1.1	1.5	38	69	7
Cales,David	13	R	26	aa	CHW	25	2.51	2.08	7.55	7.1	6.6	0.9	1.0	36	92	20
	14	R	27	a/a	CHW	59	5.79	1.81	9.36	4.4	6.6	1.5	1.1	36	69	29
Camarena,Daniel	14	L	22	aa	NYY	55	6.09	1.52	23.9	2.3	6.1	2.6	1.6	34	63	36
Caminero,Arquimed	13	R	26	a/a	MIA	54	4.67	1.22	5.1	3.9	9.0	2.3	0.7	28	61	93
	14	R	27	aaa	MIA	63	5.29	1.75	6.86	4.4	8.7	2.0	0.8	39	70	62
Campos,Leonel	13	R	26	aa	SD	31	1.07	1.09	4.61	4.9	10.5	2.1	0.0	25	89	131
	14	R	27	a/a	SD	82	6.40	1.78	9.03	5.4	9.6	1.8	0.8	39	63	67
Cargill,Collin	13	R	26	aa	MIA	56	2.17	0.95	5.56	2.7	3.4	1.3	0.3	20	78	55
	14	R	27	a/a	MIA	49	4.85	1.64	5.12	4.0	3.8	0.9	0.5	32	69	24
Carignan,Andrew	14	R	28	a/a	SF	40	5.23	2.06	6.56	8.9	6.6	0.7	0.6	33	74	37
Carpenter,David	13	R	26	a/a	LAA	61	6.99	1.69	5.17	4.9	6.2	1.3	0.7	33	57	40
	14	R	27	a/a	LAA	62	2.32	1.37	5.8	3.5	6.6	1.9	0.1	32	82	78
Carpenter,Drew	13	R	28	a/a	OAK	127	5.79	1.62	23.4	2.8	4.0	1.4	1.3	33	66	7
	14	R	29	aaa	LA	48	7.31	1.92	14.1	3.5	5.7	1.6	0.5	40	59	38
Carraway,Andrew	13	R	27	aaa	SEA	119	6.20	1.80	24.9	4.1	5.1	1.3	1.3	35	67	9
	14	R	28	aaa	SEA	125	5.63	1.65	18.7	2.3	4.7	2.1	0.9	36	66	33
Carreno,Joel	13	R	26	a/a	TOR	67	3.05	1.09	5.21	3.4	9.8	2.9	0.8	26	75	110
	14	R	27	aaa	NYM	59	4.11	1.49	12.7	3.1	6.1	1.9	0.9	33	74	48
Carson,Robert	13	L	24	aaa	NYM	44	3.49	1.43	4.39	3.3	6.3	1.9	0.5	32	76	63
	14	L	25	a/a	LA	58	5.41	1.80	6.2	4.4	6.8	1.5	1.1	37	71	32
Casey,Jarrett	14	L	27	a/a	CHW	59	2.86	1.46	7.94	4.7	3.9	0.8	0.7	26	83	23
Casilla,Jose	14	R	25	aa	SF	66	4.63	1.34	6.67	3.0	4.3	1.4	0.6	29	65	39
Castillo,Fabio	13	R	24	a/a	SF	89	5.28	1.62	10.7	4.0	7.9	2.0	0.6	37	66	69
	14	R	25	a/a	CIN	59	4.39	1.71	6.65	5.4	5.4	1.0	0.9	31	76	24
Castillo,Lendy	14	R	25	aa	CHC	41	4.73	1.92	5.4	9.1	7.3	0.8	1.0	29	77	38
Castillo,Richard	13	R	24	a/a	STL	148	4.42	1.43	24.2	3.2	4.4	1.4	1.0	29	71	25
	14	R	25	aa	COL	136	7.73	1.81	25.3	3.4	3.4	1.0	1.7	34	59	-20
Castillo,Yeiper	13	R	25	aa	CHC	62	4.77	1.52	12.7	4.9	6.3	1.3	0.7	30	68	48
	14	R	26	a/a	LAA	45	5.21	1.49	21.7	4.9	5.6	1.1	0.4	29	63	51
Cedeno,Xavier	13	L	27	aaa	WAS	34	1.59	1.28	3.61	4.2	8.9	2.1	0.6	29	91	91
	14	L	28	aaa	WAS	39	2.85	1.01	4.3	2.9	9.6	3.4	0.8	26	75	121
Celestino,Miguel	13	R	24	aa	BOS	72	7.54	1.83	8.58	4.5	7.2	1.6	1.3	37	59	27
	14	R	25	a/a	BOS	52	5.28	1.45	5.69	3.7	8.3	2.3	1.6	31	68	51
Cervenka,Hunter	13	L	23	aa	CHC	38	3.68	1.41	5.41	4.9	6.6	1.3	0.3	29	73	67
	14	L	24	aa	CHC	62	4.45	1.34	5.34	4.7	7.9	1.7	0.2	29	64	88
Chaffee,Ryan	13	R	25	aa	LAA	62	3.65	1.37	5.5	5.2	8.7	1.7	0.5	29	73	85
	14	R	26	a/a	LAA	60	4.85	1.75	6.27	5.2	9.0	1.7	0.3	39	70	78
Chafin,Andrew	13	L	23	aa	ARI	126	3.87	1.48	25.9	3.1	5.2	1.7	0.5	33	73	50
	14	L	24	a/a	ARI	148	4.56	1.59	25.1	3.4	5.7	1.7	1.0	34	73	36
Chapman,Kevin	13	L	25	aaa	HOU	51	3.73	1.69	5.07	6.5	9.1	1.4	0.4	34	77	76
	14	L	26	aaa	HOU	44	1.35	1.55	4.47	5.1	10.7	2.1	0.0	38	90	111
Church,John	13	R	27	a/a	NYM	65	3.39	1.36	4.92	3.5	7.7	2.2	0.5	32	76	79
	14	R	28	a/a	NYM	57	3.86	1.46	5.54	2.4	7.0	2.9	0.7	35	75	76
Claudio,Alexander	13	L	21	aa	TEX	32	3.77	1.42	6.4	3.3	7.0	2.1	0.7	32	75	65
	14	L	22	a/a	TEX	43	2.65	1.06	16.5	0.8	5.0	6.0	0.2	29	74	153
Clay,Caleb	13	R	25	a/a	WAS	158	3.57	1.18	23.4	1.7	4.9	2.8	0.7	29	71	72
	14	R	26	aaa	LAA	76	4.44	1.35	26.4	1.7	4.3	2.5	1.2	30	71	37
Clemens,Paul	13	R	25	aaa	HOU	30	5.25	1.42	21.2	3.4	4.0	1.2	0.3	30	60	40
	14	R	26	aaa	HOU	46	4.50	1.41	10.3	4.5	6.5	1.5	0.8	28	69	51
Cleto,Maikel	13	R	24	aaa	KC	91	6.91	1.93	12.4	7.6	7.0	0.9	0.5	34	62	45
	14	R	25	aaa	CHW	35	6.37	1.63	7.09	4.1	10.8	2.6	2.0	37	66	55
Cloyd,Tyler	13	R	26	aaa	PHI	113	5.80	1.58	26.1	2.2	6.0	2.7	2.0	34	69	24
	14	R	27	aaa	CLE	167	4.69	1.50	26.7	1.7	5.1	2.9	1.5	34	73	39
Coello,Robert	13	R	29	a/a	LAA	20	5.24	1.48	5.29	5.1	10.6	2.1	0.5	35	63	100
	14	R	30	aaa	BAL	56	2.27	1.50	5.23	6.5	8.1	1.2	0.6	27	87	68
Cole,A.J.	13	R	21	aa	WAS	45	2.57	0.97	24.6	1.9	8.2	4.4	0.6	27	76	135
	14	R	22	a/a	WAS	134	3.32	1.39	22.6	1.9	6.2	3.2	0.6	34	77	83
Coleman,Casey	13	R	26	aaa	CHC	88	4.03	1.52	9.34	4.0	5.3	1.3	0.8	30	75	35
	14	R	27	aaa	KC	68	3.06	1.38	8.15	3.8	5.3	1.4	0.5	29	79	50
Coleman,Louis	13	R	27	aaa	KC	45	2.15	1.44	7.93	3.8	7.8	2.1	0.2	34	85	85
	14	R	28	aaa	KC	40	4.56	1.37	5.94	3.6	8.8	2.4	1.3	31	71	67
Colla,Michael	13	R	27	aa	TAM	75	4.52	1.45	23	2.4	4.6	2.0	1.3	31	72	26
	14	R	28	aa	TAM	144	5.37	1.78	23.6	2.7	5.8	2.2	0.7	39	70	44
Collier,Tommy	14	R	25	aa	DET	86	6.63	1.59	22.2	4.0	3.9	1.0	1.5	29	60	-4
Collins,Tim	14	L	25	aaa	KC	42	3.06	1.07	7.15	3.4	9.3	2.8	1.2	24	78	94
Colome,Alexander	13	R	24	aaa	TAM	70	3.58	1.43	21.4	3.7	7.8	2.1	0.7	33	76	73
	14	R	25	aaa	TAM	86	4.68	1.53	24.9	3.2	6.3	1.9	0.2	35	67	69
Colon,Joseph	14	R	24	aa	CLE	138	3.91	1.48	23.7	3.5	5.3	1.5	0.5	32	74	47
Conley,Adam	13	L	23	aa	MIA	139	4.11	1.35	22.2	2.5	7.0	2.8	0.4	33	69	87
	14	L	24	aaa	MIA	60	6.12	1.57	22	3.7	5.9	1.6	0.4	34	58	55
Cooney,Tim	13	L	23	aa	STL	118	3.98	1.34	24.6	1.3	8.0	6.1	0.5	37	70	156
	14	L	24	aaa	STL	158	3.57	1.36	25.4	2.5	5.6	2.2	1.0	30	77	48
Cooper,Jordan	13	R	24	aa	CLE	72	3.33	1.20	16.2	3.7	6.0	1.6	0.7	25	74	60
	14	R	25	a/a	CLE	85	5.78	1.48	9.91	3.8	5.6	1.5	1.3	29	63	27

PITCHER	yr	t	age	lvl	org	ip	era	whip	bf/g	ctl	dom	f	hr/9	h%	s%	bpv
Cooper,Matthew	13	R	25	aa	ARI	43	4.15	1.48	4.74	5.0	5.0	1.0	0.3	28	70	49
	14	R	26	a/a	CHC	68	3.89	1.46	5.97	4.3	7.1	1.7	0.4	32	73	67
Copeland,Scott	14	R	27	a/a	TOR	165	4.75	1.61	23.6	3.4	4.5	1.4	0.8	33	71	25
Corcino,Daniel	13	R	23	aaa	CIN	129	7.57	1.89	21.7	5.3	5.5	1.0	1.6	34	61	-2
	14	R	24	a/a	CIN	149	4.75	1.44	23.5	4.4	6.2	1.4	1.3	27	71	30
Cordier,Erik	13	R	27	aaa	PIT	53	5.74	1.73	5.48	4.9	8.2	1.6	0.5	37	65	64
	14	R	28	aaa	SF	53	3.63	1.42	4.75	5.2	8.8	1.7	0.5	30	75	81
Cornelius,Jonathan	13	L	25	aa	STL	79	4.87	1.56	19.1	3.3	6.1	1.8	0.9	34	70	43
	14	L	26	a/a	STL	156	4.67	1.42	23.6	2.6	4.7	1.8	1.2	30	70	29
Cornely,John	14	R	25	aa	ATL	69	3.05	1.30	6.14	4.7	7.8	1.7	0.3	28	76	85
Corpas,Manuel	13	R	31	aaa	COL	41	6.53	1.74	8.9	3.5	5.2	1.5	1.3	35	64	13
	14	R	32	aaa	COL	48	6.70	1.91	8.05	2.1	5.4	2.6	1.5	41	67	23
Cotham,Caleb	13	R	26	a/a	NYY	124	7.10	1.90	20.9	3.9	4.9	1.3	1.2	37	63	6
	14	R	27	a/a	NYY	44	7.44	1.93	20.7	4.6	5.3	1.2	1.1	37	61	11
Couch,Keith	13	R	24	a/a	BOS	131	4.52	1.57	19.1	3.1	5.4	1.7	0.8	34	72	38
	14	R	25	aa	BOS	100	3.94	1.53	24.2	2.1	5.2	2.5	0.3	36	73	66
Crabbe,Timothy	13	R	25	a/a	CIN	153	4.22	1.55	24.8	2.8	5.4	1.9	1.0	34	75	36
	14	R	26	aaa	CIN	94	4.63	1.67	14	3.6	4.7	1.3	0.9	34	74	22
Cravy,Tyler	14	R	25	a/a	MIL	77	2.13	1.02	19.6	2.2	6.7	3.0	1.0	24	86	84
Crick,Kyle	14	R	22	aa	SF	90	4.14	1.58	17.3	5.8	9.6	1.7	0.6	33	74	79
Cruz,Luis	13	L	23	aa	HOU	17	0.60	0.56	14.4	2.1	9.7	4.6	0.0	16	88	189
	14	L	24	a/a	HOU	125	4.01	1.34	19.9	2.7	7.3	2.7	1.2	31	74	66
Cuan,Angel	14	L	25	aa	NYM	39	6.37	1.66	21.8	2.4	5.7	2.3	1.1	37	62	38
Culver,Malcom	14	R	24	a/a	KC	65	5.27	1.72	6.71	4.0	6.6	1.7	0.5	37	68	51
Cumpton,Brandon	13	R	25	a/a	PIT	132	4.30	1.49	24.6	3.3	5.1	1.5	0.4	32	70	49
	14	R	26	aaa	PIT	71	3.45	1.39	25	2.5	3.5	1.4	0.8	30	78	25
Cunniff,Brandon	14	R	26	aa	ATL	53	2.56	1.30	6.58	3.7	7.1	1.9	0.4	30	81	79
Daley,Matt	13	R	31	a/a	NYY	48	3.41	1.21	4.84	2.3	8.8	3.8	0.9	32	75	111
	14	R	32	aaa	NYY	36	6.01	1.82	5.91	2.3	8.9	3.8	2.0	42	72	56
Darnell,Logan	13	L	24	a/a	MIN	154	3.69	1.46	24.4	2.6	5.7	2.2	0.5	34	75	62
	14	L	25	aaa	MIN	115	4.61	1.59	22	4.0	5.6	1.4	1.3	31	75	20
Davies,Kyle	13	R	30	aa	MIN	28	4.53	1.39	19.9	0.7	5.5	7.8	0.7	36	68	167
	14	R	31	a/a	CLE	154	5.04	1.59	26.2	2.6	4.3	1.7	1.1	34	70	19
Davies,Zachary	14	R	21	aa	BAL	110	3.73	1.33	21.7	2.5	7.7	3.1	0.7	33	73	90
Dayton,Grant	13	L	26	aa	MIA	38	3.19	1.45	5.4	3.2	10.4	3.3	1.0	37	82	101
	14	L	27	a/a	MIA	72	3.61	1.52	6.26	3.4	7.6	2.2	1.1	34	80	56
De La Cruz,Joel	14	R	25	a/a	NYY	122	5.48	1.63	19.4	2.9	4.6	1.6	0.8	35	67	27
De La Cruz,Kelvin	13	L	25	a/a	LA	67	3.01	1.62	5.97	4.5	9.2	2.0	0.4	37	82	84
	14	L	26	aaa	BAL	50	7.07	2.09	6.59	5.8	7.0	1.2	1.7	38	69	2
De La Cruz,Luis	14	R	25	aa	SD	67	3.08	1.38	4.94	4.9	7.2	1.5	0.7	27	80	62
De la Rosa,Eury	13	L	23	aaa	ARI	50	4.97	1.54	4.93	4.3	7.4	1.7	1.0	33	69	52
	14	L	24	aaa	ARI	39	2.52	1.35	4.56	4.2	6.8	1.6	0.6	28	84	62
De La Rosa,Rubby	13	R	24	aaa	BOS	80	5.30	1.56	14.7	5.5	7.0	1.3	1.1	29	68	40
	14	R	25	aaa	BOS	60	4.55	1.47	21.4	4.0	6.9	1.7	0.2	33	66	74
De La Torre,Jose	13	R	28	aaa	BOS	52	3.74	1.43	6.55	5.1	7.6	1.5	0.4	29	73	73
	14	R	29	a/a	MIL	43	6.14	1.93	6.75	5.4	8.4	1.6	1.1	39	69	40
De Leon,Emmanuel	14	R	24	aa	PIT	48	3.76	1.68	6.97	3.5	5.2	1.5	0.3	36	77	45
De Leon,Jorge	13	R	26	a/a	HOU	68	4.16	1.14	6.54	2.4	5.2	2.2	1.1	25	66	53
	14	R	27	a/a	HOU	69	3.50	1.45	6.37	3.1	6.4	2.0	0.7	33	77	58
De los Santos,Frank	13	L	26	aaa	TAM	32	6.50	1.83	5.73	4.1	4.8	1.2	0.9	36	64	16
	14	L	27	a/a	CHW	45	5.71	1.90	7.27	4.4	3.4	0.8	0.7	35	70	3
De Paula,Jose	13	L	23	aa	SD	75	4.39	1.40	22.5	1.3	6.1	4.7	0.4	36	67	117
	14	L	24	aaa	SF	51	3.90	1.37	13.4	2.5	6.0	2.4	0.6	32	72	65
Dean,Pat	13	L	24	a/a	MIN	165	4.63	1.43	25.1	1.2	3.7	3.1	0.6	34	67	61
	14	L	25	aa	MIN	144	5.94	1.81	25.6	2.0	4.1	2.1	1.3	38	69	12
Degrom,Jacob	13	R	25	a/a	NYM	136	4.52	1.51	24.5	2.7	6.0	2.2	0.6	35	70	59
	14	R	26	aaa	NYM	38	2.19	1.24	22.2	2.0	5.6	2.7	0.4	31	83	82
Delcarmen,Manny	13	R	31	aaa	BAL	54	4.08	1.58	4.95	4.3	5.6	1.3	0.7	32	75	37
	14	R	32	aaa	WAS	60	4.04	1.64	5.85	3.7	5.8	1.6	0.3	35	74	52
DeLoach,Tyler	14	L	23	aa	LAA	35	2.84	1.04	22.7	4.3	8.5	2.0	0.8	20	76	90
Demel,Sam	13	R	28	aaa	NYY	52	2.58	1.52	6.49	4.8	8.5	1.8	0.8	32	86	68
	14	R	29	aaa	LA	46	6.05	1.65	9.86	3.2	6.3	1.9	1.5	35	66	25
Demny,Paul	13	R	24	a/a	WAS	89	6.25	1.56	20.5	3.5	7.5	2.1	1.2	34	61	50
	14	R	25	aa	WAS	41	3.10	1.55	8.08	4.3	6.3	1.4	0.6	32	82	49
Dennick,Ryan	13	L	26	a/a	CIN	123	5.38	1.60	20.1	2.9	4.7	1.6	1.1	34	68	22
	14	L	27	a/a	CIN	50	2.80	1.43	3.66	3.4	5.8	1.7	0.0	33	78	71
DePaula,Julio	14	R	31	aa	BAL	38	6.58	1.89	8.52	3.5	7.4	2.1	0.6	42	64	55
DeSclafani,Anthony	13	R	23	aa	MIA	75	4.25	1.36	24.1	1.8	6.2	3.5	0.8	34	70	84
	14	R	24	a/a	MIA	102	4.10	1.30	21.1	2.7	6.9	2.6	0.4	32	68	85
Despaigne,Odrisam	14	R	27	a/a	SD	31	6.09	1.96	21.4	5.0	9.6	1.9	0.8	43	69	63
Devenski,Christophe	14	R	24	aa	HOU	41	4.41	1.33	17.2	3.9	6.9	1.8	1.6	26	73	36
Diamond,Scott	13	L	27	aaa	MIN	41	2.95	1.20	27.5	2.1	3.2	1.5	0.9	26	79	28
	14	L	28	aaa	CIN	123	7.69	1.96	22.7	2.4	3.8	1.5	1.3	39	61	-5
Diaz,Jairo	14	R	23	aa	LAA	33	2.73	1.37	5.08	2.7	11.3	4.1	0.6	39	82	137
Diaz,Jose	13	R	29	aaa	CIN	54	2.44	1.34	5.13	4.1	7.6	1.8	1.3	27	89	54
	14	R	30	aaa	CIN	33	1.31	1.26	4.53	2.9	6.3	2.2	0.3	30	91	78
Diaz,Luis	14	R	22	aa	BOS	77	4.66	1.40	25.1	3.0	6.3	2.1	0.9	31	68	55
Dillard,Tim	13	R	30	aaa	MIL	47	5.53	1.76	5.67	5.4	4.2	0.8	0.5	32	67	24
	14	R	31	a/a	MIL	65	5.22	1.42	5.83	2.8	5.9	2.1	0.9	32	64	50
Dimock,Michael	14	R	25	aa	SD	57	3.99	1.41	6.18	2.7	8.2	3.0	1.0	34	74	82
Dodson,Zackry	14	L	24	aa	PIT	123	4.88	1.58	22.5	3.1	4.4	1.4	0.7	33	69	29
Dominguez,Jose	13	R	23	a/a	LAA	25	1.78	0.83	4.21	4.1	12.1	2.9	0.0	20	76	166
	14	R	24	aaa	LA	33	2.74	1.35	4.49	4.0	8.8	2.2	0.2	32	79	99
Donofrio,Joseph	14	R	25	a/a	STL	60	1.64	1.16	4.54	3.1	8.5	2.7	0.4	29	88	106
Doolittle,Ryan	14	R	26	aa	OAK	47	3.84	1.59	6.97	3.8	7.1	1.9	0.8	35	77	56
Doran,Robert	13	R	24	a/a	HOU	138	4.05	1.35	18.6	2.5	5.1	2.0	1.1	30	73	41
	14	R	25	aaa	CHW	126	5.85	1.69	18.9	4.0	4.5	1.1	1.0	33	66	16

PITCHER	yr	t	age	lvl	org	ip	era	whip	bf/g	ctl	dom	cmd	hr/9	h%	s%	bpv
Doyle,John	14	R	29	a/a	ATL	109	5.16	1.66	13.6	3.3	5.0	1.5	0.7	35	69	31
Drabek,Kyle	13	R	26	a/a	TOR	22	4.55	1.12	14.7	1.3	4.9	3.9	1.5	26	64	70
	14	R	27	aaa	TOR	99	5.85	1.86	14.5	3.1	4.9	1.6	1.5	37	71	4
Drake,Oliver	13	R	26	aa	BAL	31	2.16	1.18	6.53	4.0	8.7	2.2	0.4	27	83	100
	14	R	27	aa	BAL	53	3.84	1.30	4.34	3.1	9.3	3.0	0.4	34	70	111
Duffey,Tyler	14	R	24	a/a	MIN	127	4.70	1.31	25	1.8	5.7	3.2	1.2	31	67	63
Dull,Ryan	14	R	25	aa	OAK	56	3.34	1.34	5.86	2.5	7.9	3.2	0.9	33	78	87
Dunning,Jake	13	R	25	aaa	SF	48	1.45	1.30	5.85	2.4	6.7	2.8	0.4	32	91	86
	14	R	26	aaa	SF	65	4.42	1.44	7.28	3.4	5.6	1.7	0.5	31	69	53
Dupra,Brian	14	R	26	a/a	WAS	94	6.44	1.76	17.3	4.0	4.3	1.1	0.8	34	62	16
Dwyer,Christopher	13	L	25	aaa	KC	160	4.54	1.54	24	4.3	4.9	1.1	0.9	30	72	27
	14	L	26	aaa	KC	66	6.32	1.71	10.7	5.4	6.8	1.3	1.0	33	63	34
Dyer,Shane	14	R	26	aa	CIN	50	4.00	1.61	5.11	3.6	5.2	1.4	0.7	33	76	36
Edwards,Carl	14	R	23	aa	CHC	48	2.80	1.15	19	4.0	7.3	1.8	0.2	25	74	91
Edwards,Jonathan	13	R	25	aa	TEX	15	7.53	1.85	7.95	5.4	7.5	1.4	2.5	33	64	-7
	14	R	26	aa	TEX	49	5.47	1.74	6.57	6.3	8.9	1.4	0.9	34	69	57
Eickhoff,Jerad	13	R	23	aa	TEX	29	10.19	1.97	23.1	4.8	3.3	0.7	2.5	32	50	-53
	14	R	24	aa	TEX	154	5.31	1.37	24	3.3	6.8	2.1	1.3	30	64	49
Eitel,Derek	13	R	26	aa	ARI	68	4.95	1.28	6.67	4.0	6.2	1.6	1.3	25	64	42
	14	R	27	aaa	ARI	47	2.88	1.54	6.79	4.3	8.9	2.1	1.0	34	85	68
Ely,John	14	R	28	aaa	BOS	39	3.55	1.74	7.17	3.6	6.0	1.7	0.8	37	82	37
Enright,Barry	13	R	27	aaa	LAA	116	6.70	1.77	22.2	3.4	4.7	1.4	1.9	34	66	-10
	14	R	28	aaa	LA	135	5.72	1.71	22.6	2.5	4.1	1.7	1.4	35	69	5
Escalona,Edgmer	14	R	28	aaa	NYY	51	4.73	1.52	8.85	2.0	5.0	2.5	1.2	34	71	40
Escobar,Edwin	13	L	21	aa	SF	54	2.60	1.05	20.9	1.9	7.7	4.0	0.3	29	74	131
	14	L	22	aaa	BOS	138	6.14	1.67	24.8	2.9	6.5	2.2	1.3	36	65	36
Espino,Paolo	13	R	26	a/a	CLE	141	5.69	1.63	19.6	2.9	7.3	2.5	1.1	37	66	56
	14	R	27	a/a	WAS	120	4.49	1.19	19.2	1.8	6.6	3.7	0.9	30	64	91
Evans,Bryan	13	R	26	aa	MIA	79	4.47	1.30	15.4	0.9	7.3	8.1	1.1	35	68	178
	14	R	27	aaa	MIA	112	4.81	1.44	13.3	3.7	6.5	1.8	1.0	30	68	47
Eveland,Dana	14	L	31	aaa	NYM	46	3.58	1.54	16.7	2.2	8.7	3.9	0.9	39	79	101
Fassold,Cody	14	R	26	aa	ATL	49	5.02	1.65	7.6	2.9	7.9	2.7	0.4	40	68	83
Faulk,Kenny	13	L	26	aaa	DET	44	4.95	1.50	5.99	6.9	8.1	1.2	0.7	25	67	64
	14	L	27	a/a	DET	61	5.31	1.55	6.37	6.4	8.4	1.3	0.7	29	65	68
Feierabend,Ryan	13	L	28	a/a	TEX	148	5.31	1.73	23.2	2.7	4.6	1.7	1.2	36	71	14
	14	L	29	aaa	TEX	125	6.25	1.72	22.7	2.3	4.2	1.8	1.6	35	66	4
Ferguson,Andrew	13	R	25	aa	KC	96	6.45	1.59	12.4	3.6	6.1	1.7	1.1	33	59	36
	14	R	26	a/a	KC	160	3.80	1.34	24.6	2.6	5.3	2.1	1.0	30	75	45
Ferrell,Jeff	14	R	24	aa	DET	138	6.11	1.67	24.8	2.4	4.8	2.0	1.1	36	64	26
Fiers,Mike	13	R	28	aaa	MIL	29	2.67	1.48	24.7	4.1	7.4	1.8	1.2	31	88	49
	14	R	29	aaa	MIL	102	3.35	1.19	24.2	1.7	8.7	5.0	0.9	33	75	132
Fife,Stephen	13	R	27	aaa	LA	37	6.28	1.91	17.7	4.8	6.2	1.3	0.7	38	66	33
	14	R	28	aaa	LA	44	6.47	1.89	18.7	2.8	4.3	1.5	0.3	40	63	30
Figaro,Alfredo	14	R	30	aaa	MIL	70	4.92	1.84	7.81	3.3	5.3	1.6	0.9	38	74	26
Figueroa,Eduardo	13	R	25	aa	CHC	34	3.00	1.28	23.2	2.3	3.7	1.6	0.9	28	80	29
	14	R	26	aa	CHC	62	5.21	1.72	14	4.1	4.2	1.0	0.5	34	69	25
Fisher,Carlos	13	R	30	aa	TAM	57	5.13	1.87	6.33	7.1	9.3	1.3	0.9	36	73	56
	14	R	31	aaa	ATL	33	3.70	1.45	6.13	4.2	8.5	2.0	0.3	34	73	87
Fitzgerald,Justin	13	R	27	a/a	SF	110	4.48	1.56	24.1	3.3	6.7	2.0	1.0	34	73	50
	14	R	28	aa	ARI	65	5.53	1.91	20.5	4.9	5.3	1.1	0.9	36	72	17
Flande,Yohan	13	L	27	a/a	ATL	136	5.80	1.79	19.6	3.5	5.0	1.4	0.7	37	67	28
	14	L	28	aaa	COL	88	6.86	1.95	23.4	3.6	4.8	1.4	1.2	38	65	7
Fleck,Kaleb	14	R	25	aa	ARI	63	3.30	1.52	4.91	4.2	9.0	2.2	0.7	35	80	80
Fleet,Austin	13	R	26	aaa	SF	61	3.50	1.30	19.4	2.4	5.5	2.3	1.3	29	79	45
	14	R	27	a/a	SF	140	3.43	1.37	17.8	3.1	5.5	1.7	0.5	30	75	56
Flores,Jose	13	R	24	aa	CLE	66	2.90	1.28	4.61	3.3	10.0	3.0	0.1	34	76	126
	14	R	25	a/a	OAK	54	4.11	1.51	5.05	4.5	5.9	1.3	0.4	31	72	51
Floro,Dylan	14	R	24	aa	TAM	179	3.91	1.45	27.2	1.2	4.8	4.1	0.2	36	71	99
Flynn,Brian	13	L	23	a/a	MIA	161	3.31	1.34	24.8	2.5	6.9	2.7	0.5	33	76	85
	14	L	24	aaa	MIA	140	4.14	1.64	24.9	3.1	5.5	1.8	0.7	36	75	43
Foltynewicz,Mike	13	R	22	aa	HOU	103	3.22	1.29	18.4	4.4	7.4	1.7	0.7	26	77	68
	14	R	23	aaa	HOU	103	5.26	1.50	21.1	4.3	7.8	1.8	0.9	32	65	61
Font,Wilmer	13	R	23	a/a	TEX	52	1.34	1.20	4.98	6.3	10.2	1.6	0.4	21	91	107
	14	R	24	aa	TEX	31	4.53	1.57	4.69	5.3	7.3	1.4	0.7	31	72	54
Fontanez,Randy	14	R	25	aa	NYM	33	4.97	1.60	6.7	3.6	7.5	2.1	0.8	36	69	61
Fornataro,Eric	13	R	25	aaa	STL	55	6.75	1.75	6.83	3.8	5.1	1.4	0.8	36	60	27
	14	R	26	aaa	STL	56	2.76	1.27	5.21	3.2	4.4	1.4	0.4	27	79	49
Francescon,P.J.	13	R	24	aa	CHC	30	5.17	1.55	8.19	5.1	5.2	1.0	0.7	29	66	36
	14	R	25	aa	CHC	69	4.22	1.56	7.03	4.3	5.1	1.2	0.6	31	73	37
Francis,Jeff	13	L	32	aaa	COL	37	5.17	1.64	15.1	2.3	5.4	2.4	0.3	38	66	62
	14	L	33	aaa	CIN	49	4.04	1.59	26.8	2.4	6.3	2.6	0.7	37	76	63
Frankoff,Seth	14	R	26	a/a	OAK	64	3.66	1.37	5.5	3.0	7.7	2.6	0.8	33	75	79
Frazier,Parker	13	R	25	a/a	CIN	73	5.47	1.86	8.94	4.2	5.7	1.3	0.7	37	70	30
	14	R	26	a/a	CHW	70	5.22	1.72	7.53	3.3	4.7	1.4	1.1	35	71	15
Freeman,Justin	14	R	28	a/a	CIN	47	5.19	1.61	4.81	2.5	5.9	2.4	0.7	37	68	54
Frias,Carlos	13	R	24	aa	LA	16	4.97	1.56	8.76	4.0	3.8	0.9	1.3	29	71	2
	14	R	25	a/a	LA	124	4.30	1.46	25.2	1.9	4.7	2.5	0.4	34	69	62
Friedrich,Christian	14	L	27	aaa	COL	91	8.38	1.94	16.1	4.0	5.9	1.5	1.9	37	59	-6
Fuentes,Nelvin	14	L	25	a/a	CHW	64	5.06	1.57	6.42	5.2	7.7	1.5	0.8	31	68	56
Fuller,James	13	L	26	aa	NYM	18	8.35	1.64	8.93	4.5	11.2	2.5	0.5	41	45	100
	14	L	27	aa	MIN	56	3.11	1.64	6.58	5.2	8.3	1.6	0.3	35	81	73
Gagnon,Drew	13	R	23	aa	MIL	84	6.92	1.84	24.4	4.7	5.4	1.1	1.6	34	64	-1
	14	R	24	aa	MIL	155	4.74	1.43	23.5	3.8	5.9	1.6	1.3	29	70	32
Gailey,Frank	13	L	28	aa	OAK	62	3.20	1.34	6.61	1.7	6.0	3.4	0.4	34	76	91
	14	L	29	aaa	OAK	52	4.40	1.67	5.84	4.1	5.7	1.4	0.7	37	74	36
Gamboa,Eduardo	13	R	29	a/a	BAL	142	6.08	1.61	25.2	4.3	5.3	1.2	0.7	32	61	34
	14	R	30	a/a	BAL	109	4.95	1.53	24.9	4.3	6.3	1.5	0.9	31	68	43
Garces,Frank	14	L	24	aa	SD	65	2.17	1.15	5.09	3.3	8.9	2.7	0.4	29	83	109

PITCHER	yr	t	age	lvl	org	ip	era	whip	bf/g	ctl	dom	f	hr/9	h%	s%	bpv
Garcia,Luis	13	R	26	a/a	PHI	22	1.97	1.14	4.59	3.0	7.0	2.3	0.5	27	85	87
	14	R	27	aaa	PHI	47	1.19	1.28	4.9	3.3	8.0	2.4	0.0	32	90	104
Garcia,Yimi	13	R	23	aa	LA	60	3.14	0.91	4.59	2.1	10.8	5.2	1.5	24	76	146
	14	R	24	aaa	LA	61	2.62	1.17	5.18	2.2	8.5	3.9	0.6	32	79	121
Gardner,Joe	13	R	25	aa	COL	55	8.11	1.59	6.96	3.3	7.4	2.2	1.5	35	48	42
	14	R	26	aa	ATL	53	4.25	1.29	21.8	2.4	3.3	1.4	0.8	28	68	29
Garner,Perci	13	R	25	a/a	PHI	15	6.21	2.09	25.1	7.2	6.8	0.9	0.7	37	69	33
	14	R	26	aa	PHI	82	5.85	1.95	20.5	7.2	5.5	0.8	0.4	33	68	35
Garrido,Santiago	13	R	24	a/a	KC	63	3.91	1.64	6.99	5.8	5.7	1.0	0.7	30	77	35
	14	R	25	aa	TAM	58	3.92	1.65	5.51	4.5	6.2	1.4	0.6	34	77	44
Garrison,Taylor	14	R	24	aa	NYY	39	4.33	1.38	6.82	3.7	5.0	1.4	0.6	29	68	44
Garvin,Grayson	14	L	25	aa	TAM	74	4.33	1.38	15.5	1.8	6.0	3.3	0.6	34	69	84
Gast,John	13	L	24	aaa	STL	39	1.28	1.13	21.8	3.0	6.7	2.3	0.0	28	87	98
	14	L	25	aaa	STL	59	5.09	1.38	20.8	3.2	4.4	1.4	1.1	28	64	25
Gausman,Kevin	13	R	22	a/a	BAL	82	4.15	1.27	21	1.5	7.7	5.1	0.5	35	67	136
	14	R	23	aaa	BAL	43	3.69	1.45	16.8	3.6	7.7	2.1	1.2	32	79	56
Gaviglio,Sam	14	R	24	aa	STL	137	4.83	1.60	24.1	3.0	6.8	2.3	0.5	37	69	67
Geer,Josh	13	R	30	a/a	SD	104	4.10	1.65	13.3	2.4	5.3	2.2	1.0	36	78	37
	14	R	31	aa	SD	156	4.55	1.62	23	1.9	4.2	2.2	0.3	37	70	52
Geltz,Steve	13	R	26	aaa	TAM	67	3.43	0.99	6.23	3.3	8.7	2.6	1.1	21	71	92
	14	R	27	aaa	TAM	42	3.08	1.25	5.85	4.0	10.3	2.6	0.7	30	78	104
Germano,Justin	13	R	31	aaa	TOR	151	6.26	1.83	28.1	1.9	4.6	2.5	1.0	40	66	32
	14	R	32	aaa	LA	145	4.79	1.40	25.6	1.4	4.4	3.2	1.4	32	70	45
Giardina,Carmine	14	L	26	aa	LAA	57	5.86	1.72	5.25	5.0	5.7	1.1	1.1	32	67	22
Gillheeney,James	13	L	26	a/a	SEA	136	5.17	1.50	22.5	3.3	4.8	1.5	1.3	30	68	19
	14	L	27	a/a	SEA	120	5.86	1.65	19.8	3.5	7.0	2.0	1.2	36	66	42
Gilmartin,Sean	13	L	23	aaa	ATL	91	6.71	1.76	24.5	3.3	5.6	1.7	1.2	36	63	21
	14	L	24	aaa	MIN	146	4.56	1.48	24.1	2.8	6.7	2.4	0.6	35	69	70
Goeddel,Erik	13	R	25	aa	NYM	134	4.76	1.55	23.4	3.8	7.1	1.9	1.0	33	71	50
	14	R	26	aaa	NYM	64	4.55	1.62	5.76	3.7	7.5	2.0	0.7	36	72	62
Goforth,David	13	R	25	aa	MIL	47	4.24	1.26	9.52	3.8	5.8	1.5	0.3	27	64	68
	14	R	26	aa	MIL	65	4.69	1.61	5.31	4.4	5.2	1.2	0.4	33	69	44
Gomes,Brandon	14	R	30	aaa	TAM	37	4.97	1.64	6.17	3.3	7.6	2.3	1.2	37	72	52
Gomez,Leuris	13	R	27	aa	COL	42	1.95	1.31	6.99	4.0	8.6	2.2	0.0	32	83	105
	14	R	28	a/a	COL	58	6.08	1.95	7.73	6.2	7.9	1.3	0.4	38	67	54
Gomez,Roberto	14	R	25	aa	TAM	38	6.86	1.71	21.3	1.4	4.2	2.9	0.5	39	57	56
Gonzales,Marco	14	L	22	a/a	STL	84	2.97	1.16	22.4	1.9	7.8	4.1	0.8	30	78	112
Gonzalez,Alex	14	R	22	aa	TEX	73	3.37	1.41	20.7	3.2	6.6	2.1	0.5	33	76	70
Gonzalez,Juan	13	R	23	aa	COL	46	3.01	1.31	4.91	1.7	5.2	3.1	1.1	31	82	60
	14	R	24	aa	LA	70	3.23	1.58	5.7	5.5	5.2	0.9	0.2	30	79	48
Gonzalez,Miguel	14	R	28	a/a	PHI	31	2.92	1.40	5.69	5.4	9.7	1.8	0.7	29	81	85
Gonzalez,Nelson	14	R	24	aa	COL	67	5.79	1.59	6.32	3.8	5.6	1.5	0.6	33	62	43
Gonzalez,Severino	14	R	22	aa	PHI	159	5.10	1.37	24.6	1.9	5.7	3.1	1.4	32	66	54
Gorski,Darin	13	L	26	a/a	NYM	92	2.52	1.05	19.9	2.9	6.0	2.1	0.2	25	75	88
	14	L	27	a/a	NYM	100	3.18	1.34	21.9	2.6	7.6	2.9	1.3	31	83	68
Gould,Garrett	13	R	22	aa	LA	41	7.13	1.51	16.3	3.2	8.5	2.7	1.2	35	52	68
	14	R	23	aa	LA	61	7.22	1.78	17.6	3.6	5.1	1.4	1.6	35	61	3
Grace,Matt	13	L	25	aa	WAS	38	4.79	1.52	5.89	1.7	5.8	3.4	0.5	37	68	82
	14	L	26	a/a	WAS	77	1.34	1.21	6.2	2.7	5.6	2.0	0.1	29	89	79
Gracey,Scott	13	R	27	a/a	TOR	36	3.53	1.55	5.83	4.0	7.9	2.0	0.0	36	75	88
	14	R	28	aa	TOR	52	7.67	1.79	6.89	3.7	7.1	1.9	1.6	37	58	23
Graham,J.R.	13	R	23	aa	ATL	36	5.15	1.59	19.7	2.6	6.2	2.3	0.0	38	64	78
	14	R	24	aa	ATL	71	6.65	1.66	11.8	3.4	5.4	1.6	0.3	36	56	50
Granier,Drew	13	R	25	aa	OAK	72	5.99	1.90	24.4	5.4	5.7	1.1	1.1	35	69	16
	14	R	26	a/a	OAK	130	5.34	1.83	22.4	5.3	5.2	1.0	0.9	34	72	17
Graveman,Kendall	14	R	24	a/a	TOR	44	2.36	1.31	26.1	1.5	4.5	3.0	0.3	32	82	80
Gray,Jonathan	14	R	23	aa	COL	124	5.35	1.41	21.9	3.2	6.4	2.0	1.0	31	63	51
Greene,Shane	13	R	25	aa	NYY	79	4.25	1.72	25.7	2.5	6.3	2.5	0.9	39	77	50
	14	R	26	aaa	NYY	66	5.64	1.84	20.6	3.8	6.1	1.6	0.5	39	68	44
Greenwood,Nick	13	L	26	a/a	STL	95	5.57	1.71	13.1	2.9	3.4	1.2	1.1	34	69	2
	14	L	27	aaa	STL	51	3.31	1.15	7.45	1.8	5.1	2.8	0.7	28	73	74
Guaipe,Mayckol	14	R	24	aa	SEA	56	3.31	1.07	5.44	1.4	7.7	5.5	0.6	30	70	149
Guerra,Deolis	14	R	25	aaa	MIN	52	5.54	1.55	6.32	3.3	7.4	2.3	0.9	35	65	60
Guilmet,Preston	13	R	26	aaa	CLE	64	2.20	1.06	5.09	2.1	8.2	3.9	0.6	28	82	122
	14	R	27	aaa	BAL	48	4.72	1.26	4.93	2.0	7.7	3.9	1.4	31	66	89
Gurka,Jason	13	L	25	aa	BAL	40	3.58	1.51	8.59	4.2	8.4	2.0	0.6	34	77	76
	14	L	26	a/a	BAL	71	3.65	1.25	9.02	2.5	6.6	2.6	0.8	30	72	75
Hagens,Bradin	13	R	24	aa	ARI	148	4.81	1.72	25.8	4.3	4.6	1.1	0.8	33	73	21
	14	R	25	a/a	ARI	135	4.40	1.51	20.9	3.8	3.7	1.0	0.6	30	71	25
Hahn,Jesse	14	R	25	aa	SD	42	2.20	1.28	13.3	3.2	6.9	2.1	0.2	30	83	85
Hald,Kyle	14	L	25	aa	STL	137	4.31	1.52	24.8	3.0	5.5	1.8	1.1	32	75	34
Haley,Justin	14	R	23	aa	BOS	38	1.52	1.38	26.3	3.9	6.6	1.7	0.5	30	92	64
Hall,Cody	13	R	25	aa	SF	26	2.51	1.00	5.03	2.6	7.5	2.9	1.1	23	83	86
	14	R	26	aa	SF	52	3.73	1.24	4.46	2.5	7.9	3.1	0.5	32	70	102
Hamburger,Mark	14	R	27	a/a	MIN	71	4.85	1.60	14.2	3.7	5.2	1.4	0.4	34	68	44
Hancock,Justin	14	R	24	aa	SD	59	4.63	1.70	20.5	3.5	5.4	1.6	0.8	36	74	33
Hand,Donovan	13	R	27	aaa	MIL	36	3.89	1.47	7.65	3.0	7.7	2.6	1.2	34	78	61
	14	R	28	aaa	MIL	80	6.66	1.89	7.98	2.8	6.3	2.2	1.3	40	66	28
Hankins,Derek	13	R	30	a/a	DET	104	4.35	1.59	26.9	2.6	3.4	1.3	1.3	32	77	-2
	14	R	31	aaa	DET	152	7.23	1.95	25.9	2.6	3.0	1.1	1.2	38	63	-14
Hanson,Tommy	13	R	27	aaa	LAA	20	5.17	1.52	21.3	2.5	5.4	2.2	1.9	32	72	16
	14	R	28	aaa	CHW	50	7.09	1.82	23	5.8	4.5	0.8	2.0	29	64	-19
Hardy,Blaine	13	L	26	a/a	DET	92	2.21	1.21	12.3	3.3	5.9	1.8	0.9	25	87	54
	14	L	27	aaa	DET	47	3.56	1.24	9.54	2.7	7.6	2.8	0.5	31	71	95
Harlan,Thomas	14	L	24	aa	PIT	61	3.92	1.34	22.9	2.3	3.0	1.3	0.8	29	72	22
Harper,Ryne	13	R	24	aa	ATL	55	2.33	1.38	5.66	3.1	7.5	2.4	0.6	33	85	80
	14	R	25	aa	ATL	77	3.16	1.39	6.73	3.0	9.1	3.1	0.6	36	79	101
Harrell,Lucas	14	R	29	aaa	ARI	107	5.74	2.01	23.4	6.6	4.2	0.6	1.1	33	72	-1

PITCHER	yr	t	age	lvl	org	ip	era	whip	bf/g	ctl	dom	cmd	hr/9	h%	s%	bpv
Harris,Mitchell	14	R	29	a/a	STL	45	4.60	1.39	5.53	2.8	5.3	1.9	1.0	30	69	41
Harris,Will	14	R	30	aaa	ARI	46	1.11	1.34	4.42	4.0	6.3	1.6	0.6	28	96	59
Hassebrock,Blake	13	R	24	aa	OAK	16	7.43	1.67	6.11	3.9	2.3	0.6	0.5	32	52	5
	14	R	25	aa	OAK	32	8.41	2.43	8.08	2.9	4.5	1.6	1.3	46	66	-11
Hatley,Marcus	13	R	25	a/a	CHC	61	4.83	1.67	5.56	5.6	8.9	1.6	0.5	35	70	72
	14	R	26	aaa	CHC	47	5.68	1.63	4.65	2.7	8.8	3.3	1.3	39	67	73
Hauschild,Michael	14	R	24	aa	HOU	99	4.83	1.33	20.5	2.3	6.8	3.0	0.5	33	62	88
Haviland,Shawn	14	R	29	aa	OAK	146	4.92	1.57	25.7	3.5	4.3	1.2	0.9	32	70	20
Hayes,Drew	13	R	26	aa	CIN	63	7.85	2.11	6.08	5.4	7.1	1.3	1.5	40	64	11
	14	R	27	aa	CIN	71	5.06	1.67	6.16	5.3	7.7	1.5	0.7	34	69	56
Head,Louis	14	R	24	aa	CLE	36	3.43	1.53	5.45	3.9	8.2	2.1	0.7	35	79	70
Healy,Tucker	14	R	24	a/a	OAK	44	5.81	1.63	6.08	4.0	9.7	2.4	0.9	39	64	79
Heaney,Andrew	13	L	22	aa	MIA	34	3.65	1.34	23.3	2.5	5.3	2.1	0.5	31	73	61
	14	L	23	a/a	MIA	137	3.48	1.20	23	2.3	7.9	3.4	0.6	31	72	107
Heath,Deunte	13	R	28	aaa	CHW	45	3.08	1.44	6.39	3.5	5.6	1.6	0.3	32	78	59
	14	R	29	aaa	CHW	64	3.79	1.60	12.9	5.2	7.8	1.5	1.2	31	80	44
Heckathorn,Kyle	13	R	25	aaa	MIL	65	4.09	1.37	5.67	4.4	5.3	1.2	0.8	26	71	41
	14	R	26	aaa	MIL	47	6.99	1.77	7.76	4.3	4.7	1.1	1.7	32	63	-7
Heidenreich,Matthe	13	R	22	aa	HOU	55	9.21	1.95	10.4	2.6	5.0	1.9	1.7	39	53	-1
	14	R	23	aa	HOU	34	8.84	2.28	14.3	5.5	7.0	1.3	1.1	43	60	16
Hembree,Heath	13	R	24	aaa	SF	55	3.87	1.27	4.19	2.4	8.5	3.6	0.9	33	72	103
	14	R	25	aaa	BOS	46	4.91	1.62	4.25	3.7	8.6	2.3	1.1	37	72	62
Hendricks,Kyle	13	R	24	a/a	CHC	166	2.46	1.22	24.9	1.9	5.7	2.9	0.3	31	80	90
	14	R	25	aaa	CHC	103	4.35	1.36	25.3	2.1	6.9	3.2	0.5	34	67	92
Hendriks,Liam	13	R	24	aaa	MIN	98	5.34	1.48	26.4	1.3	4.6	3.4	0.8	35	64	67
	14	R	25	aaa	KC	143	2.71	1.07	24.3	0.8	6.2	7.7	0.4	31	75	189
Henry,Randy	13	R	23	aa	TEX	51	1.46	0.93	6.12	1.4	5.9	4.3	0.2	26	85	131
	14	R	24	a/a	TEX	32	6.36	1.84	6.48	2.9	4.1	1.4	0.7	38	64	20
Hensley,Steven	13	R	27	a/a	COL	51	5.49	1.91	5.88	5.5	6.5	1.2	1.9	34	76	-1
	14	R	28	aa	BAL	60	2.67	1.44	6.95	4.4	6.4	1.5	0.8	29	85	50
Heredia,Jairo	14	R	25	a/a	NYY	86	5.19	1.65	12.4	3.2	7.9	2.4	0.3	39	66	83
Hernandez,Carlos	13	L	26	a/a	OAK	152	2.97	1.34	21.8	2.5	5.0	2.0	0.3	31	78	62
	14	L	27	aa	COL	124	3.99	1.59	19.6	1.8	4.9	2.8	0.7	37	76	57
Hernandez,Chris	13	L	25	a/a	BOS	135	5.97	1.86	21.8	4.1	4.3	1.1	0.9	36	68	10
	14	L	26	aaa	BOS	117	5.50	1.81	16.4	5.0	4.5	0.9	0.5	34	68	26
Hernandez,Moises	13	R	29	aa	SEA	47	7.71	1.76	9.36	3.9	2.9	0.8	1.3	32	56	-13
	14	R	30	aa	SEA	61	7.66	2.02	9.46	3.7	4.0	1.1	1.0	39	61	0
Hernandez,Pedro	13	L	24	a/a	MIN	57	4.34	1.49	24.6	2.3	5.0	2.1	1.2	33	74	33
	14	L	25	aaa	COL	88	7.36	1.96	22.2	3.0	4.1	1.3	1.2	39	63	-2
Herron,Tyler	13	R	27	aa	WAS	46	4.10	1.70	6.35	4.3	8.5	2.0	0.5	38	75	73
	14	R	28	a/a	WAS	64	3.68	1.59	5.67	4.1	5.5	1.3	0.6	32	77	40
Heston,Chris	13	R	25	aaa	SF	109	5.64	1.65	25.5	3.5	6.5	1.9	0.9	36	66	45
	14	R	26	aaa	SF	173	3.27	1.21	24.9	2.5	5.2	2.1	0.6	28	74	61
Heyer,Kurt	14	R	23	a/a	STL	152	5.10	1.43	23.1	2.6	5.4	2.1	1.1	31	66	41
Hill,Taylor	13	R	24	a/a	WAS	80	3.45	1.44	26.3	2.0	4.5	2.3	0.8	33	78	45
	14	R	25	aaa	WAS	144	3.28	1.26	23.5	1.5	4.2	2.8	1.0	30	78	54
Hinojosa,Dalier	14	R	28	aaa	BOS	62	5.35	1.43	6.4	5.4	7.1	1.3	0.9	27	63	53
Hively,RJ	14	R	26	aa	ARI	62	3.64	1.62	5.01	4.5	6.2	1.4	0.2	34	76	58
Hobson,Cameron	13	L	24	aa	SEA	18	4.16	1.66	26.9	3.7	4.3	1.2	1.8	31	82	-10
	14	L	25	aa	SEA	129	5.38	1.74	20.3	3.3	4.1	1.2	0.7	35	69	19
Hoffman,Matthew	13	L	25	aaa	DET	35	2.73	1.62	3.88	4.4	7.0	1.6	0.6	34	85	55
	14	L	26	a/a	PHI	48	4.52	1.65	5.8	3.7	7.6	2.0	1.3	36	76	43
Holland,Neil	13	R	25	aa	WAS	51	3.59	1.36	5.17	2.0	8.8	4.5	0.6	37	74	126
	14	R	26	a/a	WAS	77	4.03	1.33	6.92	2.6	5.7	2.2	0.7	31	71	59
Holle,Gregory	13	R	25	a/a	MIL	66	4.64	1.57	5.44	3.6	6.0	1.6	0.3	34	69	56
	14	R	26	aa	MIL	35	2.89	1.12	6	1.7	4.6	2.8	0.7	27	76	71
Holmberg,David	13	L	22	aa	ARI	157	3.65	1.38	25.4	2.9	5.7	1.9	0.9	30	76	49
	14	L	23	aaa	CIN	93	4.90	1.72	23.4	3.0	4.7	1.6	0.4	37	70	38
Hooker,James	13	R	24	a/a	STL	68	4.47	1.20	5.04	2.3	8.2	3.5	0.7	31	63	106
	14	R	25	a/a	OAK	65	4.16	1.73	8.65	3.7	4.1	1.1	0.2	35	74	31
Horst,Jeremy	14	L	29	aaa	PHI	63	5.12	1.63	6.27	4.9	6.1	1.2	0.7	32	68	41
House,T.J.	13	L	24	a/a	CLE	164	4.82	1.61	26	3.1	6.4	2.1	0.7	36	70	55
	14	L	25	aaa	CLE	57	4.38	1.41	24.1	2.5	5.5	2.2	0.5	33	68	63
Houston,Daniel	13	R	27	a/a	COL	105	4.43	1.53	13.9	3.0	4.4	1.5	0.8	32	72	29
	14	R	28	a/a	COL	71	8.44	2.08	10.2	5.1	4.7	0.9	1.2	37	59	-5
Hoyt,James	13	R	27	aa	ATL	33	3.44	1.13	5.86	4.1	7.3	1.8	0.3	24	68	87
	14	R	28	aa	ATL	60	3.95	1.62	5.09	4.0	9.1	2.3	0.8	38	77	74
Humber,Philip	13	R	31	aaa	HOU	50	6.04	1.87	11.7	3.7	5.2	1.4	1.5	36	71	1
	14	R	32	aaa	OAK	69	3.98	1.54	6.83	3.6	6.5	1.8	0.9	33	76	46
Hunter,Kyle	13	L	24	aa	SEA	58	1.95	1.31	7.01	2.6	5.7	2.2	0.4	31	86	71
	14	L	25	aa	SEA	75	3.80	1.50	8.49	2.5	4.6	1.9	1.0	33	77	33
Huntzinger,Brock	13	R	25	a/a	BOS	69	2.32	1.32	5.8	3.8	6.5	1.7	0.4	29	83	69
	14	R	26	aaa	BAL	81	3.55	1.34	7.16	2.9	6.6	2.3	1.1	30	77	59
Hursh,Jason	14	R	23	aa	ATL	148	4.20	1.45	23.4	2.6	4.4	1.7	0.3	32	69	49
Hussey,John	14	R	28	aa	SD	89	5.19	1.70	10.9	2.6	4.7	1.8	0.9	36	70	26
Hynes,Colt	13	L	28	a/a	SD	47	1.70	1.11	4.53	0.4	8.8	22.6	0.2	36	85	521
	14	L	29	aaa	TOR	62	5.34	1.53	5.47	1.9	5.9	3.1	1.5	35	68	48
Ibarra,Edgar	13	L	24	a/a	MIN	61	2.21	1.24	5.24	4.2	6.5	1.5	0.4	26	83	71
	14	L	25	a/a	MIN	64	5.30	1.71	7.25	4.1	6.5	1.6	0.6	36	68	48
Ibarra,Jeffrey	13	L	26	a/a	SD	54	7.45	1.63	4.1	2.3	7.5	3.3	1.0	39	53	73
	14	L	27	aa	SD	42	3.11	1.56	4.8	3.4	8.8	2.6	1.2	36	85	67
Infante,Gregory	13	R	26	a/a	LA	40	4.44	1.72	6.43	6.3	6.9	1.1	0.5	32	74	52
	14	R	27	a/a	TOR	46	2.68	1.27	4.62	3.9	6.8	1.7	0.0	29	76	87
Irwin,Phillip	14	R	27	aaa	TEX	73	5.91	1.77	16	4.6	6.9	1.5	0.6	37	65	50
Jackson,Jay	13	R	26	a/a	MIA	105	4.73	1.41	21.1	3.2	6.3	2.0	0.8	31	67	56
	14	R	27	aaa	MIL	111	6.18	1.84	16.7	4.6	7.4	1.6	1.2	37	68	32
Jackson,Luke	13	R	22	aa	TEX	27	0.89	1.06	17.4	4.3	8.5	2.0	0.0	24	91	113
	14	R	23	a/a	TEX	123	6.29	1.47	20.4	3.8	7.6	2.0	1.2	32	58	53

PITCHER	yr	t	age	lvl	org	ip	era	whip	bf/g	ctl	dom	f	hr/9	h%	s%	bpv
Jackson,Zach	13	L	30	a/a	KC	41	1.84	1.27	4.79	1.8	2.8	1.6	0.8	28	90	26
	14	L	31	a/a	WAS	43	6.18	1.68	6.28	2.8	4.9	1.7	0.2	37	60	48
Jaime,Juan Jose	13	R	26	aa	ATL	42	5.53	1.65	5.36	6.7	12.3	1.8	0.3	37	64	111
	14	R	27	aaa	ATL	41	4.09	1.69	4.3	8.2	11.1	1.3	0.2	32	74	100
Jankowski,Jordan	14	R	25	aa	HOU	108	4.12	1.20	14.5	2.2	8.4	3.8	1.1	31	69	102
Jaye,Myles	14	R	23	aa	CHW	132	6.06	1.67	24.7	3.9	4.3	1.1	0.8	33	63	19
Jeffress,Jeremy	13	R	26	aaa	TOR	27	2.13	1.50	4.72	4.6	7.5	1.6	0.0	33	84	82
	14	R	27	aaa	MIL	42	1.89	1.45	5.93	4.3	7.8	1.8	0.0	33	85	89
Jenkins,Chad	13	R	26	a/a	TOR	37	6.16	1.63	18.1	1.5	3.4	2.2	1.8	34	66	-1
	14	R	27	aaa	TOR	44	6.58	1.55	9.16	2.1	4.4	2.1	1.4	33	59	20
Jensen,Chris	14	R	24	aa	OAK	160	3.58	1.43	26.2	3.5	4.4	1.2	0.2	30	73	49
Jimenez,Cesar	13	L	29	aaa	PHI	66	4.11	1.63	8.19	4.0	6.6	1.6	0.5	35	75	54
	14	L	30	aaa	PHI	50	1.89	1.22	5.28	3.1	6.2	2.0	0.0	29	83	87
Johnson,Brian	14	L	24	aa	BOS	118	2.29	1.08	23	2.5	6.2	2.4	0.5	26	81	84
Johnson,Cole	13	R	25	aa	MIN	39	5.14	1.43	5.92	3.5	8.8	2.5	1.4	33	67	66
	14	R	26	aa	MIN	73	4.84	1.49	6.39	2.7	7.9	2.9	0.8	36	68	80
Johnson,Erik	13	R	24	a/a	CHW	142	2.55	1.18	23.7	3.0	7.1	2.4	0.6	28	80	84
	14	R	25	aaa	CHW	106	7.25	1.98	25.3	4.9	4.5	0.9	1.1	36	63	2
Johnson,Kevin	13	R	25	a/a	LAA	63	4.21	1.55	5.26	3.1	3.8	1.2	0.5	32	72	28
	14	R	26	a/a	LAA	61	3.56	1.86	6.8	4.2	4.1	1.0	0.4	36	81	22
Johnson,Kristofer	13	L	29	aaa	PIT	136	3.13	1.44	22.2	3.1	4.4	1.4	0.4	31	78	42
	14	L	30	aaa	MIN	132	4.93	1.65	25.7	4.4	5.0	1.1	0.6	33	70	31
Johnson,Pierce	14	R	23	aa	CHC	92	2.93	1.33	21.2	5.4	7.6	1.4	0.8	25	81	64
Johnson,Steve	13	R	26	aaa	BAL	46	5.47	1.49	19.8	3.6	8.0	2.2	1.1	33	64	62
	14	R	27	aaa	BAL	38	8.58	2.32	15	7.5	5.8	0.8	2.6	36	67	-41
Jokisch,Eric	13	L	24	aa	CHC	161	4.21	1.41	25.2	3.2	6.4	2.0	0.9	31	72	54
	14	L	25	aaa	CHC	158	4.33	1.36	25.5	1.9	6.6	3.5	0.8	34	69	88
Jones,Chris	13	L	25	a/a	BAL	79	3.58	1.73	9.97	4.3	4.9	1.1	0.4	35	79	34
	14	L	26	aaa	BAL	120	4.27	1.53	14.9	2.8	5.0	1.8	0.4	34	71	52
Jones,Devin	13	R	23	aa	BAL	123	6.79	1.73	23.4	3.5	6.6	1.9	1.5	36	62	26
	14	R	24	aa	SD	37	8.13	1.85	19.4	2.8	4.2	1.5	1.3	37	55	3
Jordan,Taylor	13	R	24	aa	WAS	54	1.03	0.97	22.8	1.5	5.8	3.9	0.0	27	88	126
	14	R	25	aaa	WAS	31	4.74	1.41	21.8	2.3	6.4	2.8	0.9	33	67	67
Joseph,Don	13	L	26	aaa	KC	55	5.16	1.68	5.23	7.1	10.5	1.5	0.9	32	70	75
	14	L	27	aaa	MIA	36	5.99	2.30	6.59	8.2	6.7	0.8	1.5	37	76	3
Jungmann,Taylor	13	R	24	aa	MIL	139	5.49	1.57	23.5	5.1	4.5	0.9	0.9	28	65	21
	14	R	25	a/a	MIL	154	4.33	1.50	23.7	3.8	7.2	1.9	0.8	33	72	59
Jurrjens,Jair	13	R	27	aaa	DET	134	6.33	1.73	26.5	2.8	3.8	1.3	0.7	36	62	19
	14	R	28	aaa	COL	81	5.56	1.79	26.8	3.4	4.0	1.2	1.0	35	70	7
Kaneko,Chihiro	13	R	0	for	JPN	223	2.51	1.12	30.3	2.9	7.7	2.6	0.7	27	81	92
	14	R	0	for	JPN	184	2.37	1.14	29.1	2.5	9.0	3.6	0.6	31	81	121
Karns,Nathan	13	R	26	aa	WAS	133	4.20	1.38	24.3	3.4	8.1	2.4	1.1	32	73	68
	14	R	27	aaa	TAM	145	6.59	1.68	24.2	4.1	7.5	1.8	1.1	36	61	44
Kasparek,Kenn	13	R	28	aa	PIT	61	4.10	1.55	6.97	2.5	4.7	1.9	0.5	35	73	47
	14	R	29	a/a	PIT	49	3.06	1.29	5.63	1.5	5.4	3.6	0.4	33	76	95
Kehrt,Jeremy	13	R	28	a/a	BOS	86	6.36	2.00	15.4	3.3	5.2	1.6	0.9	41	68	20
	14	R	29	a/a	LA	78	4.71	1.69	14.1	3.0	3.7	1.2	0.5	35	72	22
Kela,Keone	14	R	21	aa	TEX	39	2.30	1.37	4.5	6.4	10.9	1.7	0.3	28	83	110
Kelly,Merrill	13	R	25	a/a	TAM	158	4.29	1.35	23.6	3.7	5.2	1.4	0.4	29	67	54
	14	R	26	aaa	TAM	114	3.51	1.49	17.5	3.1	6.9	2.2	0.9	34	79	59
Kensing,Logan	13	R	31	aaa	COL	44	3.63	1.55	4.41	4.8	5.7	1.2	1.2	29	81	23
	14	R	32	aaa	SEA	88	4.09	1.55	7.84	3.5	6.1	1.8	0.5	34	73	56
Kickham,Mike	13	L	25	aaa	SF	111	4.19	1.41	23.4	3.7	5.9	1.6	0.6	30	70	55
	14	L	26	aaa	SF	148	4.28	1.63	24.4	3.6	6.3	1.7	0.4	36	73	58
Kiekhefer,Dean	13	L	24	aa	STL	16	4.12	1.40	6.27	0.5	4.5	8.5	0.5	36	70	181
	14	L	25	a/a	STL	71	3.19	1.12	5.11	0.8	6.3	8.4	1.0	30	76	183
Kingham,Nick	13	R	22	aa	PIT	73	2.98	1.42	22.2	3.4	6.9	2.0	0.1	33	77	82
	14	R	23	a/a	PIT	159	3.51	1.25	24.9	2.7	5.4	2.0	0.4	29	72	66
Kirkman,Michael	13	L	27	aaa	TEX	30	9.25	2.04	24	6.5	5.3	0.8	1.2	35	53	5
	14	L	28	aaa	TEX	54	5.35	1.69	6.81	5.2	7.6	1.5	1.2	33	70	40
Klein,Phil	13	R	24	aa	TEX	54	3.51	1.97	8.86	8.3	10.1	1.2	0.7	36	83	66
	14	R	25	a/a	TEX	52	0.63	0.91	5.84	3.7	9.7	2.6	0.0	22	92	138
Kloess,Brandon	13	R	29	aaa	SD	101	5.12	1.73	11.2	3.4	6.7	2.0	0.8	38	71	46
	14	R	30	aaa	SD	76	5.44	1.56	7.28	4.1	4.1	1.0	1.1	29	67	11
Knebel,Corey	14	R	23	a/a	TEX	45	2.54	1.07	5.18	4.4	10.4	2.3	0.7	23	79	112
Knigge,Tyler	13	R	25	aa	PHI	66	4.88	1.51	5.93	4.2	6.2	1.5	1.2	30	70	33
	14	R	26	a/a	PHI	76	4.14	1.41	7.15	2.7	4.5	1.6	0.3	32	69	52
Knudson,Guido	14	R	25	aa	DET	61	4.79	1.60	9.69	3.8	7.5	2.0	0.6	36	70	65
Kohlscheen,Stepher	13	R	25	aa	SEA	67	3.25	1.30	6.71	3.7	9.6	2.6	1.0	31	79	90
	14	R	26	a/a	SD	70	2.40	1.17	5.5	1.4	7.3	5.0	0.7	32	83	130
Kohn,Michael	14	R	28	aaa	LAA	34	4.35	1.58	4.54	6.4	6.7	1.0	1.3	26	76	32
Kolarek,Adam	13	L	24	a/a	NYM	67	2.18	1.14	5.77	3.0	7.4	2.4	0.4	28	82	95
	14	L	25	aa	NYM	56	6.20	1.83	5.46	3.2	5.8	1.8	0.3	40	64	50
Kontos,George	13	R	28	aaa	SF	24	4.35	1.03	5.06	1.1	7.5	6.7	0.9	29	59	163
	14	R	29	aaa	SF	48	2.93	1.21	6.4	2.1	8.1	3.9	0.6	32	78	116
Kroenke,Zach	13	L	29	aaa	MIL	130	5.60	1.71	18.4	3.8	4.7	1.2	0.9	34	68	20
	14	L	30	a/a	WAS	94	7.98	2.16	23.3	3.6	3.2	0.9	1.4	39	63	-25
Kurcz,Aaron	14	R	24	aa	BOS	42	2.79	1.47	5.29	4.9	9.5	1.9	0.0	34	79	103
Kussmaul,Ryan	13	R	27	aa	CHW	33	3.41	1.20	5.82	2.4	7.8	3.3	0.8	30	74	97
	14	R	28	a/a	CHW	68	4.93	1.58	6.84	4.8	7.6	1.6	1.3	31	72	40
Laffey,Aaron	13	L	28	aaa	MIL	111	7.70	1.95	23	3.7	3.5	1.0	1.7	36	62	-26
	14	L	29	aaa	WAS	147	4.69	1.64	26.2	2.4	4.0	1.7	0.6	35	71	32
LaFromboise,Rober	13	L	27	aaa	SEA	61	3.75	1.53	5.9	2.6	7.4	2.9	0.7	37	77	78
	14	L	28	aaa	PIT	57	5.26	1.86	4.23	3.4	5.6	1.6	0.6	39	71	36
Lamb,John	13	L	23	aaa	KC	16	8.28	1.53	23.2	4.0	4.6	1.1	0.6	31	42	33
	14	L	24	aaa	KC	138	4.30	1.57	22.5	4.3	6.8	1.6	1.1	32	76	40
Lamb,Will	14	L	24	aa	TEX	33	1.42	1.51	5.5	7.7	7.5	1.0	0.4	24	92	72
Lambson,Mitchell	14	L	24	aa	HOU	33	1.53	1.00	5.48	1.4	8.2	6.0	1.2	27	95	149

PITCHER	yr	t	age	lvl	org	ip	era	whip	bf/g	ctl	dom	cmd	hr/9	h%	s%	bpv
Landazuri,Stephen	14	R	22	aa	SEA	96	4.75	1.26	20.6	3.4	6.6	2.0	1.1	27	65	54
Lannan,John	14	L	30	aaa	NYM	35	6.18	1.97	20.7	3.4	3.8	1.1	1.4	37	71	-12
Lara,Braulio Armanc	13	L	25	a/a	TAM	75	4.95	1.65	7.28	5.3	5.6	1.0	0.7	31	70	34
	14	L	26	a/a	TAM	58	7.04	1.72	5.82	5.0	7.2	1.4	0.7	35	57	50
Lara,Rainy	14	R	23	aa	NYM	109	4.22	1.39	22.9	2.0	5.2	2.6	0.9	32	72	55
Lawrence,Casey	14	R	27	aa	TOR	151	5.03	1.57	25.6	1.9	4.4	2.3	0.7	35	68	43
Layne,Tom	13	L	29	aaa	SD	46	4.61	1.79	4.33	5.2	6.3	1.2	0.2	36	72	52
	14	L	30	aaa	BOS	48	2.19	1.31	5.36	4.4	7.2	1.6	0.2	28	83	81
Leach,Brent	13	L	31	a/a	MIL	23	5.31	1.78	4.96	5.1	7.8	1.5	1.1	36	72	41
	14	L	32	a/a	MIL	64	4.31	1.58	4.57	4.8	7.7	1.6	1.3	32	77	41
Leathersich,John Vi	13	L	23	a/a	NYM	58	4.32	1.57	4.93	6.2	13.9	2.2	0.4	40	72	125
	14	L	24	a/a	NYM	54	2.97	1.30	4.67	4.1	13.3	3.3	0.4	37	77	144
LeBlanc,Wade	13	L	29	aaa	HOU	50	6.01	1.76	12	3.2	6.5	2.0	1.1	38	67	37
	14	L	30	aaa	LAA	128	4.18	1.53	25.3	2.7	6.2	2.3	0.6	35	73	60
Lee,Michael	13	R	27	a/a	ATL	134	5.01	1.78	23.6	1.6	4.3	2.7	0.8	39	72	42
	14	R	28	a/a	TOR	147	5.54	1.58	24.8	2.7	4.5	1.7	0.9	34	65	27
Lee,Zach	13	R	22	aa	LA	143	3.90	1.30	21	2.1	7.2	3.4	0.9	32	72	87
	14	R	23	aaa	LA	151	4.45	1.41	22.8	2.6	5.0	1.9	0.8	31	69	43
Leesman,Charles	13	L	26	aaa	CHW	88	5.18	1.84	25.7	5.0	6.5	1.3	1.6	34	76	12
	14	L	27	aaa	CHW	68	4.62	1.70	22	4.7	7.0	1.5	1.1	34	75	37
Leon,Arcenio	13	R	27	aa	MIL	71	7.68	2.00	9.83	8.4	4.1	0.5	1.4	28	62	-7
	14	R	28	a/a	MIL	72	4.99	1.59	6.13	3.8	5.9	1.6	0.5	34	67	50
Leon,Arnold	13	R	25	a/a	OAK	144	4.50	1.47	24.7	1.5	4.9	3.3	0.7	35	70	68
	14	R	26	aaa	OAK	145	5.00	1.62	23.8	3.1	6.3	2.1	0.6	36	69	55
Leroux,Chris	14	R	30	aaa	NYY	58	6.53	1.70	22	3.7	5.5	1.5	1.3	34	63	19
Lewis,Frederick	13	L	27	a/a	NYY	45	3.17	1.90	10	4.9	6.4	1.3	0.9	37	86	29
	14	L	28	a/a	NYY	33	9.08	2.87	6.88	9.7	6.5	0.7	0.7	45	67	8
Liberatore,Adam	13	L	26	a/a	TAM	62	4.18	1.39	5.96	3.7	8.4	2.3	0.2	34	67	97
	14	L	27	aaa	TAM	65	2.16	1.07	4.69	2.2	9.4	4.2	0.2	31	79	150
Lincoln,Brad	13	R	28	aaa	TOR	26	2.77	1.41	4.85	3.1	7.7	2.5	0.9	33	84	72
	14	R	29	aaa	PHI	123	6.57	1.79	21.1	4.8	6.2	1.3	1.2	35	64	22
Lindblom,Josh	13	R	26	aaa	TEX	108	4.00	1.30	22.2	2.8	5.1	1.8	1.3	27	74	33
	14	R	27	aaa	OAK	84	5.96	1.52	21.5	2.8	5.0	1.8	0.9	33	61	35
Lively,Ben	14	R	22	aa	CIN	72	4.37	1.40	23.4	4.3	8.5	1.9	1.0	30	71	66
Lively,Mitchell	13	R	28	aaa	SF	124	4.90	1.45	17.6	3.9	5.5	1.4	0.9	29	67	37
	14	R	29	aaa	WAS	128	6.03	1.91	19.5	4.2	5.9	1.4	0.9	38	69	25
Liz,Radhames	14	R	31	a/a	TOR	61	4.31	1.65	22.7	4.2	4.9	1.2	0.6	33	74	31
Lobstein,Kyle	13	L	24	a/a	DET	168	4.15	1.50	25.8	2.9	6.3	2.2	0.5	35	72	65
	14	L	25	aaa	DET	146	5.17	1.74	25.6	2.7	6.1	2.3	0.9	38	70	50
Locke,Jeff	14	L	27	aaa	PIT	50	4.82	1.65	24.8	4.0	4.9	1.2	0.9	33	72	25
Loewen,Adam	14	L	30	aa	PHI	103	4.32	1.63	27	5.3	4.9	0.9	0.8	30	74	27
Lollis,Matthew	13	R	23	a/a	SD	43	6.31	2.02	5.94	5.4	6.0	1.1	1.2	37	70	12
	14	R	24	aa	TAM	74	4.54	1.58	6.62	3.8	7.2	1.9	1.0	34	73	51
Long,Jaron	14	R	23	aa	NYY	69	2.87	1.21	25.3	1.5	5.5	3.7	0.3	31	76	102
Long,Nathan	13	R	27	aa	OAK	63	4.62	1.61	8.73	3.1	6.3	2.1	0.3	37	70	66
	14	R	28	aa	OAK	150	3.95	1.57	23.5	3.2	5.7	1.8	1.1	33	78	35
Loosen,Matthew	13	R	24	a/a	CHC	66	7.56	1.86	19.3	6.9	6.8	1.0	2.3	29	64	-9
	14	R	25	a/a	CHC	106	6.92	1.72	18.5	6.2	6.6	1.1	0.9	31	59	36
Lopez,Wilton	14	R	31	aaa	COL	43	5.79	1.85	8.8	1.4	5.0	3.6	1.1	41	70	53
Lorenzen,Michael	14	R	22	aa	CIN	121	3.53	1.38	21.1	3.2	5.6	1.8	0.8	30	76	48
Lorick,Jeffrey	14	L	27	aa	CHC	64	5.66	1.64	6.17	4.5	6.4	1.4	0.8	33	65	41
Lotzkar,Kyle	14	R	25	aa	TEX	66	6.55	1.89	10.3	6.0	7.1	1.2	1.1	35	66	29
Lowe,Johnnie	13	R	28	aaa	MIL	79	4.28	1.74	9.74	2.6	5.5	2.1	1.0	38	78	35
	14	R	29	a/a	MIL	46	6.94	1.87	9.45	3.8	6.4	1.7	2.4	36	68	-10
Lowe,Mark	13	R	30	aaa	WAS	29	4.02	1.75	5.46	3.4	8.3	2.5	1.1	40	80	58
	14	R	31	aaa	CLE	42	7.17	1.85	4.75	4.0	7.6	1.9	1.0	40	60	45
Ludwig,Patrick	14	R	25	aa	PIT	40	6.07	1.81	23.1	3.0	4.2	1.4	0.8	37	66	17
Lueke,Josh	13	R	29	aaa	TAM	57	0.82	1.20	5.77	2.6	9.6	3.7	0.2	34	94	136
	14	R	30	aaa	TAM	37	4.64	1.41	4.93	2.5	7.2	2.9	0.9	34	68	76
Luetge,Lucas	13	L	26	aaa	SEA	31	4.71	1.51	6.1	4.4	10.7	2.4	1.1	35	71	85
	14	L	27	aaa	SEA	62	3.58	1.48	6.38	3.8	8.1	2.1	0.8	34	78	70
Lyons,Tyler	13	L	25	aaa	STL	100	3.72	1.15	23.4	1.7	6.2	3.6	0.5	30	67	102
	14	L	26	a/a	STL	83	4.97	1.55	24.3	2.0	6.6	3.4	0.9	37	69	74
Madrigal,Warner	13	R	29	aaa	ARI	36	2.96	1.07	6.36	3.5	7.5	2.2	0.5	24	73	92
	14	R	30	a/a	WAS	38	4.40	1.72	4.8	2.7	6.9	2.5	0.8	39	75	59
Maeda,Kenta	13	R	0	for	JPN	176	2.60	1.07	26.3	2.5	7.7	3.0	1.1	25	82	88
	14	R	0	for	JPN	171	3.20	1.21	27.6	2.6	7.2	2.8	1.0	29	77	78
Magill,Matthew	13	R	24	aaa	LA	86	3.39	1.40	20.1	4.7	8.9	1.9	0.7	31	77	81
	14	R	25	aaa	LA	85	4.50	1.53	10.2	5.3	6.1	1.2	0.7	29	71	46
Mann,Brandon	14	L	30	aa	PIT	34	3.48	1.62	10.8	3.9	6.3	1.6	0.3	35	78	59
Manzueta,Jheyson	14	R	25	aa	MIA	47	5.24	1.69	7.25	4.4	4.3	1.0	0.3	33	67	32
Marimon,Sugar	13	R	25	aa	KC	148	5.38	1.60	24.3	2.9	5.6	2.0	1.6	33	71	18
	14	R	26	a/a	KC	104	3.95	1.54	23.9	3.0	5.0	1.7	0.9	33	76	34
Marinez,Jhan	13	R	25	aaa	CHW	28	8.00	1.81	6.49	6.1	7.0	1.2	3.1	28	63	-28
	14	R	26	a/a	LA	40	6.41	1.82	5.67	6.4	8.2	1.3	1.0	34	65	46
Marks,Justin	13	L	25	a/a	KC	141	5.49	1.73	24.7	4.4	6.4	1.4	0.5	36	67	47
	14	L	26	aaa	TEX	39	5.76	1.72	8.11	3.8	6.6	1.7	1.0	36	67	37
Marquis,Jason	14	R	36	aaa	PHI	47	6.02	1.58	25.7	2.8	5.2	1.8	1.2	34	63	26
Marshall,Brett	13	R	23	aaa	NYY	139	6.92	1.80	25.6	4.8	6.6	1.4	1.5	34	63	16
	14	R	24	aaa	CIN	70	7.01	1.90	20.7	6.3	6.4	1.0	1.3	33	64	17
Marte,Kelvin	14	L	27	a/a	SF	123	4.69	1.47	22	2.3	4.3	1.9	0.9	32	69	34
Martin,Cody	13	R	24	a/a	ATL	137	3.94	1.50	20.4	4.0	7.7	1.9	0.7	33	74	68
	14	R	25	aaa	ATL	156	3.92	1.45	24.7	3.2	6.9	2.1	1.0	32	76	56
Martin,Ethan	13	R	24	aaa	PHI	116	4.86	1.52	23.9	5.3	7.0	1.3	1.0	29	70	46
	14	R	25	aaa	PHI	48	4.89	1.57	7.22	4.1	7.0	1.7	0.4	34	68	64
Martin,Jarret	14	L	25	aa	LA	55	3.38	1.48	5.11	7.3	8.6	1.2	0.2	26	76	89
Martin,Rafael	14	R	30	a/a	WAS	54	1.87	1.05	5.77	2.1	7.4	3.5	0.2	29	82	122

PITCHER	yr	t	age	lvl	org	ip	era	whip	bf/g	ctl	dom	f	hr/9	h%	s%	bpv
Martinez,David	14	R	27	aaa	HOU	83	6.35	1.69	17	3.3	5.4	1.6	0.6	36	60	40
Marzec,Eric	13	R	25	aa	MIL	54	2.57	1.50	5.46	3.6	7.1	1.9	0.4	34	84	69
	14	R	26	a/a	MIL	86	3.74	1.62	10.1	3.5	5.3	1.5	0.8	34	79	34
Mateo,Marcos	13	R	29	a/a	CHC	25	2.96	1.62	5.84	4.7	5.9	1.3	0.0	34	80	61
	14	R	30	aaa	CHC	37	5.16	1.72	5.14	4.8	7.6	1.6	0.9	36	71	48
Mateo,Victor	13	R	24	aa	TAM	153	4.50	1.24	23.1	3.2	4.7	1.5	1.0	25	66	36
	14	R	25	aa	TAM	166	4.49	1.52	25.7	3.0	4.4	1.5	0.7	32	71	34
Mathis,Doug	13	R	30	aaa	PIT	121	5.34	1.75	21.2	4.4	4.6	1.1	1.0	33	70	14
	14	R	31	aaa	TAM	71	5.05	2.04	12.3	5.8	5.3	0.9	0.9	37	76	13
Mattheus,Ryan	14	R	31	aaa	WAS	40	7.78	1.81	5.49	2.9	5.1	1.8	1.3	37	57	15
Matz,Steven	14	L	23	aa	NYM	71	2.23	1.14	23.5	1.6	7.7	4.8	0.4	32	81	140
Matzek,Tyler	13	L	23	aa	COL	142	5.34	1.86	25.6	5.2	4.7	0.9	1.2	33	73	4
	14	L	24	aaa	COL	67	4.55	1.63	24.7	4.1	6.3	1.6	1.3	33	75	29
May,Trevor	13	R	24	aa	MIN	152	5.18	1.55	24.6	3.9	7.7	2.0	0.8	34	67	61
	14	R	25	aaa	MIN	98	3.63	1.34	22.7	3.7	6.8	1.8	0.4	30	72	73
Mayers,Mike	14	R	23	a/a	STL	81	3.26	1.47	24.9	2.5	5.2	2.1	0.4	34	78	58
Mazzaro,Vin	14	R	28	aaa	PIT	50	3.00	1.55	6.61	3.7	4.4	1.2	0.4	32	80	39
Mazzoni,Cory	13	R	24	aa	NYM	66	4.66	1.44	21.6	2.5	8.7	3.5	0.6	37	67	106
	14	R	25	a/a	NYM	64	4.25	1.25	23.7	2.0	7.0	3.5	0.7	32	67	94
McAllister,Zach	14	R	27	aaa	CLE	69	2.52	1.20	25.2	1.9	6.1	3.2	0.4	31	80	95
McBryde,Jeremy	13	R	26	aa	SD	61	2.84	1.05	3.89	2.3	8.9	3.9	1.0	27	78	117
	14	R	27	aaa	OAK	65	2.28	1.08	4.97	3.6	7.1	2.0	0.5	24	80	86
McCarthy,Michael	13	R	26	aa	BOS	37	7.74	1.73	17	2.3	3.6	1.6	1.1	36	54	8
	14	R	27	a/a	BOS	101	6.56	1.55	15.7	2.2	4.9	2.2	1.4	34	59	26
McClendon,Mike	13	R	28	aaa	COL	72	4.62	1.78	7.32	4.5	5.2	1.2	0.3	36	72	40
	14	R	29	a/a	COL	70	9.52	2.36	20.1	2.7	3.7	1.4	2.8	42	64	-62
McCormick,Phil	13	L	25	aa	SF	57	4.16	1.52	4.24	5.2	7.3	1.4	0.4	31	72	67
	14	L	26	aa	SF	65	4.42	1.56	5.72	4.1	6.8	1.6	0.5	34	71	58
McCoy,Patrick	13	L	25	a/a	WAS	48	6.12	1.76	4.78	2.6	5.8	2.2	1.4	38	67	25
	14	L	26	a/a	DET	45	3.66	1.30	6.18	1.9	5.2	2.8	0.7	31	73	69
McCully,Nicholas	13	R	25	a/a	CHW	120	5.26	1.45	18.4	3.7	4.5	1.2	1.4	27	67	10
	14	R	26	aa	CHW	96	7.03	1.92	20.8	4.7	2.7	0.6	1.4	33	65	-26
McFarland,Blake	14	R	26	aa	TOR	35	2.72	1.34	7.75	4.1	7.6	1.8	0.3	30	80	82
McGregor,Scott	13	R	27	a/a	STL	149	4.69	1.49	24.6	2.5	5.4	2.1	0.9	33	70	45
	14	R	28	a/a	WAS	113	6.65	1.83	21.1	3.8	4.0	1.0	1.2	35	64	-2
McGuire,Deck	13	R	24	aa	TOR	157	5.67	1.45	24.9	3.3	6.9	2.1	0.8	33	60	61
	14	R	25	a/a	OAK	150	5.44	1.58	24.4	3.3	4.9	1.5	1.1	32	67	24
Medlen,Casey	13	R	24	aa	MIL	60	4.78	1.67	5.59	5.5	6.1	1.1	1.0	31	73	31
	14	R	25	aa	MIL	38	3.44	1.54	5.77	5.3	7.5	1.4	1.2	29	82	44
Meek,Evan	13	R	30	aaa	TEX	108	6.32	1.93	15.5	4.6	4.8	1.0	1.0	36	68	7
	14	R	31	aaa	BAL	42	2.49	1.12	4.21	1.0	5.8	6.0	0.6	30	80	147
Mejia,Adalberto	14	L	21	aa	SF	108	5.05	1.46	21	2.4	6.0	2.5	0.6	34	65	64
Melville,Timothy	14	R	25	aa	KC	129	6.93	1.89	23.4	5.0	5.7	1.1	1.0	36	63	18
Mendez,Roman	13	R	23	aa	TEX	25	2.50	1.09	6.02	4.4	7.3	1.7	0.5	21	78	83
	14	R	24	aaa	TEX	31	4.41	1.76	5.74	3.4	7.0	2.1	1.2	38	78	37
Mendoza,Francisco	14	R	27	aa	TEX	65	3.65	1.52	6.27	4.8	7.0	1.5	1.1	30	80	41
Mercedes,Melvin	13	R	23	aa	DET	25	1.75	1.42	4.08	3.2	5.6	1.7	1.2	30	95	34
	14	R	24	aaa	DET	60	6.12	1.62	5.83	2.4	3.7	1.5	1.3	33	64	4
Meyer,Alex	13	R	23	aa	MIN	70	3.62	1.35	22.5	3.6	9.0	2.5	0.4	33	72	100
	14	R	24	aaa	MIN	130	4.42	1.56	21.2	4.5	8.6	1.9	0.7	34	72	70
Mikolas,Miles	13	R	25	aaa	SD	61	3.05	1.31	4.66	2.3	5.0	2.2	0.8	30	79	54
	14	R	26	aaa	TEX	45	3.69	1.44	11.9	0.6	6.0	9.5	0.7	38	76	205
Miller,Adam	14	R	30	a/a	CLE	42	6.85	1.54	6.37	3.3	7.2	2.2	1.4	33	56	42
Miller,Jim	13	R	31	aaa	NYY	63	5.53	1.72	6.68	4.5	9.6	2.2	1.8	37	73	43
	14	R	32	aaa	NYY	57	4.36	1.67	7.15	3.6	6.9	1.9	0.6	37	74	55
Miller,Justin	13	R	26	a/a	TEX	27	10.52	2.08	4.9	6.0	8.6	1.4	2.3	38	50	1
	14	R	27	aaa	DET	45	2.41	1.14	4.66	2.6	5.9	2.2	0.5	27	80	76
Miller,Quinton	13	R	24	aa	PIT	58	4.31	1.57	8.17	5.4	5.5	1.0	0.4	29	72	45
	14	R	25	aa	PIT	36	4.36	1.79	6.85	5.7	5.8	1.0	0.7	33	76	33
Miller,Trevor	13	R	22	aa	SEA	47	6.42	1.64	26	4.3	4.8	1.1	1.1	31	61	16
	14	R	23	a/a	SEA	114	4.64	1.39	14.6	3.2	6.2	1.9	0.4	32	65	67
Mills,Brad	13	L	28	aaa	TEX	98	5.25	1.56	23.7	3.1	5.0	1.6	1.1	33	68	26
	14	L	29	aaa	TOR	107	2.94	1.22	21.7	2.3	6.5	2.9	0.8	30	79	79
Milner,Hoby	14	L	23	aa	PHI	143	4.76	1.52	24.9	3.5	4.7	1.3	1.7	29	75	2
Mitchell,Bryan	13	R	22	aa	NYY	19	2.43	1.15	24.7	2.5	6.7	2.7	0.0	30	77	103
	14	R	23	a/a	NYY	103	5.17	1.65	20	4.0	7.0	1.7	1.2	35	71	38
Molina,Nestor	13	R	24	aa	CHW	36	6.20	1.83	9.93	3.2	6.1	1.9	0.7	40	65	43
	14	R	25	aa	CHW	61	5.40	1.51	6.03	3.6	5.6	1.6	1.3	31	66	27
Molleken,Dustin	14	R	30	aaa	MIL	74	6.43	1.79	6.35	5.0	8.1	1.6	1.1	37	65	43
Montero,Joan	14	R	26	aa	PIT	61	6.63	2.14	10.9	5.2	3.4	0.7	0.3	39	66	10
Montero,Rafael	13	R	23	a/a	NYM	155	2.60	1.09	22.5	1.8	7.7	4.3	0.3	30	76	133
	14	R	24	aaa	NYM	80	2.92	1.18	20	3.2	7.8	2.4	0.4	29	75	97
Montgomery,Mark	13	R	23	aaa	NYY	40	4.55	1.78	7.35	6.1	9.3	1.5	1.2	35	78	50
	14	R	24	a/a	NYY	51	2.54	1.30	5.42	4.7	7.4	1.6	0.7	26	83	70
Montgomery,Matthe	14	R	27	aa	MIA	39	6.88	2.05	12.8	3.6	4.0	1.1	0.6	40	65	11
Montgomery,Michae	13	L	24	aaa	TAM	109	5.50	1.61	24.1	3.9	5.4	1.4	0.8	33	65	35
	14	L	25	aaa	TAM	126	5.32	1.50	21.8	3.5	5.8	1.6	0.7	32	64	47
Moreno,Diego	14	R	28	aa	NYY	58	5.35	1.81	7.03	3.0	6.5	2.2	0.4	41	69	58
Morey,Robert	13	R	25	a/a	MIA	113	6.78	1.86	23.1	4.3	4.7	1.1	1.0	36	63	9
	14	R	26	a/a	MIA	57	5.72	2.02	18.4	4.4	4.3	1.0	0.5	39	71	15
Morillo,Juan	14	R	31	aa	BAL	35	6.18	2.22	7.95	8.2	7.7	0.9	0.3	39	70	47
Morimando,Shawn	14	L	22	aa	CLE	56	4.24	1.50	24.4	2.5	5.3	2.1	0.3	35	70	61
Morris,AJ	13	R	27	aa	CHC	72	6.24	1.84	10.8	5.0	5.1	1.0	0.6	35	65	27
	14	R	28	a/a	PIT	97	3.49	1.47	19.7	2.7	4.6	1.7	0.5	32	77	43
Morrow,Bryce	14	R	26	aa	SD	89	3.68	1.33	23.1	2.0	5.7	2.9	0.7	32	73	73
Mortensen,Clayton	13	R	28	aaa	KC	50	3.71	1.57	14.5	4.7	5.4	1.1	1.0	29	80	27
	14	R	29	aaa	KC	76	5.73	1.71	21.5	2.8	5.2	1.9	1.3	36	69	20
Mortensen,Jared	14	R	26	aa	TAM	55	6.72	1.81	21.2	5.2	5.6	1.1	0.8	34	62	25

PITCHER	yr	t	age	lvl	org	ip	era	whip	bf/g	ctl	dom	cmd	hr/9	h%	s%	bpv
Moscot,Jon	13	R	22	aa	CIN	31	4.25	1.72	23.5	3.7	7.2	2.0	1.2	37	79	40
	14	R	23	a/a	CIN	167	3.74	1.34	24.8	2.6	5.6	2.2	1.0	30	75	50
Moye,Andrew	13	R	26	aa	MIL	127	5.62	1.48	21	3.3	5.1	1.6	1.7	29	66	10
	14	R	27	aa	MIL	48	5.75	1.72	19.8	2.9	4.5	1.5	1.5	35	69	4
Munson,Kevin	13	R	24	a/a	ARI	55	4.68	1.26	4.21	3.5	8.9	2.5	1.1	29	65	83
	14	R	25	aaa	ARI	62	2.65	1.18	4.45	2.9	9.5	3.2	0.7	31	80	113
Murata,Toru	13	R	28	a/a	CLE	158	5.60	1.61	25	1.8	5.3	3.0	1.6	36	69	35
	14	R	29	a/a	CLE	127	6.43	1.71	21.3	2.9	4.3	1.5	1.6	34	65	-2
Murphy,Sean	13	R	25	aa	OAK	137	4.68	1.52	23.8	3.4	6.5	1.9	0.6	34	69	59
	14	R	26	a/a	OAK	93	5.67	1.69	24.7	3.5	5.6	1.6	0.8	35	66	36
Murray,Colton	14	R	24	aa	PHI	59	2.64	1.13	6.47	3.4	7.7	2.3	0.9	25	81	82
Murray,Matt	14	R	25	aa	KC	76	5.40	1.56	11.8	2.9	5.7	2.0	0.5	35	64	54
Nappo,Gregory	14	L	26	a/a	MIA	52	2.74	1.04	5.14	2.0	6.0	3.1	0.7	25	77	88
Neal,Zachary	13	R	25	aa	OAK	166	4.98	1.41	25	2.0	4.2	2.1	0.9	32	66	37
	14	R	26	a/a	OAK	150	3.65	1.35	25.1	1.2	5.0	4.1	0.8	33	75	87
Needy,James	14	R	23	aa	SD	146	3.20	1.34	23.3	3.0	6.2	2.1	0.4	31	76	72
Negrin,Yoannis	13	R	29	aaa	CHC	108	5.69	1.86	14.9	3.0	7.3	2.4	0.6	42	69	60
	14	R	30	aaa	CHC	59	7.15	2.15	11.7	6.3	5.3	0.8	0.9	38	66	8
Nelo,Hector	13	R	27	aa	LA	61	3.60	1.58	5.94	4.6	5.8	1.3	0.4	32	77	50
	14	R	28	aa	CIN	39	8.94	2.27	7.57	5.9	7.5	1.3	1.6	42	61	7
Nelson,Jimmy	13	R	24	a/a	MIL	152	3.85	1.48	24.3	4.0	8.2	2.1	0.5	34	74	79
	14	R	25	aaa	MIL	111	1.75	1.04	25.2	2.7	7.7	2.8	0.3	26	84	110
Neris,Hector	13	R	24	aa	PHI	97	5.12	1.43	8.97	3.6	7.3	2.0	1.4	30	68	45
	14	R	25	a/a	PHI	77	4.25	1.32	6.67	3.5	6.7	1.9	1.1	28	70	55
Nesbitt,Angel	14	R	24	aa	DET	32	2.46	1.14	5.33	4.0	8.0	2.0	0.8	24	83	80
Nesseth,Michael	13	R	25	a/a	PHI	51	1.66	1.24	5.44	2.7	3.8	1.4	0.4	27	88	45
	14	R	26	a/a	PHI	88	6.75	1.83	9.77	2.9	5.3	1.8	1.3	38	64	16
Newby,Kyler	13	R	28	a/a	OAK	60	3.14	1.47	5.48	3.0	6.7	2.2	0.4	34	79	71
	14	R	29	aaa	LAA	41	3.72	1.58	5.96	2.2	5.3	2.4	0.5	36	77	57
Nicasio,Juan	14	R	28	aaa	COL	36	5.56	1.86	16.7	4.0	6.4	1.6	1.3	38	72	22
Nicolino,Justin	13	L	22	aa	MIA	45	6.16	1.88	23.7	2.5	5.3	2.1	0.4	41	65	48
	14	L	23	aa	MIA	170	3.29	1.19	24.4	1.1	3.6	3.4	0.5	30	72	79
Nix,Michael	13	R	30	a/a	CHW	58	8.25	1.90	24.7	4.3	5.2	1.2	1.2	36	56	9
	14	R	31	aaa	SD	60	4.31	1.72	10	3.3	4.8	1.5	0.4	37	74	37
Nolin,Sean	13	L	24	a/a	TOR	110	3.34	1.39	23.2	2.9	8.0	2.8	0.7	34	78	86
	14	L	25	aaa	TOR	87	4.69	1.48	22.1	3.9	6.3	1.6	0.8	31	69	49
Noriega,Juan	14	R	24	aa	LA	50	3.59	1.34	5.37	2.7	6.9	2.5	0.2	33	71	90
Norris,Daniel	14	L	21	a/a	TOR	58	4.93	1.33	18.6	3.8	11.9	3.1	1.3	34	66	105
Northcraft,Aaron	13	R	23	aa	ATL	137	4.36	1.46	22.6	3.5	6.9	2.0	0.5	33	70	67
	14	R	24	a/a	ATL	130	5.36	1.67	22.5	3.8	6.7	1.8	0.6	36	67	54
Nuding,Zachary	13	R	23	a/a	NYY	134	5.57	1.81	19.4	4.3	6.0	1.4	0.9	36	70	29
	14	R	24	a/a	NYY	154	4.59	1.49	23.7	2.6	5.5	2.1	1.1	33	71	40
Nygren,James	14	R	25	a/a	MIA	70	3.99	1.39	8.2	1.7	4.3	2.6	0.9	32	73	49
O Sullivan,Sean	13	R	26	aaa	SD	115	3.68	1.45	24.5	2.3	6.5	2.9	0.5	35	75	80
	14	R	27	aaa	PHI	149	5.28	1.62	26.4	3.2	4.5	1.4	1.2	33	70	13
Oberholtzer,Brett	13	L	24	aaa	HOU	80	4.99	1.40	21.2	2.8	6.9	2.5	1.1	32	66	59
	14	L	25	aaa	HOU	31	5.01	1.35	25.9	0.9	7.5	8.8	2.7	33	75	143
Obispo,Wirfin	13	R	29	aaa	ATL	64	4.71	1.56	5.17	5.7	7.6	1.3	0.5	31	69	64
	14	R	30	aaa	PIT	48	5.08	1.69	4.81	5.4	6.5	1.2	0.4	33	68	53
O'Brien,Michael	13	R	23	aa	NYY	107	5.29	1.62	22.6	3.9	6.4	1.6	1.1	34	69	35
	14	R	24	a/a	CIN	97	4.56	1.43	15.9	3.5	6.0	1.7	1.0	30	70	43
Ogando,Nefi	14	R	25	aa	PHI	56	7.40	1.84	5.44	4.6	7.6	1.6	1.1	38	59	38
O'Grady,Dennis	14	R	25	a/a	SD	69	4.14	1.63	5.41	3.7	6.4	1.7	0.8	35	76	45
Okert,Steven	14	L	23	aa	SF	33	3.04	1.13	5.43	2.9	8.8	3.0	0.7	28	75	105
Oliver,Andrew	13	L	26	aaa	PIT	124	4.96	1.87	20.1	8.2	7.5	0.9	0.4	31	72	56
	14	L	27	aaa	PIT	64	2.94	1.38	5.6	6.6	8.8	1.3	0.4	25	79	87
Oliveros,Lester	14	R	26	a/a	MIN	66	2.11	1.26	5.36	3.9	9.4	2.4	0.0	32	81	116
Olmos,Edgar	13	L	23	aa	MIA	50	3.17	1.67	5.94	5.1	6.1	1.2	0.2	34	80	56
	14	L	24	a/a	MIA	78	4.40	1.39	6.41	3.4	5.7	1.7	0.9	29	70	46
Olmsted,Michael	13	R	26	a/a	MIL	60	7.27	1.91	5.13	7.0	7.4	1.1	1.1	33	62	30
	14	R	27	aaa	BOS	32	6.19	1.98	7.05	7.4	7.9	1.1	1.4	34	71	26
Olson,Tyler	14	L	25	aa	SEA	125	4.11	1.36	23.8	1.8	6.0	3.4	0.6	34	70	87
Oramas,Juan	13	L	23	aa	SD	56	3.49	1.33	19.2	2.5	9.2	3.6	0.7	35	75	112
	14	L	24	a/a	SD	136	4.50	1.54	22	3.0	6.7	2.2	0.8	35	72	57
O'Rourke,Ryan	13	L	25	aa	MIN	17	5.48	1.41	4.31	3.7	7.8	2.1	0.0	34	57	95
	14	L	26	a/a	MIN	42	5.27	1.50	3.53	3.7	8.9	2.4	1.2	34	67	69
Ortega,Jose	13	R	25	aaa	DET	48	2.47	1.44	5.15	6.6	8.1	1.2	0.4	26	84	76
	14	R	26	aaa	DET	58	4.63	1.73	6.13	6.0	5.7	1.0	0.7	31	74	32
Osich,Josh	13	L	25	aa	SF	30	5.09	1.35	5.62	3.5	6.9	2.0	0.5	31	61	72
	14	L	26	aa	SF	33	4.49	1.61	5.28	5.6	5.8	1.0	1.0	29	74	29
O'Sullivan,Ryan	14	R	24	aa	PHI	113	4.52	1.51	13.2	3.4	4.7	1.4	0.9	31	71	29
Owens,Henry	13	L	21	aa	BOS	30	2.08	1.14	20	4.3	11.8	2.8	0.9	27	87	118
	14	L	22	a/a	BOS	159	3.67	1.25	24.9	3.3	8.2	2.5	0.6	30	71	90
Owens,Rudy	13	L	26	aaa	HOU	17	4.42	1.94	20.2	5.0	5.6	1.1	0.0	39	75	46
	14	L	27	aaa	HOU	135	4.88	1.42	22.9	2.3	5.6	2.5	0.7	33	65	60
Palacios,Wilsen	14	R	25	aa	DET	134	5.16	1.75	23.5	3.6	4.7	1.3	1.0	35	72	15
Paredes,Willy	13	R	24	a/a	ARI	45	3.19	1.22	5.35	3.3	6.4	1.9	0.6	27	75	68
	14	R	25	a/a	ARI	67	3.08	1.57	6.65	4.1	4.9	1.2	0.4	32	81	40
Parker,Blake	13	R	28	aaa	CHC	18	2.72	1.23	4.47	5.9	10.1	1.7	0.6	23	80	99
	14	R	29	aaa	CHC	36	2.34	1.43	4.34	3.8	9.7	2.6	0.9	34	88	87
Partch,Curtis	13	R	26	a/a	CIN	37	5.19	1.59	5.05	3.9	9.0	2.3	0.7	37	67	78
	14	R	27	aaa	CIN	47	5.44	1.68	5.2	4.9	8.2	1.7	0.7	36	67	62
Paterson,Joe	13	L	27	aaa	ARI	52	1.95	1.12	4.3	2.5	7.0	2.9	0.3	28	83	101
	14	L	28	aaa	ARI	43	3.22	1.66	3.41	4.0	5.2	1.3	0.2	35	80	47
Patterson,James	13	L	24	aa	TAM	41	4.77	1.32	9.99	1.9	5.0	2.6	0.9	31	65	57
	14	L	25	a/a	TAM	74	4.65	1.42	7.85	1.9	5.7	3.1	0.9	34	68	68
Patterson,Red	13	R	26	aaa	LA	107	3.09	1.44	11.7	3.8	7.4	1.9	1.1	31	83	54
	14	R	27	aaa	LA	121	5.22	1.51	18.1	2.8	6.0	2.1	1.3	33	68	38

PITCHER	yr	t	age	lvl	org	ip	era	whip	bf/g	ctl	dom	f	hr/9	h%	s%	bpv
Patton,Spencer	13	R	25	aa	KC	18	1.87	0.95	5.65	3.1	10.5	3.3	0.5	25	83	138
	14	R	26	aaa	TEX	62	4.46	1.19	5.11	3.7	9.6	2.6	1.6	25	69	74
Pazos,James	14	L	23	aa	NYY	42	1.84	1.24	6.09	4.2	7.6	1.8	0.0	28	84	96
Peavey,Greg	13	R	25	a/a	NYM	96	4.67	1.41	8.98	3.3	5.2	1.6	0.7	30	67	44
	14	R	26	a/a	NYM	144	4.33	1.31	24.7	2.5	6.4	2.6	0.8	31	68	70
Pena,Ariel	13	R	24	aa	MIL	142	4.73	1.56	23.1	5.4	7.1	1.3	1.4	28	74	32
	14	R	25	aaa	MIL	128	5.47	1.50	22.2	5.6	8.2	1.5	1.0	29	64	57
Pena,Miguel	13	L	23	aa	BOS	18	6.76	1.45	25.2	2.5	5.1	2.0	2.1	29	58	5
	14	L	24	aa	BOS	60	8.36	1.93	22.1	3.9	5.8	1.5	1.0	39	55	21
Perez,Rafael	13	L	31	a/a	BOS	35	3.63	1.38	5.02	2.4	6.0	2.5	1.3	31	79	50
	14	L	32	aaa	PIT	60	2.60	1.47	18.3	1.9	4.0	2.1	0.5	34	83	47
Perez,Tyson	14	R	25	aa	HOU	39	2.41	1.11	5.07	3.3	5.6	1.7	0.8	23	82	60
Perez,Williams	14	R	23	aa	ATL	133	3.41	1.31	21.1	2.7	5.5	2.1	0.3	31	73	71
Pestano,Vinnie	14	R	29	aaa	LAA	38	1.75	1.23	4.09	3.5	8.6	2.5	0.2	31	86	107
Petrick,Zachary	13	R	24	aa	STL	47	4.27	1.33	21.8	2.8	6.9	2.5	0.5	32	67	80
	14	R	25	a/a	STL	134	4.44	1.38	20.8	2.7	5.2	1.9	1.0	30	70	42
Pettit,Jacob	13	L	27	a/a	BAL	148	5.82	1.59	25.1	3.1	5.1	1.6	1.1	33	64	24
	14	L	28	a/a	BAL	116	7.87	1.87	21	3.3	3.7	1.1	1.7	35	59	-19
Pike,Tyler	14	L	20	aa	SEA	49	7.83	1.85	17.6	5.6	5.6	1.0	0.8	34	56	23
Pill,Tyler	13	R	23	aa	NYM	19	7.92	2.03	23.1	3.6	7.1	2.0	0.5	44	58	52
	14	R	24	a/a	NYM	129	3.55	1.16	22.4	2.0	7.4	3.8	0.7	30	70	110
Pimentel,Carlos	13	R	24	a/a	TEX	128	5.09	1.42	19.4	3.4	7.6	2.3	1.6	31	68	47
	14	R	25	aaa	CHC	101	6.47	1.82	16.2	4.9	6.9	1.4	1.7	35	67	13
Pinder,Branden	13	R	24	aa	NYY	24	8.24	2.11	6.31	6.4	6.7	1.1	1.0	38	60	22
	14	R	25	a/a	NYY	33	2.72	1.10	5.13	2.0	6.7	3.3	0.7	28	78	96
Pineyro,Ivan	14	R	23	aa	CHC	49	6.38	1.82	20.5	4.3	6.4	1.5	1.4	36	67	19
Pino,Yohan	13	R	30	a/a	CIN	132	4.57	1.51	16.4	2.5	6.1	2.4	0.8	35	70	59
	14	R	31	aaa	MIN	73	3.49	1.25	18.5	3.4	6.4	1.9	1.3	25	78	46
Pomeranz,Drew	13	L	25	a/a	COL	91	5.77	1.61	25.2	3.5	7.5	2.2	1.0	36	65	55
	14	L	26	aaa	OAK	46	3.72	1.41	24.5	3.2	8.3	2.6	1.0	33	77	76
Portillo,Adys	14	R	23	aa	SD	56	3.56	1.61	5.37	6.7	9.8	1.5	0.3	32	77	87
Poveda,Omar	13	R	26	aaa	ATL	164	4.51	1.52	26.4	3.5	6.0	1.7	0.7	33	71	48
	14	R	27	a/a	WAS	74	6.94	1.66	22.2	2.9	6.8	2.4	1.3	37	58	43
Prado,Marcel	13	R	26	aa	BAL	29	3.04	1.39	4.94	3.2	6.8	2.1	0.4	32	78	74
	14	R	27	aa	BAL	75	5.67	1.54	8.01	4.2	5.4	1.3	0.6	31	62	41
Pressly,Ryan	14	R	26	aaa	MIN	60	3.90	1.50	7.45	3.4	7.3	2.2	0.2	36	72	83
Price,Bryan	13	R	27	a/a	CLE	75	2.51	1.15	6.33	2.0	8.8	4.4	0.6	32	81	131
	14	R	28	a/a	CLE	36	3.09	1.23	5.26	3.2	8.4	2.7	1.3	28	82	74
Pries,Jordan	14	R	24	a/a	SEA	154	4.14	1.31	23.5	2.9	6.0	2.1	0.9	29	70	57
Pryor,Stephen	14	R	25	a/a	MIN	55	4.94	1.51	5.67	6.3	6.8	1.1	1.4	24	71	32
Purke,Matt Taylor	14	L	24	aa	WAS	31	8.48	1.98	18.8	4.7	5.1	1.1	1.4	37	57	-1
Quirarte,Edwin	13	R	27	aa	SF	72	2.86	1.43	5.49	3.5	4.3	1.2	0.2	30	79	46
	14	R	28	aa	SF	84	4.01	1.47	7.03	3.3	4.2	1.3	0.4	31	72	38
Raley,Brooks	13	L	25	aaa	CHC	141	5.57	1.55	22.9	3.1	4.9	1.6	1.0	33	64	29
	14	L	26	aaa	LAA	38	6.88	2.03	13	4.7	6.5	1.4	0.4	41	64	43
Ramirez,Elvin	13	R	26	a/a	LAA	61	5.84	1.80	5.76	6.3	5.8	0.9	0.1	33	65	49
	14	R	27	a/a	CIN	41	6.62	1.75	5.81	4.6	4.6	1.0	0.6	34	60	26
Ramirez,Erasmo	13	R	23	a/a	SEA	49	3.44	1.38	25.6	2.8	7.3	2.6	0.7	33	77	75
	14	R	24	aaa	SEA	86	3.69	1.27	23.6	1.2	6.0	4.9	0.7	33	72	114
Ramirez,J.C.	13	R	25	a/a	PHI	49	4.75	1.57	6.32	4.7	6.7	1.4	0.4	32	68	58
	14	R	26	a/a	CLE	44	3.63	1.45	5.41	3.9	4.8	1.2	1.3	28	80	18
Ramirez,Noe	13	R	24	aa	BOS	29	3.48	1.18	7.65	2.5	8.0	3.2	1.3	28	77	80
	14	R	25	aa	BOS	67	2.85	1.28	6.57	2.3	6.0	2.7	0.0	32	75	93
Ramos,Jhonathan	13	L	24	aa	PIT	48	5.43	1.49	5.7	2.0	6.2	3.1	0.7	36	63	75
	14	L	25	a/a	PIT	76	4.65	1.52	8.72	2.7	4.0	1.5	1.2	31	72	15
Ramsey,Matthew	14	R	25	aa	MIA	61	1.73	1.17	5.57	4.6	9.4	2.1	0.3	26	86	109
Ranaudo,Anthony	13	R	24	a/a	BOS	140	3.66	1.28	23	3.1	6.7	2.2	0.7	29	73	70
	14	R	25	aaa	BOS	138	3.44	1.41	24.3	3.7	5.8	1.6	0.7	30	77	50
Rasmussen,Robert	13	L	24	a/a	LA	136	4.53	1.43	20.6	3.8	6.3	1.7	1.0	30	70	45
	14	L	25	aaa	TOR	43	3.64	1.35	5.12	3.8	7.6	2.0	0.0	32	70	93
Ray,Robbie	13	L	22	aa	WAS	58	4.42	1.44	22.4	3.1	7.8	2.5	0.7	34	69	79
	14	L	23	aaa	DET	100	5.14	1.66	22.5	4.0	5.5	1.4	0.6	34	68	38
Rearick,Christopher	13	L	26	aa	SD	38	2.30	1.25	4.42	2.5	8.3	3.4	0.3	33	81	116
	14	L	27	a/a	SD	44	2.91	1.18	4.37	1.8	7.9	4.4	0.8	32	78	121
Recchia,Michael	14	R	25	aa	CHW	107	3.69	1.41	23.9	3.3	6.1	1.8	1.0	30	77	45
Reed,Chris	13	L	23	aa	LA	138	4.77	1.54	20.7	4.1	5.9	1.5	0.7	32	69	46
	14	L	24	a/a	LA	158	3.91	1.33	23.5	3.2	6.4	2.0	0.7	30	72	62
Reid,Ryan	13	R	28	aaa	PIT	59	3.50	1.43	7	3.5	6.1	1.7	0.6	31	77	55
	14	R	29	aaa	NYM	70	4.44	1.79	6.69	4.0	5.6	1.4	0.4	37	74	40
Reifer,Adam	13	R	27	aaa	MIA	41	1.80	1.29	6.02	6.3	6.2	1.0	0.5	20	88	65
	14	R	28	aaa	SF	63	6.32	1.71	6.67	5.4	7.6	1.4	1.3	33	64	36
Reyes,James	13	L	24	aa	TEX	67	3.75	1.38	6.4	3.0	6.2	2.1	0.9	31	75	54
	14	L	25	a/a	TEX	56	8.15	1.78	6.48	3.0	6.2	2.1	1.5	37	54	22
Reyes,Jorge	13	R	26	aaa	SD	75	5.06	1.64	7.97	4.2	7.2	1.7	0.5	36	68	59
	14	R	27	a/a	ATL	76	4.04	1.38	6.26	4.7	6.7	1.4	0.8	27	72	56
Reynolds,Daniel	14	R	23	a/a	LAA	42	3.38	1.40	5.72	3.0	8.1	2.7	0.2	35	74	99
Rhee,Dae-Eun	13	R	24	aa	CHC	59	4.11	1.27	22.1	3.2	4.4	1.4	1.0	25	70	30
	14	R	25	a/a	CHC	153	4.12	1.48	24.3	3.5	4.6	1.3	0.6	31	72	37
Richardson,Dustin	13	L	29	aaa	LAA	56	6.38	1.76	12.8	4.9	6.1	1.2	0.4	35	61	45
	14	L	30	aaa	LAA	53	7.26	1.79	6.74	4.1	7.1	1.7	1.0	38	58	40
Riefenhauser,Charle	13	L	23	a/a	TAM	74	1.38	0.89	5.35	2.2	7.4	3.3	0.6	22	89	113
	14	L	24	aaa	TAM	58	1.71	1.25	6.02	3.8	7.0	1.8	0.5	28	89	75
Rienzo,Andre	13	R	25	aaa	CHW	113	5.32	1.62	25.1	4.3	7.5	1.7	0.8	35	67	56
	14	R	26	aaa	CHW	47	4.46	1.63	20.8	5.1	6.8	1.3	0.9	32	74	42
Rivero,Armando	14	R	26	a/a	CHC	65	2.73	1.26	5.41	4.2	11.0	2.6	0.9	30	83	104
Rivero,Felipe Javier	14	L	23	aa	WAS	44	4.26	1.47	18.7	3.3	6.4	1.9	0.8	33	72	55
Roach,Donn	13	R	24	aa	SD	143	4.10	1.39	21.4	2.5	4.2	1.7	0.5	31	70	45
	14	R	25	aaa	SD	77	4.37	1.67	18.3	4.0	4.4	1.1	0.2	34	72	38

PITCHER	yr	t	age	lvl	org	ip	era	whip	bf/g	ctl	dom	cmd	hr/9	h%	s%	bpv
Roberts,Kenneth	13	L	25	aa	COL	16	10.51	2.56	7.33	8.1	2.5	0.3	3.3	34	64	-98
	14	L	26	aa	COL	78	3.35	1.16	6.63	2.6	4.6	1.8	0.5	26	71	57
Roberts,Will	13	R	23	aa	CLE	134	4.78	1.40	24.6	2.0	5.2	2.6	0.8	33	66	59
	14	R	24	aa	CLE	161	4.70	1.42	25.3	2.0	4.6	2.4	0.7	33	67	51
Robinson,James	13	R	25	aa	HOU	49	3.91	1.41	5.49	2.6	5.6	2.1	1.2	31	77	40
	14	R	26	a/a	ATL	70	2.92	1.35	6.75	1.9	7.2	3.8	0.3	35	78	112
Robles,Hansel	14	R	24	aa	NYM	111	4.31	1.39	15.5	3.2	7.4	2.3	0.8	32	70	71
Robowski,Ryan	13	L	25	aa	DET	50	3.64	1.38	6.17	3.9	4.1	1.0	1.0	26	77	20
	14	L	26	aa	DET	78	4.67	1.50	8.61	4.0	6.8	1.7	1.1	31	71	45
Rodebaugh,Ryan	13	R	24	a/a	TEX	64	4.28	1.26	6.19	4.3	7.4	1.7	1.1	25	69	58
	14	R	25	aa	TEX	38	7.62	2.10	5.62	4.7	9.5	2.0	0.6	46	62	64
Rodgers,Brady	14	R	24	a/a	HOU	127	4.96	1.35	19.6	1.4	5.5	4.0	1.1	33	65	79
Rodriguez,Daniel	13	L	29	aaa	ATL	53	7.69	2.01	21.4	7.4	7.1	1.0	0.6	36	60	41
	14	L	30	aaa	ATL	125	6.21	1.77	19.8	3.9	6.0	1.5	1.3	36	66	22
Rodriguez,Eduardo	13	L	20	aa	BAL	60	4.68	1.34	22.5	3.4	7.8	2.3	0.8	31	66	74
	14	L	21	aa	BOS	120	4.46	1.45	23.3	2.7	7.0	2.6	0.5	35	68	78
Rodriguez,Fernandc	14	R	30	aaa	OAK	46	2.15	1.40	5.07	3.3	7.7	2.3	0.4	33	85	85
Rodriguez,Joely	14	L	23	aa	PIT	134	5.01	1.49	19.3	2.6	3.9	1.5	0.6	32	66	33
Rodriguez,Richard	14	R	24	a/a	HOU	49	3.60	1.06	7.05	1.4	8.0	5.6	0.8	30	68	149
Roe,Chaz	13	R	27	a/a	ARI	24	1.35	1.01	3.73	1.5	6.5	4.3	0.0	29	85	138
	14	R	28	aaa	MIA	64	4.07	1.31	5.62	3.1	7.6	2.5	0.6	31	69	84
Rogers,Chad	13	R	24	a/a	CIN	140	4.34	1.34	23.3	3.1	5.7	1.8	1.3	28	72	37
	14	R	25	aaa	CIN	53	4.47	1.91	7.17	6.2	4.8	0.8	1.4	32	80	-1
Rogers,Esmil	14	R	29	aaa	TOR	49	4.60	1.60	17.9	3.9	5.7	1.5	0.5	34	71	46
Rogers,Jared	13	R	25	aaa	MIA	85	5.56	1.60	22	2.6	5.3	2.1	1.2	35	67	32
	14	R	26	a/a	MIA	124	5.68	1.67	20.6	2.5	3.8	1.5	0.6	36	65	27
Rogers,Taylor	14	L	24	aa	MIN	145	3.97	1.46	25.9	2.3	5.7	2.5	0.3	35	71	73
Rollins,David	13	L	24	a/a	HOU	39	4.26	1.48	24	2.6	7.9	3.1	1.0	36	74	77
	14	L	25	aa	HOU	78	4.38	1.38	12.1	2.6	7.4	2.9	0.9	33	70	78
Romero,Enny Manu	13	L	22	a/a	TAM	148	2.89	1.32	21.9	4.3	6.0	1.4	0.5	27	79	58
	14	L	23	aaa	TAM	126	5.36	1.57	22.1	3.7	7.2	2.0	1.0	34	67	52
Romero,Ricky	13	L	29	aaa	TOR	114	8.00	2.21	26	5.7	4.9	0.9	1.2	39	64	-5
	14	L	30	aaa	TOR	38	8.13	2.67	23	11.9	5.0	0.4	1.4	35	70	-12
Rondon,Francisco	13	L	25	a/a	NYY	83	5.37	1.67	11.3	6.6	7.5	1.1	1.1	29	69	42
	14	L	26	a/a	NYY	51	4.48	1.47	7.49	5.0	5.9	1.2	1.1	27	72	32
Rondon,Jorge	13	R	25	aaa	STL	68	3.43	1.76	6.07	4.9	4.5	0.9	0.7	33	82	19
	14	R	26	aaa	STL	62	3.25	1.38	5.13	2.9	5.8	2.0	0.4	32	76	66
Rosin,Seth	13	R	25	aa	PHI	127	4.98	1.37	20.4	2.5	5.6	2.2	1.0	31	65	49
	14	R	26	a/a	PHI	58	4.64	1.65	6.06	3.1	5.5	1.8	1.1	35	74	30
Ross,Greg	14	R	25	aa	ATL	78	2.54	1.23	24.3	2.4	4.2	1.8	0.5	28	81	52
Ross,Robbie	14	L	25	aaa	TEX	60	4.84	1.51	21.8	2.4	5.1	2.1	1.2	33	70	34
Roth,Michael	13	L	23	aa	LAA	79	5.03	1.56	20.4	4.0	4.9	1.2	0.9	31	69	26
	14	L	24	aa	LAA	141	3.31	1.41	27	3.4	4.2	1.2	0.6	29	78	34
Rowen,Benjamin	13	R	25	a/a	TEX	66	0.92	1.06	5	2.6	6.3	2.4	0.2	26	92	96
	14	R	26	aaa	TEX	47	3.94	1.36	5.77	1.8	4.6	2.6	0.4	32	70	66
Rucinski,Drew	14	R	26	aa	LAA	149	4.15	1.48	24.6	2.6	6.8	2.6	0.5	35	71	77
Ruffin,Chance	13	R	25	a/a	SEA	113	4.74	1.41	15.4	2.3	5.5	2.4	1.2	32	69	45
	14	R	26	aaa	SEA	61	5.61	1.57	12.2	3.5	6.0	1.7	1.2	33	66	33
Runion,Sam	13	R	25	a/a	KC	58	5.27	1.47	6.59	2.3	5.4	2.4	0.7	34	63	57
	14	R	26	a/a	WAS	38	5.47	1.43	6.96	2.1	6.6	3.2	0.7	35	61	80
Runzler,Dan	13	L	28	aaa	SF	52	5.90	1.95	4.89	6.3	6.5	1.0	0.7	36	69	33
	14	L	29	aaa	SF	46	3.42	1.71	5.38	7.0	7.6	1.1	0.3	31	79	65
Rusin,Chris	13	L	27	aaa	CHC	121	4.36	1.42	27	2.3	4.0	1.8	0.7	31	70	36
	14	L	28	aaa	CHC	146	5.57	1.70	28.7	2.7	4.5	1.7	1.1	36	68	19
Russell,Adam	13	R	30	aaa	BAL	61	3.42	1.80	6.68	5.8	6.4	1.1	0.4	34	81	45
	14	R	31	aaa	CIN	35	5.25	1.95	6.25	5.3	6.5	1.2	0.6	38	73	36
Ryan,Kyle	14	L	23	a/a	DET	160	4.52	1.36	25.7	2.0	4.5	2.2	0.9	31	68	45
Sadler,Casey	13	R	23	a/a	PIT	136	3.83	1.31	23.5	2.7	3.8	1.4	0.7	28	72	33
	14	R	24	aaa	PIT	125	3.31	1.28	24.4	1.6	4.4	2.7	0.7	30	76	60
Salazar,Danny	13	R	23	a/a	CLE	93	3.07	1.10	17.4	2.2	10.8	4.8	0.5	33	73	161
	14	R	24	aaa	CLE	61	4.19	1.52	24	4.0	9.5	2.4	1.0	35	75	76
Salcedo,Adrian	14	R	23	aa	MIN	73	4.96	1.54	8.17	2.9	7.8	2.7	0.2	38	65	90
Sample,Tyler	14	R	25	aa	PIT	35	7.01	1.94	15	7.4	5.6	0.8	0.5	33	62	34
Sampson,Adrian	14	R	23	a/a	PIT	167	3.12	1.19	23.9	1.8	4.7	2.6	0.5	29	75	70
Sampson,Keyvius	13	R	22	a/a	SD	141	3.51	1.26	20.6	3.6	7.8	2.2	0.8	28	74	77
	14	R	23	aaa	SD	92	5.34	1.54	10.5	5.5	8.2	1.5	1.4	29	68	44
Sanabia,Alex	14	R	26	aaa	MIA	134	5.01	1.62	21.3	2.7	5.5	2.1	1.0	36	70	38
Sanchez,Aaron	14	R	22	a/a	TOR	100	4.90	1.59	20.1	5.1	6.6	1.3	0.7	31	69	50
Sanchez,Angel	14	R	25	aa	PIT	110	6.64	1.74	21.8	2.7	4.2	1.5	0.8	36	61	21
Sanchez,Jesus	13	R	26	aaa	MIL	70	3.28	1.42	6.18	2.4	5.3	2.2	0.8	32	79	51
	14	R	27	aaa	MIA	31	8.13	2.06	6.65	3.8	5.7	1.5	0.7	42	58	26
Sanchez,Raydel	14	R	24	aa	LA	65	5.81	1.48	17.6	3.1	3.0	1.0	1.4	28	63	-6
Sanchez,Victor	14	R	19	aa	SEA	125	4.38	1.30	22.4	2.2	6.5	3.0	1.1	31	69	70
Santiago,Andres	13	R	24	aa	LA	134	6.28	1.59	19.7	5.0	6.1	1.2	0.7	31	59	43
	14	R	25	aa	LA	129	4.58	1.48	21.3	3.4	5.6	1.6	1.0	31	71	36
Sappington,Mark	13	R	23	aa	LAA	26	4.62	1.79	23.7	6.8	7.8	1.1	0.4	34	73	61
	14	R	24	aa	LAA	43	8.13	2.05	23.4	7.6	5.9	0.8	0.5	35	57	33
Satterwhite,Cody	14	R	27	aa	NYM	58	2.48	1.19	4.85	3.4	7.9	2.3	0.5	28	80	92
Saupold,Warwick	13	R	23	aa	DET	129	3.98	1.51	25.4	3.6	4.6	1.3	0.9	30	76	26
	14	R	24	aa	DET	140	5.53	1.57	22.8	4.0	6.4	1.6	1.0	32	66	39
Savery,Joe	13	L	28	aaa	PHI	24	4.89	1.38	4.97	3.8	8.5	2.3	0.9	31	66	75
	14	L	29	aaa	OAK	44	3.06	1.37	4.32	3.6	6.8	1.9	0.7	30	80	62
Scahill,Rob	13	R	26	aaa	COL	46	4.95	1.54	8.73	2.1	6.5	3.1	1.3	36	71	55
	14	R	27	aaa	COL	58	5.17	1.53	6.19	2.9	5.9	2.1	1.1	33	68	39
Schlereth,Daniel	14	L	28	aaa	DET	37	7.99	2.18	4.83	8.0	6.1	0.8	0.9	36	62	17
Schlosser,Gus	13	R	25	aa	ATL	135	3.18	1.43	23	3.2	5.6	1.8	0.4	32	78	59
	14	R	26	aaa	ATL	99	4.74	1.57	17.5	4.4	5.2	1.2	0.6	31	70	36

PITCHER	yr	t	age	lvl	org	ip	era	whip	bf/g	ctl	dom	f	hr/9	h%	s%	bpv
Schugel,Andrew	14	R	25	aa	ARI	148	4.48	1.52	24.7	3.2	5.7	1.8	0.2	34	68	62
Schultz,Bo	13	R	28	a/a	ARI	105	4.16	1.44	12	3.3	4.9	1.5	0.7	30	72	39
	14	R	29	aaa	ARI	135	6.90	1.87	22.6	3.1	4.0	1.3	1.2	37	63	0
Schuster,Patrick	14	L	24	a/a	ARI	45	3.37	1.37	3.28	4.8	6.5	1.3	0.8	26	78	51
Schwartz,Blake	14	R	25	aa	WAS	38	7.59	1.96	22.9	3.5	4.3	1.2	1.4	38	62	-6
Scott,Robby	14	L	25	aa	BOS	60	2.61	1.41	7.2	2.4	6.2	2.6	0.5	34	83	73
Scribner,Evan	13	R	28	aaa	OAK	45	2.46	1.04	5.57	1.9	8.9	4.7	0.4	30	77	150
	14	R	29	aaa	OAK	47	3.30	1.16	4.68	1.8	10.2	5.7	0.7	35	73	165
Seaton,Ross	13	R	24	a/a	HOU	123	7.16	1.73	22.5	2.9	4.5	1.6	1.6	35	60	0
	14	R	25	a/a	HOU	35	5.39	1.73	13.4	4.1	5.3	1.3	1.1	34	70	20
Seidel,RJ	13	R	26	a/a	MIL	89	5.77	1.65	15.2	3.9	7.8	2.0	1.8	34	70	30
	14	R	27	a/a	COL	33	12.68	2.40	12.3	5.1	5.7	1.1	2.6	41	47	-44
Self,Derek	14	R	24	aa	WAS	40	3.56	1.49	6.9	2.7	5.6	2.1	1.5	32	83	28
Selman,Sam	14	L	24	a/a	KC	97	4.93	1.61	13	5.2	6.9	1.3	0.6	32	69	52
Serrano,Mark	13	R	28	a/a	ARI	57	3.75	1.41	13.3	2.4	5.3	2.2	0.7	32	75	53
	14	R	29	a/a	ARI	55	4.69	1.66	10.7	3.7	6.1	1.7	1.3	34	75	25
Severino,Atahualpa	13	L	29	aaa	PIT	55	4.72	1.63	6.28	3.4	6.7	2.0	1.2	35	74	38
	14	L	30	aaa	ATL	45	3.97	1.42	4.73	4.5	8.2	1.8	0.4	31	71	81
Sexton,Timothy	13	R	26	aa	SD	50	3.93	1.51	7.47	2.3	4.2	1.9	1.0	33	77	27
	14	R	27	a/a	OAK	69	6.57	1.73	10.8	2.6	5.3	2.1	0.9	38	61	37
Shackelford,Kevin	13	R	24	aa	MIL	29	1.56	1.19	5.89	2.3	6.6	2.8	0.4	30	89	92
	14	R	25	aa	MIL	50	5.94	1.78	5.76	3.3	3.8	1.2	0.7	36	66	15
Shackleford,Stephei	13	R	24	aa	SEA	28	4.01	1.73	5.54	5.1	6.3	1.2	0.4	35	76	49
	14	R	25	aa	SEA	64	3.63	1.50	6.25	4.2	8.3	2.0	0.4	34	75	80
Shelton,Matthew	14	R	26	aa	LA	87	4.35	1.57	14.1	4.6	6.2	1.3	0.7	32	73	45
Sherfy,Jimmie	14	R	23	aa	ARI	38	6.16	1.52	4.46	4.3	8.9	2.1	1.1	34	60	65
Sherriff,Ryan	13	L	23	aa	STL	27	3.49	1.67	24.2	2.8	5.0	1.8	0.0	37	77	57
	14	L	24	a/a	STL	69	3.10	1.44	6.64	2.5	5.6	2.2	0.5	33	79	63
Shirley,Thomas	14	L	26	a/a	HOU	117	2.88	1.23	15.9	2.5	6.3	2.5	0.7	29	79	75
Shreve,Chasen	13	L	23	aa	ATL	43	5.65	1.73	5.4	4.9	5.1	1.1	0.2	34	65	41
	14	L	24	a/a	ATL	64	3.05	1.09	5.44	1.7	10.4	6.2	0.6	34	73	182
Simmons,James	13	R	27	aaa	OAK	16	7.77	2.38	7.08	4.5	5.6	1.2	0.5	45	65	19
	14	R	28	a/a	WAS	106	6.60	1.60	18.7	2.9	4.8	1.7	1.4	33	60	16
Simmons,Seth	14	R	26	aa	ARI	48	1.99	1.13	5.38	3.6	8.9	2.5	0.2	28	82	112
Simms,John	14	R	22	aa	WAS	59	5.10	1.52	23.3	2.0	5.4	2.7	0.8	35	67	56
Simon,Kyle	13	R	23	aa	PHI	57	4.90	1.51	5.45	3.4	4.5	1.3	0.7	31	67	33
	14	R	24	a/a	PHI	76	4.53	1.44	7	2.5	4.1	1.6	0.4	32	67	44
Sitton,Kraig	14	L	26	aa	COL	66	5.37	1.66	6.16	3.7	4.3	1.2	1.6	31	72	-5
Smith,Blake	14	R	27	aa	LA	33	4.34	1.65	5.73	4.2	7.0	1.7	0.5	36	73	57
Smith,Carson	13	R	24	aa	SEA	50	2.50	1.18	4.55	3.2	10.9	3.4	0.2	33	78	140
	14	R	25	aaa	SEA	43	3.03	1.39	4.65	2.5	7.9	3.1	0.2	36	77	106
Smith,Chad	14	R	25	a/a	DET	47	4.11	1.56	6.05	2.1	6.0	2.8	0.4	37	73	73
Smith,Chipper	14	L	24	aa	MIA	65	4.94	1.39	19.6	4.3	6.4	1.5	1.3	27	68	36
Smith,Greg	13	L	30	a/a	PHI	116	4.34	1.60	19.7	2.0	3.3	1.6	0.8	34	74	20
	14	L	31	aaa	PHI	157	5.73	1.70	26.3	2.4	3.9	1.6	1.2	35	68	9
Smith,Josh	13	R	26	aa	CIN	160	4.71	1.56	25	3.2	6.4	2.0	1.4	33	74	35
	14	R	27	aaa	CIN	159	5.38	1.71	25.7	3.8	5.6	1.5	0.5	36	67	40
Smith,Kyle	14	R	22	aa	HOU	95	4.69	1.29	18.7	2.3	8.1	3.6	1.4	32	68	84
Smith,Murphy	13	R	26	aa	OAK	150	4.08	1.55	25.2	2.9	4.7	1.6	0.8	33	75	32
	14	R	27	aa	OAK	86	5.74	1.57	12.1	3.5	5.1	1.4	0.4	33	61	44
Smith,Nate	14	L	23	aa	LAA	62	3.57	1.38	23.8	4.3	8.3	1.9	0.5	31	74	83
Smith,Slade	14	R	24	aa	DET	52	6.53	1.89	7.37	1.8	3.5	1.9	0.7	40	64	20
Smith,Steve	13	R	27	a/a	LA	73	5.39	1.69	10.2	3.7	5.9	1.6	0.8	35	68	38
	14	R	28	a/a	LA	108	5.41	1.53	16.2	3.0	4.1	1.4	1.3	31	67	11
Smyth,Paul	13	R	26	a/a	OAK	60	2.86	1.30	5.46	3.1	6.6	2.1	0.6	30	79	72
	14	R	27	aaa	OAK	59	3.14	1.04	4.96	2.1	6.6	3.1	1.2	25	76	81
Sneed,Kramer	14	L	26	aa	LAA	138	6.17	1.73	22.5	4.5	5.7	1.3	1.3	33	66	15
Snodgrass,Jack	13	L	26	aa	SF	141	3.97	1.27	23.1	2.4	4.1	1.7	0.5	28	69	46
	14	L	27	aa	SF	131	4.33	1.52	23.8	3.0	4.6	1.5	0.1	34	69	53
Snodgress,Scott	13	L	24	aa	CHW	144	6.19	1.72	25.1	4.3	4.8	1.1	0.8	33	63	23
	14	L	25	a/a	CHW	139	4.54	1.56	21	4.0	5.1	1.3	1.0	31	73	27
Snow,Forrest	13	R	25	a/a	SEA	82	3.59	1.22	7.89	3.1	7.7	2.5	0.8	29	73	83
	14	R	26	a/a	SEA	76	4.49	1.38	16	2.9	7.2	2.5	1.1	32	70	63
Socolovich,Miguel	14	R	28	aaa	NYM	59	3.22	1.49	5.01	2.6	8.2	3.1	0.6	37	80	90
Sogard,Alexander	13	L	26	a/a	HOU	48	7.22	2.02	6.11	5.7	5.7	1.0	0.9	37	63	18
	14	L	27	aa	ARI	62	6.65	1.82	7.19	4.7	4.6	1.0	2.4	31	70	-32
Sosa,Henry	14	R	29	aaa	LA	36	3.51	1.47	22.3	2.7	5.0	1.8	0.2	34	75	58
Soto,Giovanni	14	L	23	aa	CLE	53	3.64	1.16	5.71	1.9	7.2	3.7	0.3	31	67	115
Spomer,Kurt	14	R	25	a/a	LAA	34	2.69	1.41	7.25	4.1	3.0	0.7	0.2	27	80	31
Spruill,Ezekiel	13	R	24	a/a	ARI	124	3.97	1.47	25.3	3.2	4.1	1.3	0.6	31	73	31
	14	R	25	aaa	ARI	79	6.17	1.47	12.1	2.2	6.5	2.9	1.1	34	58	62
Stange,Daniel	13	R	28	aaa	LAA	66	4.36	1.60	5.58	4.7	7.7	1.6	0.7	34	73	60
	14	R	29	aaa	WAS	59	4.64	1.91	6.38	5.5	4.7	0.9	0.3	35	74	28
Startup,Will	13	L	29	aa	DET	58	4.72	1.47	7.54	2.8	3.8	1.3	1.7	29	74	-5
	14	L	30	a/a	DET	53	6.77	1.97	6.81	4.2	4.0	0.9	1.4	36	67	-14
Stephenson,Robert	13	R	20	aa	CIN	17	6.27	1.98	20	7.1	8.9	1.2	1.5	36	71	32
	14	R	21	aa	CIN	137	5.29	1.43	21.5	4.7	8.3	1.8	1.4	28	66	52
Stewart,Zach	13	R	27	aaa	CHW	167	5.81	1.70	27	2.5	5.3	2.1	1.2	37	67	27
	14	R	28	aaa	ATL	106	5.45	1.87	24.9	3.1	3.9	1.3	0.5	38	70	19
Stilson,John	13	R	23	a/a	TOR	50	2.56	1.19	5.69	2.7	8.3	3.1	0.6	30	81	103
	14	R	24	aaa	TOR	34	4.16	1.88	6.39	5.0	7.2	1.4	0.7	38	78	44
Stinson,Josh	13	R	25	aaa	BAL	131	4.92	1.62	25.3	4.0	4.8	1.2	1.0	32	71	20
	14	R	26	aaa	BAL	85	6.48	1.53	16.9	4.1	6.6	1.6	1.8	30	61	20
Stoffel,Jason	13	R	25	a/a	HOU	70	3.81	1.41	5.78	4.0	6.3	1.6	0.3	31	72	66
	14	R	26	aaa	HOU	65	3.53	1.63	5.33	3.9	7.7	2.0	0.4	37	78	70
Stoneburner,Grahar	13	R	26	a/a	NYY	90	6.02	1.70	13.5	3.1	3.3	1.1	1.1	33	65	-2
	14	R	27	a/a	NYY	55	8.02	1.90	20	3.1	3.9	1.3	1.1	38	57	2

PITCHER	yr	t	age	lvl	org	ip	era	whip	bf/g	ctl	dom	cmd	hr/9	h%	s%	bpv
Stoppelman,Lee	14	L	24	a/a	STL	49	5.88	1.54	4.57	4.6	8.5	1.9	0.8	33	61	67
Stowell,Bryce	13	R	27	aa	CLE	45	2.94	1.32	5.21	4.2	9.8	2.3	0.4	32	78	104
	14	R	28	a/a	TAM	52	2.44	1.43	5.63	4.0	7.4	1.9	0.2	33	82	81
Straily,Dan	13	R	25	aaa	OAK	32	1.18	1.10	24.9	2.5	7.6	3.1	0.2	29	90	112
	14	R	26	aaa	CHC	118	5.47	1.58	25.9	3.8	7.5	2.0	1.4	33	68	41
Strickland,Hunter	14	R	26	aa	SF	36	2.40	0.94	3.53	1.0	9.6	9.2	0.7	30	78	240
Striz,Nate	14	R	26	aa	COL	38	9.25	2.23	6.68	5.1	5.4	1.1	1.4	41	58	-7
Stroman,Marcus	13	R	22	aa	TOR	112	3.70	1.20	22.5	2.1	9.2	4.4	1.1	32	74	117
	14	R	23	aaa	TOR	36	3.89	1.33	21.1	2.3	9.8	4.2	0.3	37	69	137
Struck,Nicholas	13	R	24	a/a	CHC	137	7.03	1.94	24.1	5.0	3.7	0.7	1.5	34	65	-18
	14	R	25	a/a	LA	108	5.14	1.63	21	3.3	4.1	1.2	0.6	34	68	24
Sturdevant,Tyler	14	R	29	a/a	CLE	58	3.38	1.31	5.17	2.9	6.4	2.2	0.7	30	76	67
Suarez,Albert	14	R	25	aa	TAM	56	4.99	1.71	23.1	3.0	4.3	1.4	0.6	36	71	25
Sulbaran,Juan	13	R	24	aa	KC	46	8.56	1.81	8.58	5.6	4.0	0.7	1.8	29	53	-19
	14	R	25	aa	KC	127	4.19	1.66	22.8	4.0	6.4	1.6	0.8	35	76	42
Sullivan,Gerald	14	R	26	a/a	SD	59	2.41	1.10	4.29	2.9	8.4	2.9	0.3	29	78	115
Summers,Matt	13	R	24	aa	MIN	22	7.40	1.80	17.2	4.8	4.3	0.9	0.4	34	56	26
	14	R	25	aa	MIN	53	8.38	1.85	8.83	3.7	7.3	2.0	0.9	40	52	47
Surkamp,Eric	13	L	26	aaa	SF	71	2.76	1.11	25.5	2.4	5.4	2.3	0.4	27	75	77
	14	L	27	aaa	CHW	79	5.28	1.69	19.7	2.6	7.9	3.1	1.1	40	70	68
Suter,Brent	14	L	25	aa	MIL	152	4.84	1.49	23.5	3.3	5.8	1.7	1.0	32	69	39
Syndergaard,Noah	13	R	21	aa	NYM	54	3.04	1.09	19.2	1.8	10.4	5.7	1.3	31	79	151
	14	R	22	aaa	NYM	133	3.58	1.32	21.2	2.3	8.8	3.8	0.6	35	73	116
Tatusko,Ryan	13	R	28	a/a	WAS	128	5.28	1.83	20.5	6.0	5.4	0.9	0.6	33	70	31
	14	R	29	aaa	WAS	79	3.63	1.38	23.7	3.6	4.2	1.2	0.7	28	75	33
Tejeda,Enosil	13	R	24	aa	CLE	41	0.95	0.92	4.61	2.7	6.7	2.5	0.0	23	89	112
	14	R	25	a/a	CLE	57	3.70	1.25	5.12	2.2	8.0	3.6	0.8	32	72	103
Tepera,Dennis	13	R	26	aa	TOR	116	5.48	1.62	15.6	4.5	6.6	1.5	1.0	33	67	38
	14	R	27	aaa	TOR	64	5.11	1.76	5.74	3.8	7.5	2.0	0.8	39	71	54
Tepesch,Nicholas	14	R	26	aaa	TEX	46	1.80	1.12	25.7	1.8	6.3	3.4	0.2	30	84	109
Texeira,Kanekoa	13	R	27	aaa	CIN	26	3.41	1.47	6.97	2.0	5.5	2.8	0.5	35	77	71
	14	R	28	aaa	ATL	70	5.79	1.87	25.4	4.9	3.3	0.7	0.9	33	70	-3
Thomas,Justin	13	L	29	aaa	OAK	84	5.09	1.73	24	3.9	5.4	1.4	0.8	35	71	29
	14	L	30	aaa	LAA	113	5.66	1.78	25.9	3.0	5.6	1.8	1.4	37	71	19
Thomas,Michael	13	L	24	aa	LA	47	4.08	1.58	6.13	4.0	8.1	2.0	0.4	36	74	75
	14	L	25	aa	LA	59	2.80	1.57	5.43	5.7	9.5	1.7	0.4	33	83	84
Thompson,Aaron	13	L	26	a/a	MIN	59	3.30	1.49	6.02	2.5	6.3	2.5	0.5	35	78	72
	14	L	27	aaa	MIN	52	5.33	1.72	5.13	4.7	6.7	1.4	1.0	34	70	37
Thompson,Jacob	13	R	24	aa	TAM	149	4.78	1.53	23.9	3.5	5.2	1.5	0.8	32	69	36
	14	R	25	a/a	TAM	52	3.33	1.65	6.8	2.6	6.3	2.4	0.4	38	80	67
Thompson,Jake	14	R	20	aa	TEX	47	3.74	1.39	21.8	4.3	8.6	2.0	0.7	31	74	79
Thompson,Taylor	13	R	26	a/a	CHW	66	4.79	1.40	6.36	2.6	6.9	2.6	0.4	34	64	83
	14	R	27	aaa	CHW	59	2.40	1.49	6.53	4.9	8.3	1.7	0.5	32	86	74
Thornton,Zachary	13	R	25	a/a	PIT	61	3.31	1.05	7.42	1.6	8.6	5.4	0.6	30	69	155
	14	R	26	aaa	NYM	67	3.30	1.30	5.11	2.6	8.1	3.1	0.5	33	75	101
Tobin,Mason	13	R	26	aaa	SF	34	5.21	1.60	4.89	4.2	4.8	1.1	0.6	32	67	32
	14	R	27	aaa	SF	34	4.19	1.66	5.64	4.5	5.6	1.2	0.6	33	75	37
Todd,Jess	13	R	27	aaa	DET	63	2.98	1.29	6.6	4.2	7.0	1.7	0.5	27	78	71
	14	R	28	aaa	ARI	72	3.94	1.46	5.84	3.3	6.2	1.9	0.6	32	74	56
Toledo,Tommy	14	R	26	aa	MIL	58	5.85	1.64	6.77	3.2	7.3	2.3	1.6	35	68	36
Tomlin,Josh	13	R	29	a/a	CLE	21	2.76	0.91	15.7	0.0	4.9	0.0	0.0	29	66	0
	14	R	30	aaa	CLE	40	2.87	1.10	26.1	2.5	5.6	2.3	1.3	24	81	53
Tonkin,Michael	13	R	24	a/a	MIN	57	3.98	1.35	4.57	2.5	8.5	3.4	0.5	35	70	109
	14	R	25	aaa	MIN	45	3.59	1.38	4.85	2.5	7.3	2.9	0.4	34	74	91
Tracy,Matthew	13	L	25	aa	NYY	64	7.38	1.95	21.7	5.8	6.9	1.2	1.2	36	62	23
	14	L	26	a/a	NYY	151	4.74	1.77	24.8	3.6	4.2	1.2	0.8	35	74	14
Treinen,Blake	13	R	25	aa	WAS	119	4.60	1.55	24.7	2.5	5.1	2.0	0.8	34	71	43
	14	R	26	aaa	WAS	81	3.99	1.39	21.2	2.2	5.5	2.5	0.5	33	71	68
Triggs,Andrew	14	R	25	a/a	KC	62	3.42	1.29	5.8	2.4	4.3	1.8	0.6	29	74	48
Troncoso,Ramon	13	R	30	aaa	CHW	25	3.17	1.36	4.91	3.3	4.7	1.4	1.1	27	81	28
	14	R	31	aaa	KC	44	5.26	1.58	8.06	2.5	4.8	1.9	0.6	35	66	42
Tropeano,Nicholas	13	R	23	aa	HOU	134	4.69	1.46	20.4	2.6	7.6	2.9	1.1	35	70	71
	14	R	24	aaa	HOU	125	3.20	1.04	20.9	2.3	7.4	3.2	0.8	26	72	100
Turley,Josh	14	L	24	aa	DET	50	4.17	1.49	23.9	2.8	4.0	1.4	1.4	30	77	7
Turley,Nikolas	13	L	24	a/a	NYY	145	5.08	1.60	22.9	5.2	7.3	1.4	0.9	31	69	47
	14	L	25	aaa	NYY	60	5.53	1.81	21.5	6.7	5.3	0.8	1.5	29	73	5
Turpen,Daniel	13	R	27	a/a	MIN	65	6.10	1.93	6.57	5.8	5.2	0.9	1.3	34	70	4
	14	R	28	aa	MIN	62	5.90	1.61	6.9	4.8	6.7	1.4	0.8	32	63	45
Urckfitz,Patrick	13	L	25	a/a	HOU	67	3.46	1.56	5.9	3.0	4.0	1.3	0.3	33	77	38
	14	L	26	a/a	HOU	54	3.05	1.46	4.88	3.4	5.8	1.7	0.4	32	79	59
Urena,Jose	14	R	23	aa	MIA	162	3.78	1.25	25.3	1.6	5.6	3.5	0.7	31	71	87
Valdez,Jose	13	R	30	aaa	HOU	39	7.38	1.97	5.38	5.4	5.7	1.1	1.1	36	62	12
	14	R	31	a/a	BOS	36	2.96	1.81	6.89	3.2	5.1	1.6	0.6	38	85	32
Valdez,Jose	14	R	24	aa	DET	57	4.53	1.53	5.28	4.0	8.3	2.1	0.9	34	72	65
Vance,Kevin	13	R	23	aa	CHW	69	5.05	1.55	7.54	5.4	9.6	1.8	0.7	33	67	78
	14	R	24	aa	CHW	62	5.21	1.59	6.4	4.8	7.5	1.6	0.5	34	66	63
Vargas,Richard	14	R	23	aa	SEA	50	5.28	1.52	5.98	5.8	7.6	1.3	0.3	30	63	70
Varner,Rett	13	R	25	a/a	MIA	73	4.21	1.60	8.07	3.6	6.4	1.8	1.1	34	77	38
	14	R	26	aaa	MIA	33	7.63	2.20	6.07	6.9	5.6	0.8	0.9	38	64	12
Vasquez,Anthony	13	L	27	aa	SEA	70	6.31	1.57	25.5	2.8	3.2	1.2	2.1	29	65	-27
	14	L	28	a/a	BAL	124	6.21	1.84	21.3	3.2	5.0	1.6	1.7	37	69	0
Veal,Donnie	13	L	29	aaa	CHW	27	3.87	1.83	7.3	6.1	7.7	1.3	0.5	36	79	55
	14	L	30	aaa	CHW	50	7.07	2.04	6.57	5.8	6.7	1.2	0.9	39	65	26
Velasquez,Jonathar	14	R	29	aa	NYM	55	4.05	1.22	5.02	2.2	6.2	2.8	0.4	31	65	89
Venditte,Patrick	14	L	29	a/a	NYY	78	3.57	1.41	8.07	2.9	7.1	2.4	1.0	32	78	64
Verdugo,Ryan	13	L	26	a/a	KC	70	5.81	1.78	18.9	4.3	5.0	1.2	1.4	34	70	5
	14	L	27	aaa	BOS	75	5.44	1.46	17	3.3	7.5	2.3	1.2	33	64	58

PITCHER	yr	t	age	lvl	org	ip	era	whip	bf/g	ctl	dom	f	hr/9	h%	s%	bpv
Verhagen,Drew	14	R	24	aaa	DET	110	4.56	1.49	25	2.1	4.1	2.0	0.5	34	68	45
Verrett,Logan	13	R	23	aa	NYM	146	4.45	1.20	24.4	1.8	7.2	4.0	1.3	30	67	91
	14	R	24	aaa	NYM	162	3.51	1.28	23.7	1.6	5.7	3.6	0.7	32	74	87
Villanueva,Elih	13	R	27	aaa	MIA	46	4.77	1.40	24.5	2.4	4.6	1.9	1.0	31	68	35
	14	R	28	aaa	MIA	137	4.97	1.62	22.5	3.2	5.1	1.6	1.0	34	71	27
Villarreal,Pedro	13	R	26	aaa	CIN	110	6.10	1.62	14.7	2.6	5.6	2.2	2.0	34	67	11
	14	R	27	aaa	CIN	56	3.66	1.42	5.69	2.1	6.4	3.0	1.0	34	77	69
Vizcaino,Arodys	14	R	24	a/a	CHC	32	4.97	1.61	4.57	4.1	7.5	1.8	0.6	35	68	62
Volstad,Chris	13	R	27	aaa	COL	128	5.15	1.77	25.5	3.1	2.9	0.9	1.0	34	72	-4
	14	R	28	aaa	LAA	39	5.63	1.56	24.6	2.5	4.2	1.7	1.3	33	66	16
Von Schamann,Duk	13	R	22	aa	LA	67	6.06	1.70	18.8	2.6	5.9	2.2	1.0	37	65	40
	14	R	23	a/a	CLE	152	4.65	1.35	23.4	2.0	3.7	1.8	1.0	30	67	29
Wada,Tsuyoshi	13	L	32	aaa	BAL	103	5.81	1.88	25.4	3.6	5.1	1.4	1.2	37	70	12
	14	L	33	aaa	CHC	114	3.71	1.48	25.7	2.6	7.0	2.7	1.3	34	80	55
Walczak,Jamie	13	R	26	aa	CIN	33	5.52	1.73	6.26	5.3	9.6	1.8	0.4	39	66	81
	14	R	27	aa	CIN	74	5.66	1.70	6.52	5.2	8.3	1.6	1.0	35	67	53
Walden,Marcus	13	R	25	aa	TOR	162	4.43	1.64	27.8	2.8	4.0	1.4	0.6	35	73	28
	14	R	26	a/a	OAK	99	5.83	1.71	12.9	3.9	4.4	1.1	0.7	34	65	20
Waldron,Tyler	13	R	24	aa	PIT	24	5.54	1.85	14.2	3.6	3.8	1.1	0.3	37	68	22
	14	R	25	a/a	PIT	41	4.06	1.39	10.2	2.5	6.0	2.4	0.6	33	71	68
Walker,Taijuan	13	R	21	a/a	SEA	141	3.30	1.25	23	3.4	9.2	2.7	0.7	31	75	100
	14	R	22	a/a	SEA	78	4.64	1.26	21.2	2.7	8.6	3.2	1.3	30	67	84
Wall,Josh	13	R	26	aaa	MIA	49	6.09	1.81	5.08	4.9	6.6	1.3	0.6	37	65	44
	14	R	27	aaa	PIT	45	3.75	1.64	5.54	3.8	6.8	1.8	0.4	36	77	62
Walters,P.J.	13	R	28	aaa	MIN	103	5.22	1.79	25.1	4.3	5.3	1.2	0.5	36	70	36
	14	R	29	a/a	TOR	142	7.05	1.83	24.4	3.4	6.0	1.8	1.6	37	63	12
Wang,Chien-Ming	13	R	33	aaa	TOR	110	4.02	1.48	26.2	2.1	3.4	1.6	0.6	33	73	31
	14	R	34	aaa	CHW	173	4.90	1.81	28.6	3.5	2.9	0.8	0.4	36	72	11
Webb,Tyler	14	L	24	a/a	NYY	56	4.89	1.48	5.99	3.5	10.3	2.9	1.0	37	68	93
Weber,Ryan	14	R	24	aa	ATL	101	5.43	1.64	14.1	1.5	4.7	3.2	0.7	38	66	62
Webster,Allen	13	R	23	aaa	BOS	105	4.39	1.19	20.1	3.7	8.3	2.3	0.8	27	64	85
	14	R	24	aaa	BOS	122	3.91	1.42	24.6	3.4	6.1	1.8	0.7	31	74	53
Werner,Andrew	13	L	26	aaa	OAK	165	6.13	1.59	27	2.1	4.8	2.3	1.0	36	61	39
	14	L	27	aa	OAK	47	7.67	1.82	15.6	4.1	5.4	1.3	1.4	35	58	9
West,Matthew	14	R	26	a/a	TEX	57	4.14	1.62	6.14	3.1	7.9	2.6	1.0	38	77	65
Wetherell,Philip	14	R	25	aa	NYY	42	5.43	1.91	7.41	4.8	5.4	1.1	0.3	38	70	37
Wheeler,Jason	14	L	24	a/a	MIN	79	3.49	1.33	25.3	2.1	5.3	2.6	1.1	31	78	54
Whelan,Kevin	13	R	29	a/a	CIN	51	7.32	1.93	5.12	7.0	9.9	1.4	2.2	35	66	21
	14	R	30	aaa	DET	43	3.79	1.48	4.55	5.0	7.9	1.6	0.0	32	72	86
White,Alex	14	R	26	aaa	HOU	64	7.17	1.88	12	4.4	6.1	1.4	1.0	37	61	24
White,Cole	13	R	25	aa	COL	48	5.82	1.98	5.08	7.0	6.0	0.9	0.6	34	70	32
	14	R	26	a/a	COL	52	4.07	1.67	4.94	6.9	5.5	0.8	0.9	27	78	28
Whiting,Boone	13	R	24	a/a	STL	136	4.15	1.43	21.5	3.0	7.2	2.4	0.8	33	72	69
	14	R	25	aaa	STL	97	4.40	1.53	20	4.0	7.4	1.9	0.7	34	72	61
Whitley,Chase	13	R	24	aaa	NYY	68	4.21	1.47	10	3.1	6.8	2.2	0.6	34	71	69
	14	R	25	aaa	NYY	31	2.40	1.09	12.2	2.4	8.6	3.6	0.0	31	75	137
Wieland,Joe	14	R	24	a/a	SD	33	2.87	1.08	21.3	1.2	6.2	5.0	0.5	30	74	133
Wilk,Adam	14	L	27	aaa	PIT	147	5.50	1.64	23.3	2.7	4.8	1.8	1.1	35	68	25
Williams,Ali	14	R	25	aa	KC	40	6.52	1.57	7.03	5.0	8.1	1.6	1.9	30	62	27
Williamson,Fabian	14	L	26	a/a	CIN	60	4.74	1.61	5.21	4.6	8.3	1.8	0.9	34	72	60
Wilson,Alex	13	R	27	aaa	BOS	17	4.92	1.58	5.34	2.9	6.5	2.3	1.2	35	72	43
	14	R	28	aaa	BOS	41	6.14	1.84	5.5	5.6	6.6	1.2	0.5	35	65	43
Wilson,Tyler	13	R	24	aa	BAL	89	4.55	1.35	23.3	2.2	5.8	2.6	1.6	30	72	41
	14	R	25	a/a	BAL	167	4.32	1.39	25.1	2.4	6.8	2.9	1.2	33	72	65
Winiarski,Cody	14	R	25	aa	CHW	45	9.91	2.09	6.55	4.5	9.0	2.0	0.7	45	49	57
Winkler,Daniel	13	R	23	aa	COL	27	4.27	1.48	22.9	3.6	6.1	1.7	1.5	30	76	28
	14	R	24	aa	COL	70	1.98	0.85	21.4	2.4	7.0	3.0	0.9	19	84	97
Wisler,Matthew	13	R	21	aa	SD	105	3.31	1.12	20.7	2.2	8.1	3.7	0.6	30	72	115
	14	R	22	a/a	SD	147	4.01	1.31	21.6	2.2	7.6	3.4	1.1	32	73	84
Wittgren,Nick	14	R	23	aa	MIA	66	4.02	1.45	5.42	1.9	6.4	3.4	0.7	35	73	82
Wojciechowski,Ashe	13	R	25	a/a	HOU	160	3.91	1.29	23.5	2.9	6.2	2.1	0.7	29	71	64
	14	R	26	aaa	HOU	76	5.22	1.61	22.4	2.5	5.7	2.3	1.2	35	70	36
Wood,Blake	13	R	28	aaa	CLE	23	3.50	1.75	4.14	6.3	8.9	1.4	0.0	36	78	84
	14	R	29	a/a	KC	33	7.03	2.36	5.9	8.8	8.0	0.9	0.9	40	70	29
Woodall,Bryan	13	R	27	a/a	ARI	62	4.40	1.54	5	3.2	7.6	2.4	1.3	34	75	52
	14	R	28	aa	ARI	38	5.18	1.51	16.6	2.9	4.9	1.7	1.2	32	68	25
Wooten,Eric	14	L	24	aa	NYY	40	5.10	1.49	24.4	2.6	4.0	1.5	0.9	32	66	24
Workman,Brandon	13	R	25	a/a	BOS	101	4.06	1.38	25	2.8	7.7	2.8	1.2	32	74	70
	14	R	26	aaa	BOS	61	5.54	1.55	24.4	2.7	6.3	2.4	1.7	33	69	29
Worley,Vance	13	R	26	aaa	MIN	58	4.63	1.63	28.7	2.7	4.1	1.5	0.5	35	71	34
	14	R	27	aaa	PIT	46	5.01	1.29	27	0.8	6.2	7.9	0.6	35	60	182
Wright,Austin	13	L	24	aa	PHI	94	6.66	1.71	15.8	5.6	6.2	1.1	1.4	31	62	19
	14	L	25	aa	PHI	48	5.98	1.94	7.14	8.5	5.9	0.7	1.1	29	70	21
Wright,Justin	13	L	24	aa	STL	59	5.70	1.73	5.37	3.7	8.0	2.2	0.8	39	67	60
	14	L	25	a/a	STL	58	3.77	1.30	5.05	3.1	6.5	2.1	0.3	31	69	79
Wright,Mike	13	R	23	a/a	BAL	150	3.75	1.47	23.9	2.4	6.9	2.9	0.7	36	75	78
	14	R	24	aaa	BAL	143	5.22	1.54	23.9	2.6	5.3	2.1	0.7	35	66	47
Wright,Steven	13	R	29	aaa	BOS	135	4.80	1.81	26.1	4.9	4.8	1.0	0.8	34	74	19
	14	R	30	aaa	BOS	100	5.01	1.51	27.1	2.4	4.7	1.9	1.2	33	69	28
Wyatt,Heath	13	R	25	aa	STL	47	3.55	1.31	5.39	1.9	5.8	3.1	0.9	32	75	73
	14	R	26	aaa	STL	66	4.65	1.34	6.13	2.3	3.8	1.7	0.6	30	65	40
Ybarra,Tyler	14	L	25	aa	TOR	53	5.76	1.57	6.12	5.4	6.0	1.1	1.7	27	67	12
Ynoa,Gabriel	14	R	21	aa	NYM	66	4.00	1.28	24.7	1.4	5.2	3.6	1.1	31	72	71
Yoon,Suk-Min	14	R	28	aaa	BAL	96	7.09	1.90	19.6	2.6	4.7	1.8	1.8	38	65	-4
Zagurski,Mike	13	L	30	aaa	OAK	53	3.49	1.48	5.1	4.4	10.3	2.4	0.6	36	78	95
	14	L	31	aaa	TOR	61	3.07	1.52	5.72	5.1	9.2	1.8	0.2	34	79	91
Zych,Tony	13	R	23	aa	CHC	56	3.69	1.44	5.07	3.5	5.4	1.6	0.4	31	74	55
	14	R	24	aa	CHC	58	5.97	1.80	5.98	2.9	4.5	1.6	0.5	38	65	31

This section provides rankings of projected skills indicators for 2015. Rather than take shots in the dark predicting league leaders in the exact number of home runs, or stolen bases, or strikeouts, the Forecaster's Leaderboards focus on the component elements of each skill.

For batters, we've ranked the top players in terms of pure power, speed, and batting average skill, breaking each down in a number of different ways to provide more insight. For pitchers, we rank some of the key base skills, differentiating between starters and relievers, and provide a few interesting cuts that might uncover some late round sleepers. And new in 2015, potential gainers/faders lists in several categories.

These are clearly not exhaustive lists of sorts and filters. If there is another cut you'd like to see, drop us a note and I'll consider it for next year's book. Also note that the database at BaseballHQ.com allows you to construct your own custom sorts and filters. Finally, remember that these are just tools. Some players will appear on multiple lists—even mutually exclusive lists—so you have to assess what makes most sense and make decisions for your specific application.

Power

Top PX, 400+ AB: Top power skills among projected full-time players.

Top PX, –300 AB: Top power skills among projected part-time players. Possible end-game options are here.

Position Scarcity: A quick scan to see which positions have deeper power options than others.

Top PX, ct% over 80%: Top power skills among the top contact hitters. Best pure power options here.

Top PX, ct% under 70%: Top power skills among the worst contact hitters. These are free-swingers who might be prone to streakiness or lower batting averages.

Top PX, FB% over 40%: Top power skills among the most extreme fly ball hitters. Most likely to convert their power into home runs.

Top PX, FB% under 35%: Top power skills among those with lesser fly ball tendencies. There may be more downside to their home run potential.

Speed

Top Spd, 400+ AB: Top speed skills among projected full-time players.

Top Spd, -300 AB: Top speed skills among projected part-time players. Possible end-game options here.

Position Scarcity: A quick scan to see which positions have deeper speed options than others.

Top Spd, OB% .330 and above: Top speed skills among those who get on base most often. Best opportunities for stolen bases here.

Top Spd, OB% under .300: Top speed skills among those who have trouble getting on base. These names may bear watching if they can improve their on base ability.

Top Spd, SBO% over 20%: Top speed skills among those who get the green light most often. Most likely to convert their speed into stolen bases.

Top Spd, SBO% under 15%: Top speed skills among those who are currently not getting the green light. There may be sleeper SBs here if given more opportunities to run.

Batting Average

Top ct%, 400+ AB: Top contact skills among projected full-time players. Contact does not always convert to higher BAs, but is still strongly correlated.

Top ct%, -300 AB: Top contact skills among projected part-time players. Possible end-gamers here.

Low ct%, 400+ AB: The poorest contact skills among projected full-time players. Potential BA killers.

Top ct%, bb% over 9%: Top contact skills among the most patient hitters. Best batting average upside here.

Top ct%, bb% under 6%: Top contact skills among the least patient hitters. These are free-swingers who might be prone to streakiness or lower batting averages.

Top ct%, GB% over 50%: Top contact skills among the most extreme ground ball hitters. A ground ball has a higher chance of becoming a hit than a non-HR fly ball so there may be some batting average upside here.

Top ct%, GB% under 40%: Top contact skills from those with lesser ground ball tendencies. These players make contact but hit more fly balls, which tend to convert to hits at a lower rate than GB.

Pitching Skills

Top Command: Leaders in projected K/BB rates.

Top Control: Leaders in fewest projected walks allowed.

Top Dominance: Leaders in projected strikeout rate.

Top Ground Ball Rate: GB pitchers tend to have lower ERAs (and higher WHIP) than fly ball pitchers.

Top Fly Ball Rate: FB pitchers tend to have higher ERAs (and lower WHIP) than ground ball pitchers.

High GB, Low Dom: GB pitchers tend to have lower K rates, but these are the most extreme examples.

High GB, High Dom: The best at dominating hitters and keeping the ball down. These are the pitchers who keep runners off the bases and batted balls in the park, a skills combination that is the most valuable a pitcher can own.

Lowest xERA: Leaders in projected skills-based ERA.

Top BPV: Two lists of top skilled pitchers. For starters, those projected to be rotation regulars (180+ IP) and fringe starters with skill (<150 IP). For relievers, those projected to be frontline closers (10+ saves) and high-skilled bullpen fillers (<9 saves).

Potential Gainers and Faders

These charts look to identify upcoming changes in performance by highlighting 2014 results that were in conflict with their corresponding skill indicators.

PX Gainers/Faders: Compares PX to xPX.

BA Gainers/Faders: Compares batter hit rate (h%) to HctX.

Dom Gainers/Faders: Compares K/9 to SwK%.

Ctl Gainers/Faders: Compares BB/9 to FpK%.

Additional details are provided on the page in which the charts appear.

Risk Management

These lists include players who've accumulated the most days on the disabled list over the past five years (Grade "F" in Health) and whose performance was the most consistent over the past three years. Also listed are the most reliable batters and pitchers overall, with a focus on positional and skills reliability. As a reminder, reliability in this context is not tied to skill level; it is a gauge of which players manage to accumulate playing time and post consistent output from year to year, whether that output is good or bad.

Mayberry Portfolio3 Plan

Players are sorted and ranked based on how they fit into the three draft tiers of the Portfolio3 Plan used in conjunction with the Mayberry Method, as updated in this year's Introduction. See page 1 for more details.

BATTER SKILLS RANKING - POWER

TOP PX, 400+ AB

NAME	POS	PX
Carter,Chris	0	214
Stanton,Giancarlo	9	208
Trout,Mike	8	199
Davis,Chris	3 5	195
Goldschmidt,Paul	3	194
Moss,Brandon	3 7 9	185
Arcia,Oswaldo	9	176
Kemp,Matt	7 8 9	170
Davis,Khristopher	7	170
Soler,Jorge	9	168
Springer,George	9	168
Cruz,Nelson	0 7	167
Gonzalez,Carlos	7	166
Upton,Justin	7	165
Encarnacion,Edwin	0 3	164
Gattis,Evan	2	164
Cabrera,Miguel	0 3	163
Alvarez,Pedro	5	163
Bautista,Jose	9	163
Rizzo,Anthony	3	163
Dickerson,Corey	7	163
Cuddyer,Michael	9	163
Ortiz,David	0	162
Abreu,Jose	0 3	162
Tulowitzki,Troy	6	160
Napoli,Mike	3	157
Trumbo,Mark	3 7	156
Belt,Brandon	3	156
McCutchen,Andrew	8	156
Baez,Javier	4 6	156
Mesoraco,Devin	2	154
Saltalamacchia,Jarrod	2	153
Votto,Joey	3	153
Martinez,J.D.	7 9	153
Duda,Lucas	3	152
Zunino,Mike	2	150
Braun,Ryan	9	148
Pearce,Steve	3 7	148
Hamilton,Josh	7	148
Lamb,Jacob	5	148

TOP PX, 300 or fewer AB

NAME	POS	PX
Gallo,Joey	5	217
Francisco,Juan	3 5	179
Van Slyke,Scott	3 7 8	173
Olt,Mike	5	172
Recker,Anthony	2	164
Ross,David	2	161
Reynolds,Mark	3 5	154
Willingham,Josh	0 7	151
Weeks,Rickie	4	146
Arencibia,J.P.	2 3	142
Ruf,Darin	3	141
Pinto,Josmil	0 2	141
Kratz,Erik	2	140
Blanks,Kyle	3	139
Mayberry,John	3	139
Phegley,Joshua	2	137
Rodriguez,Sean	0 4	137
Young,Chris	7 8	137
Soriano,Alfonso	0 9	135
Ruggiano,Justin	9	135
McKenry,Michael	2	131
Duvall,Adam	3	130
Barnes,Brandon	9	129

POSITIONAL SCARCITY

NAME	POS	PX
Carter,Chris	DH	214
Cruz,Nelson	2	167
Encarnacion,Edwin	3	164
Cabrera,Miguel	4	163
Ortiz,David	5	162
Abreu,Jose	6	162
Recker,Anthony	CA	164
Gattis,Evan	2	164
Ross,David	3	161
Mesoraco,Devin	4	154
Saltalamacchia,Jarrod	5	153
Zunino,Mike	6	150
Gomes,Yan	7	145
Arencibia,J.P.	8	142
Davis,Chris	1B	195
Goldschmidt,Paul	2	194
Moss,Brandon	3	185
Francisco,Juan	4	179
Van Slyke,Scott	5	173
Singleton,Jonathan	6	165
Encarnacion,Edwin	7	164
Cabrera,Miguel	8	163
Rizzo,Anthony	9	163
Abreu,Jose	10	162
Baez,Javier	2B	156
Weeks,Rickie	2	146
Alcantara,Arismendy	3	144
Rodriguez,Sean	4	137
Dozier,Brian	5	131
Rendon,Anthony	6	127
Valbuena,Luis	7	127
Baker,Jeff	8	125
Gallo,Joey	3B	217
Davis,Chris	2	195
Francisco,Juan	3	179
Olt,Mike	4	172
Bryant,Kris	5	165
Alvarez,Pedro	6	163
Reynolds,Mark	7	154
Lamb,Jacob	8	148
Zimmerman,Ryan	9	139
Santana,Carlos	10	136
Tulowitzki,Troy	SS	160
Baez,Javier	2	156
Ramirez,Hanley	3	134
Desmond,Ian	4	134
Peralta,Jhonny	5	123
Drew,Stephen	6	115
Flaherty,Ryan	7	113
Bogaerts,Xander	8	112
Stanton,Giancarlo	OF	208
Trout,Mike	2	199
Moss,Brandon	3	185
Arcia,Oswaldo	4	176
Van Slyke,Scott	5	173
Rasmus,Colby	6	173
Kemp,Matt	7	170
Davis,Khristopher	8	170
Soler,Jorge	9	168
Springer,George	10	168
Cruz,Nelson	11	167
Gonzalez,Carlos	12	166
Upton,Justin	13	165
Bautista,Jose	14	163
Dickerson,Corey	15	163
Cuddyer,Michael	16	163

TOP PX, Ct% over 80%

NAME	Ct%	PX
Encarnacion,Edwin	84	164
Cabrera,Miguel	82	163
Bautista,Jose	82	163
Cuddyer,Michael	81	163
Ortiz,David	81	162
Tulowitzki,Troy	84	160
Zimmerman,Ryan	82	139
Gonzalez,Adrian	82	135
Ramirez,Hanley	81	134
Arenado,Nolan	87	130
Lind,Adam	81	128
Quentin,Carlos	81	128
Fielder,Prince	83	127
Pujols,Albert	88	127
Rendon,Anthony	82	127
D Arnaud,Travis	81	127
Beltran,Carlos	81	127
Holliday,Matt	82	125
Wieters,Matt	81	124
Walker,Neil	82	123
McCann,Brian	83	123
Lawrie,Brett	81	123
Seager,Kyle	81	123
Machado,Manny	80	122
Reddick,Josh	81	121
Pillar,Kevin	83	121
Harrison,Josh	85	119
Franco,Maikel	80	118
Martinez,Victor	91	118
Betts,Mookie	85	117
Lucroy,Jonathan	86	117
Posey,Buster	86	117
Morneau,Justin	84	116
Cano,Robinson	87	116
Beltre,Adrian	87	116
Moustakas,Mike	82	113
Ramirez,Aramis	84	112
Hosmer,Eric	82	109
Cabrera,Asdrubal	80	109
Hunter,Torii	81	109

TOP PX, Ct% under 70%

NAME	Ct%	PX
Gallo,Joey	51	217
Carter,Chris	64	214
Stanton,Giancarlo	67	208
Davis,Chris	64	195
Moss,Brandon	68	185
Francisco,Juan	63	179
Arcia,Oswaldo	68	176
Van Slyke,Scott	69	173
Rasmus,Colby	67	173
Olt,Mike	60	172
Springer,George	61	168
Bryant,Kris	63	165
Singleton,Jonathan	60	165
Recker,Anthony	64	164
Alvarez,Pedro	69	163
Ross,David	62	161
Walters,Zachary	70	159
Napoli,Mike	66	157
Baez,Javier	63	156
Nieuwenhuis,Kirk	66	155
Reynolds,Mark	67	154
Saltalamacchia,Jarrod	64	153
Willingham,Josh	68	151

Top PX, FB% over 40%

NAME	FB%	PX
Gallo,Joey	53	217
Carter,Chris	50	214
Trout,Mike	45	199
Davis,Chris	41	195
Moss,Brandon	49	185
Francisco,Juan	40	179
Arcia,Oswaldo	42	176
Van Slyke,Scott	44	173
Rasmus,Colby	43	173
Olt,Mike	50	172
Springer,George	41	168
Cruz,Nelson	41	167
Bryant,Kris	45	165
Singleton,Jonathan	46	165
Encarnacion,Edwin	46	164
Recker,Anthony	49	164
Gattis,Evan	44	164
Bautista,Jose	44	163
Rizzo,Anthony	41	163
Ortiz,David	40	162
Ross,David	41	161
Tulowitzki,Troy	40	160
Belt,Brandon	43	156
McCutchen,Andrew	40	156
Baez,Javier	43	156
Reynolds,Mark	47	154
Mesoraco,Devin	40	154
Saltalamacchia,Jarrod	41	153
Duda,Lucas	47	152
Willingham,Josh	47	151
Zunino,Mike	46	150
Pearce,Steve	45	148
Cespedes,Yoenis	46	143
Arencibia,J.P.	48	142
Pinto,Josmil	40	141
Kratz,Erik	43	140
Mayberry,John	42	139
Adams,Matt	40	138
Phegley,Joshua	43	137
Rodriguez,Sean	42	137

Top PX, FB% under 35%

NAME	FB%	PX
Goldschmidt,Paul	34	194
Kemp,Matt	35	170
Cuddyer,Michael	29	163
Abreu,Jose	31	162
Votto,Joey	32	153
Lamb,Jacob	31	148
Weeks,Rickie	30	146
Puig,Yasiel	32	146
Alcantara,Arismendy	35	144
Morse,Michael	33	142
Flowers,Tyler	33	139
Zimmerman,Ryan	35	139
Freeman,Freddie	35	136
Jones,Adam	34	134
Ramirez,Hanley	34	134
Desmond,Ian	32	134
Avila,Alex	31	133
Marte,Starling	30	132
Harper,Bryce	34	132
Barnes,Brandon	33	129
Calhoun,Kole	34	128
Lind,Adam	33	128
Sanchez,Jorge Tony	32	127

BATTER SKILLS RANKING - SPEED

TOP Spd, 400+ AB

NAME	POS	Spd
Gordon,Dee	4	180
Marte,Starling	7 8	175
Hamilton,Billy	8	174
Santana,Daniel	6 8	162
Segura,Jean	6	161
Revere,Ben	8	161
Hechavarria,Adeiny	6	159
Pollock IV,A.J.	8	158
Jackson,Austin	8	158
Trout,Mike	8	151
Bourn,Michael	8	149
Fowler,Dexter	8	148
Escobar,Alcides	6	144
LeMahieu,DJ	4	144
Owings,Christopher	6	144
Pence,Hunter	9	142
Gardner,Brett	7 8	141
Eaton,Adam	8	141
Martin,Leonys	8	140
Panik,Joe	4	139
Puig,Yasiel	8 9	138
Betts,Mookie	8	138
Yelich,Christian S.	7	137
Jennings,Desmond	8	137
Odor,Rougned	4	133
Cozart,Zack	6	133
Semien,Marcus	4 5	133
Aoki,Norichika	9	132
McCutchen,Andrew	8	132
Pagan,Angel	8	131
Castillo,Rusney	8	131
Cain,Lorenzo	8 9	130
Dickerson,Corey	7	130
Upton,B.J.	8	130
Span,Denard	8	130
Alcantara,Arismendy	4 8	130
Reddick,Josh	9	129
Gomez,Carlos	8	129
Hicks,Aaron	8	129
Simmons,Andrelton	6	129

TOP Spd, 300 or fewer AB

NAME	POS	Spd
Taylor,Chris	6	165
Dyson,Jarrod	8	162
Kiermaier,Kevin	8 9	155
Gentry,Craig	8 9	154
Herrera,Dilson	4	148
Jones,James	8	144
Sierra,Moises	9	143
Young Jr.,Eric	7	142
Nunez,Eduardo	5 6	141
Gose,Anthony	8	141
Lough,David	7	141
Blanco,Gregor	7 8	138
Inciarte,Ender	7 8	135
Guyer,Brandon	7	135
Robertson,Daniel T.	7 8	133
Fuld,Sam	7 8	129
Gosselin,Phil	4	129
Herrera,Jonathan	6	128
Spangenberg,Cory	5	128
Green,Grant	7	128
Arias,Joaquin	5	128
Hernandez,Cesar	5	127
Kawasaki,Munenori	4	127

POSITIONAL SCARCITY

NAME	POS	Spd
Cespedes,Yoenis	DH	115
Forsythe,Logan	2	113
DeJesus,David	3	109
Rodriguez,Sean	4	105
Joyce,Matt	5	100
Hart,Corey	6	99
Holaday,Bryan	CA	104
Gomes,Yan	2	101
Lucroy,Jonathan	3	101
Nieto,Adrian	4	100
Cervelli,Francisco	5	99
Joseph,Caleb	6	97
Gosewisch,Tuffy	7	96
Jaso,John	8	95
Baker,Jeff	1B	124
Kelly,Don	2	119
Medica,Thomas	3	119
Goebbert,Jake	4	108
Belt,Brandon	5	107
Van Slyke,Scott	6	104
Frazier,Todd	7	101
Vogt,Stephen	8	101
Rosales,Adam	9	100
Lind,Adam	10	98
Gordon,Dee	2B	180
Herrera,Dilson	2	148
LeMahieu,DJ	3	144
Panik,Joe	4	139
Odor,Rougned	5	133
Bonifacio,Emilio	6	133
Semien,Marcus	7	133
Alcantara,Arismendy	8	130
Nunez,Eduardo	3B	141
Semien,Marcus	2	133
Spangenberg,Cory	3	128
Arias,Joaquin	4	128
Hernandez,Cesar	5	127
Escobar,Eduardo	6	123
Harrison,Josh	7	122
Machado,Manny	8	122
Franco,Maikel	9	121
Culberson,Charlie	10	121
Taylor,Chris	SS	165
Santana,Daniel	2	162
Segura,Jean	3	161
Hechavarria,Adeiny	4	159
Rutledge,Josh	5	154
Escobar,Alcides	6	144
Owings,Christopher	7	144
Nunez,Eduardo	8	141
Bourjos,Peter	OF	182
Marte,Starling	2	175
Hamilton,Billy	3	174
Dyson,Jarrod	4	162
Santana,Daniel	5	162
Revere,Ben	6	161
Pollock IV,A.J.	7	158
Jackson,Austin	8	158
Kiermaier,Kevin	9	155
Gentry,Craig	10	154
Stubbs,Drew	11	152
Trout,Mike	12	151
Bourn,Michael	13	149
Fowler,Dexter	14	148
Jones,James	15	144
Sierra,Moises	16	143

TOP Spd, .330+ OBP

NAME	OBP	Spd
Marte,Starling	349	175
Gentry,Craig	334	154
Trout,Mike	388	151
Fowler,Dexter	362	148
Gardner,Brett	340	141
Eaton,Adam	349	141
Puig,Yasiel	372	138
Blanco,Gregor	333	138
Betts,Mookie	365	138
Yelich,Christian S.	356	137
Guyer,Brandon	332	135
Aoki,Norichika	353	132
McCutchen,Andrew	394	132
Pagan,Angel	334	131
Dickerson,Corey	342	130
Span,Denard	349	130
Gomez,Carlos	340	129
Hicks,Aaron	332	129
Reyes,Jose	336	126
Altuve,Jose	344	123
Braun,Ryan	350	120
Profar,Jurickson	336	118
Springer,George	342	116
Ethier,Andre	350	115
Rendon,Anthony	353	114
Dozier,Brian	333	113
Harper,Bryce	348	113
Myers,Wil	334	111
Carpenter,Matt	374	111
Saunders,Michael	335	110
Jay,Jon	364	110
DeJesus,David	339	109
Belt,Brandon	331	107
Pedroia,Dustin	348	107
Markakis,Nick	342	107
Cuddyer,Michael	365	106
Grossman,Robert	339	106
Lowrie,Jed	332	105
Van Slyke,Scott	341	104
Zobrist,Ben	361	104

TOP Spd, OBP under .300

NAME	OBP	Spd
Jones,James	276	144
Owings,Christopher	289	144
Sierra,Moises	287	143
Nunez,Eduardo	282	141
Gose,Anthony	296	141
Robertson,Daniel T.	295	133
Cozart,Zack	275	133
Upton,B.J.	290	130
Ramirez,Jose	296	130
Alcantara,Arismendy	297	130
Simmons,Andrelton	298	129
Gosselin,Phil	293	129
Spangenberg,Cory	295	128
Green,Grant	273	128
Arias,Joaquin	287	128
Ahmed,Nick	278	126
Sardinas,Luis	289	125
Cowgill,Collin	293	124
Marisnick,Jake	276	124
Lake,Junior	277	124
Escobar,Eduardo	297	123
Franco,Maikel	278	121
Herrera,Elian	286	121

Top Spd, SBO% over 20%

NAME	SBO%	Spd
Gordon,Dee	45%	180
Marte,Starling	36%	175
Hamilton,Billy	50%	174
Dyson,Jarrod	52%	162
Santana,Daniel	24%	162
Segura,Jean	27%	161
Revere,Ben	32%	161
Pollock IV,A.J.	23%	158
Kiermaier,Kevin	21%	155
Gentry,Craig	34%	154
Stubbs,Drew	23%	152
Bourn,Michael	22%	149
Escobar,Alcides	22%	144
Jones,James	37%	144
Young Jr.,Eric	38%	142
Nunez,Eduardo	34%	141
Gose,Anthony	39%	141
Lough,David	26%	141
Martin,Leonys	30%	140
Betts,Mookie	24%	138
Inciarte,Ender	25%	135
Maybin,Cameron	22%	134
Bonifacio,Emilio	34%	133
Pagan,Angel	20%	131
Castillo,Rusney	33%	131
Cain,Lorenzo	23%	130
Upton,B.J.	23%	130
Ramirez,Jose	31%	130
Alcantara,Arismendy	26%	130
Gomez,Carlos	36%	129
Fuld,Sam	24%	129
Schafer,Jordan	44%	128
Spangenberg,Cory	36%	128
Venable,Will	23%	127
Hernandez,Cesar	20%	127
Marisnick,Jake	27%	124
Lake,Junior	23%	124
Altuve,Jose	29%	123
Cabrera,Everth	34%	123
Buxton,Byron	28%	120

Top Spd, SBO% under 15%

NAME	SBO%	Spd
Hechavarria,Adeiny	11%	159
Rutledge,Josh	14%	154
Trout,Mike	13%	151
Herrera,Dilson	12%	148
Fowler,Dexter	14%	148
Pence,Hunter	11%	142
Panik,Joe	9%	139
Puig,Yasiel	15%	138
Yelich,Christian S.	15%	137
Denorfia,Chris	14%	134
Gregorius,Didi	5%	133
Cozart,Zack	6%	133
Semien,Marcus	11%	133
McCutchen,Andrew	14%	132
Dickerson,Corey	9%	130
Reddick,Josh	6%	129
Hicks,Aaron	13%	129
Simmons,Andrelton	8%	129
Gosselin,Phil	8%	129
Iglesias,Jose	13%	128
Herrera,Jonathan	11%	128
Green,Grant	14%	128
Arias,Joaquin	6%	128

BATTER SKILLS RANKING - BATTING AVERAGE

TOP Ct%, 400+ AB

NAME	Ct%	BA
Martinez,Victor	91	315
Aoki,Norichika	91	287
Revere,Ben	91	298
Brantley,Michael	90	305
Altuve,Jose	89	309
Simmons,Andrelton	89	250
Aybar,Erick	89	276
Reyes,Jose	89	289
Span,Denard	88	293
Infante,Omar	88	276
Kinsler,Ian	88	270
Pujols,Albert	88	280
Suzuki,Kurt	88	260
Castillo,Rusney	88	272
Cabrera,Melky	88	303
Molina,Yadier	88	293
Prado,Martin	88	283
Pedroia,Dustin	87	287
Cano,Robinson	87	311
Markakis,Nick	87	277
Ramirez,Alexei	87	272
Escobar,Yunel	87	261
Beltre,Adrian	87	311
Perez,Salvador	87	283
Loney,James	87	286
Panik,Joe	87	262
Arenado,Nolan	87	289
Lucroy,Jonathan	86	291
Crisp,Coco	86	251
Posey,Buster	86	310
Sandoval,Pablo	86	280
Segura,Jean	86	267
Alonso,Yonder	86	266
Murphy,Daniel	86	288
Escobar,Alcides	86	268
Pagan,Angel	86	290
Phillips,Brandon	85	268
Murphy,David	85	266
Utley,Chase	85	268
Harrison,Josh	85	285
Betts,Mookie	85	286
Ellsbury,Jacoby	85	276
Andrus,Elvis	85	269
Encarnacion,Edwin	84	274
Morneau,Justin	84	294
Zobrist,Ben	84	276
Ramirez,Aramis	84	286
Navarro,Dioner	84	273
Pollock IV,A.J.	84	269
Tulowitzki,Troy	84	317
Lowrie,Jed	84	266
Hill,Aaron	84	261
Crawford,Carl	84	289
Peralta,David	83	274
Gennett,Scooter	83	277
McCann,Brian	83	248
Butler,Billy	83	285
Wong,Kolten	83	261
Cozart,Zack	83	234
Hechavarria,Adeiny	83	267
Eaton,Adam	83	285
Fielder,Prince	83	279
Rollins,Jimmy	83	247
Hardy,J.J.	83	252
Gillaspie,Conor	82	260
Blackmon,Charlie	82	270

LOW Ct%, 400+ AB

NAME	Ct%	BA
Springer,George	61	248
Baez,Javier	63	223
Davis,Chris	64	240
Saltalamacchia,Jarrod	64	242
Carter,Chris	64	241
Zunino,Mike	65	215
Upton,B.J.	66	212
Howard,Ryan	66	235
Napoli,Mike	66	246
Stanton,Giancarlo	67	271
Liriano,Rymer	68	239
Moss,Brandon	68	252
Arcia,Oswaldo	68	250
Alvarez,Pedro	69	237
Lamb,Jacob	70	258
Alcantara,Arismendy	71	240
Bruce,Jay	71	251
Castro,Jason	71	241
Hamilton,Josh	71	257
Martinez,J.D.	71	270
Saunders,Michael	71	250
Myers,Wil	71	267
Swisher,Nick	72	240
Trout,Mike	72	298
Upton,Justin	72	270
Duda,Lucas	72	243
Belt,Brandon	72	256
Trumbo,Mark	72	242
Granderson,Curtis	72	233
Byrd,Marlon	73	264
Gonzalez,Carlos	73	271
Hicks,Aaron	73	247
Kemp,Matt	73	286
Choo,Shin-Soo	73	260
Desmond,Ian	73	265
Grandal,Yasmani	73	246

TOP Ct%, 300 or fewer AB

NAME	Ct%	BA
Colon,Christian	89	270
Frandsen,Kevin	88	256
Pena,Brayan	88	261
Piscotty,Stephen	88	243
Izturis,Maicer	87	256
Inciarte,Ender	87	270
Aviles,Mike	87	249
Barney,Darwin	87	242
Sogard,Eric	86	240
Arias,Joaquin	86	263
Chavez,Endy	86	253
Lombardozzi,Steve	86	250
Tabata,Jose	86	259
Ruiz,Carlos	86	263
Pierzynski,A.J.	85	263
Hernandez,Enrique	85	246
Pacheco,Jordan	85	258
Ahmed,Nick	85	240
Amarista,Alexi	85	238
Lough,David	84	261
Sardinas,Luis	84	255
Robertson,Daniel T.	84	237
Nunez,Eduardo	84	248

TOP Ct%, bb% over 9%

NAME	bb%	Ct%
Martinez,Victor	10	91
Cano,Robinson	9	87
La Stella,Tommy	10	87
Hanigan,Ryan	13	86
Crisp,Coco	11	86
Posey,Buster	9	86
Utley,Chase	9	85
Betts,Mookie	10	85
Encarnacion,Edwin	12	84
Zobrist,Ben	12	84
Tulowitzki,Troy	11	84
Fuld,Sam	10	83
Kelly,Don	10	83
Fielder,Prince	14	83
Rollins,Jimmy	10	83
Jaso,John	11	82
Cabrera,Miguel	11	82
Holliday,Matt	11	82
Zimmerman,Ryan	9	82
Bautista,Jose	15	82
Morrison,Logan	9	82
Rendon,Anthony	9	82
McLouth,Nate	11	81
Polanco,Gregory	9	81
Carpenter,Matt	12	81
DeJesus,David	10	81
Ortiz,David	12	81
McGehee,Casey	9	81
Profar,Jurickson	9	81
Quentin,Carlos	10	81
Ramirez,Hanley	10	81
Descalso,Daniel	9	81
Santiago,Ramon	10	81
Mauer,Joe	12	81
Heyward,Jason	11	81
McCutchen,Andrew	12	80
Abreu,Jose	11	80
Pennington,Cliff	9	80
Sanchez,Gaby	10	80
Wright,David	9	79

TOP Ct%, bb% under 6%

NAME	bb%	Ct%
Revere,Ben	4	91
Altuve,Jose	5	89
Colon,Christian	6	89
Aybar,Erick	5	89
Frandsen,Kevin	3	88
Infante,Omar	5	88
Pena,Brayan	5	88
Castillo,Rusney	6	88
Prado,Martin	6	88
Ramirez,Alexei	4	87
Inciarte,Ender	5	87
Perez,Salvador	4	87
Aviles,Mike	4	87
Arenado,Nolan	5	87
Arias,Joaquin	3	86
Chavez,Endy	5	86
Lombardozzi,Steve	4	86
Tabata,Jose	6	86
Segura,Jean	5	86
Murphy,Daniel	5	86
Escobar,Alcides	4	86
Phillips,Brandon	5	85
Harrison,Josh	4	85

Top Ct%, GB% over 50%

NAME	GB%	Ct%
Aoki,Norichika	60	91
Revere,Ben	64	91
Colon,Christian	51	89
Frandsen,Kevin	51	88
Span,Denard	50	88
Ramirez,Jose	50	88
Inciarte,Ender	52	87
Escobar,Yunel	52	87
Arias,Joaquin	50	86
Chavez,Endy	51	86
Tabata,Jose	59	86
Segura,Jean	60	86
Suzuki,Ichiro	55	85
Andrus,Elvis	57	85
Pollock IV,A.J.	51	84
Sardinas,Luis	61	84
Robertson,Daniel T.	54	84
Nunez,Eduardo	50	84
Fuld,Sam	50	83
Peralta,David	51	83
Ramos,Wilson	56	83
Wong,Kolten	53	83
Hechavarria,Adeiny	52	83
Eaton,Adam	59	83
Hosmer,Eric	51	82
Iglesias,Jose	57	82
LeMahieu,DJ	56	82
Gonzalez,Marwin	53	82
Vazquez,Christian	57	82
Jay,Jon	52	82
Schumaker,Skip	55	81
Kendrick,Howie	56	81
Kawasaki,Munenori	58	81
Thole,Josh	54	81
Parra,Gerardo	54	81
McGehee,Casey	50	81
Presley,Alex	50	81
Holt,Brock	54	81
Young Jr.,Eric	59	81
Gordon,Dee	57	81

Top Ct%, GB% under 40%

NAME	GB%	Ct%
Infante,Omar	39	88
Kinsler,Ian	39	88
Arenado,Nolan	39	87
Sogard,Eric	39	86
Utley,Chase	40	85
Hernandez,Enrique	38	85
Encarnacion,Edwin	36	84
Lough,David	38	84
Ramirez,Aramis	39	84
Navarro,Dioner	40	84
Tulowitzki,Troy	39	84
Lowrie,Jed	32	84
Hill,Aaron	36	84
Kelly,Don	40	83
McCann,Brian	34	83
Gregorius,Didi	37	83
Vogt,Stephen	33	83
Gillaspie,Conor	39	82
Moustakas,Mike	38	82
Jaso,John	39	82
Dirks,Andy	38	82
Gonzalez,Adrian	38	82
Stewart,Chris	39	82

POTENTIAL SKILLS GAINERS AND FADERS - BATTERS

Power Gainers

Batters whose 2014 Power Index (PX) fell significantly short of their underlying power skill (xPX). If they show the same xPX skill in 2015, they are good candidates for more power output.

Power Faders

Batters whose 2014 Power Index (PX) noticeably outpaced their underlying power skill (xPX). If they show the same xPX skill in 2015, they are good candidates for less power output.

BA Gainers

Batters who had strong Hard Contact Index levels in 2014, but lower hit rates (h%). Since base hits come most often on hard contact, if these batters can make hard contact at the same strong rate again in 2015, they may get better results in terms of hit rate, resulting in a batting average improvement.

BA Faders

Batters who had weak Hard Contact Index levels in 2014, but higher hit rates (h%). Since base hits come most often on hard contact, if these batters only make hard contact at the same weak rate again in 2015, they may get worse results in terms of hit rate, resulting in a batting average decline.

PX GAINERS

NAME	PX	xPX
Sanchez, Hector	92	150
Vogt, Stephen	91	144
Moreland, Mitch	82	143
Hart, Corey	85	138
Ramirez, Aramis	90	131
Upton, B.J.	98	129
Overbay, Lyle	80	129
Crawford, Brandon	98	126
Montero, Miguel	88	124
Johnson, Reed	93	123
Moustakas, Mike	95	120
Headley, Chase	94	120
Bradley, Jackie	65	119
Baker, Jeff	92	118
Freese, David	97	117
Hill, Aaron	85	116
Gyorko, Jedd	89	115
Roberts, Brian	82	114
Wright, David	80	114
Middlebrooks, Will	70	114
Lowrie, Jed	75	112
Bogaerts, Xander	94	111
Sandoval, Pablo	85	111
Butler, Billy	79	111
Choo, Shin-Soo	99	110
Hundley, Nick	85	109
Suarez, Eugenio	72	109
Kubel, Jason	68	109
Corporan, Carlos	93	108
Almonte, Abraham	85	108
Fowler, Dexter	90	107
Parmelee, Chris	94	106
Utley, Chase	91	106
Perez, Salvador	91	106
Valencia, Danny	89	106
Gregorius, Didi	84	106
Craig, Allen	75	105

PX FADERS

NAME	PX	xPX
Santana, Daniel	113	63
Semien, Marcus	105	75
Johnson, Kelly	109	77
Coghlan, Chris	120	80
Medica, Thomas	131	82
Kiermaier, Kevin	120	82
DeJesus, David	106	82
Flowers, Tyler	131	88
Pence, Hunter	107	88
Garcia, Avisail	119	89
Alcantara, Arismendy	124	90
Snider, Travis	114	90
Gardner, Brett	112	91
Rosario, Wilin	115	92
Calhoun, Kole	123	94
Pollock IV, A.J.	128	97
Dozier, Brian	119	97
Singleton, Jonathan	152	105
Cuddyer, Michael	157	106
Weeks, Rickie	142	108
Ross, David	154	118
Pearce, Steve	180	130
Cruz, Nelson	165	131
Abreu, Jose	177	132
Dickerson, Corey	168	135
Stanton, Giancarlo	197	146
Trout, Mike	199	151
Francisco, Juan	202	156

BA GAINERS

NAME	h%	HctX
Ortiz, David	26	159
Pujols, Albert	27	139
Encarnacion, Edwin	26	137
Davis, Khristopher	28	132
LaRoche, Adam	28	126
D Arnaud, Travis	26	121
Alonso, Yonder	25	120
Lawrie, Brett	26	118
Donaldson, Josh	28	118
Alvarez, Pedro	28	118
Cabrera, Asdrubal	28	118
Santana, Carlos	25	117
Smoak, Justin	25	116
Moustakas, Mike	22	115
Perez, Salvador	28	115
McCann, Brian	23	114
Teixeira, Mark	24	114
Hill, Aaron	28	114
Montero, Miguel	28	113
Arencibia, J.P.	20	112
Trumbo, Mark	28	111
Viciedo, Dayan	26	110
Davis, Ike	27	110
Pinto, Josmil	27	110
Gonzalez, Carlos	28	109
Willingham, Josh	28	109
Rodriguez, Sean	24	108
Ackley, Dustin	27	108
Roberts, Brian	27	108
Grandal, Yasmani	28	108
Morales, Kendrys	25	106
Granderson, Curtis	27	106
Carter, Chris	27	106
Flores, Wilmer	27	106
Beltran, Carlos	26	105
Escobar, Yunel	28	105
Johnson, Reed	28	105

BA FADERS

NAME	h%	HctX
Lucas, Edward	34	55
Dyson, Jarrod	33	56
Cowgill, Collin	33	61
Gordon, Dee	35	62
Revere, Ben	33	64
Kubel, Jason	35	64
Suzuki, Ichiro	35	67
Marisnick, Jake	34	68
Tolleson, Steve	34	69
Bourn, Michael	34	70
Cain, Lorenzo	38	72
Barnes, Brandon	36	79
Flowers, Tyler	36	82
Chisenhall, Lonnie	33	83
Escobar, Alcides	33	83
Johnson, Chris	35	83
Ruggiano, Justin	39	84
Pagan, Angel	34	86
Jackson, Austin	33	86
Santana, Daniel	41	87
Eaton, Adam	36	87
Martin, Leonys	34	88
Tabata, Jose	33	88
Campbell, Eric	36	89
Panik, Joe	34	91
Weeks, Rickie	36	92
Harper, Bryce	35	92
Rios, Alex	34	92
Iannetta, Chris	34	93
Gonzalez, Marwin	33	93
Lagares, Juan	35	93
Vargas, Kennys	35	94
Holt, Brock	35	95
Altuve, Jose	36	95

PITCHER SKILLS RANKINGS - Starting Pitchers

Top Command (k/bb)

NAME	Cmd
Lee,Cliff	7.0
Hughes,Phil	5.5
Tanaka,Masahiro	5.5
Kershaw,Clayton	5.4
Petit,Yusmeiro	5.0
Zimmermann,Jordan	4.9
Price,David	4.8
Iwakuma,Hisashi	4.7
Hernandez,Felix	4.6
Sale,Chris	4.6
Strasburg,Stephen	4.6
Bumgarner,Madison	4.2
Colon,Bartolo	4.2
McCarthy,Brandon	4.1
Greinke,Zack	4.0
Ryu,Hyun-Jin	4.0
Haren,Dan	4.0
Tomlin,Josh	4.0
Pineda,Michael	4.0
Kluber,Corey	4.0
Scherzer,Max	3.9
Stroman,Marcus	3.8
Fister,Doug	3.8
Sabathia,CC	3.8
Shoemaker,Matthew	3.7
Fernandez,Jose	3.7
Hamels,Cole	3.7
Darvish,Yu	3.6
Wainwright,Adam	3.6
Wood,Alex	3.6
Teheran,Julio	3.6

Top Control (bb/9)

NAME	Ctl
Lee,Cliff	1.2
Hughes,Phil	1.4
Colon,Bartolo	1.4
Tanaka,Masahiro	1.5
Zimmermann,Jordan	1.5
Fister,Doug	1.6
Iwakuma,Hisashi	1.6
McCarthy,Brandon	1.6
Tomlin,Josh	1.7
Petit,Yusmeiro	1.8
Bergman,Christian	1.8
Arroyo,Bronson	1.8
Price,David	1.8
Kershaw,Clayton	1.9
Haren,Dan	1.9
Hendricks,Kyle	1.9
Shoemaker,Matthew	1.9
Alvarez,Henderson	1.9
Porcello,Rick	2.0
Lohse,Kyle	2.0
Hernandez,Felix	2.0
Roark,Tanner	2.0
Buehrle,Mark	2.0
Pineda,Michael	2.0
Kuroda,Hiroki	2.0
Wainwright,Adam	2.1
Bumgarner,Madison	2.1
Oberholtzer,Brett	2.1
Ryu,Hyun-Jin	2.1
Greinke,Zack	2.1
Hudson,Tim	2.2

Top Dominance (k/9)

NAME	Dom
Darvish,Yu	11.4
Sale,Chris	10.2
Strasburg,Stephen	10.1
Scherzer,Max	10.1
Kershaw,Clayton	9.9
Norris,Daniel	9.6
Salazar,Danny	9.5
Fernandez,Jose	9.4
Liriano,Francisco	9.4
Cingrani,Tony	9.4
Hernandez,Felix	9.2
Kluber,Corey	9.1
Gonzalez,Gio	9.0
Price,David	8.9
Jimenez,Ubaldo	8.9
Harvey,Matt	8.9
Wheeler,Zack	8.8
Arrieta,Jake	8.8
Petit,Yusmeiro	8.8
Syndergaard,Noah	8.8
Wood,Alex	8.7
Bumgarner,Madison	8.7
Beachy,Brandon	8.6
Hamels,Cole	8.6
Samardzija,Jeff	8.6
Greinke,Zack	8.6
Lee,Cliff	8.6
Sabathia,CC	8.6
Burnett,A.J.	8.6
Walker,Taijuan	8.6
Meyer,Alex	8.5

Top Ground Ball Rate

NAME	GB
Anderson,Brett	61
Keuchel,Dallas	59
Flande,Yohan	58
Morton,Charlie	58
Treinen,Blake	56
Cobb,Alex	56
Masterson,Justin	56
House,T.J.	55
Gray,Sonny	55
Paxton,James	55
Alvarez,Henderson	54
Cosart,Jarred	54
Ross,Tyson	54
Hernandez,Felix	54
Carroll,Scott	53
Garcia,Jaime	53
Richards,Garrett	53
Hudson,Tim	53
Burnett,A.J.	53
Peralta,Wily	53
Despaigne,Odrisamer	52
Bolsinger,Michael	52
Chatwood,Tyler	52
Gibson,Kyle	52
Hernandez,Roberto	52
Liriano,Francisco	52
Porcello,Rick	52
Kelly,Joe	52
Leake,Mike	51
Carrasco,Carlos	51
Buchanan,David	51

Top Fly Ball Rate

NAME	FB
Young,Chris	59
Ranaudo,Anthony	52
Straily,Dan	51
Odorizzi,Jake	49
Pino,Yohan	48
Baker,Scott	48
Martinez,Nicholas	47
Corcino,Daniel	47
Weaver,Jered	47
Santiago,Hector	46
Lewis,Colby	46
Tropeano,Nicholas	46
Griffin,A.J.	45
Pineda,Michael	45
Holmberg,David	45
Montero,Rafael	44
Peavy,Jake	44
Cingrani,Tony	44
Norris,Daniel	44
Duffy,Danny	44
Petit,Yusmeiro	44
Peacock,Brad	44
Wood,Travis	44
Hughes,Phil	43
Gonzales,Marco	43
Cole,A.J.	43
Nuno,Vidal	43
Fiers,Mike	43
Hand,Brad	43
Beachy,Brandon	43
Teheran,Julio	43

High GB, Low Dom

NAME	GB	Dom
Flande,Yohan	58	5.1
Morton,Charlie	58	6.2
Treinen,Blake	56	5.3
House,T.J.	55	6.5
Alvarez,Henderson	54	5.0
Cosart,Jarred	54	6.0
Carroll,Scott	53	4.5
Hudson,Tim	53	5.7
Chatwood,Tyler	52	5.4
Gibson,Kyle	52	5.6
Hernandez,Roberto	52	5.7
Porcello,Rick	52	6.0
Kelly,Joe	52	5.9
Leake,Mike	51	6.3
Buchanan,David	51	5.1
Fister,Doug	50	6.1
Perez,Martin	50	6.0
Lyles,Jordan	50	6.4
Locke,Jeff	49	6.2
Matzek,Tyler	48	6.2
Simon,Alfredo	48	6.4
Cumpton,Brandon	48	4.9
Harrison,Matt	48	5.4
Hendricks,Kyle	48	6.0
Feldman,Scott	47	5.8
Worley,Vance	46	6.1
Turner,Jacob	46	5.6
Arroyo,Bronson	45	5.3
Kendrick,Kyle	45	5.4
Chacin,Jhoulys	45	5.8
Gee,Dillon	45	6.4

High GB, High Dom

NAME	GB	Dom
Ross,Tyson	54	8.3
Hernandez,Felix	54	9.2
Burnett,A.J.	53	8.6
Liriano,Francisco	52	9.4
Carrasco,Carlos	51	8.5
Stroman,Marcus	50	8.4
Wheeler,Zack	50	8.8
Ryu,Hyun-Jin	49	8.4
Cole,Gerrit	49	8.1
Kershaw,Clayton	49	9.9
Meyer,Alex	48	8.5
Greinke,Zack	48	8.6
Samardzija,Jeff	48	8.6
Sabathia,CC	48	8.6
Johnson,Josh	47	8.4
Fernandez,Jose	47	9.4
Cueto,Johnny	47	8.1
Wood,Alex	47	8.7
Syndergaard,Noah	47	8.8
Ventura,Yordano	47	8.1
Kluber,Corey	47	9.1
Arrieta,Jake	47	8.8
Strasburg,Stephen	46	10.1
Lee,Cliff	46	8.6
Gonzalez,Gio	46	9.0
Degrom,Jacob	46	8.1
Walker,Taijuan	45	8.6
Lester,Jon	45	8.4
Bumgarner,Madison	45	8.7
Hamels,Cole	45	8.6
Rodon,Carlos	45	8.5

Lowest xERA

NAME	xERA
Kershaw,Clayton	2.44
Hernandez,Felix	2.56
Strasburg,Stephen	2.63
Sale,Chris	2.68
Darvish,Yu	2.75
Lee,Cliff	2.82
Fernandez,Jose	2.83
Greinke,Zack	2.92
Tanaka,Masahiro	2.92
Price,David	2.93
Kluber,Corey	2.94
Ryu,Hyun-Jin	2.95
Bumgarner,Madison	2.96
Iwakuma,Hisashi	2.97
Scherzer,Max	2.98
Wood,Alex	3.00
Stroman,Marcus	3.00
Cobb,Alex	3.00
Hamels,Cole	3.04
Sabathia,CC	3.05
Samardzija,Jeff	3.05
Carrasco,Carlos	3.06
Syndergaard,Noah	3.08
Cueto,Johnny	3.09
Ross,Tyson	3.10
Wainwright,Adam	3.11
Harvey,Matt	3.11
Zimmermann,Jordan	3.12
Richards,Garrett	3.12
Cole,Gerrit	3.15
Arrieta,Jake	3.15

Top BPV, 180+ IP

NAME	BPV
Kershaw,Clayton	155
Strasburg,Stephen	147
Sale,Chris	145
Hernandez,Felix	144
Darvish,Yu	138
Price,David	131
Scherzer,Max	127
Kluber,Corey	127
Bumgarner,Madison	124
Greinke,Zack	123
Iwakuma,Hisashi	120
Wood,Alex	116
Hamels,Cole	115
Zimmermann,Jordan	115
Hughes,Phil	113
Samardzija,Jeff	113
Lester,Jon	108
Cobb,Alex	105
Wainwright,Adam	104
McCarthy,Brandon	104
Cueto,Johnny	103
Cole,Gerrit	103
Arrieta,Jake	101
Sanchez,Anibal	100
Gonzalez,Gio	98
Shields,James	97
Ross,Tyson	95
Fister,Doug	95
Teheran,Julio	95
McHugh,Collin	94
Shoemaker,Matthew	94

Top BPV, <150 IP

NAME	BPV
Lee,Cliff	145
Fernandez,Jose	126
Petit,Yusmeiro	122
Sabathia,CC	119
Syndergaard,Noah	115
Pineda,Michael	103
Richards,Garrett	97
Skaggs,Tyler	96
Tomlin,Josh	92
Walker,Taijuan	90
Johnson,Josh	90
Garcia,Jaime	89
Beachy,Brandon	89
Corbin,Patrick	87
House,T.J.	83
Anderson,Brett	82
Heaney,Andrew	81
Montero,Rafael	78
Lyons,Tyler	77
Rodriguez,Wandy	77
Nelson,Jimmy	76
Kelly,Casey	75
Gonzales,Marco	75
Erlin,Robert	75
Worley,Vance	74
Ramirez,Erasmo	74
Hudson,Daniel	73
DeSclafani,Anthony	71
Cingrani,Tony	71
Pomeranz,Drew	71
Cole,A.J.	70

PITCHER SKILLS RANKINGS - Relief Pitchers

Top Command (k/bb)

NAME	Cmd
Uehara,Koji	10.9
Doolittle,Sean	6.5
Romo,Sergio	5.5
Melancon,Mark	5.5
Jansen,Kenley	5.0
Perkins,Glen	4.9
Fien,Casey	4.9
Soria,Joakim	4.8
McGee,Jake	4.7
Papelbon,Jonathan	4.7
Betances,Dellin	4.4
Maness,Michael	4.4
Vincent,Nick	4.2
Mujica,Edward	4.2
Janssen,Casey	4.2
Qualls,Chad	4.1
Kimbrel,Craig	4.1
Watson,Tony	4.0
Boxberger,Brad	4.0
Holland,Greg	4.0
O Day,Darren	4.0
Chapman,Aroldis	4.0
Medlen,Kris	4.0
Peralta,Joel	4.0
Robertson,David	3.9
Street,Huston	3.9
Benoit,Joaquin	3.9
Otero,Dan	3.8
Salas,Fernando	3.8
Reed,Addison	3.8
Hunter,Tommy	3.7

Top Control (bb/9)

NAME	Ctl
Uehara,Koji	1.0
Maness,Michael	1.3
Otero,Dan	1.4
Mujica,Edward	1.6
Fien,Casey	1.6
Melancon,Mark	1.6
Doolittle,Sean	1.7
Hunter,Tommy	1.7
Janssen,Casey	1.7
Romo,Sergio	1.8
Qualls,Chad	1.8
Soria,Joakim	1.8
Medlen,Kris	1.8
Perkins,Glen	1.9
Atchison,Scott	2.0
Papelbon,Jonathan	2.0
Watson,Tony	2.1
Greenwood,Nick	2.1
Hawkins,LaTroy	2.2
Street,Huston	2.2
Gregerson,Luke	2.2
Vincent,Nick	2.2
Storen,Drew	2.2
Abad,Fernando	2.2
Thayer,Dale	2.2
Neshek,Pat	2.3
Collmenter,Josh	2.3
O Day,Darren	2.3
Badenhop,Burke	2.3
Morin,Michael	2.3
McGee,Jake	2.4

Top Dominance (k/9)

NAME	Dom
Chapman,Aroldis	16.3
Jansen,Kenley	13.7
Kimbrel,Craig	13.5
Miller,Andrew	13.3
Boxberger,Brad	12.9
Holland,Greg	12.6
Robertson,David	12.3
Betances,Dellin	12.3
Bastardo,Antonio	11.5
Fujikawa,Kyuji	11.5
Diekman,Jake	11.4
Uehara,Koji	11.4
Giles,Kenneth	11.3
Perez,Oliver	11.2
Rosenthal,Trevor	11.2
Allen,Cody	11.1
Bedrosian,Cam	11.1
McGee,Jake	11.1
Doolittle,Sean	11.0
Frieri,Ernesto	11.0
Kelley,Shawn	11.0
Jaime,Juan	10.9
Davis,Wade	10.9
Walden,Jordan	10.7
Rondon,Bruce	10.7
Furbush,Charlie	10.7
Cecil,Brett	10.6
Capps,Carter	10.6
Fields,Joshua	10.6
Alburquerque,Al	10.6
Benoit,Joaquin	10.5

Top Ground Ball Rate

NAME	GB
Britton,Zach	69
Ziegler,Brad	66
Lopez,Javier	64
Dyson,Sam	63
Petricka,Jacob	63
Affeldt,Jeremy	62
Jeffress,Jeremy	62
Hughes,Jared	61
Maness,Michael	61
Marshall,Evan	61
Sanchez,Aaron	60
Greenwood,Nick	60
Johnson,Jim	60
Rzepczynski,Marc	60
Belisario,Ronald	60
League,Brandon	59
Familia,Jeurys	59
Qualls,Chad	59
McFarland,T.J.	59
Schlitter,Brian	58
Melancon,Mark	58
O Flaherty,Eric	58
Kintzler,Brandon	57
Badenhop,Burke	57
Hale,David	57
Wright,Jamey	56
Smith,Joe	56
Freeman,Sam	56
Avilan,Luis	56
Otero,Dan	56
Morris,Bryan	56

Top Fly Ball Rate

NAME	FB
Doolittle,Sean	54
Clippard,Tyler	53
Frieri,Ernesto	53
Bastardo,Antonio	52
Neshek,Pat	51
Peralta,Joel	51
Hoover,J.J.	51
Sipp,Tony	50
Ramirez,Neil	50
Fields,Joshua	50
Redmond,Todd	50
Feliz,Neftali	48
Uehara,Koji	48
Reed,Addison	48
Kelley,Shawn	47
Allen,Cody	47
Fien,Casey	47
Benoit,Joaquin	47
Matusz,Brian	46
McGowan,Dustin	46
Estrada,Marco	46
Soriano,Rafael	46
Rodriguez,Fernando	45
Yates,Kirby	45
Pimentel,Stolmy	45
Dunn,Mike	44
Street,Huston	44
Salas,Fernando	44
Matsuzaka,Daisuke	44
Pestano,Vinnie	43
Brach,Brad	43

High GB, Low Dom

NAME	GB	Dom
Ziegler,Brad	66	6.3
Lopez,Javier	64	5.8
Dyson,Sam	63	6.3
Petricka,Jacob	63	6.4
Hughes,Jared	61	5.6
Maness,Michael	61	5.6
Greenwood,Nick	60	4.3
League,Brandon	59	5.4
McFarland,T.J.	59	5.7
Schlitter,Brian	58	5.5
Kintzler,Brandon	57	5.7
Badenhop,Burke	57	5.6
Hale,David	57	5.3
Avilan,Luis	56	5.4
Otero,Dan	56	5.4
Atchison,Scott	54	6.0
Maholm,Paul	53	5.0
Lindstrom,Matt	52	6.0
Gomez,Jeanmar	50	5.6
Hardy,Blaine	49	6.5
Hollands,Mario	49	6.2
Hawkins,LaTroy	48	5.9
Williams,Jerome	47	6.1
Beimel,Joe	47	4.7
Bettis,Chad	47	6.4
Detwiler,Ross	47	5.5
Hunter,Tommy	46	6.4
Duensing,Brian	45	6.3
Swarzak,Anthony	44	5.4
Mikolas,Miles	42	5.6
Bueno,Francisley	42	5.6

High GB, High Dom

NAME	GB	Dom
Marshall,Evan	61	8.2
Rzepczynski,Marc	60	8.3
Familia,Jeurys	59	8.2
Melancon,Mark	58	9.0
Leone,Dominic	55	9.4
Mejia,Jenrry	55	8.8
Duke,Zach	54	8.7
Strop,Pedro	54	10.1
Parnell,Bobby	54	8.6
Medina,Yoervis	54	9.4
Wilson,Justin	53	8.3
Simmons,Shae	52	10.3
Smith,Carson	52	9.5
Webb,Daniel	52	8.4
Rodney,Fernando	51	10.0
Cecil,Brett	50	10.6
Cishek,Steve	49	10.5
Miller,Andrew	49	13.3
Chamberlain,Joba	48	8.3
Herrera,Kelvin	48	8.9
Adams,Mike	48	9.4
Axford,John	48	10.0
Kahnle,Thomas	47	9.1
Ottavino,Adam	47	9.1
Hatcher,Chris	47	8.0
Rondon,Hector	47	8.1
Grimm,Justin	47	8.3
Betances,Dellin	46	12.3
Fujikawa,Kyuji	46	11.5
Robertson,David	46	12.3
Cook,Ryan	46	8.9

Lowest xERA

NAME	xERA
Chapman,Aroldis	1.78
Kimbrel,Craig	2.04
Jansen,Kenley	2.19
Miller,Andrew	2.21
Betances,Dellin	2.28
Holland,Greg	2.29
Uehara,Koji	2.33
Melancon,Mark	2.37
Robertson,David	2.39
Boxberger,Brad	2.40
McGee,Jake	2.58
Fujikawa,Kyuji	2.61
Cishek,Steve	2.63
Doolittle,Sean	2.65
Simmons,Shae	2.65
Giles,Kenneth	2.72
Romo,Sergio	2.73
Davis,Wade	2.74
Strop,Pedro	2.82
Farquhar,Daniel	2.82
Leone,Dominic	2.82
Smith,Carson	2.85
Cecil,Brett	2.86
Benoit,Joaquin	2.86
Papelbon,Jonathan	2.87
Furbush,Charlie	2.88
Perkins,Glen	2.90
Smith,Joe	2.92
Qualls,Chad	2.92
Duke,Zach	2.94
Britton,Zach	2.95

Top BPV, 10+ Saves

NAME	BPV
Chapman,Aroldis	202
Uehara,Koji	188
Jansen,Kenley	186
Kimbrel,Craig	176
Betances,Dellin	170
Holland,Greg	165
Boxberger,Brad	164
Robertson,David	160
Doolittle,Sean	159
McGee,Jake	155
Melancon,Mark	153
Romo,Sergio	144
Cishek,Steve	135
Papelbon,Jonathan	134
Perkins,Glen	133
Benoit,Joaquin	132
Soria,Joakim	127
Allen,Cody	123
Qualls,Chad	118
Reed,Addison	117
Rodriguez,Francisco	114
Street,Huston	108
Storen,Drew	105
Rosenthal,Trevor	105
Parnell,Bobby	104
Fields,Joshua	103
Janssen,Casey	102
Rondon,Hector	100
Rodney,Fernando	99
Mejia,Jenrry	95
Britton,Zach	91

Top BPV, <10 Saves

NAME	BPV
Miller,Andrew	166
Fujikawa,Kyuji	138
Giles,Kenneth	138
Simmons,Shae	134
Davis,Wade	132
Furbush,Charlie	131
Farquhar,Daniel	126
Vincent,Nick	124
Capps,Carter	122
Peralta,Joel	122
O Day,Darren	121
Smith,Carson	119
Cecil,Brett	118
Watson,Tony	115
Duke,Zach	115
Kelley,Shawn	113
Rondon,Bruce	113
Bedrosian,Cam	111
Clippard,Tyler	111
Leone,Dominic	111
Salas,Fernando	111
Tazawa,Junichi	111
Carpenter,David	110
Grilli,Jason	110
Smith,Will	109
Gregerson,Luke	109
Fien,Casey	108
Ottavino,Adam	107
Jepsen,Kevin	106
Maness,Michael	106
Thayer,Dale	106

POTENTIAL SKILLS GAINERS AND FADERS - PITCHERS

Dom Gainers

From a pitcher's swinging-strike rate (SwK%) , we can establish a typical range in which we would expect to find their Dom (k/9). The pitchers on this list posted a 2014 Dom that was in the bottom of that expected range based on their SwK%. The names above the break line are in the bottom 10% of that range, and are the strongest candidates for Dom gains. The names below the break line are in the bottom 25%, and are also good candidates for strikeout gains.

Dom Faders

From a pitcher's swinging-strike rate (SwK%) , we can establish a typical range in which we would expect to find their Dom (k/9). The pitchers on this list posted a 2014 Dom that was in the top of that expected range based on their SwK%. The names above the break line are in the top 10% of that range, and are the strongest candidates for a Dom fade. The names below the break line are in the top 25%, and are also good candidates for a Dom fade.

Ctl Gainers

From a pitcher's first-pitch strike rate (FpK%) , we can establish a typical range in which we would expect to find their Ctl (bb/9). These pitchers posted a 2014 Ctl that was in the bottom of that expected range based on their FpK%. The names above the break line are in the bottom 10% of that range, and are the strongest candidates for Ctl gains. The names below the break line are in the bottom 25%, and are also good candidates for Ctl gains.

Ctl Faders

From a pitcher's first-pitch strike rate (FpK%) , we can establish a typical range in which we would expect to find their Ctl (bb/9). These pitchers posted a 2014 Ctl that was in the 10% of that expected range based on their FpK%, making them the strongest candidates for a Ctl fade.

DOM GAINERS

NAME	SwK	K/9
Bailey,Homer	11	7.7
Teheran,Julio	11	7.6
Estrada,Marco	11	7.6
Dickey,R.A.	11	7.2
Ventura,Yordano	11	7.8
de la Rosa,Jorge	10	6.8
Kuroda,Hiroki	10	6.6
Noesi,Hector	10	6.4
Locke,Jeff	10	6.1
Vargas,Jason	9	6.2
Nolasco,Ricky	9	6.5
Keuchel,Dallas	9	6.6
Eovaldi,Nathan	9	6.4
Hamels,Cole	13	8.7
Santana,Ervin	12	8.2
Samardzija,Jeff	12	8.3
Shoemaker,Matthew	11	8.2
Cobb,Alex	11	8.1
Jackson,Edwin	11	7.9
Zimmermann,Jordan	11	8.2
Wacha,Michael	11	7.9
Lackey,John	10	7.5
Elias,Roenis	10	7.9
Smyly,Drew	10	7.8
Lincecum,Tim	10	7.7
Hammel,Jason	10	8.1
Shields,James	10	7.1
House,T.J.	10	7.1
Peavy,Jake	10	7.0
Iwakuma,Hisashi	10	7.7
Sanchez,Anibal	10	7.3
Garza,Matt	9	6.9
Weaver,Jered	9	7.1
Wainwright,Adam	9	7.1
Verlander,Justin	9	6.9
Gausman,Kevin	9	7.0
Koehler,Tom	9	7.2

DOM FADERS

NAME	SwK	K/9
Darvish,Yu	11	11.3
Price,David	11	9.8
Arrieta,Jake	11	9.6
Wilson,C.J.	8	7.7
Happ,J.A.	8	7.6
Santiago,Hector	8	7.6
Jimenez,Ubaldo	7	8.3
Wood,Travis	7	7.6
Colon,Bartolo	6	6.7
Worley,Vance	6	6.4
Phelps,David	6	7.3
Hernandez,Felix	13	9.5
Kluber,Corey	12	10.3
Scherzer,Max	12	10.3
Strasburg,Stephen	12	10.1
Salazar,Danny	12	9.8
Kennedy,Ian	11	9.3
Wheeler,Zack	10	9.1
Lester,Jon	10	9.0
Odorizzi,Jake	10	9.3
Cole,Gerrit	10	9.0
Hughes,Phil	9	8.0
Ryu,Hyun-Jin	9	8.2
Burnett,A.J.	9	8.0
Bauer,Trevor	9	8.4
Lynn,Lance	9	8.0
Chavez,Jesse	9	8.4
Peacock,Brad	9	8.1
Quintana,Jose	9	8.0
Norris,Bud	8	7.6
Vogelsong,Ryan	8	7.4
Minor,Mike	8	7.4
Gallardo,Yovani	7	6.8

CTL GAINERS

NAME	FpK	BB/9
Nuno,Vidal	67	2.6
Miley,Wade	63	3.4
Phelps,David	62	3.7
Wilson,C.J.	59	4.4
Deduno,Samuel	58	4.1
Cahill,Trevor	57	4.5
Peacock,Brad	57	4.8
Masterson,Justin	55	4.8
Jimenez,Ubaldo	55	5.5
Lewis,Colby	66	2.5
Peavy,Jake	64	2.8
Garza,Matt	64	2.8
Wacha,Michael	64	2.8
Kennedy,Ian	64	3.1
Anderson,Chase	63	3.1
Chavez,Jesse	63	3.0
Dickey,R.A.	63	3.1
Odorizzi,Jake	61	3.2
Ventura,Yordano	61	3.4
Danks,John	61	3.4
Miller,Shelby	60	3.6
Elias,Roenis	60	3.5
Cosart,Jarred	58	3.6
Wood,Travis	57	3.9
Burnett,A.J.	56	4.0
Morales,Franklin	56	4.1
Liriano,Francisco	56	4.5

CTL FADERS

NAME	FpK	BB/9
Vargas,Jason	63	2.0
Eovaldi,Nathan	63	1.9
Shoemaker,Matthew	63	1.6
Shields,James	63	1.7
Greinke,Zack	63	1.9
Worley,Vance	63	1.8
Carrasco,Carlos	63	1.9
Alvarez,Henderson	62	1.6
Tanaka,Masahiro	62	1.4
Ryu,Hyun-Jin	62	1.7
Haren,Dan	62	1.7
Chen,Wei-Yin	61	1.7
Lester,Jon	61	2.0
House,T.J.	61	1.9
Wainwright,Adam	61	2.0
Oberholtzer,Brett	61	1.8
Teheran,Julio	60	2.1
Sanchez,Anibal	60	2.1
Leake,Mike	60	2.1
Kuroda,Hiroki	60	1.6
Collmenter,Josh	60	2.0
Arrieta,Jake	59	2.4
Cobb,Alex	59	2.5
Latos,Mat	59	2.3
Buehrle,Mark	59	2.0
Stroman,Marcus	58	1.9
McHugh,Collin	58	2.4
Nolasco,Ricky	58	2.2
Turner,Jacob	57	2.6
Hammel,Jason	57	2.2
Gallardo,Yovani	57	2.5
Buchanan,David	57	2.4
Weaver,Jered	56	2.7
Richards,Garrett	55	2.7

RISK MANAGEMENT

GRADE "F" in HEALTH

Pitchers	Pitchers
Adams,Mike	Morton,Charlie
Affeldt,Jeremy	Motte,Jason
Alburquerque,Al	Nicasio,Juan
Alvarez,Henderson	Nova,Ivan
Anderson,Brett	O Flaherty,Eric
Arroyo,Bronson	Ogando,Alexi
Atchison,Scott	Parker,Jarrod
Baker,Scott	Parnell,Bobby
Beachy,Brandon	Parra,Manny
Billingsley,Chad	Paxton,James
Broxton,Jonathan	Pelfrey,Mike
Buchholz,Clay	Perez,Martin
Bundy,Dylan	Phelps,David
Cain,Matt	Pineda,Michael
Capps,Carter	Putnam,Zach
Carrasco,Carlos	Rodriguez,Fernando
Cashner,Andrew	Rodriguez,Wandy
Casilla,Santiago	Rondon,Bruce
Chacin,Jhoulys	Sabathia,CC
Chamberlain,Joba	Scheppers,Tanner
Chatwood,Tyler	Soria,Joakim
Cobb,Alex	Stauffer,Tim
Corbin,Patrick	Thornburg,Tyler
Cueto,Johnny	Tolleson,Shawn
Danks,John	Tomlin,Josh
De Fratus,Justin	Vizcaino,Arodys
de la Rosa,Jorge	Wada,Tsuyoshi
Detwiler,Ross	Wilson,Brian
Duffy,Danny	Withrow,Chris
Familia,Jeurys	Young,Chris
Feliz,Neftali	
Fernandez,Jose	**Batters**
Floyd,Gavin	Blanks,Kyle
Fujikawa,Kyuji	Cervelli,Francisco
Garcia,Jaime	Coghlan,Chris
Garza,Matt	Crawford,Carl
Gee,Dillon	Cuddyer,Michael
Gonzalez,Miguel	DeJesus,David
Griffin,A.J.	Dirks,Andy
Happ,J.A.	Fielder,Prince
Harrison,Matt	Garcia,Avisail
Harvey,Matt	Guyer,Brandon
Hellickson,Jeremy	Hart,Corey
Henderson,Jim	Howard,Ryan
Hochevar,Luke	Iglesias,Jose
Holland,Derek	Izturis,Maicer
Hudson,Daniel	Kemp,Matt
Hutchison,Drew	Lawrie,Brett
Johnson,Josh	Ludwick,Ryan
Kazmir,Scott	Maybin,Cameron
Kelley,Shawn	Middlebrooks,Will
Kelly,Casey	Moreland,Mitch
Kintzler,Brandon	Morrison,Logan
Lackey,John	Pagan,Angel
Lee,Cliff	Profar,Jurickson
Lewis,Colby	Quentin,Carlos
Lindstrom,Matt	Ramos,Wilson
Maholm,Paul	Ross,Cody
Matsuzaka,Daisuke	Sizemore,Grady
McCarthy,Brandon	Soto,Geovany
McGowan,Dustin	Sweeney,Ryan
Medlen,Kris	Teixeira,Mark
Mejia,Jenrry	Tulowitzki,Troy
Moore,Matt	Victorino,Shane
Morales,Franklin	Votto,Joey
Morrow,Brandon	Zimmerman,Ryan

Highest Reliability Grades - Health / Experience / Consistency (Min. Grade = BBB)

CA	POS	Rel
Perez,Salvador	2	BBB

1B/DH	POS	Rel
Gonzalez,Adrian	3	AAA
Santana,Carlos	035	AAB
Carter,Chris	0	ABA
Joyce,Matt	07	ABA
Moss,Brandon	379	ABB
Wilkins,Andrew	3	ABB
Cruz,Nelson	07	BAA
Goldschmidt,Paul	3	BAB
Callaspo,Alberto	034	BBB
Napoli,Mike	3	BBB

2B	POS	Rel
Cano,Robinson	4	AAB
Zobrist,Ben	467	AAB
Gennett,Scooter	4	ABB
Goins,Ryan	4	ABB
Solarte,Yangervis	45	ABB
Kendrick,Howie	4	BAA
Kinsler,Ian	4	BAA
Murphy,Daniel	4	BAA
Cabrera,Asdrubal	46	BAB
Phillips,Brandon	4	BAB
Prado,Martin	45	BAB
Callaspo,Alberto	034	BBB
Walker,Neil	4	BBB

SS	POS	Rel
Escobar,Yunel	6	AAA
Ramirez,Alexei	6	AAA
Zobrist,Ben	467	AAB
Andrus,Elvis	6	AAB
Cozart,Zack	6	AAB
Desmond,Ian	6	AAB
Hardy,J.J.	6	AAB
Crawford,Brandon	6	ABA
Cabrera,Asdrubal	46	BAB
Aybar,Erick	6	BAB
Rollins,Jimmy	6	BAB
Simmons,Andrelton	6	BBB

3B	POS	Rel
Seager,Kyle	5	AAA
Santana,Carlos	035	AAB
Alvarez,Pedro	5	ABA

OF	POS	Rel
De Aza,Alejandro	7	AAA
Jones,Adam	8	AAA
Upton,Justin	7	AAA
Zobrist,Ben	467	AAB
Aoki,Norichika	9	AAB
Gordon,Alex	7	AAB
Holliday,Matt	7	AAB
Hunter,Torii	9	AAB
McCutchen,Andrew	8	AAB
Trout,Mike	8	AAB
Joyce,Matt	07	ABA
Ackley,Dustin	7	ABA
Blanco,Gregor	78	ABA
Grossman,Robert	79	ABA
Parra,Gerardo	79	ABA
Viciedo,Dayan	79	ABA
Moss,Brandon	379	ABB
Ethier,Andre	8	ABB
Jay,Jon	789	ABB
Smith,Seth	79	ABB
Suzuki,Ichiro	9	ABB
Cruz,Nelson	07	BAA
Heyward,Jason	9	BAA
Span,Denard	8	BAB
Crisp,Coco	8	BBB
Gomez,Carlos	8	BBB
Marte,Starling	78	BBB

RP	Rel
Kimbrel,Craig	AAA
Reed,Addison	AAA
Holland,Greg	AAB
Johnson,Jim	AAB
Papelbon,Jonathan	AAB
Cishek,Steve	ABA
Frieri,Ernesto	ABA
Romo,Sergio	ABA
Rosenthal,Trevor	ABB
Jansen,Kenley	BAA
Rodney,Fernando	BAA
Soriano,Rafael	BAA
Mujica,Edward	BBA
Rodriguez,Francisco	BBA
Villanueva,Carlos	BBA
Balfour,Grant	BBB
Perkins,Glen	BBB

SP	Rel
Buehrle,Mark	AAA
Bumgarner,Madison	AAA
Hernandez,Felix	AAA
Kendrick,Kyle	AAA
Kennedy,Ian	AAA
Leake,Mike	AAA
Lester,Jon	AAA
Lincecum,Tim	AAA
Miley,Wade	AAA
Quintana,Jose	AAA
Samardzija,Jeff	AAA
Santana,Ervin	AAA
Scherzer,Max	AAA
Shields,James	AAA
Tillman,Chris	AAA
Verlander,Justin	AAA
Wood,Travis	AAA
Kaneko,Chihiro	AAB
Keuchel,Dallas	AAB
Maeda,Kenta	AAB
Peralta,Wily	AAB
Porcello,Rick	AAB
Teheran,Julio	AAB
Archer,Chris	ABA
Collmenter,Josh	ABA
Locke,Jeff	ABA
Santiago,Hector	ABA
Gray,Sonny	ABB
Koehler,Tom	ABB
Miller,Shelby	ABB
Correia,Kevin	BAA
Dickey,R.A.	BAA
Gallardo,Yovani	BAA
Guthrie,Jeremy	BAA
Kershaw,Clayton	BAA
Kuroda,Hiroki	BAA
Lohse,Kyle	BAA
Lynn,Lance	BAA
Norris,Bud	BAA
Volquez,Edinson	BAA
Williams,Jerome	BAA
Masterson,Justin	BAB
Simon,Alfredo	BBA
Milone,Tommy	BBB

RISK MANAGEMENT

GRADE "A" in CONSISTENCY

Pitchers (min 120 IP)	Pitchers (min 120 IP)
Alvarez,Henderson	Strasburg,Stephen
Archer,Chris	Stults,Eric
Bailey,Homer	Tanaka,Masahiro
Buchanan,David	Tillman,Chris
Buehrle,Mark	Vargas,Jason
Bumgarner,Madison	Ventura,Yordano
Cain,Matt	Verlander,Justin
Cashner,Andrew	Volquez,Edinson
Chen,Wei-Yin	Wainwright,Adam
Cobb,Alex	Weaver,Jered
Collmenter,Josh	Wilson,C.J.
Colon,Bartolo	Wood,Alex
Correia,Kevin	Wood,Travis
Cueto,Johnny	
Danks,John	**Batters (min 400 AB)**
Darvish,Yu	Ackley,Dustin
Dickey,R.A.	Alcantara,Arismendy
Duffy,Danny	Alonso,Yonder
Eovaldi,Nathan	Alvarez,Pedro
Feldman,Scott	Asche,Cody
Fister,Doug	Beltre,Adrian
Gallardo,Yovani	Carter,Chris
Garza,Matt	Chisenhall,Lonnie
Gausman,Kevin	Crawford,Brandon
Gee,Dillon	Cruz,Nelson
Gibson,Kyle	Davis,Rajai
Gonzalez,Gio	De Aza,Alejandro
Greinke,Zack	Encarnacion,Edwin
Guthrie,Jeremy	Escobar,Yunel
Hamels,Cole	Gardner,Brett
Haren,Dan	Gonzalez,Adrian
Hendricks,Kyle	Heyward,Jason
Hernandez,Felix	Jones,Adam
Hudson,Tim	Kendrick,Howie
Iwakuma,Hisashi	Kinsler,Ian
Jackson,Edwin	Lawrie,Brett
Kazmir,Scott	LeMahieu,DJ
Kelly,Joe	Liriano,Rymer
Kendrick,Kyle	Machado,Manny
Kennedy,Ian	Moustakas,Mike
Kershaw,Clayton	Murphy,Daniel
Kuroda,Hiroki	Ozuna,Marcell
Lackey,John	Pagan,Angel
Latos,Mat	Plouffe,Trevor
Leake,Mike	Ramirez,Alexei
Lee,Cliff	Revere,Ben
Lester,Jon	Reyes,Jose
Locke,Jeff	Rosario,Wilin
Lohse,Kyle	Sandoval,Pablo
Lynn,Lance	Saunders,Michael
May,Trevor	Schoop,Jonathan
Miley,Wade	Seager,Kyle
Morton,Charlie	Upton,Justin
Niese,Jon	Viciedo,Dayan
Norris,Bud	Wong,Kolten
Odorizzi,Jake	Yelich,Christian S.
Paxton,James	Zimmerman,Ryan
Peavy,Jake	
Price,David	
Quintana,Jose	
Ryu,Hyun-Jin	
Sale,Chris	
Samardzija,Jeff	
Santana,Ervin	
Scherzer,Max	
Shields,James	
Simon,Alfredo	

TOP COMBINATION OF SKILLS AND RELIABILITY • Maximum of one "C" in Reliability Grade

BATTING POWER (Min. 400 AB)

PX 100+	PX	Rel
Carter,Chris	214	ABA
Trout,Mike	199	AAB
Goldschmidt,Paul	194	BAB
Moss,Brandon	185	ABB
Cruz,Nelson	167	BAA
Upton,Justin	165	AAA
Encarnacion,Edwin	164	CAA
Alvarez,Pedro	163	ABA
Bautista,Jose	163	CBB
Dickerson,Corey	163	ACB
Napoli,Mike	157	BBB
Trumbo,Mark	156	CBB
McCutchen,Andrew	156	AAB
Duda,Lucas	152	BCB
Gomez,Carlos	147	BBB
Bruce,Jay	146	AAC
Puig,Yasiel	146	ACB
Cespedes,Yoenis	143	AAC
Adams,Matt	138	ACB
Santana,Carlos	136	AAB
Gonzalez,Adrian	135	AAA
Jones,Adam	134	AAA
Desmond,Ian	134	AAB
Rosario,Wilin	134	ACA
Frazier,Todd	133	ABC
Marte,Starling	132	BBB
Jones,Garrett	131	ABC
Dozier,Brian	131	AAC
Arenado,Nolan	130	BBB
Calhoun,Kole	128	BCB
Pujols,Albert	127	CAB
Valbuena,Luis	127	ACB
Longoria,Evan	126	CBB
Holliday,Matt	125	AAB
Smith,Seth	124	ABB
Gordon,Alex	124	AAB
Walker,Neil	123	BBB
McCann,Brian	123	BBC
Seager,Kyle	123	AAA
Headley,Chase	123	BAC
Plouffe,Trevor	123	BBA
Peralta,Jhonny	123	ABC
Gyorko,Jedd	122	CBB
Machado,Manny	122	CBA
Norris,Derek	122	ACB
Reddick,Josh	121	CBB
Viciedo,Dayan	121	ABA
Asche,Cody	120	ACA
Lucroy,Jonathan	117	BBC
Cano,Robinson	116	AAB
Beltre,Adrian	116	BAA
Schoop,Jonathan	115	ACA
Upton,B.J.	114	ABC
Moustakas,Mike	113	ABA
Jennings,Desmond	111	CAB
Pence,Hunter	110	AAC
Cabrera,Asdrubal	109	BAB
Hunter,Torii	109	AAB
Heyward,Jason	109	BAA
Martin,Russell	108	BBC
Fowler,Dexter	108	CBB
Freese,David	106	CBB
De Aza,Alejandro	105	AAA
Castellanos,Nick	104	ACB
Brantley,Michael	101	AAC
Ackley,Dustin	101	ABA
Rios,Alex	100	BAC

RUNNER SPEED (Min. 400 AB)

Spd 100+	SX	Rel
Gordon,Dee	180	BCB
Marte,Starling	175	BBB
Hamilton,Billy	174	ACB
Segura,Jean	161	ABC
Revere,Ben	161	CBA
Hechavarria,Adeiny	159	ABC
Jackson,Austin	158	BAC
Trout,Mike	151	AAB
Bourn,Michael	149	CAB
Fowler,Dexter	148	CBB
LeMahieu,DJ	144	ACA
Pence,Hunter	142	AAC
Martin,Leonys	140	ACB
Puig,Yasiel	138	ACB
Jennings,Desmond	137	CAB
Cozart,Zack	133	AAB
Aoki,Norichika	132	AAB
McCutchen,Andrew	132	AAB
Dickerson,Corey	130	ACB
Upton,B.J.	130	ABC
Span,Denard	130	BAB
Reddick,Josh	129	CBB
Gomez,Carlos	129	BBB
Simmons,Andrelton	129	BBB
Machado,Manny	122	CBA
Rios,Alex	121	BAC
Lagares,Juan	120	BCB
De Aza,Alejandro	120	AAA
Andrus,Elvis	119	AAB
Ramirez,Alexei	118	AAA
Davis,Rajai	117	BCA
Cespedes,Yoenis	115	AAC
Wong,Kolten	114	ACA
Dozier,Brian	113	AAC
Prado,Martin	113	BAB
Carpenter,Matt	111	AAC
Ackley,Dustin	110	ABA
Crisp,Coco	110	BBB
Gennett,Scooter	110	ABB
Jay,Jon	110	ABB
Kinsler,Ian	109	BAA
Crawford,Brandon	109	ABA
Aybar,Erick	107	BAB
Desmond,Ian	107	AAB
Pedroia,Dustin	107	CAB
Markakis,Nick	107	BAC
Rollins,Jimmy	106	BAB
Zobrist,Ben	104	AAB
Kendrick,Howie	103	BAA
Heyward,Jason	103	BAA
Upton,Justin	102	AAA
Plouffe,Trevor	102	BBA
Lucroy,Jonathan	101	BBC
Frazier,Todd	101	ABC
Brantley,Michael	100	AAC

OVERALL PITCHING SKILL

BPV over 80	BPV	Rel
Jansen,Kenley	186	BAA
Kimbrel,Craig	176	AAA
Holland,Greg	165	AAB
Kershaw,Clayton	155	BAA
McGee,Jake	155	ACB
Melancon,Mark	153	ACB
Sale,Chris	145	CAA
Romo,Sergio	144	ABA
Hernandez,Felix	144	AAA
Cishek,Steve	135	ABA
Papelbon,Jonathan	134	AAB
Perkins,Glen	133	BBB
Benoit,Joaquin	132	ACA
Price,David	131	CAA
Scherzer,Max	127	AAA
Kluber,Corey	127	BAC
Bumgarner,Madison	124	AAA
Allen,Cody	123	ACA
Ryu,Hyun-Jin	122	CAA
Petit,Yusmeiro	122	ACB
Iwakuma,Hisashi	120	CAA
Qualls,Chad	118	BCB
Reed,Addison	117	AAA
Wood,Alex	116	ACA
Watson,Tony	115	ACB
Hamels,Cole	115	CAA
Rodriguez,Francisco	114	BBA
Hughes,Phil	113	CAB
Samardzija,Jeff	113	AAA
Clippard,Tyler	111	ACA
Gregerson,Luke	109	BCA
Lester,Jon	108	AAA
Ottavino,Adam	107	ACB
Thayer,Dale	106	ACA
Rosenthal,Trevor	105	ABB
Frieri,Ernesto	103	ABA
Smith,Joe	101	ACB
Rodney,Fernando	99	BAA
Mujica,Edward	99	BBA
Herrera,Kelvin	99	ACA
Haren,Dan	99	CAA
Gonzalez,Gio	98	CAA
Shields,James	97	AAA
Blevins,Jerry	96	ACA
Stammen,Craig	95	ACB
Ross,Tyson	95	CBB
Teheran,Julio	95	AAB
Keuchel,Dallas	92	AAB
Maeda,Kenta	91	AAB
Quintana,Jose	91	AAA
Wheeler,Zack	91	ACB
Gray,Sonny	89	ABB
Kuroda,Hiroki	88	BAA
Soriano,Rafael	85	BAA
Porcello,Rick	83	AAB
Santana,Ervin	82	AAA
Norris,Bud	81	BAA
Kennedy,Ian	81	AAA
Verlander,Justin	81	AAA
Leake,Mike	81	AAA
Lynn,Lance	81	BAA
Chavez,Jesse	80	ACB

MAYBERRY PORTFOLIO3 PLAN — BATTERS

TIER 1 Hitters
Rel BBB+; xBA score 3+; Power OR Speed score 3+

BATTERS	Age	Bats	Pos	MM	REL	MAY	R$
Trout, Mike	23	R	9	5545	AAB	121	$41
McCutchen, Andrew	28	R	9	4455	AAB	114	$38
Gomez, Carlos	29	R	9	4535	BBB	98	$36
Goldschmidt, Paul	27	R	3	5255	BAB	103	$34
Marte, Starling	26	R	79	4535	BBB	98	$33
Cano, Robinson	32	L	4	3255	AAB	95	$32
Beltre, Adrian	36	R	5	3155	BAA	89	$28
Jones, Adam	29	R	9	4345	AAA	106	$28
Gonzalez, Adrian	33	L	3	4155	AAA	100	$27
Upton, Justin	27	R	7	5335	AAA	106	$27
Desmond, Ian	29	R	6	4435	AAB	102	$25
Kendrick, Howie	31	R	4	2345	BAA	89	$24
Andrus, Elvis	26	R	6	1435	AAB	83	$24
Span, Denard	31	L	9	1555	BAB	97	$24
Heyward, Jason	25	L	8	3335	BAA	89	$24
Kinsler, Ian	33	R	4	2335	BAA	83	$24
Arenado, Nolan	24	R	5	4155	BBB	87	$23
Cruz, Nelson	35	R	07	5145	BAA	95	$22
Holliday, Matt	35	R	7	4145	AAB	89	$22
Zobrist, Ben	34	B	476	2335	AAB	83	$22
Ramirez, Alexei	33	R	6	1435	AAA	87	$22
Hunter, Torii	39	R	8	3145	AAB	83	$21
Aoki, Norichika	33	L	8	1455	AAB	95	$21
Seager, Kyle	27	L	5	4135	AAA	87	$20
Walker, Neil	29	B	4	4145	BBB	81	$19
Santana, Carlos	29	B	350	4135	AAB	83	$19
Aybar, Erick	31	B	6	1345	BAB	79	$18
Crisp, Coco	35	B	9	2435	BBB	81	$17
Prado, Martin	31	R	54	2345	BAB	85	$17
Plouffe, Trevor	29	R	5	4135	BBA	79	$14
Moustakas, Mike	26	L	5	3135	ABA	76	$13
Suzuki, Ichiro	41	L	8	0533	ABB	40	$13
Ackley, Dustin	27	L	7	3335	ABA	89	$12
Simmons, Andrelton	25	R	6	1335	BBB	69	$12
Ethier, Andre	33	L	9	3233	ABB	40	$10
Smith, Seth	32	L	78	4135	ABB	79	$9

TIER 2 Hitters
Rel BCC+; 5 PT; xBA, Power, or Speed score 3+ <$20

BATTERS	Age	Bats	Pos	MM	REL	MAY	R$
Carter, Chris*	28	R	0	5125	ABA	83	$23
Gordon, Alex*	31	L	7	4225	AAB	83	$21
Wong, Kolten	24	L	4	1435	ACA	79	$20
Murphy, Daniel	30	L	4	2245	BAA	83	$20
Adams, Matt	26	L	3	4035	ACB	69	$20
Butler, Billy	29	R	03	2035	AAC	61	$20
Peralta, Jhonny	33	R	6	4135	ABC	75	$19
Markakis, Nick	31	L	8	1235	BAC	64	$19
Gomes, Yan	27	R	2	4435	ACC	88	$18
Lagares, Juan	26	R	9	2415	BCB	66	$18
Perez, Salvador	25	R	2	2145	BBB	69	$18
Rollins, Jimmy	36	B	6	2425	BAB	79	$18
Moss, Brandon	31	L	378	5125	ABB	79	$18
Alvarez, Pedro	28	L	5	5125	ABA	83	$17
Rosario, Wilin	26	R	2	4145	ACA	85	$17

TIER 2 Hitters (Cont.)
Rel BCC+; 5 PT; xBA, Power, or Speed score 3+ <$20

BATTERS	Age	Bats	Pos	MM	REL	MAY	R$
Headley, Chase	31	B	5	4135	BAC	75	$17
Davis, Khristopher	27	R	7	5245	ACC	88	$16
Phillips, Brandon	34	R	4	1235	BAB	67	$16
De Aza, Alejandro	31	L	7	3425	AAA	93	$16
Jay, Jon	30	L	987	1235	ABB	67	$16
Duda, Lucas	29	L	3	4025	BCB	61	$16
Gennett, Scooter	25	L	4	2245	ABB	79	$15
Napoli, Mike	33	R	3	4115	BBB	64	$14
Cabrera, Asdrubal	29	B	64	3325	BAB	79	$14
LeMahieu, DJ	26	R	4	1435	ACA	79	$13
Mercer, Jordy	28	R	6	3235	ACC	72	$13
Norris, Derek	26	R	2	4225	ACB	75	$13
Castellanos, Nick	23	R	5	3125	ACB	64	$13
Hechavarria, Adeiny	26	R	6	1425	ABC	69	$13
McCann, Brian	31	L	2	4035	BBC	66	$13
Martin, Russell	32	R	2	3125	BBC	61	$12
Viciedo, Dayan	26	R	87	4025	ABA	70	$12
Asche, Cody	25	L	5	4125	ACA	73	$12
Hicks, Aaron	25	B	9	2305	BCC	53	$11
Joyce, Matt	30	L	70	4115	ABA	70	$11
Upton, B.J.	30	R	9	3505	ABC	75	$10
Jones, Garrett	34	L	3	4135	ABC	75	$10
Cozart, Zack	29	R	6	2525	AAB	89	$9
Valbuena, Luis	29	L	54	4025	ACB	64	$8
Schoop, Jonathan	23	R	4	3115	ACA	61	$8
Singleton, Jonathan	23	L	3	5105	ACC	61	$7

TIER 3 Hitters
Health>"F"; xBA score 3+; Power or Speed score 3+ <$15

BATTERS	Age	Bats	Pos	MM	REL	MAY	R$
Mesoraco, Devin	27	R	2	4045	ADD	65	$14
Lowrie, Jed	31	B	6	3335	DBC	66	$14
Gattis, Evan	28	R	2	5035	BDB	68	$14
Brown, Domonic	27	L	7	3235	ABF	68	$13
Alonso, Yonder	28	L	3	3133	CCA	33	$12
Morse, Michael	33	R	73	4033	CCF	27	$12
D'Arnaud, Travis	26	R	2	4135	ADD	65	$11
Young Jr., Eric	30	B	7	1533	CCD	34	$11
Young, Delmon	29	R	07	3233	BCB	36	$10
Inciarte, Ender	24	L	97	1533	ADA	41	$10
Kiermaier, Kevin	25	L	89	3533	ADB	46	$10
Cron, C.J.	25	R	30	4133	ADB	36	$10
Panik, Joe	24	L	4	0435	ADC	63	$10
Franco, Maikel	22	R	5	3233	AFF	29	$9
Colon, Christian	26	R	4	1453	ACB	45	$9
Turner, Justin	30	R	5	3243	BFD	32	$8
Denorfia, Chris	34	R	87	1433	ACC	36	$8
Pillar, Kevin	26	R	7	4331	ADC	11	$7
Jaso, John	31	L	20	3343	DDB	35	$7
Baker, Jeff	34	R	34	4431	BFF	10	$5
Lough, David	29	L	7	2431	ADC	10	$5
McKenry, Michael	30	R	2	4031	BFF	7	$5
Phegley, Joshua	27	R	2	4131	ACA	11	$4
Sardinas, Luis	22	B	4	0431	AFA	9	$1

* Tier 2 players should generally be less than $20. If you pay more than $20, you should be aware of the extra risk.

MAYBERRY PORTFOLIO3 PLAN — PITCHERS

TIER 1 Pitchers

Rel BBB+; xERA score 3+ and K/9 score 3+

PITCHERS	Age	Th	MM	REL	MAY	R$
Kershaw,Clayton	27	L	5505	BAA	127	$38
Hernandez,Felix	29	R	5405	AAA	126	$33
Kimbrel,Craig	27	R	5530	AAA	72	$29
Holland,Greg	29	R	5530	AAB	69	$27
Jansen,Kenley	27	R	5530	BAA	69	$26
Bumgarner,Madison	25	L	5305	AAA	120	$25
Scherzer,Max	30	R	5505	AAA	133	$24
Cishek,Steve	29	R	5530	ABA	69	$20
Perkins,Glen	32	L	5430	BBB	59	$20
Papelbon,Jonathan	34	R	5430	AAB	65	$19
Rodriguez,Francisco	33	R	5430	BBA	62	$19
Samardzija,Jeff	30	R	5305	AAA	120	$18
Lester,Jon	31	L	4305	AAA	106	$18
Rodney,Fernando	38	R	5530	BAA	69	$17
Romo,Sergio	32	R	5530	ABA	69	$17
Teheran,Julio	24	R	3305	AAB	89	$17
Reed,Addison	26	R	4530	AAA	64	$16
Rosenthal,Trevor	25	R	5531	ABB	92	$15
Lynn,Lance	28	R	3305	BAA	89	$11
Soriano,Rafael	35	R	3321	BAA	46	$11
Archer,Chris	26	R	3305	ABA	89	$10
Norris,Bud	30	R	3303	BAA	46	$10
Verlander,Justin	32	R	3305	AAA	93	$9
Kennedy,Ian	30	R	3305	AAA	93	$9
Masterson,Justin	30	R	3305	BAB	85	$4
Frieri,Ernesto	29	R	3510	ABA	15	$2

TIER 2 Pitchers

Rel BCC+; PT score 3+; xERA or K/9 score 3+   <$20

PITCHERS	Age	Th	MM	REL	MAY	R$
Zimmermann,Jordan*	29	R	4205	BAA	95	$21
Wood,Alex	24	L	5405	ACA	115	$18
Kluber,Corey	29	R	5405	BAC	110	$18
Gray,Sonny	25	R	4205	ABB	91	$16
Shields,James	33	R	3205	AAA	87	$16
Smyly,Drew	26	L	4303	BCC	44	$15
Wheeler,Zack	25	R	4405	ACB	98	$15
Kuroda,Hiroki	40	R	3105	BAA	76	$12
Quintana,Jose	26	L	3205	AAA	87	$11
Petit,Yusmeiro	30	R	4403	ACB	52	$10
Keuchel,Dallas	27	L	4105	AAB	89	$10
Ventura,Yordano	24	R	3303	BCA	42	$9
Odorizzi,Jake	25	R	2303	ACA	36	$9
Santana,Ervin	32	R	3205	AAA	87	$9
Shoemaker,Matthew	28	R	3205	ACC	72	$8
Peralta,Wily	26	R	3205	AAB	83	$8
Kaneko,Chihiro	31	R	3203	AAB	42	$8
Gallardo,Yovani	29	R	3205	BAA	83	$7
Porcello,Rick	26	R	3105	AAB	76	$7
Miley,Wade	28	L	3205	AAA	87	$6
Leake,Mike	27	R	3105	AAA	80	$6
Maeda,Kenta	27	R	3203	AAB	42	$5
Chavez,Jesse	31	R	3303	ACB	42	$5
Elias,Roenis	26	L	3203	ACB	38	$4

* Tier 2 players should generally be less than $20. If you pay more than $20, you should be aware of the extra risk.

TIER 3 Pitchers

Health > "F"; xERA score 3+   <$15

PITCHERS	Age	Th	MM	REL	MAY	R$
Benoit,Joaquin	37	R	5520	ACA	41	$15
Stroman,Marcus	24	R	5303	ADB	53	$14
Degrom,Jacob	27	R	4303	ADD	42	$14
Boxberger,Brad	27	R	5520	ADB	37	$13
Sanchez,Anibal	31	R	4305	DAB	83	$13
Ryu,Hyun-Jin	28	L	5303	CAA	58	$13
Giles,Kenneth	24	R	5511	AFF	30	$12
Fiers,Mike	30	R	3303	ADF	34	$12
Wacha,Michael	24	R	3303	DDC	31	$11
Watson,Tony	30	L	5311	ACB	35	$10
Davis,Wade	29	R	5511	ACD	36	$10
Salazar,Danny	25	R	4403	ADB	49	$10
Clippard,Tyler	30	R	4511	ACA	36	$10
Gausman,Kevin	24	R	3303	ADA	41	$9
Liriano,Francisco	31	L	4403	DBB	45	$9
O Day,Darren	32	R	5410	CCA	17	$7
Fields,Joshua	29	R	4520	BDB	31	$7
Neshek,Pat	34	R	3310	BDC	10	$7
Miller,Andrew	30	L	5500	DDB	0	$7
Leone,Dominic	23	R	5400	ADA	0	$6
Quackenbush,Kevin	26	R	4410	ADB	14	$6
Farquhar,Daniel	28	R	5510	ADA	18	$6
Walker,Taijuan	22	R	4301	DDC	10	$5
Burnett,A.J.	38	R	4305	DAB	83	$5
Carpenter,David	29	R	4411	BDD	27	$5
Herrera,Kelvin	25	R	5400	ACA	0	$4
Brach,Brad	29	R	3401	ADB	12	$4
Syndergaard,Noah	22	R	4401	AFA	14	$4
Cook,Ryan	28	R	4410	CCA	14	$4
Ottavino,Adam	29	R	4410	ACB	15	$4
Vincent,Nick	28	R	5400	CDA	0	$4
Cecil,Brett	28	L	5510	BCC	17	$4
Perez,Oliver	33	L	4510	BDB	15	$4
Cingrani,Tony	25	L	3403	BDD	37	$4
Peralta,Joel	39	R	4510	CCB	15	$4
Nathan,Joe	40	R	3420	DAB	25	$4
Strop,Pedro	30	R	5510	CCB	17	$3
Salas,Fernando	30	R	4410	DDB	12	$3
Walden,Jordan	27	R	4510	DDA	13	$3
Grimm,Justin	26	R	4310	ACD	13	$3
Ramirez,Neil	26	R	3410	ADC	11	$3
Morin,Michael	24	R	4300	BDB	0	$3
Tazawa,Junichi	29	R	4400	DDA	0	$3
Smith,Carson	25	R	5400	AFB	0	$2
Jepsen,Kevin	30	R	4410	DDC	11	$2
Dunn,Mike	30	L	4500	ADB	0	$2
Bastardo,Antonio	29	L	4500	ADA	0	$2
Wilson,Justin	27	L	3300	ACA	0	$2
Martinez,Carlos	23	R	3301	ADA	11	$2
Furbush,Charlie	29	L	5500	BDA	0	$2
Fien,Casey	31	R	3300	ADB	0	$2
Howell,J.P.	32	L	3300	DDA	0	$2
Diekman,Jake	28	L	4511	ADC	31	$2
Veras,Jose	34	R	3410	BCA	13	$2
Grilli,Jason	38	R	4510	DCB	13	$2
Blevins,Jerry	31	L	4400	ACA	0	$1
Montero,Rafael	24	R	3301	ADC	10	$1
Smith,Will	25	L	4501	ACC	15	$1
Ramos,A.J.	28	R	3501	BDB	13	$1
Pomeranz,Drew	26	L	3301	DDC	9	$1
Wilhelmsen,Tom	31	R	3301	ABC	12	$1

Universal Draft Grid

Most publications and websites provide cheat sheets with ranked player lists for different fantasy draft formats. The biggest problem with these tools is that they perpetuate the myth that players can be ranked in a linear fashion.

Since rankings are based on highly variable projections, it is foolhardy to draw conclusions that a $24 player is better than a $23 player is better than a $22 player. Yes, a first round pick is better than a 10th round pick, but within most rounds, all players are pretty much interchangeable commodities.

But typical cheat sheets don't reflect that reality. Auction sheets rank players by dollar value. Snake draft sheets rank players within round, accounting for position and categorical scarcity. But just as ADPs have a ridiculously low success rate, these cheat sheets are similarly flawed.

We have a tool at BaseballHQ.com called the Rotisserie Grid. It is a chart—that can be customized to your league parameters—which organizes players into pockets of skill, by position. It is one of the most popular tools on the site. One of the best features of this grid is that its design provides immediate insight into position scarcity.

So in the *Forecaster*, we have transitioned to this format as a sort of Universal Draft Grid.

How to use the chart

Across the top of the grid, players are sorted by position. First and third base, and second and shortstop are presented side-by-side for easy reference when considering corner and middle infielders, respectively.

The vertical axis separates each group of players into tiers based on potential fantasy impact. At the top are the Elite players; at the bottom are the Fringe players.

Auction leagues: The tiers in the grid represent rough break-points for dollar values. Elite players could be considered those that are purchased for $30 and up. Each subsequent tier is a step down of approximately $5.

Snake drafters: Tiers can be used to rank players similarly, though most tiers will encompass more than one round. Any focus on position scarcity will bump some players up a bit. For instance, with the dearth of Elite shortstops and the wealth of Elite outfielders, one might opt to draft Ian Desmond (from the Gold tier) before the Elite level Starling Marte. The reason we target scarce positions early is that there will be plenty of solid outfielders and starting pitchers later on.

To build the best foundation, you should come out of the first 10 rounds with all your middle infielders, all your corner infielders, one outfielder, at least one catcher and two pitchers (at least one closer).

The players are listed at the position where they both qualify and provide the most fantasy value. Additional position eligibility (20 games) is listed in parentheses. Listings in bold are players with high reliability grades (minimum "B" across the board).

Each player is presented with his 7-character Mayberry score. The first four digits (all on a 0-5 scale) represent skill: power, speed, batting average and playing time for batters; ERA, dominance, saves potential and playing time for pitchers. The last four alpha characters are the reliability grade (A-F): health, experience and consistency.

Within each tier, players are sorted by the first character of their Mayberry score. This means that batters are sorted by power; pitchers by ERA potential. If you need to prospect for the best skill sets among players in a given tier, target those with 4s and 5s in whatever skill you need.

CAVEATS and DISCLAIMERS

The placement of players in tiers does not represent average draft positions (ADP) or average auction values (AAV). It represents where each player's true value may lie. It is the variance between this true value and the ADP/AAV market values—or better, the value that your league-mates place on each player—where you will find your potential for profit or loss.

That means **you cannot take this chart right into your draft with you.** You have to compare these rankings with your ADPs and AAVs, and build your draft list from there. In other words, if we project Starling Marte as a "Elite" level pick but you know the other owners (or your ADPs) see him as a fourth-rounder, you can probably wait to pick him up in round 3. If you are in an auction league with owners who overvalue Cubs and Anthony Rizzo (projected at $28) gets bid past $30, you will likely take a loss should you decide to chase the bidding.

Finally, this chart is intended as a preliminary look based on current factors. For Draft Day, you will need to make your own adjustments based upon many different criteria that will impact the world between now and then. Daily updates appear online at BaseballHQ.com. A free projections update is available in March at **http://www.baseballhq.com/content/ron-shandlers-2015-baseball-forecaster**

Simulation League Cheat Sheet
Using Runs Above Replacement creates a more real-world ranking of player value, which serves simulation gamers well. Batters and pitchers are integrated, and value break-points are delineated.

Universal Draft Grid

TIER	FIRST BASE		THIRD BASE		SECOND BASE		SHORTSTOP	
Elite	Cabrera,Miguel	(5155 BAF)			Cano,Robinson	(3255 AAB)		
	Goldschmidt,Paul	**(5255 BAB)**			Altuve,Jose	(1545 AAD)		
	Abreu,Jose	(5155 ACF)						
	Martinez,Victor	(3155 CCF)						
Gold	Rizzo,Anthony	(5145 AAF)	**Beltre,Adrian**	**(3155 BAA)**	Rendon,Anthony (3)	(4445 ACD)	Tulowitzki,Troy	(5255 FDD)
	Encarnacion,Edwin	(5155 CAA)			Gordon,Dee	(1525 BCB)	**Desmond,Ian**	**(4435 AAB)**
	Gonzalez,Adrian	**(4155 AAA)**					Reyes,Jose	(2545 DAA)
	Freeman,Freddie	(4145 AAD)						
	Pujols,Albert	(4155 CAB)						
	Votto,Joey	(4155 FBF)						
Stars	Fielder,Prince	(4055 FBD)	Frazier,Todd (1)	(4335 ABC)	Dozier,Brian	(4435 AAC)	Ramirez,Hanley	(4355 DBF)
	Hosmer,Eric	(3245 BAD)	Zimmerman,Ryan (O)	(4355 FBA)	Kipnis,Jason	(3335 BAF)	Castro,Starlin	(2235 AAD)
	Morneau,Justin	(3045 CAC)	**Arenado,Nolan**	**(4155 BBB)**	**Kendrick,Howie**	**(2345 BAA)**	**Zobrist,Ben (2O)**	**(2335 AAB)**
			Donaldson,Josh	(4235 AAF)	**Kinsler,Ian**	**(2335 BAA)**	**Andrus,Elvis**	**(1435 AAB)**
			Longoria,Evan	(4225 CBB)			**Ramirez,Alexei**	**(1435 AAA)**
			Seager,Kyle	**(4135 AAA)**			Segura,Jean	(1535 ABC)
			Harrison,Josh (O)	(3445 ACD)			Escobar,Alcides	(1535 AAD)
			Wright,David	(3335 CAD)				
			Carpenter,Matt	(2235 AAC)				
Regulars	**Moss,Brandon (O)**	**(5125 ABB)**	Davis,Chris (1)	(5125 ABB)	**Walker,Neil**	**(4145 BBB)**	Peralta,Jhonny	(4135 ABC)
	Adams,Matt	(4035 ACB)	**Alvarez,Pedro**	**(5125 ABA)**	Alcantara,Arismendy (O)	(4525 ADA)	Santana,Daniel (O)	(3535 ADF)
	Belt,Brandon	(4225 DCC)	**Santana,Carlos (1)**	**(4135 AAB)**	Hill,Aaron	(3135 CBD)	**Rollins,Jimmy**	**(2425 BAB)**
	Trumbo,Mark (O)	(4125 CBB)	Machado,Manny	(4345 CBA)	**Murphy,Daniel**	**(2245 BAA)**	Owings,Christopher	(2525 CDB)
	LaRoche,Adam	(4225 CAC)	Headley,Chase	(4135 BAC)	Pedroia,Dustin	(2345 CAB)	**Aybar,Erick**	**(1345 BAB)**
	Pearce,Steve (O)	(4235 DDC)	Ramirez,Aramis	(3245 CBC)	Utley,Chase	(2335 DBB)		
	Lind,Adam	(4345 CCB)	Johnson,Chris	(3225 AAD)	**Prado,Martin (3)**	**(2345 BAB)**		
	Duda,Lucas	(4025 BCB)	Chisenhall,Lonnie	(3335 BDA)	**Gennett,Scooter**	**(2245 ABB)**		
	Butler,Billy	(2035 AAC)	Sandoval,Pablo	(2035 CBA)	Infante,Omar	(1335 CBD)		
	Mauer,Joe	(2145 DAC)			**Phillips,Brandon**	**(1235 BAB)**		
	Loney,James	(1145 AAD)			Wong,Kolten	(1435 ACA)		
Mid-Level	Van Slyke,Scott (O)	(5223 ADD)	Bryant,Kris	(5303 AFF)	Lawrie,Brett (3)	(4335 FCA)	Baez,Javier (2)	(4205 AFF)
	Napoli,Mike	**(4115 BBB)**	Lamb,Jacob	(4225 AFF)	Semien,Marcus (3)	(3425 ADC)	Bogaerts,Xander (3)	(3215 ACD)
	Teixeira,Mark	(4035 FCD)	**Plouffe,Trevor**	**(4135 BBA)**	Odor,Rougned	(2425 AFF)	Lowrie,Jed	(3335 DBC)
	Moreland,Mitch	(4135 FDB)	Asche,Cody	(4125 ACA)	Bonifacio,Emilio (O)	(1513 DCB)	**Cabrera,Asdrubal (2)**	**(3325 BAB)**
	Morse,Michael (O)	(4033 CCF)	**Moustakas,Mike**	**(3135 CBA)**	LeMahieu,DJ	(1435 ACA)	Mercer,Jordy	(3235 ACC)
	Howard,Ryan	(4015 FCC)	Castellanos,Nick	(3125 ACB)	Panik,Joe	(0435 ADC)	Miller,Bradley	(3325 ADC)
	Cron,C.J.	(4133 ADB)	Freese,David	(3025 CBB)			Rutledge,Josh	(3423 ACB)
	Alonso,Yonder	(3133 CCA)	Uribe,Juan	(2123 DDD)			Villar,Jonathan	(2503 ACB)
	Craig,Allen (O)	(2225 CBF)	McGehee,Casey	(1115 ABC)			**Hardy,J.J.**	**(2225 AAB)**
							Crawford,Brandon	**(2215 ABA)**
							Hechavarria,Adeiny	(1425 ABC)
							Cabrera,Everth	(1523 DCD)
							Simmons,Andrelton	**(1335 BBB)**
							Escobar,Yunel	(1125 AAA)
Bench	Singleton,Jonathan	(5105 ACC)	Francisco,Juan (1)	(5011 ADA)	Gyorko,Jedd	(4125 CBB)	Drew,Stephen (2)	(3213 DCF)
	Jones,Garrett	(4135 ABC)	Franco,Maikel	(3233 AFF)	Valbuena,Luis (3)	(4025 ACB)	Gregorius,Didi	(2313 ACB)
	Swisher,Nick	(4015 CBC)	Turner,Justin	(3243 BFD)	Weeks,Rickie	(4223 CCC)	Flores,Wilmer	(2023 ADB)
	Davis,Ike	(4023 CCB)	Middlebrooks,Will	(3203 FDF)	Rodriguez,Sean	(4213 ADB)	**Cozart,Zack**	**(2525 AAB)**
	Ruf,Darin	(4113 BDC)	Gillaspie,Conor	(2023 ACC)	Herrera,Dilson	(4521 AFF)	Taylor,Chris	(2503 AFB)
	Wilkins,Andrew	**(4123 ABB)**	**Dominguez,Matt**	**(2015 ABB)**	Baker,Jeff (1)	(4431 BFF)	Escobar,Eduardo (3)	(2323 ADC)
	Clark,Matthew	(4003 ACB)	Paredes,Jimmy	(2411 ACA)	Schoop,Jonathan	(3115 ACA)	Russell,Addison	(2121 AFF)
	Blanks,Kyle	(4203 FFC)	Holt,Brock (O)	(1423 ACF)	Franklin,Nick	(3303 ACB)	Gonzalez,Marwin	(2123 ADC)
	Morales,Kendrys	(3025 DBC)			Profar,Jurickson	(2321 FDD)	Ramirez,Jose	(1423 ADC)
	Morrison,Logan	(3133 FDA)			Colon,Christian	(1453 ACB)	Iglesias,Jose	(1415 FFC)
	Vogt,Stephen	(3223 ADC)			Aviles,Mike (3O)	(1223 ACA)	Nunez,Eduardo (3)	(1521 CFB)
	Sanchez,Gaby	(3223 ADC)			La Stella,Tommy	(1233 AFF)	Lindor,Francisco	(1303 AFB)
	Parmelee,Chris (O)	(3013 ADD)			**Solarte,Yangervis (3)**	**(1123 ABB)**	Amarista,Alexi (23)	(1423 ACA)
					Sogard,Eric	(1323 BDC)		
					Sanchez,Carlos	(1313 ADC)		
					Izturis,Maicer	(1321 FFB)		
Fringe	Medica,Thomas (O)	(4411 AFD)	Gallo,Joey	(5301 AFF)	Dietrich,Derek	(4111 BFB)	Flaherty,Ryan (23)	(3213 AFA)
	Mayberry,John	(4221 BDA)	Olt,Mike	(5101 ADF)	Espinosa,Danny	(3301 ACF)	Galvis,Freddy	(3201 CFA)
	Freiman,Nathan	(4021 ACC)	**Reynolds,Mark (1)**	**(4203 ABA)**	Uggla,Dan	(3101 ACC)	Suarez,Eugenio	(2301 ADB)
	Duvall,Adam	(4221 ADB)	Valencia,Danny (1)	(3021 ADD)	Forsythe,Logan	(2403 DDB)	Culberson,Charlie (23)	(2311 ADC)
	Smoak,Justin	(3003 BCC)	Johnson,Kelly (1)	(3211 ACA)	Valdespin,Jordany	(2311 AFA)	Petit,Gregorio	(2011 ACB)
	Overbay,Lyle	(3221 ADA)	Negron,Kristopher	(3401 ADA)	Tolleson,Steve (3)	(2301 ADA)	Herrera,Jonathan	(1211 BFC)
	Krauss,Marc	(3101 ACA)	Spangenberg,Cory	(1411 AFC)	Beckham,Gordon	(2213 CCB)	Pennington,Cliff	(1401 CDB)
	Bour,Justin	(2001 ACB)	Arias,Joaquin	(1521 AFB)	**Callaspo,Alberto (1)**	**(1023 BBB)**	Ahmed,Nick	(1411 ADA)
	Goebbert,Jake	(2201 ACA)	Hernandez,Cesar	(1320 ACB)	Gosselin,Phil	(1311 ACB)	Tejada,Ruben	(1111 BCD)
	Valaika,Chris	(2101 CDB)	Kelly,Don (1)	(0401 AFB)	Solano,Donovan	(1223 ADB)		
	Carp,Mike	(2011 DFF)	Garcia,Leury	(0501 ADC)	Pena,Ramiro	(1121 DFD)		
	Rosales,Adam	(2201 BDB)			Ellis,Mark	(1311 DCC)		
	Navarro Jr,Efren (O)	(1121 ACA)			Descalso,Daniel	(1111 ADA)		
					Punto,Nick	(1301 DFB)		
					Barney,Darwin	(1321 ACB)		
					Goins,Ryan	**(1111 ABB)**		
					Lucas,Edward	(1201 BDC)		
					Santiago,Ramon (3)	(1211 AFB)		
					Adrianza,Ehire	(1400 CDA)		
					Kawasaki,Munenori	(0323 AFB)		

Universal Draft Grid

TIER	CATCHER	DH	OUTFIELD	OUTFIELD
Elite		Carter,Chris (5125 ABA)	Trout,Mike (5545 AAB)	Marte,Starling (4535 BBB)
		Ortiz,David (5055 CBD)	Stanton,Giancarlo (5245 BBD)	Braun,Ryan (4345 BBD)
			McCutchen,Andrew (4455 AAB)	Brantley,Michael (3355 AAC)
			Gomez,Carlos (4535 BBB)	Ellsbury,Jacoby (2545 DBC)
Gold	Posey,Buster (1) (3155 BAD)		Dickerson,Corey (5255 ACB)	Puig,Yasiel (4445 ACB)
			Bautista,Jose (5255 CBB)	**Jones,Adam (4345 AAA)**
			Kemp,Matt (5245 FCD)	Werth,Jayson (4345 CBD)
			Upton,Justin (5335 AAA)	Pence,Hunter (3535 AAC)
			Cuddyer,Michael (5355 FCD)	Revere,Ben (0555 CBA)
Stars	Lucroy,Jonathan (3255 BBC)		Springer,George (5405 CDF)	Yelich,Christian S. (3545 ADA)
			Cruz,Nelson (5145 BAA)	**Hunter,Torii (3145 AAB)**
			Gonzalez,Carlos (5335 CCF)	Myers,Wil (3305 CCC)
			Calhoun,Kole (4245 BCB)	Davis,Rajai (2535 BCA)
			Cespedes,Yoenis (4335 AAC)	Jackson,Austin (2525 BAC)
			Holliday,Matt (4145 AAB)	Cabrera,Melky (2255 CBF)
			Martinez,J.D. (4235 BCD)	Cain,Lorenzo (2525 DCC)
			Bruce,Jay (4225 AAC)	Rios,Alex (2335 BAC)
			Gordon,Alex (4225 AAB)	Eaton,Adam (2545 DCF)
			Betts,Mookie (3545 AFF)	Hamilton,Billy (1505 ACB)
			Heyward,Jason (3335 BAA)	Martin,Leonys (1525 ACB)
			Crawford,Carl (3545 FDB)	**Span,Denard (1555 BAB)**
			Castillo,Rusney (3555 ADF)	**Aoki,Norichika (1455 AAB)**
			Blackmon,Charlie (3435 DCB)	
Regulars	Gomes,Yan (4435 ACC)		Soler,Jorge (5145 BFF)	Jennings,Desmond (3525 CAB)
	Rosario,Wilin (4145 ACA)		Davis,Khristopher (5245 ACC)	Pollock IV,A.J. (3545 DCB)
	Wieters,Matt (4035 DCC)		Harper,Bryce (4235 DBC)	**De Aza,Alejandro (3425 AAA)**
	Molina,Yadier (2155 CBC)		Ozuna,Marcell (4425 BDA)	Garcia,Avisail (3325 FFC)
	Perez,Salvador (2145 BBB)		Stubbs,Drew (4503 ABC)	Fowler,Dexter (3515 CBB)
			Tomas,Yasmani (4145 ADB)	Byrd,Marlon (3025 ACF)
			Beltran,Carlos (4235 CBC)	Polanco,Gregory (2335 AFB)
			Hamilton,Josh (4125 CBC)	Lagares,Juan (2415 BCB)
			Granderson,Curtis (4315 DBB)	**Crisp,Coco (2435 BBB)**
			Saunders,Michael (4325 CCA)	Markakis,Nick (1235 BAC)
			Gardner,Brett (3525 DCA)	Dyson,Jarrod (1513 ADB)
			Choo,Shin-Soo (3225 CAD)	**Jay,Jon (1235 ABB)**
			Peralta,David (3345 AFF)	Pagan,Angel (1533 FBA)
Mid-Level	Gattis,Evan (5035 BDB)	Walters,Zachary (4023 ADB)	Arcia,Oswaldo (5125 BDB)	Kiermaier,Kevin (3533 ADB)
	Mesoraco,Devin (4045 ADD)	Vargas,Kennys (3015 AFF)	Rasmus,Colby (5323 CBF)	Upton,B.J. (3505 ABC)
	Norris,Derek (4225 ACB)		Reddick,Josh (4325 CBB)	Murphy,David (2135 BBF)
	McCann,Brian (4035 BBC)		**Viciedo,Dayan (4025 ABA)**	Hicks,Aaron (2305 BCC)
	D Arnaud,Travis (4135 ADD)		**Joyce,Matt (4115 ABA)**	Victorino,Shane (2543 FCD)
	Grandal,Yasmani (1) (4225 CDD)		Venable,Will (3523 ABC)	**Parra,Gerardo (2233 ABA)**
	Saltalamacchia,Jarrod (4115 ACD)		Brown,Domonic (3235 ABF)	Schafer,Jordan (1513 BDA)
	Martin,Russell (3125 BBC)		Pederson,Joc (3203 ADC)	Bourn,Michael (1515 CAB)
	Ramos,Wilson (3033 FDA)		**Ackley,Dustin (3335 ABA)**	Young Jr.,Eric (1533 CCD)
	Navarro,Dioner (2135 ADF)		Liriano,Rymer (3405 AFA)	Inciarte,Ender (1533 ADA)
			Snider,Travis (3123 BDD)	**Suzuki,Ichiro (0533 ABB)**
			Young,Delmon (3233 BCB)	Gentry,Craig (0513 CDC)
Bench	Zunino,Mike (4003 BDF)	Hart,Corey (4213 FDF)	**Smith,Seth (4135 ABB)**	Dirks,Andy (2321 FDF)
	Pinto,Josmil (4023 ADB)	Boesch,Brennan (4211 ADB)	Nieuwenhuis,Kirk (4213 ADC)	Nava,Daniel (2113 BCD)
	Castro,Jason (4215 DCD)	DeJesus,David (2133 FCA)	Young,Chris (4313 BDB)	**Grossman,Robert (2203 ABA)**
	Avila,Alex (4013 BCA)		Willingham,Josh (4301 DCC)	Ross,Cody (2121 FDC)
	Flowers,Tyler (4003 ADC)		Ruggiano,Justin (4111 CDC)	Rua,Ryan (2221 AFC)
	Iannetta,Chris (4103 BDA)		Pillar,Kevin (4331 ADC)	Lough,David (2431 ADC)
	Castillo,Welington (3113 CCB)		Quentin,Carlos (4021 FDD)	Marisnick,Jake (1403 ADB)
	Jaso,John (3343 DDB)		Heisey,Chris (4413 BDA)	Gose,Anthony (1503 ACA)
	Montero,Miguel (2015 BBC)		Soriano,Alfonso (4211 ABC)	Maybin,Cameron (1513 FDB)
	Ruiz,Carlos (2133 DCD)		**Ethier,Andre (3233 ABB)**	Denorfia,Chris (1433 ACC)
	Suzuki,Kurt (1125 ACB)		Den Dekker,Matthew (2203 ACA)	Fuld,Sam (1521 DFC)
	Bethancourt,Christian (1203 ADC)		Guyer,Brandon (2533 FFA)	**Blanco,Gregor (1513 ABA)**
	Vazquez,Christian (1015 ADC)		Coghlan,Chris (2333 FDC)	Buxton,Byron (1501 DFF)
			Bourjos,Peter (2513 DFA)	
Fringe	Ross,David (5001 DFC)	Montero,Jesus (3121 ADB)	Taylor,Michael A. (4401 AFF)	McLouth,Nate (2311 CCD)
	Recker,Anthony (5001 AFB)		Barnes,Brandon (4311 ACB)	Presley,Alex (2321 CCA)
	McKenry,Michael (4031 BFF)		Raburn,Ryan (4121 BFF)	Hernandez,Enrique (2221 ADC)
	Phegley,Joshua (4131 ACA)		Sierra,Moises (3511 ADA)	Campbell,Eric (2311 ACA)
	Soto,Geovany (4011 FFD)		Lake,Junior (3401 ADC)	Smolinski,Jacob (2221 BCB)
	Arencibia,J.P. (1) (4103 ACB)		Gomes,Jonny (3201 ADC)	Sweeney,Ryan (2341 FFD)
	Susac,Andrew (4311 AFA)		Sizemore,Grady (3213 FFF)	Romero,Stefen (2101 ADD)
	Kratz,Erik (4021 BFA)		Ludwick,Ryan (3021 FDF)	Johnson,Reed (2011 BFB)
	Sanchez,Jorge Tony (4111 ADB)		Doumit,Ryan (3201 BCC)	Almonte,Abraham (2221 ACC)
	Chirinos,Robinson (3111 DFC)		Bradley,Jackie (3311 ADC)	Schafer,Logan (2311 ADA)
	Hundley,Nick (3101 CDC)		Guerrero,Alexander (3401 AFF)	Green,Grant (2211 BCA)
	Joseph,Caleb (3111 ACB)		Grichuk,Randal (3211 ADA)	Perez,Juan (2201 ACA)
	Rivera,Rene (3003 ADC)		Santana,Domingo (3301 ADA)	Tabata,Jose (1241 BDD)
	Maldonado,Martin (3001 AFD)		Kubel,Jason (3101 BDC)	Hoes,LJ (1221 ACC)
	Rupp,Cameron (3001 AFD)		Choice,Michael (3103 ACB)	Chavez,Endy (1221 BFB)
	Cervelli,Francisco (2311 FFF)		Hairston,Scott (3301 BFC)	Herrera,Elian (1401 ADB)
	Conger,Hank (2003 AFC)		Schierholtz,Nate (3221 BCC)	Piscotty,Stephen (1231 AFB)
	Corporan,Carlos (2011 AFA)		Ibanez,Raul (3111 ACD)	Robertson,Daniel T. (1411 ACB)
	Casali,Curtis (2001 AFF)		Marte,Alfredo (3211 ADC)	Schumaker,Skip (1121 CDB)
	Murphy,John (2121 AFB)		Taylor,Michael D. (3201 ACA)	Frandsen,Kevin (1121 ADA)

Universal Draft Grid

TIER	STARTING PITCHERS		RELIEF PITCHERS	
Elite	Hernandez,Felix (5405 AAA)			
	Kershaw,Clayton (5505 BAA)			
Gold	Price,David (5405 CAA)		Chapman,Aroldis (5530 DAA)	**Kimbrel,Craig** (5530 AAA)
	Sale,Chris (5505 CAA)		**Holland,Greg** (5530 AAB)	Melancon,Mark (5431 ACB)
	Strasburg,Stephen (5505 DAA)		Jansen,Kenley (5530 BAA)	
Stars	**Bumgarner,Madison** (5305 AAA)	Iwakuma,Hisashi (5205 CAA)	Cishek,Steve (5530 ABA)	Robertson,David (5530 CCA)
	Darvish,Yu (5505 DAA)	**Scherzer,Max** (5505 AAA)	Doolittle,Sean (5530 CCB)	Uehara,Koji (5530 DCA)
	Greinke,Zack (5305 DAA)	Cueto,Johnny (4305 FAA)	McGee,Jake (5530 ACB)	
	Hamels,Cole (5305 CAA)	Zimmermann,Jordan (4205 BAA)		
Regulars	Cobb,Alex (5305 FBA)	**Gray,Sonny** (4205 ABB)	Allen,Cody (5530 ACA)	**Rosenthal,Trevor** (5531 ABB)
	Kluber,Corey (5405 BAC)	Hughes,Phil (4205 CAB)	Betances,Dellin (5521 ADF)	Casilla,Santiago (4230 FCB)
	Samardzija,Jeff (5305 AAA)	**Lester,Jon** (4305 CAA)	Britton,Zach (5230 CCF)	Janssen,Casey (4230 DBB)
	Tanaka,Masahiro (5303 DAA)	Ross,Tyson (4305 CBB)	**Papelbon,Jonathan** (5430 AAB)	**Reed,Addison** (4530 AAA)
	Wood,Alex (5405 ACA)	Smyly,Drew (4303 BCC)	**Perkins,Glen** (5430 BBB)	Rondon,Hector (4330 ACC)
	Arrieta,Jake (4405 DCB)	Wainwright,Adam (4205 DAA)	**Rodney,Fernando** (5530 BAA)	Storen,Drew (4231 DCB)
	Cole,Gerrit (4305 DDB)	Wheeler,Zack (4405 ACB)	**Rodriguez,Francisco** (5430 BBA)	Street,Huston (4330 DBB)
	Fister,Doug (4105 DAA)	**Shields,James** (3205 AAA)	**Romo,Sergio** (5530 ABA)	Feliz,Neftali (2230 FDB)
	Gonzalez,Gio (4405 CAA)	Teheran,Julio (3305 AAB)		
Mid-Level	Carrasco,Carlos (5303 FCF)	**Archer,Chris** (3305 ABA)	Benoit,Joaquin (5520 ACA)	
	Lee,Cliff (5303 FAA)	Fiers,Mike (3303 ADF)	Boxberger,Brad (5520 ADB)	
	Ryu,Hyun-Jin (5303 CAA)	**Kuroda,Hiroki** (3105 DAA)	Davis,Wade (5511 ACD)	
	Stroman,Marcus (5303 ADB)	Latos,Mat (3205 DAA)	Giles,Kenneth (5511 AFF)	
	Bailey,Homer (4203 DAA)	**Lynn,Lance** (3305 BAA)	Qualls,Chad (5230 BCB)	
	Cashner,Andrew (4203 FBA)	McHugh,Collin (3205 BCF)	Smith,Joe (5211 ACB)	
	Degrom,Jacob (4303 ADD)	**Quintana,Jose** (3205 AAA)	Watson,Tony (5311 ACB)	
	Harvey,Matt (4403 FCB)	Roark,Tanner (3105 ABF)	Mejia,Jenrry (4431 FCD)	
	Petit,Yusmeiro (4403 ACB)	Wacha,Michael (3303 DDC)	**Soriano,Rafael** (3321 BAA)	
	Pineda,Michael (4301 FDB)	**Lohse,Kyle** (2105 BAA)		
	Richards,Garrett (4203 DBB)	**Miller,Shelby** (2205 ABB)		
	Sanchez,Anibal (4305 DAB)	**Tillman,Chris** (2205 AAA)		
	Alvarez,Henderson (3005 FAA)	Weaver,Jered (2205 DAA)		
Bench	Fernandez,Jose (5401 FCB)	**Kennedy,Ian** (3305 AAB)	Farquhar,Daniel (5510 ADA)	
	Sabathia,CC (5301 FAB)	Lackey,John (3205 FBA)	Gregerson,Luke (5211 BCA)	
	Keuchel,Dallas (4105 AAB)	**Leake,Mike** (3105 AAA)	Leone,Dominic (5400 ADA)	
	Liriano,Francisco (4403 DBB)	**Miley,Wade** (3205 AAA)	Miller,Andrew (5500 DDD)	
	McCarthy,Brandon (4105 FAB)	Minor,Mike (3203 CAC)	O Day,Darren (5410 CCA)	
	Salazar,Danny (4403 ADB)	Niese,Jon (3103 DAA)	Parnell,Bobby (5320 FCF)	
	Walker,Taijuan (4301 DDC)	**Norris,Bud** (3303 BAA)	Soria,Joakim (5320 FDA)	
	Buchholz,Clay (3205 FAB)	**Peralta,Wily** (3205 AAB)	Clippard,Tyler (4511 ACA)	
	Cain,Matt (3203 FAA)	**Porcello,Rick** (3105 AAB)	Fields,Joshua (4520 BDB)	
	de la Rosa,Jorge (3205 FBC)	**Santana,Ervin** (3205 AAA)	Medlen,Kris (4201 FBB)	
	Gallardo,Yovani (3205 BAA)	Shoemaker,Matthew (3205 ACC)	Quackenbush,Kevin (4410 ADB)	
	Garza,Matt (3203 FBA)	Ventura,Yordano (3303 BCA)	Hawkins,LaTroy (3020 DCB)	
	Gausman,Kevin (3303 ADA)	**Verlander,Justin** (3305 AAA)	Neshek,Pat (3310 BDC)	
	Hahn,Jesse (3201 CFF)	Chen,Wei-Yin (2103 DAA)	Putnam,Zach (3320 FDD)	
	Hammel,Jason (3203 DAC)	**Dickey,R.A.** (2205 BAA)	Shaw,Bryan (3210 ACA)	
	Haren,Dan (3203 CAA)	Duffy,Danny (2203 FCA)	**Collmenter,Josh** (2103 ABA)	
	Hendricks,Kyle (3103 ADA)	Gee,Dillon (2103 FAA)		
	Holland,Derek (3205 FBB)	Nuno,Vidal (2103 BCF)		
	Hudson,Tim (3005 DAA)	Odorizzi,Jake (2303 ACA)		
	Hutchison,Drew (3305 FCF)	Peavy,Jake (2203 DAA)		
	Kaneko,Chihiro (3203 AAB)	**Simon,Alfredo** (2105 BBA)		
	Kazmir,Scott (3305 FBA)	Wilson,C.J. (2305 CAA)		
Fringe	Burnett,A.J. (4305 DAB)	Griffin,A.J. (2101 FCC)	Bedrosian,Cam (5500 AFF)	Hunter,Tommy (4110 DCC)
	Garcia,Jaime (4201 FDB)	**Guthrie,Jeremy** (2005 BAA)	Cecil,Brett (5510 BCC)	Jepsen,Kevin (4410 DDC)
	Syndergaard,Noah (4401 AFA)	Happ,J.A. (2203 FBB)	Duke,Zach (5300 CDD)	Kelley,Shawn (4510 FDA)
	Beachy,Brandon (3301 FDA)	Hellickson,Jeremy (2203 FBC)	Fujikawa,Kyuji (5500 FDB)	Machi,Jean (4210 ADF)
	Chavez,Jesse (3303 ACB)	Hudson,Daniel (2201 FFA)	Furbush,Charlie (5500 BDA)	Medina,Yoervis (4400 ADB)
	Cingrani,Tony (3403 BDD)	Kelly,Joe (2003 DCA)	Herrera,Kelvin (5400 ACA)	Morin,Michael (4300 BDB)
	Colon,Bartolo (3103 DAA)	**Koehler,Tom** (2103 ABB)	Maness,Michael (5001 ADC)	Morris,Bryan (4111 ADA)
	Corbin,Patrick (3201 FCB)	Lewis,Colby (2203 FCF)	O Flaherty,Eric (5200 FDA)	Otero,Dan (4000 ADF)
	Elias,Roenis (3203 ACB)	Moore,Matt (2301 FBA)	Rzepczynski,Marc (5300 ADB)	Ottavino,Adam (4410 ACB)
	Heaney,Andrew (3101 ADA)	Owens,Henry (2300 AFB)	Simmons,Shae (5510 DFF)	Peralta,Joel (4510 CCB)
	House,T.J. (3103 ADB)	Parker,Jarrod (2101 FCB)	Smith,Carson (5400 AFB)	Perez,Oliver (4510 BDB)
	Maeda,Kenta (3203 AAB)	Stults,Eric (2003 CAA)	Strop,Pedro (5510 CCB)	Rondon,Bruce (4510 FFA)
	Masterson,Justin (3305 BAB)	Tropeano,Nicholas (2101 ADF)	Vincent,Nick (5400 CDA)	Salas,Fernando (4410 DDB)
	Montero,Rafael (3301 ADC)	Vargas,Jason (2105 DAA)	Adams,Mike (4410 FDA)	Sanchez,Aaron (4201 AFF)
	Morton,Charlie (3103 FCA)	Vogelsong,Ryan (2103 DAB)	Affeldt,Jeremy (4100 FDC)	Siegrist,Kevin (4500 DDF)
	Nelson,Jimmy (3201 ADB)	**Volquez,Edinson** (2205 BAA)	Alburquerque,Al (4510 FDB)	Smith,Will (4501 ACC)
	Nova,Ivan (3101 FCB)	Wada,Tsuyoshi (2203 FDF)	Atchison,Scott (4100 FDB)	Stauffer,Tim (4300 FDB)
	Paxton,James (3203 FDA)		Barrett,Aaron (4510 AFA)	Tazawa,Junichi (4400 DDA)
	Pomeranz,Drew (3301 DDC)		Bastardo,Antonio (4500 ADA)	Thayer,Dale (4310 ACA)
	Tomlin,Josh (3101 FDF)		Blevins,Jerry (4400 ACA)	Thornton,Matt (4200 CDB)
	Bauer,Trevor (2305 ACD)		Capps,Carter (4500 FDB)	Tolleson,Shawn (4400 FDF)
	Buehrle,Mark (2005 AAA)		Carpenter,David (4411 BDD)	Walden,Jordan (4510 DDA)
	Cosart,Jarred (2105 ACB)		Cook,Ryan (4410 CCA)	Ziegler,Brad (4110 ACA)
	Eovaldi,Nathan (2103 DBA)		Diekman,Jake (4511 ADC)	Abad,Fernando (3200 DDC)
	Feldman,Scott (2005 DAA)		Dunn,Mike (4500 ADB)	Badenhop,Burke (3001 ACA)
	Gonzales,Marco (2301 AFF)		Familia,Jeurys (4311 FDD)	Brach,Brad (3401 ADB)
	Gonzalez,Miguel (2103 CBB)		Grilli,Jason (4510 DCB)	Brothers,Rex (3511 ACB)
	Greene,Shane (2103 ADC)		Grimm,Justin (4310 ACD)	Broxton,Jonathan (3210 FCA)

Universal Draft Grid

TIER	STARTING PITCHERS		RELIEF PITCHERS	
Fringe (cont.)			Estrada,Marco (3201 DBA)	Scheppers,Tanner (3210 FDD)
			Fien,Casey (3300 ADB)	Sipp,Tony (3510 ADC)
			Frasor,Jason (3400 CDA)	Stammen,Craig (3201 ACB)
			Frieri,Ernesto (3510 ABA)	Torres,Carlos (3201 ACB)
			Howell,J.P. (3300 DDA)	Varvaro,Anthony (3200 ADB)
			Hughes,Jared (3000 DDB)	Veras,Jose (3410 BCA)
			Johnson,Jim (3210 AAB)	Warren,Adam (3201 ACC)
			Kintzler,Brandon (3000 FDC)	Wilhelmsen,Tom (3301 ABC)
			Kontos,George (3200 ADD)	**Balfour,Grant (2410 BBB)**
			Loup,Aaron (3211 ACB)	Black,Victor (2310 ADA)
			Martinez,Carlos (3301 ADA)	Burton,Jared (2210 DCB)
			Maurer,Brandon (3201 ADC)	Crow,Aaron (2210 ACB)
			Mujica,Edward (3110 BBA)	Delgado,Randall (2301 ADC)
			Nathan,Joe (3420 DAB)	Henderson,Jim (2410 FDA)
			Pestano,Vinnie (3500 ADC)	Petricka,Jacob (2120 ADD)
			Ramirez,Neil (3410 ADC)	Rasmus,Cory (2301 ADB)
			Ramos,A.J. (3501 BDB)	
Below Fringe	Anderson,Brett (4100 FDA)	Baker,Scott (1101 FDA)	Jeffress,Jeremy (4200 ADB)	Krol,Ian (2200 BFC)
	Johnson,Josh (4300 FCA)	Bergman,Christian (1000 DDA)	Marshall,Evan (4300 AFC)	League,Brandon (2000 ACA)
	Rodon,Carlos (3300 AFF)	Bradley,Archie (1201 BFA)	Axford,John (3500 ACA)	Lindstrom,Matt (2110 FDB)
	Skaggs,Tyler (3200 DCA)	Carroll,Scott (1000 ADC)	Belisario,Ronald (3100 ACA)	McAllister,Zach (2100 DCA)
	Anderson,Chase (2203 ADD)	Chacin,Jhoulys (1001 FCB)	Chamberlain,Joba (3310 FDC)	McFarland,T.J. (2001 ADB)
	Arroyo,Bronson (2000 FAA)	**Correia,Kevin (1003 BAA)**	Cotts,Neal (3310 ADF)	Nicasio,Juan (2100 FCB)
	Bedard,Erik (2300 DBA)	Cumpton,Brandor (1000 ADA)	Dyson,Sam (3100 ADB)	Ogando,Alexi (2300 FDB)
	Billingsley,Chad (2201 FDB)	Danks,John (1005 FBA)	Freeman,Sam (3200 ADB)	Parra,Manny (2300 FDC)
	Bolsinger,Michael (2201 ADA)	Doubront,Felix (1201 DBB)	Hatcher,Chris (3300 ADF)	Phelps,David (2301 FBA)
	Buchanan,David (2003 ADA)	Flande,Yohan (1000 ADB)	Hochevar,Luke (3200 FCC)	Ramos,Cesar (2201 ACA)
	Bundy,Dylan (2201 FFF)	Gray,Jonathan (1101 AFF)	Hoover,J.J. (3500 ADC)	Reed,Evan (2100 ADC)
	Cahill,Trevor (2201 CBB)	Hand,Brad (1101 CDA)	Jennings,Dan (3200 BDB)	Rodriguez,Fernando (2300 FDC)
	Chatwood,Tyler (2000 FDC)	Harrison,Matt (1000 FCA)	Lecure,Sam (3300 BDA)	Rogers,Esmil (2200 CCB)
	Cole,A.J. (2100 AFF)	Jimenez,Ubaldo (1403 CAC)	**Lincecum,Tim (3201 AAA)**	Russell,James (2100 ACA)
	De La Rosa,Rubby (2203 BDF)	Kelly,Casey (1200 FFF)	Lopez,Javier (3000 ADC)	Schlitter,Brian (2000 CDB)
	DeSclafani,Anthony (2100 ADB)	Kelly,Casey (1200 FFF)	Matusz,Brian (3400 BDC)	Thielbar,Caleb (2100 ADF)
	Despaigne,Odrisamer (2203 AFF)	Lobstein,Kyle (1101 ADB)	Motte,Jason (3200 FCD)	Thornburg,Tyler (2301 FDA)
	Erlin,Robert (2201 DDB)	Lobstein,Kyle (1101 ADB)	Ondrusek,Logan (3300 CDC)	Torres,Alexander (2400 ADF)
	Floyd,Gavin (2203 AFF)	Martinez,Nicholas (1200 FFF)	Ross,Robbie (3101 ACC)	**Villanueva,Carlos (2300 BBA)**
	Gibson,Kyle (2201 DDB)	Matzek,Tyler (1101 ADA)	Webb,Ryan (3100 BCA)	Webb,Daniel (2300 ADC)
	Harang,Aaron (2103 CAA)	May,Trevor (1203 ADA)	Whitley,Chase (3200 ADA)	Beimel,Joe (1000 CFF)
	Hernandez,Roberto (2003 BBC)	**Milone,Tommy (1103 BBB)**	Wilson,Brian (3500 FDF)	Bettis,Chad (1100 ADB)
	Jackson,Edwin (2203 CAA)	Noesi,Hector (1103 ACC)	Avilan,Luis (2000 ADA)	Breslow,Craig (1100 DDB)
	Kendrick,Kyle (2005 AAA)	Peacock,Brad (1303 ACB)	Belisle,Matt (2101 ACB)	Bueno,Francisley (1000 DDC)
	Locke,Jeff (2103 ABA)	Pimentel,Stolmy (1200 DDC)	Boyer,Blaine (2100 AFF)	Foltynewicz,Mike (1211 ADD)
	Lyles,Jordan (2103 DCB)	Pino,Yohan (1101 ADB)	Capuano,Chris (2201 CBA)	Gonzalez,Miguel Alfred (1201 FFF)
	Lyons,Tyler (2100 CDC)	Rienzo,Andre (1200 ADC)	Coke,Phil (2100 BDB)	Guerra,Javy (1100 CDF)
	Meyer,Alex (2300 CFC)	**Santiago,Hector (1301 ABA)**	Coleman,Louis (2300 ADD)	Hale,David (1000 ADB)
	Morrow,Brandon (2201 FCB)	Straily,Dan (1201 ACC)	Colome,Alexander (2100 DDA)	Huff,David (1000 CDC)
	Nolasco,Ricky (2105 DAB)	Turner,Jacob (1001 BCA)	Deduno,Samuel (2100 CCA)	Jaime,Juan (1500 AFA)
	Norris,Daniel (2400 CFF)	Butler,Eddie (0001 CFF)	Detwiler,Ross (2000 FBA)	Maholm,Paul (1000 FBA)
	Oberholtzer,Brett (2103 ADC)	Corcino,Daniel (0101 ADF)	Diaz,Jose (2310 AFC)	Matsuzaka,Daisuke (1201 FDD)
	Perez,Martin (2101 FCA)	Holmberg,David (0001 ADC)	Duensing,Brian (2100 ACB)	McGowan,Dustin (1201 FDB)
	Ramirez,Erasmo (2101 CDB)	Karns,Nathan (0301 ADB)	Gomez,Jeanmar (2000 BCB)	Mikolas,Miles (1000 CDB)
	Rodriguez,Wandy (2101 FCB)	Pelfrey,Mike (0000 FCD)	Greenwood,Nick (2000 ADD)	Morales,Franklin (1200 FCA)
	Tepesch,Nicholas (2001 DCC)	Ranaudo,Anthony (0001 ADF)	Gutierrez,Juan (2100 DDF)	Perez,Chris (1300 DBA)
	Treinen,Blake (2000 ADC)		Hardy,Blaine (2100 ADC)	Redmond,Todd (1201 ADB)
	Webster,Allen (2101 ADB)		Hollands,Mario (2100 BDD)	Swarzak,Anthony (1001 BCB)
	Williams,Jerome (2101 BAA)		Kahnle,Thomas (2401 BDA)	Vizcaino,Arodys (1200 FFF)

SIMULATION LEAGUE DRAFT TOP 500+

NAME	POS	RAR	NAME	POS	RAR	NAME	POS	RAR	NAME	POS	RAR
Trout,Mike	8	69.0	Longoria,Evan	5	23.0	LaRoche,Adam	3	14.6	Wainwright,Adam	P	10.9
Cabrera,Miguel	3	63.3	Kipnis,Jason	4	23.0	Lester,Jon	P	14.3	Stubbs,Drew	8	10.8
Goldschmidt,Paul	3	60.5	Mesoraco,Devin	2	23.0	Betances,Dellin	P	14.3	Hardy,J.J.	6	10.6
Tulowitzki,Troy	6	58.7	Santana,Carlos	35	22.9	Crawford,Brandon	6	14.1	Willingham,Josh	7	10.5
McCutchen,Andrew	8	58.7	Carter,Chris	0	22.8	Adams,Matt	3	14.1	Peralta,David	79	10.5
Cano,Robinson	4	54.1	Murphy,Daniel	4	22.4	Hamilton,Josh	7	13.9	Leone,Dominic	P	10.4
Abreu,Jose	3	53.4	Hamels,Cole	P	22.4	Gray,Sonny	P	13.8	Smyly,Drew	P	10.4
Stanton,Giancarlo	9	49.2	Lowrie,Jed	6	22.3	Kimbrel,Craig	P	13.7	Phillips,Brandon	4	10.4
Votto,Joey	3	48.7	Utley,Chase	4	21.7	Hill,Aaron	4	13.7	Andrus,Elvis	6	10.3
Posey,Buster	23	48.3	Ramirez,Aramis	5	21.4	Aybar,Erick	6	13.7	Ozuna,Marcell	8	10.3
Martinez,Victor	3	46.8	Harrison,Josh	579	21.3	Miller,Bradley	6	13.6	Odor,Rougned	4	10.3
Beltre,Adrian	5	44.2	Morneau,Justin	3	21.2	Mercer,Jordy	6	13.6	Saunders,Michael	9	10.2
Bautista,Jose	9	43.9	Calhoun,Kole	9	21.1	Belt,Brandon	3	13.6	Davis,Wade	P	10.2
Dickerson,Corey	7	42.9	Machado,Manny	5	21.1	Gennett,Scooter	4	13.6	Pinto,Josmil	2	10.2
Kershaw,Clayton	P	41.8	Martinez,J.D.	79	21.0	Iwakuma,Hisashi	P	13.4	Ethier,Andre	8	10.1
Encarnacion,Edwin	3	39.9	Seager,Kyle	5	20.9	Melancon,Mark	P	13.3	Teheran,Julio	P	10.1
Cuddyer,Michael	9	39.3	Frazier,Todd	35	20.9	Infante,Omar	4	13.2	McGee,Jake	P	10.1
Brantley,Michael	78	39.0	Heyward,Jason	9	20.9	Napoli,Mike	3	13.1	Gyorko,Jedd	4	10.0
Ramirez,Hanley	6	37.3	Perez,Salvador	2	20.9	Tanaka,Masahiro	P	13.1	Latos,Mat	P	9.9
Zimmerman,Ryan	57	36.6	Cespedes,Yoenis	7	20.8	Hunter,Torii	9	13.0	Pagan,Angel	8	9.9
Rendon,Anthony	45	35.9	Wieters,Matt	2	20.4	Van Slyke,Scott	378	13.0	Wacha,Michael	P	9.9
Kemp,Matt	789	35.9	Cueto,Johnny	P	20.4	Degrom,Jacob	P	13.0	Clippard,Tyler	P	9.9
Lucroy,Jonathan	2	35.5	Strasburg,Stephen	P	19.9	Davis,Chris	35	13.0	Boxberger,Brad	P	9.7
Werth,Jayson	9	35.5	Kinsler,Ian	4	19.8	Arcia,Oswaldo	9	13.0	Jay,Jon	789	9.6
Rizzo,Anthony	3	35.5	Zimmermann,Jordan	P	19.7	Alvarez,Pedro	5	12.9	Cole,Gerrit	P	9.6
Freeman,Freddie	3	34.7	Greinke,Zack	P	19.6	Arrieta,Jake	P	12.9	Escobar,Yunel	6	9.4
Upton,Justin	7	33.8	Davis,Khristopher	7	19.5	Chisenhall,Lonnie	5	12.9	Lee,Cliff	P	9.4
Puig,Yasiel	89	33.4	Price,David	P	19.4	Watson,Tony	P	12.8	Shields,James	P	9.4
Altuve,Jose	4	33.4	Bumgarner,Madison	P	19.3	Jaso,John	2	12.8	Joyce,Matt	7	9.2
Hernandez,Felix	P	33.3	Mauer,Joe	3	19.2	Johnson,Chris	5	12.8	Segura,Jean	6	9.2
Braun,Ryan	9	32.6	Rosario,Wilin	2	19.2	Ramirez,Alexei	6	12.7	Montero,Miguel	2	9.2
Ortiz,David	0	32.0	Span,Denard	8	19.1	Cabrera,Asdrubal	46	12.7	Cashner,Andrew	P	9.2
Fielder,Prince	3	30.6	Pearce,Steve	37	19.0	Bryant,Kris	5	12.6	Castillo,Rusney	8	9.2
Arenado,Nolan	5	30.5	Grandal,Yasmani	23	18.8	Morse,Michael	37	12.6	Escobar,Alcides	6	9.2
Peralta,Jhonny	6	30.4	Ellsbury,Jacoby	8	18.8	Lawrie,Brett	45	12.5	Alvarez,Henderson	P	9.1
Gonzalez,Adrian	3	30.2	Sandoval,Pablo	5	18.4	Saltalamacchia,Jarrod	2	12.4	Uribe,Juan	5	9.0
Zobrist,Ben	467	29.8	Prado,Martin	45	18.1	Markakis,Nick	9	12.4	Wong,Kolten	4	9.0
Cabrera,Melky	7	29.3	Bogaerts,Xander	56	17.9	Freese,David	5	12.4	McGehee,Casey	5	8.9
Reyes,Jose	6	29.1	Pence,Hunter	9	17.9	Giles,Kenneth	P	12.2	Gregorius,Didi	6	8.8
Sale,Chris	P	29.0	Lind,Adam	3	17.8	Myers,Wil	9	12.2	O Flaherty,Eric	P	8.8
Holliday,Matt	7	28.1	Choo,Shin-Soo	7	17.8	Eaton,Adam	8	12.1	Pollock IV,A.J.	8	8.8
Carpenter,Matt	5	27.8	Moss,Brandon	379	17.7	Jansen,Kenley	P	12.1	Cishek,Steve	P	8.6
Gomez,Carlos	8	27.3	Martin,Russell	2	17.7	Wheeler,Zack	P	12.0	Benoit,Joaquin	P	8.6
Desmond,Ian	6	27.2	Butler,Billy	3	17.4	Darvish,Yu	P	12.0	Ryu,Hyun-Jin	P	8.5
Dozier,Brian	4	26.7	Hosmer,Eric	3	17.4	Weeks,Rickie	4	12.0	Medlen,Kris	P	8.5
Gonzalez,Carlos	7	26.3	Gattis,Evan	2	17.2	Plouffe,Trevor	5	11.9	Robertson,David	P	8.4
Pedroia,Dustin	4	26.3	Headley,Chase	5	17.2	Fister,Doug	P	11.9	La Stella,Tommy	4	8.3
Castro,Starlin	6	26.1	Fowler,Dexter	8	17.0	Beltran,Carlos	9	11.9	Harvey,Matt	P	8.2
Pujols,Albert	3	26.0	Wood,Alex	P	16.8	Jackson,Austin	8	11.9	Reddick,Josh	9	8.2
Walker,Neil	4	26.0	McCann,Brian	2	16.8	Duda,Lucas	3	11.8	Ruiz,Carlos	2	8.1
Donaldson,Josh	5	25.9	Crawford,Carl	7	16.4	Samardzija,Jeff	P	11.8	Crisp,Coco	8	8.1
Kendrick,Howie	4	25.4	Norris,Derek	2	16.2	Turner,Justin	5	11.8	Semien,Marcus	45	8.1
Cruz,Nelson	7	24.9	Holland,Greg	P	16.0	Bruce,Jay	9	11.7	Miller,Andrew	P	8.1
Marte,Starling	78	24.5	Springer,George	9	15.9	Valbuena,Luis	45	11.6	Aoki,Norichika	9	8.0
Soler,Jorge	9	24.5	Lamb,Jacob	5	15.7	Iannetta,Chris	2	11.5	Castro,Jason	2	7.9
Betts,Mookie	8	24.2	Gardner,Brett	78	15.6	Tomas,Yasmani	9	11.3	O Day,Darren	P	7.8
Gomes,Yan	2	24.2	Cobb,Alex	P	15.4	Kluber,Corey	P	11.2	Quintana,Jose	P	7.8
Harper,Bryce	7	24.2	Smith,Seth	79	15.4	Smith,Joe	P	11.1	Owings,Christopher	6	7.7
Molina,Yadier	2	24.0	Rollins,Jimmy	6	15.4	Gonzalez,Gio	P	11.1	Quentin,Carlos	7	7.6
Yelich,Christian S.	7	23.8	Ross,Tyson	P	15.2	Fujikawa,Kyuji	P	11.0	Asche,Cody	5	7.5
Gordon,Alex	7	23.6	Navarro,Dioner	2	14.9	Rutledge,Josh	6	11.0	De Aza,Alejandro	7	7.4
Jones,Adam	8	23.4	Scherzer,Max	P	14.7	Ramos,Wilson	2	11.0	Herrera,Kelvin	P	7.4
Wright,David	5	23.0	D Arnaud,Travis	2	14.7	Chapman,Aroldis	P	10.9	Romo,Sergio	P	7.3

SIMULATION LEAGUE DRAFT   TOP 500+

NAME	POS	RAR	NAME	POS	RAR	NAME	POS	RAR	NAME	POS	RAR
Ventura,Yordano	P	7.3	Sanchez,Anibal	P	4.8	Familia,Jeurys	P	3.3	Sanchez,Aaron	P	1.8
Casilla,Santiago	P	7.3	Morris,Bryan	P	4.8	Frasor,Jason	P	3.3	Maurer,Brandon	P	1.7
Allen,Cody	P	7.3	Castellanos,Nick	5	4.8	Rosenthal,Trevor	P	3.3	Peralta,Wily	P	1.7
Doolittle,Sean	P	7.2	Roark,Tanner	P	4.8	Affeldt,Jeremy	P	3.2	Gallardo,Yovani	P	1.7
Avila,Alex	2	7.2	Morin,Michael	P	4.7	Hunter,Tommy	P	3.2	Kintzler,Brandon	P	1.6
Castillo,Welington	2	7.1	Stroman,Marcus	P	4.7	Phegley,Joshua	2	3.2	Ruggiano,Justin	9	1.6
Richards,Garrett	P	7.1	Trumbo,Mark	37	4.7	Loup,Aaron	P	3.2	Young,Chris	78	1.6
Rasmus,Colby	8	7.0	Cecil,Brett	P	4.7	Mujica,Edward	P	3.2	Diekman,Jake	P	1.6
Cain,Lorenzo	89	6.9	Santana,Daniel	68	4.7	Baker,Jeff	34	3.1	Pennington,Cliff	6	1.6
Storen,Drew	P	6.9	Coghlan,Chris	7	4.6	Alburquerque,Al	P	3.1	Bastardo,Antonio	P	1.6
Gregerson,Luke	P	6.9	Warren,Adam	P	4.6	Mejia,Jenrry	P	3.1	Francisco,Juan	35	1.6
Uehara,Koji	P	6.8	Marshall,Evan	P	4.6	Ziegler,Brad	P	3.1	Grilli,Jason	P	1.5
Perkins,Glen	P	6.8	Fiers,Mike	P	4.6	Simmons,Shae	P	3.1	Casali,Curtis	2	1.5
Herrera,Dilson	4	6.7	Strop,Pedro	P	4.6	Stauffer,Tim	P	3.0	Ramos,A.J.	P	1.5
Farquhar,Daniel	P	6.6	Nieuwenhuis,Kirk	7	4.5	Blevins,Jerry	P	3.0	Cabrera,Everth	6	1.5
Kuroda,Hiroki	P	6.5	Jeffress,Jeremy	P	4.5	Salazar,Danny	P	3.0	Hochevar,Luke	P	1.5
Street,Huston	P	6.5	Hahn,Jesse	P	4.5	Pestano,Vinnie	P	2.9	Ross,David	2	1.5
McKenry,Michael	2	6.5	Feliz,Neftali	P	4.5	Jepsen,Kevin	P	2.9	DeJesus,David	0	1.5
Fernandez,Jose	P	6.5	Pillar,Kevin	7	4.5	Soto,Geovany	2	2.8	Smith,Will	P	1.5
Jennings,Desmond	8	6.4	Rondon,Bruce	P	4.5	Soriano,Rafael	P	2.8	Chen,Wei-Yin	P	1.5
Otero,Dan	P	6.4	Gausman,Kevin	P	4.4	Hendricks,Kyle	P	2.8	Diaz,Jose	P	1.5
Simmons,Andrelton	6	6.4	Snider,Travis	79	4.4	Lohse,Kyle	P	2.8	Blanco,Gregor	78	1.4
Granderson,Curtis	9	6.3	Vincent,Nick	P	4.4	Guyer,Brandon	7	2.8	Putnam,Zach	P	1.4
Young,Delmon	7	6.3	Craig,Allen	39	4.4	Liriano,Francisco	P	2.8	Freeman,Sam	P	1.4
Britton,Zach	P	6.2	Escobar,Eduardo	56	4.3	Venable,Will	89	2.7	Susac,Andrew	2	1.3
Papelbon,Jonathan	P	6.2	Walden,Jordan	P	4.3	Morrison,Logan	3	2.7	Nelson,Jimmy	P	1.3
Loney,James	3	6.1	Varvaro,Anthony	P	4.3	Miley,Wade	P	2.7	Sweeney,Ryan	89	1.3
Bailey,Homer	P	6.0	Rondon,Hector	P	4.3	Torres,Carlos	P	2.7	Ruf,Darin	3	1.3
Maness,Michael	P	6.0	LeMahieu,DJ	4	4.2	Pederson,Joc	8	2.6	Lynn,Lance	P	1.2
Smith,Carson	P	6.0	Badenhop,Burke	P	4.2	Wilson,Justin	P	2.6	Taveras,Oscar	9	1.2
Hechavarria,Adeiny	6	5.8	Tazawa,Junichi	P	4.1	Russell,Addison	6	2.6	Miller,Shelby	P	1.2
Rios,Alex	9	5.8	Petit,Yusmeiro	P	4.0	Barrett,Aaron	P	2.6	Bedrosian,Cam	P	1.1
Gillaspie,Conor	5	5.7	Tolleson,Shawn	P	4.0	Viciedo,Dayan	79	2.5	Grossman,Robert	79	1.1
Shaw,Bryan	P	5.7	Martin,Leonys	8	4.0	Dietrich,Derek	4	2.5	Johnson,Josh	P	1.1
Davis,Rajai	78	5.7	Baez,Javier	46	4.0	Kontos,George	P	2.5	Qualls,Chad	P	1.1
Alonso,Yonder	3	5.6	Ackley,Dustin	7	4.0	Ramirez,Neil	P	2.5	Parra,Gerardo	79	1.1
Perez,Oliver	P	5.6	Franklin,Nick	4	4.0	Reed,Addison	P	2.5	Kratz,Erik	2	1.1
Cook,Ryan	P	5.6	Murphy,David	9	3.9	Hanigan,Ryan	2	2.4	Howard,Ryan	3	1.1
Abad,Fernando	P	5.6	Medina,Yoervis	P	3.9	Dyson,Sam	P	2.4	Rivera,Rene	2	1.1
Suzuki,Kurt	2	5.5	Colon,Christian	4	3.9	Cervelli,Francisco	2	2.4	Panik,Joe	4	1.0
Ross,Cody	79	5.5	Parnell,Bobby	P	3.8	Rodriguez,Fernando	P	2.3	Hatcher,Chris	P	1.0
Pineda,Michael	P	5.5	McHugh,Collin	P	3.8	Rua,Ryan	7	2.3	Gonzales,Marco	P	1.0
Ellis,A.J.	2	5.4	Byrd,Marlon	9	3.7	Rodriguez,Sean	4	2.3	Victorino,Shane	9	0.9
Moustakas,Mike	5	5.4	Salas,Fernando	P	3.7	Peralta,Joel	P	2.3	Jennings,Dan	P	0.9
Quackenbush,Kevin	P	5.3	Janssen,Casey	P	3.7	Gonzalez,Marwin	6	2.2	Kubel,Jason	7	0.9
Teixeira,Mark	3	5.3	Furbush,Charlie	P	3.7	Chirinos,Robinson	2	2.2	Duke,Zach	P	0.8
Brach,Brad	P	5.3	Thayer,Dale	P	3.7	Martinez,Carlos	P	2.2	Capps,Carter	P	0.8
Rzepczynski,Marc	P	5.3	Howell,J.P.	P	3.7	Hughes,Phil	P	2.2	Guerra,Javy	P	0.8
Revere,Ben	8	5.3	Alcantara,Arismendy	48	3.6	Adams,Mike	P	2.2	Lough,David	7	0.7
Neshek,Pat	P	5.2	Franco,Maikel	5	3.6	Holland,Derek	P	2.2	Izturis,Maicer	4	0.7
Brown,Domonic	7	5.2	Kiermaier,Kevin	89	3.6	Pierzynski,A.J.	2	2.1	Buxton,Byron	8	0.7
Archer,Chris	P	5.2	Garcia,Avisail	9	3.5	Atchison,Scott	P	2.0	Smolinski,Jacob	7	0.7
Broxton,Jonathan	P	5.1	Carpenter,David	P	3.5	Sanchez,Gaby	3	2.0	Nuno,Vidal	P	0.6
Keuchel,Dallas	P	5.1	Rodriguez,Francisco	P	3.5	Vazquez,Christian	2	2.0	Raburn,Ryan	79	0.6
Drew,Stephen	46	5.0	Siegrist,Kevin	P	3.5	Lecure,Sam	P	2.0	Matusz,Brian	P	0.5
Flores,Wilmer	6	5.0	Rasmus,Cory	P	3.5	Fields,Joshua	P	1.9	Valencia,Danny	35	0.5
Blackmon,Charlie	789	5.0	De Fratus,Justin	P	3.5	Tillman,Chris	P	1.9	Black,Victor	P	0.5
Machi,Jean	P	5.0	Carrasco,Carlos	P	3.5	Wilhelmsen,Tom	P	1.9	Jones,Garrett	3	0.5
Profar,Jurickson	4	5.0	Dirks,Andy	7	3.5	Thornton,Matt	P	1.9	Herrera,Jonathan	6	0.5
Rodney,Fernando	P	5.0	Ottavino,Adam	P	3.4	Grimm,Justin	P	1.8	League,Brandon	P	0.5
Moreland,Mitch	3	4.9	Paxton,James	P	3.4	Taylor,Chris	6	1.8	Stammen,Craig	P	0.5
Hughes,Jared	P	4.9	Dunn,Mike	P	3.4	Nava,Daniel	79	1.8	Collmenter,Josh	P	0.5
Gordon,Dee	4	4.8	Soria,Joakim	P	3.4	Niese,Jon	P	1.8	Walters,Zachary	0	0.5

FIRST PITCH 2015
Fantasy Baseball Forums

Read everything you want.
The best advice is live advice.

Get ready for an unforgettable experience—BaseballHQ.com's **First Pitch Forums**. These 3+ hour events are packed full of fantasy baseball talk, interactive activities and fun! Top national baseball analysts disclose competitive secrets unique to 2015: Players to watch, trends to monitor, new strategies to employ and more! Plus, they answer YOUR questions as you look for the edge that will lead to a 2015 championship.

BaseballHQ.com's Ron Shandler, Brent Hershey and Ray Murphy chair the sessions and bring a dynamic energy to every event. They are joined by experts from BaseballHQ.com as well as other sports media sources, such as ESPN.com, MLB.com, Rotowire, FanGraphs, BaseballProspectus, Mastersball, Sirius/XM Radio and more.

Don't forget
**First Pitch
Arizona:**
Nov. 6-8 in
Phoenix, at
the AFL!

2015 FIRST PITCH FORUM DATES, SITES AND REGISTRATION INFORMATION

Saturday, February 28	**CHICAGO**
Sunday, March 1	**CINCINNATI**
Friday, March 6	**WASHINGTON DC**
Saturday, March 7	**NEW YORK**
Sunday, March 8	**BOSTON**
Saturday, March 14	**LOS ANGELES**
Sunday, March 15	**SAN FRANCISCO**

NOTE: Schedule is preliminary and subject to change.

For program description and details, visit:

www.firstpitchforums.com

Registration:
$39 per person in advance
$49 per person at the door

Get Forecaster Insights
Every Single Day.

The *Baseball Forecaster* provides the core concepts in player evaluation and gaming strategy. You can maintain that edge all season long.

From spring training to the season's last pitch, **BaseballHQ.com** covers all aspects of what's happening on and off the field—all with the most powerful fantasy slant on the Internet:

- Nationally-renowned baseball analysts.
- MLB news analysis; including anticipating the *next* move.
- Dedicated columns on starting pitching, relievers, batters, and our popular Fact or Fluke? player profiles.
- Minor-league coverage beyond just scouting and lists.
- FAAB targets, starting pitcher reports, strategy articles, daily game resources, call-up profiles and more!

Plus, **BaseballHQ.com** gets personal, with customizable tools and valuable resources:

- Team Stat Tracker and Power Search tools
- Custom Draft Guide for YOUR league's parameters
- Sortable and downloadable stats and projection files
- Subscriber forums, the friendliest on the baseball Internet

Visit **www.baseballhq.com/subscribe**
to lock down your path to a 2015 championship!

Full Season subscription **$89**
(prorated at the time of order; auto-renews each October)

Draft Prep subscription **$39**
(complete access from January through April 30, 2015)

Please read our Terms of service at www.baseballhq.com/terms.html

Baseball Forecaster & BaseballHQ.com:
Your season-long championship lineup.

2015 CHEATER'S BOOKMARK

BATTING STATISTICS

Abbrv	Term	Formula / Desc.	BAD UNDER	'14 LG AVG AL	'14 LG AVG NL	BEST OVER
Avg	Batting Average	h/ab	235	254	256	280
xBA	Expected Batting Average	See glossary		267	268	
OB	On Base Average	(h+bb)/(ab+bb)	290	312	315	340
Slg	Slugging Average	total bases/ab	350	391	395	450
OPS	On Base plus Slugging	OB+Slg	650	704	711	780
bb%	Walk Rate	bb/(ab+bb)	6%	8%	8%	10%
ct%	Contact Rate	(ab-k) / ab	73%	78%	78%	83%
Eye	Batting Eye	bb/k	0.30	0.39	0.39	0.50
PX	Power Index	Normalized power skills	80	100	100	120
Spd	Speed Score	Normalized speed skills	80	100	100	120
SBO	Stolen Base Opportunity %	(sb+cs)/(singles+bb)		9%	9%	
G/F	Groundball/Flyball Ratio	gb / fb		1.3	1.3	
G	Ground Ball Per Cent	gb / balls in play		44%	45%	
L	Line Drive Per Cent	ld / balls in play		21%	21%	
F	Fly Ball Per Cent	fb / balls in play		35%	34%	
BPV	Base Performance Value	See glossary	20	40	39	55
RC/G	Runs Created per Game	See glossary	3.00	4.17	4.26	5.00
RAR	Runs Above Replacement	See glossary	0.0			10.0

PITCHING STATISTICS

Abbrv	Term	Formula / Desc.	BAD OVER	'14 LG AVG AL	'14 LG AVG NL	BEST UNDER
ERA	Earned Run Average	er*9/ip	4.75	3.82	3.66	3.00
xERA	Expected ERA	See glossary		3.78	3.64	
WHIP	Baserunners per Inning	(h+bb)/ip	1.50	1.28	1.27	1.15
BF/G	Batters Faced per Game	((ip*2.82)+h+bb)/g	28.0			
PC	Pitch Counts per Start		120	96	95	
OBA	Opposition Batting Avg	Opp. h/ab	280	252	252	235
OOB	Opposition On Base Avg	Opp. (h+bb)/(ab+bb)	350	310	309	290
BABIP	BatAvg on balls in play	(h-hr)/((ip*2.82)+h-k-hr)		296	295	
Ctl	Control Rate	bb*9/ip		2.9	2.9	2.5
hr/9	Homerun Rate	hr*9/ip		0.9	0.8	1.0
hr/f	Homerun per Fly ball	hr/fb		9%	10%	
S%	Strand Rate	(h+bb-er)/(h+bb-hr)		73%	73%	
DIS%	PQS Disaster Rate	% GS that are PQS 0/1		21%	17%	15%

Abbrv	Term	Formula / Desc.	BAD UNDER	'14 LG AVG AL	'14 LG AVG NL	BEST OVER
RAR	Runs Above Replacement	See glossary	-0.0			+10
Dom	Dominance Rate	k*9/ip		7.7	7.8	9.0
Cmd	Command Ratio	k/bb		2.6	2.6	3.3
G/F	Groundball/Flyball Ratio	gb / fb		1.23	1.39	
BPV	Base Performance Value	See glossary	50	82	86	100
DOM%	PQS Dominance Rate	% GS that are PQS 4/5		49%	54%	60%
Sv%	Saves Conversion Rate	(saves / save opps)		73%	73%	80%
REff%	Relief Effectiveness Rate	See glossary		67%	67%	80%

NOTES

Home page for year-round fanalytic coverage:
www.BaseballHQ.com

For March projections update and any other information related to this book:
www.baseballhq.com/content/ron-shandlers-2015-baseball-forecaster

For the schedule of dates and cities on our Spring 2015 First Pitch tour, including registration information:
www.FirstPitchForums.com

Facebook: **www.facebook.com/baseballhq**
Twitter: **www.twitter.com/baseballhq**
HQ staffers on Twitter:
www.twitter.com/BaseballHQ/lists/hq-staff